CLASSICS

OF

AMERICAN POLITICAL AND CONSTITUTIONAL THOUGHT

Volume 2

Reconstruction to the Present

Classics

of

American Political and Constitutional Thought

Volume 2

Reconstruction to the Present

Edited, with Introductions, by
SCOTT J. HAMMOND
KEVIN R. HARDWICK
HOWARD L. LUBERT

Hackett Publishing Company, Inc.
Indianapolis/Cambridge

12 11 10 09 08 07   1 2 3 4 5 6 7

For further information, please address:

Hackett Publishing Company, Inc.
P.O. Box 44937
Indianapolis, IN 46244-0937

www.hackettpublishing.com

Text design by Meera Dash
Composition by Scribe
Printed at Edwards Brothers, Inc.

Library of Congress Cataloging-in-Publication Data

Classics of American political and constitutional thought / edited, with introductions, by Scott J. Hammond,
    Kevin R. Hardwick, and Howard L. Lubert.
        p. cm.
    ISBN-13: 978-0-87220-786-8 (pbk. set)   ISBN-13: 978-0-87220-787-5 (cloth set)

    1. Constitutional history—United States—Sources.   2. United States—Politics and government—
Sources. I. Hammond, Scott J.   II. Hardwick, Kevin R., 1961–   III. Lubert, Howard L. (Howard Leslie),
1966–
    JK31.C54 2007
    320.473—dc22

                                                                                    2006046824

    ISBN-13 (Vol.2): 978-0-87220-885-8 (pbk.)   ISBN-13 (Vol.2): 978-0-87220-886-5 (cloth)

Acknowledgments

Many friends and colleagues have contributed in various ways to this project. In recognition of their kind support, advice, and guidance, we thank the following individuals. For providing informed opinions and needed input regarding either the content of our selections or the style of our presentation, we thank John "Chris" Arndt, Herman Belz, William Hawk, Raymond "Skip" Hyser, Iain MacLean, Charles Miller, Henry Myers, Steve Reich, Margaret Williams, Jacqueline Walker, and our anonymous reviewers. For material support as well as the occasional boost to morale, we thank all of our good colleagues in both the department of Political Science and the department of History here at James Madison University. We also thank Rob Gardner, one of our graduate assistants, for his help in transcribing text.

We are especially grateful to James Madison University for generous assistance in funding this venture. In particular, we thank Phil Bigler and the James Madison Center for a generous financial contribution that helped to underwrite a substantial portion of this project. Additionally, we thank the Provost Office, as well as Linda Halpern and the JMU summer grants program. Without all of this additional funding from our home university the final shape and substance of this project would have been decidedly different, and not for the better.

Finally, we thank the expert staff at Hackett Publishing for their good counsel, enthusiastic devotion, and inexhaustible patience. Specifically, we thank Rick Todhunter, our editor at Hackett; Fred Courtwright, our permissions guru; and Meera Dash, Hackett's managing editor, and her amazing staff of skilled and tireless copyeditors. In particular we are grateful to Carrie Wagner and her important contribution toward the completion of this project. Without them, this book would not be in your hands. Even so, we, the editors who are fortunate enough to have our name on the cover, assume full responsibility for the content of this text.

Finally, we dedicate this book to our families, without whom there would be nothing at all.

To our wives, Chereé, Jan, and Caroline, and our children,
Adriana, Neil, Carolyn, Eleanor, and Sarah

CONTENTS

2   Contractual Liberty and the Gilded Age   120

3   The Problems of Industrial Capitalism   247

4   Freedom as Power and Opportunity   370

5   The Cold War and the Limits of Dissent   494

6   The Great Society and Its Critics   592

7   Democracy's Challenges and the Price of Power   835

1

RECONSTRUCTION, RACE, AND GENDER

In the first decades of the nineteenth century, Americans redefined the foundation of citizenship. Whereas earlier generations had predicated participation in public affairs on the possession of a "stake in society," understood as possession of various degrees and kinds of property, by the 1820s most Americans embraced citizenship for all adult white males. Numerous commentators comprehended this redefinition to be a step toward a more liberal, Lockean understanding of citizenship based on possession not of property but of mature, adult reason. The assumptions of eighteenth-century thinkers, many of whom believed that rational self-government could be attained only by leisured and propertied gentlemen, gave way to the inclusiveness of Jacksonian democracy. But in the course of extending the polity to include a larger number of men, Americans also developed explicit justifications for the exclusion of other men—and women—from direct participation in public life. From the 1830s through the end of the century, articulate members of these excluded groups confronted the illiberal assumptions of mainstream society. The selections in this chapter document the evolution of that confrontation, especially with regard to women, African Americans, and Native Americans.

In the 1830s, women entered into public debate to oppose slavery. For example, Angelina and Sarah Grimké, daughters of a wealthy South Carolina slaveholder, delivered public lectures to expose the social destructiveness of slavery. As women who had experienced the evils of slavery firsthand, they were especially well positioned to argue that the sexual exploitation of female slaves by male slave owners represented a direct threat both to the sanctity of marriage and to the republican dignity of the slave owners' wives and daughters. Polite Northern opinion, however, challenged their fitness as women to participate in public and explicitly political discussions; women in early nineteenth-century America, according to evangelical clergymen and other spokesmen for conventional opinion, should be sheltered from the hurly-burly of political discourse and certainly should not speak outside the home. Sarah Grimké responded with her "Letters on the Equality of the Sexes," in which she insisted that women were competent to partake in political debate. As Grimké noted, God created woman as man's partner and companion, "like himself a *free agent*, gifted with intellect . . . able to enter into all his feelings as a moral and responsible being." Like the Grimké sisters, numerous other nineteenth-century women entered into public life to defend the purity of family and home from external corruption. Male resistance to their public presence elicited powerful liberalizing arguments in response, emphasizing women's capacity for self-government and mature reason that was every bit as proficient as that of men. By 1848, feminist activists like Elizabeth Cady Stanton and Lucretia Mott made explicit reference to the founding documents of the nation to justify their demand for public equality with men.

Native Americans and African Americans faced equally entrenched and illiberal assumptions about their lack of civil fitness. English colonists in the seventeenth and eighteenth centuries certainly possessed a deep xenophobia, which could easily translate into contempt for the "savage" races they encountered and sought to displace or dominate. At the very beginning of colonization, when the anti-English "other" against whom the colonists defined themselves was Spanish and papist, there had seemed some hope for a genuinely multicultural society to develop in the colonies. But as the "papist" threat diminished, and as Indians and Africans resisted English dominion, the bestial savage replaced the bestial Spaniard as the antithesis of English, and later American, civility.

Slavery was an entrenched institution by the beginning of the nineteenth century. Some members of the Revolutionary generation were willing to acknowledge a contradiction between slavery and the commitment to liberalism that underpinned the American political order. But even in that generation numerous slave owners were willing to defend slavery as a necessary and positive good. To reconcile slavery with American civic assumptions, such slave owners emphasized the intrinsic and childlike incapacity for self-government that they asserted was ingrained in the African character. Later generations of Southerners, under the pressure of an increasingly strident abolitionist movement, developed these arguments carefully and fully. Even when the Civil War conclusively ended slavery, many Southerners remained fully convinced that African Americans could not be safely included in public life because they were unable to make even the most basic decisions for themselves with any kind of prudential rationality. Men like Joseph Daniel Pope, who had owned slave plantations on the South Carolina coast before the war, and who reported on conditions there shortly after the war's conclusion, were convinced that freedom was disastrous both for the slaves and for their former masters. Just beneath the surface of Pope's paternalism lurked a harsh and ugly insistence on African American inferiority. Southern elites widely subscribed to Pope's racism; even in the North and West, such ideas were widely shared by many white men and women.

Just as advocates for the citizenship of African Americans confronted pervasive racist ideas of long standing, so too did advocates for Native Americans. Throughout the nineteenth century, Native American spokesmen consistently understood freedom to include maintenance of their cultural identity and political autonomy, and control over the land they required to sustain their way of life. As settlers encroached upon Native American land, and as Native Americans resisted, the federal government, and on occasion state governments, responded with military force. Before the Civil War, southern states like Georgia forcibly evicted Native Americans from their homes, relocating them to reservations in the west. After the Civil War, Native American peoples west of the Mississippi River fought vicious but losing rear guard actions to preserve their identity and way of life. By the 1890s, most Native Americans lived on reservations far removed from their ancestral homelands.

Many white commentators remained convinced that Native Americans, unlike African Americans, retained the capacity to transcend their savage existence. Thomas Jefferson, for example, had argued for the assimilation of those Native Americans willing to acculturate. For thinkers like Jefferson, savagery was not a natural, inborn feature of the essential character of Native Americans so much as it was a product of their primitive social stage of development. As the federal government gradually assumed responsibility for managing the reservations and their Native American populations, those politicians and bureaucrats who cared to trouble themselves with the fate of Native Americans advocated policies designed to encourage their "civilization." They worked hard to force Native Americans to abandon their traditional religions in favor of Christianity, foster individual ownership of property, adopt a small-farm economy, and sustain proper economic and social relationships between men and women. For most Native Americans, the cost of such assimilation was cultural death. In 1887, these policies culminated in the Dawes Act, which broke up into private lots the land belonging to almost every tribe, distributing those lots to individual Native American families. While the Dawes Act promised citizenship to those Native Americans who "adopted the habits of civilized life," its implementation was a disaster from the perspective of most of the people the act hoped to assist. Not only did the act permit the government to sell much of the tribal reservation lands to white speculators, it also led to the steady loss of vitality of Native American cultures. By 1890, as the messianic Ghost Dance revival surged over the reservations, Native American numbers and culture both ebbed to their lowest point in American history.

Walt Whitman

Selected Poems (1855–1873)

One's Self I Sing

One's-self I sing—a simple, separate Person;
Yet utter the word Democratic, the word En-masse.

Of Physiology from top to toe I sing;
Not physiognomy alone, nor brain alone, is worthy
    for the muse—I say the Form complete is wor-
    thier far;
The Female equally with the male I sing.

Of Life immense in passion, pulse, and power,
Cheerful—for freest action form'd, under the laws
    divine,
The Modern Man I sing.

To a Historian

"Historian! you who celebrate bygones!
You have explored the outward, the surface of the
    races—the life that has exhibited itself,
You have treated man as the creature of politics,
    aggregates, rulers, and priests;
But now I also, arriving, contribute something:
I, an habitué of the Alleghanies, treat man as he is
    in the influences of Nature, in himself, in his
    own inalienable rights,
Advancing, to give the spirit and the traits of new
    Democratic ages, myself, personally,
(Let the future behold them all in me—Me, so puz-
    zling and contradictory—Me, a Manhattanese,
    the most loving and arrogant of men;)
I do not tell the usual facts, proved by records and
    documents,
What I tell, (talking to every born American,)
    requires no further proof than he or she who will
    hear me, will furnish, by silently meditating alone;

I press the pulse of the life that has hitherto seldom
    exhibited itself, but has generally sought conceal-
    ment, (the great pride of man, in himself,)
I illuminate feelings, faults, yearnings, hopes—I
    have come at last, no more ashamed nor afraid;
Chanter of Personality, outlining a history yet to be,
I project the ideal man, the American of the
    future."

The Base of All Metaphysics

And now, gentlemen,
A word I give to remain in your memories and
    minds,
As base, and finale too, for all metaphysics.
(So, to the students, the old professor,
At the close of his crowded course.)
Having studied the new and antique, the Greek and
    Germanic systems,
Kant having studied and stated—Fichte and
    Schelling and Hegel,
Stated the lore of Plato—and Socrates, greater than
    Plato,
And greater than Socrates sought and stated—
    Christ divine having studied long,
I see reminiscent to-day those Greek and Germanic
    systems,
See the philosophies all—Christian churches and
    tenets see,
Yet underneath Socrates clearly see—and under-
    neath Christ the divine I see,
The dear love of man for his comrade—the attrac-
    tion of friend to friend,
Of the well-married husband and wife—of children
    and parents,
Of city for city, and land for land.

Beat! Beat! Drums!

1

Beat! beat! drums!—Blow! bugles! blow!
Through the windows—through doors—burst like a
ruthless force,
Into the solemn church, and scatter the
congregation;
Into the school where the scholar is studying;
Leave not the bridegroom quiet—no happiness
must he have now with his bride;
Nor the peaceful farmer any peace, plowing his
field or gathering his grain;
So fierce you whirr and pound, you drums—so
shrill you bugles blow.

2

Beat! beat! drums!—Blow! bugles! blow!
Over the traffic of cities—over the rumble of wheels
in the streets:
Are beds prepared for sleepers at night in the
houses? No sleepers must sleep in those beds;
No bargainers' bargains by day—no brokers or
speculators—Would they continue?
Would the talkers be talking? would the singer
attempt to sing?
Would the lawyer rise in the court to state his case
before the judge?
Then rattle quicker, heavier drums—you bugles
wilder blow.

3

Beat! beat! drums!—Blow! bugles! blow!
Make no parley—stop for no expostulation;
Mind not the timid—mind not the weeper or
prayer;
Mind not the old man beseeching the young man;
Let not the child's voice be heard, nor the mother's
entreaties;
Make even the trestles to shake the dead, where
they lie awaiting the hearses,
So strong you thump, O terrible drums—so loud
you bugles blow.

Years of the Modern

Years of the modern! years of the unperform'd!
Your horizon rises—I see it parting away for more
august dramas;
I see not America only—I see not only Liberty's
nation, but other nations preparing;
I see tremendous entrances and exits—I see new
combinations—I see the solidarity of races;
I see that force advancing with irresistible power on
the world's stage;
(Have the old forces, the old wars, played their
parts? are the acts suitable to them closed?)
I see Freedom, completely arm'd, and victorious,
and very haughty, with Law on one side, and
Peace on the other,
A stupendous Trio, all issuing forth against the idea
of caste;
—What historic denouements are these we so
rapidly approach?
I see men marching and countermarching by swift
millions;
I see the frontiers and boundaries of the old
aristocracies broken;
I see the landmarks of European kings removed;
I see this day the People beginning their landmarks,
(all others give way;)
—Never were such sharp questions ask'd as this day;
Never was average man, his soul, more energetic,
more like a God;
Lo! how he urges and urges, leaving the masses no
rest;
His daring foot is on land and sea everywhere—he
colonizes the Pacific, the archipelagoes;
With the steam-ship, the electric telegraph, the
newspaper, the wholesale engines of war,
With these, and the world-spreading factories, he
interlinks all geography, all lands;
—What whispers are these, O lands, running ahead
of you, passing under the seas?
Are all nations communing? is there going to be but
one heart to the globe?
Is humanity forming, en-masse?—for lo! tyrants
tremble, crowns grow dim;
The earth, restive, confronts a new era, perhaps a
general divine war;
No one knows what will happen next—such
portents fill the days and nights;

Years prophetical! the space ahead as I walk, as I
    vainly try to pierce it, is full of phantoms;
Unborn deeds, things soon to be, project their
    shapes around me;
This incredible rush and heat—this strange extract
    fever of dreams, O years!
Your dreams, O year, how they penetrate through
    me! (I know not whether I sleep or wake!)
The perform'd America and Europe grow dim, retir-
    ing in shadow behind me,
The unperform'd, more gigantic than ever, advance,
    advance upon me.

O Captain! My Captain!

O Captain! my Captain! our fearful trip is done,
The ship has weather'd every rack, the prize we
    sought is won,
The port is near, the bells I hear, the people all
    exulting,
While follow eyes the steady keel, the vessel grim
    and daring;
But O heart! heart! heart!
O the bleeding drops of red,

Where on the deck my Captain lies,
Fallen cold and dead.
O Captain! my Captain! rise up and hear the bells;
Rise up—for you the flag is flung—for you the
    bugle trills,
For you bouquets and ribbon'd wreaths—for you the
    shores a-crowding,
For you they call, the swaying mass, their eager
    faces turning;
Here Captain! dear father!
This arm beneath your head!
It is some dream that on the deck,
You've fallen cold and dead.
My Captain does not answer, his lips are pale and
    still,
My father does not feel my arm, he has no pulse
    nor will,
The ship is anchor'd safe and sound, its voyage
    closed and done,
From fearful trip the victor ship comes in with
    object won;
Exult O shores, and ring O bells!
But I with mournful tread,
Walk the deck my Captain lies,
Fallen cold and dead.

Angelina Grimké

Letter to Theodore Weld and John Greenleaf Whittier
(August 20, 1837)

Brookline [Mass.] 8th Mo 20—[1837]

To Theodore D. Weld and J. G. Whittier
Brethren beloved in the Lord.

As your letters came to hand at the same time and both are devoted mainly to the same subject we have concluded to answer them on one sheet and jointly. You seem greatly alarmed at the idea of our advocating the *rights of woman*. Now we will first tell you *how* we came to begin those letters in the Spectator.

Whilst we were at Newburyport we received a note from Mary Parker telling us that Wm. S. Porter had requested her to try to obtain some one to write for his paper in order that it might be better sustained. She asked him whether *she* might choose the subject and named the *province of woman*: he said yes, he would be glad to have such pieces to publish. Just at this time the Pastoral Letter came out, and Mary requested us to write something every week about *Woman* for the Spectator. We consulted together and viewed this unexpected opportunity of throwing our views before the public as providential. As I was writing to C. E. B[eecher], S. M. G. undertook it and as this paper was not an abolition paper we could not see any impropriety in embracing this opening. These letters have not been the means of *arousing* the public attention to the subject of Womans rights, it was the Pastoral Letter which did the mischief. The ministers seemed panic struck at once and commenced a most violent attack upon us. I do not say *absurd* for in truth if it can be fairly established that women *can lecture*, then why may they not preach and if *they* can preach, then woe! woe be unto that Clerical Domination which now rules the world under the various names of Gen'l Assemblies, Congregational Associations, etc. *This Letter* then roused the attention of the whole country to enquire what *right* we had to open our mouths for the dumb; the people were continually told "it is a *shame* for a *woman* to speak in the churches." Paul suffered not a *woman* to *teach* but commanded *her* to be in silence. The pulpit is too *sacred a place* for *woman's* foot etc. Now my dear brothers *this invasion of our rights* was just such an attack upon *us,* as that made upon Abolitionists generally when they were told a few years ago that *they had no right* to discuss the subject of Slavery. Did *you* take no notice of this assertion? Why no! With one heart and one voice you said, *We* will settle *this right before* we go one step further. *The time* to assert a right is *the* time when *that* right is denied. *We must establish this right* for if we do not, it will be impossible for *us* to *go on with the work of Emancipation.* But you will say that notwithstand[ing] the denial of your right you still had crowded audiences—*curiosity,* it was a new thing under the sun to see a *woman* occupy the place of a lecturer and the people were very anxious to *hear* and *see* for themselves: but you certainly *must* know that the leaven which the ministers are so assiduously working into the minds of the people *must* take effect in process of time, and *will close every church to us,* if we give the community no reasons to counteract the sophistry of priests and levities. In this State particularly there is an utter ignorance on the subject. Some few noble minds bursting thro' the trammels of educational prejudice FEEL that woman does stand on the same platform of human rights with man, but even these cannot

sustain their ground by argument, and as soon as they open their lips to assert her *rights,* their opponents throw perverted scripture into their faces and call O yea, clamor for *proof,* proof, PROOF! and this *they cannot* give and are beaten off the field in disgrace. Now we are confident that there are scores of such minds panting after light on this subject: "the children *ask* bread and no MAN give it unto them". There is an eagerness to understand our views. Now is it wrong to give those views in a series of letters in a paper NOT devoted to Abolition?

And can you not see that women *could* do, and *would* do a hundred times more for the slave if she were not fettered? Why! we are gravely told that we are out of our sphere even when we circulate petitions; out of our "appropriate sphere" when we speak to women only; and out of them when we *sing* in the churches. Silence is *our* province, submission *our* duty. If then we "give *no reason* for the hope that is in us", that we have *equal rights* with our brethren, how can we expect to be permitted *much longer to exercise those rights?* IF I know my own heart, I am NOT actuated by any selfish considerations (but I do sincerely thank our dear brother J. G. W[hittier] for the suggestion) but we are actuated by the full conviction that if we are to do any good in the Anti Slavery cause, our *right* to labor in it *must* be firmly established; *not* on the ground of Quakerism, but on the only firm bases of human rights, the Bible. Indeed I contend brethren that *this* is not *Quaker* doctrine, it is no more like *their* doctrine on Women than our Anti Slavery is like their Abolition, just about the same difference. I will explain myself. Women are regarded as equal to men on the ground of *spiritual gifts, not* on the broad ground of *humanity.* Woman may *preach*; this is a *gift*; but woman must *not* make the discipline by which *she herself* is to be governed. O that you were here that we might have a good long, *long* talk over matters and things, then I could explain myself far better. And I think we could convince you that *we* cannot push Abolitionism forward with all our might *until* we take up the stumbling block out of the road. We cannot see with brother Weld in this matter. We acknowledge the excellence of his reasons for urging us to labor in this cause of the Slave, our being Southerners, etc., but then we say how can we expect to be able to hold meetings much longer when people are so diligently taught to *despise us* for thus stepping out of the sphere of woman! Look at this instance: after we had left Groton the *Abolition* minister there, at a Lyceum meeting poured out his sarcasm and ridicule upon our heads and among other things said, he would as soon be caught robbing a hen roost as encouraging a woman to lecture. Now brethren if the leaders of the people thus speak of our labors, *how long* will we be allowed to prosecute them? Answer me this question. You may depend upon it, tho' to meet *this* question *may appear* to be turning out of our road, that *it is not*. IT IS NOT: we *must* meet it, and meet it *now* and meet it like *women* in the fear of the Lord. Why the language of the priests and levites to us women is that of Davids brother to him. "Why camest thou down hither? and with whom has thou left those few sheep in the wilderness? I know thy pride and the naughtiness of thy heart; for thou art come down that thou mightest see the battle." They utterly deny *our right* to interfere with this or any other moral reform except in the particular way *they* choose to mark out for us to walk in. If we dare to stand upright and do our duty according to the dictates of *our own* consciences, why then we are compared to Fanny Wright and so on. Why, my dear brothers can you not see the deep laid scheme of the clergy against us as lecturers? They know full well that if they can persuade the people it is a *shame* for us to speak in public, and that every time we open our mouths for the dumb we are breaking a divine command, that even if we spoke with the tongues of *men* or of angels, we should have *no hearers*. They are springing a deep mine beneath our feet, and we shall *very* soon be compelled to retreat for we shall have *no* ground to stand on. If we surrender the right to *speak* to the public this year, we must surrender the right to petition next year and the right to *write* the year after and so on. What *then* can *woman* do for the slave when she is herself under the feet of man and shamed into *silence?* Now we entreat *you* to weigh candidly the *whole subject*, and then we are sure you will see, this is no more than an abandonment of our first love than the effort made by Anti Slavery men to establish the *right* of free discussion.

With regard to brother Welds ultraism on the subject of marriage, he is quite mistaken if he fancies he has got far *ahead of us* in the human rights reform. We do *not* think his doctrine at all shocking: it is *altogether right*. But I am afraid I am *too proud* ever to exercise the right. The fact is we are living in such an artificial state of society that there are some things about which we dare not speak out, or act out the most natural and best feelings of our hearts. O! *when* shall we be "delivered from the *bondage of corruption* into the glorious liberty of the sons of God"! By the bye it will be very important to establish this right, for the men of Mass. stoutly declare that women who hold such sentiments of *equality* can never expect to be courted. They seem to hold out this as a kind of threat to deter us from asserting our rights, not *knowing whereunto this will grow*. But jesting is inconvenient says the Apostle: to business then.

Anti Slavery men are trying very hard to separate what God hath joined together. I fully believe that so far from keeping different moral reformations entirely distinct that no such attempt can ever be successful. They are bound together in a circle like the sciences; they blend with each other like the colors of the rain bow; they are the parts only of our glorious whole and that whole is Christianity, pure *practical* christianity. The fact is *I* believe—but dont be alarmed, for it is only *I*—that Men and Women will have to go out on their own responsibility, just like the prophets of old and declare the *whole* counsel of God to the people. The whole Church Government must come down, the clergy stand right in the way of reform, and I do not know but this stumbling block too must be removed *before* Slavery can be abolished, for the system is supported by *them*; it could not exist without the Church as it is called. This grand principle must be mooted, discussed and established viz. The Ministers of the Gospel are the successors of the *prophets*, not of the *priests*, the latter were types of the great eternal high priest of his Church; they were struck dumb as soon as the birth of his forerunner was announced. Zacharias could *not speak unto* the people after he had seen the vision in the temple. The Church is built *not* upon the priests at all but upon the *prophets* and *apostles*, Jesus Christ being the chief corner stone. This develops three important inferences: 1. True ministers are called like Elisha from the plough and Amos from gathering sycamore fruit, Matthew from the receipt of custom and Peter and John from their fishing nets. 2. As prophets *never were paid*, so ministers ought not to be. 3. As there were *prophetesses* as well as prophets, so there *ought* to be now *female* as well as male ministers. Just let this one principle be established and what will become of the power and sacredness of the pastoral office? Is brother Weld frightened at *my ultraism?* Please write to us soon and let us know what you think after reflecting on this letter. We are now at S. Philbricks and will we expect be here two weeks more lecturing in the neighboring towns. May the Lord bless you my dear brothers is the prayer of your sister in Jesus

A.E.G.

We never mention women's rights in our *lectures* except so far as is necessary to urge them to meet their responsibilities. We speak of their *responsibilities* and leave *them* to *infer* their *rights*. I could cross this letter all over but must not encroach on your time.

I should not be at all surprised if the public demanded of us "by what authority doest thou this thing", and if we had to lecture on this subject specifically and call upon the men "to show cause if any they had" why *women* should not open their mouths for the dumb.

I wrote to T.D.W. from Groton and left the letter to go by a private opportunity. Did he receive it?

SARAH GRIMKÉ

Letters on the Equality of the Sexes (1837)

First Letter: The Original Equality of Woman

Amesbury, 7th Mo., 11th, 1837

My Dear Friend,

In attempting to comply with thy request to give my views on the Province of Woman, I feel that I am venturing on nearly untrodden ground, and that I shall advance arguments in opposition to a corrupt public opinion, and to the perverted interpretation of Holy Writ, which has so universally obtained. But I am in search of truth; and no obstacle shall prevent my prosecuting that search, because I believe the welfare of the world will be materially advanced by every new discovery we make of the designs of Jehovah in the creation of woman. It is impossible that we can answer the purpose of our being, unless we understand that purpose. It is impossible that we should fulfill our duties, unless we comprehend them or live up to our privileges, unless we know what they are.

In examining this important subject, I shall depend solely on the Bible to designate the sphere of woman, because I believe almost every thing that has been written on this subject, has been the result of a misconception of the simple truths revealed in the Scriptures, in consequence of the false translation of many passages of Holy Writ. My mind is entirely delivered from the superstitious reverence which is attached to the English version of the Bible. King James's translators certainly were not inspired. I therefore claim the original as my standard, *believing that to have been inspired,* and I also claim to judge for myself what is the meaning of the inspired writers, because I believe it to be the solemn duty of every individual to search the Scriptures for themselves, with the aid of the Holy Spirit, and not be governed by the views of any man, or set of men.

We must first view woman at the period of her creation. "And God said, Let us make man in our own image, after our likeness; and let them have dominion over the fish of the sea, and over the fowl of the air, and over the cattle, and over all the earth. So God created man in his own image, in the image

points to the creation of man

of God created he him, male and female, created he them." [Gen. 1:26–27]. In all this sublime description of the creation of man, (which is a generic term including man and woman), there is not one particle of difference intimated as existing between them. They were both made in the image of God; dominion was given to both over every other creature, but not over each other. Created in perfect equality, they were expected to exercise the vicegerence intrusted to them by their Maker, in harmony and love.

Let us pass on now to the recapitulation of the creation of man—"The Lord God formed man of the dust of the ground, and breathed into his nostrils the breath of life; and man became a living soul. And the Lord God said, it is not good that man should be alone, I will make him an help meet for him" [Gen. 2: 7–18]. All creation swarmed with animated beings capable of natural affection, as we know they still are; it was not, therefore, merely to give man a creature susceptible of loving, obeying, and looking up to him, for all that the animals could do and did do. It was to give him a companion, in all respects his equal; one who was like himself a free agent, gifted with intellect and endowed with immortality; not a partaker merely of his animal gratifications, but able to enter into all his feelings as a moral and responsible being. If this had not been the case, how could she have been an help meet for him? I understand this as applying not only to the parties entering into the marriage contract, but to all men and women, because I believe God designed woman to be an help meet for man in every good and perfect work. She was a part of himself, as if Jehovah designed to make the oneness and identity of man and woman perfect and complete; and when the glorious work of their creation was finished, "the morning stars sand together, and all the sons of God shouted for joy" [Job 38:7].

This blissful condition was not long enjoyed by our first parents. Eve, it would seem from the history, was wandering alone amid the bowers of Paradise, when the serpent met with her. From her reply to Satan, it is evident that the command not to eat "of the tree that is in the midst of the garden," was given to both, although the term man was used when the prohibition was issued by God. "And the woman said unto the serpent, WE may eat of the fruit of the tress of the garden, but of the fruit of the tree which is in the midst of the garden, God hath said, YE shall not eat of it, neither shall YE touch it, lest YE die" [Gen. 3:3]. Here the woman was exposed to temptation from a being with whom she was unacquainted. She had been accustomed to associate with her believed partner, and to hold communion with God and with angels; but of satanic intelligence, she was in all probability entirely ignorant. Through the subtlety of the serpent, she was beguiled. And "when she saw that the tree was good for food, and that it was pleasant to the eyes, and a tree to be desired to make one wise, she took the fruit thereof and did eat" [Gen. 3:6].

We next find Adam involved in the same sin, not through the instrumentality of a supernatural agent, but through that of his equal, a being whom he must have known was liable to transgress the divine command, because he must have felt that he was himself a free agent, and that he was restrained from disobedience only by the exercise of faith and love towards his Creator. Had Adam tenderly reproved his wife, and endeavored to lead her to repentance instead of sharing in her guilt, I should be much more ready to accord to man that superiority which he claims; but as the facts stand disclosed by the sacred historian, it appears to me that to say the least, there was as much weakness exhibited by Adam as by Eve. They both fell from innocence, and consequently from happiness, but not from equality.

Let us next examine the conduct of this fallen pair, when Jehovah interrogated them respecting their fault, they both frankly confessed their guilt. "The man said, the woman whom thou gavest to be with me, she gave me of the tree and I did eat. And the woman said, the serpent beguiled me and I did eat" [Gen. 3:12]. And the Lord God said unto the woman, "Thou wilt be subject unto thy husband, he will rule over thee" [Gen 3:16]. That this is not allude to the subjection of woman to man is manifest, because the same mode of expression is used in speaking to Cain of Abel [Gen. 4:10–12]. The truth is that the curse, as it is termed, which was pronounced by Jehovah upon woman, is a simple prophecy. The Hebrew, like the French language, uses the same word to express shall and will. Our translators having been accustomed to exercise lordship over their wives, and seeing only through the medium of a perverted judgment, very naturally, though I think not very learnedly or very kindly, translated it *shall* instead of *will*, and thus converted a prediction to Eve into a command to Adam; for observe, it is addressed to the woman and not to the man. The consequence of the fall was an immediate struggle for dominion, and Jehovah foretold which would gain the ascendancy; but as he created them in his image, as that image manifestly was not lost by the fall, because it is urged in Gen. 9:6, as an argument why the life of man should not be taken by his fellow man, there is no reason to suppose that sin produced any distinction between them as moral, intellectual and responsible beings. Man might just as well have endeavored by hard labor to fulfil [sic] the prophecy, thorns and thistles will the earth bring forth to thee, as to pretend to accomplish the other, "he will rule over thee," by asserting dominion over his wife.

> Authority usurped from God, not given.
> He gave him only over beast, flesh, and fowl,
> Dominion absolute: that right he holds
> By God's donation: but man o'er woman
> He made not Lord, such title to himself
> Reserving, human left from human free.

Here then I plant myself. God created us equal;—he created us free agents;—he is our Lawgiver, our King, and our Judge, and to him alone is woman bound to be in subjection, and to him alone is she accountable for the use of those talents with which her Heavenly Father has entrusted her. One is her Master, even Christ.

Thine for the oppressed in the
bonds of womanhood,

Sarah M. Grimké

Second Letter: Women Subject Only to God

[. . .] Notwithstanding what has been urged, woman I am aware stands charged to the present day with having brought sin into the world. I shall not repel the charge by any counter assertions, although, as was before hinted, Adam's ready acquiescence with his wife's proposal, does not savor much of that

superiority *in strength of mind*, which is arrogated by man. Even admitting that Eve was the greater sinner, it seems to me man might be satisfied with the dominion he has claimed and exercised for nearly six thousand years, and that more true nobility would be manifested by endeavoring to raise the fallen and invigorate the weak, than by keeping woman in subjection. But I ask no favors for my sex. I surrender not our claim to equality. All I ask of our brethren, is that they will take their fee from off our necks, and permit us to stand upright on that ground which God designed us to occupy. If he has not given us the rights which have, as I conceive, been wrested from us, we shall soon give evidence of our inferiority, and shrink back into that obscurity, which the high souled magnanimity of man has assigned us as our appropriate sphere.

As I am unable to learn from sacred writ when woman was deprived by God of her equality with man, I shall touch upon a few points in the Scriptures, which demonstrate that no supremacy was granted to man. When God destroyed the world, except Noah and his family, by the deluge, he renewed the grant formerly made to man, and again gave him dominion upon the earth, and over all the fishes of the sea; into his hands they were delivered. But was woman, bearing the image of her God, placed under the dominion of her fellow man? Never! Jehovah could not surrender his authority to govern his own immortal creatures into the hands of a being, whom he knew, and whom his whole history proved, to be unworthy of a trust so sacred and important. God could not do it, because it is a direct contravention of his law, "Thou shalt worship the Lord thy God, and *him only* shalt thou serve" [Mt. 4:10]. If Jehovah had appointed man as the guardian, or teacher of woman, he would certainly have given some intimation of this surrender of his own prerogative. But so far from it, we find the commands of God invariably the same to man and woman; and not the slightest intimation is given in a single passage of the Bible, that God designed to point woman to man as her instructor. The tenor of his language always is, "Look unto ME, and be ye saved, all the ends of the earth, for I am God, and there is none else" [Isa. 45:22].

The lust of dominion was probably the first effect of the fall; and as there was no other intelligent being over whom to exercise it, woman was the first victim of this unhallowed passion. We afterwards see it exhibited by Cain in the murder of his brother, by Nimrod in his becoming a mighty hunter of men, and setting up a kingdom over which to reign. Here we see the origin of that Upas of slavery, which sprang up immediately after the fall, and has spread its pestilential branches over the whole face of the known world. All history attests that man has subjected woman to his will, used her as a means to promote his selfish gratification, to minister to his sensual pleasures, to be instrumental in promoting his comfort; but never has he desired to elevate her to that rank she was created to fill. He has done all he could do to debase and enslave her mind; and now he looks triumphantly on the ruin he has wrought, and says, the being he has thus deeply injured is his inferior.

Woman has been placed by John Quincy Adams, side by side with the slave, whilst he was contending for the right side of petition. I thank him for ranking us with the oppressed; for I shall not find it difficult to show, that in all ages and countries, not even excepting enlightened republican America, woman has more or less been made a *means* to promote the welfare of man, without due regard to her own happiness, and the glory of God as the end of her creation.

During the *patriarchal* ages, we find men and women engaged in the same employments—Abraham and Sarah both assisted in preparing the food which was to be set before the three men, who visited them in the plains of Mamre [Gen. 18]; but although their occupations were similar, Sarah was not permitted to enjoy the society of the holy visitant; and as we learn from Peter, that she "obeyed Abraham, calling his Lord" [1 Peter 3:6], we may presume he exercised dominion over her. We shall pass on now to Rebecca [Gen. 24]. In her history, we find another striking illustration of the low estimation in which woman was held. Eleazur is sent to seek a wife for Isaac. He finds Rebecca going down to the well to fill her pitcher. He accosts her; and she replies with all humility, "Drink, my lord." How does he endeavor to gain her favor and confidence? Does he approach her as a dignified creature, whom he was about to invite to fill an important station in his master's family, as the wife of his only son? No. He offered incense to her vanity, and "he took a golden ear-ring of half a shekel weight, and two bracelets for her hands of ten shekels weight of gold," and gave them to Rebecca.

The cupidity of man soon led him to regard woman as property, and hence we find them sold to those, who wished to marry them, as far as appears, without any regard to those sacred rights which belong to woman, as well as to man in the choice of a companion. That women were a profitable kind of property, we may gather from the description of a virtuous woman in the last chapter of Proverbs [Prov. 31:10–31]. To work willingly with her hands, to open her hands to the poor, to clothe herself with silk and purple, to look well to her household, to make fine linen and sell it, to deliver girdles to the merchant, and not to eat the bread of idleness, seems to have constituted in the view of Solomon, the perfection of a woman's character and achievements. "The spirit of that age was not favorable to intellectual improvement; but as there were wise men who formed exceptions to the general ignorance, and were destined to guide the world into more advanced states, so there was a corresponding proportion of wise women; and among the Jews, as well as other nations, we find a strong tendency to believe that women were in more immediate connection with heaven than men." L. M. Child's [Lydia Marie Child] Con. of Woman. If there be any truth in this tradition, I am at a loss to imagine in what the superiority of man consists.

Thine in the bonds of womanhood,

Sarah M. Grimké

Twelfth Letter: Legal Disabilities of Women

Concord, 9th Mo., 6th, 1837

My Dear Sister,

There are few things which present greater obstacles to the improvement and elevation of woman to her appropriate sphere of usefulness and duty, than the laws which have been enacted to destroy her independence, and crush her individuality; laws which, although they are framed for her government, she has had no voice in establishing, and which rob her of some of her *essential rights*. Woman has no political existence. With the single exception of presenting a petition to the legislative body, she is a cipher in the nation; or, if not actually so in representative

↗ representatives

governments, she is only counted, like the slaves of the South, to swell the numbers of law-makers who form decrees for her government, with little reference to her benefit, except so far as her good may promote their own. I am not sufficiently acquainted with the laws respecting women on the continent of Europe, to say anything about them. But Prof. Follen, in his essay on "The Cause of Freedom in our Country," says, "Woman, though fully possessed of that rational and moral nature which is the foundation of all rights, enjoys amongst us fewer legal rights than under the civil law of continental Europe." I shall confine myself to the laws of our country. These laws bear with peculiar rigor on married women. Blackstone, in the chapter entitled "Of husband and wife," says:—

> By marriage, the husband and wife are one person in law; that is, *the very being, or legal existence of the woman* is suspended during the marriage, or at least is incorporated and consolidated into that of the husband under whose wing, protection and cover she performs everything. For this reason, a man cannot grant anything to his wife, or enter into covenant with her; for the grant would be to suppose her separate existence, and to covenant with her would be to covenant with himself; and therefore it is also generally true, that all compacts made between husband and wife when single, are voided by the intermarriage. A woman indeed may be attorney for her husband, but that implies no separation from, but is rather a representation of, her love.

Here now, the very being of a woman, like that of a slave, is absorbed in her master. All contracts made with her, like those made with slaves by their owners, are a mere nullity. Our kind defenders have legislated away almost all our legal rights, and in the true spirit of such injustice and oppressions, have kept us in ignorance of those very laws by which we are governed. They have persuaded us, that we have no rights to investigate the laws, and that, if we did, we could not comprehend them; they alone are capable of understanding the mysteries of Blackstone, &c. But they are not backward to make us feel the practical operation of their power over our actions.

The husband is bound to provide his wife with necessaries by law, as much as himself; and if she contracts debts for them, he is obligated to pay for them; but for anything besides necessaries, he is not chargeable.

Yet a man may spend the property he has acquired by marriage at the ale-house, the gambling table, or in any other way that he pleases. Many instances of this kind have come to my knowledge; and women, who have brought their husbands handsome fortunes, have been left, in consequence of the wasteful and dissolute habits of their husbands, in straitened circumstances, and compelled to toil for the support of their families.

If the wife be indebted before marriage, the husband is bound afterwards to pay the debt; for he has adopted her and her circumstances together.

The wife's property is, I believe, equally liable for her husband's debts contracted before marriage.

If the wife is injured in her person or property, she can bring no action for redress without her husband's concurrence, and his name as well as her own: neither can she be sued, without making her husband a defendant.

This law that "a wife can bring no action," etc., is similar to the law respecting slaves. "A slave cannot bring a suit against his master, or any other person, for an injury—his master, must bring it." So if any damages are recovered for an injury committed on a wife, the husband pockets it; in the case of the slave, the master does the same.

In criminal prosecutions, the wife may be indicted and punished separately, unless there be evidence of coercion from the fact that the offense was committed in the presence, or by the command of her husband. A wife is excused from punishment for theft committed in the presence, or by the command of her husband.

It would be difficult to frame a law better calculated to destroy the responsibility of woman as a moral being, or a free agent. Her husband is supposed to possess unlimited control over her; and if she can offer the flimsy excuse that he bade her steal, she may break the eighth commandment with impunity, as far as human laws are concerned.

Our law, in general, considers man and wife as one person; yet there are some instances in which she is separately considered, as inferior to him and acting by his compulsion. Therefore, all deeds executed, and are done by her during her overture (i.e.,

Parallels between women's + slaves' struggles

marriage,) are void, except it be a fine, or like matter of record, in which case she must be solely and secretly examined, to learn if her act be voluntary.

Such a law speaks volumes of the abuse of that power which men have vested in their own hands. Still the private examination of a wife, to know whether she accedes to the disposition of property made by her husband is, in most cases, a mere form; a wife dares not do what will be disagreeable to one who is, in his own estimation, her superior, and who makes her feel, in the privacy of domestic life, that she has thwarted him. With respect to the nullity of deeds or acts done by a wife, I will mention one circumstance. A respectable woman borrowed of a female friend a sum of money to relieve her son from some distressing pecuniary embarrassment. Her husband was from home, and she assured the lender, that as soon as he returned, he would gratefully discharge the debt. She gave her note, and the lender, entirely ignorant of the law that a man is not obliged to discharge such a debt, actually borrowed the money, and lent it to the distressed and weeping mother. The father returned home, refused to pay the debt, and the person who had loaned the money was obligated to pay both principal and interest to the friend who lent it to her. Women should certainly know the laws by which they are governed, and from which they frequently suffer; yet they are kept in ignorance, nearly as profound, of their legal rights, and of the legislative enactments which are to regulate their actions, as slaves.

The husband, by the old law, might give his wife moderate correction, as he is to answer for her misbehavior. The law thought it reasonable to entrust him with this power of restraining her by domestic chastisement. The courts of law will still permit a husband to restrain a wife of her liberty, in case of any gross misbehavior.

What a mortifying proof this law affords, of the estimation in which woman is held! She is placed completely in the hands of a being subject like herself to the outbursts of passion, and therefore unworthy to be trusted with power. Perhaps I may be told respecting this law, that it is a dead letter, as I am sometimes told about the slave laws; but this is not true in either case. The slaveholder does kill his slave by moderate correction, as the law allows; and many a husband, among the poor, exercises the right given him by the law, of degrading women by personal chastisement. And among the higher ranks, if actual imprisonment is not resorted to, women are not unfrequently restrained of the liberty of going to places of worship by irreligious husbands, and of doing many other things about which, as moral and responsible beings, *they* should be the *sole* judges. Such laws remind me of the reply of some little girls at a children's meeting held recently at Ipswich. The lecturer told them that god had created four order of beings with which he had made us acquainted through the Bible. The first was angels, the second was man, the third beasts; and now, children, what is the fourth? After a pause, several girls replied, "WOMEN." [. . .]

CATHARINE A. BEECHER

Treatise on Domestic Economy (1841)

Chapter Three

Having peculiar responsibilities of American women, and the peculiar embarrassments which they are called to encounter, the following suggestions are offered, as remedies for their difficulties.

In the first place, the physical and domestic education of daughters should occupy the principal attention of mothers, in childhood; and the stimulation of the intellect should be very much reduced. As a general rule, daughters should not be sent to school before they are six years old; and, when they are sent, far more attention should be paid to their physical development, than is usually done. They should never be confined, at any employment, more than an hour at a time; and this confinement should be followed by sports in the open air. Such accommodations should be secured, that, at all seasons, and in all weathers, the teacher can every half hour send out a portion of her school, for sports. And still more care should be given to preserve pure air in the schoolroom. The close stoves, crowded condition, and poisonous air, of most schoolrooms, act as constant drains on the health and strength of young children. In addition to this, much less time should be given to school, and much more to domestic employments, especially in the wealthier classes. A little girl may begin, at five or six years of age, to assist her mother; and, if properly trained, by the time she is ten, she can render essential aid. From this time, until she is fourteen or fifteen, it should be the principal object of her education to secure a strong and healthy constitution, and a thorough practical knowledge of all kinds of domestic employments. During this period, though some attention ought to be paid to intellectual culture, it ought to be made altogether secondary in importance; and such a measure of study and intellectual excitement, as is now demanded in our best female seminaries, ought never to be allowed, until a young lady has passed the most critical period of her youth, and has a vigorous and healthful constitution fully established. The plan might be adopted, of having schools for young girls kept only in the afternoon; that their mornings might be occupied in domestic exercise, without interfering with school employments. Where a proper supply of domestic exercise cannot be afforded, the cultivation of flowers and fruits might be resorted to, as a delightful and unfailing promotive of pleasure and health.

And it is to that class of mothers, who have the best means of securing hired service, and who are the most tempted to allow their daughters to grow up with inactive habits, that their Country and the world must look for a reformation, in this respect. Whatever ladies in the wealthier classes decide shall be fashionable, will be followed by all the rest; but, while they persist in the aristocratic habits, now so common, and bring up their daughters to feel as if labor was degrading and unbecoming, the evils pointed out will never find a remedy. It is, therefore, the peculiar duty, of ladies, who have wealth, to set a proper example, in this particular, and, make it their first aim to secure a strong and healthful constitution for their daughters, by active domestic employments. All the sweeping, dusting, care of furniture and beds the clear starching, and the nice cooking, should be done by the daughters of a family, and not by hired servants. It may cost the mother more care, and she may find it needful to hire a person for the express purpose of instructing and superintending her daughters, in these employments but it should be regarded as indispensable to be secured either by the mother's agency, or by a substitute.

It is in this point of view, that the dearth of good domestics in this Country may, in its results, prove a substantial blessing. If all housekeepers, who have the means, could secure good servants, there would be little hope that so important a revolution, in the domestic customs of the wealthy classes, could be effected. And so great is the natural indolence of mankind, that the amount of exercise, needful for health, will never be secured by those who are led to it through no necessity, but merely from rational considerations. Yet the pressure of domestic troubles, from the want of good domestics, has already determined many a mother, in the wealthy classes to train her daughters to aid her in domestic service; and thus necessity is compelling mothers to do what abstract principles of expediency could never secure.

A second method of promoting the same object, is, to raise the science and practice of Domestic Economy to its appropriate place, as a regular study in female seminaries. [. . .] But it is to the mothers of our Country, that the community must look for this change. It cannot be expected, that teachers, who have their attention chiefly absorbed by the intellectual and moral interests of their pupils, should properly realize the importance of this department of education. But if mothers generally become convinced of this, their judgement and wishes will meet the respectful consideration they deserve, and the object will be accomplished.

The third method of securing a remedy for the evils pointed out, is, the endowment of female institutions, under the care of suitable trustees, who shall secure a proper course of education. The importance of this measure cannot be realized by those, who have not turned their attention to this subject; and for such, the following considerations are presented.

The endowment of colleges, and of law, medical, and divinity, schools, for the other sex, is designed to secure a thorough and proper education, for those who have the most important duties of society to perform. The men who are to, expound the laws, the men who have the care of the public health, and the men who are to communicate religious instruction, should have well-disciplined and well-informed minds; and it is mainly for this object that collegiate and professional institutions are established. Liberal and wealthy individuals contribute funds, and the legislatures of the States also lend assistance, so that every State in this Nation has from one to twenty such endowed institutions, supplied with buildings, apparatus, a library, and a faculty of learned men to carry forward a superior course of instruction. And the use of all these advantages is secured, in many cases, at an expense, no greater than is required to send a boy to a common school and pay his board there. No private school could offer these advantages, without charging such a sum, as would forbid all but the rich from securing its benefits. By furnishing such superior advantages, on low terms, multitudes are properly educated, who would otherwise remain in ignorance; and thus the professions are supplied, by men properly qualified for them.

Were there no such institutions, and no regular and appropriate course of study demanded for admission to the bar, the pulpit and to medical practice, the education of most professional men would be desultory, imperfect, and deficient. Parents and children would regulate the course of study according to their own crude notions; and, instead of having institutions which, agree in carrying on a similar course of study, each school would have its own peculiar system, and compete and conflict with every other. Meantime the public would have no means of deciding which was best nor any opportunity for learning when a professional man was properly qualified for his duties. But as it is, the diploma of a college, and the license of an appointed body of judges, must both be secured, before a young man feels that he has entered the most promising path to success in his profession.

Our Country, then, is, most abundantly supplied with endowed institutions, which secure a liberal education, on such low terms as make them accessible to all classes, and in which the interests of education are watched over, sustained, and made permanent, by an appropriate board of trustees.

But are not the most responsible of all duties committed to the charge of woman? Is it not her profession to take care of mind, body, and soul? and that, too, at the most critical of all periods of existence? And is it not as much a matter of public concern, that she should be properly qualified for her duties, as that ministers, lawyers, and physicians, should be prepared for theirs? And is it not as important, to endow institutions which shall make a superior education accessible to all classes for females, as for the other sex? And is it not equally important, that institutions for females be under the supervision of intelligent and responsible trustees, whose duty it shall be to secure a uniform and appropriate education for one sex as much as for the other? It would seem as if every mind must accord an affirmative reply, as soon as the matter is fairly considered.

As the education of females is now conducted, any man or woman who pleases, can establish a female seminary, and secure recommendations which will attract pupils. But whose business is it to see that these young females are not huddled into crowded rooms? or that they do not sleep in ill-ventilated chambers? or that they have healthful food? or that they have the requisite amount of fresh air and exercise? or that they pursue an appropriate and systematic course of study? or that their manners, principles, and morals, are properly regulated? Parents either have not the means, or else are not qualified to judge; or, if they are furnished with means and capacity, they are often restricted to a choice of the best school within reach, even when it is known to be exceedingly objectionable.

If the writer were to disclose all that can truly be told of boarding school life, and its influence on health, manners, disposition, intellect, and morals, the disclosure would both astonish and shock every rational mind. And yet she believes that such institutions are far better managed in this Country, than in any other; and that the number of those, which are subject to imputations in these respects, is much less than could reasonably be expected. But it is most surely the case, that much remains to be done, in order to supply such institutions as are needed for the proper education of American women. [. . .]

THE DECLARATION OF SENTIMENTS, SENECA FALLS (1848)

(margin note: Dec. of Indep. → same language)

When, in the course of human events, it becomes necessary for one portion of the family of man to assume among the people of the earth a position different from that which they have hitherto occupied, but one to which the laws of nature and of nature's God entitle them, a decent respect to the opinions of mankind requires that they should declare the causes that impel them to such a course.

We hold these truths to be self-evident: that all men and women are created equal; that they are endowed by their Creator with certain inalienable rights; that among these are life, liberty, and the pursuit of happiness; that to secure these rights governments are instituted, deriving their just powers from the consent of the governed. Whenever any form of government becomes destructive of these ends, it is the right of those who suffer from it to refuse allegiance to it, and to insist upon the institution of a new government, laying its foundation on such principles, and organizing its powers in such form, as to them shall seem most likely to effect their safety and happiness. Prudence, indeed, will dictate that governments long established should not be changed for light and transient causes; and accordingly all experience hath shown that mankind are more disposed to suffer, while evils are sufferable, than to right themselves by abolishing the forms to which they are accustomed. But when a long train of abuses and usurpations, pursuing invariably the same object, evinces a design to reduce them under absolute despotism, it is their duty to throw off such government, and to provide new guards for their future security. Such has been the patient sufferance of the women under this government, and such is now the necessity which constrains them to demand the equal station to which they are entitled.

The history of mankind is a history of repeated injuries and usurpations on the part of man toward woman, having in direct object the establishment of an absolute tyranny over her. To prove this, let facts be submitted to a candid world.

He has never permitted her to exercise her inalienable right to the elective franchise.

He has compelled her to submit to laws, in the formation of which she had no voice.

He has withheld from her rights which are given to the most ignorant and degraded men—both natives and foreigners.

Having deprived her of this first right of a citizen, the elective franchise, thereby leaving her without representation in the halls of legislation, he has oppressed her on all sides.

He has made her, if married, in the eye of the law, civilly dead.

He has taken from her all right in property, even to the wages she earns.

He has made her, morally, an irresponsible being, as she can commit many crimes with impunity, provided they be done in the presence of her husband. In the covenant of marriage, she is compelled to promise obedience to her husband, he becoming, to all intents and purposes, her master—the law giving him power to deprive her of her liberty, and to administer chastisement.

He has so framed the laws of divorce, as to what shall be the proper causes, and in case of separation, to whom the guardianship of the children shall be given, as to be wholly regardless of the happiness of women—the law, in all cases, going upon a false supposition of the supremacy of man, and giving all power into his hands.

After depriving her of all rights as a married woman, if single, and the owner of property, he has taxed her to support a government which recognizes her only when her property can be made profitable to it.

He has monopolized nearly all the profitable employments, and from those she is permitted to follow, she receives but a scanty remuneration. He closes against her all the avenues to wealth and distinction which he considers most honorable to himself. As a teacher of theology, medicine, or law, she is not known.

He has denied her the facilities for obtaining a thorough education, all colleges being closed against her.

He allows her in church, as well as state, but a subordinate position, claiming apostolic authority for her exclusion from the ministry, and, with some exceptions, from any public participation in the affairs of the church.

He has created a false public sentiment by giving to the world a different code of morals for men and women, by which moral delinquencies which exclude women from society, are not only tolerated, but deemed of little account in man.

He has usurped the prerogative of Jehovah himself, claiming it as his right to assign for her a sphere of action, when that belongs to her conscience and to her God.

He has endeavored, in every way that he could, to destroy her confidence in her own powers, to lessen her self-respect, and to make her willing to lead a dependent and abject life.

Now, in view of this entire disfranchisement of one-half the people of this country, their social and religious degradation—in view of the unjust laws above mentioned, and because women do feel themselves aggrieved, oppressed, and fraudulently deprived of their most sacred rights, we insist that they have immediate admission to all the rights and privileges which belong to them as citizens of the United States.

In entering upon the great work before us, we anticipate no small amount of misconception, misrepresentation, and ridicule; but we shall use every instrumentality within our power to effect our object. We shall employ agents, circulate tracts, petition the State and National legislatures, and endeavor to enlist the pulpit and the press in our behalf. We hope this Convention will be followed by a series of Conventions embracing every part of the country.

Resolutions

Whereas, the great precept of nature is conceded to be that "man shall pursue his own true and substantial happiness." Blackstone in his Commentaries remarks that this law of nature, being coeval with mankind and dictated by God himself, is, of course, superior in obligation to any other. It is binding over all the globe, in all countries and at all times; no human laws are of any validity if contrary to this, and such of them as are valid derive all their force, and all their validity, and all their authority, mediately and immediately, from this original; therefore,

Resolved, that such laws as conflict, in any way, with the true and substantial happiness of woman, are contrary to the great precept of nature and of no validity, for this is "superior in obligation to any other."

Resolved, that all laws which prevent woman from occupying such a station in society as her conscience shall dictate, or which place her in a position inferior to that of man, are contrary to the great precept of nature and therefore of no force or authority.

Resolved, that woman is man's equal, was intended to be so by the Creator, and the highest good of the race demands that she should be recognized as such.

Resolved, that the women of this country ought to be enlightened in regard to the laws under which they live, that they may no longer publish their degradation by declaring themselves satisfied with their present position, nor their ignorance, by asserting that they have all the rights they want.

Resolved, that inasmuch as man, while claiming for himself intellectual superiority, does accord to woman moral superiority, it is preeminently his duty to encourage her to speak and teach, as she has an opportunity, in all religious assemblies.

Resolved, that the same amount of virtue, delicacy, and refinement of behavior that is required of woman in the social state also be required of man, and the same transgressions should be visited with equal severity on both man and woman.

Resolved, that the objection of indelicacy and impropriety, which is so often brought against woman when she addresses a public audience, comes with a very ill grace from those who encourage, by their attendance, her appearance on the stage, in the concert, or in feats of the circus.

Resolved, that woman has too long rested satisfied in the circumscribed limits which corrupt customs and a perverted application of the Scriptures have marked out for her, and that it is time she should move in the enlarged sphere which her great Creator has assigned her.

Resolved, that it is the duty of the women of this country to secure to themselves their sacred right to the elective franchise.

Resolved, that the equality of human rights results necessarily from the fact of the identity of the race in capabilities and responsibilities.

Resolved, that the speedy success of our cause depends upon the zealous and untiring efforts of both men and women, for the overthrow of the monopoly of the pulpit, and for the securing to woman an equal participation with men in the various trades, professions, and commerce.

Resolved, therefore, that, being invested by the Creator with the same capabilities and same consciousness of responsibility for their exercise, it is demonstrably the right and duty of woman, equally with man, to promote every righteous cause by every righteous means; and especially in regard to the great subjects of morals and religion, it is self-evidently her right to participate with her brother in teaching them, both in private and in public, by writing and by speaking, by any instrumentalities proper to be used, and in any assemblies proper to be held; and this being a self-evident truth growing out of the divinely implanted principles of human nature, any custom or authority adverse to it, whether modern or wearing the hoary sanction of antiquity, is to be regarded as a self-evident falsehood, and at war with mankind.

ELIZABETH CADY STANTON

Address to the New York State Legislature (1854)

To the Legislature of the State of New York:

"The thinking minds of all nations call for change. There is a deep-lying struggle in the whole fabric of society; a boundless grinding collision of the New with the Old."

The tyrant, Custom, has been summoned before the bar of Common Sense. His Majesty no longer awes the multitude—his sceptre is broken—his crown is trampled in the dust—the sentence of death is pronounced upon him. All nations, ranks and classes have, in turn, questioned and repudiated his authority; and now, that the monster is chained and caged, timid woman, on tiptoe, comes to look him in the facet and to demand of her brave sires and sons, who have struck stout blows for liberty, if, in this change of dynasty, she, too, shall find relief.

Yes, gentlemen, in republican America, in the 19th century, we, the daughters of the revolutionary heroes of 1761, demand at your hands the redress of our grievances—a revision of your state constitution—a new code of laws. Permit us then, as briefly as possible, to call your attention to the legal disabilities under which we labor.

1st. Look at the position of woman as woman. It is not enough for us that by your laws we are permitted to live and breathe, to claim the necessaries of life from our legal protectors—to pay the penalty of our crimes; we demand the full recognition of all our rights as citizens of the Empire State. We are persons; native, free-born citizens; property-holders, tax-payers; yet are we denied the exercise of our right to the elective franchise. We support ourselves, and, in part, your schools, colleges, churches, your poor-houses, jails, prisons, the army, the navy, the whole machinery of government, and yet we have no voice in your councils. We have every qualification required by the constitution, necessary to the legal voter, but the one of sex. We are moral, virtuous and intelligent, and in all respects quite equal to the proud white man himself, and yet by your laws we are classed with idiots, lunatics, and negroes; and though we do not feel honored by the place assigned us, yet, in fact, our legal position is lower than that of either; for the negro can be raised to the dignity of a voter if he possess himself of $250; the lunatic can vote in his moments of sanity, and the idiot, too, if he be a male one, and not more than nine-tenths a fool; but we, who have guided great movements of charity, established missions, edited journals, published works on history, economy, and statistics; who have governed nations, led armies, filled the professor's chair, taught philosophy and mathematics to the savants of our age, discovered planets, piloted ships across the sea, are denied the most sacred rights of citizens, because, forsooth, we came not into this republic crowned with the dignity of manhood! Woman is theoretically absolved from all allegiance to the laws of the State. Sec. 1, Bill of Rights, 2 R.S., 301, says that no authority can, on any pretense whatever, be exercised over the citizens of this state but such as is or shall be derived from, and granted by, the people of this state.

Now, gentlemen, we would fain know by what authority you have disfranchised one-half the people of this state? You who have so boldly taken possession of the bulwarks of this republic, show us your credentials, and thus prove your exclusive right to govern, not only yourselves, but us. Judge Hurlbut, who has long occupied a high place at the bar in this state, and who recently retired with honor from the bench of the Supreme Court, in his profound work on human rights, has pronounced your present position rank usurpation. Can it be that here, where are acknowledged no royal blood, no apostolic descent, that you, who have declared that all men were created equal—that governments derive their just powers from the consent of the governed, would willingly build up an aristocracy that places the ignorant and vulgar above the educated and refined—the alien and the ditch-digger above the authors and poets of the day—an aristocracy that would raise the sons above the mothers that bore them? Would that the men who can sanction a constitution so opposed to the genius of this government, who can enact and execute laws so degrading to womankind, had sprung, Minerva-like, from the brains of their fathers, that the matrons of this republic need not blush to own their sons!

Woman's position, under our free institutions, is much lower than under the monarchy of England. "In England the idea of woman holding official station is not so strange as in the United States. The Countess of Pembroke, Dorset, and Montgomery held the office of hereditary sheriff of Westmoreland, and exercised it in person. At the assizes at Appleby, she sat with the judges on the bench. In a reported case, it is stated by counsel, and substantially assented to by the court, that a woman is capable of serving in almost all the offices of the kingdom, such as those of queen, marshal, great chamberlain and constable of England, the champion of England, commissioner of sewers, governor of work-house, sexton, keeper of the prison, of the gatehouse of the dean and chapter of Westminster, returning officer for members of parliament, and constable, the latter of which is in some respects judicial. The office of jailor is frequently exercised by a woman. In the United States a woman may administer on the effects of her deceased husband, and she has occasionally held a subordinate place in the post: office department. She has therefore a sort of postmortem, postmistress notoriety; but with the exception of handling letters of administration and letters mailed, she is the submissive creature of the old common law." True, the unmarried woman has a right to the property she inherits and the money she earns, but she is taxed without representation. And here again you place the negro, so unjustly degraded by you, in a superior position to your own wives and mothers; for colored males, if possessed of a certain amount of property and certain other qualifications, can vote, but if they do not have these qualifications they are not subject to direct taxation; wherein they have the advantage of woman, she being subject to taxation for whatever amount she may possess (Constitution of N.Y., Article 2, Sec. 2). But, say you, are not all women sufficiently represented by their fathers, husbands and brothers? Let your statute books answer the question.

Again we demand, in criminal cases, that most sacred of all rights, trial by a jury of our own peers. The establishment of trial by jury is of so early a date that its beginning is lost in antiquity; but the right of trial by a jury of one's own peers is a great, progressive step of advanced civilization. No rank of men have ever been satisfied with being tried by jurors higher or lower in the civil or political scale than themselves; for jealousy on the one hand, and contempt on the other, has ever effectually blinded the eyes of justice. Hence, all along the pages of history, we find the king, the noble, the peasant, the cardinal, the priest, the layman, each in turn protesting against the authority of the tribunal before which they were summoned to appear. Charles the First refused to recognize the competency of the tribunal which condemned him: For how, said he, can subjects judge a king? The stern descendants of our Pilgrim Fathers refused to answer for their crimes before an English Parliament. For how, said they, can a king judge rebels? And shall woman here consent to be tried by her liege lord, who has dubbed himself law-maker, judge, juror, and sheriff, too?—whose power, though sanctioned by Church and State, has no foundation in justice and equity, and is a bold assumption of our inalienable rights. In England a parliament-lord could challenge a jury where a knight was not empanelled [sic]; an alien could demand a jury composed half of his own country-men; or, in some special cases, juries were even con-stituted entirely of women. Having seen that man fails to do justice to woman in her best estate, to the virtuous, the noble, the true of our sex, should we trust to his tender mercies, the weak, the ignorant, the morally insane? It is not to be denied that the interests of man and woman in the present undevel-oped state of the race, and under the existing social arrangements, are and must be antagonistic. The nobleman cannot make just laws for the peasant; the slaveholder for the slave; neither can man make and execute just laws for woman; because in each case, the one in power fails to apply the immutable princi-ples of right to any grade but his own. Shall an erring woman be dragged before a bar of grim-visaged judges, lawyers, and jurors, there to be grossly ques-tioned in public on subjects which women scarce breathe in secret to one another? Shall the most sacred relations of life be called up and rudely scanned by men who, by their own admission, are so coarse that women could not meet them even at the polls without contamination? And yet shall she find there no woman's face or voice to pity and defend? Shall the frenzied mother who, to save herself and child from exposure and disgrace, ended the life that had but just begun, be dragged before such a tribu-nal to answer for her crime? How can man enter into the feelings of that mother? How can he judge of the mighty agonies of soul that impelled her to such an outrage of maternal instincts? How can he weigh the mountain of sorrow that crushed that mother's heart

when she wildly tossed her helpless babe into the cold waters of the midnight sea? Where is he who by false vows thus blasted this trusting woman? Had that helpless child no claims on his protection? Ah, he is freely abroad in the dignity of manhood, in the pulpit, on the bench, in the professor's chair. The imprisonment of his victim and the death of his child, detract not a tithe from his standing and com-placency. His peers made the law, and shall lawmak-ers lay nets for those of their own rank? Shall laws which come from the logical brain of man take cog-nizance of violence done to the moral and affectional nature which predominates, as is said, in woman? Statesmen of New York, whose daughters, guarded by your affection, and lapped amidst luxuries which your indulgence spreads, care more for their nodding plumes and velvet trains than for the statute laws by which their persons and properties are held—who, blinded by custom and prejudice to the degraded position which they and their sisters occupy in the civil scale, haughtily claim that they already have all rights they want, how, think ye, you would feel to see a daughter summoned for such a crime—and remember these daughters are but human—before such a tribunal? Would it not, in that hour, be some consolation to see that she was surrounded by the wise and virtuous of her own sex; by those who had known the depth of a mother's love and the misery of a lover's falsehood; to know that to these she could make her confession, and from them receive her sen-tence? If so then listen to our just demands and, make such a change in your laws as will secure to every woman tried in your courts, an impartial jury. At this moment among the hundreds of women who are shut up in prisons in this state, not one has enjoyed that most sacred of all rights—that right which you would die to defend for yourselves—trial by a jury of one's peers.

2d. Look at the position of woman as wife. Your laws relating to marriage—founded as they are on the old common law of England, a compound of bar-barous usages, but partially modified by progressive civilization—are in the open violation of our enlight-ened ideas of justice, and of the holiest feelings of our nature. If you take the highest view of marriage, as a Divine relation, which love alone can constitute and sanctify, then of course human legislation can only recognize it. Man can neither bind nor loose its ties, for that prerogative belongs to God alone, who makes man and woman, and the laws of attraction by which they are united. But if you regard marriage as a civil contract, then let it be subject to the same laws which control all other contracts. Do not make it a kind of half-human, half-divine institution, which you may build up but cannot regulate. Do not, by your special legislation for this one kind of contract, involve yourselves in the grossest absurdities and contradictions.

So long as by your laws no man can make a contract for a horse or piece of land until he is twenty-one years of age, and by which contract he is not bound if any deception has been practiced, or if the party contracting has not fulfilled his part of the agreement—so long as the parties in all mere civil contracts retain their identity and all the power and independence they had before contracting, with the full right to dissolve all partnerships and contracts for any reason, at the will and option of the parties themselves, upon what principle of civil jurisprudence do you permit the boy of fourteen and the girl of twelve, in violation of every natural law, to make a contract more momentous in importance than any other, and then hold them to it, come what may, the whole of their natural lives, in spite of disappointment, deception and misery? Then, too, the signing of this contract is instant civil death to one of the parties. The woman who but yesterday was sued on banded knee, who stood so high in the scale of being as to make an agreement on equal terms with a proud Saxon man, to-day has no civil existence, no social freedom. The wife who inherits no property holds about the same legal position that does the slave on the southern plantation. She can own nothing, sell nothing. She has no right even to the wages she earns; her person, her time, her services are the property of another. She cannot testify, in many cases, against her husband. She can get no redress for wrongs in her own name in any court of justice. She can neither sue nor be sued. She is not held morally responsible for any crime committed in the presence of her husband, so completely is her very existence supposed by the law to be merged in that of another. Think of it; your wives may be thieves, libelers, burglars, incendiaries, and for crimes like these they are not held amenable to the laws of the land, if they but commit them in your dread presence. For them, alas! there is no higher law than the will of man. Herein

behold the bloated conceit of these Petruchios of the law, who seem to say:

Nay, look not big, nor stamp, nor stare, nor fret, I will be master of what is mine own; She is my goods, my chattels; she is my house, My household stuff, my field, my barn, my horse, my ox, my ass, my anything; And here she stands, touch her whoever dare; I'll bring my action on the proudest he, That stops my way, in Padua.

How could man ever look thus on woman? She, at whose feet Socrates learned wisdom—she, who gave to the world a Saviour, and witnessed alike the adoration of the Magi and the agonies of the cross. How could such a being, so blessed and honored, ever become the ignoble, servile, cringing slave, with whom the fear of man could be paramount to the sacred dictates of conscience and the holy love of Heaven? By the common law of England, the spirit of which has been but too faithfully incorporated into our statute law, a husband has a right to whip his wife with a rod not larger than his thumb, to shut her up in a room, and administer whatever moderate chastisement he may deem necessary to insure obedience to his wishes, and for her healthful moral development! He can forbid all persons harboring or trusting her on his account. He can deprive her of all social intercourse with her nearest and dearest friends. If by great economy she accumulates a small sum, which for future need she deposit, little by little, in a savings bank, the husband has a right to draw it out, at his option, to use it as he may see fit.

"Husband is entitled to wife's credit or business talents (whenever their intermarriage may have occurred); and goods purchased by her on her own credit, with his consent, while cohabiting with him, can be seized and sold in execution against him for his own debts, and this, though she carry on business in her own name."—7 Howard's Practice Reports, 105, Lovett agt. Robinson and Whitbeck, sheriff, etc.

"No letters of administration shall be granted to a person convicted of infamous crime; nor to any one incapable by law of making a contract; nor to a person not a citizen of the United States, unless such person reside within this State; nor to any one who is under twenty-one years of age; nor to any person who shall be adjudged incompetent by the surrogate to execute duties of such trust, by reason of drunkenness, improvidence, or want of understanding, nor any married woman; but where a married woman is entitled to administration, the same may be granted to her husband in her right and behalf."

There is nothing that an unruly wife might do against which the husband has not sufficient protection in the law. But not so with the wife. If she have a worthless husband, a confirmed drunkard, a villain, or a vagrant, he has still all the rights of a man, a husband and a father. Though the whole support of the family be thrown upon the wife, if the wages she earns be paid to her by her employer, the husband can receive them again. If, by unwearied industry and perseverance, she can earn for herself and children a patch of ground and a shed to cover them, the husband can strip her of all her hard earnings, turn her and her little ones out in the cold northern blast, take the clothes from their backs, the bread from their mouths; all this by your laws may he do, and has he done, oft and again, to satisfy the rapacity of that monster in human form, the rumseller.

But the wife who is so fortunate as to have inherited property, has, by the new law in this state, been redeemed from her lost condition. She is no longer a legal nonentity. This property law, if fairly construed, will overturn the whole code relating to woman and property. The right to property implies the right to buy and sell, to will and bequeath, and herein is the dawning of a civil existence for woman, for now the "femme covert" must have the right to make contracts. So, get ready, gentlemen; the "little justice" will be coming to you one day deed in hand, for your acknowledgment. When he asks you "if you sign without fear or compulsion," say yes, boldly, as we do. Then, too, the right to will is ours. Now what becomes of the "tenant for life?" Shall he, the happy husband of a millionaire, who has lived in yonder princely mansion in the midst of plenty and elegance, be cut down in a day to the use of one-third of this estate and a few hundred a year, as long as he remains her widower? And should he, in spite of this bounty on celibacy, impelled by his affections, marry again, choosing for a wife a woman as poor as himself, shall he be thrown penniless on the cold world—this child of fortune, enervated by ease and luxury, henceforth to be dependent wholly on his own resources? Poor man! He would be rich, though, in the sympathies of many women who have passed through just such an ordeal. But what is property

without the right to protect that property by law? It is mockery to say a certain estate is mine, if, without my consent, you have the right to tax me when and how you please, while I have no voice in making the tax-gatherer, the legislator or the law. The right to property will, of necessity, compel us in due time to the exercise of our right to the elective franchise, and then naturally follows the right to hold office.

3d. Look at the position of woman as widow. Whenever we attempt to point out the wrongs of the wife, those who would have us believe that the laws cannot be improved, point us to the privileges, powers and claims of the widow. Let us look into these a little. Behold in yonder humble house a married pair, who, for long years, have lived together, childless and alone. Those few acres of well-tilled land, with the small white house that looks so cheerful through its vines and flowers, attest the honest thrift and simple taste of its owners. This man and woman, by their hard days labor, have made this home their own. Here they live in peace and plenty, happy in the hope that they may dwell together securely under their own vine and fig tree for the few years that remain to them, and that under the shadow of these trees, planted by their own hands, and in the midst of their household goods, so loved and familiar, here may take their last farewell of earth. But, alas for human hopes! the husband dies, and without will, and the stricken widow, at one fell blow, loses the companion of her youth, her house and home, and half the little sum she had in bank. For the law, which takes no cognizance of widows left with twelve children and not one cent, instantly spies out this widow, takes account of her effects, and announces to her the startling intelligence that but one-third of the house and lot, and one-half the personal property, are hers. The law has other favorites with whom she must share the hard-earned savings of years. In this dark hour of grief, the coarse minions of the law gather round the widow's hearth-stone, and, in the name of justice, outrage all natural sense of right; mock at the sacredness of human love, and with cold familiarity proceed to place a moneyed value on the old arm chair, in which, but a few brief hours since, she closed the eyes that had ever beamed on her with kindness and affection; on the solemn clock in the corner, that told the hour he passed away; on every garment with which his form and presence were associated, and on every article of comfort and convenience that the house contained, even down to the knives and forks and spoons—and the widow saw it all—and when the work was done, she gathered up what the law allowed her and went forth to seek her another home! This is the much-talked of widow's dower. Behold the magnanimity of the law in allowing the widow to retain a life interest in one-third the landed estate, and one-half the personal property of her husband, and taking the lion's share to itself! Had she died first, the house and land would all have been the husband's still. No one would have dared to intrude upon the privacy of his home or to molest him in his sacred retreat of sorrow.

How, I ask you, can that be called justice, which makes such a distinction as this between man and woman?

By management, economy and industry, our widow is able, in a few years, to redeem her house and home. But the law never loses sight of the purse, no matter how low in the scale of being its owner may be. It sends its officers round every year to gather in the harvest for the public crib, and no widow who owns a piece of land two feet square ever escapes this reckoning. Our widow, too, who has now twice earned her home, has her annual tax to pay also—a tribute of gratitude that she is permitted to breathe the free air of this republic, where "taxation without representation," by such worthies as John Hancock and Samuel Adams, has been declared "intolerable tyranny." Having glanced at the magnanimity of the law in its dealings with the widow, let us see how the individual man, under the influence of such laws, doles out justice to his helpmate. The husband has the absolute right to will away his property as he may see fit. If he has children, he can divide his property among them, leaving his wife her third only of the landed estate, thus making her a dependent on the bounty of her own children. A man with thirty thousand dollars in personal property, may leave his wife but a few hundred a year, as long as she remains his widow.

The cases are without number where women, who have lived in ease and elegance, at the death of their husbands have, by will, been reduced to the bare necessaries of life. The man who leaves his wife the sole guardian of his property and children is an exception to the general rule. Man has ever manifested a wish that the world should indeed be a blank

to the companion whom he leaves behind him. The Hindoo [sic] makes that wish a law, and burns the widow on the funeral pile of her husband; but the civilized man, impressed with a different view of the sacredness of life, takes a less summary mode of drawing his beloved partner after him; he does it by the deprivation and starvation of the flesh, and the humiliation and mortification of the spirit. In bequeathing to the wife just enough to keep soul and body together, man seems to lose sight of the fact that woman, like himself, takes great pleasure in acts of benevolence and charity. It is but just, therefore, that she should have it in her power to give during her life, and to will away at her death, as her benevolence or obligations might prompt her to do.

4th. Look at the position of woman as mother. There is no human love so generous, strong and steadfast as that of the mother for her child; yet behold how cruel and ruthless are your laws touching this most sacred relation.

Nature has clearly made the mother the guardian of the child; but man, in his inordinate love of power, does continually set nature and nature's laws at open defiance. The father may apprentice his child, bind him out to a trade or labor, without the mother's consent—yea, in direct opposition to her most earnest entreaties, her prayers and tears.

He may apprentice his son to a gamester or rumseller, and thus cancel his debts of honor. By the abuse of this absolute power, he may bind his daughter to the owner of a brothel, and, by the degradation of his child, supply his daily wants; and such things, gentlemen, have been done in our very midst. Moreover, the father, about to die, may bind out all his children wherever and to whomsoever he may see fit, and thus, in fact, will away the guardianship of all his children from the mother. The Revised Statutes of New York provide that "every father, whether of full age or a minor, of a child to be born, or of any living child under the age of twenty-one years, and unmarried, may by his deed or last will, duly executed, dispose of the custody and tuition of such child during its minority, or for any less time, to any person or persons, in possession or remainder." 2 R.S., page 150, sec. 1.

Thus, by your laws, the child is the absolute property of the father, wholly at his disposal in life or at death.

preference given to father

In case of separation, the law gives the children to the father; no matter what his character or condition. At this very time we can point you to noble, virtuous, well educated mothers in this state, who have abandoned their husbands for their profligacy and confirmed drunkenness. All these have been robbed of their children, who are in the custody of the husband, under the care of his relatives, whilst the mothers are permitted to see them but at stated intervals. But, said one of these mothers, with a grandeur of attitude and manner worthy the noble Roman matron in the palmiest days of that republic, I would rather never see my child again, than be the medium to hand down the low, animal nature of its father, to stamp degradation on the brow of another innocent being. It is enough that one child of his shall call me mother. If you are far sighted statesmen, and do wisely judge of the interests of this commonwealth, you will so shape your future laws as to encourage woman to take the high moral ground that the father of her children must be great and good.

Instead of your present laws, which make the mother and her children the victims of vice and license, you might rather pass laws prohibiting to all drunkards, libertines and fools, the rights of husbands and fathers. Do not the hundreds of laughing idiots that are crowding into our asylums, appeal to the wisdom of our statesmen for some new laws on marriage—to the mothers of this day for a higher, purer morality?

Again, as the condition of the child always follows that of the mother, and as by the abuse of your laws the father may beat the mother, so may he the child. What mother cannot bear me witness to untold sufferings which cruel, vindictive fathers have visited upon their helpless children? Who ever saw a human being that would not abuse unlimited power? Base and ignoble must that man be, who, let the provocation be what it may, would strike a woman; but he who would lacerate a trembling child is unworthy the name of man. A mother's love can be no protection to a child; she cannot appeal to you to save it from a father's cruelty, for the laws take no cognizance of the mother's most grievous wrongs. Neither at home nor abroad can a mother protect her son. Look at the temptations that surround the paths of our youth at every step; look at the gambling and drinking saloons, the club rooms, the dens of infamy and abomination that infest all our villages and cities—slowly but surely sapping the very foundations of all virtue and strength.

By your laws, all these abominable resorts are permitted. It is folly to talk of a mother molding the character of her son, when all mankind, backed up by law and public sentiment, conspire to destroy her influence. But when woman's moral power shall speak through the ballot-box, then shall her influence be seen and felt; then, in our legislative debates, such questions as the canal tolls on salt, the improvement of rivers and harbors, and the claims of Mr. Smith for damages against the state, would be secondary to the consideration of the legal existence of all these public resorts, which lure our youth on to excessive indulgence and destruction.

Many times and oft it has been asked us, with unaffected seriousness, "what do you women want? what are you aiming at?" Many have manifested a laudable curiosity to know what the wives and daughters could complain of in republican America, where their sires and sons have so bravely fought for freedom and gloriously secured their independence, trampling all tyranny, bigotry and caste in the dust, and declaring to a waiting world the divine truth that all men are created equal. What can woman want under such a government? Admit a radical difference in sex and you demand different spheres—water for fish, and air for birds.

It is impossible to make the southern planter believe that his slave feels and reasons just as he does—that injustice and subjection are as galling as to him—that the degradation of living by the will of another, the mere dependent on his caprice, at the mercy of his passions, is as keenly felt by him as his master. If you can force on his unwilling vision a vivid picture of the negro's wrongs and for a moment touch his soul, his logic brings him instant consolation. He says, the slave does not feel this as I would. Here, gentlemen, is our difficulty: When we plead our cause before the law makers and savants of the republic, they cannot take in the idea that men and women are alike; and so long as the mass rest in this delusion, the public mind will not be so much startled by the revelations made of the injustice and degradation of woman's position as by the fact that she should at length wake up to a sense of it.

It's not wrong if you don't think you're equal

If you, too, are thus deluded, what avails it that we show by your statute books that your laws are unjust—that woman is the victim of avarice and power? What avails it that we point out the wrongs of woman in social life; the victim of passion and lust? You scorn the thought that she has any natural love of freedom burning in her breast, any clear perception of justice urging her on to demand her rights.

Would to God you could know the burning indignation that fills woman's soul when she turns over the pages of your statute books, and sees there how like feudal barons you freemen hold your women. Would that you could know the humiliation she feels for her sex, when she thinks of all the beardless boys in your law offices, learning these ideas of one-sided justice—taking their first lessons in contempt for all womankind—being indoctrinated into the incapacities of their mothers, and the lordly, absolute rights of man over all women, children and property, and to know that these are to be our future Presidents, Judges, Husbands and Fathers; in sorrow we exclaim, alas! for that nation whose sons bow not in loyalty to woman. The mother is the first object of the child's veneration and love, and they who root out this holy sentiment, dream not of the blighting effect it has on the boy and the man. The impression left on law students, fresh from your statute books, is most unfavorable to woman's influence; hence you see but few lawyers chivalrous and high-toned in their sentiments toward woman. They cannot escape the legal view which, by constant reading, has become familiarized to their minds: "Femme covert," "dower," "widow's claims," "protection," "incapacities," "incumbrance," is written on the brow every woman they meet.

But if gentlemen, you take the ground that the sexes are alike, and, therefore, you are our faithful representatives—then why all these special laws for woman? Would not one code answer for all of like needs and wants? Christ's golden rule is better than all the special legislation that the ingenuity of man can devise: "Do unto others as you would have others do unto you" [Matt. 7:12]. This, men are brethren, is all we ask at your hands. We ask no better laws than those you have made for yourselves. We need no other protection than that which your present laws secure to you.

In conclusion, then, let us say, in behalf of the women of this state, we ask for all that you have asked for yourselves in the progress of your development, since the May Flower cast anchor side [sic] Plymouth rock; and simply on the ground that the rights of every human being are the same and identical. You may say that the mass of the women of this State do not make the demand; it comes from a few sour, disappointed old maids and childless women.

You are mistaken; the mass speak through us. A very large majority of the women of this state support themselves and their children, and many their husbands too. Go into any village you please, of three or four thousand inhabitants, and you will find as many as fifty men or more, whose only business is to discuss religion and politics, as they watch the trains come and go at the depot, or the passage of a canal boat through a lock; to laugh at the vagaries of some drunken brother, or the capers of a monkey dancing to the music of his master's organ. All these are supported by their mothers, wives or sisters.

Now, do you candidly think these wives do not wish to control the wages they earn—to own the land they buy—the houses they build? to have at their disposal their own children, without being subject to the constant interference and tyranny of an idle, worthless profligate? Do you suppose that any woman is such a pattern of devotion and submission that she willingly stitches all day for the small sum of fifty cents, that she may enjoy the unspeakable privilege, in obedience to your laws, of paying for her husband's tobacco and rum? Think you the wife of the confirmed, beastly drunkard would consent to share with him her home and bed, if law and public sentiment would release her from such gross companionship? Verily, no! Think you the wife, with whom endurance has ceased to be a virtue, who, through much suffering has lost all faith in the justice of both Heaven and earth, takes the law in her own hand, severs the unholy bond and turns her back forever upon him whom she once called husband, consents to the law that in such an hour tears her child from her—all that she has left on earth to love and cherish? The drunkards' wives speak through us, and they number 50,000. Think you that the woman who has worked hard all her days, in helping her husband to accumulate a large property, consents to the law that places this wholly at his disposal? Would not the mother, whose only child is bound out for a term of years, against her expressed wishes, deprive the father of this absolute power if she could?

For all these, then, we speak. If to this long list you add all the laboring women who are loudly demanding remuneration for their unending toil—those women who teach in our seminaries, academies and common schools for a miserable pittance; the widows, who are taxed without mercy; the unfortunate ones in our work houses, poor houses, and prisons; who are they that we do not now represent? But a small class of fashionable butterflies, who, through the short summer days, seek the sunshine and the flowers; but the cool breezes of autumn and the hoary frosts of winter will soon chase all these away; then, they too will need and seek protection, and through other lips demand, in their turn, justice and equity at your hands.

RED CLOUD

Speech (1866)

Friends, it has been our misfortune to welcome the white man. We have been deceived. He brought with him some shining things that pleased our eyes; he brought weapons more effective than our own: above all, he brought the spirit water that makes one forget for a time old age, weakness, and sorrow. But I wish to say to you that if you would possess these things for yourselves, you must begin anew and put away the wisdom of your fathers. You must lay up food, and forget the hungry. When your house is built, your storeroom filled, then look around for a neighbor whom you can take at a disadvantage, and seize all that he has! Give away only what you do not want; or rather, do not part with any of your possessions unless in exchange for another's.

My countrymen, shall the glittering trinkets of this rich man, his deceitful drink that overcomes the mind, shall these things tempt us to give up our homes, our hunting grounds, and the honorable teaching of our old men? Shall we permit ourselves to be driven to and fro—to be herded like the cattle of the white man?

Speech for War (1866)

Hear ye, Dakotas! When the Great Father at Washington sent us his chief soldier [General Harney] to ask for a path through our hunting grounds, a way for his iron road to the mountains and the western sea, we were told that they wished merely to pass through our country, not to tarry among us, but to seek for gold in the far west. Our old chiefs thought to show their friendship and good will, when they allowed this dangerous snake in our midst. They promised to protect the wayfarers.

Yet before the ashes of the council fire are cold, the Great Father is building his forts among us. You have heard the sound of the white soldier's ax upon the Little Piney. His presence here is an insult and a threat. It is an insult to the spirits of our ancestors. Are we then to give up their sacred graves to be plowed for corn? Dakotas, I am for war!

Cooper Union Address (1870)

My Brothers and my Friends who are before me today: God Almighty has made us all, and He is here to hear what I have to say to you today. The Great Spirit made us both. He gave us lands and He gave you lands. You came here and we received you as brothers. When the Almighty made you, He made you all white and clothed you. When He made us He made us with red skins and poor. When you first came we were very many and you were few. Now you are many and we are few. You do not know who appears before you to speak. He is a representative of the original American race, the first people of this continent. We are good, and not bad. The reports which you get about us are all on one side. You hear of us only as murderers and thieves. We are not so. If we had more lands to give to you we would give them, but we have no more. We are driven into a very little island, and we want you, our dear friends, to help us with the Government of the United States. The Great Spirit made us poor and ignorant. He made you rich and wise and skillful in things which we know nothing about. The good Father made you to eat tame game and us to eat wild game. Ask any one who has gone through to California. They will tell you we have treated them well. You have children. We, too, have children, and we wish to bring them up well. We ask you to help us do it. At the mouth of Horse Creek, in 1852, the Great Father made a treaty with us. We agreed to let him pass through our territory unharmed for fifty-five years. We kept our word. We committed no murders, no depredations, until the troops came there. When the troops were sent there trouble and disturbance arose. Since that time there have been various goods sent from time to time to us, but only once did they reach us, and soon the Great Father took away the only good man he had sent us, Col. Fitzpatrick. The Great Father said we must go to farming, and some of our men went to farming near Fort Laramie, and were treated very badly indeed. We came to Washington to see our Great Father that peace might be continued. The Great Father that made us both wishes peace to be kept; we want to keep peace. Will you help us? In 1868 men came out and brought papers. We could not read them, and they did not tell us truly what was in them. We thought the treaty was to remove the forts, and that we should then cease from fighting. But they wanted to send us traders on the Missouri. We did not want to go on the Missouri, but wanted traders where we were. When I reached Washington the Great Father explained to me what the treaty was, and showed me that the interpreters had deceived me. All I want is right and justice. I have tried to get from the Great Father what is right and just. I have not altogether succeeded. I want you to help me to get what is right and just. I represent the whole Sioux nation, and they will be bound by what I say. I am no Spotted Tail, to say one thing one day and be bought for a pin the next. Look at me. I am poor and naked, but I am the Chief of the nation. We do not want riches, but we want to train our children right. Riches would do us no good. We could not take them with us to the other world. We do not want riches, we want peace and love.

The riches that we have in this world, Secretary Cox said truly, we cannot take with us to the next world. Then I wish to know why Commissioners are sent out to us who do nothing but rob us and get the riches of this world away from us! I was brought up among the traders, and those who came out there in the early times treated me well and I had a good time with them. They taught us to wear clothes and to use tobacco and ammunition. But, by and by, the Great Father sent out a different kind of men; men who cheated and drank whisky; men who were so bad that the Great Father could not keep them at home and so sent them out there. I have sent a great many words to the Great Father but they never reached him. They were drowned on the way, and I was afraid the words I spoke lately to the Great Father would not reach you, so I came to speak to you myself; and now I am going away to my home. I want to have men sent out to my people whom we know and can trust. I am glad I have come here. You belong in the East and I belong in the West, and I am glad I have come here and that we could understand one another. I am very much obliged to you for listening to me. I go home this afternoon. I hope you will think of what I have said to you. I bid you all an affectionate farewell.

SPOTTED TAIL

Speech (1866)

"Hay, hay, hay! Alas, alas!" Thus speaks the old man, when he knows that his former vigor and freedom is gone from him forever. So we may exclaim today, Alas! There is a time appointed to all things. Think for a moment how many multitudes of the animal tribes we ourselves have destroyed! Look upon the snow that appears today—tomorrow it is water! Listen to the dirge of the dry leaves, that were green and vigorous but a few moons before! We are a part of this life and it seems that our time is come.

Yet note how the decay of one nation invigorates another. This strange white man—consider him, his gifts are manifold! His tireless brain, his busy hand do wonders for his race. Those things which we despise he holds as treasures; yet he is so great and so flourishing that there must be some virtue and truth in his philosophy. I wish to say to you, my friends: Be not moved alone by heated arguments and thoughts of revenge! These are for the young. We are young no longer; let us think well, and give counsel as old men!

Speech (1876)

My friends that have come here to see me; you have brought to me words from the Great Father at Washington, and I have considered them now for seven days, and have made up my mind. I have considered the matter of these messages and words sent out by the Great Father to me.

This is the fifth time that you have come. At the time of the first treaty that was made on Horse Creek—the one we call the "great treaty"—there was provision made to borrow the overland road of the Indians, and promises made at the time of the treaty, though I was a boy at the time; they told me it was to last fifty years. These promises have not been kept. All the Dakotas that lived in this country were promised these things together at that time. All the words

have proved to be false. The next conference was the one held with General Manydear, when there was no promises made in particular, nor for any amount to be given us, but we had a conference with him and made friends and shook hands.

Then after that there was a treaty made by General Sherman, General Sanborn, and General Harney. At that time the general told us we should have annuities and goods from that treaty for thirty-five years. He said this, but yet he didn't tell the truth. At that time General Sherman told me the country was mine, and that I should select any place I wished for my reservation and live in it. I told the general I would take the land from the headwaters of the White River to the Missouri, and he assented to it.

My friends, I will show you well his words today. When he promised us we should have annuities for thirty-five years he told us there should be an issue of goods in the spring when the grass began to grow, and also another issue of goods every fall. He said we should raise cattle; that they would give us cows to raise cattle with, and mares to raise horses with, and that they would give us yokes of oxen to haul logs with; that they would give us large wagons to haul goods with, in order that we might earn money in that way. He said also, there should be issues of such things as we needed to learn the arts with, besides that there should be money given to every one. He told us that we should each have $15 for an annuity. I told him that was a bad amount—that we didn't understand money, and that it should be $20, and he assented to that. He told me that these things should be carried out; for me to go to the mouth of the Whetstone River and locate with my people and these things should be fulfilled, but it was not true. When these promises failed to be carried out, I went myself to see the Great Father, and went into his house and told him these things. The Great Father told me to go home, to select any place in my country I choose, and to go there and live with my people. I came home and selected this place to move here and settle. Then persons came to me, after I had settled, and said I must move from this place, and I came back here again and located the agency. You told me to come here and locate my agency and I should receive the fulfillment of these promises. You gave me some very small cows, some very bad cattle, and some old wagons that were worn out. Again: you came last summer to talk about the country, and we said we would consider the matter; we said we would leave the matter to the Great Father for settlement. In answer to that reply of ours, he has sent you out this summer. You have now come to visit our land, and we now ask you how many years there are for us to live?

My friends, you that sit before me are traders and merchants. You have come here to trade. You have not come here to turn anything out of the way without payment for it. When a man has a possession that he values, and another party comes to buy it, he brings with him such good things as the people that own it desire to have. My friends, your people have both intellect and hearts. You use these to consider in what way you had best live. My people, who are here before you today, are precisely the same. If you have much of anything you use it for your own benefit and in order that your children shall have food and clothing, and my people also are the same. I see that my friends before me are men of age and dignity. Men of that kind have good judgment to consider well what they do. I infer from this you are here to consider what shall be good for my people for a long time to come. I think that each of you have selected somewhere a good piece of land for himself, with the intention of living on it, that he may there raise up his children. My people, that you see here before you, are not different; they also live upon the earth and upon the things that come to them from above. We have the same thoughts and desires in that respect that white people have. The people that you see before you are not men of a different country, but this is their country, where they were born and where they have acquired all their property; their children, their horses, and other property were all raised here in this country. You have come here to buy this country of ours, and it would be well if you came with the things you propose to give us—the good price you propose to pay for it in your hands, so we could see the price you propose to pay for it, then our hearts would be glad. My people have grown up together with these white men, who have married into our tribe. A great many of them have grown up with their children; a great many of us have learned to speak their language; our children are with theirs in our school, and we want to be considered all one people with them.

My friends, when you get back to the Great Father, we wish you to tell him to send us goods; to send us oxen; to give us wagons, so we can earn money by hauling goods that may come to the railroad, and haul our own provisions. My friends, this seems to me to be a very hard day. You have come here to buy our country, and there is, at the time you come, half our country at war, and we have come upon very difficult times. This war did not spring up here in our land; this war was brought upon us by the children of the Great Father who came to take our land from us without price, and who, in our land, do a great many evil things. The Great Father and his children are to blame for this trouble. We have here a store-house to hold our provisions the Great Father sends us, but he sends very little provision to put in our store-house. When our people become displeased with their provision and have gone north to hunt in order that they might live, the Great Father's children are fighting them. It has been our wish to live here in our country peaceably, and do such things as may be for the welfare and good of our people, but the Great Father has filled it with soldiers who think only of our death. Some of our people who have gone from here hunt in order they may have a change, and others who have gone north to hunt, have been attacked by the soldiers from the other side, and now when they are willing to come back the soldiers stand between them to keep them from coming home. It seems to me there is a better way than this. When people come to trouble, it is better for both parties to come together without arms and talk it over and find some peaceful way to settle it.

My friends, you have come to me today, and mentioned two countries to me. One of them I know of old—the Missouri River. It is not possible for me to go there. When I was there before we had a great deal of trouble. I left, also, one hundred of my people buried there. The other country you have mentioned is one I have never seen since I was born, but I agree to go and look at it. If it is possible to go with fifty of my young men, I will go down there and look at it. When men have a difficult business to settle it is not possible it should be well settled in one day; it takes at least twelve moons to consider it. In the meantime I want you to see to it that my people are well fed.

My friends, since I have lived in this country I have never had any evil thoughts. My only end has been to cultivate the ground and raise such things as may be for the good of my people. You are not different; you are good men; you are friends of the Great Father at Washington. My people also are good people, and we are friends of the Great Father in Washington. When this trouble first raised, the Great Father sent out word to stop the sale of ammunition at the stores. The ammunition my people needed to kill game, and the result has been great suffering to my people. It seems as if the wish of the Great Father was that my people should go into the ground, but notwithstanding we are all of sincere purpose to do what we can for the good of our people.

SATANTA

Medicine Lodge Speech (1867)

You, the Commissioners, have come from afar to listen to our grievances. My heart is glad, and I hide nothing from you. I understood that you were coming down to see us. I moved away from those disposed for war, and I also came along to see you. The Kiowas and Comanches have not been fighting. We were away down South when we heard you were coming to see us. The Cheyennes are those who have been fighting with you. They did it in broad daylight, so that all could see them. If I had been fighting I would have done it by day and not in the dark.

Two years ago I made peace with Gen's. Harney, Sanborn and Col. Leavenworth, at the mouth of the Little Arkansas. That peace I have never broken.

When the grass was growing in the spring a large body of soldiers came along on the Santa Fe road. I had not done anything and therefore I was not afraid. All the chiefs of the Kiowas, Comanches and Arrapahoes are here today; they have come to listen to good words. We have been waiting here a long time to see you, and are getting tired.

All the land south of the Arkansas belongs to the Kiowas and Comanches, and I don't want to give away any of it. I love the land and the buffalo, and will not part with it. I want you to understand well what I say. Write it on paper. Let the Great Father see it, and let me hear what he has to say. I want you to understand, also, that the Kiowas and Comanches don't want to fight, and have not been fighting since we made the treaty. I hear a good deal of good talk from the gentlemen whom the Great Father sends us, but they never do what they say. I don't want any of the Medicine lodges within the country. I want the children raised as I was.

When I make peace, it is a long and lasting one; there is no end to it. We thank you for your presents. All the head men and braves are happy. They will do what you want them, for they know you are doing the best you can. I and they will do our best also. When I look upon you I know you are all big chiefs. While you are in this country we go to sleep happy and are not afraid.

I have heard that you intend to settle us on a reservation near the mountains. I don't want to settle. I love to roam over the prairies. I feel free and happy; but when we settle down we grow pale and die. I have laid aside my lance, bow and shield, and yet I feel safe in your presence. I have told you the truth. I have no little lies hid about me; but I don't know how it is with the Commissioners. Are they as clear as I am?

A long time ago this land belonged to our fathers; but when I go up to the river I see camps of soldiers on its banks. These soldiers cut down my timber, they kill my buffalo; and when I see that my heart feels like bursting; I feel sorry. I have spoken.

Blackfoot

Speech (1873)

What you have said we have listened to and we think it is true. At Laramie the treaty was made. We did not feel right. We had made a long journey and were tired and sick. They gave us some horses. They thought they were doing a big thing, and making us a big present. But the horses were wild like the antelope. We caught them with the lasso. They jumped and kicked; we held on tight to them, but they got away from us; we were sick hunting them, and when we got home nearly all of them were gone. The commissioners told me that we should have plenty of food given us for forty years. They were big men who talked with us; they were not drunk when they told us. We were men and heard them, and so it ought to be written in the treaty. I told the commissioners at Laramie that I had seen the Sioux commit a great massacre; they killed many white men. But the Sioux are still there and still kill white men. When you whip the Sioux come and tell us of it. You are afraid of the Sioux. Two years ago I went with the soldiers; they were very brave; they were going through the Sioux country to Powder River and Tongue River. We got to Prior Creek, just below here in the Crow country. I wanted to go ahead into the Sioux country, but the soldiers got scared and turned back. I was there and so were others who are here; they know what I say is true. The soldiers said they were going to Tongue River, but they got frightened at the Sioux and turned back. The soldiers were the whirlwind; they went toward the Sioux country, but the whirlwind turned back. Last summer the soldiers went to Prior Creek again; again they said they were going through the Sioux country, but they saw a few Sioux; they were afraid of them; they got scared.

See all these old women! They have no clothing; the young men have no good blankets. We would like the Nez Percés, when they raise camp, to come here; they die with the Crows; they help to fight the Sioux. The last commission told us we could eat buffalo a long time. While we are here, the Flathead Indians take our horses. I would like you to take our part and stop them.

CRAZY HORSE

Last Words (1877)

I was not hostile to the white man. Sometimes my young men would attack the Indians who were their enemies and took their ponies. They did it in return. We had buffalo for food, and their hides for clothing and our tepees. We preferred hunting to a life of idleness on the reservations, where we were driven against our will. At times we did not get enough to eat, and we were not allowed to leave the reservation to hunt. We preferred our own way of living. We were no expense to the government then. All we wanted was peace and to be left alone. Soldiers were sent out in the winter, who destroyed our villages. [He referred to the winter before when his village was destroyed by Colonel Reynolds, Third Cavalry.] Then "Long Hair" [Custer] came in the same way.

They say we massacred him, but he would have done the same to us had we not defended ourselves and fought to the last. Our first impulse was to escape with our squaws and papooses, but we were so hemmed in that we had to fight. After that I went up on Tongue River with a few of my people and lived in peace. But the government would not let me alone. Finally, I came back to Red Cloud agency. Yet I was not allowed to remain quiet. I was tired of fighting. I went to Spotted Tail agency and asked that chief and his agent to let me live there in peace. I came here with the agent [Lee] to talk with big white chief, but was not given a chance. They tried to confine me, I tried to escape, and a soldier ran his bayonet into me. I have spoken.

CHIEF JOSEPH

Surrender to General Howard (1877)

Tell General Howard I know his heart. What he told me before I have in my heart. I am tired of fighting. Our chiefs are killed. Looking Glass is dead. Too-hul-hul-sote is dead. The old men are all dead. It is the young men who say yes or no. He who led on the young men is dead. It is cold and we have no blankets. The little children are freezing to death. My people, some of them, have run away to the hills, and have no blankets, no food; no one knows where they are—perhaps freezing to death. I want to have time to look for my children and see how many of them I can find. Maybe I shall find them among the dead. Hear me, my chiefs. I am tired; my heart is sick and sad. From where the sun now stands I will fight no more forever.

Sitting Bull

Powder River Council Speech (1875)

Behold, my friends, the spring is come; the earth has gladly received the embraces of the sun, and we shall soon see the results of their love! Every seed is awakened, and all animal life. It is through this mysterious power that we too have our being, and we therefore yield to our neighbors, even to our animal neighbors, the same right as ourselves to inhabit this vast land.

Yet hear me, friends! we have now to deal with another people, small and feeble when our forefathers first met with them, but now great and overbearing. Strangely enough, they have a mind to till the soil, and the love of possessions is a disease in them. These people have made many rules that the rich may break, but the poor may not! They have a religion in which the poor worship, but the rich will not! They even take tithes of the poor and weak to support the rich and those who rule. They claim this mother of ours, the Earth, for their own use, and fence their neighbors away from her, and deface her with their buildings and their refuse. They compel her to produce out of season, and when sterile she is made to take medicine in order to produce again. All this is sacrilege.

This nation is like a spring freshet; it overruns its banks and destroys all who are in its path. We cannot dwell side by side. Only seven years ago we made a treaty by which we were assured that the buffalo country should be left to us forever. Now they threaten to take that from us also. My brothers, shall we submit? or shall we say to them: "First kill me, before you can take possession of my fatherland!"

Response to U.S. Government (1878)

For sixty-four years you have kept me and my people and treated us bad. What have we done that you should want us to stop? We have done nothing. It is all the people on your side that have started us to do all these depredations. We could not go anywhere else, and so we took refuge in this country. It was on this side of the country we learned to shoot, and that is the reason why I came back to it again. I would like to know why you came here. In the first place, I did not give you the country, but you followed me from one place to another, so I had to leave and come over to this country. I was born and raised in this country with the Red River Half-Breeds, and I intend to stop with them. I was raised hand in hand with the Red River Half-Breeds, and we are going over to that part of the country, and that is the reason why I have come over here. [Shaking hands with the British officers.] That is the way I was raised, in the hands of these people here, and that is the way I intend to be with them. You have got ears, and you have got eyes to see with them, and you see how I live with these people. You see me? Here I am! If you think I am a fool you are a bigger fool than I am. This house is a medicine-house. You come here to tell us lies, but we don't want to hear them. I don't wish any such language used to me; that is, to tell me such lies in my Great Mother's house. Don't you say two more words. Go back home where you came from. This country is mine, and I intend to stay here, and to raise this country full of grown people. See these people here. We were raised with them. [Again shaking hands with the British officers.] That is enough; so no more. You see me shaking hands with these people.

The part of the country you gave me you ran me out of. I have now come here to stay with these people, and I intend to stay here. I wish you to go back, and to "take it easy" going back. [As Sitting Bull got up to leave this meeting, a U. S. government representative asked, "Shall I say to the President that you refuse the offers that he has made to you? Are we to understand from what you have said that you refuse those offers?" Sitting Bull answered: "I could tell you more, but that is all I have to tell you. If we told you more—why, you would not pay any attention to it. That is all I have to say. This part of the country does not belong to your people. You belong on the other side; this side belongs to us." Nevertheless, in July 1881, Sitting Bull—with his people hungry and ill, and Canada regarding them as unwanted refugees—surrendered at Fort Buford, Montana.]

Remarks in Prison at Ft. Randall (1882)

I have lived a long time, and I have seen a great deal, and I have always had a reason for everything I have done. Every act of my life has had an object in view, and no man can say that I have neglected facts or failed to think.

I am one of the last chiefs of the independent Sioux nation, and the place I hold among my people was held by my ancestors before me. If I had no place in the world, I would not be here, and the fact of my existence entitles me to exercise any influence I possess. I am satisfied that I was brought into this life for a purpose; otherwise, why am I here?

This land belongs to us, for the Great Spirit gave it to us when he put us here. We were free to come and go, and to live in our own way. But white men, who belong to another land, have come upon us, and are forcing us to live according to their ideas. That is an injustice; we have never dreamed of making white men live as we live.

White men like to dig in the ground for their food. My people prefer to hunt the buffalo as their fathers did. White men like to stay in one place. My people want to move their tepees here and there to the different hunting grounds. The life of white men is slavery. They are prisoners in towns or farms. The life my people want is a life of freedom. I have seen nothing that a white man has, houses or railways or clothing or food, that is as good as the right to move in the open country, and live in our own fashion. Why has our blood been shed by your soldiers?

[Sitting Bull drew a square on the ground with his thumb nail. The Indians craned their necks to see what he was doing.]

There! Your soldiers made a mark like that in our country, and said that we must live there. They fed us well, and sent their doctors to heal our sick. They said that we should live without having to work. But they told us that we must go only so far in this direction, and only so far in that direction. They gave us meat, but they took away our liberty. The white men had many things that we wanted, but we could see that they did not have the one thing we liked best,—freedom. I would rather live in a tepee and go without meat when game is scarce than give up my privileges as a free Indian, even though I could have all that white men have. We marched across the lines of our reservation, and the soldiers followed us. They attacked our village, and we killed them all. What would you do if your home was attacked? You would stand up like a brave man and defend it. That is our story. I have spoken.

Speech (undated)

What treaty that the whites have kept has the red man broken? Not one. What treaty that the whites ever made with us red men have they kept? Not one. When I was a boy the Sioux owned the world. The sun rose and set in their lands. They sent ten thousand horsemen to battle. Where are the warriors today? Who slew them? Where are our lands? Who owns them? What white man can say I ever stole his lands or a penny of his money? Yet they say I am a thief. What white woman, however lonely, was ever when a captive insulted by me? Yet they say I am a bad Indian. What white man has ever seen me drunk? Who has ever come to me hungry and gone unfed? Who has ever seen me beat my wives or abuse my children? What law have I broken? Is it wrong for me to love my own? Is it wicked in me because my skin is red; because I am a Sioux; because I was born where my fathers lived; because I would die for my people and my country?

WOKOVA [JACK WILSON]

Messiah Letter (undated)

When you get home you must make a dance to continue five days. Dance four successive nights, and the last night keep up the dance until the morning of the fifth day, when all must bathe in the river and then disperse to their homes. You must all do in the same way.

I, Jack Wilson, love you all, and my heart is full of gladness for the gifts you have brought me. When you get home I shall give you a good cloud which will make you feel good. I give you a good spirit and give you all good paint. [. . .]

There will be a good deal of snow this year and some rain. In the fall there will be such a rain as I have never given you before.

Grandfather says, when your friends die you must not cry. You must not hurt anybody or do harm to anyone. You must not fight. Do right always. It will give you satisfaction in life. [. . .]

Do not tell the white people about this. Jesus is now upon the earth. He appears like a cloud. The dead are still alive again. I do not know when they will be here; maybe this fall or in the spring. When the time comes there will be no more sickness and everyone will be young again.

Do not refuse to work for the whites and do not make any trouble with them until you leave them. When the earth shakes do not be afraid. It will not hurt you.

I want you to dance every six weeks. Make a feast of the dance and have food that everybody may eat. Then bathe in the water. That is all. You will receive good words again from me some time. Do not tell lies.

KICKING BEAR

Kicking Bear's Vision (1890)

My brothers, I bring to you the promise of a day in which there will be no white man to lay his hand on the bridle of the Indian's horse; when the red men of the prairie will rule the world and not be turned from the hunting-grounds by any man. I bring you word from your fathers, the ghosts, that they are now marching to join you, led by the Messiah who came once to live on earth with the white men, but was cast out and killed by them. I have seen the wonders of the spirit-land, and have talked with the ghosts. I traveled far and am sent back with a message to tell you to make ready for the coming of the Messiah and return of the ghosts in the spring.

In my tepee on the Cheyenne reservation I arose after the corn-planting, sixteen moons ago, and prepared for my journey. I had seen many things and had been told by a voice to go forth and meet the ghosts, for they were to return and inhabit the earth. I traveled far on the cars of the white men, until I came to the place where the railroad stopped. There I met two men, Indians, whom I had never seen before, but who greeted me as a brother and gave me meat and bread. They had three horses, and we rode without talking for four days, for I knew they were to be witnesses to what I should see. Two suns had we traveled, and had passed the last signs of the white man—for no white man had ever had the courage to travel so far—when we saw a strange and fierce-looking black man, dressed in skins. He was living alone, and had medicine with which he could do what he wished. He would wave his hands and make great heaps of money; another motion, and we saw many spring wagons, already painted and ready to hitch horses to; yet another motion of the hands, and there sprung up before us great herds of buffalo. The black man spoke and told us that he was the friend of the Indian; that we should remain with him and go no farther, and we might take what we wanted of the money, and spring wagons, and the buffalo. But our hearts were turned away from the black man, my brothers, and we left him and traveled for two days more.

On the evening of the fourth day, when we were weak and faint from our journey, we looked for a camping-place, and were met by a man dressed like an Indian, but whose hair was long and glistening like the yellow money of the white man. His face was very beautiful to see, and when he spoke my heart was glad and I forgot my hunger and the toil I had gone through. And he said, "How, my children. You have done well to make this long journey to come to me. Leave your horses and follow me." And our hearts sang in our breasts and we were glad. He led the way up a great ladder of small clouds, and we followed him up through an opening in the sky. My brothers, the tongue of Kicking Bear is straight and he cannot tell all that he saw, for he is not an orator, but the forerunner and herald of the ghosts. He whom we followed took us to the Great Spirit and his wife, and we lay prostrate on the ground, but I saw that they were dressed as Indians. Then from an opening in the sky we were shown all the countries of the earth and the camping-grounds of our fathers since the beginning; all were there, the tepees, and the ghosts of our fathers, and great herds of buffalo, and a country that smiled because it was rich and the white man was not there. Then he whom we had followed showed us his hands and feet, and there were wounds in them which had been made by the whites when he went to them and they crucified him. And he told us that he was going to come again on earth, and this time he would remain and live with the Indians, who were his chosen people.

Then we were seated on rich skins, of animals unknown to me, before the open door of the tepee of the Great Spirit, and told how to say the prayers and perform the dances I am now come to show my brothers. And the Great Spirit spoke to us saying:

"Take this message to my red children and tell it to them as I say it. I have neglected the Indians for many moons, but I will make them my people now if they obey me in this message. The earth is getting old, and I will make it new for my chosen people, the

Indians, who are to inhabit it, and among them will be all those of their ancestors who have died, their fathers, mothers, brothers, cousins and wives—all those who hear my voice and my words through the tongues of my children. I will cover the earth with new soil to a depth of five times the height of a man, and under this new soil will be buried the whites, and all the holes and the rotten places will be filled up. The new lands will be covered with sweet-grass and running water and trees, and herds of buffalo and ponies will stray over it, that my red children may eat and drink, hunt and rejoice. And the sea to the west I will fill up so that no ships may pass over it, and the other seas will I make impassable. And while I am making the new earth the Indians who have heard this message and who dance and pray and believe will be taken up in the air and suspended there, while the wave of new earth is passing; then set down among the ghosts of their ancestors, relatives, and friends. Those of my children who doubt will be left in undesirable places, where they will be lost and wander around until they believe and learn the songs and the dance of the ghosts. And while my children are dancing and making ready to join the ghosts, they shall have no fear of the white man, for I will take from the whites the secret of making gunpowder, and the powder they now have on hand will not burn when it is directed against the red people, my children, who know the songs and the dances of the ghosts; but that powder which my children, the red men, have, will burn and kill when it is directed against the whites and used by those who believe.

And if a red man die at the hands of the whites while he is dancing, his spirit will only go to the end of the earth and there join the ghosts of his fathers and return to his friends next spring. Go then, my children, and tell these things to all the people and make all ready for the coming of the ghosts."

We were given food that was rich and sweet to taste, and as we sat there eating, there came up through the clouds a man, tall as a tree and thin like a snake, with great teeth sticking out of his mouth, his body covered with short hair, and we knew at once it was the Evil Spirit. And he said to the Great Spirit, "I want half the people of the earth." And the Great Spirit answered and said, "No, I cannot give you any; I love them all too much." The Evil Spirit asked again and was again refused, and asked the third time, and the Great Spirit then told him that he could have the whites to do what he liked with, but that he would not let him have any Indians, as they were his chosen people for all future time. Then we were shown the dances and taught the songs that I am bringing to you, my brothers, and were led down the ladder of clouds by him who had taken us up. We found our horses and rode back to the railroad, the Messiah flying along in the air with us and teaching us the songs for the new dances. At the railroad he left us and told us to return to our people, and tell them, and all the people of the red nations, what we had seen; and he promised us that he would return to the clouds no more, but would remain at the end of the earth and lead the ghosts of our fathers to meet us when the next winter is passed.

North Carolina Freedmen's Address (1865)

To the Constitutional Convention of North Carolina and the Legislature to assemble thereafter:—

Assembled as delegates from different portions of the State of North Carolina, and representing a large body of the colored population, we most respectfully and humbly beg leave to present to you, and through you to the people of the State, something of our situation and our wants as a people.

Earnestly disclaiming all wish to forestall your action or to dictate in the solemn and important duties which have been intrusted to you at this most critical period, and confiding in your justice, wisdom, and patriotism to guard the interests of all classes, and more particularly of that class which, being more helpless, will most need your just and kind consideration, we but exercise the right guaranteed to the humblest citizen in thus petitioning.

It is with reverent and grateful acknowledgment of the Divine power and interposition, that we accept the precious boon of freedom, resulting, as it has, from a prolonged and sanguinary struggle between two great powers; and finally decreed as it has been by the national will, we look forward with confidence to see the decree ratified by the whole people of this State.

Though it was impossible for us to be indifferent spectators of such a struggle, you will do us the justice to admit that we have remained throughout obedient and passive, acting such part only as has been assigned us, and calmly waiting upon Providence. Our brethren have fought on the side of the Union, while we have been obliged to serve in the camp, to build fortifications, and raise subsistence for the Confederate army. Do you blame us that we have, meantime, prayed for the freedom of our race?

Just emerging from bondage, under which our race has groaned for two hundred and fifty years, and suffering from its consequent degradation, we are fully conscious that we possess no power to control legislation in our behalf, and that we must depend wholly upon moral appeal to the hearts and consciences of the people of our State.

Born upon the same soil, and brought up in an intimacy of relationship unknown to any other state of society, we have formed attachments for the white race which must be as enduring as life, and we can conceive of no reason that our God-bestowed freedom should now sever the kindly ties which have so long united us.

We are fully conscious that we cannot long expect the presence of government agents, or of the troops, to secure us against evil treatment from unreasonable prejudice and unjust men. Yet we have no desire to look abroad for protection and sympathy. We know we must find both at home and among the people of our own State, and merit them by our industry, sobriety, and respectful demeanor, or suffer long and grievous evils.

We acknowledge with gratitude that there are those among former slave masters who have promptly conceded our freedom, and have manifested a just

and humane disposition towards their former slaves. We think no such persons, or very few at least, have lost their working-hands by desertion.

At the same time, it must be known to you that many planters have either kept the freedman in doubt, have wholly denied his freedom, or have grudgingly conceded it; and while doing so have expelled his family from the plantations which they perhaps cleared and enriched by their toil through long and weary years. Some have withheld a just compensation, or have awarded such pay as would not support the laborer and his family. Others have driven their hands away without any pay at all, or even a share of the crops they have raised. Women with families of children, whose husbands have been sold, have died, or have wrongfully deserted them, have in some cases been driven away from the homes where, under slavery, they have spent a lifetime of hard service. Is it just or Christian thus to thrust out upon the cold world helpless families to perish? These grosser forms of evil we believe will correct themselves under wise and humane legislation; but we do most respectfully urge that some suitable measures may be adopted to prevent unscrupulous and avaricious employers from the practice of these and other similar acts of injustice towards our people.

Our first and engrossing concern in our new relation is, how we may provide shelter and an honorable subsistence for ourselves and families. You will say, work; but without your just and considerate aid, how shall we secure adequate compensation for our labor? If the friendly relations which we so much desire shall prevail, must there not be mutual co-operation? As our longer degradation cannot add to your comfort, make us more obedient as servants, or more useful as citizens, will you not aid us by wise and just legislation to elevate ourselves?

We desire education for our children, that they may be made useful in all the relations of life. We most earnestly desire to have the disabilities under which we formerly labored removed, and to have all the oppressive laws which make unjust discriminations on account of race or color wiped from the statutes of the State. We invoke your protection for the sanctity of our family relations. Is this asking too much? We most respectfully and earnestly pray that some provision may be made for the care of the great number of orphan children and the helpless and infirm, who, by the new order of affairs, will be thrown upon the world without protection; also that you will favor, by some timely and wise measures, the reunion of families which have long been broken up by war or by the operations of slavery.

Though associated with many memories of suffering, as well as of enjoyment, we have always loved our homes, and dreaded, as the worst of evils, a forcible separation from them. Now that freedom and a new career are before us, we love this land and people more than ever before. Here we have toiled and suffered; our parents, wives, and children are buried here; and in this land we will remain, unless forcibly driven away.

Finally, praying for such encouragement to our industry as the proper regulation of the hours of labor and the providing of the means of protection against rapacious and cruel employers, and for the collection of just claims, we commit our cause into your hands, invoking Heaven's choicest blessings upon your deliberations and upon the State.

J. H. Harris,
John R. Good,
George A. Rue,
Isham Swett,
J. Randolph, Jr.,
Committee.

Civil Rights Act of 1875 (March 1, 1875)

Whereas, it is essential to just government we recognize the equality of all men before the law, and hold that it is the duty of government in its dealings with the people to mete out equal and exact justice to all, of whatever nativity, race, color, or persuasion, religious or political; and it being the appropriate object of legislation to enact great fundamental principles into law: Therefore,

Be it enacted by the Senate and House of Representatives of the United States of American in Congress assembled, That all persons within the jurisdiction of the United States shall be entitled to the full and equal enjoyment of the accommodations, advantages, facilities, and privileges of inns, public conveyances on land or water, theaters, and other places of public amusement; subject only to the conditions and limitations established by law, and applicable alike to citizens of every race and color, regardless of any previous condition of servitude.

Sec. 2. That any person who shall violate the foregoing section by denying to any citizen, except for reasons by law applicable to citizens of every race and color, and regardless of any previous condition of servitude, the full enjoyment of any of the accommodations, advantages, facilities, or privileges in said section enumerated, or by aiding or inciting such denial,

shall, for every offense, forfeit and pay the sum of five hundred dollars to the person aggrieved thereby, to be recovered in an action of debt, with full costs; and shall also, for every such offense, be deemed guilty of a misdemeanor, and, upon conviction thereof, shall be fined not less than five hundred nor more than one thousand dollars, or shall be imprisoned not less than thirty days nor more than one year: Provided, that all persons may elect to sue for the State under their rights at common law and by State statutes; and having so elected to proceed in the one mode or the other, their right to proceed in the other jurisdiction shall be barred. But this proviso shall not apply to criminal proceedings, either under this act or the criminal law of any State: And provided further, That a judgment for the penalty in favor of the party aggrieved, or a judgment upon an indictment, shall be a bar to either prosecution respectively.

Sec. 3. That the district and circuit courts of the United States shall have, exclusively of the courts of the several States, cognizance of all crimes and offenses against, and violations of, the provisions of this act; and actions for the penalty given by the preceding section may be prosecuted in the territorial, district, or circuit courts of the United States wherever the defendant may be found, without regard to the other party; and the district attorneys, marshals, and deputy marshals of the United States, and commissioners appointed by the circuit and territorial courts of the United States, with powers of arresting and imprisoning or bailing offenders against the laws of the United States, are hereby specially authorized and required to institute proceedings against every person who shall violate the provisions of this act, and cause him to be arrested and imprisoned or bailed, as the case may be, for trial before such court of the United States, or territorial court, as by law has cognizance of the offense, except in respect of the right of action accruing to the person aggrieved; and such district attorneys shall cause such proceedings to be prosecuted to their termination as in other cases: Provided, That nothing contained in this section shall be construed to deny or defeat any right of civil action accruing to any person, whether by reason of this act or otherwise; and any district attorney who shall willfully fail to institute and prosecute the proceedings herein required, shall, for every such offense, forfeit and pay the sum of five hundred dollars to the person aggrieved thereby, to be recovered by an action of debt, with full costs, and shall, on conviction thereof, be deemed guilty of a misdemeanor, and be fined not

less than one thousand nor more than five thousand dollars: And provided further, That a judgment for the penalty in favor of the party aggrieved against any such district attorney, or a judgment upon an indictment against any such district attorney, shall be a bar to either prosecution respectively.

Sec. 4. That no citizen possessing all other qualification which are or may be prescribed by law shall be disqualified for service as grand or petit juror in any court of the United States, or of any State, on account of race, color, or previous condition of servitude; and any officer or other person charged with any duty in the selection or summoning of jurors who shall exclude or fail to summon any citizen for the cause aforesaid shall, on conviction thereof, be deemed guilty of a misdemeanor, and be fined not more than five thousand dollars.

Sec. 5. That all cases arising under the provisions of this act in the courts of the United States shall be reviewable by the Supreme Court of the United States, without regard to the sum in controversy, under the same provisions and regulations as are now provided by law for the review of other causes in said court.

Approved, March 1, 1875.

SUSAN B. ANTHONY

Speech in Defense of Equal Suffrage (1873)

Is It a Crime for a Citizen of the United States to Vote?

Friends and Fellow-citizens: I stand before you tonight, under indictment for the alleged crime of having voted at the last Presidential election, without having a lawful right to vote. It shall be my work this evening to prove to you that in thus voting, I not only committed no crime, but, instead, simply exercised my citizen's right, guaranteed to me and all United States citizens by the National Constitution, beyond the power of any State to deny.

Our democratic-republican government is based on the idea of the natural right of every individual member thereof to a voice and a vote in making and executing the laws. We assert the province of government to be to secure the people in the enjoyment of their unalienable rights. We throw to the winds the old dogma that governments can give rights. Before governments were organized, no one denies that each individual possessed the right to protect his own life, liberty and property. And when 100 or 1,000,000 people enter into a free government, they do not barter away their natural rights; they simply pledge themselves to protect each other in the enjoyment of them, through prescribed judicial and legislative tribunals. They agree to abandon the methods of brute force in the adjustment of their differences, and adopt those of civilization.

Nor can you find a word in any of the grand documents left us by the fathers that assumes for government the power to create or to confer rights. The Declaration of Independence, the United States Constitution, the constitutions of the several states and the organic laws of the territories, all alike propose to protect the people in the exercise of their God-given rights. Not one of them pretends to bestow rights.

"All men are created equal, and endowed by their Creator with certain unalienable rights. Among these are life, liberty and the pursuit of happiness. That to secure these, governments are instituted among men, deriving their just powers from the consent of the governed."

Here is no shadow of government authority over rights, nor exclusion of any from their full and equal enjoyment. Here is pronounced the right of all men, and "consequently," as the Quaker preacher said, "of all women," to a voice in the government. And here, in this very first paragraph of the declaration, is the assertion of the natural right of all to the ballot; for, how can "the consent of the governed" be given, if the right to vote be denied. Again:

"That whenever any form of government becomes destructive of these ends, it is the right of the people to alter or abolish it, and to institute a new government, laying its foundations on such principles, and organizing its powers in such forms as to them shall seem most likely to effect their safety and happiness."

Surely, the right of the whole people to vote is here clearly implied. For however destructive in their happiness this government might become, a disfranchised class could neither alter nor abolish it, nor institute a new one, except by the old brute force method of insurrection and rebellion. One-half of the people of this nation to-day are utterly powerless to blot from the statute books an unjust law, or to write there a new and a just one. The women, dissatisfied as they are with this form of government, that enforces taxation without representation,—that compels them to obey laws to which they have never given their consent,—that imprisons and hangs them without a trial by a jury of their peers, that robs them, in marriage, of the custody of their own persons, wages and children,—are this half of the people left wholly at the mercy of the other half, in direct violation of the spirit and letter of the declarations of the framers of this government, every one of which was based on the immutable principle of equal rights to all. By those declarations, kings, priests, popes, aristocrats, were all alike dethroned, and placed on a common level politically, with the lowliest born subject or serf. By them, too, me, as such, were deprived of their divine right to rule, and placed on a political level with women. By the practice of those declarations all class and caste distinction will be abolished; and slave, serf, plebeian, wife, woman, all alike, bound from their subject position to the proud platform of equality.

The preamble of the federal constitution says:

"We, the people of the United States, in order to form a more perfect union, establish justice, insure domestic tranquility, provide for the common defense, promote the general welfare and secure the blessings of liberty to ourselves and our posterity, do ordain and established this constitution for the United States of America."

It was we, the people, not we, the white male citizens, nor yet we, the male citizens; but we, the whole people, who formed this Union. And we formed it, not to give the blessings or liberty, but to secure them; not to the half of ourselves and the half of our posterity, but to the whole people—women as well as men. And it is downright mockery to talk to women of their enjoyment of the blessings of liberty while they are denied the use of the only means of securing them provided by this democratic republican government—the ballot.

The early journals of Congress show that when the committee reported to that body the original articles of confederation, the very first article which became the subject of discussion was that respecting equality of suffrage. Article 4th said: "The better to secure and perpetuate mutual friendship and intercourse between the people of the different States of this Union, the free inhabitants of each of the States, (paupers, vagabonds and fugitives from justice excepted,) shall be entitled to all the privileges and immunities of the free citizens of the several States."

Thus, at the very beginning, did the fathers see the necessity of the universal application of the great principle of equal rights to all—in order to produce the desired result—a harmonious union and a homogeneous people.

Luther Martin, attorney-general of Maryland, in his report to the Legislature of that State of the convention that framed the United States Constitution, said:

"Those who advocated the equality of suffrage took the matter up on the original principles of government: that the reason why each individual man in forming a State government should have an equal vote, is because each individual, before he enters into government, is equally free and equally independent."

James Madison said:

"Under every view of the subject, it seems indispensable that the mass of the citizens should not be without a voice in making the laws which they are to obey, and in choosing the magistrate who are to administer them." Also, "Let it be remembered, finally, that it has ever been the pride and the boast of America that the rights for which she contended were the rights of human nature."

And these assertions of the framers of the United States Constitution of the equal and natural rights of all the people to a voice in the government, have been affirmed and reaffirmed by the leading statesmen of the nation, throughout the entire history of our government.

Thaddeus Stevens, of Pennsylvania, said in 1866:

"I have made up my mind that elective franchise is one of the inalienable rights meant to be secured by the declaration of independence."

B. Gratz Brown, of Missouri, in the three day's discussion in the United States Senate in 1866, on Senator Cowan's motion to strike "male" from the District of Columbia suffrage bill, said:

"Mr. President, I say here on the floor of the American Senate, I stand for universal suffrage; and as a matter of fundamental principle, do not recognize the right of society to limit on any ground of race or sex. I will go farther and say, that I recognize the right of franchise as being intrinsically a natural right. I do not believe that society is authorized to impose any limitation upon it that do not spring out of the necessities of the social state itself. Sir, I have been shocked, in the course of this debate, to hear Senators declare this right only a conventional and political arrangement, a privilege yielded to you and me and others; not a right in any sense, only a concession! Mr. President, I do not hold my liberties by any such tenure. On the contrary, I believe that whenever you establish that doctrine, whenever you crystallize that idea in the public mind of this country, you ring the death knell of American liberties."

Charles Summer, in his brave protests against the fourteenth and fifteenth amendments, insisted that, so soon as by the thirteenth amendment the slaves became free men, the original powers of the United States Constitution guaranteed to them equal rights—the right to vote and to be voted for. In closing one of his great speeches he said:

"I do not hesitate to say that when the slaves of our country became citizens they took their place in the body politic as a component part of the people, entitled to equal rights, and under the protection of these two guardian principles: First—That all just government stand on the consent of the governed; and second, that taxation without representation is tyranny; and these rights it is the duty of Congress to guarantee as essential to the ideal of a Republic."

The preamble of the Constitution of the State of New York declares the same purpose. It says: "We, the people of the State of New York, grateful to Almighty God for our freedom, in order to secure its blessings, do establish this Constitution."

Here is not the slightest intimation either of receiving freedom from the United States Constitution, or of the State conferring the blessings of liberty upon the people; and the same is true of every one of the thirty-six State Constitutions. Each and all, alike declare rights God-given, and that to secure the people in the enjoyment of their inalienable rights, is their one and only object in ordaining and establishing government. And all of the State Constitutions are equally emphatic in their recognition of the ballot as the means of securing the people in the enjoyment of these rights.

Article 1 of the New York State Constitution says: "No member of this State shall be disfranchised or deprived of the rights or privileges secured to any citizen thereof, unless by the law of the land, or the judgement of his peers."

And so carefully guarded is the citizen's right to vote, that the Constitution makes special mention of all who may be excluded. It says:

"Laws may be passed excluding from the right of suffrage all persons who have been or may be convicted of bribery, larceny or any infamous crime."

In naming the various employments that shall not affect the residence of voters—the 3d section of article 2d says "that being kept at any alms house, or other asylum, at public expense, nor being confined at any public prison, shall deprive a person of his residence," and hence his vote. Thus is the right of voting most sacredly hedged about. The only seeming permission in the New York State Constitution for the disfranchisement of women is in section 1st of article 2d, which says: "Every male citizen of the age of twenty-one years shall be entitled to vote."

But I submit that in view of the explicit assertions of the equal right of the whole people, both in the preamble and previous article of the constitution, this omission of the adjective "female" in the second, should not be construed into a denial; but, instead, counted as of no effect. Mark the direct prohibition: "No member of this State shall be disfranchised, unless by the law of the land, or the judgment of his peers." "The law of the land," is the United States Constitution: and there is no provision in that document that can be fairly construed into a permission to the States to deprive any class of their citizens of their right to vote. Hence New York can get no power from that source to disfranchise one entire half of her members. Nor has "the judgment of their peers" been pronounced against women exercising their right to vote; no disfranchised person is allowed to be judge or juror and none but disfranchised persons can be women's peers; nor has the legislature passed laws excluding them on account of idiocy or lunacy; nor yet the courts convicted them of bribery, larceny, or any infamous crime. Clearly, then, there is no constitutional ground for the exclusion of women from the ballot-box in the State of New York. No barriers whatever stand to-day between women and the exercise of their right to vote save those of precedent and prejudice.

The clauses of the United States Constitution, cited by our opponents as giving power to the States to disfranchise any classes of citizens they shall please, are contained in sections 2d and 4th of article 1st. The second says: "The House of Representatives shall be composed of members chosen every second year by the people of the several States; and the electors in each State shall have the qualifications requisite for electors of the most numerous branch of the State Legislature."

This cannot be construed into a concession to the States of the power to destroy the right to become an elector, but simply to prescribe what shall be the qualification, such as competency of intellect, maturity of age, length of residence, that shall be deemed necessary to enable them to make an intelligent choice of candidates. If, as our opponents assert, the last clause of this section makes it the duty of the United States to protect citizens in the several States against higher or different qualifications for electors for representatives in Congress, than for members of Assembly, then must the first clause make it equally imperative for the national government to interfere with the States, and forbid them from arbitrarily cutting off the right of one-half of the people to become electors altogether. Section 4th says:

"The time, places and manner of holding elections for Senators and Representatives shall be prescribed in each State by the Legislative thereof; but Congress may at any time, by law, make or alter such regulations, except as to the places by choosing Senators."

Here is conceded the power only to prescribed times, places and manner of holding the elections; and even with these Congress may interfere, with all excepting the mere place of choosing Senators. Thus you see, there is not the slightest permission in either section for the States to discriminate against the right of any class of citizens to vote. Surely, to regulate cannot be to annihilate! nor to qualify to wholly deprive. And to this principle every true Democrat and Republican said amen, when applied to black men by Senator Sumner in his great speeches for EQUAL RIGHTS TO ALL from 1865 to 1869; and when, in 1871, I asked that Senator to declare the power of the United States Constitution to protect women in their right to vote—as he had done for black men—he handed me a copy of all his speeches during that reconstruction period, and said:

"Miss Anthony, put sex where I have race or color, and you have here the best and strongest argument I can make for woman. There is not a doubt but women have the constitutional right to vote, and I will never vote for a sixteenth amendment to guarantee it to them. I voted for both the fourteenth and fifteenth under protest; would never have done it but for the pressing emergency of that hour; would have insisted that the power of the original Constitution to protect all citizens in the equal enjoyment of their rights should have been vindicated through the courts. But the newly made freedmen had neither the intelligence, wealth nor time to wait that slow process. Women possess all these in an eminent degree, and I insist that they shall appeal to the courts, and through them establish the power of our American magna charta, to protect every citizen of the Republic." But, friends, when in accordance with Senator Summer's counsel, I went to the ballot-box, last November, and exercised my citizen's right to vote, the courts did not wait for me to appeal to them—they appealed to me, and indicted me on the charge of having voted illegally.

Senator Summer, putting sex where he did color, said:

"Qualifications cannot be in their nature permanent or insurmountable. Sex cannot be a qualification any more than size, race, color, or previous condition of servitude. A permanent or insurmountable qualification is equivalent to a deprivation of the suffrage. In other words, it is the tyranny of taxation without representation, against which our revolutionary mothers, as well as fathers, rebelled."

For any State to make sex a qualification that must ever result in the disfranchisement of one entire half of the people, is to pass a bill of attainder, or an ex post facto law, and is therefore a violation of the supreme law of the land. By it, the blessings of liberty are forever withheld from women and their female posterity. To them, this government has no just powers derived from the consent of the governed. To them this government is not a democracy. It is not a republic. It is an odious aristocracy; a hateful obligarchy of sex. The most hateful aristocracy ever established on the face of the globe. An obligarchy of wealth, where the rich govern the poor; an obligarchy of learning, where the educated govern the ignorant; or even an obligarchy of race, where the Saxon rules the African, might be endured; but this obligarchy of sex, which makes father, brothers, husband, sons, the obligarchs over the mother and sisters, the wife and daughters of every household; which ordains all men sovereigns, all women subjects, carries dissension, discord and rebellion into every home of the nation. And this most odious aristocracy exists, too, in the face of Section 4, of Article 4, which says: "The United States shall guarantee to every State in the Union a republican form of government."

What, I ask you, is the distinctive difference between the inhabitants of a monarchical and those of a republican form of government, save that in the monarchical the people are subjects, helpless, powerless, bound to obey laws made by superiors—while in the republican, the people are citizens, individual sovereigns, all clothed with equal power, to make and unmake both their laws and law makers, and the moment you deprive a person of his right to a voice in the government, you degrade him from the status of a citizen of the republic, to that of a subject, and it matters very little to him whether his monarch be an individual tyrant, as is the Czar of Russia, or a 15,000,000 headed monster, as here in the United States; he is a powerless subject, serf or slave; not a free and independent citizen in any sense.

But is urged, the use of the masculine pronouns he, his and him, in all the constitutions and laws, is proof that only men were meant to be included in their provisions. If you insist on this version of the letter of the law, we shall insist that you be consistent, and accept the other horn of the dilemma, which would compel you to exempt women from taxation for the support of the government, and from penalties for the violation of laws.

A year and a half ago I was at Walla, Walla, Washington Territory. I saw there a theatrical company, called the "Pixley Sisters," playing before crowded houses, every night of the whole week of the territorial fair. The eldest of those three fatherless girls was scarce eighteen. Yet every night a United States officer stretched out his long fingers, and clutched six dollars of the proceeds of the exhibition of those orphan girls, who, but a few years before, were half starvelings in the streets of Olympia, the capital of the far-off northwest territory. So the poor widow, who keeps a boarding house, manufacturers shirts, or sells apples and peanuts on the street corners of our cities, is compelled to pay taxes from her scanty pittance. I would that the women of this republic, at once, resolve, never again to submit of taxation, until their right to vote be recognized. Amen.

Miss Sarah E. Wall, of Worcester, Mass., twenty years ago, took this position. For several years, the officers of the law distrained her property, and sold it to meet the necessary amount; still she persisted, and would not yield an iota, though every foot of her lands should be struck off under the hammer. And now, for several years, the assessor has left her name off the tax list, and the collector passed her by without a call.

Mrs. J. S. Weeden, of Viroqua, Wis., for the past six years, has refused to pay her taxes, though the annual assessment is $75.

Mrs. Ellen Van Valkenburg, of Santa Cruz, Cal., who sued the County Clerk for refusing to register her name, declares she will never pay another dollar of tax until allowed to vote; and all over the country, women property holders are waking up to the injustice of taxation without representation, and ere long will refuse, en masse, to submit to the imposition.

There is no she, or her, or hers, in the tax laws.

The statute of New York reads:

"Every person shall be assessed in the town or ward where he resides when the assessment is made, or the lands owned by him." "Every collector shall call at least once on the person taxed, or at his usual place of residence, and shall demand payment of the taxes charged on him. If any one shall refues to pay the tax imposed on him, the collector shall levy the same by distress and sale of his property."

The same is true of all the criminal laws: "No person shall be compelled to be a witness against himself."

The same with the law of May 31st, 1870, the 19th section of which I am charged with having violated; not only are all the pronouns in it masculine, but everybody knows that that particular section was intended expressly to hinder the rebels from voting. It reads "If any person shall knowingly vote without his having a lawful right." Precisely so with all the papers served on me—the U.S. Marshal's warrant, the bail-bond, the petition for habeas corpus, the bill of indictment—not one of them had a feminine pronoun printed in it; but, to make them applicable to me, the Clerk of the Court made a little carat at the left of "he" and placed an "s" over it, thus making she out of he. Then the letters "is" were scratched out, the little carat under and "er" over, to make her out of his, and I insist if government officials may thus manipulate the pronouns to tax, fine, imprison and hang women, women may take the same liberty with them to secure to themselves their right to a voice in the government.

So long as any classes of men were denied their right to vote, the government made a show of consistency, by exempting them from taxation. When a property qualification of $250 was required of black men in New York, they were not compelled to pay taxes, so long as they were content to report themselves worth less than that sum; but the moment the black man died, and his property fell to his widow or daughter, the black woman's name would be put on the assessor's list, and she be compelled to pay taxes on the same property exempted to her husband. The same is true of ministers in New York. So long as the minister lives, he is exempted from taxation on $1,500 of property, but the moment the breath goes out of his body, his widow's name will go down on the assessor's list, and she will have to pay taxes on the $1,500. So much for the special legislation in favor of women.

In all the penalties and burdens of the government, (except the military,) women are reckoned as citizens, equally with men. Also, in all privileges and immunities, save those of the jury box and ballot box, the two fundamental privileges on which rest all the others. The United States government not only taxes, fines, imprisons and hangs women, but it allows them to pre-empt lands, register ships, and take out passport and naturalization papers. Not only does the law permit single women and widows to the right of naturalization, but Section 2 says: "A married woman may be naturalized without the concurrence of her husband." (I wonder the fathers were not afraid of creating discord in the families of foreigners); and again: "When an alien, having complied with the law, and declared his intention to become a citizen, dies before he is actually naturalized, his widow and children shall be considered citizens, entitled to all rights and privileges as such, on taking the required oath." If a foreign born woman by becoming a naturalized citizen, is entitled to all the rights and privileges of citizenship, is not a native born woman, by her national citizenship, possessed of equal rights and privileges?

The question of the masculine pronouns, yes and nouns, too, has been settled by the United States Supreme Court, in the Case of Silver versus Ladd, December, 1868, in a decision as to whether a woman was entitled to lands, under the Oregon donation law of 1850. Elizabeth Cruthers, a widow, settled upon a claim, received patents. She died, and her son was heir. He died. Then Messrs. Ladd Nott took possession, under the general pre-emption law, December, 1861. The administrator, E. P. Silver, applied for a writ of ejectment at the land office in Oregon City. Both the Register and Receiver decided that an unmarried woman could not hold land under that law. The Commissioner of the General Land Office, at Washington, and the Secretary of the Interior, also gave adverse opinions. Here patents were issued to Ladd Nott, and duly recorded. Then a suit was brought to set aside Ladd's patent, and it was carried through all the State Courts and the Supreme Court of Oregon, each, in turn, giving adverse decisions. At last, in the United States Supreme Court, Associate Justice Miller reversed the decisions of all the lower tribunals, and ordered the land back to the heirs of Mrs. Cruthers. The Court said:

"In construing a benevolent statute of the government, made for the benefit of its own citizens, inviting and encouraging them to settle on its distant public lands, the words a single man, and unmarried man may, especially if aided by the context and other parts of the statute, be taken in a generic sense. Held, accordingly, that the Fourth Section of the Act of Congress, of September 27th, 1850, granting by way of donation, lands in Oregon Territory, to every white settler or occupant, American half-breed Indians included, embraced within the term single man an unmarried woman."

And the attorney, who carried this question to its final success, is now the United States senator elect from Oregon, Hon. J. H. Mitchell, in whom the cause of equal rights to women has an added power on the floor of the United States Senate.

Though the words persons, people, inhabitants, electors, citizens, are all used indiscriminately in the national and state constitutions, there was always a conflict of opinion, prior to the war, as to whether they were synonymous terms, as for instance:

"No person shall be a representative who shall not have been seven years a citizen, and who shall not, when elected, be an inhabitant of that state in which he is chosen. No person shall be a senator who shall not have been a citizen of the United States, and an inhabitant of that state in which he is chosen."

But, whatever there was for a doubt, under the old regime, the adoption of the fourteenth amendment settled that question forever, in its first sentence: "All persons born or naturalized in the United States and subject to the jurisdiction thereof, are citizens of the United States and of the state wherein they reside."

And the second settles the equal status of all persons—all citizens:

"No states shall make or enforce any law which shall abridge the privileges or immunities of citizens; nor shall any state deprive any person of life, liberty or property, without due process of law, nor deny to any person within its jurisdiction the equal protection of the laws."

The only question left to be settled, now, is: Are women persons? And I hardly believe any of our opponents will have the hardihood to say they are not. Being persons, then, women are citizens, and no state has a right to make any new law, or to enforce any old law, that shall abridge their privileges or immunities. Hence, every discrimination against women in the constitutions and laws of the several states, is to-day null and void, precisely as is every one against negroes.

Is the right to vote one of the privileges or immunities of citizens? I think the disfranchised ex-rebels, and the ex-state prisoners will agree with me, that it is not only one of the them, but the one without which all the others are nothing. Seek the first kingdom of the ballot, and all things else shall be given thee, is the political injunction.

Webster, Worcester and Bouvier all define citizen to be a person, in the United States, entitled to vote and hold office.

Prior to the adoption of the thirteenth amendment, by which slavery was forever abolished, and black men transformed from property to persons, the judicial opinions of the country had always been in harmony with these definitions. To be a person was to be a citizen, and to be a citizen was to be a voter.

Associate Justice Washington, in defining the privileges and immunities of the citizen, more than fifty years ago, said: "they included all such privileges as were fundamental in their nature. And among them is the right to exercise the elective franchise, and to hold office."

Even the "Dred Scott" decision, pronounced by the abolitionists and republicans infamous, because it virtually declared "black men had no rights white men were bound to respect," gave this true and logical conclusion, that to be one of the people was to be a citizen and a voter.

Chief Judge Daniels said:

"There is not, it is believed, to be found in the theories of writers on government, or in any actual experiment heretofore tried, an exposition of the term citizen, which has not been considered as conferring the actual possession and enjoyment of the perfect right of acquisition and enjoyment of an entire equality of privileges, civil and political."

Associate Justice Taney said:

"The words people of the United States, and citizens, are synonymous terms, and mean the same thing. They both describe the political body, who, according to our republican institutions, form the sovereignty, and who hold the power and conduct the government, through their representatives. They are what we familiarly call the sovereign people, and every citizen is one of this people, and a constituent member of this sovereignty."

Thus does Judge Taney's decision, which was such a terrible ban to the black man, while he was a slave, now, that he is a person, no longer property, pronounce him a citizen possessed of an entire equality of privileges, civil and political. And not only the black man, but the black woman, and all women as well.

And it was not until after the abolition of slavery, by which the negroes became free men, hence citizens, that the United States Attorney, General Bates, rendered a contrary opinion. He said:

"The constitution uses the word citizen only to express the political quality, (not equality mark,) of the individual in his relation to the nation; to declare that he is a member of the body politic, and bound to it by the reciprocal obligations of allegiance on the one side, and protection on the other. The phrase, a citizen of the United States, without addition or qualification, means neither more nor less than a member of the nation."

Then, to be a citizen of this republic, is no more than to be a subject of an empire. You and I, and all true and patriotic citizens must repudiate this base conclusion. We all know that American citizenship, without addition or qualification, means the possession of equal rights, civil and political. We all know that the crowing glory of every citizen of the United States is, that he can either give or withhold his vote from every law and every legislator under the government.

Did "I am Roman citizen," mean nothing more than that I am a "member" of the body politic of the republic of Rome, bound to it by the reciprocal obligations of allegiance on the one side, and protection on the other? Ridiculously absurd question, you say. When you, young man, shall travel abroad, among the monarchies of the old world, and there proudly boast yourself an "American citizen," will you thereby declare yourself neither more nor less than a "member" of the American nation?

And this opinion of Attorney General Bates, that a black citizen was not a voter, made merely to suit the political exigency of the republican party, in that transition hour between emancipation and enfranchisement, was no less in-famous, in spirit or purpose, than was the decision of Judge Taney, that a black man was not one of the people, rendered in the interest and the behest of the old democratic party, in its darkest hour of subjection to the slave power. Nevertheless, all of the adverse arguments, adverse congressional reports and judicial opinions, thus far, have been based on this purely partisan, time-serving opinion of General Bates, that the normal condition of the citizen of the United States is that of disfranchisement. That only such classes of citizens as have had special legislative guarantee have a legal right to vote.

And if this decision of Attorney General Bates was infamous, as against black men, but yesterday plantation slaves, what shall we pronounce upon Judge Bingham, in the house of Representatives, and Carpenter, in the Senate of the United States, for citing it against the women of the entire nation, vast numbers of whom are the peers of those honorable gentlemen, themselves, in moral!! intellect, culture, wealth, family-paying taxes on large estates, and contributing equally with them and their sex, in every direction, to the growth, prosperity and well-being of the republic? And what shall be said of the judicial opinions of Judges Carter, Jameson, McKay and Sharswood, all based upon this aristocratic, monarchial idea, of the right of one class to govern another?

I am proud to mention the names of the two United States Judges who have given opinions honorable to our republican idea, and honorable to themselves—Judge Howe, of Wyoming Territory, and Judge Underwood, of Virginia.

The former gave it as his opinion a year ago, when the Legislature seemed likely to revoke the law enfranchising the women of that territory, that, in case they succeeded, the women would still possess the right to vote under the fourteenth amendment.

Judge Underwood, of Virginia, in noting the recent decision of Judge Carter, of the Supreme Court of the District of Columbia to women the right to vote, under the fourteenth and fifteenth amendment, says:

"If the people of the United States, by amendment of their constitution, could expunge, without any explanatory or assisting legislation, an adjective of five letters from all state and local constitutions, and thereby raise millions of our most ignorant fellow-citizens to all of the rights and privileges of electors, why should not the same people, by the same amendment, expunge an adjective of four letters from the same state and local constitutions, and thereby raise other millions of more educated and better informed citizens to equal rights and privileges, without explanatory or assisting legislation?"

If the fourteenth amendment does not secure to all citizens the right to vote, for what purpose was the grand old charter of the fathers lumbered with its unwieldy proportions? The republican party, and Judges Howard and Bingham, who drafted the document, pretended it was to do something for black men; and if that something was not to secure them in their right to vote and hold office, what could it have been? For, by the thirteenth amendment, black men had become people, and hence were entitled to all the privileges and immunities of the government, precisely as were the women of the country, and foreign men not naturalized. According to Associate Justice Washington, they already had the "Protection of the government, the enjoyment of life and liberty, with the right to acquire and possess property of every kind, and to pursue and obtain happiness and safety, subject to such restraints as the government may justly prescribe for the general welfare of the whole; the right of a citizen of one state to pass through or to reside in any other state for the purpose of trade, agriculture, professional pursuit, or otherwise; to claim the benefit of the writ of habeas corpus, to institute and maintain actions of any kind in the courts of the state; to take, hold, and dispose of property, either real or personal, and an exemption from higher taxes or impositions than are paid by the other citizens of the state."

Thus, you see, those newly freed men were in possession of every possible right, privilege and immunity of the government, except that of suffrage, and hence, needed no constitutional amendment for any other purpose. What right, I ask you, has the Irishman the day after he receives his naturalization papers that he did not possess the day before, save the right to vote and hold office? And the Chinamen, now crowding our Pacific coast, are in precisely the same position. What privilege or immunity has California or Oregon the constitutional right to deny them, save that of the ballot? Clearly, then if the fourteenth amendment was not to secure to black men their right to vote, it did nothing for them, since they possessed everything else before. But, if it was meant to be a prohibition of the states, to deny or abridge their right to vote—which I fully believe—then it did the same for all persons, white women included, born or naturalized in the United States; for the amendment does not say all male persons of African descent, but all persons are citizens.

The second section is simply a threat to punish the states, by reducing their representation on the floor of Congress, should they disfranchise any of their male citizens, on account of color, and does not allow of the inference that the states may disfranchise from any, or all other causes, nor in any wise weaken or invalidate the universal guarantee of the first section. What rule of law or logic would allow the conclusion, that the prohibition of a crime to one person, on severe pains and penalties, was a sanction of that crime to any and all other persons save that one?

But, however much the doctors of the law may disagree, as to whether people and citizens, in the original constitution, were once and the same, or whether the privileges and immunities in the fourteenth amendment include the right of suffrage, the question of the citizen's right to vote is settled forever by the fifteenth amendment. "The citizen's right to vote shall not be denied by the United States, nor any state thereof; on account of race, color, or previous condition of servitude." How can the state deny or abridge the right of the citizen, if the citizen does not possess it? There is no escape from the conclusion, that to vote is the citizen's right, and the specifications of race, color, or previous condition of servitude can, in no way, impair the force of the emphatic assertion, that the citizen's right to vote shall not be denied or abridged.

The political strategy of the second section of the fourteenth amendment, failing to coerce the rebel states into enfranchising their negroes, and the necessities of the republican party demanding their votes throughout the South, to ensure the re-election of Grant in 1872, that party was compelled to place this positive prohibition of the fifteenth amendment upon the United States and all the states thereof.

If we once establish the false principle, that United States citizenship does not carry with it the right to vote in every state in this Union, there is no end to the petty freaks and cunning devices, that will be resorted to, to exclude one and another class of citizens from the right of suffrage.

It will not always be men combining to disfranchise all women; native born men combining to abridge the rights of all naturalized citizens, as in Rhode Island. It will not always be the rich and educated who may combine to cut off the poor and ignorant; but we may live to see the poor, hardworking, uncultivated day laborers, foreign and native born, learning the power of the ballot and their vast majority of numbers, combine and amend state constitutions so as to disfranchise the Vanderbilts and A. T. Stewarts, the Conklings and Fentons. It is poor rule that won't work more ways than one. Establish this precedent, admit the right to deny suffrage to the states, and there is no power to foresee the confusion, discord and disruption that may await us. There is, and can be, but one safe principle of government— equal rights to all. And any and every discrimination against any class, whether on account of color, race, nativity, sex, property, culture, can but imbitter and disaffect that class, and thereby endanger the safety of the whole people.

Clearly, then, the national government must not only define the rights of citizens, but it must stretch out its powerful hand and protect them in every state in this Union.

But if you will insist that the fifteenth amendment's emphatic interdiction against robbing United States citizens of their right to vote, "on account of race, color, or previous condition of servitude," is a recognition of the right, either of the United States, or any state, to rob citizens of that right, for any or all other reason, I will prove to you that the class of citizens for which I now plead, and to which I belong, may be, and sure, by all the principles of our government, and many of the laws of the states, included under the term "previous condition of servitude."

First.—The married women and their legal status. What is servitude? "The condition of a slave." What is a slave? "A person who is robbed of the proceeds of his labor; a person who is subject to the will of another."

By the law of Georgia, South Carolina, and all the states of the South, the negro had no right to the custody and control of his person. He belonged to his master. If he was disobedient, the master had the right to use correction. If the negro didn't like the correction, and attempted to run away, the master had a right to use coercion to bring him back.

By the law of every state in this Union to-day, North as well as South, the married woman has no right to the custody and control of her person. The wife belongs to her husband; and if she refuses obedience to his will, he may use moderate correction, and if she doesn't like his moderate correction, and attempts to leave his "bed and board," the husband may use moderate coercion to bring her back. The little word "moderate," you see, is the saving clause for the wife, and would doubtless be overstepped should offended husband administer his correction with the "cat-o'-nine-tails," or accomplish his coercion with blood-hounds.

Again, the slave had no right to the earnings of his hands, they belonged to his master; no right to the custody of his children, they belonged to his master; no right to sue or be sued, or testify in the courts. If he committed a crime, it was the master who must sue or be sued.

In many of the states there has been special legislation, giving to married women the right to property inherited, or received by bequest, or earned by the pursuit of any avocation outside of the home; also, giving her the right to sue and be sued in matters pertaining to such separate property; but not a single state of this Union has eve[r] secured the wife in the enjoyment of her right to the joint ownership of the joint earnings of the marriage copartnership. And since, in the nature of things, the vast majority of married women never earn a dollar, by work outside of their families, nor inherit a dollar from their fathers, it follows that from the day of their marriage to the day of the death of their husbands, not one of them ever has a dollar, except it shall please her husband to let her have it.

In some of the states, also, there have been laws passed giving to the mother a joint right with the father in the guardianship of the children. But twenty years ago, when our woman's rights movement commenced, by the laws of the State of New York, and all the states, the father had the sole custody and control of the children. No matter if he were a brutal, drunken libertine, he had the legal right, without the mother's consent, to apprentice her sons to rum-sellers, or her daughters to brothel keepers. He could even will away an unborn child, to some other person than the mother. And in many of the states the law still prevails, and the mothers are still utterly powerless under the common law.

I doubt if there is, to-day, a State in this Union where a married woman can sue or be sued for slander of character, and until quite recently there was not one in which she could sue or be sued for injury of person. However damaging to the wife's reputation any slander may be, she is wholly powerless to institute legal proceedings against her accuser, unless her husband shall join with her; and how often have we heard of the husband conspiring with some outside barbarian to blast the good name of his wife? A married woman cannot testify in courts in cases of joint interest with her husband. A good farmer's wife near Earlville, Ill., who had all the rights she wanted, went to a dentist of the village and had a full set of false teeth, both upper and under. The dentist pronounced them an admirable fit, and the wife declared they gave her fits to wear them; that she could neither chew nor talk with them in her mouth. The dentist sued the husband; his counsel brought the wife as witness; the judge ruled her off the stand; saying "a married woman cannot be a witness in matters of joint interest between herself and her husband." Think of it, ye good wives, the false teeth in your mouths are joint interest with your husbands, about which you are legally incompetent to speak!! If in our frequent and shocking railroad accidents a married woman is injured in her person, in nearly all of the States, it is her husband who must sue the company, and it is to her husband that the damages, if there are any, will be awarded. In Ashfield, Mass., supposed to be the most advanced of any State in the Union in all things, humanitarian as well as intellectual, a married woman was severely injured by a defective sidewalk. Her husband sued the corporation and recovered $13,000 damages. And those $13,000 belong to him bona fide; and whenever that unfortunate wife wishes a dollar of it to supply her needs she must ask her husband for it; and if the man be of a narrow, selfish, nighardly nature, she will have to hear him say, every time, "What have you done, my dear, with the twenty-five cents I gave you yesterday?" Isn't such a position, ask you, humiliating enough to be called "servitude?" That husband, as would any other husband, in nearly every State of this Union, sued and obtained damages for the loss of the services of his wife, precisely as the master, under the old slave regime, would have done, had his slave been thus injured, and precisely as he himself would have done had it been his ox, cow or horse instead of his wife.

There is an old saying that "a rose by any other name would smell as sweet," and I submit it the deprivation by law of the ownership of one's own person, wages, property, children, the denial of the right as an individual, to sue and be sued, and to testify in the courts, is not a condition of servitude most bitter and absolute, though under the sacred name of marriage?

Does any lawyer doubt my statement of the legal status of married women? I will remind him of the fact that the old common law of England prevails in every State in this Union, except where the Legislature has enacted special laws annulling it. And I am ashamed that not one State has yet blotted from its statue books the old common law of marriage, by which Blackstone, summed up in the fewest words possible, is made to say, "husband and wife are one, and that one is the husband."

Thus may all married women, wives and widows, by the laws of the several States, be technically included in the fifteenth amendment's specification of "condition of servitude," present or previous. And not only married women, but I will also prove to you that by all the great fundamental principles of our free government, the entire womanhood of the nation is in a "condition of servitude" as surely as were our revolutionary fathers, when they rebelled against old King George. Women are taxed without representation, governed without their consent, tried, convicted and punished without a jury of their peers. And is all this tyranny any less humiliating and degrading to women under our democratic-republican government to-day than it was to men under their aristocratic, monarchical government one hundred years ago? There is not an utterance of old John Adams, John Hancock or Patrick Henry, but finds a living response in the soul of every intelligent, patriotic woman of the nation. Bring to me a common-sense woman property holder, and I will show you one whose soul is fired with all the indignation of 1776 every time the tax-gatherer presents himself at her door. You will not find one such but feels her condition of servitude as galling as did James Otis when he said:

"The very act of taxing exercised over those who are not represented appears to me to be depriving them of one of their most essential rights, and if continued, seems to be in effect an entire disfranchisement of every civil right. For, what one civil right is worth a rush after a man's property is subject to be taken from him at pleasure without his consent? If a man is not his own assessor in person, or by deputy, his liberty is gone, or he is wholly at the mercy of others."

What was the three-penny tax on tea, or the paltry tax on paper and sugar to which our revolutionary fathers were subjected, when compared with the taxation of the women of this Republic? The orphaned Pixley sisters, six dollars a day, and even the women, who are proclaiming the tyranny of our taxation without representation, from city to city throughout the country, are often compelled to pay a tax for the poor privilege of defending our rights. And again, to show that disfranchisement was precisely the slavery of which the fathers complained, allow me to cite to you old Ben. Franklin, who in those olden times was admitted to be good authority, not merely in domestic economy, but in political as well; he said:

"Every man of the commonalty, except infants, insane persons and criminals, is, of common right and the law of God, a freeman and entitled to the free enjoyment of liberty. That liberty or freedom consists in having an actual share in the appointment of those who are to frame the laws, and who are to be the guardians of every man's life, property and peace. For the all of one man is as dear to him as the all of another; and the poor man has an equal right, but more need to have representatives in the Legislature that the rich one. That they who have no voice or vote in the electing of representatives, do not enjoy liberty, but are absolutely enslaved to those who have votes and their representatives; for to be enslaved is to

have governors whom other men have set over us, and to be subject to laws made by the representatives of others, without having had representatives of our own to give consent in our behalf."

Suppose I read it with the feminine gender:

"That women who have no voice nor vote in the electing of representatives, do not enjoy liberty, but are absolutely enslaved to men who have votes and their representatives; for to be enslaved is to have governors whom men have set over us, and to be subject to the laws made by the representatives of men, without having representatives of our own to give consent in our behalf."

And yet one more authority; that of Thomas Paine, than whom not one of the Revolutionary patriots more ably vindicated the principles upon which our government is founded:

"The right of voting for representatives is the primary right by which other rights are protected. To take away this right is to reduce man to a state of slavery; for slavery consists in being subject to the will of another; and he that has not a vote in the election of representatives is in this case. The proposal, therefore, to disfranchise any class of men is as criminal as the proposal to take away property."

Is anything further needed to prove woman's condition of servitude sufficiently orthodox to entitle her to the guaranties of the fifteenth amendment?

Is there a man who will not agree with me, that to talk of freedom without the ballot, is mockery—is slavery—to the women of this Republic, precisely as New England's orator Wendell Phillips, at the close of the late war, declared it to be to the newly emancipated black men?

I admit that prior to the rebellion, by common consent, the right to enslave, as well as to disfranchise both native and foreign born citizens, was conceded to the States. But the one grand principle, settled by the war and the reconstruction legislation, is the supremacy of national power to protect the citizens of the United States in their right to freedom and the elective franchise, against any and every interference on the part of the several States. And again and again, have the American people asserted the triumph of this principle, by their overwhelming majorities for Lincoln and Grant.

The one issue of the last two Presidential elections was, whether the fourteenth and fifteenth amendments should be considered the irrevocable will of the people; and the decision was, they shall be—and that it is only the right, but the duty of the National Government to protect all United States citizens in the full enjoyment and free exercise of all their privileges and immunities against any attempt of any State to deny or abridge.

And in this conclusion Republican and Democrats alike agree.

Senator Frelinghuysen said:

"The heresy of State rights has been completely buried in these amendments, that as amended, the Constitution confers not only national but State citizenship upon all persons born or naturalized within our limits."

The Call for the national Republican convention said:

"Equal suffrage has been engrafted on the national Constitution; the privileges and immunities of American citizenship have become a part of the organic law."

The national Republican platform said:

"Complete liberty and exact equality in the enjoyment of all civil, political and public rights, should be established and maintained throughout the Union by efficient and appropriate State and federal legislation."

If that means anything, it is that Congress should pass a law to require the States to protect women in their equal political rights, and that the States should enact laws making it the duty of inspectors of elections to receive women's votes on precisely the same conditions they do those of men.

Judge Stanley Mathews—a substantial Ohio democrat—in his preliminary speech at the Cincinnati convention, said most emphatically:

"The constitutional amendments have established the political equality of all citizens before the law."

President Grant, in his message to Congress March 30th, 1870, on the adoption of the fifteenth amendment, said: "A measure which makes at once four millions of people voters, is indeed a measure, of greater importance than any act of the kind from the foundation of the Government to the present time."

How could four millions negroes be made voter if two millions were not included?

The California State Republican convention said:

"Among the many practical and substantial triumphs of the principles achieved by the Republican party during the past twelve years, it enumerated with pride and pleasure, the prohibiting of any State from abridging the privileges of any citizen of the Republic, the declaring the civil and political equality of every citizen, and the establishing all these principles in the federal constitution by amendments thereto, as the permanent law."

Benjamin F. Butler, in a recent letter to me, said:

"I do not believe anybody in Congress doubts that the Constitution authorizes the right of women to vote, precisely as if authorizes trial by jury and many other like rights guaranteed to citizens."

And again, General Butler said:

"It is not laws we want; there are plenty of laws—good enough, too. Administrative ability to enforce law is the great want of the age, in this country especially. Everybody talks of law, law. If everybody would insist on the enforcement of law, the government would stand on a firmer basis, and question would settle themselves."

And it is upon this just interpretation of the United States Constitution that our National Woman Suffrage Association which celebrates the twenty-fifth anniversary of the woman's rights movement in New York on the 6th of May next, has based all its arguments and action the past five years.

We no longer petition Legislature or Congress to give us the right to vote. We appeal to the women everywhere to exercise their too long neglected "citizen's right to vote." We appeal to the inspectors of election everywhere to receive the votes of all United States citizens as it is their duty to do. We appeal to United States commissioners and marshals to arrest the inspectors who reject the names and votes of United States citizens, as it is their duty to do, and leave those alone who, like our eighth ward inspectors, perform their duties faithfully and well.

We ask the juries to fail to return verdicts of "guilty" against honest, law-abiding, tax-paying United States citizens for offering their votes at our elections. Or against intelligent, worthy young men, inspectors of elections, for receiving and counting such citizens votes.

We ask the judges to render true and unprejudiced opinions of the law, and wherever there is room for a doubt to give its benefit on the side of liberty and equal rights to women, remembering that "the true rule of interpretation under our national constitution, especially since its amendments, is that anything for human rights is constitutional, everything against human right unconstitutional."

And it is on this line that we propose to fight our battle for the ballot—all peaceably, but nevertheless persistently through to complete triumph, when all United States citizens shall be recognized as equals before the law.

Statement at the Close of Her Trial (1873)

JUDGE HUNT: (Ordering the defendant to stand up), "Has the prisoner anything to say why sentence shall not be pronounced?"

MISS ANTHONY: Yes, your honor, I have many things to say; for in your ordered verdict of guilty, you have trampled under foot every vital principle of our government. My natural rights, my civil rights, my political rights, my judicial rights, are all alike ignored. Robbed of the fundamental privilege of citizenship, I am degraded from the status of a citizen to that of a subject; and not only myself individually, but all of my sex, are, by your honor's verdict, doomed to political subjection under this, so-called, form of government.

JUDGE HUNT: The Court cannot listen to a rehearsal of arguments the prisoner's counsel has already consumed three hours in presenting.

MISS ANTHONY: May it please your honor, I am not arguing the question, but simply stating the reasons why sentence cannot, in justice, be pronounced against me. Your denial of my citizen's right to vote, is the denial of my right of consent as one of the governed, the denial of my right of representation as one of the taxed, the denial of my right to a trial by a jury of my peers as an offender against the law, therefore, the denial of my sacred rights to life, liberty, property, and—

JUDGE HUNT: The Court cannot allow the prisoner to go on.

MISS ANTHONY: But your honor will not deny me this one and only poor privilege of protest against this high-handed outrage upon my citizen's rights. May it please the Court to remember that since the day of my arrest last November, this is the first time that either myself or any person of my disfranchised class has been allowed a word of defense before judge or jury—

JUDGE HUNT: The prisoner must sit down—the Court cannot allow it.

MISS ANTHONY: All of my prosecutors, from the 8th ward corner grocery politician, who entered the compliant, to the United States Marshal, Commissioner, District Attorney, District Judge, your honor on the bench, not one is my peer, but each and all are my political sovereigns; and had your honor submitted my case to the jury, as was clearly your duty, even then I should have had just cause of protest, for not one of those men was my peer; but, native or foreign born, white or black, rich or poor, educated or ignorant, awake or asleep, sober or drunk, each and every man of them was my political superior; hence, in no sense, my peer. Even, under such circumstances, a commoner of England, tried before a jury of Lords, would have far less cause to complain than should I, a woman, tried before a jury of men. Even my counsel, the Hon. Henry R. Selden, who has argued my cause so ably, so earnestly, so unanswerably before your honor, is my political sovereign. Precisely as no disfranchised person is entitled to sit upon a jury, and no woman is entitled to the franchise, so, none but a regularly admitted lawyer is allowed to practice in the courts, and no woman can gain admission to the bar—hence, jury, judge, counsel, must all be of the superior class.

JUDGE HUNT: The Court must insist—the prisoner has been tried according to the established forms of law.

MISS ANTHONY: Yes, your honor, but by forms of law all made by men, interpreted by men, administered by men, in favor of men, and against women; and hence, your honor's ordered verdict of guilty; against a United States citizen for the exercise of "that citizen's right to vote," simply because that citizen was a woman and not a man. But, yesterday, the same man made forms of law, declared it a crime punishable with $1,000 fine and six months imprisonment, for you, or me, or you of us, to give a cup of cold water, a crust of bread, or a night's shelter to a panting fugitive as he was tracking his way to Canada. And every man or woman in whose veins coursed a drop of human sympathy violated that wicked law, reckless of consequences, and was justified in so doing. As then, the slaves who got their freedom must take it over, or under, or through the unjust forms of law, precisely so, now, must women, to get their right to a voice in this government, take it; and I have taken mine, and mean to take it at every possible opportunity.

Judge Hunt: The Court orders the prisoner to sit down. It will not allow another word.

Miss Anthony: When I was brought before your honor for trial, I hoped for a broad and liberal interpretation of the Constitution and its recent amendments, that should declare all United States citizens under its [protection] equality of rights. [. . .] But failing to get this justice—failing, even, to get a trial by a jury not of my peers—I ask not leniency at your hands—but rather the full rigors of the law:

Judge Hunt: The Court must insist—

(Here the prisoner sat down.)

Judge Hunt: The prisoner will stand up.

(Here Miss Anthony arose again.)

The sentence of the Court is that you pay a fine of one hundred dollars and the costs of the prosecution.

Miss Anthony: May it please your honor, I shall never pay a dollar of your unjust penalty. All the stock in trade I possess is a $10,000 debt, incurred by publishing my paper—The Revolution—four years ago, the sole object of which was to educate all women to do precisely as I have done, rebel against your manmade, unjust, unconstitutional forms of law, that tax, fine, imprison and hang women, while they deny them the right of representation in the government; and I shall work on with might and main to pay every dollar of that honest debt, but not a penny shall go to this unjust claim. And I shall earnestly and persistently continue to urge all women to the practical recognition of the old revolutionary maxim, that "Resistance to tyranny is obedience to God."

Judge Hunt: Madam, the Court will not order you committed until the fine is paid.

J. E. Brown

Remarks before the Senate on Woman Suffrage (1887)

I believe that the Creator intended that the sphere of the males and females of our races should be different, and that their duties and obligations, while they differ materially, are equally important and equally honorable, and that each sex is equally well qualified by natural endowments for the discharge of the important duties which pertain to each, and that each sex is equally competent to discharge those duties.

We find an abundance of evidence, both in the works of nature and in the Divine revelation, to establish the fact that the family properly regulated is the foundation and pillar of society, and is the most important of any other human institution.

In the Divine economy it is provided that the man shall be the head of the family, and shall take upon himself the solemn obligation of providing for and protecting the family.

While the man is contending with the sterner duties of life, the whole time of the noble, affectionate, and true woman is required in the discharge of the delicate and difficult duties assigned her in the family circle, in her church relations, and in the society where her lot is cast. When the husband returns home weary and worn in the discharge of the difficult and laborious tasks assigned him, he finds in the good wife solace and consolation, which is nowhere else afforded. If he is despondent and distressed, she cheers his heart with words of kindness; if he is sick or languishing, she soothes, comforts, and ministers to him as no one but an affectionate wife can do. If his burdens are onerous, she divides their weight by the exercise of her love and her sympathy.

If it were proper to reverse the order of nature and assign woman to the sterner duties devolved upon the male sex, and to attempt to assign man to the more refining, delicate, and ennobling duties of the woman, man would be found entirely incompetent to the discharge of the obligations which nature has devolved upon the gentler sex, and society must be greatly injured by the attempted change. But if we are told that the object of this movement is not to reverse this order of nature but only to devolve upon the gentler sex a portion of the more rigorous duties imposed by nature upon the stronger sex, we reply that society must be injured, as the woman would not be able to discharge those duties so well, by reason of her want of physical strength, as the male, upon whom they are devolved, and to the extent that the duties are to be divided, the male would be infinitely less competent to discharge the delicate and sacred trusts which nature has assigned to the female.

But it has been said that the present law is unjust to woman; that she is often required to pay tax on the property she holds without being permitted to take part in framing or administering the laws by which her property is governed, and that she is taxed without representation. That is a great mistake.

It may be very doubtful whether the male or female sex in the present state of things has more influence in the administration of the affairs of the Government and the enactment of the laws by which we are governed.

While the woman does not discharge military duty, nor does she attend courts and serve on juries, nor does she labor in the public streets, bridges, or highways, nor does she engage actively and publicly in the discussion of political affairs, nor does she enter the crowded precincts of the ballot-box to deposit her suffrage, still the intelligent, cultivated, noble woman is a power behind the throne. All her influence is in favor of morality, justice, and fair dealing, all her efforts and counsel are in favor of good government, wise and wholesome regulations, and a faithful administration of the laws. Such a woman, by her gentleness, kindness, and Christian bearing, impresses her counsels and her views upon her father, her husband, her brothers, her sons, and her other male friends who imperceptibly yield to her influence many times without even being conscious of it. She rules not with a rod of iron, but with the queenly scepter; she binds not with hooks of steel, but with silken cords; she governs not by physical efforts, but by moral suasion and feminine purity and delicacy. Her dominion is one of love, not of arbitrary power.

We are satisfied, therefore, that the pure, cultivated, and pious ladies of this country now exercise a very powerful, but quiet, imperceptible influence in popular affairs, much greater than they can ever again exercise if female suffrage should be enacted and they should be compelled actively to take part in the affairs of state and the corruptions of party politics.

[. . .] It has been frequently urged with great earnestness by those who advocate woman suffrage that the ballot is necessary to the women to enable them to protect themselves in securing occupations, and to enable them to realize the same compensation for the like labor which is received by men. This argument is plausible, but upon a closer examination it will be found to possess but little real force. The price of labor is and must continue to be governed by the law of supply and demand, and the person who has the most physical strength to labor, and the most pursuits requiring such strength open for employment, will always command the higher prices.

Ladies make excellent teachers in public schools; many of them are every way the equals of their male competitors, and still they secure less wages than males. The reason is obvious. The number of ladies who offer themselves as teachers is much larger than the number of males who are willing to teach. The larger number of females offer to teach because other more profitable occupations are not open to them. The smaller number of males offer to teach because other more profitable occupations are open to most males who are competent to teach. The result is that the competition for positions of teachers to be filled by ladies is so great as to reduce the price; but as males can not be employed at that price, and are necessary in certain places in the schools, those seeking their services have to pay a higher price for them.

Persons having a larger number of places open to them with fewer competitors command higher wages than those who have a smaller number of places open to them with more competitors. This is the law of society. It is the law of supply and demand, which cannot be changed by legislation. Then it follows that the ballot can not enable those who have to compete with the larger number to command the same prices as those who compete with the smaller number in the labor market. As the Legislature has no power to regulate in practice that of which the advocates of woman suffrage complain, the ballot in the hands of females could not aid its regulation.

MARY PUTNAM JACOBI

"Common Sense" Applied to Woman Suffrage (1894)

No political experiment is more recent, has had so far a shorter span of duration, than that of universal manhood suffrage. Only little by little have been abolished the restrictions of church membership, of education, and of modest property qualification, which formerly prevailed throughout the United States. The farthest limit of possible extension of masculine franchise was reached when, at the close of the Civil War, the right of suffrage was bestowed on the newly emancipated slaves.

Until, practically, to-day the inequalities of political rights have been along lines of social class distinction. The well-born, the powerful, the educated, the rich, have ruled. The poor, the ignorant, the helpless have submitted. Macaulay declares that the upper and middle orders are the natural representatives of the human race. Whether advisably or not, it is they who have been the representatives. Thus it has happened that women, though unenfranchised, and submitted to the personal sovereignty of the men of their own families and own class, have enjoyed superiority to and even actual supremacy over thousands of men in lower classes. But to-day, for the first time, classes have been indistinguishably fused; all previous lines of cleavage have been consolidated into one great line of demarcation, which makes a political class out of a sex. For the first time, all political right, privilege, and power reposes undisguisedly on the one brutal fact of sex, unsupported, untempered, unalloyed by any attribute of education, any justification of intelligence, any glamour of wealth, any prestige of birth, any insignia of actual power. For the first time, all women, no matter how well born, how well educated, how intelligent, how rich, how serviceable to the State, have been rendered the political inferiors of men, no matter how base-born, how poverty-stricken, how ignorant, how vicious, how brutal. The pauper in the almshouse may vote, the lady who devotes herself to getting that almshouse made habitable may not. The tramp who begs cold victuals in the kitchen may vote; the heiress who feeds him, and endows a university may not. Communities are agitated and Legislatures convulsed to devise means to secure the right of suffrage to the illiterate voter. And the writers, journalists, physicians, teachers, the wives and daughters and the companions of the best educated men in the State, are left in silence; blotted out, swamped, obliterated behind this cloud of often besotted ignorance. To-day, the immigrants pouring in through the open gates of our seaport towns—the Indian when settled in severalty,—the negro hardly emancipated from the degradation of two hundred years of slavery,—may all share in the Sovereignty of the State. The white woman—the American woman,—the woman in whose veins runs the blood of those heroic colonists who founded our country, of those women who helped to sustain the courage of their husbands in the Revolutionary War; the woman who may have given the flower of her youth and health in the service of our Civil War—this woman is excluded. To-day women constitute the only class of sane people excluded from the franchise, the only class deprived of political representation, except the tribal Indians and the Chinese.

So lax in these facile days has become the conception of power, so loose and confused the Idea of Sovereignty, that we are often advised not to press our claim, because it really makes no difference who rules. Because, it is said, in a democracy, sovereignty is so minutely subdivided that the infinitesimal crumbs which fall to each man's portion are not worth scrambling for. But we refuse to think of the Republic as a barnyard filled with insignificant fowl! If the right to rule has been removed from certain men on account of their inadequacy, it has been transferred to Man, and to such part of the human race as can by their strength of soul make good its claim to such lofty right. Of such humanity we are a part. And while among those to whom at present is exclusively entrusted the power are thousands, admitted on all sides to be unworthy of it, there are among us thousands of women intrinsically fitted for those functions of citizenship which can only by an eclipse of political faith be despised.

Our Constitutional Conventions only meet once in twenty years; but the problem of Rights is of no such intermittent recurrence. It recurs all the time,—daily; it is involved in every transaction effected between human beings, at home or abroad, in business or in politics, in national issues, in municipal difficulties, in family dissensions. Rules for the solution of this problem are expounded every week in the churches, and laid down every day in the law courts. No personal or social ideal is possible without a conception of Rights, and every lofty character manifests its superiority to the herd, by the clearness with which it recognizes the existence of Rights, and by the unflinching tenacity with which it insists upon their maintenance.

Hence the danger, the vast and subtle danger, of so educating one half the population of a free State, that it has no vivid conception of Rights. Why should we wonder at the low tone which habitually prevails at present in relation to public affairs, when the women who stand as guardians at the fountain sources and household shrines of thought are trained to believe that there are no Rights, but only Privileges, Expediences, Immunities? Can those who cower before the public ridicule which greets the

enunciation of the Rights of Women; who are habituated to stifle generous impulses for their own larger freedom at the authoritative dictation of the men they see in power,—can such women be relied upon to serve the nation's heart for generous deeds?

Thus it is that, although we believe our demand to be fully in accord with public utility, and to meet some of the most serious wants of the time, we should be false to our trust did we rest this claim primarily upon expediency. We hope to show that the concession of suffrage to woman will be practically useful in innumerable directions; but we should unworthily belittle our case did we seek to introduce it on the ground that it could be made subservient to anything else. We demand the suffrage as a Right—not in a metaphysical sense,—but because we do fulfil all the essential conditions which the State has proclaimed necessary to qualify for the electorate. We demand it, because to-day, and not a thousand years ago,—because in the State of New York, and not in France or Germany or Austria,—women are recognized by law and custom to be persons, and to possess intelligence entirely equal to the average intelligence of those who already exercise the suffrage. We demand it, on no new principle, but on the double principle which runs through all our institutions, namely: that all the intelligence in the State must be enlisted for its welfare, and that all the weakness in the community must be represented for its own defence. There are women among us of intelligence, of wealth, of leisure, of high character, who only demand the opportunity to serve the State nobly, as they have already shown their ability to promote the welfare of the community in public affairs. And there are other women among us—hard working, patient, industrious,—who require the suffrage, and the opportunities of the suffrage, and the immense practical education of the suffrage, to enable them to better advance the interests of their own affairs. And there are poor and weak women among us, defenceless except so far as they may be touched by an occasional enthusiasm of philanthropy, who require the status of a definite representation—a medium through which they can make their wants known—which shall do for them, as the suffrage alone has been able to do for other masses of the poor and weak: give them means to defend themselves, enable them to take the initial step in rising out of otherwise easily-forgotten misery. In a community where the definition of a social unit is the person who casts one vote, every one who casts no vote is reckoned as less than a unit,—and hence suffers in the social estimate and in her own. Her power for work is lessened, and its recompense correlatively diminished.

It is to these same poor and working women that objection is most often made when we demand equal suffrage, and when we embrace in our demand all classes of women,—*because* the suffrage is now exercised by all classes of men. It is said that these women, adding an inherent weakness of sex to the weaknesses of ignorance and poverty, will be, even more than the men of their families, subject to corrupt influence, liable to be induced to sell their votes to the party, or even to the private agents, who will offer the highest price for them. It is even whispered that there is, in large cities, a class of women, whose names dare not be mentioned out loud, who would be solidly voted by the police,—and that *therefore* all the honest and virtuous women of the State must remain disfranchised! Was ever covert insult so distinctly offered to American womanhood!

It has been proposed, on other occasions, to accord special legal recognition to those unfortunate women: to subject them to slavery even more stringent than that in which they are now bound: to record their names upon the municipal archives, not in order that their defencelessness might be represented, but so that the men who are their accomplices in degradation might be protected. Other women, from the shelter of happy and honored homes, have successfully resisted this iniquitous proposal, and no such archaic infamy as yet stains the legislature of this State. But do not these facts, does not the prompt reference to such conditions, the moment a demand arises for political freedom, and political representation for women, itself indicate the ultimate outcome, the last and darkest effect, of the general social inequality of women?

We fully believe that the great reason why the lot of masses of toiling women is so miserable, is because on the one hand women have never been accustomed to band together for self-development and self-protection; and on the other hand, because women enjoying personal protection have not been accustomed to think of the affairs of masses of women

and children as their especial concern. The assumption still holds in theory, though daily contradicted by facts,—that all the concerns of women are adequately provided for by the solicitude of their own families. Yet it is perfectly well known, that society was obliged to enact laws to protect the women and children working in factories; not only against the greed of the employers of the so-called enlightened classes, but against the brutal insistence of the husbands and fathers who tried to work them to death.

In theory, women are always protected at home. In fact, laws are constantly being required for their special protection. Why is it desirable to leave such legal or social protection to be secured, if at all, by tedious and roundabout methods,—through petitions, and through the efforts of other people, whose warmest enthusiasm can hardly ever equal the energy of those who speak for themselves? Why should not the women have the right to speak for themselves, and by their own mouths to make their own wants known?

Herein lies the true solution of the problem of the illiterate vote. The influence of the women who are now busily engaged in civilizing the hordes of uncivilized people in our midst, will be utilized, not only to kindle the lagging interest of the men of their own class, but to so guide ignorant women voters, that they could be made to counterbalance, when necessary, the votes of ignorant and interested men. Here is a broad channel for the missionary enthusiasm of women, now too often allowed to run to waste in the sands of foreign heathendom. Success in such direction is rendered possible by the secrecy of the ballot, which the persistent efforts of public-spirited men have secured. Every effort to improve the purity of the ballot facilitates the participation of women in the suffrage. It is an omen of splendid augury that this very Committee before which our amendment is brought, is also charged with the grave duty of devising measures for the better protection of the ballot. We could ask no better introduction to the voters of this State for the cause of Equal Suffrage, than such intimate, such inseparable association with the cause of Purity of the Suffrage.

In bringing this cause of Equal Suffrage before this Convention, we are supported by the approval of thousands of men and women, who join us, because they believe either that the demand is just, or that it is timely, or that it is favorable to their own interests, or that it is ultimately conducive to the best interests of the State. Confessedly, however, the demand does not receive unanimous support. Did it do so, it would be irresistible, while we are aware that the success of our petition is trembling in the balance. But a unanimous demand for anything would also be unprecedented to the point of the miraculous.

There are some undesirable peculiarities about women, due to special conditions of circumstance, training, and environment, which would tend to disappear where changes in such environments were conducive to the greater development of strength. This, indeed, is the fundamental reason for desiring such changes; since no living creature or class of creatures can have a more fundamental desire than the just desire to grow, to become more effective in whatever is given them to do. There are other peculiarities about women which are, on the contrary, most desirable to conserve, and which nature cannot fail to conserve, and even intensify, with every increase in development and opportunity. All such qualities originate in and centre round the function of maternity—the special relations of women to their children, the special protection due to the mother from the father of their children, and which justifies a correlative degree of individual subordination. The laws of New York, as they stand to-day, establish with great clearness these complex relations of women. Women are accorded their individual rights and responsibilities as persons; and the right and responsibility to guard the persons and the inheritance of their children; they are given a right to maintenance to the extent to which their own industrial capacity is lessened by the care of their children; and in view of this, they are constrained to follow the domicile of their husbands so long as he acquits himself of his own responsibility.

We do believe that this special relation of women to children, in which the heart of the world has always felt there was something sacred, serves to impress upon women certain tendencies, to endow them with certain virtues which not only contribute to the charm which their anxious friends fear might be destroyed, but which will render them of special value in public affairs. Their conservatism, their economy, their horror of waste, their interest in personal character, the very simplicity of their judgment, their preoccupation with direct and living issues, are all qualities generated by the special circumstances which have surrounded women, and must continue to surround them. These can not be broken down by the fact of sharing the suffrage, for they lie far deeper than any political condition; they exist in the very nature of things.

A single phrase, often, but none too often repeated, sums up this aspect of the case. To the extent to which women resemble men, they require the same liberties; to the extent to which they differ, they require their own representation, and the State requires their special influence. Under the new, the extremely new regime of universal manhood suffrage, the State has become like a mining camp on the frontier. We claim that it should be reconstituted as a household, where, if man is at the head, for the protection and the defence, woman shall have her equal place as the mother, the daughter, the caretaker, the administrator, the conserver. We do not propose, after all, to change the existing sphere of women. Political status reflects and sanctions social change—it cannot create it. Political activities may become an occupation—but not political rights. How many women would engage in politics were they so empowered—how many would accept office, were they elected, it is impossible to foresee, and it is absolutely useless to discuss. We are not here to seek privileges for a few—but equal opportunity for all. We are not here to demand the maximum responsibilities in the gift of the State, but only the minimum rights. If women engage to-day in a hundred pursuits outside their households, it is not the suffrage which is the cause of this, for they do not possess the suffrage. The same causes, industrial and intellectual, which have led to a social expansion which is almost a revolution, will continue to operate; but the suffrage, while it will not weaken, can hardly intensify their influence. Women will not be sent into a new place by possession of the ballot. Like men, they will vote in the places where they already stand—in the mart, the factory, the place of business; but also in the schoolroom, the library, the hospital, and—far more often than all—in the household. If, in capacity, taste, and opportunity, women have in this half century, approximated towards the capacities of men, it is not in order to be men that they now desire to vote. It is because they are—and are fully satisfied to be—women.

Morrison R. Waite

United States v. Cruikshank (1875)

Mr. Chief Justice WAITE delivered the opinion of the Court.

This case comes here with a certificate by the judges of the Circuit Court for the District of Louisiana that they were divided in opinion upon a question which occurred at the hearing. It presents for our consideration an indictment containing sixteen counts, divided into two series of eight counts each, based upon sect. 6 of the Enforcement Act of May 31, 1870. That section is as follows:

That if two or more persons shall band or conspire together, or go in disguise upon the public highway, or upon the premises of another, with intent to violate any provision of this act, or to injure, oppress, threaten, or intimidate any citizen, with intent to prevent or hinder his free exercise and enjoyment of any right or privilege granted or secured to him by the constitution or laws of the United States, or because of his having exercised the same, such persons shall be held guilty of felony, and, on conviction thereof, shall be fined or imprisoned, or both, at the discretion of the court, the fine not to exceed $5,000, and the imprisonment not to exceed ten years; and shall, moreover, be thereafter ineligible to, and disabled from holding, any office or place of honor, profit, or trust created by the constitution or laws of the United States.

The question certified arose upon a motion in arrest of judgment after a verdict of guilty generally upon the whole sixteen counts, and is stated to be, whether "the said sixteen counts of said indictment are severally good and sufficient in law, and contain charges of criminal matter indictable under the laws of the United States."

The general charge in the first eight counts is that of "banding," and in the second eight, that of "conspiring" together to injure, oppress, threaten, and intimidate Levi Nelson and Alexander Tillman, citizens of the United States, of African descent and persons of color, with the intent thereby to hinder and prevent them in their free exercise and enjoyment of rights and privileges "granted and secured" to them "in common with all other good citizens of the United States by the constitution and laws of the United States." [. . .]

We have in our political system a government of the United States and a government of each of the several States. Each one of these governments is distinct from the others, and each has citizens of its own who owe it allegiance, and whose rights, within its jurisdiction, it must protect. The same person may be at the same time a citizen of the United States and a citizen of a State, but his rights of citizenship under one of these governments will be different from those he has under the other. *Slaughter-House Cases* [1873].

Citizens are the members of the political community to which they belong. They are the people who compose the community, and who, in their associated capacity, have established or submitted themselves to the dominion of a government for the promotion of their general welfare and the protection of their individual as well as their collective rights. In the formation of a government, the people may confer upon it such powers as they choose. The government, when so formed, may, and when called upon should, exercise all the powers it has for the protection of the rights of its citizens and the people within its jurisdiction; but it can exercise no other. The duty of a government to afford protection is limited always by the power it possesses for that purpose.

Experience made the fact known to the people of the United States that they required a national government for national purposes. The separate governments of the separate States, bound together by the articles of confederation alone, were not sufficient for the promotion of the general welfare of the people in respect to foreign nations, or for their complete protection as citizens of the confederated States. For this reason, the people of the United States [. . .]

ordained and established the government of the United States, and defined its powers by a constitution, which they adopted as its fundamental law, and made its rule of action.

The government thus established and defined is to some extent a government of the States in their political capacity. It is also, for certain purposes, a government of the people. Its powers are limited in number, but not in degree. Within the scope of its powers, as enumerated and defined, it is supreme and above the States; but beyond, it has no existence. It was erected for special purposes, and endowed with all the powers necessary for its own preservation and the accomplishment of the ends its people had in view. It can neither grant nor secure to its citizens any right or privilege not expressly or by implication placed under its jurisdiction.

The people of the United States resident within any State are subject to two governments: one State, and the other National; but there need be no conflict between the two. The powers which one possesses, the other does not. They are established for different purposes, and have separate jurisdictions. Together they make one whole, and furnish the people of the United States with a complete government, ample for the protection of all their rights at home and abroad. True, it may sometimes happen that a person is amenable to both jurisdictions for one and the same act. Thus, if a marshal of the United States is unlawfully resisted while executing the process of the courts within a State, and the resistance is accompanied by an assault on the officer, the sovereignty of the United States is violated by the resistance, and that of the State by the breach of peace, in the assault. So, too, if one passes counterfeited coin of the United States within a State, it may be an offence against the United States and the State: the United States, because it discredits the coin; and the State, because of the fraud upon him to whom it is passed. This does not, however, necessarily imply that the two governments possess powers in common, or bring them into conflict with each other. It is the natural consequence of a citizenship which owes allegiance to two sovereignties, and claims protection from both. The citizen cannot complain, because he has voluntarily submitted himself to such a form of government. He owes allegiance to the two departments, so to speak, and within their respective spheres must pay the penalties which each exacts for disobedience to its laws. In return, he can demand protection from each within its own jurisdiction.

The government of the United States is one of delegated powers alone. Its authority is defined and limited by the Constitution. All powers not granted to it by that instrument are reserved to the States or the people. No rights can be acquired under the constitution or laws of the United States, except such as the government of the United States has the authority to grant or secure. All that cannot be so granted or secured are left under the protection of the States.

We now proceed to an examination of the indictment, to ascertain whether the several rights, which it is alleged the defendants intended to interfere with, are such as had been in law and in fact granted or secured by the constitution or laws of the United States.

The first and ninth counts state the intent of the defendants to have been to hinder and prevent the citizens named in the free exercise and enjoyment of their "lawful right and privilege to peaceably assemble together with each other and with other citizens of the United States for a peaceful and lawful purpose." The right of the people peaceably to assemble for lawful purposes existed long before the adoption of the Constitution of the United States. In fact, it is, and always has been, one of the attributes of citizenship under a free government. It "derives its source," to use the language of Chief Justice Marshall, in *Gibbons v. Ogden* [1824], "from those laws whose authority is acknowledged by civilized man throughout the world." It is found wherever civilization exists. It was not, therefore, a right granted to the people by the Constitution. The government of the United States when established found it in existence, with the obligation on the part of the States to afford it protection. As no direct power over it was granted to Congress, it remains, according to the ruling in *Gibbons v. Ogden*, subject to State jurisdiction. Only such existing rights were committed by the people to the protection of Congress as came within the general scope of the authority granted to the national government.

The First Amendment to the Constitution prohibits Congress from abridging "the right of the people to assemble and to petition the government for a redress of grievances." This, like the other amendments proposed and adopted at the same time, was not intended to limit the powers of the State governments in respect to their own citizens, but to operate upon the National government alone. *Barron v. The City of Baltimore* [1833]. It is now too late to question the correctness of this construction. As was said by the late Chief Justice, in *Twitchell v. The Commonwealth* [1869], "the scope and application of these amendments are no longer subjects of discussion here." They left the authority of the States just where they found it, and added nothing to the already existing powers of the United States.

The particular amendment now under consideration assumes the existence of the right of the people to assemble for lawful purposes, and protects it against encroachment by Congress. The right was not created by the amendment; neither was its continuance guaranteed, except as against congressional interference. For their protection in its enjoyment, therefore, the people must look to the States. The power for that purpose was originally placed there, and it has never been surrendered to the United States.

The right of the people peaceably to assemble for the purpose of petitioning Congress for a redress of grievances, or for any thing else connected with the powers or the duties of the national government, is an attribute of national citizenship, and, as such, under the protection of, and guaranteed by, the United States. The very idea of a government, republican in form, implies a right on the part of its citizens to meet peaceably for consultation in respect to public affairs and to petition for a redress of grievances. If it had been alleged in these counts that the object of the defendants was to prevent a meeting for such a purpose, the case would have been within the statute, and within the scope of the sovereignty of the United States. Such, however, is not the case. The offence, as stated in the indictment, will be made out, if it be shown that the object of the conspiracy was to prevent a meeting for any lawful purpose whatever.

The second and tenth counts are equally defective. The right there specified is that of "bearing arms for a lawful purpose." This is not a right granted by the Constitution. Neither is it in any manner dependent upon that instrument for its existence. The Second Amendment declares that it shall not be infringed; but this, as has been seen, means no more than that it shall not be infringed by Congress. This is one of the amendments that has no other effect than to restrict the powers of the national government, leaving the people to look for their protection against any violation by their fellow-citizens of the rights it recognizes, to what is called, in *The City of New York v. Miln* [1837], the "powers which relate to merely municipal legislation, or what was, perhaps, more properly called internal police," "not surrendered or restrained" by the Constitution of the United States.

The third and eleventh counts are even more objectionable. They charge the intent to have been to deprive the citizens named, they being in Louisiana, "of their respective several lives and liberty of person without due process of law." This is nothing else than alleging a conspiracy to falsely imprison or murder citizens of the United States, being within the territorial jurisdiction of the State of Louisiana. The rights of life and personal liberty are natural rights of man. "To secure these rights," says the Declaration of Independence, "governments are instituted among men, deriving their just powers from the consent of the governed." The very highest duty of the States, when they entered into the Union under the Constitution, was to protect all persons within their boundaries in the enjoyment of these "unalienable rights with which they were endowed by their Creator." Sovereignty, for this purpose, rests alone with the States. It is no more the duty or within the power of the United States to punish for a conspiracy to falsely imprison or murder within a State, than it would be to punish for false imprisonment or murder itself.

The Fourteenth Amendment prohibits a State from depriving any person of life, liberty, or property, without due process of law; but this adds nothing to the rights of one citizen as against another. It simply furnishes an additional guaranty against any encroachment by the States upon the fundamental rights which belong to every citizen as a member of society. As was said by Mr. Justice Johnson, in *Bank of Columbia v. Okely* [1819], it secures "the individual from the arbitrary exercise of the powers of government, unrestrained by the established principles of private rights and distributive justice." These counts in the indictment do not call for the exercise of any of the powers conferred by this provision in the amendment.

The fourth and twelfth counts charge the intent to have been to prevent and hinder the citizens named, who were of African descent and persons of color, in "the free exercise and enjoyment of their several right and privilege to the full and equal benefit of all laws and proceedings, then and there, before that time, enacted or ordained by the said State of Louisiana and by the United States; and then and there, at that time, being in force in the said State and District of Louisiana aforesaid, for the security of their respective persons and property, then and there, at that time enjoyed at and within said State and District of Louisiana by white persons, being citizens of said State of Louisiana and the United States, for the protection of the persons and property of said white citizens." There is no allegation that this was done because of the race or color of the persons conspired against. When stripped of its verbiage, the case as presented amounts to nothing more than that the defendants conspired to prevent certain citizens of the United States, being within the State of Louisiana, from enjoying the equal protection of the laws of the State and of the United States.

The Fourteenth Amendment prohibits a State from denying to any person within its jurisdiction the equal protection of the laws; but this provision does not, any more than the one which precedes it, and which we have just considered, add any thing to the rights which one citizen has under the Constitution against another. The equality of the rights of citizens is a principle of republicanism. Every republican government is in duty bound to protect all its citizens in the enjoyment of this principle, if within its power. That duty was originally assumed by the States; and it still remains there. The only obligation resting upon the United States is to see that the States do not deny the right. This the amendment guarantees, but no more. The power of the national government is limited to the enforcement of this guaranty.

No question arises under the Civil Rights Act of April 9, 1866, which is intended for the protection of citizens of the United States in the enjoyment of certain rights, without discrimination on account of race, color, or previous condition of servitude, because, as has already been stated, it is nowhere alleged in these counts that the wrong contemplated against the rights of these citizens was on account of their race or color. [. . .]

The sixth and fourteenth counts state the intent of the defendants to have been to hinder and prevent the citizens named, being of African descent, and colored, "in the free exercise and enjoyment of their several and respective right and privilege to vote at any election to be thereafter by law had and held by the people in and of the said State of Louisiana, or by the people of and in the parish of Grant aforesaid." In *Minor v. Happersett* [1874], we decided that the Constitution of the United States has not conferred the right of suffrage upon any one, and that the United States have no voters of their own creation in the States. In *United States v. Reese et al.* [1875], we hold that the Fifteenth Amendment has invested the citizens of the United States with a new constitutional right, which is, exemption from discrimination in the exercise of the elective franchise on account of race, color, or previous condition of servitude. From this it appears that the right of suffrage is not a necessary attribute of national citizenship; but that exemption from discrimination in the exercise of that right on account of race, etc., is. The right to vote in the States comes from the States; but the right of exemption from the prohibited discrimination comes from the United States. The first has not been granted or secured by the Constitution of the United States; but the last has been.

Inasmuch, therefore, as it does not appear in these counts that the intent of the defendants was to prevent these parties from exercising their right to vote on account of their race, etc., it does not appear that it was their intent to interfere with any right granted or secured by the constitution or laws of the United States. We may suspect that race was the cause of the hostility; but it is not so averred. This is material to a description of the substance of the offence, and cannot be supplied by implication. Every thing essential must be charged positively, and not inferentially. The defect here is not in form, but in substance.

The seventh and fifteenth counts are no better than the sixth and fourteenth. The intent here charged is to put the parties named in great fear of bodily harm, and to injure and oppress them, because, being and having been in all things qualified, they had voted "at an election before that time had and held according to law by the people of the said State of Louisiana, in said State, to wit, on the fourth day of November, A.D. 1872, and at divers other elections by the people of the State, also before that time had and held according to law." There is nothing to show that the elections voted at were any other than State elections, or that the conspiracy was formed on account of the race of the parties against whom the conspirators were to act. The charge as made is really of nothing more than a conspiracy to commit a breach of the peace within a State. Certainly it will not be claimed that the United States have the power or are required to do mere police du[t]y in the States. If a State cannot protect itself against domestic violence, the United States may, upon the call of the executive, when the legislature cannot be convened, lend their assistance for that purpose. This is a guaranty of the Constitution (art. 4, sect. 4); but it applies to no case like this.

We are, therefore, of the opinion that the first, second, third, fourth, sixth, seventh, ninth, tenth, eleventh, twelfth, fourteenth, and fifteenth counts do not contain charges of a criminal nature made indictable under the laws of the United States, and that consequently they are not good and sufficient in law. They do not show that it was the intent of the defendants, by their conspiracy, to hinder or prevent the enjoyment of any right granted or secured by the Constitution.

We come now to consider the fifth and thirteenth and the eighth and sixteenth counts, which may be brought together for that purpose. The intent charged in the fifth and thirteenth is "to hinder and prevent the parties in their respective free exercise and enjoyment of the rights, privileges, immunities, and protection granted and secured to them respectively as citizens of the United States, and as citizens of said State of Louisiana," "for the reason that they, . . . being then and there citizens of said State and of the United States, were persons of African descent and race, and persons of color, and not white citizens thereof"; and in the eighth and sixteenth, to hinder and prevent them "in their several and respective free exercise and enjoyment of every, each, all, and singular the several rights and privileges granted and secured to them by the constitution and laws of the United States." The same general statement of the rights to be interfered with is found in the fifth and thirteenth counts.

According to the view we take of these counts, the question is not whether it is enough, in general, to describe a statutory offence in the language of the statute, but whether the offence has here been described at all. The statute provides for the punishment of those who conspire "to injure, oppress, threaten, or intimidate any citizen, with intent to prevent or hinder his free exercise and enjoyment of any right or privilege granted or secured to him by the constitution or laws of the United States." These counts in the indictment charge, in substance, that the intent in this case was to hinder and prevent these citizens in the free exercise and enjoyment of "every, each, all, and singular" the rights granted them by the Constitution, etc. There is no specification of any particular right. The language is broad enough to cover all. [. . .]

In criminal cases, prosecuted under the laws of the United States, the accused has the constitutional right "to be informed of the nature and cause of the accusation." Amend. VI. In *United States v. Mills* [1833], this was construed to mean, that the indictment must set forth the offence "with clearness and all necessary certainty, to apprise the accused of the crime with which he stands charged"; and in *United States v. Cook* [1872], that "every ingredient of which the offence is composed must be accurately and clearly alleged." It is an elementary principle of criminal pleading, that where the definition of an offence, whether it be at common law or by statute, "includes generic terms, it is not sufficient that the indictment shall charge the offence in the same generic terms as in the definition; but it must state the [specifics]—it must descend to particulars." [. . .] The object of the indictment is, first, to furnish the accused with such a description of the charge against him as will enable him to make his defence, and avail himself of his conviction or acquittal for protection against a further prosecution for the same cause; and, second, to inform the court of the facts alleged, so that it may decide whether they are sufficient in law to support a conviction, if one should be had. For this, facts are to be stated, not conclusions of law alone. A crime is made up of acts and intent; and these must be set forth in the indictment, with reasonable particularity of time, place, and circumstances. [. . .]

The conclusion is irresistible, that these counts are too vague and general. They lack the certainty and precision required by the established rules of criminal pleading. It follows that they are not good and sufficient in law. They are so defective that no judgment of conviction should be pronounced upon them.

The order of the Circuit Court arresting the judgment upon the verdict is, therefore, affirmed; and the cause remanded, with instructions to discharge the defendants.

JOSEPH P. BRADLEY

The Civil Rights Cases (1883)

Justice BRADLEY delivered the opinion of the Court.

It is obvious that the primary and important question in all the cases is the constitutionality of the law; for if the law is unconstitutional none of the prosecutions can stand.

The sections of the law referred to provide as follows:

Section 1. That all persons within the jurisdiction of the United States shall be entitled to the full and equal enjoyment of the accommodations, advantages, facilities, and privileges of inns, public conveyances on land or water, theaters, and other places of public amusement; subject only to the conditions and limitations established by law, and applicable alike to citizens of every race and color, regardless of any previous condition of servitude.

Sec. 2. That any person who shall violate the foregoing section by denying to any citizen, except for reasons by law applicable to citizens of every race and color, and regardless of any previous condition of servitude, the full enjoyment of any of the accommodations, advantages, facilities, or privileges in said section enumerated, or by aiding or inciting such denial, shall, for every such offense, forfeit and pay the sum of $500 to the person aggrieved thereby, to be recovered in an action of debt, with full costs; and shall, also, for every such offense, be deemed guilty of a misdemeanor, and upon conviction thereof shall be fined not less than $500 nor more than $1,000, or

shall be imprisoned not less than 30 days nor more than one year: Provided, that all persons may elect to sue for the penalty aforesaid, or to proceed under their rights at common law and by state statutes; and having so elected to proceed in the one mode or the other, their right to proceed in the other jurisdiction shall be barred. But this provision shall not apply to criminal proceedings, either under this act or the criminal law of any state: And provided, further, that a judgment for the penalty in favor of the party aggrieved, or a judgment upon an indictment, shall be a bar to either prosecution respectively.

[. . .] Has Congress constitutional power to make such a law? Of course, no one will contend that the power to pass it was contained in the Constitution before the adoption of the last three amendments. The power is sought, first, in the Fourteenth Amendment, and the views and arguments of distinguished senators, advanced while the law was under consideration, claiming authority to pass it by virtue of that amendment, are the principal arguments adduced in favor of the power. [. . .]

The first section of the Fourteenth Amendment (which is the one relied on), after declaring who shall be citizens of the United States, and of the several states, is prohibitory in its character, and prohibitory upon the states. It declares that "no state shall make or enforce any law which shall abridge the privileges or immunities of citizens of the United States; nor shall any state deprive any person of life, liberty, or property without due process of law; nor deny to any person within its jurisdiction the equal protection of the laws." It is state action of a particular character that is prohibited. Individual invasion of individual rights is not the subject matter of the amendment. It has a deeper and broader scope. It nullifies and makes void all state legislation, and state action of every kind, which impairs the privileges and immunities of citizens of the United States, or which injures them in life, liberty, or property without due process of law, or which denies to any of them the equal protection of the laws. It not only does this, but, in order that the national will, thus declared, may not be a mere *brutum fulmen*, the last section of the amendment invests Congress with power to enforce it by appropriate legislation. To enforce what? To enforce the prohibition. To adopt appropriate legislation for correcting the effects of such prohibited state law and state acts, and thus to render them effectually null, void, and innocuous. This is the legislative power conferred upon Congress, and this is the whole of it. It does not invest Congress with power to legislate upon subjects which are within the domain of state legislation; but to provide modes of relief against state legislation, or state action, of the kind referred to. It does not authorize Congress to create a code of municipal law for the regulation of private rights; but to provide modes of redress against the operation of state laws, and the action of state officers, executive or judicial, when these are subversive of the fundamental rights specified in the amendment. Positive rights and privileges are undoubtedly secured by the Fourteenth Amendment; but they are secured by way of prohibition against state laws and state proceedings affecting those rights and privileges, and by power given to Congress to legislate for the purpose of carrying such prohibition into effect; and such legislation must necessarily be predicated upon such supposed state laws or state proceedings, and be directed to the correction of their operation and effect. A quite full discussion of this aspect of the amendment may be found in *United States v. Cruikshank* [1876]. [. . .]

And so in the present case, until some state law has been passed, or some state action through its officers or agents has been taken, adverse to the rights of citizens sought to be protected by the Fourteenth Amendment, no legislation of the United States under said amendment, nor any proceeding under such legislation, can be called into activity, for the prohibitions of the amendment are against state laws and acts done under state authority. Of course, legislation may and should be provided in advance to meet the exigency when it arises, but it should be adapted to the mischief and wrong which the amendment was intended to provide against; and that is, state laws or state action of some kind adverse to the rights of the citizen secured by the amendment. Such legislation cannot properly cover the whole domain of rights appertaining to life, liberty, and property, defining them and providing for their vindication. That would be to establish a code of municipal law regulative of all private rights between man and man in society. It would be to make Congress take the place of the state legislatures and to supersede them. It is absurd to affirm that, because the rights of life, liberty, and property (which include all civil rights that men have) are by the amendment sought to be protected against invasion on the part of the state without due process of law, Congress may, therefore, provide due process of law for their vindication in every case; and that, because the denial by a state to any persons of the equal protection of the laws is prohibited by the amendment, therefore Congress may establish laws for their equal protection. In fine, the legislation which Congress is authorized to adopt in this behalf is not general legislation upon the rights of the citizen, but corrective legislation; that is, such as may be necessary and proper for counteracting such laws as the states may adopt or enforce, and which by the amendment they are prohibited from making or enforcing, or such acts and proceedings as the states may commit or take, and which by the amendment they are prohibited from committing or taking. It is not necessary for us to state, if we could, what legislation would be proper for Congress to adopt. It is sufficient for us to examine whether the law in question is of that character.

An inspection of the law shows that it makes no reference whatever to any supposed or apprehended violation of the Fourteenth Amendment on the part of the states. It is not predicated on any such view. It proceeds *ex directo* to declare that certain acts committed by individuals shall be deemed offenses, and shall be prosecuted and punished by proceedings in the courts of the United States. It does not profess to be corrective of any constitutional wrong committed by the states; it does not make its operation to depend upon any such wrong committed. It applies equally to cases arising in states which have the justest laws respecting the personal rights of citizens, and whose authorities are ever ready to enforce such laws as to those which arise in states that may have violated the prohibition of the amendment. In other words, it steps into the domain of local jurisprudence, and lays down rules for the conduct of individuals in society towards each other, and imposes sanctions for the enforcement of those rules, without referring in any manner to any supposed action of the state or its authorities.

If this legislation is appropriate for enforcing the prohibitions of the amendment, it is difficult to see where it is to stop. Why may not Congress, with equal show of authority, enact a code of laws for the enforcement and vindication of all rights of life, liberty, and property? If it is supposable that the states may deprive persons of life, liberty, and property without due process of law, (and the amendment itself does suppose this,) why should not Congress proceed at once to prescribe due process of law for the protection of every one of these fundamental rights, in every possible case, as well as to prescribe equal privileges in inns, public conveyances, and theaters. The truth is that the implication of a power to legislate in this manner is based upon the assumption that if the states are forbidden to legislate or act in a particular way on a particular subject, and power is conferred upon Congress to enforce the prohibition, this gives Congress power to legislate generally upon that subject, and not merely power to provide modes of redress against such state legislation or action. The assumption is certainly unsound. It is repugnant to the Tenth Amendment of the Constitution, which declares that powers not delegated to the United States by the Constitution, nor prohibited by it to the states, are reserved to the states respectively or to the people. [. . .]

In this connection it is proper to state that civil rights, such as are guarantied by the Constitution against state aggression, cannot be impaired by the wrongful acts of individuals, unsupported by state authority in the shape of laws, customs, or judicial or executive proceedings. The wrongful act of an individual, unsupported by any such authority, is simply a private wrong, or a crime of that individual; an invasion of the rights of the injured party, it is true, whether they affect his person, his property, or his reputation; but if not sanctioned in some way by the state, or not done under state authority, his rights remain in full force, and may presumably be vindicated by resort to the laws of the state for redress. An individual cannot deprive a man of his right to vote, to hold property, to buy and to sell, to sue in the courts, or to be a witness or a juror; he may, by force or fraud, interfere with the enjoyment of the right in a particular case; he may commit an assault against the person, or commit murder, or use ruffian violence at the polls, or slander the good name of a fellow citizen; but unless protected in these wrongful acts by some shield of state law or state authority, he cannot destroy or injure the right; he will only render himself amenable to satisfaction or punishment; and amenable therefor to the laws of the state where the wrongful acts are committed. Hence, in all those cases where the Constitution seeks to protect the rights of the citizen against discriminative and unjust laws of the state by prohibiting such laws, it is not individual offenses, but abrogation and denial of rights, which it denounces, and for which it clothes the Congress with power to provide a remedy. This abrogation and denial of rights, for which the states alone were or could be responsible, was the great seminal and fundamental wrong which was intended to be remedied. And the remedy to be provided must necessarily be predicated upon that wrong. It must assume that in the cases provided for, the evil or wrong actually committed rests upon some state law or state authority for its excuse and perpetration. [. . .]

Of course, these remarks do not apply to those cases in which Congress is clothed with direct and plenary powers of legislation over the whole subject, accompanied with an express or implied denial of such power to the states, as in the regulation of commerce with foreign nations, among the several states, and with the Indian tribes, the coining of money, the establishment of post-offices and post-roads, the declaring of war, etc. In these cases Congress has power to pass laws for regulating the subjects specified, in every detail, and the conduct and transactions of individuals respect thereof. But where a subject is not submitted to the general legislative power of Congress, but is only submitted thereto for the purpose of rendering effective some prohibition against particular state legislation or state action in reference to that subject, the power given is limited by its object, and any legislation by Congress in the matter must necessarily be corrective in its character, adapted to counteract and redress the operation of such prohibited state laws or proceedings of state officers.

If the principles of interpretation which we have laid down are correct, as we deem them to be (and they are in accord with the principles laid down in the cases before referred to, as well as in the recent case of *United States v. Harris*), decided at the last term of this court, it is clear that the law in question cannot be sustained by any grant of legislative power made to Congress by the Fourteenth Amendment. That amendment prohibits the states from denying to any person the equal protection of the laws, and declares that Congress shall have power to enforce, by appropriate legislation, the provisions of the amendment. The law in question, without any reference to adverse state legislation on the subject, declares that all persons shall be entitled to equal accommodation and privileges of inns, public conveyances, and places of public amusement, and imposes a penalty upon any individual who shall deny to any citizen such equal accommodations and privileges. This is not corrective legislation; it is primary and direct; it takes immediate and absolute possession of the subject of the right of admission to inns, public conveyances, and places of amusement. It supersedes and displaces state legislation on the same subject, or only allows it permissive force. It ignores such legislation, and assumes that the matter is one that belongs to the domain of national regulation. Whether it would not have been a more effective protection of the rights of citizens to have clothed Congress with plenary power over the whole subject, is not now the question. What we have to decide is, whether such plenary power has been conferred upon Congress by the Fourteenth Amendment, and, in our judgment, it has not. [. . .]

[T]he power of Congress to adopt direct and primary, as distinguished from corrective, legislation on the subject in hand, is sought, in the second place, from the Thirteenth Amendment, which abolishes slavery. This amendment declares "that neither slavery, nor involuntary servitude, except as a punishment for crime, whereof the party shall have been duly convicted, shall exist within the United States, or any place subject to their jurisdiction"; and it gives Congress power to enforce the amendment by appropriate legislation.

This amendment, as well as the Fourteenth, is undoubtedly self-executing without any ancillary legislation, so far as its terms are applicable to any existing state of circumstances. By its own unaided force and effect it abolished slavery, and established universal freedom. Still, legislation may be necessary and proper to meet all the various cases and circumstances to be affected by it, and to prescribe proper modes of redress for its violation in letter or spirit. And such legislation may be primary and direct in its character; for the amendment is not a mere prohibition of state laws establishing or upholding slavery, but an absolute declaration that slavery or involuntary servitude shall not exist in any part of the United States.

It is true that slavery cannot exist without law any more than property in lands and goods can exist without law, and therefore the Thirteenth Amendment may be regarded as nullifying all state laws which establish or uphold slavery. But it has a reflex character also, establishing and decreeing universal civil and political freedom throughout the United States; and it is assumed that the power vested in Congress to enforce the article by appropriate legislation, clothes Congress with power to pass all laws necessary and proper for abolishing all badges and incidents of slavery in the United Stated; and upon this assumption it is claimed that this is sufficient authority for declaring by law that all persons shall have equal accommodations and privileges in all inns, public conveyances, and places of public amusement; the argument being that the denial of such equal accommodations and privileges is in itself a subjection to a species of servitude within the meaning of the amendment. Conceding the major proposition to be true, that Congress has a right to enact all necessary and proper laws for the obliteration and prevention of slavery, with all its badges and incidents, is the minor proposition also true, that the denial to any person of admission to the accommodations and privileges of an inn, a public conveyance, or a theater, does subject that person to any form of servitude, or tend to fasten upon him any badge of slavery? If it does not, then power to pass the law is not found in the Thirteenth Amendment. [. . .]

The long existence of African slavery in this country gave us very distinct notions of what it was, and what were its necessary incidents. Compulsory service of the slave for the benefit of the master, restraint of his movements except by the master's will, disability to hold property, to make contracts, to have a standing in court, to be a witness against a white person, and such like burdens and incapacities were the inseparable incidents of the institution. Severer punishments for crimes were imposed on the slave than on free persons guilty of the same offenses. Congress, as we have seen, by the civil rights bill of 1866, passed in view of the Thirteenth Amendment, before the Fourteenth was adopted, undertook to wipe out these burdens and disabilities, the necessary incidents of slavery, constituting its substance and visible from; and to secure to all citizens of every race and color, and without regard to previous servitude, those fundamental rights which are the essence of civil freedom, namely, the same right to make and enforce contracts, to sue, be parties, give evidence, and to inherit, purchase, lease, sell, and convey property, as is enjoyed by white citizens. Whether this legislation was fully authorized by the Thirteenth Amendment alone, without the support which it afterwards received from the Fourteenth Amendment, after the adoption of which it was reenacted with some additions, it is not necessary to inquire. It is referred to for the purpose of showing that at that time (in 1866) Congress did not assume, under the authority given by the Thirteenth Amendment, to adjust what may be called the social rights of men and races in the community; but only to declare and vindicate those fundamental rights which appertain to the essence of citizenship, and the enjoyment or deprivation of which constitutes the essential distinction between freedom and slavery. We must not forget that the province and scope of the Thirteenth and Fourteenth Amendments are different: the former simply abolished slavery; the latter prohibited the states from abridging the privileges or immunities of citizens of the United States, from depriving them of life, liberty, or property without due process of law, and from denying to any the equal protection of the laws. The amendments are different, and the powers of Congress under them are different. What Congress has power to do under one, it may not have power to do under the other. Under the Thirteenth Amendment, it has only to do with slavery and its incidents. Under the Fourteenth Amendment, it has power to counteract and render nugatory all state laws and proceedings which have the effect to abridge any of the privileges or immunities [. . .] [and] deprive them of life, liberty, or property without due process of law, or to deny to any of them the equal protection of the laws. Under the Thirteenth Amendment the legislation, so far as necessary or proper to eradicate all forms and incidents of slavery and involuntary servitude, may be direct and primary, operating upon the acts of individuals, whether sanctioned by state legislation or not; under the Fourteenth, as we have already shown, it must necessarily be, and can only be, corrective in its character, addressed to counteract and afford relief against state regulations or proceedings.

The only question under the present head, therefore, is, whether the refusal to any persons of the accommodations of an inn, or a public conveyance, or a place of public amusement, by an individual, and without any sanction or support from any state law or regulation, does inflict upon such persons any manner of servitude, or form of slavery, as those terms are understood in this country? Many wrongs may be obnoxious to the prohibitions of the Fourteenth Amendment which are not, in any just sense, incidents or elements of slavery. Such, for example, would be the taking of private property without due process of law; or allowing persons who have committed certain crimes (horse-stealing, for example) to be seized and hung by the *posse comitatus* without regular trial; or denying to any person, or class of persons, the right to pursue any peaceful avocations allowed to others. What is called class legislation would belong to this category, and would be obnoxious to the prohibitions of the Fourteenth Amendment, but would not to the prohibitions of the Fourteenth when not involving the idea of any subjection of one man to another. The Thirteenth Amendment has respect, not to distinctions of race, or class, or color, but to slavery. The Fourteenth Amendment extends its protection to races and classes, and prohibits any state legislation which has the effect of denying to any race or class, or to any individual, the equal protection of the laws. [. . .]

After giving to these questions all the consideration which their importance demands, we are forced to the conclusion that such an act of refusal has nothing to do with slavery or involuntary servitude, and that if it is violative of any right of the party, his redress is to be sought under the laws of the state; or, if those laws are adverse to his rights and do not protect him, his remedy will be found in the corrective legislation which Congress has adopted, or may adopt, for counteracting the effect of state laws, or state action, prohibited by the Fourteenth Amendment. It would be running the slavery argument into the ground to make it apply to every act of discrimination which a person may see fit to make as to the guests he will entertain, or as to the people he will take into his coach or cab or car, or admit to his concert or theater, or deal with in other matters of intercourse or business. Innkeepers and public carriers, by the laws of all the states, so far as we are aware, are bound, to the extent of their facilities, to furnish proper accommodation to all unobjectionable persons who in good faith apply for them. If the laws themselves make any unjust discrimination, amenable to the prohibitions of the Fourteenth Amendment, Congress has full power to afford a remedy under that amendment and in accordance with it.

When a man has emerged from slavery, and by the aid of beneficent legislation has shaken off the inseparable concomitants of that state, there must be some stage in the progress of his elevation when he takes the rank of a mere citizen, and ceases to be the special favorite of the laws, and when his rights as a citizen, or a man, are to be protected in the ordinary modes by which other men's rights are protected. There were thousands of free colored people in this country before the abolition of slavery, enjoying all the essential rights of life, liberty, and property the same as white citizens; yet no one, at that time, thought that it was any invasion of their personal status as freemen because they were not admitted to all the privileges enjoyed by white citizens, or because they were subjected to discriminations in the enjoyment of accommodations in inns, public conveyances, and places of amusement. Mere discriminations on account of race or color were not regarded as badges of slavery. If, since that time, the enjoyment of equal rights in all these respects has become established by constitutional enactment, it is not by force of the Thirteenth Amendment, (which merely abolishes slavery,) but by force of the Fourteenth and Fifteenth Amendments.

On the whole, we are of opinion that no countenance of authority for the passage of the law in question can be found in either the Thirteenth or Fourteenth Amendment of the Constitution; and no other ground of authority for its passage being suggested, it must necessarily be declared void, at least so far as its operation in the several states is concerned. [. . .]

JOHN MARSHALL HARLAN

The Civil Rights Cases, Dissent (1883)

Justice HARLAN, dissenting.

The opinion in these cases proceeds, as it seems to me, upon grounds entirely too narrow and artificial. The substance and spirit of the recent amendments of the Constitution have been sacrificed by a subtle and ingenious verbal criticism. "It is not the words of the law but the internal sense of it that makes the law. The letter of the law is the body; the sense and reason of the law is the soul." Constitutional provisions, adopted in the interest of liberty, and for the purpose of securing, through national legislation, if need be, rights inhering in a state of freedom, and belonging to American citizenship, have been so construed as to defeat the ends the people desired to accomplish, which they attempted to accomplish, and which they supposed they had accomplished by changes in their fundamental law. By this I do not mean that the determination of these cases should have been materially controlled by considerations of mere expediency or policy. I mean only, in this form, to express an earnest conviction that the court has departed from the familiar rule requiring, in the interpretation of constitutional provisions, that full effect be given to the intent with which they were adopted. [. . .]

The Thirteenth Amendment, my brethren concede, did something more than to prohibit slavery as an institution, resting upon distinctions of race, and upheld by positive law. They admit that it established and decreed universal civil freedom throughout the United States. But did the freedom thus established involve nothing more than exemption from actual slavery? Was nothing more intended than to forbid one man from owning another as property? Was it the purpose of the nation simply to destroy the institution, and then remit the race, theretofore held in bondage, to the several states for such protection, in their civil rights, necessarily growing out of freedom, as those states, in their discretion, choose to provide? Were the states, against whose solemn protest the institution was destroyed, to be left perfectly free, so far as national interference was concerned, to make or allow discriminations against that race, as such, in the enjoyment of those fundamental rights that inhere in a state of freedom? Had the Thirteenth Amendment stopped with the sweeping declaration, in its first section, against the existence of slavery and involuntary servitude, except for crime, Congress would have had the power, by implication, according to the doctrines of *Prigg v. Com* [1842], repeated in *Strauder v. West Virginia* [1880], to protect the freedom thus established, and consequently to secure the enjoyment of such civil rights as were fundamental in freedom. But that it can exert its authority to that extent is now made clear, and was intended to be made clear, by the express grant of power contained in the second section of that amendment.

That there are burdens and disabilities which constitute badges of slavery and servitude, and that the express power delegated to Congress to enforce, by appropriate legislation, the Thirteenth Amendment, may be exerted by legislation of a direct and primary character, for the eradication, not simply of the institution, but of its badges and incidents, are propositions which ought to be deemed indisputable. They lie at the very foundation of the civil rights act of 1866. Whether that act was fully authorized by the Thirteenth Amendment alone, without the support which it afterwards received from the Fourteenth Amendment, after the adoption of which it was reenacted with some additions, the court, in its opinion, says it is unnecessary to inquire. But I submit, with all respect to my brethren, that its constitutionality is conclusively shown by other portions of their opinion. It is expressly conceded by them that the Thirteenth Amendment established freedom; that there are burdens and disabilities, the necessary incidents of slavery, which constitute its substance and visible form; that Congress, by the act of 1866, passed in view of the Thirteenth Amendment, before the Fourteenth was adopted, undertook to remove certain burdens and disabilities, the necessary incidents of slavery, and to secure to all citizens of every race and color, and without regard to previous servitude, those fundamental rights which are the essence of civil freedom, namely, the same right to make and enforce contracts, to sue, be parties, give evidence, and to inherit, purchase, lease, sell, and convey property as is enjoyed by white citizens; that under the Thirteenth Amendment Congress has to do with slavery and its incidents; and that legislation, so far as necessary or proper to eradicate all forms and incidents of slavery and involuntary servitude, may be direct and primary, operating upon the acts of individuals, whether sanctioned by state legislation or not. These propositions being conceded, it is impossible, as it seems to me, to question the constitutional validity of the civil rights act of 1866. I do not contend that the Thirteenth Amendment invests Congress with authority, by legislation, to regulate the entire body of the civil rights which citizens enjoy, or may enjoy, in the several states. But I do hold that since slavery, as the court has repeatedly declared, was the moving or principal cause of the adoption of that amendment, and since that institution rested wholly upon the inferiority, as a race, of those held in bondage, their freedom necessarily involved immunity from, and protection against, all discrimination against them, because of their race, in respect of such civil rights as belong to freemen of other races. Congress, therefore, under its express power to enforce that amendment, by appropriate legislation, may enact laws to protect that people against the deprivation, on account of their race, of any civil rights enjoyed by other freemen in the same state; and such legislation may be of a direct and primary character, operating upon states, their officers and agents, and also upon, at least, such individuals and corporations as exercise public functions and wield power and authority under the state. [. . .]

What has been said is sufficient to show that the power of Congress under the Thirteenth Amendment is not necessarily restricted to legislation against slavery as an institution upheld by positive law, but may be exerted to the extent at least of protecting the race, so liberated, against discrimination, in respect of legal rights belonging to freemen, where such discrimination is based upon race. [. . .]

I also submit whether it can be said—in view of the doctrines of this court as announced in *Munn v. Illinois* [1877], that the management of places of public amusement is a purely private matter, with which government has no rightful concern. In the *Munn* Case the question was whether the state of Illinois could fix, by law, the maximum of charges for the storage of grain in certain warehouses in that state—the private property of individual citizens. After quoting a remark attributed to Lord Chief Justice Hale, to the effect that when private property is "affected with a public interest it ceases to be *juris privati* only," the court says:

> Property does become clothed with a public interest when used in a manner to make it of public consequence and affect the community at large. When, therefore, one devotes his property to a use in which the public has an interest, he in effect grants to the public an interest in that use, and must submit to be controlled by the public for the common good to the extent of the interest he has thus created. He may withdraw his grant by discontinuing the use, but, so long as he maintains the use, he must submit to the control.

The doctrines of *Munn v. Illinois* have never been modified by this court, and I am justified, upon the authority of that case, in saying that places of public amusement, conducted under the authority of the law, are clothed with a public interest, because used in a manner to make them of public consequence and to affect the community at large. The law may therefore regulate, to some extent, the mode in which they shall be conducted, and consequently the public have rights in respect of such places which may be vindicated by the law. It is consequently not a matter purely of private concern.

Congress has not, in these matters, entered the domain of state control and supervision. It does not assume to prescribe the general conditions and limitations under which inns, public conveyances, and places of public amusement shall be conducted or managed. It simply declares in effect that since the nation has established universal freedom in this country for all time, there shall be no discrimination, based merely upon race or color, in respect of the legal rights in the accommodations and advantages of public conveyances, inns, and places of public amusement.

I am of opinion that such discrimination is a badge of servitude, the imposition of which Congress may prevent under its power, through appropriate legislation, to enforce the Thirteenth Amendment; and consequently, without reference to its enlarged power under the Fourteenth Amendment, the act of March 1, 1875, is not, in my judgment, repugnant to the Constitution.

It remains now to consider these cases with reference to the power Congress has possessed since the adoption of the Fourteenth Amendment.

Before the adoption of the recent amendments it had become, as we have seen, the established doctrine of this court that negroes, whose ancestors had been imported and sold as slaves, could not become citizens of a state, or even of the United States, with the rights and privileges guaranteed to citizens by the national Constitution; further, that one might have all the rights and privileges of a citizen of a state without being a citizen in the sense in which that word was used in the national Constitution, and without being entitled to the privileges and immunities of citizens of the several states. Still further, between the adoption of the Thirteenth Amendment and the proposal by Congress of the Fourteenth Amendment, on June 16, 1866, the statute-books of several of the states, as we have seen, had become loaded down with enactments which, under the guise of apprentice, vagrant, and contract regulations, sought to keep the colored race in a condition, practically, of servitude. It was openly announced that whatever rights persons of that race might have as freemen, under the guaranties of the national Constitution, they could not become citizens of a state, with the rights belonging to citizens, except by the consent of such state; consequently, that their civil rights, as citizens of the state, depended entirely upon state legislation. To meet this new peril to the black race, that the purposes of the nation might not be doubted or defeated, and by way of further enlargement of the power of Congress, the Fourteenth Amendment was proposed for adoption. [. . .]

Remembering that this court, in the *Slaughter-House Cases* [1873], declared that the one pervading purpose found in all the recent amendments, lying at the foundation of each, and without which none of them would have been suggested, was "the freedom of the slave race, the security and firm establishment of that freedom, and the protection of the newly-made freeman and citizen from the oppression of those who had formerly exercised unlimited dominion over him"—that each amendment was addressed primarily to the grievances of that race—let us proceed to consider the language of the Fourteenth Amendment. Its first and fifth sections are in these words:

> Section 1. All persons born or naturalized in the United States, and subject to the jurisdiction thereof, are citizens of the United States and of the state wherein they reside. No state shall make or enforce any law which shall abridge the privileges or immunities of citizens of the United States; nor shall any state deprive any person of life, liberty, or property without due process of law; nor deny to any person within its jurisdiction the equal protection of the laws.
>
> Sec. 5. That Congress shall have power to enforce, by appropriate legislation, the provisions of this article.

[. . .] But when, under what circumstances, and to what extent may Congress, by means of legislation, exert its power to enforce the provisions of this amendment? The logic of the opinion of the majority of the court—the foundation upon which its whole reasoning seems to rest—is that the general government cannot, in advance of hostile state laws or hostile state proceedings, actively interfere for the protection of any of the rights, privileges, and immunities

secured by the Fourteenth Amendment. It is said that such rights, privileges, and immunities are secured by way of prohibition against state laws and state proceedings affecting such rights and privileges, and by power given to Congress to legislate for the purpose of carrying such prohibition into effect; also, that congressional legislation must necessarily be predicated upon such supposed state laws or state proceedings, and be directed to the correction of their operation and effect. [. . .]

The assumption that this amendment consists wholly of prohibitions upon state laws and state proceedings in hostility to its provisions, is unauthorized by its language. The first clause of the first section . . . is of a distinctly affirmative character. In its application to the colored race, previously liberated, it created and granted, as well citizenship of the United States, as citizenship of the state in which they respectively resided. It introduced all of that race, whose ancestors had been imported and sold as slaves, at once, into the political community known as the "People of the United States." They became, instantly, citizens of the United States, and of their respective states. Further, they were brought, by this supreme act of the nation, within the direct operation of that provision of the Constitution which declares that "the citizens of each state shall be entitled to all privileges and immunities of citizens in the several states." Article 4, 2.

The citizenship thus acquired by that race, in virtue of an affirmative grant by the nation, may be protected, not alone by the judicial branch of the government, but by congressional legislation of a primary direct character; this, because the power of Congress is not restricted to the enforcement of prohibitions upon state laws or state action. It is, in terms distinct and positive, to enforce "the provisions of this article" of amendment; not simply those of a prohibitive character, but the provisions,—all of the provisions,—affirmative and prohibitive, of the amendment. It is, therefore, a grave misconception to suppose that the fifth section of the amendment has reference exclusively to express prohibitions upon state laws or state action. If any right was created by that amendment, the grant of power, through appropriate legislation, to enforce its provisions authorizes Congress, by means of legislation operating throughout the entire Union, to guard, secure, and protect that right.

It is, therefore, an essential inquiry what, if any, right, privilege, or immunity was given by the nation to colored persons when they were made citizens of the state in which they reside? Did the national grant of state citizenship to that race, of its own force, invest them with any rights, privileges, and immunities whatever? That they became entitled, upon the adoption of the Fourteenth Amendment, "to all privileges and immunities of citizens in the several states," within the meaning of section 2 of article 4 of the Constitution, no one, I suppose, will for a moment question. What are the privileges and immunities to which, by that clause of the Constitution, they became entitled? To this it may be answered, generally, upon the authority of the adjudged cases, that they are those which are fundamental in citizenship in a free government, "common to the citizens in the latter states under their constitutions and laws by virtue of their being citizens."

Of that provision it has been said, with the approval of this court, that no other one in the Constitution has tended so strongly to constitute the citizens of the United States one people.

Although this court has wisely forborne any attempt, by a comprehensive definition, to indicate all the privileges and immunities to which the citizens of each state are entitled of right to enjoy in the several states, I hazard nothing, in view of former adjudications, in saying that no state can sustain her denial to colored citizens of other states, while within her limits, of privileges or immunities, fundamental in republican citizenship, upon the ground that she accords such privileges and immunities only to her white citizens and withholds them from her colored citizens. The colored citizens of other states, within the jurisdiction of that state, could claim, under the Constitution, every privilege and immunity which that state secures to her white citizens. Otherwise, it would be in the power of any state, by discriminating class legislation against its own citizens of a particular race or color, to withhold from citizens of other states, belonging to that proscribed race, when within her limits, privileges and immunities of the character regarded by all courts as fundamental in citizenship; and that, too, when the constitutional guaranty is that the citizens of each state shall be entitled to "all privileges and immunities of citizens of the several states." [. . .]

But what was secured to colored citizens of the United States—as between them and their respective states—by the grant to them of state citizenship? With what rights, privileges, or immunities did this grant from the nation invest them? There is one, if there be no other—exemption from race discrimination in respect of any civil right belonging to citizens of the white race in the same state. That, surely, is their constitutional privilege when within the jurisdiction of other states. And such must be their constitutional right, in their own state, unless the recent amendments be "splendid baubles," thrown out to delude those who deserved fair and generous treatment at the hands of the nation. Citizenship in this country necessarily imports equality of civil rights among citizens of every race in the same state. It is fundamental in American citizenship that, in respect of such rights, there shall be no discrimination by the state, or its officers, or by individuals, or corporations exercising public functions or authority, against any citizen because of his race or previous condition of servitude. In *United States v. Cruikshank* [1876], it was said that "the equality of rights of citizens is a principle of republicanism." And in *Ex parte Virginia* [1879], the emphatic language of this court is that "one great purpose of these amendments was to raise the colored race from that condition of inferiority and servitude in which most of them had previously stood, into perfect equality of civil rights with all other persons within the jurisdiction of the states." So, in *Strauder v. West Virginia* [1880], the court, alluding to the Fourteenth Amendment, said: "This is one of a series of constitutional provisions having a common purpose, namely, securing to a race recently emancipated, a race that through many generations had been held in slavery, all the civil rights that the superior race enjoy." [. . .]

Much light is thrown upon this part of the discussion by the language of this court in reference to the Fifteenth Amendment. In *United States v. Cruikshank* it was said:

> In *United States v. Reese* [1876], we held that the Fifteenth Amendment has invested the citizens of the United States with a new constitutional right, which is exemption from discrimination in the exercise of the elective franchise on account of race, color, or previous condition of servitude.

From this it appears that the right of suffrage is not a necessary attribute of national citizenship, but that exemption from discrimination in the exercise of that right on account of race, etc., is. The right to vote in the states comes from the states; but the right of exemption from the prohibited discrimination comes from the United States. The first has not been granted or secured by the Constitution of the United States, but the last has been.

Here, in language at once clear and forcible, is stated the principle for which I contend. It can hardly be claimed that exemption from race discrimination, in respect of civil rights, against those to whom state citizenship was granted by the nation, is any less for the colored race a new constitutional right, derived from and secured by the national Constitution, than is exemption from such discrimination in the exercise of the elective franchise. It cannot be that the latter is an attribute of national citizenship, while the other is not essential in national citizenship, or fundamental in state citizenship.

If, then, exemption from discrimination in respect of civil rights is a new constitutional right, secured by the grant of state citizenship to colored citizens of the United States, why may not the nation, by means of its own legislation of a primary direct character, guard, protect, and enforce that right? It is a right and privilege which the nation conferred. It did not come from the states in which those colored citizens reside. It has been the established doctrine of this court during all its history, accepted as vital to the national supremacy, that Congress, in the absence of a positive delegation of power to the state legislatures, may by legislation enforce and protect any right derived from or created by the national Constitution. [. . .]

This court has always given a broad and liberal construction to the Constitution, so as to enable Congress, by legislation, to enforce rights secured by that instrument. The legislation Congress may enact, in execution of its power to enforce the provisions of this amendment, is that which is appropriate to protect the right granted. Under given circumstances, that which the court characterizes as corrective legislation might be sufficient. Under other circumstances primary direct legislation may be required. But it is for Congress, not the judiciary, to say which is best adapted to the end to be attained. [. . .] "The

sound construction of the Constitution," said Chief Justice Marshall, "must allow to the national legislature that discretion, with respect to the means by which the powers it confers are to be carried into execution, which will enable that body to perform the high duties assigned to it in the manner most beneficial to the people. Let the end be legitimate, let it be within the scope of the Constitution, and all means which are appropriate, which are plainly adapted to that end, which are not prohibited, but consistent with the letter and spirit of the Constitution, are constitutional." *McCulloch v. Maryland* [1819].

Must these rules of construction be now abandoned? Are the powers of the national legislature to be restrained in proportion as the rights and privileges, derived from the nation, are more valuable? Are constitutional provisions, enacted to secure the dearest rights of freemen and citizens, to be subjected to that rule of construction, applicable to private instruments, which requires that the words to be interpreted must be taken most strongly against those who employ them? Or shall it be remembered that "a constitution of government, founded by the people for themselves and their posterity, and for objects of the most momentous nature — for perpetual union, for the establishment of justice, for the general welfare, and for a perpetuation of the blessings of liberty — necessarily requires that every interpretation of its powers should have a constant reference to these objects? No interpretation of the words in which those powers are granted can be a sound one which narrows down their ordinary import so as to defeat those objects." 1 Story, Const. 422.

The opinion of the court, as I have said, proceeds upon the ground that the power of Congress to legislate for the protection of the rights and privileges secured by the Fourteenth Amendment cannot be brought into activity except with the view, and as it may become necessary, to correct and annul state laws and state proceedings in hostility to such rights and privileges. In the absence of state laws or state action, adverse to such rights and privileges, the nation may not actively interfere for their protection and security. Such I understand to be the position of my brethren. If the grant to colored citizens of the United States of citizenship in their respective states imports exemption from race discrimination, in their states, in respect of the civil rights belonging to citizenship, then, to hold that the amendment remits that right to the states for their protection, primarily, and stays the hands of the nation, until it is assailed by state laws or state proceedings, is to adjudge that the amendment, so far from enlarging the powers of Congress—as we have heretofore said it did—not only curtails them, but reverses the policy which the general government has pursued from its very organization. Such an interpretation of the amendment is a denial to Congress of the power, by appropriate legislation, to enforce one of its provisions. In view of the circumstances under which the recent amendments were incorporated into the Constitution, and especially in view of the peculiar character of the new rights they created and secured, it ought not to be presumed that the general government has abdicated its authority, by national legislation, direct and primary in its character, to guard and protect privileges and immunities secured by that instrument. Such an interpretation of the Constitution ought not to be accepted if it be possible to avoid it. Its acceptance would lead to this anomalous result: that whereas, prior to the amendments, Congress, with the sanction of this court, passed the most stringent laws—operating directly and primarily upon states, and their officers and agents, as well as upon individuals—in vindication of slavery and the right of the master, it may not now, by legislation of a like primary and direct character, guard, protect, and secure the freedom established, and the most essential right of the citizenship granted, by the constitutional amendments. I venture, with all respect for the opinion of others, to insist that the national legislature may, without transcending the limits of the Constitution, do for human liberty and the fundamental rights of American citizenship, what it did, with the sanction of this court, for the protection of slavery and the rights of the masters of fugitive slaves. If fugitive slave laws, providing modes and prescribing penalties whereby the master could seize and recover his fugitive slave, were legitimate exertions of an implied power to protect and enforce a right recognized by the Constitution, why shall the hands of Congress be tied, so that—under an express power, by appropriate legislation, to enforce a constitutional provision, granting citizenship—it may not, by means of direct legislation, bring the whole power of this nation to bear upon states and their officers, and

upon such individuals and corporations exercising public functions, as assume to abridge, impair, or deny rights confessedly secured by the supreme law of the land?

It does not seem to me that the fact that, by the second clause of the first section of the Fourteenth Amendment, the states are expressly prohibited from making or enforcing laws abridging the privileges and immunities of citizens of the United States, furnishes any sufficient reason for holding or maintaining that the amendment was intended to deny Congress the power, by general, primary, and direct legislation, of protecting citizens of the United States, being also citizens of their respective states, against discrimination, in respect to their rights as citizens, founded on race, color, or previous condition of servitude. Such an interpretation of the amendment is plainly repugnant to its fifth section, conferring upon Congress power, by appropriate legislation, to enforce, not merely the provisions containing prohibitions upon the states, but all of the provisions of the amendment, including the provisions, express and implied, of the grant of citizenship in the first clause of the first section of the article. This alone is sufficient for holding that Congress is not restricted to the enactment of laws adapted to counteract and redress the operation of state legislation, or the action of state officers of the character prohibited by the amendment. It was perfectly well known that the great danger to the equal enjoyment by citizens of their rights, as citizens, was to be apprehended, not altogether from unfriendly state legislation, but from the hostile action of corporations and individuals in the states. And it is to be presumed that it was intended, by that section, to clothe Congress with power and authority to meet that danger. If the rights intended to be secured by the act of 1875 are such as belong to the citizen, in common or equally with other citizens in the same state, then it is not to be denied that such legislation is appropriate to the end which Congress is authorized to accomplish, viz., to protect the citizen, in respect of such rights, against discrimination on account of his race. As to the prohibition in the Fourteenth Amendment upon the making or enforcing of state laws abridging the privileges of citizens of the United States, it was impossible for any state to have enforced laws of that character. The judiciary could have annulled all such legislation under the provision that the Constitution shall be the supreme law of the land, anything in the Constitution or laws of any state to the contrary notwithstanding. The states were already under an implied prohibition not to abridge any privilege or immunity belonging to citizens of the United States as such. Consequently, the prohibition upon state laws hostile to the rights belonging to citizens of the United States, was intended only as an express limitation on the powers of the states, and was not intended to diminish, in the slightest degree, the authority which the nation has always exercised, of protecting, by means of its own direct legislation, rights created or secured by the Constitution. The purpose not to diminish the national authority is distinctly negatived by the express grant of power, by legislation, to enforce every provision of the amendment, including that which, by the grant of citizenship in the state, secures exemption from race discrimination in respect of the civil rights of citizens. [. . .]

But the court says that Congress did not, in the act of 1866, assume, under the authority given by the Thirteenth Amendment, to adjust what may be called the social rights of men and races in the community. I agree that government has nothing to do with social, as distinguished from technically legal, rights of individuals. No government ever has brought, or ever can bring, its people into social intercourse against their wishes. Whether one person will permit or maintain social relations with another is a matter with which government has no concern. I agree that if one citizen chooses not to hold social intercourse with another, he is not and cannot be made amenable to the law for his conduct in that regard; for no legal right of a citizen is violated by the refusal of others to maintain merely social relations with him, even upon grounds of race. What I affirm is that no state, nor the officers of any state, nor any corporation or individual wielding power under state authority for the public benefit or the public convenience, can, consistently either with the freedom established by the fundamental law, or with that equality of civil rights which now belongs to every citizen, discriminate against freemen or citizens, in their civil rights, because of their race, or because they once labored under disabilities imposed upon them as a race. The rights which Congress, by the act

of 1875, endeavored to secure and protect are legal, not social, rights. The right, for instance, of a colored citizen to use the accommodations of a public highway upon the same terms as are permitted to white citizens is no more a social right than his right, under the law, to use the public streets of a city, or a town, or a turnpike road, or a public market, or a post-office, or his right to sit in a public building with others, of whatever race, for the purpose of hearing the political questions of the day discussed. Scarcely a day passes without our seeing in this court-room citizens of the white and black races sitting side by side watching the progress of our business. It would never occur to any one that the presence of a colored citizen in a court-house or court-room was an invasion of the social rights of white persons who may frequent such places. [. . .]

My brethren say that when a man has emerged from slavery, and by the aid of beneficent legislation has shaken off the inseparable concomitants of that state, there must be some stage in the progress of his elevation when he takes the rank of a mere citizen, and ceases to be the special favorite of the laws, and when his rights as a citizen, or a man, are to be protected in the ordinary modes by which other men's rights are protected. It is, I submit, scarcely just to say that the colored race has been the special favorite of the laws. What the nation, through Congress, has sought to accomplish in reference to that race is, what had already been done in every state in the Union for the white race, to secure and protect rights belonging to them as freemen and citizens; nothing more. The one underlying purpose of congressional legislation has been to enable the black race to take the rank of mere citizens. The difficulty has been to compel a recognition of their legal right to take that rank, and to secure the enjoyment of privileges belonging, under the law, to them as a component part of the people for whose welfare and happiness government is ordained. At every step in this direction the nation has been confronted with class tyranny, which a contemporary English historian says is, of all tyrannies, the most intolerable, "for it is ubiquitous in its operation, and weighs, perhaps, most heavily on those whose obscurity or distance would withdraw them from the notice of a single despot." Today it is the colored race which is denied, by corporations and individuals wielding public authority, rights fundamental in their freedom and citizenship. At some future time it may be some other race that will fall under the ban. If the constitutional amendments be enforced, according to the intent with which, as I conceive, they were adopted, there cannot be, in this republic, any class of human beings in practical subjection to another class, with power in the latter to dole out to the former just such privileges as they may choose to grant. The supreme law of the land has decreed that no authority shall be exercised in this country upon the basis of discrimination, in respect of civil rights, against freemen and citizens because of their race, color, or previous condition of servitude. To that decree—for the due enforcement of which, by appropriate legislation, Congress has been invested with express power—every one must bow, whatever may have been, or whatever now are, his individual views as to the wisdom or policy, either of the recent changes in the fundamental law, or of the legislation which has been enacted to give them effect.

For the reasons stated I feel constrained to withhold my assent to the opinion of the court.

HORACE GRAY

Elk v. Wilkins (1884)

Justice GRAY delivered the opinion of the Court.

This is an action brought by an Indian, in the circuit court of the United States for the district of Nebraska, against the registrar of one of the wards of the city of Omaha, for refusing to register him as a qualified voter therein. The petition was as follows:

John Elk, plaintiff, complains of Charles Wilkins, defendant, and avers that [. . .] he, the plaintiff, is an Indian, and was born within the United States; that more than one year prior to the grievances hereinafter complained of he had severed his tribal relation to the Indian tribes, and had fully and completely surrendered himself to the jurisdiction of the United States, and still so continues subject to the jurisdiction of the United States; and avers that, under and by virtue of the Fourteenth Amendment to the Constitution of the United States, he is a citizen of the United States, and entitled to the right and privilege of citizens of the United States. That on the sixth day of April, 1880, there was held in the city of Omaha [. . .] a general election for the election of members of the city council and other officers for said city. That the defendant, Charles Wilkins, held the office of and acted as registrar in the Fifth ward of said city, and that as such registrar it was the duty of such defendant to register the names of all persons entitled to exercise the elective franchise in said ward of said city at said general election. That this plaintiff was a citizen of and had been a bona fide resident of the state of Nebraska for more than six months prior to said sixth day of April, 1880 [. . .] and was in every way qualified, under the laws of the state of Nebraska and of the city of Omaha, to be registered as a voter, and to cast a vote at said election, and complied with the laws of the city and state in that behalf.

That on or about the fifth day of April, 1880, and prior to said election, this plaintiff presented himself to said Charles Wilkins, as such registrar, at his office, for the purpose of having his name registered as a qualified voter, as provided by law, and complied with all the provisions of the statutes in that regard, and claimed that, under the Fourteenth and Fifteenth Amendments to the Constitution of the United States, he was a citizen of the United States, and was entitled to exercise the elective franchise, regardless of his race and color; and that said Wilkins, designedly, corruptly, willfully, and maliciously, did then and there refuse to register this plaintiff, for the sole reason that the plaintiff was an Indian, and therefore not a citizen of the United States, and not, therefore, entitled to vote, and on account of his race and color. [. . .]

By the constitution of the state of Nebraska, art. 7, 1, "every male person of the age of twenty-one years or upwards, belonging to either of the following classes, who shall have resided in the state six months, and in the county, precinct, or ward for the term provided by law, shall be an elector: First, citizens of the United States; second, persons of foreign birth who shall have declared their intention to become citizens, conformably to the laws of the United States on the subject of naturalization, at least thirty days prior to an election." By the statutes of Nebraska, every male person of the age of 21 years or upward, belonging to either of the two classes so defined in the Constitution of the state, who shall have resided in the state 6 months [. . .] shall be an elector. [. . .]

The plaintiff, in support of his action, relies on the first clause of the first section of the fourteenth article of amendment of the Constitution of the United States, by which "all persons born or naturalized in the United States, and subject to the jurisdiction thereof, are citizens of the United States and of the state wherein they reside;" and on the fifteenth article of amendment, which provides that "the right of citizens of the United States to vote shall not be denied or abridged by the United States or by any state on account of race, color, or previous condition of servitude." This being a suit at common law in which the matter in dispute exceeds $500, arising under the Constitution of the United States, the circuit court had jurisdiction. [. . .] The judgment of that court, dismissing the action with costs, must have proceeded upon the merits, for if the dismissal had been for want of jurisdiction, no costs could have been awarded. And the only point argued by the defendant in this court is whether the petition sets forth facts enough to constitute a cause of action. The decision of this point, as both parties assume in their briefs, depends upon the question whether the legal conclusion, that under and by virtue of the Fourteenth Amendment of the Constitution the plaintiff is a citizen of the United States, is supported by the facts alleged in the petition and admitted by the demurrer, to-wit: The plaintiff is an Indian, and was born in the United States, and has severed his tribal relation to the Indian tribes, and fully and completely surrendered himself to the jurisdiction of the United States, and still continues to be subject to the jurisdiction of the United States, and is a bona fide resident of the state of Nebraska and city of Omaha. The petition, while it does not show of what Indian tribe the plaintiff was a member, yet, by the allegations that he "is an Indian, and was born within the United States," and that "he had severed his tribal relations to the Indian tribes," clearly implies that he was born a member of one of the Indian tribes within the limits of the United States which still exists and is recognized as a tribe by the government of the United States. Though the plaintiff alleges that he "had fully and completely surrendered himself to the jurisdiction of the United States," he does not allege that the United States accepted his surrender, or that he has ever been naturalized, or taxed, or in any way recognized or treated as a citizen by the state or by the United States. Nor is it contended by his counsel that there is any statute or treaty that makes him a citizen.

The question then is, whether an Indian, born a member of one of the Indian tribes within the United States, is, merely by reason of his birth within the United States, and of his afterwards voluntarily separating himself from his tribe and taking up his residence among white citizens, a citizen of the United States, within the meaning of the first section of the Fourteenth Amendment of the Constitution. Under the Constitution of the United States, as originally established, "Indians not taxed" were excluded from the persons according to whose numbers representatives and direct taxes were apportioned among the several states; and Congress had and exercised the power to regulate commerce with the Indian tribes, and the members thereof, whether within or without the boundaries of one of the states of the Union. The Indian tribes, being within the territorial limits of the United States, were not, strictly speaking, foreign states; but they were alien nations, distinct political communities, with whom the United States might and habitually did deal, as they thought fit, either through treaties made by the president and senate, or through acts of Congress in the ordinary forms of legislation. The members of those tribes owed immediate allegiance to their several tribes, and were not part of the people of the United States. They were in a dependent condition, a state of pupilage, resembling that of a ward to his guardian. Indians and their property, exempt from taxation by treaty or statute of the United States, could not be taxed by any state. General acts of Congress did not apply to Indians, unless so expressed as to clearly manifest an intention to include them.

The alien and dependent condition of the members of the Indian tribes could not be put off at their own will without the action or assent of the United States. They were never deemed citizens of the United States, except under explicit provisions of treaty or statute to that effect, either declaring a certain tribe, or such members of it as chose to remain behind on the removal of the tribe westward, to be citizens, or authorizing individuals of particular tribes to become citizens on application to a court of the United States for naturalization and satisfactory proof of fitness for civilized life. [. . .]

Chief Justice Taney, in the passage cited for the plaintiff from his opinion in [*Dred*] *Scott v. Sandford* [1857], did not affirm or imply that either the Indian tribes, or individual members of those tribes, had the right, beyond other foreigners, to become citizens of their own will, without being naturalized by the United States. His words were: "They" (the Indian tribes) "may without doubt, like the subjects of any foreign government, be naturalized by the authority of Congress, and become citizens of a state, and of the United States; and if an individual should leave his nation or tribe, and take up his abode among the white population, he would be entitled to all the rights and privileges which would belong to an emigrant from any other foreign people." But an emigrant from any foreign state cannot become a citizen of the United States without a formal renunciation of his old allegiance, and an acceptance by the United States of that renunciation through such form of naturalization as may be required law.

The distinction between citizenship by birth and citizenship by naturalization is clearly marked in the provisions of the Constitution, by which "no person, except a natural-born citizen, or a citizen of the United States at the time of the adoption of this Constitution, shall be eligible to the office of president;" and "the Congress shall have power to establish an uniform rule of naturalization." Const. art. 2, 1; art. 1, 8. By the Thirteenth Amendment of the Constitution slavery was prohibited. The main object of the opening sentence of the Fourteenth Amendment was to settle the question, upon which there had been a difference of opinion throughout the country and in this court, as to the citizenship of free negroes, and to put it beyond doubt that all persons, white or black, and whether formerly slaves or not, born or naturalized in the United States, and owing no allegiance to any alien power, should be citizens of the United States and of the state in which they reside. *Slaughter-House Cases* [1873]; *Strauder v. West Virginia* [1880]

This section contemplates two sources of citizenship, and two sources only: birth and naturalization. The persons declared to be citizens are "all persons born or naturalized in the United States, and subject to the jurisdiction thereof." The evident meaning of these last words is, not merely subject in some respect or degree to the jurisdiction of the United States, but completely subject to their political jurisdiction, and owing them direct and immediate allegiance. And the words relate to the time of birth in the one case, as they do to the time of naturalization in the other. Persons not thus subject to the jurisdiction of the United States at the time of birth cannot become so afterwards, except by being naturalized, either individually, as by proceedings under the naturalization acts; or collectively, as by the force of a treaty by which foreign territory is acquired. Indians born within the territorial limits of the United States, members of, and owing immediate allegiance to, one of the Indian tribes, (an alien though dependent power,) although in a geographical sense born in the United States, are no more "born in the United States and subject to the jurisdiction thereof," within the meaning of the first section of the Fourteenth Amendment, than the children of subjects of any foreign government born within the domain of that government, or the children born within the United States, of ambassadors or other public ministers of foreign nations. This view is confirmed by the second section of the Fourteenth Amendment, which provides that "representatives shall be apportioned among the several states according to their respective numbers, counting the whole number of persons in each state, excluding Indians not taxed." Slavery having been abolished, and the persons formerly held as slaves made citizens, this clause fixing the apportionment of representatives has abrogated so much of the corresponding clause of the original Constitution as counted only three-fifths of such persons. But Indians not taxed are still excluded from the count, for the reason that they are not citizens. Their absolute exclusion from the basis of representation, in which all other persons are now included, is wholly inconsistent with their being considered citizens. So the further provision of the second section for a proportionate reduction of the basis of the representation of any state in which the right to vote for presidential electors, representatives in Congress, or executive or judicial officers or members of the legislature of a state, is denied, except for participation in rebellion or other crime, to "any of the male inhabitants of such state, being twenty-one years of age and citizens of the United States," cannot apply to a denial of the elective franchise to Indians not taxed, who form no part of the people entitled to representation. [. . .]

Since the ratification of the Fourteenth Amendment, Congress has passed several acts for naturalizing Indians of certain tribes, which would have been superfluous if they were, or might become without any action of the government, citizens of the United States. By the act of July 15, 1870, for instance, it was provided that if at any time thereafter any of the Winnebago Indians in the state of Minnesota should desire to become citizens of the United States, they should make application to the district court of the United States for the district of Minnesota, and in open court make the same proof, and take the same oath of allegiance as is provided by law for the naturalization of aliens, and should also make proof, to the satisfaction of the court, that they were sufficiently intelligent and prudent to control their affairs and interests, that they had adopted the habits of civilized life, and had for at least five years before been able to support themselves and their families; and thereupon they should be declared by the court to be citizens of the United States, the declaration entered of record, and a certificate thereof given to the applicant; and the secretary of the interior, upon presentation of that certificate, might issue to them patents in fee-simple, with power of alienation, of the lands already held by them in severalty, and might cause to be paid to them their proportion of the money and effects of the tribe held in trust under any treaty or law of the United States; and thereupon such persons should cease to be members of the tribe; and the lands so patented to them should be subject to levy, taxation, and sale in like manner with the property of other citizens. By the act of March 3, 1873, similar provision was made for the naturalization of any adult members of the Miami tribe in Kansas, and of their minor children. [. . .]

The law upon the question before us has been well stated by Judge Deady in the district court of the United States for the district of Oregon. In giving judgment against the plaintiff in a case resembling the case at bar, he said: "Being born a member of "an independent political community"—the Chinook—he was not born subject to the jurisdiction of the United States—not born in its allegiance." *McKay v. Campbell*, 2 Sawy. 118, 134. And in a later case he said: "But an Indian cannot make himself a citizen of the United States without the consent and co-operation of the government. The fact that he has abandoned his nomadic life or tribal relations, and adopted the habits and manners of civilized people, may be a good reason why he should be made a citizen of the United States, but does not of itself make him one. To be a citizen of the United States is a political privilege which no one, not born to, can assume without its consent in some form. The Indians in Oregon, not being born subject to the jurisdiction of the United States, were not born citizens thereof, and I am not aware of any law or treaty by which any of them have been made so since." *United States v. Osborne* [1880]. Upon the question whether any action of a state can confer rights of citizenship on Indians of a tribe still recognized by the United States as retaining its tribal existence, we need not, and do not, express an opinion, because the state of Nebraska is not shown to have taken any action affecting the condition of this plaintiff. The plaintiff, not being a citizen of the United States under the Fourteenth Amendment of the Constitution, has been deprived of no right secured by the Fifteenth Amendment, and cannot maintain this action.

Judgment affirmed.

John Marshall Harlan

Elk v. Wilkins, Dissent (1884)

Justice Harlan, dissenting.

Mr. Justice Woods and myself feel constrained to express our dissent from the interpretation which our brethren give to that clause of the Fourteenth Amendment which provides that "all persons born or naturalized in the United States, and subject to the jurisdiction thereof, are citizens of the United States and of the state wherein they reside." [. . .]

It is said that the petition contains no averment that Elk was taxed in the state in which he resides, or had ever been treated by her as a citizen. It is evident that the court would not have held him to be a citizen of the United States, even if the petition had contained a direct averment that he was taxed; because its judgment, in legal effect, is that, although born within the territorial limits of the United States, he could not, if at his birth a member of an Indian tribe, acquire national citizenship by force of the Fourteenth Amendment, but only in pursuance of some statute or treaty providing for his naturalization. It would, therefore, seem unnecessary to inquire whether he was taxed at the time of his application to be registered as a voter; for, if the words "all persons born . . . in the United States and subject to the jurisdiction thereof" were not intended to embrace Indians born in tribal relations, but who subsequently became bona fide residents of the several states, then, manifestly, the legal status of such Indians is not altered by the fact that they are taxed in those states. While denying that national citizenship, as conferred by that Amendment, necessarily depends upon the inquiry whether the person claiming it is taxed in the state of his residence, or has property therein from which taxes may be derived, we submit that the petition does sufficiently show that the plaintiff was taxed, that is, belongs to the class which, by the laws of Nebraska, are subject to taxation. [. . .]

At the adoption of the Constitution there were, in many of the states, Indians, not members of any tribe, who constituted a part of the people for whose benefit the state governments were established. This is apparent from that clause of article 1, 3, which requires, in the apportionment of representatives and direct taxes among the several states "according to their respective numbers," the exclusion of "Indians not taxed." This implies that there were, at that time, in the United States, Indians who were taxed; that is, were subject to taxation by the laws of the state of which they were residents. Indians not taxed were those who held tribal relations, and therefore were not subject to the authority of any state, and were subject only to the authority of the United States, under the power conferred upon Congress in reference to Indian tribes in this country. The same provision is retained in the Fourteenth Amendment; for, now, as at the adoption of the Constitution, Indians in the several states, who are taxed by their laws, are counted in establishing the basis of representation in Congress. By the act of April 9, 1866, entitled "An act to protect all persons in the United States in their civil rights, and furnish means for their vindication," it is provided that "all persons born in the United States, and not subject to any foreign power, excluding Indians not taxed, are hereby declared to be citizens of the United States." This, so far as we are aware, is the first general enactment making persons of the Indian race citizens of the United States. Numerous statutes and treaties previously provided for all the individual members of particular Indian tribes becoming, in certain contingencies, citizens of the United States. But the act of 1866 reached Indians not in tribal relations. Beyond question, by that act, national citizenship was conferred directly upon all persons in this country, of whatever race (excluding only "Indians not taxed") who were born within the territorial limits of the United States, and were not subject to any foreign power. Surely every one must admit that an Indian residing in one of the states, and subject to taxation there, became, by force alone of the act of 1866, a citizen of the United States, although he may have been, when born, a member of a tribe. The exclusion of Indians not taxed evinced a purpose to include those subject to taxation in the state of their residence. Language could not express that purpose with more distinctness than does the act of 1866. Any doubt upon the subject, in respect to persons of the Indian race residing in the United States or territories, and not members of a tribe, will be removed by an examination of the debates, in which many distinguished statesmen and lawyers participated in the senate of the United States when the act of 1866 was under consideration.

In the bill as originally reported from the judiciary committee there were no words excluding "Indians not taxed" from the citizenship proposed to be granted. Attention being called to this fact, the friends of the measure disclaimed any purpose to make citizens of those who were in tribal relations, with governments of their own. In order to meet that objection, while conforming to the wishes of those desiring to invest with citizenship all Indians permanently separated from their tribes, and who, by reason of their residence away from their tribes, constituted a part of the people under the jurisdiction of the United States, Mr. Trumbull, who reported the bill, modified it by inserting the words "excluding Indians not taxed." What was intended by that modification appears from the following language used by him in debate: "Of course we cannot declare the wild Indians who do not recognize the government of the United States, who are not subject to our laws, with whom we make treaties, who have their own laws, who have their own regulations, whom we do not intend to interfere with or punish for the commission of crimes one upon the other, to be the subjects of the United States in the sense of being citizens. They must be excepted. The Constitution of the United States excludes them from the enumeration of the population of the United States when it says that Indians not taxed are to be excluded. It has occurred to me that, perhaps, the amendment would meet the views of all gentlemen, which used these constitutional words, and said that all persons born in the United States, excluding Indians not taxed, and not subject to any foreign power, shall be deemed citizens of the United States." Cong. Globe, (1st Sess. 39th Congress,) p. 527. In replying to the objections urged by Mr. Hendricks to the bill even as amended, Mr. Trumbull said: "Does the senator from Indiana want the wild roaming Indians, not taxed, not subject to our authority, to be citizens of the United States-persons that are not to be counted, in our government? If he does not, let him not object to this amendment that brings in even [only] the Indian when he shall have cast off his wild habits, and submitted to the laws of organized society and become a citizen." Id. 528.

The entire debate shows, with singular clearness, indeed, with absolute certainty, that no senator who participated in it, whether in favor of or in opposition to the measure, doubted that the bill as passed admitted, and was intended to admit, to national citizenship Indians who abandoned their tribal relations and became residents of one of the states or territories, within the full jurisdiction of the United States. It was so interpreted by President Johnson, who, in his veto message, said: "By the first section of the bill all persons born in the United States, and not subject to any foreign power, excluding Indians not taxed, are declared to be citizens of the United States. This provision comprehends the Chinese of the Pacific states, Indians subject to taxation, the people called gypsies, as well as the entire race designated as blacks, persons of color, negroes, mulattoes, and persons of African blood. Every individual of those races, born in the United States, is, by the bill, made a citizen of the United States."

It would seem manifest, from this brief review of the history of the act of 1866, that one purpose of that legislation was to confer national citizenship upon a part of the Indian race in this country—such of them, at least, as resided in one of the states or territories, and were subject to taxation and other public burdens. And it is to be observed that, whoever was included within the terms of the grant contained in that act, became citizens of the United States without any record of their names being made. The citizenship conferred was made to depend wholly upon the existence of the facts which the statute declared to be a condition precedent to the grant taking effect. At the same session of the Congress which passed the act of 1866, the Fourteenth Amendment was approved and submitted to the states for adoption. Those who sustained the former urged the adoption of the latter. An examination of the debates, pending the consideration of the amendment, will show that there was no purpose on the part of those who framed it, or of those who sustained it by their votes, to abandon the policy inaugurated by the act of 1866, of admitting to national citizenship such Indians as were separated from their tribes and were residents of one of the states or territories outside of any reservation set apart for the exclusive use and occupancy of Indian tribes. [. . .]

It seems to us that the Fourteenth Amendment, insofar as it was intended to confer national citizenship upon persons of the Indian race, is robbed of its vital force by a construction which excludes from such citizenship those who, although born in tribal relations, are within the complete jurisdiction of the United States. There were, in some of our states and territories at the time the amendment was submitted by Congress, many Indians who had finally left their tribes and come within the complete jurisdiction of the United States. They were as fully prepared for citizenship as were or are vast numbers of the white and colored races in the same localities. Is it conceivable that the statesmen who framed, the Congress which submitted, and the people who adopted that amendment intended to confer citizenship, national and state, upon the entire population in this country of African descent, (the larger part of which was shortly before held in slavery,) and, by the same constitutional provision, to exclude from such citizenship Indians who had never been in slavery, and who, by becoming bona fide residents of states and territories within the complete jurisdiction of the United States, had evinced a purpose to abandon their former mode of life, and become a part of the people of the United States? If this question be answered in the negative, as we think it must be, then we are justified in withholding our assent to the doctrine which excludes the plaintiff from the body of citizens of the United States upon the ground that his parents were, when he was born, members of an Indian tribe; for, if he can be excluded upon any such ground, it must necessarily follow that the Fourteenth Amendment did not grant citizenship even to Indians who, although born in tribal relations, were, at its adoption, severed from their tribes, subject to the complete jurisdiction as well of the United States as of the state or territory in which they resided.

Our brethren, it seems to us, construe the Fourteenth Amendment as if it read: "All persons born subject to the jurisdiction of, or naturalized in, the United States, are citizens of the United States and of the state in which they reside;" whereas the amendment, as it is, implies in respect of persons born in this country that they may claim the rights of national citizenship from and after the moment they become subject to the complete jurisdiction of the United States. This would not include the children born in this country of a foreign minister, for the reason that, under the fiction of extraterritoriality as recognized by international law, such minister, "though actually in a foreign country, is considered still to remain within the territory of his own state," and, consequently, he continues "subject to the laws of his own country, both with respect to his personal status and his rights of property; and his children, though born in a foreign country, are considered as natives." Nor was plaintiff born without the jurisdiction of the United States in the same sense that the subject of a foreign state, born within the territory of that state, may be said to have been born without the jurisdiction of our government. For, according to the decision in *Cherokee Nation v. Georgia* [1831], the tribe of which the parents of plaintiff were members was not "a foreign state, in the sense of the Constitution," but a domestic dependent people, "in a state of pupilage," and "so completely under the sovereignty and dominion of the United States, that any attempt to acquire their lands, or to form a political connection with them, would be considered an invasion of our territory and an act of hostility." They occupied territory which the court, in that case, said composed "a part of the United States," the title to which this nation asserted independent of their will. "In all our intercourse with foreign nations," said Chief Justice Marshall in the same case, "in our commercial regulations, in any attempt at intercourse between Indians and foreign nations, they are considered as within the jurisdictional limits of the United States, subject to many of those restraints which are imposed upon our citizens. . . . They look to our government for protection; rely upon its kindness and its power; appeal to it for relief to their wants; and address the president as their great father." And, again, in *United States v. Rogers* [1846], this court, speaking by Chief Justice Taney, said that it was "too firmly and clearly established to admit of dispute that the Indian tribes, residing within the territorial limits of the United States, are subject to their authority." Born, therefore, in the territory, under the dominion and within the jurisdictional limits of the United States, plaintiff has acquired, as was his undoubted right, a residence in one of the states, with her consent, and is subject to taxation and to all other burdens imposed by her upon residents of every race. If he did not acquire national citizenship on abandoning his tribe and becoming, by residence in one of the states, subject to the complete jurisdiction of the United States, then the Fourteenth Amendment has wholly failed to accomplish, in respect of the Indian race, what, we think, was intended by it; and there is still in this country a despised and rejected class of persons with no nationality whatever, who, born in our territory, owing no allegiance to any foreign power, and subject, as residents of the states, to all the burdens of government, are yet not members of any political community, nor entitled to any of the rights, privileges, or immunities of citizens of the United States.

George Washington Cable

The Freedman's Case in Equity (1885)

The greatest social problem before the American people to-day is, as it has been for a hundred years, the presence among us of the negro.

No comparable entanglement was ever drawn round itself by any other modern nation with so serene a disregard of its ultimate issue, or with a more distinct national responsibility. The African slave was brought here by cruel force, and with everybody's consent except his own. Everywhere the practice was favored as a measure of common aggrandizement. When a few men and women protested, they were mobbed in the public interest, with the public consent. There rests, therefore, a moral responsibility on the whole nation never to lose sight of the results of African-American slavery until they cease to work mischief and injustice.

It is true these responsibilities may not fall everywhere with the same weight; but they are nowhere entirely removed. The original seed of trouble was sown with the full knowledge and consent of the nation. The nation was to blame; and so long as evils spring from it, their correction must be the nation's duty.

The late Southern slave has within two decades risen from slavery to freedom, from freedom to citizenship, passed on into political ascendency, and fallen again from that eminence. The amended Constitution holds him up in his new political rights as well as a mere constitution can. On the other hand, certain enactments of Congress, trying to reach further, have lately been made void by the highest court of the nation. And another thing has happened. The popular mind in the old free States, weary of strife at arm's length, bewildered by its complications, vexed by many a blunder, eager to turn to the cure of other evils, and even tinctured by that race feeling whose grosser excesses it would so gladly see suppressed, has retreated from its uncomfortable dictational attitude and thrown the whole matter over to the States of the South. Here it rests, no longer a main party issue, but a group of questions which are to be settled by each of these States separately in the light of simple equity and morals, and which the genius of American government does not admit of being forced upon them from beyond their borders. Thus the whole question, become secondary in party contest, has yet reached a period of supreme importance.

Before slavery ever became a grave question in the nation's politics,—when it seemed each State's private affair, developing unmolested,—it had two different fates in two different parts of the country. In one, treated as a question of public equity, it withered away. In the other, overlooked in that aspect, it petrified and became the corner-stone of the whole social structure; and when men sought its overthrow as a national evil, it first brought war upon the land, and then grafted into the citizenship of one of the most intelligent nations in the world six millions of people from one of the most debased races on the globe.

And now this painful and wearisome question, sown in the African slave-trade, reaped in our civil war, and garnered in the national adoption of millions of an inferior race, is drawing near a second seed-time. For this is what the impatient proposal to make it a dead and buried issue really means. It means to recommit it to the silence and concealment of the covered furrow. Beyond that incubative retirement no suppressed moral question can be pushed; but all such questions, ignored in the domain of private morals, spring up and expand once more into questions of public equity; neglected as matters of public equity, they blossom into questions of national interest; and, despised in that guise, presently yield the red fruits of revolution.

This question must never again bear that fruit. There must arise, nay, there has arisen, in the South itself, a desire to see established the equities of the issue; to make it no longer a question of endurance between one group of States and another, but between the moral debris of an exploded evil and the duty, necessity, and value of planting society firmly upon universal justice and equity. This, and this only, can give the matter final burial. True, it is still a question between States; but only secondarily, as something formerly participated in, or as it concerns every householder to know that what is being built against his house is built by level and plummet. It is the interest of the Southern States first, and *consequently* of the whole land, to discover clearly these equities and the errors that are being committed against them.

If we take up this task, the difficulties of the situation are plain. We have, first, a revision of Southern State laws which has forced into them the recognition of certain human rights discordant with the sentiments of those who have always called themselves the community; second, the removal of the entire political machinery by which this forcing process was effected; and, third, these revisions left to be interpreted and applied under the domination of these antagonistic sentiments. These being the three terms of the problem, one of three things must result. There will arise a system of vicious evasions eventually ruinous to public and private morals and liberty,

or there will be a candid reconsideration of the sentiments hostile to these enactments, or else there will be a division, some taking one course and some the other.

This is what we should look for from our knowledge of men and history; and this is what we find. The revised laws, only where they could not be evaded, have met that reluctant or simulated acceptance of their narrowest letter which might have been expected—a virtual suffocation of those principles of human equity which the unwelcome decrees do little more than shadow forth. But in different regions this attitude has been made in very different degrees of emphasis. In some the new principles have grown, or are growing, into the popular conviction, and the opposing sentiments are correspondingly dying out. There are even some limited districts where they have received much practical acceptance. While, again, other sections lean almost wholly toward the old sentiments; an easy choice, since it is the conservative, the unyielding attitude, whose strength is in the absence of intellectual and moral debate.

Now, what are the gains, what the losses of these diverse attitudes? Surely these are urgent questions to any one in our country who believes it is always a losing business to be in the wrong. Particularly in the South, where each step in this affair is an unprecedented experience, it will be folly if each region, small or large, does not study the experiences of all the rest. And yet this, alone, would be superficial; we would still need to do more. We need to go back to the roots of things and study closely, analytically, the origin, the present foundation, the rationality, the rightness, of those sentiments surviving in us which prompt an attitude qualifying in any way peculiarly the black man's liberty among us. Such a treatment will be less abundant in incident, less picturesque; but it will be more thorough.

First, then, what are these sentiments? Foremost among them stands the idea that he is of necessity an alien. He was brought to our shores a naked, brutish, unclean, captive, pagan savage, to be and remain a kind of connecting link between man and the beasts of burden. The great changes to result from his contact with a superb race of masters were not taken into account. As a social factor he was intended to be as purely zero as the brute at the other end of his plow-line. The occasional mingling of his blood with that of the white man worked no change in the sentiment; one, two, four, eight, multiplied upon or divided into zero, still gave zero for the result. Generations of American nativity made no difference; his children and children's children were born in sight of our door, yet the old notion held fast. He increased to vast numbers, but it never wavered. He accepted our dress, language, religion, all the fundamentals of our civilization, and became forever expatriated from his own land; still he remained, to us, an alien. Our sentiment went blind. It did not see that gradually, here by force and there by choice, he was fulfilling a host of conditions that earned at least a solemn moral right to that naturalization which no one at first had dreamed of giving him. Frequently he even bought back the freedom of which he had been robbed, became a tax-payer, and at times an educator of his children at his own expense; but the old idea of alienism passed laws to banish him, his wife, and children by thousands from the state, and threw him into loathsome jails as a common felon for returning to his native land.

It will be wise to remember that these were the acts of an enlightened, God-fearing people, the great mass of whom have passed beyond all earthly accountability. They were our fathers. I am the son and grandson of slave-holders. These were their faults; posterity will discover ours; but these things must be frankly, fearlessly taken into account if we are ever to understand the true interests of our peculiar state of society.

Why, then, did this notion that the man of color must always remain an alien stand so unshaken? We may readily recall how, under ancient systems, he rose not only to high privileges, but often to public station and power. Singularly, with us the trouble lay in a modern principle of liberty. The whole idea of American government rested on all men's equal, inalienable right to secure their life, liberty, and the pursuit of happiness by governments founded in their own consent. Hence, our Southern forefathers, shedding their blood, or ready to shed it, for this principle, yet proposing in equal good conscience to continue holding the American black man and mulatto and quadroon in slavery, had to anchor that conscience, their conduct, and their laws in the conviction that the man of African tincture was, not by his master's arbitrary assertion merely, but by nature and

unalterably, an alien. If that hold should break, one single wave of irresistible inference would lift our whole Southern social fabric and dash it upon the rocks of negro emancipation and enfranchisement. How was it made secure? Not by books, though they were written among us from every possible point of view, but, with the mass of our slave-owners, by the calm hypothesis of a positive, intuitive knowledge. To them the statement was an axiom. They abandoned the methods of moral and intellectual reasoning, and fell back upon this assumption of a God-given instinct, nobler than reason, and which it was an insult to a freeman to ask him to prove on logical grounds.

Yet it was found not enough. The slave multiplied. Slavery was a dangerous institution. Few in the South to-day have any just idea how often the slave plotted for his freedom. Our Southern ancestors were a noble, manly people, springing from some of the most highly intelligent, aspiring, upright, and refined nations of the modern world; from the Huguenot, the French Chevalier, the Old Englander, the New Englander. Their acts were not always right; whose are? But for their peace of mind they had to believe them so. They therefore spoke much of the negro's contentment with that servile condition for which nature had designed him. Yet there was no escaping the knowledge that we dared not trust the slave caste with any power that could be withheld from them. So the perpetual alien was made also a perpetual menial, and the belief became fixed that this, too, was nature's decree, not ours.

Thus we stood at the close of the civil war. There were always a few Southerners who did not justify slavery, and many who cared nothing whether it was just or not. But what we have described was the general sentiment of good Southern people. There was one modifying sentiment. It related to the slave's spiritual interests. Thousands of pious masters and mistresses flatly broke the shameful laws that stood between their slaves and the Bible. Slavery was right; but religion, they held, was for the alien and menial as well as for the citizen and master. They could be alien and citizen, menial and master, in church as well as out; and they were.

Yet over against this lay another root of to-day's difficulties. This perpetuation of the alien, menial relation tended to perpetuate the vices that naturally cling to servility, dense ignorance and a hopeless separation from true liberty; and as we could not find it in our minds to blame slavery with this perpetuation, we could only assume as a further axiom that there was, by nature, a disqualifying moral taint in every drop of negro blood. The testimony of an Irish, German, Italian, French, or Spanish beggar in a court of justice was taken on its merits; but the colored man's was excluded by law wherever it weighed against a white man. The colored man was a pre-judged culprit. The discipline of the plantation required that the difference between master and slave be never lost sight of by either. It made our master caste a solid mass, and fixed a common master-hood and subserviency between the ruling and the serving race.[1] Every one of us grew up in the idea that he had, by birth and race, certain broad powers of police over any and every person of color.

All at once the tempest of war snapped off at the ground every one of these arbitrary relations, without removing a single one of the sentiments in which they stood rooted. Then, to fortify the freedman in the tenure of his new rights, he was given the ballot. Before this grim fact the notion of alienism, had it been standing alone, might have given way. The idea that slavery was right did begin to crumble almost at once. "As for slavery," said an old Creole sugar-planter and former slave-owner to me, "it was damnable." The revelation came like a sudden burst of light. It is one of the South's noblest poets who has but just said:

> I am a Southerner;
> I love the South; I dared for her
> To fight from Lookout to the sea,
> With her proud banner over me:
> But from my lips thanksgiving broke,
> As God in battle-thunder spoke,
> And that Black Idol, breeding drouth
> And dearth of human sympathy
> Throughout the sweet and sensuous South,
> Was, with its chains and human yoke,

> Blown hellward from the cannon's mouth,
> While Freedom cheered behind the smoke![2]

With like readiness might the old alien relation have given way if we could only, while letting that pass, have held fast by the other old ideas. But they were all bound together. See our embarrassment. For more than a hundred years we had made these sentiments the absolute essentials to our self-respect. And yet if we clung to them, how could we meet the freedman on equal terms in the political field? Even to lead would not compensate us; for the fundamental profession of American politics is that the leader is servant to his followers. It was too much. The ex-master and ex-slave—the quarter-deck and the fore-castle, as it were—could not come together. But neither could the American mind tolerate a continuance of martial law. The agonies of reconstruction followed.

The vote, after all, was a secondary point, and the robbery and bribery on one side, and whipping and killing on the other, were but huge accidents of the situation. The two main questions were really these: on the freedman's side, how to establish republican State government under the same recognition of his rights that the rest of Christendom accorded him; and on the former master's side, how to get back to the old semblance of republican State government, and—allowing that the freedman was *de facto* a voter—still to maintain a purely arbitrary superiority of all whites over all blacks, and a purely arbitrary equality of all blacks among themselves as an alien, menial, and dangerous class.

Exceptionally here and there some one in the master caste did throw off the old and accept the new ideas, and, if he would allow it, was instantly claimed as a leader by the newly liberated thousands around him. But just as promptly the old master race branded him also an alien reprobate, and in ninety-nine cases out of a hundred, if he had not already done so, he soon began to confirm by his actions the brand on his cheek. However, we need give no history here of the dreadful episode of reconstruction. Under an experimentative truce its issues rest to-day upon the pledge of the wiser leaders of the master

---

1.   The old Louisiana Black Code says, "That free people of color ought never to . . . presume to conceive themselves equal to the white; but, on the contrary, that they ought to yield to them in every occasion, and never speak or answer to them but with respect, under the penalty of imprisonment according to the nature of the offense." (Section 21, p. 164.)

---

2.   Maurice Thompson, in the "Independent."

class: Let us but remove the hireling demagogue, and we will see to it that the freedman is accorded a practical, complete, and cordial recognition of his equality with the white man before the law. As far as there has been any understanding at all, it is not that the originally desired ends of reconstruction have been abandoned, but that the men of North and South have agreed upon a new, gentle, and peaceable method for reaching them; that, without change as to the ends in view, compulsory reconstruction has been set aside and a voluntary reconstruction is on trial.

It is the fashion to say we paused to let the "feelings engendered by the war" pass away, and that they are passing. But let not these truths lead us into error. The sentiments we have been analyzing, and upon which we saw the old compulsory reconstruction go hard aground—these are not the "feelings engendered by the war." We must disentangle them from the "feelings engendered by the war," and by reconstruction. They are older than either. But for them slavery would have perished of itself, and emancipation and reconstruction been peaceful revolutions.

Indeed, as between master and slave, the "feelings engendered by the war" are too trivial, or at least were too short-lived, to demand our present notice. One relation and feeling the war destroyed: the patriarchal tie and its often really tender and benevolent sentiment of dependence and protection. When the slave became a freedman the sentiment of alienism became for the first time complete. The abandonment of this relation was not one-sided; the slave, even before the master, renounced it. Countless times, since reconstruction began, the master has tried, in what he believed to be everybody's interest, to play on that old sentiment. But he found it a harp without strings. The freedman could not formulate, but he could see, all our old ideas of autocracy and subserviency, of master and menial, of an arbitrarily fixed class to guide and rule, and another to be guided and ruled. He rejected the overture. The old master, his well-meant condescensions slighted, turned away estranged, and justified himself in passively withholding that simpler protection without patronage which any one American citizen, however exalted, owes to any other, however humble. Could the freedman in the bitterest of those days have consented to throw himself upon just that one old relation, he could have found a physical security for himself and his house such as could not, after years of effort, be given him by constitutional amendments, Congress, United States marshals, regiments of regulars, and ships of war. But he could not; the very nobility of the civilization that had held him in slavery had made him too much a man to go back to that shelter; and by his manly neglect to do so he has proved to us who once ruled over him that, be his relative standing among the races of men what it may, he is worthy to be free.

To be a free man is his still distant goal. Twice he has been a freedman. In the days of compulsory reconstruction he was freed in the presence of his master by that master's victorious foe. In these days of voluntary reconstruction he is virtually freed by the consent of his master, but the master retaining the exclusive right to define the bounds of his freedom. Many everywhere have taken up the idea that this state of affairs is the end to be desired and the end actually sought in reconstruction as handed over to the States. I do not charge such folly to the best intelligence of any American community; but I cannot ignore my own knowledge that the average thought of some regions rises to no better idea of the issue. The belief is all too common that the nation, having aimed at a wrong result and missed, has left us of the Southern States to get now such other result as we think best. I say this belief is not universal. There are those among us who see that America has no room for a state of society which makes its lower classes harmless by abridging their liberties, or, as one of the favored class lately said to me, has "got 'em so they don't give no trouble." There is a growing number who see that the one thing we cannot afford to tolerate at large is a class of people less than citizens; and that every interest in the land demands that the freedman be free to become in all things, as far as his own personal gifts will lift and sustain him, the same sort of American citizen he would be if, with the same intellectual and moral caliber, he were white.

Thus we reach the ultimate question of fact. Are the freedman's liberties suffering any real abridgment? The answer is easy. The letter of the laws, with but few exceptions, recognizes him as entitled to every right of an American citizen; and to some it may seem unimportant that there is scarcely one public relation of life in the South where he is not arbitrarily and unlawfully compelled to hold toward the white man the attitude of an alien, a menial, and a probable reprobate, by reason of his race and color. One of the marvels of future history will be that it was counted a small matter, by a majority of our nation, for six millions of people within it, made by its own decree a component part of it, to be subjected to a system of oppression so rank that nothing could make it seem small except the fact that they had already been ground under it for a century and a half.

Examine it. It proffers to the freedman a certain security of life and property, and then holds the respect of the community, that dearest of earthly boons, beyond his attainment. It gives him certain guarantees against thieves and robbers, and then holds him under the unearned contumely of the mass of good men and women. It acknowledges in constitutions and statutes his title to an American's freedom and aspirations, and then in daily practice heaps upon him in every public place the most odius distinctions, without giving ear to the humblest plea concerning mental or moral character. It spurns his ambition, tramples upon his languishing self-respect, and indignantly refuses to let him either buy with money, or earn by any excellence of inner life or outward behavior, the most momentary immunity from these public indignities even for his wife and daughters. Need we cram these pages with facts in evidence, as if these were charges denied and requiring to be proven? They are simply the present avowed and defended state of affairs peeled of its exteriors.

Nothing but the habit, generations old, of enduring it could make it endurable by men not in actual slavery. Were we whites of the South to remain every way as we are, and our six million blacks to give place to any sort of whites exactly their equals, man for man, in mind, morals, and wealth, provided only that they had tasted two years of American freedom, and were this same system of tyrannies attempted upon them, there would be as bloody an uprising as this continent has ever seen. We can say this quietly. There is not a scruple's weight of present danger. These six million freedmen are dominated by nine million whites immeasurably stronger than they, backed by the virtual consent of thirty-odd millions more. Indeed, nothing but the habit of oppression could make such oppression possible to a people of the intelligence and virtue of our Southern whites, and the invitation to practice it on millions of any

other than the children of their former slaves would be spurned with a noble indignation.

Suppose, for a moment, the tables turned. Suppose the courts of our Southern States, while changing no laws requiring the impaneling of jurymen without distinction as to race, etc., should suddenly begin to draw their thousands of jurymen all black, and well-nigh every one of them counting not only himself, but all his race, better than any white man, Assuming that their average of intelligence and morals should be not below that of jurymen as now drawn, would a white man, for all that, choose to be tried in one of those courts? Would he suspect nothing? Could one persuade him that his chances of even justice were all they should be, or all they would be were the court not evading the law in order to sustain an outrageous distinction against him because of the accidents of his birth? Yet only read white man for black man, and black man for white man, and that—I speak as an eye-witness—has been the practice for years, and is still so to-day; an actual emasculation, in the case of six million people both as plaintiff and defendant, of the right of trial by jury.

In this and other practices the outrage falls upon the freedman. Does it stop there? Far from it. It is the first premise of American principles that whatever elevates the lower stratum of the people lifts all the rest, and whatever holds it down holds all down. For twenty years, therefore, the nation has been working to elevate the freedman. It counts this one of the great necessities of the hour. It has poured out its wealth publicly and privately for this purpose. It is confidently expected that it will soon bestow a royal gift of millions for the reduction of the illiteracy so largely shared by the blacks. Our Southern States are, and for twenty years have been, taxing themselves for the same end. The private charities alone of the other States have given twenty millions in the same good cause. Their colored seminaries, colleges, and normal schools dot our whole Southern country, and furnish our public colored schools with a large part of their teachers. All this and much more has been or is being done in order that, for the good of himself and everybody else in the land, the colored man may be elevated as quickly as possible from all the debasements of slavery and semi-slavery to the full stature and integrity of citizenship. And it is in the face of all this that the adherent of the old regime stands in the way to every public privilege and place—steamer landing, railway platform, theater, concert-hall, art display, public library, public school, court-house, church, everything—flourishing the hot branding-iron of ignominious distinctions. He forbids the freedman to go into the water until *he* is satisfied that he knows how to swim, and for fear he should learn hangs mill-stones about his neck. This is what we are told is a small matter that will settle itself. Yes, like a roosting curse, until the outraged intelligence of the South lifts its indignant protest against this stupid firing into our own ranks.

I say the outraged intelligence of the South; for there are thousands of Southern-born white men and women in the minority in all these places—in churches, courts, schools, libraries, theaters, concert-halls, and on steamers and railway carriages—who see the wrong and folly of these things, silently blush for them, and withhold their open protests only because their belief is unfortunately stronger in the futility of their counsel than in the power of a just cause. I do not justify their silence; but I affirm their sincerity and their goodly numbers. Of late years, when condemning these evils from the platform in Southern towns, I have repeatedly found that those who I had earlier been told were the men and women in whom the community placed most confidence and pride—they were the ones who, when I had spoken, came forward with warmest hand-grasps and expressions of thanks, and pointedly and cordially justified my every utterance. And were they the young South? Not by half! The gray-beards of the old times have always been among them, saying in effect, not by any means as converts, but as fellow-discoverers, "Whereas we were blind, now we see."

Another sort among our good Southern people make a similar but feebler admission, but with the time-worn proviso that expediency makes a more imperative demand than law, justice, or logic, and demands the preservation of the old order. Somebody must be outraged, it seems; and if not the freedman, then it must be a highly refined and enlightened race of people constantly offended and grossly discommoded, if not imposed upon, by a horde of tatterdemalions, male and female, crowding into a participation in their reserved privileges. Now, look at this plea. It is simply saying in another way that though the Southern whites far outnumber the blacks, and though we hold every element of power in greater degree than the blacks, and though the larger part of us claim to be sealed by nature as an exclusive upper class, and though we have the courts completely in our own hands, with the police on our right and the prisons on our left, and though we justly claim to be an intrepid people, and though we have a superb military experience, with ninety-nine hundredths of all the military equipment and no scarcity of all the accessories, yet with all the facts behind us we cannot make and enforce that intelligent and approximately just assortment of persons in public places and conveyances on the merits of exterior decency that is made in all other enlightened lands. On such a plea are made a distinction and separation that not only are crude, invidious, humiliating, and tyrannous, but which do not reach their ostensible end or come near it; and all that saves such a plea from being a confession of driveling imbecility is its utter speciousness. It is advanced sincerely; and yet nothing is easier to show than that these distinctions on the line of color are really made not from any necessity, but simply for their own sake—to preserve the old arbitrary supremacy of the master class over the menial without regard to the decency or indecency of appearance or manners in either the white individual or the colored.

See its every-day working. Any colored man gains unquestioned admission into innumerable places the moment he appears as the menial attendant of some white person, where he could not cross the threshold in his own right as a well-dressed and well-behaved master of himself. The contrast is even greater in the case of colored women. There could not be a system which when put into practice would more offensively condemn itself. It does more: it actually creates the confusion it pretends to prevent. It blunts the sensibilities of the ruling class themselves. It waives all strict demand for painstaking in either manners or dress of either master or menial, and, for one result, makes the average Southern railway coach more uncomfortable than the average of railway coaches elsewhere. It prompts the average Southern white passenger to find less offense in the presence of a profane, boisterous, or unclean white person than in that of a quiet, well-behaved colored man or woman attempting to travel on an equal footing with him without a white master or mistress. The holders of the old sentiments hold the opposite choice in scorn. It is only when we go on to say that there are regions where the riotous expulsion of a decent and peaceable colored person is preferred to his inoffensive company, that it may seem necessary to bring in evidence. And yet here again it is *primâ facie* evidence; for the following extract was printed in the Selma (Alabama) "Times" not six months ago, and not as a complaint, but as a boast:

> A few days since, a negro minister, of this city, boarded the east-bound passenger train on the E. T., V. & G. Railway and took a seat in the coach occupied by white passengers. Some of the passengers complained to the conductor and brakemen, and expressed considerable dissatisfaction that they were forced to ride alongside of a negro. The railroad officials informed the complainants that they were not authorized to force the colored passenger into the coach set apart for the negroes, and they would lay themselves liable should they do so. The white passengers then took the matter in their own hands and ordered the ebony-hued minister to take a seat in the next coach. He positively refused to obey orders, whereupon the white men gave him a sound flogging and forced him to a seat among his own color and equals. We learned yesterday that the vanquished preacher was unable to fill his pulpit on account of the severe chastisement inflicted upon him. Now [says the delighted editor] the query that puzzles is, "Who did the flogging?"

And as good an answer as we can give is that likely enough they were some of the men for whom the whole South has come to a halt to let them get over the "feelings engendered by the war." Must such men, such acts, such sentiments, stand alone to represent us of the South before an enlightened world? No. I say, as a citizen of an extreme Southern State, a native of Louisiana, an ex-Confederate soldier, and a lover of my home, my city, and my State, as well as of my country, that this is not the best sentiment in the South, nor the sentiment of her best intelligence; and that it would not ride up and down that beautiful land dominating and domineering were it not for its tremendous power as the *traditional* sentiment of a conservative people. But is not silent endurance criminal? I cannot but repeat my own words, spoken near the scene and about the time of this event.

Speech may be silver and silence golden; but if a lump of gold is only big enough, it can drag us to the bottom of the sea and hold us there while all the world sails over us.

The laws passed in the days of compulsory reconstruction requiring "equal accommodations," etc., for colored and white persons were freedmen's follies. On their face they defeated their ends; for even in theory they at once reduced to half all opportunity for those more reasonable and mutually agreeable self-assortments which public assemblages and groups of passengers find it best to make in all other enlightened countries, making them on the score of conduct, dress, and price. They also led the whites to overlook what they would have seen instantly had these invidious distinctions been made against themselves: that their offense does not vanish at the guarantee against the loss of physical comforts. But we made, and are still making, a mistake beyond even this. For years many of us have carelessly taken for granted that these laws were being carried out in some shape that removed all just ground of complaint. It is common to say, "We allow the man of color to go and come at will, only let him sit apart in a place marked off for him." But marked off how? So as to mark him instantly as a menial. Not by railings and partitions merely, which, raised against any other class in the United States with the same invidious intent, would be kicked down as fast as put up, but by giving him besides, in every instance and without recourse, the most uncomfortable, uncleanest, and unsafest place; and the unsafety, uncleanness, and discomfort of most of these places are a shame to any community pretending to practice public justice. If any one can think the freedman does not feel the indignities thus heaped upon him, let him take up any paper printed for colored men's patronage, or ask any colored man of known courageous utterance. Hear them:

> We ask not Congress, nor the Legislature, nor any other power, to remedy these evils, but we ask the people among whom we live. Those who *can* remedy them if they *will*. Those who have a high sense of honor and a deep moral feeling. Those who have one vestige of human sympathy left. . . . Those are the ones we ask to protect us in our weakness and ill-treatments. . . . As soon as the colored man is treated by the white man as a *man*,

that harmony and pleasant feeling which should characterize all races which dwell together, shall be the bond of peace between them.

Surely their evidence is good enough to prove their own feelings. We need not lean upon it here for anything else. I shall not bring forward a single statement of fact from them or any of their white friends who, as teachers and missionaries, share many of their humiliations, though my desk is covered with them. But I beg to make the same citation from my own experience that I made last June in the far South. It was this: One hot night in September of last year I was traveling by rail in the State of Alabama. At rather late bed-time there came aboard the train a young mother and her little daughter of three or four years. They were neatly and tastefully dressed in cool, fresh muslins, and as the train went on its way they sat together very still and quiet. At the next station there came aboard a most melancholy and revolting company. In filthy rags, with vile odors and the clanking of shackles and chains, nine penitentiary convicts chained to one chain, and ten more chained to another, dragged laboriously into the compartment of the car where in one corner sat this mother and child, and packed it full, and the train moved on. The keeper of the convicts told me he should take them in that car two hundred miles that night. They were going to the mines. My seat was not in that car, and I staid in it but a moment. It stank insufferably. I returned to my own place in the coach behind, where there was, and had all the time been, plenty of room. But the mother and child sat on in silence in that foul hole, the conductor having distinctly refused them admission elsewhere because they were of African blood, and not because the mother was, but because she was *not*, engaged at the moment in menial service. Had the child been white, and the mother not its natural but its hired guardian, she could have sat anywhere in the train, and no one would have ventured to object, even had she been as black as the mouth of the coal-pit to which her loathsome fellow-passengers were being carried in chains.

Such is the incident as I saw it. But the illustration would be incomplete here were I not allowed to add the comments I made upon it when in June last I recounted it, and to state the two opposite tempers in which my words were received. I said: "These are the facts. And yet you know and I know we belong to communities that, after years of hoping for, are at last taking comfort in the assurance of the nation's highest courts that no law can reach and stop this shameful foul play until we choose to enact a law to that end ourselves. And now the east and north and west of our great and prosperous and happy country, and the rest of the civilized world, as far as it knows our case, are standing and waiting to see what we will write upon the white page of to-day's and to-morrow's history, now that we are simply on our honor and on the mettle of our far and peculiarly famed Southern instinct. How long, then, shall we stand off from such ringing moral questions as these on the flimsy plea that they have a political value, and, scrutinizing the Constitution, keep saying. 'Is it so nominated in the bond? I cannot find it; 'tis not in the bond.'"

With the temper that promptly resented these words through many newspapers of the neighboring regions there can be no propriety in wrangling. When regions so estranged from the world's thought carry their resentment no further than a little harmless invective, it is but fair to welcome it as a sign of progress. If communities nearer the great centers of thought grow impatient with them, how shall we resent the impatience of these remoter ones when their oldest traditions are, as it seems to them, ruthlessly assailed? There is but one right thing to do: it is to pour in upon them our reiterations of the truth without malice and without stint.

But I have a much better word to say. It is for those who, not voiced by the newspapers around them, showed, both then and constantly afterward in public and private during my two days' subsequent travel and sojourn in the region, by their cordial, frequent, specific approval of my words, that a better intelligence is longing to see the evils of the old regime supplanted by a wiser and more humane public sentiment and practice. And I must repeat my conviction that if the unconscious habit of oppression were not already there, a scheme so gross, irrational, unjust, and inefficient as our present caste distinctions could not find place among a people so generally intelligent and high-minded. I ask attention to their bad influence in a direction not often noticed.

In studying, about a year ago, the practice of letting out public convicts to private lessees to serve out their sentences under private management, I found that it does not belong to all our once slave States nor to all our once seceded States. Only it is no longer in practice outside of them. Under our present condition in the South, it is beyond possibility that the individual black should behave mischievously without offensively rearousing the old sentiments of the still dominant white man. As we have seen, too, the white man virtually monopolizes the jury-box. Add another fact: the Southern States have entered upon a new era of material development. Now, if with these conditions in force the public mind has been captivated by glowing pictures of the remunerative economy of the convict-lease system, and by the seductive spectacle of mines and railways, turnpikes and levees, that everybody wants and nobody wants to pay for, growing apace by convict labor that seems to cost nothing, we may almost assert beforehand that the popular mind will—not so maliciously as unreflectingly—yield to the tremendous temptation to hustle the misbehaving black man into the State prison under extravagant sentence, and sell his labor to the highest bidder who will use him in the construction of public works. For ignorance of the awful condition of these penitentiaries is extreme and general, and the hasty, half-conscious assumption naturally is, that the culprit will survive this term of sentence, and its fierce discipline "teach him to behave himself."

But we need not argue from cause to effect only. Nor need I repeat one of the many painful rumors that poured in upon me the moment I began to investigate this point. The official testimony of the prisons themselves is before the world to establish the conjectures that spring from our reasoning. After the erroneous takings of the census of 1880 in South Carolina had been corrected, the population was shown to consist of about twenty blacks to every thirteen whites. One would therefore look for a preponderance of blacks on the prison lists; and inasmuch as they are a people only twenty years ago released from servile captivity, one would not be surprised to see that preponderance large. Yet, when the actual numbers confront us, our speculations are stopped with a rude shock; for what is to account for the fact that in 1881 there were committed to the State prison at Columbia, South Carolina, 406 colored persons and but 25 whites? The proportion of blacks sentenced to the whole black population was one to every 1488; that of the whites to the white population was but one to every 15,644. In Georgia the white inhabitants decidedly outnumber the blacks; yet in the State penitentiary, October 20, 1880, there were 115 whites and 1071 colored; or if we reject the summary of its tables and refer to the tables themselves (for the one does not agree with the other), there were but 102 whites and 1083 colored. Yet of 52 pardons granted in the two years then closing, 22 were to whites and only 30 to blacks. If this be a dark record, what shall we say of the records of lynch law? But for them there is not room here.

A far pleasanter aspect of our subject shows itself when we turn from courts and prisons to the school-house. And the explanation is simple. Were our educational affairs in the hands of that not high average of the community commonly seen in jury-boxes, with their transient sense of accountability and their crude notions of public interests, there would most likely be no such pleasant contrast. But with us of the South, as elsewhere, there is a fairly honest effort to keep the public-school interests in the hands of the State's most highly trained intelligence. Hence our public educational work is a compromise between the unprogressive prejudices of the general mass of the whites and the progressive intelligence of their best minds. Practically, through the great majority of our higher educational officers, we are fairly converted to the imperative necessity of elevating the colored man intellectually, and are beginning to see very plainly that the whole community is sinned against in every act or attitude of oppression, however gross or however refined.

Yet one thing must be said. I believe it is wise that all have agreed not to handicap education with the race question, but to make a complete surrender of that issue, and let it find adjustment elsewhere first and, in the schools last. And yet, in simple truth and justice and in the kindest spirit, we ought to file one exception for that inevitable hour when the whole question must be met. There can be no more real justice in pursuing the freedman's children with humiliating arbitrary distinctions and separations in the school-houses than in putting them upon him in other places. If, growing out of their peculiar mental structure, there are good and just reasons for their isolation, by all means let them be proved and known;

but it is simply tyrannous to assume them without proof. I know that just here looms up the huge bugbear of Social Equality. Our eyes are filled with absurd visions of all Shantytown pouring its hordes of unwashed imps into the company and companionship of our own sunny-headed darlings. What utter nonsense! As if our public schools had no gauge of cleanliness, decorum, or moral character! Social equality? What a godsend it would be if the advocates of the old Southern regime could only see that the color line points straight in the direction of social equality by tending toward the equalization of all whites on one side of the line and of all blacks on the other. We may reach the moon some day, not social equality; but the only class that really effects anything toward it are the makers and holders of arbitrary and artificial social distinctions interfering with society's natural self-distribution. Even the little children everywhere are taught, and begin to learn almost with their A B C, that they will find, and must be guided by, the same variations of the social scale in the public school as out of it; and it is no small mistake to put them or their parents off their guard by this cheap seperation on the line of color.

But some will say this is not a purely artificial distinction. We hear much about race instinct. The most of it, I fear, is pure twaddle. It may be there is such a thing. We do not know. It is not proved. And even if it were established, it would not necessarily be a proper moral guide. We subordinate instinct to society's best interests as apprehended in the light of reason. If there is such a thing, it behaves with strange malignity toward the remnants of African blood in individuals principally of our own race, and with singular indulgence to the descendants of—for example—Pocahontas. Of mere race *feeling* we all know there is no scarcity. Who is stranger to it? And as another man's motive of private preference no one has a right to forbid it or require it. But as to its being an instinct, one thing is plain: if there is such an instinct, as far from excusing the malignant indignities practiced in its name, it furnishes their final condemnation; for it stands to reason that just in degree as it is a real thing it will take care of itself.

It has often been seen to do so, whether it is real or imaginary. I have seen in New Orleans a Sunday-school of white children every Sunday afternoon take possession of its two rooms immediately upon their being vacated by a black school of equal or somewhat larger numbers. The teachers of the colored school are both white and black, and among the white teachers are young ladies and gentlemen of the highest social standing. The pupils of the two schools are alike neatly attired, orderly, and in every respect inoffensive to each other. I have seen the two races sitting in the same public high-school and grammar school rooms, reciting in the same classes and taking recess on the same ground at the same time, without one particle of detriment that any one ever pretended to discover, although the fiercest enemies of the system swarmed about it on every side. And when in the light of these observations I reflect upon the enormous educational task our Southern States have before them, the inadequacy of their own means for performing it, the hoped-for beneficence of the general Government, the sparseness with which so much of our Southern population is distributed over the land, the thousands of school districts where, consequently, the multipication of schools must involve both increase of expense and reduction of efficiency, I must enter some demurer to the enforcement of the tyrannous sentiments of the old regime until wise experiments have established better reasons than I have yet heard given.

What need to say more? The question is answered. Is the freedman a free man? No. We have considered his position in a land whence nothing can, and no man has a shadow of right to, drive him and where he is multiplying as only oppression can multiply a people. We have carefully analyzed his relations to the finer and prouder race, with which he shares the ownership and citizenship of a region large enough for ten times the number of both. Without accepting one word of his testimony, we have shown that the laws made for his protection against the habits of suspicion and oppression in his late master are being constantly set aside, not for their defects, but for such merit as they possess. We have shown that the very natural source of these oppressions is the surviving sentiments of an extinct and now universally execrated institution; sentiments which no intelligent or moral people should harbor a moment after the admission that slavery was a moral mistake. We have shown the outrageousness of these tyrannies in some of their workings, and how distinctly they antagonize every State and national interest involved in the elevation of the colored race. Is it not well to have done so? For, I say again, the question has reached a moment of special importance. The south stands on her honor before the clean equities of the issue. It is no longer whether constitutional amendments, but whether the eternal principles of justice are violated. And the answer must—it shall—come from the South. And it shall be practical. It will not cost much. We have had a strange experience: the withholding of simple rights has cost us much blood; such concessions of them as we have made have never yet cost them a drop. The answer is coming. Is politics in the way? Then let it clear the track or get run over, just as it prefers. But, as I have said over and over to my bretheren in the South, I take upon me to say again here, that there is a moral and intellectual intelligence there which is not going to be much longer beguiled out of its moral right of way by questions of political punctilio, but will seek that plane of universal justice and equity which it is every people's duty before God to seek, not along the line of politics,—God forbid!—but across it and across it and across it as many times as it may lie across the path, until the whole people of every once slave-holding State can stand up as one man, saying "Is the freedman a free man?" and the whole world shall answer, "Yes."

The Dawes Severalty Act (1887)

Chap. 119.—An act to provide for the allotment of lands in severalty to Indians on the various reservations, and to extend the protection of the laws of the United States and the Territories over the Indians, and for other purposes.

Be it enacted by the Senate and House of Representatives of the United States of America in Congress assembled, That in all cases where any tribe or band of Indians has been, or shall hereafter be, located upon any reservation created for their use, either by treaty stipulation or by virtue of an act of Congress or executive order setting apart the same for their use, the President of the United States be, and he hereby is, authorized, whenever in his opinion any reservation or any part thereof of such Indians is advantageous for agricultural and grazing purposes, to cause said reservation, or any part thereof, to be surveyed, or resurveyed if necessary, and to allot the lands in said reservation in severalty to any Indian located thereon in quantities as follows:

To each head of a family, one-quarter of a section;
To each single person over eighteen years of age, one-eighth of a section;
To each orphan child under eighteen years of age, one-eighth of a section; and

To each other single person under eighteen years now living, or who may be born prior to the date of the order of the President directing an allotment of the lands embraced in any reservation, one-sixteenth of a section: *Provided,* That in case there is not sufficient land in any of said reservations to allot lands to each individual of the classes above named in quantities as above provided, the lands embraced in such reservation or reservations shall be allotted to each individual of each of said classes pro rata in accordance with the provisions of this act: *And provided further,* That where the treaty or act of Congress setting apart such reservation provides for the allotment of lands in severalty in quantities in excess of those herein provided, the President, in making allotments upon such reservation, shall allot the lands to each individual Indian belonging thereon in quantity as specified in such treaty or act: *And provided further,* That when the lands allotted are only valuable for grazing purposes, an additional allotment of such grazing lands, in quantities as above provided, shall be made to each individual.

Sec. 2. That all allotments set apart under the provisions of this act shall be selected by the Indians, heads of families selecting for their minor children, and the agents shall select for each orphan child, and in such manner as to embrace the improvements of the Indians making the selection. Where the improvements of two or more Indians have been made on the same legal subdivision of land, unless they shall otherwise agree, a provisional line may be run dividing said lands between them, and the amount to which each is entitled shall be equalized in the assignment of the remainder of the land to which they are entitled under this act: *Provided*, That if any one entitled to an allotment shall fail to make a selection within four years after the President shall direct that allotments may be made on a particular reservation, the Secretary of the Interior may direct the agent of such tribe or band, if such there be, and if there be no agent, then a special agent appointed for that purpose, to make a selection for such Indian, which election shall be allotted as in cases where selections are made by the Indians, and patents shall issue in like manner.

Sec. 3. That the allotments provided for in this act shall be made by special agents appointed by the President for such purpose, and the agents in charge of the respective reservations on which the allotments are directed to be made, under such rules and regulations as the Secretary of the Interior may from time to time prescribe, and shall be certified by such agents to the Commissioner of Indian Affairs, in duplicate, one copy to be retained in the Indian Office and the other to be transmitted to the Secretary of the Interior for his action, and to be deposited in the General Land Office.

Sec. 4. That where any Indian not residing upon a reservation, or for whose tribe no reservation has been provided by treaty, act of Congress, or executive order, shall make settlement upon any surveyed or unsurveyed lands of the United States not otherwise appropriated, he or she shall be entitled, upon application to the local land-office for the district in which the lands are located, to have the same allotted to him or her, and to his or her children, in quantities and manner as provided in this act for Indians residing upon reservations; and when such settlement is made upon unsurveyed lands, the grant to such Indians shall be adjusted upon the survey of the lands so as to conform thereto; and patents shall be issued to them for such lands in the manner and with the

restrictions as herein provided. And the fees to which the officers of such local land-office would have been entitled had such lands been entered under the general laws for the disposition of the public lands shall be paid to them, from any moneys in the Treasury of the United States not otherwise appropriated, upon a statement of an account in their behalf for such fees by the Commissioner of the General Land Office, and a certification of such account to the Secretary of the Treasury by the Secretary of the Interior.

Sec. 5. That upon the approval of the allotments provided for in this act by the Secretary of the Interior, he shall cause patents to issue therefor in the name of the allottees, which patents shall be of the legal effect, and declare that the United States does and will hold the land thus allotted, for the period of twenty-five years, in trust for the sole use and benefit of the Indian to whom such allotment shall have been made, or, in case of his decease, of his heirs according to the laws of the State or Territory where such land is located, and that at the expiration of said period the United States will convey the same by patent to said Indian, or his heirs as aforesaid, in fee, discharged of said trust and free of all charge or incumbrance whatsoever: *Provided*, That the President of the United States may in any case in his discretion extend the period. And if any conveyance shall be made of the lands set apart and allotted as herein provided, or any contract made touching the same, before the expiration of the time above mentioned, such conveyance or contract shall be absolutely null and void: *Provided*, That the law of descent and partition in force in the State or Territory where such lands are situated shall apply thereto after patents therefor have been executed and delivered, except as herein otherwise provided; and the laws of the State of Kansas regulating the descent and partition of real estate shall, so far as practicable, apply to all lands in the Indian Territory which may be allotted in severalty under the provisions of this act: *And provided further*, That at any time after lands have been allotted to all the Indians of any tribe as herein provided, or sooner if in the opinion of the President it shall be for the best interests of said tribe, it shall be lawful for the Secretary of the Interior to negotiate with such Indian tribe for the purchase and release by said tribe, in conformity with the treaty or statute under which such reservation is held, of such portions of its reservation not allotted as such tribe shall, from time to time, consent to sell, on such terms and conditions as shall be considered just and equitable between the United States and said tribe of Indians, which purchase shall not be complete until ratified by Congress, and the form and manner of executing such release shall also be prescribed by Congress: *Provided however,*

That all lands adapted to agriculture, with or without irrigation so sold or released to the United States by any Indian tribe shall be held by the United States for the sole purpose of securing homes to actual settlers and shall be disposed of by the United States to actual and bona fide settlers only in tracts not exceeding one hundred and sixty acres to any one person, on such terms as Congress shall prescribe, subject to grants which Congress may make in aid of education: *And provided further,* That no patents shall issue therefor except to the person so taking the same as and for a homestead, or his heirs, and after the expiration of five years occupancy thereof as such homestead; and any conveyance of said lands so taken as a homestead, or any contract touching the same, or lien thereon, created prior to the date of such patent, shall be null and void. And the sums agreed to be paid by the United States as purchase money for any portion of any such reservation shall be held in the Treasury of the United States for the sole use of the tribe or tribes of Indians; to whom such reservations belonged; and the same, with interest thereon at three per cent per annum, shall be at all times subject to appropriation by Congress for the education and civilization of such tribe or tribes of Indians or the members thereof. The patents aforesaid shall be recorded in the General Land Office, and afterward delivered, free of charge, to the allottee entitled thereto. And if any religious society or other organization is now occupying any of the public lands to which this act is applicable, for religious or educational work among the Indians, the Secretary of the Interior is hereby authorized to confirm such occupation to such society or organization, in quantity not exceeding one hundred and sixty acres in any one tract, so long as the same shall be so occupied, on such terms as he shall deem just; but nothing herein contained shall change or alter any claim of such society for religious or educational purposes heretofore granted by law. And hereafter in the employment

of Indian police, or any other employees in the public service among any of the Indian tribes or bands affected by this act, and where Indians can perform the duties required, those Indians who have availed themselves of the provisions of this act and become citizens of the United States shall be preferred.

Sec. 6. That upon the completion of said allotments and the patenting of the lands to said allottees, each and every member of the respective bands or tribes of Indians to whom allotments have been made shall have the benefit of and be subject to the laws, both civil and criminal, of the State or Territory in which they may reside; and no Territory shall pass or enforce any law denying any such Indian within its jurisdiction the equal protection of the law. And every Indian born within the territorial limits of the United States to whom allotments shall have been made under the provisions of this act, or under any law or treaty, and every Indian born within the territorial limits of the United States who has voluntarily taken up, within said limits, his residence separate and apart from any tribe of Indians therein, and has adopted the habits of civilized life, is hereby declared to be a citizen of the United States, and is entitled to all the rights, privileges, and immunities of such citizens, whether said Indian has been or not, by birth or otherwise, a member of any tribe of Indians within the territorial limits of the United States without in any manner impairing or otherwise affecting the right of any such Indian to tribal or other property.

Sec. 7. That in cases where the use of water for irrigation is necessary to render the lands within any Indian reservation available for agricultural purposes, the Secretary of the Interior be, and he is hereby, authorized to prescribe such rules and regulations as he may deem necessary to secure a just and equal distribution thereof among the Indians residing upon any such reservations; and no other appropriation or grant of water by any riparian proprietor shall be authorized or permitted to the damage of any other riparian proprietor.

Sec. 8. That the provision of this act shall not extend to the territory occupied by the Cherokees, Creeks, Choctaws, Chickasaws, Seminoles, and Osage, Miamies and Peorias, and Sacs and Foxes, in the Indian Territory, nor to any of the reservations of the Seneca Nation of New York Indians in the State of New York, nor to that strip of territory in the State of Nebraska adjoining the Sioux Nation on the south added by executive order.

Sec. 9. That for the purpose of making the surveys and resurveys mentioned in section two of this act, there be, and hereby is, appropriated, out of any moneys in the Treasury not otherwise appropriated, the sum of one hundred thousand dollars, to be repaid proportionately out of the proceeds of the sales of such land as may be acquired from the Indians under the provisions of this act.

Sec. 10. That nothing in this act contained shall be so construed as to affect the right and power of

Congress to grant the right of way through any lands granted to an Indian, or a tribe of Indians, for railroads or other highways, or telegraph lines, for the public use, or to condemn such lands to public uses, upon making just compensation.

Sec. 11. That nothing in this act shall be so construed as to prevent the removal of the Southern Ute Indians from their present reservation in Southwestern Colorado to a new reservation by and with the consent of a majority of the adult male members of said tribe.

Approved, February 8, 1887.

HENRY B. BROWN

Plessy v. Ferguson (1896)

Justice BROWN delivered the opinion of the Court.

This case turns upon the constitutionality of an act of the general assembly of the state of Louisiana, passed in 1890, providing for separate railway carriages for the white and colored races. [. . .]

The constitutionality of this act is attacked upon the ground that it conflicts both with the Thirteenth Amendment of the Constitution, abolishing slavery, and the Fourteenth Amendment, which prohibits certain restrictive legislation on the part of the states.

1. That it does not conflict with the Thirteenth Amendment, which abolished slavery and involuntary servitude, except a punishment for crime, is too clear for argument. Slavery implies involuntary servitude—a state of bondage; the ownership of mankind as a chattel, or, at least, the control of the labor and services of one man for the benefit of another, and the absence of a legal right to the disposal of his own person, property, and services. This amendment was said in the *Slaughter-House Cases* [1873], to have been intended primarily to abolish slavery, as it had been previously known in this country, and that it equally forbade Mexican peonage or the Chinese coolie trade, when they amounted to slavery or involuntary servitude, and that the use of

the word "servitude" was intended to prohibit the use of all forms of involuntary slavery, of whatever class or name. It was intimated, however, in that case, that this amendment was regarded by the statesmen of that day as insufficient to protect the colored race from certain laws which had been enacted in the Southern states, imposing upon the colored race onerous disabilities and burdens, and curtailing their rights in the pursuit of life, liberty, and property to such an extent that their freedom was of little value; and that the Fourteenth Amendment was devised to meet this exigency.

So, too, in the *Civil Rights Cases* [1883], it was said that the act of a mere individual, the owner of an inn, a public conveyance or place of amusement, refusing accommodations to colored people, cannot be justly regarded as imposing any badge of slavery or servitude upon the applicant, but only as involving an ordinary civil injury, properly cognizable by the laws of the state, and presumably subject to redress by those laws until the contrary appears. "It would be running the slavery question into the ground," said Mr. Justice Bradley, "to make it apply to every act of discrimination which a person may see fit to make as to the guests he will entertain, or as to the people he will take into his coach or cab or car, or admit to his concert or theater, or deal with in other matters of intercourse or business."

A statute which implies merely a legal distinction between the white and colored races—a distinction which is founded in the color of the two races, and which must always exist so long as white men are distinguished from the other race by color—has no tendency to destroy the legal equality of the two races, or re-establish a state of involuntary servitude. Indeed, we do not understand that the Thirteenth Amendment is strenuously relied upon by the plaintiff in error in this connection.

2. By the Fourteenth Amendment, all persons born or naturalized in the United States, and subject to the jurisdiction thereof, are made citizens of the United States and of the state wherein they reside; and the states are forbidden from making or enforcing any law which shall abridge the privileges or immunities of citizens of the United States, or shall deprive any person of life, liberty, or property without due process of law, or deny to any person within their jurisdiction the equal protection of the laws. [. . .]

The object of the amendment was undoubtedly to enforce the absolute equality of the two races before the law, but, in the nature of things, it could not have been intended to abolish distinctions based upon color, or to enforce social, as distinguished from political, equality, or a commingling of the two races upon terms unsatisfactory to either. Laws permitting, and even requiring, their separation, in places where they are liable to be brought into contact, do not necessarily imply the inferiority of either race to the other, and have been generally, if not universally, recognized as within the competency of the state legislatures in the exercise of their police power. The most common instance of this is connected with the establishment of separate schools for white and colored children, which have been held to be a valid exercise of the legislative power even by courts of states where the political rights of the colored race have been longest and most earnestly enforced. [. . .]

Laws forbidding the intermarriage of the two races may be said in a technical sense to interfere with the freedom of contract, and yet have been universally recognized as within the police power of the state.

The distinction between laws interfering with the political equality of the negro and those requiring the separation of the two races in schools, theaters, and railway carriages has been frequently drawn by this court. Thus, in *Strauder v. West Virginia* [1880], it was held that a law of West Virginia limiting to white male persons 21 years of age, and citizens of the state, the right to sit upon juries, was a discrimination which implied a legal inferiority in civil society, which lessened the security of the right of the colored race, and was a step towards reducing them to a condition of servility. Indeed, the right of a colored man that, in the selection of jurors to pass upon his life, liberty, and property, there shall be no exclusion of his race, and no discrimination against them because of color, has been asserted in a number of cases. [. . .] So, where the laws of a particular locality or the charter of a particular railway corporation has provided that no person shall be excluded from the cars on account of color, we have held that this meant that persons of color should travel in the same car as white ones, and that the enactment was not satisfied by the company providing cars assigned exclusively to people of color, though they were as good as those which they assigned exclusively to white persons.

Upon the other hand, where a statute of Louisiana required those engaged in the transportation of passengers among the states to give to all persons traveling within that state, upon vessels employed in that business, equal rights and privileges in all parts of the vessel, without distinction on account of race or color, and subjected to an action for damages the owner of such a vessel who excluded colored passengers on account of their color from the cabin set aside by him for the use of whites, it was held to be, so far as it applied to interstate commerce, unconstitutional and void. *Hall v. De Cuir* [1877]. The court in this case, however, expressly disclaimed that it had anything whatever to do with the statute as a regulation of internal commerce, or affecting anything else than commerce among the states. [. . .]

Much nearer, and, indeed, almost directly in point, is the case of the *Louisville, New Orleans & Railway v. Mississippi* [1890], wherein the railway company was indicted for a violation of a statute of Mississippi, enacting that all railroads carrying passengers should provide equal, but separate, accommodations for the white and colored races, by providing two or more passenger cars for each passenger train, or by dividing the passenger cars by a

[handwritten margin note, left side:] argument → separate" does not imply inferiority

partition, so as to secure separate accommodations. The case was presented in a different aspect from the one under consideration, inasmuch as it was an indictment against the railway company for failing to provide the separate accommodations, but the question considered was the constitutionality of the law. In that case, the supreme court of Mississippi had held that the statute applied solely to commerce within the state, and, that being the construction of the state statute by its highest court, was accepted as conclusive. "If it be a matter," said the court, "respecting commerce wholly within a state, and not interfering with commerce between the states, then, obviously, there is no violation of the commerce clause of the federal Constitution. . . . No question arises under this section as to the power of the state to separate in different compartments interstate passengers, or affect, in any manner, the privileges and rights of such passengers. All that we can consider is whether the state has the power to require that railroad trains within her limits shall have separate accommodations for the two races. That affecting only commerce within the state is no invasion of the power given to Congress by the commerce clause."

A like course of reasoning applies to the case under consideration, since the supreme court of Louisiana [. . .] held that the statute in question did not apply to interstate passengers, but was confined in its application to passengers traveling exclusively within the borders of the state. [. . .] In the present case no question of interference with interstate commerce can possibly arise, since the East Louisiana Railway appears to have been purely a local line, with both its termini within the state of Louisiana. [. . .]

While we think the enforced separation of the races, as applied to the internal commerce of the state, neither abridges the privileges or immunities of the colored man, deprives him of his property without due process of law, nor denies him the equal protection of the laws, within the meaning of the Fourteenth Amendment, we are not prepared to say that the conductor, in assigning passengers to the coaches according to their race, does not act at his peril, or that the provision of the second section of the act that denies to the passenger compensation in damages for a refusal to receive him into the coach in which he properly belongs is a valid exercise of the legislative power. Indeed, we understand it to be conceded by the state's attorney that such part of the act as exempts from liability the railway company and its officers is unconstitutional. The power to assign to a particular coach obviously implies the power to determine to which race the passenger belongs, as well as the power to determine who, under the laws of the particular state, is to be deemed a white, and who a colored, person. This question, though indicated in the brief of the plaintiff in error, does not properly arise upon the record in this case, since the only issue made is as to the unconstitutionality of the act, so far as it requires the railway to provide separate accommodations, and the conductor to assign passengers according to their race.

It is claimed by the plaintiff in error that, in an mixed community, the reputation of belonging to the dominant race, in this instance the white race, is "property," in the same sense that a right of action or of inheritance is property. Conceding this to be so, for the purposes of this case, we are unable to see how this statute deprives him of, or in any way affects his right to, such property. If he be a white man, and assigned to a colored coach, he may have his action for damages against the company for being deprived of his so-called "property." Upon the other hand, if he be a colored man, and be so assigned, he has been deprived of no property, since he is not lawfully entitled to the reputation of being a white man.

In this connection, it is also suggested by the learned counsel for the plaintiff in error that the same argument that will justify the state legislature in requiring railways to provide separate accommodations for the two races will also authorize them to require separate cars to be provided for people whose hair is of a certain color, or who are aliens, or who belong to certain nationalities, or to enact laws requiring colored people to walk upon one side of the street, and white people upon the other, or requiring white men's houses to be painted white, and colored men's black, or their vehicles or business signs to be of different colors, upon the theory that one side of the street is as good as the other, or that a house or vehicle of one color is as good as one of another color. The reply to all this is that every exercise of the police power must be reasonable, and extend only to such laws as are enacted in good faith for the promotion of the public good, and not for the annoyance or oppression of a particular class. [. . .]

So far, then, as a conflict with the Fourteenth Amendment is concerned, the case reduces itself to the question whether the statute of Louisiana is a reasonable regulation, and with respect to this there must necessarily be a large discretion on the part of the legislature. In determining the question of reasonableness, it is at liberty to act with reference to the established usages, customs, and traditions of the people, and with a view to the promotion of their comfort, and the preservation of the public peace and good order. Gauged by this standard, we cannot say that a law which authorizes or even requires the separation of the two races in public conveyances is unreasonable, or more obnoxious to the Fourteenth Amendment than the acts of Congress requiring separate schools for colored children in the District of Columbia, the constitutionality of which does not seem to have been questioned, or the corresponding acts of state legislatures.

We consider the underlying fallacy of the plaintiff's argument to consist in the assumption that the enforced separation of the two races stamps the colored race with a badge of inferiority. If this be so, it is not by reason of anything found in the act, but solely because the colored race chooses to put that construction upon it. The argument necessarily assumes that if, as has been more than once the case, and is not unlikely to be so again, the colored race should become the dominant power in the state legislature, and should enact a law in precisely similar terms, it would thereby relegate the white race to an inferior position. We imagine that the white race, at least, would not acquiesce in this assumption. The argument also assumes that social prejudices may be overcome by legislation, and that equal rights cannot be secured to the negro except by an enforced commingling of the two races. We cannot accept this proposition. If the two races are to meet upon terms of social equality, it must be the result of natural affinities, a mutual appreciation of each other's merits, and a voluntary consent of individuals. As was said by the court of appeals of New York in *People v. Gallagher*, 93 N.Y. 438, 448: "This end can neither be accomplished nor promoted by laws which conflict with the general sentiment of the community upon whom they are designed to operate. When the government, therefore, has secured to each of its citizens equal rights before the law, and equal opportunities for improvement and progress, it has accomplished the end for which it was organized, and performed all of the functions respecting social advantages with which it is endowed." Legislation is powerless to eradicate racial instincts, or to abolish distinctions based upon physical differences, and the attempt to do so can only result in accentuating the difficulties of the present situation. If the civil and political rights of both races be equal, one cannot be inferior to the other civilly or politically. If one race be inferior to the other socially, the Constitution of the United States cannot put them upon the same plane.

It is true that the question of the proportion of colored blood necessary to constitute a colored person, as distinguished from a white person, is one upon which there is a difference of opinion in the different states; some holding that any visible admixture of black blood stamps the person as belonging to the colored race; others, that it depends upon the preponderance of blood; and still others, that the predominance of white blood must only be in the proportion of three-fourths. But these are questions to be determined under the laws of each state, and are not properly put in issue in this case. Under the allegations of his petition, it may undoubtedly become a question of importance whether, under the laws of Louisiana, the petitioner belongs to the white or colored race.

The judgment of the court below is therefore affirmed.

John Marshall Harlan

Plessy v. Ferguson, Dissent (1896)

Mr. Justice HARLAN, dissenting.

[. . .] While there may be in Louisiana persons of different races who are not citizens of the United States, the words in the act "white and colored races" necessarily include all citizens of the United States of both races residing in that state. So that we have before us a state enactment that compels, under penalties, the separation of the two races in railroad passenger coaches, and makes it a crime for a citizen of either race to enter a coach that has been assigned to citizens of the other race.

Thus, the state regulates the use of a public highway by citizens of the United States solely upon the basis of race.

However apparent the injustice of such legislation may be, we have only to consider whether it is consistent with the Constitution of the United States. [. . .]

In respect of civil rights, common to all citizens, the Constitution of the United States does not, I think, permit any public authority to know the race of those entitled to be protected in the enjoyment of such rights. Every true man has pride of race, and under appropriate circumstances, when the rights of others, his equals before the law, are not to be affected, it is his privilege to express such pride and to take such action based upon it as to him seems proper. But I deny that any legislative body or judicial tribunal may have regard to the race of citizens when the civil rights of those citizens are involved. Indeed, such legislation as that here in question is inconsistent not only with that equality of rights which pertains to citizenship, national and state, but with the personal liberty enjoyed by every one within the United States.

The Thirteenth Amendment does not permit the withholding or the deprivation of any right necessarily inhering in freedom. It not only struck down the institution of slavery as previously existing in the United States, but it prevents the imposition of any burdens or disabilities that constitute badges of slavery or servitude. It decreed universal civil freedom in this country. This court has so adjudged. But, that amendment having been found inadequate to the protection of the rights of those who had been in slavery, it was followed by the Fourteenth Amendment, which added greatly to the dignity and glory of American citizenship, and to the security of personal liberty, by declaring that "all persons born or naturalized in the United States, and subject to the jurisdiction thereof, are citizens of the United States and of the state wherein they reside," and that "no state shall make or enforce any law which shall abridge the privileges or immunities of citizens of the United States; nor shall any state deprive any person of life, liberty or property without due process of law, nor deny to any person within its jurisdiction the equal protection of the laws." These two amendments, if enforced according to their true intent and meaning, will protect all the civil rights that pertain to freedom and citizenship. Finally, and to the end that no citizen should be denied, on account of his race, the privilege of participating in the political control of his country, it was declared by the Fifteenth Amendment that "the right of citizens of the United States to vote shall not be denied or abridged by the United States or by any state on account of race, color or previous condition of servitude."

These notable additions to the fundamental law were welcomed by the friends of liberty throughout the world. They removed the race line from our governmental systems. They had, as this court has said, a common purpose, namely, to secure "to a race recently emancipated, a race that through many generations have been held in slavery, all the civil rights that the superior race enjoy." They declared, in legal effect, this court has further said, "that the law in the states shall be the same for the black as for the white; that all persons, whether colored or white, shall stand equal before the laws of the states; and in regard to the colored race, for whose protection the amendment was primarily designed, that no discrimination shall be made against them by law because of their color." We also said: "The words of the amendment, it is true, are prohibitory, but they contain a necessary implication of a positive immunity or right, most valuable to the colored race—the right to exemption from unfriendly legislation against them distinctively as colored; exemption from legal discriminations, implying inferiority in civil society, lessening the security of their enjoyment of the rights which others enjoy; and discriminations which are steps towards reducing them to the condition of a subject race." It was, consequently, adjudged that a state law that excluded citizens of the colored race from juries, because of their race, however well qualified in other respects to discharge the duties of jurymen, was repugnant to the Fourteenth Amendment. *Strauder v. West Virginia* [1880]. [. . .]

It was said in argument that the statute of Louisiana does not discriminate against either race, but prescribes a rule applicable alike to white and colored citizens. But this argument does not meet the difficulty. Every one knows that the statute in question had its origin in the purpose, not so much to exclude white persons from railroad cars occupied by blacks, as to exclude colored people from coaches occupied by or assigned to white persons. Railroad corporations of Louisiana did not make discrimination among whites in the matter of accommodation for travelers. The thing to accomplish was, under the guise of giving equal accommodation for whites and blacks, to compel the latter to keep to themselves while traveling in railroad passenger coaches. No one would be so wanting in candor as to assert the contrary. The fundamental objection, therefore, to the statute, is that it interferes with the personal freedom of citizens. "Personal liberty," it has been well said, "consists in the power of locomotion, of changing situation, or removing one's person to whatsoever places one's own inclination may direct, without imprisonment or restraint, unless by due course of law." 1 Bl[ackstone] [*Commentaries*] 134. If a white man and a black man choose to occupy the same public conveyance on a public highway, it is their right to do so; and no government, proceeding alone on grounds of race, can prevent it without infringing the personal liberty of each.

It is one thing for railroad carriers to furnish, or to be required by law to furnish, equal accommodations for all whom they are under a legal duty to carry. It is quite another thing for government to forbid citizens of the white and black races from traveling in the same public conveyance, and to punish officers of railroad companies for permitting persons of the two races to occupy the same passenger coach. If a state can prescribe, as a rule of civil conduct, that whites and blacks shall not travel as passengers in the same railroad coach, why may it not so regulate the use of the streets of its cities and towns as to compel white citizens to keep on one side of a street, and black citizens to keep on the other? Why may it not, upon like grounds, punish whites and blacks who ride together in street cars or in open vehicles on a public road or street? Why may it not require sheriffs to assign whites to one side of a court room, and blacks to the other? And why may it not also prohibit the commingling of the two races in the galleries of legislative halls or in public assemblages convened for the consideration of the political questions of the day? Further, if this statute of Louisiana is consistent with the personal liberty of citizens, why may not the state require the separation in railroad coaches of native and naturalized citizens of the United States, or of Protestants and Roman Catholics?

The answer given at the argument to these questions was that regulations of the kind they suggest would be unreasonable, and could not, therefore, stand before the law. Is it meant that the determination of questions of legislative power depends upon the inquiry whether the statute whose validity is questioned is, in the judgment of the courts, a reasonable one, taking all the circumstances into consideration? A statute may be unreasonable merely because a sound public policy forbade its enactment. But I do not understand that the courts have anything to do with the policy or expediency of legislation. A statute may be valid, and yet, upon grounds of public policy, may well be characterized as unreasonable. Mr. Sedgwick correctly states the rule when he says that, the legislative intention being clearly ascertained, "the courts have no other duty to perform than to execute the legislative will, without any regard to their views as to the wisdom or justice of the particular enactment." Sedg. *St. & Const. Law*, 324. There is a dangerous tendency in these latter days to enlarge the functions of the courts, by means of judicial interference with the will of the people as expressed by the legislature. Our institutions have the distinguishing characteristic that the three departments of government are co-ordinate and separate. Each much keep within the limits defined by the Constitution. And the courts best discharge their duty by executing the will of the law-making power, constitutionally expressed, leaving the results of legislation to be dealt with by the people through their representatives. Statutes must always have a reasonable construction. Sometimes they are to be construed strictly, sometimes literally, in order to carry out the legislative will. But, however construed, the intent of the legislature is to be respected if the particular statute in question is valid, although the courts, looking at the public interests, may conceive the statute to be both unreasonable and impolitic. If the power exists to enact a statute, that ends the matter so far as the courts are concerned. The adjudged cases in which statutes have been held to be void, because unreasonable, are those in which the means employed by the legislature were not at all germane to the end to which the legislature was competent.

The white race deems itself to be the dominant race in this country. And so it is, in prestige, in achievements, in education, in wealth, and in power. So, I doubt not, it will continue to be for all time, if it remains true to its great heritage, and holds fast to the principles of constitutional liberty. But in view of the Constitution, in the eye of the law, there is in this country no superior, dominant, ruling class of citizens. There is no caste here. Our Constitution is color-blind, and neither knows nor tolerates classes among citizens. In respect of civil rights, all citizens are equal before the law. The humblest is the peer of the most powerful. The law regards man as man, and takes no account of his surroundings or of his color when his civil rights as guaranteed by the supreme law of the land are involved. It is therefore to be regretted that this high tribunal, the final expositor of the fundamental law of the land, has reached the conclusion that it is competent for a state to regulate the enjoyment by citizens of their civil rights solely upon the basis of race.

In my opinion, the judgment this day rendered will, in time, prove to be quite as pernicious as the decision made by this tribunal in the *Dred Scott Case* [1857].

It was adjudged in that case that the descendants of Africans who were imported into this country, and

sold as slaves, were not included nor intended to be included under the word "citizens" in the Constitution, and could not claim any of the rights and privileges which that instrument provided for and secured to citizens of the United States; that, at time of the adoption of the Constitution, they were "considered as a subordinate and inferior class of beings, who had been subjugated by the dominant race, and, whether emancipated or not, yet remained subject to their authority, and had no rights or privileges but such as those who held the power and the government might choose to grant them." The recent amendments of the Constitution, it was supposed, had eradicated these principles from our institutions. But it seems that we have yet, in some of the states, a dominant race—a superior class of citizens—which assumes to regulate the enjoyment of civil rights, common to all citizens, upon the basis of race. The present decision, it may well be apprehended, will not only stimulate aggressions, more or less brutal and irritating, upon the admitted rights of colored citizens, but will encourage the belief that it is possible, by means of state enactments, to defeat the beneficent purposes which the people of the United States had in view when they adopted the recent amendments of the Constitution, by one of which the blacks of this country were made citizens of the United States and of the states in which they respectively reside, and whose privileges and immunities, as citizens, the states are forbidden to abridge. Sixty millions of whites are in no danger from the presence here of eight millions of blacks. The destinies of the two races, in this country, are indissolubly linked together, and the interests of both require that the common government of all shall not permit the seeds of race hate to be planted under the sanction of law. What can more certainly arouse race hate, what more certainly create and perpetuate a feeling of distrust between these races, than state enactments which, in fact, proceed on the ground that colored citizens are so inferior and degraded that they cannot be allowed to sit in public coaches occupied by white citizens? That, as all will admit, is the real meaning of such legislation as was enacted in Louisiana.

The sure guaranty of the peace and security of each race is the clear, distinct, unconditional recognition by our governments, national and state, of every right that inheres in civil freedom, and of the equality before the law of all citizens of the United

States, without regard to race. State enactments regulating the enjoyment of civil rights upon the basis of race, and cunningly devised to defeat legitimate results of the war, under the pretense of recognizing equality of rights, can have no other result than to render permanent peace impossible, and to keep alive a conflict of races, the continuance of which must do harm to all concerned. This question is not met by the suggestion that social equality cannot exist between the white and black races in this country. That argument, if it can be properly regarded as one, is scarcely worthy of consideration; for social equality no more exists between two races when traveling in a passenger coach or a public highway than when members of the same races sit by each other in a street car or in the jury box, or stand or sit with each other in a political assembly, or when they use in common the streets of a city or town, or when they are in the same room for the purpose of having their names placed on the registry of voters, or when they approach the ballot box in order to exercise the high privilege of voting.

There is a race so different from our own that we do not permit those belonging to it to become citizens of the United States. Persons belonging to it are, with few exceptions, absolutely excluded from our country. I allude to the Chinese race. But, by the statute in question, a Chinaman can ride in the same passenger coach with white citizens of the United States, while citizens of the black race in Louisiana, many of whom, perhaps, risked their lives for the preservation of the Union, who are entitled, by law, to participate in the political control of the state and nation, who are not excluded, by law or by reason of their race, from public stations of any kind, and who have all the legal rights that belong to white citizens, are yet declared to be criminals, liable to imprisonment, if they ride in a public coach occupied by citizens of the white race. It is scarcely just to say that a colored citizen should not object to occupying a public coach assigned to his own race. He does not object, nor, perhaps, would he object to separate coaches for his race if his rights under the law were recognized. But he does object, and he ought never to cease objecting, that citizens of the white and black races can be adjudged criminals because they sit, or claim the right to sit, in the same public coach on a public highway. The arbitrary separation of citizens, on the basis of race, while they are

on a public highway, is a badge of servitude wholly inconsistent with the civil freedom and the equality before the law established by the Constitution. It cannot be justified upon any legal grounds.

If evils will result from the commingling of the two races upon public highways established for the benefit of all, they will be infinitely less than those that will surely come from state legislation regulating the enjoyment of civil rights upon the basis of race. We boast of the freedom enjoyed by our people above all other peoples. But it is difficult to reconcile that boast with a state of the law which, practically, puts the brand of servitude and degradation upon a large class of our fellow citizens—our equals before the law. The thin disguise of "equal" accommodations for passengers in railroad coaches will not mislead any one, nor atone for the wrong this day done.

The result of the whole matter is that while this court has frequently adjudged, and at the present term has recognized the doctrine, that a state cannot, consistently with the Constitution of the United States, prevent white and black citizens, having the required qualifications for jury service, from sitting in the same jury box, it is now solemnly held that a state may prohibit white and black citizens from sitting in the same passenger coach on a public highway, or may require that they be separated by a "partition" when in the same passenger coach. May it not now be reasonably expected that astute men of the dominant race, who affect to be disturbed at the possibility that the integrity of the white race may be corrupted, or that its supremacy will be imperiled, by contact on public highways with black people, will endeavor to procure statutes requiring white and black jurors to be separated in the jury box by a "partition," and that, upon retiring from the court room to consult as to their verdict, such partition, if it be a movable one, shall be taken to their consultation room, and set up in such way as to prevent black jurors from coming too close to their brother jurors of the white race. If the "partition" used in the court room happens to be stationary, provision could be made for screens with openings through which jurors of the two races could confer as to their verdict without coming into personal contact with each other. I cannot see but that, according to the principles this day announced, such state legislation, although conceived in hostility to, and enacted for the purpose of humiliating, citizens of the United States of a particular race, would be held to be consistent with the constitution.

I do not deem it necessary to review the decisions of state courts to which reference was made in argument. Some, and the most important, of them, are wholly inapplicable, because rendered prior to the adoption of the last amendments of the Constitution, when colored people had very few rights which the dominant race felt obliged to respect. Others were made at a time when public opinion, in many localities, was dominated by the institution of slavery; when it would not have been safe to do justice to the black man; and when, so far as the rights of blacks were concerned, race prejudice was, practically, the supreme law of the land. Those decisions cannot be guides in the era introduced by the recent amendments of the supreme law, which established universal civil freedom, gave citizenship to all born or naturalized in the United States, and residing here, obliterated the race line from our systems of governments, national and state, and placed our free institutions upon the broad and sure foundation of the equality of all men before the law.

I am of opinion that the state of Louisiana is inconsistent with the personal liberty of citizens, white and black, in that state, and hostile to both the spirit and letter of the Constitution of the United States. If laws of like character should be enacted in the several states of the Union, the effect would be in the highest degree mischievous. Slavery, as an institution tolerated by law, would, it is true, have disappeared from our country; but there would remain a power in the states, by sinister legislation, to interfere with the full enjoyment of the blessings of freedom, to regulate civil rights, common to all citizens, upon the basis of race, and to place in a condition of legal inferiority a large body of American citizens, now constituting a part of the political community, called the "People of the United States," for whom, and by whom through representatives, our government is administered. Such a system is inconsistent with the guaranty given by the Constitution to each state of a republican form of government, and may be stricken down by congressional action, or by the courts in the discharge of their solemn duty to maintain the supreme law of the land, anything in the Constitution or laws of any state to the contrary notwithstanding.

For the reason stated, I am constrained to withhold my assent from the opinion and judgment of the majority.

BOOKER T. WASHINGTON

Who Is Permanently Hurt? (1896)

The United States Supreme Court has recently handed down a decision declaring the separate coach law, or "Jim Crow" car law constitutional. What does this mean? Simply that the separation of colored and white passengers as now practiced in certain Southern States, is lawful and constitutional.

This separation may be good law, but it is not good common sense. The difference in the color of the skin is a matter for which nature is responsible. If the Supreme Court can say that it is lawful to compel all persons with black skins to ride in one car, and all with white skins to ride in another, why may it not say that it is lawful to put all yellow people in one car and all white people, whose skin is sun burnt, in another car. Nature has given both their color; or why cannot the courts go further and decide that all men with bald heads must ride in one car and all with red hair still in another. Nature is responsible for all these conditions.

But the colored people do not complain so much of the separation, as of the fact that the accommodations, with almost no exceptions, are not equal, still the same price is charged the colored passengers as is charged the white people.

Now the point of all this article is not to make a complaint against the white man or the "Jim Crow Car" law, but it is simply to say that such an unjust law injures the white man, and inconveniences the negro. No race can wrong another race simply because it has the power to do so, without being permanently injured in morals, and its ideas of justice. The negro can endure the temporary inconvenience, but the injury to the white man is permanent. It is the one who inflicts the wrong that is hurt, rather than the one on whom the wrong is inflicted. It is for the white man to save himself from this degradation that I plead.

If a white man steals a negro's ballot, it is the white man who is permanently injured. Physical death comes to the negro lynched—death of the morals—death of the soul—comes to the white man who perpetrates the lynching.

The Best Labor in the World (1898)

Many persons who have never lived in the South and want to move to the South, get the idea that the presence of the negro in the South in large numbers is a disadvantage.

I have just returned from a visit to the State of Vermont. While there I attended a convention in which the subject of domestic help was discussed. Several persons in the meeting stated that they had tried to get satisfactory help among all the representatives of foreign countries who flock to America; in despair they sent South for negro help, and in every instance they stated that the result had been satisfactory.

It may be that I, a member of the negro race, cannot speak without bias on this subject, but I believe I can do so. I believe I have grown to the point where I can love a white man as much as I can love a black man. I believe that I can sympathize with a Southern white man as much as I can sympathize with a Northern white man. To me "a man is but a man for a' that and a' that."

The negro race has several characteristics which the average Northern or Western man does not appreciate or know. In the first place, with few exceptions, the Northern people see the worst side of negro life in the colored people who are in the Northern cities and towns. The negro race should not be judged by these.

The negro race has a genuine interest in this country—in the South. It is his home, and he is going to remain in the South. He is not here to grab a few dollars and then return to some foreign country. Then the negro, when treated right, can be trusted when made to feel that confidence is put in him. During our late war no Southern or Northern soldier who confided in the negro was betrayed. Even where an individual negro is inclined to be dishonest on general principles, when valuables are entrusted to him he will not betray the trust except in rare instances. The negro is used to the climate and the soil of the South, and he is at his best when cultivating this soil. If he is treated fairly, paid good wages and is paid promptly, there is no farm laborer in this country that will excel him.

The negro is not given to strikes and lock-outs. He believes in letting each individual be free to work where and for whom he pleases. He has the physical strength to endure hard labor, and he is not ashamed or afraid to work.

The negro, like the white man, has his faults, but he can be educated out of them. He is too quick to spend his money for gew-gaws. He likes to go on excursions, he likes to go to town on Saturday, but these faults, if dealt with in the right way, can soon be cured.

It is very seldom that the black man on the farm becomes a drunkard. He likes his whiskey on Saturday and Sunday, perhaps, but he seldom becomes a drunkard. On this, as on all subjects, the negro is willing to take the advice of anyone who gets and deserves his confidence.

The charge is often made that the educated negro will not work. Some years ago there seemed to be some foundation for this charge. Soon after his freedom, when the negro was intoxicated with his new ideas of liberty, not knowing what it meant, and when he did not feel the responsibilities of freedom, many negroes had the idea that to get education was to be put into a condition where labor would not be necessary. But all this is changing. In 1881, when I started the Tuskegee Normal and Industrial Institute at Tuskegee, Ala., parents would not send their children because they said they did not want their children taught to work. Now a revolution has been wrought in this matter. Here at Tuskegee we have about 1000 students, and every one of them is learning some trade or industry. Every parent who sends his son or daughter requests that they be taught some industry in connection with their academic training. So great is the demand from all parts of the South for this that we are compelled to refuse admission to hundreds each year. For example, our students cultivate 700 acres of land each year. Not only this, but they are being taught farming, dairying, horticulture, truck gardening, etc., and there is a positive enthusiasm about it. Of the forty-two buildings on our grounds, all except four have been erected by the labor of the students. While erecting a building some are taught brick masonry, others brickmaking, plastering, carpentry, tin-smithing, etc. In all we have twenty-six different industries in constant operation. I ask any white school in the country to show a better record in regard to labor. When the negro is properly taught he learns to love labor instead of despising it. The negro throughout the South is beginning to see the dignity and beauty in labor.

He who would succeed with negro labor must let the negro see that he is treated as a man, not as a brute. If he is given a decent house for himself and family, and not made to work an unreasonable number of hours during the day, he will repay anyone in high profits who thus treats him and at nearly one-half the cost paid to Northern white farm help.

Sooner or later this country is going to realize that it has at its very doors the best labor that the world has seen.

The vast unoccupied lands in the South, with its mellow climate and the strong and willing arm of the negro, are simply waiting for those with capital, foresight and faith to step in and occupy.

Conditions at the South are too often misunderstood by Northern and Western people in another direction. Those who get their information from newspaper dispatches alone are likely to get the impression that there is continual friction between the white and colored people in the South. The fact is that the newspaper reports, as a rule, give the worst side. Outbreaks of lawlessness are widely reported, while the evidences of friendly relations now to be found in every part of the South are seldom referred to. In most sections of the South there is little, if any, trouble between the two races. As the colored people continue to grow in intelligence, property, thrift and character there will be less trouble. And still more will friction disappear as the white people grow in the same direction. Within the last few months I have attended several county fairs. In each case I found both the white and colored people making exhibits together, and there was the most friendly rivalry. In one case the fair was in charge of the colored people, but the white people made exhibits and some of them acted as judges. In another case colored people were awarded first prizes over their white competitors; one colored man won the prize for the best bushel of corn and another for the best cow.

At the Tuskegee Normal and Industrial Institute a few days ago we had the annual opening of our new agricultural hall. The secretary of agriculture, a republican, was present and spoke; the governor of Alabama, a democrat and ex-Confederate soldier, was present and spoke; also the State commissioner of agriculture. Besides, there were hundreds of the best white farmers, together with hundreds of colored people. There was the most friendly feeling shown throughout the day. These are only a few of the many evidences of the growing friendship of the two races.

An Open Letter to the Louisiana Constitutional Convention
(1898)

To the Louisiana State Constitutional Convention: In addressing you this letter, I know that I am running the risk of appearing to meddle with something that does not concern me. But since I know that nothing but sincere love for our beautiful Southland, which I hold as near to my heart as any of you can, and a sincerer love for every black and white man within her borders, is the only thing actuating me to write, I am willing to be misjudged, if need be, if I can accomplish a little good.

But I do not believe that you, gentlemen of the Convention, will misinterpret my motives. What I say will, I believe, be considered in the same earnest spirit in which I write.

I am no politician; on the other hand, I have always advised my race to give attention to acquiring property, intelligence and character, as the necessary bases of good citizenship, rather than to mere political agitation. But the question upon which I write is out of the region of ordinary politics; it affects the civilization of two races, not for a day alone, but for a very long time to come; it is up in the region of duty of man to man, of Christian to Christian.

Since the war, no State has had such an opportunity to settle for all time the race question, so far as it concerns politics, as is now given in Louisiana. Will your Convention set an example to the world in this respect? Will Louisiana take such high and just grounds in respect to the Negro that no one can doubt that the South is as good a friend to the Negro as he possesses elsewhere? In all this, gentlemen of the Convention, I am not pleading for the Negro alone, but for the morals, the higher life of the white man, as well. For the more I study this question, the more I am convinced that it is not so much a question as to what the white man will do with the Negro, as to what the Negro will do with the white man's civilization.

The Negro agrees with you that it is necessary to the salvation of the South that restriction be put upon the ballot. I know that you have two serious problems before you; ignorant and corrupt government on the one hand, and on the other, a way to restrict the ballot so that control will be in the hands of the intelligent, without regard to race. With the sincerest sympathy with you in your efforts to find a way out of the difficulty, I want to suggest that no State in the South can make a law that will provide an opportunity or temptation for an ignorant white man to vote and withhold the same opportunity from an ignorant colored man, without injuring both men. No State can make a law that can thus be executed, without dwarfing for all time the morals of the white man in the South. Any law controlling the ballot, that is not absolutely just and fair to both races, will work more permanent injury to the whites than to the blacks.

The Negro does not object to an educational or property test, but let the law be so clear that no one clothed with State authority will be tempted to perjure and degrade himself, by putting one interpretation upon it for the white man and another for the black man. Study the history of the South, and you will find that where there has been the most dishonesty in the matter of voting, there you will find to-day the lowest moral condition of both races. First, there was the temptation to act wrongly with the Negro's ballot. From this it was an easy step to dishonesty with the white man's ballot, to the carrying of concealed weapons, to the murder of a Negro, and then to the murder of a white man, and then to lynching. I entreat you not to pass such a law as will prove an eternal millstone about the neck of your children.

No man can have respect for government and officers of the law, when he knows, deep down in his heart, that the exercise of the franchise is tainted with fraud.

The road that the South has been compelled to travel during the last thirty years has been strewn with thorns and thistles. It has been as one groping through the long darkness into the light. The time is not distant when the world will begin to appreciate the real character of the burden that was imposed upon the South when 4,500,000 ex-slaves, ignorant and impoverished, were given the franchise. No people had ever been given such a problem to solve. History had blazed no path through the wilderness that could be followed. For thirty years, we wandered in the wilderness. We are beginning to get out. But there is but one road out, and all makeshifts, expedients, "profit and loss calculations," but lead into the swamps, quicksands, quagmires and jungles. There is a highway that will lead both races out into the pure, beautiful sunshine, where there will be nothing to hide and nothing to explain, where both races can grow strong and true and useful in every fibre of their being. I believe that your Convention will find this highway; that it will enact a fundamental law which will be absolutely just and fair to white and black alike.

I beg of you, further, that in the degree that you close the ballot-box against the ignorant, that you open the school house. More than one half of the people of your State are Negroes. No State can long prosper when a large percentage of its citizenship is in ignorance and poverty, and has no interest in government. I beg of you that you do not treat us as alien people. We are not aliens. You know us; you know that we have cleared your forests, tilled your fields, nursed your children and protected your families. There is an attachment between us that few understand. While I do not presume to be able to advise you, yet it is in my heart to say that if your Convention would do something that would prevent, for all time, strained relations between the two races, and would permanently settle the matter of political relations in our Southern States, at least, let the very best educational opportunities be provided for both races; and add to this the enactment of an election law that shall be incapable of unjust discrimination, at the same time providing that in proportion as the ignorant secure education, property and character, they will be given the right of citizenship. Any other course will take from one-half your citizens interest in the State, and hope and ambition to become intelligent producers and taxpayers—to become useful and virtuous citizens. Any other course will tie the white citizens of Louisiana to a body of death.

The Negroes are not unmindful of the fact that the white people of your State pay the greater proportion of the school taxes, and that the poverty of the State prevents it from doing all that it desires for public education; yet I believe you will agree with me, that ignorance is more costly to the State than education; that it will cost Louisiana more not to educate her Negroes than it will cost to educate them. In connection with a generous provision for public schools, I believe that nothing will so help my own people in your State as provision at some institution for the highest academic and normal training, in connection with thorough training in agriculture, mechanics and domestic economy. The fact is that 90 per cent of our people depend upon the common occupations for their living, and outside of the cities 85 per cent depend upon agriculture for support. Notwithstanding this, our people have been educated since the war in everything else but the very thing that most of them live by. First-class training in agriculture, horticulture, dairying, stock-raising, the mechanical arts and domestic economy, will make us intelligent producers, and not only help us to contribute our proportion as taxpayers, but will result in retaining much money in the State that now goes outside for that which can be produced in the State. An institution that will give this training of the hand, along with the highest mental culture, will soon convince our people that their salvation is in the ownership of property, industrial and business development, rather than in mere political agitation.

The highest test of the civilization of any race is in its willingness to extend a helping hand to the less fortunate. A race, like an individual, lifts itself up by lifting others up. Surely no people ever had a greater chance to exhibit the highest Christian fortitude and magnanimity than is now presented to the people of Louisiana. It requires little wisdom or statesmanship to repress, to crush out, to retard the hopes and aspirations of a people, but the highest and most profound statesmanship is shown in guiding and stimulating a people so that every fibre in the body, mind and soul shall be made to contribute in the highest degree to the usefulness and nobility of the State. It is along this line that I pray God the thoughts and activities of your Convention be guided. Respectfully submitted,

Booker T. Washington

W. E. B. Du Bois

The Negro Problem: On the "Talented Tenth" (1903)

The Negro race, like all races, is going to be saved by its exceptional men. The problem of education, then, among Negroes must first of all deal with the Talented Tenth; it is the problem of developing the Best of this race that they may guide the Mass away from the contamination and death of the Worst, in their own and other races. Now the training of men is a difficult and intricate task. Its technique is a matter for educational experts, but its object is for the vision of seers. If we make money the object of man-training, we shall develop money-makers but not necessarily men; if we make technical skill the object of education, we may possess artisans but not, in nature, men. Men we shall have only as we make manhood the object of the work of the schools—intelligence, broad sympathy, knowledge of the world that was and is, and of the relation of men to it—this is the curriculum of that Higher Education which must underlie true life. On this foundation we may build bread winning, skill of hand and quickness of brain, with never a fear lest the child and man mistake the means of living for the object of life.

If this be true—and who can deny it—three tasks lay before me; first to show from the past that the Talented Tenth as they have risen amon American Negroes have been worthy of leadership; secondly, to show how these men may be educated and developed; and thirdly, to show their relation to the Negro problem.

From the very first it has been the educated and intelligent of the Negro people that have led and elevated the mass, and the sole obstacles that nullified and retarded their efforts were slavery and race prejudice. [. . .]

And so we come to the present—a day of cowardice and vacillation, or strident wide-voiced wrong and faint hearted compromise; of double-faced dallying with Truth and Right. Who are to-day guiding the work of the Negro people? The "exceptions" of course. And yet so sure as this Talented Tenth is pointed out, the blind worshippers of the average cry out in alarm: "these are exceptions, look here at death, disease and crime—these are the happy rule." Of course they are the rule, because a silly nation made them the rule: Because for three long centuries this people lynched Negroes who dared to be brave, raped black women who dared to be virtuous, crushed dark-hued youth who dared to be ambitious, and encouraged and made to flourish servility and lewdness and apathy. But not even this was able to crush all manhood and chastity and aspiration from black folk. A saving remnant continually survives and persists, continually aspires, continually shows itself in thrift and ability and character. Exceptional it is to be sure, but this is its chiefest promise; it shows the capability of Negro blood, the promise of black men. [. . .]

Can the masses of the Negro people be in any possible way more quickly raised than by the effort and example of this aristocracy of talent and character? Was there ever a nation on God's fair earth civilized from the bottom upward? Never; it is, ever was and ever will be from the top downward that culture filters. The Talented Tenth rises and pulls all that are worth the saving up to their vantage ground.

All men cannot go to college but some men must; every isolated group or nation must have its yeast, must have for the talented few centers of training where men are not so mystified and befuddled by the hard and necessary toil of earning a living, as to have no aims higher than their bellies, and no God greater than Gold. [. . .]

The main question, so far as the Southern Negro is concerned, is: What under the present circumstance, must a system of education do in order to raise the Negro as quickly as possible in the scale of civilization? The answer to this question seems to me clear: It must strengthen the Negro's character, increase his knowledge and teach him to earn a living [. . .] [O]ur system of training must set before itself two great aims—the one dealing with knowledge and character, the other part seeking to give the child the technical knowledge necessary for him to earn a living under the present circumstances. These objects are accomplished in part by the opening of the common schools on the one, and of the industrial schools on the other. But only in part, for there must also be trained those who are to teach these schools—men and women of knowledge and culture and technical skill who understand modern civilization, and have the training and aptitude to impart it to the children under them. There must be teachers, and teachers of teachers, and to attempt to establish any sort of a system of common and industrial school training, without *first* (and I say *first* advisedly) without *first* providing for the higher training of the very best teachers, is simply throwing your money to the winds. . . . Nothing, in these latter days, has so dampened the faith of thinking Negroes in recent educational movements, as the fact that such movements have been accompanied by ridicule and denouncement and decrying of those very institutions of higher training which made the Negro public school possible, and make Negro industrial schools thinkable. . . .

I would not deny, or for a moment seem to deny, the paramount necessity of teaching the Negro to work, and to work steadily and skillfully; or seem to depreciate in the slightest degree the important part industrial schools must play in the accomplishment of these ends, but I *do* say, and insist upon it, that it is industrialism drunk with its vision of success, to imagine that its own work can be accomplished without providing for the training of broadly cultured men and women to teach its own teachers, and to teach the teachers of the public schools. [. . .]

I am an earnest advocate of manual training and trade teaching for black boys, and for white boys, too. I believe that next to the founding of Negro colleges the most valuable addition to Negro education since the war, has been industrial training for black boys. Nevertheless, I insist that the object of all true education is not to make men carpenters, it is to make carpenters men; there are two means of making the carpenter a man, each equally important: the first is to give the group and community in which he works, liberally trained teachers and leaders to teach him and his family what life means; the second is to give him sufficient intelligence and technical skill to make him an efficient workman; the first object demands the Negro college and college-bred men—not a quantity of such colleges, but a few of excellent quality; not too many college-bred men, but enough to leaven the lump, to inspire the masses, to raise the Talented Tenth to leadership. [. . .]

Men of America, the problem is plain before you. Here is a race transplanted through the criminal foolishness of your fathers. Whether you like it or not the millions are here, and here they will remain. If you do not lift them up, they will pull you down. Education and work are the levers to uplift a people. Work alone will not do it unless inspired by the right ideals and guided by intelligence. Education must not simply teach work—it must teach Life. The Talented Tenth of the Negro race must be made leaders of thought and missionaries of culture among their people. No others can do this work and Negro colleges must train men for it. The Negro race, like all other races, is going to be saved by its exceptional men.

CHARLOTTE PERKINS GILMAN

Our Androcentric Culture (1911)

Chapter One—As to Humanness

Human life of any sort is dependent upon what Kropotkin calls "mutual aid," and human progress keeps step absolutely with that interchange of specialized services which makes society organic. The nomad, living on cattle as ants live on theirs, is less human than the farmer, raising food by intelligently applied labor; and the extension of trade and commerce, from mere village market-places to the world-exchanges of to-day, is extension of humanness as well.

Humanity, thus considered, is not a thing made at once and unchangeable, but a stage of development; and is still, as Wells describes it, "in the making." Our humanness is seen to lie not so much in what we are individually, as in our relations to one another; and even that individuality is but the result of our relations to one another. It is in what we do and how we do it, rather than in what we are. Some, philosophically inclined, exalt "being" over "doing." To them this question may be put: "Can you mention any form of life that merely 'is,' without doing anything?"

Taken separately and physically, we are animals, genus homo; taken socially and psychically, we are, in varying degree, human; and our real history lies in the development of this humanness.

Our historic period is not very long. Real written history only goes back a few thousand years, beginning with the stone records of ancient Egypt. During this period we have had almost universally what is here called an Androcentric Culture. The history, such as it was, was made and written by men.

The mental, the mechanical, the social development, was almost wholly theirs. We have, so far, lived and suffered and died in a man-made world. So general, so unbroken, has been this condition, that to mention it arouses no more remark than the statement of a natural law. We have taken it for granted, since the dawn of civilization, that "mankind" meant men-kind, and the world was theirs.

Women we have sharply delimited. Women were a sex, "the sex," according to chivalrous toasts; they were set apart for special services peculiar to femininity. As one English scientist put it, in 1888, "Women are not only not the race—they are not even half the race, but a subspecies told off for reproduction only."

This mental attitude toward women is even more clearly expressed by Mr. H. B. Marriot-Watson in his article on "The American Woman" in the "Nineteenth Century" for June, 1904, where he says: "Her constitutional restlessness has caused her to abdicate those functions which alone excuse or explain her existence." This is a peculiarly happy and condensed expression of the relative position of women during our androcentric culture. The man was accepted as the race type without one dissentient voice; and the woman—a strange, diverse creature, quite disharmonious in the accepted scheme of things—was excused and explained only as a female. [. . .]

This is a book about men—as such. It differentiates between the human nature and the sex nature. It will not go so far as to allege man's masculine traits to be all that excuse, or explain his existence: but it will point out what are masculine traits as distinct from human ones, and what has been the effect on our human life of the unbridled dominance of one sex. [. . .]

The task here undertaken is of this sort. It seeks to show that what we have all this time called "human nature" and deprecated, was in great part only male nature, and good enough in its place; that what we have called "masculine" and admired as such, was in large part human, and should be applied to both sexes: that what we have called "feminine" and condemned, was also largely human and applicable to both. Our androcentric culture is so shown to have been, and still to be, a masculine culture in excess, and therefore undesirable. [. . .]

Chapter Two— The Man-Made Family

Industry, at its base, is a feminine function. The surplus energy of the mother does not manifest itself in noise, or combat, or display, but in productive industry. Because of her mother-power she became the first inventor and laborer; being in truth the mother of all industry as well as all people.

Man's entrance upon industry is late and reluctant; as will be shown later in treating his effect on economics. In this field of family life, his effect was as follows:

Establishing the proprietary family at an age when the industry was primitive and domestic; and thereafter confining the woman solely to the domestic area, he thereby confined her to primitive industry. The domestic industries, in the hands of women, constitute a survival of our remotest past. Such work was "woman's work" as was all the work then known; such work is still considered woman's work because they have been prevented from doing any other.

The term "domestic industry" does not define a certain kind of labor, but a certain grade of labor. Architecture was a domestic industry once—when every savage mother set up her own tepee. To be confined to domestic industry is no proper distinction of womanhood; it is an historic distinction, an economic distinction, it sets a date and limit to woman's industrial progress.

In this respect the man-made family has resulted in arresting the development of half the field. We have a world wherein men, industrially, live in the twentieth century; and women, industrially, live in the first—and back of it. [. . .]

This abnormal restriction of women has necessarily injured motherhood. The man, free, growing in the world's growth, has mounted with the centuries, filling an ever wider range of world activities. The woman, bound, has not so grown; and the child is born to a progressive fatherhood and a stationary motherhood. Thus the man-made family reacts unfavorably upon the child. We rob our children of half their social heredity by keeping the mother in an inferior position; however legalized, hallowed, or ossified by time, the position of a domestic servant is inferior.

It is for this reason that child culture is at so low a level, and for the most part utterly unknown. Today, when the forces of education are steadily working nearer to the cradle, a new sense is wakening of the importance of the period of infancy, and its wiser treatment; yet those who know of such a movement are few, and of them some are content to earn easy praise—and pay—by belittling right progress to gratify the prejudices of the ignorant.

The whole position is simple and clear; and easily traceable to its root. Given a proprietary family, where the man holds the woman primarily for his satisfaction and service—then necessarily he shuts her up and keeps her for these purposes. Being so kept, she cannot develop humanly, as he has, through social contact, social service, true social life. (We may note in passing, her passionate fondness for the child-game called "society" she has been allowed to entertain herself withal; that poor simiacrum of real social life, in which people decorate themselves and madly crowd together, chattering, for what is called "entertainment.") Thus checked in social development, we have but a low grade motherhood to offer our children; and the children, reared in the primitive conditions thus artificially maintained, enter life with a false perspective, not only toward men and women, but toward life as a whole.

The child should receive in the family, full preparation for his relation, to the world at large. His whole life must be spent in the world, serving it well or ill; and youth is the time to learn how. But the androcentric home cannot teach him. We live to-day in a democracy—the man-made family is a despotism. It may be a weak one; the despot may be dethroned and overmastered by his little harem of one; but in that case she becomes the despot—that is all. The male is esteemed "the head of the family;" it belongs to him; he maintains it; and the rest of the world is a wide hunting ground and battlefield wherein he competes with other males as of old.

The girl-child, peering out, sees this forbidden field as belonging wholly to men-kind; and her relation to it is to secure one for herself—not only that she may love, but that she may live. He will feed, clothe and adorn her—she will serve him; from the subjection of the daughter to that of the wife she steps; from one home to the other, and never enters the world at all—man's world.

The boy, on the other hand, considers the home as a place of women, an inferior place, and longs to grow up and leave it—for the real world. He is quite right. The error is that this great social instinct, calling for full social exercise, exchange, service, is considered masculine, whereas it is human, and belongs to boy and girl alike.

The child is affected first through the retarded development of his mother, then through the arrested condition of home industry; and further through the wrong ideals which have arisen from these conditions. A normal home, where there was human equality between mother and father, would have a better influence.

We must not overlook the effect of the proprietary family on the proprietor himself. He, too, has been held back somewhat by this reactionary force. In the process of becoming human we must learn to recognize justice, freedom, human rights; we must learn self-control and to think of others; have minds that grow and broaden rationally; we must learn the broad mutual interservice and unbounded joy of social intercourse and service. The petty despot of the man-made home is hindered in his humanness by too much manness.

For each man to have one whole woman to cook for and wait upon him is a poor education for democracy. The boy with a servile mother, the man with a servile wife, cannot reach the sense of equal rights we need to-day. Too constant consideration of the master's tastes makes the master selfish; and the assault upon his heart direct, or through that proverbial side-avenue, the stomach, which the dependent woman needs must make when she wants anything, is bad for the man, as well as for her.

We are slowly forming a nobler type of family; the union of two based on love and recognized by law, maintained because of its happiness and use. We are even now approaching a tenderness and permanence of love, high pure enduring love; combined with the broad deep-rooted friendliness and comradeship of equals; which promises us more happiness in marriage than we have yet known. It will be good for all the parties concerned—man, woman and child: and promote our general social progress admirably.

If it needs "a head" it will elect a chairman pro tem. Friendship does not need "a head." Love does not need "a head." Why should a family? [. . .]

Chapter Ten—
Law and Government

It is easy to assume that men are naturally the law-makers and law-enforcers, under the plain historic fact that they have been such since the beginning of the patriarchate.

Back of law lies custom and tradition. Back of government lies the correlative activity of any organized group. What group-insects and group-animals evolve unconsciously and fulfill by their social instincts, we evolve consciously and fulfill by arbitrary systems called laws and governments. In this, as in all other fields of our action, we must discriminate between the humanness of the function in process of development, and the influence of the male or female upon it. Quite apart from what they may like or dislike as sexes, from their differing tastes and faculties, lies the much larger field of human progress, in which they equally participate.

On this plane the evolution of law and government proceeds somewhat as follows:—The early woman-centered group organized on maternal lines of common love and service. The early combinations of men were first a grouped predacity—organized hunting; then a grouped belligerency,—organized warfare.

By special development some minds are able to perceive the need of certain lines of conduct over others, and to make this clear to their fellows; whereby, gradually, our higher social nature establishes rules and precedents to which we personally agree to submit. The process of social development is one of progressive co-ordination.

From independent individual action for individual ends, up to interdependent social action for social ends we slowly move; the "devil" in the play being the old Ego, which has to be harmonized with the new social spirit. This social process, like all others, having been in masculine hands, we may find in it the same marks of one-sided Specialization so visible in our previous studies.

The coersive attitude is essentially male. In the ceaseless age-old struggle of sex combat he developed the desire to overcome, which is always stimulated by resistance; and in this later historic period of his supremacy, he further developed the habit of dominance and mastery. We may instance the contrast between the conduct of a man when "in love" and while courting; in which period he falls into the natural position of his sex towards the other—namely, that of a wooer, and his behavior when, with marriage, they enter the artificial relation of the master male and servile female. His "instinct of dominance" does not assert itself during the earlier period, which was a million times longer than the latter, it only appears in the more modern and arbitrary relation. [. . .]

The use of force is natural to the male; while as a human being he must needs legislate somewhat in the interests of the community, as a male being he sees no necessity for other enforcement than by penalty. To violently oppose, to fight, to trample to the earth, to triumph in loud bellowings of savage joy,—these are the primitive male instincts; and the perfectly natural social instinct which leads to peaceful persuasion, to education, to an easy harmony of action, are contemptuously ranked as "feminine," or as "philanthropic,"—which is almost as bad. "Men need stronger measures" they say proudly. Yes, but four-fifths of the world are women and children!

As a matter of fact the woman, the mother, is the first co-ordinator, legislator, administrator and executive. From the guarding and guidance of her cubs and kittens up to the longer, larger management of human youth, she is the first to consider group interests and co-relate them.

As a father the male grows to share in these original feminine functions, and with us, fatherhood having become socialized while motherhood has not, he does the best he can, alone, to do the world's mother-work in his father way.

In study of any long established human custom it is very difficult to see it clearly and dispassionately. Our minds are heavily loaded with precedent, with race-custom, with the iron weight called authority. These heavy forces reach their most perfect expression in the absolutely masculine field of warfare. The absolute authority; the brainless, voiceless obedience; the relentless penalty. Here we have male coercion at its height; law and government wholly arbitrary. The result is as might be expected, a fine machine of destruction. But destruction is not a human process—merely a male process of eliminating the unfit.

The female process is to select the fit; her elimination is negative and painless. [. . .]

In masculine administration of the laws we may follow the instinctive love of battle down through the custom of "trial by combat"—only recently outgrown, to our present method, where each contending party hires a champion to represent him, and these fight it out in a wordy war, with tricks and devices of complex ingenuity, enjoying this kind of struggle as they enjoy all other kinds.

It is the old masculine spirit of government as authority which is so slow in adapting itself to the democratic idea of government as service. That it should be a representative government they grasp, but representative of what? of the common will, they say; the will of the majority;—never thinking that it is the common good, the common welfare, that government should represent.

It is the inextricable masculinity in our idea of government which so revolts at the idea of women as voters. "To govern:" that means to boss, to control, to have authority; and that only, to most minds. They cannot bear to think of the woman as having control over even their own affairs; to control is masculine, they assume. Seeing only self-interest as a natural impulse, and the ruling powers of the state as a sort of umpire, an authority to preserve the rules of the game while men fight it out forever; they see in a democracy merely a wider range of self interest, and a wider, freer field to fight in.

The law dictates the rules, the government enforces them, but the main business of life, hitherto, has been esteemed as one long fierce struggle; each man seeking for himself. To deliberately legislate for the service of all the people, to use the government as the main engine of that service, is a new process, wholly human, and difficult of development under an androcentric culture. [. . .]

As human beings both male and female stand alike useful and honorable, and should in our government be alike used and honored; but as creatures of sex, the female is fitter than the male for administration of constructive social interests. The change in governmental processes which marks our times is a change in principle. Two great movements convulse the world to-day, the woman's movement and the labor movement. Each regards the other as of less moment than itself. Both are parts of the same world-process.

We are entering upon a period of social consciousness. Whereas so far almost all of us have seen life only as individuals, and have regarded the growing strength and riches of the social body as merely so much the more to fatten on; now we are beginning to take an intelligent interest in our social nature, to understand it a little, and to begin to feel the vast increase of happiness and power that comes of real Human Life.

In this change of systems a government which consisted only of prohibition and commands; of tax collecting and making war; is rapidly giving way to a system which intelligently manages our common interests, which is a growing and improving method of universal service. Here the socialist is perfectly right in his vision of the economic welfare to be assured by the socialization of industry, though that is but part of the new development; and the individualist who opposes socialism, crying loudly for the advantage of "free competition" is but voicing the spirit of the predacious male.

So with the opposers to the suffrage of women. They represent, whether men or women, the male viewpoint. They see the woman only as a female, utterly absorbed in feminine functions, belittled and ignored as her long tutelage has made her, and they see the man as he sees himself, the sole master of human affairs for as long as we have historic record.

This, fortunately, is not long. We can now see back of the period of his supremacy, and are beginning to see beyond it. We are well under way already in a higher stage of social development, conscious, well-organized, wisely managed, in which the laws shall be simple and founded on constructive principles instead of being a set of ring-regulations within which people may fight as they will; and in which the government shall be recognized in its full use; not only the sternly dominant father, and the wisely servicable mother, but the real union of all people to sanely and economically manage their affairs.

Chapter Twelve—
Politics and Warfare

[. . .] There are many to-day who hold that politics need not be at all connected with warfare, and others who hold that politics is warfare front start to finish.

In order to dissociate the two ideas completely let us give a paraphrase of the above definition, applying it to domestic management;—that part of ethics which has to do with the regulation and government of a family; the preservation of its safety, peace and prosperity; the defense of its existence and rights against any strangers' interference or control; the augmentation of its strength and resources, and the protection of its members in their rights; with the preservation and improvement of their morals.

All this is simple enough, and in no way masculine; neither is it feminine, save in this; that the tendency to care for, defend and manage a group, is in its origin maternal.

In every human sense, however, politics has left its maternal base far in the background; and as a field of study and of action is as well adapted to men as to women. There is no reason whatever why men should not develop great ability in this department of ethics, and gradually learn how to preserve the safety, peace and prosperity of their nation; together with those other services as to resources, protection of citizens, and improvement of morals.

Men, as human beings, are capable of the noblest devotion and efficiency in these matters, and have often shown them; but their devotion and efficiency have been marred in this, as in so many other fields, by the constant obtrusion of an ultra-masculine tendency. [. . .]

We have been much misled as to warfare by our androcentric literature. With a history which recorded nothing else; a literature which praised and an art which exalted it; a religion which called its central power "the God of Battles"—never the God of Workshops, mind you!—with a whole complex social structure man-prejudiced from center to circumference, and giving highest praise and honor to the Soldier; it is still hard for its to see what warfare really is in human life.

Someday we shall have new histories written, histories of world progress, showing the slow uprising, the development, the interservice of the nations; showing the faint beautiful dawn of the larger spirit of world-consciousness, and all its benefitting growth.

We shall see people softening, learning, rising; see life lengthen with the possession of herds, and widen in rich prosperity with agriculture. Then industry, blossoming, fruiting, spreading wide; art, giving light and joy; the intellect developing with companionship and human intercourse; the whole spreading tree of social progress, the trunk of which is specialized industry, and the branches of which comprise every least and greatest line of human activity and enjoyment. This growing tree, springing up wherever conditions of peace and prosperity gave it a chance, we shall see continually hewed down to the very root by war.

To the later historian will appear throughout the ages, like some Hideous Fate, some Curse, some predetermined check, to drag down all our hope and joy and set life forever at its first steps over again, this Red Plague of War.

The instinct of combat, between males, worked advantageously so long as it did not injure the female or the young. It is a perfectly natural instinct, and therefore perfectly right, in its place; but its place is in a pre-patriarchal era. So long as the animal mother was free and competent to care for herself and her young; then it was an advantage to have "the best man win;" that is the best stag or lion; and to have the vanquished die, or live in sulky celibacy, was no disadvantage to any one but himself.

Humanity is on a stage above this plan. The best man in the social structure is not always the huskiest. When a fresh horde of ultra-male savages swarmed down upon a prosperous young civilization, killed off the more civilized males and appropriated the more civilized females; they did, no doubt, bring in a fresh physical impetus to the race; but they destroyed the civilization.

The reproduction of perfectly good savages is not the main business of humanity. Its business is to grow, socially; to develop, to improve; and warfare, at its best, retards human progress; at its worst, obliterates it.

Combat is not a social process at all; it is a physical process, a subsidiary sex process, purely masculine, intended to improve the species by the elimination of the unfit. Amusingly enough, or absurdly enough; when applied to society, it eliminates the fit, and leaves the unfit to perpetuate the race! [. . .]

In politics the military ideal, the military processes, are so predominant as to almost monopolise "that part of ethics." The science of government, the plain wholesome business of managing a community for its own good; doing its work, advancing its prosperity, improving its morals—this is frankly understood and accepted as a fight from start to finish. Marshall your forces and try to get in, this is the political campaign. When you are in, fight to stay in, and to keep the other fellow out. Fight for your own hand, like an animal; fight for your master like any hired bravo; fight always for some desired "victory"—and "to the victors belong the spoils."

This is not by any means the true nature of politics. It is not even a fair picture of politics to-day; in which man, the human being, is doing noble work for humanity; but it is the effect of man, the male, on politics.

Life, to the "male mind" (we have heard enough of the "female mind" to use the analogue!) is a fight, and his ancient military institutions and processes keep up the delusion.

As a matter of fact life is growth. Growth comes naturally, by multiplication of cells, and requires three factors to promote it; nourishment, use, rest. Combat is a minor incident of life; belonging to low levels, and not of a developing influence socially.

The science of politics, in a civilized community, should have by this time a fine accumulation of simplified knowledge for diffusion in public schools; a store of practical experience in how to promote social advancement most rapidly, a progressive economy and ease of administration, a simplicity in theory and visible benefit in practice, such as should make every child an eager and serviceable citizen. [. . .]

2

CONTRACTUAL LIBERTY AND THE GILDED AGE

Economic transformation in the decades after the Civil War instigated a spirited, multilayered national conversation about the relationship between a democratic public order and economic development. The documents in this chapter illuminate the evolution of that conversation in the years between the end of the Civil War and the turn of the twentieth century. Americans have always maintained an uneasy alliance between economic life and political liberty. For many of the Founders (especially in the circles surrounding Thomas Jefferson and James Madison), economic liberty was important because it promoted particular values, including political liberty, equality, and independence. Indeed, they routinely linked property with liberty. As John Dickinson put it, we *cannot be* HAPPY, *without being* FREE—[and] cannot be free, *without being secure in our property.*" Happiness and freedom were grounded in property and a government of laws.

But those eighteenth-century statesmen who thought this way were also wary of wealth and the means by which it was accumulated. The way people earn money mattered because it shaped and conditioned their civil dispositions. Jefferson, for instance, linked the virtues necessary for a robust republic to the life of the yeoman farmer. "Those who labour in the earth are the chosen people of God," he wrote, while ascribing to manufacturing the characteristics of venality, subservience, dependence, and corruption. "It is the manners and spirit of a people which preserve a republic in vigour," he warned, seeing in a manufacturing and commercial economy the "canker" that would eventually eat to the nation's "laws and constitution."

Jefferson's thoughts on political economy did not go unchallenged, in the eighteenth century or in the decades that followed. Alexander Hamilton and the Federalist Party, and in the following generation Henry Clay and the Whigs, advocated government promotion of domestic manufacturing. The Civil War gave a huge boost to domestic manufacturing, stimulating expansion in industries ranging from metals, railroad, and textiles, to meatpacking and chemicals. After secession, and well into Reconstruction, statesmen in Washington tended to the Hamiltonian side of the argument, instituting a climate at the federal level friendly to economic development. Jeffersonian concerns about the civic consequences of different kinds of work receded, as the U.S. economy, and economic productivity, increased with monumental speed.

The scale of economic expansion in the United States in the decades after the Civil War can scarcely be overstated. By the 1880s, the American economy had been transformed. The number of miles of railroad track in the United States tripled between 1860 and 1880 (and again by 1920). As a consequence, American regional markets were linked together more tightly than ever before, which in turn permitted efficient and dramatic increases in the scope and scale of domestic commerce. To meet the massive demand for steel and building supplies, the coal and steel industries and others expanded as well, and consolidated production in a small number of integrated and corporately managed firms. Large factories became the norm, overtaking smaller industry. The spectacular growth and industrialization of the economy in these decades gave rise to what Mark Twain called the Gilded Age, a period of enormous wealth, greed, and corruption.

This period in American history also witnessed profound social and cultural changes. Until 1880, the vast majority of immigrants were Protestants from northern and western Europe (the exception being an influx of Irish Catholics during the 1840s and 1850s). Beginning in 1881, that pattern changed. Suddenly, large numbers of unskilled, single men—mostly Catholic and Jewish from southern, central, and eastern Europe—began to swell the ranks of immigrants. Driven from their homelands by persecution and poverty, drawn to America by promises of liberty and economic prosperity, these new immigrants settled primarily in large cities, including Philadelphia, Boston, Detroit, Chicago, and especially New York.

Rapid industrialization and urbanization exacerbated existing social problems and brought profound new ones. Mass poverty and unemployment, oppressive working conditions, inadequate or nonexistent housing (New York City's infamous tenements, for example), public health crises, crime, the concentration of wealth, the link between wealth and political power—these and other issues forced their way on to the public agenda. Publicized by the influential writings of journalists and critics like Jacob Riis, and inflamed by events like the Haymarket Riot, the social conditions of the Gilded Age elicited two overarching responses.

One broad strain of thought inverted the relationship between economy and citizenship that dominated the Founding. Confronting the changes they witnessed transforming America, many social critics celebrated the pursuit of wealth. Property, which early generations had viewed as instrumentally important to political liberty, was in this view merely one form of capital among many, and wealth itself became the primary value. Its primacy received legitimacy from the newfound belief that the pursuit of wealth was agreeable to God's will. Moreover, proponents of this line of argument suggested that the pursuit of wealth by self-interested individuals would necessarily advance civilization. This change produced in the Gilded Age a new understanding of progress, along with a new understanding of Christianity—one that promoted the pursuit of riches as godly—as well as a new understanding about the nexus between the commercial and ethical lives of individuals.

The unification of Christianity to the pursuit of wealth is amply illustrated by Russell Conwell's "Acres of Diamonds" speech. A lecturer, lawyer, clergyman, and philanthropist, Conwell delivered this popular speech more than 6,000 times, earning in the process more than $8 million. Challenging what he perceived to be a prejudice against "a Christian man . . ." attaining wealth, Conwell responded, "I say that you ought to get rich, and it is your duty to get rich." At the same time, Conwell attached to that duty an obligation to use one's riches to do good. For Conwell, following I Timothy, it is not money in itself that is the root of all evil, but rather the *love* of money.

In promoting the pursuit of wealth and a commitment to philanthropy, Conwell expressed a belief echoed by Andrew Carnegie, whose essay "Gospel of Wealth" became the moniker used to describe the era's prevailing political attitude. Like Conwell, Carnegie believed that the rich obtained their wealth through hard work, thrift, and determination, the characteristics on which progress depended. And like Conwell, Carnegie believed that charity should be directed *not* to the alleviation of individuals living in poverty, but instead to social institutions that would promote the progress of the human race (hospitals, universities, public libraries, and so on). Conwell justified such direction in charitable giving by arguing that "While we should sympathize with God's poor . . . let us remember there is not a poor person in the United States who was not made poor by his own shortcomings."

This assumption—that the poor deserve to be poor, and that they retard human progress—was the cornerstone of a related response to the era's problems: laissez-faire, or Social Darwinism. Exemplified forcefully in the writings of William Graham Sumner, Social Darwinism defended the minimalist or "watchman" state, a position based on more than mere prudential grounds. The strong and fit *should* prevail. For Sumner, this was not simply a descriptive fact. The Social Darwinist saw in this principle a moral imperative. Society would only improve if unfettered strength and ability were encouraged. Talent, egoism, and ruthless ambition are what stimulate progress, and benighted anxieties over the less capable can only result in preventing the ascent of humanity. Social Darwinists like Sumner thus seemed to go further than Conwell and Carnegie, embracing the cold rationalism of human relations based on contract and questioning the very notion of a "public good." This strong prejudice toward a largely unregulated market economy would come to dominate the Supreme Court's commerce clause's jurisprudence, a jurisprudence represented in its *United States v. E. C. Knight Company* (1895) and *Lochner v. New York* (1905) rulings and compellingly criticized by Justice Oliver Wendell Holmes' dissent in the latter.

It's worth noting, too, that often mixed in with the economic theory of laissez-faire lay a racist nativism. Many commentators seized upon the seemingly scientific rationalism of Social Darwinism to justify what they asserted was a natural racial typology of humanity. The blame for social ills, in this view, did not simply rest with morally weak individuals incapable of navigating the natural laws of supply and demand. Rather, the blame lay with genetically inferior races, whose influx into the nation was a pestilence that had to be kept at bay. In 1882 Congress enacted the Chinese Exclusion Act, ushering in a long period in American immigration policy aimed at eliminating or severely limiting immigration from Asia, Africa, and elsewhere. This attitude toward immigration was supported by "scientific" publications, like Frederick Hoffman's *Race Traits and Tendencies of the American Negro* (1896), which purported to prove a natural hierarchy among races and thus justified policies, such as laws against interracial marriage, that would produce weaker "mongrel" races. Modern genetics, it should be emphasized, now tells us that in fact there is only one human race. But in the late nineteenth and early twentieth centuries, the veneer of science lent polite credibility to a malignant and deep-seated racism the extended everywhere throughout the United States.

The socioeconomic ills of the period elicited a second response, one diametrically opposed to the advocates of laissez-faire. Critics like W. E. B. Du Bois objected to the "ideals of material prosperity" that dominated American culture. "Is not life more than meat, and the body more than raiment?" asked Du Bois, who like Conwell, knew his scripture. Du Bois recognized in this "triumphant materialism" a prevailing norm that would "keep brown and black men in their 'places.'" His eye was keen, for Social Darwinism affected public and private attitudes toward issues of race, a fact made evident in the Court's notorious *Plessy v. Ferguson* (1896) decision (see Chapter 1).

More generally, critics of laissez-faire rejected it for promoting a Hobbesian state, one that promoted liberty at the expense of equality, that rejected the ideals of universal suffrage and democracy, that viewed civilization as a collection of radically alienated individuals competing in a world of scarcity, and one that viewed the principal role of the state as preventing the outbreak of "war of all against all." Such critics, men like Henry George and Lester Frank Ward, advocated the idea of the fraternity of humankind. Interestingly, these critics, too, embraced the ideals of scientific knowledge and evolution, but unlike the Darwinists, they understood evolution in terms far larger than Hobbes' collision of wills. The fit would survive, but the fittest of all were those who acted collectively and cooperatively, and not as ruthless atoms driven by narrow interests and small desires. Critics like George and Ward blamed unfettered free enterprise combined with evangelical Christianity for fomenting competition and inequality, rather than cooperation, brotherhood, and equality. Human progress was possible, but it depended on social planning. The "Holy Trinity of Science"—reason, observation, and experience— would provide the knowledge needed to uplift all people and thus promote the human interest.

Russell Conwell

Acres of Diamonds (c. 1870)[1]

I am astonished that so many people should care to hear this story over again. Indeed, this lecture has become a study in psychology; it often breaks all rules of oratory, departs from the precepts of rhetoric, and yet remains the most popular of any lecture I have delivered in the fifty-seven years of my public life. I have sometimes studied for a year upon a lecture and made careful research, and then presented the lecture just once—never delivered it again. I put too much work on it. But this had no work on it—thrown together perfectly at random, spoken offhand without any special preparation, and it succeeds when the thing we study, work over, adjust to a plan, is an entire failure.

The "Acres of Diamonds" which I have mentioned through so many years are to be found in this city, and you are to find them. Many have found them. And what man has done, man can do. I could not find anything better to illustrate my thought than a story I have told over and over again, and which is now found in books in nearly every library.

In 1870 we went down the Tigris River. We hired a guide at Bagdad to show us Persepolis, Nineveh and Babylon, and the ancient countries of Assyria as far as the Arabian Gulf. He was well acquainted with the land, but he was one of those guides who love to entertain their patrons; he was like a barber that tells you many stories in order to keep your mind off the scratching and the scraping. He told me so many stories that I grew tired of his telling them and I refused to listen—looked away whenever he commenced; that made the guide quite angry.

I remember that toward evening he took his Turkish cap off his head and swung it around in the air. The gesture I did not understand and I did not dare look at him for fear I should become the victim of another story. But, although I am not a woman, I did look, and the instant I turned my eyes upon that worthy guide he was off again. Said he, "I will tell you a story now which I reserve for my particular friends!" So then, counting myself a particular friend, I listened, and I have always been glad I did.

He said there once lived not far from the River Indus an ancient Persian by the name of Al Hafed. He said that Al Hafed owned a very large farm with orchards, grain fields and gardens. He was a contented and wealthy man—contented because he was wealthy, and wealthy because he was contented. One day there visited this old farmer one of those ancient Buddhist priests, and he sat down by Al Hafed's fire and told that old farmer how this world of ours was made.

He said that this world was once a mere bank of fog, which is scientifically true, and he said that the Almighty thrust his finger into the bank of fog and then began slowly to move his finger around and gradually to increase the speed of his finger until at last he whirled that bank of fog into a solid ball of fire, and it went rolling through the universe, burning its way through other cosmic banks of fog, until it condensed the moisture without, and fell in floods of rain upon the heated surface and cooled the outward crust. Then the internal flames burst through the cooling crust and threw up the mountains and made the hills and the valleys of this wonderful world of ours. If this internal melted mass burst out and cooled very quickly it became granite; that which cooled less quickly became silver, and less quickly, gold; and after gold diamonds were made. Said the old priest, "A diamond is a congealed drop of sunlight."

This is a scientific truth also. You all know that a diamond is pure carbon, actually deposited sunlight—and he said another thing I would not forget:

---

1. [The first delivery of Conwell's speech is unknown. It began as part of a speech titled "Lessons of Travel," which incorporated the themes of what would later become popularly known as "Acres of Diamonds." Students of rhetoric trace the speech to the early or mid-1870s. We do know that the speech was delivered over 6,000 times, mostly within the time frame spanning 1900–1925.]

he declared that a diamond is the last and highest of God's mineral creations, as a woman is the last and highest of God's animal creations. I suppose that is the reason why the two have such a liking for each other. And the old priest told Al Hafed that if he had a handful of diamonds he could purchase a whole country, and with a mine of diamonds he could place his children upon thrones through the influence of their great wealth.

Al Hafed heard all about diamonds and how much they were worth, and went to his bed that night a poor man—not that he had lost anything, but poor because he was discontented and discontented because he thought he was poor. He said: "I want a mine of diamonds!" So he lay awake all night, and early in the morning sought out the priest.

Now I know from experience that a priest when awakened early in the morning is cross. He awoke that priest out of his dreams and said to him, "Will you tell me where I can find diamonds?" The priest said, "Diamonds? What do you want with diamonds?" "I want to be immensely rich," said Al Hafed, " but I don't know where to go." "Well," said the priest, "if you will find a river that runs over white sand between high mountains, in those sands you will always see diamonds." "Do you really believe that there is such a river?" "Plenty of them, plenty of them; all you have to do is just go and find them, then you have them." Al Hafed said, "I will go." So he sold his farm, collected his money at interest, left his family in charge of a neighbor, and away he went in search of diamonds.

He began very properly, to my mind, at the Mountains of the Moon. Afterwards he went around into Palestine, then wandered on into Europe, and at last, when his money was all spent, and he was in rags, wretchedness and poverty, he stood on the shore of that bay in Barcelona, Spain, when a tidal wave came rolling in through the Pillars of Hercules and the poor, afflicted, suffering man could not resist the awful temptation to cast himself into that incoming tide, and he sank beneath its foaming crest, never to rise in this life again.

When that old guide had told me that very sad story, he stopped the camel I was riding and went back to fix the baggage on one of the other camels, and I remember thinking to myself, "Why did he reserve that for his particular friends?" There seemed to be no beginning, middle or end—nothing to it. That was the first story I ever heard told or read in which the hero was killed in the first chapter. I had but one chapter of that story and the hero was dead.

When the guide came back and took up the halter of my camel again, he went right on with the same story. He said that Al Hafed's successor led his camel out into the garden to drink, and as that camel put its nose down into the clear water of the garden brook Al Hafed's successor noticed a curious flash of light from the sands of the shallow stream, and reaching in he pulled out a black stone having an eye of light that reflected all the colors of the rainbow, and he took that curious pebble into the house and left it on the mantel, then went on his way and forgot all about it.

A few days after that, this same old priest who told Al Hafed how diamonds were made, came in to visit his successor, when he saw that flash of light from the mantel. He rushed up and said, "Here is a diamond— here is a diamond! Has Al Hafed returned?" "No, no; Al Hafed has not returned and that is not a diamond; that is nothing but a stone; we found it right out here in our garden." "But I know a diamond when I see it," said he; "that is a diamond!"

Then together they rushed to the garden and stirred up the white sands with their fingers and found others more beautiful, more valuable diamonds than the first, and thus, said the guide to me, were discovered the diamond mines of Golconda, the most magnificent diamond mines in all the history of mankind, exceeding the Kimberley in its value. The great Kohinoor diamond in England's crown jewels and the largest crown diamond on earth in Russia's crown jewels, which I had often hoped she would have to sell before they had peace with Japan, came from that mine, and when the old guide had called my attention to that wonderful discovery he took his Turkish cap off his head again and swung it around in the air to call my attention to the moral.

Those Arab guides have a moral to each story, though the stories are not always moral. He said had Al Hafed remained at home and dug in his own cellar or in his own garden, instead of wretchedness, starvation, poverty and death—a strange land, he would have had "acres of diamonds"—for every acre, yes, every shovelful of that old farm afterwards revealed the gems which since have decorated the crowns of monarchs. When he had given the moral to his story, I saw why he had reserved this story for his "particular friends." I didn't tell him I could see it; I was not going to tell that old Arab that I could see it. For it was that mean old Arab's way of going around such a thing, like a lawyer, and saying indirectly what he did not dare say directly, that there was a certain young man that day traveling down the Tigris River that might better be at home in America. I didn't tell him I could see it. [. . .]

[. . .] Ninety out of every hundred people here have made that mistake this very day. I say you ought to be rich; you have no right to be poor. To live in Philadelphia and not be rich is a misfortune, and it is doubly a misfortune, because you could have been rich just as well as be poor. Philadelphia furnishes so many opportunities. You ought to be rich. But persons with certain religious prejudice will ask, "How can you spend your time advising the rising generation to give their time to getting money—dollars and cents—the commercial spirit?"

Yet I must say that you ought to spend time getting rich. You and I know there are some things more valuable than money; of course, we do. Ah, yes! By a heart made unspeakably sad by a grave on which the autumn leaves now fall, I know there are some things higher and grander and sublimer than money. Well does the man know, who has suffered, that there are some things sweeter and holier and more sacred than gold. Nevertheless, the man of common sense also knows that there is not any one of those things that is not greatly enhanced by the use of money. Money is power.

Love is the grandest thing on God's earth, but fortunate the lover who has plenty of money. Money is power: money has powers; and for a man to say, "I do not want money," is to say, "I do not wish to do any good to my fellowmen." It is absurd thus to talk. It is absurd to disconnect them. This is a wonderfully great life, and you ought to spend your time getting money, because of the power there is in money. And yet this religious prejudice is so great that some people think it is a great honor to be one of God's poor. I am looking in the faces of people who think just that way.

I heard a man once say in a prayer-meeting that he was thankful that he was one of God's poor, and then I silently wondered what his wife would say to that speech, as she took in washing to support the man while he sat and smoked on the veranda. I don't want to see any more of that kind of God's poor. Now, when a man could have been rich just as well, and he is now weak because he is poor, he has done some great wrong; he has been untruthful to himself; he has been unkind to his fellowmen. We ought to get rich if we can by honorable and Christian methods, and these are the only methods that sweep us quickly toward the goal of riches.

I remember, not many years ago, a young theological student who came into my office and said to me that he thought it was his duty to come in and "labor with me." I asked him what had happened, and he said: "I feel it is my duty to come in and speak to you, sir, and say that the Holy Scriptures declare that money is the root of all evil." I asked him where he found that saying, and he said he found it in the Bible. I asked him whether he had made a new Bible, and he said, no, he had not gotten a new Bible, that it was in the old Bible. "Well," I said, "if it is in my Bible, I never saw it. Will you please get the textbook and let me see it?"

He left the room and soon came stalking in with his Bible open, with all the bigoted pride of the narrow sectarian, who founds his creed on some misinterpretation of Scripture, and he puts the Bible down on the table before me and fairly squealed into my ear, "There it is. You can read it for yourself." I said to him, "Young man, you will learn, when you get a little older, that you cannot trust another denomination to read the Bible for you." I said, "Now, you belong to another denomination. Please read it to me, and remember that you are taught in a school where emphasis is exegesis." So he took the Bible and read it: "The love of money is the root of all evil." Then he had it right.

The Great Book has come back into the esteem and love of the people, and into the respect of the greatest minds of earth, and now you can quote it and rest your life and your death on it without more fear. So, when he quoted right from the Scriptures he quoted the truth. "The love of money is the root of all evil." Oh, that it is. It is the worship of the means instead of the end. Though you cannot reach the end without the means. When a man makes an idol of the money instead of the purposes for which it may be used, when he squeezes the dollar until the eagle squeals, then it is made the root of all evil. Think, if you only had the money, what you could do for your wife, your child, and for your home and your city. Think how soon you could endow the Temple College yonder if you only had the money and the disposition to give it; and yet, my friend, people say you and I should not spend the time getting rich. How inconsistent the whole thing is. We ought to be rich, because money has power.

I think the best thing for me to do is to illustrate this, for if I say you ought to get rich, I ought, at least, to suggest how it is done. We get a prejudice against rich men because of the lies that are told about them. The lies that are told about Mr. Rockefeller because he has two hundred million dollars—so many believe them; yet how false is the representation of that man to the world. How little we can tell what is true nowadays when newspapers try to sell their papers entirely on some sensation! The way they lie about the rich men is something terrible, and I do not know that there is anything to illustrate this better than what the newspapers now say about the city of Philadelphia.

A young man came to me the other day and said, "If Mr. Rockefeller, as you think, is a good man, why is it that everybody says so much against him?" It is because he has gotten ahead of us; that is the whole of it—just gotten ahead of us. Why is it Mr. Carnegie is criticized so sharply by an envious world! Because he has gotten more than we have. If a man knows more than I know, don't I incline to criticize somewhat his learning? Let a man stand in a pulpit and preach to thousands, and if I have fifteen people in my church, and they're all asleep, don't I criticize him? We always do that to the man who gets ahead of us. Why, the man you are criticizing has one hundred millions, and you have fifty cents, and both of you have just what you are worth.

One of the richest men in this country came into my home and sat down in my parlor and said: "Did you see all those lies about my family in the papers?" "Certainly I did; I knew they were lies when I saw them." "Why do they lie about me the way they do?" "Well," I said to him, "if you will give me your check for one hundred millions, I will take all the lies along with it." "Well," said he, "I don't see any sense in their thus talking about my family and myself. Conwell, tell me frankly, what do you think the American

people think of me?" "Well," said I, "they think you are the blackest hearted villain that ever trod the soil!" "But what can I do about it?" There is nothing he can do about it, and yet he is one of the sweetest Christian men I ever knew. If you get a hundred millions you will have the lies; you will be lied about, and you can judge your success in any line by the lies that are told about you. I say that you ought to be rich.

But there are ever coming to me young men who say, "I would like to go into business, but I cannot" "Why not?" "Because I have no capital to begin on." Capital, capital to begin on! What! young man! Living in Philadelphia and looking at this wealthy generation, all of whom began as poor boys, and you want capital to begin on? It is fortunate for you that you have no capital. I am glad you have no money. I pity a rich man's son. A rich man's son in these days of ours occupies a very difficult position. They are to be pitied. A rich man's son cannot know the very best things in human life. He cannot. The statistics of Massachusetts show us that not one out of seventeen rich men's sons ever die rich. They are raised in luxury, they die in poverty. Even if a rich man's son retains his father's money, even then he cannot know the best things of life.

A young man in our college yonder asked me to formulate for him what I thought was the happiest hour in a man's history, and I studied it long and came back convinced that the happiest hour that any man ever sees in any earthly matter is when a young man takes his bride over the threshold of the door, for the first time, of the house he himself has earned and built, when he turns to his bride and with an eloquence greater than any language of mine, he sayeth to his wife, "My loved one, I earned this home myself; I earned it all. It is all mine, and I divide it with thee." That is the grandest moment a human heart may ever see. But a rich man's son cannot know that. He goes into a finer mansion, it may be, but he is obliged to go through the house and say, "Mother gave me this, mother gave me that, my mother gave me that, my mother gave me that," until his wife wishes she had married his mother.

Oh, I pity a rich man's son. I do. Until he gets so far along in his dudeism that he gets his arms up like that and can't get them down. Didn't you ever see any of them astray at Atlantic City? I saw one of these scarecrows once and I never tire thinking about it. I was at Niagara Falls lecturing, and after the lecture I went to the hotel, and when I went up to the desk there stood there a millionaire's son from New York. He was an indescribable specimen of anthropologic potency. He carried a goldheaded cane under his arm—more in its head than he had in his. I do not believe I could describe the young man if I should try. But still I must say that he wore an eye-glass he could not see through; patent leather shoes he could not walk in, and pants he could not sit down in— dressed like a grasshopper!

Well, this human cricket came up to the clerk's desk just as I came in. He adjusted his unseeing eye-glass in this wise and lisped to the clerk, because it's "Hinglish, you know," to lisp: "Thir, thir, will you have the kindness to fuhnish me with thome papah and thome envelopehs!" The clerk measured that man quick, and he pulled out a drawer and took some envelopes and paper and cast them across the counter and turned away to his books.

You should have seen that specimen of humanity when the paper and envelopes came across the counter—he whose wants had always been anticipated by servants. He adjusted his unseeing eye-glass and he yelled after that clerk:

"Come back here, thir, come right back here. Now, thir, will you order a thervant to take that papah and thothe envelopehs and carry them to yondah dethk." Oh, the poor, miserable, contemptible American monkey! He couldn't carry paper and envelopes twenty feet. I suppose he could not get his arms down. I have no pity for such travesties of human nature. If you have no capital, I am glad of it. You don't need capital; you need common sense, not copper cents.

A. T. Stewart, the great princely merchant of New York, the richest man in America in his time, was a poor boy; he had a dollar and a half and went into the mercantile business. But he lost eighty-seven and a half cents of his first dollar and a half because he bought some needles and thread and buttons to sell, which people didn't want.

Are you poor? It is because you are not wanted and are left on your own hands. There was the great lesson. Apply it whichever way you will it comes to every single person's life, young or old. He did not know what people needed, and consequently bought something they didn't want, and had the goods left

on his hands a dead loss. A. T. Stewart learned there the great lesson of his mercantile life and said "I will never buy anything more until I first learn what the people want; then I'll make the purchase." He went around to the doors and asked them what they did want, and when he found out what they wanted, he invested his sixty-two and a half cents and began to supply a "known demand." I care not what your profession or occupation in life may be; I care not whether you are a lawyer, a doctor, a housekeeper, teacher or whatever else, the principle is precisely the same. We must know what the world needs first and then invest ourselves to supply that need, and success is almost certain.

A. T. Stewart went on until he was worth forty millions. "Well," you will say, "a man can do that in New York, but cannot do it here in Philadelphia." The statistics very carefully gathered in New York in 1889 showed one hundred and seven millionaires in the city worth over ten millions apiece. It was remarkable and people think they must go there to get rich. Out of that one hundred and seven millionaires only seven of them made their money in New York, and the others moved to New York after their fortunes were made, and sixty-seven out of the remaining hundred made their fortunes in towns of less than six thousand people, and the richest man in the country at that time lived in a town of thirty-five hundred inhabitants, and always lived there and never moved away. It is not so much where you are as what you are. But at the same time if the largeness of the city comes into the problem, then remember it is the smaller city that furnishes the great opportunity to make the millions of money. [. . .]

In our city especially, there are great opportunities for manufacturing, and the time has come when the line is drawn very sharply between the stockholders of the factory and their employees. Now, friends, there has also come a discouraging gloom upon this country and the laboring men are beginning to feel that they are being held down by a crust over their heads through which they find it impossible to break, and the aristocratic moneyowner-himself is so far above that he will never descend to their assistance. That is the thought that is in the minds of our people. But, friends, never in the history of our country was there an opportunity so great for the poor man to get rich as there is now and in the city of Philadelphia.

The very fact that they get discouraged is what prevents them from getting rich. That is all there is to it. The road is open, and let us keep it open between the poor and the rich.

I know that the labor unions have two great problems to contend with, and there is only one way to solve them. The labor unions are doing as much to prevent its solving as are capitalists today, and there are positively two sides to it. The labor union has two difficulties; the first one is that it began to make a labor scale for all classes on a par, and they scale down a man that can earn five dollars a day to two and a half a day, in order to level up to him an imbecile that cannot earn fifty cents a day. That is one of the most dangerous and discouraging things for the working man. He cannot get the results of his work if he do better work or higher work or work longer; that is a dangerous thing, and in order to get every laboring man free and every American equal to every other American, let the laboring man ask what he is worth and get it—not let any capitalist say to him: "You shall work for me for half of what you are worth"; nor let any labor organization say: "You shall work for the capitalist for half your worth."

Be a man, be independent, and then shall the laboring man find the roar ever open from poverty to wealth.

The other difficulty that the labor union has to consider, and this problem they have to solve themselves, is the kind of orators who come and talk to them about the oppressive rich. I can in my dreams recite the oration I have heard again and again under such circumstances. My life has been with the laboring man. I am a laboring man myself. I have often, in their assemblies, heard the speech of the man who has been invited to address the labor union. The man gets up before the assembled company of honest laboring men and he begins by saying: "Oh, ye honest, industrious laboring men, who have furnished all the capital of the world, who have built all the palaces and constructed all the railroads and covered the ocean with her steamships. Oh, you laboring men! You are nothing but slaves; you are ground down in the dust by the capitalist who is gloating over you as he enjoys his beautiful estates and as he has his banks filled with gold, and every dollar he owns is coined out of the heart's blood of the honest laboring man." Now, that is a lie, and you know it is a lie; and

yet that is the kind of speech that they are hearing all the time, representing the capitalists as wicked and the laboring man so enslaved.

Why, how wrong it is! Let the man who loves his flag and believes in American principles endeavor with all his soul to bring the capitalists and the laboring man together until they stand side by side, and arm in arm, and work for the common good of humanity.

He is an enemy to his country who sets capital against labor or labor against capital.

Suppose I were to go down through this audience and ask you to introduce me to the great inventors who live here in Philadelphia. "The inventors of Philadelphia," you would say, "why, we don't have any in Philadelphia. It is too slow to invent anything." But you do have just as great inventors, and they are here in this audience, as ever invented a machine. But the probability is that the greatest inventor to benefit the world with his discovery is some person, perhaps some lady, who thinks she could not invent anything.

Did you ever study the history of invention and see how strange it was that the man who made the greatest discovery did it without any previous idea that he was an inventor? Who are the great inventors? They are persons with plain, straightforward common sense, who saw a need in the world and immediately applied themselves to supply that need. If you want to invent anything, don't try to find it in the wheels in your head nor the wheels in your machine, but first find out what the people need, and then apply yourself to that need, and this leads to invention on the part of people you would not dream of before. The great inventors are simply great men; the greater the man the more simple the man; and the more simple a machine, the more valuable it is.

Did you ever know a really great man? His ways are so simple, so common, so plain, that you think any one could do what he is doing. So it is with the great men the world over. If you know a really great man, a neighbor of yours, you can go right up to him and say, "How are you, Jim, good morning, Sam." Of course you can, for they are always so simple.

When I wrote the life of General Garfield, one of his neighbors took me to his back door, and shouted, "Jim, Jim, Jim!" and very soon "Jim" came to the door and General Garfield let me in—one of the grandest men of our century. The great men of the world are ever so. I was down in Virginia and went up to an educational institution and was directed to a man who was setting out a tree. I approached him and said, "Do you think it would be possible for me to see General Robert E. Lee, the President of the University?" He said, "Sir, I am General Lee." Of course, when you meet such a man, so noble a man as that, you will find him a simple, plain man. Greatness is always just so modest and great inventions are simple.

[. . .] Great men, I have said, are very simple men. Just as many great men here as are to be found anywhere. The greatest error in judging great men is that we think that they always hold an office. The world knows nothing of its greatest men. Who are the great men of the world? The young man and young woman may well ask the question. It is not necessary that they should hold an office, and yet that is the popular idea. That is the idea we teach now in our high schools and common schools, that the great men of the world are those who hold some high office, and unless we change that very soon and do away with that prejudice, we are going to change to an empire. There is no question about it. We must teach that men are great only on their intrinsic value, and not on the position they may incidentally happen to occupy. And yet, don't blame the young men saying that they are going to be great when they get into some official position.

I ask this audience again who of you are going to be great? Says a young man: "I am going to be great." "When are you going to be great?" "When I am elected to some political office." Won't you learn the lesson, young man that it is prima facie evidence of littleness to hold public office under our form of government? Think of it. This is a government of the people, and by the people, and for the people, and not for the officeholder, and if the people in this country rule as they always should rule, an officeholder is only the servant of the people, and the Bible says that "the servant cannot be greater than his master."

The Bible says that "he that is sent cannot be greater than he who sent him." In this country the people are the masters, and the officeholders can never be greater than the people; they should be honest servants of the people, but they are not our greatest men. Young man, remember that you never heard of a great man holding any political office in this

country unless he took that office at an expense to himself. It is a loss to every great man to take a public office in our country. Bear this in mind, young man, that you cannot be made great by a political election.

Another young man says, "I am going to be a great man in Philadelphia some time." "Is that so? When are you going to be great?" "When there comes another war! When we get into difficulty with Mexico, or England, or Russia, or Japan, or with Spain again over Cuba, or with New Jersey, I will march up to the cannon's mouth, and amid the glistening bayonets I will tear down their flag from its staff, and I will come home with stars on my shoulders, and hold every office in the gift of the government, and I will be great." "No, you won't! No, you won't; that is no evidence of true greatness, young man." But don't blame that young man for thinking that way; that is the way he is taught in the high school. That is the way history is taught in college. He is taught that the men who held the office did all the fighting.

I remember we had a Peace Jubilee here in Philadelphia soon after the Spanish War. Perhaps some of these visitors think we should not have had it until now in Philadelphia, and as the great procession was going up Broad Street I was told that the tally-ho coach stopped right in front of my house, and on the coach was Hobson, and all the people threw up their hats and swung their handkerchiefs, and shouted "Hurrah for Hobson!" I would have yelled too, because he deserves much more of his country than he has ever received. But suppose I go into the high school tomorrow and ask, "Boys, who sunk the Merrimac?" If they answer me "Hobson," they tell me seven-eighths of a lie—seven-eighths of a lie, because there were eight men who sunk the Merrimac. The other seven men, by virtue of their position, were continually exposed to the Spanish fire while Hobson, as an officer, might reasonably be behind the smoke-stack.

Why, my friends, in this intelligent audience gathered here tonight I do not believe I could find a single person that can name the other seven men who were with Hobson. Why do we teach history in that way? We ought to teach that however humble the station a man may occupy, if he does his full duty in his place, he is just as much entitled to the American people's honor as is a king upon a throne. We do teach it as a mother did her little boy in New York when he said, "Mamma, what great building is that?" "That is General Grant's tomb." "Who was General Grant?" "He was the man who put down the rebellion." Is that the way to teach history?

Do you think we would have gained a victory if it had depended on General Grant alone. Oh, no. Then why is there a tomb on the Hudson at all? Why, not simply because General Grant was personally a great man himself, but that tomb is there because he was a representative man and represented two hundred thousand men who went down to death for this nation and many of them as great as General Grant. That is why that beautiful tomb stands on the heights over the Hudson.

I remember an incident that will illustrate this, the only one that I can give tonight. I am ashamed of it, but I don't dare leave it out. I close my eyes now, I look back through the years to 1863; I can see my native town in the Berkshire Hills, I can see that cattle-show ground filled with people; I can see the church there and the town hall crowded, and hear bands playing, and see flags flying and handkerchiefs streaming—well do I recall at this moment that day.

The people had turned out to receive a company of soldiers, and that company came marching up on the Common. They had served out one term in the Civil War and had reenlisted, and they were being received by their native townsmen. I was but a boy, but I was captain of that company, puffed out with pride on that day—why, a cambric needle would have burst me all to pieces.

As I marched on the Common at the head of my company, there was not a man more proud than I. We marched into the town hall and then they seated my soldiers down in the center of the house and I took my place down on the front seat, and then the town officers filed through the great throng of people, who stood close and packed in that little hall. They came up on the platform, formed a half circle around it, and the mayor of the town, the "chairman of the selectmen" in New England, took his seat in the middle of that half circle.

He was an old man, his hair was gray; he never held an office before in his life. He thought that an office was all he needed to be a truly great man, and when he came up he adjusted his powerful spectacles and glanced calmly around the audience with amazing dignity. Suddenly his eyes fell upon me, and then the good old man came right forward and invited me to come up on the stand with the town officers. Invited me up on the stand! No town officer ever took notice of me before I went to war. Now, I should not say that. One town officer was there who advised the teachers to "whale" me, but I mean no "honorable mention."

So I was invited up on the stand with the town officers. I took my seat and let my sword fall on the floor, and folded my arms across my breast and waited to be received. Napoleon the Fifth! Pride goeth before destruction and a fall. When I had gotten my seat and all became silent through the hall, the chairman of the selectmen arose and came forward with great dignity to the table, and we all supposed he would introduce the Congregational minister, who was the only orator in the town, and who would give the oration to the returning soldiers.

But, friends, you should have seen the surprise that ran over that audience when they discovered that this old farmer was going to deliver that oration himself. He had never made a speech in his life before, but he fell into the same error that others have fallen into, he seemed to think that the office would make him an orator. So he had written out a speech and walked up and down the pasture until he had learned it by heart and frightened the cattle, and he brought that manuscript with him, and, taking it from his pocket, he spread it carefully upon the table. Then he adjusted his spectacles to be sure that he might see it, and walked far back on the platform and then stepped forward like this. He must have studied the subject much, for he assumed an elocutionary attitude; he rested heavily upon his left heel, slightly advanced the right foot, threw back his shoulders, opened the organs of speech, and advanced his right hand at an angle of forty-five.

As he stood in this elocutionary attitude this is just the way that speech went, this is it precisely. Some of my friends have asked me if I do not exaggerate it, but I could not exaggerate it. Impossible! This is the way it went; although I am not here for the story but the lesson that is back of it:

"Fellow citizens." As soon as he heard his voice, his hand began to shake like that, his knees began to tremble, and then he shook all over. He coughed and choked and finally came around to look at his manuscript. Then he began again "Fellow citizens: We—are—we are—we are—we are—We are very happy—we are very happy—we are very happy—to welcome back to their native town these soldiers who have fought and bled—and come back again to their native town. We are especially—we are especially— we are especially—we are especially pleased to see with us today this young hero (that meant me) this young hero who in imagination (friends, remember, he said 'imagination,' for if he had not said that, I would not be egotistical enough to refer to it), this young hero who, in imagination, we have seen leading his troops—leading—we have seen leading—we have seen leading his troops on to the deadly breach. We have seen his shining—his shining—we have seen his shining—we have seen his shining—his shining sword—flashing in the sunlight as he shouted to his troops, 'Come on!'"

Oh dear, dear, dear, dear! How little that good, old man knew about war. If he had known anything about war, he ought to have known what any soldier in this audience knows is true, that it is next to a crime for an officer of infantry ever in time of danger to go ahead of his men. I, with my shining sword flashing in the sunlight, shouting to my troops: "Come on." I never did it. Do you suppose I would go ahead of my men to be shot in the front by the enemy and in the back by my own men? That is no place for an officer. The place for the officer is behind the private soldier in actual fighting.

How often, as a staff officer, I rode down the line when the rebel cry and yell was coming out of the woods, sweeping along over the fields, and shouted, "Officers to the rear! Officers to the rear!" and then every officer goes behind the line of battle, and the higher the officer rank, the farther behind he goes. Not because he is any the less brave, but because the laws of war require that to be done. If the general came up on the front line and were killed you would lose your battle anyhow, because he has the plan of the battle in his brain, and must be kept in comparative safety.

I, with my "shining sword flashing in the sunlight." Ah! There sat in the hall that day men who had given that boy their last hardtack, who had carried him on their backs through deep rivers. But some were not there; they had gone down to death for their country. The speaker mentioned them, but they were but little noticed, and yet they had gone down to death for their country, gone down for a cause they believed was right and still believe was right, though I grant to the other side the same that I ask for myself. Yet these men who had actually died for their country were little noticed, and the hero of the hour was this boy.

Why was he the hero? Simply because that man fell into the same foolishness. This boy was an officer, and those were only private soldiers. I learned a lesson that I will never forget. Greatness consists not in holding some office; greatness really consists in doing some great deed with little means, in the accomplishment of vast purposes from the private ranks of life, that is true greatness.

He who can give to this people better streets, better homes, better schools, better churches, more religion, more of happiness, more of God, he that can be a blessing to the community in which he lives tonight will be great anywhere, but he who cannot be a blessing where he now lives will never be great anywhere on the face of God's earth. "We live in deeds, not years, in feeling, not in figures on a dial; in thoughts, not breaths; we should count time by heart throbs, in the cause of right." Bailey says: "He most lives who thinks most."

If you forget everything I have said to you, do not forget this, because it contains more in two lines than all I have said. Baily says: "He most lives who thinks most, who feels the noblest, and who acts the best."

Mark Twain

The Curious Republic of Gondour (1875)

As soon as I had learned to speak the language a little, I became greatly interested in the people and the system of government.

I found that the nation had at first tried universal suffrage pure and simple, but had thrown that form aside because the result was not satisfactory. It had seemed to deliver all power into the hands of the ignorant and non-taxpaying classes; and of a necessity the responsible offices were filled from these classes also.

A remedy was sought. The people believed they had found it; not in the destruction of universal suffrage but in the enlargement of it. It was an odd idea, and ingenious. You must understand, the constitution gave every man a vote; therefore that vote was a vested right and could not be taken away. But the constitution did not say that certain individuals might not be given two votes, or ten! So an amendatory clause was inserted in a quiet way; a clause which authorized the enlargment of the suffrage in certain cases to be specified by statute. To offer to "limit" the suffrage might have made instant trouble; the offer to "enlarge" it had a pleasant aspect.

But of course the newspapers soon began to suspect; and then out they came! It was found, however, that for once—and for the first time in the history of the republic—property, character, and intellect were able to wield a political influence; for once, money, virtue, and intelligence took a vital and a united interest in a political question. For once these powers went to the "primaries" in strong force; for once the best men in the nation were put forward as candidates for that parliament whose business it should be to enlarge the suffrage. The weightiest half of the press quickly joined forces with the new movement, and left the other half to rail about the proposed "destruction of the liberties" of the bottom layer of society, the hitherto governing class of the community.

The victory was complete. The new law was framed and passed. Under it every citizen, howsoever poor or ignorant, possessed one vote, so universal suffrage still reigned; but if a man possessed a good common-school education and no money, he had two votes; a high-school education gave him four; if he had property likewise, to the value of 3,000 *sacos*, he wielded one more vote; for every 50,000 *sacos* a man added to his property, he was entitled to another vote; a university education entitled a man to nine votes, even though he owned no property. Therefore, learning being more prevalent and more easily acquired than riches; educated men became a wholesome check upon wealthy men, since they could outvote them. Learning goes usually with uprightness, broad views, and humanity; so the learned voters, possessing the balance of power, became the vigilant and efficient protectors of the great lower rank of society.

And now a curious thing developed itself—a sort of emulation whose object was voting power! Whereas formerly a man was honored only according to the amount of money he possessed, his grandeur was measured now by the number of votes he wielded. A man with only one vote was conspicuously respectful to his neighbor who possessed three. And if he was a man above the commonplace, he was as conspicuously energetic in his determination to acquire three for himself. This spirit of emulation invaded all ranks. Votes based upon capital were commonly called "mortal" votes, because they could be lost; those based upon learning were called "immortal," because they were permanent, and because of their customarily imperishable character they were naturally more valued than the other sort. I say "customarily" for the reason that these votes were not absolutely imperishable, since insanity could suspend them.

Under this system, gambling and speculation almost ceased in the republic. A man honored as the possessor of great voting power could not afford to risk the loss of it upon a doubtful chance.

It was curious to observe the manners and customs which the enlargement plan produced. Walking the street with a friend one day, he delivered a careless bow to a passerby, and then remarked that that person possessed only one vote and would probably never earn another; he was more respectful to the next acquaintance he met; he explained that this salute was a four-vote bow. I tried to "average" the importance of the people he accosted after that by the nature of his bows, but my success was only partial, because of the somewhat greater homage paid to the immortals than to the mortals.

My friend explained. He said there was no law to regulate this thing, except that most powerful of all laws, custom. Custom had created these varying bows, and in time they had become easy and natural. At this moment he delivered himself of a very profound salute, and then said, "Now there's a man who began life as a shoemaker's apprentice and without education; now he swings twenty-two mortal votes and two immortal ones; he expects to pass a high-school examination this year and climb a couple of votes higher among the immortals; mighty valuable citizen."

By and by my friend met a venerable personage, and not only made him a most elaborate bow but also took off his hat. I took off mine, too, with a mysterious awe. I was beginning to be infected.

"What grandee is that?"

"That is our most illustrious astronomer. He hasn't any money, but is fearfully learned. Nine immortals is *his* political weight! He would swing 150 votes if our system were perfect."

"Is there any altitude of mere moneyed grandeur that you take off your hat to?"

"No. Nine immortal votes is the only power we uncover for—that is, in civil life. Very great officials receive that mark of homage, of course."

It was common to hear people admiringly mention men who had begun life on the lower levels and in time achieved great voting power. It was also common to hear youths planning a future of ever so many votes for themselves. I heard shrewd mammas speak of certain young men as good "catches" because they possessed such-and-such a number of votes. I knew of more than one case where an heiress was married to a youngster who had but one vote; the argument being that he was gifted with such excellent parts that in time he would acquire a good voting strength, and perhaps in the long run be able to outvote his wife, if he had luck.

Competitive examinations were the rule in all official grades. I remarked that the questions asked the candidates were wild, intricate, and often required a sort of knowledge not needed in the office sought.

"Can a fool or an ignoramus answer them?" asked the person I was talking with.

"Certainly not."

"Well, you will not find any fools or ignoramuses among our officials."

I felt rather cornered, but made shift to say—

"But these questions cover a good deal more ground than is necessary."

"No matter; if candidates can answer these it is tolerably fair evidence that they can answer nearly any other question you choose to ask them."

There were some things in Gondour which one could not shut his eyes to. One was that ignorance and incompetence had no place in the government. Brains and property managed the state. A candidate for office must have marked ability, education, and high character, or he stood no sort of chance of election. If a hod carrier possessed these, he could succeed; but the mere fact that he was a hod carrier could not elect him, as in previous times.

It was now a very great honor to be in the parliament or in office; under the old system such distinction had only brought suspicion upon a man and made him a helpless mark for newspaper contempt and scurrility. Officials did not need to steal now, their salaries being vast in comparison with the pittances paid in the days when parliaments were created by hod carriers, who viewed official salaries from a hod-carrying point of view and compelled that view to be respected by their obsequious servants. Justice was wisely and rigidly administered; for a judge, after once reaching his place through the specified line of promotions, was a permanency during good behavior. He was not obliged to modify his judgments according to the effect they might have upon the temper of a reigning political party.

The country was mainly governed by a ministry which went out with the administration that created it. This was also the case with the chiefs of the great departments. Minor officials ascended to their several positions through well-earned promotions and not by a jump from gin-mills or the needy families and friends of members of parliament. Good behavior measured their terms of office.

The head of the government, the Grand Caliph, was elected for a term of twenty years. I questioned the wisdom of this. I was answered that he could do no harm, since the ministry and the parliament governed the land, and he was liable to impeachment for misconduct. This great office had twice been ably filled by women, women as aptly fitted for it as some of the sceptered queens of history. Members of the cabinet, under many administrations, had been women.

I found that the pardoning power was lodged in a court of pardons, consisting of several great judges. Under the old *régime*, this important power was vested in a single official, and he usually took care to have a general jail delivery in time for the next election.

I inquired about public schools. There were plenty of them, and of free colleges, too. I inquired about compulsory education. This was received with a smile, and the remark—

"When a man's child is able to make himself powerful and honored according to the amount of education he acquires, don't you suppose that that parent will apply the compulsion himself? Our free schools and free colleges require no law to fill them."

There was a loving pride of country about this person's way of speaking which annoyed me. I had long been unused to the sound of it in my own. The Gondour national airs were forever dinning in my ears; therefore I was glad to leave that country and come back to my dear native land, where one never hears that sort of music.

MORRISON R. WAITE

Munn v. Illinois (1877)

Mr. Chief Justice WAITE delivered the opinion of the Court.

The question to be determined in this case is whether the general assembly of Illinois can, under the limitations upon the legislative power of the States imposed by the Constitution of the United States, fix by law the maximum of charges for the storage of grain in warehouses at Chicago and other places in the State having not less than one hundred thousand inhabitants, "in which grain is stored in bulk, and in which the grain of different owners is mixed together, or in which grain is stored in such a manner that the identity of different lots or parcels cannot be accurately preserved."

It is claimed that such a law is repugnant—

1. To that part of sect. 8, art. 1, of the Constitution of the United States which confers upon Congress the power "to regulate commerce with foreign nations and among the several States;" [. . .]

3. To that part of Amendment 14 which ordains that no State shall "deprive any person of life, liberty, or property, without due process of law, nor deny to any person within its jurisdiction the equal protection of the laws."

We will consider the last of these objections first.

Every statute is presumed to be constitutional. The courts ought not to declare one to be unconstitutional unless it is clearly so. If there is doubt, the expressed will of the legislature should be sustained.

The Constitution contains no definition of the word "deprive," as used in the Fourteenth Amendment. To determine its signification, therefore, it is necessary to ascertain the effect which usage has given it, when employed in the same or a like connection.

While this provision of the amendment is new in the Constitution of the United States, as a limitation upon the powers of the States, it is old as a principle of civilized government. It is found in Magna Charta, and, in substance if not in form, in nearly or quite all the constitutions that have been from time to time adopted by the several States of the Union. By the Fifth Amendment, it was introduced into the

Constitution of the United States as a limitation upon the powers of the national government, and by the Fourteenth, as a guaranty against any encroachment upon an acknowledged right of citizenship by the legislatures of the States. [. . .]

When one becomes a member of society, he necessarily parts with some rights or privileges which, as an individual not affected by his relations to others, he might retain. "A body politic," as aptly defined in the preamble of the constitution of Massachusetts, "is a social compact by which the whole people covenants with each citizen, and each citizen with the whole people, that all shall be governed by certain laws for the common good." This does not confer power upon the whole people to control rights which are purely and exclusively private, but it does authorize the establishment of laws requiring each citizen to so conduct himself, and so use his own property, as not unnecessarily to injure another. This is the very essence of government, and has found expression in the maxim *sic utere tuo ut alienum non laedas*. From this source come the police powers, which, as was said by Mr. Chief Justice Taney in the *License Cases* [1847], "are nothing more or less than the powers of government inherent in every sovereignty . . . that is to say . . . the power to govern men and things." Under these powers, the government regulates the conduct of its citizens one towards another, and the manner in which each shall use his own property, when such regulation becomes necessary for the public good. In their exercise, it has been customary in England from time immemorial, and in this country from its first colonization, to regulate ferries, common carriers, hackmen, bakers, millers, wharfingers, innkeepers, etc., and, in so doing, to fix a maximum of charge to be made for services rendered, accommodations furnished, and articles sold. To this day, statutes are to be found in many of the States upon some or all these subjects; and we think it has never yet been successfully contended that such legislation came within any of the constitutional prohibitions against interference with private property. With the Fifth Amendment in force, Congress, in 1820, conferred power upon the city of Washington "to regulate . . . the rates of wharfage at private wharves . . . the sweeping of chimneys, and to fix the rates of fees therefor, . . . and the weight and quality of bread," and, in 1848, "to make all necessary regulations respecting hackney carriages and the rates of fare of the same, and the rates of hauling by cartmen, wagoners, carmen, and draymen, and the rates of commission of auctioneers."

From this it is apparent that, down to the time of the adoption of the Fourteenth Amendment, it was not supposed that statutes regulating the use, or even the price of the use, of private property necessarily deprived an owner of his property without due process of law. Under some circumstances they may, but not under all. The amendment does not change the law in this particular; it simply prevents the States from doing that which will operate as such a deprivation.

This brings us to inquire as to the principles upon which this power of regulation rests, in order that we may determine what is within and what without its operative effect. Looking, then, to the common law, from whence came the right which the Constitution protects, we find that, when private property is "affected with a public interest, it ceases to be *juris privati* only." This was said by Lord Chief Justice Hale more than two hundred years ago, in his treatise *De Portibus Maris*, and has been accepted without objection as an essential element in the law of property ever since. Property does become clothed with a public interest when used in a manner to make it of public consequence and affect the community at large. When, therefore, one devotes his property to a use in which the public has an interest, he, in effect, grants to the public an interest in that use, and must submit to be controlled by the public for the common good, to the extent of the interest he has thus created. He may withdraw his grant by discontinuing the use, but, so long as he maintains the use, he must submit to the control.

Thus, as to ferries, Lord Hale says, in his treatise *De Jure Maris*, the king has

a right of franchise or privilege, that no man may set up a common ferry for all passengers without a prescription time out of mind, or a charter from the king. He may make a ferry for his own use or the use of his family, but not for the common use of all the king's subjects passing that way, because it doth in consequence tend to a common charge, and is become a thing if public interest and use, and every man for his passage pays a toll, which is a common charge, and every ferry ought to be under a public regulation, *viz.*, that it give attendance at due times, keep a boat in due order, and take but reasonable toll; for if he fail in these, he is finable.

So if one owns the soil and landing-places on both banks of a stream, he cannot use them for the purposes of a public ferry except upon such terms and conditions as the body politic may from time to time impose, and this because the common good requires that all public ways shall be under the control of the public authorities. This privilege or prerogative of the king, who in this connection only represents and gives another name to the body politic, is not primarily for his profit, but for the protection of the people and the promotion of the general welfare. [. . .]

In later times, the same principle came under consideration in the Supreme Court of Alabama. That court was called upon in 1841 to decide whether the power granted to the city of Mobile to regulate the weight and price of bread was unconstitutional, and it was contended that "it would interfere with the right of the citizen to pursue his lawful trade or calling in the mode his judgment might dictate;" but the court said,

> there is no motive . . . for this interference on the part of the legislature with the lawful actions of individuals, or the mode in which private property shall be enjoyed, unless such calling affects the public interest or private property is employed in a manner which directly affects the body of the people. Upon this principle, in this State, tavern keepers are licensed, . . . and the County Court is required, at least once a year, to settle the rates of innkeepers. Upon the same principle is founded the control which the legislature has always exercised in the establishment and regulation of mills, ferries, bridges, turnpike roads, and other kindred subjects. *Mobile v. Yuille*, 3 Ala. N. S. 140.

Enough has already been said to show that, when private property is devoted to a public use, it is subject to public regulation. It remains only to ascertain whether the warehouses of these plaintiffs in error, and the business which is carried on there, come within the operation of this principle.

For this purpose, we accept as true the statements of fact contained in the elaborate brief of one of the counsel of the plaintiffs in error. From these it appears that the great producing region of the West and Northwest sends its grain by water and rail to Chicago, where the greater part of it is shipped by vessel for transportation to the seaboard by the Great Lakes, and some of it is forwarded by railway to the Eastern ports. . . . Vessels, to some extent, are loaded in the Chicago harbor, and sailed through the St. Lawrence directly to Europe. . . . The quantity [of grain] received in Chicago has made it the greatest grain market in the world. This business has created a demand for means by which the immense quantity of grain can be handled or stored, and these have been found in grain warehouses, which are commonly called elevators, because the grain is elevated from the boat or car, by machinery operated by steam, into the bins prepared for its reception, and elevated from the bins, by a like process, into the vessel or car which is to carry it on. . . . In this way, the largest traffic between the citizens of the country north and west of Chicago and the citizens of the country lying on the Atlantic coast north of Washington is in grain which passes through the elevators of Chicago. In this way, the trade in grain is carried on by the inhabitants of seven or eight of the great States of the West with four or five of the States lying on the seashore, and forms the largest part of interstate commerce in these States. The grain warehouses or elevators in Chicago are immense structures, holding from 300,000 to 1,000,000 bushels at one time, according to size. They are divided into bins of large capacity and great strength. . . . They are located with the river harbor on one side and the railway tracks on the other, and the grain is run through them from car to vessel, or boat to car, as may be demanded in the course of business. It has been found impossible to preserve each owner's grain separate, and this has given rise to a system of inspection and grading by which the grain of different owners is mixed, and receipts issued for the number of bushels which are negotiable, and redeemable in like kind, upon demand. This mode of conducting the business was inaugurated more than twenty years ago, and has grown to immense proportions. The railways have found it impracticable to own such elevators, and public policy forbids the transaction of such business by the carrier; the ownership has, therefore, been by private individuals, who have embarked their capital and devoted their industry to such business as a private pursuit.

In this connection, it must also be borne in mind that, although in 1874 there were in Chicago fourteen warehouses adapted to this particular business, and owned by about thirty persons, nine business firms controlled them, and that the prices charged and received for storage were such "as have been from year to year agreed upon and established by the different elevators or warehouses in the city of Chicago, and which rates have been annually published in one or more newspapers printed in said city, in the month of January in each year, as the established rates for the year then next ensuing such publication." Thus, it is apparent that all the elevating facilities through which these vast productions "of seven or eight great States of the West" must pass on the way "to four or five of the States on the seashore" may be a "virtual" monopoly.

Under such circumstances, it is difficult to see why, if the common carrier, or the miller, or the ferryman, or the innkeeper, or the wharfinger, or the baker, or the cartman, or the hackney-coachman, pursues a public employment and exercises "a sort of public office," these plaintiffs in error do not. They stand, to use again the language of their counsel, in the very "gateway of commerce," and take toll from all who pass. Their business most certainly "tends to a common charge, and is become a thing of public interest and use." Every bushel of grain for its passage "pays a toll, which is a common charge," and, therefore, according to Lord Hale, every such warehouseman "ought to be under public regulation, *viz.*, that he . . . take but reasonable toll." Certainly, if any business can be clothed "with a public interest, and cease to be *juris privati* only," this has been. It may not be made so by the operation of the constitution of Illinois or this statute, but it is by the facts.

We also are not permitted to overlook the fact that, for some reason, the people of Illinois, when they revised their constitution in 1870, saw fit to make it the duty of the general assembly to pass laws "for the protection of producers, shippers, and receivers of grain and produce," art. 13, sect. 7; and by sect. 5 of the same article, to require all railroad companies receiving and transporting grain in bulk or otherwise to deliver the same at any elevator to which it might be consigned, that could be reached by any track that was or could be used by such company, and that all railroad companies should permit connections to be made with their tracks, so that any public warehouse, etc., might be reached by the cars on their railroads. This indicates very clearly that, during the twenty years in which this peculiar business had been assuming its present "immense proportions," something had occurred which led the whole body of the people to suppose that remedies such as are usually employed to prevent abuses by virtual monopolies might not be inappropriate here. For our purposes, we must assume that, if a state of facts could exist that would justify such legislation, it actually did exist when the statute now under consideration was passed. For us, the question is one of power, not of expediency. If no state of circumstances could exist to justify such a statute, then we may declare this one void because it is in excess of the legislative power of the State. But if it could, we must presume it did. Of the propriety of legislative interference within the scope of legislative power the legislature is the exclusive judge. [. . .]

We know that this is a power which may be abused, but that is no argument against its existence. For protection against abuses by legislatures, the people must resort to the polls, not to the courts. [. . .]

We come now to consider the effect upon this statute of the power of Congress to regulate commerce.

It was very properly said in the case of the *State Tax on Railway Gross Receipts*, 15 Wall. 293, that "it is not everything that affects commerce that amounts to a regulation of it, within the meaning of the Constitution." The warehouses of these plaintiffs in error are situated, and their business carried on, exclusively within the limits of the State of Illinois. They are used as instruments by those engaged in State as well as those engaged in interstate commerce, but they are no more necessarily a part of commerce itself than the dray or the cart by which, but for them, grain would be transferred from one railroad station to another. Incidentally they may become connected with interstate commerce, but not necessarily so. Their regulation is a thing of domestic concern, and, certainly, until Congress acts in reference to their interstate relations, the State may exercise all the powers of government over them even though in so doing it may indirectly operate upon commerce outside its immediate jurisdiction. We do not say that a case may not arise in which it will be found that a State, under the form of regulating its own affairs, has encroached upon the exclusive domain of Congress in respect to interstate commerce, but we do say that, upon the facts as they are represented to us in this record, that has not been done. [. . .]

We conclude, therefore, that the statute in question is not repugnant to the Constitution of the United States. [. . .]

Judgment affirmed.

STEPHEN FIELD

Munn v. Illinois, Dissent (1877)

Mr. Justice FIELD.

I am compelled to dissent from the decision of the Court in this case, and from the reasons upon which that decision is founded. The principle upon which the opinion of the majority proceeds is, in my judgment, subversive of the rights of private property, heretofore believed to be protected by constitutional guaranties against legislative interference, and is in conflict with the authorities cited in its support.

The defendants had constructed their warehouse and elevator in 1862 with their own means, upon ground leased by them for that purpose, and, from that time until the filing of the information against them, had transacted the business of receiving and storing grain for hire. The rates of storage charged by them were annually established by arrangement with the owners of different elevators in Chicago, and were published in the month of January. In 1870, the State of Illinois adopted a new constitution, and, by it, "all elevators or storehouses where grain or other property is stored for a compensation, whether the property stored be kept separate or not, are declared to be public warehouses."

In April, 1871, the legislature of the State passed an act to regulate these warehouses, thus declared to be public, and the warehousing and inspection of grain, and to give effect to this article of the Constitution. By that act, public warehouses, as defined in the Constitution, were divided into three classes, the first of which embraced all warehouses, elevators, or granaries located in cities having not less than one hundred thousand inhabitants in which grain was stored in bulk and the grain of different owners was mixed together or stored in such manner that the identity of different lots or parcels could not be accurately preserved. To this class, the elevator of the defendants belonged. The act prescribed the maximum of charges which the proprietor, lessee, or manager of the warehouse was allowed to make for storage and handling of grain, including the cost of receiving and delivering it, for the first thirty days or any part thereof, and for each succeeding fifteen days or any part thereof, and it required him to procure from the Circuit Court of the county a license to transact business as a public warehouseman, and to give a bond to the people of the State in the penal sum of $10,000 for the faithful performance of his duty as such warehouseman of the first class, and for his full and unreserved compliance with all laws of the State in relation thereto. [. . .] The maximum of charges prescribed by the act for the receipt and storage of grain was different from that which the defendants had previously charged and which had been agreed to by the owners of the grain. More extended periods of storage were required of them than they formerly gave for the same charges. [. . .] The defendants, deeming that they had a right to use their own property in such manner as they desired, not inconsistent with the equal right of others to a like use, and denying the power of the legislature to fix prices for the use of their property and their services in connection with it, refused to comply with the act by taking out the license and giving the bond required, but continued to carry on the business and to charge for receiving and storing grain such prices as they had been accustomed to charge and as had been agreed upon between them and the owners of the grain. For thus transacting their business without procuring a license as required by the act, they were prosecuted and fined, and the judgment against them was affirmed by the Supreme Court of the State.

The question presented, therefore, is one of the greatest importance—whether it is within the competency of a State to fix the compensation which an individual may receive for the use of his own property in his private business and for his services in connection with it. [. . .]

The validity of the legislation was, among other grounds, assailed in the State court as being in conflict with that provision of the State Constitution which declares that no person shall be deprived of life, liberty, or property without due process of law, and with that provision of the Fourteenth Amendment of the Federal Constitution which imposes a similar restriction upon the action of the State. The State court held, in substance, that the constitutional provision was not violated so long as the owner was not deprived of the title and possession of his property. . . . In this court, the legislation was also assailed on the same ground, our jurisdiction arising upon the clause of the Fourteenth Amendment, ordaining that no State shall deprive any person of life, liberty, or property without due process of law. But it would seem from its opinion that the court holds that property loses something of its private character when employed in such a way as to be generally useful. The doctrine declared is that property "becomes clothed with a public interest when used in a manner to make it of public consequence and affect the community at large," and, from such clothing, the right of the legislature is deduced to control the use of the property and to determine the compensation which the owner may receive for it. When Sir Matthew Hale and the sages of the law in his day spoke of property as affected by a public interest, and ceasing from that cause to be *juris privati* solely, that is, ceasing to be held merely in private right, they referred to property dedicated by the owner to public uses, or to property the use of which was granted by the government, or in connection with which special privileges were conferred. Unless the property was thus dedicated, or some right bestowed by the government was held with the property, either by specific grant or by prescription or so long a time as to

imply a grant originally, the property was not affected by any public interest so as to be taken out of the category of property held in private right. But it is not in any such sense that the terms "clothing property with a public interest" are used in this case. From the nature of the business under consideration—the storage of grain—which, in any sense in which the words can be used, is a private business in which the public are interested only as they are interested in the storage of other products of the soil or in articles of manufacture, it is clear that the court intended to declare that, whenever one devotes his property to a business which is useful to the public—"affects the community at large"—the legislature can regulate the compensation which the owner may receive for its use, and for his own services in connection with it. "When, therefore," says the court, "one devotes his property to a use in which the public has an interest, he, in effect, grants to the public an interest in that use, and must submit to be controlled by the public for the common good, to the extent of the interest he has thus created. He may withdraw his grant by discontinuing the use, but, so long as he maintains the use, he must submit to the control." The building used by the defendants was for the storage of grain; in such storage, says the court, the public has an interest; therefore, the defendants, by devoting the building to that storage, have granted the public an interest in that use, and must submit to have their compensation regulated by the legislature.

If this be sound law, if there be no protection, either in the principles upon which our republican government is founded or in the prohibitions of the Constitution against such invasion of private rights, all property and all business in the State are held at the mercy of a majority of its legislature. The public has no greater interest in the use of buildings for the storage of grain than it has in the use of buildings for the residences of families, nor, indeed, anything like so great an interest, and, according to the doctrine announced, the legislature may fix the rent of all tenements used for residences, without reference to the cost of their erection. If the owner does not like the rates prescribed, he may cease renting his houses. He has granted to the public, says the court, an interest in the use of the buildings, and "he may withdraw his grant by discontinuing the use, but, so long as he maintains the use, he must submit to the control."

The public is interested in the manufacture of cotton, woollen, and silken fabrics, in the construction of machinery, in the printing and publication of books and periodicals, and in the making of utensils of every variety, useful and ornamental; indeed, there is hardly an enterprise or business engaging the attention and labor of any considerable portion of the community in which the public has not an interest in the sense in which that term is used by the court in its opinion, and the doctrine which allows the legislature to interfere with and regulate the charges which the owners of property thus employed shall make for its use, that is, the rates at which all these different kinds of business shall be carried on, has never before been asserted, so far as I am aware, by any judicial tribunal in the United States.

The doctrine of the State court that no one is deprived of his property, within the meaning of the constitutional inhibition, so long as he retains its title and possession, and the doctrine of this court that, whenever one's property is used in such a manner as to affect the community at large, it becomes by that fact clothed with a public interest, and ceases to be *juris privati* only, appear to me to destroy, for all useful purposes, the efficacy of the constitutional guaranty. All that is beneficial in property arises from its use and the fruits of that use, and whatever deprives a person of them deprives him of all that is desirable or valuable in the title and possession. If the constitutional guaranty extends no further than to prevent a deprivation of title and possession, and allows a deprivation of use, and the fruits of that use, it does not merit the encomiums it has received. Unless I have misread the history of the provision now incorporated into all our State constitutions, and by the Fifth and Fourteenth Amendments into our Federal Constitution, and have misunderstood the interpretation it has received, it is not thus limited in its scope, and thus impotent for good. It has a much more extended operation than either court, State, or Federal has given to it. The provision, it is to be observed, places property under the same protection as life and liberty. Except by due process of law, no State can deprive any person of either. The provision has been supposed to secure to every individual the essential conditions for the pursuit of happiness, and, for that reason, has not been heretofore, and should never be, construed in any narrow or restricted sense. [. . .]

The power of the State over the property of the citizen under the constitutional guaranty is well defined. The State may take his property for public uses, upon just compensation being made therefor. It may take a portion of his property by way of taxation for the support of the government. It may control the use and possession of his property, so far as may be necessary for the protection of the rights of others, and to secure to them the equal use and enjoyment of their property. The doctrine that each one must so use his own as not to injure his neighbor—*sic utere tuo ut alienum non laedas*—is the rule by which every member or society must possess and enjoy his property, and all legislation essential to secure this common and equal enjoyment is a legitimate exercise of State authority. Except in cases where property may be destroyed to arrest a conflagration or the ravages of pestilence, or be taken under the pressure of an immediate and overwhelming necessity to prevent a public calamity, the power of the State over the property of the citizen does not extend beyond such limits.

It is true that the legislation which secures to all protection in their rights, and the equal use and enjoyment of their property, embraces an almost infinite variety of subjects. Whatever affects the peace, good order, morals, and health of the community comes within its scope, and everyone must use and enjoy his property subject to the restrictions which such legislation imposes. What is termed the police power of the State, which, from the language often used respecting it, one would suppose to be an undefined and irresponsible element in government, can only interfere with the conduct of individuals in their intercourse with each other, and in the use of their property, so far as may be required to secure these objects. The compensation which the owners of property, not having any special rights or privileges from the government in connection with it, may demand for its use, or for their own services in union with it, forms no element of consideration in prescribing regulations for that purpose. If one construct a building in a city, the State, or the municipality exercising a delegated power from the State, may require its walls to be of sufficient thickness for the uses intended; it may forbid the employment of inflammable materials in its construction, so as not to endanger the safety of his neighbors; if designed as a theatre, church, or public hall, it may prescribe ample means of egress, so as to afford facility for escape in case of accident; it may forbid the storage in it of powder, nitroglycerine, or other explosive material; it may require its occupants daily to remove decayed vegetable and animal matter which would otherwise accumulate and engender disease; it may exclude from it all occupations and business calculated to disturb the neighborhood or infect the air. Indeed, there is no end of regulations with respect to the use of property which may not be legitimately prescribed, having for their object the peace, good order, safety, and health of the community, thus securing to all the equal enjoyment of their property; but, in establishing these regulations, it is evident that compensation to the owner for the use of his property, or for his services in union with it, is not a matter of any importance; whether it be one sum or another does not affect the regulation either in respect to its utility or mode of enforcement. One may go, in like manner, through the whole round of regulations authorized by legislation, State or municipal, under what is termed the police power, and in no instance will he find that the compensation of the owner for the use of his property has any influence in establishing them. It is only where some right or privilege is conferred by the government or municipality upon the owner, which he can use in connection with his property or by means of which the use of his property is rendered more valuable to him, or he thereby enjoys an advantage over others, that the compensation to be received by him becomes a legitimate matter of regulation. Submission to the regulation of compensation in such cases is an implied condition of the grant, and the State, in exercising its power of prescribing the compensation, only determines the conditions upon which its concession shall be enjoyed. When the privilege ends, the power of regulation ceases.

Jurists and writers on public law find authority for the exercise of this police power of the State and the numerous regulations which it prescribes in the doctrine already stated, that everyone must use and enjoy his property consistently with the rights of others and the equal use and enjoyment by them of their property. [. . .] In his Commentaries, after speaking of the protection afforded by the Constitution to private property, Chancellor Kent says:

But though property be thus protected, it is still to be understood that the lawgiver has the right to prescribe the mode and manner of using it, *so far as may be necessary to prevent the abuse of the right, to the injury or annoyance of others, or of the public.* The government may, by general regulations, interdict such uses of property as would create nuisances and become dangerous to the lives, or health, or peace, or comfort of the citizens. Unwholesome trades, slaughterhouses, operations offensive to the senses, the deposit of powder, the application of steam power to propel cars, the building with combustible materials, and the burial of the dead, may all be interdicted by law in the midst of dense masses of population, *on the general and rational principle that every person ought so to use his property as not to injure his neighbors, and that private interests must be made subservient to the general interests of the community.* 2 Kent 340.

The Italics in these citations are mine. The citations show what I have already stated to be the case, that the regulations which the State, in the exercise of its police power, authorizes with respect to the use of property are entirely independent of any question of compensation for such use, or for the services of the owner in connection with it.

There is nothing in the character of the business of the defendants as warehousemen which called for the interference complained of in this case. Their buildings are not nuisances; their occupation of receiving and storing grain infringes upon no rights of others, disturbs no neighborhood, infects not the air, and in no respect prevents others from using and enjoying their property as to them may seem best. The legislation in question is nothing less than a bold assertion of absolute power by the State to control at its discretion the property and business of the citizen, and fix the compensation he shall receive. The will of the legislature is made the condition upon which the owner shall receive the fruits of his property and the just reward of his labor, industry, and enterprise. "That government," says Story, "can scarcely be deemed to be free where the rights of property are left solely dependent upon the will of a legislative body without any restraint. The fundamental maxims of a free government seem to require that the rights of personal liberty and private property should be held sacred." *Wilkeson v. Leland*, 2 Pet. 657. The decision of the court in this case gives unrestrained license to legislative will.

The several instances mentioned by counsel in the argument, and by the court in its opinion in which legislation has fixed the compensation which parties may receive for the use of their property and services do not militate against the views I have expressed of the power of the State over the property of the citizen. They were mostly cases of public ferries, bridges, and turnpikes, of wharfingers, hackmen, and draymen, and of interest on money. In all these cases except that of interest on money, which I shall presently notice, there was some special privilege granted by the State or municipality; and no one, I suppose, has ever contended that the State had not a right to prescribe the conditions upon which such privilege should be enjoyed. [. . .] The conditions upon which the privilege shall be enjoyed being stated or implied in the legislation authorizing its grant, no right is, of course, impaired by their enforcement. The recipient of the privilege, in effect, stipulates to comply with the conditions. It matters not how limited the privilege conferred, its acceptance implies an assent to the regulation of its use and the compensation for it. The privilege which the hackman and drayman have to the use of stands on the public streets, not allowed to the ordinary coachman or laborer with teams, constitutes a sufficient warrant for the regulation of their fares. In the case of the warehousemen of Chicago, no right or privilege is conferred by the government upon them, and hence no assent of theirs can be alleged to justify any interference with their charges for the use of their property. [. . .]

The principal authority cited in support of the ruling of the court is that of *Alnutt v. Inglis*, decided by the King's Bench, and reported in 12 East. But that case, so far from sustaining the ruling, establishes, in my judgment, the doctrine that everyone has a right to charge for his property, or for its use, whatever he pleases unless he enjoys in connection with it some right or privilege from the government not accorded to others; and, even then, it only decides what is above stated in the quotations from Sir Matthew Hale, that he must submit, so long as he retains the right or privilege, to reasonable rates. In that case, the London Dock Company, under certain acts of

Parliament, possessed the exclusive right of receiving imported goods into their warehouses before the duties were paid, and the question was whether the company was bound to receive them for a reasonable reward, or whether it court arbitrarily fix its compensation. In deciding the case, the Chief Justice, Lord Ellenborough, said:

> There is no doubt that the general principle is favored, both in law and justice, that every man may fix what price he pleases upon his own property, or the use of it; but if, for a particular purpose, the public have right to resort to his premises and make use of them, and he have a monopoly in them for that purpose, if he will take the benefit of that monopoly, he must, as an equivalent, perform the duty attached to it on reasonable terms.

And, coming to the conclusion that the company's warehouses were invested with "the monopoly of a public privilege," he held that, by law, the company must confine itself to take reasonable rates, and added that, if the crown should thereafter think it advisable to extend the privilege more generally to other persons and places, so that the public would not be restrained from exercising a choice of warehouses for the purpose, the company might be enfranchised from the restriction which attached to a monopoly; but, so long as its warehouses were the only places which could be resorted to for that purpose, the company was bound to let the trade have the use of them for a reasonable hire and reward. The other judges of the court placed their concurrence in the decision upon the ground that the company possessed a legal monopoly of the business, having the only warehouses where goods imported could be lawfully received without previous payment of the duties. From this case, it appears that it is only where some privilege in the bestowal of the government is enjoyed in connection with the property that it is affected with a public interest in any proper sense of the terms. It is the public privilege conferred with the use of the property which creates the public interest in it.

In the case decided by the Supreme Court of Alabama, where a power granted to the city of Mobile to license bakers and to regulate the weight and price of bread was sustained so far as regulating the weight of the bread was concerned, no question was made as to the right to regulate the price. There is no doubt of the competency of the State to prescribe the weight of a loaf of bread, as it may declare what weight shall constitute a pound or a ton. But I deny the power of any legislature under our government to fix the price which one shall receive for his property of any kind. If the power can be exercised as to one article, it may as to all articles, and the prices of everything, from a calico gown to a city mansion, may be the subject of legislative direction. [. . .]

It requires no comment to point out the radical differences between the cases of public mills and interest on money and that of the warehouses in Chicago. No prerogative or privilege of the crown to establish warehouses was ever asserted at the common law. The business of a warehouseman was, at common law, a private business, and is so in its nature. It has no special privileges connected with it, nor did the law ever extend to it any greater protection than it extended to all other private business. No reason can be assigned to justify legislation interfering with the legitimate profits of that business that would not equally justify an intermeddling with the business of every man in the community, so soon, at least, as his business became generally useful.

I am of opinion that the judgment of the Supreme Court of Illinois should be reversed.

Terence V. Powderly and Robert Schilling

The Constitution of the Knights of Labor (1878)

The recent alarming development and aggression of aggregated wealth, which, unless checked, will invariably lead to the pauperization and hopeless degradation of the toiling masses, render it imperative, if we desire to enjoy the blessings of life, that a check should be placed upon its power and upon unjust accumulation, and a system adopted which will secure to the laborer the fruits of his toil. And as this much-desired object can only be accomplished by the thorough unification of labor and the united efforts of those who obey the divine injunction that "In the sweat of thy brow shalt thou eat bread," we have formed the ——— with a view of securing the organization and direction, by cooperative effort, of the power of the industrial classes; and we submit to the world the objects sought to be accomplished by our organization, calling upon all who believe in securing "the greatest good to the greatest number" to aid and assist us:

1. To bring within the folds of organization every department of productive industry, making knowledge a standpoint for action and industrial and moral worth, not wealth, the true standard of individual and national greatness.

2. To secure to the toilers a proper share of the wealth that they create; more of the leisure that rightfully belongs to them; more societary advantages; more of the benefits, privileges, and emoluments of the world; in a word, all those rights and privileges necessary to make them capable of enjoying, appreciating, defending, and perpetuating the blessings of good government.

3. To arrive at the true condition of the producing masses in their educational, moral, and financial condition by demanding from the various governments the establishment of Bureaus of Labor Statistics.

4. The establishment of cooperative institutions, productive and distributive.

5. The reserving of the public lands—the heritage of the people—for the actual settler—not another acre for railroads or speculators.

6. The abrogation of all laws that do not bear equally upon capital and labor; the removal of unjust technicalities, delays, and discriminations in the

administration of justice; and the adopting of measures providing for the health and safety of those engaged in mining, manufacturing, or building pursuits.

7. The enactment of laws to compel chartered corporations to pay their employees weekly, in full, for labor performed during the preceding week, in the lawful money of the country.

8. The enactment of laws giving mechanics and laborers a first lien on their work for their full wages.

9. The abolishment of the contract system on national, state, and municipal work.

10. The substitution of arbitration for strikes, whenever and wherever employers and employees are willing to meet on equitable grounds.

11. The prohibition of the employment of children in workshops, mines, and factories before attaining their fourteenth year.

12. To abolish the system of letting out by contract the labor of convicts in our prisons and reformatory institutions.

13. To secure for both sexes equal pay for equal work.

14. The reduction of the hours of labor to eight per day, so that the laborers may have more time for social enjoyment and intellectual improvement and be enabled to reap the advantages conferred by the labor-saving machinery which their brains have created.

15. To prevail upon governments to establish a purely national circulating medium, based upon the faith and resources of the nation and issued directly to the people, without the intervention of any system of banking corporations, which money shall be a legal tender in payment of all debts, public or private.

HENRY GEORGE

Progress and Poverty (1879)

The Problem

The present century has been marked by a prodigious increase in wealth-producing power. The utilisation of steam and electricity, the introduction of improved processes and labour-saving machinery, the greater subdivison and grander scale of production, the wonderful facilitation of exchanges, have multiplied enormously the effectiveness of labour.

At the beginning of this marvellous era it was natural to expect, and it was expected, that labour-saving inventions would lighten the toil and improve the condition of the labourer; that the enormous increase in the power of producing wealth would make real poverty a thing of the past. Could a man of the last century—a Franklin or a Priestley—have seen, in a vision of the future, the steamship taking the place of the sailing vessel, the railroad train of the waggon, the reaping machine of the scythe, the threshing machine of the flail; could he have heard the throb of the engines that in obedience to human will, and for the satisfaction of human desire, exert a power greater than that of all the men and all the beasts of burden of the earth combined; [. . .] Plainly, in the sight of the imagination, he would have beheld these new forces elevating society from its very foundations, lifting the very poorest above the possibility of want, exempting the very lowest from anxiety for the material needs of life; he would have seen these slaves of the lamp of knowledge taking on themselves the traditional curse, these muscles of iron and sinews of steel making the poorest labourer's life a holiday, in which every high quality and noble impulse could have scope to grow.

And out of these bounteous material conditions he would have seen arising, as necessary sequences, moral conditions realising the golden age of which mankind have always dreamed. Youth no longer stunted and starved; age no longer harried by avarice; the child at play with the tiger; the man with the muck-rake drinking in the glory of the stars! Foul things fled, fierce things tame; discord turned to harmony! For how could there be greed where all had enough? How could the vice, the crime, the ignorance, the brutality, that spring from poverty and the fear of poverty, exist where poverty had vanished? Who should crouch where all were freemen, who oppress where all were peers? [. . .]

It is true that disappointment has followed disappointment, and that discovery upon discovery, and invention after invention, have neither lessened the toil of those who most need respite, nor brought plenty to the poor. But there have been so many things to which it seemed this failure could be laid, that up to our time the new faith has hardly weakened. We have better appreciated the difficulties to be overcome; but not the less trusted that the tendency of the times was to overcome them.

Now, however, we are coming into collision with facts which there can be no mistaking. From all parts of the civilised world come complaints of industrial depression; of labour condemned to involuntary idleness; of capital massed and wasting; of pecuniary distress among business men; of want and suffering and anxiety among the working classes. All the dull, deadening pain, all the keen, maddening anguish, that to great masses of men are involved in the words "hard times," afflict the world to-day. This state of things, common to communities differing so widely in situation, in political institutions, in fiscal and financial systems, in density of population and in social organisation, can hardly be accounted for by local causes. There is distress where large standing armies are maintained, but there is also distress where the standing armies are nominal; there is distress where protective tariffs stupidly and wastefully hamper trade, but there is also distress where trade is nearly free; there is distress where autocratic government yet prevails, but there is also distress where political power is wholly in the hands of the people; in countries where paper is money, and in countries where gold and silver are the only currency. Evidently, beneath all such things as these, we must infer a common cause.

That there is a common cause, and that it is either what we call material progress, or something closely connected with material progress, becomes more than an inference when it is noted that the phenomena we class together and speak of as industrial depression, are but intensifications of phenomena which always accompany material progress, and which show themselves more clearly and strongly as material progress goes on. Where the conditions to which material progress everywhere tends are most fully realised—that is to say, where population is densest, wealth greatest, and the machinery of production and exchange most highly developed—we find the deepest poverty, the sharpest struggle for existence, and the most enforced idleness.

It is to the newer countries—that is, to the countries where material progress is yet in its earlier stages—that labourers emigrate in search of higher wages, and capital flows in search of higher interest. It is the older countries—that is to say, the countries where material progress has reached later stages—that widespread destitution is found in the midst of the greatest abundance. Go into one of the new communities where Anglo-Saxon vigour is just beginning the race of progress; where the machinery of production and exchange is yet rude and inefficient; where the increment of wealth is not yet great enough to enable any class to live in ease and luxury; where the best house is but a cabin of logs or a cloth and paper shanty, and the richest man is forced to daily work—and though you will find an absence of wealth and all its concomitants, you will find no beggars. There is no luxury, but there is no destitution. No one makes an easy living, nor a very good living; but every one *can* make a living, and no one able and willing to work is oppressed by the fear of want.

But just as such a community realises the conditions which all civilised communities are striving for, and advances in the scale of material progress—just as closer settlement and a more intimate connection with the rest of the world, and greater utilisation of labour-saving machinery, make possible greater economies in production and exchange, and wealth in consequence increases, not merely in the aggregate, but in proportion to population—so does poverty take a darker aspect. Some get an infinitely better and easier living, but others find it hard to get a living at all. The "tramp" comes with the locomotive, and almshouses and prisons are as surely the marks of "material progress" as are costly dwellings, rich warehouses, and magnificent churches. Upon streets lighted with gas and patrolled by uniformed policemen, beggars wait for the passer-by, and in the shadow of college, and library, and museum, are gathering the more hideous Huns and fiercer Vandals of whom Macaulay prophesied.

This fact—the great fact that poverty and all its concomitants show themselves in communities just as they develop into the conditions toward which material progress tends—proves that the social difficulties existing wherever a certain stage of progress has been reached, do not arise from local circumstances, but are, in some way or another, engendered by progress itself. [. . .]

This association of poverty with progress is the great enigma of our times. It is the central fact from which spring industrial, social, and political difficulties that perplex the world, and with which statesmanship and philanthropy and education grapple in vain. From it come the clouds that overhang the future of the most progressive and self-reliant nations. It is the riddle which the Sphinx of Fate puts to our civilisation, and which not to answer is to be destroyed. So long as all the increased wealth which modern progress brings goes but to build up great fortunes, to increase luxury, and make sharper the contrast between the House of Have and the House of Want, progress is not real and cannot be permanent. The reaction must come. The tower leans from its foundations, and every new story but hastens the final catastrophe. To educate men who must be condemned to poverty is but to make them restive; to base on a state of most glaring social inequality political institutions under which men are theoretically equal, is to stand a pyramid on its apex. [. . .]

The Laws of Distribution

[. . .] [C]apital instead of first is last; instead of being the employer of labour, it is in reality employed by labour. There must be land before labour can be exerted, and labour must be exerted before capital can be produced. Capital is a result of labour, and is used by labour to assist it in further production. Labour is the active and initial force, and labour is therefore the employer of capital. Labour can only be exerted upon land, and it is from land that the matter which it transmutes into wealth must be

drawn. Land, therefore, is the condition precedent, the field and material of labour. The natural order is land, labour, capital, and, instead of starting from capital as our initial point, we should start from land.

There is another thing to be observed. Capital is not a necessary factor in production. Labour exerted upon land can produce wealth without the aid of capital, and in the necessary genesis of things must so produce wealth before capital can exist. Therefore the law of rent and the law of wages must correlate each other and form a perfect whole without reference to the law of capital, as otherwise these laws would not fit the cases which can readily be imagined, and which to some degree actually exist, in which capital takes no part in production. And as capital is, as is often said, but stored-up labour, it is but a form of labour, a subdivision of the general term labour, and its law must be subordinate to, and independently correlate with, the law of wages, so as to fit cases in which the whole produce is divided between labour and capital, without any deduction for rent. [. . .]

The term rent, in its economic sense—that is, when used, as I am using it, to distinguish that part of the produce which accrues to the owners of land or other natural capabilities by virtue of their ownership—differs in meaning from the word rent as commonly used. In some respects this economic meaning is narrower than the common meaning; in other respects it is wider.

It is narrower in this: In common speech, we apply the word rent to payments for the use of buildings, machinery, fixtures, etc., as well as to payments for the use of land or other natural capabilities; and in speaking of the rent of a house or the rent of a farm, we do not separate the price for the use of the improvements from the price for the use of the bare land. But in the economic meaning of rent payments for the use of any of the products of human exertion are excluded, and of the lumped payments for the use of houses, farms, etc., only that part is rent which constitutes the consideration for the use of the land—that part paid for the use of buildings or other improvements being properly interest, as it is a consideration for the use of capital.

[. . .] [R]ent or land value does not arise from the productiveness or utility of land. It in no wise represents any help or advantage given to production, but simply the power of securing a part of the results of production. No matter what are its capabilities, land can yield no rent and have no value until some one is willing to give labour or the results of labour for the privilege of using it; and what any one will thus give depends not upon the capacity of the land but upon its capacity as compared with that of land that can be had for nothing. I may have very rich land, but it will yield no rent and have no value so long as there is other land as good to be had without cost. But when this other land is appropriated, and the best land to be had for nothing is inferior, either in fertility, situation, or other quality, my land will begin to have a value and yield rent. And though the productiveness of my land may decrease, yet if the productiveness of the land to be had without charge decreases in greater proportion, the rent I can get, and consequently the value of my land, will steadily increase. Rent, in short, is the price of monopoly, arising from the reduction to individual ownership of natural elements which human exertion can neither produce nor increase. [. . .]

Perhaps it may conduce to a fuller understanding of the law of rent to put it in this form: The ownership of a natural agent of production will give the power of appropriating so much of the wealth produced by the exertion of labour and capital upon it as exceeds the return which the same application of labour and capital could secure in the least productive occupation in which they freely engage.

This, however, amounts to precisely the same thing, for there is no occupation in which labour and capital can engage which does not require the use of land; and, furthermore, the cultivation or other use of land will always be carried to as low a point of remuneration, all things considered, as is freely accepted in any other pursuit. [. . .]

The law of rent is, in fact, but a deduction from the law of competition, and amounts simply to the assertion that as wages and interest tend to a common level, all that part of the general production of wealth which exceeds what the labour and capital employed could have secured for themselves, if applied to the poorest natural agent in use, will go to landowners in the shape of rent. It rests, in the last analysis, upon the fundamental principle, which is to political economy what the attraction of gravitation is to physics—that men will seek to gratify their desires with the least exertion. [. . .]

This, then, is the law of rent. [. . .]

The Problem Solved

The great problem, of which these recurring seasons of industrial depression are but peculiar manifestations, is now, I think, fully solved, and the social phenomena which all over the civilised world appal the philanthropist and perplex the statesman, which hang with clouds the future of the most advanced races, and suggest doubts of the reality and ultimate goal of what we have fondly called progress, are now explained.

> The reason why, in spite of the increase of productive power, wages constantly tend to a minimum which will give but a bare living, is that, with increase in productive power, rent tends to even greater increase, thus producing a constant tendency to the forcing down of wages.

In every direction, the direct tendency of advancing civilisation is to increase the power of human labour to satisfy human desires—to extirpate poverty, and to banish want and the fear of want. All the things in which progress consists, all the conditions which progressive communities are striving for, have for their direct and natural result the improvement of the material (and consequently the intellectual and moral) condition of all within their influence. The growth of population, the increase and extension of exchanges, the discoveries of science, the march of invention, the spread of education, the improvement of government, and the amelioration of manners, considered as material forces, have all a direct tendency to increase the productive power of labour—not of some labour, but of all labour; not in some departments of industry, but in all departments of industry; for the law of the production of wealth in society is the law of "each for all, and all for each."

But labour cannot reap the benefits which advancing civilisation thus brings, because they are intercepted. Land being necessary to labour, and being reduced to private ownership, every increase in the productive power of labour but increases rent—the price that labour must pay for the opportunity to utilise its powers; and thus all the advantages gained by the march of progress go to the owners of land, and wages do not increase. Wages cannot increase; for the greater the earnings of labour the greater the price that labour must pay out of its earnings for the opportunity to make any earnings at all. The mere labourer has thus no more interest in the general advance of productive power than the Cuban slave has in advance in the price of sugar. And just as an advance in the price of sugar may make the condition of the slave worse, by inducing the master to drive him harder, so may the condition of the free labourer be positively, as well as relatively, changed for the worse by the increase in the productive power of his labour. For, begotten of the continuous advance of rents, arises a speculative tendency, which discounts the effect of future improvements by a still further advance of rent, and thus tends, where this has not occurred from the normal advance of rent, to drive wages down to the slave point—the point at which the labourer can just live.

And thus robbed of all the benefits of the increase in productive power, labour is exposed to certain effects of advancing civilisation which, without the advantages that naturally accompany them, are positive evils, and of themselves tend to reduce the free labourer to the helpless and degraded condition of the slave.

For all the improvements which add to productive power as civilisation advances, consist in, or necessitate, a still further subdivision of labour, and the efficiency of the whole body of labourers is increased at the expense of the independence of the constituents. The individual labourer acquires knowledge of, and skill in, but an infinitesimal part of the varied processes which are required to supply even the commonest wants. The aggregate produce of the labour of a savage tribe is small, but each member is capable of an independent life. He can build his own habitation, hew out or stitch together his own canoe, make his own clothing, manufacture his own weapons, snares, tools, and ornaments. He has all the knowledge of nature possessed by his tribe—knows what vegetable productions are fit for food, and where they may be found; knows the habits and resorts of beasts, birds, fishes, and insects; can pilot himself by the sun or the stars, by the turning of blossoms or the mosses on the trees; is, in short, capable of supplying all his wants. He may be cut off from his fellows and still live; and thus possesses an independent power which makes him a free contracting party in his relations to the community of which he is a member.

Compare with this savage the labourer in the lowest ranks of civilised society, whose life is spent in producing but one thing, or oftener but the infinitesimal part of one thing, out of the multiplicity of things that constitute the wealth of society and go to supply even the most primitive wants; who not only cannot make even the tools required for his work, but often works with tools that he does not own and can never hope to own. Compelled to even closer and more continuous labour than the savage, and gaining by it no more than the savage gets—the mere necessaries of life—he loses the independence of the savage. He is not only unable to apply his own powers to the direct satisfaction of his own wants, but, without the concurrence of many others, he is unable to apply them indirectly to the satisfaction of his wants. He is a mere link in an enormous chain of producers and consumers, helpless to separate himself, and helpless to move, except as they move. The worse his position in society, the more dependent is he on society; the more utterly unable does he become to do anything for himself. The very power of exerting his labour for the satisfaction of his wants passes from his own control, and may be taken away or restored by the actions of others, or by general causes over which he has no more influence than he has over the motions of the solar system. The primeval curse comes to be looked upon as a boon, and men think, and talk, and clamour and legislate as though monotonous manual labour in itself were a good and not an evil, an end and not a means. Under such circumstances, the man loses the essential quality of manhood—the godlike power of modifying and controlling conditions. He becomes a slave, a machine, a commodity—a thing, in some respects, lower than the animal.

I am no sentimental admirer of the savage state. I do not get my ideas of the untutored children of nature from Rousseau, or Chateaubriand or Cooper. I am conscious of its material and mental poverty, and its low and narrow range. I believe that civilisation is not only the natural destiny of man, but the enfranchisement, elevation, and refinement of all his powers, and think that it is only in such moods as may lead him to envy the cud-chewing cattle that a man who is free to the advantages of civilisation could look with regret upon the savage state. But, nevertheless, I think no one who will open his eyes to the facts can resist the conclusion that there are in the heart of our civilisation large classes with whom the veriest savage could not afford to exchange. It is my deliberate opinion that if, standing on the threshold of being, one were given the choice of entering life as a Terra del Fuegan, a black fellow of Australia, an Esquimaux in the Arctic Circle, or among the lowest classes in such a highly civilised country as Great Britain, he would make infinitely the better choice in selecting the lot of the savage. For those classes who in the midst of wealth are condemned to want, suffer all the privations of the savage, without the sense of personal freedom; they are condemned to more than his narrowness and littleness, without opportunity for the growth of his rude virtues; if their horizon is wider, it is but to reveal blessings that they cannot enjoy.

There are some to whom this may seem like exaggeration, but it is only because they have never suffered themselves to realise the true condition of those classes upon whom the iron heel of modern civilisation presses with full force. As De Tocqueville observes, in one of his letters to Mme. Swetchine, "we so soon become used to the thought of want that we do not feel, that an evil which grows greater to the sufferer the longer it lasts becomes less to the observer by the very fact of its duration;" and perhaps the best proof of the justice of this observation is that in cities where there exists a pauper class and a criminal class, where young girls shiver as they sew for bread, and tattered and barefooted children make a home in the streets, money is regularly raised to send missionaries to the heathen! Send missionaries to the heathen! It would be laughable if it were not so sad. Baal no longer stretches forth his hideous, sloping arms; but in Christian lands mothers slay their infants for a burial fee! And I challenge the production from any authentic accounts of savage life of such descriptions of degradation as are to be found in official documents of highly civilised countries — in reports of Sanitary Commissioners and of inquiries into the condition of the labouring poor. [. . .]

Look over the world to-day. In countries the most widely differing — under conditions the most diverse as to government, as to industries, as to tariffs, as to currency — you will find distress among the working classes; but everywhere that you thus find distress and destitution in the midst of wealth, you will find that the land is monopolised; that instead of being treated as the common property of the whole people, it is treated as the private property of individuals; that, for its use by labour, large revenues are extorted from the earnings of labour. Look over the world to-day, comparing different countries with each other, and you will see that it is not the abundance of capital or the productiveness of labour that makes wages high or low; but the extent to which the monopolisers of land can, in rent, levy tribute upon the earnings of labour. Is it not a notorious fact, known to the most important, that new countries, where the aggregate wealth is small, but where land is cheap, are always better countries for the labouring classes than the rich countries, where land is dear? Wherever you find land relatively low, will you not find wages relatively high? And wherever land is high, will you not find wages low? As land increases in value, poverty deepens and pauperism appears. In the new settlements, where land is cheap, you will find no beggars, and the inequalities in condition are very slight. In the great cities, where land is so valuable that it is measured by the foot, you will find the extremes of poverty and of luxury. And this disparity in condition between the two extremes of the social scale may always be measured by the price of land. [. . .] The principle is as universal and as obvious. That rent *must* reduce wages, is as clear as that the greater the subtractor the less the remainder. That rent *does* reduce wages, any one, wherever situated, can see by merely looking around him. [. . .]

In all our long investigation we have been advancing to this simple truth: That as land is necessary to the exertion of labour in the production of wealth, to command the land which is necessary to labour is to command all the fruits of labour save enough to enable labour to exist. We have been advancing as through an enemy's country, in which every step must be secured, every position fortified, and every by-path explored; for this simple truth, in its application to social and political problems, is hid from the great masses of men partly by its very simplicity, and in greater part by widespread fallacies and erroneous habits of thought which lead them to look in every direction but the right one for an explanation of the evils which oppress and threaten the civilised world. And back of these elaborate fallacies and misleading theories is an active, energetic power, a power that in every country, be its political forms what they may, writes laws and moulds thought—the power of a vast and dominant pecuniary interest.

But so simple and so clear is this truth, that to fully see it once is always to recognise it. There are pictures which though looked at again and again, present only a confused labyrinth of lines or scroll work—a landscape, trees, or something of the kind—until once the attention is called to the fact that these things make up a face or a figure. This relation once recognised is always afterwards clear. It is so in this case. In the light of this truth all social facts group themselves in an orderly relation and the most diverse phenomena are seen to spring from one great principle. It is not in the relations of capital and labour; it is not in the pressure of population against subsistence that an explanation of the unequal development of our civilisation is to be found. The great cause of inequality in the distribution of wealth is inequality in the ownership of land. The ownership of land is the great fundamental fact which ultimately determines the social, the political, and consequently the intellectual and moral condition of a people. And it must be so. For land is the habitation of man, the storehouse upon which he must draw for all his needs, the material to which his labour must be applied for the supply of all his desires; for even the products of the sea cannot be taken, the light of the sun enjoyed, or any of the forces of nature utilised, without the use of land or its products. On the land we are born, from it we live, to it we return again—children of the soil as truly as is the blade of grass or the flower of the field. Take away from man all that belongs to land, and he is but a disembodied spirit. Material progress cannot rid us of our dependence upon land; it can but add to the power of producing wealth from land; and hence, when land is monopolised, it might go on to infinity without increasing wages or improving the condition of those who have but their labour. It can but add to the value of land and the power which its possession gives. Everywhere, in all times, among all peoples, the possession of land is the base of aristocracy, the foundation of great fortunes, the source of power. As said the Brahmins, ages ago—

To whomsoever the soil at any time belongs, to him belong the fruits of it. White parasols and elephants mad with pride are the flowers of a grant of land. [. . .]

The Remedy

[. . .] [I]n the United States, if we were to reduce public expenditures to the lowest possible point, and meet them by revenue taxation, the benefit could certainly not be greater than that which railroads have brought. There would be more wealth left in the hands of the people as a whole, just as the railroads have put more wealth in the hands of the people as a whole, but the same inexorable laws would operate as to its distribution. The condition of those who live by their labour would not ultimately be improved.

A dim consciousness of this pervades—or, rather, is beginning to pervade—the masses, and constitutes one of the grave political difficulties that are closing in around the American republic. Those who have nothing but their labour, and especially the proletarians of the cities—a growing class—care little about the prodigality of government, and in many cases are disposed to look upon it as a good thing—"furnishing employment," or "putting money in circulation." Tweed, who robbed New York as a guerilla chief might levy upon a captured town (and who was but a type of the new banditti who are grasping the government of all our cities), was undoubtedly popular with a majority of the voters, though his thieving was notorious, and his spoils were blazoned in big diamonds and lavish personal expenditure. After his indictment, he was triumphantly elected to the Senate; and, even when a recaptured fugitive, was frequently cheered on his way from court to prison. He had robbed the public treasury of many millions, but the proletarians felt that he had not robbed them. And the verdict of political economy is the same as theirs.

Let me be clearly understood. I do not say that governmental economy is not desirable; but simply that reduction in the expenses of government can have no direct effect in extirpating poverty and increasing wages as long as land is monopolised.

Although this is true, yet even with sole reference to the interests of the lowest class, no effort should be spared to keep down useless expenditure. The more complex and extravagant government becomes, the more it gets to be a power distinct from and independent of the people, and the more difficult does it become to bring questions of real public policy to a popular decision. Look at our elections in the United

States—upon what do they turn? The most momentous problems are pressing upon us, yet so great is the amount of money in politics, so large are the personal interests involved, that the most important questions of government are but little considered. The average American voter has prejudices, party feelings, general notions of a certain kind, but he gives to the fundamental questions of government not much more thought than a street car horse does to the profits of the line. Were this not the case, so many hoary abuses could not have survived and so many new ones been added. Anything that tends to make government simple and inexpensive tends to put it under control of the people, and to bring questions of real importance to the front. But no reduction in the expenses of government can of itself cure or mitigate the evils that arise from a constant tendency to the unequal distribution of wealth. [. . .]

[A]s soon as land acquires a value, wages, as we have seen, do not depend upon the real earnings or product of labour, but upon what is left to labour after rent is taken out; and when land is all monopolised, as it is everywhere except in the newest communities, rent must drive wages down to the point at which the poorest paid class will be just able to live and reproduce, and thus wages are forced to a minimum fixed by what is called the standard of comfort—that is, the amount of necessaries and comforts which habit leads the working classes to demand as the lowest on which they will consent to maintain their numbers. This being the case, industry, skill, frugality, and intelligence can only avail the individual in so far as they are superior to the general level—just as in a race speed can only avail the runner in so far as it exceeds that of his competitors. If one man work harder, or with superior skill or intelligence than ordinary, he will get ahead; but if the average of industry, skill, or intelligence is brought up to the higher point, the increased intensity of application will secure but the old rate of wages, and he who would get ahead must work harder still. [. . .]

We have traced the unequal distribution of wealth which is the curse and menace of modern civilisation to the institution of private property in land. We have seen that as long as this institution exists no increase in productive power can permanently benefit the masses; but, on the contrary, must tend to still further depress their condition. We have examined all the remedies, short of the abolition of private property in land, which are currently relied on or proposed for the relief of poverty and the better distribution of wealth, and have found them all inefficacious or impracticable.

There is but one way to remove an evil—and that is, to remove its cause. Poverty deepens as wealth increases, and wages are forced down while productive power grows, because land, which is the source of all wealth and the field of all labour, is monopolised. To extirpate poverty, to make wages what justice commands they should be, the full earnings of the labourer, we must therefore substitute for the individual ownership of land a common ownership. Nothing else will go to the cause of the evil—in nothing else is there the slightest hope.

This, then, is the remedy for the unjust and unequal distribution of wealth apparent in modern civilisation, and for all the evils which flow from it:

We must make land common property.

Justice of the Remedy

[. . .] The recognition of individual proprietorship of land is the denial of the natural rights of other individuals—it is a wrong which *must* show itself in the inequitable division of wealth. For as labour cannot produce without the use of land, the denial of the equal right to the use of land is necessarily the denial of the right of labour to its own produce. If one man can command the land upon which others must labour, he can appropriate the produce of their labour as the price of his permission to labour. The fundamental law of nature, that her enjoyment by man shall be consequent upon his exertion, is thus violated. The one receives without producing; the others produce without receiving. The one is unjustly enriched; the others are robbed. To this fundamental wrong we have traced the unjust distribution of wealth which is separating modern society into the very rich and the very poor. It is the continuous increase of rent—the price that labour is compelled to pay for the use of land, which strips the many of the wealth they justly earn, to pile it up in the hands of the few who do nothing to earn it. [. . .]

The right to exclusive ownership of anything of human production is clear. No matter how many the hands through which it has passed, there was at the beginning of the line, human labour—some one who having procured or produced it by his exertions, had to it a clear title as against all the rest of mankind, and which could justly pass from one to another by sale or gift. But at the end of what string of conveyances or grants can be shown or supposed a like title to any part of the material universe? To improvements such an original title can be shown; but it is a title only to the improvements, and not to the land itself. If I clear a forest, drain a swamp, or fill a morass, all I can justly claim is the value given by these exertions. They give me no right to the land itself, no claim other than to my equal share with every other member of the community in the value which is added to it by the growth of the community.

But it will be said: There are improvements which in time become indistinguishable from the land itself! Very well; then the title to the improvements becomes blended with the title to the land; the individual right is lost in the common right. It is the greater that swallows up the less, not the less that swallows up the greater. Nature does not proceed from man, but man from nature, and it is into the bosom of nature that he and all his works must return again. [. . .]

Now, as I think I have conclusively proved, it is the same cause which has in every age degraded and enslaved the labouring masses, that is working in the civilised world to-day. Personal liberty—that is to say, the liberty to move about—is everywhere conceded, while of political and legal inequality there are in the United States no vestiges, and in the most backward civilised countries but few. But the great cause of inequality remains, and is manifesting itself in the unequal distribution of wealth. The essence of slavery is that it takes from the labourer all he produces save enough to support an animal existence, and to this minimum the wages of free labour, under existing conditions, unmistakably tend. Whatever be the increase of productive power, rent steadily tends to swallow up the gain, and more than the gain.

Thus the condition of the masses in every civilised country is, or is tending to become, that of virtual slavery under the forms of freedom. And it is probable that of all kinds of slavery this is the most cruel and relentless. For the labourer is robbed of the produce of his labour and compelled to toil for a mere subsistence; but his taskmasters, instead of human beings, assume the form of imperious necessities. Those to whom his labour is rendered and from whom his wages are received are often driven in their turn—contact between the labourers and the ultimate beneficiaries of their labour is sundered, and individuality is lost. The direct responsibility of master to slave, a responsibility which exercises a softening influence upon the great majority of men, does not arise; it is not one human being who seems to drive another to unremitting and ill-requited toil but "the inevitable laws of supply and demand," for which no one in particular is responsible. The maxims of Cato the Censor—maxims which were regarded with abhorrence even in an age of cruelty and universal slaveholding—that after as much work as possible is obtained from a slave he should be turned out to die, become the common rule; and even the selfish London, New York, and Boston, among people who have given, and would give again, money and blood to free the slave, where no one could abuse a beast in public without arrest and punishment, barefooted and ragged children may be seen running around the streets even in the winter time, and in squalid garrets and noisome cellars women work away their lives for wages that fail to keep them in proper warmth and nourishment. Is it any wonder that to the slaveholders of the South the demand for the abolition of slavery seemed like the cant of hypocrisy? [. . .]

Application of the Remedy

It is an axiom of statesmanship, which the successful founders of tyranny have understood and acted upon—that great changes can best be brought about under old forms. We, who would free men, should heed the same truth. It is the natural method. When nature would make a higher type, she takes a lower one and develops it. This, also, is the law of social growth. Let us work by it. With the current we may glide fast and far. Against it, it is hard pulling and slow progress.

I do not propose either to purchase or to confiscate private property in land. The first would be unjust;

the second, needless. Let the individuals who now hold it still retain, if they want to, possession of what they are pleased to call *their* land. Let them continue to call it *their* land. Let them buy and sell, and bequeath and devise it. We may safely leave them the shell, if we take the kernel. *It is not necessary to confiscate land; it is only necessary to confiscate rent.*

Nor to take rent for public uses is it necessary that the State should bother with the letting of lands, and assume the chances of the favouritism, collusion, and corruption that might involve. It is not necessary that any new machinery should be created. The machinery already exists. Instead of extending it, all we have to do is to simplify and reduce it. By leaving to landowners a percentage of rent, which would probably be much less than the cost and loss involved in attempting to rent lands through State agency, and by making use of this existing machinery, we may, without jar or shock, assert the common right to land by taking rent for public uses.

We already take some rent in taxation. We have only to make some changes in our modes of taxation to take it all.

What I, therefore, propose, as the simple yet sovereign remedy, which will raise wages, increase the earnings of capital, extirpate pauperism, abolish poverty, give remunerative employment to whoever wishes it, afford free scope to human powers, lessen crime, elevate morals, and taste, and intelligence, purify government and carry civilisation to yet nobler heights, is—*to appropriate rent by taxation.*

In this way, the State may become the universal landlord without calling herself so, and without assuming a single new function. In form, the ownership of land would remain just as now. No owner of land need be dispossessed, and no restriction need be placed upon the amount of land any one could hold. For, rent being taken by the State in taxes, land, no matter in whose name it stood, or in what parcels it was held, would be really common property, and every member of the community would participate in the advantages of its ownership.

Now, insomuch as the taxation of rent, or land values, must necessarily be increased just as we abolish other taxes, we may put the proposition into practical form by proposing—

To abolish all taxation save that upon land values.

As we have seen, the value of land is at the beginning of society nothing, but as society develops by the increase of population and the advance of the arts, it becomes greater and greater. In every civilised country, even the newest, the value of the land taken as a whole is sufficient to bear the entire expenses of government. In the better developed countries it is much more than sufficient. Hence it will not be enough to merely place all taxes upon the value of land. It will be necessary, where rent exceeds the present governmental revenues, to commensurately increase the amount demanded in taxation, and to continue this increase as society progresses and rent advances. But this is so natural and easy a matter, that it may be considered as involved, or at least understood, in the proposition to put all taxes on the value of land. That is the first step, upon which the practical struggle must be made. When the hare is once caught and killed, cooking him will follow as a matter of course. When the common right to land is so far appreciated that all taxes are abolished save those which fall upon rent, there is no danger of much more than is necessary to induce them to collect the public revenues being left to individual landholders.

Experience has taught me (for I have been for some years endeavouring to popularise this proposition) that wherever the idea of concentrating all taxation upon land values finds lodgment sufficient to induce consideration, it invariably makes way, but that there are few of the classes most to be benefited by it, who at first, or even for a long time afterwards, see its full significance and power. It is difficult for working men to get over the idea that there is a real antagonism between capital and labour. It is difficult for small farmers and homestead owners to get over the idea that to put all taxes on the value of land would be to unduly tax them. It is difficult for both classes to get over the idea that to exempt capital from taxation would be to make the rich richer, and the poor poorer. These ideas spring from confused thought. But behind ignorance and prejudice there is a powerful interest, which has hitherto dominated literature, education, and opinion. A great wrong always dies hard, and the great wrong which in every civilised country condemns the masses of men to poverty and want will not die without a bitter struggle. [. . .]

The Law of Human Progress

The poverty which in the midst of abundance pinches and embrutes men, and all the manifold evils which flow from it, spring from a denial of justice. In permitting the monopolisation of the opportunities which nature freely offers to all, we have ignored the fundamental law of justice—for so far as we can see, when we view things upon a large scale, justice seems to be the supreme law of the universe. But by sweeping away this injustice and asserting the rights of all men to natural opportunities, we shall conform ourselves to the law—we shall remove the great cause of unnatural inequality in the distribution of wealth and power; we shall abolish poverty; tame the ruthless passions of greed; dry up the springs of vice and misery; light in dark places the lamp of knowledge; give new vigour to invention and a fresh impulse to discovery; substitute political strength for political weakness; and make tyranny and anarchy impossible.

The reform I have proposed accords with all that is politically, socially, or morally desirable. It has the qualities of a true reform, for it will make all other reforms easier. What is it but the carrying out in letter and spirit of the truth enunciated in the Declaration of Independence—the "self-evident" truth that is the heart and soul of the Declaration—*"That all men are created equal; that they are endowed by their Creator with certain inalienable rights; that among them are life, liberty, and the pursuit of happiness!"*

These rights are denied when the equal right to land—on which and by which men alone can live—is denied. Equality of political rights will not compensate for the denial of the equal right to the bounty of nature. Political liberty, when the equal right to land is denied, becomes, as population increases and invention goes on, merely the liberty to compete for employment at starvation wages. This is the truth that we have ignored. And so there come beggars in our streets and tramps on our roads; and poverty enslaves men whom we boast are political sovereigns; and want breeds ignorance that our schools cannot enlighten; and citizens vote as their masters dictate; and the demagogue usurps the part of the statesman; and gold weighs in the scales of justice; and in high places sit those who do not pay to civic virtue even the compliment of hypocrisy; and the pillars of the republic that we thought so strong already bend under an increasing strain.

We honour Liberty in name and in form. We set up her statues and sound her praises. But we have not fully trusted her. And with our growth so grow her demands. She will have no half service!

Liberty! it is a word to conjure with, not to vex the ear in empty boastings. For liberty means justice, and justice is the natural law—the law of health and symmetry and strength, of fraternity and co-operation.

They who look upon liberty as having accomplished her mission when she has abolished hereditary privileges and given men the ballot, who think of her as having no further relations to the everyday affairs of life, have not seen her real grandeur—to them the poets who have sung of her must seem rhapsodists, and her martyrs fools! As the sun is the lord of life, as well as of light; as his beams not merely pierce the clouds, but support all growth, supply all motion, and call forth from what would otherwise be a cold and inert mass, all the infinite diversities of being and beauty, so is liberty to mankind. It is not for an abstraction that men have toiled and died; that in every age the witnesses of Liberty have stood forth, and the martyrs of Liberty have suffered.

We speak of Liberty as one thing, and virtue, wealth, knowledge, invention, national strength and national independence as other things. But, of all these Liberty is the source, the mother, the necessary condition. She is to virtue what light is to colour; to wealth what sunshine is to grain; to knowledge what eyes are to sight. She is the genius of invention, the brawn of national strength, the spirit of national independence. Where Liberty rises, there virtue grows, wealth increases, knowledge expands, invention multiplies human powers, and in strength and spirit the freer nation rises among her neighbours as Saul amid his brethren—taller and fairer. Where Liberty sinks, there virtue fades, wealth diminishes, knowledge is forgotten, invention ceases, and empires once mighty in arms and arts become a helpless prey to freer barbarians! [. . .]

Our primary social adjustment is a denial of justice. In allowing one man to own the land on which and from which other men must live, we have made them his bondsmen in a degree which increases as material progress goes on. This is the subtle alchemy that in ways they do not realise is extracting from the masses in every civilised country the fruits of their weary toil; that is instituting a harder and more hopeless slavery in place of that which has been destroyed; that is bringing political despotism out of political freedom, and must soon transmute democratic institutions into anarchy. [. . .]

Can it be that the gifts of the Creator may be thus misappropriated with impunity? Is it a light thing that labour should be robbed of its earnings while greed rolls in wealth—that the many should want while the few are surfeited? Turn to history, and on every page may be read the lesson that such wrong never goes unpunished; that the Nemesis that follows injustice never falters nor sleeps! Look around to-day. Can this state of things continue? May we even say, "After us the deluge!" Nay; the pillars of the state are trembling even now, and the very foundations of society begin to quiver with pent-up forces that glow underneath. The struggle that must either revivify, or convulse in ruin, is near at hand, if it be not already begun.

The fiat has gone forth! With steam and electricity, and the new powers born of progress, forces have entered the world that will either compel us to a higher plane or overwhelm us as nation after nation, as civilisation after civilisation, have been overwhelmed before. It is the delusion which precedes destruction that sees in the popular unrest with which the civilised world is feverishly pulsing, only the passing effect of ephemeral causes. Between democratic ideas and the aristocratic adjustments of society there is an irreconcilable conflict. Here in the United States, as there in Europe, it may be seen arising. We cannot go on permitting men to vote and forcing them to tramp. We cannot go on educating boys and girls in our public schools and then refusing them the right to earn an honest living. We cannot go on prating of the inalienable rights of man and then denying the inalienable right to the bounty of the Creator. Even now, in old bottles the new wine begins to ferment, and elemental forces gather for the strife!

But if, while there is yet time, we turn to Justice and obey her, if we trust Liberty and follow her, the dangers that now threaten must disappear, the forces that now menace will turn to agencies of elevation. Think of the powers now wasted; of the infinite fields of knowledge yet to be explored; of the possibilities of which the wondrous inventions of this century give

us but a hint. With want destroyed; with greed changed to noble passions; with the fraternity that is born of equality taking the place of the jealousy and fear that now array men against each other; with mental power loosed by conditions that give to the humblest comfort and leisure; and who shall measure the heights to which our civilisation may soar? Words fail the thought! It is the Golden Age of which poets have sung and high-raised seers have told in metaphor! It is the glorious vision which has always haunted man with gleams of fitful splendour. It is what he saw whose eyes at Patmos were closed in a trance. It is the culmination of Christianity—the City of God on earth, with its walls of jasper and its gates of pearl! It is the reign of the Prince of Peace!

Conclusion

[. . .] The great fact which Science in all her branches shows is the universality of law. Wherever he can trace it, whether in the fall of an apple or in the revolution of binary suns, the astronomer sees the working of the same law, which operates in the minutest divisions in which we may distinguish space as it does in the immeasurable distances with which his science deals. Out of that which lies beyond his telescope comes a moving body and again it disappears. So far as he can trace its course the law is ignored. Does he say that this is an exception? On the contrary, he says that this is merely a part of its orbit that he has seen; that beyond the reach of his telescope the law holds good. He makes his calculations, and after centuries they are proved.

Now, if we trace out the laws which govern human life in society, we find that in the largest as in the smallest community they are the same. We find that what seem at first sight like divergences and exceptions, are but manifestations of the same principles. And we find that everywhere we can trace it, the social law runs into and conforms with the moral law; that in the life of a community, justice infallibly brings its reward and injustice its punishment. [. . .]

The laws which Political Economy discovers, like the facts and relations of physical nature, harmonise with what seems to be the law of mental development—not a necessary and involuntary progress, but a progress in which the human will is an initiatory force. But in life, as we are cognisant of it, mental development can go but a little way. The mind hardly begins to awake ere the bodily powers decline—it but becomes dimly conscious of the vast fields before it, but begins to learn and use its strength, to recognise relations and extend its sympathies, when, with the death of the body, it passes away. Unless there is something more, there seems here a break, a failure. Whether it be a Humboldt or a Herschel, a Moses who looks from Pisgah, a Joshua who leads the host, or one of those sweet and patient souls who in narrow circles live radiant lives, there seems, if mind and character here developed can go no further, a purposelessness inconsistent with what we can see of the linked sequence of the universe.

By a fundamental law of our minds—the law, in fact, upon which Political Economy relies in all her deductions—we cannot conceive of a means without an end; a contrivance without an object. Now, to all nature, so far as we come in contact with it in this world, the support and employment of the intelligence that is in man furnishes such an end and object. But unless man himself may rise to or bring forth something higher his existence is unintelligible. So strong is this metaphysical necessity that those who deny to the individual anything more than this life are compelled to transfer the idea of perfectibility to the race. But as we have seen (and the argument could have been made much more complete) there is nothing whatever to show any essential race improvement. Human progress is not the improvement of human nature. The advances in which civilisation consists are not secured in the constitution of man, but in the constitution of society. They are thus not fixed and permanent, but may at any time be lost—nay are constantly tending to be lost. And further than this, if human life does not continue beyond what we see of it here, then we are confronted with regard to the race with the same

difficulty as with the individual. For it is as certain that the race must die as it is that the individual must die. We know that there have been geologic conditions under which human life was impossible on this earth. We know that they must return again. Even now, as the earth circles on her appointed orbit, the northern ice cap slowly thickens, and the time gradually approaches when its glaciers will flow again, and austral seas, sweeping northward, bury the seats of present civilisation under ocean wastes, as it may be they now bury what was once as high a civilisation as our own. And beyond these periods, science discerns a dead earth, an exhausted sun—a time when, clashing together, the solar system shall resolve itself into a gaseous form, again to begin immeasurable mutations.

What then is the meaning of life—of life absolutely and inevitably bounded by death? To me it only seems intelligible as the avenue and vestibule to another life. And its facts seem only explainable upon a theory which cannot be expressed but in myth and symbol, and which, everywhere and at all times, the myths and symbols in which men have tried to portray their deepest perceptions do in some form express. [. . .]

Though Truth and Right seem often overborne, we may not see it all. How can we see it all? All that is passing, even here, we cannot tell. The vibrations of matter which gives the sensations of light and colour become to us indistinguishable when they pass a certain point. It is only within a like range that we have cognisance of sounds. Even animals have senses which we have not. And, here? Compared with the solar system our earth is but an indistinguishable speck; and the solar system itself shrivels into nothingness when gauged with the star depths. Shall we say that what passes from *our* sight passes into oblivion? No; not into oblivion. Far, far beyond our ken the eternal laws must hold their sway. [. . .]

CARROLL D. WRIGHT

The Factory System as an Element in Civilization (1882)

The influences which led to the institution of the factory system are as diverse in their nature, almost, as the ramifications of the system itself. These influences, however, are not shrouded in any mystery but are clearly defined; and their power, not only abstractly but concretely, is fully recognizable in the origin of the system.

The factory system is of recent origin and is entirely the creation of influences existing or coming into existence during the last half of the eighteenth century. These influences were both direct and subtle in their character but all-important in their place and in their combination. As a great fact, the system originated in no preconceived plan, nor did it spring from any spasmodic exercise of human wisdom; on the contrary, "it was formed and shaped by the irresistible force of circumstances, fortunately aided and guided by men who were able to profit by circumstances." To borrow the expression of Cooke Taylor,

> Those who were called the fathers of the system were not such demons as they have sometimes been described, nor yet were they perfect angels; they were simply men of great intelligence, industry, and enterprise; they have bequeathed the system to this age with the imperfections incident to every human institution, and the task of harmonizing their innovation with existing institutions, and with the true spirit of righteousness belongs really to the great employers of labor rather than to the professed teachers of morality. It is too late to inquire whether the system ought or ought not to have been established; for established it is, and established it will remain in spite of all the schemes of the socialists or the insane panaceas of quack economists.

In its origin the factory system found its application in the textile trades of England, and we are very apt now, when the term is used, to confine it in our minds to the production of cotton and woolen goods, although it has in reality embraced nearly all lines of the products of machinery.

A factory is an establishment where several workmen are collected together for the purpose of obtaining greater and cheaper conveniences for labor than they could procure individually at their homes; for producing results by their combined efforts which they could not accomplish separately; and for saving the loss of time which the carrying of an article from place to place, during the several processes necessary to complete its manufacture, would occasion.

The principle of a factory is that each laborer, working separately, is controlled by some associating principle, which directs his producing powers to effect a common result, which it is the object of all collectively to attain. Factories are, therefore, the legitimate outgrowth of the universal tendency to association which is inherent in our nature, and by the development of which every advance in human improvement and human happiness has been gained. [. . .]

Inventions were the material forces, powerful, indeed, as agents in building the factory system. What were the spiritual forces, so to speak? The inner, subtle but also powerful agencies at work to render the material forces successful? A body without a spirit is but dead matter. This is certainly true in one sense of all the mechanical bodies which have served as expressions of mind. A machine is really embodied action; a grand combination of inventions must embody not only all the actions represented but the spirit of the age, for without this they are powerless. [. . .]

[A] new system, which has found its most rapid extension in the United States, has enabled the manufacturers of this country, with our wonderful stores of raw materials at hand, to become the successful rivals in the mechanic arts of any country that desires to compete with them. It has changed the conditions of masses of people; it has become an active element in the processes of civilization, and has changed the character of legislation and of national policy everywhere.

Is this great, powerful, and growing system a power for good or for evil? Does it mean the elevation of the race or its retrogression?

When we speak of civilization we have in mind the progress of society toward a more perfect state, as indicated by the growth of a long period of time; we do not simply contemplate specific reforms or special evils but the trend of all social influences.

When we speak of the factory system we are apt to let our thoughts dwell upon the evils that we know or imagine belong to it; this is certainly true when civilization and the factory system are suggested in the same sentence. This is wrong, for we should contemplate the factory system in its general influence upon society and especially upon that portion of society most intimately connected with the factory.

My position is that the system has been and is a most potent element in promoting civilization. I assume, of course, and the assumption is in entire harmony with my thoughts, that the civilization of the nineteenth century is better than that of the eighteenth. An examination into the conditions existing under the factory system and those of the domestic or individual system which preceded it fully sustains this position.

None of the systems of labor which existed prior to the present or factory system were particularly conducive to a higher civilization. Wages have been paid for services rendered since the wants of men induced one to serve another, yet the wage system is of recent origin as a system. It arose out of the feudal system of labor and was the first fruits of the efforts of men to free themselves from villenage. The origin of the wage system cannot be given a birthday as can the factory system. It is true, however, that the wage system rendered the factory system possible, and they have since grown together. The first may give way to some other method for dividing the profits of production, but the factory system perfected, must, whether under socialistic or whatever political system, remain, until disintegration is the rule in society.

The feudal and slave systems had nothing in them from which society could draw the forces necessary to growth; on the contrary, they reflected the most depressing influences and were actually the allies of retrogression. The domestic system, which claims the eighteenth century almost entirely, was woven into the two systems which existed before and came

after it; in fact, it has not yet disappeared. It is simple fact, however, when we say that the factory system set aside the domestic system of industry; it is idyllic sentiment when we say that the domestic system surpassed the former, and nothing but sentiment.

There is something poetic in the idea of the weaver of old England, before the spinning machinery was invented, working at his loom in his cottage, with his family about him, some carding, others spinning the wool or the cotton for the weaver, and writers and speakers are constantly bewailing the departure of such scenes.

I am well aware that I speak against popular impression, and largely against popular sentiment, when I assert that the factory system in every respect is vastly superior as an element in civilization to the domestic system which preceded it; that the social and moral influences of the present outshine the social and moral influences of the old. The hue and cry against the prevailing system has not been entirely genuine on either side of the Atlantic. Abuses have existed, great and abominable enough, but not equal to those which have existed in the imagination of men who would have us believe that virtue is something of the past.

The condition of the workers of society has never been the ideal condition, and the worker is too often the victim of the contemptible selfishness which tempts a man to commit the crime of robbing the operative of his just share in the results of his toil. The evils of the factory system are sufficient to call out all the sentiments of justice and philanthropy which enable us to deal with wrong and oppression; all this I do not dispute, but I claim that with all its faults and attendant evils the factory system is a vast improvement upon the domestic system of industry in almost every respect, not only with reference to the individual and the family but to society and the state.

The usual mistake is to consider the factory system as the creator of evils, and not only evils, but of evil disposed persons. This can hardly be shown to be true, although it is that the system may congregate evils or evil disposed persons, and thus give the appearance of creating that which already existed. [. . .]

Do not construe what I say against the domestic system of industry as in the least antagonistic to the family, for I am one of those who believe that its integrity is the integrity of the nation; that the sacredness of its compacts is the sacredness and the preservation and the extension of the race; that the inviolability of its purity and its peace is the most emphatic source of anxiety of lawmakers; and that any tendency, whether societary or political, toward its decay or even toward its disrespect, deserves the immediate condemnation and active opposition of all citizens as the leading cause of irreligion and of national disintegration.

It should not be forgotten that

the term factory system, in technology, designates the combined operation of many orders of work people . . . in tending with assiduous skill a series of productive machines continually propelled by a central power. This definition includes such organizations as cotton mills, flax mills, silk and woolen mills, and many other works; but it excludes those in which the mechanisms do not form a connected series, nor are dependent on one prime mover.

It involves in its strictest sense "the idea of a vast automatum, composed of various mechanical and intellectual organs, acting in uninterrupted concert for the production of a common object, all of them being subordinated to a self-regulated moving force."

So a factory becomes a scientific structure, its parts harmonious, the calculations requisite for their harmony involving the highest mathematical skill, and in the factory the operative is always the master of the machine and never the machine the master of the operative. [. . .]

The spasmodic nature of work under the domestic system caused much disturbance, for handworking is always more or less discontinuous from the caprice of the operative, while much time must be lost in gathering and returning materials. For these and obvious reasons a hand weaver could very seldom turn off in a week much more than one-half what his loom could produce if kept continuously in action during the working hours of the day at the rate which the weaver in his working paroxysms impelled it.

The regular order maintained in the factory cures this evil of the old system and enables the operative to know with reasonable certainty the wages he is to receive at the next payday. His life and habits become more orderly, and he finds, too, that as he has left the closeness of his home shop for the usually clean and well-lighted factory, he imbibes more freely of the health giving tonic of the atmosphere. It is commonly supposed that cotton factories are crowded with operatives. From the nature of things the spinning and weaving rooms cannot be crowded. The spinning mules, in their advancing and retreating locomotion, must have five or six times the space to work in that the actual bulk of the mechanism requires, and where the machinery stands the operative cannot.

In the weaving rooms there can be no crowding of persons. During the agitation for factory legislation in the early part of this century, it was remarked before a committee of the House of Commons "that no part of a cotton mill is one-tenth part as crowded, or the air in it one-tenth part as impure, as the House of Commons with a moderate attendance of members." This is true today; the poorest factory in this country is as good a place to breathe in as Representatives Hall during sessions, or the ordinary schoolroom. In this respect the new system of labor far surpasses the old.

Bad air is one of the surest influences to intemperance, and it is clearly susceptible of proof that intemperance does not exist, and has not existed to such alarming degrees, under the new as under the old system; certainly the influence of bad air has not been as potent.

The regularity required in mills is such as to render persons who are in the habit of getting intoxicated unfit to be employed there, and many manufacturers object to employing persons guilty of the vice; yet, notwithstanding all the efforts which have been made to stop the habit, the beer-drinking operatives of factory towns still constitute a most serious drawback to the success of industrial enterprises, but its effects are not so ruinous under the new as under the old system. [. . .]

I am constantly obliged, in my everyday labors, to refute the assertion that wages under the factory system are growing lower and lower. The reverse is the truth, which is easily demonstrated; the progress of improvement in machinery may have reduced the price paid for a single article, yard, or pound of product, or for the services of a skilled and intelligent operative, but the same improvement has enabled the workman to produce in a greater proportion and always with a less expenditure of muscular labor and in less time, and it has enabled a low grade of labor to increase its earnings. At the same time, a greater number have been benefited, either in consumption or production, by the improvement.

Experience has not only evolved but proven a law in this respect, which is, the more the factory system is perfected, the better will it reward those engaged in it, if not in increased wages to skill, certainly in higher wages to less skill.

Better morals, better sanitary conditions, better health, better wages, these are the practical results of the factory system, as compared with that which preceded it, and the results of all these have been a keener intelligence. Under the domestic system there existed no common centers of thought and action. Religious bigotry has fought against the new order because it tends to destroy the power of the church. Association kills such power in time. [. . .]

The factory brings mental friction, contact, which could not exist under the old system. Take our own factories in New England, today, fed as they are by French Canadian operatives; when they go back to their own land, as many do, they carry with them the results, whatever they are, of contact with a new system, and the effects of such contact will tell upon their children if not upon themselves. The factory brings progress and intelligence; it establishes at the centers, the public hall for the lyceum and the concert; and even literary institutions have been the result of the direct influence of the system.

Such things could not, in the nature of conditions, find a lodgement under the domestic system. It is in evidence that "the book trade of Great Britain flourishes and fades with its manufactures in vital sympathy, while it is nearly indifferent to the good or bad state of its agriculture."

While the factory system is superior in almost every respect to the individual system, the former is not free from positive evils because human nature is not perfect. These evils are few compared to the magnitude of the benefits of the system, but they should be kept constantly in mind, that public sentiment may be strong enough some day to remove them, in fact, it is removing them.

Whatever there was that was good in the old household plan of labor—so far as keeping the family together at all times and working under the care of the head—was temporarily lost when the factory system took its place, insofar as the old workers entered the factories. This evil, like most others attendant upon the new order, has been greatly exaggerated. The workers under the old system strenuously opposed the establishment of the new, and this led to the employment of great numbers of parish children, a feature of employment which was eagerly fostered by parish officers. Yet, while the working of young children in mills is something to be condemned in our own time, when it began it placed them in a far better condition than they had ever been in, or could have expected to be in, for it made them self-supporting.

The children have been excluded from the factories in all countries, gradually, till the laws of most states, European and American, prohibit their employment under fourteen years of age.

A great evil which even now attracts attention, and in our own country too, is the employment of married women. This occurs more generally with Irish and Canadian women, and too often is the result of the indolence or cupidity of the father. Employers have done much to check this evil, which is not so much an evil to the present as to the future generations. It is bad enough for the present. It robs the young of the care of their natural protectors, it demoralizes the older children, it makes home dreary and robs it of its amenities. The factory mother's hours of labor in the mills are as long as those of others, and then comes the thousand and one duties of the home, in which, although she may be aided by members of the family, there is little rest.

No ten-hour law can reach the overworked housewife in any walk of life, certainly not when she is a factory worker. Her employment in the mills is a crime to her offspring and, logically, a crime to the state; and the sooner law and sentiment make it impossible for her to stand at the loom, the sooner the character of mill operatives will be elevated. I count their employment with the consequent train of evils, the worst, and the very worst of the evils of a system which is the grandeur of the age, in an industrial point of view.

It is gratifying to know that in Massachusetts cotton mills only about 8 percent of the females employed are married women. This is equally true of English factories, and I believe that in both countries the number is gradually decreasing. So, too, the number of operatives who live in individual homes is increasing.

The employment of children is an evil which has been stimulated as much by the actions of parents as by mill owners.

These evils, however, have been the result of development rather than of inauguration, and thus will disappear as education, in its broad sense, takes the place of ignorance.

The evil effects of the kind of labor performed in mills, so far as health is concerned, have been considerable, while less than those attending the household system. All employments have features not conducive to health. These features or conditions are incidental and cannot be separated from the employment. In mining coal, for instance, the nature of the occupation is bad in nearly all respects; but coal must be had, and there is never any lack of miners. What, then, shall be done?

Operators are in duty bound, of course, to make all evils, whether incidental or artificial, as light as possible, and should introduce every improvement which will lighten the burden of any class who, by their mental incapacity or other causes, are content to seek employment in the lowest grades of labor. Machinery is constantly elevating the grades of labor and the laborer. The working of mines, even, is today an easy task compared to what it was a few years ago. The workers themselves have much responsibility on their own shoulders so far as the healthfulness or unhealthfulness of an occupation is concerned.

Let the children of factory workers everywhere be educated in the rudiments of sanitary science, and then let law say that bad air shall be prohibited, and I believe the vexed temperance question will not trouble us to the extent it has. Drunkenness and intemperance are not the necessary accompanying evils of the factory system and never have been; but wherever corporations furnish unhealthy home surroundings, there the evils of intemperance will be more or less felt in all the directions in which the results of rum find their wonderful ramifications.

The domestic system of labor could not deal with machinery; machinery really initiated the factory system; that is, the latter is the result of machinery. But machinery has done something more—it has brought with it new phases of civilization—for while it means the factory system in one sense, it is the type and representative of the civilization of this period, because it embodies, so far as mechanics are concerned, the concentrated, clearly wrought-out thought of the age. While books represent thought, machinery is the embodiment of thought.

Industry and poverty are not handmaidens, and, as poverty is lessened, good morals thrive. If labor, employment of the mind, is an essential to good morals, then the highest kind of employment, that requiring the most application and the best intellectual effort, means the best morals. This condition, I take courage to assert, is superinduced eventually by the factory system, for by it the operative is usually employed in a higher grade of labor than that which occupied him in his previous condition. For this reason the present system of productive industry is constantly narrowing the limits of the class that occupies the bottom step of social order.

One of the inevitable results of the factory is to enable men to secure a livelihood in less hours than of old; this is grand in itself, for as the time required to earn a living grows shorter, our civilization grows up. That system which demands of a man all his time for the earning of mere subsistence is demoralizing in all respects. [. . .]

The fact that the lowest grade of operatives can now be employed in mills does not signify more ignorance but, as I have said, a raising of the lowest to higher employments, and, as the world progresses in its refinement, the lowest, which is high comparatively, seems all the lower. Society will bring all up, unless society is compelled to take up what is called a simpler system of labor. We should not forget that growth in civilization means complication, not simplification, nor that the machine is the servant of the workman, and not his competitor. [. . .]

The softening of the misery caused by the change in systems has occurred, but in subtle ways. Transition stages are always harsh upon the generation that experiences them; the great point is that they should be productive of good results in the end. The mind recoils at the contemplation of the conditions which the vast increase of population would have imposed without the factory system.

It is a sad law, perhaps, but it is an invariable law, that industry, in its march, takes no account of the positions that it overturns, nor of the destinies that it modifies. We must keep step with its progress or be left upon the road. It always accomplishes its work, which is to make better goods at a lower price, to supply more wants and also those of a better order, not with regard for any class but having in view the whole human race. Industry is this, or it is not industry; true to its instincts it has no sentiment in it, unless it is for its own interest; and yet such is the harmony of things, when they are abandoned to their natural course, notwithstanding the selfishness of industry, directed to its own good, it turns finally to secure the good of all, and while requiring service for itself, it serves at the same time by virtue of its resources and its power.

Recent writers, notwithstanding all the facts of history, find a solution for whatever difficulties result from the production of goods under the factory system, in the dispersion of congregated labor, and a return to simple methods when they would have the machines owned and manipulated as individual property, under individual enterprise; but it is safe to assert that "a people who have once adopted the large system of production, are not likely to recede from it"; labor is more productive on the system of large industrial enterprises; the produce is greater in proportion to the labor employed; the same number of persons can be supported equally well with less toil and greater leisure; and in the moral aspect of the question, something better is aimed at as the good of industrial improvement than to disperse the workers of society over the earth to be employed in pent-up houses and the sin-breeding small shops of another age, where there would be scarcely any community of interest or necessary mental communion with other human beings. "If public spirit, generous sentiments, or true justice and equality are desired, association, not isolation of interests, is the school in which these excellences are nurtured."

It is from such influences we discern the elevation of an increased proportion of working people from the position of unskilled to that of skilled laborers and the opening of an adequate field of remunerative employment to women, two of the most important improvements which could be desired in the condition of the working classes. Since, therefore, the extension of the factory system tends strongly toward both these results, it may be considered as one of the

features of the present age, which is the most favorable to their more permanent advancement.

It is also true that the factory system has stamped itself most emphatically upon the written law of all countries where it has taken root, as well as upon the social and moral laws which lie at the bottom of the forces which make written law what it is. With the exception of laws relating to the purely commercial features of the factory system, the legislation which that system has produced has been stimulated by the evils which have grown with it.

It is the worst phases of society which gauge the legislation requisite for its protection. Laws other than those for the regulation of trade and the protection of rights as to property, by definition of rights, are made for the restraint of the evil disposed and do not disturb those whose motives and actions are right; so if it were not for the evils which creep into existence with every advance society makes, laws would remain unwritten because not needed. We have a way of judging by the worst examples.

The social battles which men have fought have been among the severest for human rights, and they mark eras in social conditions as clearly as do field contests in which more human lives have been lost, perhaps, but in which no greater human interests have been involved.

At the time of the institution of the factory system, there was upon the statute books of England but few laws relating to master and man; those which did exist were largely of criminal bearing, establishing punishment for various shortcomings of the men; but with the coming of the new system, the evils of poor law abuses came into full view, and while pauper children were vastly better off in the factories than in the parish poorhouses, they attracted attention and became the subjects of parliamentary protection. For the first time, there appeared some of the consequences of congregated labor, or rather the effects of the congregation of one class of labor appeared. A whole generation of operatives were growing up under conditions of comparative physical degeneracy, of mental ignorance and moral corruption, all of which existed before, but which the factory system brought into strong light.

And now the great question began to be asked, "Has the nation any right to interfere? Shall society suffer that individuals may profit?" Shall the next and succeeding generations be weakened, morally and intellectually, that estates may be enlarged? [. . .] I know of no trust more sacred than that given into the hands of the captains of industry, for they deal with human beings in close relations; not through the media of speech or exhortation but of positive association, and by this they can make or mar. Granted that the material is often poor, the intellects often dull; then all the more sacred the trust and all the greater the responsibility. The rich and powerful manufacturer with the adjuncts of education and good business training holds in his hand something more than the means of subsistence for those he employs, he holds their moral well-being in his keeping, insofar as it is in his power to mold their morals. He is something more than a producer, he is an instrument of God for the upbuilding of the race.

This may sound like sentiment; I am willing to call it sentiment, but I know it means the best material prosperity, and that every employer who has been guided by such sentiments has been rewarded

twofold; first, in witnessing the wonderful improvement of his people, and, second, in seeing his dividends increase and the wages of the operatives increase with his dividends.

The factory system of the future will be run on this basis. The instances of such are multiplying rapidly now, and whenever it occurs, the system outstrips the pulpit in the actual work of the gospel, that is, in the work of humanity. It needs no gift of prophecy to foretell the future of a system which has in it more possibilities for good for the masses who must work for day wages than any scheme which has yet been devised by philanthropy alone.

To make the system what it will be, the factory itself must be rebuilt and so ordered in all its appointments that the great question for the labor reformer shall be how to get people out of their homes and into the factory. The agitation of such a novel proposition will bring all the responsibility for bad conditions directly home to the individual, and then the law can handle the difficulty.

WILLIAM GRAHAM SUMNER

What Social Classes Owe Each Other (1883)

right around
Gilded Age

Introduction

We are told every day that great social problems stand before us and demand a solution, and we are assailed by oracles, threats, and warnings in reference to those problems. There is a school of writers who are playing quite a *rôle* as the heralds of the coming duty and the coming woe. They assume to speak, for a large, but vague and undefined, constituency, who set the task, exact a fulfillment, and threaten punishment for default. The task or problem is not specifically defined. Part of the task which devolves on those who are subject to the duty is to define the problem. They are told only that something is the matter: that it behooves them to find out what it is, and how to

correct it, and then to work out the cure. All this is more or less truculently set forth.

After reading and listening to a great deal of this sort of assertion I find that the question forms itself with more and more distinctness in my mind: Who are those who assume to put hard questions to other people and to demand a solution of them? How did they acquire the right to demand that others should solve their world-problems for them? Who are they who are held to consider and solve all questions, and how did they fall under this duty?

So far as I can find out what the classes are who are respectively endowed with the rights and duties of posing and solving social problems, they are as follows: Those who are bound to solve the problems are the rich, comfortable, prosperous, virtuous, respectable, educated, and healthy; those whose right it is to set the problems are those who have been less fortunate or less successful in the struggle for existence. The problem itself seems to be, How shall the latter be made as comfortable as the former? To solve this problem, and make us all equally well off, is assumed to be the duty of the former class; the penalty, if they fail of this, is to be bloodshed and destruction. If they cannot make everybody else as well off as themselves, they are to be brought down to the same misery as others.

During the last ten years I have read a great many books and articles, especially by German writers, in which an attempt has been made to set up "the State" as an entity having conscience, power, and will sublimated above human limitations, and as constituting a tutelary genius over us all. I have never been able to find in history or experience anything to fit this concept. I once lived in Germany for two years, but I certainly saw nothing of it there then. Whether the State which Bismarck is moulding will fit the notion is at best a matter of faith and hope. My notion of the State has dwindled with growing experience of life. As an abstraction, the State is to me only All-of-us. In practice—that is, when it exercises will or adopts a line of action—it is only a little group of men chosen in a very haphazard way by the majority of us to perform certain services for all of us. The majority do not go about their selection very rationally, and they are almost always disappointed by the results of their own operation. Hence "the State," instead of offering resources of wisdom, right reason, and pure moral sense beyond what the average of us possess, generally offers much less of all those things. Furthermore, it often turns out in practice that "the State" is not even the known and accredited servants of the State, but, as has been well said, is only some obscure clerk, hidden in the recesses of a Government bureau, into whose power the chance has fallen for the moment to pull one of the stops which control the Government machine. In former days it often happened that "The State" was a barber, a fiddler, or a bad woman. In our day it often happens that "the State" is a little functionary on whom a big functionary is forced to depend. [. . .]

The little group of public servants who, as I have said, constitute the State, when the State determines on anything, could not do much for themselves or anybody else by their own force. If they do anything, they must dispose of men, as in an army, or of capital, as in a treasury. But the army, or police, or *posse comitatus*, is more or less All-of-us, and the capital in the treasury is the product of the labor and saving of All-of-us. Therefore, when the State means power-to-do it means All-of-us, as brute force or as industrial force.

If anybody is to benefit from the action of the State it must be Some-of-us. If, then, the question is raised, What ought the State to do for labor, for trade, for manufactures, for the poor, for the learned professions? etc., etc.—that is, for a class or an interest—it is really the question, What ought All-of-us to do for Some-of-us? But Some-of-us are included in All-of-us, and, so far as they get the benefit of their own efforts, it is the same as if they worked for themselves, and they may be cancelled out of All-of-us. Then the question which remains is, What ought Some-of-us to do for Others-of-us? or, What do social classes owe to each other?

I now propose to try to find out whether there is any class in society which lies under the duty and burden of fighting the battles of life for any other class, or of solving social problems for the satisfaction of any other class; also, whether there is any class which has the right to formulate demands on "society"—that is, on other classes; also, whether there is anything but a fallacy and a superstition in the notion that "the State" owes anything to anybody except peace, order, and the guarantees of rights. [. . .]

On a New Philosophy: That Poverty Is the Best Policy

It is commonly asserted that there are in the United States no classes, and any allusion to classes is resented. On the other hand, we constantly read and hear discussions of social topics in which the existence of social classes is assumed as a simple fact. "The poor," "the weak," "the laborers," are expressions which are used as if they had exact and well-understood definition. Discussions are made to bear upon the assumed rights, wrongs, and misfortunes of certain social classes; and all public speaking and writing consists, in a large measure, of the discussion of general plans for meeting the wishes of classes of people who have not been able to satisfy their own desires. These classes are sometimes discontented, and sometimes not. Sometimes they do not know that anything is amiss with them until the "friends of humanity" come to them with offers of aid. Sometimes they are discontented and envious. They do not take their achievements as a fair measure of their rights. They do not blame themselves or their parents for their lot, as compared with that of other people. Sometimes they claim that they have a right to everything of which they feel the need for their happiness on earth. To make such a claim against God and Nature would, of course, be only to say that we claim a right to live on earth if we can. But God and Nature have ordained the chances and conditions of life on earth once for all. The case cannot be reopened. We cannot get a revision of the laws of human life. We are absolutely shut up to the need and duty, if we would learn how to live happily, of investigating the laws of Nature, and deducing the rules of right living in the world as it is. These are very wearisome and commonplace tasks. They consist in labor and self-denial repeated over and over again in learning and doing. When the people whose claims we are considering are told to apply themselves to these tasks they become irritated and feel almost insulted. They formulate their claims as rights against society—that is, against some other men. In their view they have a right, not only to *pursue* happiness, but to *get* it; and if they fail to get it, they think they have a claim to the aid of other men—that is, to the labor and self-denial of other men—to get it for them. They find orators and poets who tell them that they have grievances, so long as they have unsatisfied desires.

Now, if there are groups of people who have a claim to other people's labor and self-denial, and if there are other people whose labor and self-denial are liable to be claimed by the first groups, then there certainly are "classes," and classes of the oldest and most vicious type. For a man who can command another man's labor and self-denial for the support of his own existence is a privileged person of the highest species conceivable on earth. Princes and paupers meet on this plane, and no other men are on it all. On the other hand, a man whose labor and self-denial may be diverted from his maintenance to that of some other man is not a free man, and approaches more or less toward the position of a slave. Therefore

we shall find that, in all the notions which we are to discuss, this elementary contradiction, that there are classes and that there are not classes, will produce repeated confusion and absurdity. We shall find that, in our efforts to eliminate the old vices of class government, we are impeded and defeated by new products of the worst class theory. We shall find that all the schemes for producing equality and obliterating the organization of society produce a new differentiation based on the worst possible distinction—the right to claim and the duty to give one man's effort for another man's satisfaction. We shall find that every effort to realize equality necessitates a sacrifice of liberty. [. . .]

Certain ills belong to the hardships of human life. They are natural. They are part of the struggle with Nature for existence. We cannot blame our fellow-men for our share of these. My neighbor and I are both struggling to free ourselves from these ills. The fact that my neighbor has succeeded in this struggle better than I constitutes no grievance for me. Certain other ills are due to the malice of men, and to the imperfections or errors of civil institutions. These ills are an object of agitation, and a subject for discussion. The former class of ills is to be met only by manly effort and energy; the latter may be corrected by associated effort. The former class of ills is constantly grouped and generalized, and made the object of social schemes. We shall see, as we go on, what that means. The second class of ills may fall on certain social classes, and reform will take the form of interference by other classes in favor of that one. The last fact is, no doubt, the reason why people have been led, not noticing distinctions, to believe that the same method was applicable to the other class of ills. The distinction here made between the ills which belong to the struggle for existence and those which are due to the faults of human institutions is of prime importance.

It will also be important, in order to clear up our ideas about the notions which are in fashion, to note the relation of the economic to the political significance of assumed duties of one class to another. That is to say, we may discuss the question whether one class owes duties to another by reference to the economic effects which will be produced on the classes and society; or we may discuss the political expediency of formulating and enforcing rights and duties respectively between the parties. In the former case we might assume that the givers of aid were willing to give it, and we might discuss the benefit or mischief of their activity. In the other case we must assume that some at least of those who were forced to give aid did so unwillingly. Here, then, there would be a question of rights. The question whether voluntary charity is mischievous or not is one thing; the question whether legislation which forces one man to aid another is right and wise, as well as economically beneficial, is quite another question. Great confusion and consequent error is produced by allowing these two questions to become entangled in the discussion. Especially we shall need to notice the attempts to apply legislative methods of reform to the ills which belong to the order of Nature.

There is no possible definition of "a poor man." A pauper is a person who cannot earn his living; whose producing powers have fallen positively below his necessary consumption; who cannot, therefore, pay his way. A human society needs the active co-operation and productive energy of every person in it. A man who is present as a consumer, yet who does not contribute either by land, labor, or capital to the work of society, is a burden. On no sound political theory ought such a person to share in the political power of the State. He drops out of the ranks of workers and producers. Society must support him. It accepts the burden, but he must be cancelled from the ranks of the rulers likewise. So much for the pauper. About him no more need be said. But he is not the "poor man." The "poor man" is an elastic term, under which any number of social fallacies may be hidden.

Neither is there any possible definition of "the weak." Some are weak in one way, and some in another; and those who are weak in one sense are strong in another. In general, however, it may be said that those whom humanitarians and philanthropists call the weak are the ones through whom the productive and conservative forces of society are wasted. They constantly neutralize and destroy the finest efforts of the wise and industrious, and are a deadweight on the society in all its struggles to realize any better things. Whether the people who mean no harm, but are weak in the essential powers necessary to the performance of one's duties in life, or those who are malicious and vicious, do the more mischief, is a question not easy to answer. [. . .]

The humanitarians, philanthropists, and reformers, looking at the facts of life as they present themselves, find enough which is sad and unpromising in the condition of many members of society. They see wealth and poverty side by side. They note great inequality of social position and social chances. They eagerly set about the attempt to account for what they see, and to devise schemes for remedying what they do not like. In their eagerness to recommend the less fortunate classes to pity and consideration they forget all about the rights of other classes; they gloss over all the faults of the classes in question, and they exaggerate their misfortunes and their virtues. They invent new theories of property, distorting rights and perpetuating injustice, as anyone is sure to do who sets about the readjustment of social relations with the interests of one group distinctly before his mind, and the interests of all other groups thrown into the background. When I have read certain of these discussions I have thought that it must be quite disreputable to be respectable, quite dishonest to own property, quite unjust to go one's own way and earn one's own living, and that the only really admirable person was the good-for-nothing. The man who by his own effort raises himself above poverty appears, in these discussions, to be of no account. The man who has done nothing to raise himself above poverty finds that the social doctors flock about him, bringing the capital which they have collected from the other class, and promising him the aid of the State to give him what the other had to work for. In all these schemes and projects the organized intervention of society through the State is either planned or hoped for, and the State is thus made to become the protector and guardian of certain classes. The agents who are to direct the State action are, of course, the reformers and philanthropists. [. . .] Here it may suffice to observe that, on the theories of the social philosophers to whom I have referred, we should get a new maxim of judicious living: Poverty is the best policy. If you get wealth, you will have to support other people; if you do not get wealth, it will be the duty of other people to support you.

No doubt one chief reason for the unclear and contradictory theories of class relations lies in the fact that our society, largely controlled in all its organization by one set of doctrines, still contains survivals of old social theories which are totally inconsistent with the former. In the Middle Ages men were united by custom and prescription into associations, ranks, guilds, and communities of various kinds. These ties endured as long as life lasted. Consequently society was dependent, throughout all its details, on status, and the tie, or bond, was sentimental. In our modern state, and in the United States more than anywhere else, the social structure is based on contract, and status is of the least importance. Contract, however, is rational—even rationalistic. It is also realistic, cold, and matter-of-fact. A contract relation is based on a sufficient reason, not on custom or prescription. It is not permanent. It endures only so long as the reason for it endures. In a state based on contract sentiment is out of place in any public or common affairs. It is relegated to the sphere of private and personal relations, where it depends not at all on class types, but on personal acquaintance and personal estimates. The sentimentalists among us always seize upon the survivals of the old order. They want to save them and restore them. Much of the loose thinking also which troubles us in our social discussions arises from the fact that men do not distinguish the elements of status and of contract which may be found in our society.

Whether social philosophers think it desirable or not, it is out of the question to go back to status or to the sentimental relations which once united baron and retainer, master and servant, teacher and pupil, comrade and comrade. That we have lost some grace and elegance is undeniable. That life once held more poetry and romance is true enough. But it seems impossible that any one who has studied the matter should doubt that we have gained immeasurably, and that our farther gains lie in going forward, not in going backward. The feudal ties can never be restored. If they could be restored they would bring back personal caprice, favoritism, sycophancy, and intrigue. A society based on contract is a society of free and independent men, who form ties without favor or obligation, and co-operate without cringing or intrigue. A society based on contract, therefore, gives the utmost room and chance for individual development, and for all the self-reliance and dignity of a free man. That a society of free men, co-operating under contract, is by far the strongest society which has ever yet existed; that no such society has ever yet developed the full measure of strength of which it is

capable; and that the only social improvements which are now conceivable lie in the direction of more complete realization of a society of free men united by contract, are points which cannot be controverted. It follows, however, that one man, in a free state, cannot claim help from, and cannot be charged to give help to, another. To understand the full meaning of this assertion it will be worth while to see what a free democracy is.

That a Free Man Is a Sovereign, but That a Sovereign Cannot Take "Tips"

A free man, a free country, liberty, and equality are terms of constant use among us. They are employed as watchwords as soon as any social questions come into discussion. It is right that they should be so used. They ought to contain the broadest convictions and most positive faiths of the nation, and so they ought to be available for the decision of questions of detail.

In order, however, that they may be so employed successfully and correctly it is essential that the terms should be correctly defined, and that their popular use should conform to correct definitions. No doubt it is generally believed that the terms are easily understood, and present no difficulty. Probably the popular notion is, that liberty means doing as one has a mind to, and that it is a metaphysical or sentimental good. A little observation shows that there is no such thing in this world as doing as one has a mind to. There is no man, from the tramp up to the President, the Pope, or the Czar, who can do as he has a mind to. [. . .] [L]iberty is not a metaphysical or sentimental thing at all. It is positive, practical, and actual. It is produced and maintained by law and institutions, and is, therefore, concrete and historical. Sometimes we speak distinctively of civil liberty; but if there be any liberty other than civil liberty—that is, liberty under law—it is a mere fiction of the schoolmen, which they may be left to discuss.

Even as I write, however, I find in a leading review the following definition of liberty: Civil liberty is "the result of the restraint exercised by the sovereign people on the more powerful individuals and classes of the community, preventing them from availing themselves of the excess of their power to the detriment of the other classes." This definition lays the foundation for the result which it is apparently desired to reach, that "a government by the people can in no case become a paternal government, since its law-makers are its mandatories and servants carrying out its will, and not its fathers or its masters." Here we have the most mischievous fallacy under the general topic which I am discussing distinctly formulated. In the definition of liberty it will be noticed that liberty is construed as the act of the sovereign people against somebody who must, of course, be differentiated from the sovereign people. Whenever "people" is used in this sense for anything less than the total population, man, woman, child, and baby, and whenever the great dogmas which contain the word "people" are construed under the limited definition of "people," there is always fallacy.

History is only a tiresome repetition of one Story. Persons and classes have sought to win possession of the power of the State in order to live luxuriously out of the earnings of others. [. . .]

What history shows is, that rights are safe only when guaranteed against all arbitrary power, and all class and personal interest. Around an autocrat there has grown up an oligarchy of priests and soldiers. In time a class of nobles has been developed, who have broken into the oligarchy and made an aristocracy. Later the *demos*, rising into an independent development, has assumed power and made a democracy. Then the mob of a capital city has overwhelmed the democracy in an ochlocracy. Then the "idol of the people," or the military "savior of society," or both in one, has made himself autocrat, and the same old vicious round has recommenced. Where in all this is liberty? There has been no liberty at all, save where a state has known how to break out, once for all, from this delusive round; to set barriers to selfishness, cupidity, envy, and lust, in *all* classes, from highest to lowest, by laws and institutions; and to create great organs of civil life which can eliminate, as far as possible, arbitrary and personal elements from the adjustment of interests and the definition of rights. Liberty is an affair of laws and institutions which bring rights and duties into equilibrium. It is not at all an affair of selecting the proper class to rule. [. . .]

The notion of civil liberty which we have inherited is that of *a status created for the individual by laws and institutions, the effect of which is that each man is guaranteed the use of all his own powers exclusively for his own welfare.* It is not at all a matter of elections, or universal suffrage, or democracy. All institutions are to be tested by the degree to which they guarantee liberty. It is not to be admitted for a moment that liberty is a means to social ends, and that it may be impaired for major considerations. Any one who so argues has lost the bearing and relation of all the facts and factors in a free state. A human being has a life to live, a career to run. He is a centre of powers to work, and of capacities to suffer. What his powers may be—whether they can carry him far or not; what his chances may be, whether wide or restricted; what his fortune may be, whether to suffer much or little—are questions of his personal destiny which he must work out and endure as he can; but for all that concerns the bearing of the society and its institutions upon that man, and upon the sum of happiness to which he can attain during his life on earth, the product of all history and all philosophy up to this time is summed up in the doctrine, that he should be left free to do the most for himself that he can, and should be guaranteed the exclusive enjoyment of all that he does. If the society—that is to say, in plain terms, if his fellow-men, either individually, by groups, or in a mass—impinge upon him otherwise than to surround him with neutral conditions of security, they must do so under the strictest responsibility to justify themselves. Jealousy and prejudice against all such interferences are high political virtues in a free man. It is not at all the function of the State to make men happy. They must make themselves happy in their own way, and at their own risk. The functions of the State lie entirely in the conditions or chances under which the pursuit of happiness is carried on, so far as those conditions or chances can be affected by civil organization. Hence, liberty for labor and security for earnings are the ends for which civil institutions exist, not means which may be employed for ulterior ends.

Now, the cardinal doctrine of any sound political system is, that rights and duties should be in equilibrium. A monarchical or aristocratic system is not immoral, if the rights and duties of persons and classes are in equilibrium, although the rights and duties of different persons and classes are unequal. An immoral political system is created whenever there are privileged classes—that is, classes who have arrogated to themselves rights while throwing the duties upon others. In a democracy all have equal political rights. That is the fundamental political principle. A democracy, then, becomes immoral, if all have not equal political duties. This is unquestionably the doctrine which needs to be reiterated and inculcated beyond all others, if the democracy is to be made sound and permanent. Our orators and writers never speak of it, and do not seem often to know anything about it; but the real danger of democracy is, that the classes which have the power under it will assume all the rights and reject all the duties—that is, that they will use the political power to plunder those-who-have. Democracy, in order to be true to itself, and to develop into a sound working system, must oppose the same cold resistance to any claims for favor on the ground of poverty, as on the ground of birth and rank. It can no more admit to public discussion, as within the range of possible action, any schemes for coddling and helping wage-receivers than it could entertain schemes for restricting political power to wage-payers: It must put down schemes for making "the rich" pay for whatever "the poor" want, just as it tramples on the old theories that only the rich are fit to regulate society. One needs but to watch our periodical literature to see the danger that democracy will be construed as a system of favoring a new privileged class of the many and the poor. [. . .]

A free man in a free democracy has no duty whatever toward other men of the same rank and standing, except respect, courtesy, and good-will. We cannot say that there are no classes, when we are speaking politically, and then say that there are classes, when we are telling A what it is his duty to do for B. In a free state every man is held and expected to take care of himself and his family, to make no trouble for his neighbor, and to contribute his full share to public interests and common necessities. If he fails in this he throws burdens on others. He does not thereby acquire rights against the others. On the contrary, he only accumulates obligations toward

them; and if he is allowed to make his deficiencies a ground of new claims, he passes over into the position of a privileged or petted person—emancipated from duties, endowed with claims. This is the inevitable result of combining democratic political theories with humanitarian social theories. It would be aside from my present purpose to show, but it is worth noticing in passing, that one result of such inconsistency must surely be to undermine democracy, to increase the power of wealth in the democracy, and to hasten the subjection of democracy to plutocracy; for a man who accepts any share which he has not earned in another man's capital cannot be an independent citizen.

It is often affirmed that the educated and wealthy have an obligation to those who have less education and property, just because the latter have political equality with the former, and oracles and warnings are uttered about what will happen if the uneducated classes who have the suffrage are not instructed at the care and expense of the other classes. In this view of the matter universal suffrage is not a measure for *strengthening* the State by bringing to its support the aid and affection of all classes, but it is a new burden, and, in fact, a peril. Those who favor it represent it as a peril. This doctrine is politically immoral and vicious. When a community establishes universal suffrage, it is as if it said to each new-comer, or to each young man: "We give you every chance that any one else has. Now come along with us; take care of yourself, and contribute your share to the burdens which we all have to bear in order to support social institutions." Certainly, liberty, and universal suffrage, and democracy are not pledges of care and protection, but they carry with them the exaction of individual responsibility. The State gives equal rights and equal chances just because it does not mean to give anything else. It sets each man on his feet, and gives him leave to run, just because it does not mean to carry him. Having obtained his chances, he must take upon himself the responsibility for his own success or failure. [. . .]

Lester Frank Ward

Mind as Social Factor (1884)

After many centuries of exclusive study of the soul the thinkers of the world turned their attention for some centuries more to the study of the intellect. During all this time, the true influence of mind as a social factor was left quite out of view. At last there rose up the scientific philosophy which essayed to explain the nature of mind. Its dependence upon organisation in general and upon brain in particular was proved by scientific experimentation, and the domain of metaphysics became that of psychology. Mind was shown to be a function of body and psychology became a department of biology. Man has now taken his true position in the animal world as a product of development. Brain, which alone raises him above other animals, has been developed in the same manner as the other anatomical characters. The brain is the organ of the mind, its physical seat and cause. Mind is therefore a natural product of evolution, and its achievements are to be classed and studied along with all other natural phenomena. Such is the scientific conception of mind.

The modern scientist places all objects in the midst of an infinite series of antecedents and consequents. Organic forms as well as inorganic must take their places in this series—the animal no less than the plant, the man no less than the beast. Mind itself is a link of this endless chain. Its activities consist in the transmission of the properties of its antecedents to its consequents. The quantity of force in the universe is constant. No power can increase or dimnish it. All attempts on the part of the creatures of this constant and unchangeable force to modify its normal effects are not less vain because such creatures happen to have acquired the faculty of observing the changes going on in nature.

The protracted study of nature's processes leads to admiration of them, and the belief has become prevalent that they are not only unalterable but also in some way necessarily beneficent. Nature has made great progress in developing organised beings and is assumed to be still working in this direction.

The natural method is always the true method, and to find it out is the aim of all scientific investigation. Out of this earnest and laudable strife to discover the true method of nature has grown, logically enough, the assumption that when found it must be something of great worth. It is commonly supposed that the highest wisdom of man is to learn and then to follow the ways of nature. Those dissatisfied people who would improve upon the natural course of events are rebuked as meddlers with the unalterable. Their systems are declared utopian, their laws *bruta fulmina*. All efforts in this direction are held to be trifling and are stigmatised as so many ignorant attempts to nullify the immutable laws of nature.

This general mode of reasoning is carried into all departments of human life.

In government every attempt to improve the condition of the state is condemned and denounced. Curiously enough, here the claim is illogically made that such measures are harmful. In fact, unfortunately for the whole theory, they have often been proved to be so. But this, of course, proves their efficacy. This glaring inconsistency is, however, overlooked, and government is implored, not to adopt wise and successful measures, but to refrain from adopting any, to let society alone, and thus allow the laws of nature to work out their beneficent results.

In commerce and trade absolute freedom is insisted upon. Free trade is the watchword of this entire school. The laws of trade, they maintain, are natural laws. As such they must be better than any human rules. And here again we find, them insisting that regulation is injurious to trade, although it is at the same time declared to be nugatory.

In social affairs these doctrines are carried to their extreme logical outcome. The laws of nature as they manifest themselves in society must be left wholly untouched. The passions of men will neutralise and regulate themselves. Competition can be depended upon to correct abuses. The seller must be allowed to exaggerate and misstate the nature of his wares. This has the effect to sharpen the wits of the buyer, and this develops the brain. To dilute, adulterate, or even poison food and medicine for personal gain is not objectionable, since the destruction thereby of a few unwary consumers only proves their unfitness to survive in society. As in general commerce, so in private business, competition must be free. If a dealer, by selling at a loss, can hold out until all his competitors have been driven from the field, in order then to recover more than his losses by the monopoly he will enjoy, his right to do this must not be questioned. It is under such conditions and by the aid of such discipline that man and society have developed.

Education must be that of experience. Knowledge must be gained by efforts to avoid the consequences of ignorance already felt. The intellectual development of the child must be an epitome of that of the race. It is thus only that nature operates, and surely nature is greater and wiser than man.

All schemes of social reform are unscientific. Public charities tend to bolster up unworthy elements in society that nature has declared unfit to survive. Temperance reforms tend only to abridge individual liberty—for even the liberty to destroy one's self should be respected. Philanthropy is zeal without knowledge, while humanitarianism is fanaticism.

This general class of views antedated by many years the publication by Spencer and Darwin of their formulated doctrines of the "survival of the fittest" and "natural selection". But it cannot be denied that these doctrines, supported as they were by facts fresh from nature, have greatly strengthened this habit of thought. Nature's method is now much better known than formerly, and it is now well understood that an utterly soulless competition constitutes its fundamental characteristic. Surely man cannot go astray in following in the footsteps of nature. Let him learn from the animal world. He has descended from some of the humble stocks which he is now studying. Nature's plan has raised him from the condition of a beast to that of a rational being. It has created and developed society and civilisation. Unless tampered with by "reformers" all the operations of society would be competitive. Competition is the law of nature out of which progress results. Sociology, as its founder insisted, must be based on biology, and the true sociologist must understand this biologic law. Those who propose to apply methods to society which are opposed to the methods of nature are supposed to be ignorant of these fundamental truths and are called empiricists, "meddlers," and "tinkers".

Such, I say, is the tenor and tendency of modern scientific thought. I do not say that all scientific men hold these views. I merely maintain that leading ones have formulated and inculcated them as natural deductions from the established facts of science, and that the public mind is rapidly assimilating them, while scarcely any attempts are being made to check their advance.[1]

Is there any way of answering these arguments? Can the *laissez faire* doctrine be successfully met? That all attempts to do this have been timidly made—cannot be denied. That these have been few and feeble is equally certain. While there has existed in the minds of many rational persons a vague sense of some hidden fallacy in all this reasoning, none have felt competent to formulate their objections with sufficient clearness and force to warrant pitting them against the resistless stream of concurrent science and philosophy of the nineteenth century. There has, however, been developing of late a more or less marked apprehension with regard to the possible consequences of this mode of thought. The feeling is distinct in the best minds, and to a large extent in the public mind, that the tendency of modern ideas is nihilistic. It is clear that if they become universally accepted they must work stagnation in society. The *laissez faire* doctrine is a gospel of inaction, the scientific creed is struck with sterility, the policy of resigning all into the hands of Nature is a surrender.

But this recognition is by no means proof that the prevalent opinions are false. At best it can only suggest this on the ground that true doctrines should be progressive. But this would be a *petitio principii*. Nature is not optimistic, still less anthropocentric. For aught we know, the laws of nature are such as make a recognition of strict scientific truth a positive

---

1. The social philosophy of Mr. Herbert Spencer possesses this tone throughout, and his disciples, particularly in America, delight in going even farther than their master. The most extreme statement of the *laissez faire* doctrine known to me is that of Prof. W. G. Sumner, in his recent work, *Social Classes*.

barrier to social advancement. The argument we have been considering must be refuted, if at all, by legitimate counter-argument.

The present attempt to meet some parts of this argument is made in full consciousness of its strength as a factor in modern thought and with due deference to the great names that stand committed to it. The scientific facts which its defenders have brought to its support are, in the main, incontestable. To answer by denying these would be to abjure science and deserve contempt. The method of nature has been correctly interpreted. The doctrines of the survival of the fittest and natural selection are perfectly true doctrines. The law of competition is the fundamental law. It is unquestionably true that progress, not only in primary organic development, but also in society, has resulted from the action of this law.

After conceding all this, the attempt, notwithstanding, to stem the tide of modern scientific thought must, indeed, seem a hopeless one. At the outset it must be frankly acknowledged that if the current views are unsound the fault is not chargeable to science. If there is any defect it must he in the inferences drawn from the facts and not in the facts themselves. To what extent, then, is the *laissez faire* doctrine, as defined and popularly accepted, an inference? If the method of nature is correctly formulated by that doctrine, wherein lies the fallacy when it is applied to man and to society?

In order to grapple at once with the whole problem let me answer these questions by the open charge that the modern scientific philosophers fail to recognise the true value of the *psychic factor*. Just as the metaphysicians lost their bearings by an empty worship of mind and made philosophy a plaything, so the modern evolutionists have missed their mark by degrading mind to a level with mechanical force. They seem thus about to fling away the grand results that the doctrine of evolution cannot otherwise fail to achieve. Far be it from me to appeal to the prejudices of the enemies of science by casting opprobrium upon scientific deductions, but when I consider the tendencies which are now so unmistakable, and which are so certainly the consequence of the protracted study, on the part of leading scientists, of the unquestionable methods of nature, I think I can, though holding precisely opposite opinions, fully sympathise with Carlyle in characterising the philosophy of evolution as a "gospel of dirt".

But I need not longer dwell upon the blighting influence of this construction of the known laws of nature. Let us approach the kernel of the problem.

The *laissez faire* doctrine fails to recognise that, in the development of mind, a virtually *new power* was introduced into the world. To say that this has been done is no startling announcement. It is no more than has taken place many times in the course of the evolution of living and feeling beings out of the tenuous nebulae of space. For, while it is true that nature makes no leaps, while, so long as we consider their beginning, all the great steps in evolution are due to minute increments repeated through vast periods, still, when we survey the whole field, as we must do to comprehend the scheme, and contrast the extremes, we find that nature has been making a series of enormous strides, and reaching from one plane of development to another. It is these independent achievements of evolution that the true philosopher must study.

Not to mention the great steps in the cosmical history of the solar system and of the earth, we must regard the evolution of protoplasm, the "physical basis of life," as one of those gigantic strides which thenceforth completely revolutionised the surface of our planet. The development of the cell as the unit of organisation was another such stride. The origin of vertebrate life introduced a new element, and the birth of man wrought still another transformation. These are only a few of nature's revolutions. Many more will suggest themselves. And although, in no single one of these cases can it be said at what exact point the new essence commenced to exist, although the development of all these several expressions of Nature's method of concentrating her hitherto diffused forces was accomplished through an unbroken series of minute transitional increments continued through eons of time, still, it is not a whit less true that each of these grand products of evolution, when at length fully formed, constituted a new cosmic energy, and proceeded to stamp all future products and processes with a character hitherto wholly unknown upon the globe.

It is in this sense, and in this only, that I claim the development of mind—of the thinking, reasoning, inventing faculty of the human brain—as another, and one of the best marked, of the great cosmic strides that have characterised the course of evolution and belong to the legitimate methods of nature.

It is, for example, only to a limited extent and in the most general way that we can apply the same canons to the organic as to the inorganic world. It is usually, but falsely, supposed that the student of biology need know nothing of physics, the assumption being that they have nothing in common. While this error is fatal to all fundamental acquaintance with the laws of life, it well illustrates the immensity of the advance from one realm to the other. The same could be said, in varying degrees of obviousness, of every one of the ascending steps to which reference has been made. I freely admit that the theologians and metaphysicians commit the most fatal error in treating the soul, or mind, as independent of the body, but this enormous fallacy is scarcely greater than that of the modern evolutionist, who, finding out their dependence, ignores the *magnitude* of the step by which mind was made a property of body, and proceeds as though no new factor had entered into the world.

But all this may be regarded as mere generality. Let us come to something more specific.

It has always been a marvel to my comprehension that wise men and philosophers, when smitten with the specious logic of the *laissez faire* school, can close their eyes to the most obtrusive fact that civilisation presents. In spite of the influence of philosophy, all forms of which have thus far been negative and nihilistic, the human animal, with his growing intellect, has still ever realised the power that is vouchsafed through mind, and has ever exercised that power. Philosophy would have long since robbed him of it and caused his early extermination from the earth but for the persistence, through heredity, of the impulse to exercise in self-preservation every power in his possession; by which practice alone he first gained his ascendancy ages before philosophy began.

The great fact, then, to which I allude is that, in spite of all philosophy, whether mythologic, metaphysical, or naturalistic, declaring that man must and can do nothing, he has, from the very dawn of his intelligence, been transforming the entire surface of the planet he inhabits. No other animal performs anything comparable to what man performs. This is solely because no other possesses the developed psychic faculty.

If we analyse mind into its two departments, sense and intellect, we shall see that it is through this latter faculty that these results are accomplished. If we inquire more closely into the mode by which intellect operates, we shall find that it serves as a guiding power to those natural forces with which it is acquainted (and no others), directing them into channels of human advantage. If we seek for a single term by which to characterise with precision the nature of this process, we find this in *Invention*. The essential characteristic of all intellectual action is invention.

Glancing now at the *ensemble* of human achievement, which may be collectively called civilisation, we readily see that it is all the result of this inventive process. All practical art is merely the product of successful invention, and it requires no undue expansion of the term, nor extraordinary power of generalisation, to see in all human institutions only modified forms of arts, and true products of the intellectual, or inventive, faculty.

But what is the general result of all this? An entirely new dispensation has been given to the world. All the materials and forces of nature have been thus placed completely under the control of one of the otherwise least powerful of the creatures inhabiting the earth. He has only to know them in order to become their master. Nature has thus been made the servant of man. Thus only has man succeeded in peopling the entire globe while all other animals are restricted to narrow faunal areas. He has also peopled certain portions far more densely than any other species could have done, and he seems destined to continue multiplying his numbers for a long time yet in the future. But this quantitative proof is even less telling than the qualitative. When we confine our attention to the *élite* of mankind we do not need to have the ways specified in detail by which the powers of mind have exalted the intellectual being above all other products of creation. At the present moment the most dense and the most enlightened populations of the globe occupy what are termed temperate latitudes, which means latitudes in which for from three to five months each year vegetation ceases entirely, the waters are locked in ice, and the temperature frequently sinks far below the zero of the Fahrenheit thermometer. Imagine the thin-skinned, furless animal man subsisting in such a climate. Extinguish his fires, banish his clothing, blot out the habitations that deck the civilised landscape.

How long would the puny race survive? But these are not products of nature, they are products of *art*, the wages of thought—fruits of the intellect.

When a well-clothed philosopher on a bitter winter's night sits in a warm room well lighted for his purpose and writes on paper with pen and ink in the arbitrary characters of a highly developed language the statement that civilisation is the result of natural laws, and that man's duty is to let nature alone so that untrammeled it may work out a higher civilisation, he simply ignores every circumstance of his existence and deliberately closes his eyes to every fact within the range of his faculties. If man had acted upon his theory there would have been no civilisation, and our philosopher would have remained a troglodyte.

But how shall we distinguish this human, or anthropic, method from the method of nature? Simply by reversing all the definitions. Art is the antithesis of nature. If we call one the natural method we must call the other the artificial method. If nature's process is rightly named natural selection, man's process is artificial selection. The survival of the fittest is simply the survival of the strong, which implies, and might as well be called, the destruction of the weak. And if nature progresses through the destruction of the weak, man progresses through the *protection* of the weak. This is the essential distinction.

In human society the psychic power has operated to secure the protection of the weak in two distinct ways: first, by increasing the supply of the necessities of life, and, secondly, by preventing the destruction of life through the enemies of man. The immediate instrumentality through which the first of these processes is carried on is art, the product of invention. The second process takes place through the establishment of positive institutions.

It is difficult to say which of these agencies has been most effective. Both were always indispensable, and therefore all comparison is unprofitable.

Art operates to protect the weak against adverse surroundings. It is directed against natural forces, chiefly physical. By thus defeating the destructive influences of the elements and hostile forms of life, and by forcing nature to yield an unnatural supply of man's necessities, many who would have succumbed from inability to resist these adverse agencies—the feebler members of society—were able to survive, and population increased and expanded. While no one openly denies this, there is a tendency either to ignore it in politico-economic discussions, or to deny its application to them as an answer to naturalistic arguments.

If, on the other hand, we inquire into the nature of human institutions, we shall perceive that they are of three kinds, tending to protect the weak in three ways, or ascending degrees. These three successively higher means through which this end is attained are, first, Justice, second, Morality, and third, Charity. These forms of action have been reached through the development, respectively, of the three corresponding sentiments: Equity, Beneficence, and Benevolence.

All of these altruistic sentiments are wholly unknown, or known only in the merest embryo, to all animals below man, and therefore no such means of protection exist among them. They are strictly human, or anthropic. Many evolutionists fail to recognise this. Some sociologists refuse to admit it. They look about and see so much injustice, immorality and rapacity that they are led to suppose that only natural methods are in operation in society. This is a great mistake. In point of fact, the keener the sense of justice the more conspicuous the diminishing number of violations of it come to appear, and conversely, the obviousness of injustice proves the general prevalence of justice. It is the same with morality and philanthropy.

If we consider the effect of these three codes of human conduct in the direction of enabling the weaker ones to survive we shall see that it has been immense. Out of the first has arisen government, the chief value and function of which has always been and still is such protection. Great systems of jurisprudence have been elaborated, engrossing the attention of a large portion of the population of enlightened as well as of barbaric states. To say that these have been failures because often weighted with grave defects is to misinterpret history and misunderstand society. No one could probably be found to gainsay that the moral law of society has exerted a salutary influence, yet its aim is strictly altruistic, opposed to the law of the survival of the fittest, and wholly in the direction of enabling those to survive who would not survive without its protection. Finally, the last sentiment to be developed, and doubtless the highest, is so universally recognised as peculiar to man that his very name has been given to it—the sentiment of *humanity*. Yet the mode of protecting the weak arising out of this sentiment is the one that has been most seriously called in question by the naturalistic school. It must be admitted that humanitarian institutions have done far less good than either juridical or ethical institutions. The sentiment itself is of recent origin, the product only of highly developed and greatly refined mental organisation. It exists to an appreciable degree only in a minute fraction of the most enlightened populations. It is rarely directed with judgment; no fixed, self-enforcing code of conduct, as in the other cases, having had time to take shape. The institutions estahhshed to enforce it are for the most part poorly supported, badly managed, and often founded on a total misconception of human nature and of the true mode of attaining the end in view. Hence they are specially open to attack. But if ever humanitarian sentiments become diffused throughout the body politic, become the object of deep study, as have those of justice and right, it may be confidently predicted that society will prove itself capable of caring for the most unfortunate of its members in a manner that shall not work demoralisation.

In all these ways man, through his intelligence, has laboured successfully to resist the law of nature. His success is conclusively demonstrated by a comparison of his condition with that of other species of animals. No other cause can be assigned for his superiority. How can the naturalistic philosophers shut their eyes to such obvious facts? Yet, what is their attitude? They condemn all attempts to protect the weak, whether by private or public methods. They claim that it deteriorates the race by enabling the unfit to survive and transmit their inferiority. This is true only in certain cases of hereditary diseases or mental deficiencies, which should be taken account of by man because they are not by nature. Nothing is easier than to show that the unrestricted competition of nature does not secure the survival of the fittest possible, but only of the actually fittest, and in every attempt man makes to obtain something fitter than this actual fittest he succeeds, as witness improved breeds of animals and grafts of fruits. Now, the human method of protecting the weak deals in some such way with men. It not only increases the number but improves the quality.

But "government," at least, must *laisser faire*. It must not "meddle" with natural laws. The laws of trade, business, social intercourse, are natural laws, immutable and indestructible. All interference with them is vain. The fallacy here is a *non sequitur*. It may be readily granted that these laws are immutable and indestructible. Were this not the case it would certainly be hopeless to interfere with their action. But every mechanical invention proves that nothing is easier than to interfere successfully with the operation of these uniform natural forces. They have only to be first thoroughly understood and then they are easily *controlled*. To *destroy* a force is one thing, to control its action is quite another. Those who talk in this way involve themselves in the most palpable inconsistency. They must not be allowed to stop where they do. They must go on and carry their strictures to a logical conclusion. They must deny to government the right to protect its citizens from injustice. This is a clear interference with the natural laws of society. They must deny to society the right to enforce its code of morals. Nothing is more unnatural. They must suppress the healing art which keeps the sick from dying as they do among animals. Nor is this all. They must condemn all interference with physical laws and natural forces. To dam a stream must be characterised as a "vain" attempt to overcome a natural law. The wind must be left free to blow where it will, and not be forced against the fan of a wind-mill. The vapour of heated water must be allowed to float off naturally into the air and not be pent up in a steam-boiler and thence conducted into the cylinder of a steam-engine. All these things and every other device of inventive man are so many attempts to "violate" the laws of nature, which is declared impossible.

What then remains of the *laissez faire* doctrine? Nothing but this: That it is useless, and may be dangerous, to attempt to control natural forces until their character is first well understood. This is a proposition which is true for every department of force, and does not involve the surrender of the whole domain of sociology after it has been demonstrated that society is a theatre of forces.

The truth thus comes forth from a rational study of nature and human society that social progress has been due only in very slight degree to natural evolution as accomplished through the survival of the fittest, and its chief success has resulted from the reduction of competition in the struggle for existence and the protection of the weaker members. Such competition, in so far as it has been permitted to operate, has tended to lower the standard of the fittest and to check advancement. It is not, of course, claimed that the natural method has ever been fully overcome. It has always operated, and still operates, powerfully in many ways. It has been chiefly in the simpler departments of physical and mechanical phenomena that the psychic, or anthropic, method has superseded it. The inventive arts have been the result. Vital forces have yielded to some extent to the influence of mind in bringing about improved stocks of animals and vegetables, and even certain social laws have come under rational control through the establishment of institutions. Still, every step in this progress has been contested. It was not enough that the intellect was feeble and ill-fitted to grapple with such problems. It was not enough that ignorance of nature's laws should cause unnumbered failures. A still stronger barrier was presented by the intellect itself in the form of positive error embodied in philosophy. As already remarked, philosophy has always been negative and nihilistic, and has steadily antagonised the common sense of mankind. It is only quite recently that there has come into existence anything like a truly *positive* philosophy, *i.e.*, a philosophy of *action*. The intellectual power of enlightened man has at length become sufficient to grasp the problems of social life. A large body of truth has been accumulated by which to be guided in their solution. Positive error in the drawing of false conclusions from established facts is now the chief obstacle. Rational interpretation has come to prevail in all the lower departments of phenomena. It is chiefly in the complex departments of psychic and social action that error still holds sway. Nothing remains to be done but to apply the established canons of science to these higher fields of activity. Here there is still competition. Here the weaker still go to the wall. Here the strong are still the fittest to survive. Here Nature still practises her costly selection which always involves the destruction of the defenceless. The demand is for still further reduction of competition, still greater interference with the operations of natural forces, still more complete control of the laws of nature, and still more absolute supremacy of the psychic over the natural method of evolution.

These ends will be secured in proportion as the true nature of mind is understood. When nature comes to be regarded as passive and man as active, instead of the reverse as now, when human action is recognised as the most important of all forms of action, and when the power of the human intellect over vital, psychic and social phenomena is practically conceded, then, and then only, can man justly claim to have risen out of the animal and fully to have entered the human stage of development.

SAMUEL GOMPERS

Letter to Judge Peter Grosscup (1894)

Dear Sir:

I have the honor to acknowledge the receipt of your favor of the 31st ult., the contents of which I have carefully noted. Possibly I should have written you earlier, but more important matters demanded my immediate consideration. I hope, however, that you have suffered no inconvenience or pain of injustice done you by reason of this delay.

You say that I have misquoted you in my article in the *North American Review* in attributing to you the following words in your Decoration Day address at Galesburg: "The growth of labor organizations must be restrained by law." Upon closer examination you will find that I did not use the word "restrained," but "checked." However, this makes little material difference, except to show that unintentionally one man may misquote another.

The words I quoted I saw in several newspaper accounts of your address, and I am exceedingly pleased that you favor me with a printed copy of it, which I have read with much interest. In perusing that address I find that you said (page 12): "Restore to each individual by *the enforcement of law*, not simply his right but if possible a returning sense of duty to control his own personality and property. *Let us set a limit to the field of organization.*

Of course this citation from the printed address you send me does not contain the words I attributed to you, but you say in your letter that I will not find either that you used the words or that you "expressed that sentiment." To my untutored mind there may not be that grave difference which your legal learning can discern in limiting by law the field of organization and checking its growth by law.

I doubt that the thinking world will hold me chargeable of having done you a grave injustice, and I feel convinced after a perusal of your address that both in fact and in spirit you gave utterance to the sentiment I attribute to you, and which you either fail to remember or regret.

You say that, as you stated in your charge to the grand jury, you believe in labor organizations within such lawful and reasonable limits as will make them a service to the laboring man and not a menace to the lawful institutions of the country. I have had the pleasure of reading your charge to the grand jury, and have only partially been able to discover how far you believe in labor organizations.

You would certainly have no objection officially or personally to workingmen organizing, and in their meetings discuss perhaps "the origin of man," benignly smiling upon each other and declaring that all existing things are right, going to their wretched homes to find some freedom in sleep from gnawing hunger. You would have them extol the virtues of monopolists and wreckers of the people's welfare. You would not have them consider seriously the fact that more than 2 million of their fellows are unemployed, and though willing and able, cannot find the opportunity to work in order that they may sustain themselves, their wives, and their children. You

would not have them consider seriously the fact that Pullman has grown so rich from the toil of his workmen that he can riot in luxury, while he heartlessly turns these very workmen out of their tenements into the streets and leave[s] [them] to the tender mercies of corporate greed. Nor would you have them ponder upon the hundreds of other Pullmans of different names.

You know, or ought to know, that the introduction of machinery is turning into idleness thousands faster than new industries are founded, and yet, machinery certainly should not be either destroyed or hampered in its full development. The laborer is a man, he is made warm by the same sun and made cold—yes, colder—by the same winter as you are. He has a heart and brain, and feels and knows the human and paternal instinct for those depending upon him as keenly as do you.

What shall the workers do? Sit idly by and see the vast resources of nature and the human mind be utilized and monopolized for the benefit of the comparative few? No. The laborers must learn to think and act, and soon, too, that only by the power of organization and common concert of action can either their manhood be maintained, their rights to life (work to sustain it) be recognized, and liberty and rights secured.

Since you say that you favor labor organizations within certain limits, will you kindly give to thousands of your anxious fellow citizens what you believe the workers could and should do in their organizations to solve this great problem? Not what they should not do. You have told us that.

I am not one of those who regards the entire past as a failure. I recognize the progress made and the improved conditions of which nearly the entire civilized world are the beneficiaries. I ask you to explain, however, that if the wealth of the whole world is, as you say, "preeminently and beneficially the nation's wealth," how is it that thousands of able-bodied, willing, earnest men and women are suffering the pangs of hunger? We may boast of our wealth and civilization, but to the hungry man and woman and child our progress is a hollow mockery, our civilization a sham, and our "national wealth" a chimera.

You recognize that the industrial forces set in motion by steam and electricity have materially changed the structure of our civilization. You also admit that a system has grown up where the accumulations of the individual have passed from his control into that of representative combinations and trusts, and that the tendency in this direction is on the increase. How, then, can you consistently criticize the workingmen for recognizing that as individuals they can have no influence in deciding what the wages, hours of toil, and conditions of employment shall be?

You evidently have observed the growth of corporate wealth and influence. You recognize that wealth, in order to become more highly productive, is concentrated into fewer hands, and controlled by representatives and directors, and yet you sing the old siren song that the workingman should depend entirely upon his own "individual effort."

The school of laissez-faire, of which you seem to be a pronounced advocate, has produced great men in advocating the theory of each for himself and his Satanic majesty taking the hindermost, but the most pronounced advocates of your school of thought in economics have, when practically put to the test, been compelled to admit that combination and organization of the toiling masses are essential both to prevent the deterioration and to secure an improvement in the condition of the wage earners.

If, as you say, the success of commercial society depends upon the full play of competition, why do not you and your confreres turn your attention and direct the shafts of your attacks against the trusts and corporations, business wreckers and manipulators in the food products—the necessities of the people. Why garland your thoughts in beautiful phrase when speaking of these modern vampires, and steep your pen in gall when writing of the laborers' efforts to secure some of the advantages accruing from the concentrated thought and genius of the ages?

You charge that before a boy can learn a trade he must receive a permit from the union and assume obligations which the union imposes. I am sure you have read the current history of industry but superficially, or you would certainly have discovered that with the introduction of modern methods of production, the apprenticeship system has almost been entirely eliminated. Professors, the learned men concerned in the welfare of our people, insist upon a maintenance of a technical knowledge of crafts and trades. They are endeavoring to substitute manual training schools in order that the youth of our country may be supplied with a knowledge of the trades and crafts of which modern methods of production have deprived them.

For the sake of your argument, let me admit that what you may say in connection with this matter is true. I ask you whether it is not true that before a boy can properly learn your trade, is it not necessary for him to enter a term of apprenticeship? Of course, you have a more euphonious name for it, student life, I believe. Would judges permit anyone to practise law in their courts where justice is dispensed (with) unless he could produce his working card? Pardon, I mean his diploma.

One becomes enraptured in reading the beauty of your description of modern progress. Could you have had in mind the miners of Spring Valley or Pennsylvania, or the clothing workers of the sweatshops of New York or Chicago when you grandiloquently dilate,

> Who is not rich today when compared with his ancestors of a century ago? The steamboat and the railroad bring to his breakfast table the coffees of Java and Brazil, the fruits from Florida and California, and the steaks from the plains. The loom arrays him in garments and the factories furnish him with a dwelling that the richest contemporaries of his grandfather would have envied. With health and industry he is a prince.

Probably you have not read within the past year of babes dying of starvation at their mothers' breasts. More than likely the thousands of men lying upon the bare stones night after night in the City Hall of Chicago last winter escaped your notice. You may not have heard of the cry for bread that was sounded through this land of plenty by thousands of honest men and women. But should these and many other painful incidents have passed you by unnoticed, I am fearful that you may learn of them with keener thoughts with the coming sleets and blasts of winter.

You say that "labor cannot afford to attack capital." Let me remind you that labor has no quarrel with capital, as such. It is merely the possessors of capital who refuse to accord to labor the recognition, the right, the justice which is the laborers' due with whom we contend.

See what is implied by your contemptuous reference to the laborer when you ask, "Will the conqueror destroy his trophy?" Who ever heard of a conqueror marching unitedly with his *trophy*, as you would have them? But if by your comparison you mean that the conqueror is the corporation, the trust, the capitalist class, and ask then whether they would destroy their *trophy*, I would have you ask the widows and orphans of the thousands of men killed annually through the avarice of railroad corporations refusing to avail themselves of modern appliances in coupling and other improvements on their railroads.

Inquire from the thousands of women and children whose husbands or fathers were suffocated, or crushed in the mines through the rapacious greed of stockholders clamoring for more dividends. Investigate the sweating dens of the large cities. Go to the mills, factories, through the country. Visit the modern tenement houses or hovels in which thousands of workers are compelled to eke out an existence. Ask these whether the conqueror (monopoly) cares whether his trophy (the laborers) is destroyed or preserved. Ascertain from employers whether the laborer is not regarded the same as a machine, thrown out as soon as all the work possible has been squeezed out of him.

Are you aware that all the legislation ever secured for the ventilation or safety of mines, factory, or workshop is the result of the efforts of organized labor? Do you know that the trade unions were the shield for the seven-year-old children from being the conqueror's trophy until they become somewhat older? And that the reformatory laws now on the statute books protecting or defending the trophies of both sexes, young and old from the fond care of the conquerors were wrested from congresses, legislatures, and parliaments despite the Pullmans, the Jeffries, the Ricks, the Tafts, the Williams, the Woods, or the Grosscups.

By what right, sir, do you assume that the labor organizations do not conduct their affairs within lawful limits, or that they are a menace to the lawful institutions of the country? Is it because some thoughtless or overzealous member at a time of great excitement and smarting under a wrong may violate under a law or commit an improper act? Would you apply the same rule to the churches, the other moral agencies and organizations that you do to the organizations of labor? If you did, the greatest moral force of life today, the trade unions, would certainly stand out the clearest, brightest, and purest. Because a certain class (for which you and a number of your colleagues on the bench seem to be the special pleaders) have a monopoly in their lines of trade, I submit that this is no good reason for their claim to have a monopoly on true patriotism or respect for the lawful institutions of the country.

But speaking of law reminds me of the higher law of the land. The Constitution prescribes that all rights not specifically granted to the general government are reserved to the states. There is another provision prohibiting the President from sending armed forces into any state except for the purpose of maintaining "a republican form of government," and then only upon the requisition of the legislature of the state, or of the governor when the legislature is not in session. Yet when, during the recent railroad strike, the President sent the troops into Illinois, it was not in compliance with the request of the legislature of that state, nor of the governor, but in spite of his protest. Yes, even when the governor remonstrated he was practically told by the President to stop arguing the law upon the question. Pardon the simplicity of my inquiry, but does not the law require that its limits shall be observed by a president, a judge, equally as by a labor organization?

If I remember aright you based the injunctions recently issued by you upon the provisions of the Interstate Commerce Law, a law enacted by Congress upon the demand of the farmers and shippers of our country to protect them against the unjust and outrageous discriminations imposed by the railroads. Where in the law can you find one word to justify your course applying to workingmen organized and engaged in a strike?

Read the discussions in Congress when that law was under consideration. You will not find a remote reference to the application of the laws as you construe it. In fact, I am informed upon excellent authority that when the law was before the Senate in the form of a bill, Senator Morgan of Alabama, proposed an amendment which, if adopted, would have had the effect of empowering judges to issue an order of the nature you have in the recent railroad strike; but it was not adopted; it was defeated. How then in the face of this you can issue your omnibus restraining order passes the comprehension of ordinary men.

In his last report to Congress, the pastmaster general recommended the passage of a law by Congress declaring that any train in which there should be but one pouch of mail matter should be considered a mail train, thus recognizing that there was no law by which other than regular "mail trains" come under the operation of the postal laws. Hence it is not a grave stretch of the imagination to regard this latest court-made law as an invention to break the strike.

I am not versed in the law, but somewhere I read that Blackstone says that a law which is not based on justice is not law, and presumably judges who distort law so that injustice is done are not the ablest or purest devotees of the "blind goddess." I do not quote this for the purpose of converting your mind to some degree of impartiality for labor, but merely to show what a sycophantic knave Blackstone was.

Year by year man's liberties are trampled underfoot at the bidding of corporations and trusts, rights are invaded, and law perverted. In all ages, wherever a tyrant has shown himself, he has always found some willing judge to clothe that tyranny in the robes of legality, and modern capitalism has proven no exception to the rule.

You may not know that the labor movement as represented by the trades unions stand for right, for justice, for liberty. You may not imagine that the issuance of an injunction depriving men of a legal as well as a natural right to protect themselves, their wives, and little ones must fail of its purpose. Repression or oppression never yet succeeded in crushing the truth or redressing a wrong.

In conclusion let me assure you that labor will organize and more compactly than ever and upon practical lines; and despite relentless antagonism, achieve for humanity a nobler manhood, a more beautiful womanhood, and a happier childhood.

IDA B. WELLS

On Lynching (1894)

A Red Record

The student of American sociology will find the year 1894 marked by a pronounced awakening of the public conscience to a system of anarchy and outlawry which had grown during a series of ten years to be so common, that scenes of unusual brutality failed to have any visible effect upon the humane sentiments of the people of our land.

Beginning with the emancipation of the Negro, the inevitable result of unbribled power exercised for two and a half centuries, by the white man over the Negro, began to show itself in acts of conscienceless outlawry. During the slave regime, the Southern white man owned the Negro body and soul. It was to his interest to dwarf the soul and preserve the body. Vested with unlimited power over his slave, to subject him to any and all kinds of physical punishment,

the white man was still restrained from such punishment as tended to injure the slave by abating his physical powers and thereby reducing his financial worth. While slaves were scourged mercilessly, and in countless cases inhumanly treated in other respects, still the white owner rarely permitted his anger to go so far as to take a life, which would entail upon him a loss of several hundred dollars. The slave was rarely killed, he was too valuable; it was easier and quite as effective, for discipline or revenge, to sell him "Down South."

But Emancipation came and the vested interests of the white man in the Negro's body were lost. The white man had no right to scourge the emancipated Negro, still less has he a right to kill him. But the Southern white people had been educated so long in that school of practice, in which might makes right, that they disdained to draw strict lines of action in dealing with the Negro. In slave times the Negro was kept subservient and submissive by the frequency and severity of the scourging, but, with freedom, a new system of intimidation came into vogue; the Negro was not only whipped and scourged; he was killed.

Not all nor nearly all of the murders done by white men, during the past thirty years in the South, have come to light, but the statistics as gathered and preserved by white men, and which have not been questioned, show that during these years more than ten thousand Negroes have been killed in cold blood, without the formality of judicial trial and legal execution. And yet, as evidence of the absolute impunity with which the white man dares to kill a Negro, the same record shows that during all these years, and for all these murders only three white men have been tried, convicted, and executed. As no white man has been lynched for the murder of colored people, these three executions are the only instances of the death penalty being visited upon white men for murdering Negroes.

Naturally enough the commission of these crimes began to tell upon the public conscience, and the Southern white man, as a tribute to the nineteenth century civilization, was in a manner compelled to give excuses for his barbarism. His excuses have adapted themselves to the emergency, and are aptly outlined by that greatest of all Negroes, Frederick Douglass, in an article of recent date, in which he shows that there have been three distinct eras of Southern barbarism, to account for which three distinct excuses have been made.

The first excuse given to the civilized world for the murder of unoffending Negroes was the necessity of the white man to repress and stamp out alleged "race riots." For years immediately succeeding the war there was an appalling slaughter of colored people, and the wires usually conveyed to northern people and the world the intelligence, first, that an insurrection was being planned by Negroes, which, a few hours later, would prove to have been vigorously resisted by white men, and controlled with a resulting loss of several killed and wounded. It was always a remarkable feature in these insurrections and riots that only Negroes were killed during the rioting, and that all the white men escaped unharmed.

From 1865 to 1872, hundreds of colored men and women were mercilessly murdered and the almost invariable reason assigned was that they met their death by being alleged participants in an insurrection or riot. But this story at last wore itself out. No insurrection ever materialized; no Negro rioter was ever apprehended and proven guilty, and no dynamite ever recorded the black man's protest against oppression and wrong. It was too much to ask thoughtful people to believe this transparent story, and the southern white people at last made up their minds that some other excuse must be had.

Then came the second excuse, which had its birth during the turbulent times of Reconstruction. By an amendment to the Constitution the Negro was given the right of franchise, and, theoretically at least, his ballot became his invaluable emblem of citizenship. In a government "of the people, for the people, and by the people," the Negro's vote became an important factor in all matters of state and national politics. But this did not last long. The southern white man would not consider that the Negro had any right which a white man was bound to respect, and the idea of a republican form of government in the southern states grew into general contempt. It was maintained that "This is a white man's government," and regardless of numbers the white man should rule. "No Negro domination" became the new legend on the sanguinary banner of the sunny South, and under it rode the Ku Klux Klan, the Regulators, and the lawless mobs, which for any cause chose to murder one man or a dozen as suited their purpose best. It was a long, gory campaign; the blood chills and the heart almost loses faith in Christianity when one thinks of Yazoo, Hamburg, Edgefield, Copiah, and the countless massacres of defenseless Negroes, whose only crime was the attempt to exercise their right to vote.

But it was a bootless strife for colored people. The government which had made the Negro a citizen found itself unable to protect him. It gave him the right to vote, but denied him the protection which should have maintained that right. Scourged from his home; hunted through the swamps; hung by midnight raiders, and openly murdered in the light of day, the Negro clung to his right of franchise with a heroism which would have wrung admiration from the hearts of savages. He believed that in that small white ballot there was a subtle something which stood for manhood as well as citizenship, and thousands of brave black men went to their graves, exemplifying the one by dying for the other.

The white man's victory soon became complete by fraud, violence, intimidation and murder. The franchise vouchsafed to the Negro grew to be a "barren ideality," and regardless of numbers, the colored people found themselves voiceless in the councils of those whose duty it was to rule. With no longer the fear of "Negro Domination" before their eyes, the white man's second excuse became valueless. With the Southern governments all subverted and the Negro actually eliminated from all participation in state and national elections, there could be no longer an excuse for killing Negroes to prevent "Negro Domination."

Brutality still continued; Negroes were whipped, scourged, exiled, shot and hung whenever and wherever it pleased the white man so to treat them, and as the civilized world with increasing persistency held the white people of the South to account for its outlawry, the murderers invented the third excuse—that Negroes had to be killed to avenge their assaults upon women. There could be framed no possible excuse more harmful to the Negro and more unanswerable if true in its sufficiency for the white man.

Humanity abhors the assailant of womanhood, and this charge upon the Negro at once placed him beyond the pale of human sympathy. With such unanimity, earnestness and apparent candor was this charge made and reiterated that the world has accepted the story that the Negro is a monster which the Southern white man has painted him. And to-day, the Christian world feels, that while lynching is a crime, and lawlessness and anarchy the certain precursors of a nation's fall, it can not by word or deed, extend sympathy or help to a race of outlaws, who might mistake their plea for justice and deem it an excuse for their continued wrongs.

The Negro has suffered much and is willing to suffer more. He recognizes that the wrongs of two centuries can not be righted in a day, and he tries to bear his burden with patience for to-day and be hopeful for to-morrow. But there comes a time when the veriest worm will turn, and the Negro feels to-day that after all the work he has done, all the sacrifices he has made, and all the suffering he has endured, if he did not, now, defend his name and manhood from this vile accusation, he would be unworthy even of

the contempt of mankind. It is to this charge he now feels he must make answer.

If the Southern people in defense of their lawlessness, would tell the truth and admit that colored men and women are lynched for almost any offense, from murder to a misdemeanor, there would not now be the necessity for this defense. But when they intentionally, maliciously and constantly belie the record and bolster up these falsehoods by the words of legislators, preachers, governors and bishops, then the Negro must give to the world his side of the awful story.

A word as to the charge itself. In considering the third reason assigned by the Southern white people for the butchery of blacks, the question must be asked, what the white man means when he charges the black man with rape. Does he mean the crime which the statutes of the civilized states describe as such? Not by any means. With the Southern white man, any mesalliance existing between a white woman and a colored man is a sufficient foundation for the charge of rape. The Southern white man says that it is impossible for a voluntary alliance to exist between a white woman and a colored man, and therefore, the fact of an alliance is a proof of force. In numerous instances where colored men have have been lynched on the charge of rape, it was positively known at the time of lynching, and indisputably proven after the victim's death, that the relationship sustained between the man and woman was voluntary and clandestine, and that in no court of law could even the charge of assault have been successfully maintained.

It was for the assertion of this fact, in the defense of her own race, that the writer hereof became an exile; her property destroyed and her return to her home forbidden under penalty of death, for writing the following editorial which was printed in her paper, the Free Speech, in Memphis, Tenn., May 21, 1892:

"Eight Negroes lynched since last issue of the 'Free Speech' one at Little Rock, Ark., last Saturday morning where the citizens broke (?) into the penitentiary and got their man; three near Anniston, Ala., one near New Orleans; and three at Clarksville, Ga., the last three for killing a white man, and five on the same old racket—the new alarm about raping white women. The same programme of hanging, then shooting bullets into the lifeless bodies was carried out to the letter. Nobody in this section of the country believes the old threadbare lie that Negro men rape white women. If Southern white men are not careful, they will over-reach themselves and public sentiment will have a reaction; a conclusion will then be reached which will be very damaging to the moral reputation of their women."

But threats cannot suppress the truth, and while the Negro suffers the soul deformity, resultant from two and a half centuries of slavery, he is no more guilty of this vilest of all vile charges than the white man who would blacken his name.

During all the years of slavery, no such charge was ever made, not even during the dark days of the rebellion, when the white man, following the fortunes of war went to do battle, for the maintenance of slavery. While the master was away fighting to forge the fetters upon the slave, he left his wife and children with no protectors save the Negroes themselves. And yet during those years of trust and peril, no Negro proved recreant to his trust and no white man returned to a home that had been dispoiled.

Likewise during the period of alleged "insurrection," and alarming "race riots," it never occurred to the white man, that his wife and children were in danger of assault. Nor in the Reconstruction era, when the hue and cry was against "Negro Domination," was there ever a thought that the domination would ever contaminate a fireside or strike to death the virtue of womanhood. It must appear strange indeed, to every thoughtful and candid man, that more than a quarter of a century elapsed before the Negro began to show signs of such infamous degeneration.

In his remarkable apology for lynching, Bishop Haygood, of Georgia, says: "No race, not the most savage, tolerates the rape of woman, but it may be said without reflection upon any other people that the Southern people are now and always have been most sensitive concerning the honor of their women—their mothers, wives, sisters and daughters." It is not the purpose of this defense to say one word against the white women of the South. Such need not be said, but it is their misfortune that the chivalrous white men of that section, in order to escape the deserved execration of the civilized world, should shield themselves by their cowardly and infamously false excuse, and call into question that very honor about which their distinguished priestly apologist claims they are most sensitive. To justify their own barbarism they assume a chivalry which they do not possess. True chivalry respects all womanhood, and no one who reads the record, as it is written in the faces of the million mulattoes in the South, will for a minute conceive that the southern white man had a very chivalrous regard for the honor due the women of his own race or respect for the womanhood which circumstances placed in his power. That chivalry which is "most sensitive concerning the honor of women" can hope for but little respect from the civilized world, when it confines itself entirely to the women who happen to be white. Virtue knows no color line, and the chivalry which depends upon complexion of skin and texture of hair can command no honest respect.

When emancipation came to the Negroes, there arose in the northern part of the United States an almost divine sentiment among the noblest, purest and best white women of the North, who felt called to a mission to educate and Christianize the millions of southern ex-slaves. From every nook and corner of the North, brave young white women answered that call and left their cultured homes, their happy associations and their lives of ease, and with heroic determination went to the South to carry light and truth to the benighted blacks. It was a heroism no less than that which calls for volunteers for India, Africa and the Isles of the sea. To educate their unfortunate charges; to teach them the Christian virtues and to inspire in them the moral sentiments manifest in their own lives, these young women braved dangers whose record reads more like fiction than fact. They became social outlaws in the South. The peculiar sensitiveness of the southern white men for women, never shed its protecting influence about them. No friendly word from their own race cheered them in their work; no hospitable doors gave them the companionship like that from which they had come. No chivalrous white man doffed his hat in honor or respect. They were "Nigger teachers"—unpardonable offenders in the social ethics of the South, and were insulted, persecuted and ostracized, not by Negroes, but by the white manhood which boasts of its chivalry toward women.

And yet these northern women worked on, year after year, unselfishly, with a heroism which amounted almost to martyrdom. Threading their way through dense forests, working in schoolhouse, in the cabin and in the church, thrown at all times and in all places among the unfortunate and lowly Negroes, whom they had come to find and to serve, these northern women, thousands and thousands of them, have spent more than a quarter of a century in giving to the colored people their splendid lessons for home and heart and soul. Without protection, save that which innocence gives to every good woman, they went about their work, rearing no assault and suffering none. Their chivalrous protectors were hundreds of miles away in their northern homes, and yet they never feared any "great dark faced mobs," they dared night or day to "go beyond their own roof trees." They never complained of assaults, and no mob was ever called into existence to avenge crimes against them. Before the world adjudges the Negro a moral monster, a vicious assailant of womanhood and a menace to the sacred precincts of home, the colored people ask the consideration of the silent record of gratitude, respect, protection and devotion of the millions of the race in the South, to the thousands of northern white women who have served as teachers and missionaries since the war.

The Negro may not have known what chivalry was, but he knew enough to preserve inviolate the womanhood of the South which was entrusted to his hands during the war. The finer sensibilities of his soul may have been crushed out by years of slavery, but his heart was full of gratitude to the white women of the North, who blessed his home and inspired his soul in all these years of freedom. Faithful to his trust in both of these instances, he should now have the impartial ear of the civilized world, when he dares to speak for himself as against the infamy wherewith he stands charged.

It is his regret, that, in his own defense, he must disclose to the world that degree of dehumanizing brutality which fixes upon America the blot of a national crime. Whatever faults and failings other nations may have in their dealings with their own subjects or with other people, no other civilized nation stands condemned before the world with a series of crimes so peculiarly national. It becomes a painful duty of the Negro to reproduce a record which shows that a large portion of the American people avow anarchy, condone murder and defy the contempt of civilization.

These pages are written in no spirit of vindictiveness, for all who give the subject consideration must concede that far too serious is the condition of that civilized government in which the spirit of unrestrained outlawry constantly increases in violence, and casts its blight over a continually growing area of territory. We plead not for the colored people alone, but for all victims of the terrible injustice which puts men and women to death without form of law. During the year 1894, there were 132 persons executed in the United States by due form of law, while in the same year, 197 persons were put to death by mobs who gave the victims no opportunity to make a lawful defense. No comment need be made upon a condition of public sentiment responsible for such alarming results.

The purpose of the pages which follow shall be to give the record which has been made, not by colored men, but that which is the result of compilations made by white men, of reports sent over the civilized world by white men in the South. Out of their own mouths shall the murderers be condemned. For a number of years the Chicago Tribune, admittedly one of the leading journals of America, has made a specialty of the compilation of statistics touching upon lynching. The data compiled by that journal and published to the world January 1st, 1894, up to the present time has not been disputed. In order to be safe from the charge of exaggeration, the incidents hereinafter reported have been confined to those vouched for by the Tribune.

Examples of Lynchings

Burned at the Stake

Arriving here at 12 o'clock the train was met by a surging mass of humanity 10,000 strong. The Negro was placed upon a carnival float in mockery of a king upon his throne, and, followed by an immense crowd, was escorted through the city so that all might see the most inhuman monster known in current history. The line of march was up Main street to the square, around the square down Clarksville street to Church street, thence to the open prairies about 300 yards from the Texas & Pacific depot. Here Smith was placed upon a scaffold, six feet square and ten feet high, securely bound, within the view of all beholders. Here the victim was tortured for fifty minutes by red-hot iron brands thrust against his quivering body. Commencing at the feet the brands were placed against him inch by inch until they were thrust against the face. Then, being apparently dead, kerosene was poured upon him, cottonseed hulls placed beneath him and set on fire. In less time than it takes to relate it, the tortured man was wafted beyond the grave to another fire, hotter and more terrible than the one just experienced.

Curiosity seekers have carried away already all that was left of the memorable event, even to pieces of charcoal. The cause of the crime was that Henry Vance when a deputy policeman, in the course of his duty was called to arrest Henry Smith for being drunk and disorderly. The Negro was unruly, and Vance was forced to use his club. The Negro swore vengeance, and several times assaulted Vance. In his greed for revenge, last Thursday, he grabbed up the little girl and committed the crime. The father is prostrated with grief and the mother now lies at death's door, but she has lived to see the slayer of her innocent babe suffer the most horrible death that could be conceived.

Torture beyond Description

Words to describe the awful torture inflicted upon Smith cannot be found. The Negro, for a long time after starting on the journey to Paris, did not realize his plight. At last when he was told that he must die by slow torture he begged for protection. His agony was awful. He pleaded and writhed in bodily and mental pain. Scarcely had the train reached Paris than this torture commenced. His clothes were torn off piecemeal and scattered in the crowd, people catching the shreds and putting them away as mementos. The child's father, her brother, and two uncles then gathered about the Negro as he lay fastened to the torture platform and thrust hot irons into his quivering flesh. It was horrible—the man dying by slow torture in the midst of smoke from his own burning flesh. Every groan from the fiend, every contortion of his body was cheered by the thickly packed crowd of 10,000 persons. The mass of beings 600 yards in diameter, the scaffold being the center. After burning the feet and legs, the hot irons—plenty of

fresh ones being at hand—were rolled up and down Smith's stomach, back, and arms. Then the eyes were burned out and irons were thrust down his throat.

The men of the Vance family having wreaked vengeance, the crowd piled all kinds of combustible stuff around the scaffold, poured oil on it and set it afire. The Negro rolled and tossed out of the mass, only to be pushed back by the people nearest him. He tossed out again, and was roped and pulled back. Hundreds of people turned away, but the vast crowd still looked calmly on. People were here from every part of this section. They came from Dallas, Fort Worth, Sherman, Denison, Bonbam, Texarkana, Fort Smith, Ark., and a party of fifteen came from Hempstead county, Arkansas, where he was captured. Every train that came in was loaded to its utmost capacity, and there were demands at many points for special trains to bring the people here to see the unparalleled punishment for an unparalleled crime. When the news of the burning went over the country like wildfire, at every country town anvils boomed forth the announcement.

Lynched Because the Jury Acquitted Him

The entire system of the judiciary of this country is in the hands of white people. To this add the fact of the inherent prejudice against colored people, and it will be clearly seen that a white jury is certain to find a Negro prisoner guilty if there is the least evidence to warrant such a finding.

Meredith Lewis was arrested in Roseland, La., in July of last year. A white jury found him not guilty of the crime of murder wherewith he stood charged. This did not suit the mob. A few nights after the verdict was rendered, and he declared to be innocent, a mob gathered in his vicinity and went to his house. He was called, and suspecting nothing, went outside. He was seized and hurried off to a convenient spot and hanged by the neck until he was dead for the murder of a woman of which the jury had said he was innocent.

[. . .] [T]he finding of the dead body of a Negro, suspended, between heaven and earth to the limb of a tree, is of so slight importance that neither the civil authorities nor press agencies consider the matter worth investigating. July 21st, in Shelby county, Tenn., a colored man by the name of Charles Martin was lynched. July 30th, at Paris, Mo., a colored man named William Steen shared the same fate. December 28th, Mack Segars was announced to have been lynched at Brantley, Alabama. August 31st, at Yarborough, Texas, and on September 19th, at Houston, a colored man was found lynched, but so little attention was paid to the matter that not only was no record made as to why these last two men were lynched, but even their names were not given. The dispatches simply stated that an unknown Negro was found lynched in each case.

There are friends of humanity who feel their souls shrink from any compromise with murder, but whose deep and abiding reverence for womanhood causes them to hesitate in giving their support to this crusade against Lynch Law, out of fear that they may encourage the miscreants whose deeds are worse than murder. But to these friends it must appear certain that these five men could not have been guilty of any terrible crime. They were simply lynched by parties of men who had it in their power to kill them, and who chose to avenge some fancied wrong by murder, rather than submit their grievances to court.

Lynched Because They Were Saucy

At Moberly, Mo., February 18th and at Fort Madison, S.C., June 2d, both in 1892, a record was made in the line of lynching which should certainly appeal to every humanitarian who has any regard for the sacredness of human life. John Hughes, of Moberly, and Isaac Lincoln, of Fort Madison, and Will Lewis in Tullahoma, Tenn., suffered death for no more serious charge than that they "were saucy to white people." In the days of slavery it was held to be a very serious matter for a colored person to fail to yield the sidewalk at the demand of a white person, and it will not be surprising to find some evidence of this intolerance existing in the days of freedom. But the most that could be expected as a penalty for acting or speaking saucily to a white person would be a slight physical chastisement to make the Negro "know his place" or an arrest and fine. But Missouri, Tennessee and South Carolina chose to make precedents in their cases and as a result both men, after being charged with their offense and apprehended, were

taken by a mob and lynched. The civil authorities, who in either case would have been very quick to satisfy the aggrieved white people had they complained and brought the prisoners to court, by imposing proper penalty upon them, did not feel it their duty to make any investigation after the Negroes were killed. They were dead and out of the way and as no one would be called upon to render an account for their taking off, the matter was dismissed from the public mind.

The Remedy

It is a well established principle of law that every wrong has a remedy. Herein rests our respect for law. The Negro does not claim that all of the one thousand black men, women and children, who have been hanged, shot and burned alive during the past ten years, were innocent of the charges made against them. We have associated too long with the white man not to have copied his vices as well as his virtues. But we do insist that the punishment is not the same for both classes of criminals. In lynching, opportunity is not given the Negro to defend himself against the unsupported accusations of white men and women. The word of the accuser is held to be true and the excited bloodthirsty mob demands that the rule of law be reversed and instead of proving the accused to be guilty, the victim of their hate and revenge must prove himself innocent. No evidence he can offer will satisfy the mob; he is bound hand and foot and swung into eternity. Then to excuse its infamy, the mob almost invariably reports the monstrous falsehood that its victim made a full confession before he was hanged.

With all military, legal and political power in their hands, only two of the lynching States have attempted a check by exercising the power which is theirs. Mayor Trout, of Roanoke, Virginia, called out the militia in 1893, to protect a Negro prisoner, and in so doing nine men were killed and a number wounded. Then the mayor and militia withdrew, left the Negro to his fate and he was promptly lynched. The business men realized the blow to the town's were given light sentences, the highest being one of twelve financial interests, called the mayor home, the grand jury indicted and prosecuted the ringleaders of the mob. They months in State prison. The day he arrived at the penitentiary, he was pardoned by the governor of the State.

The only other real attempt made by the authorities to protect a prisoner of the law, and which was more successful, was that of Gov. McKinley, of Ohio, who sent the militia to Washington Courthouse, O., in October, 1894, and five men were killed and twenty wounded in maintaining the principle that the law must be upheld.

In South Carolina, in April, 1893, Gov. Tillman aided the mob by yielding up to be killed, a prisoner of the law, who had voluntarily placed himself under the Governor's protection. Public sentiment by its representatives has encouraged Lynch Law, and upon the revolution of this sentiment we must depend for its abolition.

Therefore, we demand a fair trial by law for those accused of crime, and punishment by law after honest conviction. No maudlin sympathy for criminals is solicited, but we do ask that the law shall punish all alike. We earnestly desire those that control the forces which make public sentiment to join with us in the demand. Surely the humanitarian spirit of this country which reaches out to denounce the treatment of the Russian Jews, the Armenian Christians, the laboring poor of Europe, the Siberian exiles and the native women of India—will no longer refuse to lift its voice on this subject. If it were known that the cannibals or the savage Indians had burned three human beings alive in the past two years, the whole of Christendom would be roused, to devise ways and means to put a stop to it. Can you remain silent and inactive when such things are done in our own community and country? Is your duty to humanity in the United States less binding?

What can you do, reader, to prevent lynching, to thwart anarchy and promote law and order throughout our land?

1st. You can help disseminate the facts contained in this book by bringing them to the knowledge of every one with whom you come in contact, to the end that public sentiment may be revolutionized. Let the facts speak for themselves, with you as a medium.

2d. You can be instrumental in having churches, missionary societies, Y. M. C. A.'s, W. C. T. U.'s and all Christian and moral forces in connection with your religious and social life, pass resolutions of condemnation and protest every time a lynching takes place; and see that they are sent to the place where these outrages occur.

3d. Bring to the intelligent consideration of Southern people the refusal of capital to invest where lawlessness and mob violence hold sway. Many labor organizations have declared by resolution that they would avoid lynch infested localities as they would the pestilence when seeking new homes. If the South wishes to build up its waste places quickly, there is no better way than to uphold the majesty of the law by enforcing obedience to the same, and meting out the same punishment to all classes of criminals, white as well as black. "Equality before the law," must become a fact as well as a theory before America is truly the "land of the free and the home of the brave."

4th. Think and act on independent lines in this behalf, remembering that after all, it is the white man's civilization and the white man's government which are on trial. This crusade will determine whether that civilization can maintain itself by itself, or whether anarchy shall prevail; whether this Nation shall write itself down a success at self government, or in deepest humiliation admit its failure complete; whether the precepts and theories of Christianity are professed and practiced by American white people as Golden Rules of thought and action, or adopted as a system of morals to be preached to heathen until they attain to the intelligence which needs the system of Lynch Law.

5th. Congressman Blair offered a resolution in the House of Representatives, August, 1894. The organized life of the country can speedily make this a law by sending resolutions to Congress indorsing Mr. Blair's bill and asking Congress to create the commission. In no better way can the question be settled, and the Negro does not fear the issue. The following is the resolution:

"Resolved, By the House of Representatives and Senate in congress assembled. That the committee on labor be instructed to investigate and report the number, location and date of all alleged assaults by males upon females throughout the country during the ten years last preceding the passing of this joint resolution, for or on account of which organized but unlawful violence has been inflicted or attempted to be inflicted. Also to ascertain and report all facts of organized but unlawful violence to the person, with the attendant facts and circumstances, which have been inflicted upon accused persons alleged to have been guilty of crimes punishable by due process of law which have taken place in any part of the country within the ten years last preceding the passage of this resolution. Such investigation shall be made by the usual methods and agencies of the Department of Labor, and report made to Congress as soon as the work can be satisfactorily done, and the sum of $25,000, or so much thereof as may be necessary, is hereby appropriated to pay the expenses out of any money in the treasury not otherwise appropriated."

The belief has been constantly expressed in England that in the United States, which has produced Wm. Lloyd Garrison, Henry Ward Beecher, James Russell Lowell, John G. Whittier and Abraham Lincoln there must be those of their descendants who would take hold of the work of inaugurating an era of law and order. The colored people of this country who have been loyal to the flag believe the same, and strong in that belief have begun this crusade. To those who still feel they have no obligation in the matter, we commend the following lines of Lowell on "Freedom."

Men! whose boast it is that ye
Come of fathers brave and free,
If there breathe on earth a slave
Are ye truly free and brave?

If ye do not feel the chain,
When it works a brother's pain,
Are ye not base slaves indeed.
Slaves unworthy to be freed?

Women! who shall one day bear
Sons to breathe New England air,
If ye hear without a blush,
Deeds to make the roused blood rush
Like red lava through your veins,
For your sisters now in chains,—
Answer! are ye fit to be
Mothers of the brave and free?

Is true freedom but to break
Fetters for our own dear sake,
And, with leathern hearts, forget
That we owe mankind a debt?
No! true freedom is to share
All the chains our brothers wear,
And, with heart and hand, to be
Earnest to make others free!

There are slaves who fear to speak
For the fallen and the weak;
They are slaves who will not choose
Hatred, scoffing, and abuse.
Rather than in silence shrink
From the truth they needs must think;
They are slaves who dare not be
In the right with two or three.

BOOKER T. WASHINGTON

Atlanta Exposition Address (1895)

→ post 13th Am.

A ship lost at sea for many days suddenly sighted a friendly vessel. From the mast of the unfortunate vessel was seen a signal, "Water, water; we die of thirst!" The answer from the friendly vessel at once came back, "Cast down your bucket where you are." A second time the signal, "Water, water; send us water!" ran up from the distressed vessel, and was answered, "Cast down your bucket where you are." And a third and fourth signal for water was answered, "Cast down your bucket where you are." The captain of the distressed vessel, at last heeding the injunction, cast down his bucket, and it came up full of fresh, sparkling water from the mouth of the Amazon River. To those of my race who depend on bettering their condition in a foreign land or who underestimate the importance of cultivating friendly relations with the Southern white man, who is their next door neighbour, I would say: "Cast down your bucket where you are"—cast it down in making friends in every manly way of the people of all races by whom we are surrounded.

Cast it down in agriculture, mechanics, in commerce, in domestic service, and in the professions. And in this connection it is well to bear in mind that whatever other sins the South may be called to bear, when it comes to business, pure and simple, it is in the South that the Negro is given a man's chance in the commercial world, and in nothing is this Exposition more eloquent than in emphasizing this chance. Our greatest danger is that in the great leap from slavery to freedom we may overlook the fact that the masses of us are to live by the productions of our hands, and fail to keep in mind that we shall prosper in proportion as we learn to dignify and glorify common labour, and put brains and skill into the common occupations of life; shall prosper in proportion as we learn to draw the line between the superficial and the substantial, the ornamental gewgaws of life and the useful. No race can prosper till it learns that there is as much dignity in tilling a field as in writing a poem. It is at the bottom of life we must begin, and not at the top. Nor should we permit our grievances to overshadow our opportunities.

To those of the white race who look to the incoming of those of foreign birth and strange tongue and habits for the prosperity of the South, were I permitted I would repeat what I say to my own race, "Cast down your bucket where you are." Cast it down among the eight millions of Negroes whose habits you know, whose fidelity and love you have tested in days when to have proved treacherous meant the ruin of your firesides. Cast down your bucket among these people who have, without strikes and labour wars, tilled your fields, cleared your forests, builded your railroads and cities, and brought forth treasures from the bowels of the earth, and helped make possible this magnificent representation of the progress of the South. Casting down your bucket among my people, helping and encouraging them as you are doing on these grounds, and to education of head, hand, and heart, you will find that they will buy your surplus land, make blossom the waste places in your fields, and run your factories. While doing this, you can be sure in the future, as in the past, that you and your families will be surrounded by the most patient, faithful, law-abiding, and unresentful people that the

world has seen. As we have proved our loyalty to you in the past, in nursing your children, watching by the sick-bed of your mothers and fathers, and often following them with tear-dimmed eyes to their graves, so in the future, in our humble way, we shall stand by you with a devotion that no foreigner can approach, ready to lay down our lives, if need be, in defense of yours, interlacing our industrial, commercial, civil, and religious life with yours in a way that shall make the interests of both races one. In all things that are purely social we can be as separate as the fingers, yet one as the hand in all things essential to mutual progress.

There is no defense or security for any of us except in the highest intelligence and development of all. If anywhere there are efforts tending to curtail the fullest growth of the Negro, let these efforts be turned into stimulating, encouraging, and making him the most useful and intelligent citizen. Effort or means so invested will pay a thousand per cent interest. These efforts will be twice blessed—"blessing him that gives and him that takes." There is no escape through law of man or God from the inevitable: *economic*

The laws of changeless justice bind
   Oppressor with oppressed;
And close as sin and suffering joined
   We march to fate abreast.

Nearly sixteen millions of hands will aid you in pulling the load upward, or they will pull against you the load downward. We shall constitute one-third and more of the ignorance and crime of the South, or one-third its intelligence and progress; we shall contribute one-third to the business and industrial prosperity of the South, or we shall prove a veritable body of death, stagnating, depressing, retarding every effort to advance the body politic. *alternatives*

In conclusion, may I repeat that nothing in thirty years has given us more hope and encouragement, and drawn us so near to you of the white race, as this opportunity offered by the Exposition; and here bending, as it were, over the altar that represents the results of the struggles of your race and mine, both starting practically empty-handed three decades ago, I pledge that in your effort to work out the great and intricate problem which God has laid at the doors of the South, you shall have at all times the patient, sympathetic help of my race; only let this be constantly in mind, that, while from representations in these buildings of the product of field, of forest, of mine, of factory, letters, and art, much good will come, yet far above and beyond material benefits will be that higher good, that, let us pray God, will come, in a blotting out of sectional differences and racial animosities and suspicions, in a determination to administer absolute justice, in a willing obedience among all classes to the mandates of law. This, coupled with our material prosperity, will bring into our beloved South a new heaven and a new earth.

W. E. B. Du Bois

The Souls of Black Folk (1903)

Of Mr. Booker T. Washington and Others

From birth till death enslaved; in word, in deed, unmanned!
. . . .
Hereditary bondsmen! Know ye not
Who would be free themselves must strike the blow?　　　　　　　Byron.

Easily the most striking thing in the history of the American Negro since 1876 is the ascendancy of Mr. Booker T. Washington. It began at the time when war memories and ideals were rapidly passing; a day of astonishing commercial development was dawning; a sense of doubt and hesitation overtook the freedmen's sons,—then it was that his leading began.

Mr. Washington came, with a simple definite programme, at the psychological moment when the nation was a little ashamed of having bestowed so much sentiment on Negroes, and was concentrating its energies on Dollars. His programme of industrial education, conciliation of the South, and submission and silence as to civil and political rights, was not wholly original; the Free Negroes from 1830 up to wartime had striven to build industrial schools,—and the American Missionary Association had from the first taught various trades; and Price and others had sought a way of honorable alliance with the best of the Southerners. But Mr. Washington first indissolubly linked these things; he put enthusiasm, unlimited energy, and perfect faith into this programme, and changed it from a by-path into a veritable Way of Life. And the tale of the methods by which he did this is a fascinating study of human life.

It startled the nation to hear a Negro advocating such a programme after many decades of bitter complaint; it startled and won the applause of the South, it interested and won the admiration of the North; and after a confused murmur of protest, it silenced if it did not convert the Negroes themselves.

To gain the sympathy and cooperation of the various elements comprising the white South was Mr. Washington's first task; and this, at the time Tuskegee was founded, seemed, for a black man, well-nigh impossible. And yet ten years later it was done in the word spoken at Atlanta: "In all things purely social we can be as separate as the five fingers,

---

1.　[In his introduction to *The Souls of Black Folk*, Du Bois explains, "Before each chapter, as now printed, stands a bar of the Sorrow Songs,—some echo of haunting melody from the only American music which welled up from black souls in the dark past."]

and yet one as the hand in all things essential to mutual progress." This "Atlanta Compromise" is by all odds the most notable thing in Mr. Washington's career. The South interpreted it in different ways: the radicals received it as a complete surrender of the demand for civil and political equality; the conservatives, as a generously conceived working basis for mutual understanding. So both approved it, and to-day its author is certainly the most distinguished Southerner since Jefferson Davis, and the one with the largest personal following.

Next to this achievement comes Mr. Washington's work in gaining place and consideration in the North. Others less shrewd and tactful had formerly essayed to sit on these two stools and had fallen between them; but as Mr. Washington knew the heart of the South from birth and training, so by singular insight he intuitively grasped the spirit of the age which was dominating the North. And so thoroughly did he learn the speech and thought of triumphant commercialism, and the ideals of material prosperity, that the picture of a lone black boy poring over a French grammar amid the weeds and dirt of a neglected home soon seemed to him the acme of absurdities. One wonders what Socrates and St. Francis of Assisi would say to this.

And yet this very singleness of vision and thorough oneness with his age is a mark of the successful man. It is as though Nature must needs make men narrow in order to give them force. So Mr. Washington's cult has gained unquestioning followers, his work has wonderfully prospered, his friends are legion, and his enemies are confounded. To-day he stands as the one recognized spokesman of his ten million fellows, and one of the most notable figures in a nation of seventy millions. One hesitates, therefore, to criticize a life which, beginning with so little, has done so much. And yet the time is come when one may speak in all sincerity and utter courtesy of the mistakes and shortcomings of Mr. Washington's career, as well as of his triumphs, without being thought captious or envious, and without forgetting that it is easier to do ill than well in the world.

The criticism that has hitherto met Mr. Washington has not always been of this broad character. In the South especially has he had to walk warily to avoid the harshest judgments,—and naturally so, for he is dealing with the one subject of deepest sensitiveness to that section. Twice—once when at the Chicago celebration of the Spanish-American War he alluded to the color-prejudice that is "eating away the vitals of the South," and once when he dined with President Roosevelt—has the resulting Southern criticism been violent enough to threaten seriously his popularity. In the North the feeling has several times forced itself into words, that Mr. Washington's counsels of submission overlooked certain elements of true manhood, and that his educational programme was unnecessarily narrow. Usually, however, such criticism has not found open expression, although, too, the spiritual sons of the Abolitionists have not been prepared to acknowledge that the schools founded before Tuskegee, by men of broad ideals and self-sacrificing spirit, were wholly failures or worthy of ridicule. While, then, criticism has not failed to follow Mr. Washington, yet the prevailing public opinion of the land has been but too willing to deliver the solution of a wearisome problem into his hands, and say, "If that is all you and your race ask, take it."

Among his own people, however, Mr. Washington has encountered the strongest and most lasting opposition, amounting at times to bitterness, and even to-day continuing strong and insistent even though largely silenced in outward expression by the public opinion of the nation. Some of this opposition is, of course, mere envy; the disappointment of displaced demagogues and the spite of narrow minds. But aside from this, there is among educated and thoughtful colored men in all parts of the land a feeling of deep regret, sorrow, and apprehension at the wide currency and ascendancy which some of Mr. Washington's theories have gained. These same men admire his sincerity of purpose, and are willing to forgive much to honest endeavor which is doing something worth the doing. They cooperate with Mr. Washington as far as they conscientiously can; and, indeed, it is no ordinary tribute to this man's tact and power that, steering as he must between so many diverse interests and opinions, he so largely retains the respect of all.

But the hushing of the criticism of honest opponents is a dangerous thing. It leads some of the best of the critics to unfortunate silence and paralysis of effort, and others to burst into speech so passionately and intemperately as to lose listeners. Honest and earnest criticism from those whose interests are most nearly touched,—criticism of writers by readers, of government by those governed, of leaders by those led,—this is the soul of democracy and the safeguard of modern society. If the best of the American Negroes receive by outer pressure a leader whom they had not recognized before, manifestly there is here a certain palpable gain. Yet there is also irreparable loss,—a loss of that peculiarly valuable education which a group receives when by search and criticism it finds and commissions its own leaders. The way in which this is done is at once the most elementary and the nicest problem of social growth. History is but the record of such group-leadership; and yet how infinitely changeful is its type and character! And of all types and kinds, what can be more instructive than the leadership of a group within a group?—that curious double movement where real progress may be negative and actual advance be relative retrogression. All this is the social student's inspiration and despair.

Now in the past the American Negro has had instructive experience in the choosing of group leaders, founding thus a peculiar dynasty which in the light of present conditions is worth while studying. When sticks and stones and beasts form the sole environment of a people, their attitude is largely one of determined opposition to and conquest of natural forces. But when to earth and brute is added an environment of men and ideas, then the attitude of the imprisoned group may take three main forms,—a feeling of revolt and revenge; an attempt to adjust all thought and action to the will of the greater group; or, finally, a determined effort at self-realization and self-development despite environing opinion. The influence of all of these attitudes at various times can be traced in the history of the American Negro, and in the evolution of his successive leaders.

Before 1750, while the fire of African freedom still burned in the veins of the slaves, there was in all leadership or attempted leadership but the one motive of revolt and revenge,—typified in the terrible Maroons, the Danish blacks, and Cato of Stono, and veiling all the Americas in fear of insurrection. The liberalizing tendencies of the latter half of the eighteenth century brought, along with kindlier relations between black and white, thoughts of ultimate adjustment and assimilation. Such aspiration was especially voiced in the earnest songs of Phyllis, in the martyrdom of Attucks, the fighting of Salem and Poor, the intellectual accomplishments of Banneker and Derham, and the political demands of the Cuffes.

Stern financial and social stress after the war cooled much of the previous humanitarian ardor. The disappointment and impatience of the Negroes at the persistence of slavery and serfdom voiced itself in two movements. The slaves in the South, aroused undoubtedly by vague rumors of the Haitian revolt, made three fierce attempts at insurrection,—in 1800 under Gabriel in Virginia, in 1822 under Vesey in Carolina, and in 1831 again in Virginia under the terrible Nat Turner. In the Free States, on the other hand, a new and curious attempt at self-development was made. In Philadelphia and New York color-prescription led to a withdrawal of Negro communicants from white churches and the formation of a peculiar socio-religious institution among the Negroes known as the African Church,—an organization still living and controlling in its various branches over a million of men.

Walker's wild appeal against the trend of the times showed how the world was changing after the coming of the cotton-gin. By 1830 slavery seemed hopelessly fastened on the South, and the slaves thoroughly cowed into submission. The free Negroes of the North, inspired by the mulatto immigrants from the West Indies, began to change the basis of their demands; they recognized the slavery of slaves, but insisted that they themselves were freemen, and sought assimilation and amalgamation with the nation on the same terms with other men. Thus, Forten and Purvis of Philadelphia, Shad of Wilmington, Du Bois of New Haven, Barbadoes of Boston, and others, strove singly and together as men, they said, not as slaves; as "people of color," not as "Negroes." The trend of the times, however, refused them recognition save in individual and exceptional cases, considered them as one with all the despised blacks, and they soon found themselves striving to keep even the rights they formerly had of voting and working and moving as freemen. Schemes of migration and colonization arose among them; but these they refused to entertain, and they eventually turned to the Abolition movement as a final refuge.

Here, led by Remond, Nell, Wells-Brown, and Douglass, a new period of self-assertion and self-development dawned. To be sure, ultimate freedom and assimilation was the ideal before the leaders, but the assertion of the manhood rights of the Negro by himself was the main reliance, and John Brown's raid was the extreme of its logic. After the war and emancipation, the great form of Frederick Douglass, the greatest of American Negro leaders, still led the host. Self-assertion, especially in political lines, was the main programme, and behind Douglass came Elliot, Bruce, and Langston, and the Reconstruction politicians, and, less conspicuous but of greater social significance, Alexander Crummell and Bishop Daniel Payne.

Then came the Revolution of 1876, the suppression of the Negro votes, the changing and shifting of ideals, and the seeking of new lights in the great night. Douglass, in his old age, still bravely stood for the ideals of his early manhood,—ultimate assimilation *through* self-assertion, and on no other terms. For a time Price arose as a new leader, destined, it seemed, not to give up, but to re-state the old ideals in a form less repugnant to the white South. But he passed away in his prime. Then came the new leader. Nearly all the former ones had become leaders by the silent suffrage of their fellows, had sought to lead their own people alone, and were usually, save Douglass, little known outside their race. But Booker T. Washington arose as essentially the leader not of one race but of two,—a compromiser between the South, the North, and the Negro. Naturally the Negroes resented, at first bitterly, signs of compromise which surrendered their civil and political rights, even though this was to be exchanged for larger chances of economic development. The rich and dominating North, however, was not only weary of the race problem, but was investing largely in Southern enterprises, and welcomed any method of peaceful cooperation. Thus, by national opinion, the Negroes began to recognize Mr. Washington's leadership; and the voice of criticism was hushed.

Mr. Washington represents in Negro thought the old attitude of adjustment and submission; but adjustment at such a peculiar time as to make his programme unique. This is an age of unusual economic development, and Mr. Washington's programme naturally takes an economic cast, becoming a gospel of Work and Money to such an extent as apparently almost completely to overshadow the higher aims of life. Moreover, this is an age when the more advanced races are coming in closer contact with the less developed races, and the race-feeling is therefore intensified; and Mr. Washington's programme practically accepts the alleged inferiority of the Negro races. Again, in our own land, the reaction from the sentiment of war time has given impetus to race-prejudice against Negroes, and Mr. Washington withdraws many of the high demands of Negroes as men and American citizens. In other periods of intensified prejudice all the Negro's tendency to self-assertion has been called forth; at this period a policy of submission is advocated. In the history of nearly all other races and peoples the doctrine preached at such crises has been that manly self-respect is worth more than lands and houses, and that a people who voluntarily surrender such respect, or cease striving for it, are not worth civilizing.

In answer to this, it has been claimed that the Negro can survive only through submission. Mr. Washington distinctly asks that black people give up, at least for the present, three things,—

First, political power,

Second, insistence on civil rights,

Third, higher education of Negro youth,—and concentrate all their energies on industrial education, the accumulation of wealth, and the conciliation of the South. This policy has been courageously and insistently advocated for over fifteen years, and has been triumphant for perhaps ten years. As a result of this tender of the palm-branch, what has been the return? In these years there have occurred:

1. The disfranchisement of the Negro.
2. The legal creation of a distinct status of civil inferiority for the Negro.
3. The steady withdrawal of aid from institutions for the higher training of the Negro.

These movements are not, to be sure, direct results of Mr. Washington's teachings; but his propaganda has, without a shadow of doubt, helped their speedier accomplishment. The question then comes: Is it possible, and probable, that nine millions of men can make effective progress in economic lines if they are deprived of political rights, made a servile caste, and allowed only the most meagre chance for developing their exceptional men? If history and reason give any distinct answer to these questions, it is an emphatic *No*. And Mr. Washington thus faces the triple paradox of his career:

1. He is striving nobly to make Negro artisans business men and property-owners; but it is utterly impossible, under modern competitive methods, for workingmen and property-owners to defend their rights and exist without the right of suffrage.

2. He insists on thrift and self-respect, but at the same time counsels a silent submission to civic inferiority such as is bound to sap the manhood of any race in the long run.

3. He advocates common-school and industrial training, and depreciates institutions of higher learning; but neither the Negro common-schools, nor Tuskegee itself, could remain open a day were it not for teachers trained in Negro colleges, or trained by their graduates.

This triple paradox in Mr. Washington's position is the object of criticism by two classes of colored Americans. One class is spiritually descended from Toussaint the Savior, through Gabriel, Vesey, and Turner, and they represent the attitude of revolt and revenge; they hate the white South blindly and distrust the white race generally, and so far as they agree on definite action, think that the Negro's only hope lies in emigration beyond the borders of the United States. And yet, by the irony of fate, nothing has more effectually made this programme seem hopeless than the recent course of the United States toward weaker and darker peoples in the West Indies, Hawaii, and the Philippines,—for where in the world may we go and be safe from lying and brute force?

The other class of Negroes who cannot agree with Mr. Washington has hitherto said little aloud. They deprecate the sight of scattered counsels, of internal disagreement; and especially they dislike making their just criticism of a useful and earnest man an excuse for a general discharge of venom from small-minded opponents. Nevertheless, the questions involved are so fundamental and serious that it is difficult to see how men like the Grimkes, Kelly Miller, J. W. E. Bowen, and other representatives of this group, can much longer be silent. Such men feel in conscience bound to ask of this nation three things:

1. The right to vote.
2. Civic equality.
3. The education of youth according to ability.

They acknowledge Mr. Washington's invaluable service in counselling patience and courtesy in such demands; they do not ask that ignorant black men vote when ignorant whites are debarred, or that any reasonable restrictions in the suffrage should not be applied; they know that the low social level of the mass of the race is responsible for much discrimination against it, but they also know, and the nation knows, that relentless color-prejudice is more often a cause than a result of the Negro's degradation; they seek the abatement of this relic of barbarism, and not its systematic encouragement and pampering by all agencies of social power from the Associated Press to the Church of Christ. They advocate, with Mr. Washington, a broad system of Negro common schools supplemented by thorough industrial training; but they are surprised that a man of Mr. Washington's insight cannot see that no such educational system ever has rested or can rest on any other basis than that of the well-equipped college and university, and they insist that there is a demand for a few such institutions throughout the south to train the best of the Negro youth as teachers, professional men, and leaders.

This group of men honor Mr. Washington for his attitude of conciliation toward the white South; they accept the "Atlanta Compromise" in its broadest interpretation; they recognize, with him, many signs of promise, many men of high purpose and fair judgment, in this section; they know that no easy task has been laid upon a region already tottering under heavy burdens. But, nevertheless, they insist that the way to truth and right lies in straightforward honesty, not in indiscriminate flattery; in praising those of the South who do well and criticizing uncompromisingly those who do ill; in taking advantage of the opportunities at hand and urging their fellows to do the same, but at the same time in remembering that only a firm adherence to their higher ideals and aspirations will ever keep those ideals within the realm of possibility. They do not expect that the free right to vote, to enjoy civic rights, and to be educated, will come in a moment; they do not expect to see the bias and prejudices of years disappear at the blast of a trumpet; but they are absolutely certain that the way for a people to gain their reasonable rights is not by voluntarily throwing them away and insisting that they do not want them; that the way for a people to gain respect is not by continually belittling and ridiculing themselves; that, on the contrary, Negroes must insist continually, in season and out of season, that voting is necessary to modern manhood, that color discrimination is barbarism, and that black boys need education as well as white boys.

In failing thus to state plainly and unequivocally the legitimate demands of their people, even at the cost of opposing an honored leader, the thinking classes of American Negroes would shirk a heavy responsibility,—a responsibility to themselves, a responsibility to the struggling masses, a responsibility to the darker races of men whose future depends so largely on this American experiment, but especially a responsibility to this nation,—this common Fatherland. It is wrong to encourage a man or a people in evil-doing; it is wrong to aid and abet a national crime simply because it is unpopular not to do so. The growing spirit of kindliness and reconciliation between the North and South after the frightful differences of a generation ago ought to be a source of deep congratulation to all, and especially to those whose mistreatment caused the war; but if that reconciliation is to be marked by the industrial slavery and civic death of those same black men, with permanent legislation into a position of inferiority, then those black men, if they are really men, are called upon by every consideration of patriotism and loyalty to oppose such a course by all civilized methods, even though such opposition involves disagreement with Mr. Booker T. Washington. We have no right to sit silently by while the inevitable seeds are sown for a harvest of disaster to our children, black and white.

First, it is the duty of black men to judge the South discriminatingly. The present generation of Southerners are not responsible for the past, and they should not be blindly hated or blamed for it. Furthermore, to no class is the indiscriminate endorsement of the recent course of the South toward Negroes more nauseating than to the best thought of the South. The South is not "solid"; it is a land in the ferment of social change, wherein forces of all kinds are fighting for supremacy; and to praise the ill the South is to-day perpetrating is just as wrong as to condemn the good. Discriminating and broad-minded criticism is what the South needs,—needs it for the sake of her own white sons and daughters, and for the insurance of robust, healthy mental and moral development.

To-day even the attitude of the Southern whites toward the blacks is not, as so many assume, in all cases the same; the ignorant Southerner hates the Negro, the workingmen fear his competition, the moneymakers wish to use him as a laborer, some of the educated see a menace in his upward development, while others—usually the sons of the masters—wish to help him to rise. National opinion has enabled this last class to maintain the Negro common schools, and to protect the Negro partially in property, life, and limb. Through the pressure of the moneymakers, the Negro is in danger of being reduced to semi-slavery, especially in the country districts; the workingmen, and those of the educated who fear the Negro, have united to disfranchise him, and some have urged his deportation; while the passions of the ignorant are easily aroused to lynch and abuse any black man. To praise this intricate whirl of thought and prejudice is nonsense; to inveigh indiscriminately against "the South" is unjust; but to use the same breath in praising Governor Aycock, exposing Senator Morgan, arguing with Mr. Thomas Nelson Page, and denouncing Senator Ben Tillman, is not only sane, but the imperative duty of thinking black men.

It would be unjust to Mr. Washington not to acknowledge that in several instances he has opposed movements in the South which were unjust to the Negro; he sent memorials to the Louisiana and Alabama constitutional conventions, he has spoken against lynching, and in other ways has openly or silently set his influence against sinister schemes and unfortunate happenings. Notwithstanding this, it is equally true to assert that on the whole the distinct impression left by Mr. Washington's propaganda is, first, that the South is justified in its present attitude toward the Negro because of the Negro's degradation; secondly, that the prime cause of the Negro's failure to rise more quickly is his wrong education in the past; and, thirdly, that his future rise depends primarily on his own efforts. Each of these propositions is a dangerous half-truth. The supplementary truths must never be lost sight of: first, slavery and race-prejudice are potent if not sufficient causes of the Negro's position; second, industrial and common-school training were necessarily slow in planting because they had to await the black teachers trained by higher institutions,—it being extremely doubtful if any essentially different development was possible, and certainly a Tuskegee was unthinkable before 1880; and, third, while it is a great truth to say that the Negro must strive and strive mightily to help himself, it is equally true that unless his striving be not simply seconded, but rather aroused and encouraged, by the initiative of the richer and wiser envisioning group, he cannot hope for great success.

In his failure to realize and impress this last point, Mr. Washington is especially to be criticized. His doctrine has tended to make the whites, North and South, shift the burden of the Negro problem to the Negro's shoulders and stand aside as critical and rather pessimistic spectators; when in fact the burden belongs to the nation, and the hands of none of us are clean if we bend not our energies to righting these great wrongs.

The South ought to be led, by candid and honest criticism, to assert her better self and do her full duty to the race she has cruelly wronged and is still wronging. The North—her co-partner in guilt—cannot salve her conscience by plastering it with gold. We cannot settle this problem by diplomacy and suaveness, by "policy" alone. If worse come to worst, can the moral fibre of this country survive the slow throttling and murder of nine millions of men?

The black men of America have a duty to perform, a duty stern and delicate,—a forward movement to oppose a part of the work of their greatest leader. So far as Mr. Washington preaches Thrift, Patience, and Industrial Training for the masses, we must hold up his hands and strive with him, rejoicing in his honors and glorying in the strength of this Joshua called of God and of man to lead the headless host. But so far as Mr. Washington apologizes for injustice, North or South, does not rightly value the privilege and duty of voting, belittles the emasculating effects of caste distinctions, and opposes the higher training and ambition of our brighter minds,—so far as he, the South, or the Nation, does this,—we must unceasingly and firmly oppose them. By every civilized and peaceful method we must strive for the rights which the world accords to men, clinging unwaveringly to those great words which the sons of the Fathers would fain forget: "We hold these truths to be self-evident: That all men are created equal; that they are endowed by their Creator with certain unalienable rights; that among these are life, liberty, and the pursuit of happiness."

The Development of a People (1904)

In the realm of physical health the teachings of Nature, with its stern mercy and merciful punishment, are showing men gradually to avoid the mistake of unhealthful homes, and to clear fever and malaria away from parts of earth otherwise so beautiful. Death that arises from foul sewage, bad plumbing or vitiated air we no longer attribute to "Acts of God," but to "Misdeeds of Man," and so work to correct this loss. But if we have escaped Medievalism to some extent in the care of physical health, we certainly have not in the higher realm of the economic and spiritual development of people. Here the world rests, and is largely contented to rest, in a strange fatalism. Nations and groups and social classes are born and reared, reel sick unto death, or tear forward in frenzied striving. We sit and watch and moralize, and judge our neighbors or ourselves foredoomed to failure or success, not because we know or have studied the causes of a people's advance, but rather because we instinctively dislike certain races, and instinctively like our own.

This attitude cannot long prevail. The solidarity of human interests in a world which is daily becoming physically smaller, cannot afford to grope in darkness as to the causes and incentives to human advance when the advance of all depends increasingly on the advance of each. Nor is it enough here to have simply the philanthropic impulse—simply a rather blind and aimless desire to do good.

If then we would grapple intelligently with the greater problems of human development in society, we must sit and study and learn even when the mad impulse of aimless philanthropy is striving within, and we find it easier to labor blindly, rather than to wait intelligently.

In no single set of human problems is this striving after intelligence, after real facts and clear thinking, more important than in answering the many questions that concern the American Negro. And especially is this true since the basic axiom upon which all intelligent and decent men, North and South, white and black, must agree, is that the best interests of every single American demand that *every Negro make the best of himself.*

But what is good and better and best in the measure of human advance? and how shall we compare the present with the past, nation with nation, and group with group, so as to gain real intelligent insight into conditions and needs, and enlightened guidance? Now this is extremely difficult in matters of human development, because we are so ignorant of the ordinary facts relating to conditions of life, and because, above all, criteria of life and the objects of living are so diverse.

And yet the desire for clear judgment and rational advance, even in so intricate a problem as that of the races in the United States, is not hopeless. First of all, the most hopeful thing about the race problem to-day is, that people are beginning to recognize its intricacy and be justly suspicious of any person who insists that the race problem is simply this or simply that—realizing that it is not simply anything. It is as complex as human nature, and you do well to distrust the judgment of any man who thinks, however honestly, that any one simple remedy will cure evils that arise from the whirling wants and longings and passions of writhing human souls.

Not only do we to-day recognize the Negro problems as intricate, but we are beginning to see that they are pressing—asking, *demanding* solution; not to be put off by half measures, not answered by being handed down in thinly disguised yet even larger form to our children. With these intricate and pressing problems before us, we ask searchingly and often for the light; and here again we are baffled. An honest gentleman from the South informs us that there are fully as many illiterate Negroes today in the South as there were at Emancipation. We gasp with astonishment, and as we are asking "Where then is all our money and effort gone?" another gentleman from the South, apparently just as honest, tells us that whereas nine-tenths of the Negroes in 1870 could *not* read and write, to-day fully three-fifths of them *can*; or, again, the Negroes themselves exult over the ownership of three hundred million dollars worth of real estate, while the critic points out that the Negroes are a burden to the South, since forming a third of the population they own but one-twenty-fifth of the property.

Such seemingly contradictory propositions and others even more glaring, we hear every day, and it is small wonder that persons without leisure to weigh the evidence find themselves curiously in the dark at times and anxious for reliable interpretation of the real facts.

Much of this befogging of the situation is apparent rather than real. As a matter of fact, the statements referred to are not at all contradictory. There are to-day more illiterate Negroes than in 1870, but there are six times as many who can read and write. The real underlying problem is dynamic, not static. Is the educational movement in the right direction, and is it as rapid as is safe? or, in other words, What is satisfactory advance in education? Ought a people to learn to read and write in one generation or in a hundred years? How far can we hasten the growth of intelligence, avoiding stagnation on the one hand, and abnormal forcing on the other? Or take the question of property ownership; it is probably true that only a twenty-fifth of the total property of the South belongs to the Negro, and that the Negro property of the land exceeds three hundred million. Here, again, brute figures mean little, and the comparison between black and white is misleading. The basic question is, How soon after a social revolution like emancipation ought one reasonably to expect the appearance of habits of thrift and the accumulation of property? Moreover, how far is the accumulating of wealth indicative of general advance in moral habits and sound character, or how far is it independent of them or in spite of them?

In other words, if we are to judge intelligently or clearly of the development of a people, we must allow ourselves neither to be dazzled by figures nor misled by inapt comparisons, but we must seek to know what human advancement historically considered has meant and what it means to-day, and from such criteria we may then judge the condition, development and needs of the group before us. I want then to mention briefly the steps which groups of men have usually taken in their forward struggling, and to ask which of these steps the Negroes of the United States have taken and how far they have gone. In such comparisons we cannot, unfortunately, have the aid of exact statistics, for actual measurement of social phenomena is peculiar to the nineteenth century—that is, to an age when the culture Nations were full-grown, and we can only roughly indicate conditions in the days of their youth. A certain youth and childhood is common to all men in their mingled striving. Everywhere, glancing across the seas of human history, we note it. The average American community of to-day has grown by a slow, intricate and hesitating advance through four overlapping eras. First, there is the struggle for sheer physical existence—a struggle still waging among the submerged tenth, but settled for a majority of the community long years ago. Above this comes the accumulation for future subsistence—the saving and striving and transmuting of goods for use in days to come—a stage reached to-day tentatively for the middle classes and to an astounding degree by a few. Then in every community there goes on from the first, but with larger and larger emphasis as the years fly, some essay to train the young into the tradition of the fathers—their religion, thought and tricks of doing. And, finally, as the group meets other groups and comes into larger spiritual contact with nations, there is that transference and sifting and accumulation of the elements of human culture which makes for wider civilization and higher development. These four steps of subsistence, accumulation, education and culture-contact are not disconnected, discreet [sic] stages. No nation ever settles its problems of poverty and then turns to educating children; or first accumulates its wealth and then its culture. On the contrary, in every stage of a nation's growing all these efforts are present, and we designate any particular age of a people's development as (for instance) a struggle for existence, because, their conscious effort is more largely expended in this direction than in others; but despite this we all know, or ought to know, that no growing nation can spend its whole effort on to-day's food lest accumulation and training of children and learning of their neighbors—lest all these things so vitally necessary to advance be neglected, and the people,

full-bellied though they be, stagnate and die because in one mighty struggle to live they forget the weightier objects of life.

We all know these very obvious truths, and yet despite ourselves certain mechanical conceptions of society creep into our everyday thought. We think of growing men as cogs in some vast factory—we would stop these wheels and set these others going, hasten that department and retard this; but this conception applied to struggling men is mischievously wrong. You cannot stop the education of children in order to feed their fathers; the children continue to grow—something they are bound to learn. What then shall it be: truth, or half-truth, good or bad? So, too, a people may be engaged in the pressing work of accumulating and saving for future needs—storing grain and cotton, building houses, leveling land; but all the time they are learning something from inevitable contact with men and nations and thoughts—you cannot stop this learning; you cannot postpone it. What then shall this learning—this contact with culture—be? a lesson of fact or fable? of growth or debauchery? the inspiration of the schools or the degradation of the slums? Something it must be, but what? The growth of society is an ever-living, many-sided, bundle of activities, some of which are emphasized at different ages, none of which can be neglected without peril, all of which demand guidance and direction. As they receive this, the nation grows; as they do not, it stagnates and dies.

Whence now must the guidance and direction come? It can come only from four great sources: the precepts of parents, the sight of Seers, the opinion of the majority, and the tradition of the grandfathers; or, in other words, a nation or group of people can be taught the things it must learn in its family circles, at the feet of teachers and preachers, by contact with surrounding society, by reverence for the dead Hand—for that mighty accumulation of customs and traditions handed down generation after generation.

And thus I come to the center of my theme. How far do these great means of growth operate among American Negroes and influence their development in the main lines of human advancement?

Let me take you journeying across mountains and meadows, threading the hills of Maryland, gliding over the broad fields of Virginia, climbing the blue ridge of Carolina and seating ourselves in the cotton kingdom. I would not like you to spend a day or a month here in this little town; I should much rather you would spend ten years, if you are really studying the problem; for casual visitors get casual ideas, and the problems here are the growth of centuries.

From the depot and the cluster of doubtful houses that form the town, pale crimson fields with tell-tale gullies stretch desolately away. The whole horizon looks shabby, and there is a certain awful leisure in the air that makes a westerner wonder when work begins. A neglected and uncertain road wanders up from the depot, past several little stores and a post-office, and then stops hesitatingly and melts away into crooked paths across the washed-out cotton fields. But I do not want you to see so much of the physical as of the spiritual town, and first you must see the color line. It stands at the depot with "waiting room for white people" and "waiting room for colored people," and then the uninitiated might lose sight of it; but it is there, there and curiously wandering, but continuous and never ending. And in that little town, as in a thousand others, they have an eleventh commandment, and it reads "Thou shalt not Cross the Line." Men may at times break the sixth commandment and the seventh, and it makes but little stir. But when the eleventh is broken, *the world heaves.* And yet you must not think the town inhabited by anything inhuman. Simple, good hearted folks are there—generosity and hospitality, politeness and charity, dim strivings and hard efforts—a human world, aye, even lovable at times; and one cannot argue about that strange line—it is simply so.

Were you there in person I could not take you easily across the line into the world I want to study. But in spirit let me lead you across. In one part of the town are sure to be clustered the majority of the Negro cabins; there is no strict physical separation; on some streets whites and blacks are neighbors, and yet the general clustering by color is plain. I want to take you among the houses of the colored people, and I start not with the best, but with the worst: a little one-room box with a family of eight. The cabin is dirty, ill-smelling and cheerless; the furniture is scanty, old and worn. The man works when he has no whiskey to drink, which is comparatively seldom. The woman washes and squanders and squanders and washes. I am not sure that the couple were ever married formally, but still they'll stick together in all

probability for life, despite their quarreling. There are five children, and the nameless child of the eldest daughter makes the last member of the family. Three of the children can spell and read a bit, but there's little need of it. The rest of the family are in ignorance, dark and dense. Here is a problem of home and family. One shudders at it almost hopelessly, or flares in anger and says: why do these people live like animals? Why don't they work and strive to do? If the stranger be from the North he looks suspiciously at the color line and shakes his head. If he be from the South he looks at it thankfully and stamps his foot. And these two attitudes are in some respects typical. We look around for the forces keeping this family down, or with fatalistic resignation conclude that nothing better is to be expected of black people. Exactly the same attitude with which the man of a century or so ago fought disease: looked about for the witch, or wondered at the chastening of the Lord; but withal continued to live in the swamps. There are forces in the little town to keep Negroes down, but they do not wholly explain the condition of this family. There are differences in human capabilities, but that they are not based on color can be seen in a dozen Negro homes up the street. What we have in degraded homes like this is a plain survival from the past.

What was slavery and the slave trade? Turn again with me even at the risk of hearing a twice-told tale and, as we have journeyed in space to this little southern town, so journey again in time, back through that curious crooked way along which civilization has wandered looking for the light. There was the nineteenth century—a century of material prosperity, of systematic catering to human wants, that men might eat, drink, be clothed and transported through space. And with this came the physical freeing of the soul through the wonders of science and the spread of democracy. Such a century was a legitimate offspring of the eighteenth century, of the years from 1700 to 1800, when our grandfathers' grandfathers lived—that era of revolution and heart searching that gave the world George Washington and the French Revolution. Behind the eighteenth century looms the age of Louis XIV of France, an age of mighty leaders: Richelieu, Gustavus Adolphus, and Oliver Cromwell. Thus we come back on the world's way, through three centuries of imperialism, revolution and commercial democracy, to two great centuries which prepared Europe for the years from 1600 to 1900—the century of the Protestant Reformation and the century of the Renaissance. The African Slave trade was the child of the Renaissance. We do not realize this; we think of the slave trade as a thing apart, the incident of a decade or a century, and yet let us never forget that from the year 1442, when Antonio Gonzales first looked upon the river of Gold, until 1807, when Great Britain first checked the slave trade, for three hundred and sixty-five years Africa was surrendered wholly to the cruelty and rapacity of the Christian man-dealer, and for full five hundred years and more this frightful heart disease of the Dark Continent destroyed the beginnings of Negro civilization, overturned governments, murdered men, disrupted families and poisoned the civilized world. Do you want an explanation of the degradation of this pitiful little nest perched in the crimson soil of Georgia? Ask your fathers and your father's fathers, for they know. Nay, you need not go back even to their memories.

In 1880 a traveler crossed Africa from Lake Nyassa to Lake Tanganyika. He saw the southern end of the lake peopled with large and prosperous villages. The next traveler who followed in 1890 found not a solitary human being—nothing but burned homes and bleaching skeletons. He tells us that the Wa-Nkonde tribe to which these people belonged, was, until this event, one of the most prosperous tribes in East Central Africa. Their people occupied a country of exceptional fertility and beauty. Three rivers, which never failed in the severest drought, ran through their territory, and their crops were the richest and most varied in the country. They possessed herds of cattle and goats; they fished in the lake with nets; they wrought iron into many-patterned spear-heads with exceptional ingenuity and skill; and that even artistic taste had begun to develop among them was evident from the ornamental work of their huts, which were unique for clever construction and beauty of design. This people, in short, by their own inherent ability and the natural resources of their country, were on the high road to civilization. Then came the overthrow. Arab traders mingled with them, settled peacefully among them, obeyed their laws, and gained their confidence. The number of the traders slowly increased; the power of the chief was slowly

undermined, until, at last, with superior weapons and reinforcements, every vestige of the tribe was swept away and their lands laid in red ruins. Fourteen villages they razed from the ground and, finally, seizing more slaves than they could transport, drove the rest into the tall dry grass and set it on fire; and in the black forest was silence.

This took place in the nineteenth century during your lives, in the midst of modern missionary effort. But worse was the tale of the eighteenth century and the seventeenth century and the sixteenth century, and this whole dark crime against a human race began in 1442 when the historic thirty Negroes landed in Lisbon.

Systematic man-hunting was known in ancient times, but it subsided as civilization advanced, until the Mohammedan fanatics swept across Africa. Arabian slavery, however, had its mitigations. It was patriarchal house service; the slave might hope to rise and, once admitted to the household of faith, he became in fact, and not merely in theory, a man and a brother. The domestic slavery of the African tribes represented that first triumph of humanity that leads the savage to spare his foe's life and use his labor. Such slaves could and did rise to freedom and preferment; they became parts of the new tribe. It was left to Christian slavery to improve on all this—to make slavery a rigid unending caste by adding to bondage the prejudice of race and color. Marauding bands traversed the forests, fell upon native villages, slew the old and young and drove the rest in herds to the slave market; tribe was incited against tribe, and nation against nation. As Mr. Stanley tells us,

> While a people were thus subject to capture and expatriation, it was clearly impossible that any intellectual or moral progress could be made. The greater number of those accessible from the coast were compelled to study the best methods of avoiding the slaver and escaping his force and his wiles; the rest only thought of the arts of kidnapping their innocent and unsuspecting fellow creatures. Yet, contradictory as it may appear to us, there were not wanting at the same time zealous men who devoted themselves to Christianity. In Angola, Congo and Mozambique, and far up the Zambesi, missionaries erected churches and cathedrals, appointed bishops and priests who converted and baptized; while at the mouth of

the Congo, the Niger and the Zambesi their countrymen built slave bar racoons, and anchored their murderous slave ships. Europeans legalized and sanctioned the slave trade; the public conscience of the period approved it; the mitred heads of the church blessed the slave gangs as they marched to the shore, and the tax-collector received the levy per head as lawful revenue.

The development of the trade depended largely upon the commercial nations, and, as they put more and more ruthless enterprise into the traffic, it grew and flourished. First came the Portuguese as the world's slave trader, secured in their monopoly by the Bull of Demarcation issued by Pope Alexander VI. Beginning in 1442 they traded a hundred and fifty years, until Portugal was reduced to a province of Spain in 1580 and her African settlements neglected. Immediately the thrifty Dutch began to monopolize the trade, and held it for a century, until Oliver Cromwell deprived them of it. The celebrated Dutch West India Company intrigued with native states and gained a monopoly of the trade in Negroes from 1630 to 1668. They whirled a stream of cargoes over the great seas, filled the West Indies, skirted the coasts of America and, sailing up the curving river to Jamestown, planted the Negro problems in Virginia in 1619. Then the English scented gain and bestirred themselves mightily.

Two English slave ships sailed from Plymouth in the middle of the sixteenth century, but the great founder of the English slave trade was Sir John Hawkins. Queen Elizabeth had some scruples at the trade in human beings, and made Hawkins promise to seize only those who were willing to go with him—a thing which he easily promised and easily forgot. This Sir John Hawkins was a strange product of his times. Brave, ruthless, cruel and religious: a pirate, a man-stealer and a patriot. He sailed to Africa in the middle of the sixteenth century, and immediately saw profits for English gain. He burned villages, murdered the natives and stole slaves, and then, urging his crew to love one another and serve God daily, he sailed merrily westward to the Spanish West Indies in the good ship called the "Jesus," and compelled the Spaniards to buy slaves at the muzzle of his guns.

Thus the English slave trade began under Queen Elizabeth, was encouraged under James I, who had made the translation of our Bible, and renewed by Oliver Cromwell, the great Puritan, who fought for it and seized the island of Jamaica as a slave market. So kings, queens and countries encouraged the trade, and the English soon became the world's greatest slave traders. New manufactures suitable to the trade were introduced into England, and the trade brought so much gold to Great Britain that they named the pieces "guineas" after the slave coast. Four million dollars a year went from England, in the eighteenth century, to buy slaves. Liverpool, the city where the trade centered, had, in 1783, nine hundred slave ships in the trade, and in eleven years they carried $76,000,000 worth of slaves to America, and they did this on a clear profit of $60,000,000.

These vast returns seduced the conscience of Europe. [Samuel] Boswell, the biographer of Dr. Johnson, called the slave trade "an important necessary branch of commerce," and probably the best people of England were of this opinion, and were surprised and indignant when [Thomas] Clarkson and [William] Wilberforce began their campaign.

Gradually aroused by repeated and seemingly hopeless assaults, the conscience of England awoke and forbade the trade, in 1807, after having guided and cherished it for one hundred and fifty years. She called for aid from America, and America apparently responded in the statutes of 1808. But, true to her reputation as the most lawless nation on earth, America made no attempt to enforce the law in her own territory for a generation, and, after that, refused repeatedly and doggedly to prevent the slave trade of the world from sailing peacefully under the American flag for fifty years—up until the very outbreak of the civil war. Thus, from 1442 to 1860, nearly half a millennium, the Christian world fattened on the stealing of human souls.

Nor was there any pretence of charity in the methods of their doing. The capture of the slaves was organized deceit, murder and force; the shipping of them was far worse than the modern shipping of horses and cattle. Of this middle passage across the sea in slow sailing ships, with brutal sailors and little to eat, it has often been said "that never in the world before was so much wretchedness condensed in so little room." The Negroes, naked and in irons, were chained to each other hand and foot, and stowed so close that they were not allowed more than a foot and a half each. Thus, crammed together like herrings in a barrel, they contracted putrid and fatal disorders, so that those who came to inspect them in the morning had frequently to pick dead slaves out of their rows and unchain their corpses from the bodies of their wretched mates. Blood and filth covered the floors, the hot air reeked with contagion, and the death rate among the slaves often reached fifty per cent, not to speak of the decimation when once they reached the West Indian plantations.

The world will never know the exact number of slaves transported to America. Several thousand came in the fifteenth century, tens of thousands in the sixteenth, and hundreds of thousands in the seventeenth. In the eighteenth century more than two and one-half millions of slaves were transported, and in 1790 Negroes were crossing the ocean at the rate of sixty thousand a year. Dunbar thinks that nearly fifteen millions were transported in all.

Such was the traffic that revolutionized Africa. Instead of man-hunting being an incident of tribal wars, war became the incident of man-hunting. From the Senegal to St. Paul de Loanda winding, beaten tracks converged to the sea from every corner of the Dark Continent, covered with the blood of the foot-sore, lined with the bleaching bones of the dead, and echoing with the wails of the conquered, the bereaved and the dying. The coast stood bristling with forts and prisons to receive the human cattle. Across the blue waters of the Atlantic two hundred and fifty ships a year hurried to the west, with their crowded, half-suffocated cargoes. And during all this time Martin Luther had lived and died, Calvin had preached, Raphael had painted and Shakespeare and Milton sung; and yet for four hundred years the coasts of Africa and America were strewn with the dying and the dead, four hundred years the sharks followed the scurrying ships, four hundred years Ethiopia stretched forth her hands unto God. All this you know, all this you have read many a time. I tell it again, lest you forget.

What was slavery to the slave trade? Not simply forced labor, else we are all in bondage. Not simply toil without pay, even that is not unknown in America. No, the dark damnation of slavery in America was the destruction of the African family and of all just ideals of family life. No one pretends that the family life of African tribes had reached modern standards—barbarous nations have barbarous ideals. But this does not mean that they have no ideals at all. The patriarchal clan-life of the Africans, with its polygamy protected by custom, tradition and legal penalty, was infinitely superior to the shameless promiscuity of the West Indian plantations, the unhallowed concubinage of Virginia, or the prostitution of Louisiana. And these ideals slavery broke and scattered and flirted to the winds and left ignorance and degradation in their train.

When the good New England clergyman thought it a shame that slaves should herd like animals, without a legal marriage bond, he devised a quaint ceremony for them in which Sally promised Bob to cleave to him. For life? Oh no. As long as "God in his providence" kept them on the same plantation. This was in New England where there was a good deal more conscience than in Georgia. What ideal of family life could one reasonably expect Bob and Sally to have? The modern American family (considering the shame of divorce) has not reached perfection; yet it is the result of long training and carefully fostered ideals and persistent purging of the socially unfit.

As I study this family in the little southern town, in all its degradation and unclearness, I cannot but see a plain case of cause and effect. If you degrade people the result is degradation, and you have no right to be surprised at it. Nor am I called upon to apologize for these people, or to make fun of their dumb misery. For their condition there is an apology due, witness High Heaven; but not from me.

Upon the town we have visited, upon the state, upon this section, the awful incubus of the past broods like a writhing sorrow, and when we turn our faces from that past, we turn it not to forget but to remember; viewing degradation with fear and not contempt, with awe and not criticism, bowing our head and straining willing ears to the iron voice

. . . of Nature merciful and stern.
I teach by killing, let others learn.

But the Negroes of the South are not all upon this low level. From this Nadir they stretch slowly, resolutely upward, by infinite gradation, helped now by the hand of a kindly master or a master's son, now by the sacrifice of friends; always by the ceaseless energy of a people who will never submit to burial alive.

Look across the street of your little southern town: here is a better house—a mother and father, two sons and a girl. They are hard-working people and good people. They read and write a little and, though they are slow and good natured, they are seldom idle. And yet they are unskilled, without foresight, always in debt and living from hand to mouth. Hard pressed they may sink into crime; encouraged they may rise to comfort, but never to wealth. Why? Because they and their fathers have been trained this way. What does a slave know of saving? What can he know of forethought? What could he learn even of skill, save in exceptional cases? In other words, slavery must of necessity send into the world of work a mass of unskilled laborers who have no idea of what thrift means; who have been a part of a great economic organization but had nothing to do with its organizing; and so when they are suddenly called to take a place in a greater organization, in which free individual initiative is a potent factor, they cannot, for they do not know how; they lack skill and, more than that, they lack ideals!

And so we might go on: past problems of work and wages, of legal protection, of civil rights and of education, up to this jaunty, little yellow house on a cross street with a flower-bed struggling sturdily with the clay, with vines and creepers and a gleam of white curtains and a decorous parlor. If you enter this house you may not find it altogether up to your ideals. A Dutch housekeeper would find undiscovered corners, and a fastidious person might object to the general scheme of decoration. And yet, compared with the homes in the town, white or black, the house is among the best. It may be the home of a Negro butcher who serves both sides the color line, or of a small grocer, a carpenter, a school teacher or a preacher. Whatever this man may be, he is a leader in a peculiar sense—the ideal-maker in his group of people. The white world is there, but it is the other side of the color line; it is seen distinctly and from afar. Of white and black there is no mingling in church and school, in general gatherings. The black world is isolated and alone; it gets its ideals, its larger thoughts, its notions of life, from these local leaders; they set the tone to that all-powerful spiritual world that surrounds and envelopes the souls of men; their standards of living, their interpretation of sunshine and rain and human hearts, their thoughts of love

and labor, their aspirations and dim imaginings—all that makes life *life*.

Not only does this group leader guide a mass of men isolated in space, but also isolated in time. For we must remember that not only did slavery overthrow the Negro family and teach few lessons of thrift and foresight; it also totally broke a nation from all its traditions of the past in every realm of life. I fear I cannot impress upon you the full meaning of such a revolution. A nation that breaks suddenly with its past is almost fatally crippled. No matter how crude or imperfect that past may be, with all its defects, it is the foundation upon which generations to come must build. Beauty and finish and architectural detail are not required of it, but the massive weight of centuries of customs and traditions it must have. The slave trade, a new climate, a new economic regime, a new language and a new religion separated the American Negro as completely from his fatherland as it is possible for human agencies to do. The result is curious. There is a certain swaying in the air, a tilting and a crumbling, a vast difficulty of adjustment—of making the new ideas of work and wealth, of authority and right, fit in and hitch themselves to something gone; to the authority of the fathers, the customs of the past in a nation without grandfathers. So, then, the Negro group leader not only sets present standards, but he supplies in a measure the lack of past standards, and his leading is doubly difficult, since with Emancipation there came a second partial breaking with the past. The leader of the masses must discriminate between the good and bad in the past; he must keep the lesson of work and reject the lesson of concubinage; he must add more lessons of moral rectitude to the old religious fervor; he must, in fine, stand to this group in the light of the interpreter of the civilization of the twentieth century to the minds and hearts of people who, from sheer necessity, can but dimly comprehend it. And this man—I care not what his vocation may be—preacher, teacher, physician, or artisan, this person is going to solve the Negro problem; for that problem is at bottom the clash of two different standards of culture, and this priest it is who interprets the one to the other.

Let me for a moment recapitulate. In the life of advancing peoples there must go on simultaneously a struggle for existence, accumulation of wealth, education of the young, and a development in culture and the higher things of life. The more backward the nation the larger sum of effort goes into the struggle for existence; the more forward the nation the larger and broader is the life of the spirit. For guidance, in taking these steps in civilization, the nation looks to four sources: the precepts of parents, the sight of seers, the opinion of the majority and the traditions of the past.

Here, then, is a group of people in which every one of these great sources of inspiration is partially crippled: the family group is struggling to recover from the debauchery of slavery; and the number of the enlightened leaders must necessarily be small; the surrounding and more civilized white majority is cut off from its natural influence by the color line; and the traditions of the past are either lost, or largely traditions of evil and wrong.

Any one looking the problem squarely in the face might conclude that it was unjust to expect progress, or the signs of progress, until many generations had gone by. Indeed, we must not forget that those people who claimed to know the Negro best, freely and confidently predicted during the abolition controversy—

1. That free Negroes would not, and could not, work effectively.
2. That the freedman who did work, would not save.
3. That it was impossible to educate Negroes.
4. That no members of the race gave signs of ability and leadership.
5. That the race was morally degenerate.

Not only was this said, it was sincerely and passionately believed, by honorable men who, with their forefathers, had lived with the Negro three hundred years. And yet to-day the Negro in one generation forms the chief laboring force of the most rapidly developing part of the land. He owns twelve million acres of land, two hundred and fifty million dollars worth of farm property, and controls as owner or renter five hundred millions. Nearly three-fifths of the Negroes have learned to read and write. An increasing number have given evidence of ability and thoughtfulness—not, to be sure, of transcendent genius, but of integrity, large knowledge and common-sense. And finally there can be to-day no reasonable dispute but that the number of efficient, law-abiding and morally upright black people in this land is far larger than it ever was before, and is daily growing. Now these obvious and patent facts do not by any means indicate the full solution of the problem. There are still hosts of idle and unreliable Negro laborers; the race still, as a whole, has not learned the lesson of thrift and saving; fully seventy-five per cent are still fairly designated as ignorant. The number of group leaders of ability and character is far behind the demand, and the development of a trustworthy upper class has, as is usually true, been accompanied by the differentiation of a dangerous class of criminals.

What the figures of Negro advancement mean is, that the development has been distinctly and markedly in the right direction, and that, given justice and help, no honest man can doubt the outcome. The giving of justice means the recognition of desert wherever it appears; the right to vote on exactly the same terms as other people vote; the right to the equal use of public conveniences and the educating of youth in the public schools. On these points, important as they are, I will not dwell. I am more interested here in asking how these struggling people may be actually helped. I conceive that such help may take any one of four forms:—

1. Among a people deprived of guiding traditions, they may be furnished trained guidance in matters of civilization and ideals of living.
2. A people whose family life is not strongly established must have put before them and brought home to them the morals of sane and sanitary living.
3. The mass of Negro children must have the keys of knowledge put into their hands by good elementary schools.
4. The Negro youth must have the opportunity to learn the technical skill of modern industry.

All these forms of help are important. No one of them can be neglected without danger of increasing complications as time flies, and each one of them are lines of endeavor in which the Negro cannot be reasonably expected to help himself without aid from others. For instance, it cannot be seriously expected that a race of freedmen would have the skill necessary for modern industry. They cannot teach themselves what they themselves do not know, and consequently a legitimate and crying need of the south is the establishment of industrial schools. The public school system is one of the foundation stones of free republican government. Negro children, as well as other children, have a right to ask of the nation knowledge of reading, writing and the rules of number, together with some conception of the world in time and space. Not one Negro child in three is to-day receiving any such training or has any chance to receive it, and a decent public school system in the South, aided by the national government, is something that must come in the near future, if you expect the race problem to be settled.

Here then are two great needs: public schools and industrial schools. How are schools of any sort established? By furnishing teachers. Given properly equipped teachers and your schools are a foregone success; without them, I care not how much you spend on buildings and equipment, the schools are a failure. It is here that Negro colleges, like Atlanta University, show their first usefulness.

But, in my list of ways in which the Negro may legitimately be helped to help himself, I named two other avenues of aid, and I named them first because to my mind they are even of more importance than popular education. I mean the moral uplift of a people. Now moral uplift comes not primarily from schools, but from strong home life and high social ideals. I have spoken of the Negroes' deficiency in these lines and the reason of that deficiency. Here, then, is a chance for help, but how? Not by direct teaching, because that is often ineffective and it is precluded in the South by the color line. It can be done, to my mind, only by group leadership; by planting in every community of Negroes black men with ideals of life and thrift and civilization, such as must in time filter through the masses and set examples of moral living and correct thinking to the great masses of Negroes who spend but little of their life in schools. After all the education of men comes but in small degree from schools; it comes mostly from the fireside, from companionships, from your social set, from the opinion of each individual's little world. This is even more true of the Negro. His world is smaller. He is shut in to himself by prejudice; he has, by reason of his poverty, little time for school. If he is to learn, he must learn from his group leaders, his daily companions, his social surroundings, his own dark world of striving, longing and dreaming. Here, then, you must plant the seed of civilization. Here you must place men educated, not merely in the technique of teaching or skill of hand, but above and beyond that into a thorough understanding of their age and the demands and meaning of modern culture. In so far as the college of to-day stands for the transmission from age to age of all that is best in the world's deeds, thoughts and traditions, in so far it is a crying necessity that a race, ruthlessly torn from its traditions and trained for centuries awry, should receive back through the higher culture of its gifted children some of the riches of the great system of culture into which it has been thrust. If the meaning of modern life cannot be taught at Negro hearthsides because the parents themselves are untaught, then its ideals can be forced into the centres of Negro life only by the teaching of higher institutions of learning and the agency of thoroughly educated men.

Melville Fuller

United States v. E. C. Knight Company (1895)

Mr. Chief Justice FULLER, after stating the case, delivered the opinion of the Court.

By the purchase of the stock of the four Philadelphia refineries, with shares of its own stock, the American Sugar Refining Company acquired nearly complete control of the manufacture of refined sugar within the United States. The bill charged that the contracts under which these purchases were made constituted combinations in restraint of trade, and that, in entering into them, the defendants combined and conspired to restrain the trade and commerce in refined sugar among the several States and with foreign nations, contrary to the act of Congress of July 2, 1890.

The relief sought was the cancellation of the agreements under which the stock was transferred; the redelivery of the stock to the parties respectively, and an injunction against the further performance of the agreements and further violations of the act. [. . .]

The fundamental question is whether, conceding that the existence of a monopoly in manufacture is established by the evidence, that monopoly can be directly suppressed under the act of Congress in the mode attempted by this bill.

It cannot be denied that the power of a State to protect the lives, health, and property of its citizens, and to preserve good order and the public morals, "the power to govern men and things within the limits of its dominion," is a power originally and always belonging to the States, not surrendered by them to the general government nor directly restrained by the Constitution of the United States, and essentially exclusive. The relief of the citizens of each State from the burden of monopoly and the evils resulting from the restraint of trade among such citizens was left with the States to deal with, and this court has recognized their possession of that power even to the extent of holding that an employment or business carried on by private individuals, when it becomes a matter of such public interest and importance as to create a common charge or burden upon the citizen—in other words, when it becomes a practical monopoly to which the citizen is compelled to resort and by means of which a tribute can be exacted from the community—is subject to regulation by state legislative power. On the other hand, the power of Congress to regulate commerce among the several States is also exclusive. The Constitution does not provide that interstate commerce shall be free, but, by the grant of this exclusive power to regulate it, it was left free except as Congress might impose restraints. Therefore it has been determined that the failure of Congress to exercise this exclusive power in any case is an expression of its will that the subject shall be free from restrictions or impositions upon it by the several States, and if a law passed by a State in the exercise of its acknowledged powers comes into conflict with that will, the Congress and the State cannot occupy the position of equal opposing sovereignties, because the Constitution declares its supremacy and that of the laws passed in pursuance thereof, and that which is not supreme must yield to that which is supreme. "Commerce, undoubtedly, is traffic," said Chief Justice Marshall, "but it is something more; it is intercourse. It describes the commercial intercourse between nations and parts of nations in all its branches, and is regulated by prescribing rules for carrying on that intercourse." That which belongs to commerce is within the jurisdiction of the United States, but that which does not belong to commerce is within the jurisdiction of the police power of the State. *Gibbons v. Ogden* [1824].

The argument is that the power to control the manufacture of refined sugar is a monopoly over a necessary of life, to the enjoyment of which by a large part of the population of the United States interstate commerce is indispensable, and that, therefore, the general government, in the exercise of the power to regulate commerce, may repress such monopoly directly and set aside the instruments which have created it. But this argument cannot be confined to necessaries of life merely, and must include all articles of general consumption. Doubtless the power to control the manufacture of a given thing involves in a certain sense the control of its disposition, but this is a secondary, and not the primary, sense, and although the exercise of that power may result in bringing the operation of commerce into play, it does not control it, and affects it only incidentally and indirectly. Commerce succeeds to manufacture, and is not a part of it. The power to regulate commerce is the power to prescribe the rule by which commerce shall be governed, and is a power independent of the power to suppress monopoly. But it may operate in repression of monopoly whenever that comes within the rules by which commerce is governed or whenever the transaction is itself a monopoly of commerce.

It is vital that the independence of the commercial power and of the police power, and the delimitation between them, however sometimes perplexing, should always be recognized and observed, for while the one furnishes the strongest bond of union, the other is essential to the preservation of the autonomy of the States, as required by our dual form of government, and acknowledged evils, however grave and urgent they may appear to be, had better be borne than the risk be run, in the effort to suppress them, of more serious consequences by resort to expedients of even doubtful constitutionality.

It will be perceived how far-reaching the proposition is that the power of dealing with a monopoly directly may be exercised by the general government whenever interstate or international commerce may be ultimately affected. The regulation of commerce applies to the subjects of commerce, and not to matters of internal police. Contracts to buy, sell, or exchange goods to be transported among the several States, the transportation and its instrumentalities, and articles bought, sold, or exchanged for the purposes of such transit among the States, or put in the way of transit, may be regulated, but this is because they form part of interstate trade or commerce. The fact that an article is manufactured for export to another State does not, of itself, make it an article of interstate commerce, and the intent of the manufacturer does not determine the time when the article or product passes from the control of the State and belongs to commerce. [. . .]

Does the owner's state of mind in relation to the goods, that is, his intent to export them, and his partial preparation to do so, exempt them from taxation? This is the precise question for solution. [. . .] There must be a point of time when they cease to be governed exclusively by the domestic law and begin to be governed and protected by the national law of commercial regulation, and that moment seems to us to be a legitimate one for this purpose, in which they commence their final movement from the State of their origin to that of their destination. [. . .]

And again, in *Kidd v. Pearson* [1888], where the question was discussed whether the right of a State to enact a statute prohibiting within its limits the manufacture of intoxicating liquors, except for certain purposes, could be overthrown by the fact that the manufacturer intended to export the liquors when made, it was held that the intent of the manufacturer did not determine the time when the article or product passed from the control of the State and belonged to commerce, and that, therefore, the statute, in omitting to except from its operation the manufacture of intoxicating liquors within the limits of the State for export, did not constitute an unauthorized interference with the right of Congress to regulate commerce. And Mr. Justice Lamar remarked:

No distinction is more popular to the common mind, or more clearly expressed in economic and political literature, than that between manufacture and commerce. Manufacture is transformation—the fashioning of raw materials into a change of form for use. The functions of commerce are different. The buying and selling and the transportation incidental thereto constitute commerce, and the regulation of commerce in the constitutional sense embraces the regulation at least of such transportation. . . . If it be held that the term includes the regulation of all such manufactures as are intended to be the subject of commercial transactions in the future, it is impossible to deny that it would also include all productive industries that contemplate the same thing. The result would be that Congress would be invested, to the exclusion of the States, with the power to regulate not only manufactures, but also agriculture, horticulture, stock raising, domestic fisheries, mining—in short, every branch of human industry. For is there one of them that does not contemplate, more or less clearly, an interstate or foreign market? Does not the wheat grower of the Northwest or the cotton planter of the South, plant, cultivate, and harvest his crop with an eye on the prices at Liverpool, New York, and Chicago? The power being vested in Congress and denied to the States, it would follow as an inevitable result that the duty would devolve on Congress to regulate all of these delicate, multiform and vital interests—interests which in their nature are and must be local in all the details of their successful management. . . . A situation more paralyzing to the state governments, and more provocative of conflicts between the general government and the States, and less likely to have been what the framers of the Constitution intended it would be difficult to imagine.

Contracts, combinations, or conspiracies to control domestic enterprise in manufacture, agriculture, mining, production in all its forms, or to raise or lower prices or wages might unquestionably tend to restrain external as well as domestic trade, but the restraint would be an indirect result, however inevitable and whatever its extent, and such result would not necessarily determine the object of the contract, combination, or conspiracy. [. . .]

Slight reflection will show that, if the national power extends to all contracts and combinations in manufacture, agriculture, mining, and other productive industries whose ultimate result may affect external commerce, comparatively little of business operations and affairs would be left for state control.

It was in the light of well settled principles that the act of July 2, 1890, was framed. Congress did not attempt thereby to assert the power to deal with monopoly directly as such, or to limit and restrict the rights of corporations created by the States or the citizens of the States in the acquisition, control, or disposition of property, or to regulate or prescribe the price or prices at which such property or the products thereof should be sold, or to make criminal the acts of persons in the acquisition and control of property which the States of their residence or creation sanctioned or permitted. Aside from the provisions applicable where Congress might exercise municipal power, what the law struck at was combinations, contracts, and conspiracies to monopolize trade and commerce among the several States or with foreign nations; but the contracts and acts of the defendants related exclusively to the acquisition of the Philadelphia refineries and the business of sugar refining in Pennsylvania, and bore no direct relation to commerce between the States or with foreign nations. The object was manifestly private gain in the manufacture of the commodity, but not through the control of interstate or foreign commerce. It is true that the bill alleged that the products of these refineries were sold and distributed among the several States, and that all the companies were engaged in trade or commerce with the several States and with foreign nations; but this was no more than to say that trade and commerce served manufacture to fulfill its function. Sugar was refined for sale, and sales were probably made at Philadelphia for consumption, and undoubtedly for resale by the first purchasers throughout Pennsylvania and other States, and refined sugar was also forwarded by the companies to other States for sale. Nevertheless it does not follow that an attempt to monopolize, or the actual monopoly of, the manufacture was an attempt, whether executory or consummated, to monopolize commerce, even though, in order to dispose of the product, the instrumentality of commerce was necessarily invoked. There was nothing in the proofs to indicate any intention to put a restraint upon trade or commerce, and the fact, as we have seen, that trade or commerce might be indirectly affected was not enough to entitle complainants to a decree. [. . .]

The Circuit Court declined, upon the pleadings and proofs, to grant the relief prayed, and dismissed the bill, and we are of opinion that the Circuit Court of Appeals did not err in affirming that decree.

Decree affirmed.

John Marshall Harlan

United States v. E. C. Knight Company, Dissent (1895)

Mr. Justice HARLAN dissenting.

Prior to the 4th day of March, 1892, the American Sugar Refining Company, a corporation organized under a general statute of New Jersey for the purpose of buying, manufacturing, refining, and *selling sugar in different parts of the country*, had obtained the control of all the sugar refineries in the United States except five, of which four were owned and operated by Pennsylvania corporations—the E. C. Knight Company, the Franklin Sugar Refining Company, Spreckels' Sugar Refining Company, and the Delaware Sugar House—and the other, by the Revere Sugar Refinery of Boston. These five corporations were all in active competition with the American Sugar Refining Company and with each other. The product of the Pennsylvania companies was about thirty-three percent, and that of the Boston company about two percent, of the entire quantity of sugar refined in the United States.

In March, 1899, by means of contracts or arrangements with stockholders of the four Pennsylvania companies, the New Jersey corporation—using for that purpose its own stock—purchased the stock of those companies, and thus obtained absolute control of the entire business of sugar refining in the United States except that done by the Boston company, which is too small in amount to be regarded in this discussion.

"The object," the court below said, "in purchasing the Philadelphia refineries was to obtain a greater influence or *more perfect control* over *the business* of refining *and selling* sugar *in this country*." This characterization of the object for which this stupendous combination was formed is properly accepted in the opinion of the court as justified by the proof. I need not therefore analyze the evidence upon this point. In its consideration of the important constitutional question presented, this court assumes on the record before us that the result of the transactions disclosed by the pleadings and proof was the creation of a monopoly in the manufacture of a necessary of life.

If this combination, so far as its operations necessarily or directly affect interstate commerce, cannot be restrained or suppressed under some power granted to Congress, it will be cause for regret that the patriotic statesmen who framed the Constitution did not foresee the necessity of investing the national government with power to deal with gigantic monopolies holding in their grasp, and injuriously controlling in their own interest, the entire trade *among the States* in food products that are essential to the comfort of every household in the land.

The court holds it to be vital in our system of government to recognize and give effect to both the commercial power of the nation and the police powers of the States, to the end that the Union be strengthened and the autonomy of the States preserved. In this view I entirely concur. Undoubtedly, the preservation of the just authority of the States is an object of deep concern to every lover of his country. No greater calamity could befall our free institutions than the destruction of that authority, by whatever means such a result might be accomplished. [. . .] But it is equally true that the preservation of the just authority of the General Government is essential as well to the safety of the States as to the attainment of the important ends for which that government was ordained by the People of the United States, and the destruction of that authority would be fatal to the peace and wellbeing of the American people. The Constitution which enumerates the powers committed to the nation for objects of interest to the people of all the States should not, therefore, be subjected to an interpretation so rigid, technical, and narrow that those objects cannot be accomplished. [. . .]

Congress is invested with power to regulate commerce with foreign nations and among the several States. The power to regulate is the power to prescribe the rule by which the subject regulated is to be governed. It is one that must be exercised whenever necessary throughout the territorial limits of the several States. The power to make these regulations "is complete in itself, may be exercised to its utmost extent, and acknowledges no limitations other than are prescribed in the Constitution." It is plenary because vested in Congress "as absolutely as it would be in a single government having in its constitution the same restrictions on the exercise of the power as are found in the Constitution of the United States." It may be exercised "whenever the subject exists." *Gibbons v. Ogden* [1824]. In his concurring opinion in that case, Mr. Justice Johnson observed that the grant to Congress of the power to regulate commerce carried with it the whole subject, leaving nothing for the State to act upon, and that, "if there was anyone object riding over every other in the adoption of the Constitution, it was to keep commercial intercourse among the States free from *all* invidious and partial restraints. In all commercial regulations, we are one and the same people." [. . .]

What is commerce among the States? The decisions of this court fully answer the question. "Commerce, undoubtedly, is traffic, but it is something more: it is intercourse." It does not embrace the completely interior traffic of the respective States— that which is "carried on between man and man in a State, or between different parts of the same State and which does not extend to or affect other States"—but it does embrace "every species of commercial intercourse" between the United States and foreign nations and among the States, and therefore it includes such traffic or trade, buying, selling, and interchange of commodities as directly affects or necessarily involves the interests of the People of the United States. "Commerce, as the word is used in the Constitution, is a unit," and cannot stop at the external boundary line of each State, but may be introduced into the interior. [. . .] The genius and character of the whole government seem to be that its action is to be applied to all the external concerns of the nation, and to those internal concerns which affect the States generally.

These principles were announced in *Gibbons v. Ogden*, and have often been approved. It is the settled doctrine of this court that interstate commerce embraces something more than the mere physical transportation of articles of property, and the vehicles or vessels by which such transportation is effected. In *County of Mobile v. Kimball* [1880], it

was said that "commerce with foreign countries and among the States, strictly considered, consists in intercourse and traffic, including, in these terms, navigation and the transportation and transit of persons and property, as well as the purchase, sale, and exchange of commodities."

In *Kidd v. Pearson* [1888], it was said that "the buying and selling, and the transportation *incidental thereto* constitute commerce." Interstate commerce does not, therefore, consist in transportation simply. It includes the purchase and sale of articles that are intended to be transported from one State to another—every species of commercial intercourse among the States and with foreign nations.

In the light of these principles, determining as well the scope of the power to regulate commerce among the States as the nature of such commerce, we are to inquire whether the act of Congress of July 2, 1890, is repugnant to the Constitution.

By that act every contract, combination in the form of trust *or otherwise,* or conspiracy, in restraint of trade or commerce *among the several States* or with foreign nations, is declared to be illegal, and every person making any such contract, or engaging in any such combination or conspiracy, is to be deemed guilty of a misdemeanor, and punishable, on conviction, by a fine not exceeding five thousand dollars, or by imprisonment not exceeding one year, or by both said punishments in the discretion of the court. § 1. It is also made a misdemeanor, punishable in like manner, for any person to monopolize, or attempt to monopolize, or combine or conspire with any other person or persons to monopolize, any part of the trade or commerce *among the several States* or with foreign nations. [. . .]

It would seem to be indisputable that no *combination* of corporations or individuals can, *of right,* impose unlawful restraints upon *interstate* trade, whether upon transportation or upon such interstate intercourse and traffic as precede transportation, any more than it can, *of right,* impose unreasonable restraints upon the completely internal traffic of a State. The supposition cannot be indulged that this general proposition will be disputed. If it be true that a *combination* of corporations or individuals may, so far as the power of Congress is concerned, subject interstate trade, in any of its stages, to unlawful restraints, the conclusion is inevitable that the

Constitution has failed to accomplish one primary object of the Union, which was to place commerce *among the States* under the control of the common government of all the people, and thereby relieve or protect it against burdens or restrictions imposed, by whatever authority, for the benefit of particular localities or special interests. [. . .]

A leading case on the question as to what combinations are illegal as being in general restraint of trade is *Richardson v. Buhl,* 77 Michigan 632, which related to certain agreements connected with the business and operations of the Diamond Match Company. From the report of the case, it appears that that company was organized under the laws of Connecticut for the purpose of uniting in one corporation all the match manufactories in the United States, and to monopolize and control the business of making all the friction matches in the country and establish the price thereof. To that end, it became necessary, among other things, to buy many plants that had become established or were about to be established, as well as the property used in connection therewith. Chief Justice Sherwood of the Supreme Court of Michigan said:

The sole object of the corporation is to make money by having it in its power to raise the price of the article, or diminish the quantity to be made and used, at its pleasure. Thus, both the supply of the article and the price thereof are made to depend upon the action of a half dozen individuals, more or less, to satisfy their cupidity and avarice, who may happen to have the controlling interest in this corporation—an artificial person, governed by a single motive or purpose, which is to accumulate money regardless of the wants or necessities of over 60,000,000 people. The article thus completely under their control for the last fifty years has come to be regarded as one of necessity not only in every household in the land, but one of daily use by almost every individual in the country. It is difficult to conceive of a monopoly which can affect a greater number of people, or one more extensive in its effect on the country, than that of the Diamond Match Company. It was to aid that company in its purposes and in carrying out its object that the contract in this case was made between those parties which we are now asked to aid in enforcing. Monopoly in trade, or in any kind of business in this country, is

odious to our form of government. It is sometimes permitted to aid the government in carrying on a great public enterprise or public work under governmental control in the interest of the public. Its tendency is, however, destructive of free institutions and repugnant to the instincts of a free people, and contrary to the whole scope and spirit of the Federal Constitution, and is not allowed to exist under express provisions in several of our state constitutions. . . . All combinations among persons or corporations for the purpose of raising or controlling the prices of merchandise, or any of the necessaries of life, are monopolies and intolerable, and ought to receive the condemnation of all courts.

In the same case, Mr. Justice Champlin, with whom Mr. Justice Campbell concurred, said:

There is no doubt that all the parties to this suit were active participants in perfecting the combination called "The Diamond Match Company," and that the present dispute grows out of that transaction and is the fruit of the scheme by which all competition in the manufacture of matches was stifled, opposition in the business crushed, and the whole business of the country in that line engrossed by the Diamond Match Company. Such a vast combination as has been entered into under the above name is a menace to the public. Its object and direct tendency is to prevent free and fair competition, and control prices throughout the national domain. It is no answer to say that this monopoly has, in fact, reduced the price of friction matches. That policy may have been necessary to crush competition. The fact exists that it rests in the discretion of this company at any time to raise the price to an exorbitant degree. Such combinations have frequently been condemned by courts as unlawful and against public policy.

This extended reference to adjudged cases relating to unlawful restraints upon the interior traffic of a State has been made for the purpose of showing that a combination such as that organized under the name of the American Sugar Refining Company has been uniformly held by the courts of the States to be against public policy and illegal because of its necessary tendency to impose improper restraints upon trade. And such, I take it, would be the judgment of any Circuit Court of the United States in a case between parties in which it became necessary to determine the question. The judgments of the state courts rest upon general principles of law, and not necessarily upon statutory provisions expressly condemning restraints of trade imposed by or resulting from combinations. Of course, in view of the authorities, it will not be doubted that it would be competent for a State, under the power to regulate its domestic commerce and for the purpose of protecting its people against fraud and injustice, to make it a public offence punishable by fine and imprisonment for individuals or corporations to make contracts, form combinations, or engage in conspiracies, which unduly restrain trade or commerce carried on within its limits, and also to authorize the institution of proceedings for the purpose of annulling contracts of that character, as well as of preventing or restraining such combinations and conspiracies.

But there is a trade among the several States which is distinct from that carried on within the territorial limits of a State. The regulation and control of the former is committed by the national Constitution to Congress. Commerce among the States, as this court has declared, is a unit, and, in respect of that commerce, this is one country and we are one people. It may be regulated by rules applicable to every part of the United States, and state lines and state jurisdiction cannot interfere with the enforcement of such rules. The jurisdiction of the general government extends over every foot of territory within the United States. Under the power with which it is invested, Congress may remove unlawful obstructions, of whatever kind, to the free course of trade among the States. In so doing, it would not interfere with the " autonomy of the States," because the power thus to protect interstate commerce is expressly given by the people of all the States. [. . .] It is the Constitution, the supreme law of the land, which invests Congress with power to protect commerce among the States against burdens and exactions arising from unlawful restraints by whatever authority imposed. Surely a right secured or granted by that instrument is under the protection of the government which that instrument creates. Any combination, therefore, that disturbs or unreasonably obstructs freedom in buying and selling articles manufactured to be sold to persons in other States or to

be carried to other States—a freedom that cannot exist if the right to buy and sell is fettered by unlawful restraints that crush out competition—affects, not incidentally, but directly, the people of all the States, and the remedy for such an evil is found only in the exercise of powers confided to a government which, this court has said, was the government of all, exercising powers delegated by all, representing all, acting for all. *McCulloch v. Maryland* [1819]. [. . .]

It may be admitted that an act which did nothing more than forbid, and which had no other object than to forbid, the mere refining of sugar in any State would be in excess of any power granted to Congress. But the act of 1890 is not of that character. It does not strike at the manufacture simply of articles that are legitimate or recognized subjects of commerce, but at *combinations* that unduly restrain, because they monopolize, *the buying and selling of articles* which are to go into interstate commerce. [. . .]

In *Kidd v. Pearson*, we recognized, as had been done in previous cases, the distinction between the mere transportation of articles of interstate commerce and the *purchasing* and *selling* that *precede transportation*. It is said that manufacture precedes commerce, and is not a part of it. But it is equally true that, when manufacture ends, that which has been manufactured becomes a subject of commerce; that buying and selling succeed manufacture, come into existence after the process of manufacture is completed, precede transportation, and are as much commercial intercourse, where articles are bought to be carried from one State to another, as is the manual transportation of such articles after they have been so purchased. The distinction was recognized by this court in *Gibbons v. Ogden*, where the principal question was whether commerce included navigation. Both the court and counsel recognized buying and selling or barter *as included in commerce*. Chief Justice Marshall said that the mind can scarcely conceive a system for regulating commerce, which was "*confined* to prescribing rules for the conduct of individuals in the actual employment of buying and selling, or of barter."

The power of Congress covers and protects the absolute freedom of such intercourse and trade among the States as may or must succeed manufacture and precede transportation from the place of purchase. This would seem to be conceded, for the

court in the present case expressly declare that "contracts to buy, sell, or exchange goods *to be transported
among the several States*, the transportation and its
instrumentalities, and articles bought, sold, or
exchanged for the purpose of such transit among the
States, or put in the way of transit, *may be regulated*,
but this is *because they form part of interstate trade or
commerce.*" Here is a direct admission—one which
the settled doctrines of this court justify—that contracts to buy and the purchasing of goods *to be transported from one State to another*, and transportation,
with its instrumentalities, are all *parts* of interstate
trade or commerce. Each part of such trade is then
under the protection of Congress. And yet, by the
opinion and judgment in this case, if I do not misapprehend them, Congress is without power to protect
the commercial intercourse that such purchasing
necessarily involves against the restraints and burdens arising from the existence of combinations that
meet purchasers, from whatever State they come,
with the threat—for it is nothing more nor less than
a threat—that they *shall not* purchase what they
desire to purchase, *except at the prices fixed by such
combinations*. A citizen of Missouri has the right to
go in person, or send orders, to Pennsylvania and
New Jersey for the purpose of purchasing refined
sugar. But of what value is that right if he is confronted in those States by a vast *combination* which
absolutely controls the price of that article by reason
of its having acquired all the sugar refineries in the
United States in order that they may fix prices in
their own interest exclusively?

In my judgment, the citizens of the several States
composing the Union are entitled, of right, to buy
goods in the State where they are manufactured, or
in any other State, without being confronted by an
illegal combination whose business extends throughout the whole country, which by the law everywhere
is an enemy to the public interests, and which prevents such buying, except at prices arbitrarily fixed by
it. I insist that the free course of trade among the
States cannot coexist with such combinations. When
I speak of trade, I mean the buying and selling of articles of every kind that are recognized articles of interstate commerce. Whatever improperly obstructs the
free course of interstate intercourse and trade, as
involved in the buying and selling of articles to be
carried from one State to another, may be reached by

Congress under its authority to regulate commerce
among the States. The exercise of that authority so as
to make trade among the States in all recognized articles of commerce absolutely free from unreasonable
or illegal restrictions imposed by combinations is justified by an express grant of power to Congress, and
would redound to the welfare of the whole country. I
am unable to perceive that any such result would
imperil the autonomy of the States, especially as that
result cannot be attained through the action of any
one State. [. . .]

In committing to Congress the control of commerce with foreign nations and among the several
States, the Constitution did not define the means
that may be employed to protect the freedom of commercial intercourse and traffic established for the
benefit of all the people of the Union. It wisely for-
bore to impose any limitations upon the exercise of
that power except those arising from the general
nature of the government, or such as are embodied
in the fundamental guarantees of liberty and property. It gives to Congress, in express words, authority
to enact all laws necessary and proper for carrying
into execution the power to regulate commerce, and
whether an act of Congress, passed to accomplish an
object to which the general government is competent, is within the power granted must be determined
by the rule announced through Chief Justice Marshall three-quarters of a century ago, and which has
been repeatedly affirmed by this court. That rule is:

> The sound construction of the Constitu-
> tion must allow to the national legislature
> the discretion with respect to the means by
> which the powers it confers are to be car-
> ried into execution, which will enable that
> body to perform the high duties assigned
> to it in the manner most beneficial to the
> people. Let the end be legitimate, let it be
> within the scope of the Constitution, and
> all means which are appropriate, which
> are plainly adapted to that end, which are
> not prohibited, but consistent with the let-
> ter and spirit of the Constitution, are con-
> stitutional. *McCulloch v. Maryland*

The end proposed to be accomplished by the act of
1890 is the protection of trade and commerce among
the States against unlawful restraints. Who can say

that that end is not legitimate or is not within the scope of the Constitution? The means employed are the suppression, by legal proceedings, of combinations, conspiracies, and monopolies which, by their inevitable and admitted tendency, improperly restrain trade and commerce among the States. Who can say that such means are not appropriate to attain the end of freeing commercial intercourse among the States from burdens and exactions imposed upon it by combinations which, under principles long recognized in this country as well as at the common law, are illegal and dangerous to the public welfare? What clause of the Constitution can be referred to which prohibits the means thus prescribed in the act of Congress?

It may be that the means employed by Congress to suppress combinations that restrain interstate trade and commerce are not all or the best that could have been devised. But Congress, under the delegation of authority to enact laws necessary and proper to carry into effect a power granted, is not restricted to the employment of those means "without which the end would be entirely unattainable." "To have prescribed the means," this court has said,

by which government should, in all future time, execute its powers would have been to change entirely the character of that instrument, and give it the properties of a legal code. It would have been an unwise attempt to provide by immutable rules for exigencies which, if foreseen at all, must have been seen dimly, and which can be best provided for as they occur. To have declared that the best means shall not be used, but those alone without which the power given would be nugatory, would have been to deprive the legislature of the capacity to avail itself of experience, to exercise its reason, and to accommodate its legislation to circumstances.

Again:

Where the law is not prohibited, and is really calculated to effect any of the objects entrusted to the government, to undertake here to inquire into the degree of its necessity would be to pass the line which circumscribes the judicial department and to tread on legislative ground. *McCulloch v. Maryland*.

By the act of 1890, Congress subjected to forfeiture "any property owned under any contract or by any combination, or pursuant to any conspiracy (and being the subject thereof) mentioned in section one of this act and being in the course of transportation from one State to another, or to a foreign country." It was not deemed wise to subject such property to forfeiture before transportation began or after it ended. If it be suggested that Congress might have prohibited the *transportation* from the State in which they are manufactured of any articles, by whomsoever at the time owned, that had been manufactured by combinations formed to monopolize some designated part of trade or commerce among the States, my answer is that it is not within the functions of the judiciary to adjudge that Congress shall employ particular means in execution of a given power simply because such means are, in the judgment of the courts, best conducive to the end sought to be accomplished. Congress, in the exercise of its discretion as to choice of means conducive to an end to which it was competent, determined to reach that end through civil proceedings instituted to prevent or restrain these obnoxious combinations in their attempts to burden interstate commerce by obstructions that interfere *in advance of transportation* with the free course of trade between the people of the States. In other words, Congress sought to prevent the coming into existence of combinations the purpose or tendency of which was to impose unlawful restraints upon interstate commerce. [. . .]

The question here relates to restraints upon the freedom of interstate trade and commerce imposed by illegal combinations. After the fullest consideration I have been able to bestow upon this important question, I find it impossible to refuse my assent to this proposition: whatever a State may do to protect its completely interior traffic or trade against unlawful restraints, the general government is empowered to do for the protection of the people of all the States—for this purpose, one people—against unlawful restraints imposed upon interstate traffic or trade in articles that are to enter into commerce among the several States. If, as already shown, a State may prevent or suppress a *combination*, the effect of which is to subject its domestic trade to the restraints necessarily arising from their obtaining the absolute control of the sale of a particular article in general use by the community, there ought to be no hesitation in allowing to Congress the right to suppress a similar combination that imposes a like unlawful restraint upon interstate trade and traffic in that article. While the States retain, because they have never surrendered, full control of their completely internal traffic, it was not intended by the framers of the Constitution that any part of interstate commerce should be excluded from the control of Congress. Each State can reach and suppress combinations so far as they unlawfully restrain its interior trade, while the national government may reach and suppress them so far as they unlawfully restrain trade among the States. [. . .]

It is said that there are no proofs in the record which indicate an *intention* upon the part of the American Sugar Refining Company and its associates to put a restraint upon trade or commerce. Was it necessary that formal proof be made that the persons engaged in this combination admitted, in words, that they intended to restrain trade or commerce? Did anyone expect to find in the written agreements which resulted in the formation of this combination a distinct expression of a purpose to restrain interstate trade or commerce? Men who form and control these combinations are too cautious and wary to make such admissions orally or in writing. Why, it is conceded that the object of this combination was to obtain control of the business of making and selling refined sugar throughout the entire country. Those interested in its operations will be satisfied with nothing less than to have the whole population of America pay tribute to them. That object is disclosed upon the very face of the transactions described in the bill. And it is proved—indeed, is conceded—that that object has been accomplished to the extent that the American Sugar Refining Company now controls ninety-eight percent of all the sugar refining business in the country, and therefore controls the price of that article everywhere. Now the *mere existence* of a combination having such an object and possessing such extraordinary power is itself, under settled principles of law—there being no adjudged case to the contrary in this country—a direct restraint of trade in the article for the control of the sales of which in this country that combination was organized. And that restraint is felt in all the States for the reason, known to all, that the article in question goes, was intended

to go, and must always go, into commerce among the several States, and into the homes of people in every condition of life.

A decree recognizing the freedom of commercial intercourse as embracing the right to buy goods to be transported from one State to another, without buyers being burdened by unlawful restraints imposed by combinations of corporations or individuals, so far from disturbing or endangering, would tend to preserve the autonomy of the States, and protect the people of all the States against dangers so portentous as to excite apprehension for the safety of our liberties. If this be not a sound interpretation of the Constitution, it is easy to perceive that interstate traffic, so far as it involves the price to be paid for articles necessary to the comfort and well being of the people in all the States, may pass under the absolute control of overshadowing combinations having financial resources without limit and an audacity in the accomplishment of their objects that recognizes none of the restraints of moral obligations controlling the action of individuals; combinations governed entirely by the law of greed and selfishness—so powerful that no single State is able to overthrow them and give the required protection to the whole country, and so all-pervading that they threaten the integrity of our institutions.

We have before us the case of a combination which absolutely controls, or may, at its discretion, control the price of all refined sugar in this country. Suppose another *combination*, organized for private gain and to control prices, should obtain possession of all the large flour mills in the United States; another, of all the grain elevators; another, of all the oil territory; another, of all the salt-producing regions; another, of all the cotton mills, and another, of all the great establishments for slaughtering animals and the preparation of meats. What power is competent to protect the people of the United States against such dangers except a national power—one that is capable of exerting its sovereign authority throughout every part of the territory and over all the people of the nation?

To the general government has been committed the control of commercial intercourse among the States, to the end that it may be free at all times from any restraints except such as Congress may impose or permit for the benefit of the whole country. The common government of all the people is the only one that can adequately deal with a matter which directly and injuriously affects the entire Commerce of the country, which concerns equally all the people of the Union, and which, it must be confessed, cannot be adequately controlled by any one State. Its authority should not be so weakened by construction that it cannot reach and eradicate evils that, beyond all question, tend to defeat an object which that government is entitled, by the Constitution, to accomplish. "Powerful and ingenious minds," this court has said,

> taking as postulates that the powers expressly granted to the government of the Union are to be contracted by construction into the narrowest possible compass, and that the original powers of the States are retained if any possible construction will retain them, may, by a course of well digested but refined and metaphysical reasoning founded on these premises, explain away the Constitution of our country and leave it a magnificent structure indeed to look at, but totally unfit for use. They may so entangle and perplex the understanding as

to obscure principles which were before thought quite plain, and induce doubts where, if the mind were to pursue its own course, none would be perceived. *Gibbons v. Ogden.*

While a decree annulling the contracts under which the combination in question was formed may not, in view of the facts disclosed, be effectual to accomplish the object of the act of 1890, I perceive no difficulty in the way of the court's passing a decree declaring that that combination imposes an unlawful restraint upon trade and commerce among the States and perpetually enjoining it from further prosecuting any business pursuant to the unlawful agreements under which it was formed or by which it was created. Such a decree would be within the scope of the bill, and is appropriate to the end which Congress intended to accomplish, namely, to protect the freedom of commercial intercourse among the States against combinations and conspiracies which impose unlawful restraints upon such intercourse.

For the reasons stated, I dissent from the opinion and judgment of the Court.

KATHARINE LEE BATES

America the Beautiful (1893, 1904, 1913)[1]

O beautiful for spacious skies,
For amber waves of grain,
For purple mountain majesties
Above the fruited plain!
America! America!
God shed his grace on thee
And crown thy good with brotherhood
From sea to shining sea!

O beautiful for pilgrim feet
Whose stern, impassioned stress
A thoroughfare for freedom beat
Across the wilderness!
America! America!
God mend thine every flaw,
Confirm thy soul in self-control,
Thy liberty in law!

O beautiful for heroes proved in liberating strife.
Who more than self the country loved
And mercy more than life!
America! America!
May God thy gold refine

---

1. [This poem, originally written in 1893, was modified twice by Bates, eventually producing this final form by 1913. The poem was inspired by a hike to the summit of Pike's Peak in Colorado.]

Till all success be nobleness
And every gain divine!

O beautiful for patriot dream
That sees beyond the years
Thine alabaster cities gleam
Undimmed by human tears!
America! America!
God shed his grace on thee
And crown thy good with brotherhood
From sea to shining sea!

O beautiful for halcyon skies,
For amber waves of grain,
For purple mountain majesties
Above the enameled plain!
America! America!
God shed his grace on thee
Till souls wax fair as earth and air
And music-hearted sea!

O beautiful for pilgrims feet,
Whose stern impassioned stress
A thoroughfare for freedom beat
Across the wilderness!

America! America!
God shed his grace on thee
Till paths be wrought through
Wilds of thought
By pilgrim foot and knee!

O beautiful for glory-tale
Of liberating strife
When once and twice,
For man's avail
Men lavished precious life!
America! America!
God shed his grace on thee
Till selfish gain no longer stain
The banner of the free!

O beautiful for patriot dream
That sees beyond the years
Thine alabaster cities gleam
Undimmed by human tears!
America! America!
God shed his grace on thee
Till nobler men keep once again
Thy whiter jubilee!

John Phillip Sousa

The Stars and Stripes Forever (1897)

Let martial note in triumph float,
And liberty extend its mighty hand.
A flag appears, 'mid thund'rous cheers,
The banner of the Western land.
The emblem of the brave and true,
Its folds protect no tyrant crew,
The red and white and starry blue
Is freedom's shield and hope.

Other nations may deem their flags the best,
And cheer them with fervid elation.
But the flag of the North and South and West
Is the flag of flags, the flag of freedom's nation.

Chorus:
Let eagle shriek from lofty peak
The never-ending watchword of our land.
Let summer breeze waft through the trees
The echo of the chorus grand.
Sing out for liberty and light,
Sing out for freedom and the right.
Sing out for Union and its might,
Oh, patriotic sons!

Hurrah for the flag of the free;
May it wave as our standard forever.
The gem of the land and the sea,

The banner of the right.
Let despots remember the day
When our fathers, with mighty endeavor,
Proclaimed as they marched to the fray,
That by their might, and by their right,
It waves forever!

Other nations may deem their flags the best,
And cheer them with fervid elation.
But the flag of the North and South and West
Is the flag of flags, the flag of freedom's nation.

ANDREW CARNEGIE

The Gospel of Wealth (1889)

The problem of our age is the proper administration of wealth, so that the ties of brotherhood may still bind together the rich and poor in harmonious relationship. The conditions of human life have not only been changed, but revolutionized, within the past few hundred years. In former days there was little difference between the swelling, dress, food, and environment of the chief and those of his retainers. The Indians are to-day where civilized man then was. When visiting the Sioux, I was led to the wigwam of the chief. It was just like the others in external appearance, and even within the difference was trifling between it and those of the poorest of his braves. The contrast between the palace of the millionaire and the cottage of the laborer with us today measures the change which has come with civilization.

This change, however, is not to be deplored, but welcomed as highly beneficial. It is well, nay, essential for the progress of the race, that the houses of some should be homes for all that is highest and best in literature and the arts, and for all the refinements of civilization, rather than that none should be so. Much better this great irregularity than universal squalor. Without wealth there can be no Maecenas. The "good old times" were not good old times. Neither master nor servant was as well situated then as today. A relapse to old conditions would be disastrous to both—not the least so to him who serves—and would sweep away civilization with it. But whether the change be for good or ill, it is upon us, beyond our power to alter, and therefore to be accepted and made the best of. It is waste of time to criticize the inevitable.

It is easy to see how the change has come. One illustration will serve for almost every phase of the cause. In the manufacture of products we have the whole story. It applies to all combinations of human industry, as stimulated and enlarged by the inventions of this scientific age. Formerly articles were manufactured at the domestic hearth or in small shops which formed part of the household. The master and his apprentices worked side by side, the latter living with the master, and therefore subject to the same conditions. When these apprentices rose to be masters, there was little or no change in their mode of life, and they, in turn, educated in the same routine succeeding apprentices. There was, substantially, social equality, and even political equality, for those engaged in industrial pursuits had then little or no political voice in the State.

But the inevitable result of such a mode of manufacture was crude articles at high prices. Today the world obtains commodities of excellent quality at prices which even the generation preceding this would have deemed incredible. In the commercial world similar causes have produced similar results, and the race is benefited thereby. The poor enjoy what the rich could not before afford. What were the luxuries have become the necessaries of life. The laborer has now more comforts than the farmer had a few generations ago. The farmer has more luxuries than the landlord had, and is more richly clad and better housed. The landlord has books and pictures rarer, and appointments more artistic, than the King could then obtain.

The price we pay for this salutary change is, no doubt, great. We assemble thousands of operatives in the factory, in the mine, and in the counting-house, of whom the employer can know little or nothing, and to whom the employer is little better than a myth. All intercourse between them is at an end. Rigid Castes are formed, and, as usual, mutual ignorance breeds mutual distrust. Each Caste is without sympathy for the other, and ready to credit anything disparaging in regard to it. Under the law of competition, the employer of thousands is forced into the strictest economies, among which the rates paid to labor figure prominently, and often there is friction between the employer and the employed, between capital and labor, between rich and poor. Human society loses homogeneity.

The price which society pays for the law of competition, like the price it pays for cheap comforts and luxuries, is also great; but the advantages of this law are also greater still, for it is to this law that we owe our wonderful material development which brings improved conditions in its train. But, whether the law be benign or not, we must say of it, as we say of the change in the conditions of men to which we have referred: It is here; we cannot evade it; no substitutes for it have been found; and while the law may be sometimes hard for the individual, it is best for the race, because it insures the survival of the fittest in every department. We accept and welcome, therefore, as conditions to which we must accommodate ourselves, great inequality of environment, the concentration of business, industrial and commercial, in the hands of a few, and the law of competition between these, as being not only beneficial, but essential for the future progress of the race. Having accepted these, it follows that there must be great scope for the exercise of special ability in the merchant and in the manufacturer who has to conduct affairs upon a great scale. That this talent for organisation and management is rare among men is proved by the fact that it invariably secures for its possessor enormous rewards, no matter where or under what laws or conditions. The experienced in affairs always rate the MAN whose services can be obtained as a partner as not only the first consideration, but such as to render the question of his capital scarcely worth considering, for such men soon create capital; while, without the special talent required, capital soon takes

wings. Such men become interested in firms or corporations using millions; and estimating only simple interest to be made upon the capital invested, it is inevitable that their income must exceed their expenditures, and that they must accumulate wealth. Nor is there any middle ground which such men can occupy, because the great manufacturing or commercial concern which does not earn at least interest upon its capital soon becomes bankrupt. It must either go forward or fall behind: to stand still is impossible. It is a condition essential for its successful operation that it should be thus far profitable, and even that, in addition to interest on capital, it should make profit. It is a law, as certain as any of the others named, that men possessed of this peculiar talent for affairs, under the free play of economic forces, must, of necessity, soon be in receipt of more revenue than can be judiciously expended upon themselves; and this law is as beneficial for the race as the others.

Objections to the foundations upon which society is based are not in order, because the condition of the race is better with these than it has been with any others which have been tried. Of the effect of any new substitutes proposed we cannot be sure. The Socialist or Anarchist who seeks to overturn present conditions is to be regarded as attacking the foundation upon which civilization itself rests, for civilization took its start from the day that the capable, industrious workman said to his incompetent and lazy fellow, "If thou dost not sow, thou shalt not reap," and thus ended primitive Communism by separating the drones from the bees. One who studies this subject will soon be brought face to face with the conclusion that upon the sacredness of property civilization itself depends—the right of the laborer to his hundred dollars in the savings bank, and equally the legal right of the millionaire to his millions. To those who propose to substitute Communism for this intense Individualism the answer, therefore, is: The race has tried that. All progress from that barbarous day to the present time has resulted from its displacement. Not evil, but good, has come to the race from the accumulation of wealth by those who have the ability and energy that produce it. But even if we admit for a moment that it might be better for the race to discard its present foundation, Individualism,—that it is a nobler ideal that man should labor, not for himself alone, but in and for a brotherhood of his fellows, and share with them all in common, realizing Swedenborg's idea of Heaven, where, as he says, the angels derive their happiness, not from laboring for self, but for each other,—even admit all this, and a sufficient answer is, This is not evolution, but revolution. It necessitates the changing of human nature itself—a work of eons, even if it were good to change it, which we cannot know. It is not practicable in our day or in our age. Even if desirable theoretically, it belongs to another and long-succeeding sociological stratum. Our duty is with what is practicable now; with the next step possible in our day and generation. It is criminal to waste our energies in endeavoring to uproot, when all we can profitably or possibly accomplish is to bend the universal tree of humanity a little in the direction most favorable to the production of good fruit under existing circumstances. We might as well urge the destruction of the highest existing type of man because he failed to reach our ideal as to favor the destruction of Individualism, Private Property, the Law of Accumulation of Wealth, and the Law of Competition; for these are the highest results of human experience, the soil in which society so far has produced the best fruit. Unequally or unjustly, perhaps, as these laws sometimes operate, and imperfect as they appear to the Idealist, they are, nevertheless, like the highest type of man, the best and most valuable of all that humanity has yet accomplished.

We start, then, with a condition of affairs under which the best interests of the race are promoted, but which inevitably gives wealth to the few. Thus far, accepting conditions as they exist, the situation can be surveyed and pronounced good. The question then arises,—and, if the foregoing be correct, it is the only question with which we have to deal,—What is the proper mode of administering wealth after the laws upon which civilization is founded have thrown it into the hands of the few? And it is of this great question that I believe I offer the true solution. It will be understood that *fortunes* are here spoken of, not moderate sums saved by many years of effort, the returns from which are required for the comfortable maintenance and education of families. This is not *wealth*, but only *competence*, which it should be the aim of all to acquire.

There are but three modes in which surplus wealth can be disposed of. It can be left to the families of the decedents; or it can be bequeathed for public purposes; or, finally, it can be administered during their lives by its possessors. Under the first and second modes most of the wealth of the world that has reached the few has hitherto been applied. Let us in turn consider each of these modes. The first is the most injudicious. In monarchical countries, the estates and the greatest portion of the wealth are left to the first son, that the vanity of the parent may be gratified by the thought that his name and title are to descend to succeeding generations unimpaired. The condition of this class in Europe today teaches the futility of such hopes or ambitions. The successors have become impoverished through their follies or from the fall in the value of land. Even in Great Britain the strict law of entail has been found inadequate to maintain the status of an hereditary class. Its soil is rapidly passing into the hands of the stranger. Under republican institutions the division of property among the children is much fairer, but the question which forces itself upon thoughtful men in all lands is: Why should men leave great fortunes to their children? If this is done from affection, is it not misguided affection? Observation teaches that, generally speaking, it is not well for the children that they should be so burdened. Neither is it well for the state. Beyond providing for the wife and daughters moderate sources of income, and very moderate allowances indeed, if any, for the sons, men may well hesitate, for it is no longer questionable that great sums bequeathed oftener work more for the injury than for the good of the recipients. Wise men will soon conclude that, for the best interests of the members of their families and of the state, such bequests are an improper use of their means.

It is not suggested that men who have failed to educate their sons to earn a livelihood shall cast them adrift in poverty. If any man has seen fit to rear his sons with a view to their living idle lives, or, what is highly commendable, has instilled in them the sentiment that they are in a position to labor for public ends without reference to pecuniary consideration, then, of course, the duty of the parent is to see that such are provided for *in moderation*. There are instances of millionaires' sons unspoiled by wealth, who, being rich, still perform great services in the community. Such are the very salt of the earth, as valuable as, unfortunately, they are rare; still it is not the exception, but the rule, that men must regard, and, looking at the usual result of enormous sums conferred upon legatees, the thoughtful man must shortly say, "I would as soon leave to my son a curse as the almighty dollar," and admit to himself that it is not the welfare of the children, but family pride, which inspires these enormous legacies.

As to the second mode, that of leaving wealth at death for public uses, it may be said that this is only a means for the disposal of wealth, provided a man is content to wait until he is dead before it becomes of much good in the world. Knowledge of the results of legacies bequeathed is not calculated to inspire the brightest hopes of much posthumous good being accomplished. The cases are not few in which the real object sought by the testator is not attained, nor are they few in which his real wishes are thwarted. In many cases the bequests are so used as to become only monuments of his folly. It is well to remember that it requires the exercise of not less ability than that which acquired the wealth to use it so as to be really beneficial to the community. Besides this, it may fairly be said that no man is to be extolled for doing what he cannot help doing, nor is he to be thanked by the community to which he only leaves wealth at death. Men who leave vast sums in this way may faintly be thought men who would not have left it at all, had they been able to take it with them. The memories of such cannot be held in grateful remembrance, for there is not grace in their gifts. It is not to be wondered at that such bequests seems so generally to lack the blessing.

The growing disposition to tax more and more heavily large estates left at death is a cheering indication of the growth of a salutary change in public opinion. The State of Pennsylvania now takes—subject to some exceptions—one-tenth of the property left by its citizens. The budget presented in the British Parliament the other day proposes to increase the death-duties; and, most significant of all, the new tax is to be a graduated one. Of all forms of taxation, this seems the wisest. Men who continue hoarding great sums all their lives, the proper use of which for the public ends would work good to the community, should be made to feel that the community, in the form of the state, cannot thus be deprived of its proper share. By taxing estates heavily at death the state marks its condemnation of the selfish millionaire's unworthy life.

It is desirable that nations should go much further in this direction. Indeed, it is difficult to set bounds to the share of a rich man's estate which should go at his death to the public through the agency of the state, and by all means such taxes should be graduated, beginning at nothing upon moderate sums to dependents, and increasing rapidly as the amounts swell, until of the millionaire's hoard, as of Shylock's, at least:

——The other half
Comes to the privy coffer of the state.

This policy would work powerfully to induce the rich man to attend to the administration of wealth during his life, which is the end that society should always have in view, as being that by far most fruitful for the people. Nor need it be feared that this policy would sap the root of enterprise and render men less anxious to accumulate, for to the class whose ambition it is to leave great fortunes and be talked about after their death, it will attract even more attention, and, indeed, be a somewhat nobler ambition to have enormous sums paid over to the state from their fortunes.

There remains, then, only one mode of using great fortunes; but in this we have the true antidote for the temporary unequal distribution of wealth, the reconciliation of the rich and the poor—a reign of harmony—another ideal, differing, indeed, from that of the Communist in requiring only the further evolution of existing conditions, not the total overthrow of our civilization. It is founded upon the present most intense individualism, and the race is prepared to put it in practice by degrees whenever it pleases. Under its sway we shall have an ideal state, in which the surplus wealth of the few will become, in the best sense, the property of the many, because administered for the common good, and this wealth, passing through the hands of the few, can be made a much more potent force for the elevation of our race than if it had been distributed in small sums to the people themselves. Even the poorest can be made to see this, and to agree that great sums gathered by some of their fellow-citizens and spent for public purposes, from which the masses reap the principal benefit, are more valuable to them than if scattered among them through the course of many years in trifling amounts.

If we consider what results flow from the Cooper Institute, for instance, to the best portion of the race in New York not possessed of means, and compare these with those which would have arisen for the good of the masses from an equal sum distributed by Mr. Cooper in his lifetime in the form of wages, which is the highest form of distribution, being for work done and not for charity, we can form some estimate of the possibilities for the improvement of the race which lie embedded in the present law of the accumulation of wealth. Much of this sum, if distributed in small quantities among the people, would have been wasted in the indulgence of appetite, some of it in excess, and it may be doubted whether even the part put to the best use, that of adding to the comforts of the home, would have yielded results for the race, as a race, at all comparable to those which are flowing and are to flow from the Cooper Institute from generation to generation. Let the advocate of violent or radical change ponder well this thought.

We might even go so far as to take another instance, that of Mr. Tilden's bequest of five millions of dollars for a free library in the city of New York, but in referring to this one cannot help saying involuntarily, How much better if Mr. Tilden had devoted the last years of his own life to the proper administration of this immense sum; in which case neither legal contest nor any other cause of delay could have interfered with his aims. But let us assume that Mr. Tilden's millions finally become the means of giving to this city a noble public library, where the treasures of the world contained in books will be open to all forever, without money and without price. Considering the good of that part of the race which congregates in and around Manhattan Island, would its permanent benefit have been better promoted had these millions been allowed to circulate in small sums through the hands of the masses? Even the most strenuous advocate of Communism must entertain a doubt upon this subject. Most of those who think will probably entertain no doubt whatever.

Poor and restricted are our opportunities in is life; narrow our horizon; our best work most imperfect; but rich men should be thankful for one inestimable boon. They have it in their power during their lives to busy themselves in organizing benefactions from which the masses of their fellows will derive lasting advantage, and thus dignify their own lives. The highest life is probably to be reached, not by such imitation of the life of Christ as Count Tolstoi gives us, but, while animated by Christ's spirit, by recognizing the changed conditions of this age, and adopting modes of expressing this spirit suitable to the changed conditions under which we live; still laboring for the good of our fellows, which was the essence of his life and teaching, but laboring in a different manner.

This, then, is held to be the duty of the man of Wealth: First, to set an example of modest, unostentatious living, shunning display or extravagance; to provide moderately for the legitimate wants of those dependent upon him, and after doing so to consider all surplus revenues which come to him simply as trust funds, which he is called upon to administer, and strictly bound as a matter of duty to administer in the manner which, in his judgment, is best calculated to produce the most beneficial results for the community—the man of wealth thus becoming the mere agent and trustee for his poorer brethren, bringing to their service his superior wisdom, experience, and ability to administer, doing for them better than they would or could do for themselves.

We are met here with the difficulty of determining what are moderate sums to leave to members of the family; what is modest, unostentatious living; what is the test of extravagance. There must be different standards for different conditions. The answer is that it is as impossible to name exact amounts or actions as it is to define good manners, good taste, or the rules of propriety; but, nevertheless, these are verities, well known although undefinable. Public sentiment is quick to know and to feel what offends these. So in the case of wealth. The rule in regard to good taste in the dress of men or women applies here. Whatever makes one conspicuous offends the canon. If any family be chiefly known for display, for extravagance in home, table, equipage, for enormous sums ostentatiously spent in any form upon itself,—if these be its chief distinctions, we have no difficulty in estimating its nature or culture. So likewise in regard to the use or abuse of its surplus wealth, or to generous, freehanded cooperation in good public uses, or to unabated efforts to accumulate and hoard to the last, whether they administer or bequeath. The verdict rests with the best and most enlightened public sentiment. The community will surely judge, and its judgments will not often be wrong.

The best uses to which surplus wealth can be put have already been indicated. Those who would administer wisely must, indeed, be wise, for one of the serious obstacles to the improvement of our race is indiscriminate charity. It were better for mankind that the millions of the rich were thrown into the sea than so spent as to encourage the slothful, the drunken, the unworthy. Of every thousand dollars spent in so called charity to-day, it is probable that $950 is unwisely spent; so spent, indeed, as to produce the very evils which it proposes to mitigate or cure. A well-known writer of philosophic books admitted the other day that he had given a quarter of a dollar to a man who approached him as he was coming to visit the house of his friend. He knew nothing of the habits of this beggar; knew not the use that would be made of this money, although he had every reason to suspect that it would be spent improperly. This man professed to be a disciple of Herbert Spencer; yet the quarter-dollar given that night will probably work more injury than all the money which its thoughtless donor will ever be able to give in true charity will do good. He only gratified his own feelings, saved himself from annoyance,—and this was probably one of the most selfish and very worst actions of his life, for in all respects he is most worthy.

In bestowing charity, the main consideration should be to help those who will help themselves; to provide part of the means by which those who desire to improve may do so; to give those who desire to rise the aids by which they may rise; to assist, but rarely or never to do all. Neither the individual nor the race is improved by alms-giving. Those worthy of assistance, except in rare cases, seldom require assistance. The really valuable men of the race never do, except in cases of accident or sudden change. Every one has, of course, cases of individuals brought to his own knowledge where temporary assistance can do genuine good, and these he will not overlook. But the amount which can be wisely given by the individual for individuals is necessarily limited by his lack of knowledge of the circumstances connected with each. He is the only true reformer who is as careful and as anxious not to aid the unworthy as he is to aid the worthy, and, perhaps, even more so, for in alms-giving more injury is probably done by rewarding vice than by relieving virtue.

The rich man is thus almost restricted to following the examples of Peter Cooper, Enoch Pratt of Baltimore, Mr. Pratt of Brooklyn, Senator Stanford, and others, who know that the best means of benefiting the community is to place within its reach the ladders upon which the aspiring can rise—parks, and means of recreation, by which men are helped in body and minds; works of art, certain to give pleasure and improve the public taste, and public institutions of various kinds, which will improve the general condition of the people;—in this manner returning their surplus wealth to the mass of their fellows in the forms best calculated to do them lasting good.

Thus is the problem of Rich and Poor to be solved. The laws of accumulation will be left free; the laws of distribution free. Individualism will continue, but the millionaire will be but a trustee for the poor; intrusted for a season with a great part of the increased wealth of the community, but administering it for the community far better than it could or would have done for itself. The best minds will thus have reached a stage in the development of the race in which it is clearly seen that there is no mode of disposing of surplus wealth creditable to thoughtful and earnest men into whose hands it flows save by using it year by year for the general good. This day already dawns. But a little while, and although, without incurring the pity of their fellows, men may die sharers in great business enterprises from which their capital cannot be or has not been withdrawn, and is left chiefly at death for public uses, yet the man who dies leaving behind him millions of available wealth, which was his to administer during life, will pass away "unwept, unhonored, and unsung," no matter to what uses he leaves the dross which he cannot take with him. Of such as these the public verdict will then be: "The man who dies thus rich dies disgraced."

Such, in my opinion, is the true Gospel concerning Wealth, obedience to which is destined some day to solve the problem of the Rich and the Poor, and to bring "Peace on earth, among men Good-Will."

George D. Herron

Address before the Minnesota Congregational Club (1890)

I am appointed to present to you, this evening, what I understand to be the message of Jesus to men of wealth, and to apply that message to the problems of society which the best thought and truest sympathy of our times are reaching out to solve. I assume, in what I shall say, that I am addressing an audience of Christ's disciples.

In their essence, the social problems of to-day are not different from those of yesterday, they are as old as society itself. They date back to the infancy of the race, when sin couched at the door of Adam's eldest son, to spring up within his heart as hatred for his younger groaner. Ever since Cain—whom President Hitchcock calls "that first godless political economist"—killed his brother Abel, the associability of human beings for good and common ends has been a problem; a problem, be it kept in mind, born in a heart of covetousness, and set by the hand of hate for the race to solve. Cain's murder of his brother Abel was the first bald, brutal assertion of self-interest as the law of human life—an assertion always potential with murder; an assertion whose acceptance involves the triumph of the brute man over the God-imaged man; an assertion which the divine heart of humanity has always denied; a theory of society which will be remembered as a frightful dream of the past when the race recovers its moral sanity. Cain's hands were the first to group and wield competition as the weapon of progress; a weapon from which no economic theorists have ever been able to wash the blood of human suffering. When Cain replied to God, "Am I my brothers keeper?" he stated the question to which all past and present problems of man's earthly existence are reducible. The search for the final and comprehensive answer to Cain's question has been the race's sacred sorrow; and obedience to such an answer would carry in it the perfect solvent of all the problems that perplex the minds and hearts of men.

History and prophecy have always pointed toward a time of industrial peace and social brotherhood. The most unselfish aspirations of the noblest men have been along the line of the social unity of the race. About this hope statesman and philosophers have woven their sublimest theories of society and government. It has been the highest inspiration of poetry. It is the end toward which Moses and Plato looked. It is the lofty strain borne along from prophet to prophet through Israel's glory and shame. Outside of Biblical prophecy there is no purer expression of this ancient hope than in John Stuart Mill's autobiography: I yet looked forward," he said, to a time [. . .] when the division of the produce of labor, instead of depending, as in so great a degree it now does, on the accident of birth, will be made by an acknowledged principle of justice; and when it will no longer be, or be thought to be, impossible for human beings to exert themselves strenuously in procuring benefits which are not to be exclusively their own, but to be shared by society to which they belong."

And yet, with all the history and prophecy, the schools and temples, the philosophy and poetry, the governments and civilizations, the day of brotherhood seems no nearer than generations ago. The hope grows faint with age. The problems of society are still unsolved.

The question of Cain is the master question of our age. It has grown articulate with the greed and cruelty of history. It threatens our American day and nation with the crisis of the centuries. It must be answered; and answered with justice and righteousness. The blood of Abel cries out through toiling millions. The expectation of the poor shall not forever perish in hopeless toiling and longing for better days. As John Ruskin says, "There are voices of battle and famine through all the earth, which must be heard some day, whoever keeps silence." No arrogant reply as to the historic and legal rights of private and corporate property will silence these voices.

The natural development of our civilization will not unfold the solution of our industrial problems. When we watch the mammoth enginery of this modern civilization through the assurances of a partisan press, or the mercenary declamation of the politician who estimates the moral stupidity of the people by his own, the movements of its great wheels seem wonderfully safe and perfect; but when we, in our sober, honest, thoughtful moments, view it through the sympathies and purposes of the divine Man of Sorrows, we see torn, bleeding, mangled, sorrowing, famishing multitudes beneath the wheels of its remorseless enginery; we see that greed and not love is the power that moves our civilization; we see politics, commerce, and the social club moving on the economic assumption that selfishness is the only considerable social force, and assuming that civilization can advance only through the equal balancing of warring selfish interests; we see men valuing brute cunning and the low instinct of shrewdness more than whiteness of soul. A civilization based on self-interest, and securing itself through competition, has no power within itself to secure justice. We speak to pitiless forces when we appeal to its processes to right the wrongs and inequalities of society. The world is not to be saved by civilization. It is civilization that needs saving. A civilization basing itself upon self-interest has a more dangerous foundation than dynamite. It is built upon falsehood. It carries in it the elements of anarchy because it has no ground in moral realities. It is atheistic because it treats God and his righteousness as external to itself. It is nihilistic because it thrives on destruction. It is a civilization which Bishop Huntington declares "leads by a sure course to barbarism." It is a civilization tinder whose procession John Stuart Mill affirms the very idea of "justice, or any proportionality between success and merit, or between success and exertion," to be "so chimerical as to be relegated to the region of romance." The end to which the civilization of the present tends is material, and not moral; it tends to the enslavement of society and the smothering of its highest life. Civilization is the flower of the character of the dominant classes; it is an effect more than a cause; its forces originate in character; its activities are the expression of the people's being. No civilization can be made righteous, or can make itself righteous, by any restraints or regulations external to itself. A righteous civilization can have no other source than the inward righteousness of those who originate and control its forces.

There is no power in abstract truth, either economic, ethical, or theological, to cure our social ills. Economic laws naturally deal with things external to man's being; with principles which will be accepted or rejected according to inward forces of character which they can obey, but cannot control. Ethical truth taught to an unspiritualized race, or generation, or civilization, is a childish waste of time and strength. There is no ethics apart from religion. The springs of human virtue are all in God. There is no ethical truth other than the expression of the will of God. Socrates, Plato, and Shakespeare seem to have understood this better than some of us who teach our fellow-men to-day. Nearly all the warnings of the Old and New Testament, which we so self-assuringly address to so-called unbelievers, were addressed in the first place to those who presumed themselves to be already in the kingdom of God: to those in the temple services and the churches. The ethical instructions of Jesus and the Apostles were all based upon and developed from the cross. Theological truth has repeatedly shown its barrenness of the fruit of righteousness. The darkest crimes of history have been committed by the conservators of religion. A jealousy for theological truth often accompanies a hatred of duty. The Pharisees were so orthodox that they crucified Christ for heresy. They alone possessed the oracles of God. Yet the truth did not save them from greedy, heartless, malignant, hypocritical lives. A slavish and enslaving conservatism has always joined hands with an indifferent worldlyism for the crucifixion of God's perennial revelations of incarnate truth. I suspect the devil knows more truth than any of us; and he is all the more devilish for knowing it. Truth that does not strike its roots in love is a curse; and the truer the truth the more accursed its results. There is a pregnant thought, which the Church has yet to learn, in a saying of Mozoomdar's in his "Oriental Christ:" "Unless our creeds fertilize the world, and our lives furnish meat and drink to mankind, the curse uttered on barrenness will descend on us."

We cannot look to the State to solve our social woes and grant our social hopes. All the great political prophets, from Moses to Milton, and from Milton to Sumner and Mulford, recognize that the people are the makers of the State rather than the State the makers of the people. The State is the expression of the highest common thought of the people; it is the work of the people's faith. Hegel says "the State is the realization of the moral idea" of the people. The people must be righteous before the State can be righteous. If we agree with Milton that the State ought to be but as one huge Christian personage, one mighty growth or suture of an honest man," then the Christian State must be the offspring of a Christian people. If we regard the State, with Sumner, as a grand moral institution, it must be moral because the people build it with their moral thought and purpose. The best and strongest institutions have been powerless to restrain people whose moral conceptions they did not embody. The Mosaic legislation was never fully enforced. Roman law could find no expression in the thought and life of later Rome. Alfred the Great incorporated the Ten Commandments and Golden Rule in the early English constitution, but they are yet far from being the laws of English industrial and social life. Laws written on tables of stone and printed in statute books are but the playthings of politicians if they are not written in people's hearts. Laws cannot make men unselfish. They can restrain; but all legal righteousness is but temporary. Police righteousness is not divine righteousness. Force-justice is unreal justice. The State cannot, by any possible process, make the rich man unselfish, or the poor man thrifty. The State cannot establish justice and righteousness on the earth; but justice and righteousness must establish the State.

The heart of all our social disputes is what Mulford calls "the crude assertion of an enlightened self-interest as a law of human activity." This assertion is the essence of the gospel which Professor Sumner proclaimed from his chair in a great Christian University. Social classes, he decided, owe each other nothing; benevolence is simply barter, and "the yearning after equality the offspring of envy and covetousness." This is a gospel which would have caused the proclaimer to be mobbed in the streets of Athens in the days of Pericles; a gospel which would have astounded Moses, and seemed ancient and barbarous to Abraham. The supremacy of the law of self-interest is the conclusion of Herbert Spencer's materialistic philosophy; and of the wretched pessimism of Hartmann and Schopenhauer. It is the principle upon which Cain slew his brother. It was the seductive whisper of the serpent in Eve's ear. It is the principle upon which crime is committed. It is the principle upon which the capitalist acts who treats labor as no more than a commodity subject to the lowest market rate and the law of supply and demand. It is the principle upon which railroads are bonded and bankrupted for private ends. It is the law by which the New England deacon chattels his money upon the Dakota farmer's meager possessions at a usurious and impoverishing rate of interests—a deed which will not be obscured from the eyes of a just God by the endowment of a chair in a denominational college. It is the principle upon which a Chicago financier proceeds, with no more moral justification than the highwayman's robbery of an express train, to "corner" the pork market, and thus force from the mouths of toiling families a million and a half of dollars into his private treasury—a deed for which the giving of some thousands to found city missions and orphans' homes will be no atonement in the reckoning of the God who judges the world in righteousness and not by the ethics of the stock exchange. The law of self-interest is the eternal falsehood which mothers all social and private woes; for sin is pure individualism—the assertion of self against God and humanity.

God's answer to Cain's question, God's solvent of the social problems of our day, is the cross. And the cross is more than a historic event. It is the law by which God acts, and expects men to act. It is the creed of God which will never be revised. It is the principle upon which creation and history proceed. It was the assertion intensified which God has been making through all history, of self-sacrifice as the law of human development and achievement. Self-sacrifice is the law which God asserts in Christ over against the law of self-interest which Satan asserts in Cain. The trial in progress is Christ *versus* Cain. The decision to which the times are hastening us is, Shall Christ or Cain reign in our American civilization? And well may the heavens await our decision in silent and awful wonder, for we are deciding the destiny of the earth!

The message of Jesus to every man, rich or poor, weak or strong, ignorant or wise, is the cross. In whatever form he puts it, whether in parable or principle, miracle or command, the cross is the heart of every man: not a cross, but his cross—the cross of absolute self-renunciation which he carried in his heart. In Christ's teachings the cross was something else than an arbitrary contrivance for populating heaven. The Gospel of our Lord knows of no reconciliation by the cross that does not begin with a reconciliation to the cross. Being reconciled to God has a vaster meaning than being reconciled to the comfortable reception of certain benefits from God's hand. It means the apprehension of the law of God's life as the law of our lives. And sacrifice is the law of the life of God. The creation involved an infinite sacrifice. Out of the travail of God humanity was born. Before earth's sinning, sorrowing ages began, with infinite sorrow God consented within himself to their beginning. The sorrow of Gethsemane was in God's heart before he breathed life into man; and the suffering of the crow continues in the Father-heart till sin vanishes from the hearts of his children.

The moral progress of the race has been through sacrifice. It is the divine order of culture. The race's divine types are always dying that the race may live. The world has thriven on the sufferings of those who have loved it and given themselves for it. Every new truth which men have learned has been read in the blaze of martyr fires. Every great reform has been won at unreckonable cost. A Calvary is the tribute Freedom always claims from men. Every commercial privilege which an American enjoys was purchased on Golgotha. We are not our own; and that which we have is not ours. Every breath of our bodies and every opportunity of our hands, hearts, and brains was bought for us with immeasurable sacrifice. Our little lives are surcharged with the blood-bought wealth of the centuries; and not one of us, if we could live to the age of Methuselah, and held in our grasp the wealth of the continents, could begin to pay the future the debt we owe the past. Sacrifice is not life's accident, but life's law. No man has a moral right to live other than a sacrificial life in this world of sin and sacrifice. Lotze affirms that no life is moral which is not self-sacrificed in the service of others. No Christian is true to his Christ, nor has grasped the meaning of the cross, who is not a vicarious sufferer for his fellow-men. The cross was not our release from, but our obligation to, sacrifice. And wherever there is a heart throbbing with the passion of Jesus there will be a life straitened till its mission be accomplished. Wherever there is a soul pulsing with the life of God there will always be sacrificial hands uplifting humanity to higher things.

Now, the reason this message of the cross has so much larger an application to men of wealth is that they have the larger opportunities and possessions to sacrifice. They have the weapons of love. Christ offers no different terms of discipleship to any American man of wealth than he offered to Matthew at his custom-table. The centuries have not bulged the needle's eye. It is as hard to enter now as when Christ mentioned its smallness to the rich Pharisees. Christ was infinitely pitiful to the weak, the poor, the thriftless, the sinful, the ignorant; but to those who sought to hallow covetousness with religious forms, and convert piety into a cloak for greed, he had but wrath and scorn and scourges. The simple fact of our industrial situation is that the men of wealth in our American churches can begin to solve our pressing social problems any time they choose, by simply being disciples of the Lord Christ. As the Father sent Christ into the world to sacrifice himself in the service of man, so Christ sends the corporation manager, the merchant, the mill owner, the mine operator, the street-railway president, to be a living sacrifice in the service of men. Christ was under no more obligation to consecrate himself wholly to the world-saving, man-uplifting business than every business man in America. The uniqueness of Christ's work has no bearing upon this fact. The claim of God to Christ's service is the claim that rests upon us all. The Lord did not die to give us an opportunity for self-seeking. We are not here on a vacation from God. He sends every man of wealth forth to be a savior of his fellow-men; and the business man who fails to be a little Christ to the world has made a disastrous and irreparable business failure. A man of business has no more right to make personal profit the supreme purpose of his store, his shop, his capital, his factory, big railway, than Jesus had to work miracles for personal profit. We have no more moral right than our Lord to direct our social, domestic, or financial affairs for personal ends. The Christian has no more right to an unconsecrated horse, or house, or dress, than Christ to an unconsecrated cross. We are not on own; we are bought with a price; and nothing short of an unreserved surrender of self-interest to God's interest in humanity is moral or just. Not to be self-sacrificing in others' service is injustice. To be unloving, even to the unlovable, is to be ungodly.

The day is coming when the homes, the shops, the stores, the social clubs, the newspapers, the corporations, the political caucuses, that have not for their sacred purpose the making of men divine will be regarded as out of place in a world that has been redeemed by the Son of God and nourished by the life-blood of his saints. There is no such thing as a secular affair in the universe of God. There is nothing but moral anarchy outside of the realm of God's authority. God recognizes nothing as having a right to exist apart from a vital relation to himself. There is no affair which engages human passions, brains, hearts, hands, that is not a religious matter. Nothing has a moral right to an existence on the earth which has any other basic purpose than the uplifting and sustaining of men in righteousness. The basing of commerce, or education, or politics, or society, on the modem atheistic and mercantile idea of secularity is an assumption that violates the lesson of history, and is intolerable to the Scriptures. Christ is King! Unto him every knee shall bow. The freedom of the race is to be reached only through yielding to Christ's moral despotism. As President Valentine has said, "There is nothing under the stars that is not amenable to his authority." There are no exemptions provided for stock exchanges, or wholesale establishments, or railway corporations, or social leaders, or politicians, or teachers of natural sciences. Whatsoever ye do, in word or deed, do all in the name of the Lord Jesus. We have no moral right to dress simply with a view to pleasing ourselves; eat as we please; live in the kind of homes we please; ride in the carriages we please; have the company we please; buy the books, pictures, jewelry, luxuries, we please—no more than Christ had.

I am aware that what I am saying is irritating to this practical, anti-theocratic age an age which has small sense of the divineness of things. We have little practical use for things we cannot buy or sell; things that do not minister to our bodily comfort and social pride. We are apt to measure even the religious value of men by their market value. We are willing enough that Christ should have been crucified for us, but are angered at the thought of being crucified for him. It is so much easier to worship Christ than go up and share with him his cross. It is so much easier to be obsequious in saying Lord, Lord, than it is to do the things he tells us; so much easier to subscribe to creeds and repeat rituals than renounce selfish ownership to one's possessions and deny one's self. But only a crucified Christianity will ever be able to win a selfish world to the crucified Christ. And there is no other name under heaven given among men whereby society and civilization can be saved. Not until the race shall have been crucified with Christ's crucifixion will it assemble with clasped hands and free spirits around the throne of the Lamb.

Men first quarreled with God, and they have been quarreling with each other ever since. And the reconciliation of men to each other must proceed through their reconciliation to God as he is revealed in Christ. Social unity must be the result of God-oneness and God-in-ness. It will be the outgrowth of the incarnation of the divine sacrificial Christ-life in the life of humanity. When men touch each other with the touch of God, and love each other with the love of God, and serve each other with the sacrificial heart of God, then the race will be one concordant family. The solvent of every problem of society is the love of God. And the cross is the weapon which God took from his own heart to break open our hearts that he might pour therein the life-renewing balm of his love. Our hope for social freedom will reach its fulfillment, not through social mechanisms, but through our acting, as Frederick Maurice says, "in the faith that the constraining love of Christ is the mightiest power in the universe." Society is to be saved by men and women who shall pour their lives and possessions as streams of love and service into the great current of Christ's redeeming light, whose onflowing is healing the nations. The whole question of labor and capital, and all the problems of our day, can be restated in this form: Is the Gospel of Jesus livable? God is calling to-day for able men who are willing to be financially crucified in order to establish the world's market on a Golden Rule basis. He is calling for noble women who are willing to be socially crucified to make society the agency for uplifting instead of crushing the poor and ignorant and weak. "Whoever," says Benjamin Franklin, "introduces into the public affairs the principles of primitive Christianity will change the face of the world." It is for this work that God would anoint you, O Christian business men of America! History has never presented to man an opportunity richer than yours. You can make the market as sacred as the church. You can make the whirl of industrial wheels like the joyous music of worship. You can be the knights of the noblest chivalry the world has ever seen; not going forth "to recover the tomb of a buried god," as Ruskin said of the crusaders of Richard Lionheart, but to fulfill the commands of the eternal Christ. And where you go, flowers of hope will spring in your footprints. You can bear the weak in your arms, and set the captives of poverty free. You can cause the deserts of human despair to blossom with the gladness of fulfilled prophecy, and hush the voices of discontent in the sweetness of fruitful toil. You can give work to the wage-less; teach the thrifty and ignorant; seat the poor in the best pews of your churches. You need not strive nor cry, nor wear plumes and flaunt banners; but you can be the heralds of a new civilization, the creators of a Christian industry whose peaceful procession will reach round the globe. You need carry no crosses of wood or gold or silver; but you can bury the cross of your Christ deep within your hearts, and stretch forth consecrated hands to realize the life of humanity by raising it into the idealism of Jesus. You can draw the world's trades and traffics within the onsweep of Christ's redemptive purpose. You can

plant everlasting peace underneath the feet of men, so that there shall be no more strife; and light earth's night of toil with skies of love, so that there shall be no more night. You can be the makers of the new earth wherein dwelleth righteousness in which [they] will be at last human because it is divine, and divine because it is human.

God's new day of judgment is surely and swiftly dawning. Voices from out [of] the future are crying repentance unto this mammon-worshiping generation. The ax is laid at the root of the trees. Now John Baptists are arising who will speak truth and justice to the Herods of finance, though their ecclesiastical heads be the price of the message.

In the lead of human progress I see the matchless figure of the Son of God—

"Toiling up new Calvaries ever with the
cross that turns not back."

Let us close about him, O brother men,
and keep step with the march of the cross!

"Till upon earth's grateful sod
Rests the city of our God."

THE POPULIST PARTY PLATFORM (1892)

Assembled upon the 116th anniversary of the Declaration of Independence, the People's Party of America, in their first national convention, invoking upon their action the blessing of Almighty God, put forth in the name and on behalf of the people of this country, the following preamble and declaration of principles:

Preamble

The conditions which surround us best justify our co-operation; we meet in the midst of a nation brought to the verge of moral, political, and material ruin. Corruption dominates the ballot-box, the Legislatures, the Congress, and touches even the ermine of the bench. The people are demoralized; most of the States have been compelled to isolate the voters at

the polling places to prevent universal intimidation and bribery. The newspapers are largely subsidized or muzzled, public opinion silenced, business prostrated, homes covered with mortgages, labor impoverished, and the land concentrating in the hands of capitalists. The urban workmen are denied the right to organize for self-protection, imported pauperized labor beats down their wages, a hireling standing army, unrecognized by our laws, is established to shoot them down, and they are rapidly degenerating into European conditions. The fruits of the toil of millions are boldly stolen to build up colossal fortunes for a few, unprecedented in the history of mankind; and the possessors of these, in turn, despise the Republic and endanger liberty. From the same prolific womb of governmental injustice we breed the two great classes—tramps and millionaires.

The national power to create money is appropriated to enrich bond-holders; a vast public debt payable in legal-tender currency has been funded into gold-bearing bonds, thereby adding millions to the burdens of the people.

Silver, which has been accepted as coin since the dawn of history, has been demonetized to add to the purchasing power of gold by decreasing the value of all forms of property as well as human labor, and the supply of currency is purposely abridged to fatten usurers, bankrupt enterprise, and enslave industry. A vast conspiracy against mankind has been organized on two continents, and it is rapidly taking possession of the world. If not met and overthrown at once it forebodes terrible social convulsions, the destruction of civilization, or the establishment of an absolute despotism.

We have witnessed for more than a quarter of a century the struggles of the two great political parties for power and plunder, while grievous wrongs have been inflicted upon the suffering people. We charge that the controlling influences dominating both these parties have permitted the existing dreadful conditions to develop without serious effort to prevent or restrain them. Neither do they now promise us any substantial reform. They have agreed together to ignore, in the coming campaign, every issue but one. They propose to drown the outcries of a plundered people in the uproar of a sham battle over the tariff, so that capitalists, corporations, national banks, rings, trusts, watered stock, the demonetization of silver and the oppressions the usurers may all be lost sight of. They suppose to sacrifice our homes, lives, and children on the altar of mammon; to destroy of multitude in order to secure corruption funds from the millionaires.

Assembled on the anniversary of the birthday of the nation, and filled with the spirit of the grand general and chief who established our independence, we seek to restore government of the Republic to the hands of the "plain people," with which class it originated. We assert our purposes to be identical with the purposes of the National Constitution; to form a more perfect union and establish justice, insure domestic tranquility, provide for the common defence, promote the general welfare, and secure the signs of liberty for ourselves and our posterity.

We declare that this Republic can only endure as a free government while built upon love of the people for each other and the nation; that it cannot be pinned together by bayonets; that the Civil War is over and that every passion and resentment which grew out of it must die with it, and we must be in fact, as we are in name, united brotherhood of free men.

Our country finds itself confronted by conditions for which there is no precedent in history of the world; our annual agricultural productions amount to billions of dollars in value, which must, within a few weeks or months, be exchanged for billions dollars' worth of commodities consumed in their production; the existing currency supply is wholly inadequate to make this change; the results are falling prices, the formation of combines and rings, the impoverishment of the producing class. We pledge ourselves that if given power we will labor to correct these evils by wise and reasonable legislation, in accordance with the terms of our Constitution.

We believe that the power of government—in other words, of the people—should be expanded (as in the case of the postal service) as rapidly and as far as the good sense of an intelligent people and the teachings of experience shall justify, to the end that oppression, injustice, and poverty shall eventually cease in the land.

While our sympathies as a party of reform are naturally upon the side of every proposition which will tend to make men intelligent, virtuous, and temperate, we nevertheless regard these questions, important as they are, as secondary to the great issues now pressing for solution, and upon which not only our individual prosperity but the very existence of free institutions depend; and we ask all men to first help us to determine whether we are to have a republic to administer before we differ as to the conditions upon which it is to be administered, believing that the forces of reform this day organized will never cease to move forward until every wrong is righted and equal rights and equal privileges securely established for all the men and women of this country.

Platform

We declare, therefore—

First.—That the union of the labor forces of the United States this day consummated shall be permanent and perpetual; may its spirit enter into all hearts for the salvation of the Republic and the uplifting of mankind.

Second.—Wealth belongs to him who creates it, and every dollar taken from industry without an equivalent is robbery "If any will not work, neither shall he eat." The interests of rural and civil labor are the same; their enemies are identical.

Third.—We believe that the time has come when the railroad corporations will either own the people or the people must own the railroads; and should the government enter upon the work of owning and managing all railroads, we should favor an amendment to the constitution by which all persons engaged in the government service shall be placed under a civil-service regulation of the most rigid character, so as to prevent the increase of the power of the national administration by the use of such additional government employees.

Finance.—We demand a national currency, safe, sound, and flexible issued by the general government only, a full legal tender for all debts, public and private, and that without the use of banking corporations; a just, equitable, and efficient means of distribution direct to the people, at a tax not to exceed 2 per cent per annum, to be provided as set forth in the sub-treasury plan of the Farmers' Alliance, or a better system; also by payments in discharge of its obligations for public improvements.

1. We demand free and unlimited coinage of silver and gold at the present legal ratio of 16 to 1.
2. We demand that the amount of circulating medium be speedily increased to not less than $50 per capita.
3. We demand a graduated income tax.
4. We believe that the money of the country should be kept as much as possible in the hands of the people, and hence we demand that all State and national revenues shall be limited to the necessary expenses of the government, economically and honestly administered.
5. We demand that postal savings banks be established by the government for the safe deposit of the earnings of the people and to facilitate exchange.

Transportation.—Transportation being a means of exchange and a public necessity, the government should own and operate the railroads in the interest of the people. The telegraph and telephone, like the post-office system, being a necessity for the transmission of news, should be owned and operated by the government in the interest of the people.

Land.—The land, including all the natural sources of wealth, is the heritage of the people, and should not be monopolized for speculative purposes, and alien ownership of land should be prohibited. All land now held by railroads and other corporations in excess of their actual needs, and all lands now owned by aliens should be reclaimed by the government and held for actual settlers only.

Expression of Sentiments

Your Committee on Platform and Resolutions beg leave unanimously to report the following:

Whereas, Other questions have been presented for our consideration, we hereby submit the following, not as a part of the Platform of the People's Party, but as resolutions expressive of the sentiment of this Convention.

1. RESOLVED, *That we demand a free ballot and a fair count in all elections, and pledge ourselves to secure it to every legal voter without Federal intervention, through the adoption by the States of the unperverted Australian or secret ballot system.*
2. RESOLVED, *That the revenue derived from a graduated income tax should be applied to the reduction of the burden of taxation now levied upon the domestic industries of this country.*
3. RESOLVED, *That we pledge our support to fair and liberal pensions to ex-Union soldiers and sailors.*
4. RESOLVED, *That we condemn the fallacy of protecting American labor under the present system, which opens our ports to the pauper and criminal classes of the world and crowds out our wage-earners; and we denounce the present ineffective laws against contract labor, and demand the further restriction of undesirable emigration.*

5. RESOLVED, *That we cordially sympathize with the efforts of organized workingmen to shorten the hours of labor, and demand a rigid enforcement of the existing eight-hour law on Government work, and ask that a penalty clause be added to the said law.*

6. RESOLVED, *That we regard the maintenance of a large standing army of mercenaries, known as the Pinkerton system, as a menace to our liberties, and we demand its abolition; and we condemn the recent invasion of the Territory of Wyoming by the hired assassins of plutocracy, assisted by Federal officers.*

7. RESOLVED, *That we commend to the favorable consideration of the people and the reform press the legislative system known as the initiative and referendum.*

8. RESOLVED, *That we favor a constitutional provision limiting the office of President and Vice-President to one term, and providing for the election of Senators of the United Stales by a direct vote of the people.*

9. RESOLVED, *That we oppose any subsidy or national aid to any private corporation for any purpose.*

10. RESOLVED, *That this convention sympathizes with the Knights of Labor and their righteous contest with the tyrannical combine of clothing manufacturers of Rochester, and declare it to be a duty of all who hate tyranny and oppression to refuse to purchase the goods made by the said manufacturers, or to patronize any merchants who sell such goods.*

OLIVER WENDELL HOLMES

The Path of Law (1897)

When we study law we are not studying a mystery but a well known profession. We are studying what we shall want in order to appear before judges, or to advise people in such a way as to keep them out of court. The reason why it is a profession, why people will pay lawyers to argue for them or to advise them is that in societies like ours the command of the public force is intrusted to the judges in certain cases, and the whole power of the state will be put forth, if necessary, to carry out their judgments and decrees. People want to know under what circumstances and how far they will run the risk of coming against what is so much stronger than themselves, and hence it becomes a business to find out when this danger is to be feared. The object of our study, then, is prediction, the prediction of the incidence of the public force through the instrumentality of the courts.

The means of the study are a body of reports, of treatises, and of statutes, in this country and in England, extending back for six hundred years, and now increasing annually by hundreds. In these sibylline leaves are gathered the scattered prophecies of the past upon the cases in which the axe will fall. These are what properly have been called the oracles of the law. Far the most important and pretty nearly the whole meaning of every new effort of legal thought is to make these prophecies more precise, and to generalize them into a thoroughly connected system. The process is one, from a lawyer's statement of a case, eliminating as it does all the dramatic elements with which his client's story has clothed it, and retaining only the facts of legal import, up to the final analyses and abstract universals of theoretic jurisprudence. The reason why a lawyer does not mention that his client wore a white hat when he made a contract, while Mrs. Quickly would be sure to dwell upon it along with the parcel gilt goblet and the sea-coal fire, is that he foresees that the public force will act in the same way whatever his client had upon his head. It is to make the prophecies easier to be remembered and to be understood that the teachings of the decisions of the past are put into general propositions and gathered into text-books, or that statutes are passed in a general form. The primary rights and duties with which jurisprudence busies itself again are nothing but prophecies. One of the many evil effects of the confusion between legal and moral ideas, about which I shall have something to say in a moment, is that theory is apt to get the cart before the horse, and to consider the right or the duty as something existing apart from and independent of the consequences of its breach, to which certain sanctions are added afterward. But, as I shall try to show, a legal duty so called is nothing but a prediction that if a man does or omits certain things he will be made to suffer in this or that way by judgment of the court;—and so of a legal right.

The number of our predictions when generalized and reduced to a system is not unmanageably large. They present themselves as a finite body of dogma which may be mastered within a reasonable time. It is a great mistake to be frightened by the ever increasing number of reports. The reports of a given jurisdiction in the course of a generation take up pretty much the whole body of the law, and restate it from the present point of view. We could reconstruct the corpus from them if all that went before were burned. The use of the earlier reports is mainly historical, a use about which I shall have something to say before I have finished.

I wish, if I can, to lay down some first principles for the study of this body of dogma or systematized prediction which we call the law, for men who want to use it as the instrument of their business to enable them to prophesy in their turn, and, as bearing upon the study, I wish to point out an ideal which as yet our law has not attained.

The first thing for a business-like understanding of the matter is to understand its limits, and therefore I think it desirable at once to point out and dispel a confusion between morality and law, which sometimes rises to the height of conscious theory, and more often and indeed constantly is making trouble in detail without reaching the point of consciousness. You can see very plainly that a bad man has as much reason as a good one for wishing to avoid an encounter with the public force, and therefore you can see the practical importance of the distinction between morality and law. A man who cares nothing for an ethical rule which is believed and practiced by his neighbors is likely nevertheless to care a good deal to avoid being made to pay money, and will want to keep out of jail if he can.

I take it for granted that no hearer of mine will misinterpret what I have to say as the language of cynicism. The law is the witness and external deposit of our moral life. Its history is the history of the moral development of the race. The practice of it, in spite of popular jests, tends to make good citizens and good men. When I emphasize the difference between law and morals I do so with reference to a single end, that of learning and understanding the law. For that purpose you must definitely master its specific marks, and it is for that that I ask you for the moment to imagine yourselves indifferent to other and greater things.

I do not say that there is not a wider point of view from which the distinction between law and morals becomes of secondary or no importance, as all mathematical distinctions vanish in presence of the infinite. But I do say that that distinction is of the first importance for the object which we are here to consider,—a right study and mastery of the law as a business with well understood limits, a body of dogma enclosed within definite lines. I have just shown the practical reason for saying so. If you want to know the law and nothing else, you must look at it as a bad man, who cares only for the material consequences which such knowledge enables him to predict, not as a good one, who finds his reasons for conduct, whether inside the law or outside of it, in the vaguer sanctions of conscience. The theoretical importance of the distinction is no less, if you would reason on your subject aright. The law is full of phraseology drawn from morals, and by the mere force of language continually invites us to pass from one domain to the other without perceiving it, as we are sure to do unless we have the boundary constantly before our minds. The law talks about rights, and duties, and malice, and intent, and negligence, and so forth, and nothing is easier, or, I may say, more common in legal reasoning, than to take these words in their moral sense, at some stage of the argument, and so to drop into fallacy. For instance, when we speak of the rights of man in a moral sense, we mean to mark the limits of interference with individual freedom which we think are prescribed by conscience, or by our ideal, however reached. Yet it is certain that many laws have been enforced in the past, and it is likely that some are enforced now, which are condemned by the most enlightened opinion of the time, or which at all events pass the limit of interference as many consciences would draw it. Manifestly, therefore, nothing but confusion of thought can result from assuming that the rights of man in a moral sense are equally rights in the sense of the Constitution and the law. No doubt simple and extreme cases can be put of imaginable laws which the statute-making power would not dare to enact, even in the absence of written constitutional prohibitions, because the community would rise in rebellion and fight; and this gives some plausibility to the proposition that the law, if not a part of morality, is limited by it. But this limit of power is not coextensive with any system of morals. For the most part it falls far within the lines of any such system, and in some cases may extend beyond them, for reasons drawn from the habits of a particular people at a particular time. I once heard the late Professor Agassiz say that a German population would rise if you added two cents to the price of a glass of beer. A statute in such a case would be empty words, not because it was wrong, but because it could not be enforced. No one will deny that wrong statutes can be and are enforced, and we should not all agree as to which were the wrong ones.

The confusion with which I am dealing besets confessedly legal conceptions. Take the fundamental question. What constitutes the law? You will find some text writers telling you that it is something different from what is decided by the courts of Massachusetts or England, that it is a system of reason, that it is a deduction from principles of ethics or admitted axioms or what not, which may or may not coincide with the decisions. But if we take the view of our friend the bad man we shall find that he does not care two straws for the axioms or deductions, but that he does want to know what the Massachusetts or English courts are likely to do in fact. I am much of his mind. The prophecies of what the courts will do in fact, and nothing more pretentious, are what I mean by the law.

Take again a notion which as popularly understood is the widest conception which the law contains—the notion of legal duty, to which already I have referred. We fill the word with all the content which we draw from morals. But what does it mean to a bad man? Mainly, and in the first place, a prophecy that if he does certain things he will be subjected to disagreeable consequences by way of imprisonment or compulsory payment of money. But from his point of view, what is the difference between being fined and being taxed a certain sum for doing a certain thing? That his point of view is the test of legal principles is shown by the many discussions which have arisen in the courts on the very question whether a given statutory liability is a penalty or a tax. On the answer to this question depends the decision whether conduct is legally wrong or right, and also whether a man is under compulsion or free. Leaving the criminal law on one side, what is the difference between the liability under the mill acts or statutes authorizing a taking by eminent domain and the liability for what we call a wrongful conversion of property where restoration is out of the question? In both cases the party taking another man's property has to pay its fair value as assessed by a jury, and no more. What significance is there in calling one taking right and another wrong from the point of view of the law? It does not matter, so far as the given consequence, the compulsory payment, is concerned, whether the act to which it is attached is described in terms of praise or in terms of blame, or whether the law purports to prohibit it or allow it. If it matters at all, still speaking from the bad man's point of view, it must be because in one case and not in the other some further disadvantages, or at least some further consequences, are attached to the act by the law. The only other disadvantages thus attached to it which I ever have been able to think of are to be found in two somewhat insignificant legal doctrines, both of which might be abolished without much disturbance. One is, that a contract to do a prohibited act is unlawful, and the other, that, if one of two or more joint wrongdoers has to pay all the damages, he cannot recover contribution from his fellows. And that I believe is all. You see how the vague circumference of the notion of duty shrinks and at the same time grows more precise when we wash it with cynical acid and expel everything except the object of our study, the operations of the law.

Nowhere is the confusion between legal and moral ideas more manifest than in the law of contract. Among other things, here again the so called primary rights and duries are invested with a mystic significance beyond what can be assigned and explained. The duty to keep a contract at common law means a prediction that you must pay damages if you do not keep it—and nothing else. If you commit a tort, you are liable to pay a compensatory sum. If you commit a contract, you are liable to pay a compensatory sum unless the promised event comes to pass, and that is all the difference. But such a mode of looking at the matter stinks in the nostrils of those who think it advantageous to get as much ethics into the law as they can. It was good enough for Lord Coke, however, and here, as in many other cases, I am content to abide with him. In *Bromage v. Genning*,[1] a prohibition was sought in the King's Bench against a suit in the marches of Wales for the specific performance of a covenant to grant a lease, and Coke said that it would subvert the intention of the covenant or, since he intends it to be at his election either to lose the damages or to make the lease. Sergeant Harris for the plaintiff confessed that he moved the matter against his conscience, and a prohibition was granted. This goes further than we should go now, but it shows what I venture to say has been the common law point of view from the beginning, although Mr. Harriman, in his very able little book upon Contracts has been misled, as I humbly think, to a different conclusion.

I have spoken only of the common law, because there are some cases in which a logical justification can be found for speaking of civil liabilities as imposing duties in an intelligible sense. These are the relatively few in which equity will grant an injunction, and will enforce it by putting the defendant in prison or otherwise punishing him unless he complies with the order of the court. But I hardly think it advisable to shape general theory from the exception, and I think it would be better to cease troubling ourselves about primary rights and sanctions altogether, than to describe our prophecies concerning the liabilities commonly imposed by the law in those inappropriate terms.

I mentioned, as other examples of the use by the law of words drawn from morals, malice, intent, and negligence. It is enough to take malice as it is used in the law of civil liability for wrongs—what we lawyers call the law of torts—to show you that it means something different in law from what it means in morals, and also to show how the difference has been obscured by giving to principles which have little or nothing to do with each other the same name. Three hundred years ago a parson preached a sermon and told a story out of Fox's Book of Martyrs of a man who had assisted at the torture of one of the saints, and afterward died, suffering compensatory inward torment. It happened that Fox was wrong. The man was alive and chanced to hear the sermon, and thereupon he sued the parson. Chief Justice Wray instructed the jury that the defendant was not liable, because the story was told innocently, without malice. He took malice in the moral sense, as importing a malevolent motive. But nowadays no one doubts that a man may be liable, without any malevolent motive at all, for false statements manifestly calculated to inflict temporal damage. In stating the case in pleading, we still should call the defendant's conduct malicious; but, in my opinion at least, the word means nothing about motives, or even about the defendant's attitude toward the future, but only signifies that the tendency of his conduct under the known circumstances was very plainly to cause the plaintiff temporal harm.[2]

In the law of contract the use of moral phraseology has led to equal confusion, as I have shown in part already, but only in part. Morals deal with the actual internal state of the individual's mind, what he actually intends. From the time of the Romans down to now, this mode of dealing has affected the language of the law as to contract, and the language used has reacted upon the thought. We talk about a contract as a meeting of the minds of the parties, and thence it is inferred in various cases that there is no contract because their minds have not met; that is, because they have intended different things or because one party has not known of the assent of the other. Yet nothing is more certain than that parties

---

1. I Roll. Rep. 368.

2. See *Hanson v. Globe Newspaper Co.*, 159 Mass. 293, 302.

may be bound by a contract to things which neither of them intended, and when one does not know of the other's assent. Suppose a contract is executed in due form and in writing to deliver a lecture, mentioning no time. One of the parties thinks that the promise will be construed to mean at once, within a week. The other thinks that it means when he is ready. The court says that it means within a reasonable time. The parties are bound by the contract as it is interpreted by the court, yet neither of them meant what the court declares that they have said. In my opinion no one will understand the true theory of contract or be able even to discuss some fundamental questions intelligently until he has understood that all contracts are formal, that the making of a contract depends not on the agreement of two minds in one intention, but on the agreement of two sets of external signs—not on the parties' having *meant* the same thing but on their having *said* the same thing. Furthermore, as the signs may be addressed to one sense or another—to sight or to hearing—on the nature of the sign will depend the moment when the contract is made. If the sign is tangible, for instance, a letter, the contract is made when the letter of acceptance is delivered. If it is necessary that the minds of the parties meet, there will be no contract until the acceptance can be read—none, for example, if the acceptance be snatched from the hand of the offerer by a third person.

This is not the time to work out a theory in detail, or to answer many obvious doubts and questions which are suggested by these general views. I know of none which are not easy to answer, but what I am trying to do now is only by a series of hints to throw some light on the narrow path of legal doctrine, and upon two pitfalls which, as it seems to me, lie perilously near to it. Of the first of these I have said enough. I hope that my illustrations have shown the danger, both to speculation and to practice, of confounding morality with law, and the trap which legal language lays for us on that side of our way. For my own part, I often doubt whether it would not be a gain if every word of moral significance could be banished from the law altogether, and other words adopted which should convey legal ideas uncolored by anything outside the law. We should lose the fossil records of a good deal of history and the majesty got from ethical associations, but by ridding ourselves of an unnecessary confusion we should gain very much in the clearness of our thought.

So much for the limits of the law. The next thing which I wish to consider is what are the forces which determine its content and its growth. You may assume, with Hobbes and Bentham and Austin, that all law emanates from the sovereign, even when the first human beings to enunciate it are the judges, or you may think that law is the voice of the Zeitgeist, or what you like. It is all one to my present purpose. Even if every decision required the sanction of an emperor with despotic power and a whimsical turn of mind, we should be interested none the less, still with a view to prediction, in discovering some order, some rational explanation, and some principle of growth for the rules which he laid down. In every system there are such explanations and principles to be found. It is with regard to them that a second fallacy comes in, which I think it important to expose.

The fallacy to which I refer is the notion that the only force at work in the development of the law is logic. In the broadest sense, indeed, that notion would be true. The postulate on which we think about the universe is that there is a fixed quantitative relation between every phenomenon and its antecedents and consequents. If there is such a thing as a phenomenon without these fixed quantitative relations, it is a miracle. It is outside the law of cause and effect, and as such transcends our power of thought, or at least is something to or from which we cannot reason. The condition of our thinking about the universe is that it is capable of being thought about rationally, or, in other words, that every part of it is effect and cause in the same sense in which those parts are with which we are most familiar. So in the broadest sense it is true that the law is a logical development, like everything else. The danger of which I speak is not the admission that the principles governing other phenomena also govern the law, but the notion that a given system, ours, for instance, can be worked out like mathematics from some general axioms of conduct. This is the natural error of the schools, but it is not confined to them. I once heard a very eminent judge say that he never let a decision go until he was absolutely sure that it was right. So judicial dissent often is blamed, as if it meant simply that one side or the other were not doing their sums right, and, if they would take more trouble, agreement inevitably would come.

This mode of thinking is entirely natural. The training of lawyers is a training in logic. The processes of analogy, discrimination, and deduction are those in which they are most at home. The language of judicial decision is mainly the language of logic. And the logical method and form flatter that longing for certainty and for repose which is in every human mind. But certainty generally is illusion, and repose is not the destiny of man. Behind the logical form lies a judgment as to the relative worth and importance of competing legislative grounds, often an inarticulate and unconscious judgment, it is true, and yet the very root and nerve of the whole proceeding. You can give any conclusion a logical form. You always can imply a condition in a contract. But why do you imply it? It is because of some belief as to the practice of the community or of a class, or because of some opinion as to policy, or, in short, because of some attitude of yours upon a matter not capable of exact quantitative measurement, and therefore not capable of founding exact logical conclusions. Such matters really are battle grounds where the means do not exist for determinations that shall be good for all time, and where the decision can do no more than embody the preference of a given body in a given time and place. We do not realize how large a part of our law is open to reconsideration upon a slight change in the habit of the public mind. No concrete proposition is self-evident, no matter how ready we may be to accept it, not even Mr. Herbert Spencer's. Every man has a right to do what he wills, provided he interferes not with a like right on the part of his neighbors.

Why is a false and injurious statement privileged, if it is made honestly in giving information about a servant? It is because it has been thought more important that information should be given freely, than that a man should be protected from what under other circumstances would be an actionable wrong. Why is a man at liberty to set up a business which he knows will ruin his neighbor? It is because the public good is supposed to be best sub served by free competition. Obviously such judgments of relative importance may vary in different times and places. Why does a judge instruct a jury that an employer is not liable to an employee for an injury received in the course of his employment unless he is negligent, and why do the jury generally find for the plaintiff if the case is allowed to go to them? It is because the traditional policy of our law is to confine liability to cases where a prudent man might have foreseen the injury, or at least the danger, while the inclination of a very large part of the community is to make certain classes of persons insure the safety of those with whom they deal. Since the last words were written, I have seen the requirement of such insurance put forth as part of the programme of one of the best known labor organizations. There is a concealed, half conscious battle on the question of legislative policy, and if any one thinks that it can be settled deductively, or once for all, I only can say that I think he is theoretically wrong, and that I am certain that his conclusion will not be accepted in practice *semper ubique et ab omnibus.*

Indeed, I think that even now our theory upon this matter is open to reconsideration, although I am not prepared to say how I should decide if a reconsideration were proposed. Our law of torts comes from the old days of isolated, ungeneralized wrongs, assaults, slanders, and the like, where the damages might be taken to lie where they fell by legal judgment. But the torts with which our courts are kept busy to-day are mainly the incidents of certain well known businesses. They are injuries to person or property by railroads, factories, and the like. The liability for them is estimated, and sooner or later goes into the price paid by the public. The public really pays the damages, and the question of liability, if pressed far enough, is really the question how far it is desirable that the public should insure the safety of those whose work it uses. It might be said that in such cases the chance of a jury finding for the defendant is merely a chance, once in a while rather arbitrarily interrupting the regular course of recovery, most likely in the case of an unusually conscientious plaintiff, and therefore better done away with. On the other hand, the economic value even of a life to the community can be estimated, and no recovery, it may be said, ought to go beyond that amount. It is conceivable that some day in certain cases we may find ourselves imitating, on a higher plane, the tariff for life and limb which we see in the Leges Barbarorum.

I think that the judges themselves have failed adequately to recognize their duty of weighing considerations of social advantage. The duty is inevitable, and the result of the often proclaimed judicial aversion to deal with such considerations is simply to leave the very ground and foundation of judgments inarticulate, and often unconscious, as I have said. When socialism first began to be talked about, the comfortable classes of the community were a good deal frightened. I suspect that this fear has influenced judicial action both here and in England, yet it is certain that it is not a conscious factor in the decisions to which I refer. I think that something similar has led people who no longer hope to control the legislatures to look to the courts as expounders of the Constitutions, and that in some courts new principles have been discovered outside the bodies of those instruments, which may be generalized into acceptance of the economic doctrines which prevailed about fifty years ago, and a wholesale prohibition of what a tribunal of lawyers does not think about right. I cannot but believe that if the training of lawyers led them habitually to consider more definitely and explicitly the social advantage on which the rule they lay down must be justified, they sometimes would hesitate where now they are confident, and see that really they were taking sides upon debatable and often burning questions.

JOHN PETER ALTGELD

Address to the Laboring Order of Chicago (1899)

You are to be congratulated on the success of your celebration. Two great demonstrations in Chicago alone are vying with each other in honoring Labor Day. These vast assemblages represent sturdy manhood and womanhood. They represent honest toil of every kind, and they represent strong patriotism and desirable citizenship. The law has set apart this day in recognition of the nobility of labor, and, as the governor of this great state, I have come to pay homage to that force which lays the foundation of empires, which builds cities, builds railroads, develops agriculture, supports schools, founds industries, creates commerce, and moves the world.

It is wisely directed labor that has made our country the greatest ever known and has made Chicago the wonder of mankind. I say wisely directed labor, for without wise direction labor is fruitless. The pointing out and the doing are inseparably connected. More than this, ahead of the directing, there must go the genius which originates and conceives, the genius which takes the risk and moves a league forward. All three are necessary to each other. Weaken either, and there are clouds in the sky. Destroy either, and the hammer of industry ceases to be heard.

Glance over this majestic city, see its workshops, its warehouses, its commercial palaces, its office temples, and the thousand other structures that show the possibilities of human achievement and tell who did all this. You say the laboring men; yes, that is correct. But I tell you that if the gods keep a record of our doings, they have set down the men who originated all this, and then dared to make a forward step in building, as among the greatest of laborers.

We are at present in the midst of a great industrial and commercial depression. Industry is nearly at a standstill all over the earth. The consumptive power, or rather the purchasing power, of the world has been interfered with, producing not only a derangement but a paralysis, not only stopping further production but preventing the proper distribution of what there is already created; so that we have the anomalous spectacle of abundant food products, on the one hand, and hungry men without bread, on the other; abundant fabrics, on the one hand, and industrious, frugal men going half-clad, on the other. Employer and employee are affected alike.

There are thousands of honest, industrious, and frugal men who walk the streets all day in search of work, and even bread, and there are many hundreds of the most enterprising employers who sweat by day and walk the floor by night trying to devise means to keep the sheriff away from the establishment. You are not responsible for this condition. Men here and in Europe who call themselves statesmen have inaugurated policies of which this is a natural result. Considering the increase in population, the increase in the industries and commercial activity of the world, as well as the increased area over which business was done, there has in recent years been a practical reduction in the volume of the money of the world of from 33 to 40 percent, and there had of necessity to follow a shrinkage in the value of property to a corresponding extent.

This has been going on for a number of years, and as it has progressed it has become harder and harder for the debtor to meet his obligations; for the value of his property kept falling while his debt did not fall. Consequently, every little while, a lot of debtors who could no longer stand the strain succumbed. The result was that each time there was a flurry in financial circles. By degrees these failures became more frequent, until, finally, people who had money took alarm and withdrew it from circulation. This precipitated a panic and with it a harvest of bankruptcy. No doubt there were secondary causes that contributed, but this one cause was sufficient to create the distress that we see.

If for some years to come there should not be sufficient blood in the industrial and commercial world to make affairs healthy, then you must console yourselves with the thought that our country, with all the other great nations, has been placed on a narrow gold basis, and you will not be troubled with any of these cheap dollars that the big newspapers claim you did not want. The present depression, resulting from a lack of ready money in the world, shows how indispensable capital is to labor—all the wheels of industry stand still the moment it is withdrawn. It also shows that, while the interests of the employer and the employee may be antagonistic on the subject of wages, they are the same in every other respect; neither can do anything without the other—certain it is that the employee cannot prosper unless the employer does. On the other hand, if the purchasing power of the employee is destroyed, the employer must soon be without a market for his goods.

The great American market was due to the purchasing power of the laboring classes. If this should

in the end be destroyed, it will change entirely the character of our institutions. Whenever our laboring classes are reduced to a condition where they can buy only a few coarse articles of food and clothing, then our glory will have departed.

Still another thing has been made more clear than before, and that is that the employers, as a rule, are not great capitalists of the country. As a rule, they are enterprising men who borrow idle capital and put it to some use; and whenever they are suddenly called on to pay up and are not able to borrow elsewhere, they are obliged to shut down.

There are many advanced thinkers who look forward to a new industrial system that shall be an improvement on the present and under which the laborer shall come nearer getting his share of the benefits resulting from invention and machinery than under the present system. All lovers of their kind would hail such a system with joy. But we are forced to say that it is not yet at hand. As we must have bread and must have clothing, we are obliged to cling to the old system for the present, and probably for a long time to come, until the foundations can be laid for a better one by intelligent progress. Classes, like individuals, have their bright and their dark days, and just now there seems to be a long, dark day ahead of you. It will be a day of suffering and distress, and I must say to you there seems to be no way of escaping it, and I therefore counsel you to face it squarely and bear it with that heroism and fortitude with which an American citizen should face and bear calamity.

It has been suggested that the state and different branches of government should furnish employment during the winter to idle men. Certainly everything that can be done in this line will be done, but I must warn you not to expect too much from this source. The powers of government are so hedged about with constitutional provisions that much cannot be done. The state at present has no work to. do. The parks can employ only a few men. The city has work for more men, but it is also limited in its funds. The great drainage canal may, and probably will, give employment to a considerable number of men; but, after all, you must recognize that these things will be only in the nature of makeshifts; only to tide over; only to keep men and their families from starving. And on this point let me say it will be the duty of all public officials to see to it that no man is permitted to starve on the soil of Illinois, and provision will be made to that end.

But all this is temporary. The laborer must look to ways and means that are permanent for the improvement of his condition when the panic is over, and these measures must be along the line of and in harmony with the institutions of this century and must move by a gradual and steady development. Nothing that is violently done is of permanent advantage to the workingman. He can only prosper when his labor is in demand, and his labor can be in demand only when his employer prospers and there is nothing to interfere with consumption.

The world has been slow to accord labor its due. For thousands of years pillage, plunder, and organized robbery, called warfare, were honorable pursuits, and the man who toiled in order that all might live was despised. In the flight of time, it was but yesterday that the labor of the earth was driven with the lash and either sold on the block like cattle or tied by an invisible chain to the soil, and was forbidden to even wander outside his parish. In the yesterday of time, even the employers of labor were despised. The men who conducted great industries, who carried on commerce, who practiced the useful arts, the men who made the earth habitable were looked down upon by a class that considered it honorable to rob the toiler of his bread—a class which, while possessing the pride of the eagle, had only the character of the vulture.

Great has been the development since then. This century brought upon its wings higher ideas, more of truth and more of common sense, and it announced to mankind that he is honorable who creates; that he should be despised who can only consume; that he is the benefactor of the race who gives it additional thought, an additional flower, an additional loaf of bread, an additional comfort; and he is a curse to his kind who tramples down what others build or, without compensation, devours what others create. The century brought with it still greater things. Not only did it lift the employer to a position of honor, influence, and power but it tore away parish boundaries, it cut the chains of the serf, it burned the auction block, where the laborer and his children were sold. And it brought ideas; it taught the laboring man to extend his hand to his fellow laborer; it taught him to organize and not only to read but to investigate, to inquire,

to discuss, to consider, and to look ahead; so that today the laborer and his cause, at least theoretically, command the homage of all civilized men, and the greatest states in Christendom have set apart a day to be annually observed as a holiday in honor of labor.

The children of Israel were forty years in marching from the bondage of Egypt to the freer atmosphere of Palestine, and a halo of glory envelops their history. In the last forty years the children of Toil have made a forward march which is greater than any ever made in the wilderness. True, the land is not conquered. You have simply camped upon that higher plane where you can more clearly see the difficulties of the past, and where, in the end, you may hope for a higher justice and a happier condition for yourselves and your children; but a great deal remains to be done. In a sense, you are just out of the wilderness.

You ask along what lines, then, shall we proceed when the times get better in order to improve our condition? I answer along lines which harmonize, not only with nature's laws but with the laws of the land. Occupying, as I do, a position which makes me in a sense a conservator of all interests and classes, I desire to see the harmonious prosperity of all; and let me say to you that, until all the active interests of the land prosper again, there can be no general demand for your services and, consequently, no healthy prosperity. What I wish to point out is the absolute necessity of each class or interest being able to take care of itself in the fierce struggle for existence. You have not yet fully reached this state.

In the industrial world, as well as in the political world, only those forces survive which can maintain themselves and which are so concentrated that their influence is immediately and directly felt. A scattered force, no matter how great, is of no account in the sharp contests of the age. This is an age of concentration. Everywhere there is concentration and combination of capital and of those factors which today rule the world. The formation of corporations has greatly accelerated this movement, and no matter what is said about it, whether we approve it or not, it is the characteristic feature of our civilization and grows out of increased invention, the speedy communication between different parts of the world, and the great industrial generalship and enterprise of the time. It is questionable whether this tendency to combination could have been stopped in any way. It is certain, without this concentration of force, the gigantic achievements of our times would have been an impossibility. Combination and concentration are the masters of the age.

Let the laborer learn from this and act accordingly. Faultfinding and idle complaint are useless. Great forces, like great rivers, cannot be stopped. You must be able to fight your own battles. For the laborer to stand single-handed before giant combinations of power means annihilation. The world gives only when it is obliged to and respects only those who compel its respect.

Government was created by power and has always been controlled by power. Do not imagine that it is sufficient if you have justice and equity on your side, for the earth is covered with the graves of justice and equity that failed to receive recognition because there was no influence or force to compel it, and it will be so until the millennium. Whenever you demonstrate that you are an active, concentrated power, moving along lawful lines, then you will be felt in government. Until then, you will not. This is an age of law as well as of force, and no force succeeds that does not move along legal lines.

The laboring men of the world always have been, and are today, the support and principal reliance of the government. They support its flags in time of war, and their hands earn the taxes in time of peace. Their voice is for fair play, and no great government was ever destroyed by the laboring classes. Treason and rebellion never originated with them but always came from the opposite source.

Early in our history there occurred what was called Shays's Rebellion, but they were not wage workers who created it. Then came the so-called Whisky Rebellion, created not by day laborers. During the War of 1812, a convention was held in the East which practically advocated a dissolution of the Union, but wage workers were not among its members. The great rebellion of 1861 was not fomented by the laboring classes but by those classes which ate the bread that others toiled for. It was a rebellion by those who had long been prominent as leaders, who largely controlled the wealth of the country, who boasted of aristocratic society, and many of whom had been educated at the expense of the country whose flag they fired on. While, on the other hand, the great armies which put down this rebellion and supported the flag were composed of men who had literally earned their bread by the sweat of their brows.

It is true that at times a number of laborers, more or less ignorant, who thought they were being robbed of the fruits of their toil have indulged in rioting, and, while they have always lost by it and while they cannot be too severely condemned, yet they do not stand alone in this condemnation; for there have been many broadcloth mobs in this country, and in different sections of it, whose actions were lawless and as disgraceful as that of any labor mob that ever assembled. I must congratulate organized labor upon its freedom from turbulence. Rioting is nearly always by an ignorant class outside of all organizations and which, in most cases, was brought into the community by conscienceless men to defeat organized labor. There should be a law compelling a man who brings this class of people into our midst to give bond for their support and their good behavior, for at present they are simply a disturbing element. They threaten the peace of society and bring reproach on the cause of labor.

The lesson I wish to impress upon you is that in business, in the industries, in government, everywhere, only those interests and forces survive that can maintain themselves along legal lines; and if you permanently improve your condition it must be by intelligently and patriotically standing together all over the country. Every plan must fail unless you do this.

At present you are to a great extent yet a scattered force, sufficiently powerful, if collected, to make yourselves heard and felt; to secure not only a fair hearing but a fair decision of all questions. Unite this power and you will be independent; leave it scattered and you will fail. Organization is the result of education as well as an educator. Let all the men of America who toil with their hands once stand together and no more complaints will be heard about unfair treatment. The progress of labor in the future must be along the line of patriotic association, not simply in localities but everywhere. And let me caution you that every act of violence is a hindrance to your progress.

There will be men among you ready to commit it. They are your enemies. There will be sneaks and Judas Iscariots in your ranks, who will for a mere pittance act as spies and try to incite some of the more hotheaded of your number to deeds of violence in order that these reptiles may get the credit of exposing you. They are your enemies. Cast them out of your ranks. Remember that any permanent prosperity must be based upon intelligence and upon conditions which are permanent.

And let me say to you again, in conclusion, this fall and this winter will be a trying time to you. The record of the laborers of the earth is one of patriotism. They have maintained the government, they have maintained the schools and churches, and it behooves you now to face the hardships that are upon you and see that your cause is not injured by grave indiscretions. Make the ignorant understand that government is strong and that life and property will be protected and law and order will be maintained, and that, while the day is dark now, the future will place the laborer in a more exalted position than he has ever occupied.

RUFUS PECKHAM

Lochner v. New York (1905)

Mr. Justice PECKHAM delivered the opinion of the Court.

The indictment, it will be seen, charges that the plaintiff in error violated the one hundred and tenth section of article 8, chapter 415, of the Laws of 1897, known as the labor law of the State of New York, in that he wrongfully and unlawfully required and permitted an employee working for him to work more than sixty hours in one week. [. . .] The mandate of the statute that "no employee shall be required or permitted to work," is the substantial equivalent of an enactment that "no employee shall contract or agree to work," more than ten hours per day, and, as there is no provision for special emergencies, the statute is mandatory in all cases. It is not an act merely fixing the number of hours which shall constitute a legal day's work, but an absolute prohibition upon the employer's permitting, under any circumstances, more than ten hours' work to be done in his establishment. The employee may desire to earn the extra money which would arise from his working more than the prescribed time, but this statute forbids the employer from permitting the employee to earn it.

The statute necessarily interferes with the right of contract between the employer and employees concerning the number of hours in which the latter may labor in the bakery of the employer. The general right to make a contract in relation to his business is part of the liberty of the individual protected by the Fourteen Amendment of the Federal Constitution. *Allgeyer v. Louisiana* [1897]. Under that provision, no State can deprive any person of life, liberty or property without due process of law. The right to purchase or to sell labor is part of the liberty protected by this amendment unless there are circumstances which exclude the right. There are, however, certain powers, existing in the sovereignty of each State in the Union, somewhat vaguely termed police powers, the exact description and limitation of which have not been attempted by the courts. Those powers, broadly stated and without, at present, any attempt at a more specific limitation, relate to the safety, health, morals and general welfare of the public. Both property and liberty are held on such reasonable conditions as may be imposed by the governing power of the State in the exercise of those powers, and with such conditions the Fourteen Amendment was not designed to interfere.

The State therefore has power to prevent the individual from making certain kinds of contracts, and, in regard to them, the Federal Constitution offers no protection. If the contract be one which the State, in the legitimate exercise of its police power, has the right to prohibit, it is not prevented from prohibiting it by the Fourteenth Amendment. Contracts in violation of a statute, either of the Federal or state government, or a contract to let one's property for immoral purposes, or to do any other unlawful act, could obtain no protection from the Federal Constitution as coming under the liberty of person or of free contract. Therefore, when the State, by its legislature, in the assumed exercise of its police powers, has passed an act which seriously limits the right to labor or the right of contract in regard to their means of livelihood between persons who are *sui juris* (both employer and employee), it becomes of great importance to determine which shall prevail—the right of the individual to labor for such time as he may choose or the right of the State to prevent the individual from laboring or from entering into any contract to labor beyond a certain time prescribed by the State.

This court has recognized the existence and upheld the exercise of the police powers of the States in many cases which might fairly be considered as border ones, and it has, in the course of its determination of questions regarding the asserted invalidity of such statutes on the ground of their violation of the rights secured by the Federal Constitution, been guided by rules of a very liberal nature, the application of which has resulted, in numerous instances, in upholding the validity of state statutes thus assailed. Among the later cases where the state law has been upheld by this court is that of *Holden v. Hardy* [1898]. A provision in the act of the legislature of Utah was there under consideration, the act limiting the employment of workmen in all underground mines or workings to eight hours per day "except in cases of emergency, where life or property is in imminent danger." It also limited the hours of labor in smelting and other institutions for the reduction or refining of ores or metals to eight hours per day except in like cases of emergency. The act was held to be a valid exercise of the police powers of the State. A review of many of the cases on the subject, decided by this and other courts, is given in the opinion. It was held that the kind of employment, mining, smelting, etc., and the character of the employees in such kinds of labor, were such as to make it reasonable and proper for the State to interfere to prevent the employees from being constrained by the rules laid down by the proprietors in regard to labor. [. . .]

It must, of course, be conceded that there is a limit to the valid exercise of the police power by the State. There is no dispute concerning this general proposition. Otherwise the Fourteenth Amendment would have no efficacy, and the legislatures of the States would have unbounded power, and it would be enough to say that any piece of legislation was enacted to conserve the morals, the health or the safety of the people; such legislation would be valid no matter how absolutely without foundation the claim might be. The claim of the police power would be a mere pretext—become another and delusive name for the supreme sovereignty of the State to be exercised free from constitutional restraint. This is not contended for. In every case that comes before this court, therefore, where legislation of this character is concerned and where the protection of the Federal Constitution is sought, the question necessarily arises: is this a fair, reasonable and appropriate exercise of the police power of the State, or is it an unreasonable, unnecessary and arbitrary interference with the right of the individual to his personal liberty or to enter into those contracts in relation to labor which may seem to him appropriate or necessary for the support of himself and his family? Of course, the liberty of contract relating to labor includes both parties to it. The one has as much right to purchase as the other to sell labor.

This is not a question of substituting the judgment of the court for that of the legislature. If the act be within the power of the State, it is valid although the judgment of the court might be totally opposed to the enactment of such a law. But the question would still remain: is it within the police power of the State?, and that question must be answered by the court.

The question whether this act is valid as a labor law, pure and simple, may be dismissed in a few words. There is no reasonable ground for interfering with the liberty of person or the right of free contract by determining the hours of labor in the occupation of a baker. There is no contention that bakers as a class are not equal in intelligence and capacity to men in other trades or manual occupations, or that they are able to assert their rights and care for themselves without the protecting arm of the State, interfering with their independence of judgment and of action. They are in no sense wards of the State. Viewed in the light of a purely labor law, with no reference whatever to the question of health, we think that a law like the one before us involves neither the safety, the morals, nor the welfare of the public, and that the interest of the public is not in the slightest degree affected by such an act. The law must be upheld, if at all, as a law pertaining to the health of the individual engaged in the occupation of a baker. It does not affect any other portion of the public than those who are engaged in that occupation. Clean and wholesome bread does not depend upon whether the baker works but ten hours per day or only sixty hours a week. The limitation of the hours of labor does not come within the police power on that ground.

It is a question of which of two powers or rights shall prevail—the power of the State to legislate or the right of the individual to liberty of person and freedom of contract. The mere assertion that the subject relates though but in a remote degree to the public health does not necessarily render the enactment valid. The act must have a more direct relation, as a means to an end, and the end itself must be appropriate and legitimate, before an act can be held to be valid which interferes with the general right of an individual to be free in his person and in his power to contract in relation to his own labor. [. . .]

We think the limit of the police power has been reached and passed in this case. There is, in our judgment, no reasonable foundation for holding this to be necessary or appropriate as a health law to safeguard the public health or the health of the individuals who are following the trade of a baker. If this statute be valid, and if, therefore, a proper case is made out in which to deny the right of an individual, *sui juris*, as employer or employee, to make contracts for the labor of the latter under the protection of the provisions of the Federal Constitution, there would seem to be no length to which legislation of this nature might not go. [. . .]

We think that there can be no fair doubt that the trade of a baker, in and of itself, is not an unhealthy one to that degree which would authorize the legislature to interfere with the right to labor, and with the right of free contract on the part of the individual, either as employer or employee. In looking through statistics regarding all trades and occupations, it may be true that the trade of a baker does not appear to be as healthy as some other trades, and is also vastly more healthy than still others. To the common understanding, the trade of a baker has never been regarded as an unhealthy one. Very likely, physicians would not recommend the exercise of that or of any other trade as a remedy for ill health. Some occupations are more healthy than others, but we think there are none which might not come under the power of the legislature to supervise and control the hours of working therein if the mere fact that the occupation is not absolutely and perfectly healthy is to confer that right upon the legislative department of the Government. It might be safely affirmed that almost all occupations more or less affect the health. There must be more than the mere fact of the possible existence of some small amount of unhealthiness to warrant legislative interference with liberty. It is unfortunately true that labor, even in any department, may possibly carry with it the seeds of unhealthiness. But are we all, on that account, at the mercy of legislative majorities? A printer, a tinsmith, a locksmith, a carpenter, a cabinetmaker, a dry goods clerk, a bank's, a lawyer's or a physician's clerk, or a clerk in almost any kind of business, would all come under the power of the legislature on this assumption. No trade, no occupation, no mode of earning one's living could escape this all-pervading power, and the acts of the legislature in limiting the hours of labor in all employments would be valid although such limitation might seriously cripple the ability of the laborer to support himself and his family. [. . .]

It is also urged, pursuing the same line of argument, that it is to the interest of the State that its population should be strong and robust, and therefore any legislation which may be said to tend to make people healthy must be valid as health laws, enacted under the police power. If this be a valid argument and a justification for this kind of legislation, it follows that the protection of the Federal Constitution from undue interference with liberty of person and freedom of contract is visionary wherever the law is sought to be justified as a valid exercise of the police power. Scarcely any law but might find shelter under such assumptions, and conduct, properly so called, as well as contract, would come under the restrictive sway of the legislature. Not only the hours of employees, but the hours of employers, could be regulated, and doctors, lawyers, scientists, all professional men, as well as athletes and artisans, could be forbidden to fatigue their brains and bodies by prolonged hours of exercise, lest the fighting strength of the State be impaired. [. . .] The act is not, within any fair meaning of the term, a health law, but is an illegal interference with the rights of individuals, both employers and employees, to make contracts regarding labor upon such terms as they may think best, or which they may agree upon with the other parties to such contracts. Statutes of the nature of that under review, limiting the hours in which grown and intelligent men may labor to earn their living, are mere meddlesome interferences with the rights of the individual, and they are not saved from condemnation by the claim that they are passed in the exercise of the police power and upon the subject of the health of the individual whose rights are interfered with, unless there be some fair ground, reasonable in and of itself, to say that there is material danger to the public health or to the health of the employees if the hours of labor are not curtailed. If this be not clearly the case, the individuals whose rights are thus made the subject of legislative interference are under the protection of the Federal Constitution regarding their liberty of contract as well as of person, and the legislature of the State has no power to limit their right as proposed in this statute. [. . .]

It was further urged on the argument that restricting the hours of labor in the case of bakers was valid because it tended to cleanliness on the part of the workers, as a man was more apt to be cleanly when not overworked, and, if cleanly, then his "output" was also more likely to be so. What has already been said applies with equal force to this contention. We do not admit the reasoning to be sufficient to justify the claimed right of such interference. The State in that case would assume the position of a supervisor, or *pater familias*, over every act of the individual, and its right of governmental interference with his hours of labor, his hours of exercise, the character thereof, and the extent to which it shall be carried would be recognized and upheld. In our judgment, it is not possible, in fact, to discover the connection between the number of hours a baker may work in the bakery and the healthful quality of the bread made by the workman. The connection, if any exists, is too shadowy and thin to build any argument for the interference of the legislature. If the man works ten hours a day, it is all right, but if ten and a half or eleven, his health is in danger and his bread may be unhealthful, and, therefore, he shall not be permitted to do it. This, we think, is unreasonable, and entirely arbitrary. When assertions such as we have adverted to become necessary in order to give, if possible, a plausible foundation for the contention that the law is a "health law," it gives rise to at least a suspicion that there was some other motive dominating the legislature than the purpose to subserve the public health or welfare. [. . .]

It is manifest to us that the limitation of the hours of labor as provided for in this section of the statute under which the indictment was found, and the plaintiff in error convicted, has no such direct relation to, and no such substantial effect upon, the health of the employee as to justify us in regarding the section as really a health law. It seems to us that the real object and purpose were simply to regulate the hours of labor between the master and his employees (all being men *sui juris*) in a private business, not dangerous in any degree to morals or in any real and substantial degree to the health of the employees. Under such circumstances, the freedom of master and employee to contract with each other in relation to their employment, and in defining the same, cannot be prohibited or interfered with without violating the Federal Constitution.

Reversed.

Oliver Wendell Holmes

Lochner v. New York, Dissent (1905)

Mr. Justice HOLMES dissenting.

I regret sincerely that I am unable to agree with the judgment in this case, and that I think it my duty to express my dissent.

This case is decided upon an economic theory which a large part of the country does not entertain. If it were a question whether I agreed with that theory, I should desire to study it further and long before making up my mind. But I do not conceive that to be my duty, because I strongly believe that my agreement or disagreement has nothing to do with the right of a majority to embody their opinions in law. It is settled by various decisions of this court that state constitutions and state laws may regulate life in many ways which we, as legislators, might think as injudicious, or, if you like, as tyrannical, as this, and which, equally with this, interfere with the liberty to contract. Sunday laws and usury laws are ancient examples. A more modern one is the prohibition of lotteries. The liberty of the citizen to do as he likes so long as he does not interfere with the liberty of others to do the same, which has been a shibboleth for some well known writers, is interfered with by school laws, by the Post Office, by every state or municipal institution which takes his money for purposes thought desirable, whether he likes it or not. The Fourteenth Amendment does not enact Mr. Herbert Spencer's *Social Statics.* The other day, we sustained the Massachusetts vaccination law. *Jacobson v. Massachusetts* [1905]. United States and state statutes and decisions cutting down the liberty to contract by way of combination are familiar to this court. *Northern Securities Co. v. United States* [1904]. Two years ago, we upheld the prohibition of sales of stock on margins or for future delivery in the constitution of California. *Otis v. Parker* [1903]. The decision sustaining an eight hour law for miners is still recent. *Holden v. Hardy* [1898]. Some of these laws embody convictions or prejudices which judges are likely to share. Some may not. But a constitution is not intended to embody a particular economic theory, whether of paternalism and the organic relation of the citizen to the State or of *laissez faire.* It is made for people of fundamentally differing views, and the accident of our finding certain opinions natural and familiar or novel and even shocking ought not to conclude our judgment upon the question whether statutes embodying them conflict with the Constitution of the United States.

General propositions do not decide concrete cases. The decision will depend on a judgment or intuition more subtle than any articulate major premise. But I think that the proposition just stated, if it is accepted, will carry us far toward the end. Every opinion tends to become a law. I think that the word liberty in the Fourteenth Amendment is perverted when it is held to prevent the natural outcome of a dominant opinion, unless it can be said that a rational and fair man necessarily would admit that the statute proposed would infringe fundamental principles as they have been understood by the traditions of our people and our law. It does not need research to show that no such sweeping condemnation can be passed upon the statute before us. A reasonable man might think it a proper measure on the score of health. Men whom I certainly could not pronounce unreasonable would uphold it as a first installment of a general regulation of the hours of work. Whether in the latter aspect it would be open to the charge of inequality I think it unnecessary to discuss.

3

THE PROBLEMS OF INDUSTRIAL CAPITALISM

From Thomas Jefferson to Abraham Lincoln, one important strain of American political thought perceived a vital connection between economic independence, ownership of productive property, and skilled labor on the one hand, and the civic qualities necessary to sustain republican self-government on the other. The person who possessed a farm, a store, a profession, or tools and the knowledge and skill to use them was most likely to cultivate the personal attributes of responsible citizenship. Economic independence made a person less vulnerable to the machinations of demagogues. Commitment to one's livelihood gave a person a powerful interest in the vitality and well-being of one's community. The ability to make one's own way in the world gave a person the confidence to think for oneself, while the work ethic gave one the incentive to engage in projects of self-improvement. Wise government, therefore, pursued policies designed to encourage Americans to develop an economic "competency." The bounty of America, most politicians and statesmen agreed, permitted any properly self-reliant individual who sought to strive for the ownership of a farm or small business the realistic opportunity of achieving it.

After the Civil War American entrepreneurs, with substantial public assistance, constructed a vast and interlocking network of railroads that permitted the emergence of regional and then national integrated markets. Integrated markets, and the development of bureaucratic innovations necessary to coordinate them, permitted businesses to realize the benefits of economies of scale. From the 1870s well into the twentieth century, modern corporations, massive by comparison to any economic enterprises that had preceded them, increasingly dominated the American economy. In the new economy labor was simply one of the factors of production, something like land, raw materials, and capital, that had to be managed efficiently. As fewer Americans were able to achieve or sustain an independent competency, American politicians, intellectuals, religious authorities, and citizens had to grapple with the civic implications and consequences. The older economy, which had seemed well adapted to a republican polity, atrophied, and with it the vitality of the ethos of independence and self-sufficiency it had sustained. By the beginning of the twentieth century, Americans struggled to develop a civic alternative. The task before us, said Woodrow Wilson in 1907, was to make "a new translation of our morals into the terms of our modern life, where individuality seems for the time being lost in complex organizations."

Moreover, the vitality of the new industrial and corporate economy impelled Americans beyond their own national borders. The acquisition of Spanish territories, most importantly the Philippines, Guam, and Puerto Rico, followed the United States' victory in the 1898 Spanish-American War. Subsequent aggressive American intervention in Central America and the Far East, motivated in part by corporate interests, secured for the United States prominence as a world power. As the United States Army and Navy worked to secure possession of what to many seemed like a growing American empire, facing in the Philippines especially a ferocious native resistance, statesmen and critics at home debated the expanse and nature of American government abroad. Anti-imperialist critics warned, "free government is hard and absolutism easy—a dangerous lesson in a Republic. Liberty and absolutism cannot exist together." Others, like the bitingly satiric humorist Mark Twain, condemned the tight connection between imperial aggression and the expansion of corporate markets. "The Blessings-of-Civilization Trust, wisely and cautiously administered, is a Daisy," Twain remarked. "There is more money in it, more territory, more sovereignty, and other kinds of emolument, than there is in any other game that is played."

Even as some Americans celebrated the "gospel of wealth" and, like William Graham Sumner, relished the Social Darwinist "struggle for survival," others decried the conditions of life entailed by the new economy and its attendant cultural transformations. Thorstein Veblen, the ever angular economist, considered "pecuniary emulation" and "conspicuous consumption" as the hollow consequence of America's rapidly expanding affluence. The evident economic vitality of the United States, Veblen suggested, had produced a vulgar society increasingly attached to limitless acquisition, voracious consumption, and monumentally careless waste. Henry Adams, a scholar, social critic, and descendant of U.S. presidents, ruminated on the meaning of new forms of power, harnessed from nature, shaping a barren new culture blindly set in opposition against the spiritual power of a higher order of things. Veblen and Adams both criticized the transformed culture of the United States for what they took to be its new, and debilitating, materialism.

More famously and effectively, other observers focused on the deep poverty and human misery increasingly evident in post–Civil War America. The novelist Upton Sinclair, for example, produced a scathing commentary on life for working men and women in the new industrial and corporate economy. Jurgis, Sinclair's Polish immigrant protagonist in *The Jungle*, possessed a fiercely energetic work ethic. In earlier decades his character would have admirably fit him to develop both economic independence and civic responsibility. In the new world of the Chicago meatpacking industry, Jurgis' vigor represented an opportunity for artful managers to speed up the work, resulting in misery for older, worn-out, or less physically gifted coworkers. The new economy, as experienced by Jurgis and people like him, created a class of laboring citizens characterized by exhaustion, helplessness, poverty, and ultimately depravity. Socialist reformers like Eugene Debs and W. E. B. Du Bois drew upon a vast reservoir of popular resentment, most immediately at the inhumanity of contemporary industrial working conditions. Their anger, however, also drew upon deep perceptions of loss, as they contemplated the rapidly diminishing vitality of the civic ideals of Lincoln's America. Christian reformers like Walter Rauschenbusch confronted the reality of profound human suffering, stemming not from individual evil but rather from the very structure of human relationships as ordered by the new economy. Rauschenbusch was drawn to Socialism for religious reasons, in the process rejecting as deeply misguided the religious conclusions of men like Russell Conwell.

Building on the work of earlier generations of activists, Progressive reformers insisted that meaningful response to the new social and economic conditions of the United States must include civic equality for women. Some, like Jane Addams, expanded and developed the analyses of earlier advocates for woman suffrage. Addams started with the traditional notion that women had a special obligation to tend to the domestic sphere of home and family, but she insisted that in the face of thoroughgoing social and economic change, women of necessity had to be politically active if they were to fulfill their proper domestic role. "If woman would keep on with her old business of caring for her house and rearing her children," Addams wrote, "she will have to have some conscience in regard to public affairs lying quite outside of her immediate household." Addams' analysis drew deeply from her profound experience as a Progressive activist. She was a cofounder of Hull House, a "settlement house" project emulating a similar movement previously established in Great Britain and dedicated to the assistance of the working class and inner-city poor. She worked at Hull House to support education, fine arts, and organized sports within otherwise deprived urban environments. One of the most prominent reformers during the Progressive Era, she became the first woman to receive the Nobel Peace Prize for her humanitarian efforts.

A more radical voice was that of Margaret Sanger, who insisted that women had a bedrock right to ownership of their own bodies, and especially over reproductive choice. "Woman," wrote Sanger, "had chained herself to her place in society and the family through the maternal functions of her nature, and only chains thus strong could have bound her to her lot as a brood animal for the masculine civilizations of the world." Birth control, Sanger envisioned, would allow women "to decide for themselves whether they shall become mothers, under what conditions and when," a choice that "is for woman the key to the temple of liberty." Sanger's rhetoric of self-ownership and spiritual self-development resonated with ideals deeply seated in the American political tradition, and blossomed in subsequent decades following the Second World War. And yet Sanger was very much a product of her times. Her thought drew inspiration not just from the liberalism of the early republic, with its emphasis on individual autonomy, independence, and self-ownership, but also from the cutting edge of early twentieth-century social science. She promoted eugenics, arguing in 1922 that birth control represented "the application of intelligent guidance over the reproductive power." Thus she was an advocate for forced sterilization of "the unfit" and the "inferior classes," and she incorporated attitudes influenced by racist elements within the popular Social Darwinist movement into her promotion of woman rights. "The most urgent problem today is how to limit and discourage the over-fertility of the mentally and physically defective," she suggested. "Possibly drastic and Spartan methods may be forced upon American society if it continues complacently to encourage the chance and chaotic breeding that has resulted from our stupid, cruel sentimentalism."

The great Progressive politicians of the early twentieth century, men as diverse as Theodore Roosevelt, Woodrow Wilson, and Robert La Follette, recognized the depth of the challenge that the evolving corporate capitalist economy posed to American political institutions. Both Roosevelt and Wilson perceived that meaningful social and economic change was necessary to foreclose the socialist alternative so forcefully advocated by reformers like Debs and Sinclair. But in rejecting socialism, both insisted that a forceful national state must take responsibility for regulating the economy. Influenced by the writings of influential Progressives like Herbert Croly, both Roosevelt and Wilson understood the central political issues of their time within the context of the transition from free-market capitalism to an economy dominated by the alliance between large industrial corporations and the activist state. Even as American statesmen struggled to retain in some viable form the older individualism, they abandoned the laissez-faire liberalism of the late nineteenth century, and laid the groundwork for a thoroughgoing, active role for the national government in the economic affairs of the United States and its people.

This shift toward the modern administrative state, however, ran headlong into a federal judiciary—particularly the Supreme Court—that philosophically and constitutionally objected to more active government. That's not to say that the Court never upheld state or federal legislation aimed at regulating economic activity, such as work hours, workplace safety, mergers, and so forth. The Court's ruling in *Muller v. Oregon* (1908) shows that the Court could be persuaded that such legislation—in this case a state law setting maximum work hours for women—was consistent with the Constitution. But *Muller* also reveals the Court's underlying presumption of the unconstitutionality of governmental economic regulation. Indeed, the case arguably turns on prevailing cultural prejudices. The state's law in this case could stand because *women* were different. Such laws covering men, such as the New York law in *Lochner v. New York* (1905), failed to find favor with the Court. Moreover, some laws, such as minimum wage laws, were consistently struck down by the Court. Thus, while this period of American political history witnessed the birth of a more active, positivist state, the Progressive aspiration for the state would not finally mature until the New Deal politics of the 1930s.

THORSTEIN VEBLEN

Theory of the Leisure Class (1899)

Pecuniary Emulation

Wherever the institution of private property is found, even in a slightly developed form, the economic process bears the character of a struggle between men for the possession of goods. It has been customary in economic theory, and especially among those economists who adhere with least faltering to the body of modernised classical doctrines, to construe this struggle for wealth as being substantially a struggle for subsistence. Such is, no doubt, its character in large part during the earlier and less efficient phases of industry. Such is also its character in all cases where the "niggardliness of nature" is so strict as to afford but a scanty livelihood to the community in return for strenuous and unremitting application to the business of getting the means of subsistence. But in all progressing communities an advance is presently made beyond this early stage of technological development. Industrial efficiency is presently carried to such a pitch as to afford something appreciably more than a bare livelihood to those engaged in the industrial process. It has not been unusual for economic theory to speak of the further struggle for wealth on this new industrial basis as a competition for an increase of the comforts of life,—primarily for an increase of the physical comforts which the consumption of goods affords.

The end of acquisition and accumulation is conventionally held to be the consumption of the goods accumulated—whether it is consumption directly by the owner of the goods or by the household attached to him and for this purpose identified with him in theory. This is at least felt to be the economically legitimate end of acquisition, which alone it is incumbent on the theory to take account of. Such consumption may of course be conceived to serve the consumer's physical wants—his physical comfort—or his so-called higher wants—spiritual, aesthetic, intellectual, or what not; the latter class of wants being served indirectly by an expenditure of goods, after the fashion familiar to all economic readers.

But it is only when taken in a sense far removed from its naïve meaning that consumption of goods can be said to afford the incentive from which accumulation invariably proceeds. The motive that lies at the root of ownership is emulation; and the same motive of emulation continues active in the further development of the institution to which it has given rise and in the development of all those features of the social structure which this institution of ownership touches. The possession of wealth confers honour; it is an invidious distinction. Nothing equally cogent can be said for the consumption of goods, nor for any other conceivable incentive to acquisition, and especially not for any incentive to the accumulation of wealth. [. . .]

Property set out with being booty held as trophies of the successful raid. So long as the group had departed but little from the primitive communal organisation, and so long as it still stood in close contact with other hostile groups, the utility of things or persons owned lay chiefly in an invidious comparison between their possessor and the enemy from whom they were taken. The habit of distinguishing between the interests of the individual and those of the group to which he belongs is apparently a later growth. Invidious comparison between the possessor of the honorific booty and his less successful neighbours within the group was no doubt present early as an element of the utility of the things possessed, though this was not at the outset the chief element of their value. The man's prowess was still primarily the group's prowess, and the possessor of the booty felt himself to be primarily the keeper of the honour of his group. This appreciation of exploit from the communal point of view is met with also at later stages of social growth, especially as regards the laurels of war.

But so soon as the custom of individual ownership begins to gain consistency, the point of view taken in making the invidious comparison on which private property rests will begin to change. Indeed, the one change is but the reflex of the other. The initial phase of ownership, the phase of acquisition by naïve seizure and conversion, begins to pass into the subsequent stage of an incipient organisation of industry on the basis of private property (in slaves); the horde develops into a more or less self-sufficing industrial community; possessions then come to be valued not so much as evidence of successful foray, but rather as evidence of the prepotence of the possessor of these goods over other individuals within the community. The invidious comparison now becomes primarily a comparison of the owner with the other members of the group. Property is still of the nature of trophy, but, with the cultural advance, it becomes more and more a trophy of successes scored in the game of ownership carried on between the members of the group under the quasi-peaceable methods of nomadic life.

Gradually, as industrial activity further displaces predatory activity in the community's everyday life and in men's habits of thought, accumulated property more and more replaces trophies of predatory exploit as the conventional exponent of prepotence and success. With the growth of settled industry, therefore, the possession of wealth gains in relative importance and effectiveness as a customary basis of repute and esteem. Not that esteem ceases to be awarded on the basis of other, more direct evidence of prowess; not that successful predatory aggression or warlike exploit ceases to call out the approval and admiration of the crowd, or to stir the envy of the less successful competitors; but the opportunities for gaining distinction by means of this direct manifestation of superior force grow less available both in scope and frequency. At the same time opportunities for industrial aggression, and for the accumulation of property by the quasi-peaceable methods of nomadic industry, increase in scope and availability. And it is even more to the point that property now becomes the most easily recognised evidence of a reputable degree of success as distinguished from heroic or signal achievement. It therefore becomes the conventional basis of esteem. Its possession in some amount becomes necessary in order to [have] any reputable standing in the community. It becomes indispensable to accumulate, to acquire property, in order to

retain one's good name. When accumulated goods have in this way once become the accepted badge of efficiency, the possession of wealth presently assumes the character of an independent and definitive basis of esteem. The possession of goods, whether acquired aggressively by one's own exertion or passivly by transmission through inheritance from others, becomes a conventional basis of reputability. The possession of wealth, which was at the outset valued simply as an evidence of efficiency, becomes, in popular apprehension, itself a meritorious act. Wealth is now itself intrinsically honourable and confers honour on its possessor. [. . .]

So far as concerns the present question, the end sought by accumulation is to rank high in comparison with the rest of the community in point of pecuniary strength. So long as the comparison is distincly unfavourable to himself, the normal, average individual will live in chronic dissatisfaction with his present lot; and when he has reached what may be called the normal pecuniary standard of the community, or of his class in the community, this chronic dissatisfaction will give place to a restless straining to place a wider and ever-widening pecuniary interval between himself and this average standard. The invidious comparison can never become so favourable to the individual making it that he would not gladly rate himself still higher relatively to his competitors in the struggle for pecuniary reputability. [. . .]

[. . .] Under the régime of individual ownership the most available means of visibly achieving a purpose is that afforded by the acquisition and accumulation of goods; and as the self-regarding antithesis between man and man reaches fuller consciousness, the propensity for achievement—the instinct of workmanship—tends more and more to shape itself into a straining to excel others in pecuniary achievement. Relative success, tested by an invidious pecuniary comparison with other men, becomes the conventional end of action. The currently accepted legitimate end of effort becomes the achievement of a favourable comparison with other men; and therefore the repugnance to futility to a good extent coalesces with the incentive of emulation. It acts to accentuate the struggle for pecuniary reputability by visiting with a sharper disapproval all shortcoming and all evidence of shortcoming in point of pecuniary success. Purposeful effort comes to mean, primarily, effort directed to or resulting in a more creditable showing of accumulated wealth. Among the motives which lead men to accumulate wealth, the primacy, both in scope and intensity, therefore, continues to belong to this motive of pecuniary emulation. [. . .]

Conspicuous Consumption

[. . .] During the earlier stages of economic development, consumption of goods without stint, especially consumption of the better grades of goods,—ideally all consumption in excess of the subsistence minimum,—pertains normally to the leisure class. This restriction tends to disappear, at least formally, after the later peaceable stage has been reached, with private ownership of goods and an industrial system based on wage labour or on the petty household economy. But during the earlier quasi-peaceable stage, when so many of the traditions through which the institution of a leisure class has affected the economic life of later times were taking form and consistency, this principle has had the force of a conventional law. It has served as the norm to which consumption has tended to conform, and any appreciable departure from it is to be regarded as an aberrant form, sure to be eliminated sooner or later in the further course of development.

The quasi-peaceable gentleman of leisure, then, not only consumes of the staff of life beyond the minimum required for subsistence and physical efficiency, but his consumption also undergoes a specialisation as regards the quality of the goods consumed. He consumes freely and of the best, in food, drink, narcotics, shelter, services, ornaments, apparel, weapons and accoutrements, amusements, amulets, and idols or divinities. In the process of gradual amelioration which takes place in the articles of his consumption, the motive principle and the proximate aim of innovation is no doubt the higher efficiency of the improved and more elaborate products for personal comfort and well-being. But that does not remain the sole purpose of their consumption. The canon of reputability is at hand and seizes upon such innovations as are, according to its standard, fit to survive. Since the consumption of these more excellent goods is an evidence of wealth, it becomes honorific; and conversely, the failure to consume in due quantity and quality becomes a mark of inferiority and demerit. [. . .]

In the giving of costly entertainments other motives, of a more genial kind, are of course also present. The custom of festive gatherings probably originated in motives of conviviality and religion; these motives are also present in the later development, but they do not continue to be the sole motives. The latter-day leisure-class festivities and entertainments may continue in some slight degree to serve the religious need and in a higher degree the needs of recreation and conviviality, but they also serve an invidious purpose; and they serve it none the less effectually for having a colourable non-invidious ground in these more avowable motives. But the economic effect of these social amenities is not therefore lessened, either in the vicarious consumption of goods or in the exhibition of difficult and costly achievements in etiquette.

As wealth accumulates, the leisure class develops further in function and structure, and there arises a differentiation within the class. There is a more or less elaborate system of rank and grades. This differentiation is furthered by the inheritance of wealth and the consequent inheritance of gentility. With the inheritance of gentility goes the inheritance of obligatory leisure; and gentility of a sufficient potency to entail a life of leisure may be inherited without the complement of wealth required to maintain a dignified leisure. Gentle blood may be transmitted without goods enough to afford a reputably free consumption at one's ease. Hence results a class of impecunious gentlemen of leisure. [. . .] These lower grades, especially the impecunious, or marginal, gentlemen of leisure, affiliate themselves by a system of dependence or fealty to the great ones; by so doing they gain an increment of repute, or of the means with which to lead a life of leisure, from their patron. They become his courtiers or retainers, servants; and being fed and countenanced by their patron they are indices of his rank and vicarious consumers of his superfluous wealth. Many of these affiliated gentlemen of leisure are at the same time lesser men of substance in their own right; so that some of them are scarcely at all, others only partially, to be rated as vicarious consumers. [. . .]

[. . .] Many of these again, and also many of the other aristocracy of less degree, have in turn attached to their persons a more or less comprehensive group of vicarious consumers in the persons of their wives and children, their servants, retainers, etc. [. . .]

With the disappearance of servitude, the number of vicarious consumers attached to any one gentleman tends, on the whole, to decrease. The like is of course true, and perhaps in a still higher degree, of the number of dependents who perform vicarious leisure for him. In a general way, though not wholly nor consistently, these two groups coincide. The dependent who was first delegated for these duties was the wife, or the chief wife; and, as would be expected, in the later development of the institution, when the number of persons by whom these duties are customarily performed gradually narrows, the wife remains the last. In the higher grades of society a large volume of both these kinds of service is required; and here the wife is of course still assisted in the work by a more or less numerous corps of menials. But as we descend the social scale, the point is presently reached where the duties of vicarious leisure and consumption devolve upon the wife alone. In the communities of the Western culture, this point is at present found among the lower middle class.

And here occurs a curious inversion. It is a fact of common observation that in this lower middle class there is no pretence of leisure on the part of the head of the household. Through force of circumstances it has fallen into disuse. But the middle-class wife still carries on the business of vicarious leisure, for the good name of the household and its master. In descending the social scale in any modern industrial community, the primary fact—the conspicuous leisure of the master of the household—disappears at a relatively high point. The head of the middle-class household has been reduced by economic circumstances to turn his hand to gaining a livelihood by occupations which often partake largely of the character of industry, as in the case of the ordinary business man of to-day. But the derivative fact—the vicarious leisure and consumption rendered by the wife, and the auxiliary vicarious performance of leisure by menials—remains in vogue as a conventionality which the demands of reputability will not suffer to be slighted. It is by no means an uncommon spectacle to find a man applying himself to work with the utmost assiduity, in order that his wife may in due

form render for him that degree of vicarious leisure which the common sense of the time demands. [. . .]

The leisure rendered by the wife in such cases is, of course, not a simple manifestation of idleness or indolence. It almost invariably occurs disguised under some form of work or household duties or social amenities, which prove on analysis to serve little or no ulterior end beyond showing that she does not and need not occupy herself with anything that is gainful or that is of substantial use. As has already been noticed under the head of manners, the greater part of the customary round of domestic cares to which the middle-class housewife gives her time and effort is of this character. Not that the results of her attention to household matters, of a decorative and mundificatory character, are not pleasing to the sense of men trained in middle-class proprieties; but the taste to which these effects of household adornment and tidiness appeal is a taste which has been formed under the selective guidance of a canon of propriety that demands just these evidences of wasted effort. The effects are pleasing to us chiefly because we have been taught to find them pleasing. There goes into these domestic duties much solicitude for a proper combination of form and colour, and for other ends that are to be classed as æsthetic in the proper sense of the term; and it is not denied that effects having some substantial æsthetic value are sometimes attained. Pretty much all that is here insisted on is that, as regards these amenities of life, the housewife's efforts are under the guidance of traditions that have been shaped by the law of conspicuously wasteful expenditure of time and substance. If beauty or comfort is achieved,—and it is a more or less fortuitous circumstance if they are,—they must be achieved by means and methods that commend themselves to the great economic law of wasted effort. The more reputable, "presentable" portion of middle-class household paraphernalia are, on the one hand, items of conspicuous consumption, and on the other hand, apparatus for putting in evidence the vicarious leisure rendered by the housewife.

The requirement of vicarious consumption at the hands of the wife continues in force even at a lower point in the pecuniary scale than the requirement of vicarious leisure. At a point below which little if any pretence of wasted effort, in ceremonial cleanness and the like, is observable, and where there is assuredly no conscious attempt at ostensible leisure, decency still requires the wife to consume some goods conspicuously for the reputability of the household and its head. So that, as the latter-day outcome of this evolution of an archaic institution, the wife, who was at the outset the drudge and chattel of the man, both in fact and in theory, — the producer of goods for him to consume, — has become the ceremonial consumer of goods which he produces. But she still quite unmistakably remains his chattel in theory; for the habitual rendering of vicarious leisure and consumption is the abiding mark of the un-free servant.

This vicarious consumption practised by the household of the middle and lower classes can not be counted as a direct expression of the leisure-class scheme of life, since the household of this pecuniary grade does not belong within the leisure class. It is rather that the leisure-class scheme of life here comes to an expression at the second remove. The leisure class stands at the head of the social structure in point of reputability; and its manner of life and its standards of worth therefore afford the norm of reputability for the community. The observance of these standards, in some degree of approximation, becomes incumbent upon all classes lower in the scale. In modern civilized communities the lines of demarcation between social classes have grown vague and transient, and wherever this happens the norm of reputability imposed by the upper class extends its coercive influence with but slight hindrance down through the social structure to the lowest strata. The result is that the members of each stratum accept as their ideal of decency the scheme of life in vogue in the next higher stratum, and bend their energies to live up to that ideal. On pain of forfeiting their good name and their self-respect in case of failure, they must conform to the accepted code, at least in appearance. [. . .]

No class of society, not even the most abjectly poor, foregoes all customary conspicuous consumption. The last items of this category of consumption are not given up except under stress of the direst necessity. Very much of squalor and discomfort will be endured before the last trinket or the last pretence of pecuniary decency is put away. There is no class and no country that has yielded so abjectly before the pressure of physical want as to deny themselves all gratification of this higher or spiritual need. [. . .]

It is also noticeable that the serviceability of consumption as a means of repute, as well as the insistence on it as an element of decency, is at its best in those portions of the community where the human contact of the individual is widest and the mobility of the population is greatest. Conspicuous consumption claims a relatively larger portion of the income of the urban than of the rural population, and the claim is also more imperative. The result is that, in order to keep up a decent appearance, the former habitually live hand-to-mouth to a greater extent than the latter. So it comes, for instance, that the American farmer and his wife and daughters are notoriously less modish in their dress, as well as less urbane in their manners, than the city artisan's family with an equal income. It is not that the city population is by nature much more eager for the peculiar complacency that comes of a conspicuous consumption, nor has the rural population less regard for pecuniary decency. But the provocation to this line of evidence, as well as its transient effectiveness, are more decided in the city. This method is therefore more readily resorted to, and in the struggle to outdo one another the city population push their normal standard of conspicuous consumption to a higher point, with the result that a relatively greater expenditure in this direction is required to indicate a given degree of pecuniary decency in the city. The requirement of conformity to this higher conventional standard becomes mandatory. The standard of decency is higher, class for class, and this requirement of decent appearance must be lived up to on pain of losing caste.

Consumption becomes a larger element in the standard of living in the city than in the country. Among the country population its place is to some extent taken by savings and home comforts known through the medium of neighbourhood gossip sufficiently to serve the like general purpose of pecuniary repute. These home comforts and the leisure indulged in — where the indulgence is found — are of course also in great part to be classed as items of conspicuous consumption; and much the same is to be said of the savings. The smaller amount of the savings laid by by the artisan class is no doubt due, in some measure, to the fact that in the case of the artisan the savings are a less effective means of advertisement, relative to the environment in which he is placed, than are the savings of the people living on farms and in the small villages. Among the latter, everybody's affairs, especially everybody's pecuniary status, are known to everybody else. Considered by itself simply—taken in the first degree—this added provocation to which the artisan and the urban labouring classes are exposed may not very seriously decrease the amount of savings; but in its cumulative action, through raising the standard of decent expenditure, its deterrent effect on the tendency to save cannot but be very great. [. . .]

But there are other standards of repute and other, more or less imperative, canons of conduct, besides wealth and its manifestation, and some of these come in to accentuate or to qualify the broad, fundamental canon of conspicuous waste. Under the simple test of effectiveness for advertising, we should expect to find leisure and the conspicuous consumption of goods dividing the field of pecuniary emulation pretty evenly between them at the outset. Leisure might then be expected gradually to yield ground and tend to obsolescence as the economic development goes forward, and the community increases in size; while the conspicuous consumption of goods should gradually gain in importance, both absolutely and relatively, until it had absorbed all the available product, leaving nothing over beyond a bare livelihood. But the actual course of development has been somewhat different from this ideal scheme. Leisure held the first place at the start, and came to hold a rank very much above wasteful consumption of goods, both as a direct exponent of wealth and as an element in the standard of decency, during the quasi-peaceable culture. From that point onward, consumption has gained ground, until, at present, it unquestionably holds the primacy, though it is still far from absorbing the entire margin of production above the subsistence minimum.

The early ascendency of leisure as a means of reputability is traceable to the archaic distinction between noble and ignoble employments. Leisure is honourable and becomes imperative partly because it shows exemption from ignoble labour. The archaic differentiation into noble and ignoble classes is based on an invidious distinction between employments as honorific or debasing; and this traditional distinction grows into an imperative canon of decency during the early quasi-peaceable stage. Its ascendency is furthered by the fact that leisure is still fully as effective

an evidence of wealth as consumption. Indeed, so effective is it in the relatively small and stable human environment to which the individual is exposed at that cultural stage, that, with the aid of the archaic tradition which deprecates all productive labour, it gives rise to a large impecunious leisure class, and it even tends to limit the production of the community's industry to the subsistence minimum. This extreme inhibition of industry is avoided because slave labour, working under a compulsion more rigorous than that of reputability, is forced to turn out a product in excess of the subsistence minimum of the working class. The subsequent relative decline in the use of conspicious leisure as a basis of repute is due partly to an increasing relative effectiveness of consumption as an evidence of wealth; but in part it is traceable to another force, alien, and in some degree antagonistic, to the usage of conspicuous waste. [. . .]

Throughout the entire evolution of conspicuous expenditure, whether of goods or of services or human life, runs the obvious implication that in order to effectually mend the consumer's good fame it must be an expenditure of superfluities. In order to be reputable it must be wasteful. No merit would accrue from the consumption of the bare necessaries of life, except by comparison with the abjectly poor who fall short even of the subsistence minumum; and no standard of expenditure could result from such a comparison, except the most prosaic and unattractive level of decency. A standard of life would still be possible which should admit of invidious comparison in other respects than that of opulence; as, for instance, a comparison in various directions in the manifestation of moral, physical, intellectual, or aesthetic force. Comparison in all these directions is in vogue to-day; and the comparison made in these respects is commonly so inextricably bound up with the pecuniary comparison as to be scarcely distinguishable from the latter. This is especially true as regards the current rating of expressions of intellectual and aesthetic force or proficiency; so that we frequently interpret as aesthetic or intellectual a difference which in substance is pecuniary only.

The use of the term "waste" is in one respect an unfortunate one. As used in the speech of everyday life the word carries an undertone of deprecation. It is here used for want of a better term that will adequately describe the same range of motives and of phenomena, and it is not to be taken in an odious sense, as implying an illegitimate expenditure of human products or of human life. In the view of economic theory the expenditure in question is no more and no less legitimate than any other expenditure. It is here called "waste" because this expenditure does not serve human life or human well-being on the whole, not because it is waste or misdirection of effort or expenditure as viewed from the standpoint of the individual consumer who chooses it. If he chooses it, that disposes of the question of its relative utility to him, as compared with other forms of consumption that would not be deprecated on account of their wastefulness. Whatever form of expenditure the consumer chooses, or whatever end he seeks in making his choice, has utility to him by virtue of his preference. As seen from the point of view of the individual consumer, the question of wastefulness does not arise within the scope of economic theory proper. The use of the word "waste" as a technical term, therefore, implies no deprecation of the motives or of the ends sought by the consumer under this canon of conspicuous waste.

But it is, on other grounds, worth noting that the term "waste" in the language of everyday life implies deprecation of what is characterised as wasteful. This common-sense implication is itself an outcropping of the instinct of workmanship. The popular reprobation of waste goes to say that in order to be at peace with himself the common man must be able to see in any and all human effort and human enjoyment an enhancement of life and well-being on the whole. In order to meet with unqualified approval, any economic fact must approve itself under the test of impersonal usefulness—usefulness as seen from the point of view of the generically human. Relative or competitive advantage of one individual in comparison with another does not satisfy the economic conscience, and therefore competitive expenditure has not the approval of this conscience.

In strict accuracy nothing should be included under the head of conspicuous waste but such expenditure as is incurred on the ground of an invidious pecuniary comparison. But in order to bring any given item or element in under this head it is not necessary that it should be recognised as waste in this sense by the person incurring the expenditure. It frequently happens that an element of the standard of living which set out with being primarily wasteful, ends with becoming, in the apprehension of the consumer, a necessary of life; and it may in this way become as indispensable as any other item of the consumer's habitual expenditure. [. . .]

[. . .] Customary expenditure must be classed under the head of waste in so far as the custom on which it rests is traceable to the habit of making an invidious pecuniary comparison—in so far as it is conceived that it could not have become customary and prescriptive without the backing of this principle of pecuniary reputability or relative economic success.

It is obviously not necessary that a given object of expenditure should be exclusively wasteful in order to come in under the category of conspicuous waste. An article may be useful and wasteful both, and its utility to the consumer may be made up of use and waste in the most varying proportions. Consumable goods, and even productive goods, generally show the two elements in combination, as constituents of their utility; although, in a general way, the element of waste tends to predominate in articles of consumption, while the contrary is true of articles designed for productive use. Even in articles which appear at first glance to serve for pure ostentation only, it is always possible to detect the presence of some, at least ostensible, useful purpose; and on the other hand, even in special machinery and tools contrived for some particular industrial process, as well as in the rudest appliances of human industry, the traces of conspicuous waste, or at least of the habit of ostentation, usually become evident on a close scrutiny. It would be hazardous to assert that a useful purpose is ever absent from the utility of any article or of any service, however obviously its prime purpose and chief element is conspicuous waste; and it would be only less hazardous to assert of any primarily useful product that the element of waste is in no way concerned in its value, immediately or remotely.

The Pecuniary Standard of Living

[. . .] [T]he conspicuously wasteful honorific expenditure that confers spiritual well-being may become more indispensable than much of that expenditure which ministers to the "lower" wants of physical well-being or sustenance only. It is notoriously just as difficult to recede from a "high" standard of living as it is to lower a standard which is already relatively low; although in the former case the difficulty is a moral one, while in the latter it may involve a material deduction from the physical comforts of life.

But while retrogression is difficult, a fresh advance in conspicuous expenditure is relatively easy; indeed, it takes place almost as a matter of course. In the rare cases where it occurs, a failure to increase one's visible consumption when the means for an increase are at hand is felt in popular apprehension to call for explanation, and unworthy motives of miserliness are imputed to those who fall short in this respect. A prompt response to the stimulus, on the other hand, is accepted as the normal effect. This suggests that the standard of expenditure which commonly guides our efforts is not the average, ordinary expenditure already achieved; it is an ideal of consumption that lies just beyond our reach, or to reach which requires some strain. The motive is emulation—the stimulus of an invidious comparison which prompts us to outdo those with whom we are in the habit of classing ourselves. Substantially the same proposition is expressed in the commonplace remark that each class envies and emulates the class next above it in the social scale, while it rarely compares itself with those below or with those who are considerably in advance. [. . .]

A standard of living is of the nature of habit. It is an habitual scale and method of responding to given stimuli. The difficulty in the way of receding from an accustomed standard is the difficulty of breaking a habit that has once been formed. The relative facility with which an advance in the standard is made means that the life process is a process of unfolding activity and that it will readily unfold in a new direction whenever and wherever the resistance to self-expression decreases. But when the habit of expression along such a given line of low resistance has once been formed, the discharge will seek the accustomed outlet even after a change has taken place in the environment whereby the external resistance has appreciably risen. That heightened facility of expression in a given direction which is called habit may offset a considerable increase in the resistance offered by external circumstances to the unfolding of life in the given direction. As between the various habits, or habitual modes and directions of

expression, which go to make up an individual's standard of living, there is an appreciable difference in point of the degree of imperativeness with which the discharge seeks a given direction. [. . .]

In general, the longer the habituation, the more unbroken the habit and the more nearly it coincides with previous habitual forms of the life process, the more persistently will the given habit assert itself. The habit will be stronger if the particular traits of human nature which its action involves, or the particular aptitudes that find exercise in it, are traits or aptitudes that are already largely and profoundly concerned in the life process or that are intimately bound up with the life history of the particular racial stock.

The varying degrees of ease with which different habits are formed by different persons, as well as the varying degrees of reluctance with which different habits are given up, goes to say that the formation of specific habits is not a matter of length of habituation simply. Inherited aptitudes and traits of temperament count for quite as much as length of habituation in deciding what range of habits will come to dominate any individual's scheme of life. And the prevalent type of transmitted aptitudes, or in other words the type of temperament belonging to the dominant ethnic element in any community, will go far to decide what will be the scope and form of expression of the community's habitual life process. [. . .]

Men differ in respect of transmitted aptitudes, or in respect of the relative facility with which they unfold their life activity in particular directions; and the habits which coincide with or proceed upon a relatively strong specific aptitude or a relatively great specific facility of expression become of great consequence to the man's well-being. The part played by this element of aptitude in determining the relative tenacity of the several habits which constitute the standard of living goes to explain the extreme reluctance with which men give up any habitual expenditure in the way of conspicuous consumption. The aptitudes or propensities to which a habit of this kind is to be referred as its ground are those aptitudes whose exercise is comprised in emulation; and the propensity for emulation—for invidious comparison—is of ancient growth and is a pervading trait of human nature. It is easily called into vigorous activity in any new form, and it asserts itself with great insistence under any form under which it has once found habitual expression. When the individual has once formed the habit of seeking expression in a given line of honorific expenditure,—when a given set of stimuli have come to be habitually responded to in activity of a given kind and direction under the guidance of these alert and deep-reaching propensities of emulation,—it is with extreme reluctance that such an habitual expenditure is given up. And on the other hand, whenever an accession of pecuniary strength puts the individual in a position to unfold his life process in larger scope and with additional reach, the ancient propensities of the race will assert themselves in determining the direction which the new unfolding of life is to take. And those propensities which are already actively in the field under some related form of expression, which are aided by the pointed suggestions afforded by a current accredited scheme of life, and for the exercise of which the material means and opportunities are readily available,—these will especially have much to say in shaping the form and direction in which the new accession to the individual's aggregate force will assert itself. That is to say, in concrete terms, in any community where conspicuous consumption is an element of the scheme of life, an increase in an individual's ability to pay is likely to take the form of an expenditure for some accredited line of conspicuous consumption.

With the exception of the instinct of self-preservation, the propensity for emulation is probably the strongest and most alert and persistent of the economic motives proper. In an industrial community this propensity for emulation expresses itself in pecuniary emulation; and this, so far as regards the Western civilised communities of the present, is virtually equivalent to saying that it expresses itself in some form of conspicuous waste. The need of conspicuous waste, therefore, stands ready to absorb any increase in the community's industrial efficiency or output of goods, after the most elementary physical wants have been provided for. Where this result does not follow, under modern conditions, the reason for the discrepancy is commonly to be sought in a rate of increase in the individual's wealth too rapid for the habit of expenditure to keep abreast of it; or it may be that the individual in question defers the

conspicuous consumption of the increment to a later date—ordinarily with a view to heightening the spectacular effect of the aggregate expenditure contemplated. As increased industrial efficiency makes it possible to procure the means of livelihood with less labour, the energies of the industrious members of the community are bent to the compassing of a higher result in conspicuous expenditure, rather than slackened to a more comfortable pace. The strain is not lightened as industrial efficiency increases and makes a lighter strain possible, but the increment of output is turned to use to meet this want, which is indefinitely expansible, after the manner commonly imputed in economic theory to higher or spiritual wants. It is owing chiefly to the presence of this element in the standard of living that J. S. Mill was able to say that "hitherto it is questionable if all the mechanical inventions yet made have lightened the day's toil of any human being."

The accepted standard of expenditure in the community or in the class to which a person belongs largely determines what his standard of living will be. It does this directly by commending itself to his common sense as right and good, through his habitually contemplating it and assimilating the scheme of life in which it belongs; but it does so also indirectly through popular insistence on conformity to the accepted scale of expenditure as a matter of propriety, under pain of disesteem and ostracism. To accept and practise the standard of living which is in vogue is both agreeable and expedient, commonly to the point of being indispensable to personal comfort and to success in life. The standard of living of any class, so far as concerns the element of conspicuous waste, is commonly as high as the earning capacity of the class will permit—with a constant tendency to go higher. The effect upon the serious activities of men is therefore to direct them with great singleness of purpose to the largest possible acquisition of wealth, and to discountenance work that brings no pecuniary gain. At the same time the effect on consumption is to concentrate it upon the lines which are most patent to the observers whose good opinion is sought; while the inclinations and aptitudes whose exercise does not involve a honorific expenditure of time or substance tend to fall into abeyance through disuse. [. . .]

Industrial Exemption and Conservatism

The life of man in society, just like the life of other species, is a struggle for existence, and therefore it is a process of selective adaptation. The evolution of social structure has been a process of natural selection of institutions. The progress which has been and is being made in human institutions and in human character may be set down, broadly, to a natural selection of the fittest habits of thought and to a process of enforced adaptation of individuals to an environment which has progressively changed with the growth of the community and with the changing institutions under which men have lived. Institutions are not only themselves the result of a selective and adaptive process which shapes the prevailing or dominant types of spiritual attitude and aptitudes; they are at the same time special methods of life and of human relations, and are therefore in their turn efficient factors of selection. So that the changing institutions in their turn make for a further selection of individuals endowed with the fittest temperament, and a further adaptation of individual temperament and habits to the changing environment through the formation of new institutions. [. . .]

For the present purpose, however, the question as to the nature of the adaptive process—whether it is chiefly a selection between stable types of temperament and character, or chiefly an adaptation of men's habits of thought to changing circumstances—is of less importance than the fact that, by one method or another, institutions change and develop. Institutions must change with changing circumstances, since they are of the nature of an habitual method of responding to the stimuli which these changing circumstances afford. The development of these institutions is the development of society. The institutions are, in substance, prevalent habits of thought with respect to particular relations and particular functions of the individual and of the community; and the scheme of life, which is made up of the aggregate of institutions in force at a given time or at a given point in the development of any society, may, on the psychological side, be broadly characterised as a prevalent spiritual attitude or a prevalent theory of life. As

regards its generic features, this spiritual attitude or theory of life is in the last analysis reducible to terms of a prevalent type of character.

The situation of to-day shapes the institutions of tomorrow through a selective, coercive process, by acting upon men's habitual view of things, and so altering or fortifying a point of view or a mental attitude handed down from the past. The institutions—that is to say the habits of thought—under the guidance of which men live are in this way received from an earlier time; more or less remotely earlier, but in any event they have been elaborated in and received from the past. Institutions are products of the past process, are adapted to past circumstances, and are therefore never in full accord with the requirements of the present. In the nature of the case, this process of selective adaptation can never catch up with the progressively changing situation in which the community finds itself at any given time; for the environment, the situation, the exigencies of life which enforce the adaptation and exercise the selection, change from day to day; and each successive situation of the community in its turn tends to obsolescence as soon as it has been established. When a step in the development has been taken, this step itself constitutes a change of situation which requires a new adaptation; it becomes the point of departure for a new step in the adjustment, and so on interminably.

It is to be noted then, although it may be a tedious truism, that the institutions of to-day—the present accepted scheme of life—do not entirely fit the situation of to-day. At the same time, men's present habits of thought tend to persist indefinitely, except as circumstances enforce a change. These institutions which have so been handed down, these habits of thought, points of view, mental attitudes and aptitudes, or what not, are therefore themselves a conservative factor. This is the factor of social inertia, psychological inertia, conservatism.

Social structure changes, develops, adapts itself to an altered situation, only through a change in the habits of thought of the several classes of the community; or in the last analysis, through a change in the habits of thought of the individuals which make up the community. The evolution of society is substantially a process of mental adaptation on the part of individuals under the stress of circumstances which will no longer tolerate habits of thought formed under and conforming to a different set of circumstances in the past. For the immediate purpose it need not be a question of serious importance whether this adaptive process is a process of selection and survival of persistent ethnic types or a process of individual adaptation and an inheritance of acquired traits.

Social advance, especially as seen from the point of view of economic theory, consists in a continued progressive approach to an approximately exact "adjustment of inner relations to outer relations"; but this adjustment is never definitively established, since the "outer relations" are subject to constant change as a consequence of the progressive change going on in the "inner relations." But the degree of approximation may be greater or less, depending on the facility with which an adjustment is made. A readjustment of men's habits of thought to conform with the exigencies of an altered situation is in any case made only tardily and reluctantly, and only under the coercion exercised by a situation which has made the accredited views untenable. The readjustment of institutions and habitual views to an altered environment is made in response to pressure from without; it is of the nature of a response to stimulus. Freedom and facility of readjustment, that is to say capacity for growth in social structure, therefore depends in great measure on the degree of freedom with which the situation at any given time acts on the individual members of the community—the degree of exposure of the individual members to the constraining forces of the environment. If any portion or class of society is sheltered from the action of the environment in any essential respect, that portion of the community, or that class, will adapt its views and its scheme of life more tardily to the altered general situation; it will in so far tend to retard the process of social transformation. The wealthy leisure class is in such a sheltered position with respect to the economic forces that make for change and readjustment. And it may be said that the forces which make for a readjustment of institutions, especially in the case of a modern industrial community, are, in the last analysis, almost entirely of an economic nature.

[. . .] The group is made up of individuals, and the group's life is the life of individuals carried on in at least ostensible severalty. The group's accepted scheme of life is the consensus of views held by the body of these individuals as to what is right, good, expedient, and beautiful in the way of human life. In the redistribution of the conditions of life that comes of the altered method of dealing with the environment, the outcome is not an equable change in the facility of life throughout the group. The altered conditions may increase the facility of life for the group as a whole, but the redistribution will usually result in a decrease of facility or fulness of life for some members of the group. An advance in technical methods, in population, or in industrial organisation will require at least some of the members of the community to change their habits of life, if they are to enter with facility and effect into the altered industrial methods; and in doing so they will be unable to live up to the received notions as to what are the right and beautiful habits of life.

Any one who is required to change his habits of life and his habitual relations to his fellow-men will feel the discrepancy between the method of life required of him by the newly arisen exigencies, and the traditional scheme of life to which he is accustomed. It is the individuals placed in this position who have the liveliest incentive to reconstruct the received scheme of life and are most readily persuaded to accept new standards; and it is through the need of the means of livelihood that men are placed in such a position. The pressure exerted by the environment upon the group, and making for a readjustment of the group's scheme of life, impinges upon the members of the group in the form of pecuniary exigencies; and it is owing to this fact—that external forces are in great part translated into the form of pecuniary or economic exigencies—it is owing to this fact that we can say that the forces which count toward a readjustment of institutions in any modern industrial community are chiefly economic forces; or more specifically, these forces take the form of pecuniary pressure. Such a readjustment as is here contemplated is substantially a change in men's views as to what is good and right, and the means through which a change is wrought in men's apprehension of what is good and right is in large part the pressure of pecuniary exigencies.

Any change in men's views as to what is good and right in human life makes its way but tardily at the best. Especially is this true of any change in the direction of what is called progress; that is to say, in the direction of divergence from the archaic position—from the position which may be accounted the point of departure at any step in the social evolution of the community. Retrogression, reapproach to a standpoint to which the race has been long habituated in the past, is easier. This is especially true in case the development away from this past standpoint has not been due chiefly to a substitution of an ethnic type whose temperament is alien to the earlier standpoint.

The cultural stage which lies immediately back of the present in the life history of Western civilisation is what has here been called the quasi-peaceable stage. At this quasi-peaceable stage the law of status is the dominant feature in the scheme of life. There is no need of pointing out how prone the men of to-day are to revert to the spiritual attitude of mastery and of personal subservience which characterises that stage. It may rather be said to be held in an uncertain abeyance by the economic exigencies of to-day, than to have been definitively supplanted by a habit of mind that is in full accord with these later-developed exigencies. The predatory and quasi-peaceable stages of economic evolution seem to have been of long duration in the life history of all the chief ethnic elements which go to make up the populations of the Western culture. The temperament and the propensities proper to those cultural stages have, therefore, attained such a persistence as to make a speedy reversion to the broad features of the corresponding psychological constitution inevitable in the case of any class or community which is removed from the action of those forces that make for a maintenance of the later-developed habits of thought.

It is a matter of common notoriety that when individuals, or even considerable groups of men, are segregated from a higher industrial culture and exposed to a lower cultural environment, or to an economic situation of a more primitive character, they quickly show evidence of reversion toward the spiritual features which characterise the predatory type; and it seems probable that the dolicho-blond type of European man is possessed of a greater facility for such reversion to barbarism than the other ethnic elements with which that type is associated in the Western culture. Examples of such a reversion on a small scale abound in the later history of migration and colonisation. Except for the fear of offending that chauvinistic patriotism which is so characteristic a feature of the predatory culture, and the presence of which is frequently the most striking mark of reversion in modern communities, the case of the American colonies might be cited as an example of such a reversion on an unusually large scale, though it was not a reversion of very large scope.

The leisure class is in great measure sheltered from the stress of those economic exigencies which prevail in any modern, highly organised industrial community. The exigencies of the struggle for the means of life are less exacting for this class than for any other; and as a consequence of this privileged position we should expect to find it one of the least responsive of the classes of society to the demands which the situation makes for a further growth of institutions and a readjustment to an altered industrial situation. The leisure class is the conservative class. The exigencies of the general economic situation of the community do not freely or directly impinge upon the members of this class. They are not required under penalty of forfeiture to change their habits of life and their theoretical views of the external world to suit the demands of an altered industrial technique, since they are not in the full sense an organic part of the industrial community. Therefore these exigencies do not readily produce, in the members of this class, that degree of uneasiness with the existing order which alone can lead any body of men to give up views and methods of life that have become habitual to them. The office of the leisure class in social evolution is to retard the movement and to conserve what is obsolescent. This proposition is by no means novel; it has long been one of the commonplaces of popular opinion.

The prevalent conviction that the wealthy class is by nature conservative has been popularly accepted without much aid from any theoretical view as to the place and relation of that class in the cultural development. When an explanation of this class conservatism is offered, it is commonly the invidious one that the wealthy class opposes innovation because it has a vested interest, of an unworthy sort, in maintaining the present conditions. The explanation here put forward imputes no unworthy motive. The opposition of the class to changes in the cultural scheme is instinctive, and does not rest primarily on an interested calculation of material advantages; it is an instinctive revulsion at any departure from the accepted way of doing and of looking at things—a revulsion common to all men and only to be overcome by stress of circumstances. All change in habits of life and of thought is irksome. The difference in this respect between the wealthy and the common run of mankind lies not so much in the motive which prompts to conservatism as in the degree of exposure to the economic forces that urge a change. The members of the wealthy class do not yield to the demand for innovation as readily as other men because they are not constrained to do so. [. . .]

[. . .] The fact that the usages, actions, and views of the well-to-do leisure class acquire the character of a prescriptive canon of conduct for the rest of society, gives added weight and reach to the conservative influence of that class. It makes it incumbent upon all reputable people to follow their lead. So that, by virtue of its high position as the avatar of good form, the wealthier class comes to exert a retarding influence upon social development far in excess of that which the simple numerical strength of the class would assign it. Its prescriptive example acts to greatly stiffen the resistance of all other classes against any innovation, and to fix men's affections upon the good institutions handed down from an earlier generation. [. . .]

From this proposition it follows that the institution of a leisure class acts to make the lower classes conservative by withdrawing from them as much as it may of the means of sustenance, and so reducing their consumption, and consequently their available energy, to such a point as to make them incapable of the effort required for the learning and adoption of new habits of thought. The accumulation of wealth at the upper end of the pecuniary scale implies privation at the lower end of the scale. It is a commonplace that, wherever it occurs, a considerable degree of privation among the body of the people is a serious obstacle to any innovation.

This direct inhibitory effect of the unequal distribution of wealth is seconded by an indirect effect tending to the same result. As has already been seen, the imperative example set by the upper class in fixing the canons of reputability fosters the practice of conspicuous consumption. [. . .]

The relation of the leisure (that is, propertied non-industrial) class to the economic process is a pecuniary relation—a relation of acquisition, not of production; of exploitation, not of serviceability. Indirectly their economic office may, of course, be of the utmost importance to the economic life process; and it is by no means here intended to depreciate the economic function of the propertied class or of the captains of industry. The purpose is simply to point out what is the nature of the relation of these classes to the industrial process and to economic institutions. Their office is of a parasitic character, and their interest is to divert what substance they may to their own use, and to retain whatever is under their hand. The conventions of the business world have grown up under the selective surveillance of this principle of predation or parasitism. They are conventions of ownership; derivatives, more or less remote, of the ancient predatory culture. But these pecuniary institutions do not entirely fit the situation of to-day, for they have grown up under a past situation differing somewhat from the present. Even for effectiveness in the pecuniary way, therefore, they are not as apt as might be. The changed industrial life requires changed methods of acquisition; and the pecuniary classes have some interest in so adapting the pecuniary institutions as to give them the best effect for acquisition of private gain that is compatible with the continuance of the industrial process out of which this gain arises. Hence there is a more or less consistent trend in the leisure-class guidance of institutional growth, answering to the pecuniary ends which shape leisure-class economic life.

The effect of the pecuniary interest and the pecuniary habit of mind upon the growth of institutions is seen in those enactments and conventions that make for security of property, enforcement of contracts, facility of pecuniary transactions, vested interests. Of such bearing are changes affecting bankruptcy and receiverships, limited liability, banking and currency, coalitions of labourers or employers, trusts and pools. The community's institutional furniture of this kind is of immediate consequence only to the propertied classes, and in proportion as they are propertied; that is to say, in proportion as they are to be ranked with the leisure class. But indirectly these conventions of business life are of the gravest consequence for the industrial process and for the life of the community. And in guiding the institutional growth in this respect, the pecuniary classes, therefore, serve a purpose of the most serious importance to the community, not only in the conservation of the accepted social scheme, but also in shaping the industrial process proper.

The immediate end of this pecuniary institutional structure and of its amelioration is the greater facility of peaceable and orderly exploitation; but its remoter effects far outrun this immediate object. Not only does the more facile conduct of business permit industry and extra-industrial life to go on with less perturbation; but the resulting elimination of disturbances and complications calling for an exercise of astute discrimination in everyday affairs acts to make the pecuniary class itself superfluous. As fast as pecuniary transactions are reduced to routine, the captain of industry can be dispensed with. This consummation, it is needless to say, lies yet in the indefinite future. The ameliorations wrought in favour of the pecuniary interest in modern institutions tend, in another field, to substitute the "soulless" joint-stock corporation for the captain, and so they make also for the dispensability of the great leisure-class function of ownership. Indirectly, therefore, the bent given to the growth of economic institutions by the leisure-class influence is of very considerable industrial consequence.

Jane Addams

Chicago Liberty Address (1899)

None of us who has been reared and nurtured in America can be wholly without the democratic instinct. It is not a question with any of us of having it or not having it; it is merely a question of trusting it or not trusting it. For good or ill we suddenly find ourselves bound to an international situation. The question practically reduces itself to this: Do we mean to democratize the situation? Are we going to trust our democracy, or are we going to weakly imitate the policy of other governments, which have never claimed a democratic basis?

The political code, as well as the moral law, has no meaning and becomes absolutely emptied of its contents if we take out of it all relation to the world and concrete cases, and it is exactly in such a time as this that we discover what we really believe. We may make a mistake in politics as well as in morals by forgetting that new conditions are ever demanding the evolution of a new morality, along old lines but in larger measure. Unless the present situation extends our nationalism into internationalism, unless it has thrust forward our patriotism into humanitarianism we cannot meet it.

We must also remember that peace has come to mean a larger thing. It is no longer merely absence of war, but the unfolding of life processes which are making for a common development. Peace is not merely something to hold congresses about and to discuss as an abstract dogma. It has come to be a rising tide of moral feeling, which is slowly engulfing all pride of conquest and making war impossible.

Under this new conception of peace it is perhaps natural that the first men to formulate it and give it international meaning should have been working-men, who have always realized, however feebly and vaguely they may have expressed it, that it is they who in all ages have borne the heaviest burden of privation and suffering imposed on the world by the military spirit.

The first international organization founded not to promote a colorless peace, but to advance and develop the common life of all nations was founded in London in 1864 by workingmen and called simply "The International Association of Workingmen." They recognized that a supreme interest raised all workingmen above the prejudice of race, and united them by wider and deeper principles than those by which they were separated into nations. That as religion, science, art, had become international, so now at last labor took its position as an international interest. A few years later, at its third congress, held in Brussels in 1868, the internationals recommended in view of the Franco-German war, then threatening, that "the workers resist all war as systematic murder," and in case of war a universal strike be declared.

This is almost exactly what is now happening in Russia. The peasants are simply refusing to drill and fight and the czar gets credit for a peace manifesto the moral force of which comes from the humblest of his subjects. It is not, therefore, surprising that as long ago as last December, the organized workingmen of America recorded their protest against the adoption of an imperialistic policy.

In the annual convention of the American Federation of Labor, held that month in Kansas City, resolutions were adopted indorsing the declaration made by President Gompers in his opening address: "It has always been the hewers of wood and the carriers of water, the wealth producers, whose mission it has been not only to struggle for freedom, but to be ever vigilant to maintain the liberty of freedom achieved, and it behooves the representatives of the grand army of labor in convention assembled to give vent to the alarm we feel from the dangers threatening us and our entire people, to enter our solemn and emphatic protest against what we already feel; that, with the success of imperialism the decadence of our republic will have already set in."

There is a growing conviction among workingmen of all countries that, whatever may be accomplished by a national war, however high the supposed moral aim of such a war, there is one inevitable result—an increased standing army, the soldiers of which are non-producers and must be fed by the workers. The Russian peasants support an army of 1,000,000, the German peasants sow and reap for 500,000 more. The men in these armies spend their muscular force in drilling, their mental force in thoughts of warfare. The mere hours of idleness conduce mental and moral deterioration.

The appeal to the fighting instinct does not end in mere warfare, but arouses these brutal instincts latent in every human being. The countries with the large standing armies are likewise the countries with national hospitals for the treatment of diseases which should never exist, of large asylums for the care of children which should never have been born. These institutions, as well as the barracks, again increase the taxation, which rests, in the last analysis, upon producers, and, at the same time, withdraws so much of their product from the beneficent development of their national life. No one urges peaceful association with more fervor than the workingman. Organization is his only hope, but it must be kept distinct from militarism, which can never be made a democratic instrument.

Let us not make the mistake of confusing moral issues sometimes involved in warfare with warfare itself. Let us not glorify the brutality. The same strenuous endeavor, the same heroic self-sacrifice, the same fine courage and readiness to meet death, may be displayed without the accompaniment of killing our fellow men. With all Kipling's insight he has, over and over, failed to distinguish between war and imperialism on the one hand and the advance of civilization on the other.

To "protect the weak" has always been the excuse of the ruler and tax-gatherer, the chief, the king, the baron; and now, at last, of "the white man." The form of government is not necessarily the function itself. Government is not something extraneous, consisting of men who wear gold lace and sit on high stools and write rows of figures in books. We forget that an ideal government is merely an adjustment between men concerning their mutual relations towards those general matters which concern them all; that the office of an outside and alien people must always be to collect taxes and to hold a negative law and order. In its first attempt to restore mere order and quiet, the outside power inevitably breaks down the framework of the nascent government itself, the more virile and initiative forces are destroyed; new relations must in the end be established, not only with the handicap of smart animosity on the part of the conquered, but with the loss of the most able citizens among them.

Some of us were beginning to hope that we were getting away from the ideals set by the civil war, that we had made all the presidents we could from men who had distinguished themselves in that war, and were coming to seek another type of man. That we were ready to accept the peace ideal, to be proud of our title as a peace nation; to recognize that the man who cleans a city is greater than he who bombards it, and the man who irrigates a plain greater than he who lays it waste. Then came the Spanish war, with its gilt and lace and tinsel, and again the moral issues are confused with exhibitions of brutality.

For ten years I have lived in a neighborhood which is by no means criminal, and yet during last October and November we were startled by seven murders within a radius of ten blocks. A little investigation of details and motives, the accident of a personal acquaintance with two of the criminals, made it not in the least difficult to trace the murders back to the influence of war. Simple people who read of carnage and bloodshed easily receive its suggestions. Habits of self-control which have been but slowly and imperfectly acquired quickly break down under the stress.

Psychologists intimate that action is determined by the selection of the subject upon which the attention is habitually fixed. The newspapers, the theatrical posters, the street conversations for weeks had to do with war and bloodshed. The little children on the street played at war, day after day, killing Spaniards. The humane instinct, which keeps in abeyance the tendency to cruelty, the growing belief that the life of each human being—however hopeless or degraded, is still sacred—gives way, and the barbaric instinct asserts itself.

It is doubtless only during a time of war that the men and women of Chicago could tolerate whipping for children in our city prison, and it is only during such a time that the introduction in the legislature of a bill for the re-establishment of the whipping post could be possible. National events determine our ideals, as much as our ideals determine national events.

Mark Twain

To the Person Sitting in the Darkness (1901)

(New York: Anti-Imperialist League of New York, 1901)

Extending the Blessings of Civilization to our Brother who Sits in Darkness has been a good trade and has paid well, on the whole; and there is money in it yet, if carefully worked—but not enough, in my judgement, to make any considerable risk advisable. The People that Sit in Darkness are getting to be too scarce—too scarce and too shy. And such darkness as is now left is really of but an indifferent quality, and not dark enough for the game. The most of those People that Sit in Darkness have been furnished with more light than was good for them or profitable for us. We have been injudicious.

The Blessings-of-Civilization Trust, wisely and cautiously administered, is a Daisy. There is more money in it, more territory, more sovereignty, and other kinds of emolument, than there is in any other game that is played. But Christendom has been playing it badly of late years, and must certainly suffer by it, in my opinion. She has been so eager to get every stake that appeared on the green cloth, that the People who Sit in Darkness have noticed it—they have noticed it, and have begun to show alarm. They have become suspicious of the Blessings of Civilization. More—they have begun to examine them. This is not well. The Blessings of Civilization are all right, and a good commercial property; there could not be a better, in a dim light. In the right kind of a light, and at a proper distance, with the goods a little out of focus, they furnish this desirable exhibit to the Gentlemen who Sit in Darkness:

LOVE,

JUSTICE,

GENTLENESS,

CHRISTIANITY,

PROTECTION TO THE WEAK,

TEMPERANCE,

LAW AND ORDER,

LIBERTY,

EQUALITY,

HONORABLE DEALING,

MERCY,

EDUCATION,

—and so on.

There. Is it good? Sir, it is pie. It will bring into camp any idiot that sits in darkness anywhere. But not if we adulterate it. It is proper to be emphatic upon that point. This brand is strictly for Export—apparently. *Apparently.* Privately and confidentially, it is nothing of the kind. Privately and confidentially, it is merely an outside cover, gay and pretty and attractive, displaying the special patterns of our Civilization which we reserve for Home Consumption, while *inside* the bale is the Actual Thing that the Customer Sitting in Darkness buys with his blood and tears and land and liberty. That Actual Thing is, indeed, Civilization, but it is only for Export. Is there a difference between the two brands? In some of the details, yes.

We all know that the Business is being ruined. The reason is not far to seek. It is because our Mr. McKinley, and Mr. Chamberlain, and the Kaiser, and the Czar and the French have been exporting the Actual Thing *with the outside cover left off.* This is bad for the Game. It shows that these new players of it are not sufficiently acquainted with it.

It is a distress to look on and note the mismoves, they are so strange and so awkward. Mr. Chamberlain manufactures a war out of materials so inadequate and so fanciful that they make the boxes grieve and the gallery laugh, and he tries hard to persuade himself that it isn't purely a private raid for cash, but has a sort of dim, vague respectability about it somewhere, if he could only find the spot; and that, by and by, he can scour the flag clean again after he has finished dragging it through the mud, and make it shine and flash in the vault of heaven once more as it had shone and flashed there a thousand years in the world's respect until he laid his unfaithful hand upon it. It is bad play—bad. For it exposes the Actual Thing to Them that Sit in Darkness, and they say: "What! Christian against Christian? And only for money? Is *this* a case of magnanimity, forbearance, love, gentleness, mercy, protection of the weak—this strange and over-showy onslaught of an elephant upon a nest of field-mice, on the pretext that the mice had squeaked an insolence at him—conduct which 'no self-respecting government could allow to pass unavenged?' as Mr. Chamberlain said. Was that a good pretext in a small case, when it had not been a good pretext in a large one?—for only recently Russia had affronted the elephant three times and survived alive and unsmitten. Is this Civilization and Progress? Is it something better than we already possess? These harryings and burnings and desert-makings in the Transvaal—is this an improvement on our darkness? Is it, perhaps, possible that there are two kinds of Civilization—one for home consumption and one for the heathen market?"

Then They that Sit in Darkness are troubled, and shake their heads; and they read this extract from a letter of a British private, recounting his exploits in one of Methuen's victories, some days before the affair of Magersfontein, and they are troubled again:

> We tore up the hill and into the intrenchments, and the Boers saw we had them; so they dropped their guns and went down on their knees and put up their hands clasped, and begged for mercy. And we gave it them—*with the long spoon.*

The long spoon is the bayonet. See *Lloyd's Weekly*, London, of those days. The same number—and the same column—contains some quite unconscious satire in the form of shocked and bitter upbraidings of the Boers for their brutalities and inhumanities!

Next, to our heavy damage, the Kaiser went to playing the game without first mastering it. He lost a couple of missionaries in a riot in Shantung, and in his account he made an overcharge for them. China had to pay a hundred thousand dollars apiece for them, in money; twelve miles of territory, containing several millions of inhabitants and worth twenty million dollars; and to build a monument, and also a Christian church; whereas the people of China could have been depended upon to remember the missionaries without the help of these expensive memorials. This was all bad play. Bad, because it would not, and could not, and will not now or ever, deceive the Person Sitting in Darkness. He knows that it was an overcharge. He knows that a missionary is like any other man: he is worth merely what you can supply his place for, and no more. He is useful, but so is a doctor, so is a sheriff, so is an editor; but a just Emperor does not charge war-prices for such. A diligent, intelligent, but obscure missionary, and a diligent, intelligent country editor are worth much, and we know it; but they are not worth the earth. We esteem such an editor, and we are sorry to see him go; but, when he goes, we should consider twelve miles of territory, and a church, and a fortune, over-compensation for his loss. I mean, if he was a Chinese editor, and we had to settle for him. It is no proper figure for an editor or a missionary; one can get shop-worn kings for less. It was bad play on the Kaiser's part. It got this property, true; but it *produced the Chinese revolt*, the indignant uprising of China's traduced patriots, the Boxers. The results have been expensive to Germany, and to the other Disseminators of Progress and the Blessings of Civilization.

The Kaiser's claim was paid, yet it was bad play, for it could not fail to have an evil effect upon Persons Sitting in Darkness in China. They would muse upon the event, and be likely to say: "Civilization is gracious and beautiful, for such is its reputation; but can we afford it? There are rich Chinamen, perhaps they could afford it; but this tax is not laid upon them, it is laid upon the peasants of Shantung; it is they that must pay this mighty sum, and their wages are but four cents a day. Is this a better civilization than ours, and holier and higher and nobler? Is not this rapacity? Is not this extortion? Would Germany charge America two hundred thousand dollars for two missionaries, and shake the mailed fist in her face, and send warships, and send soldiers, and say: 'Seize twelve miles of territory, worth twenty millions of dollars, as additional pay for the missionaries; and make those peasants build a monument to the missionaries, and a costly Christian church to remember them by?' And later would Germany say to her soldiers: 'March through America and slay, *giving no quarter*; make the German face there, as has been our Hun-face here, a terror for a thousand years; march through the Great Republic and slay, slay, slay, carving a road for our offended religion through its heart and bowels?' Would Germany do like this to America, to England, to France, to Russia? Or only to China the helpless—imitating the elephant's assault upon the field-mice? Had we better invest in this Civilization—this Civilization which called

Napoleon a buccaneer for carrying off Venice's bronze horses, but which steals our ancient astronomical instruments from our walls, and goes looting like common bandits—that is, all the alien soldiers except America's; and (Americans again excepted) storms frightened villages and cables the result to glad journals at home every day: 'Chinese losses, 450 killed; ours, *one officer and two men wounded.* Shall proceed against neighboring village to-morrow, where a *massacre* is reported.' Can we afford Civilization?"

And, next, Russia must go and play the game injudiciously. She affronts England once or twice—with the Person Sitting in Darkness observing and noting; by moral assistance of France and Germany, she robs Japan of her hard-earned spoil, all swimming in Chinese blood—Port Arthur—with the Person again observing and noting; then she seizes Manchuria, raids its villages, and chokes its great river with the swollen corpses of countless massacred peasants—that astonished Person still observing and noting. And perhaps he is saying to himself: "It is yet *another* Civilized Power, with its banner of the Prince of Peace in one hand and its loot-basket and its butcher-knife in the other. Is there no salvation for us but to adopt Civilization and lift ourselves down to its level?"

And by and by comes America, and our Master of the Game plays it badly—plays it as Mr. Chamberlain was playing it in South Africa. It was a mistake to do that; also, it was one which was quite unlooked for in a Master who was playing it so well in Cuba. In Cuba, he was playing the usual and regular *American* game, and it was winning, for there is no way to beat it. The Master, contemplating Cuba, said: "Here is an oppressed and friendless little nation which is willing to fight to be free; we go partners, and put up the strength of seventy million sympathizers and the resources of the United States: play!" Nothing but Europe combined could call that hand: and Europe cannot combine on anything. There, in Cuba, he was following our great traditions in a way which made us very proud of him, and proud of the deep dissatisfaction which his play was provoking in Continental Europe. Moved by a high inspiration, he threw out those stirring words which proclaimed that forcible annexation would be "criminal aggression;" and in that utterance fired another "shot heard round the world." The memory of that fine saying will be outlived by the remembrance of no act of his but one—that he forgot it within the twelvemonth, and its honorable gospel along with it.

For, presently, came the Philippine temptation. It was strong; it was too strong, and he made that bad mistake: he played the European game, the Chamberlain game. It was a pity; it was a great pity, that error: that one grievous error, that irrevocable error. For it was the very place and time to play the American game again. And at no cost. Rich winnings to be gathered in, too; rich and permanent; indestructible; a fortune transmissible forever to the children of the flag. Not land, not money, not dominion—no, something worth many times more than that dross: our share, the spectacle of a nation of long harassed and persecuted slaves set free through our influence; our posterity's share, the golden memory of that fair deed. The game was in our hands. If it had been played according to the American rules, Dewey would have sailed away from Manila as soon as he had destroyed the Spanish fleet—after putting up a sign on shore guaranteeing foreign property and life against damage by the Filipinos, and warning the Powers that interference with the emancipated patriots would be regarded as an act unfriendly to the United States. The Powers cannot combine, in even a bad cause, and the sign would not have been molested.

Dewey could have gone about his affairs elsewhere, and left the competent Filipino army to starve out the little Spanish garrison and send it home, and the Filipino citizens to set up the form of government they might prefer, and deal with the friars and their doubtful acquisitions according to Filipino ideas of fairness and justice—ideas which have since been tested and found to be of as high an order as any that prevail in Europe or America.

But we played the Chamberlain game, and lost the chance to add another Cuba and another honorable deed to our good record.

The more we examine the mistake, the more clearly we perceive that it is going to be bad for the Business. The Person Sitting in Darkness is almost sure to say: "There is something curious about this—curious and unaccountable. There must be two Americas: one that sets the captive free, and one that takes a once-captive's new freedom away from him, and picks a quarrel with him with nothing to found it on; then kills him to get his land."

The truth is, the Person Sitting in Darkness *is* saying things like that; and for the sake of the Business we must persuade him to look at the Philippine matter in another and healthier way. We must arrange his opinions for him. I believe it can be done; for Mr. Chamberlain has arranged England's opinion of the South African matter, and done it most cleverly and successfully. He presented the facts—some of the facts—and showed those confiding people what the facts meant. He did it statistically, which is a good way. He used the formula: "Twice 2 are 14, and 2 from 9 leaves 35." Figures are effective; figures will convince the elect.

Now, my plan is a still bolder one than Mr. Chamberlain's, though apparently a copy of it. Let us be franker than Mr. Chamberlain; let us audaciously present the whole of the facts, shirking none, then explain them according to Mr. Chamberlain's formula. This daring truthfulness will astonish and dazzle the Person Sitting in Darkness, and he will take the Explanation down before his mental vision has had time to get back into focus. Let us say to him:

"Our case is simple. On the 1st of May, Dewey destroyed the Spanish fleet. This left the Archipelago in the hands of its proper and rightful owners, the Filipino nation. Their army numbered 30,000 men, and they were competent to whip out or starve out the little Spanish garrison; then the people could set up a government of their own devising. Our traditions required that Dewey should now set up his warning sign, and go away. But the Master of the Game happened to think of another plan—the European plan. He acted upon it. This was, to send out an army—ostensibly to help the native patriots put the finishing touch upon their long and plucky struggle for independence, but really to take their land away from them and keep it. That is, in the interest of Progress and Civilization. The plan developed, stage by stage, and quite satisfactorily. We entered into a military alliance with the trusting Filipinos, and they hemmed in Manila on the land side, and by their valuable help the place, with its garrison of 8,000 or 10,000 Spaniards, was captured—a thing which we could not have accomplished unaided at that time. We got their help by—by ingenuity. We knew they were fighting for their independence, and that they had been at it for two years. We knew they supposed that we also were fighting in their worthy cause—just as we had helped the Cubans fight for Cuban independence—and we allowed them to go on thinking so. *Until Manila was ours and we could get along without them.* Then we showed our hand. Of course, they were surprised—that was natural; surprised and disappointed; disappointed and grieved. To them it looked un-American; uncharacteristic; foreign to our established traditions. And this was natural, too; for we were only playing the American Game in public—in private it was the European. It was neatly done, very neatly, and it bewildered them. They could not understand it; for we had been so friendly—so affectionate, even—with those simple-minded patriots! We, our own selves, had brought back out of exile their leader, their hero, their hope, their Washington—Aguinaldo; brought him in a warship, in high honor, under the sacred shelter and hospitality of the flag; brought him back and restored him to his people, and got their moving and eloquent gratitude for it. Yes, we had been so friendly to them, and had heartened them up in so many ways! We had lent them guns and ammunition; advised with them; exchanged pleasant courtesies with them; placed our sick and wounded in their kindly care; entrusted our Spanish prisoners to their humane and honest hands; fought shoulder to shoulder with them against "the common enemy" (our own phrase); praised their courage, praised their gallantry, praised their mercifulness, praised their fine and honorable conduct; borrowed their trenches, borrowed strong positions which they had previously captured from the Spaniard; petted them, lied to them—officially proclaiming that our land and naval forces came to give them their freedom and displace the bad Spanish Government—fooled them, used them until we needed them no longer; then derided the sucked orange and threw it away. We kept the positions which we had beguiled them of; by and by, we moved a force forward and overlapped patriot ground—a clever thought, for we needed trouble, and this would produce it. A Filipino soldier, crossing the ground, where no one had a right to forbid him, was shot by our sentry. The badgered patriots resented this with arms, without waiting to know whether Aguinaldo, who was absent, would approve or not. Aguinaldo did not

approve; but that availed nothing. What we wanted, in the interest of Progress and Civilization, was the Archipelago, unencumbered by patriots struggling for independence; and the War was what we needed. We clinched our opportunity. It is Mr. Chamberlain's case over again—at least in its motive and intention; and we played the game as adroitly as he played it himself."

At this point in our frank statement of fact to the Person Sitting in Darkness, we should throw in a little trade-taffy about the Blessings of Civilization—for a change, and for the refreshment of his spirit—then go on with our tale:

"We and the patriots having captured Manila, Spain's ownership of the Archipelago and her sovereignty over it were at an end—obliterated—annihilated—not a rag or shred of either remaining behind. It was then that we conceived the divinely humorous idea of *buying* both of these spectres from Spain! [It is quite safe to confess this to the Person Sitting in Darkness, since neither he nor any other sane person will believe it.] In buying those ghosts for twenty millions, we also contracted to take care of the friars and their accumulations. I think we also agreed to propagate leprosy and smallpox, but as to this there is doubt. But it is not important; persons afflicted with the friars do not mind the other diseases.

"With our Treaty ratified, Manila subdued, and our Ghosts secured, we had no further use for Aguinaldo and the owners of the Archipelago. We forced a war, and we have been hunting America's guest and ally through the woods and swamps ever since."

At this point in the tale, it will be well to boast a little of our war-work and our heroisms in the field, so as to make our performance look as fine as England's in South Africa; but I believe it will not be best to emphasize this too much. We must be cautious. Of course, we must read the war-telegrams to the Person, in order to keep up our frankness; but we can throw an air of humorousness over them, and that will modify their grim eloquence a little, and their rather indiscreet exhibitions of gory exultation. Before reading to him the following display heads of the dispatches of November 18, 1900, it will be well to practice on them in private first, so as to get the right tang of lightness and gaiety into them:

"Administration weary of protracted hostilities!"
"Real war ahead for filipino rebels!"[1]
"Will show no mercy!"
"Kitchener's plan adopted!"

Kitchener knows how to handle disagreeable people who are fighting for their homes and their liberties, and we must let on that we are merely imitating Kitchener, and have no national interest in the matter, further than to get ourselves admired by the Great Family of Nations, in which august company our Master of the Game has bought a place for us in the back row.

Of course, we must not venture to ignore our General MacArthur's reports—oh, why do they keep on printing those embarrassing things?—we must drop them trippingly from the tongue and take the chances:

"During the last ten months our losses have been 268 killed and 750 wounded; Filipino loss, *three thousand two hundred and twenty-seven killed*, and 694 wounded."

We must stand ready to grab the Person Sitting in Darkness, for he will swoon away at this confession, saying: "Good God, those 'niggers' spare their wounded, and the Americans massacre theirs!"

We must bring him to, and coax him and coddle him, and assure him that the ways of Providence are best, and that it would not become us to find fault with them; and then, to show him that we are only imitators, not originators, we must read the following passage from the letter of an American soldier-lad in the Philippines to his mother, published in *Public Opinion*, of Decorah, Iowa, describing the finish of a victorious battle:

"We never left one alive. If one was wounded, we would run our bayonets through him."

Having now laid all the historical facts before the Person Sitting in Darkness, we should bring him to again, and explain them to him. We should say to him:

"They look doubtful, but in reality they are not. There have been lies; yes, but they were told in a good cause. We have been treacherous; but that was only in order that real good might come out of apparent evil. True, we have crushed a deceived and confiding people; we have turned against the weak and the friendless who trusted us; we have stamped out a just and intelligent and well-ordered republic; we have stabbed an ally in the back and slapped the face of a guest; we have bought a Shadow from an enemy that hadn't it to sell; we have robbed a trusting friend of his land and his liberty; we have invited our clean young men to shoulder a discredited musket and do bandit's work under a flag which bandits have been accustomed to fear, not to follow; we have debauched America's honor and blackened her face before the world; but each detail was for the best. We know this. The Head of every State and Sovereignty in Christendom and ninety per cent of every legislative body in Christendom, including our Congress and our fifty State Legislatures, are members not only of the church, but also of the Blessings-of-Civilization Trust. This world-girdling accumulation of trained morals, high principles, and justice, cannot do an unright thing, an unfair thing, an ungenerous thing, an unclean thing. It knows what it is about. Give yourself no uneasiness; it is all right."

Now then, that will convince the Person. You will see. It will restore the Business. Also, it will elect the Master of the Game to the vacant place in the Trinity of our national gods; and there on their high thrones the Three will sit, age after age, in the people's sight, each bearing the Emblem of his service: Washington, the Sword of the Liberator; Lincoln, the Slave's Broken Chains; the Master, the Chains Repaired.

It will give the Business a splendid new start. You will see.

Everything is prosperous, now; everything is just as we should wish it. We have got the Archipelago, and we shall never give it up. Also, we have every reason to hope that we shall have an opportunity before very long to slip out of our Congressional contract with Cuba and give her something better in the place of it. It is a rich country, and many of us are already beginning to see that the contract was a sentimental mistake. But now—right now—is the best time to do some profitable rehabilitating work—work that will set us up and make us comfortable, and discourage gossip. We cannot conceal from ourselves that, privately, we are a little troubled about our uniform. It

1. "Rebels!" Mumble that funny word—Don't let the Person catch it distinctly.

is one of our prides; it is acquainted with honor; it is familiar with great deeds and noble; we love it, we revere it; and so this errand it is on makes us uneasy. And our flag—another pride of ours, our chiefest! We have worshipped it so; and when we have seen it in far lands—glimpsing it unexpectedly in that strange sky, waving its welcome and benediction to us—we have caught our breath, and uncovered our heads, and couldn't speak, for a moment, for the thought of what it was to us and the great ideals it stood for. Indeed, we *must* do something about these things; we must not have the flag out there, and the uniform. They are not needed there; we can manage in some other way. England manages, as regards the uniform, and so can we. We have to send soldiers— we can't get out of that—but we can disguise them. It is the way England does in South Africa. Even Mr. Chamberlain himself takes pride in England's honorable uniform, and makes the army down there wear an ugly and odious and appropriate disguise, of yellow stuff such as quarantine flags are made of, and which are hoisted to warn the healthy away from

unclean disease and repulsive death. This cloth is called khaki. We could adopt it. It is light, comfortable, grotesque, and deceives the enemy, for he cannot conceive of a soldier being concealed in it.

And as for a flag for the Philippine Province, it is easily managed. We can have a special one—our States do it: we can have just our usual flag, with the white stripes painted black and the stars replaced by the skull and cross-bones.

And we do not need that Civil Commission out there. Having no powers, it has to invent them, and that kind of work cannot be effectively done by just anybody; an expert is required. Mr. Croker can be spared. We do not want the United States represented there, but only the Game.

By help of these suggested amendments, Progress and Civilization in that country can have a boom, and it will take in the Persons who are Sitting in Darkness, and we can resume Business at the old stand.

Mark Twain

International Workers of the World

Manifesto on Organizing the Industrial Workers of the World (1905)

Social Relations and groupings only reflect mechanical and industrial conditions. The great facts of present industry are the displacement of human skill by machines and the increase of capitalist power through the concentration in the possession of the tools with which wealth is produced and distributed.

Because of these facts trade division among laborers and competition among capitalists are alike disappearing. Class divisions grow ever more fixed and class antagonisms more sharp. Trade lines have been swallowed up in a common servitude of all workers to the machines which they tend. New machines, ever replacing less productive ones, wipe out whole trades and plunge new bodies of workers into the

ever-growing army of tradeless, hopeless unemployed. As human beings and human skill are displaced by mechanical progress, the capitalists need use the workers only during the period when muscles and nerves respond most intensely. The moment the laborer no longer yields the maximum profits he is thrown upon the scrap pile, to starve alongside the discarded machine. A dead line has been drawn, and an age limit established, to cross which, in this world of monopolized opportunities, means condemnation to industrial death.

The worker, wholly separated from the land and the tools, with his skill of craftmanship rendered useless, is sunk in the uniform mass of wage slaves. He sees his power of resistance broken by craft divisions, perpetuated from outgrown industrial stages. His wages constantly grow less as his hours grow longer and monopolized prices grow higher. Shifted hither and thither by the demands of profit-takers, the laborer's home no longer exists. In this hopeless condition he is forced to accept whatever humiliating conditions his master may impose. He is subjected to a physical and intellectual examination more searching than was the chattel slave when sold upon the auction block. Laborers are no longer classified by differences in trade skill, but the employer assigns them according to the machines to which they are attached. These divisions, far from representing differences in skill or interests among the laborers, are imposed by the employers so that the workers may be pitted against one another and spurred to greater exertion in the shop, and that all resistance to capitalist tyranny may be weakened by artificial distinctions.

While encouraging these outgrown divisions among the workers the capitalists carefully adjust themselves to the new conditions. They wipe out all differences among themselves and present a united front in their war on labor. Through employers' associations, they seek to crush, with brutal force, by the injunctions of the judiciary, and the use of military power, all efforts at resistance. Or when the other policy seems more profitable, they conceal daggers beneath the Civic Federation and hoodwink and betray those whom they would rule and exploit.

Both methods depend for success upon the blindness and internal dissensions of the working class. The employers' line of battle and methods of warfare correspond to the solidarity of the mechanical and industrial concentration, while laborers still form their fighting organizations on lines of long-gone trade divisions. The battles of the past emphasize this lesson. The textile workers of Lowell, Philadelphia, and Fall River; the butchers of Chicago, weakened by the disintegrating effects of trade divisions; the machinists on the Sante Fe, unsupported by their fellow workers subject to the same masters; the long-struggling miners of Colorado, hampered by the lack of unity and solidarity upon the industrial battlefield; all bear witness to the helplessness and impotency of labor as it is presently organized.

This worn out and corrupt system offers no promise of improvement and adaptation. There is no silver lining to the clouds of darkness and despair settling down upon the world of labor.

This system offers only a perpetual struggle for slight relief within wage slavery. It is blind to the possibility of establishing an industrial democracy, wherein there shall be no wage slavery, but where the workers will own the tools which they operate, and the product which they alone will enjoy. It shatters the ranks of the workers into fragments, rendering them helpless and impotent on the industrial battlefield. Separation of craft from craft renders industrial and financial solidarity impossible. Union men scab upon union men; hatred of worker for worker is engendered, and the workers are delivered helpless and disintegrated into the hands of the capitalists.

Craft jealousy leads to the attempt to create trade monopolies. Prohibitive initiation fees are established that force men to become scabs against their will. Men whom manliness or circumstances have driven from one trade are thereby fined when they seek to transfer membership to the union of a new craft.

Craft divisions foster political ignorance among the workers, thus dividing their class at the ballot box, as well as in the shop, mine and factory.

Craft unions may be and have been used to assist employers in the establishment of monopolies and the raising of prices. One set of workers is thus used to make harder the conditions of life for another body of laborers.

Craft divisions hinder the growth of class-consciousness of the workers, foster the idea of harmony of interests between employing exploiter and employed slave. They permit the association of the misleaders of the workers with the capitalists in the Civic Federations, where plans are made for the perpetuation of capitalism, and the permanent enslavement of the workers through the wage system.

Previous efforts for the betterment of the working class have proven abortive because limited in scope and disconnected in action.

Universal economic evils afflicting the working class can be eradicated only by a universal working-class movement. Such a movement of the working class is impossible while separate craft and wage agreements are made favoring the employer against other crafts in the same industry, and while energies are wasted in fruitless jurisdiction struggles which serve only to further the personal aggrandizement of union officials.

A movement to fulfill these conditions must consist of one great industrial union embracing all industries—providing for craft autonomy locally, industrial autonomy internationally and working class unity generally.

It must be founded on the class struggle, and its general administration must be conducted in harmony with the recognition of the irrepressible conflict between the capitalist class and the working class. It should be established as the economic organization of the working class, without affiliation with any political party.

All power should rest in the collective membership.

Local, national and general administration, including union labels, buttons, badges, transfer cards, initiation fees, and per capita tax should be uniform throughout.

All members must hold membership in the local, national or international union covering the industry in which they are employed, but transfers of membership between unions, local, national, or international, should be universal.

Workingmen bringing union cards from industrial unions in foreign countries should be freely admitted into the organization.

The general administration should issue a publication representing the entire union and its principles which should reach all members in every industry at regular intervals.

A central defense fund, to which all members contribute equally, should be established and maintained.

All workers, therefore, who agree with the principles herein set forth, will meet in convention at Chicago the 27th day of June, 1905, for the purpose of forming an economic organization of the working class along the lines marked out in this manifesto.

Representation in the convention shall be based upon the number of workers whom a delegate represents. No delegate, however, shall be given representation in the convention on the numerical basis of an organization unless he has credentials—bearing the seal of his union, local, national, or international, and the signatures of the officers thereof—authorizing him to install his union as a working part of the proposed economic organization in the industrial department in which it logically belongs in the general plan of the organization. Lacking this authority, the delegate shall represent himself as an individual.

Adopted at Chicago, January 2, 3 and 4, 1905.

A. G. Swing	Joseph Schmidt
A. M. Simmons	John Guild
W. Shurtleff	Daniel McDonald
Frank M. McCabe	Eugene V. Debs
John M. O'Neil	Thomas J. Hagerty
George Estes	Thomas J. DeYoung
William D. Haywood	Fred D. Henion
Mother Jones	W. J. Bradley
Ernest Untermann	Charles O. Sherman
W. L. Hall	M. E. White
Charles H. Moyer	William J. Pinkerton
Clarence Smith	Frank Kraffs
William Ernest Trautmann	J. E. Fityzgerald
	Frank Bohn

Upton Sinclair

The Jungle (1906)

Chapter Two

Jurgis talked lightly about work, because he was young. They told him stories about the breaking down of men, there in the stockyards of Chicago, and of what had happened to them afterward—stories to make your flesh creep, but Jurgis would only laugh. He had only been there four months, and he was young, and a giant besides. There was too much health in him. He could not even imagine how it would feel to be beaten. "That is well enough for men like you," he would say, "silpnas, puny fellows — but my back is broad."

Jurgis was like a boy, a boy from the country. He was the sort of man the bosses like to get hold of, the sort they make it a grievance they cannot get hold of. When he was told to go to a certain place, he would go there on the run. When he had nothing to do for the moment, he would stand round fidgeting, dancing, with the overflow of energy that was in him. If he were working in a line of men, the line always moved too slowly for him, and you could pick him out by his impatience and restlessness. That was why he had been picked out on one important occasion; for Jurgis had stood outside of Brown and Company's "Central Time Station" not more than half an hour, the second day of his arrival in Chicago, before he had been beckoned by one of the bosses. Of this he was very proud, and it made him more disposed than ever to laugh at the pessimists. In vain would they all tell him that there were men in that crowd from which he had been chosen who had stood there a month — yes, many months — and not been chosen yet. "Yes," he would say, "but what sort of men? Broken-down tramps and good-for-nothings, fellows who have spent all their money drinking, and want to get more for it. Do you want me to believe that with these arms" — and he would clench his fists and hold them up in the air, so that you might see the rolling muscles — that with these arms people will ever let me starve?"

"It is plain," they would answer to this, "that you have come from the country, and from very far in the country." And this was the fact, for Jurgis had never seen a city, and scarcely even a fair-sized town, until he had set out to make his fortune in the world and earn his right to Ona. His father, and his father's father before him, and as many ancestors back as legend could go, had lived in that part of Lithuania known as Brelovicz, the Imperial Forest. This is a great tract of a hundred thousand acres, which from time immemorial has been a hunting preserve of the nobility. There are a very few peasants settled in it, holding title from ancient times; and one of these was Antanas Rudkus, who had been reared himself, and had reared his children in turn, upon half a dozen acres of cleared land in the midst of a wilderness.

There had been one son besides Jurgis, and one sister. The former had been drafted into the army; that had been over ten years ago, but since that day nothing had ever been heard of him. The sister was married, and her husband had bought the place when old Antanas had decided to go with his son.

It was nearly a year and a half ago that Jurgis had met Ona, at a horse fair a hundred miles from home. Jurgis had never expected to get married — he had laughed at it as a foolish trap for a man to walk into; but here, without ever having spoken a word to her, with no more than the exchange of half a dozen smiles, he found himself, purple in the face with embarrassment and terror, asking her parents to sell her to him for his wife — and offering his father's two horses he had been sent to the fair to sell. But Ona's father proved as a rock — the girl was yet a child, and he was a rich man, and his daughter was not to be had in that way. So Jurgis went home with a heavy heart, and that spring and summer toiled and tried hard to forget. In the fall, after the harvest was over, he saw that it would not do, and tramped the full fortnight's journey that lay between him and Ona.

He found an unexpected state of affairs — for the girl's father had died, and his estate was tied up with creditors; Jurgis' heart leaped as he realized that now the prize was within his reach. There was Elzbieta Lukoszaite, Teta, or Aunt, as they called her, Ona's stepmother, and there were her six children, of all ages. There was also her brother Jonas, a dried-up little man who had worked upon the farm. They were people of great consequence, as it seemed to Jurgis, fresh out of the woods; Ona knew how to read, and knew many other things that he did not know, and now the farm had been sold, and the whole family was adrift — all they owned in the world being about seven hundred rubles which is half as many dollars. They would have had three times that, but it had gone to court, and the judge had decided against them, and it had cost the balance to get him to change his decision.

Ona might have married and left them, but she would not, for she loved Teta Elzbieta. It was Jonas who suggested that they all go to America, where a friend of his had gotten rich. He would work, for his part, and the women would work, and some of the children, doubtless — they would live somehow. Jurgis, too, had heard of America. That was a country where, they said, a man might earn three rubles a day; and Jurgis figured what three rubles a day would mean, with prices as they were where he lived, and decided forthwith that he would go to America and marry, and be a rich man in the bargain. In that country, rich or poor, a man was free, it was said; he did not have to go into the army, he did not have to pay out his money to rascally officials—he might do as he pleased, and count himself as good as any other man. So America was a place of which lovers and young people dreamed. If one could only manage to get the price of a passage, he could count his troubles at an end.

It was arranged that they should leave the following spring, and meantime Jurgis sold himself to a contractor for a certain time, and tramped nearly four hundred miles from home with a gang of men to work upon a railroad in Smolensk. This was a fearful experience, with filth and bad food and cruelty and overwork; but Jurgis stood it and came out in fine trim, and with eighty rubles sewed up in his coat. He did not drink or fight, because he was thinking all the time of Ona; and for the rest, he was a quiet, steady man, who did what he was told to, did not lose his temper often, and when he did lose it made the offender anxious that he should not lose it again. When they paid him off he dodged the company gamblers and dramshops, and so they tried to kill him; but he escaped, and tramped it home, working at odd jobs, and sleeping always with one eye open.

So in the summer time they had all set out for America. At the last moment there joined them Marija Berczynskas, who was a cousin of Ona's. Marija was an orphan, and had worked since childhood for a rich farmer of Vilna, who beat her regularly. It was only at the age of twenty that it had occurred to Marija to try her strength, when she had risen up and nearly murdered the man, and then come away.

There were twelve in all in the party, five adults and six children—and Ona, who was a little of both. They had a hard time on the passage; there was an agent who helped them, but he proved a scoundrel, and got them into a trap with some officials, and cost them a good deal of their precious money, which they clung to with such horrible fear. This happened to them again in New York—for, of course, they knew nothing about the country, and had no one to tell them, and it was easy for a man in a blue uniform to lead them away, and to take them to a hotel and keep them there, and make them pay enormous charges to get away. The law says that the rate card shall be on the door of a hotel, but it does not say that it shall be in Lithuanian.

It was in the stockyards that Jonas' friend had gotten rich, and so to Chicago the party was bound. They knew that one word, Chicago and that was all they needed to know, at least, until they reached the city. Then, tumbled out of the cars without ceremony, they were no better off than before; they stood staring down the vista of Dearborn Street, with its big black buildings towering in the distance, unable to realize that they had arrived, and why, when they said "Chicago," people no longer pointed in some direction, but instead looked perplexed, or laughed, or went on without paying any attention. They were pitiable in their helplessness; above all things they stood in deadly terror of any sort of person in official uniform, and so whenever they saw a policeman they would cross the street and hurry by. For the whole of the first day they wandered about in the midst of deafening confusion, utterly lost; and it was only at night that, cowering in the doorway of a house, they were finally discovered and taken by a policeman to the station. In the morning an interpreter was found, and they were taken and put upon a car, and taught a new word—"stockyards." Their delight at discovering that they were to get out of this adventure without losing another share of their possessions it would not be possible to describe.

They sat and stared out of the window. They were on a street which seemed to run on forever, mile after mile—thirty-four of them, if they had known it—and each side of it one uninterrupted row of wretched little two-story frame buildings. Down every side street they could see, it was the same—never a hill and never a hollow, but always the same endless vista of ugly and dirty little wooden buildings. Here and there would be a bridge crossing a filthy creek, with hard-baked mud shores and dingy sheds and docks along it; here and there would be a railroad crossing, with a tangle of switches, and locomotives puffing, and rattling freight cars filing by; here and there would be a great factory, a dingy building with innumerable windows in it, and immense volumes of smoke pouring from the chimneys, darkening the air above and making filthy the earth beneath. But after each of these interruptions, the desolate procession would begin again—the procession of dreary little buildings.

A full hour before the party reached the city they had begun to note the perplexing changes in the atmosphere. It grew darker all the time, and upon the earth the grass seemed to grow less green. Every minute, as the train sped on, the colors of things became dingier; the fields were grown parched and yellow, the landscape hideous and bare. And along with the thickening smoke they began to notice another circumstance, a strange, pungent odor. They were not sure that it was unpleasant, this odor; some might have called it sickening, but their taste in odors was not developed, and they were only sure that it was curious. Now, sitting in the trolley car, they realized that they were on their way to the home of it—that they had traveled all the way from Lithuania to it. It was now no longer something far off and faint, that you caught in whiffs; you could literally taste it, as well as smell it—you could take hold of it, almost, and examine it at your leisure. They were divided in their opinions about it. It was an elemental odor, raw and crude; it was rich, almost rancid, sensual, and strong. There were some who drank it in as if it were an intoxicant; there were others who put their handkerchiefs to their faces. The new emigrants were still tasting it, lost in wonder, when suddenly the car came to a halt, and the door was flung open, and a voice shouted—"Stockyards!"

They were left standing upon the corner, staring; down a side street there were two rows of brick houses, and between them a vista: half a dozen chimneys, tall as the tallest of buildings, touching the very sky—and leaping from them half a dozen columns of smoke, thick, oily, and black as night. It might have come from the center of the world, this smoke, where the fires of the ages still smolder. It came as if self-impelled, driving all before it, a perpetual explosion. It was inexhaustible; one stared, waiting to see it stop, but still the great streams rolled out. They spread in vast clouds overhead, writhing, curling; then, uniting in one giant river, they streamed away down the sky, stretching a black pall as far as the eye could reach.

Then the party became aware of another strange thing. This, too, like the color, was a thing elemental; it was a sound, a sound made up of ten thousand little sounds. You scarcely noticed it at first—it sunk into your consciousness, a vague disturbance, a trouble. It was like the murmuring of the bees in the spring, the whisperings of the forest; it suggested endless activity, the rumblings of a world in motion. It was only by an effort that one could realize that it was made by animals, that it was the distant lowing of ten thousand cattle, the distant grunting of ten thousand swine.

They would have liked to follow it up, but, alas, they had no time for adventures just then. The policeman on the corner was beginning to watch them; and so, as usual, they started up the street. Scarcely had they gone a block, however, before Jonas was heard to give a cry, and began pointing excitedly across the street. Before they could gather the meaning of his breathless ejaculations he had bounded away, and they saw him enter a shop, over which was a sign: "J. Szedvilas, Delicatessen." When he came out again it was in company with a very stout gentleman in shirt sleeves and an apron, clasping Jonas by both hands and laughing hilariously. Then Teta Elzbieta recollected suddenly that Szedvilas had been the name of the mythical friend who had made his fortune in America. To find that he had been making it in the delicatessen business was an extraordinary piece of good fortune at this juncture; though it was well on in the morning, they had not breakfasted, and the children were beginning to whimper.

Thus was the happy ending to a woeful voyage. The two families literally fell upon each other's necks—for it had been years since Jokubas Szedvilas had met a man from his part of Lithuania. Before half the day they were lifelong friends. Jokubas understood all the pitfalls of this new world, and could explain all of its mysteries; he could tell them the things they ought to have done in the different emergencies—and what was still more to the point, he could tell them what to do now. He would take them to poni Aniele, who kept a boarding-house the other side of the yards; old Mrs. Jukniene, he explained, had not what one would call choice accommodations, but they might do for the moment. To this Teta Elzbieta hastened to respond that nothing could be too cheap to suit them just then; for they were quite terrified over the sums they had had to expend. A very few days of practical experience in this land of high wages had been sufficient to make clear to them the cruel fact that it was also a land of high prices, and that in it the poor man was almost as poor as in any other corner of the earth; and so there vanished in a night all the wonderful dreams of wealth that had been haunting Jurgis. What had made the discovery all the more painful was that they were spending, at American prices, money which they had earned at home rates of wages—and so were really being cheated by the world! The last two days they had all but starved themselves—it made them quite sick to pay the prices that the railroad people asked them for food.

Yet, when they saw the home of the Widow Jukniene they could not but recoil, even so. In all their journey they had seen nothing so bad as this. Poni Aniele had a four-room flat in one of that wilderness of two-story frame tenements that lie "back of the yards." There were four such flats in each building, and each of the four was a "boarding-house" for the occupancy of foreigners—Lithuanians, Poles, Slovaks, or Bohemians. Some of these places were kept by private persons, some were cooperative. There would be an average of half a dozen boarders to each room—sometimes there were thirteen or fourteen to one room, fifty or sixty to a flat. Each one of the occupants furnished his own accommodations—that is, a mattress and some bedding. The mattresses would be spread upon the floor in rows—and there would be nothing else in the place except a stove. It was by no means unusual for two men to own the same mattress in common, one working by day and using it by night, and the other working at night and using it in the daytime. Very frequently a lodging house keeper would rent the same beds to double shifts of men.

Mrs. Jukniene was a wizened-up little woman, with a wrinkled face. Her home was unthinkably filthy; you could not enter by the front door at all, owing to the mattresses, and when you tried to go up the backstairs you found that she had walled up most of the porch with old boards to make a place to keep her chickens. It was a standing jest of the boarders that Aniele cleaned house by letting the chickens loose in the rooms. Undoubtedly this did keep down the vermin, but it seemed probable, in view of all the circumstances, that the old lady regarded it rather as feeding the chickens than as cleaning the rooms. The truth was that she had definitely given up the idea of cleaning anything, under pressure of an attack of rheumatism, which had kept her doubled up in one corner of her room for over a week; during which time eleven of her boarders, heavily in her debt, had concluded to try their chances of employment in Kansas City. This was July, and the fields were green. One never saw the fields, nor any green thing whatever, in Packingtown; but one could go out on the road and "hobo it," as the men phrased it, and see the country, and have a long rest, and an easy time riding on the freight cars.

Such was the home to which the new arrivals were welcomed. There was nothing better to be had—they might not do so well by looking further, for Mrs. Jukniene had at least kept one room for herself and her three little children, and now offered to share this with the women and the girls of the party. They could get bedding at a secondhand store, she explained; and they would not need any, while the weather was so hot—doubtless they would all sleep on the sidewalk such nights as this, as did nearly all of her guests. "Tomorrow," Jurgis said, when they were left alone, "tomorrow I will get a job, and perhaps Jonas will get one also; and then we can get a place of our own."

Later that afternoon he and Ona went out to take a walk and look about them to see more of this district which was to be their home. In back of the yards the dreary two-story frame houses were scattered farther apart, and there were great spaces bare—that seemingly had been overlooked by the great sore of a city as it spread itself over the surface of the prairie. These bare places were grown up with dingy, yellow weeds, hiding innumerable tomato cans; innumerable children played upon them, chasing one another here and there, screaming and fighting. The most uncanny thing about this neighborhood was the number of the children; you thought there must be a school just out, and it was only after long acquaintance that you were able to realize that there was no school, but that these were the children of the neighborhood—that there were so many children to the block in Packingtown that nowhere on its streets could a horse and buggy move faster than a walk!

It could not move faster anyhow, on account of the state of the streets. Those through which Jurgis and Ona were walking resembled streets less than they did a miniature topographical map. The roadway was commonly several feet lower than the level of the houses, which were sometimes joined by high board walks; there were no pavements—there were mountains and valleys and rivers, gullies and ditches, and great hollows full of stinking green water. In these pools the children played, and rolled about in the mud of the streets; here and there one noticed them digging in it, after trophies which they had stumbled on. One wondered about this, as also about the swarms of flies which hung about the scene, literally blackening the air, and the strange, fetid odor which assailed one's nostrils, a ghastly odor, of all the dead things of the universe. It impelled the visitor to questions and then the residents would explain, quietly, that all this was "made" land, and that it had been "made" by using it as a dumping ground for the city garbage. After a few years the unpleasant effect of this would pass away, it was said; but meantime, in hot weather—and especially when it rained—the flies were apt to be annoying. Was it not unhealthful? the stranger would ask, and the residents would answer, "Perhaps; but there is no telling."

A little way farther on, and Jurgis and Ona, staring open-eyed and wondering, came to the place where this "made" ground was in process of making. Here was a great hole, perhaps two city blocks square, and with long files of garbage wagons creeping into it. The place had an odor for which there are no polite words; and it was sprinkled over with children, who raked in it from dawn till dark. Sometimes visitors from the packing houses would wander out to see this "dump," and they would stand by and debate as to whether the children were eating the food they got, or merely collecting it for the chickens at home. Apparently none of them ever went down to find out.

Beyond this dump there stood a great brickyard, with smoking chimneys. First they took out the soil to make bricks, and then they filled it up again with garbage, which seemed to Jurgis and Ona a felicitous arrangement, characteristic of an enterprising country like America. A little way beyond was another great hole, which they had emptied and not yet filled up. This held water, and all summer it stood there, with the near-by soil draining into it, festering and stewing in the sun; and then, when winter came, somebody cut the ice on it, and sold it to the people of the city. This, too, seemed to the newcomers an economical arrangement; for they did not read the newspapers, and their heads were not full of troublesome thoughts about "germs."

They stood there while the sun went down upon this scene, and the sky in the west turned blood-red, and the tops of the houses shone like fire. Jurgis and Ona were not thinking of the sunset, however—their backs were turned to it, and all their thoughts were of Packingtown, which they could see so plainly in the distance. The line of the buildings stood clear-cut and black against the sky; here and there out of the mass rose the great chimneys, with the river of smoke streaming away to the end of the world. It was a study in colors now, this smoke; in the sunset light it was black and brown and gray and purple. All the sordid suggestions of the place were gone—in the twilight it was a vision of power. To the two who stood watching while the darkness swallowed it up, it seemed a dream of wonder, with its talc of human energy, of things being done, of employment for thousands upon thousands of men, of opportunity and freedom, of life and love and joy. When they came away, arm in arm, Jurgis was saying, "Tomorrow I shall go there and get a job!"

Chapter Four

Promptly at seven the next morning Jurgis reported for work. He came to the door that had been pointed out to him, and there he waited for nearly two hours. The boss had meant for him to enter, but had not said this, and so it was only when on his way out to hire another man that he came upon Jurgis. He gave him a good cursing, but as Jurgis did not understand a word of it he did not object. He followed the boss, who showed him where to put his street clothes, and waited while he donned the working clothes he had bought in a secondhand shop and brought with him in a bundle; then he led him to the "killing beds." The work which Jurgis was to do here was very simple, and it took him but a few minutes to learn it. He was provided with a stiff besom, such as is used by street sweepers, and it was his place to follow down the line the man who drew out the smoking entrails from the carcass of the steer; this mass was to be swept into a trap, which was then closed, so that no one might slip into it. As Jurgis came in, the first cattle of the morning were just making their appearance; and so, with scarcely time to look about him, and none to speak to any one, he fell to work. It was a sweltering day in July, and the place ran with steaming hot blood—one waded in it on the floor. The stench was almost overpowering, but to Jurgis it was nothing. His whole soul was dancing with joy—he was at work at last! He was at work and earning money! All day long he was figuring to himself. He was paid the fabulous sum of seventeen and a half cents an hour; and as it proved a rush day and he worked until nearly seven o'clock in the evening, he went home to the family with the tidings that he had earned more than a dollar and a half in a single day! [. . .]

Chapter Five

[. . .] This was the first time in his life that he had ever really worked, it seemed to Jurgis; it was the first time that he had ever had anything to do which took all he had in him. Jurgis had stood with the rest up in the gallery and watched the men on the killing beds, marveling at their speed and power as if they had been wonderful machines; it somehow never occurred to one to think of the flesh-and-blood side of it—that is, not until he actually got down into the pit and took off his coat. Then he saw things in a different light, he got at the inside of them. The pace they set here, it was one that called for every faculty of a man—from the instant the first steer fell till the sounding of the noon whistle, and again from half-past twelve till heaven only knew what hour in the late afternoon or evening, there was never one instant's rest for a man, for his hand or his eye or his brain. Jurgis saw how they managed it; there were portions of the work which determined the pace of the rest, and for these they had picked men whom they paid high wages, and whom they changed frequently. You might easily pick out these pacemakers, for they worked under the eye of the bosses, and they worked like men possessed. This was called "speeding up the gang," and if any man could not keep up with the pace, there were hundreds outside begging to try.

Yet Jurgis did not mind it; he rather enjoyed it. It saved him the necessity of flinging his arms about and fidgeting as he did in most work. He would laugh to himself as he ran down the line, darting a glance now and then at the man ahead of him. It was not the pleasantest work one could think of, but it was necessary work; and what more had a man the right to ask than a chance to do something useful, and to get good pay for doing it?

So Jurgis thought, and so he spoke, in his bold, free way; very much to his surprise, he found that it had a tendency to get him into trouble. For most of the men here took a fearfully different view of the thing. He was quite dismayed when he first began to find it out—that most of the men hated their work. It seemed strange, it was even terrible, when you came to find out the universality of the sentiment; but it was certainly the fact—they hated their work. They hated the bosses and they hated the owners; they hated the whole place, the whole neighborhood—even the whole city, with an all-inclusive hatred, bitter and fierce. Women and little children would fall to cursing about it; it was rotten, rotten as hell—everything was rotten. When Jurgis would ask them what they meant, they would begin to get suspicious, and content themselves with saying, "Never mind, you stay here and see for yourself."

One of the first problems that Jurgis ran upon was that of the unions. He had had no experience with unions, and he had to have it explained to him that the men were banded together for the purpose of fighting for their rights. Jurgis asked them what they meant by their rights, a question in which he was quite sincere, for he had not any idea of any rights that he had, except the right to hunt for a job, and do as he was told when he got it. Generally, however, this harmless question would only make his fellow workingmen lose their tempers and call him a fool. There was a delegate of the butcher-helpers' union who came to see Jurgis to enroll him; and when Jurgis found that this meant that he would have to part with some of his money, he froze up directly, and the delegate, who was an Irishman and only knew a few words of Lithuanian, lost his temper and began to threaten him. In the end Jurgis got into a fine rage, and made it sufficiently plain that it would take more than one Irishman to scare him into a union. Little by little he gathered that the main thing the men wanted was to put a stop to the habit of "speeding-up"; they were trying their best to force a lessening of the pace, for there were some, they said, who could not keep up with it, whom it was killing. But Jurgis had no sympathy with such ideas as this—he could do the work himself, and so could the rest of them, he declared, if they were good for anything. If they couldn't do it, let them go somewhere else. Jurgis had not studied the books, and he would not have known how to pronounce "laissez faire"; but he had been round the world enough to know that a man has to shift for himself in it, and that if he gets the worst of it, there is nobody to listen to him holler.

Yet there have been known to be philosophers and plain men who swore by Malthus in the books, and would, nevertheless, subscribe to a relief fund in time of a famine. It was the same with Jurgis, who consigned the unfit to destruction, while going about all day sick at heart because of his poor old father, who was wandering somewhere in the yards begging for a chance to earn his bread. Old Antanas had been a worker ever since he was a child; he had run away from home when he was twelve, because his father beat him for trying to learn to read. And he was a faithful man, too; he was a man you might leave alone for a month, if only you had made him understand what you wanted him to do in the meantime. And now here he was, worn out in soul and body, and with no more place in the world than a sick dog. He had his home, as it happened, and some one who would care for him if he never got a job; but his son could not help thinking, suppose this had not been the case. Antanas Rudkus had been into every building in Packingtown by this time, and into nearly every room; he had stood mornings among the crowd of applicants till the very policemen had come to know his face and to tell him to go home and give it up. He had been likewise to all the stores and saloons for a mile about, begging for some little thing to do; and everywhere they had ordered him out, sometimes with curses, and not once even stopping to ask him a question.

So, after all, there was a crack in the fine structure of Jurgis' faith in things as they are. The crack was wide while Dede Antanas was hunting a job—and it was yet wider when he finally got it. For one evening the old man came home in a great state of excitement, with the tale that he had been approached by a man in one of the corridors of the pickle rooms of Durham's, and asked what he would pay to get a job. He had not known what to make of this at first; but the man had gone on with matter-of-fact frankness to say that he could get him a job, provided that he were willing to pay one-third of his wages for it. Was he a boss? Antanas had asked; to which the man had

replied that that was nobody's business, but that he could do what he said.

Jurgis had made some friends by this time, and he sought one of them and asked what this meant. The friend, who was named Tamoszius Kuszleika, was a sharp little man who folded hides on the killing beds, and he listened to what Jurgis had to say without seeming at all surprised. They were common enough, he said, such cases of petty graft. It was simply some boss who proposed to add a little to his income. After Jurgis had been there awhile he would know that the plants were simply honeycombed with rottenness of that sort—the bosses grafted off the men, and they grafted off each other; and some day the superintendent would find out about the boss, and then he would graft off the boss. Warming to the subject, Tamoszius went on to explain the situation. Here was Durham's, for instance, owned by a man who was trying to make as much money out of it as he could, and did not care in the least how he did it; and underneath him, ranged in ranks and grades like an army, were managers and superintendents and foremen, each one driving the man next below him and trying to squeeze out of him as much work as possible. And all the men of the same rank were pitted against each other; the accounts of each were kept separately, and every man lived in terror of losing his job, if another made a better record than he. So from top to bottom the place was simply a seething caldron of jealousies and hatreds; there was no loyalty or decency anywhere about it, there was no place in it where a man counted for anything against a dollar. And worse than there being no decency, there was not even any honesty. The reason for that? Who could say? It must have been old Durham in the beginning; it was a heritage which the self-made merchant had left to his son, along with his millions.

Jurgis would find out these things for himself, if he stayed there long enough; it was the men who had to do all the dirty jobs, and so there was no deceiving them; and they caught the spirit of the place, and did like all the rest. Jurgis had come there, and thought he was going to make himself useful, and rise and become a skilled man; but he would soon find out his error—for nobody rose in Packingtown by doing good work. You could lay that down for a rule—if you met a man who was rising in Packingtown, you met a knave. That man who had been sent to Jurgis' father by the boss, he would rise; the man who told tales and spied upon his fellows would rise; but the man who minded his own business and did his work—why, they would "speed him up" till they had worn him out, and then they would throw him into the gutter.

Jurgis went home with his head buzzing. Yet he could not bring himself to believe such things—no, it could not be so. Tamoszius was simply another of the grumblers. He was a man who spent all his time fiddling; and he would go to parties at night and not get home till sunrise, and so of course he did not feel like work. Then, too, he was a puny little chap; and so he had been left behind in the race, and that was why he was sore. And yet so many strange things kept coming to Jurgis' notice every day!

He tried to persuade his father to have nothing to do with the offer. But old Antanas had begged until he was worn out, and all his courage was gone; he wanted a job, any sort of a job. So the next day he went and found the man who had spoken to him, and promised to bring him a third of all he earned; and that same day he was put to work in Durham's cellars. It was a "pickle room," where there was never a dry spot to stand upon, and so he had to take nearly the whole of his first week's earnings to buy him a pair of heavy-soled boots. He was a "squeedgie" man; his job was to go about all day with a long-handled mop, swabbing up the floor. Except that it was damp and dark, it was not an unpleasant job, in summer.

Now Antanas Rudkus was the meekest man that God ever put on earth; and so Jurgis found it a striking confirmation of what the men all said, that his father had been at work only two days before he came home as bitter as any of them, and cursing Durham's with all the power of his soul. For they had set him to cleaning out the traps; and the family sat round and listened in wonder while he told them what that meant. It seemed that he was working in the room where the men prepared the beef for canning, and the beef had lain in vats full of chemicals, and men with great forks speared it out and dumped it into trucks, to be taken to the cooking room. When they had speared out all they could reach, they emptied the vat on the floor, and then with shovels scraped up the balance and dumped it into the truck. This floor was filthy, yet they set Antanas with his mop slopping the "pickle" into a hole that connected with a sink, where it was caught and used over again forever; and if that were not enough, there was a trap in the pipe, where all the scraps of meat and odds and ends of refuse were caught, and every few days it was the old man's task to clean these out, and shovel their contents into one of the trucks with the rest of the meat!

This was the experience of Antanas; and then there came also Jonas and Marija with tales to tell. Marija was working for one of the independent packers, and was quite beside herself and outrageous with triumph over the sums of money she was making as a painter of cans. But one day she walked home with a pale-faced little woman who worked opposite to her, Jadvyga Marcinkus by name, and Jadvyga told her how she, Marija, had chanced to get her job. She had taken the place of an Irishwoman who had been working in that factory ever since any one could remember. For over fifteen years, so she declared. Mary Dennis was her name, and a long time ago she had been seduced, and had a little boy; he was a cripple, and an epileptic, but still he was all that she had in the world to love, and they had lived in a little room alone somewhere back of Halsted Street, where the Irish were. Mary had had consumption, and all day long you might hear her coughing as she worked; of late she had been going all to pieces, and when Marija came, the "forelady" had suddenly decided to turn her off. The forelady had to come up to a certain standard herself, and could not stop for sick people, Jadvyga explained. The fact that Mary had been there so long had not made any difference to her—it was doubtful if she even knew that, for both the forelady and the superintendent were new people, having only been there two or three years themselves. Jadvyga did not know what had become of the poor creature; she would have gone to see her, but had been sick herself. She had pains in her back all the time, Jadvyga explained, and feared that she had womb trouble. It was not fit work for a woman, handling fourteen-pound cans all day.

It was a striking circumstance that Jonas, too, had gotten his job by the misfortune of some other person. Jonas pushed a truck loaded with hams from the smoke rooms on to an elevator, and thence to the packing rooms. The trucks were all of iron, and heavy, and they put about threescore hams on each of them, a load of more than a quarter of a ton. On the uneven floor it was a task for a man to start one of these trucks, unless he was a giant; and when it was once started he naturally tried his best to keep it going. There was always the boss prowling about, and if there was a second's delay he would fall to cursing; Lithuanians and Slovaks and such, who could not understand what was said to them, the bosses were wont to kick about the place like so many dogs. Therefore these trucks went for the most part on the run; and the predecessor of Jonas had been jammed against the wall by one and crushed in a horrible and nameless manner.

All of these were sinister incidents; but they were trifles compared to what Jurgis saw with his own eyes before long. One curious thing he had noticed, the very first day, in his profession of shoveller of guts; which was the sharp trick of the floor bosses whenever there chanced to come a "slunk" calf. Any man who knows anything about butchering knows that the flesh of a cow that is about to calve, or has just calved, is not fit for food. A good many of these came every day to the packing houses—and, of course, if they had chosen, it would have been an easy matter for the packers to keep them till they were fit for food. But for the saving of time and fodder, it was the law that cows of that sort came along with the others, and whoever noticed it would tell the boss, and the boss would start up a conversation with the government inspector, and the two would stroll away. So in a trice the carcass of the cow would be cleaned out, and entrails would have vanished; it was Jurgis' task to slide them into the trap, calves and all, and on the floor below they took out these "slunk" calves, and butchered them for meat, and used even the skins of them.

One day a man slipped and hurt his leg; and that afternoon, when the last of the cattle had been disposed of, and the men were leaving, Jurgis was ordered to remain and do some special work which this injured man had usually done. It was late, almost dark, and the government inspectors had all gone, and there were only a dozen or two of men on the floor. That day they had killed about four thousand cattle, and these cattle had come in freight trains from far states, and some of them had got hurt. There were some with broken legs, and some with gored sides; there were some that had died, from what cause no one could say; and they were all to be disposed of,

here in darkness and silence. "Downers," the men called them; and the packing house had a special elevator upon which they were raised to the killing beds, where the gang proceeded to handle them, with an air of businesslike nonchalance which said plainer than any words that it was a matter of everyday routine. It took a couple of hours to get them out of the way, and in the end Jurgis saw them go into the chilling rooms with the rest of the meat, being carefully scattered here and there so that they could not be identified. When he came home that night he was in a very somber mood, having begun to see at last how those might be right who had laughed at him for his faith in America.

Chapter Seven

All summer long the family toiled, and in the fall they had money enough for Jurgis and Ona to be married according to home traditions of decency. In the latter part of November they hired a hall, and invited all their new acquaintances, who came and left them over a hundred dollars in debt.

It was a bitter and cruel experience, and it plunged them into an agony of despair. Such a time, of all times for them to have it, when their hearts were made tender! Such a pitiful beginning it was for their married life; they loved each other so, and they could not have the briefest respite! It was a time when everything cried out to them that they ought to be happy; when wonder burned in their hearts, and leaped into flame at the slightest breath. They were shaken to the depths of them, with the awe of love realized—and was it so very weak of them that they cried out for a little peace? They had opened their hearts, like flowers to the springtime, and the merciless winter had fallen upon them. They wondered if ever any love that had blossomed in the world had been so crushed and trampled!

Over them, relentless and savage, there cracked the lash of want; the morning after the wedding it sought them as they slept, and drove them out before daybreak to work. Ona was scarcely able to stand with exhaustion; but if she were to lose her place they would be ruined, and she would surely lose it if she were not on time that day. They all had to go, even little Stanislovas, who was ill from overindulgence in sausages and sarsaparilla. All that day he stood at his lard machine, rocking unsteadily, his eyes closing in spite of him; and he all but lost his place even so, for the foreman booted him twice to waken him.

It was fully a week before they were all normal again, and meantime, with whining children and cross adults the house was not a pleasant place to live in. Jurgis lost his temper very little, however, all things considered. It was because of Ona; the least glance at her was always enough to make him control himself.

She was so sensitive—she was not fitted for such a life as this; and a hundred times a day, when he thought of her, he would clench his hands and fling himself again at the task before him. She was too good for him, he told himself, and he was afraid, because she was his. So long he had hungered to possess her, but now that the time had come he knew that he had not earned the right; that she trusted him so was all her own simple goodness, and no virtue of his. But he was resolved that she should never find this out, and so was always on the watch to see that he did not betray any of his ugly self; he would take care even in little matters, such as his manners, and his habit of swearing when things went wrong. The tears came so easily into Ona's eyes, and she would look at him so appealingly—it kept Jurgis quite busy making resolutions, in addition to all the other things he had on his mind. It was true that more things were going on at this time in the mind of Jurgis than ever had in all his life before.

He had to protect her, to do battle for her against the horror he saw about them. He was all that she had to look to, and if he failed she would be lost; he would wrap his arms about her, and try to hide her from the world. He had learned the ways of things about him now. It was a war of each against all, and the devil take the hindmost. You did not give feasts to other people, you waited for them to give feasts to you. You went about with your soul full of suspicion and hatred; you understood that you were environed by hostile powers that were trying to get your money, and who used all the virtues to bait their traps with. The storekeepers plastered up their windows with all sorts of lies to entice you; the very fences by the way-side, the lampposts and telegraph poles, were pasted over with lies. The great corporation which employed you lied to you, and lied to the whole country—from top to bottom it was nothing but one gigantic lie. [. . .]

Their children were not as well as they had been at home; but how could they know that there was no sewer to their house, and that the drainage of fifteen years was in a cesspool under it? How could they know that the pale-blue milk that they bought around the corner was watered, and doctored with formaldehyde besides? When the children were not well at home, Teta Elzbieta would gather herbs and cure them; now she was obliged to go to the drug-store and buy extracts—and how was she to know that they were all adulterated? How could they find out that their tea and coffee, their sugar and flour, had been doctored; that their canned peas had been colored with copper salts, and their fruit jams with aniline dyes? And even if they had known it, what good would it have done them, since there was no place within miles of them where any other sort was to be had? The bitter winter was coming, and they had to save money to get more clothing and bedding; but it would not matter in the least how much they saved, they could not get anything to keep them warm. All the clothing that was to be had in the stores was made of cotton and shoddy, which is made by tearing old clothes to pieces and weaving the fiber again. If they paid higher prices, they might get frills and fanciness, or be cheated; but genuine quality they could not obtain for love nor money. [. . .]

There was no heat upon the killing beds; the men might exactly as well have worked out of doors all winter. For that matter, there was very little heat anywhere in the building, except in the cooking rooms and such places—and it was the men who worked in these who ran the most risk of all, because whenever they had to pass to another room they had to go through ice-cold corridors, and sometimes with nothing on above the waist except a sleeveless undershirt. On the killing beds you were apt to be covered with blood, and it would freeze solid; if you leaned against a pillar, you would freeze to that, and if you put your hand upon the blade of your knife, you would run a chance of leaving your skin on it. The men would tie up their feet in newspapers and old sacks, and these would be soaked in blood and frozen, and then soaked again, and so on, until by nighttime a man would be walking on great lumps the size of the feet of an elephant. Now and then, when the bosses were not looking, you would see them plunging their feet and ankles into the steaming hot carcass of the steer, or darting across the room to the hot-water jets. The crudest thing of all was that nearly all of them—all of those who used knives—were unable to wear gloves, and their arms would be white with frost and their hands would grow numb, and then of course there would be accidents. Also the air would be full of steam, from the hot water and the hot blood, so that you could not see five feet before you; and then, with men rushing about at the speed they kept upon the killing beds, and all with butcher knives, like razors, in their hands—well, it was to be counted as a wonder that there were not more men slaughtered than cattle. [. . .]

Home was not a very attractive place—at least not this winter. They had only been able to buy one stove, and this was a small one, and proved not big enough to warm even the kitchen in the bitterest weather. This made it hard for Teta Elzbieta all day, and for the children when they could not get to school. At night they would sit huddled round this stove, while they ate their supper off their laps; and then Jurgis and Jonas would smoke a pipe, after which they would all crawl into their beds to get warm, after putting out the fire to save the coal. Then they would have some frightful experiences with the cold. They would sleep with all their clothes on, including their overcoats, and put over them all the bedding and spare clothing they owned; the children would sleep all crowded into one bed, and yet even so they could not keep warm. The outside ones would be shivering and sobbing, crawling over the others and trying to get down into the center, and causing a fight. This old house with the leaky weatherboards was a very different thing from their cabins at home, with great thick walls plastered inside and outside with mud; and the cold which came upon them was a living thing, a demon-presence in the room. They would waken in the midnight hours, when everything was black; perhaps they would hear it yelling outside, or perhaps there would be deathlike stillness—and that would be worse yet. They could feel the cold as it crept in through the cracks, reaching out for them with its icy, death-dealing fingers; and they would crouch and cower, and try to hide from it, all in vain. It would come, and it would come; a grisly thing, a specter born in the black caverns of terror; a power primeval, cosmic, shadowing the tortures of the lost souls flung out to chaos and destruction. It was cruel iron-hard; and hour after hour they would cringe in its grasp, alone, alone. There would be no one to hear them if they cried out; there would be no help, no mercy. And so on until morning—when they would go out to another day of toil, a little weaker, a little nearer to the time when it would be their turn to be shaken from the tree.

David J. Brewer

Muller v. Oregon (1908)

Mr. Justice Brewer delivered the opinion of the Court.

On February 19, 1903, the legislature of the State of Oregon passed an act the first section of which is in these words:

Sec. 1. That no female [shall] be employed in any mechanical establishment, or factory, or laundry in this State more than ten hours during any one day. The hours of work may be so arranged as to permit the employment of females at any time so that they shall not work more than ten hours during the twenty-four hours of any one day.

Sec. 3 made a violation of the provisions of the prior sections a misdemeanor subject to a fine of not less than $10 nor more than $25. On September 18, 1905, an information was filed in the circuit court of the State for the County of Multnomah, charging that the defendant on the 4th day of September, A.D. 1905, in the county of Multnomah and State of Oregon, then and there being the owner of a laundry, known as the Grand Laundry, in the city of Portland, and the employer of females therein, did then and there unlawfully permit and suffer one Joe Haselbock, he, the said Joe Haselbock, then and there being an overseer, superintendent, and agent of said Curt Muller, in the said Grand Laundry, to require a female, to-wit, one Mrs. E. Gotcher, to work more than ten hours in said laundry on said 4th day of September, A.D. 1905, contrary to the statutes in such cases made and provided, and against the peace and dignity of the State of Oregon.

A trial resulted in a verdict against the defendant, who was sentenced to pay a fine of $10. The Supreme Court of the State affirmed the conviction, whereupon the case was brought here on writ of error.

The single question is the constitutionality of the statute under which the defendant was convicted so far as it affects the work of a female in a laundry. That it does not conflict with any provisions of the state constitution is settled by the decision of the Supreme Court of the State. The contentions of the defendant, now plaintiff in error, are thus stated in his brief:

(1) Because the statute attempts to prevent persons *sui juris* from making their own contracts, and thus violates the provisions of the Fourteenth Amendment. . . .

(2) Because the statute does not apply equally to all persons similarly situated, and is class legislation.

(3) The statute is not a valid exercise of the police power. The kinds of work prescribed are not unlawful, nor are they declared to be immoral or dangerous to the public health; nor can such a law be sustained on the ground that it is designed to protect women on account of their sex. There is no necessary or reasonable connection between the limitation prescribed by the act and the public health, safety, or welfare. [. . .]

We held in *Lochner v. New York* [1905], that a law providing that no laborer shall be required or permitted to work in bakeries more than sixty hours in a week or ten hours in a day was not, as to men, a legitimate exercise of the police power of the State, but an unreasonable, unnecessary, and arbitrary interference with the right and liberty of the individual to contract in relation to his labor, and, as such, was in conflict with, and void under, the Federal Constitution. That decision is invoked by plaintiff in error as decisive of the question before us. But this assumes that the difference between the sexes does not justify a different rule respecting a restriction of the hours of labor. [. . .]

It may not be amiss, in the present case, before examining the constitutional question, to notice the course of legislation, as well as expressions of opinion from other than judicial sources. In the brief filed by Mr. Louis D. Brandeis for the defendant in error is a very copious collection of all these matters, an epitome of which is found in the margin. [. . .]

The legislation and opinions referred to in the margin may not be, technically speaking, authorities, and in them is little or no discussion of the constitutional question presented to us for determination, yet they are significant of a widespread belief that woman's physical structure, and the functions she performs in consequence thereof, justify special legislation restricting or qualifying the conditions under which she should be permitted to toil. Constitutional questions, it is true, are not settled by even a consensus of present public opinion, for it is the peculiar value of a written constitution that it places in unchanging form limitations upon legislative action, and thus gives a permanence and stability to popular government which otherwise would be lacking. At the same time, when a question of fact is debated and debatable, and the extent to which a special constitutional limitation goes is affected by the truth in respect to that fact, a widespread and long-continued belief concerning it is worthy of consideration. We take judicial cognizance of all matters of general knowledge.

It is undoubtedly true, as more than once declared by this Court, that the general right to contract in relation to one's business is part of the liberty of the individual, protected by the Fourteenth Amendment to the Federal Constitution; yet it is equally well settled that this liberty is not absolute, and extending to all contracts, and that a State may, without conflicting with the provisions of the Fourteen Amendment, restrict in many respects the individual's power of contract. Without stopping to discuss at length the extent to which a State may act in this respect, we refer to the following cases in which the question has been considered: *Allgeyer v.*

Louisiana [1897]; *Holden v. Hardy* [1898]; *Lochner v. New York* [1905].

That woman's physical structure and the performance of maternal functions place her at a disadvantage in the struggle for subsistence is obvious. This is especially true when the burdens of motherhood are upon her. Even when they are not, by abundant testimony of the medical fraternity, continuance for a long time on her feet at work, repeating this from day to day, tends to injurious effects upon the body, and, as healthy mothers are essential to vigorous offspring, the physical wellbeing of woman becomes an object of public interest and care in order to preserve the strength and vigor of the race.

Still again, history discloses the fact that woman has always been dependent upon man. He established his control at the outset by superior physical strength, and this control in various forms, with diminishing intensity, has continued to the present. As minors, though not to the same extent, she has been looked upon in the courts as needing especial care that her rights may be preserved. Education was long denied her, and while now the doors of the schoolroom are opened and her opportunities for acquiring knowledge are great, yet, even with that and the consequent increase of capacity for business affairs, it is still true that, in the struggle for subsistence, she is not an equal competitor with her brother. Though limitations upon personal and contractual rights may be removed by legislation, there is that in her disposition and habits of life which will operate against a full assertion of those rights. She will still be where some legislation to protect her seems necessary to secure a real equality of right. Doubtless there are individual exceptions, and there are many respects in which she has an advantage over him; but, looking at it from the viewpoint of the effort to maintain an independent position in life, she is not upon an equality. Differentiated by these matters from the other sex, she is properly placed in a class by herself, and legislation designed for her protection may be sustained even when like legislation is not

necessary for men, and could not be sustained. It is impossible to close one's eyes to the fact that she still looks to her brother, and depends upon him. Even though all restrictions on political, personal, and contractual rights were taken away, and she stood, so far as statutes are concerned, upon an absolutely equal plane with him, it would still be true that she is so constituted that she will rest upon and look to him for protection; that her physical structure and a proper discharge of her maternal functions—having in view not merely her own health, but the wellbeing of the race—justify legislation to protect her from the greed, as well as the passion, of man. The limitations which this statute places upon her contractual powers, upon her right to agree with her employer as to the time she shall labor, are not imposed solely for her benefit, but also largely for the benefit of all. Many words cannot make this plainer. The two sexes differ in structure of body, in the functions to be performed by each, in the amount of physical strength, in the capacity for long-continued labor, particularly when done standing, the influence of vigorous health upon the future wellbeing of the race, the self-reliance which enables one to assert full rights, and in the capacity to maintain the struggle for subsistence. This difference justifies a difference in legislation, and upholds that which is designed to compensate for some of the burdens which rest upon her.

We have not referred in this discussion to the denial of the elective franchise in the State of Oregon, for, while that may disclose a lack of political equality in all things with her brother, that is not of itself decisive. The reason runs deeper, and rests in the inherent difference between the two sexes and in the different functions in life which they perform.

For these reasons, and without questioning in any respect the decision in *Lochner v. New York*, we are of the opinion that it cannot be adjudged that the act in question is in conflict with the Federal Constitution so far as it respects the work of a female in a laundry, and the judgment of the Supreme Court of Oregon is affirmed.

Eugene V. Debs

Speech at Indianapolis (1909)

The Class Struggle

We are entering tonight upon a momentous campaign. The struggle for political supremacy is not between political parties merely, as appears upon the surface, but at bottom it is a life and death struggle between two hostile economic classes, the one the capitalist, and the other the working class.

The capitalist class is represented by the Republican, Democratic, Populist and Prohibition parties, all of which stand for private ownership of the means of production, and the triumph of any one of which will mean continued wage-slavery to the working class.

As the Populist and Prohibition sections of the capitalist party represent minority elements which propose to reform the capitalist system without disturbing wage-slavery, a vain and impossible task, they will be omitted from this discussion with all the credit due the rank and file for their good intentions.

The Republican and Democratic parties, or, to be more exact, the Republican-Democratic Party, represent the capitalist class in the class struggle. They are the political wings of the capitalist system and such differences as arise between them relate to spoils and not to principles.

With either of these parties in power one thing is always certain and that is that the capitalist class is in the saddle and the working class under the saddle.

Under the administration of both these parties the means of production are private property, production is carried forward for capitalist profit purely, markets are glutted and industry paralyzed, workingmen become tramps and criminals while injunctions, soldiers and riot guns are brought into action to preserve "law and order" in the chaotic carnival of capitalistic anarchy.

Deny it as may the cunning capitalists who are clear-sighted enough to perceive it, or ignore it as may the torpid workers who are too blind and unthinking to see it, the struggle in which we are engaged today is a class struggle, and as the toiling millions come to see and understand it and rally to the political standard of their class, they will drive all capitalist parties of whatever name into the same party, and the class struggle will then be so clearly revealed that the hosts of labor will find their true place in the conflict and strike the united and decisive blow that will destroy slavery and achieve their full and final emancipation.

In this struggle the workingmen and women and children are represented by the Socialist Party and it is my privilege to address you in the name of that revolutionary and uncompromising party of the working class.

Attitude of the Workers

What shall be the attitude of the workers of the United States in the present campaign? What part shall they take in it? What party and what principles shall they support by their ballots? And why?

These are questions the importance of which are not sufficiently recognized by workingmen or they would not be the prey of parasites and the service tools of scheming politicians who use them at election time to renew their masters' lease of power and perpetuate their own ignorance, poverty and shame.

In answering these questions I propose to be as frank and candid as plain-meaning words will allow, for I have but one object in this discussion and that object is not office, but the truth, and I shall state it as I see it, if I have to stand alone.

But I shall not stand alone, for the party that has my allegiance and may have my life, the Socialist Party, the party of the working class, the party of emancipation, is made up of men and women who know their rights and scorn to compromise with their oppressors; who want no votes that can be bought and no support under any false pretense whatsoever.

The Socialist Party stands squarely upon its proletarian principles and relies wholly upon the forces of industrial progress and the education of the working class.

The Socialist Party buys no votes and promises no office. Not a farthing is spent for whiskey or cigars. Every penny in the campaign fund is the voluntary offerings of workers and their sympathizers and every penny is used for education.

What other parties can say the same?

Ignorance alone stands in the way of Socialist success. The capitalist parties understand this and use their resources to prevent the workers from seeing the light.

Intellectual darkness is essential to industrial slavery.

Capitalist parties stand for Slavery and Night.

The Socialist Party is the herald of Freedom and Light.

Capitalist parties cunningly contrive to divide the workers upon dead issues.

The Socialist Party is uniting them upon the living issue:

Death to Wage Slavery!

When industrial slavery is as dead as the issues of the Siamese-twin capitalist parties the Socialist Party will have fulfilled its mission and enriched history.

And now to our questions:

First, all workingmen and women owe it to themselves, their class and their country to take an active and intelligent interest in political affairs.

The Ballot

The ballot of united labor expresses the people's will and the people's will is the supreme law of a free nation.

The ballot means that labor is no longer dumb, that at last it has a voice, that it may be heard and if united shall be heeded.

Centuries of struggle and sacrifice were required to wrest this symbol of freedom from the mailed clutch of tyranny and place it in the hand of labor as the shield and lance of attack and defense.

The abuse and not the use of it is responsible for its evils.

The divided vote of labor is the abuse of the ballot and the penalty is slavery and death.

The united vote of those who toil and have not will vanquish those who have and toil not, and solve forever the problem of democracy.

The Historic Struggle of Classes

Since the race was young there have been class struggles. In every state of society, ancient and modern, labor has been exploited, degraded and in subjection.

Civilization has done little for labor except to modify the forms of its exploitation.

Labor has always been the mudsill of the social fabric—is so now and will be until the class struggle ends in class extinction and free society.

Society has always been and is now built upon exploitation—the exploitation of a class—the working class, whether slaves, serfs or wage-laborers, and the exploited working class in subjection have always been, instinctively or consciously, in revolt against their oppressors.

Through all the centuries the enslaved toilers have moved slowly but surely toward their final freedom.

The call of the Socialist Party is to the exploited class, the workers in all useful trades and professions, all honest occupations, from the most menial service to the highest skill, to rally beneath their own standard and put an end to the last of the barbarous class struggles by conquering the capitalist government, taking possession of the means of production and making them the common property of all, abolishing wage-slavery and establishing the co-operative commonwealth.

Capitalist Parties

They are precisely alike and I challenge their most discriminating partisans to tell them apart in relation to labor.

The Republican and Democratic parties are alike capitalist parties—differing only in being committed to different sets of capitalist interests—they have the same principles under varying colors, are equally corrupt and are one in their subservience to capital and their hostility to labor.

The ignorant workingman who supports either of these parties forges his own fetters and is the unconscious author of his own misery. He can and must be made to see and think and act with his fellows in supporting the party of his class and this work of education is the crowning virtue of the Socialist movement. [. . .]

The Socialist Party

In what has been said of other parties I have tried to show why they should not be supported by the common people, least of all by workingmen, and I think I have shown clearly enough that such workers as do support them are guilty, consciously or unconsciously, of treason to their class. They are voting into power the enemies of labor and are morally responsible for the crimes thus perpetrated upon their fellow-workers and sooner or later they will have to suffer the consequences of their miserable acts.

The Socialist Party is not, and does not pretend to be, a capitalist party. It does not ask, nor does it expect the votes of the capitalist class. Such capitalists as do support it do so seeing the approaching doom of the capitalist system and with a full understanding that the Socialist Party is not a capitalist party, nor a middle class party, but a revolutionary working class party, whose historic mission it is to conquer capitalism on the political battle-field, take control of government and through the public powers take possession of the means of wealth production, abolish wage-slavery and emancipate all workers and all humanity.

The people are as capable of achieving their industrial freedom as they were to secure their political liberty, and both are necessary to a free nation.

The capitalist system is no longer adapted to the needs of modern society. It is outgrown and fetters the forces of progress. Industrial and commercial competition are largely of the past. The handwriting blazes on the wall. Centralization and combination are the modern forces in industrial and commercial life. Competition is breaking down and co-operation is supplanting it.

The hand tools of early times are used no more. Mammoth machines have taken their places. A few thousand capitalists own them and many millions of workingmen use them.

All the wealth the vast army of labor produces above its subsistence is taken by the machine owning capitalists, who also own the land and the mills, the factories, railroads and mines, the forests and fields and all other means of production and transportation.

Hence wealth and poverty, millionaires and beggars, castles and caves, luxury and squalor, painted parasites on the boulevard and painted poverty among the red lights.

Hence strikes, boycotts, riots, murder, suicide, insanity, prostitution on a fearful and increasing scale.

The capitalist parties can do nothing. They are a part, an iniquitous part, of the foul and decaying system.

There is no remedy for the ravages of death.

Capitalism is dying and its extremities are already decomposing. The blotches upon the surface show that the blood no longer circulates. The time is near when the cadaver will have to be removed and the atmosphere purified.

In contrast with the Republican and Democratic conventions, where politicians were the puppets of plutocrats, the convention of the Socialist Party consisted of workingmen and women fresh from their labors, strong, clean, wholesome, self-reliant, ready to do and dare for the cause of labor, the cause of humanity.

Proud indeed am I to have been chosen by such a body of men and women to bear aloft the proletarian standard in this campaign, and heartily do I endorse the clear and cogent platform of the party which appeals with increasing force and eloquence to the whole working class of the country.

To my associate upon the national ticket I give my hand with all my heart. Ben Hanford typifies the working class and fitly represents the historic mission and revolutionary character of the Socialist Party.

Closing Words

These are stirring days for living men. The day of crisis is drawing near and Socialists are exerting all their power to prepare the people for it.

The old order of society can survive but little longer. Socialism is next in order. The swelling minority sounds warning of the impending change. Soon that minority will be the majority and then will come the co-operative commonwealth.

Every workingman should rally to the standard of his class and hasten the full-orbed day of freedom.

Every progressive Democrat must find his way in our direction, and if he will but free himself from prejudice and study the principles of Socialism he will soon be a sturdy supporter of our party.

Every sympathizer with labor, every friend of justice, every lover of humanity should support the Socialist Party as the only party that is organized to abolish industrial slavery, the prolific source of the giant evils that afflict the people.

Who with a heart in his breast can look upon Colorado without keenly feeling the cruelties and crimes of capitalism! Repression will not help her. Brutality will only brutalize her. Private ownership and wage-slavery are the curse of Colorado. Only Socialism will save Colorado and the nation.

The overthrow of capitalism is the object of the Socialist Party. It will not fuse with any other party and it would rather die than compromise.

The Socialist Party comprehends the magnitude of its task and has the patience of preliminary defeat and the faith of ultimate victory.

The working class must be emancipated by the working class.

Woman must be given her true place in society by the working class.

Child labor must be abolished by the working class.

Society must be reconstructed by the working class.

The working class must be employed by the working class.

The fruits of labor must be enjoyed by the working class.

War, bloody war, must be ended by the working class.

These are the principles and objects of the Socialist Party and we fearlessly proclaim them to our fellowmen.

We know our cause is just and that it must prevail.

With faith and hope and courage we hold our heads erect and with dauntless spirit marshal the working class for the march from Capitalism to Socialism, from Slavery to Freedom, from Barbarism to Civilization.

JANE ADDAMS

Why Women Should Vote (1915)

For many generations it has been believed that woman's place is within the walls of her own home, and it is indeed impossible to imagine the time when her duty there shall be ended or to forecast any social change which shall release her from that paramount obligation.

1

This paper is an attempt to show that many women to-day are failing to discharge their duties to their own households properly simply because they do not perceive that as society grows more complicated it, is necessary that woman shall extend her sense of responsibility to many things outside of her own home if she would continue to preserve the home in its entirety. One could illustrate in many ways. A woman's simplest duty, one would say, is to keep her house clean and wholesome and to feed her children properly. Yet if she lives in a tenement house, as so many of my neighbors do, she cannot fulfill these simple obligations by her own efforts because she is utterly dependent upon the city administration for the conditions which render decent living possible. Her basement will not be dry, her stairways will not be fireproof, her house will not be provided with sufficient windows to give light and air, nor will it be equipped with sanitary plumbing, unless the Public Works Department sends inspectors who constantly insist that these elementary decencies be provided. Women who live in the country sweep their own dooryards and may either feed the refuse of the table to a flock of chickens or allow it innocently to decay in the open air and sunshine. In a crowded city quarter, however, if the street is not cleaned by the city authorities no amount of private sweeping will keep the tenement free from grime; if the garbage is not properly collected and destroyed a tenement house mother may see her children sicken and die of diseases from which she alone is powerless to shield them, although her tenderness and devotion are unbounded. She cannot even secure untainted meat for her household, she cannot provide fresh fruit, unless the meat has been inspected by city officials, and the decayed fruit, which is so often placed upon sale in the tenement districts, has been destroyed in the interests of public health. In short, if woman would keep on with her old business of caring for her house and rearing her children she will have to have some conscience in regard to public affairs lying quite outside of her immediate household. The individual conscience and devotion are no longer effective.

2

Chicago one spring had a spreading contagion of scarlet fever just at the time that the school nurses had been discontinued because business men had pronounced them too expensive. If the women who sent their children to the schools had been sufficiently public-spirited and had been provided with an implement through which to express that public spirit they would have insisted that the schools be supplied with nurses in order that their own children might be protected from contagion. In other words, if women would effectively continue their old avocations they must take part in the slow upbuilding of that code of legislation which is alone sufficient to protect the home from the dangers incident to modern life. One might instance the many deaths of children from contagious diseases the germs of which

had been carried in tailored clothing. Country doctors testify as to the outbreak of scarlet fever in remote neighborhoods each autumn, after the children have begun to wear the winter overcoats and cloaks which have been sent from infected city sweatshops. That their mothers charter was the unexpected enthusiasm and help which came from large groups of foreign-born women. The Scandinavian women represented in many Lutheran Church societies said quite simply that in the old country they had had the municipal franchise upon the same basis as men for many years; all the women living under the British Government, in England, Australia or Canada, pointed out that Chicago women were asking now for what the British women had long ago. But the most unexpected response came from the foreign colonies in which women had never heard such problems discussed and took the prospect of the municipal ballot as a simple device—which it is—to aid them in their daily struggle with adverse city conditions. The Italian women said that the men engaged in railroad construction were away all summer and did not know anything about their household difficulties. Some of them came to Hull-House one day to talk over the possibility of a public wash-house. They do not like to wash in their own tenements; they had never seen a washing-tub until they came to America, and find it very difficult to use it in the restricted space of their little kitchens and to hang the clothes within the house to dry. They say that in the Italian villages the women all go to the streams together; in the town they go to the public wash-house; and washing, instead of being lonely and disagreeable, is made pleasant by cheerful conversation. It is asking a great deal of these women to change suddenly all their habits of living, and their contention that the tenement house kitchen is too small for laundry work is well taken. If women in Chicago knew the needs of the Italian colony they would realize that any change bringing cleanliness and fresh air into the Italian household would be a very sensible and hygienic measure. It is, perhaps, asking a great deal that the members of the City Council should understand this, but surely a comprehension of the needs of these women and efforts toward ameliorating their lot might be regarded as matters of municipal obligation on the part of voting women.

3

The same thing is true of the Jewish women in their desire for covered markets which have always been a municipal provision in Russia and Poland. The vegetables piled high upon the wagons standing in the open markets of Chicago become covered with dust and soot. It seems to these women a violation of the most rudimentary decencies and they sometimes say quite simply: "If women had anything to say about it they would change all that."

4

If women follow only the lines of their traditional activities, here are certain primary duties which belong to even the most conservative women, and which no one woman or group of women can adequately discharge unless they join the more general movements looking toward social amelioration through legal enactment.

5

The first of these, of which this article has already treated, is woman's responsibility for the members of her own household that they may be properly fed and clothed and surrounded by hygienic conditions. The second is a responsibility for the education of children: (a) that they may be provided with good books; (b) that they may be kept free from vicious influences on the street; (c) that when working they may be protected by adequate child-labor legislation.

6

(a) The duty of a woman toward the schools which her children attend is so obvious that it is not necessary to dwell upon it. But even this simple obligation cannot be effectively carried out without some form of social organization, as the mothers' school clubs and mothers' congresses testify, and to which the most conservative women belong because they feel the need of wider reading and discussion concerning the many problems of childhood. It is, therefore, perhaps natural that the public should have been more willing to accord a vote to women in school matters than in any other, and yet women have never been members of a Board of Education in sufficient numbers to influence largely actual school curiculi. If they had been, kindergartens, domestic science courses and school playgrounds would be far more numerous than they are. More than one woman has been convinced of the need of the ballot by the futility of her efforts in persuading a business man that young children need nurture in something besides the three r's. Perhaps, too, only women realize the influence which the school might exert upon the home if a proper adaptation to actual needs were considered. An Italian girl who has had lessons in cooking at the public school will help her mother to connect the entire family with American food and household habits. That the mother has never baked bread in Italy—only mixed it in her own house and then taken it out to the village oven—makes it all the more necessary that her daughter should understand the complications of a cooking-stove. The same thing is true of the girl who learns to sew in the public school, and more than anything else, perhaps, of the girl who receives the first simple instruction in the care of little children, that skillful care which every tenement house baby requires if he is to be pulled through his second summer. The only time, to my knowledge, that lessons in the care of children were given in the public schools of Chicago was one summer when the vacation schools were being managed by a volunteer body of women. The instruction was eagerly received by the Italian girls, who had been "little mothers" to younger children ever since they could remember.

7

As a result of this teaching I recall a young girl who carefully explained to her Italian mother that the reason the babies in Italy were so healthy and the babies in Chicago were so sickly was not, as her mother had always firmly insisted, because her babies in Italy had goat's milk and her babies in America had cow's milk, but because the milk in Italy was clean and the milk in Chicago was dirty. She said that when you milked your own goat before the door you knew that the milk was clean, but when you bought milk from the grocery store after it had been carried for many miles in the country, "you couldn't tell whether or not it was fit for the baby to drink until the men from the City Hall, who had watched it all the way, said that it was all right." She also informed her mother that the "City Hall wanted to fix up the milk so that it couldn't make the baby sick, but that they hadn't quite-enough votes for it yet." The Italian mother believed what her child had been taught in the big school; it seemed to her quite as natural that the city should be concerned in providing pure milk for her younger children as that it should provide big schools and teachers for her older children. She reached this naive conclusion because she had never heard those arguments which make it seem reasonable that a woman should be given the school franchise, but no other.

8

(b) But women are also beginning to realize that children need attention outside of school hours; that much of the petty vice in cities is merely the love of pleasure gone wrong, the over-strained boy or girl seeking improper recreation and excitement. It is obvious that a little study of the needs of children, a sympathetic understanding of the conditions under which they go astray, might save hundreds of them. Women traditionally have had an opportunity to observe the plays of children and the needs of youth, and yet in Chicago, at least, they had done singularly little in this vexed problem of juvenile delinquency until they helped to inaugurate the Juvenile Court movement a dozen years ago. The Juvenile Court Committee, made up largely of women, paid the salaries of the probation officers connected with the court for the first six years of its existence, and after the salaries were cared for by the county the same organization turned itself into a Juvenile Protective League, and through a score of paid officers are doing valiant service in minimizing some of the dangers of city life which boys and girls encounter.

9

This Protective League, however, was not formed until the women had had a civic training through their semi-official connection with the juvenile Court. This is, perhaps, an illustration of our inability to see the duty "next to hand" until we have become alert through our knowledge of conditions in connection with the larger duties. We would all agree that social amelioration must come about through the efforts of many people who are moved thereto by the compunction and stirring of the individual conscience, but we are only beginning to understand that the individual conscience will respond to the special challenge largely in proportion as the individual is able to see the social conditions because he has felt responsible for their improvement. Because this body of women assumed a public responsibility they have seen to it that every series of pictures displayed in the five-cent theatre is subjected to a careful censorship before it is produced, and those series suggesting obscenity and criminality have been practically eliminated. The police department has performed this and many other duties to which it was oblivious before, simply because these women have made it realize that it is necessary to protect and purify those places of amusement which are crowded with young people every night. This is but the negative side of the policy pursued by the public authorities in the fifteen small parks of Chicago, each of which is provided with balls in which young people may meet nightly for social gatherings and dances. The more extensively the modern city endeavors on the one hand to control and on the other hand to provide recreational facilities for its young people, the more necessary it is that women should assist in their direction and extension. After all, a care for wholesome and innocent amusement is what women have for many years assumed. When the reaction comes on the part of taxpayers, women's votes may be necessary to keep the city to its beneficent obligations toward its own young people.

10

(c) As the education of her children has been more and more transferred to the school, so that even children four years old go to the kindergarten, the woman has been left in a household of constantly-narrowing interests, not only because the children are away, but also because one industry after another is slipping from the household into the factory. Ever since steam power has been applied to the processes of weaving and spinning woman's traditional work has been carried on largely outside of the home. The clothing and household linen are not only spun and woven, but also usually sewed by machinery; the preparation of many foods has also passed into the factory and necessarily a certain number of women have been obliged to follow their work there, although it is doubtful, in spite of the large number of factory girls, whether women now are doing as large a proportion of the world's work as they used to do. Because many thousands of those working in factories and shops are girls between the ages of fourteen and twenty-two, there is a necessity that older women should be interested in the conditions of industry. The very fact that these girls are not going to remain in industry permanently makes it more important that some one should see to it that they shall not be incapacitated for their future family life because they work for exhausting hours and under insanitary conditions.

11

If woman's sense of obligation had enlarged as the industrial conditions changed she might naturally and almost imperceptibly have inaugurated movements for social amelioration in the line of factory legislation and shop sanitation. That she has not done so is doubtless due to the fact that her conscience is slow to recognize any obligation outside of her own family circle, and because she was so absorbed in her own household that she failed to see what the conditions outside actually were. It would be interesting to know how far the consciousness that she had no vote and could not change matters operated in this direction. After all, we see only those things to which our attention has been drawn, we feel responsibility for those things which are brought to us as matters of responsibility. If conscientious women were convinced that it was a civic duty to be informed in regard to these grave industrial affairs,

and then to express the conclusions which they had reached by depositing a piece of paper in a ballot-box, one cannot imagine that they would shirk simply because the action ran counter to old traditions.

12

To those of my readers who would admit that although woman has no right to shirk her old obligations, that all of these measures could be secured more easily through her influence upon the men of her family than through the direct use of the ballot, I should like to tell a little story. I have a friend in Chicago who is the mother of four sons and the grandmother of twelve grandsons who are voters. She is a woman of wealth, of secured social position, of sterling character and clear intelligence, and may, therefore, quite fairly be cited as a "woman of influence." Upon one of her recent birthdays, when she was asked how she had kept so young, she promptly replied: "Because I have always advocated at least one unpopular cause." It may have been in pursuance of this policy that for many years she has been an ardent advocate of free silver, although her manufacturing family are all Republicans! I happened to call at her house on the day that Mr. McKinley was elected President against Mr. Bryan for the first time. I found my friend much disturbed. She said somewhat bitterly that she had at last discovered what the much-vaunted influence of woman was worth; that she had implored each one of her sons and grandsons; had entered into endless arguments and moral appeals to induce one of them to represent her convictions by voting for Mr. Bryan; that, although sincerely devoted to her, each one had assured her that his convictions forced him to vote the Republican ticket! She said that all she had been able to secure was the promise from one of the grandsons, for whom she had an especial tenderness because he bore her husband's name, that he would not vote at all. He could not vote for Bryan, but out of respect for her feeling he would refrain from voting for McKinley. My friend said that for many years she had suspected that women could influence men only in regard to those things in which men were not deeply concerned, but when it came to persuading a man to a woman's view in affairs of politics or business it was absolutely useless. I contended that a woman had no right to persuade a man to vote against his own convictions; that I respected the men of her family for following their own judgement regardless of the appeal which the honored head of the house had made to their chivalric devotion. To this she replied that she would agree with that point of view when a woman had the same opportunity as a man to register her convictions by vote. I believed then as I do now, that nothing is gained when independence of judgment is assailed by "influence," sentimental or otherwise, and that we test advancing civilization somewhat by our power to respect differences and by our tolerance of another's honest conviction.

13

This is, perhaps, the attitude of many busy women who would be glad to use the ballot to further public measures in which they are interested and for which they have been working for years. It offends the taste of such a woman to be obliged to use indirect "influence" when she is accustomed to well-bred, open action in other affairs, and she very much resents the time spent in persuading a voter to take her point of view, and possibly to give up his own, quite as honest and valuable as hers, although different because resulting from a totally different experience. Public-spirited women who wish to use the ballot, as I know them, do not wish to do the work of men nor to take over men's affairs. They simply want an opportunity to do their own work and to take care of those affairs which naturally and historically belong to women, but which are constantly being overlooked and slighted in our political institutions. In a complex community like the modern city all points of view need to be represented; the resultants of diverse experiences need to be pooled if the community would make for sane and balanced progress. If it would meet fairly each problem as it arises, whether it be connected with a freight tunnel having to do largely with business men, or with the increasing death fate among children under five years of age, a problem in which women are vitally concerned, or with the question of more adequate streetcar transfers, in which both men and women might be said to be equally interested, it must not ignore the judgments of its entire adult population. To turn the administration of our civic affairs wholly over to men may mean that the American city will continue to push forward in its commercial and industrial development, and continue to lag behind in those things which make a city healthful and beautiful. After all, woman's traditional function has been to make her dwelling-place both clean and fair. Is that dreariness in city life, that lack of domesticity which the humblest farm dwelling presents, due to a withdrawal of one of the naturally co-operating forces? If women have in any sense been responsible for the gentler side of life which softens and blurs some of its harsher conditions, may they not have a duty to perform in our American cities? In closing, may I recapitulate that if woman would fulfill her traditional responsibility to her own children; if she would educate and protect from danger factory children who must find their recreation on the street; if she would bring the cultural forces to bear upon our materialistic civilization; and if she would do it all with the dignity and directness fitting one who carries on her immemorial duties, then she must bring herself to the use of the ballot—that latest implement for self-government. May we not fairly say that American women need this implement in order to preserve the home?

Herbert Croly

The Promise of American Life (1909)

Chapter One: What Is the Promise of American Life?

The average American is nothing if not patriotic. "The Americans are filled," says Mr. Emil Reich in his "Success among the Nations," "with such an implicit and absolute confidence in their Union and in their future success that any remark other than laudatory is inacceptable to the majority of them. We have had many opportunities of hearing public speakers in America cast doubts upon the very existence of God and of Providence, question the historic nature or veracity of the whole fabric of Christianity; but never has it been our fortune to catch the slightest whisper of doubt, the slightest want of faith, in the chief God of America—unlimited belief in the future of America." Mr. Reich's method of emphasis may not be very happy, but the substance of what he says is true. The faith of Americans in their own country is religious, if not in its intensity, at any rate in its almost absolute and universal authority. It pervades the air we breathe. As children we hear it asserted or implied in the conversation of our elders. Every new stage of our educational training provides some additional testimony on its behalf. Newspapers and novelists, orators and playwrights, even if they are little else, are at least loyal preachers of the Truth. The skeptic is not controverted; he is overlooked. It constitutes the kind of faith which is the implication, rather than the object, of thought, and consciously or unconsciously it enters largely into our personal lives as a formative influence. We may distrust and dislike much that is done in the name of our country by our fellow-countrymen; but our country itself, its democratic system, and its prosperous future are above suspicion.

Of course, Americans have no monopoly of patriotic enthusiasm and good faith. Englishmen return thanks to Providence for not being born anything but an Englishman, in churches and alehouses as well as in comic operas. The Frenchman cherishes and proclaims the idea that France is the most civilized modern country and satisfies best the needs of a man of high social intelligence. The Russian, whose political and social estate does not seem enviable to his foreign contemporaries, secretes a vision of a mystically glorified Russia, which condemns to comparative insipidity the figures of the "Pax Britannica" and of "La Belle France" enlightening the world. Every nation, in proportion as its nationality is thoroughly alive, must be leavened by the ferment of some such faith. But there are significant differences between the faith of, say, an Englishman in the British Empire and that of an American in the Land of Democracy. The contents of an Englishman's national idea tends to be more exclusive. His patriotism is anchored to the historical achievements of Great Britain and restricted thereby. As a good patriot he is bound to be more preoccupied with the inherited fabric of national institutions and traditions than he is with the ideal and more than national possibilities of the future. This very loyalty to the national fabric does, indeed, imply an important ideal content; but the national idealism of an Englishman, a German, or even a Frenchman, is heavily mortgaged to his own national history and cannot honestly escape the debt. [. . .]

The higher American patriotism, on the other hand, combines loyalty to historical tradition and precedent with the imaginative projection of an ideal national Promise. The Land of Democracy has always appealed to its more enthusiastic children chiefly as a land of wonderful and more than national possibilities. "Neither race nor tradition," says Professor Hugo Münsterberg in his volume on "The Americans," "nor the actual past, binds the American to his countrymen, but rather the future which together they are building." This vision of a better future is not, perhaps, as unclouded for the present generation of Americans as it was for certain former generations; but in spite of a more friendly acquaintance with all

sorts of obstacles and pitfalls, our country is still figured in the imagination of its citizens as the Land of
Promise. They still believe that somehow and sometime something better will happen to good Americans than has happened to men in any other country;
and this belief, vague, innocent, and uninformed
though it be, is the expression of an essential constituent in our national ideal. [. . .]

An America which was not the Land of Promise,
which was not informed by a prophetic outlook and
a more or less constructive ideal, would not be the
America bequeathed to us by our forefathers. In cherishing the Promise of a better national future the
American is fulfilling rather than imperiling the substance of the national tradition.

When, however, Americans talk of their country
as the Land of Promise, a question may well be raised
as to precisely what they mean. They mean, of
course, in general, that the future will have something better in store for them individually and collectively than has the past or the present; but a very
superficial analysis of this meaning discloses certain
ambiguities. What are the particular benefits which
this better future will give to Americans either individually or as a nation? And how is this Promise to be
fulfilled? Will it fulfill itself, or does it imply certain
responsibilities? If so, what responsibilities? |When
we speak of a young man's career as promising, we
mean that his abilities and opportunities are such
that he is likely to become rich or famous or powerful; and this judgment does not of course imply, so
far as we are concerned, any responsibility. It is
merely a prophecy based upon past performances
and proved qualities. But the career, which from the
standpoint of an outsider is merely an anticipation,
becomes for the young man himself a serious task.
For him, at all events, the better future will not
merely happen. He will have to do something to
deserve it. It may be wrecked by unforeseen obstacles, by unsuspected infirmities, or by some critical
error of judgment. So it is with the Promise of American life. From the point of view of an immigrant this
Promise may consist of the anticipation of a better
future, which he can share merely by taking up his
residence on American soil; but once he has become
an American; the Promise can no longer remain
merely an anticipation. It becomes in that case a
responsibility, which requires for its fulfillment a
certain land of behavior on the part of himself and
his fellow-Americans. And when we attempt to
define the Promise of American life, we are obliged,
also, to describe the kind of behavior which the fulfillment of the Promise demands. [. . .]

To conceive the better American future as a consummation which will take care of itself,—as the
necessary result of our customary conditions, institutions, and ideas,—persistence in such a conception is
admirably designed to deprive American life of any
promise at all. The better future which Americans
propose to build is nothing if not an idea which must
in certain essential respects emancipate them from
their past. American history contains much matter
for pride and congratulation, and much matter for
regret and humiliation. On the whole, it is a past of
which the loyal American has no reason to feel
ashamed, chiefly because it has throughout been
made better than it was by the vision of a better
future; and the American of to-day and tomorrow
must remain true to that traditional vision. He must
be prepared to sacrifice to that traditional vision even
the traditional American ways of realizing it. Such a
sacrifice is, I believe, coming to be demanded; and
unless it is made, American life will gradually cease
to have any specific Promise.

The only fruitful promise of which the life of any
individual or any nation can be possessed, is a promise determined by an ideal. Such a promise is to be
fulfilled, not by sanguine anticipations, not by a conservative imitation of past achievements, but by
laborious, single-minded, clear-sighted, and fearless
work. [. . .]

If [. . .] promise is anything more than a vision of
power and success, that addition must derive its value
from a purpose; because in the moral world the
future exists only as a workshop in which a purpose is
to be realized. Each of the several leading European
nations is possessed of a specific purpose determined
for the most part by the pressure of historical circumstances; but the American nation is committed
to a purpose which is not merely of historical manufacture. It is committed to the realization of the democratic ideal; and if its Promise is to be fulfilled, it
must be prepared to follow whithersoever that ideal
may lead. [. . .]

No more explicit expression has ever been given
to the way in which the Land of Promise was first

conceived by its children than in the "Letters of an American Farmer." This book was written by a French immigrant, Hector St. John de Crèvecœur before the Revolution, and is informed by an intense consciousness of the difference between conditions in the Old and in the New World. "What, then, is an American, this new man?" asks the Pennsylvanian farmer. He is either a European or the descendant of a European; hence the strange mixture of blood, which you will find in no other country. . . .

"He becomes an American by being received in the broad lap of our great *Alma Mater*. Here individuals of all nations are melted into a new race of men, whose labors and prosperity will one day cause great changes in the world. Here the rewards of his industry follow with equal steps the progress of his labor; this labor is founded on the basis of *self-interest*; can it want a stronger allurement? Wives and children, who before in vain demanded a morsel of bread, now fat and frolicsome, gladly help their father to clear those fields, whence exuberant crops are to arise to feed them all; without any part being claimed either by a despotic prince, a rich abbot, or a mighty lord. . . . The American is a new man, who acts upon new principles; he must therefore entertain new ideas and form new opinions. From involuntary idleness, servile dependence, penury, and useless labor, he has passed to toils of a very different nature rewarded by ample subsistence. This is an American." [. . .]

America has been peopled by Europeans primarily because they expected in that country to make more money more easily. To the European immigrant—that is, to the aliens who have been converted into Americans by the advantages of American life—the Promise of America has consisted largely in the opportunity which it offered of economic independence and prosperity. Whatever else the better future, of which Europeans anticipate the enjoyment in America, may contain, these converts will consider themselves cheated unless they are in a measure relieved of the curse of poverty.

This conception of American life and its Promise is as much alive to-day as it was in 1780. Its expression has no doubt been modified during four generations of democratic political independence, but the modification has consisted of an expansion and a development rather than of a transposition. The native American, like the alien immigrant, conceives

the better future which awaits himself and other men in America as fundamentally a future in which economic prosperity will be still more abundant and still more accessible than it has yet been either here or abroad. No alteration or attenuation of this demand has been permitted. With all their professions of Christianity their national idea remains thoroughly worldly. They do not want either for themselves or for their descendants an indefinite future of poverty and deprivation in this world, redeemed by beatitude in the next. The Promise, which bulks so large in their patriotic outlook, is a promise of comfort and prosperity for an ever increasing majority of good Americans. At a later stage of their social development they may come to believe that they have ordered a larger supply of prosperity than the economic factory is capable of producing. Those who are already rich and comfortable, and who are keenly alive to the difficulty of distributing these benefits over a larger social area, may come to tolerate the idea that poverty and want are an essential part of the social order. But as yet this traditional European opinion has found few echoes in America, even among the comfortable and the rich. The general belief still is that Americans are not destined to renounce, but to enjoy.

Let it be immediately added, however, that this economic independence and prosperity has always been absolutely associated in the American mind with free political institutions. The "American Farmer" traced the good fortune of the European immigrant in America, not merely to the abundance of economic opportunity, but to the fact that a ruling class of abbots and lords had no prior claim to a large share of the products of the soil. He did not attach the name of democracy to the improved political and social institutions of America, and when the political differences between Great Britain and her American colonies culminated in the Revolutionary War, the converted "American Farmer" was filled with anguish at this violent assertion of the "New Americanism." Nevertheless he was fully alive to the benefits which the immigrant enjoyed from a larger dose of political and social freedom; and so, of course, have been all the more intelligent of the European converts to Americanism. A certain number of them, particularly during the early years, came over less for the purpose of making money than for that of escaping from European political and religious persecution. America has always been conventionally conceived, not merely as a land of abundant and accessible economic opportunities, but also as a refuge for the oppressed; and the immigrant ships are crowded both during times of European famine and during times of political revolution and persecution.

Inevitably, however, this aspect of the American Promise has undergone certain important changes since the establishment of our national independence. When the colonists succeeded in emancipating themselves from political allegiance to Great Britain, they were confronted by the task of organizing a stable and efficient government without encroaching on the freedom, which was even at that time traditionally associated with American life. The task was by no means an easy one, and required for its performance the application of other political principles than that of freedom. The men who were responsible for this great work were not, perhaps, entirely candid in recognizing the profound modifications in their traditional ideas which their constructive political work had implied; but they were at all events fully aware of the great importance of their addition to the American idea. That idea, while not ceasing to be at bottom economic, became more than ever political and social in its meaning and contents. The Land of Freedom became in the course of time also the Land of Equality. The special American political system, the construction of which was predicted in the "Farmer's" assertion of the necessary novelty of American modes of thought and action, was made explicitly, if not uncompromisingly, democratic; and the success of this democratic political system was indissolubly associated in the American mind with the persistence of abundant and widely distributed economic prosperity. Our democratic institutions became in a sense the guarantee that prosperity would continue to be abundant and accessible. In case the majority of good Americans were not prosperous, there would be grave reasons for suspecting that our institutions were not doing their duty.

The more consciously democratic Americans became, however, the less they were satisfied with a conception of the Promised Land, which went no farther than a pervasive economic prosperity guaranteed by free institutions. The amelioration promised to aliens and to future Americans was to possess its moral and social aspects. The implication was, and still is, that by virtue of the more comfortable and less trammeled lives which Americans were enabled to lead, they would constitute a better society and would become in general a worthier set of men. The confidence which American institutions placed in the American citizen was considered equivalent to a greater faith in the excellence of human nature. In our favored land political liberty and economic opportunity were by a process of natural education inevitably making for individual and social amelioration. [. . .]

The increased momentum of American life, both in its particles and its mass, unquestionably has a considerable moral and social value. It is the beginning, the only possible beginning, of a better life for the people as individuals and for society. So long as the great majority of the poor in any country are inert and are laboring without any hope of substantial rewards in this world, the whole associated life of that community rests on an equivocal foundation. Its moral and social order is tied to an economic system which starves and mutilates the great majority of the population, and under such conditions its religion necessarily becomes a spiritual drug, administered for the purpose of subduing the popular discontent and relieving the popular misery. The only way the associated life of such a community can be radically improved is by the leavening of the inert popular mass. Their wants must be satisfied, and must be sharpened and increased with the habit of satisfaction. During the past hundred years every European state has made a great stride in the direction of arousing its poorer citizens to be more wholesomely active, discontented, and expectant; but our own country has succeeded in traveling farther in this direction than has any other, and it may well be proud of its achievement. That the American political and economic system has accomplished so much on behalf of the ordinary man does constitute the fairest hope that men have been justified in entertaining of a better worldly order; and any higher social achievement, which America may hereafter reach, must depend upon an improved perpetuation of this process. The mass of mankind must be aroused to still greater activity by a still more abundant satisfaction of their needs, and by a consequent increase of their aggressive discontent. [. . .]

The better future, whatever else it may bring, must bring at any rate a continuation of the good things of the past. The drama of its fulfillment must find an appropriate setting in the familiar American social and economic scenery. No matter how remote the end may be, no matter what unfamiliar sacrifices may eventually be required on its behalf, the substance of the existing achievement must constitute a veritable beginning, because on no other condition can the attribution of a peculiar Promise to American life find a specific warrant. On no other condition would our national Promise constitute more than an admirable but irrelevant moral and social aspiration.

The moral and social aspiration proper to American life is, of course, the aspiration vaguely described by the word democratic; and the actual achievement of the American nation points towards an adequate and fruitful definition of the democratic ideal. Americans are usually satisfied by a most inadequate verbal description of democracy, but their national achievement implies one which is much more comprehensive and formative. In order to be true to their past, the increasing comfort and economic independence of an ever increasing proportion of the population must be secured, and it must be secured by a combination of individual effort and proper political organization. Above all, however, this economic and political system must be made to secure results of moral and social value. It is the seeking of such results which converts democracy from a political system into a constructive social ideal; and the more the ideal significance of the American national Promise is asserted and emphasized, the greater will become the importance of securing these moral and social benefits.

The fault in the vision of our national future possessed by the ordinary American does not consist in the expectation of some continuity of achievement. It consists rather in the expectation that the familiar benefits will continue to accumulate automatically. In his mind the ideal Promise is identified with the processes and conditions which hitherto have very much simplified its fulfillment, and he fails sufficiently to realize that the conditions and processes are one thing and the ideal Promise quite another. Moreover, these underlying social and economic conditions are themselves changing, in such wise that hereafter the ideal Promise, instead of being automatically fulfilled, may well be automatically stifled. [. . .]

Economic conditions have been profoundly modified, and American political and social problems have been modified with them. The Promise of American life must depend less than it did upon the virgin wilderness and the Atlantic Ocean, for the virgin wilderness has disappeared, and the Atlantic Ocean has become merely a big channel. The same results can no longer be achieved by the same easy methods. Ugly obstacles have jumped into view, and ugly obstacles are peculiarly dangerous to a person who is sliding down hill. The man who is clambering up hill is in a much better position to evade or overcome them. Americans will possess a safer as well as a worthier vision of their national Promise as soon as they give it a house on a hill-top rather than in a valley. [. . .]

A numerous and powerful group of reformers has been collecting whose whole political policy and action is based on the conviction that the "common people" have not been getting the Square Deal to which they are entitled under the American system; and these reformers are carrying with them a constantly increasing body of public opinion. A considerable proportion of the American people is beginning to exhibit economic and political, as well as personal, discontent. A generation ago the implication was that if a man remained poor and needy, his poverty was his own fault, because the American system was giving all its citizens a fair chance. Now, however, the discontented poor are beginning to charge their poverty to an unjust political and economic organization, and reforming agitators do not hesitate to support them in this contention. Manifestly a threatened obstacle has been raised against the anticipated realization of our national Promise. Unless the great majority of Americans not only have, but believe they have, a fair chance, the better American future will be dangerously compromised. [. . .]

The more enlightened reformers are conscious of the additional dignity and value which the popularity of reform has bestowed upon the American idea, but they still fail to realize the deeper implications of their own programme. In abandoning the older conception of an automatic fulfillment of our national destiny, they have abandoned more of the traditional American point of view than they are aware. The traditional

American optimistic fatalism was not of accidental origin, and it cannot be abandoned without involving in its fall some other important ingredients in the accepted American tradition. Not only was it dependent on economic conditions which prevailed until comparatively recent times, but it has been associated with certain erroneous but highly cherished political theories. It has been wrought into the fabric of our popular economic and political ideas to such an extent that its overthrow necessitates a partial revision of some of the most important articles in the traditional American creed.

The extent and the character of this revision may be inferred from a brief consideration of the effect upon the substance of our national Promise of an alteration in its proposed method of fulfillment. The substance of our national Promise has consisted, as we have seen, of an improving popular economic condition, guaranteed by democratic political institutions, and resulting in moral and social amelioration. These manifold benefits were to be obtained merely by liberating the enlightened self-interest of the American people. The beneficent result followed inevitably from the action of wholly selfish motives— provided, of course, the democratic political system of equal rights was maintained in its integrity. The fulfillment of the American Promise was considered inevitable because it was based upon a combination of self-interest and the natural goodness of human nature. On the other hand, if the fulfillment of our national Promise can no longer be considered inevitable, if it must be considered as equivalent to a conscious national purpose instead of an inexorable national destiny, the implication necessarily is that the trust reposed in individual self-interest has been in some measure betrayed. No preestablished harmony can then exist between the free and abundant satisfaction of private needs and the accomplishment of a morally and socially desirable result. The Promise of American life is to be fulfilled—not merely by a maximum amount of economic freedom, but by a certain measure of discipline; not merely by the abundant satisfaction of individual desires, but by a large measure of individual subordination and self-denial. And this necessity of subordinating the satisfaction of individual desires to the fulfillment of a national purpose is attached particularly to the absorbing occupation of the American people,—the occupation, viz.: of accumulating wealth. The automatic fulfillment of the American national Promise is to be abandoned, if at all, precisely because the traditional American confidence in individual freedom has resulted in a morally and socially undesirable distribution of wealth.

In making the concluding statement of the last paragraph I am venturing, of course, upon very debatable ground. Neither can I attempt in this immediate connection to offer any justification for the statement which might or should be sufficient to satisfy a stubborn skeptic. I must be content for the present with the bare assertion that the prevailing abuses and sins, which have made reform necessary, are all of them associated with the prodigious concentration of wealth, and of the power exercised by wealth, in the hands of a few men. I am far from believing that this concentration of economic power is wholly an undesirable thing, and I am also far from believing that the men in whose hands this power is concentrated deserve, on the whole, any exceptional moral reprobation for the manner in which it has been used. In certain respects they have served their country well, and in almost every respect their moral or immoral standards are those of the great majority of their fellow-countrymen. But it is none the less true that the political corruption, the unwise economic organization, and the legal support afforded to certain economic privileges are all under existing conditions due to the malevolent social influence of individual and incorporated American wealth; and it is equally true that these abuses, and the excessive "money power" with which they are associated, have originated in the peculiar freedom which the American tradition and organization have granted to the individual. Up to a certain point that freedom has been and still is beneficial. Beyond that point it is not merely harmful; it is by way of being fatal. Efficient regulation there must be; and it must be regulation which will strike, not at the symptoms of the evil, but at its roots. The existing concentration of wealth and financial power in the hands of a few irresponsible men is the inevitable outcome of the chaotic individualism of our political and economic organization, while at the same time it is inimical to democracy, because it tends to erect political abuses and social inequalities into a system. The inference which follows may be disagreeable, but it is not to be escaped. In becoming responsible for the subordination of the individual to the demand of a dominant and constructive national purpose, the American state will in effect be making itself responsible for a morally and socially desirable distribution of wealth.

The consequences, then, of converting our American national destiny into a national purpose are beginning to be revolutionary. When the Promise of American life is conceived as a national ideal, whose fulfillment is a matter of artful and laborious work, the effect thereof is substantially to identify the national purpose with the social problem. What the American people of the present and the future have really been promised by our patriotic prophecies is an attempt to solve that problem. They have been promised on American soil comfort, prosperity, and the opportunity for self-improvement; and the lesson of the existing crisis is that such a Promise can never be redeemed by an indiscriminate individual scramble for wealth. The individual competition, even when it starts under fair conditions and rules, results, not only, as it should, in the triumph of the strongest, but in the attempt to perpetuate the victory; and it is this attempt which must be recognized and forestalled in the interest of the American national purpose. The way to realize a purpose is, not to leave it to chance, but to keep it loyally in mind, and adopt means proper to the importance and the difficulty of the task. No voluntary association of individuals, resourceful and disinterested though they be, is competent to assume the responsibility. The problem belongs to the American national democracy, and its solution must be attempted chiefly by means of official national action. [. . .]

Chapter Five:
The Contemporary Situation

[. . .] Although nobody in 1870 suspected it, the United States was entering upon a new phase of its economic career; and the new economy was bringing with it radical social changes. Even before the outbreak of the Civil War the rich and fertile states of the Middle West had become well populated. They had passed from an almost exclusively agricultural economy to one which was much more largely urban and

industrial. The farms had become well-equipped; large cities were being built up; factories of various kinds were being established; and most important of all, the whole industrial organization of the country was being adjusted to transportation by means of the railroad. An industrial community, which was, comparatively speaking, well-organized and well-furnished with machinery, was taking the place of the agricultural community of 1830–1840, which was incoherent and scattered and which lacked everything except energy and opportunity. Such an increase of organization, capital, and equipment necessarily modified the outlook and interests of the people of the Middle West. While still retaining many of their local traits, their point of view had been approaching in certain respects that of the inhabitants of the East. They had ceased to be pioneers. [. . .]

After 1870, the pioneer farmer was much less dependent than he had been upon local conditions and markets, and upon the unaided exertions of himself and his neighbors. He bought and sold in the markets of the world. [. . .] The pioneer had enjoyed his day, and his day was over. The Jack-of-all-trades no longer possessed an important economic function. The average farmer was, of course, still obliged to be many kinds of a rough mechanic, but for the most part he was nothing more than a farmer. Unskilled labor began to mean labor which was insignificant and badly paid. Industrial economy demanded the expert with his high and special standards of achievement. The railroads and factories could not be financed and operated without the assistance of well-paid and well-trained men, who could do one or two things remarkably well, and who did not pretend to do much of anything else. These men had to retain great flexibility and an easy adaptability of intelligence, because American industry and commerce remained very quick in its movements. The machinery which they handled was less permanent, and was intended to be less permanent than the machinery which was considered economical in Europe. But although they had to avoid routine and business rigidity on the penalty of utter failure, still they belonged essentially to a class of experts. Like all experts, they had to depend, not upon mere energy, untutored enthusiasm, and good-will, but upon careful training and single-minded devotion to a special task, and at the same time proper provision had to be made for coördinating the results of this highly specialized work. More complete organization necessarily accompanied specialization. The expert became a part of a great industrial machine. His individuality tended to disappear in his work. His interests became those of a group. Imperative economic necessities began to classify the individuals composing American society in the same way, if not to the same extent, that they had been classified in Europe.

This was a result which had never entered into the calculations of the pioneer Democrat. He had disliked specialization, because, as he thought, it narrowed and impoverished the individual: and he distrusted permanent and official forms of organization, because, as he thought, they hampered the individual. His whole political, social, and economic outlook embodied a society of energetic, optimistic, and prosperous democrats, united by much the same interests, occupations, and point of view. Each of these democrats was to be essentially an all-round man. His conception of all-round manhood was somewhat limited; but it meant at least a person who was expansive in feeling, who was enough of a business man successfully to pursue his own interests, and enough of a politician to prevent any infringement or perversion of his rights. [. . .] [F]or a long time the vision remained sufficiently true. The typical American democrat described by De Tocqueville corresponded very well with the vision of the pioneer; and he did not disappear during the succeeding generation. For many years millions of Americans of much the same pattern were rewarded for their democratic virtue in an approximately similar manner. Of course some people were poor, and some people were rich; but there was no class of the very rich, and the poverty of the poor was generally their own fault. Opportunity knocked at the door of every man, and the poor man of to-day was the prosperous householder of to-morrow. For a long time American social and economic conditions were not merely fluid, but consistent and homogeneous, and the vision of the pioneer was fulfilled. Nevertheless, this condition was essentially transient. It contained within itself the seeds of its own dissolution and transformation; and this transformation made headway just as soon as, and just as far as, economic conditions began to prefer the man who was capable of specializing his work, and of organizing it with the work of his fellows. [. . .]

Before seeking to trace the consequences and the significance of this specialized organization of American practical affairs, we must examine its origin with some care. An exact and complete understanding thereof will in itself afford an unmistakable hint of the way in which its consequences are to be appraised, and wherever necessary, corrected. The great and increasing influence of the new unofficial leaders has been due not only to economic conditions and to individual initiative, but to the nature of our political ideas and institutions. The traditional American theory was that the individual should have a free hand. In so far as he was subject to public regulation and control such control should be exercised by local authorities, whereof the result would be a happy combination of individual prosperity and public weal. But this expectation, as we have seen, has proved to be erroneous. While it has, indeed, resulted in individual prosperity, the individual who has reaped most of the prosperity is not the average, but the special man; and however the public may have benefited from the process, the benefit is mixed with so many drawbacks that, even if it may not be wholly condemned, it certainly cannot be wholly approved. The plain fact is that the individual in freely and energetically pursuing his own private purposes has not been the inevitable public benefactor assumed by the traditional American interpretation of democracy. No doubt he has incidentally accomplished, in the pursuit of his own aggrandizement, certain manifest public benefits; but wherever public and private advantages have conflicted, he has naturally preferred the latter. And under our traditional political system there was, until recently, no effective way of correcting his preference.

As long as the economic opportunities of American life consisted chiefly in the appropriation and improvement of uncultivated land, the average energetic man had no difficulty in obtaining his fair share of the increasing American economic product; but the time came when such opportunities, although still important, were dwarfed by other opportunities, incident to the development of a more mature economic system. These opportunities, which were, of course, connected with the manufacturing, industrial, and technical development of the country, demanded under American conditions a very special type of man—the man who would bring to his task not merely energy, but unscrupulous devotion, originality, daring, and in the course of time a large fund of instructive experience. [. . .]

The industrious and thrifty farmer could be tolerably sure of a modest competence, due partly to his own efforts, and partly to the increased value of his land in a more populous community; but the business man had no such security. In his case it was war to the knife. He was presented with a choice between aggressive daring business operations, and financial insignificance or ruin. [. . .]

If, however, the fluid and fluctuating nature of American economic conditions and the fierceness of American competitive methods turned business into a state of dangerous and aggressive warfare, the steady and enormous expansion of the American markets made the rewards of victory correspondingly great. Not only was the population of the country increasing at an enormous rate, but the demand for certain necessary products, services, and commodities was increasing at a higher rate than the population. The American people were still a most homogeneous collection of human beings. They wanted very much the same things; they wanted more of these things year after year; and they immediately rewarded any cheapening of the product by buying it in much larger quantities. The great business opportunities of American life consisted, consequently, in supplying some popular or necessary article or service at a cheaper price than that at which any one else could furnish it; and the great effort of American business men was, of course, to obtain some advantage over their competitors in producing such an article or in supplying such a service. The best result of this condition was a constant improvement in the mechanism of production. Cheapness was found to depend largely upon the efficient use of machinery, and the efficient use of machinery was found to depend upon constant wear and quick replacement by a better machine. But while the economic advantage of the exhausting use and the constant improvement of machinery was the most important economic discovery of the American business man, he was also encouraged by his surroundings to seek economies in other and less legitimate ways. It was all very well to multiply machines and make them more efficient, but similar improvements were open to competitors. The great object was to obtain some advantage which was denied to your competitors. Then the business man could not only secure his own position, but utterly rout and annihilate his adversaries. [. . .]

The great American industrial leaders have accumulated fortunes for which there is also no precedent on the part of men who exercise no official political power. These inequalities are the result of the organization of American industry on almost a national scale,—an organization which was brought about as a means of escape from the intolerable evils of unregulated competition. Every aspect of American business methods has helped to make them inevitable, and the responsibility for them must be distributed over the whole business and social fabric. But in spite of the fact that they have originated as the inevitable result of American business methods and political ideas and institutions, they constitute a serious problem for a democracy to face; and this problem has many different aspects. Its most serious aspect is constituted by the sheer size of the resulting inequalities. The rich men and the big corporations have become too wealthy and powerful for their official standing in American life. They have not obeyed the laws. They have attempted to control the official makers, administrators, and expounders of the law. They have done little to allay and much to excite the resentment and suspicion. In short, while their work has been constructive from an economic and industrial standpoint, it has made for political corruption and social disintegration. Children, as they are, of the traditional American individualistic institutions, ideas, and practices, they have turned on their parents and dealt them an ugly wound. Either these economic monsters will destroy the system of ideas, institutions, and practices out of which they have issued or else be destroyed by them. [. . .]

Not only did he no longer give as much time to politics as he formerly did, but as his business increased in size and scope, he found his own interests by way of conflicting at many points with the laws of his country and with its well-being. He did not take this conflict very seriously. He was still reflected in the mirror of his own mind as a patriotic and a public-spirited citizen; but at the same time his ambition was to conquer, and he did not scruple to sacrifice both the law and the public weal to his own prosperity. All unknowingly he began to testify to a growing and a decisive division between the two primary interests of American life,—between the interest of the individual business man and the interest of the body politic; and he became a living refutation of the amiable theories of the Jacksonian Democrat that the two must substantially coincide. The business man had become merely a business man, and the conditions which had made him less of a politician had also had its effect upon the men whose business was that of politics. Just as business had become specialized and organized, so politics also became subject to specialization and organization. The appearance of the "Captain of Industry" was almost coincident with the appearance of the "Boss."

There has been a disposition to treat the "Boss" chiefly as the political creature of the corrupt corporation; and it is undoubtedly true that one of the most important functions of the municipal and state "Bosses" has been that of conducting negotiations with the corporations. But to consider the specialized organization of our local politics as the direct result of specialized organization of American business is wholly to misunderstand its significance. The two processes are the parallel effects of the same conditions and ideas working in different fields. Business efficiency under the conditions prevailing in our political and economic fabric demanded the "Captain of Industry." Political efficiency under our system of local government demanded the "Boss." The latter is an independent power who has his own special reasons for existence. He put in an embryonic appearance long before the large corporations had obtained anything like their existing power in American politics; and he will survive in some form their reduction to political insignificance. He has been a genuine and within limits a useful product of the American democracy; and it would be fatal either to undervalue or to misunderstand him. [. . .]

The state constitutions were all very much influenced by the Federal instrument, but in the copies many attempts were made to improve upon the model. The Democracy had come to believe that the Federal Constitution tended to encourage independence and even special efficiency on the part of Federal officials; and it proposed to correct such an erroneous tendency in the more thoroughly democratic state governments. [. . .]

The more "democratic" these constitutions became, the more clearly the Democracy showed its disposition to distrust its own representatives, and to deprive them of any chance of being genuinely representative.

The object of the Jacksonian Democrat in framing constitutions of this kind was to keep political power in the hands of the "plain people," and to forestall the domination of administrative and legislative specialists. The effect was precisely the opposite. They afforded the political specialist a wonderful opportunity. The ordinary American could not pretend to give as much time to politics as the smooth operation of this complicated machine demanded; and little by little there emerged in different parts of the country a class of politicians who spent all their time in nominating and electing candidates to these numerous offices. The officials so elected, instead of being responsible to the people, were responsible to the men to whom they owed their offices; and their own individual official power was usually so small that they could not put what little independence they possessed to any good use. As a matter of fact, they used their official powers chiefly for the benefit of their creators. They appointed to office the men whom the "Bosses" selected. They passed the measures which the machine demanded. In this way the professional politician gradually obtained a stock of political goods wherewith to maintain and increase his power. Reenforced by the introduction of the spoils system first into the state and then into the Federal civil services, a process of local political organization began after 1830 to make rapid headway. Local leaders appeared in different parts of the country who little by little relieved the farmer and the business man of the cares and preoccupations of government. In the beginning the most efficient of these politicians were usually Jacksonian Democrats, and they ruled both in the name of the people and by virtue of a sturdy popular following. They gradually increased in power, until in the years succeeding the war they became the dominant influence in local American politics, and had won the right to be called something which they would never have dared to call themselves, viz. a governing class. [. . .]

American democracy was divided politically into a multitude of small groups, organized chiefly for the purpose of securing the local and individual interests of these groups and their leaders, and supported by local and personal feeling, political patronage, and petty "graft." These groups were associated with both parties, and merely made the use of partisan ties and cries to secure the cooperation of more disinterested voters. The result was that so far as American political representation was merely local, it was generally corrupt, and it was always selfish. The leader's power depended absolutely on an appeal to the individual, neighborhood, and class interests of his followers. They were the "people"; he was the popular tribune. He could not retain his power for a month, in case he failed to subordinate every larger interest to the flattery, cajolery, and nourishment of his local clan. Thus the local representative system was poisoned at its source. The alderman, the assemblyman, or the congressman, even if he were an honest man, represented little more than the political powers controlling his district; and to be disinterested in local politics was usually equivalent to being indifferent. [. . .]

His secretiveness and his unpopularity point to one of the most important functions of the municipal and state "Bosses," to which as yet only incidental reference has been made. The "Boss" became the man who negotiated with the corporations, and through whom they obtained what they wanted. [. . .]

This alliance between the political machines and the big corporations—particularly those who operate railroads or control municipal franchises—was an alliance between two independent and coordinate powers in the kingdom of American practical affairs. The political "Boss" did not create the industrial leader for his own good purposes. Neither did the industrial leader create the machine and its "Boss," although he has done much to confirm the latter's influence. Each of them saw an opportunity to turn to his own account the individualistic "freedom" of American politics and industry. Each of them was enabled by the character of our political traditions to obtain an amount of power which the originators of those political ideas never anticipated, and which, if not illegal, was entirely outside the law. It so happened that the kind of power which each obtained was very useful to the other. A corporation which derived its profits from public franchises, or from a business transacted in many different states, found the purchase of a local or state machine well within its means and well according to its interests. The professional politicians who had embarked in politics as a business and who were making what they could out

of it for themselves and their followers, could not resist this unexpected and lucrative addition to their market. But it must be remembered that the alliance was founded on interest rather than association, on mutual agreement rather than on any effective subordination one to another. A certain change in conditions might easily make their separate interests diverge, and abstract all the profits from their traffic. [. . .] If anything happened, for instance, to make inter-state railroad corporations less dependent on the state governments, they would no longer need the expense of subsidizing the state machines. There are signs at the present time that these interests are diverging, and that such alliances will be less dangerous in the future than they have been in the past. But even if the alliance is broken, the peculiar unofficial organization of American industry and politics will persist, and will constitute, both in its consequences and its significance, two of our most important national problems.

It would be as grave a mistake, however, absolutely to condemn this process of political organization as it would absolutely to condemn the process of industrial organization. The huge corporation and the political machine were both created to satisfy a real and a permanent need—the needs of specialized leadership and associated action in these two primary American activities. That in both of these cases the actual method of organization has threatened vital public interests, and even the very future of democracy has been due chiefly to the disregard by the official American political system of the necessity and the consequences of specialized leadership and associated action. The political system was based on the assumption that the individualism it encouraged could be persuaded merely by the power of words to respect the public interest, that public officials could be deprived of independence and authority for the real benefit of the "plain people," and that the "plain people" would ask nothing from the government but their legal rights. These assumptions were all erroneous; and when associated action and specialized leadership became necessary in local American politics, the leaders and their machine took advantage of the defective official system to build up an unofficial system, better suited to actual popular needs. The "people" wanted the government to do something for them, and the politicians made their living and served their country by satisfying the want. To be sure, the "people" they benefited were a small minority of the whole population whose interests were far from being the public interest; but it was none the less natural that the people, whoever they were, should want the government to do more for them than to guarantee certain legal rights, and it was inevitable that they should select leaders who could satisfy their positive, if selfish, needs. [. . .]

One other decisive instance of this specialized organization of American activity remains to be considered—that of the labor unions. The power which the unions have obtained in certain industrial centers and the tightness of their organization would have seemed anomalous to the good Jacksonian Democrat. From his point of view the whole American democracy was a kind of labor union whose political constitution provided for a substantially equal division of the products of labor; and if the United States had remained as much of an agricultural community as it was in 1830, the Jacksonian system would have preserved a much higher degree of serviceability. [. . .]

But when the mechanic or the day-laborer gathered into the cities, he soon discovered that life in a democratic state by no means deprived him of special class interests. No doubt he was at worst paid better than his European analogues, because the demand for labor in a new country was continually outrunning the supply; but on occasions he was, like his employer, threatened with merciless competition. The large and continuous stream of foreign immigrants, whose standards of living were in the beginning lower than those which prevailed in this country, were, particularly in hard times, a constant menace not merely to his advancement, but to the stability of his economic situation; and he began to organize partly for the purpose of protecting himself against such competition. During the past thirty years the work of organization has made enormous strides; and it has been much accelerated by the increasing industrial power of huge corporations. The mechanic and the laborer have come to believe that they must meet organization with organization, and discipline with discipline. Their object in forming trade associations has been militant. Their purpose has been to conquer a larger share of the economic product by aggressive associated action.

They have been very successful in accomplishing their object. In spite of the flood of alien immigration the American laborer has been able to earn an almost constantly increasing wage, and he devoutly thinks that his unions have been the chief agency of his stronger economic position. He believes in unionism, consequently, as he believes in nothing else. He is, indeed, far more aggressively preoccupied with his class, as contrasted with his individual interests, than are his employers. He has no respect for the traditional American individualism as applied to his own social and economic standing. Whenever he has had the power, he has suppressed competition as ruthlessly as have his employers. [. . .]

The most serious danger to the American democratic future which may issue from aggressive and unscrupulous unionism consists in the state of mind of which mob-violence is only one expression. The militant unionists are beginning to talk and believe as if they were at war with the existing social and political order—as if the American political system was as inimical to their interests as would be that of any European monarchy or aristocracy. The idea is being systematically propagated that the American government is one which favors the millionaire rather than the wage-earner; and the facts which either superficially or really support this view are sufficiently numerous to win for it an apparently increasing number of adherents. The union laborer is tending to become suspicious, not merely of his employer, but of the constitution of American society. His morals are becoming those of men engaged in a struggle for life. The manifestations of this state of mind in action are not very numerous. although on many occasions they they have worn a sufficiently sinister aspect. But they are numerous enough to demand serious the literature popular among the unionists is a literature, not merely of discontent, but sometimes of revolt.

Whether this aggressive unionism will ever become popular enough to endanger the foundations of the American political and social order, I shall not predict. The practical dangers resulting from it at any one time are largely neutralized by the mere size of the country and its extremly complicated social and industrial economy. The menace it contains to the nation as a whole can hardly become very critical as long as so large a proportion of the American voters are land-owning farmers. But while the general national well-being seems sufficiently protected for the present against the aggressive assertion of the class interests of the unionists, the local public interest of particular states and cities cannot be considered as anywhere near so secure; and in any event the existence of aggressive discontent on the part of the unionists must constitute a serious problem for the American legislator and statesman. [. . .]

The large corporations and the unions occupy in certain respects a similar relation to the American political system. Their advocates both believe in associated action for themselves and in competition for their adversaries. They both demand governmental protection and recognition, but resent the notion of efficient governmental regulation. They have both reached their existing power, partly because of the weakness of the state governments, to which they are legally subject, and they both are opposed to any interference by the Federal government—except exclusively on their own behalf. Yet they both have become so very powerful that they are frequently too strong for the state governments, and in different ways they both traffic for their own benefit with the politicians, who so often control those governments. Here, of course, the parallelism ends and the divergence begins. The corporations have apparently the best of the situation, because existing institutions are more favorable to the interests of the corporations than to the interests of the unionists; but on the other hand, the unions have the immense advantage of a great and increasing numerical strength. They are beginning to use the suffrage to promote a class interest, though how far they will travel on this perilous path remains doubtful. In any event, it is obvious that the development in this country of two such powerful and unscrupulous and well-organized special interests has created a condition which the founders of the Republic never anticipated, and which demands as a counterpoise a more effective body of national opinion, and a more powerful organization of the national interest.

The corporation, the politician, and the union laborer are all illustrations of the organization of men representing fundamental interests for special purposes. The specialization of American society has not, however, stopped with its specialized organization. A similar process has been taking place in the different professions, arts, and trades; and of these much the most important is the gradual transformation of the function of the lawyer in the American political system. He no longer either performs the same office or occupies the same place in the public mind as he did before the Civil War; and the nature and meaning of this change cannot be understood without some preliminary consideration of the important part which American lawyers have played in American political history.

The importance of that part is both considerable and peculiar—as is the debt of gratitude which the American people owe to American lawyers. They founded the Republic, and they have always governed it. Some few generals, and even one colonel, have been elected to the Presidency of the United States; and occasionally business men of one kind or another have prevailed in local politics; but really important political action in our country has almost always been taken under the influence of lawyers. On the whole, American laws have been made by lawyers; they have been executed by lawyers; and, of course, they have been expounded by lawyers. Their predominance has been practically complete; and so far as I know, it has been unprecedented. [. . .]

The American would claim, of course, that the unprecedented prominence of the lawyer in American politics is to be explained on the ground that the American government is a government by law. The lawyer is necessarily of subordinate importance in any political system tending towards absolutism. He is even of subordinate importance in a liberal system such as that of Great Britain, where Crown and Parliament, acting together, have the power to enact any desired legislation. The Federal Constitution, on the other hand, by establishing the Supreme Court as the interpreter of the Fundamental Law, and as a separate and independent department of the government, really made the American lawyer responsible for the future of the country. In so far as the Constitution continues to prevail, the Supreme Court becomes the final arbiter of the destinies of the United States. Whenever its action can be legally invoked, it can, if necessary, declare the will of either or both the President and Congress of no effect; and inasmuch as almost every important question of public policy raises corresponding questions of Constitutional interpretation, its possible or actual influence dominates American political discussion. Thus the lawyer, when consecrated as Justice of the Supreme Court, has become the High Priest of our political faith. He sits in the sanctuary and guards the sacred rights which have been enshrined in the ark of the Constitution. [. . .]

The statesman, who is not a lawyer, suffers under many disadvantages—not the least of which is the suspicion wherewith he is regarded by his legal fellow-statesmen. When they talk about a government by law, they really mean a government by lawyers; and they are by way of believing that government by anybody but lawyers is really unsafe.

The Constitution bestowed upon the American lawyer a constructive political function; and this function has been confirmed and even enlarged by American political custom and practice. The work of finally interpreting the Federal Constitution has rarely been either conceived or executed in a merely negative spirit. The construction, which successive generations of Supreme Court Justices have placed upon the instrument, has tended to enlarge its scope, and make it a legal garment, which was being better cut to fit the American political and economic organism. In its original form, and to a certain extent in its present form, the Constitution was in many respects an ambiguous document which might have been interpreted along several different lines; and the Supreme Court in its official expositions has been influenced by other than strictly legal and verbal reasons—by considerations of public welfare or by general political ideas. But such constructive interpretations have been most cautiously and discreetly admitted. In proclaiming them, the Supreme Court has usually represented a substantial consensus of the better legal opinion of the time; and constructions of this kind are accepted and confirmed only when any particular decision is the expression of some permanent advance or achievement in political thinking by the American lawyer. It becomes consequently of the utmost importance that American lawyers should really represent the current of national political opinion. The Supreme Court has been, on the whole, one of the great successes of the American political system, because the lawyers, whom it represented, were themselves representative of the ideas and interests of the bulk of their fellow-countrymen; and if for any reason they become less representative, a dangerous division would be created between the body

of American public opinion and its official and final legal expositors. If the lawyers have any reason to misinterpret a serious political problem, the difficulty of dealing therewith is much increased, because in addition to the ordinary risks of political therapeutics there will be added that of a false diagnosis by the family doctor. The adequacy of the lawyers training, the disinterestedness of their political motives, the fairness of their mental outlook, and the closeness of their contact with the national public opinion—all become matters of grave public concern.

It can be fairly asserted that the qualifications of the American lawyer for his traditional task as the official interpreter and guide of American constitutional democracy have been considerably impaired. Whatever his qualifications have been for the task (and they have, perhaps, been overestimated) they are no longer as substantial as they were. Not only has the average lawyer become a less representative citizen, but a strictly legal training has become a less desirable preparation for the candid consideration of contemporary political problems.

Since 1870 the lawyer has been traveling in the same path as the business man and the politician. He has tended to become a professional specialist, and to give all his time to his specialty. The greatest and most successful American lawyers no longer become legislators and statesmen as they did in the time of Daniel Webster. They no longer obtain the experience of men and affairs which an active political life brings with it. Their professional practice, whenever they are successful, is so remunerative and so exacting that they cannot afford either the time or the money which a political career demands. The most eminent American lawyers usually remain lawyers all their fives; and if they abandon private practice at all, it is generally for the purpose of taking a seat on the Bench. Like nearly all other Americans they have found rigid specialization a condition of success.

A considerable proportion of our legislators and executives continue to be lawyers, but the difference is that now they are more likely to be less successful lawyers. Knowledge of the law and a legal habit of mind still have a great practical value in political work; and the professional politicians, who are themselves rarely men of legal training, need the services of lawyers whose legal methods are not attenuated by scruples. Lawyers of this class occupy the same relation to the local political "Bosses" as the European lawyer used to occupy in the court of the absolute monarch. He phrases the legislation which the ruler decides to be of private or public benefit; and he acts frequently as his employer's official mouthpiece and special pleader. [. . .]

The tendency of the legally trained mind is inevitably and extremely conservative. So far as reform consists in the enforcement of the law, it is, of course, supported by the majority of successful lawyers; but so far as reform has come to mean a tendency to political or economic reorganization, it has to face the opposition of the bulk of American legal opinion. The existing political order has been created by lawyers; and they naturally believe somewhat obsequiously in a system for which they are responsible, and from which they benefit. This government by law, of which they boast, is not only a government by lawyers, but is a government in the interest of litigation. It makes legal advice more constantly essential to the corporation and the individual than any European political system. The lawyer, just as much as the millionaire and the politician, has reaped a bountiful harvest from the inefficiency and irresponsibility of American state governments, and from the worship of individual rights.

They have corporations in Europe, but they have nothing corresponding to the American corporation lawyer. The ablest American lawyers have been retained by the special interests. In some cases they have been retained to perform tasks which must have been repugnant to honest men; but that is not the most serious aspect of the situation. The retainer which the American legal profession has accepted from the corporations inevitably increases its natural tendency to a blind conservatism; and its influence has been used not for the purpose of extricating the large corporations from their dubious and dangerous legal situation, but for the purpose of keeping them entangled in its meshes. At a time when the public interest needs a candid reconsideration of the basis and the purpose of the American legal system, they have either opposed or contributed little to the essential work, and in adopting this course they have betrayed the interests of their more profitable clients—the large corporations themselves—whose one chance of perpetuation depends upon political and legal reconstruction. [. . .]

The changes which have been taking place in industrial and political and social conditions have all tended to impair the consistency of feeling characteristic of the first phase of American national democracy. Americans are divided from one another much more than they were during the Middle Period by differences of interest, of intellectual outlook, of moral and technical standards, and of manner of life. Grave inequalities of power and deep-lying differences of purpose have developed in relation of the several primary American activities. The millionaire, the "Boss," the union laborer, and the lawyer, have all taken advantage of the loose American political organization to promote somewhat unscrupulously their own interests, and to obtain special sources of power and profit at the expense of a wholesome national balance. But the foregoing examples of specialized organization and purposes do not stand alone. They are the most conspicuous and the most troublesome because of the power wielded by those particular classes, and because they can claim for their purposes the support of certain aspects of the American national tradition. Yet the same process has been taking place in all the other departments of American social and intellectual life. Technical experts of all kinds—engineers, men of letters, and artists—have all of them been asserting much more vigorously their own special interests and purposes. In so asserting themselves they cannot claim the support of the American national democratic convention. On the contrary, the proclamation of high technical standards and of insistent individual purposes is equivalent to a revolt from the traditions of the Middle Period, which were all in favor of cheap work and the average worker. But different as is the situation of these technical experts, the fundamental meaning of their self-assertion is analogous to that of the millionaire and the "Boss." The vast incoherent mass of the American people is falling into definite social groups, which restrict and define the mental outlook and social experience of their members. The all-round man of the innocent Middle Period has become the exception. The earlier homogeneity of American society has been impaired, and no authoritative and edifying, but conscious, social ideal has as yet taken its place.

The specialized organization of American industry, politics, and labor, and the increasingly severe special discipline imposed upon the individual, are not to be considered as evils. On the contrary, they are indications of greater practical efficiency, and they contain a promise of individual moral and intellectual emancipation. But they have their serious and perilous aspects, because no sufficient provision has been made for them in the national democratic tradition. What it means is that the American nation is being confronted by a problem which the earlier national democracy expected to avoid—the social problem. By the social problem is usually meant the problem of poverty; but grave inequalities of wealth are merely the most dangerous and distressing expression of fundamental differences among the members of a society of interest and of intellectual and moral standards. In its deepest aspect, consequently, the social problem is the problem of preventing such divisions from dissolving the society into which they enter—of keeping such a highly differentiated society fundamentally sound and whole.

In this country the solution of the social problem demands the substitution of a conscious social ideal for the earlier instinctive homogeneity of the American nation. That homogeneity has disappeared never to return. We should not want it to return, because it was dependent upon too many sacrifices of individual purpose and achievement. But a democracy cannot dispense with the solidarity which it imparted to American life, and in one way or another such solidarity must be restored. There is only one way in which it can be restored, and that is by means of a democratic social ideal, which shall give consistency to American social life, without entailing any essential sacrifice of desirable individual and class distinctions. I have used the word "restoration" to describe this binding and healing process; but the consistency which would result from the loyal realization of a comprehensive coherent democratic social ideal would differ radically from the earlier American homogeneity of feeling. The solidarity which it would impart to American society would have its basis in feeling and its results in good fellowship; but it must always remain a promise and constructive ideal rather than a finished performance. The social problem must, as long as societies continue to endure, be solved afresh by almost every generation; and the one chance of progress depends both upon an invincible loyalty to a constructive social ideal and

upon a correct understanding by the new generation of the actual experience of its predecessors. [. . .]

Chapter Six:
Reform and the Reformers

[. . .] No substantial progress had been made in the direction of reform until it began to be understood that here, also, a national responsibility existed, which demanded an exercise of the powers of the central government. Reform is both meaningless and powerless unless the Jeffersonian principle of non-interference is abandoned. The experience of the last generation plainly shows that the American economic and social system cannot be allowed to take care of itself, and that the automatic harmony of the individual and the public interest, which is the essence of the Jeffersonian democratic creed, has proved to be an illusion. Interference with the natural course of individual and popular action there must be in the public interest; and such interference must at least be sufficient to accomplish its purposes. The house of the American democracy is again by way of being divided against itself, because the national interest has not been consistently asserted as against special and local interests; and again, also, it can be reunited only by being partly reconstructed on better foundations. If reform does not and cannot mean restoration, it is bound to mean reconstruction.

The reformers have come partly to realize that the Jeffersonian policy of drift must be abandoned. They no longer expect the American ship of state by virtue of its own righteous framework to sail away to a safe harbor in the Promised Land. They understand that there must be a vigorous and conscious assertion of the public as opposed to private and special interests, and that the American people must to a greater extent than they have in the past subordinate the latter to the former. They behave as if the American ship of state will hereafter require careful steering; and a turn or two at the wheel has given them some idea of the course they must set. On the other hand, even the best of them have not learned the name of its ultimate destination, the full difficulties of the navigation, or the stern discipline which may eventually be imposed upon the ship's crew. They do not realize, that is, how thoroughly Jeffersonian individualism must be abandoned for the benefit of a genuinely individual and social consummation; and they do not realize how dangerous and fallacious a chart their cherished principle of equal rights may well become. In reviving the practice of vigorous national action for the achievement of a national purpose, the better reformers have, if they only knew it, been looking in the direction of a much more trustworthy and serviceable political principle. The assumption of such a responsibility implies the rejection of a large part of the Jeffersonian creed, and a renewed attempt to establish in its place the popularity of its Hamiltonian rival. On the other hand, it involves no less surely the transformation of Hamiltonianism into a thoroughly democratic political principle. None of these inferences have, however, as yet been generally drawn, and no leading reformer has sought to give reform its necessary foundation of positive political principle. [. . .]

Chapter Seven: Reconstruction; Its Conditions and Purposes

[. . .] If a people, in becoming more of a nation, become for that very reason more of a democracy, the realization of the democratic purpose is not rendered any easier, but democracy is provided with a simplified, a consistent, and a practicable programme. An alliance is established thereby between the two dominant political and social forces in modern life. The suspicion with which aggressive advocates of the national principle have sometimes regarded democracy would be shown to have only a conditional justification; and the suspicion with which many ardent democrats have regarded aggressive nationalism would be similarly disarmed. A democrat, so far as the statement is true, could trust the fate of his cause in each particular state to the friends of national progress. Democracy would not need for its consummation the ruin of the traditional political fabrics; but so far as those political bodies were informed by genuinely national ideas and aspirations, it could await confidently the process of national development. In fact, the first duty of a good democrat would be that of rendering to his country loyal patriotic service. Democrats would abandon the task of making over the world to suit their own purposes, until they had come to a better understanding with their own countrymen. One's democracy, that is, would begin at home and it would for the most part stay at home; and the cause of national well-being would derive invaluable assistance from the loyal coöperation of good democrats. [. . .]

Americans have always been both patriotic and democratic, just as they have always been friendly both to liberty and equality, but in neither case have they brought the two ideas or aspirations into mutually helpful relations. As democrats they have often regarded nationalism with distrust, and have consequently deprived their patriotism of any sufficient substance and organization. As nationalists they have frequently regarded essential aspects of democracy with a wholly unnecessary and embarrassing suspicion. They have been after a fashion Hamiltonian, and Jeffersonian after more of a fashion; but they have never recovered from the initial disagreement between Hamilton and Jefferson. If there is any truth in the idea of a constructive relation between democracy and nationality this disagreement must be healed. They must accept both principles loyally and unreservedly; and by such acceptance their "noble national theory" will obtain a wholly unaccustomed energy and integrity. The alliance between the two principles will not leave either of them intact; but it will necessarily do more harm to the Jeffersonian group of political ideas than it will to the Hamiltonian. The latter's nationalism can be adapted to democracy without an essential injury to itself, but the former's democracy cannot be nationalized without being transformed. The manner of its transformation has already been discussed in detail. It must cease to be a democracy of indiscriminate individualism, and become one of selected individuals who are obliged constantly to justify their selection; and its members must be united not by a sense of joint irresponsibility, but by a sense of joint responsibility for the success of their political and social ideal. They must become, that is, a democracy devoted to the welfare of the whole people by means of a conscious labor of individual and social improvement; and that is precisely the sort of democracy which demands for its realization the aid of the Hamiltonian nationalistic organization and principle.

Chapter Thirteen: Conclusions—The Individual and National Purpose

It is, then, essential to recognize that the individual American will never obtain a sufficiently complete chance of self-expression, until the American nation has earnestly undertaken and measurably achieved the realization of its collective purpose. As we shall see presently, the cure for this individual sterility lies partly with the individual himself or rather with the man who proposes to become an individual; and under any plan of economic or social organization, the man who proposes to become an individual is a condition of national as well as individual improvement. It is none the less true that any success in the achievement of the national purpose will contribute positively to the liberation of the individual, both by diminishing his temptations, improving his opportunities, and by enveloping him in an invigorating rather than an enervating moral and intellectual atmosphere.

It is the economic individualism of our existing national system which inflicts the most serious damage on American individuality; and American individual achievement in politics and science and the arts will remain partially impoverished as long as our fellow-countrymen neglect or refuse systematically to regulate the distribution of wealth in the national interest. I am aware, of course, that the prevailing American conviction is absolutely contradictory of the foregoing assertion. Americans have always associated individual freedom with the unlimited popular enjoyment of all available economic opportunities. Yet it would be far more true to say that the popular enjoyment of practically unrestricted economic opportunities is precisely the condition which makes for individual bondage. Neither does the bondage which such a system fastens upon the individual exist only in the case of those individuals who are victimized by the pressure of unlimited economic competition. Such victims exist, of course, in large numbers, and they will come to exist in still larger numbers hereafter. [. . .] [A man's individuality] does not depend merely on the display [. . .] of superior enterprise and energy, although, of course, he may and should be as enterprising and as energetic as he

can. It depends upon the actual excellence of the work in every respect,—an excellence which can best be achieved by the absorbing and exclusive pursuit of that alone. A man's individuality is projected into his work. He does not stop when he has earned enough money, and he does not cease his improvements when they cease to bring in an immediate return. He is identified with his job, and by means of that identification his individuality becomes constructive. His achievement, just because of its excellence, has an inevitable and an unequivocal social value. The quality of a man's work reunites him with his fellows. He may have been in appearance just as selfish as a man who spends most of his time in making money, but if his work has been thoroughly well done, he will, in making himself an individual, have made an essential contribution to national fulfillment. [. . .] The man whose motive is that of money-making will not make the work any more excellent than is demanded by the largest possible returns; and frequently the largest possible returns are to be obtained by indifferent work or by work which has absolutely no social value. The ordinary mercenary purpose always compels a man to stop at a certain point, and consider something else than the excellence of his achievement. It does not make the individual independent, except in so far as independence is merely a matter of cash in the bank; and for every individual on whom it bestows excessive pecuniary independence, there are many more who are by that very circumstance denied any sort of liberation. Even pecuniary independence is usually purchased at the price of moral and intellectual bondage. Such genuine individuality as can be detected in the existing social system is achieved not because of the prevailing money-making motive, but in spite thereof.

The ordinary answer to such criticisms is that while the existing system may have many faults, it certainly has proved an efficient means of releasing individual energy; whereas the exercise of a positive national responsibility for the wholesome distribution of wealth would tend to deprive the individual of any sufficient initiative. The claim is that the money-making motive is the only one which will really arouse the great majority of men, and to weaken it would be to rob the whole economic system of its momentum. Just what validity this claim may have cannot, with our present experience, be definitely settled. That to deprive individuals suddenly of the opportunities they have so long enjoyed would be disastrous may be fully admitted. It may also be admitted that any immediate and drastic attempt to substitute for the present system a national regulation of the distribution of wealth or a national responsibility for the management even of monopolies or semi-monopolies would break down and would do little to promote either individual or social welfare. But to conclude from any such admissions that a systematic policy of promoting individual and national amelioration should be abandoned is wholly unnecessary. That the existing system has certain practical advantages, and is a fair expression of the average moral standards of to-day is not only its chief merit, but also its chief and inexcusable defect. What a democratic nation must do is not to accept human nature as it is, but to move in the direction of its improvement. The question it must answer is: How can it contribute to the increase of American individuality? The defender of the existing system must be able to show either (1) that it does contribute to the increase of American individuality; or that (2) whatever its limitations, the substitution of some better system is impossible. [. . .]

The proposed economic policy of reform, in so far as it were successful, would also tend to stimulate labor to more efficiency, and to diminish its grievances. The state would be lending assistance to the effort of the workingman to raise his standard of living, and to restrict the demoralizing effect of competition among laborers who cannot afford to make a stand on behalf of their own interest. It should, consequently, increase the amount of economic independence enjoyed by the average laborer, diminish his "class consciousness" by doing away with his class grievances, and intensify his importance to himself as an individual. It would in every way help to make the individual workingman more of an individual. His class interest would be promoted by the nation in so far as such promotion was possible, and could be adjusted to a general policy of national economic construction. His individual interest would be left in his own charge; but he would have much more favorable opportunities of redeeming the charge by the excellence of his individual work than he has under the existing system. His condition would doubtless still remain in certain respects unsatisfactory, for the purpose of a democratic nation must remain unfulfilled just in so far as the national organization of labor does not enable all men to compete on approximately equal terms for all careers. But a substantial step would be made towards its improvement, and the road marked, perhaps, for still further advance.

Again, however, must the reader be warned that the important thing is the constructive purpose, and not the means proposed for its realization. Whenever the attempt at its realization is made, it is probable that other and unforeseen measures will be found necessary; and even if a specific policy proposed were successfully tried, this would constitute merely an advance towards the ultimate end. The ultimate end is the complete emancipation of the individual, and that result depends upon his complete disinterestedness. He must become interested exclusively in the excellence of his work; and he can never become disinterestedly interested in his work as long as heavy responsibilities and high achievements are supposed to be rewarded by increased pay. The effort equitably to adjust compensation to earnings is ultimately not only impossible, but undesirable, because it necessarily would foul the whole economic organization — so far as its efficiency depended on a generous rivalry among individuals. The only way in which work can be made entirely disinterested is to adjust its compensation to the needs of a normal and wholesome human life.

John Dewey

The Influence of Darwin on Philosophy (1910)

[. . .] We live in the twilight of intellectual transition. One must add the rashness of the prophet to the stubbornness of the partizan to venture a systematic exposition of the influence upon philosophy of the Darwinian method. At best, we can but inquire as to its general bearing—the effect upon mental temper and complexion, upon that body of half-conscious, half-instinctive intellectual aversions and preferences which determine, after all, our more deliberate intellectual enterprises. In this vague inquiry there happens to exist as a kind of touchstone a problem of long historic currency that has also been much discussed in Darwinian literature. I refer to the old problem of design *versus* chance, mind *versus* matter, as the causal explanation, first or final, of things.

As we have already seen, the classic notion of species carried with it the idea of purpose. In all living forms, a specific type is present directing the earlier stages of growth to the realization of its own perfection. Since this purposive regulative principle is not visible to the senses, it follows that it must be an ideal or rational force. Since, however, the perfect form is gradually approximated through the sensible changes, it also follows that in and through a sensible realm a rational ideal force is working out its own ultimate manifestation. These inferences were extended to nature: (*a*) She does nothing in vain; but all for an ulterior purpose. (*b*) Within natural sensible events there is therefore contained a spiritual causal force, which as spiritual escapes perception, but is apprehended by an enlightened reason. (*c*) The manifestation of this principle brings about a subordination of matter and sense to its own realization, and this ultimate fulfillment is the goal of nature and of man. The design argument thus operated in two directions. Purposefulness accounted for the intelligibility of nature and the possibility of science, while the absolute or cosmic character of this purposefulness gave sanction and worth to the moral and religious endeavors of man. Science was underpinned and morals authorized by one and the same

principle, and their mutual agreement was eternally guaranteed.

This philosophy remained, in spite of skeptical and polemic outbursts, the official and the regnant philosophy of Europe for over two thousand years. The expulsion of fixed first and final causes from astronomy, physics, and chemistry had indeed given the doctrine something of a shock. But, on the other hand, increased acquaintance with the details of plant and animal life operated as a counterbalance and perhaps even strengthened the argument from design. The marvelous adaptations of organisms to their environment, of organs to the organism, of unlike parts of a complex organ—like the eye—to the organ itself; the fore-shadowing by lower forms of the higher; the preparation in earlier stages of growth for organs that only later had their functioning—these things were increasingly recognized with the progress of botany, zoology, paleontology, and embryology. Together, they added such prestige to the design argument that by the late eighteenth century it was, as approved by the sciences of organic life, the central point of theistic and idealistic philosophy.

The Darwinian principle of natural selection cut straight under this philosophy. If all organic adaptations are due simply to constant variation and the elimination of those variations which are harmful in the struggle for existence that is brought about by excessive reproduction, there is no call for a prior intelligent causal force to plan and preordain them. Hostile critics charged Darwin with materialism and with making chance the cause of the universe.

Some naturalists, like Asa Gray, favored the Darwinian principle and attempted to reconcile it with design. Gray held to what may be called design on the installment plan. If we conceive the "stream of variations" to be itself intended, we may suppose that each successive variation was designed from the first to be selected. In that case, variation, struggle, and selection simply define the mechanism of "secondary causes" through which the "first cause" acts; and the doctrine of design is none the worse off because we know more of its *modus operandi*.

Darwin could not accept this mediating proposal. He admits or rather he asserts that it is "impossible to conceive this immense and wonderful universe including man with his capacity of looking far backwards and far into futurity as the result of blind chance or necessity."[1] But nevertheless he holds that since variations are in useless as well as useful directions, and since the latter are sifted out simply by the stress of the conditions of struggle for existence, the design argument as applied to living beings is unjustifiable; and its lack of support there deprives it of scientific value as applied to nature in general. [. . .]

Darwin concluded that the impossibility of assigning the world to chance as a whole and to design in its parts indicated the insolubility of the question. Two radically different reasons, however, may be given as to why a problem is insoluble. One reason is that the problem is too high for intelligence; the other is that the question in its very asking makes assumptions that render the question meaningless. The latter alternative is unerringly pointed to in the celebrated case of design *versus* chance. Once admit that the sole verifiable or fruitful object of knowledge is the particular set of changes that generate the object of study together with the consequences that then flow from it, and no intelligible question can be asked about what, by assumption, lies outside. To assert—as is often asserted—that specific values of particular truth, social bonds and form of beauty, if they can be shown to be generated by concretely knowable conditions, are meaningless and in vain; to assert that they are justified only when they and their particular causes and effects have all at once been gathered up into some inclusive first cause and some exhaustive final goal, is intellectual atavism. Such argumentation is reversion to the logic that explained the extinction of fire by water through the formal essence of aqueousness and the quenching of thirst by water through the final cause of aqueousness. Whether used in the case of the special event or that of life as a whole, such logic only abstracts some aspect of the existing course of events in order to reduplicate it as a petrified eternal principle by

which to explain the very changes of which it is the formalization.

When Henry Sidgwick casually remarked in a letter that as he grew older his interest in what or who made the world was altered into interest in what kind of a world it is anyway, his voicing of a common experience of our own day illustrates also the nature of that intellectual transformation effected by the Darwinian logic. Interest shifts from the wholesale essence back of special changes to the question of how special changes serve and defeat concrete purposes; shifts from an intelligence that shaped things once for all to the particular intelligence which things are even now shaping; shifts from an ultimate goal of good to the direct increments of justice and happiness that intelligent administration of existent conditions may beget and that present carelessness or stupidity will destroy or forego.

In the second place, the classic type of logic inevitably set philosophy upon proving that life *must* have certain qualities and values—no matter how experience presents the matter—because of some remote cause and eventual goal. The duty of wholesale justification inevitably accompanies all thinking that makes the meaning of special occurrences depend upon something that once and for all lies behind them. The habit of derogating from present meanings and uses prevents our looking the facts of experience in the face; it prevents serious acknowledgment of the evils they present and serious concern with the goods they promise but do not as yet fulfill. It turns thought to the business of finding a wholesale transcendent remedy for the one and guarantee for the other. One is reminded of the way many moralists and theologians greeted Herbert Spencer's recognition of an unknowable energy from which welled up the phenomenal physical process without and the conscious operations within. Merely because Spencer labeled his unknowable energy "God," this faded piece of metaphysical goods was greeted as an important and grateful concession to the reality of the spiritual realm. Were it not for the deep hold of the habit of seeking justification for ideal values in the remote and transcendent, surely this reference of them to an unknowable absolute would be despised in comparison with the demonstrations of experience that knowable energies are daily generating about us precious values.

---

1. "Life and Letters," Vol. I, p. 282; cf. 285.

The displacing of this wholesale type of philosophy will doubtless not arrive by sheer logical disproof, but rather by growing recognition of its futility. Were it a thousand times true that opium produces sleep because of its dormitive energy, yet the inducing of sleep in the tired, and the recovery to waking life of the poisoned, would not be thereby one least step forwarded. And were it a thousand times dialectically demonstrated that life as a whole is regulated by a transcendent principle to a final inclusive goal, none the less truth and error, health and disease, good and evil, hope and fear in the concrete, would remain just what and where they now are. To improve our education, to ameliorate our manners, to advance our politics, we must have recourse to specific conditions of generation.

Finally, the new logic introduces responsibility into the intellectual life. To idealize and rationalize the universe at large is after all a confession of inability to master the courses of things that specifically concern us. As long as mankind suffered from this impotency, it naturally shifted a burden of responsibility that it could not carry over to the more competent shoulders of the transcendent cause. But if insight into specific conditions of value and into specific consequences of ideas is possible, philosophy must in time become a method of locating and interpreting the more serious of the conflicts that occur in life, and a method of projecting ways for dealing with them: a method of moral and political diagnosis and prognosis.

The claim to formulate *a priori* the legislative constitution of the universe is by its nature a claim that may lead to elaborate dialectic developments. But it is also one that removes these very conclusions from subjection to experimental test, for, by definition, these results make no differences in the detailed course of events. But a philosophy that humbles its pretensions to the work of projecting hypotheses for the education and conduct of mind, individual and social, is thereby subjected to test by the way in which the ideas it propounds work out in practice. In having modesty forced upon it, philosophy also acquires responsibility.

Doubtless I seem to have violated the implied promise of my earlier remarks and to have turned both prophet and partizan. But in anticipating the direction of the transformations in philosophy to be wrought by the Darwinian genetic and experimental logic, I do not profess to speak for any save those who yield themselves consciously or unconsciously to this logic. No one can fairly deny that at present there are two effects of the Darwinian mode of thinking. On the one hand, there are many making sincere and vital efforts to revise our traditional philosophic conceptions in accordance with its demands. On the other hand, there is as definitely a recrudescence of absolutistic philosophies; an assertion of a type of philosophic knowing distinct from that of the sciences, one which opens to us another kind of reality from that to which the sciences give access; an appeal through experience to something that essentially goes beyond experience. This reaction affects popular creeds and religious movements as well as technical philosophies. The very conquest of the biological sciences by the new ideas has led many to proclaim an explicit and rigid separation of philosophy from science.

Old ideas give way slowly; for they are more than abstract logical forms and categories. They are habits, predispositions, deeply engrained attitudes of aversion and preference. Moreover, the conviction persists—though history shows it to be a hallucination—that all the questions that the human mind has asked are questions that can be answered in terms of the alternatives that the questions themselves present. But in fact intellectual progress usually occurs through sheer abandonment of questions together with both of the alternatives they assume—an abandonment that results from their decreasing vitality and a change of urgent interest. We do not solve them: we get over them. Old questions are solved by disappearing, evaporating, while new questions corresponding to the changed attitude of endeavor and preference take their place. Doubtless the greatest dissolvent in contemporary thought of old questions, the greatest precipitant of new methods, new intentions, new problems, is the one effected by the scientific revolution that found its climax in the "Origin of Species."

Woodrow Wilson

Fourth of July Address on the Declaration of Independence
(1907)

It is common to think of the Declaration of Independence as a highly speculative document; but no one can think it so who has read it. It is a strong, rhetorical statement of grievances against the English government. It does indeed open with the assertion that all men are equal and that they have certain inalienable rights, among them the right to life, liberty and the pursuit of happiness. It asserts that governments were instituted to secure these rights, and can derive their just powers only from the consent of the governed; and it solemnly declares that "whenever any government becomes destructive of these ends, it is the right of the people to alter or to abolish it, and to institute a new government, laying its foundations in such principles, and organizing its powers in such forms, as to them shall seem most likely to effect their safety and happiness." But this would not afford a general theory of government to formulate policies upon. No doubt we are meant to have liberty, but each generation must form its own conception of what liberty is. No doubt we shall always wish to be given leave to pursue happiness as we will, but we are not yet sure where or by what method we shall find it. That we are free to adjust government to these ends we know. But Mr. Jefferson and his colleagues in the Continental Congress prescribed the law of adjustment for no generation but their own. They left us to say whether we thought the government they had set up was founded on "such principles," its powers organized in "such forms" as seemed to us most likely to effect our safety and happiness. They did not attempt to dictate the aims and objects of any generation but their own. [. . .]

The genius of the new republic was expressed among these men as it was expressed eleven years later among the men who framed the Constitution of the United States, by practical capacity, thoughtful indeed and holding at its heart clear-cut, unmistakable conceptions of what government of free men ought to be, but not fanciful, a thing of action rather than of theory, suited to meet an exigency, not a mere turn in debate. We do not live in times as critical as theirs. We are not engaged in making a nation. But we are engaged in purging and preserving a nation, and an analysis of our duty in the situation in which we stand is in many ways more difficult than that which they attempted, the remedies to be applied left less obvious to our choice. They gave us the nation: we owe them, not empty eulogy, but the sincere flattery of imitation. If we are their descendants either in blood or in spirit, let us distinguish our ancestry from that of others by clear wisdom in counsel and fearless action taken upon plain principle.

No one now needs to be told what the principle of the American Revolution was: it was the principle of individual liberty. Though those men who signed the Declaration of Independence were no theorists but practical statesmen, a very definite conception of what the government of enlightened men ought to be lay back of everything they did, and that conception they held with a passionate conviction. They believed government to be a means by which the individual could realize at once his responsibility and his freedom from unnecessary restraint. Government should guard his rights, but it must not undertake to exercise them for him.

No doubt the most interesting spokesman of that conception was that eminent Virginian, that unique and singular author of the Declaration of Independence. No doubt Thomas Jefferson was an astute politician; no doubt he was a most interesting philosopher; certainly he was a most inscrutable man. It would be impossible to make a consistent picture of him that should include all sides of his varied genius and singular character. He took leave, like all great men of affairs, to be inconsistent and do what circumstances required, approaching the perfection of theory by the tedious in directions of imperfect practice, but the main base of his theories was the base upon which all thoughtful men in his day founded their thinking about politics and intended to found their measures also. He believed consistently and profoundly in the right of the individual to a free opportunity, and in the right of the nation to an unhampered development, and was ready to support every law or arrangement which promised to secure the people against any sort of monopoly in taking part in that development. Moreover, he knew that government was a thing conducted by individuals, men whose weaknesses and passions did not differ from the weaknesses and passions of the men whom they governed; and that government must operate upon individuals whose tangled rights and opportunities no government could look into too curiously or seek to control too intimately without intolerable consequences of paternalism and petty tyranny. Every man who signed the Declaration of Independence believed, as Mr. Jefferson did, that free men had a much more trustworthy capacity in taking care of themselves than any government had ever shown or was ever likely to show, in taking care of them; and upon that belief American government was built.

So far as the Declaration of Independence was a theoretical document, that is its theory. Do we still hold it? Does the doctrine of the Declaration of Independence still live in our principles of action, in the things we do, in the purposes we applaud, in the measures we approve? It is not a question of piety. We are not bound to adhere to the doctrines held by the signers of the Declaration of Independence: we are as free as they were to make and unmake governments. We are not here to worship men or a document. But neither are we here to indulge in a mere rhetorical and uncritical eulogy. Every Fourth of July should be a time for examining our standards, our purposes, for determining afresh what principles, what forms of power we think most likely to effect our safety and happiness. That and that alone is the obligation the Declaration lays upon us. It is no fetish; its words lay no compulsion upon the thought of any free man; but it was drawn by men who thought, and it obliges those who receive its benefits to *think* likewise.

What then do we think of our safety and of our happiness, — of the principles of action and the forms of power we are using to secure them? That we have come to a new age and a new attitude towards questions of government, no one can doubt, — to new definitions of constitutional power, new conceptions of legislative object, new schemes of individual and corporate regulation. Upon what principle of change do we act? Do we act upon definite calculations of purpose, or do we but stumble hesitatingly upon expedients? To what statements of principle would a declaration of our reasons and purposes commit us before the world: to those the signers of the Declaration of Independence would have avowed, or to others very different and not at all novel in the political history of the world? This is not a party question: there is apparently little difference between parties in regard to it. It is a national question, — a question touching the political principles of America. We ought not to hesitate to avow a change, if change there is to be; but we should be ashamed to act in radical fashion and not know that there was a change. Precedent is at least a guide by which to determine our direction.

There is much in our time that would cause men of the principles of Mr. Jefferson the bitterest disappointment. Individual opportunity is not unhampered. The nation has had in every respect an extraordinary material development, but the chief instrumentalities of that development have been at least virtually monopolized, and the people, though they created the opportunity and contributed the labor, have not shared the benefits of that development as they might have shared them. This has not been due to the operation of our institutions; it has been due to the operation of human nature, which is alike under all institutions and which has perhaps had freer play under our institutions than it would have had under any others, as Mr. Jefferson wished that it should have. Moreover, there is no doubt that we shall set all things right; but it is important we should inquire the way and not set them right by methods which may bring new trouble upon us, if the old methods will suffice for our safety and happiness. What were those methods? What was the spirit of the nation at its inception, — in 1776 when the great declaration of its intentions was framed, and in 1787 when it made deliberate choice of its form of government?

There is no difficulty in answering these questions; the answers to them have lain before us since we were children, in every book that spoke of our history or of our character as a nation. Let us use them as a mirror into which to look in order to make test whether we shall recognize our own features, disguised as they are by change of circumstance, in our present habit, as we live.

The most obvious characteristic of the men who gave the nation voice and power was their profound regard for law. That conviction is upon the surface and at the heart of everything they said or did in support of their purpose. They did not fling off from the mother country because they wanted new rights, but because the rights they had time out of mind enjoyed as free men under the laws and constitution of England, and the rights they had been promised as colonists in a new country with a life of its own, had been arbitrarily disregarded and withdrawn, and they knew not what ancient and undoubted liberties and privileges they could count upon. They wanted, not less law nor even better law, but law they could rely upon and live by. Their case was a case for legality, for the established understandings of law, upon which they knew that liberty had immemorially depended. There is no longer any need to debate what liberty really is; the question has been tried out again and again, both in theory and in practice, — in the council chamber and on the field of battle, where the air was calm and where it thrilled with passion, — and by no race more thoroughly than by that from which we derived our law; and we may say that we know. Affairs swing this way and that, sometimes with revolutionary force, as interests wage war for advantage, but we know where the midpoint of perfect poise lies and seek constantly to turn our lines of policy towards it. Liberty consists in the best possible adjustment between the power of the government and the privilege of the individual; and only law can effect that adjustment. Where liberty is, there must be a perfect understanding between the individual and those who would control him; and if either he or they can disregard the understanding, there is license or anarchy. It was in that knowledge that the founders of our government loved the law.

These same men, therefore, who revered law and depended upon its grants and definitions for their security and happiness, were deeply jealous of too much law. It is easy to talk of "society," of "communities," of "the people," but the fact is that these are but names we give to bodies made up of individuals. It is easy also to speak of "governments" as if they were forces set apart from us and above us; but governments also consist of individuals of like nature with ourselves. That is the reason, the very interesting and important reason, which the founders of our government needed not to have explained to whem [them], why control of our affairs by the government and the regulation of our relations to each other by the law are two very different things and lead to sharply contrasted results. The history of liberty in the past, from which we may possibly gather some intimation of its history in the future, has been a history of resistance to too much governmental control and a careful discovery of the best forms and the most prudent degrees of legal regulations; and it is clear that the law which the signers of the Declaration of Independence loved was something which they regarded, not as a body of powers possessed by a government, but as a body of rules regulating the complex game of life, no more favorable to control than was necessary to make it a safeguard of individual privilege and a guarantee of equal rights. Too much law was too much government; and too much government was too little individual privilege, — as too much individual privilege in its turn was selfish license.

Now let us hold this mirror up to ourselves and see if we recognize in it the image of our own minds. In that mirror we see a conception of government which frankly puts the individual in the foreground, thinking of him as the person to be at once protected and heartened to make a free use of himself; the responsible administrator of his own liberties and his own responsibilities; and of government as the umpire; and which depends upon law for nothing else than a clear establishment of the rules of the game. That is hardly our notion. We are indeed in love with law, — more in love with it than were the makers of the government, — but hardly in love with it as a government of mere regulation. For us it is an instrument of reconstruction and control. The individual has eluded us, we seem to say, has merged and hidden himself in corporations and associations, through the intricacies of whose structure we have not time to thread our way in search of him; we will therefore meet the circumstances as we find them, treat him not as an integer but as a fraction, and deal with the association, not with the individual. We will prohibit corporations to do this or to do that, to be this or to be that, and punish them either with fine or with dissolution if they disobey. The morals of business and of law we will frankly accept as corporate morals, and we will not set these corporations, these new individuals of our modern law, to watch and sue one another for infractions of the law: they might combine, and there is no sufficient motive for them to check one another in illegal practices. Neither can we depend upon individuals: they are now too minute and weak. The moralizer and disciplinarian of corporations can in the nature of the case be none other than the government itself, and, because corporations spread from state to state, can be none other than the government of the United States.

It is amusing how we extend this new theory of law into some of the new details of our life,—extend it at any rate in our thinking, if not in our legislation. We hear it suggested on every side, for example, that the true and effective way to stop the driving of automobiles along our highways at excessive rates of speed is to lock up the automobiles themselves whenever the speed laws are violated, so that for a long time at least it may not be used again. I suppose we shall some day see officers of the law arresting electric cars and steam locomotives for the offences which their motormen and engineers have committed, and the faults of men everywhere corrected by locking up their tools. The trouble is that the tools are wanted, and the lives of all of us are inconvenienced if they are taken away. Even the automobile is useful, when used with sanity and caution. And there is exactly the same serious trouble about the way we now deal with our corporations, punishing inanimate things instead of persons. When we fine them, we merely take that much money out of their business,—that is, out of the business of the country,—and put it into the public treasury, where there is generally already a surplus and where it is likely to be idle. When we dissolve them, we check and hamper legitimate undertakings and embarrass the business of the country much more than we should embarrass it were we to arrest locomotives and impound electric cars, the necessary vehicles of our intercourse. And all the while we know perfectly well that the iniquities we levy fines for were conceived and executed by particular individuals who go

unpunished, unchecked even, in the enterprises which have led to the action of the courts. And so from one body of hidden individuals we turn to another, and say, "Go to, we will instruct the government to regulate this thing in place of boards of directors: if necessary, we will instruct the government to transact the business which these corporations have made the government interfere with on account of bad practices. We shall then have honesty: for are not the men who compose the government men of our own choice, our servants for our common business?"

It needs no prophet to predict that too much government lies that way, and nothing but too much government,—and no increased efficiency or improved business to be had in the bargain. And beyond too much government lies the old programme, repeated and repeated again and again every time the like thing has happened: a new struggle for liberty, a new eagerness for emancipation from the law that dictates, into the freedom of the law that umpires. No doubt the old cycle must some time be gone through again; but we ought not to be the people to go through it. We have had too much light: we have furnished the world with doctrines and example in this kind, and we cannot afford to illustrate our own principles by our mistakes after having illustrated them by our successes. Shall we return to our old standards, or shall we attempt arrangements which we know our children will be obliged to reject?

Can we return to our old standards in this strange and altered day, when all the face of circumstances seems changed and nothing remains as it was in the time when the government was hopefully set up? Undoubtedly we can. Not everything is changed: the biggest item of all remains unaltered,—human nature itself; and it is nothing to daunt a free people,—free to think and free to act, that the circumstances in which that old, unalterable nature now expresses itself are so complex and singular. The difficulty of the task is part of its desirability: it is a new enterprise upon which to stretch our powers and make proof of our sanity and strength. It is the task of making a new translation of our morals into the terms of our modern life, where individuality seems for the time being lost in complex organizations, and then making a new translation of our laws to match our new translation of morals. It is the task of finding the individual in the maize [maze] of modern social, commercial and industrial conditions; finding him with the probe of morals and with the probe of law. One really responsible man in jail, one real originator of the schemes and transactions which are contrary to public interest legally lodged in the penitentiary would be worth more than a thousand corporations mulcted in fines, if reform is to be genuine and permanent.

It is only in this way that we can escape socialism. If the individual is lost to our law, he is lost to our politics and to our social structure. If he is merged in the business group, he is merged in the state, the association that includes all others. Unless we can single him out again and make him once more the subject and object of law, we shall have to travel still further upon the road of government regulation which we have already traveled so far, and that road leads to state ownership. We have not even tried to extend the old roads into this vast new area of business and of corporate enterprise, which recent years have seen open up like a new continent of mind and achievement; and until we have tried, we cannot claim legitimate descent from the founders of the government. We have abandoned their principles without even making trial of their efficacy in a new situation. [. . .] We know that the vast majority of our business transactions are sound, the vast majority of our business men honest. In order to clear the way of unjust suspicion, give credit where credit is due, condemnation where condemnation [is due]; let us set ourselves to work to single out individuals and real personal responsibility, and we shall both lighten the difficulty of government and make a new platform of life. Governmental supervision there must be, but of the kind there has always been in District Attorneys' offices; not the kind that seeks to determine the processes of business, but the kind that brings home to individuals the obligations of the law.

It would be a happy emancipation. We should escape the burden of too much government, and we should regain our self-respect, our self-confidence, our sense of individual integrity; we should think straightway with regard to the moral aspect of conduct, and we should escape perplexities with regard to our political future; we should once more have the exhilarating freedom of governing our own lives, the law standing as umpire, not as master.

By such means we should prove ourselves indeed the spiritual descendants of the signers of the Declaration of Independence. It is fashionable, it is easy, to talk about Jeffersonian principles of government. Men of all kinds and of the most opposite doctrines call themselves by Mr. Jefferson's name; and it must be admitted that it is easy to turn many of Mr. Jefferson's opinions this way or that. But no man's name settles any principle, and Mr. Jefferson was originating no novel doctrine, announcing no discoveries in politics, when he wrote the Declaration of Independence. What it contains is in fact the common-place of political history. There can be no liberty if the individual is not free: there is no such thing as corporate liberty. There is no other possible formula for a free government than this: that the laws must deal with individuals, allowing them to choose their own lives under a definite personal responsibility to a common government set over them; and that government must regulate, not as a superintendent does, but as a judge does; it must safeguard, it must not direct.

These thoughts ought still to linger in the very air of this place. The first English settlers came here while the breath of the "spacious times of great Elizabeth" was still in every man's lungs, and the quickening impulse of enterprise and adventure. The great Tudor queen had known how to deal with mettlesome men: she had given them leave to do what they pleased in the world, if only they would remember always her sovereignty and their allegiance, and deal always with each other's rights as the law commanded. The things which government fostered and sought to manage never throve in America, amongst the French colonists in Canada and the South, and amongst the Dutch and Danes on the North and South Rivers; but the free English energy throve like a thing bred for the wilderness. That breath of individual liberty has never gone out of our lungs. Too much government still suffocates us. We do not respect ourselves as much as fractions, as we do as integers. The future, like the past, is for individual energy and initiative; for men, not for corporations or for governments; and the law that has this ancient principle at its heart is the law that will endure.

Address to the Jefferson Club of Los Angeles (1911)

[. . .] [A]s I was coming here this evening and reflected upon the name of this association, my thoughts naturally went back to that great man whose name you have adopted. And I asked myself, what would Jefferson say if a number of men of the Democratic faith were gathered together in the year 1911, if he were present? Jefferson was the author of the Declaration of Independence. But the Declaration of Independence, so far as I recollect, did not mention any of the issues of the year 1911. I am constantly reminding audiences that I have the pleasure of addressing that the rhetorical introduction of the Declaration of Independence is the least part of it. That was the theoretical expression of the views of which the rest of the document was meant to give teeth and substance to. The Declaration of Independence is a long enumeration of the issues of the year 1776, of exactly the things that were then supposed to be radical matters of discontent among the people living in America—the things which they meant to remedy, to remedy in the spirit of the introductory paragraphs, but which the introductory paragraphs themselves did not contain.

Now, the business of every true Jeffersonian is to translate the terms of those abstract portions of the Declaration of Independence into the language and the problems of his own day. If you want to understand the real Declaration of Independence, do not repeat the preface. Make a new table of contents, make a new set of counts in the indictment, make a new statement of the things you mean to set right, and then call all the civilized world to witness, as that great document does, that you mean to settle these things in the spirit of liberty, but also in the spirit of justice and responsibility. If you remember how that great document calls on all mankind to witness that we are not doing this thing in the spirit of insurgents but in the spirit of free men, men who have the true interests of humanity at heart—now, in a similar spirit, how are we going to realize the conceptions of the author of the Declaration of Independence in our own day? If Jefferson were here I am sure that he would reargue the whole matter from the principles

which he held so dear, and the chief principle which Jefferson held dear was this: that whatever was done must be done in the interests of the people as a whole. By this it was meant that every public servant must adjust his conception of public need not to the interests of particular classes, not to the interests of particular circumstances but to the interests of the general body of the nation, without regard to class, without regard in particular to any principles that might have been set up. It is our duty, therefore, to re conceive our politics and our policies in the common interest. Men have talked as if you could get action in politics by a sort of correlation of forces, by putting all the antagonistic forces in such a position as to run at one another, as if by contest you could work out concord, as if by rivalry you should achieve peace. The process is out of the question. Men must revise their thinking and revise their purposes, and alter their standards before you will settle the fundamental questions of our politics.

Let us look at the two things that have been giving us the most trouble. One of them is the political machine. We are not antagonistic to political organizations. [. . .]

What we call the machine is the instrumentality by which big business controls politics. That is all that it is. It is inimical to the very spirit of democracy that any group of persons, no matter how important their occupation may be to the community at large, should control the politics of the nation. "Democracy" and "control" are absolutely antagonistic terms—contradictory terms. Anybody less than a majority who organizes control in the democracy is its enemy.

So that whenever you organize control by an interest, even though it may be in some aspects the legitimate interest of a single class, you are cutting at the very root of the whole structure. [. . .]

The only way to defend yourself against improper legislation in America is to let Americans know it is improper and it will stop. The great antiseptic in America is public information and public opinion. You can clarify and purify the worst things in our life by simply letting the eyes of honest Americans have access to them. So that we are driven to the conclusion that these interests design to accomplish things which they do not care to have exposed to the public view. They want privileges which are exclusive—they want those things which they alone should enjoy—they want protections to which they are not justly entitled.

Look at the other thing that is giving us trouble—it is simply another side of the same picture. Look at the corporations.

We are not hostile to corporations if corporations will prove that they are as much interested in the general welfare and the general development as we are. We are not opposed to anybody who is serving the public—who is honestly serving the public by giving them honest service and at a reasonable rate, not with the primary idea of squeezing and exploiting the public, but with the primary idea of serving the public. America is not jealous of wealth, but it is jealous of ill-gotten wealth. America is willing to give largess of infinite fortune to anybody who will serve her, but she is very chary, if she could have her own way, of giving fortunes to anybody who will impose upon her. [. . .] The alliance of these men with politics is the most demoralizing thing that could possibly descend upon any country. And it has descended upon us. Those are the things that need correction, in our politics, and these are the things to which a man who acted in the Jeffersonian spirit would have to address himself.

The question is not whether all men are born free and equal or not. Suppose they were born so, you know they are not. They may have been born free and equal, but they are neither free nor equal if things of this sort can go on and continue to go on so that the problem of [the] Jeffersonian is to discredit and break up the machine. How to dissolve the partnership between the machine and the corporations—that is the problem of modern democracy. [. . .]

We ought to be afraid of thinking of our own generation only, when we ought to think of the long future of America. Because I, for one, feel, as I am sure you do, that I would have reason to be ashamed of having sprung from a great race of Americans if I do not do everything in my power to make the future of America greater than her past. Born of a free people, we, above all other men, are under bonds to prove ourselves worthy of freedom. And not only that, but to hand the freedom on, enhanced, glorified, purified, in order that America may not look back for her credit upon the days of her making and of her birth, but look forward for her credit to the things that she will do in the advancement of the rights of mankind.

The New Freedom (1912)

The Old Order Changeth

There is one great basic fact which underlies all the questions that are discussed on the political platform at the present moment. That singular fact is that nothing is done in this country as it was done twenty years ago.

We are in the presence of a new organization of society. Our life has broken away from the past. The life of America is not the life that it was twenty years ago; it is not the life that it was ten years ago. We have changed our economic conditions, absolutely, from top to bottom; and, with our economic society, the organization of our life. The old political formulas do not fit the present problems; they read now like documents taken out of a forgotten age. The older cries sound as if they belonged to a past age which men have almost forgotten. Things which used to be put into the party platforms of ten years ago would sound antiquated if put into a platform now. We are facing the necessity of fitting a new social organization, as we did once fit the old organization, to the happiness and prosperity of the great body of citizens; for we are conscious that the new order of society has not been made to fit and provide the convenience or prosperity of the average man. The life of the nation has grown infinitely varied. It does not center now upon questions of governmental structure or of the distribution of governmental powers. It centers upon questions of the very structure and operation of society itself, of which government is only the instrument. Our development has run so fast and so far along the lines sketched in the earlier day of constitutional definition, has so crossed and interlaced those lines, has piled upon them such novel structures of trust and combination, has elaborated within them a life so manifold, so full of forces which transcend the boundaries of the country itself and fill the eyes of the world, that a new nation seems to have been created which the old formulas do not fit or afford a vital interpretation of.

We have come upon a very different age from any that preceded us. We have come upon an age when we do not do business in the way in which we used to do business,—when we do not carry on any of the operations of manufacture, sale, transportation, or communication as men used to carry them on. There is a sense in which in our day the individual has been submerged. In most parts of our country men work, not for themselves, not as partners in the old way in which they used to work, but generally as employees,—in a higher or lower grade,—of great corporations. There was a time when corporations played a very minor part in our business affairs, but now they play the chief part, and most men are the servants of corporations.

You know what happens when you are the servant of a corporation. You have in no instance access to the men who are really determining the policy of the corporation. If the corporation is doing the things that it ought not to do, you really have no voice in the matter and must obey the orders, and you have oftentimes with deep mortification to co-operate in the doing of things which you know are against the public interest. Your individuality is swallowed up in the individuality and purpose of a great organization. . . .

Yesterday, and ever since history began, men were related to one another as individuals. To be sure there were the family, the Church, and the State, institutions which associated men in certain wide circles of relationship. But in the ordinary concerns of life, in the ordinary work, in the daily round, men dealt freely and directly with one another. To-day, the everyday relationships of men are largely with great impersonal concerns, with organizations, not with other individual men.

Now this is nothing short of a new social age, a new era of human relationships, a new stage-setting for the drama of life.

In this new age we find, for instance, that our laws with regard to the relations of employer and employee are in many respects wholly antiquated and impossible. They were framed for another age, which nobody now living remembers, which is, indeed, so remote from our life that it would be difficult for many of us to understand it if it were described to us. The employer is now generally a corporation or a huge company of some kind; the employee is one of hundreds or of thousands brought together, not by individual masters whom they know and with whom they have personal relations, but by agents of one sort or another. Workingmen are marshaled in great numbers for the performance of a multitude of particular tasks under a common discipline. They generally use dangerous and powerful machinery, over whose repair and renewal they have no control. New rules must be devised with regard to their obligations and their rights, their obligations to their employers and their responsibilities to one another. Rules must be devised for their protection, for their compensation when injured, for their support when disabled.

There is something very new and very big and very complex about these new relations of capital and labor. A new economic society has sprung up, and we must effect a new set of adjustments. We must not pit power against weakness. The employer is generally, in our day, as I have said, not an individual, but a powerful group; and yet the workingman when dealing with his employer is still, under our existing law, an individual. [. . .]

[W]e are all caught in a great economic system which is heartless. The modern corporation is not engaged in business as an individual. When we deal with it, we deal with an impersonal element, an immaterial piece of society. [. . .] American enterprise is not free; the man with only a little capital is finding it harder to get into the field, more and more impossible to compete with the big fellow. Why? Because the laws of this country do not prevent the strong from crushing the weak. That is the reason, and because the strong have crushed the weak the strong dominate the industry and the economic life of this country. No man can deny that the lines of endeavor have more and more narrowed and stiffened; no man who knows anything about the development of industry in this country can have failed to observe that the larger kinds of credit are more and more difficult to obtain, unless you obtain them upon the terms of uniting your efforts with those who already control the industries of the country; and nobody can fail to observe that any man who tries to set himself up in competition with any process of manufacture which has been taken under the control of large combinations of capital will presently find himself either squeezed out or obliged to sell and allow himself to be absorbed. [. . .]

What this country needs above everything else is a body of laws which will look after the men who are on the make rather than the men who are already made. Because the men who are already made are not going to live indefinitely, and they are not always kind enough to leave sons as able and as honest as they are.

The originative part of America, the part of America that makes new enterprises, the part into which the ambitious and gifted workingman makes his way up, the class that saves, that plants, that organizes, that presently spreads its enterprises until they have a national scope and character,—that middle class is being more and more squeezed out by the processes which we have been taught to call processes of prosperity. Its members are sharing prosperity, no doubt; but what alarms me is that they are not *originating* prosperity. No country can afford to have its prosperity originated by a small controlling class. The treasury of America does not lie in the brains of the small body of men now in control of the great enterprises that have been concentrated under the direction of a very small number of persons. The treasury of America lies in those ambitions, those energies, that cannot be restricted to a special favored class. It depends upon the inventions of unknown men, upon the originations of unknown men, upon the ambitions of unknown men. Every country is renewed out of the ranks of the unknown, not out of the ranks of those already famous and powerful and in control. [. . .]

We used to think in the old-fashioned days when life was very simple that all that government had to do was to put on a policeman's uniform, and say,

"Now don't anybody hurt anybody else." We used to say that the ideal of government was for every man to be left alone and not interfered with, except when he interfered with somebody else; and that the best government was the government that did as little governing as possible. That was the idea that obtained in Jefferson's time. But we are coming now to realize that life is so complicated that we are not dealing with the old conditions, and that the law has to step in and create new conditions under which we may live, the conditions which will make it tolerable for us to live.

Monopoly, or Opportunity?

[. . .] I take my stand absolutely, where every progressive ought to take his stand, on the proposition that private monopoly is indefensible and intolerable. And there I will fight my battle. And I know how to fight it. Everybody who has even read the newspapers knows the means by which these men built up their power and created these monopolies. Any decently equipped lawyer can suggest to you statutes by which the whole business can be stopped. What those gentlemen do not want is this: they do not want to be compelled to meet all comers on equal terms. I am perfectly willing that they should beat any competitor by fair means; but I know the foul means they have adopted, and I know that they can be stopped by law. If they think that coming into the market upon the basis of mere efficiency, upon the mere basis of knowing how to manufacture goods better than anybody else and to sell them cheaper than anybody else, they can carry the immense amount of water that they have put into their enterprises in order to buy up rivals, then they are perfectly welcome to try it. But there must be no squeezing out of the beginner, no crippling his credit; no discrimination against retailers who buy from a rival; no threats against concerns who sell supplies to a rival; no holding back of raw material from him; no secret arrangements against him. All the fair competition you choose, but no unfair competition of any kind. And then when unfair competition is eliminated, let us see these gentlemen carry their tanks of water on their backs. All that I ask and all I shall fight for is that they shall come into the field against merit and brains everywhere. [. . .]

I have been told by a great many men that the idea I have, that by restoring competition you can restore industrial freedom, is based upon a failure to observe the actual happenings of the last decades in this country; because, they say, it is just free competition that has made it possible for the big to crush the little.

I reply, it is not free competition that has done that; it is illicit competition. It is competition of the kind that the law ought to stop, and can stop,—this crushing of the little man. [. . .]

A People's Vital Energies

[. . .] What is liberty?

I have long had an image in my mind of what constitutes liberty. Suppose that I were building a great piece of powerful machinery, and suppose that I should so awkwardly and unskillfully assemble the parts of it that every time one part tried to move it would be interfered with by the others, and the whole thing would buckle up and be choked. Liberty for the several parts would consist in the best possible assembling and adjustment of them all, would it not? If you want the great piston of the engine to run with absolute freedom, give it absolutely perfect alignment and adjustment with the other parts of the machine, so that it is free, not because it is let alone or isolated, but because it has been associated most skillfully and carefully with the other parts of the great structure. [. . .]

Human freedom consists in perfect adjustments of human interests and human activities and human energies.

Now, the adjustments necessary between individuals, between individuals and the complex institutions amidst which they live, and between those institutions and the government, are infinitely more intricate today than ever before. . . . Life has become complex; there are many more elements, more parts, to it than ever before. And, therefore, it is harder to keep everything adjusted,—and harder to find out where the trouble lies when the machine gets out of order.

You know that one of the interesting things that Mr. Jefferson said in those early days of simplicity which marked the beginnings of our government was that the best government consisted in as little governing as possible. And there is still a sense in which that is true. It is still intolerable for the government to interfere with our individual activities except where it is necessary to interfere with them in order to free them. But I feel confident that if Jefferson were living in our day he would see what we see: that the individual is caught in a great confused nexus of all sorts of complicated circumstances, and that to let him alone is to leave him helpless as against the obstacles with which he has to contend; and that, therefore, law in our day must come to the assistance of the individual. It must come to his assistance to see that he gets fair play; that is all, but that is much. Without the watchful interference, the resolute interference, of the government, there can be no fair play between individuals and such powerful institutions as the trusts. Freedom to-day is something more than being let alone. The program of a government of freedom must in these days be positive, not negative merely.

Well, then, in this new sense and meaning of it, are we preserving freedom in this land of ours, the hope of all the earth? [. . .]

The answer must be, I am sure, that we have been in a fair way of failure,—tragic failure. And we stand in danger of utter failure yet except we fulfill speedily the determination we have reached, to deal with the new and subtle tyrannies according to their deserts. Don't deceive yourselves for a moment as to the power of the great interests which now dominate our development. They are so great that it is almost an open question whether the government of the United States can dominate them or not. Go one step further, make their organized power permanent, and it may be too late to turn back. The roads diverge at the point where we stand. They stretch their vistas out to regions where they are very far separated from one another; at the end of one is the old tiresome scene of government tied up with special interests; and at the other shines the liberating light of individual initiative, of individual liberty, of individual freedom, the light of untrammeled enterprise. I believe that that light shines out of the heavens itself that God has created. I believe in human liberty as I believe in the wine of life. There is no salvation for men in the pitiful condescensions of industrial masters. Guardians have no place in a land of freemen. Prosperity guaranteed by trustees has no prospect of endurance. Monopoly means the atrophy of enterprise. If monopoly persists, monopoly will always sit at the helm of the government. I do not expect to see monopoly restrain itself. If there are men in this country big enough to own the government of the United States, they are going to own it; what we have to determine now is whether we are big enough, whether we are men enough, whether we are free enough, to take possession again of the government which is our own. We haven't had free access to it, our minds have not touched it by way of guidance, in half a generation, and now we are engaged in nothing less than the recovery of what was made with our own hands, and acts only by our delegated authority. . . . You know what the vitality of America consists of. Its vitality does not lie in New York, nor in Chicago; it will not be sapped by anything that happens in St. Louis. The vitality of America lies in the brains, the energies, the enterprise of the people throughout the land; in the efficiency of their factories and in the richness of the fields that stretch beyond the borders of the town; in the wealth which they extract from nature and originate for themselves through the inventive genius characteristic of all free American communities.

That is the wealth of America, and if America discourages the locality, the community, the self-contained town, she will kill the nation. A nation is as rich as her free communities; she is not as rich as her capital city or her metropolis. [. . .]

We have carried in our minds, after you had thought you had obscured and blurred them, the ideals of those men who first set their foot upon America, those little bands who came to make a foothold in the wilderness, because the great teeming nations that they had left behind them had forgotten what human liberty was, liberty of thought, liberty of religion, liberty of residence, liberty of action.

Since their day the meaning of liberty has deepened. But it has not ceased to be a fundamental demand of the human spirit, a fundamental necessity for the life of the soul. And the day is at hand when it shall be realized on this consecrated soil,—a New Freedom,—a Liberty widened and deepened to match the broadened life of man in modern America, restoring to him in very truth the control of his government, throwing wide all gates of lawful enterprise, unfettering his energies, and warming the generous impulses of his heart,—a process of release, emancipation, and inspiration, full of a breath of life as sweet and wholesome as the airs that filled the sails of the caravels of Columbus and gave the promise and boast of magnificent Opportunity in which America *dare not fail.*

THEODORE ROOSEVELT

An Autobiography (1913)

The Square Deal

One of the vital questions with which as President I had to deal was the attitude of the Nation toward the great corporations. Men who understand and practice the deep underlying philosophy of the Lincoln school of American political thought are necessarily Hamiltonian in their belief in a strong and efficient National Government and Jeffersonian in their belief in the people as the ultimate authority, and in the welfare of the people as the end of Government. The men who first applied the extreme Democratic theory in American life were, like Jefferson, ultra individualists, for at that time what was demanded by our people was the largest liberty for the individual. During the century that had elapsed since Jefferson became President the need had been exactly reversed. There had been in our country a riot of individualistic materialism, under which complete freedom for the individual—that ancient license which President Wilson a century after the term was excusable has called the "New" Freedom—turned out in practice to mean perfect freedom for the strong to wrong the weak. The total absence of governmental control had led to a portentous growth in the financial and industrial world both of natural individuals and of artificial individuals—that is, corporations. In no other country in the world had such enormous fortunes been gained. In no other country in the world was such power held by the men who had gained these fortunes; and these men almost always worked through, and by means of, the giant corporations which they controlled. The power of the mighty industrial overlords of the country had increased with giant strides, while the methods of controlling them, or checking abuses by them on the part of the people, through the Government, remained archaic and therefore practically impotent. The courts, not unnaturally, but most regrettably, and to the grave detriment of the people and of their own standing, had for a quarter of a century been on the whole the agents of reaction, and by conflicting decisions which, however, in their sum were hostile to the interests of the people, had left both the nation and the several States well-nigh impotent to deal with the great business combinations. Sometimes they forbade the Nation to interfere, because such interference trespassed on the rights of the States; sometimes they forbade the States to interfere (and often they were wise in this), because to do so would trespass on the rights of the Nation; but always, or well-nigh always, their action was negative action against the interests of the people, ingeniously devised to limit their power against wrong, instead of affirmative action giving to the people power to right wrong. They had rendered these decisions sometimes as upholders of property rights against human rights, being especially zealous in securing the rights of the very men who were most competent to take care of themselves; and sometimes in the name of liberty, in the name of the so-called "new freedom," in reality the old, old "freedom," which secured to the powerful the freedom to prey on the poor and the helpless.

One of the main troubles was the fact that the men who saw the evils and who tried to remedy them attempted to work in two wholly different ways, and the great majority of them in a way that offered little promise of real betterment. They tried (by the Sherman law method) to bolster up an individualism already proved to be both futile and mischievous; to remedy by more individualism the concentration that was the inevitable result of the already existing individualism. They saw the evil done by the big combinations, and sought to remedy it by destroying them and restoring the country to the economic conditions of the middle of the nineteenth century. This was a hopeless effort, and those who went into it, although they regarded themselves as radical progressives, really represented a form of sincere rural toryism. They confounded monopolies with big business combinations, and in the effort to prohibit both alike, instead of where possible prohibiting one and drastically controlling the other, they succeeded merely in preventing any effective control of either.

On the other hand, a few men recognized that corporations and combinations had become indispensable in the business world, that it was folly to try to prohibit them, but that it was also folly to leave them without thoroughgoing control. These men realized that the doctrines of the old *laissez-faire* economists, of the believers in unlimited competition, unlimited individualism, were in the actual state of affairs false and mischievous. They realized that the Government must now interfere to protect labor, to subordinate the big corporation to the public welfare, and to shackle cunning and fraud exactly as centuries before it had interfered to shackle the physical force which does wrong by violence.

The big reactionaries of the business world and their allies and instruments among politicians and newspaper editors took advantage of this division of opinion, and especially of the fact that most of their opponents were on the wrong path; and fought to keep matters absolutely unchanged. These men demanded for themselves an immunity from governmental control which, if granted, would have been as wicked and as foolish as immunity to the barons of the twelfth century. Many of them were evil men. Many others were just as good men as were some of these same barons; but they were as utterly unable as any medieval castle-owner to understand what the public interest really was. There have been aristocracies which have played a great and beneficent part at stages in the growth of mankind; but we had come to the stage where for our people what was needed was a real democracy; and of all forms of tyranny the least attractive and the most vulgar is the tyranny of mere wealth, the tyranny of a plutocracy.

When I became President, the question as to the *method* by which the United States Government was to control the corporations was not yet important. The absolutely vital question was whether the Government had power to control them at all. This question had not yet been decided in favor of the United States Government. It was useless to discuss methods of controlling big business by the National Government until it was definitely settled that the National Government had the power to control it. A decision of the Supreme Court had, with seeming definiteness, settled that the National Government had not the power.

This decision I caused to be annulled by the court that had rendered it; and the present power of the National Government to deal effectively with the trusts is due solely to the success of the Administration in securing this reversal of its former decision by the Supreme Court. . . .

The true way of dealing with monopoly is to prevent it by administrative action before it grows so powerful that even when courts condemn it they shrink from destroying it. The Supreme Court in the Tobacco and Standard Oil cases, for instance, used very vigorous language in condemning these trusts; but the net result of the decision was of positive advantage to the wrongdoers, and this has tended to bring the whole body of our law into disrepute in quarters where it is of the very highest importance that the law be held in respect and even in reverence. My effort was to secure the creation of a Federal Commission which should neither excuse nor tolerate monopoly, but prevent it when possible and uproot it when discovered; and which should in addition effectively control and regulate all big combinations, and should give honest business certainty as to what the law was and security as long as the law was obeyed. Such a Commission would furnish a steady expert control, a control adapted to the problem; and dissolution is neither control nor regulation, but is purely negative; and negative remedies are of little permanent avail. Such a Commission would have complete power to examine into every big corporation engaged or proposing to engage in business between the States. It would have the power

to discriminate sharply between corporations that are doing well and those that are doing ill; and the distinction between those who do well and those who do ill would be defined in terms so clear and unmistakable that no one could misapprehend them. Where a company is found seeking its profits through serving the community by stimulating production, lowering prices or improving service, while scrupulously respecting the rights of others (including its rivals, its employees, its customers, and the general public), and strictly obeying the law, then no matter how large its capital, or how great the volume of its business it would be encouraged to still more abundant production, or better service, by the fullest protection that the Government could afford it. On the other hand, if a corporation were found seeking profit through injury or oppression of the community, by restricting production through trick or device, by plot or conspiracy against competitors, or by oppression of wage-workers, and then extorting high prices for the commodity it had made artificially scarce, it would be prevented from organizing if its nefarious purpose could be discovered in time, or pursued and suppressed by all the power of Government whenever found in actual operation. Such a commission, with the power I advocate, would put a stop to abuses of big corporations and small corporations alike; it would draw the line on conduct and not on size; it would destroy monopoly, and make the biggest business man in the country conform squarely to the principles laid down by the American people, while at the same time giving fair play to the little man and certainty of knowledge as to what was wrong and what was right both to big man and little man. [. . .]

By the time I became President I had grown to feel with deep intensity of conviction that governmental agencies must find their justification largely in the way in which they are used for the practical betterment of living and working conditions among the mass of the people. I felt that the fight was really for the abolition of privilege; and one of the first stages in the battle was necessarily to fight for the rights of the workingman. For this reason I felt most strongly that all that the government could do in the interest of labor should be done. [. . .]

Because of things I have done on behalf of justice to the workingman, I have often been called a

Socialist. Usually I have not taken the trouble even to notice the epithet. I am not afraid of names, and I am not one of those who fear to do what is right because some one else will confound me with partisans with whose principles I am not in accord. Moreover, I know that many American Socialists are high-minded and honorable citizens, who in reality are merely radical social reformers. They are oppressed by the brutalities and industrial injustices which we see everywhere about us. When I recall how often I have seen Socialists and ardent non-Socialists working side by side for some specific measure of social or industrial reform, and how I have found opposed to them on the side of privilege many shrill reactionaries who insist on calling all reformers Socialists, I refuse to be panic-stricken by having this title mistakenly applied to me.

None the less, without impugning their motives, I do disagree most emphatically with both the fundamental philosophy and the proposed remedies of the Marxian Socialists. These Socialists are unalterably opposed to our whole industrial system. They believe that the payment of wages means everywhere and inevitably an exploitation of the laborer by the employer, and that this leads inevitably to a class war between those two groups, or, as they would say, between the capitalists and the proletariat. They assert that this class war is already upon us and can only be ended when capitalism is entirely destroyed and all the machines, mills, mines, railroads and other private property used in production are confiscated, expropriated or taken over by the workers. They do not as a rule claim—although some of the sinister extremists among them do—that this class war is a war of blood and bullets, but they do claim that there is and must be a continual struggle between two great classes, whose interests are opposed and cannot be reconciled. In this war they insist that the whole government—National, State and local—is on the side of the employers and is used by them against the workmen, and that our law and even our common morality are class weapons, like a policeman's club or a Gatling gun.

I have never believed, and do not to-day believe, that such a class war is upon us, or need ever be upon us; nor do I believe that the interests of wage-earners and employers cannot be harmonized, compromised and adjusted. It would be idle to deny that wage-earners have certain different economic interests from, let us say, manufacturers or importers, just as farmers have different interests from sailors, and fishermen from bankers. There is no reason why any of these economic groups should not consult their group interests by any legitimate means and with due regard to the common, overlying interests of all. I do not even deny that the majority of wage-earners, because they have less property and less industrial security than others and because they do not own the machinery with which they work (as does the farmer) are perhaps in greater need of acting together than are other groups in the community. But I do insist (and I believe that the great majority of wage-earners take the same view) that employers and employees have overwhelming interests in common, both as partners in industry and as citizens of the Republic, and that where these interests are apart they can be adjusted by so altering our laws and their interpretation as to secure to all members of the community social and industrial justice.

I have always maintained that our worst revolutionaries to-day are those reactionaries who do not see and will not admit that there is any need for change. Such men seem to believe that the four and a half million Progressive voters, who in 1912 registered their solemn protest against our social and industrial injustices, are "anarchists," who are not willing to let ill enough alone. If these reactionaries had lived at an earlier time in our history, they would have advocated Sedition Laws, opposed free speech and free assembly, and voted against free schools, free access by settlers to the public lands, mechanics lien laws, the prohibition of truck stores and the abolition of imprisonment for debt; and they are the men who to-day oppose minimum wage laws, insurance of workmen against the ills of industrial life and the reform of our legislators and our courts, which can alone render such measures possible. Some of these reactionaries are not bad men, but merely shortsighted and belated. It is these reactionaries, however, who, by "standing pat" on industrial injustice, incite inevitably to industrial revolt, and it is only we who advocate political and industrial democracy who render possible the progress of our American industry on large constructive lines with a minimum of friction because with a maximum of justice. [. . .]

Walter Rauschenbusch

Christianizing the Social Order (1912)

Our business life is the seat and source of our present troubles. So much ought to be plain to all who care to see. It is in commerce and industry that we encounter the great collective inhumanities that shame our Christian feeling, such as child labor and the bloody total of industrial accidents. Here we find the friction between great classes of men which makes whole communities hot with smoldering hate or sets them ablaze with lawlessness. To commerce and industry we are learning to trace the foul stream of sex prostitution, poverty, and political corruption. Just as an epidemic of typhoid fever would call for an analysis of the water supply, so these chronic conditions call for a moral analysis of the economic order and justify the presumption that it is fundamentally unchristian. Business men themselves concede that it is; some by calmly denying that Christian principles have anything to do with business; others by sadly confessing that Christianity ought to govern business, but that it would mean loss or ruin to put Christian ethics in practice.

Business life is the unregenerate section of our social order. If by some magic it could be plucked out of our total social life in all its raw selfishness, and isolated on an island, unmitigated by any other factors of our life, that island would immediately become the object of a great foreign mission crusade for all Christendom. Our argument, therefore, will now concentrate on this unredeemed portion of the social order.

Our first need is to analyze our economic system so that we may understand wherein and why it is fundamentally unchristian. Most of us have accepted our economic system as we accept our stomach, without understanding its workings. Nor is it easy to understand the moral essentials of this huge and complicated social machinery. We have no such historical perspective of it as our great-grandchildren will have when they study the Great Industrial Transition of the Twentieth Century in college. We are like a swimmer in a stormy sea. To negotiate the next wave is the great object of his concern, but whether that wave is part of a tidal current sweeping him toward shore or out to sea, his narrow horizon does not tell him. So amid the swift changes of our age we find it hard to distinguish between incidental troubles and the essential drifts of our economic system. [. . .]

The reign of competition is a reign of fear. The rate of mortality for small business concerns is higher than infant mortality. If all the leaden weight of fear of all business men who watch a vanishing margin of profit through the year could be gathered up and set before us in some dramatic form, it would palsy our joy in life. Business panics merely render this chronic condition acute and make men high up who have been secure in prosperity feel the same sufferings which others have felt who went down before them. A reign of fear is never a reign of God. Fear makes children lie and businessmen cheat. In competition the worst man sets the pace, and good men follow because they are afraid. A capable mind with no bowels of mercy to hinder who can wring the last ounce of strength from his men, and who put women and children to work wherever men can be displaced, can outbid a morally sensitive man unless the latter has some counterbalancing advantage elsewhere. In a cooperating group the efficiency and courage of the best members of the team hold the rest up to their level; in commercial competition the greed and inhumanity of the worst infect the rest through the medium of fear. For this reason considerations of humanity have often had so little response from communities of businessmen composed largely of Christian persons. Individually they are kind-hearted men; but as members of a competitive social order they are driven by fear and forgetful of mercy. Workmen complain when their employers speed up the machinery, which compels them to keep up with its pace or be hurt. But their employers are also slaves of a huger machine, and many of them are seeking with laboring breath to keep up with a treadmill that will mangle them if they do not.

The objection will be raised that the instinct of competition is inherent in human life and that its free play is a necessary factor in the evolution of the race. That is quite true. Life would lose much of its zest and of its educational value if competition were eliminated from it. But there is no danger whatever that it will be.

Young men will always compete for the love of woman (and sometimes that game is reversed); students will compete for educational honors; workmen will compete for leadership within their group; statesmen will compete for popularity and power. When the ablest are honored and promoted, it benefits all. A superior type is thereby placed in a conspicuous position, and the rest are more or less modeled after it. The unsuccessful competitors may suffer all the pangs of disappointed, ambition, but they are not usually impoverished or disgraced. A college boy who fails to win a prize is not on that account reduced to high school rank. A workman who fails to be promoted to the position of foreman does not lose his old job. Such emulation advances some without ruining the rest. For that kind of competition an economic system founded wholly on cooperation would offer splendid chances, with more publicity and fame for the winners than is now offered in business life. [. . .]

For a century the doctrine of salvation by competition was the fundamental article in the working creed of the capitalistic nations. It was the "natural theology" of industry, and no political economy was orthodox that did not preach it. Governments felt it would be a sin to interfere while competitors were having a Donnybrook Fair. In theory it is still in effect in our country. Businessmen are indignant when workingmen refuse to permit unrestrained competition among themselves. Government is supposed to punish combinations "in restraint of trade." But in practice competition is being hemmed in and tied up on all hands. None of the big leaders of business believe in it. If they do, their faith is even farther removed from their works than usually. The doctrine of competition was once historically useful because it helped to clear away an outgrown economic system and to substitute larger cooperating groups for the little groups of the handicraft system. But that work has

been done, and to-day competition has itself become an antiquated method which ties its down to petty and inefficient forms of teamwork. The polliwog is through with its tail and gills, and is anxious to grow legs and lungs, and sit on a stone in the pride of its froghood. But legislators, lawyers, and old gentlemen generally are anxiously trying to coax back the vanishing tail. The only valid defense for the wastefulness and inefficiency of the competitive system is that it protects the consumer against the voracity of the monopolist. That end is wholly laudable, but we shall have to find more effective means of attaining it than moving back the clock-hands that destiny is driving forward.

Business is abandoning competition because it is inefficient, and larger and more powerful forms of association and teamwork are being wrought out. Christianity should help to end competition because it is immoral. Its murderous effect in England at the beginning of the capitalistic era is a matter of record. It has had much the same effect every time it invaded a new country or community. It is a shortsighted and suicidal policy. One nation after the other has had to hog-tie competition by government interference, inspection, and paternalism in the interests of safety and humanity. Competition as a principle is a denial of fraternity. In so far as it is allowed to do its unrestrained work, it establishes the law of tooth and nail, and brings back the age of savage warfare where every man's hand is against every man. It dechristianizes the social order. Whatever progress was achieved under the competitive system was secured, not by the competitive element in it, but by the fact that it allowed so large an application of the forces of association and teamwork. It behooves us to find forms of organization that will expand the present narrow areas of cooperation and make them nation wide. [. . .]

Men who are in the same line of work must be so organized that they can emulate while they cooperate. Commercial competition has developed in our commercial communities the lower instincts of selfishness, covetousness, and craft. A Christian social order must be such that it will develop and educate mutual interest and good will, and equip workmates with that sense of comradeship and solidarity to which they are entitled. [. . .]

Let us sum up the case of Christianity against Capitalism.

We saw that the distinctive characteristic of the capitalistic system is that the industrial outfit of society is owned and controlled by a limited group, while the mass of the industrial workers is without ownership or power over the system within which they work. A small group of great wealth and power is set over against a large group of propertyless men. Given this line-up, the rest follows with the inevitableness of a process in physics or chemistry.

Wherever the capitalist class remains in unorganized and small units, they will struggle for the prizes held out by modern industry. Capitalism in its youth threw off the restraints upon competition created by the older social order, and a fierce, free fight followed. Wherever the competitive principle is still in operation, it intensifies natural emulation by the size of the stakes it offers, enables the greedy and cunning to set the pace for the rest, makes men immoral by fear, and puts the selfish impulses in control. The charge of Christianity against cooperative capitalism is that it is unfraternal, the opposite of cooperation and teamwork.

Capitalism gives the owners and managers of industry autocratic power over the workers. The dangers always inherent in the leadership of the strong are intensified by the fact that in capitalistic industry, this power is unrestrained by democratic checks and fortified by almost absolute ownership of the means of production and life. [. . .] The practice of mutualism has always worked this way. Most sin is preying, and every new social relation begets its cannibalism. No one will "make the ephah small" or "falsify the balances" until there is buying and selling, "withhold the pledge" until there is loaning, "keep back the hire of the laborers" until there is a wage system, "justify the wicked for a reward" until men submit their disputes to a judge. The rise of the state makes possible counterfeiting, smuggling, peculation, and treason. Commerce tempts the pirate, the forger, and the embezzler. Every new fiduciary relation is a fresh opportunity for breach of trust. Today the factory system makes it possible to work children to death on the double-quick, speculative building gives the jerry-builder his chance, long-range investment spawns the get-rich-quick concern, and the trust movement opens the door to the bubble promoter.

The springs of the older sin seem to be drying up. Our forced-draught pace relieves us of the superabundance of energy that demands an explosive outlet. Spasms of violent feeling go with a sluggish habit of life, and are as out of place to-day as are the hard-drinking habits of our Saxon ancestors. We are too busy to give rein to spite. The stresses and lures of civilized life leave slender margin for the gratification of animosities. In quiet, side-tracked communities there is still much old-fashioned hatred, leading to personal clash, but elsewhere the cherishing of malice is felt to be an expensive luxury. Moreover, brutality, lust, and cruelty are on the wane. In this country, it is true, statistics show a widening torrent of bloody crime, but the cause is the weakening of law rather than an excess of bile. Outer civilized peoples seem to be turning away from the sins of passion.

The darling sins that are blackening the face of our time are incidental to the ruthless pursuit of private ends, and hence quite "without prejudice." The victims are used or sacrificed not at all from personal ill-will, but because they can serve as pawns in somebody's little game. Like the wayfarers run down by the automobilist, they are offered up to the God of Speed. The essence of the wrongs that infest our articulated society is betrayal rather than aggression. Having perforce to build men of willow into a social fabric that calls for oak, we see on all hands monstrous treacheries,—adulterators, peculators, doodlers, grafters, violating the trust others have placed its them. The little finger of Chicane has come to be thicker than the loins of Violence.

The sinister opportunities presented in this webbed social life have been seized unhesitatingly, because such treasons have not yet become infamous. The man who picks pockets with a railway rebate, murders with an adulterant instead of a bludgeon, burglarizes with a rake-off instead of a jimmy, cheats with a company prospectus instead of a deck of cards, or scuttles his town instead of his ship, does not feel on his brow the brand of a malefactor. The shedder of blood, the oppressor of the widow and the fatherless, long ago became odious, but latter-day treacheries fly no skull-and-crossbones flag at the masthead. The qualities which differentiate them from the primitive sin and procure them such indulgence may be clearly defined.

The stealings and slayings that lurk in the complexities of our social relations are not deeds of the dive, the dark alley, the lonely road, and the midnight hour. They require no nocturnal prowling with muffled step and bated breath, no weapon or offer of violence. Unlike the old-time villain, the latter-day malefactor does not wear a slouch hat and a comforter, breathe forth curses and an odor of gin, go about his nefarious work with clenched teeth and an evil scowl. In the supreme moment his lineaments are not distorted with rage, or lust, or malevolence. One misses the dramatic setting, the time-honored insignia of turpitude. Fagin and Bill Sykes and Simon Legree are vanishing types. Gamester, murderer, body-snatcher, and kidnapper may appeal to a Hogarth, but what challenge finds his pencil in the countenance of the doodler, the savings-bank wrecker, or the ballot-box stuffer? Among our criminals of greed, one begins to meet the "grand style" of the great criminals of ambition. Macbeth or Richard III. The modern high-powered dealer of woe wears immaculate linen, carries a silk hat and a lighted cigar, sins with a calm countenance and a serene soul, leagues or months from the evil he causes. [. . .]

The grading of sinners according to badness of character goes on the assumption that the wickedest man is the most dangerous. This would he true if men were abreast in their opportunities to do harm. In that case the blackest villain would be the worst scourge of society. But the fact is that the patent ruffian is confined to the social basement, and enjoys few opportunities. He can assault or molest, to be sure; but he cannot betray. Nobody depends on him, so he cannot commit breach of trust,—that arch sin of our time. He does not hold in his hand the safety or welfare or money of the public. He is the clinker, not the live coal; vermin, not beast of prey. To-day the villain most in need of curbing is the respectable, exemplary, trusted personage who, strategically placed at the focus of a spider-web of fiduciary relations, is able from his office-chair to pick a thousand pockets, poison a thousand sick, pollute a thousand minds, or imperil a thousand lives. It is the great-scale, high-voltage sinner that needs the shackle. [. . .]

[. . .] [T]he master class in large domains of industry have exacted excessive toil, and have paid neither a just return for the work done nor sufficient to support life normally. The working class is everywhere in a state of unrest and embattlement. By great sacrifices it has tried to organize in order to strengthen its position against these odds, but the master class has hampered or suppressed the organizations of labor. This line-up of two antagonistic classes is the historical continuation of the same line-up which we see in chattel slavery and feudal serfdom. In recent years the development of corporations has added a new difficulty by depersonalizing the master. The whole situation contradicts the spirit of American institutions. It is the last entrenchment of the despotic principle. It tempts the class in power to be satisfied with a semi-morality in their treatment of the working class. It is not Christian.

The capitalist class serves society in the capacity of the middleman, and modern conditions make this function more important than ever before. But under the capitalistic organization this wholesome function is not under public control, and the relations created call out the selfish motives and leave the higher motives of human nature dormant. Under competition business readily drifts into the use of tricky methods, sells harmful or adulterated goods, and breaks down the moral self-restraint of the buyer. Under monopoly the middleman is able to practice extortion on the consumer. The kindly and friendly relations that abound in actual business life between the dealer and the consumer are due to the personal character of the parties and the ineradicable social nature of man, and are not created by the nature of business itself.

In all the operations of capitalistic industry and commerce the aim that controls and directs is not the purpose to supply human needs, but to make a profit for those who direct industry. This in itself is an irrational and unchristian adjustment of the social order, for it sets money up as the prime aim, and human life as something secondary, or as a means to secure money. The supremacy of profit in capitalism stamps it as a mammonistic organization with which Christianity can never be content. "Profit" commonly contains considerable elements of just reward for able work; it may contain nothing but that; but where it is large and dissociated from hard work, it is traceable to some kind of monopoly privilege and power, either the power to withhold part of the earnings of the workers by the control of the means of production, or the ability to throw part of the expenses of business on the community, or the power to overcharge the public. In so far as profit is derived from these sources, it is tribute collected by power from the helpless, a form of legalized graft, and a contradiction of Christian relations.

Thus our capitalistic commerce and industry lies alongside of the home, the school, the Church, and the democratized States as an unregenerate part of the social order, not based on freedom, love, and mutual service, as they are, but on autocracy, antagonism of interests, and exploitation. Such a verdict does not condemn the moral character of the men in business. On the contrary, it gives a remarkable value to every virtue they exhibit in business, for every act of honesty, justice, and kindness in a triumph over hostile conditions, a refusal of Christianity and humanity to be chilled by low temperature or scorched by the flame of high-pressure temptation. Our business life has been made endurable only by the high qualities of the men and women engaged in it. These personal qualities have been created by the home, the school, and the Church. The State has also made Business tolerable by pulling a few of the teeth and shortening the tether of greed. Thus moral forces generated outside of Capitalism have invaded its domain and supplied the moral qualities without which it would have collapsed. But capitalistic business in turn is invading the regenerate portions of the social order, paralyzing their activities, breaking down the respect for the higher values, desecrating the holy, and invading God's country. [. . .]

Immediately after the Methodist General Conference, in December, 1908, the Federal Council of the Churches of Christ in America was organized at Philadelphia, representing and uniting thirty-three Protestant denominations. This organization marked an epoch in the history of American Protestantism. But no other session created so profound an interest as that devoted to "Social Service." The report of the Commission was heard with tense feeling, which broke into prolonged and enthusiastic applause at the close. The Bill of Rights adopted by the Methodist Convention was presented with some changes and adopted without the slightest disposition to halt it at any point. The following declaration, therefore, has stood since 1908 as the common sense of the Protestant churches of America:

"We deem it the duty of all Christian people to concern themselves directly which certain practical industrial problems. To us it seems that the churches must stand:

For equal rights and complete justice for all men in all stations of life.

For the right of all men to the opportunity for self-maintenance, a right ever to be wisely and strongly safeguarded against encroachments of every kind.

For the right of workers to some protection against the hardships, often resulting from the swift crises of industrial change.

For the principle of conciliation and arbitration in industrial dissensions.

For the protection of the worker from dangerous machinery, occupational disease, injuries, and mortality.

For the abolition of child labor.

For such regulations of the conditions of toil for women as shall safeguard the physical and moral health of the community.

For the suppression of the 'sweating system.'

For the gradual and reasonable reduction of the hours of labor to the lowest practicable point and for that degree of measure for all which is a condition of the highest human life.

For a release from employment one day in seven.

For a living wage as a minimum in every industry, and for the highest wage that each industry can afford.

For the most equitable division of the products of industry that can ultimately be devised.

For suitable provision for the old age of the workers and for those incapacitated by injury.

For the abatement of poverty.

To the toilers of America and to those who by organized effort are seeking to lift the crushing burdens of the poor, and to reduce the hardships and uphold the dignity of labor, this Council sends the greeting of human brotherhood and the pledge of sympathy and of help in a cause which belongs to all who follow Christ."

Emma Goldman

Anarchism: What It Really Stands For (1911)

Anarchy.

Ever reviled, accursed, ne'er understood,
Thou art the grisly terror of our age.
"Wreck of all order," cry the multitude,
"Art thou, and war and murder's endless rage."
O, let them cry. To them that ne'er have striven
The truth that lies behind a word to find,
To them the word's right meaning was not given.
They shall continue blind among the blind.
But thou, O word, so clear, so strong, so pure,
Thou sayest all which I for goal have taken.
I give thee to the future! Thine secure
When each at least unto himself shall waken.
Comes it in sunshine? In the tempest's thrill?
I cannot tell—but it the earth shall see!
I am an Anarchist! Wherefore I will
Not rule, and also ruled I will not be!

John Henry Mackay.

The history of human growth and development is at the same time the history of the terrible struggle of every new idea heralding the approach of a brighter dawn. In its tenacious hold on tradition, the Old has never hesitated to make use of the foulest and cruelest means to stay the advent of the New, in whatever form or period the latter may have asserted itself. Nor need we retrace our steps into the distant past to realize the enormity of opposition, difficulties, and hardships placed in the path of every progressive idea. The rack, the thumbscrew, and the knout are still with us; so are the convict's garb and the social wrath, all conspiring against the spirit that is serenely marching on.

Anarchism could not hope to escape the fate of all other ideas of innovation. Indeed, as the most revolutionary and uncompromising innovator, Anarchism must needs meet with the combined ignorance and venom of the world it aims to reconstruct.

To deal even remotely with all that is being said and done against Anarchism would necessitate the writing of a whole volume. I shall therefore meet only two of the principal objections. In so doing, I shall attempt to elucidate what Anarchism really stands for.

The strange phenomenon of the opposition to Anarchism is that it brings to light the relation between so-called intelligence and ignorance. And yet this is not so very strange when we consider the relativity of all things. The ignorant mass has in its favor that it makes no pretense of knowledge or tolerance. Acting, as it always does, by mere impulse, its reasons are like those of a child. "Why?" "Because." Yet the opposition of the uneducated to Anarchism deserves the same consideration as that of the intelligent man.

What, then, are the objections? First, Anarchism is impractical, though a beautiful ideal. Second, Anarchism stands for violence and destruction, hence it must be repudiated as vile and dangerous. Both the intelligent man and the ignorant mass judge not from a thorough knowledge of the subject, but either from hearsay or false interpretation.

A practical scheme, says Oscar Wilde, is either one already in existence, or a scheme that could be carried out under the existing conditions; but it is exactly the existing conditions that one objects to, and any scheme that could accept these conditions is wrong and foolish. The true criterion of the practical, therefore, is not whether the latter can keep intact the wrong or foolish; rather is it whether the scheme has vitality enough to leave the stagnant waters of the old, and build, as well as sustain, new life. In the light of this conception, Anarchism is indeed practical. More than any other idea, it is helping to do away with the wrong and foolish; more than any other idea, it is building and sustaining new life.

The emotions of the ignorant man are continuously kept at a pitch by the most blood-curdling stories about Anarchism. Not a thing too outrageous to be employed against this philosophy and its exponents. Therefore Anarchism represents to the unthinking what the proverbial bad man does to the child,—a black monster bent on swallowing everything; in short, destruction and violence.

Destruction and violence! How is the ordinary man to know that the most violent element in society is ignorance; that its power of destruction is the very thing Anarchism is combating? Nor is he aware that Anarchism, whose roots, as it were, are part of nature's forces, destroys, not healthful tissue, but parasitic growths that feed on the life's essence of society. It is merely clearing the soil from weeds and sagebrush, that it may eventually bear healthy fruit.

Someone has said that it requires less mental effort to condemn than to think. The widespread mental indolence, so prevalent in society, proves this to be only too true. Rather than to go to the bottom of any given idea, to examine into its origin and meaning, most people will either condemn it altogether, or rely on some superficial or prejudicial definition of non-essentials.

Anarchism urges man to think, to investigate, to analyze every proposition; but that the brain capacity of the average reader be not taxed too much, I also shall begin with a definition, and then elaborate on the latter.

ANARCHISM:—The philosophy of a new social order based on liberty unrestricted by man-made law; the theory that all forms of government rest on violence, and are therefore wrong and harmful, as well as unnecessary.

The new social order rests, of course, on the materialistic basis of life; but while all Anarchists agree that the main evil today is an economic one, they maintain that the solution of that evil can be brought about only through the consideration of *every phase* of life,—individual, as well as the collective; the internal, as well as the external phases.

A thorough perusal of the history of human development will disclose two elements in bitter conflict with each other; elements that are only now beginning to be understood, not as foreign to each other, but as closely related and truly harmonious, if only placed in proper environment: the individual and social instincts. The individual and society have waged a relentless and bloody battle for ages, each striving for supremacy, because each was blind to the value and importance of the other. The individual and social instincts,—the one a most potent factor for individual endeavor, for growth, aspiration, self-realization; the other an equally potent factor for mutual helpfulness and social well-being.

The explanation of the storm raging within the individual, and between him and his surroundings, is not far to seek. The primitive man, unable to understand his being, much less the unity of all life, felt himself absolutely dependent on blind, hidden forces ever ready to mock and taunt him. Out of that attitude grew the religious concepts of man as a mere speck of dust dependent on superior powers on high, who can only be appeased by complete surrender. All the early sagas rest on that idea, which continues to be the *Leitmotiv* of the biblical tales dealing with the relation of man to God, to the State, to society. Again and again the same motif, *man is nothing, the powers are everything*. Thus Jehovah would only endure man on condition of complete surrender. Man can have all the glories of the earth, but he must not become conscious of himself. The State, society, and moral laws all sing the same refrain: Man can have all the glories of the earth, but he must not become conscious of himself.

Anarchism is the only philosophy which brings to man the consciousness of himself; which maintains that God, the State, and society are non-existent, that their promises are null and void, since they can be fulfilled only through man's subordination. Anarchism is therefore the teacher of the unity of life; not merely in nature, but in man. There is no conflict between the individual and the social instincts, any more than there is between the heart and the lungs: the one the receptacle of a precious life essence, the other the repository of the element that keeps the essence pure and strong. The individual is the heart of society, conserving the essence of social life; society is the lungs which are distributing the element to keep the life essence—that is, the individual—pure and strong.

"The one thing of value in the world," says Emerson, "is the active soul; this every man contains within him. The soul active sees absolute truth and utters truth and creates." In other words, the individual instinct is the thing of value in the world. It is the true soul that sees and creates the truth alive, out of which is to come a still greater truth, the re-born social soul.

Anarchism is the great liberator of man from the phantoms that have held him captive; it is the arbiter and pacifier of the two forces for individual and social harmony. To accomplish that unity, Anarchism has declared war on the pernicious influences which have so far prevented the harmonious blending of individual and social instincts, the individual and society.

Religion, the dominion of the human mind; Property, the dominion of human needs; and Government, the dominion of human conduct, represent the stronghold of man's enslavement and all the horrors it entails. Religion! How it dominates man's mind, how it humiliates and degrades his soul. God is everything, man is nothing, says religion. But out of that nothing God has created a kingdom so despotic, so tyrannical, so cruel, so terribly exacting that naught but gloom and tears and blood have ruled the world since gods began. Anarchism rouses man to rebellion against this black monster. Break your mental fetters, says Anarchism to man, for not until you think and judge for yourself will you get rid of the dominion of darkness, the greatest obstacle to all progress.

Property, the dominion of man's needs, the denial of the right to satisfy his needs. Time was when property claimed a divine right, when it came to man with the same refrain, even as religion, "Sacrifice! Abnegate! Submit!" The spirit of Anarchism has lifted man from his prostrate position. He now stands erect, with his face toward the light. He has learned to see the insatiable, devouring, devastating nature of property, and he is preparing to strike the monster dead.

"Property is robbery," said the great French Anarchist Proudhon. Yes, but without risk and danger to the robber. Monopolizing the accumulated efforts of man, property has robbed him of his birthright, and has turned him loose a pauper and an outcast. Property has not even the time-worn excuse that man does not create enough to satisfy all needs. The A B C student of economics knows that the productivity of labor within the last few decades far exceeds normal demand. But what are normal demands to an abnormal institution? The only demand that property recognizes is its own gluttonous appetite for greater wealth, because wealth means power; the power to subdue, to crush, to exploit, the power to enslave, to outrage, to degrade. America is particularly boastful of her great power, her enormous national wealth. Poor America, of what avail is all her wealth, if the individuals comprising the nation are wretchedly poor? If they live in squalor, in filth, in crime, with hope and joy gone, a homeless, soilless army of human prey.

It is generally conceded that unless the returns of any business venture exceed the cost, bankruptcy is inevitable. But those engaged in the business of producing wealth have not yet learned even this simple lesson. Every year the cost of production in human life is growing larger (50,000 killed, 100,000 wounded in America last year); the returns to the masses, who help to create wealth, are ever getting smaller. Yet America continues to be blind to the inevitable bankruptcy of our business of production. Nor is this the only crime of the latter. Still more fatal is the crime of turning the producer into a mere particle of a machine, with less will and decision than his master of steel and iron. Man is being robbed not merely of the products of his labor, but of the power of free initiative, of originality, and the interest in, or desire for, the things he is making.

Real wealth consists in things of utility and beauty, in things that help to create strong, beautiful bodies and surroundings inspiring to live in. But if man is doomed to wind cotton around a spool, or dig coal, or build roads for thirty years of his life, there can be no talk of wealth. What he gives to the world is only gray and hideous things, reflecting a dull and hideous existence,—too weak to live, too cowardly to die. Strange to say, there are people who extol this deadening method of centralized production as the proudest achievement of our age. They fail utterly to realize that if we are to continue in machine subserviency, our slavery is more complete than was our bondage to the King. They do not want to know that centralization is not only the death-knell of liberty, but also of health and beauty, of art and science, all these being impossible in a clock-like, mechanical atmosphere.

Anarchism cannot but repudiate such a method of production: its goal is the freest possible expression of all the latent powers of the individual. Oscar Wilde defines a perfect personality as "one who develops under perfect conditions, who is not wounded, maimed, or in danger." A perfect personality, then, is only possible in a state of society where man is free to choose the mode of work, the conditions of work, and the freedom to work. One to whom the making of a table, the building of a house, or the tilling of the soil, is what the painting is to the artist and the discovery to the scientist,—the result of inspiration, of intense longing, and deep interest in work as a creative force. That being the ideal of Anarchism, its economic arrangements must consist of voluntary productive and distributive associations, gradually developing into free communism, as the best means of producing with the least waste of human energy. Anarchism, however, also recognizes the right of the individual, or numbers of individuals, to arrange at all times for other forms of work, in harmony with their tastes and desires.

Such free display of human energy being possible only under complete individual and social freedom, Anarchism directs its forces against the third and greatest foe of all social equality; namely, the State, organized authority, or statutory law,—the dominion of human conduct.

Just as religion has fettered the human mind, and as property, or the monopoly of things, has subdued and stifled man's needs, so has the State enslaved his spirit, dictating every phase of conduct. "All government in essence," says Emerson, "is tyranny." It matters not whether it is government by divine right or majority rule. In every instance its aim is the absolute subordination of the individual.

Referring to the American government, the greatest American Anarchist, David Thoreau, said: "Government, what is it but a tradition, though a recent one, endeavoring to transmit itself unimpaired to posterity, but each instance losing its integrity; it has not the vitality and force of a single living man. Law never made man a whit more just; and by means of their respect for it, even the well disposed are daily made agents of injustice."

Indeed, the keynote of government is injustice. With the arrogance and self-sufficiency of the King who could do no wrong, governments ordain, judge, condemn, and punish the most insignificant offenses, while maintaining themselves by the greatest of all offenses, the annihilation of individual liberty. Thus Ouida is right when she maintains that "the State only aims at instilling those qualities in its public by which its demands are obeyed, and its exchequer is filled. Its highest attainment is the reduction of mankind to clockwork. In its atmosphere all those finer and more delicate liberties, which require treatment and spacious expansion,

inevitably dry up and perish. The State requires a tax-paying machine in which there is no hitch, an exchequer in which there is never a deficit, and a public, monotonous, obedient, colorless, spiritless, moving humbly like a flock of sheep along a straight high road between two walls."

Yet even a flock of sheep would resist the chicanery of the State, if it were not for the corruptive, tyrannical, and oppressive methods it employs to serve its purposes. Therefore Bakunin repudiates the State as synonymous with the surrender of the liberty of the individual or small minorities,—the destruction of social relationship, the curtailment, or complete denial even, of life itself, for its own aggrandizement. The State is the altar of political freedom and, like the religious altar, it is maintained for the purpose of human sacrifice.

In fact, there is hardly a modern thinker who does not agree that government, organized authority, or the State, is necessary *only* to maintain or protect property and monopoly. It has proven efficient in that function only.

Even George Bernard Shaw, who hopes for the miraculous from the State under Fabianism, nevertheless admits that "it is at present a huge machine for robbing and slave-driving of the poor by brute force." This being the case, it is hard to see why the clever prefacer wishes to uphold the State after poverty shall have ceased to exist.

Unfortunately, there are still a number of people who continue in the fatal belief that government rests on natural laws, that it maintains social order and harmony, that it diminishes crime, and that it prevents the lazy man from fleecing his fellows. I shall therefore examine these contentions.

A natural law is that factor in man which asserts itself freely and spontaneously without any external force, in harmony with the requirements of nature. For instance, the demand for nutrition, for sex gratification, for light, air, and exercise, is a natural law. But its expression needs not the machinery of government, needs not the club, the gun, the handcuff, or the prison. To obey such laws, if we may call it obedience, requires only spontaneity and free opportunity. That governments do not maintain themselves through such harmonious factors is proven by the terrible array of violence, force, and coercion all governments use in order to live. Thus Blackstone is right when he says, "Human laws are invalid, because they are contrary to the laws of nature."

Unless it be the order of Warsaw after the slaughter of thousands of people, it is difficult to ascribe to governments any capacity for order or social harmony. Order derived through submission and maintained by terror is not much of a safe guaranty; yet that is the only "order" that governments have ever maintained. True social harmony grows naturally out of solidarity of interests. In a society where those who always work never have anything, while those who never work enjoy everything, solidarity of interests is non-existent; hence social harmony is but a myth. The only way organized authority meets this grave situation is by extending still greater privileges to those who have already monopolized the earth, and by still further enslaving the disinherited masses. Thus the entire arsenal of government—laws, police, soldiers, the courts, legislatures, prisons,—is strenuously engaged in "harmonizing" the most antagonistic elements in society.

The most absurd apology for authority and law is that they serve to diminish crime. Aside from the fact that the State is itself the greatest criminal, breaking every written and natural law, stealing in the form of taxes, killing in the form of war and capital punishment, it has come to an absolute standstill in coping with crime. It has failed utterly to destroy or even minimize the horrible scourge of its own creation.

Crime is naught but misdirected energy. So long as every institution of today, economic, political, social, and moral, conspires to misdirect human energy into wrong channels; so long as most people are out of place doing the things they hate to do, living a life they loathe to live, crime will be inevitable, and all the laws on the statutes can only increase, but never do away with, crime. What does society, as it exists today, know of the process of despair, the poverty, the horrors, the fearful struggle the human soul must pass on its way to crime and degradation. Who that knows this terrible process can fail to see the truth in these words of Peter Kropotkin:

"Those who will hold the balance between the benefits thus attributed to law and punishment and the degrading effect of the latter on humanity; those who will estimate the torrent of depravity poured abroad in human society by the informer, favored by the Judge even, and paid for in clinking cash by governments, under the pretext of aiding to unmask crime; those who will go within prison walls and there see what human beings become when deprived of liberty, when subjected to the care of brutal keepers, to coarse, cruel words, to a thousand stinging, piercing humiliations, will agree with us that the entire apparatus of prison and punishment is an abomination which ought to be brought to an end."

The deterrent influence of law on the lazy man is too absurd to merit consideration. If society were only relieved of the waste and expense of keeping a lazy class, and the equally great expense of the paraphernalia of protection this lazy class requires, the social tables would contain an abundance for all, including even the occasional lazy individual. Besides, it is well to consider that laziness results either from special privileges, or physical and mental abnormalities. Our present insane system of production fosters both, and the most astounding phenomenon is that people should want to work at all now. Anarchism aims to strip labor of its deadening, dulling aspect, of its gloom and compulsion. It aims to make work an instrument of joy, of strength, of color, of real harmony, so that the poorest sort of a man should find in work both recreation and hope.

To achieve such an arrangement of life, government, with its unjust, arbitrary, repressive measures, must be done away with. At best it has but imposed one single mode of life upon all, without regard to individual and social variations and needs. In destroying government and statutory laws, Anarchism proposes to rescue the self-respect and independence of the individual from all restraint and invasion by authority. Only in freedom can man grow to his full stature. Only in freedom will he learn to think and move, and give the very best in him. Only in freedom will he realize the true force of the social bonds which knit men together, and which are the true foundation of a normal social life.

But what about human nature? Can it be changed? And if not, will it endure under Anarchism?

Poor human nature, what horrible crimes have been committed in thy name! Every fool, from king to policeman, from the flatheaded parson to the visionless dabbler in science, presumes to speak authoritatively of human nature. The greater the mental charlatan, the more definite his insistence on the wickedness and weaknesses of human nature. Yet how can any one speak of it today, with every soul in a prison, with every heart fettered, wounded, and maimed?

John Burroughs has stated that experimental study of animals in captivity is absolutely useless. Their character, their habits, their appetites undergo a complete transformation when torn from their soil in field and forest. With human nature caged in a narrow space, whipped daily into submission, how can we speak of its potentialities?

Freedom, expansion, opportunity, and, above all, peace and repose, alone can teach us the real dominant factors of human nature and all its wonderful possibilities.

Anarchism, then, really stands for the liberation of the human mind from the dominion of religion; the liberation of the human body from the dominion of property; liberation from the shackles and restraint of government. Anarchism stands for a social order based on the free grouping of individuals for the purpose of producing real social wealth; an order that will guarantee to every human being free access to the earth and full enjoyment of the necessities of life, according to individual desires, tastes, and inclinations.

This is not a wild fancy or an aberration of the mind. It is the conclusion arrived at by hosts of intellectual men and women the world over; a conclusion resulting from the close and studious observation of the tendencies of modern society: individual liberty and economic equality, the twin forces for the birth of what is fine and true in man.

As to methods. Anarchism is not, as some may suppose, a theory of the future to be realized through divine inspiration. It is a living force in the affairs of our life, constantly creating new conditions. The methods of Anarchism therefore do not comprise an iron-clad program to be carried out under all circumstances. Methods must grow out of the economic needs of each place and clime, and of the intellectual and temperamental requirements of the individual. The serene, calm character of a Tolstoy will wish different methods for social reconstruction than the intense, overflowing personality of a Michael Bakunin or a Peter Kropotkin. Equally so it must be apparent that the economic and political needs of Russia will dictate more drastic measures than would England or America. Anarchism does not stand for military drill and uniformity; it does,

however, stand for the spirit of revolt, in whatever form, against everything that hinders human growth. All Anarchists agree in that, as they also agree in their opposition to the political machinery as a means of bringing about the great social change.

"All voting," says Thoreau, "is a sort of gaming, like checkers, or backgammon, a playing with right and wrong; its obligation never exceeds that of expediency. Even voting for the right thing is doing nothing for it. A wise man will not leave the right to the mercy of chance, nor wish it to prevail through the power of the majority." A close examination of the machinery of politics and its achievements will bear out the logic of Thoreau.

What does the history of parliamentarism show? Nothing but failure and defeat, not even a single reform to ameliorate the economic and social stress of the people. Laws have been passed and enactments made for the improvement and protection of labor. Thus it was proven only last year that Illinois, with the most rigid laws for mine protection, had the greatest mine disasters. In States where child labor laws prevail, child exploitation is at its highest, and though with us the workers enjoy full political opportunities, capitalism has reached the most brazen zenith.

Even were the workers able to have their own representatives, for which our good Socialist politicians are clamoring, what chances are there for their honesty and good faith? One has but to bear in mind the process of politics to realize that its path of good intentions is full of pitfalls: wire-pulling, intriguing, flattering, lying, cheating; in fact, chicanery of every description, whereby the political aspirant can achieve success. Added to that is a complete demoralization of character and conviction, until nothing is left that would make one hope for anything from such a human derelict. Time and time again the people were foolish enough to trust, believe, and support with their last farthing aspiring politicians, only to find themselves betrayed and cheated.

It may be claimed that men of integrity would not become corrupt in the political grinding mill. Perhaps not; but such men would be absolutely helpless to exert the slightest influence in behalf of labor, as indeed has been shown in numerous instances. The State is the economic master of its servants. Good men, if such there be, would either remain true to their political faith and lose their economic support, or they would cling to their economic master and be utterly unable to do the slightest good. The political arena leaves one no alternative, one must either be a dunce or a rogue.

The political superstition is still holding sway over the hearts and minds of the masses, but the true lovers of liberty will have no more to do with it. Instead, they believe with Stirner that man has as much liberty as he is willing to take. Anarchism therefore stands for direct action, the open defiance of, and resistance to, all laws and restrictions, economic, social, and moral. But defiance and resistance are illegal. Therein lies the salvation of man. Everything illegal necessitates integrity, self-reliance, and courage. In short, it calls for free, independent spirits, for "men who are men, and who have a bone in their backs which you cannot pass your hand through."

Universal suffrage itself owes its existence to direct action. If not for the spirit of rebellion, of the defiance on the part of the American revolutionary fathers, their posterity would still wear the King's coat. If not for the direct action of a John Brown and his comrades, America would still trade in the flesh of the black man. True, the trade in white flesh is still going on; but that, too, will have to be abolished by direct action. Trade-unionism, the economic arena of the modern gladiator, owes its existence to direct action. It is but recently that law and government have attempted to crush the trade-union movement, and condemned the exponents of man's right to organize to prison as conspirators. Had they sought to assert their cause through begging, pleading, and compromise, trade-unionism would today be a negligible quantity. In France, in Spain, in Italy, in Russia, nay even in England (witness the growing rebellion of English labor unions), direct, revolutionary, economic action has become so strong a force in the battle for industrial liberty as to make the world realize the tremendous importance of labor's power. The General Strike, the supreme expression of the economic consciousness of the workers, was ridiculed in America but a short time ago. Today every great strike, in order to win, must realize the importance of the solidaric general protest.

Direct action, having proven effective along economic lines, is equally potent in the environment of the individual. There a hundred forces encroach upon his being, and only persistent resistance to them will finally set him free. Direct action against the authority in the shop, direct action against the authority of the law, direct action against the invasive, meddlesome authority of our moral code, is the logical, consistent method of Anarchism.

Will it not lead to a revolution? Indeed, it will. No real social change has ever come about without a revolution. People are either not familiar with their history, or they have not yet learned that revolution is but thought carried into action.

Anarchism, the great leaven of thought, is today permeating every phase of human endeavor. Science, art, literature, the drama, the effort for economic betterment, in fact every individual and social opposition to the existing disorder of things, is illumined by the spiritual light of Anarchism. It is the philosophy of the sovereignty of the individual. It is the theory of social harmony. It is the great, surging, living truth that is reconstructing the world, and that will usher in the Dawn.

Elihu Root

Experiments in Government (1913)

When proposals are made to change these institutions there are certain general considerations which should be observed.

The first consideration is that free government is impossible except through prescribed and established governmental institutions, which work out the ends of government through many separate human agents, each doing his part in obedience to law. Popular will cannot execute itself directly except through a mob. Popular will cannot get itself executed through an irresponsible executive, for that is simple autocracy. An executive limited only by the direct expression of popular will cannot be held to responsibility against his will, because, having possession of all the powers of government, he can prevent any true, free, and general expression adverse to himself, and unless he yields voluntarily he can be overturned only by a revolution. [. . .]

We should, therefore, reject every proposal which involves the idea that the people can rule merely by voting, or merely by voting and having one man or group of men to execute their will.

A second consideration is that in estimating the value of any system of governmental institutions due regard must be had to the true functions of government and to the limitations imposed by nature upon what it is possible for government to accomplish. We all know of course that we cannot abolish all the evils in this world by statute or by the enforcement of statutes, nor can we prevent the inexorable law of nature which decrees that suffering shall follow vice, and all the evil passions and folly of mankind. Law cannot give to depravity the rewards of virtue, to indolence the rewards of industry, to indifference the rewards of ambition, or to ignorance the rewards of learning. The utmost that government can do is measurably to protect men, not against the wrong they do themselves but against wrong done by others, and to promote the long, slow process of educating mind and character to a better knowledge and nobler standards of life and conduct. We know all this, but when we see how much misery there is in the world and instinctively cry out against it, and when we see some things that government may do to mitigate it, we are apt to forget how little after all it is possible for any government to do, and to hold the particular government of the time and place to a standard of responsibility which no government can possibly meet. The chief motive power which has moved mankind along the course of development which we call the progress of civilization has been the sum total of intelligent selfishness in a vast number of individuals, each working for his own support, his own gain, his own betterment. [. . .]

A third consideration is that it is not merely useless but injurious for government to attempt too much. It is manifest that to enable it to deal with the new conditions I have described we must invest government with authority to interfere with the individual conduct of the citizen to a degree hitherto unknown in this country. When government undertakes to give the individual citizen protection by regulating the conduct of others towards him in the field where formerly he protected himself by his freedom of contract, it is limiting the liberty of the citizen whose conduct is regulated and taking a step in the direction of paternal government. While the new conditions of industrial life make it plainly necessary that many such steps shall be taken, they should be taken only so far as they are necessary and are effective. Interference with individual liberty by government should be jealously watched and restrained, because the habit of undue interference destroys that independence of character without which in its citizens no free government can endure.

We should not forget that while institutions receive their form from national character they have a powerful reflex influence upon that character. Just so far as a nation allows its institutions to be moulded by its weaknesses of character rather than by its strength it creates an influence to increase weakness at the expense of strength.

The habit of undue interference by government in private affairs breeds the habit of undue reliance upon government in private affairs at the expense of individual initiative, energy, enterprise, courage, independent manhood.

The strength of self-government and the motive power of progress must be found in the characters of the individual citizens who make up a nation. Weaken individual character among a people by comfortable reliance upon paternal government and a nation soon becomes incapable of free self-government and fit only to be governed: the higher and nobler qualities of national life that make for ideals and effort and achievement become atrophied and the nation is decadent.

A fourth consideration is that in the nature of things all government must be imperfect because men are imperfect. Every system has its shortcomings and inconveniences; and these are seen and felt as they exist in the system under which we live, while the shortcomings and inconveniences of other systems are forgotten or ignored.

It is not unusual to see governmental methods reformed and after a time, long enough to forget the evils that caused the change, to have a new movement for a reform which consists in changing back to substantially the same old methods that were cast out by the first reform.

Robert La Follette

Address on Free Speech in Wartime (1917)

Mr. President:

I rise to a question of personal privilege. I have no intention of taking the time of the Senate with a review of the events which led to our entrance into the war except in so far as they bear upon the question of personal privilege to which I am addressing myself.

Six Members of the Senate and fifty Members of the House voted against the declaration of war. Immediately there was let loose upon those Senators and Representatives a flood of invective and abuse from newspapers and individuals who had been clamoring for war, unequaled, I believe in the history of civilized society.

Prior to the declaration of war every man who had ventured to oppose our entrance into it had been condemned as a coward or worse, and even the President had by no means been immune from these attacks.

Since the declaration of war the triumphant war press has pursued those Senators and Representatives who voted against war with malicious falsehood and recklessly libelous attacks, going to the extreme limit of charging them with treason against their country.

This campaign of libel and character assassination directed against the Members of Congress who opposed our entrance into the war has been continued down to the present hour, and I have upon my desk newspaper clippings, some of them libels upon me alone, some directed as well against other Senators who voted in opposition to the declaration of war. One of these newspaper reports most widely circulated represents a Federal judge in the state of Texas as saying, in a charge to a grand jury—I read the article as it appeared in the newspaper and the headline with which it is introduced:

District Judge Would Like to Take Shot at Traitors in Congress
(A.P.) Houston, Texas, Oct. 1,
Judge Waller T. Burns, of the United States district court, in charging a Federal grand jury at the beginning of the October term today, after calling by name Senators Stone of Missouri, Hardwick of Georgia, Vardaman of Mississippi, Gronna of North Dakota, Gore of Oklahoma, and La Follette of Wisconsin, said: "If I had a wish, I would

wish that you men had jurisdiction to return bills of indictment against these men. They ought to be tried promptly and fairly, and I believe this court could administer the law fairly; but I have a conviction, as strong as life, that this country should stand them up against an adobe wall tomorrow and give them what they deserve. If any man deserves death, it is a traitor. I wish that I could pay for the ammunition. I would like to attend the execution, and if I were in the firing squad I would not want to be the marksman who had the blank shell.". . .

If this newspaper clipping were a single or exceptional instance of lawless defamation, I should not trouble the Senate with a reference to it. But, Mr. President, it is not.

In this mass of newspaper clippings which I have here upon my desk, and which I shall not trouble the Senate to read unless it is desired I find other Senators, as well as myself, accused of the highest crimes of which any man can be guilty—treason and disloyalty—and, sir, accused not only with no evidence to support the accusation, but without the suggestion that such evidence anywhere exists. It is not claimed that Senators who opposed the declaration of war have since that time acted with any concerted purpose either regarding war measures or any others. They have voted according to their individual opinions, have often been opposed to each other on bills which have come before the Senate since the declaration of war, and, according to my recollection, have never all voted together since that time upon any single proposition upon which the Senate has been divided.

I am aware, Mr. President, that in pursuance of this campaign of vilification and attempted intimidation, requests from various individuals and certain organizations have been submitted to the Senate for my expulsion from this body, and that such requests have been referred to and considered by one of the committees of the Senate.

If I alone had been made the victim of these attacks, I should not take one moment of the Senate's time for their consideration, and I believe that other Senators who have been unjustly and unfairly assailed, as I have been, hold the same attitude upon this that I do. Neither the clamor of the mob nor the voice of power will ever turn me by the breadth of a hair from the course I mark out for myself, guided by

such knowledge as I can obtain and controlled and directed by a solemn conviction of right and duty.

The purpose of this campaign [is] to throw the country into a state of terror, to coerce public opinion, to stifle criticism, and suppress discussion.

But, sir, it is not alone Members of Congress that the war party in this country has sought to intimidate. The mandate seems to have gone forth to the sovereign people of this country that they must be silent while those things are being done by their Government which most vitally concern their well-being, their happiness, and their lives. Today and for weeks past honest and law-abiding citizens of this country are being terrorized and outraged in their rights by those sworn to uphold the laws and protect the rights of the people. I have in my possession numerous affidavits establishing the fact that people are being unlawfully arrested, thrown into jail, held incommunicado for days, only to be eventually discharged without ever having been taken into court, because they have committed no crime. Private residences are being invaded, loyal citizens of undoubted integrity and probity arrested, cross-examined, and the most sacred constitutional rights guaranteed to every American citizen are being violated.

It appears to be the purpose of those conducting this campaign to throw the country into a state of terror, to coerce public opinion, to stifle criticism, and suppress discussion of the great issues involved in this war.

I think all men recognize that in time of war the citizen must surrender some rights for the common good which he is entitled to enjoy in time of peace. But sir, the right to control their own Government according to constitutional forms is not one of the rights that the citizens of this country are called upon to surrender in time of war.

Rather in time of war the citizen must be more alert to the preservation of his right to control his Government. He must be most watchful of the encroachment of the military upon the civil power. He must beware of those precedents in support of arbitrary action by administration officials which, excused on the plea of necessity in war time, become the fixed rule when the necessity has passed and normal conditions have been restored.

More than all, the citizen and his representative in Congress in time of war must maintain his right of free speech. More than in times of peace it is necessary that the channels for free public discussion of governmental policies shall be open and unclogged. I believe, Mr. President, that I am now touching upon the most important question in this country today—and that is the right of the citizens of this country and their representatives in Congress to discuss in an orderly way frankly and publicly and without fear, from the platform and through the press, every important phase of this war; its causes, and manner in which it should be conducted, and the terms upon which peace should be made. The belief which is becoming widespread in this land that this most fundamental right is being denied to the citizens of this country is a fact, the tremendous significance of which those in authority have not yet begun to appreciate. I am contending, Mr. President, for the great fundamental right of the sovereign people of this country to make their voice heard and have that voice heeded upon the great questions arising out of this war, including not only how the war shall be prosecuted but the conditions upon which it may be terminated with a due regard for the rights and the honor of this Nation and the interests of humanity.

I am contending for this right because the exercise of it is necessary to the welfare, to the existence, of this Government, to the successful conduct of this war, and to a peace which shall be enduring for the best interest of this country.

Suppose success attends the attempt to stifle all discussion of the issues of this war, all discussions of the terms upon which it should be concluded, all discussion of the objects and purposes to be accomplished by it, and concede the demand of the war-mad press and war extremists that they monopolize the right of public utterance upon these questions unchallenged, what think you would be the consequences to this country not only during the war but after the war?

It is no answer to say that when the war is over the citizen may once more resume his rights and feel some security in his liberty and his person. As I have already tried to point out, now is precisely the time when the country needs the counsel of all its citizens. In time of war even more than in time of peace, whether citizens happen to agree with the ruling administration or not, these precious fundamental personal rights—free speech, free press, and right of assemblage so explicitly and emphatically guaranteed by the Constitution should be maintained inviolable. There is no rebellion in the land, no martial law, no courts are closed, no legal processes suspended, and there is no threat even of invasion.

But more than this, if every preparation for war can be made the excuse for destroying free speech and a free press and the right of the people to assemble together for peaceful discussion, then we may well despair of ever again finding ourselves for a long period in a state of peace. . . . The destruction of rights now occurring will be pointed to then as precedents for a still further invasion of the rights of the citizen. [. . .]

Mr. President, our Government, above all others, is founded on the right of the people freely to discuss all matters pertaining to their Government, in war not less than in peace. It is true, sir, that Members of the House of Representatives are elected for two years, the President for four years, and the Members of the Senate for six years, and during their temporary official terms these officers constitute what is called the Government. But back of them always is the controlling sovereign power of the people, and when the people can make their will known, the faithful officer will obey that will. Though the right of the people to express their will by ballot is suspended during the term of office of the elected official, nevertheless the duty of the official to obey the popular will continue throughout his entire term of office. How can that popular will express itself between elections except by meetings, by speeches, by publications, by petitions, and by addresses to the representatives of the people? Any man who seeks to set a limit upon those rights, whether in war or peace, aims a blow at the most vital part of our Government. And then as the time for election approaches and the official is called to account for his stewardship—not a day, not a week, not a month, before the election, but a year or more before it, if the people choose— they must have the right to the freest possible discussion of every question upon which their representative has acted, of the merits of every measure he has supported or opposed, of every vote he has cast and every speech that he has made. And before this great fundamental right every other must, if necessary, give way, for in no other manner can representative government be preserved.

WILLIAM RUFUS DAY

Hammer v. Dagenhart (1918)

Mr. Justice DAY delivered the opinion of the Court.

A bill was filed in the United States District Court for the Western District of North Carolina by a father in his own behalf and as next friend of his two minor sons, one under the age of fourteen years and the other between the ages of fourteen and sixteen years, employees in a cotton mill at Charlotte, North Carolina, to enjoin the enforcement of the act of Congress intended to prevent interstate commerce in the products of child labor.

The District Court held the act unconstitutional and entered a decree enjoining its enforcement. This appeal brings the case here. [. . .]

The attack upon the act rests upon three propositions: first: it is not a regulation of interstate and foreign commerce; second: it contravenes the Tenth Amendment to the Constitution; third: it conflicts with the Fifth Amendment to the Constitution.

The controlling question for decision is: is it within the authority of Congress in regulating commerce among the States to prohibit the transportation in interstate commerce of manufactured goods, the product of a factory in which, within thirty days prior to their removal therefrom, children under the age of fourteen have been employed or permitted to work, or children between the ages of fourteen and sixteen years have been employed or permitted to work more than eight hours in any day, or more than six days in any week, or after the hour of seven o'clock P.M. or before the hour of 6 o'clock a.m.?

The power essential to the passage of this act, the Government contends, is found in the commerce clause of the Constitution, which authorizes Congress to regulate commerce with foreign nations and among the States.

In *Gibbons v. Ogden* [1824], Chief Justice Marshall, speaking for this court and defining the extent and nature of the commerce power, said, "It is the power to regulate; that is, to prescribe the rule by which commerce is to be governed." In other words,

the power is one to control the means by which commerce is carried on, which is directly the contrary of the assumed right to forbid commerce from moving, and thus destroy it as to particular commodities. But it is insisted that adjudged cases in this court establish the doctrine that the power to regulate given to Congress incidentally includes the authority to prohibit the movement of ordinary commodities, and therefore that the subject is not open for discussion. The cases demonstrate the contrary. They rest upon the character of the particular subjects dealt with, and the fact that the scope of governmental authority, state or national, possessed over them is such that the authority to prohibit is as to them but the exertion of the power to regulate.

The first of these cases is *Champion v. Ames* [1903], the so-called *Lottery Case*, in which it was held that Congress might pass a law having the effect to keep the channels of commerce free from use in the transportation of tickets used in the promotion of lottery schemes. In *Hipolite Egg Co. v. United States* [1911], this court sustained the power of Congress to pass the Pure Food and Drug Act, which prohibited the introduction into the States by means of interstate commerce of impure foods and drugs. In *Hoke v. United States* [1913], this court sustained the constitutionality of the so-called "White Slave Traffic Act," whereby the transportation of a woman in interstate commerce for the purpose of prostitution was forbidden. [. . .]

In each of these instances, the use of interstate transportation was necessary to the accomplishment of harmful results. In other words, although the power over interstate transportation was to regulate, that could only be accomplished by prohibiting the use of the facilities of interstate commerce to effect the evil intended.

This element is wanting in the present case. The thing intended to be accomplished by this statute is the denial of the facilities of interstate commerce to those manufacturers in the States who employ children within the prohibited ages. The act, in its effect, does not regulate transportation among the States, but aims to standardize the ages at which children may be employed in mining and manufacturing within the States. The goods shipped are, of themselves, harmless. The act permits them to be freely shipped after thirty days from the time of their removal from the factory. When offered for shipment, and before transportation begins, the labor of their production is over, and the mere fact that they were intended for interstate commerce transportation does not make their production subject to federal control under the commerce power. [. . .]

The making of goods and the mining of coal are not commerce, nor does the fact that these things are to be afterwards shipped or used in interstate commerce make their production a part thereof. [. . .]

Over interstate transportation or its incidents, the regulatory power of Congress is ample, but the production of articles intended for interstate commerce is a matter of local regulation.

When the commerce begins is determined not by the character of the commodity, nor by the intention of the owner to transfer it to another state for sale, nor by his preparation of it for transportation, but by its actual delivery to a common carrier for transportation, or the actual commencement of its transfer to another state. This principle has been recognized often in this court. If it were otherwise, all manufacture intended for interstate shipment would be brought under federal control to the practical exclusion of the authority of the States, a result certainly not contemplated by the framers of the Constitution when they vested in Congress the authority to regulate commerce among the States. *Kidd v. Pearson* [1888].

It is further contended that the authority of Congress may be exerted to control interstate commerce in the shipment of child-made goods because of the effect of the circulation of such goods in other States where the evil of this class of labor has been recognized by local legislation, and the right to thus employ child labor has been more rigorously restrained than in the State of production. In other words, that the unfair competition thus engendered may be controlled by closing the channels of interstate commerce to manufacturers in those States where the local laws do not meet what Congress deems to be the more just standard of other States.

There is no power vested in Congress to require the States to exercise their police power so as to prevent possible unfair competition. Many causes may cooperate to give one State, by reason of local laws or conditions, an economic advantage over others. The Commerce Clause was not intended to give to Congress a general authority to equalize such conditions. In some of the States, laws have been passed fixing minimum wages for women, in others, the local law regulates the hours of labor of women in various employments. Business done in such States may be at an economic disadvantage when compared with States which have no such regulations; surely, this fact does not give Congress the power to deny transportation in interstate commerce to those who carry on business where the hours of labor and the rate of compensation for women have not been fixed by a standard in use in other States and approved by Congress.

The grant of power to Congress over the subject of interstate commerce was to enable it to regulate such commerce, and not to give it authority to control the States in their exercise of the police power over local trade and manufacture.

The grant of authority over a purely federal matter was not intended to destroy the local power always existing and carefully reserved to the States in the Tenth Amendment to the Constitution.

Police regulations relating to the internal trade and affairs of the States have been uniformly recognized as within such control. "This," said this court in *United States v. Dewitt*, 9 Wall. 41, 45, "has been so frequently declared by this court, results so obviously from the terms of the Constitution, and has been so fully explained and supported on former occasions that we think it unnecessary to enter again upon the discussion."

In the judgment which established the broad power of Congress over interstate commerce, Chief Justice Marshall said: "They [inspection laws] act upon the subject before it becomes an article of foreign commerce, or of commerce among the states, and prepare it for that purpose. They form a portion of that immense mass of legislation which embraces everything within the territory of a state not surrendered to the general government, all which can be most advantageously exercised by the states themselves. Inspection laws, quarantine laws, health laws of every description, as well as laws for regulating the internal commerce of a state and those which respect turnpike roads, ferries, etc., are component parts of this mass."

And in *Dartmouth College v. Woodward*, [1819], the same great judge said: "That the framers of the Constitution did not intend to restrain the states in the regulation of their civil institutions, adopted for internal government, and that the instrument they have given us is not to be so construed may be admitted."

That there should be limitations upon the right to employ children in mines and factories in the interest of their own and the public welfare, all will admit. That such employment is generally deemed to require regulation is shown by the fact that the brief of counsel states that every State in the Union has a law upon the subject, limiting the right to thus employ children. In North Carolina, the State wherein is located the factory in which the employment was had in the present case, no child under twelve years of age is permitted to work.

It may be desirable that such laws be uniform, but our Federal Government is one of enumerated powers; "this principle," declared Chief Justice Marshall in *McCulloch v. Maryland* [1819] "is universally admitted."

A statute must be judged by its natural and reasonable effect. The control by Congress over interstate commerce cannot authorize the exercise of authority not entrusted to it by the Constitution. The maintenance of the authority of the States over matters purely local is as essential to the preservation of our institutions, as is the conservation of the supremacy of the federal power in all matters entrusted to the Nation by the Federal Constitution.

In interpreting the Constitution, it must never be forgotten that the Nation is made up of States to which are entrusted the powers of local government. And to them and to the people the powers not expressly delegated to the National Government are reserved. The power of the States to regulate their

purely internal affairs by such laws as seem wise to the local authority is inherent, and has never been surrendered to the general government. To sustain this statute would not be, in our judgment, a recognition of the lawful exertion of congressional authority over interstate commerce, but would sanction an invasion by the federal power of the control of a matter purely local in its character, and over which no authority has been delegated to Congress in conferring the power to regulate commerce among the States.

We have neither authority nor disposition to question the motives of Congress in enacting this legislation. The purposes intended must be attained consistently with constitutional limitations, and not by an invasion of the powers of the States. This court has no more important function than that which devolves upon it the obligation to preserve inviolate the constitutional limitations upon the exercise of authority, federal and state, to the end that each may continue to discharge, harmoniously with the other, the duties entrusted to it by the Constitution.

In our view, the necessary effect of this act is, by means of a prohibition against the movement in interstate commerce of ordinary commercial commodities, to regulate the hours of labor of children in factories and mines within the States, a purely state authority. Thus, the act in a two-fold sense is repugnant to the Constitution. It not only transcends the authority delegated to Congress over commerce, but also exerts a power as to a purely local matter to which the federal authority does not extend. The far-reaching result of upholding the act cannot be more plainly indicated than by pointing out that, if Congress can thus regulate matters entrusted to local authority by prohibition of the movement of commodities in interstate commerce, all freedom of commerce will be at an end, and the power of the States over local matters may be eliminated, and, thus, our system of government be practically destroyed.

For these reasons, we hold that this law exceeds the constitutional authority of Congress. It follows that the decree of the District Court must be

Affirmed.

Oliver Wendell Holmes

Hammer v. Dagenhart, Dissent (1918)

Mr. Justice HOLMES, dissenting.

The single question in this case is whether Congress has power to prohibit the shipment in interstate or foreign commerce of any product of a cotton mill situated in the United States in which, within thirty days before the removal of the product, children under fourteen have been employed or children between fourteen and sixteen have been employed more than eight hours in a day, or more than six days in any week, or between seven in the evening and six in the morning. The objection urged against the power is that the States have exclusive control over their methods of production, and that Congress cannot meddle with them, and, taking the proposition in the sense of direct intermeddling, I agree to it, and suppose that no one denies it. But if an act is within the powers specifically conferred upon Congress, it seems to me that it is not made any less constitutional because of the indirect effects that it may have, however obvious it may be that it will have those effects, and that we are not at liberty upon such grounds to hold it void.

The first step in my argument is to make plain what no one is likely to dispute—that the statute in question is within the power expressly given to Congress if considered only as to its immediate effects, and that, if invalid, it is so only upon some collateral ground. The statute confines itself to prohibiting the carriage of certain goods in interstate or foreign commerce. Congress is given power to regulate such commerce in unqualified terms. It would not be argued today that the power to regulate does not include the power to prohibit. Regulation means the prohibition of something, and when interstate commerce is the matter to be regulated, I cannot doubt that the regulation may prohibit any part of such commerce that Congress sees fit to forbid. At all events, it is established by the *Lottery Case* and others that have followed it that a law is not beyond the regulative power of Congress merely because it

prohibits certain transportation out and out. *Champion v. Ames* [1903]. So I repeat that this statute, in its immediate operation, is clearly within the Congress' constitutional power.

The question, then, is narrowed to whether the exercise of its otherwise constitutional power by Congress can be pronounced unconstitutional because of its possible reaction upon the conduct of the States in a matter upon which I have admitted that they are free from direct control. I should have thought that that matter had been disposed of so fully as to leave no room for doubt. I should have thought that the most conspicuous decisions of this Court had made it clear that the power to regulate commerce and other constitutional powers could not be cut down or qualified by the fact that it might interfere with the carrying out of the domestic policy of any State.

The manufacture of oleomargarine is as much a matter of state regulation as the manufacture of cotton cloth. Congress levied a tax upon the compound when colored so as to resemble butter that was so great as obviously to prohibit the manufacture and sale. In a very elaborate discussion, the present Chief Justice excluded any inquiry into the purpose of an act which, apart from that purpose, was within the power of Congress. *McCray v. United States* [1904]. Fifty years ago, a tax on state banks the obvious purpose and actual effect of which was to drive them, or at least their circulation, out of existence was sustained although the result was one that Congress had no constitutional power to require. The Court made short work of the argument as to the purpose of the act. "The judicial cannot prescribe to the legislative department of the government limitations upon the exercise of its acknowledged powers." *Veazie Bank v. Fenno* [1869]. So it well might have been argued that the corporation tax was intended, under the guise of a revenue measure, to secure a control not otherwise belonging to Congress, but the tax was sustained, and the objection, so far as noticed, was disposed of by citing *McCray v. United States. Flint v. Stone Tracy Co.* [1911]. And to come to cases upon interstate commerce, notwithstanding *United States v. E. C. Knight Co.* [1895], the Sherman Act has been made an instrument for the breaking up of combinations in restraint of trade and monopolies, using the power to regulate commerce as a foothold, but not proceeding because that commerce was the end actually in mind. The objection that the control of the States over production was interfered with was urged again and again, but always in vain. *Standard Oil Co. v. United States* [1910].

The Pure Food and Drug Act which was sustained in *Hipolite Egg Co. v. United States* [1911], with the intimation that "no trade can be carried on between the States to which it [the power of Congress to regulate commerce] does not extend," applies not merely to articles that the changing opinions of the time condemn as intrinsically harmful, but to others innocent in themselves, simply on the ground that the order for them was induced by a preliminary fraud. It does not matter whether the supposed evil precedes or follows the transportation. It is enough that, in the opinion of Congress, the transportation encourages the evil. I may add that, in the cases on the so-called White Slave Act, it was established that the means adopted by Congress as convenient to the exercise of its power might have the character of police regulations. *Hoke v. United States* [1913]. [. . .]

The notion that prohibition is any less prohibition when applied to things now thought evil I do not understand. But if there is any matter upon which civilized countries have agreed—far more unanimously than they have with regard to intoxicants and some other matters over which this country is now emotionally aroused—it is the evil of premature and excessive child labor. I should have thought that, if we were to introduce our own moral conceptions where in my opinion they do not belong, this was preeminently a case for upholding the exercise of all its powers by the United States.

But I had thought that the propriety of the exercise of a power admitted to exist in some cases was for the consideration of Congress alone, and that this Court always had disavowed the right to intrude its judgment upon questions of policy or morals. It is not for this Court to pronounce when prohibition is necessary to regulation—if it ever may be necessary—to say that it is permissible as against strong drink, but not as against the product of ruined lives.

The Act does not meddle with anything belonging to the States. They may regulate their internal affairs and their domestic commerce as they like. But when they seek to send their products across the state line, they are no longer within their rights. If there were no Constitution and no Congress, their power to cross the line would depend upon their neighbors. Under the Constitution, such commerce belongs not to the States, but to Congress to regulate. It may carry out its views of public policy whatever indirect effect they may have upon the activities of the States. Instead of being encountered by a prohibitive tariff at her boundaries, the State encounters the public policy of the United States, which it is for Congress to express. The public policy of the United States is shaped with a view to the benefit of the nation as a whole. If, as has been the case within the memory of men still living, a State should take a different view of the propriety of sustaining a lottery from that which generally prevails, I cannot believe that the fact would require a different decision from that reached in *Champion v. Ames.* Yet, in that case, it would be said with quite as much force as in this that Congress was attempting to intermeddle with the State's domestic affairs. The national welfare, as understood by Congress, may require a different attitude within its sphere from that of some self-seeking State. It seems to me entirely constitutional for Congress to enforce its understanding by all the means at its command.

Margaret Sanger

Women and the New Race (1920)

Woman's Error and Her Debt

The most far-reaching social development of modern times is the revolt of woman against sex servitude. The most important force in the remaking of the world is a free motherhood. Beside this force, the elaborate international programmes of modern statesmen are weak and superficial. Diplomats may formulate leagues of nations and nations may pledge their utmost strength to maintain them, statesmen may dream of reconstructing the world out of alliances, hegemonies and spheres of influence, but woman, continuing to produce explosive populations, will convert these pledges into the proverbial scraps of paper; or she may, by controlling birth, lift motherhood to the plane of a voluntary, intelligent function, and remake the world. When the world is thus remade, it will exceed the dream of statesman, reformer and revolutionist.

Only in recent years has woman's position as the gentler and weaker half of the human family been emphatically and generally questioned. Men assumed that this was woman's place; woman herself accepted it. It seldom occurred to anyone to ask whether she would go on occupying it forever.

Upon the mere surface of woman's organized protests there were no indications that she was desirous of achieving a fundamental change in her position. She claimed the right of suffrage and legislative regulation of her working hours, and asked that her property rights be equal to those of the man. None of these demands, however, affected directly the most vital factors of her existence. Whether she won her point or failed to win it, she remained a dominated weakling in a society controlled by men.

Woman's acceptance of her inferior status was the more real because it was unconscious. She had chained herself to her place in society and the family through the maternal functions of her nature, and only chains thus strong could have bound her to her lot as a brood animal for the masculine civilizations of the world. In accepting her role as the "weaker and gentler half," she accepted that function. In turn, the acceptance of that function fixed the more firmly her rank as an inferior.

Caught in this "vicious circle," woman has, through her reproductive ability, founded and perpetuated the tyrannies of the Earth. Whether it was the tyranny of a monarchy, an oligarchy or a republic, the one indispensable factor of its existence was, as it is now, hordes of human beings—human beings so plentiful as to be cheap, and so cheap that ignorance was their natural lot. Upon the rock of an unenlightened, submissive maternity have these been founded; upon the product of such a maternity have they flourished.

No despot ever flung forth his legions to die in foreign conquest, no privilege-ruled nation ever erupted across its borders, to lock in death embrace with another, but behind them loomed the driving power of a population too large for its boundaries and its natural resources.

No period of low wages or of idleness with their want among the workers, no peonage or sweatshop, no child-labor factory, ever came into being, save from the same source. Nor have famine and plague been as much "acts of God" as acts of too prolific mothers. They, also, as all students know, have their basic causes in over-population.

The creators of over-population are the women, who, while wringing their hands over each fresh horror, submit anew to their task of producing the multitudes who will bring about the *next* tragedy of civilization.

While unknowingly laying the foundations of tyrannies and providing the human tinder for racial conflagrations, woman was also unknowingly creating slums, filling asylums with insane, and institutions with other defectives. She was replenishing the ranks of the prostitutes, furnishing grist for the criminal courts and inmates for prisons. Had she planned deliberately to achieve this tragic total of human waste and misery, she could hardly have done it more effectively.

Woman's passivity under the burden of her disastrous task was almost altogether that of ignorant resignation. She knew virtually nothing about her reproductive nature and less about the consequences of her excessive child-bearing. It is true that, obeying the inner urge of their natures, *some* women revolted. They went even to the extreme of infanticide and abortion. Usually their revolts were not general enough. They fought as individuals, not as a mass. In the mass they sank back into blind and hopeless subjection. They went on breeding with staggering rapidity those numberless, undesired children who become the clogs and the destroyers of civilizations.

To-day, however, woman is rising in fundamental revolt. Even her efforts at mere reform are, as we shall see later, steps in that direction. Underneath each of them is the feminine urge to complete freedom. Millions of women are asserting their right to voluntary motherhood. They are determined to decide for themselves whether they shall become mothers, under what conditions and when. This is the fundamental revolt referred to. It is for woman the key to the temple of liberty.

Even as birth control is the means by which woman attains basic freedom, so it is the means by which she must and will uproot the evil she has wrought through her submission. As she has unconsciously and ignorantly brought about social disaster, so must and will she consciously and intelligently *undo* that disaster and create a new and a better order.

The task is hers. It cannot be avoided by excuses, nor can it be delegated. It is not enough for woman to point to the self-evident domination of man. Nor does it avail to plead the guilt of rulers and the exploiters of labor. It makes no difference that she does not formulate industrial systems nor that she is an instinctive believer in social justice. In her submission lies her error and her guilt. By her failure to withhold the multitudes of children who have made inevitable the most flagrant of our social evils, she incurred a debt to society. Regardless of her own wrongs, regardless of her lack of opportunity and regardless of all other considerations, *she* must pay that debt.

She must not think to pay this debt in any superficial way. She cannot pay it with palliatives—with child-labor laws, prohibition, regulation of prostitution and agitation against war. Political nostrums and social panaceas are but incidentally and superficially useful. They do not touch the source of the social disease.

War, famine, poverty and oppression of the workers will continue while woman makes life cheap. They will cease only when she limits her reproductivity and human life is no longer a thing to be wasted.

Two chief obstacles hinder the discharge of this tremendous obligation. The first and the lesser is the legal barrier. Dark-Age laws would still deny to her the knowledge of her reproductive nature. Such knowledge is indispensable to intelligent motherhood and she must achieve it, despite absurd statutes and equally absurd moral canons.

The second and more serious barrier is her own ignorance of the extent and effect of her submission. Until she knows the evil her subjection has wrought to herself, to her progeny and to the world at large, she cannot wipe out that evil.

To get rid of these obstacles is to invite attack from the forces of reaction which are so strongly entrenched in our present-day society. It means warfare in every phase of her life. Nevertheless, at whatever cost, she must emerge from her ignorance and assume her responsibility.

New Morality

[. . .] Woman was and is condemned to a system under which the lawful rapes exceed the unlawful ones a million to one. She has had nothing to say as to whether she shall have strength sufficient to give a child a fair physical and mental start in life; she has had as little to do with determining whether her own body shall be wrecked by excessive child-bearing. She has been adjured not to complain of the burden of caring for children she has not wanted. Only the married woman who has been constantly loved by the most understanding and considerate of husbands has escaped these horrors. Besides the wrongs done to women in marriage, those involved in promiscuity, infidelities and rapes become inconsequential in nature and in number.

Out of woman's inner nature, in rebellion against these conditions, is rising the new morality. Let it be realized that this creation of new sex ideals is a challenge to the church. Being a challenge to the church, it is also, in less degree, a challenge to the state. The woman who takes a fearless stand for the incoming sex ideals must expect to be assailed by reactionaries of every kind. Imperialists and exploiters will fight hardest in the open, but the ecclesiastic will fight longest in the dark. He understands the situation best of all; he best knows what reaction he has to fear from the morals of women who have attained liberty. For, be it repeated, the church has always known and feared the spiritual potentialities of woman's freedom.

And in this lies the answer to the question why the opponent of birth control raises the moral issue. Sex morals for women have been one-sided; they have been purely negative, inhibitory and repressive. They have been fixed by agencies which have sought to keep women enslaved; which have been determined, even as they are now, to use woman solely as an asset to the church, the state and the man. Any means of freedom which will enable women to live and think for themselves first, will be attacked as immoral by these selfish agencies.

What effect will the practice of birth control have upon woman's moral development? [. . .] It will free her to understand the cravings and soul needs of herself and other women. It will enable her to develop her love nature separate from and independent of her maternal nature.

It goes without saying that the woman whose children are desired and are of such number that she can not only give them adequate care but keep herself mentally and spiritually alive, as well as physically fit, can discharge her duties to her children much better than the overworked, broken and querulous mother of a large, unwanted family.

Thus the way is open to her for a twofold development; first, through her own full rounded life, and next, through her loving, unstrained, full-hearted relationship with her offspring. The bloom of mother love will have an opportunity to infuse itself into her soul and make her, indeed, the fond, affectionate guardian of her offspring that sentiment now

pictures her but hard facts deny her the privilege of being. She will preserve also her love life with her mate in its ripening perfection. She will want children with a deeper passion, and will love them with a far greater love.

In spite of the age-long teaching that sex life in itself is unclean, the world has been moving to a realization that a great love between a man and woman is a holy thing, freighted with great possibilities for spiritual growth. The fear of unwanted children removed, the assurance that she will have a sufficient amount of time in which to develop her love life to its greatest beauty, with its comradeship in many fields—these will lift woman by the very soaring quality of her innermost self to spiritual heights that few have attained. Then the coming of eagerly desired children will but enrich life in all its avenues, rather than enslave and impoverish it as do unwanted ones to-day.

What healthier grounds for the growth of sound morals could possibly exist than the ample spiritual life of the woman just depicted? Free to follow the feminine spirit, which dwells in the sanctuary of her nature, she will, in her daily life, give expression to that high idealism which is the fruit of that spirit when it is unhampered and unviolated. The love for her mate will flower in beauty of deeds that are pure because they are the natural expression of her physical, mental and spiritual being. The love for desired children will come to blossom in a spirituality that is high because it is free to reach the heights.

The moral force of woman's nature will be unchained—and of its own dynamic power will uplift her to a plane unimagined by those holding fast to the old standards of church morality. Love is the greatest force of the universe; freed of its bonds of submission and unwanted progeny, it will formulate and compel of its own nature observance to standards of purity far beyond the highest conception of the average moralist. The feminine spirit, animated by joyous, triumphant love, will make its own high tenets of morality. Free womanhood, out of the depths of its rich experiences, will observe and comply with the inner demands of its being. The manner in which it learns to do this best may be said to be the moral law of woman's being. [. . .]

The Pivot of Civilization (1922)

A New Truth Emerges

[. . .] The Birth Control movement was launched because it was in this form that the whole relation of woman and child—eternal emblem of the future of society—could be most effectively dramatized. The amazing growth of this movement dates from the moment when in my home a small group organized the first Birth Control League. Since then we have been criticized for our choice of the term "Birth Control" to express the idea of modern scientific contraception. I have yet to hear any criticism of this term that is not based upon some false and hypocritical sense of modesty, or that does not arise out of a semi-prurient misunderstanding of its aim. On the other hand: nothing better expresses the idea of purposive, responsible, and self-directed guidance of the reproductive powers.

Those critics who condemn Birth Control as a negative, destructive idea, concerned only with self-gratification, might profitably open the nearest dictionary for a definition of "control." There they would discover that the verb "control" means to exercise a directing, guiding, or restraining influence;—to direct, to regulate, to counteract. Control is guidance, direction, foresight. It implies intelligence, forethought and responsibility. They will find in the Standard Dictionary a quotation from Lecky to the effect that, "The greatest of all evils in politics is power without control." In what phase of life is not "power without control" an evil? Birth Control, therefore, means not merely the limitation of births, but the application of intelligent guidance over the reproductive power. It means the substitution of reason and intelligence for the blind play of instinct.

The term "Birth Control" had the immense practical advantage of compressing into two short words the answer to the inarticulate demands of millions of men and women in all countries. At the time this slogan was formulated, I had not yet come to the complete realization of the great truth that had been thus crystallized. It was the response to the overwhelming, heart-breaking appeals that came by every mail for aid and advice, which revealed a great truth that lay dormant, a truth that seemed to spring into full vitality almost over night—that could never again be crushed to earth! [. . .] Birth Control affords an approach to the study of humanity because it cuts through the limitations of current methods. It is economic, biological, psychological and spiritual in its aspects. It awakens the vision of mankind moving and changing, of humanity growing and developing, coming to fruition, of a race creative, flowering into beautiful expression through talent and genius.

As a social program, Birth Control is not merely concerned with population questions. In this respect, it is a distinct step in advance of earlier Malthusian doctrines, which concerned themselves chiefly with economics and population. Birth Control concerns itself with the spirit no less than the body. It looks for the liberation of the spirit of woman and through woman of the child. To-day, motherhood is wasted, penalized, tortured. Children brought into the world by unwilling mothers suffer an initial handicap that cannot be measured by cold statistics. Their lives are blighted from the start. To substantiate this fact, I have chosen to present the conclusions of reports on Child Labor and records of defect and delinquency published by organizations with no bias in favor of Birth Control. The evidence is before us. It crowds in upon us from all sides. But prior to this new approach, no attempt had been made to correlate the effects of the blind and irresponsible play of the sexual instinct with its deep-rooted causes.

The duty of the educator and the intellectual creator of public opinion is, in this connection, of the greatest importance. For centuries official moralists, priests, clergymen and teachers, statesmen and politicians have preached the doctrine of glorious and divine fertility. To-day, we are confronted with the world-wide spectacle of the realization of this doctrine. It is not without significance that the moron and the imbecile set the pace in living up to this teaching, and that the intellectuals, the educators, the archbishops, bishops, priests, who are most insistent on it, are the staunchest adherents in their own lives of celibacy and non-fertility. It is time to point out to the champions of unceasing and indiscriminate fertility the results of their teaching. [. . .]

Certain fundamental convictions should be made clear here. The program for Birth Control is not a charity. It is not aiming to interfere in the private lives of poor people, to tell them how many children they should have, nor to sit in judgment upon their fitness to become parents. It aims, rather, to awaken responsibility, to answer the demand for a scientific means by which and through which each human life may be self-directed and self-controlled. The exponent of Birth Control, in short, is convinced that social regeneration, no less than individual regeneration, must come from within. Every potential parent, and especially every potential mother, must be brought to an acute realization of the primary and individual responsibility of bringing children into this world. Not until the parents of this world are given control over their reproductive faculties will it be possible to improve the quality of the generations of the future, or even to maintain civilization at its present level. Only when given intelligent mastery of the procreative powers can the great mass of humanity be aroused to a realization of responsibility of parenthood. We have come to the conclusion, based on widespread investigation and experience, that education for parenthood must be based upon the needs and demands of the people themselves. An idealistic code of sexual ethics, imposed from above, a set of rules devised by high-minded theorists who fail to take into account the living conditions and desires of the masses, can never be of the slightest value in effecting change in the customs of the people. Systems so imposed in the past have revealed their woeful inability to prevent the sexual and racial chaos into which the world has drifted.

The universal demand for practical education in Birth Control is one of the most hopeful signs that the masses themselves to-day possess the divine spark of regeneration. It remains for the courageous and the enlightened to answer this demand, to kindle the spark, to direct a thorough education in sex hygiene based upon this intense interest.

Birth Control is thus the entering wedge for the educator. In answering the needs of these thousands upon thousands of submerged mothers, it is possible to use their interest as the foundation for education in prophylaxis, hygiene and infant welfare. The potential mother can then be shown that maternity need not be slavery but may be the most effective avenue to self-development and self-realization. Upon this basis only may we improve the quality of the race.

The lack of balance between the birth rate of the "unfit" and the "fit," admittedly the greatest present menace to civilization, can never be rectified by the inauguration of a cradle competition between these two classes. The example of the inferior classes, the fertility of the feeble-minded, the mentally defective, the poverty-stricken, should not be held up for emulation to the mentally and physically fit, and therefore less fertile, parents of the educated and well-to-do classes. On the contrary, the most urgent problem to-day is how to limit and discourage the over-fertility of the mentally and physically defective. Possibly drastic and Spartan methods may be forced upon American society if it continues complacently to encourage the chance and chaotic breeding that has resulted from our stupid, cruel sentimentalism.

To effect the salvation of the generations of the future—nay of the generations of to-day—our greatest need, first of all, is the ability to face the situation without flinching; to cooperate in the formation of a code of sexual ethics based upon a thorough biological and psychological understanding of human nature; and then to answer the questions and the needs of the people with all the intelligence and honesty at our command. If we can summon the bravery to do this, we shall best be serving the pivotal interests of civilization.

To conclude this introduction: my initiation, as I have confessed, was primarily an emotional one. My interest in Birth Control was awakened by experience. Research and investigation have followed. Our effort has been to raise our program from the plane of the emotional to the plane of the scientific. Any social progress, it is my belief, must purge itself of sentimentalism and pass through the crucible of science. We are willing to submit Birth Control to this test. It is part of the purpose of this book to appeal to the scientist for aid, to arouse that interest which will result in widespread research and investigation. I believe that my personal experience with this idea must be that of the race at large. We must temper our emotion and enthusiasm with the impersonal determination of science. We must unite in the task of creating an instrument of steel, strong but supple, if we are to triumph finally in the war for human emancipation.

A Moral Necessity

Orthodox opposition to Birth Control is formulated in the official protest of the National Council of Catholic Women against the resolution passed by the New York State Federation of Women's Clubs which favored the removal of all obstacles to the spread of information regarding practical methods of Birth Control. The Catholic statement completely embodies traditional opposition to Birth Control. It affords a striking contrast by which we may clarify and justify the ethical necessity for this new instrument of civilization as the most effective basis for practical and scientific morality. "The authorities at Rome have again and again declared that all positive methods of this nature are immoral and forbidden," states the National Council of Catholic Women. "There is no question of the lawfulness of birth restriction through abstinence from the relations which result in conception. The immorality of Birth Control as it is practiced and commonly understood, consists in the evils of the particular method employed. These are all contrary to the moral law because they are unnatural, being a perversion of a natural function. Human faculties are used in such a way as to frustrate the natural end for which these faculties were created. This is always intrinsically wrong—as wrong as lying and blasphemy. No supposed beneficial consequence can make good a practice which is, in itself, immoral. [. . .]"

The Catholic position has been stated in an even more extreme form by Archbishop Patrick J. Hayes of the archdiocese of New York. In a "Christmas Pastoral" this dignitary even went to the extent of declaring that "even though some little angels in the flesh, through the physical or mental deformities of their parents, may appear to human eyes hideous, misshapen, a blot on civilized society, we must not lose sight of this Christian thought that under and within such visible malformation, lives an immortal soul to be saved and glorified for all eternity among the blessed in heaven."[1]

With the type of moral philosophy expressed in this utterance, we need not argue. It is based upon traditional ideas that have had the practical effect of making this world a vale of tears. Fortunately such words carry no weight with those who can bring free and keen as well as noble minds to the consideration of the matter. To them the idealism of such an utterance appears crude and cruel. The menace to civilization of such orthodoxy, if it be orthodoxy, lies in the fact that its powerful exponents may be for a time successful not merely in influencing the conduct of their adherents but in checking freedom of thought and discussion. To this, with all the vehemence of emphasis at our command, we object. From what Archbishop Hayes believes concerning the future blessedness in Heaven of the souls of those who are born into this world as hideous and misshapen beings he has a right to seek such consolation as may be obtained; but we who are trying to better the conditions of this world believe that a healthy, happy human race is more in keeping with the laws of God, than disease, misery and poverty perpetuating itself generation after generation. Furthermore, while conceding to Catholic or other churchmen full freedom to preach their own doctrines, whether of theology or morals, nevertheless when they attempt to carry these ideas into legislative acts and force their opinions and codes upon the non-Catholics, we consider such action an interference with the principles of democracy and we have a right to protest.

Religious propaganda against Birth Control is crammed with contradiction and fallacy. It refutes itself. Yet it brings the opposing views into vivid contrast. In stating these differences we should make clear that advocates of Birth Control are not seeking to attack the Catholic church. We quarrel with that church, however, when it seeks to assume authority over non-Catholics and to dub their behavior immoral because they do not conform to the dictatorship of Rome. The question of bearing and rearing children we hold is the concern of the mother and the potential mother. If she delegates the responsibility, the ethical education, to an external authority, that is her affair. We object, however, to the State or the Church which appoints itself as arbiter and dictator in this sphere and attempts to force unwilling women into compulsory maternity.

---

1. Quoted in daily press, December 19, 1921.

Henry Adams

The Education of Henry Adams (1918)

The Dynamo and the Virgin (1900)

Until the Great Exposition of 1900 closed its doors in November, Adams[1] haunted it, aching to absorb knowledge, and helpless to find it. He would have liked to know how much of it could have been grasped by the best-informed man in the world. While he was thus meditating chaos, Langley[2] came by, and showed it to him. At Langley's behest, the Exhibition dropped its superfluous rags and stripped itself to the skin, for Langley knew what to study, and why, and how; while Adams might as well have stood outside in the night, staring at the Milky Way. Yet Langley said nothing new, and taught nothing that one might not have learned from Lord Bacon, three hundred years before; but though one should have known the "Advancement of Science" as well as one knew the "Comedy of Errors," the literary knowledge counted for nothing until some teacher should show how to apply it. Bacon took a vast deal of trouble in teaching King James I and his subjects, American or other, towards the year 1620, that true science was the development or economy of forces; yet an elderly American in 1900 knew neither the formula nor the forces; or even so much as to say to himself that his historical business in the Exposition concerned only the economies or developments of force since 1893, when he began the study at Chicago.

Nothing in education is so astonishing as the amount of ignorance it accumulates in the form of inert facts. Adams had looked at most of the accumulations of art in the storehouses called Art Museums;

yet he did not know how to look at the art exhibits of 1900. He had studied Karl Marx and his doctrines of history with profound attention, yet he could not apply them at Paris. Langley, with the ease of a great master of experiment, threw out of the field every exhibit that did not reveal a new application of force, and naturally threw out, to begin with, almost the whole art exhibit. Equally, he ignored almost the whole industrial exhibit. He led his pupil directly to the forces. His chief interest was in new motors to make his airship feasible, and he taught Adams the astonishing complexities of the new Daimler motor, and of the automobile, which, since 1893, had become a nightmare at a hundred kilometres an hour, almost as destructive as the electric tram which was only ten years older; and threatening to become as terrible as the locomotive steam-engine itself, which was almost exactly Adams's own age.

Then he showed his scholar the great hall of dynamos, and explained how little he knew about electricity or force of any kind, even of his own special sun, which spouted heat in inconceivable volume, but which, as far as he knew, might spout less or more, at any time, for all the certainty he felt in it. To him, the dynamo itself was but an ingenious channel for conveying somewhere the heat latent in a few tons of poor coal hidden in a dirty engine-house carefully kept out of sight; but to Adams the dynamo became a symbol of infinity. As he grew accustomed to the great gallery of machines, he began to feel the forty-foot dynamos as a moral force, much as the early Christians felt the Cross. The planet itself seemed less impressive, in its old-fashioned, deliberate, annual or daily revolution, than this huge wheel, revolving within arm's-length at some vertiginous speed, and barely murmuring—scarcely humming an audible warning to stand a hair's-breadth further for respect of power—while it would not wake the baby lying close against its frame. Before the end, one began to pray to it; inherited instinct taught the natural expression of man before silent and infinite

---

1. [Like Julius Caesar, Henry Adams refers to himself in the third person.]

2. [Samuel Pierpont Langley (1834–1906), American scientist and aviation pioneer. Appointed Secretary of the Smithsonian Institute in 1887.]

force. Among the thousand symbols of ultimate energy, the dynamo was not so human as some, but it was the most expressive.

Yet the dynamo, next to the steam-engine, was the most familiar of exhibits. For Adams's objects its value lay chiefly in its occult mechanism. Between the dynamo in the gallery of machines and the engine-house outside, the break of continuity amounted to abysmal fracture for a historian's objects. No more relation could he discover between the steam and the electric current than between the Cross and the cathedral. The forces were interchangeable if not reversible, but he could see only an absolute *fiat* in electricity as in faith. Langley could not help him. Indeed, Langley seemed to be worried by the same trouble, for he constantly repeated that the new forces were anarchical, and specially that he was not responsible for the new rays, that were little short of parricidal in their wicked spirit towards science. His own rays, with which he had doubled the solar spectrum, were altogether harmless and beneficent; but Radium denied its God—or, what was to Langley the same thing, denied the truths of his Science. The force was wholly new.

A historian who asked only to learn enough to be as futile as Langley or Kelvin, made rapid progress under this teaching, and mixed himself up in the tangle of ideas until he achieved a sort of Paradise of ignorance vastly consoling to his fatigued senses. He wrapped himself in vibrations and rays which were new, and he would have hugged Marconi and Branly had he met them, as he hugged the dynamo; while he lost his arithmetic in trying to figure out the equation between the discoveries and the economies of force. The economies, like the discoveries, were absolute, supersensual, occult; incapable of expression in horse-power. What mathematical equivalent could he suggest as the value of a Branly coherer? Frozen air, or the electric furnace, had some scale of measurement, no doubt, if somebody could invent a thermometer adequate to the purpose; but X-rays had played no part whatever in man's consciousness, and the atom itself had figured only as a fiction of thought. In these seven years man had translated himself into a new universe which had no common scale of measurement with the old. He had entered a supersensual world, in which he could measure nothing except by chance collisions of movements imperceptible to his senses, perhaps even imperceptible to his instruments, but perceptible to each other, and so to some known ray at the end of the scale. Langley seemed prepared for anything, even for an indeterminable number of universes interfused— physics stark mad in metaphysics.

Historians undertake to arrange sequences,— called stories, or histories—assuming in silence a relation of cause and effect. These assumptions, hidden in the depths of dusty libraries, have been astounding, but commonly unconscious and childlike; so much so, that if any captious critic were to drag them to light, historians would probably reply, with one voice, that they had never supposed themselves required to know what they were talking about. Adams, for one, had toiled in vain to find out what he meant. He had even published a dozen volumes of American history for no other purpose than to satisfy himself whether, by the severest process of stating, with the least possible comment, such facts as seemed sure, in such order as seemed rigorously consequent, he could fix for a familiar moment a necessary sequence of human movement. The result had satisfied him as little as at Harvard College. Where he saw sequence, other men saw something quite different, and no one saw the same unit of measure. He cared little about his experiments and less about his statesmen, who seemed to him quite as ignorant as himself and, as a rule, no more honest; but he insisted on a relation of sequence, and if he could not reach it by one method, he would try as many methods as science knew. Satisfied that the sequence of men led to nothing and that the sequence of their society could lead no further, while the mere sequence of time was artificial, and the sequence of thought was chaos, he turned at last to the sequence of force; and thus it happened that, after ten years' pursuit, he found himself lying in the Gallery of Machines at the Great Exposition of 1900, his historical neck broken by the sudden irruption of forces totally new.

Since no one else showed much concern, an elderly person without other cares had no need to betray alarm. The year 1900 was not the first to upset schoolmasters. Copernicus and Galileo had broken many professorial necks about 1600; Columbus had stood the world on its head towards 1500; but the nearest approach to the revolution of 1900 was that of

310, when Constantine set up the Cross. The rays that Langley disowned, as well as those which he fathered, were occult, supersensual, irrational; they were a revelation of mysterious energy like that of the Cross; they were what, in terms of mediæval science, were called immediate modes of the divine substance.

The historian was thus reduced to his last resources. Clearly if he was bound to reduce all these forces to a common value, this common value could have no measure but that of their attraction on his own mind. He must treat them as they had been felt; as convertible, reversible, interchangeable attractions on thought. He made up his mind to venture it; he would risk translating rays into faith. [. . .]

Here opened another totally new education, which promised to be by far the most hazardous of all. The knife-edge along which he must crawl, like Sir Lancelot in the twelfth century, divided two kingdoms of force which had nothing in common but attraction. They were as different as a magnet is from gravitation, supposing one knew what a magnet was, or gravitation, or love. The force of the Virgin was still felt at Lourdes, and seemed to be as potent as X-rays; but in America neither Venus nor Virgin ever had value as force—at most as sentiment. No American had ever been truly afraid of either.

This problem in dynamics gravely perplexed an American historian. The Woman had once been supreme; in France she still seemed potent, not merely as a sentiment, but as a force. Why was she unknown in America? For evidently America was ashamed of her, and she was ashamed of herself, otherwise they would not have strewn fig-leaves so profusely all over her. When she was a true force, she was ignorant of fig-leaves, but the monthly-magazine-made American female had not a feature that would have been recognized by Adam. The trait was notorious, and often humorous, but any one brought up among Puritans knew that sex was sin. In any previous age, sex was strength. Neither art nor beauty was needed. Every one, even among Puritans, knew that neither Diana of the Ephesians nor any of the Oriental goddesses was worshipped for her beauty. She was goddess because of her force; she was the animated dynamo; she was reproduction—the greatest and most mysterious of all energies; all she needed was to be fecund. [. . .] All this was to American

thought as though it had never existed. The true American knew something of the facts, but nothing of the feelings; he read the letter, but he never felt the law. Before this historical chasm, a mind like that of Adams felt itself helpless; he turned from the Virgin to the Dynamo as though he were a Branly coherer. On one side, at the Louvre and at Chartres, as he knew by the record of work actually done and still before his eyes, was the highest energy ever known to man, the creator of four-fifths of his noblest art, exercising vastly more attraction over the human mind than all the steam-engines and dynamos ever dreamed of; and yet this energy was unknown to the American mind. An American Virgin would never dare command; an American Venus would never dare exist.

The question, which to any plain American of the nineteenth century seemed as remote as it did to Adams, drew him almost violently to study, once it was posed; and on this point Langleys were as useless as though they were Herbert Spencers or dynamos. The idea survived only as art. There one turned as naturally as though the artist were himself a woman. Adams began to ponder, asking himself whether he knew of any American artist who had ever insisted on the power of sex, as every classic had always done; but he could think only of Walt Whitman; Bret Harte, as far as the magazines would let him venture; and one or two painters, for the flesh-tones. All the rest had used sex for sentiment, never for force; to them, Eve was a tender flower, and Herodias an unfeminine horror. American art, like the American language and American education, was as far as possible sexless. Society regarded this victory over sex as its greatest triumph, and the historian readily admitted it, since the moral issue, for the moment, did not concern one who was studying the relations of unmoral force. He cared nothing for the sex of the dynamo until he could measure its energy. [. . .]

Once St. Gaudens[3] took him down to Amiens, with a party of Frenchmen, to see the cathedral. Not until they found themselves actually studying the sculpture of the western portal, did it dawn on

---

3. [Augustus Saint-Gaudens (1848–1907), American sculptor.]

Adams's mind that, for his purposes, St. Gaudens on that spot had more interest to him than the cathedral itself. Great men before great monuments express great truths, provided they are not taken too solemnly. Adams never tired of quoting the supreme phrase of his idol Gibbon, before the Gothic cathedrals: "I darted a contemptuous look on the stately monuments of superstition." Even in the footnotes of his history, Gibbon had never inserted a bit of humor more human than this, and one would have paid largely for a photograph of the fat little historian, on the background of Notre Dame of Amiens, trying to persuade his readers—perhaps himself—that he was darting a contemptuous look on the stately monument, for which he felt in fact the respect which every man of his vast study and active mind always feels before objects worthy of it; but besides the humor, one felt also the relation. Gibbon ignored the Virgin, because in 1789 religious monuments were out of fashion. In 1900 his remark sounded fresh and simple as the green fields to ears that had heard a hundred years of other remarks, mostly no more fresh and certainly less simple. Without malice, one might find it more instructive than a whole lecture of Ruskin. One sees what one brings, and at that moment Gibbon brought the French Revolution. Ruskin brought reaction against the Revolution. St. Gaudens had passed beyond all. He liked the stately monuments much more than he liked Gibbon or Ruskin; he loved their dignity; their unity; their scale; their lines; their lights and shadows; their decorative sculpture; but he was even less conscious than they of the force that created it all—the Virgin, the Woman—by whose genius "the stately monuments of superstition" were built, through which she was expressed. He would have seen more meaning in Isis with the cow's horns, at Edfoo, who expressed the same thought. The art remained, but the energy was lost even upon the artist.

Yet in mind and person St. Gaudens was a survival of the 1500; he bore the stamp of the Renaissance, and should have carried an image of the Virgin round his neck, or stuck in his hat, like Louis XI. In mere time he was a lost soul that had strayed by chance into the twentieth century, and forgotten where it came from. He writhed and cursed at his ignorance, much as Adams did at his own, but in the opposite sense. St. Gaudens was a child of Benvenuto Cellini, smothered in an American cradle. Adams was a quintessence of Boston, devoured by curiosity to think like Benvenuto. St. Gaudens's art was starved from birth, and Adams's instinct was blighted from babyhood. Each had but half of a nature, and when they came together before the Virgin of Amiens they ought both to have felt in her the force that made them one; but it was not so. To Adams she became more than ever a channel of force; to St. Gaudens she remained as before a channel of taste.

For a symbol of power, St. Gaudens instinctively preferred the horse, as was plain in his horse and Victory of the Sherman monument. Doubtless Sherman also felt it so. The attitude was so American that, for at least forty years, Adams had never realized that any other could be in sound taste. How many years had he taken to admit a notion of what Michael Angelo and Rubens were driving at? He could not say; but he knew that only since 1895 had he begun to feel the Virgin or Venus as force, and not everywhere even so. At Chartres—perhaps at Lourdes—possibly at Cnidos if one could still find there the divinely naked Aphrodite of Praxiteles—but otherwise one must look for force to the goddesses of Indian mythology. The idea died out long ago in the German and English stock. St. Gaudens at Amiens was hardly less sensitive to the force of the female energy than Matthew Arnold at the Grande Chartreuse. Neither of them felt goddesses as power—only as reflected emotion, human expression, beauty, purity, taste, scarcely even as sympathy. They felt a railway train as power; yet they, and all other artists, constantly complained that the power embodied in a railway train could never be embodied in art. All the steam in the world could not, like the Virgin, build Chartres.

Yet in mechanics, whatever the mechanicians might think, both energies acted as interchangeable forces on man, and by action on man all known force may be measured. Indeed, few men of science measured force in any other way. After once admitting that a straight line was the shortest distance between two points, no serious mathematician cared to deny anything that suited his convenience, and rejected no symbol, unproved or unproveable, that helped him to accomplish work. The symbol was force, as a compass-needle or a triangle was force, as the mechanist might prove by losing it, and nothing could be gained by ignoring their value. Symbol or energy, the Virgin had acted as the greatest force the Western world ever felt, and had drawn man's activities to herself more strongly than any other power, natural or supernatural, had ever done; the historian's business was to follow the track of the energy; to find where it came from and where it went to; its complex source and shifting channels; its values, equivalents, conversions. It could scarcely be more complex than radium; it could hardly be deflected, diverted, polarized, absorbed more perplexingly than other radiant matter. Adams knew nothing about any of them, but as a mathematical problem of influence on human progress, though all were occult, all reacted on his mind, and he rather inclined to think the Virgin easiest to handle.

The pursuit turned out to be long and tortuous, leading at last into the vast forests of scholastic science. From Zeno to Descartes, hand in hand with Thomas Aquinas, Montaigne, and Pascal, one stumbled as stupidly as though one were still a German student of 1860. Only with the instinct of despair could one force one's self into this old thicket of ignorance after having been repulsed at a score of entrances more promising and more popular. Thus far, no path had led anywhere, unless perhaps to an exceedingly modest living. Forty-five years of study had proved to be quite futile for the pursuit of power; one controlled no more force in 1900 than in 1850, although the amount of force controlled by society had enormously increased. The secret of education still hid itself somewhere behind ignorance, and one fumbled over it as feebly as ever. In such labyrinths, the staff is a force almost more necessary than the legs; the pen becomes a sort of blindman's dog, to keep him from falling into the gutters. The pen works for itself, and acts like a hand, modelling the plastic material over and over again to the form that suits it best. The form is never arbitrary, but is a sort of growth like crystallization, as any artist knows too well; for often the pencil or pen runs into side-paths and shapelessness, loses its relations, stops or is bogged. Then it has to return on its trail, and recover, if it can, its line of force. The result of a year's work depends more on what is struck out than on what is left in; on the sequence of the main lines of thought, than on their play or variety. [. . .]

The Height of Knowledge (1902)

America has always taken tragedy lightly. Too busy to stop the activity of their twenty-million-horse-power society, Americans ignore tragic motives that would have overshadowed the Middle Ages; and the world learns to regard assassination as a form of hysteria, and death as neurosis, to be treated by a rest-cure. Three hideous political murders, that would have fattened the Eumenides with horror, have thrown scarcely a shadow on the White House.

[. . .] Honestly, the lessons at education were becoming too trite. Hay[4] himself, probably for the first time, felt half glad that Roosevelt should want him to stay in office, if only to save himself the trouble of quitting; but to Adams all was pure loss. On that side, his education had been finished at school. His friends in power were lost, and he knew life too well to risk total wreck by trying to save them.

As far as concerned Roosevelt, the chance was hopeless. To them at sixty-three, Roosevelt at forty-three could not be taken seriously in his old character, and could not be recovered in his new one. Power when wielded by abnormal energy is the most serious of facts, and all Roosevelt's friends know that his restless and combative energy was more than abnormal. Roosevelt, more than any other man living within the range of notoriety, showed the singular primitive quality that belongs to ultimate matter—the quality that mediæval theology assigned to God—he was pure act. With him wielding unmeasured power with immeasurable energy, in the White House, the relation of age to youth—of teacher to pupil—was altogether out of place; and no other was possible. Even Hay's relation was a false one, while Adams's ceased of itself. History's truths are little valuable now; but human nature retains a few of its archaic, proverbial laws, and the wisest courtier that ever lived—Lucius Seneca himself—must have remained in some shade of doubt what advantage he should get from the power of his friend

---

4. [John Milton Hay (1838–1905), Secretary of State under William McKinley and Theodore Roosevelt. Formerly ambassador to Great Britain and assistant personal secretary to Abraham Lincoln, he cowrote with John Nicolay a 10-volume biography of Lincoln.]

and pupil Nero Claudius, until, as a gentleman past sixty, he received Nero's filial invitation to kill himself. Seneca closed the vast circle of his knowledge by learning that a friend in power was a friend lost—a fact very much worth insisting upon—while the gray-headed moth that had fluttered through many moth-administrations and had singed his wings more or less in them all, though he now slept nine months out of the twelve, acquired an instinct of self-preservation that kept him to the north side of La Fayette Square, and, after a sufficient habitude of Presidents and Senators, deterred him from hovering between them.

Those who seek education in the paths of duty are always deceived by the illusion that power in the hands of friends is an advantage to them. As far as Adams could teach experience, he was bound to warn them that he had found it an invariable disaster. Power is poison. Its effect on Presidents had been always tragic, chiefly as an almost insane excitement at first, and a worse reaction afterwards; but also because no mind is so well balanced as to bear the strain of seizing unlimited force without habit or knowledge or it; and finding it disputed with him by hungry packs of wolves and hounds whose lives depend on snatching the carrion. Roosevelt enjoyed a singularly direct nature and honest intent, but he lived naturally in restless agitation that would have worn out most tempers in a month, and his first year of Presidency showed chronic excitement that made a friend tremble. The effect of unlimited power on limited mind is worth noting in Presidents because it must represent the same process in society, and the power of self-control must have limit somewhere in face of the control of the infinite.

Here, education seemed to see its first and last lesson, but this is a matter of psychology which lies far down in the depths of history and of science; it will recur in other forms. The personal lesson is different. Roosevelt was lost, but this seemed no reason why Hay and Lodge should also be lost, yet the result was mathematically certain. With Hay, it was only the steady decline of strength, and the necessary economy of force; but with Lodge it was law of politics. He could not help himself, for his position as the President's friend and independent statesman at once was false, and he must be unsure in both relations.

To a student, the importance of Cabot Lodge[5] was great—much greater than that of the usual Senator—but it hung on his position in Massachusetts rather than on his control of Executive patronage; and his standing in Massachusetts was highly insecure. Nowhere in America was society so complex or change so rapid. No doubt the Bostonian had always been noted for a certain chronic irritability—a sort of Bostonitis—which, in its primitive Puritan forms, seemed due to knowing too much of his neighbors, and thinking too much of himself. Many years earlier William M. Evarts had pointed out to Adams the impossibility of uniting New England behind a New England leader. The trait led to good ends—such as admiration of Abraham Lincoln and George Washington—but the virtue was exacting; for New England standards were various, scarcely reconcilable with each other, and constantly multiplying in number, until balance between them threatened to become impossible. The old ones were quite difficult enough—State Street and the banks exacted one stamp; the old Congregational clergy another; Harvard College, poor in votes, but rich in social influence, a third; the foreign element, especially the Irish, held aloof, and seldom consented to approve any one; the new socialist class, rapidly growing, promised to become more exclusive than the Irish. New power was disintegrating society, and setting independent centres of force to work, until money had all it could do to hold the machine together. No one could represent it faithfully as a whole. [. . .]

Double standards are inspiration to "men of letters, but they are apt to be fatal to politicians. Adams had no reason to care whether his standards were popular or not, and no one else cared more than he; but Roosevelt and Lodge were playing a game in which they were always liable to find the shifty sands of American opinion yield suddenly under their feet. With this game an elderly friend had long before carried acquaintance as far as he wished. There was nothing in it for him but the amusement of the pugilist or acrobat. The larger study was lost in the

---

5. [Henry Cabot Lodge (1850–1924), U.S. Senator from 1893 to 1924.]

division of interests and the ambitions of fifth-rate men; but foreign affairs dealt only with large units, and made personal relation possible with Hay which could not be maintained with Roosevelt or Lodge. As an affair of pure education the point is worth notice from young men who are drawn into politics. The work of domestic progress is done by masses of mechanical power—steam, electric, furnace, or other—which have to be controlled by a score or two of individuals who have shown capacity to manage it. The work of internal government has become the task of controlling these men, who are socially as remote as heathen gods, alone worth knowing, but never known, and who could tell nothing of political value if one skinned them alive. Most of them have nothing to tell, but are forces as dumb as their dynamos, absorbed in the development or economy of power. They are trustees for the public, and whenever society assumes the property, it must confer on them that title; but the power will remain as before, whoever manages it, and will then control society without appeal, as it controls its stokers and pit-men. Modern politics is, at bottom, a struggle not of men but of forces. The men become every year more and more creatures of force, massed about central power-houses. The conflict is no longer between the men, but between the motors that drive the men, and the men tend to succumb to their own motive forces.

This is a moral that man strongly objects to admit, especially in mediaeval pursuits like politics and poetry, nor is it worth while for a teacher to insist upon it. What he insists upon is only that, in domestic politics, every one works for an immediate object, commonly for some private job, and invariably in a near horizon, while in foreign affairs the outlook is far ahead, over a field as wide as the world. There the merest scholar could see what he was doing. For history, international relations are the only sure standards of movement; the only foundation for a map. For this reason, Adams had always insisted that international relation was the only sure base for a chart of history.

He cared little to convince any one of the correctness of his view, but as teacher he was bound to explain it, and as friend he found it convenient. The Secretary of State has always stood as much alone as the historian. Required to look far ahead and round

him, he measures forces unknown to party managers, and has found Congress more or less hostile ever since Congress first sat. The Secretary of State exists only to recognize the existence of a world which Congress would rather ignore; of obligations which Congress repudiates whenever it can; of bargains which Congress distrusts and tries to turn to its advantage or to reject. Since the first day the Senate existed, it has always intrigued against the Secretary of State whenever the Secretary has been obliged to extend his functions beyond the appointment of Consuls in Senators' service.

This is a matter of history which any one may approve or dispute as he will; but as education it gave new resources to an old scholar, for it made of Hay the best schoolmaster since 1865. Hay had become the most imposing figure ever known in the office. He had an influence that no other Secretary of State ever possessed, as he had a nation behind him such as history had never imagined. He needed to write no state papers; he wanted no help, and he stood far above counsel or advice; but he could instruct an attentive scholar as no other teacher in the world could do; and Adams sought only instruction— wanted only to chart the international channel for fifty years to come; to triangulate the future; to obtain his dimension, and fix the acceleration of movement in politics since the year 1200, as he was trying to fix it in philosophy and physics; in finance and force.

Hay had been so long at the head at foreign affairs that at last the stream of events favored him. With infinite effort he had achieved the astonishing diplomatic feat of inducing the Senate, with only six negative votes, to permit Great Britain to renounce, without equivalent, treaty rights which she had for fifty years defended tooth and nail. This unprecedented triumph in his negotiations with the Senate enabled him to carry one step further his measures for general peace. About England the Senate could make no further effective opposition, for England was won, and Canada alone could give trouble. The next difficulty was with France, and there the Senate blocked advance, but England assumed the task, and, owing to political changes in France, effected the object—a combination which, as late as 1901, had been visionary. The next, and far more difficult step, was to bring Germany into the combine; while, at the end of the vista, most unmanageable of all, Russia remained to be satisfied and disarmed. This was the instinct of what might be named McKinley-ism; the system of combinations, consolidations, trusts, realized at home, and realizable abroad.

With the system, a student nurtured in ideas of the eighteenth century had nothing to do, and made not the least pretence of meddling; but nothing forbade him to study, and he noticed to his astonishment that this capitalistic scheme of combining governments, like railways or furnaces, was in effect precisely the socialist scheme of Jaurès and Bebel.[6] That John Hay, of all men, should adopt a socialist policy seemed an idea more absurd than conservative Christian anarchy, but paradox had become the only orthodoxy in politics as in science. When one saw the field, one realized that Hay could not help himself, nor could Bebel. Either Germany must destroy England and France to create the next inevitable unification as a system of continent against continent—or she must pool interests. Both schemes in turn were attributed to the Kaiser; one or the other he would have to choose; opinion was balanced doubtfully on their merits; but, granting both to be feasible, Hay's and McKinley's statesmanship turned on the point of persuading the Kaiser to join what might be called the Coal-power combination, rather than build up the only possible alternative, a Gun-power combination by merging Germany in Russia. Thus Bebel and Jaurès, McKinley and Hay, were partners.

The problem was pretty—even fascinating—and, to an old Civil-War private soldier in diplomacy, as rigorous as a geometrical demonstration. As the last possible lesson in life, it had all sorts of ultimate values. Unless education marches on both feet—theory and practice—it risks going astray; and Hay was probably the most accomplished master of both then living. He knew not only the forces but also the men, and he had no other thought than his policy.

Probably this was the moment of highest knowledge that a scholar could ever reach. He had under his eyes the whole educational staff of the Government at a time when the Government had just reached the heights of highest activity and influence.

---

6. [August Bebel (1840–1913) and Jean Jaurès (1859–1914), nineteenth-century socialists.]

Since 1860, education had done its worst, under the greatest masters and at enormous expense to the world, to train these two minds to catch and comprehend every spring of international action, not to speak of personal influence; and the entire machinery of politics in several great countries had little to do but supply the last and best information. Education could be carried no further.

With its effects on Hay, Adams had nothing to do; but its effects on himself were grotesque. Never had the proportions of his ignorance looked so appalling. He seemed to know nothing—to be groping in darkness—to be falling forever in space; and the worst depth consisted in the assurance, incredible as it seemed, that no one knew more. He had, at least, the mechanical assurance of certain values to guide him—like the relative intensities of his Coal-powers, and relative inertia of his Gun-powers—but he conceived that had he known, besides the mechanics, every relative value of persons, as well as he knew the inmost thoughts of his own Government—had the Czar and the Kaiser and the Mikado turned schoolmasters, like Hay and taught him all they knew, he would still have known nothing. They knew nothing themselves. Only by comparison of their ignorance could the student measure his own.

Darwinism (1867–1868)

Politics, diplomacy, law, art, and history had opened no outlet for future energy or effort, but a man must do something, even in Portland Place, when winter is dark and winter evenings are exceedingly long. At that moment Darwin was convulsing society. The geological champion of Darwin was Sir Charles Lyell, and the Lyells were intimate at the Legation. Sir Charles constantly said of Darwin, what Palgrave said of Tennyson, that the first time he came to town, Adams should be asked to meet him, but neither of them ever came to town, or ever cared to meet a young American, and one could not go to them because they were known to dislike intrusion. The only Americans who were not allowed to intrude were the half-dozen in the Legation. Adams was content to read Darwin, especially his "Origin of Species" and his "Voyage of the Beagle." He was a Darwinist before the letter; a predestined follower of the tide; but he was hardly trained to follow Darwin's evidences. Fragmentary the British mind might be, but in those days it was doing a great deal of work in a very un-English way, building up so many and such vast theories on such narrow foundations as to shock the conservative, and delight the frivolous. The atomic theory; the correlation and conservation of energy; the mechanical theory of the universe; the kinetic theory of gases, and Darwin's Law of Natural Selection, were examples of what a young man had to take on trust. Neither he nor any one else knew enough to verify them; in his ignorance of mathematics, he was particularly helpless; but this never stood in his way. The ideas were new and seemed to lead somewhere—to some great generalization which would finish one's clamor to be educated. That a beginner should understand them all, or believe them all, no one could expect, still less exact. Henry Adams was Darwinist because it was easier than not, for his ignorance exceeded belief, and one must know something in order to contradict even such trifles as Tyndall and Huxley.[7]

By rights, he should have been also a Marxist, but some narrow trait of the New England nature seemed to blight socialism, and he tried in vain to make himself a convert. He did the next best thing; he became a Comteist[8] within the limits of evolution. He was ready to become anything but quiet. As though the world had not been enough upset in his time, he was eager to see it upset more. He had his wish, but he lost his hold on the results by trying to understand them.

He never tried to understand Darwin; but he still fancied he might get the best part of Darwinism from the easier study of geology; a science which suited idle minds as well as though it were history. Every curate in England dabbled in geology and hunted for vestiges of Creation. Darwin hunted only for vestiges of Natural Selection, and Adams followed him, although he cared nothing about Selection, unless perhaps for the indirect amusement of upsetting curates. He felt, like nine men in ten, an instinctive belief in Evolution, but he felt no more concern in Natural than in unnatural Selection, though he seized with greediness the new volume on the "Antiquity of Man" which Sir Charles Lyell published in 1863 in order to support Darwin by wrecking the Garden of Eden. Sir Charles next brought out, in 1866, a new edition of his "Principles," then the highest text-book of geology; but here the Darwinian doctrine grew in stature. Natural Selection led back to Natural Evolution, and at last to Natural Uniformity. This was a vast stride. Unbroken Evolution under uniform conditions pleased every one—except curates and bishops; it was the very best substitute for religion; a safe, conservative, practical, thoroughly Common-Law deity. Such a working system for the universe suited a young man who had just helped to waste five or ten thousand million dollars and a million lives, more or less, to enforce unity and uniformity on people who objected to it; the idea was only too seductive in its perfection; it had the charm of art. Unity and Uniformity were the whole motive of philosophy, and if Darwin, like a true Englishman, preferred to back into it—to reach God *a posteriori*—rather than start from it, like Spinoza, the difference of method taught only the moral that the best way of reaching unity was to unite. Any road was good that arrived.

Life depended on it. One had been, from the first, dragged hither and thither like a French poodle on a string, following always the strongest pull, between one form of unity or centralization and another. The proof that one had acted wisely because of obeying the primordial habit of nature flattered one's self-esteem. Steady, uniform, unbroken evolution from lower to higher seemed easy. So, one day when Sir Charles came to the Legation to inquire about getting his "Principles" properly noticed in America, young Adams found nothing simpler than to suggest that he could do it himself if Sir Charles would tell him what to say. Youth risks such encounters with the universe before one succumbs to it, yet even he was surprised at Sir Charles's ready assent, and still more so at finding himself, after half an hour's conversation, sitting down to clear the minds of American geologists about the principles of their profession. This was getting on fast; Arthur Pendennis had never gone so far.

---

7. [Thomas Huxley (1825–1895) and John Tyndall (1820–1893), leading scientists of nineteenth-century Great Britain, who were advocates of evolution.]

8. [Cometians, who were followers of French intellectual Auguste Comte (1798–1857), founder of positivism.]

The geologists were a hardy class, not likely to be much hurt by Adams's learning, nor did he throw away much concern on their account. He undertook the task chiefly to educate, not them, but himself, and if Sir Isaac Newton had, like Sir Charles Lyell, asked him to explain for Americans his last edition of the "Principia," Adams would have jumped at the chance. Unfortunately the mere reading such works for amusement is quite a different matter from studying them for criticism. Ignorance must always begin at the beginning. Adams must inevitably have begun by asking Sir Isaac for an intelligible reason why the apple fell to the ground. He did not know enough to be satisfied with the fact. The Law of Gravitation was so-and-so, but what was Gravitation? and he would have been thrown quite off his base if Sir Isaac had answered that he did not know. [. . .]

[. . .] Objections fatal to one mind are futile to another, and as far as concerned the article, the matter ended there, although the glacial epoch remained a misty region in the young man's Darwinism. Had it been the only one, he would not have fretted about it; but uniformity often worked queerly and sometimes did not work as Natural Selection at all. Finding himself at a loss for some single figure to illustrate the Law of Natural Selection, Adams asked Sir Charles for the simplest case of uniformity on record. Much to his surprise Sir Charles told him that certain forms, like *Terebratula*, appeared to be identical from the beginning to the end of geological time. Since this was altogether too much uniformity and much too little selection, Adams gave up the attempt to begin at the beginning, and tried starting at the end—himself. Taking for granted that the vertebrates would serve his purpose, he asked Sir Charles to introduce him to the first vertebrate. Infinitely to his bewilderment, Sir Charles informed him that the first vertebrate was a very respectable fish, among the earliest of all fossils, which had lived, and whose bones were still reposing, under Adams's own favorite Abbey on Wenlock Edge.

By this time, in 1867, Adams had learned to know Shropshire familiarly, and it was the part of his diplomatic education which he loved best. Like Catherine Olney in "Northanger Abbey," he yearned for nothing so keenly as to feel at home in a thirteenth-century Abbey, unless it were to haunt a fifteenth-century Prior's House, and both these joys were his at

Wenlock. With companions or without, he never tired of it. [. . .]

That here, on the Wenlock Edge of time, a young American, seeking only frivolous amusement, should find a legitimate parentage as modern as though just caught in the Severn below, astonished him as much as though he had found Darwin himself. In the scale of evolution, one vertebrate was as good as another. For anything he, or any one else, knew, nine hundred and ninety-nine parts of evolution out of a thousand lay behind or below the *Pteraspis*. To an American in search of a father, it mattered nothing whether the father breathed through lungs, or walked on fins, or on feet. Evolution of mind was altogether another matter and belonged to another science, but whether one traced descent from the shark or the wolf was immaterial even in morals. This matter had been discussed for ages without scientific result. La Fontaine and other fabulists maintained that the wolf, even in morals, stood higher than man; and in view of the late civil war, Adams had doubts of his own on the facts of moral evolution:—[. . .]

That *Pteraspis* and shark were his cousins, great-uncles, or grandfathers, in no way troubled him, but that either or both of them should be older than evolution itself seemed to him perplexing; nor could he at all simplify the problem by taking the sudden back-somersault into Quincy Bay in search of the fascinating creature he had called a horseshoe, whose huge dome of shell and sharp spur of tail had so alarmed him as a child. [. . .]

Cousinship had limits but no one knew enough to fix them. When the vertebrate vanished in Siluria, it disappeared instantly and forever. Neither vertebra nor scale nor print reappeared, nor any trace of ascent or descent to a lower type. The vertebrate began in the Ludlow shale, as complete as Adams himself—in some respects more so—at the top of the column of organic evolution: and geology offered no sort of proof that he had ever been anything else. Ponder over it as he might, Adams could see nothing in the theory of Sir Charles but pure inference, precisely like the inference of Paley, that, if one found a watch, one inferred a maker. He could detect no more evolution in life since the *Pteraspis* than he could detect it in architecture since the Abbey. All he could prove was change. Coal-power alone asserted evolution—of power—and only by violence could be forced to assert selection of type.

All this seemed trivial to the true Darwinian, and to Sir Charles it was mere defect in the geological record. Sir Charles labored only to heap up the evidences of evolution; to cumulate them till the mass became irresistible. With that purpose, Adams gladly studied and tried to help Sir Charles, but, behind the lesson of the day, he was conscious that, in geology as in theology, he could prove only Evolution that did not evolve; Uniformity that was not uniform; and Selection that did not select. To other Darwinians— except Darwin—Natural Selection seemed a dogma to be put in the place of the Athanasian creed;[9] it was a form of religious hope; a promise of ultimate perfection. Adams wished no better; he warmly sympathized in the object; but when he came to ask himself what he truly thought, he felt that he had no Faith; that whenever the next new hobby should be brought out, he should surely drop off from Darwinism like a monkey from a perch; that the idea of one Form, Law, Order, or Sequence had no more value for him than the idea of none; that what he valued most was Motion, and that what attracted his mind was Change.

Psychology was to him a new study, and a dark corner of education. As he lay on Wenlock Edge, with the sheep nibbling the grass close about him as they or their betters had nibbled the grass—or whatever there was to nibble—in the Silurian kingdom of Pteraspis, he seemed to have fallen on an evolution far more wonderful than that of fishes. He did not like it; he could not account for it; and he determined to stop it. Never since the days of his *Limulus* ancestry had any of his ascendants thought thus. Their modes of thought might be many, but their thought was one. Out of his millions of millions of ancestors, back to the Cambrian mollusks, every one had probably lived and died in the illusion of Truths which did not amuse him, and which had never changed. Henry Adams was the first in an infinite series to discover and admit to himself that he really did not care whether truth was, or was not, true. He did not even care that it should be proved true, unless the process were new and amusing. He was a Darwinian for fun.

From the beginning of history, this attitude had been branded as criminal—worse than crime—sacrilege! Society punished it ferociously and justly, in self-defence. Mr. Adams, the father, looked on it as moral weakness; it annoyed him; but it did not annoy him nearly so much as it annoyed his son, who had no need to learn from Hamlet the fatal effect of the pale cast of thought on enterprises great or small. He had no notion of letting the currents of his action be turned awry by this form of conscience. To him, the current of his time was to be his current, lead where it might. He put psychology under lock and key; he insisted on maintaining his absolute standards; on aiming at ultimate Unity. The mania for handling all the sides of every question, looking into every window, and opening every door, was, as Bluebeard judiciously pointed out to his wives, fatal to their practical usefulness in society. One could not stop to chase doubts as though they were rabbits. One had no time to paint and putty the surface of Law, even though it were cracked and rotten. For the young men whose lives were cast in the generation between 1867 and 1900, Law should be Evolution from lower to higher, aggregation of the atom in the mass, concentration of multiplicity in unity, compulsion of anarchy in order; and he would force himself to follow wherever it led, though he should sacrifice five thousand millions more in money, and a million more lives.

As the path ultimately led, it sacrificed much more than this; but at the time, he thought the price he named a high one, and he could not foresee that science and society would desert him in paying it. He, at least, took his education as a Darwinian in good faith. The Church was gone, and Duty was dim, but Will should take its place, founded deeply in interest and law. This was the result of five or six years in England; a result so British as to be almost the equivalent of an Oxford degree.

9. [A Christian statement of belief attributed to St. Athanasius (fourth century) and affirming the nature of the Trinity.]

4

FREEDOM AS POWER AND OPPORTUNITY

In June 1928, Herbert Hoover accepted his party's presidential nomination. "We in America today," he proclaimed, expressing a prevailing perception of the day, "are nearer to the final triumph over poverty than ever before in the history of this land." Hoover, like much of the electorate who had voted for him, had reason to be optimistic. For many Americans, the "Roaring Twenties" were a time of prosperity. Wages in many industries rose throughout the decade, allowing Americans to buy an increasing quantity of consumer goods. Liberty and progress seemed evident everywhere. After a seventy-year struggle, women nationwide finally exercised the suffrage. Flappers pushed the boundaries of female decorum and sexuality. America buzzed, as electricity lit the cities, radio broadcasted to a mass audience, and movies shaped a new popular culture. Skyscrapers redefined the skylines of American cities. The Model T and other automobiles lent unprecedented personal mobility to the increasing number of Americans who owned them. Both rapidly became popular symbols for the limitless possibilities to American freedom, wealth, and power. Indeed, just one year prior to Hoover's declaration Charles Lindbergh became the first person to fly nonstop and solo between North America and Europe. It was a heady time in America.

That exhilarating confidence ended abruptly on October 28, 1929, as panicked investors began a record sell-off of stock shares. "Black Monday" was followed by "Black Tuesday." The market entered a free fall, ushering in the Great Depression, an unparalleled period of economic hardship in American history. The stock market collapse was, in fact, merely symptomatic of larger macroeconomic problems, and conditions would grow considerably worse over the next few years. By 1932, more than 15 million American workers—at least 25 percent of the workforce—were unemployed. The gross national product plunged, as did wages for those lucky enough to find work. Banks failed nationwide. Farmers were hit hard by sharply falling prices, by a seven-year drought, and by fierce dust storms. Some took up arms in an effort to prevent banks from foreclosing on their property. A "Bonus Expeditionary Force" of 20,000 unemployed World War I veterans took up camp in Washington to protest their pensions, only to be driven out by a federal army. It's no surprise that Americans made "Brother Can You Spare a Dime" a hit.

In fact, the full story about the 1920s is more complicated than the name Roaring Twenties implies. Not all Americans prospered. Whole sectors of the economy, including farming, textiles, and mining, had faced hard times since the early years of the decade. The Ku Klux Klan's membership and influence peaked in this period, signifying the reality that liberty in America was decidedly a racial affair. Xenophobia grew, and with the Klan calling for "100 percent Americanism," Congress in 1924 and 1929 passed laws effectively banning non-Western, "non-white" immigration. Fear of anarchy and communism, though diminished after the Red Scare (1919–20), as well as a religious fundamentalism, remained political forces that, bound up with this renewed nativism, found expression in the Scopes, Gitlow, and Sacco and Vanzetti trials. In short, the reality and zeitgeist, or spirit of the age, were discordant. Nonetheless, the decade's zeitgeist was defined by an exuberant belief in the nation's future and seemingly boundless cultural and economic progress—a belief that perhaps was a reaction to the recent horrors of the First World War (the "war to end all wars").

The profound economic shock of the Great Depression fostered equally profound political and social change. The 1932 election swept Franklin Roosevelt into the White House and the Democrat

Party into public offices at all levels of government, a hold on power it would maintain for decades. Campaigning on a platform that asserted government's responsibility to provide economic security to all Americans, Roosevelt led a constitutional revolution in American politics.

Roosevelt's commitment to a strong governmental role in social and economic policy was not unprecedented. Progressives had for years been calling on government to fight economic hardship and for a bureaucracy of experts to run the new administrative state. But it took the Great Depression to change popular thinking, clearing the way for sweeping political change. For despite the Progressives' arguments and modest political successes, throughout the first three decades of the century the prevailing view held liberty to be a negative concept; that is, most Americans understood liberty in terms of an individual's freedom *from* social and political interference. Government was to play only a minimal role in socioeconomic affairs. Thus while Hoover rejected unadulterated laissez faire, he still spoke for much of the nation in envisioning a society of "rugged individuals" competing in a minimally regulated market. It was in the marketplace that people, governed by the natural laws of supply and demand and freely contracting with each other, exhibited the idea of the free individual.

Of course, Progressives were not all of one stripe. The more egalitarian of them, like John Dewey, argued simultaneously for greater governmental responsibility for the economic welfare of all Americans and for more political democracy. Dewey's importance is especially notable and goes beyond specific policy prescriptions; his writings present a particular notion about the proper nature and function of social inquiry. Dewey eschewed the traditional emphasis on metaphysics, rejecting the claim that truth and good are fixed principles to be discovered. He maintained instead that such concepts have meaning only within particular historical and social contexts. Additionally, he held—and here the influence of Darwin is evident—that there is no guiding hand behind the relationship between humans and the natural world. In other words, there is no permanent "good" that humans must strive to discover and toward which they must always move. Like all species, humans adapt to their environment, understanding that environment will allow humans to manage it in a way beneficial to the species. Achieving this understanding is the purpose of scientific and social science inquiry, inquiry that would serve as the basis for social and political action. In sum, Dewey argued that we should consider the consequences of ideas and theories, and measure their value by their practical effects.

But, Dewey argued, culture tends to be conservative. Rather than genuine, socially transformative inquiry, "traditions, moth-eaten slogans and catchwords" perpetuate old, prevailing norms, even when those norms are no longer consistent with the public good. Looking around, Dewey concluded that the political institutions that once helped promote democracy in an agrarian America were inadequate in industrial America. The "natural" law of unregulated markets now produced great social and political anxiety. Greater public regulation of the economy, he concluded, was needed to promote democracy and social justice.

What prevented the public from adopting new policies that would reconcile the public good with this new economic environment? Dewey's answer was "the eclipse of the public." As the population grew increasingly diverse it had grown increasingly fragmented, and the idea of "the public" had given way to numerous, competing publics. Needed was a renewed sense of a public purpose, a "Great Community" in which citizens, informed by published, disseminated, and easily accessible social science inquiry would shape public policy for their good. The emergence of this great, that is, truly democratic community required "continuous inquiry," the habituation of people to constant, serious attention to public affairs. As people were educated to this practice of social inquiry, their sense of ownership in and identity from the community would develop. Collectively, as a public, they would make policy to fit their needs and to promote economic and social justice.

Progressives like Dewey faced resistance from other (less egalitarian) Progressives like Walter Lippman. Lippman challenged Dewey's assumption that under the right conditions, ordinary citizens were capable of governing themselves—that mass democracy could produce a sense of community and good government. Most people, Lippman argued, were incapable of the type of reasoned inquiry necessary to create and administer policies for the public good. Instead, they were shortsighted, poorly informed, and too often governed by emotion. As a result, they were incapable of truly independent thought and susceptible to manipulation by political and media leaders. In short, there was no truly independent, authentic "voice of the people." Other, perhaps more sympathetic critics, like Reinhold Niebuhr (see Chapter 5) discounted the notion that "social conservatism is [due] to ignorance," arguing instead that "the traditionalism which the social sciences face is based upon the economic interest of the dominant social classes who are trying to maintain their special privileges in society." For Niebuhr, group conflict was an inevitable part "of the process of gaining social justice."

What's especially noteworthy about FDR, as evidenced in his Commonwealth Club Address, is his appropriation of the American Founders to defend the interventionist or positive state. While remaining committed to the Founders' core values, he interprets these abstract commitments in the context of a new industrial economy and through a new understanding of the social contract. "[W]e have now to apply the earlier concepts of American government to the conditions of today," he claims, concluding that "the new terms of the old social contract" obligate government to ensure that all citizens enjoy the basic necessities required for freedom and happiness.

Although Roosevelt's New Deal received overwhelming electoral support, his policies still faced stiff opposition—most importantly, from laissez-faire advocates on the bench. For example, in 1935 and 1936 the Supreme Court struck down a provision of the National Industrial Recovery Act, a retirement program for railroad workers, and a policy for farm subsidies under the Agricultural Adjustment Act. Roosevelt responded aggressively after his 1936 landslide reelection. On February 5, 1937, he proposed that Congress increase the number of seats on the Supreme Court. This "Court packing" plan proved to be highly controversial, precipitating a political crisis. The crisis subsided when, in spring 1937, the Court reversed course—the famous "switch in time that saved nine"—in its liberty of contract and commerce clause jurisprudence.

While Roosevelt embraced the Progressive ideal of "enlightened administration," an active national government dedicated to solving socioeconomic problems, and while he advocated the idea of mass democracy, he avoided the Progressive tendency to equate democracy with majoritarianism. Instead, Roosevelt's new "liberalism" emphasized rights, an emphasis that the Court likewise had begun to make in its rulings. In its famous World War I First Amendment rulings, the Court offered a narrow interpretation of free speech. Moreover, the Court continued to hold that the national Bill of Rights was not binding on state governments. The Court's Fourteenth Amendment jurisprudence finally began to change with *Gitlow v. New York* (1925), and the robust debate over how—and whether—to apply the Bill of Rights to the states (a process called "incorporation") is mapped out in a number of cases included in this chapter. Finally, while rights gained new political and legal respect during the New Deal era, progress was halting and inconsistent. In particular, African Americans continued to press, with increased vigor, for equal civil, political, and economic rights, in part through an emphasis on more effective political organization.

Eugene V. Debs

Speech to the Court (1918)

Your Honor, years ago I recognized my kinship with all living beings, and I made up my mind that I was not one bit better than the meanest on earth. I said then, and I say now, that while there is a lower class, I am in it, and while there is a criminal element I am of it, and while there is a soul in prison, I am not free.

I listened to all that was said in this court in support and justification of this prosecution, but my mind remains unchanged. I look upon the Espionage Law as a despotic enactment in flagrant conflict with democratic principles and with the spirit of free institutions. [. . .]

Your Honor, I have stated in this court that I am opposed to the social system in which we live; that I believe in a fundamental change—but if possible by peaceable and orderly means. [. . .]

Standing here this morning, I recall my boyhood. At fourteen I went to work in a railroad shop; at sixteen I was firing a freight engine on a railroad. I remember all the hardships and privations of that earlier day, and from that time until now my heart has been with the working class. I could have been in Congress long ago. I have preferred to go to prison. [. . .]

I am thinking this morning of the men in the mills and the factories; of the men in the mines and on the railroads. I am thinking of the women who for a paltry wage are compelled to work out their barren lives; of the little children who in this system are robbed of their childhood and in their tender years are seized in the remorseless grasp of Mammon and forced into the industrial dungeons, there to feed the monster machines while they themselves are being starved and stunted, body and soul. I see them dwarfed and diseased and their little lives broken and blasted because in this high noon of Christian civilization money is still so much more important than the flesh and blood of childhood. In very truth gold is god today and rules with pitiless sway in the affairs of men.

In this country—the most favored beneath the bending skies—we have vast areas of the richest and most fertile soil, material resources in inexhaustible abundance, the most marvelous productive machinery on earth, and millions of eager workers ready to apply their labor to that machinery to produce in abundance for every man, woman, and child—and if there are still vast numbers of our people who are the victims of poverty and whose lives are an unceasing struggle all the way from youth to old age, until at last death comes to their rescue and lulls these hapless victims to dreamless sleep, it is not the fault of the Almighty: it cannot be charged to nature, but it is due entirely to the outgrown social system in which we live that ought to be abolished not only in the interest of the toiling masses but in the higher interest of all humanity. [. . .]

I believe, Your Honor, in common with all Socialists, that this nation ought to own and control its own industries. I believe, as all Socialists do, that all things that are jointly needed and used ought to be jointly owned—that industry, the basis of our social life, instead of being the private property of a few and operated for their enrichment, ought to be the common property of all, democratically administered in the interest of all. [. . .]

I am opposing a social order in which it is possible for one man who does absolutely nothing that is useful to amass a fortune of hundreds of millions of dollars, while millions of men and women who work all the days of their lives secure barely enough for a wretched existence.

This order of things cannot always endure. I have registered my protest against it. I recognize the feebleness of my effort, but, fortunately, I am not alone. There are multiplied thousands of others who, like myself, have come to realize that before we may truly enjoy the blessings of civilized life, we must reorganize society upon a mutual and cooperative basis; and to this end we have organized a great economic and political movement that spreads over the face of all the earth.

There are today upwards of sixty millions of Socialists, loyal, devoted adherents to this cause, regardless of nationality, race, creed, color, or sex. They are all making common cause. They are spreading with tireless energy the propaganda of the new social order. They are waiting, watching, and working hopefully through all the hours of the day and the night. They are still in a minority. But they have learned how to be patient and to bide their time. They feel—they know, indeed—that the time is coming, in spite of all opposition, all persecution, when this emancipating gospel will spread among all the peoples, and when this minority will become the triumphant majority and, sweeping into power, inaugurate the greatest social and economic change in history.

In that day we shall have the universal commonwealth—the harmonious cooperation of every nation with every other nation on earth. [. . .]

Your Honor, I ask no mercy and I plead for no immunity. I realize that finally the right must prevail. I never so clearly comprehended as now the great struggle between the powers of greed and exploitation on the one hand and upon the other the rising hosts of industrial freedom and social justice.

I can see the dawn of the better day for humanity. The people are awakening. In due time they will and must come to their own.

When the mariner, sailing over tropic seas, looks for relief from his weary watch, he turns his eyes toward the southern cross, burning luridly above the tempest-vexed ocean. As the midnight approaches, the southern cross begins to bend, the whirling worlds change their places, and with starry finger-points the Almighty marks the passage of time upon the dial of the universe, and though no bell may beat the glad tidings, the lookout knows that the midnight is passing and that relief and rest are close at hand. Let the people everywhere take heart of hope, for the cross is bending, the midnight is passing, and joy cometh with the morning.

OLIVER WENDELL HOLMES

Schenck v. United States (1919)

Mr. Justice HOLMES delivered the opinion of the Court.

This is an indictment in three counts. The first charges a conspiracy to violate the Espionage Act of June 15, 1917, by causing and attempting to cause insubordination, etc., in the military and naval forces of the United States, and to obstruct the recruiting and enlistment service of the United States, when the United States was at war with the German Empire, to-wit, that the defendant wilfully conspired to have printed and circulated to men who had been called and accepted for military service under the Act of May 18, 1917, a document set forth and alleged to be calculated to cause such insubordination and obstruction. The count alleges overt acts in pursuance of the conspiracy, ending in the distribution of the document set forth. The second count alleges a conspiracy to commit an offense against the United States, to-wit, to use the mails for the transmission of matter declared to be non-mailable by title 12, 2, of the Act of June 15, 1917, to-wit, the above mentioned document, with an averment of the same overt acts. The third count charges an unlawful use of the mails for the transmission of the same matter and otherwise as above. The defendants were found guilty on all the counts. They set up the First Amendment to the Constitution forbidding Congress to make any law abridging the freedom of speech, or of the press, and bringing the case here on that ground have argued some other points also of which we must dispose. [. . .]

The document in question upon its first printed side recited the first section of the Thirteenth Amendment, said that the idea embodied in it was violated by the conscription act and that a conscript is little better than a convict. In impassioned language it intimated that conscription was despotism in its worst form and a monstrous wrong against humanity in the interest of Wall Street's chosen few. It said, "Do not submit to intimidation," but in form at least confined itself to peaceful measures such as a petition for the repeal of the act. The other and later printed side of the sheet was headed "Assert Your Rights." It stated reasons for alleging that any one violated the Constitution when he refused to recognize "your right to assert your opposition to the draft," and went on, "If you do not assert and support your rights, you are helping to deny or disparage rights which it is the solemn duty of all citizens and residents of the United States to retain." It described the arguments on the other side as coming from cunning politicians and a mercenary capitalist press, and even silent consent to the conscription law as helping to support an infamous conspiracy. It denied the power to send our citizens away to foreign shores to shoot up the people of other lands, and added that words could not express the condemnation such cold-blooded ruthlessness deserves, etc., etc., winding up, "You must do your share to maintain, support and uphold the rights of the people of this country." Of course the document would not have been sent unless it had been intended to have some effect, and we do not see what effect it could be expected to have upon persons subject to the draft except to influence them to obstruct the carrying of it out. The defendants do not deny that the jury might find against them on this point.

But it is said, suppose that that was the tendency of this circular, it is protected by the First Amendment to the Constitution. Two of the strongest expressions are said to be quoted respectively from well-known public men. It well may be that the prohibition of laws abridging the freedom of speech is not confined to previous restraints, although to prevent them may have been the main purpose, as intimated in *Patterson v. Colorado* [1907]. We admit that in many places and in ordinary times the defendants in saying all that was said in the circular would have been within their constitutional rights. But the character of every act depends upon the circumstances in which it is done. *Aikens v. Wisconsin* [1904]. The

most stringent protection of free speech would not protect a man in falsely shouting fire in a theatre and causing a panic. It does not even protect a man from an injunction against uttering words that may have all the effect of force. *Gompers v. Buck's Stove & Range Co.* [1911]. The question in every case is whether the words used are used in such circumstances and are of such a nature as to create a clear and present danger that they will bring about the substantive evils that Congress has a right to prevent. It is a question of proximity and degree. When a nation is at war many things that might be said in time of peace are such a hindrance to its effort that their utterance will not be endured so long as men fight and that no Court could regard them as protected by any constitutional right. It seems to be admitted that if an actual obstruction of the recruiting service were proved, liability for words that produced that effect might be enforced. The statute of 1917 in section 4 (Comp. St. 1918, 10212d) punishes conspiracies to obstruct as well as actual obstruction. If the act, (speaking, or circulating a paper) its tendency and the intent with which it is done are the same, we perceive no ground for saying that success alone warrants making the act a crime. Indeed that case might be said to dispose of the present contention if the precedent covers all media concludendi. But as the right to free speech was not referred to specially, we have thought fit to add a few words.

It was not argued that a conspiracy to obstruct the draft was not within the words of the Act of 1917. The words are "obstruct the recruiting or enlistment service," and it might be suggested that they refer only to making it hard to get volunteers. Recruiting heretofore usually having been accomplished by getting volunteers the word is apt to call up that method only in our minds. But recruiting is gaining fresh supplies for the forces, as well by draft as otherwise. It is put as an alternative to enlistment or voluntary enrollment in this act. The fact that the Act of 1917 was enlarged by the amending Act of May 16, 1918, of course, does not affect the present indictment and would not, even if the former act had been repealed.

Judgments affirmed.

John H. Clarke

Abrams v. United States (1919)

Mr. Justice Clarke delivered the opinion of the Court.

On a single indictment, containing four counts, the five plaintiffs in error, hereinafter designated the defendants, were convicted of conspiring to violate provisions of the Espionage Act of Congress (section 3, title I, of Act June 15, 1917, c. 30, 40 Stat. 219, as amended by Act May 16, 1918, c. 75, 40 Stat. 553 [Comp. St. 1918, 10212c]).

Each of the first three counts charged the defendants with conspiring, when the United States was at war with the Imperial Government of Germany, to unlawfully utter, print, write and publish: In the first count, "disloyal, scurrilous and abusive language about the form of government of the United States;" in the second count, language "intended to bring the form of government of the United States into contempt, scorn, contumely, and disrepute;" and in the third count, language "intended to incite, provoke and encourage resistance to the United States in said war." The charge in the fourth count was that the defendants conspired "when the United States was at war with the Imperial German Government, [. . .] unlawfully and willfully, by utterance, writing, printing and publication to urge, incite and advocate curtailment of production of things and products, to wit, ordnance and ammunition, necessary and essential to the prosecution of the war." The offenses were charged in the language of the act of Congress.

It was charged in each count of the indictment that it was a part of the conspiracy that the defendants would attempt to accomplish their unlawful purpose by printing, writing and distributing in the city of New York many copies of a leaflet or circular, printed in the English language, and of another printed in the Yiddish language, copies of which, properly identified, were attached to the indictment.

All of the five defendants were born in Russia. They were intelligent, had considerable schooling, and at the time they were arrested they had lived in the United States terms varying from five to ten years, but none of them had applied for naturalization.

Four of them testified as witnesses in their own behalf, and of these three frankly avowed that they were "rebels," "revolutionists," "anarchists," that they did not believe in government in any form, and they declared that they had no interest whatever in the government of the United States. The fourth defendant testified that he was a "Socialist" and believed in "a proper kind of government, not capitalistic," but in his classification the government of the United States was "capitalistic."

It was admitted on the trial that the defendants had united to print and distribute the described circulars and that 5,000 of them had been printed and distributed about the 22d day of August, 1918. The group had a meeting place in New York City, in rooms rented by defendant Abrams, under an assumed name, and there the subject of printing the circulars was discussed about two weeks before the defendants were arrested. The defendant Abrams, although not a printer, on July 27, 1918, purchased the printing outfit with which the circulars were printed, and installed it in a basement room where the work was done at night. The circulars were distributed, some by throwing them from a window of a building where one of the defendants was employed and others secretly, in New York City.

The defendants pleaded "not guilty," and the case of the government consisted in showing the facts we have stated, and in introducing in evidence copies of the two printed circulars attached to the indictment, a sheet entitled "Revolutionists Unite for Action," written by the defendant Lipman, and found on him when he was arrested, and another paper, found at the headquarters of the group, and for which Abrams assumed responsibility.

Thus the conspiracy and the doing of the overt acts charged were largely admitted and were fully established.

On the record thus described it is argued, somewhat faintly, that the acts charged against the defendants were not unlawful because within the protection of that freedom of speech and of the press which is guaranteed by the First Amendment to the Constitution of the United States, and that the entire Espionage Act is unconstitutional because in conflict with that amendment.

This contention is sufficiently discussed and is definitely negatived in *Schenck v. United States* [1919] and *Baer v. United States* [1919], and in *Frohwerk v. United States* [1919]. [. . .]

The first of the two articles attached to the indictment is conspicuously headed, "The Hypocrisy of the United States and her Allies." After denouncing President Wilson as a hypocrite and a coward because troops were sent into Russia, it proceeds to assail our government in general, saying: "His [the President's] shameful, cowardly silence about the intervention in Russia reveals the hypocrisy of the plutocratic gang in Washington and vicinity."

It continues:

He [the President] is too much of a coward to come out openly and say: We capitalistic nations cannot afford to have a proletarian republic in Russia.

Among the capitalistic nations Abrams testified the United States was included.

Growing more inflammatory as it proceeds, the circular culminates in:

The Russian Revolution cries: Workers of the World! Awake! Rise! Put down your enemy and mine!

Yes friends, there is only one enemy of the workers of the world and that is CAPITALISM.

This is clearly an appeal to the "workers" of this country to arise and put down by force the government of the United States which they characterize as their "hypocritical," "cowardly" and "capitalistic" enemy.

It concludes:

Awake! Awake, you Workers of the World!

REVOLUTIONISTS.

The second of the articles was printed in the Yiddish language and in the translation is headed, "Workers—Wake Up." After referring to "his Majesty, Mr. Wilson, and the rest of the gang, dogs of all colors!" it continues:

Workers, Russian emigrants, you who had the least belief in the honesty of our government, which defendants admitted referred to the United States government—

must now throw away all confidence, must spit in the face the false, hypocritic, military propaganda which has fooled you so relentlessly, calling forth your sympathy, your help, to the prosecution of the war.

The purpose of this obviously was to persuade the persons to whom it was addressed to turn a deaf ear to patriotic appeals in behalf of the government of the United States, and to cease to render it assistance in the prosecution of the war. [. . .]

Again, the spirit becomes more bitter as it proceeds to declare that—

America and her Allies have betrayed [the Workers]. Their robberish aims are clear to all men. The destruction of the Russian Revolution, that is the politics of the march to Russia.

Workers, our reply to the barbaric intervention has to be a general strike! An open challenge only will let the government know that not only the Russian Worker fights for freedom, but also here in America lives the spirit of Revolution.

This is not an attempt to bring about a change of administration by candid discussion, for no matter what may have incited the outbreak on the part of the defendant anarchists, the manifest purpose of such a publication was to create an attempt to defeat the war plans of the government of the United States, by bringing upon the country the paralysis of a general strike, thereby arresting the production of all munitions and other things essential to the conduct of the war.

This purpose is emphasized in the next paragraph, which reads:

Do not let the government scare you with their wild punishment in prisons, hanging and shooting. We must not and will not betray the splendid fighters of Russia. Workers, up to fight.

After more of the same kind, the circular concludes:

Woe unto those who will be in the way of progress. Let solidarity live!

It is signed, "The Rebels."

That the interpretation we have put upon these articles, circulated in the greatest port of our land, from which great numbers of soldiers were at the time taking ship daily, and in which great quantities of war supplies of every kind were at the time being manufactured for transportation overseas, is not only the fair interpretation of them, but that it is the meaning which their authors consciously intended should be conveyed by them to others is further shown by the additional writings found in the meeting place of the defendant group and on the person of one of them. One of these circulars is headed: "Revolutionists! Unite for Action!" [. . .]

[W]hile the immediate occasion for this particular outbreak of lawlessness, on the part of the defendant alien anarchists, may have been resentment caused by our government sending troops into Russia as a strategic operation against the Germans on the eastern battle front, yet the plain purpose of their propaganda was to excite, at the supreme crisis of the war, disaffection, sedition, riots, and, as they hoped, revolution, in this country for the purpose of embarrassing and if possible defeating the military plans of the government in Europe. A technical distinction may perhaps be taken between disloyal and abusive language applied to the form of our government or language intended to bring the form of our government into contempt and disrepute, and language of like character and intended to produce like results directed against the President and Congress, the agencies through which that form of government must function in time of war. But it is not necessary to a decision of this case to consider whether such distinction is vital or merely formal, for the language of these circulars was obviously intended to provoke and to encourage resistance to the United States in the war, as the third count runs, and, the defendants, in terms, plainly urged and advocated a resort to a general strike of workers in ammunition factories for the purpose of curtailing the production of ordnance and munitions necessary and essential to the prosecution of the war as is charged in the fourth count. Thus it is clear not only that some evidence but that much persuasive evidence was before the jury tending to prove that the defendants were guilty as charged in both the third and fourth counts of the indictment and under the long established rule of law hereinbefore stated the judgment of the District Court must be

Affirmed.

OLIVER WENDELL HOLMES

Abrams v. United States, Dissent (1919)

Mr. Justice HOLMES, dissenting.

This indictment is founded wholly upon the publication of two leaflets which I shall describe in a moment. The first count charges a conspiracy pending the war with Germany to publish abusive language about the form of government of the United States, laying the preparation and publishing of the first leaflet as overt acts. The second count charges a conspiracy pending the war to publish language intended to bring the form of government into contempt, laying the preparation and publishing of the two leaflets as overt acts. The third count alleges a conspiracy to encourage resistance to the United States in the same war and to attempt to effectuate the purpose by publishing the same leaflets. The fourth count lays a conspiracy to incite curtailment of production of things necessary to the prosecution of the war and to attempt to accomplish it by publishing the second leaflet to which I have referred.

The first of these leaflets says that the President's cowardly silence about the intervention in Russia reveals the hypocrisy of the plutocratic gang in Washington. It intimates that "German militarism combined with allied capitalism to crush the Russian revolution"—goes on that the tyrants of the world fight each other until they see a common enemy—working class enlightenment, when they combine to crush it; and that now militarism and capitalism combined, though not openly, to crush the Russian revolution. It says that there is only one enemy of the workers of the world and that is capitalism; that it is a crime for workers of America, etc., to fight the workers' republic of Russia, and ends "Awake! Awake, you workers of the world! Revolutionists." A note adds "It is absurd to call us pro-German. We hate and despise German militarism more than do you hypocritical tyrants. We have more reason for denouncing German militarism than has the coward of the White House."

The other leaflet, headed "Workers—Wake Up," with abusive language says that America together with the Allies will march for Russia to help the Czecko-Slovaks in their struggle against the Bolsheviki, and that this time the hypocrites shall not fool the Russian emigrants and friends of Russia in America. It tells the Russian emigrants that they now must spit in the face of the false military propaganda by which their sympathy and help to the prosecution of the war have been called forth and says that with the money they have lent or are going to lend "they will make bullets not only for the Germans but also for the Workers Soviets of Russia," and further, "Workers in the ammunition factories, you are producing bullets, bayonets, cannon to murder not only the Germans, but also your dearest, best, who are in Russia fighting for freedom." It then appeals to the same Russian emigrants at some length not to consent to the "inquisitionary expedition in Russia," and says that the destruction of the Russian revolution is "the politics of the march to Russia." [. . .]

No argument seems to be necessary to show that these pronunciamentos in no way attack the form of government of the United States, or that they do not support either of the first two counts. What little I have to say about the third count may be postponed until I have considered the fourth. With regard to that it seems too plain to be denied that the suggestion to workers in the ammunition factories that they are producing bullets to murder their dearest, and the further advocacy of a general strike, both in the second leaflet, do urge curtailment of production of things necessary to the prosecution of the war within the meaning of the Act of May 16, 1918. But to make the conduct criminal that statute requires that it should be "with intent by such curtailment to cripple or hinder the United States in the prosecution of the war." It seems to me that no such intent is proved.

I am aware of course that the word "intent" as vaguely used in ordinary legal discussion means no more than knowledge at the time of the act that the consequences said to be intended will ensue. Even less than that will satisfy the general principle of civil and criminal liability. A man may have to pay damages, may be sent to prison, at common law might be hanged, if at the time of his act he knew facts from which common experience showed that the consequences would follow, whether he individually could foresee them or not. But, when words are used exactly, a deed is not done with intent to produce a consequence unless that consequence is the aim of the deed. It may be obvious, and obvious to the actor, that the consequence will follow, and he may be liable for it even if he regrets it, but he does not do the act with intent to produce it unless the aim to produce it is the proximate motive of the specific act, although there may be some deeper motive behind.

It seems to me that this statute must be taken to use its words in a strict and accurate sense. They would be absurd in any other. A patriot might think that we were wasting money on aeroplanes, or making more cannon of a certain kind than we needed, and might advocate curtailment with success, yet even if it turned out that the curtailment hindered and was thought by other minds to have been obviously likely to hinder the United States in the prosecution of the war, no one would hold such conduct a crime. I admit that my illustration does not answer all that might be said but it is enough to show what I think and to let me pass to a more important aspect of the case. I refer to the First Amendment to the Constitution that Congress shall make no law abridging the freedom of speech.

I never have seen any reason to doubt that the questions of law that alone were before this Court in the cases of *Schenck, Frohwerk,* and *Debs* were rightly decided. I do not doubt for a moment that by the same reasoning that would justify punishing persuasion to murder, the United States constitutionally may punish speech that produces or is intended to produce a clear and imminent danger that it will bring about forthwith certain substantive evils that the United States constitutionally may seek to prevent. The power undoubtedly is greater in time of war than in time of peace because war opens dangers that do not exist at other times.

But as against dangers peculiar to war, as against others, the principle of the right to free speech is always the same. It is only the present danger of immediate evil or an intent to bring it about that warrants Congress in setting a limit to the expression of opinion where private rights are not concerned. Congress certainly cannot forbid all effort to change the mind of the country. Now nobody can suppose that the surreptitious publishing of a silly leaflet by an unknown man, without more, would present any immediate danger that its opinions would hinder the success of the government arms or have any appreciable tendency to do so. Publishing those opinions for the very purpose of obstructing, however, might indicate a greater danger and at any rate would have the quality of an attempt. So I assume that the second leaflet if published for the purposes alleged in the fourth count might be punishable. But it seems pretty clear to me that nothing less than that would bring these papers within the scope of this law. An actual intent in the sense that I have explained is necessary to constitute an attempt, where a further act of the same individual is required to complete the substantive crime, for reasons given in *Swift & Co. v. United States* [1905]. It is necessary where the success of the attempt depends upon others because if that intent is not present the actor's aim may be accomplished without bringing about the evils sought to be checked. An intent to prevent interference with the revolution in Russia might have been satisfied without any hindrance to carrying on the war in which we were engaged.

I do not see how anyone can find the intent required by the statute in any of the defendant's words. The second leaflet is the only one that affords even a foundation for the charge, and there, without invoking the hatred of German militarism expressed in the former one, it is evident from the beginning to the end that the only object of the paper is to help Russia and stop American intervention there against the popular government—not to impede the United States in the war that it was carrying on. To say that two phrases taken literally might import a suggestion of conduct that would have interference with the war as an indirect and probably undesired effect seems to me by no means enough to show an attempt to produce that effect.

I return for a moment to the third count. That charges an intent to provoke resistance to the United States in its war with Germany. Taking the clause in the statute that deals with that in connection with the other elaborate provisions of the Act, I think that resistance to the United States means some forcible act of opposition to some proceeding of the United States in pursuance of the war. I think the intent must be the specific intent that I have described and for the reasons that I have given I think that no such intent was proved or existed in fact. I also think that there is no hint at resistance to the United States as I construe the phrase.

In this case sentences of twenty years imprisonment have been imposed for the publishing of two leaflets that I believe the defendants had as much right to publish as the Government has to publish the Constitution of the United States now vainly invoked by them. Even if I am technically wrong and enough can be squeezed from these poor and puny anonymities to turn the color of legal litmus paper; I will add, even if what I think the necessary intent were shown; the most nominal punishment seems to me all that possible could be inflicted, unless the defendants are to be made to suffer not for what the indictment alleges but for the creed that they avow—a creed that I believe to be the creed of ignorance and immaturity when honestly held, as I see no reason to doubt that it was held here but which, although made the subject of examination at the trial, no one has a right even to consider in dealing with the charges before the Court.

Persecution for the expression of opinions seems to me perfectly logical. If you have no doubt of your premises or your power and want a certain result with all your heart you naturally express your wishes in law and sweep away all opposition. To allow opposition by speech seems to indicate that you think the speech impotent, as when a man says that he has squared the circle, or that you do not care whole heartedly for the result, or that you doubt either your power or your premises. But when men have realized that time has upset many fighting faiths, they may come to believe even more than they believe the very foundations of their own conduct that the ultimate good desired is better reached by free trade in ideas—that the best test of truth is the power of the thought to get itself accepted in the competition of the market, and that truth is the only ground upon which their wishes safely can be carried out. That at any rate is the theory of our Constitution. It is an experiment, as all life is an experiment. Every year if not every day we have to wager our salvation upon some prophecy based upon imperfect knowledge. While that experiment is part of our system I think that we should be eternally vigilant against attempts to check the expression of opinions that we loathe and believe to be fraught with death, unless they so imminently threaten immediate interference with the lawful and pressing purposes of the law that an immediate check is required to save the country. I wholly disagree with the argument of the Government that the First Amendment left the common law as to seditious libel in force. History seems to me against the notion. I had conceived that the United States through many years had shown its repentance for the Sedition Act of 1798 by repaying fines that it imposed. Only the emergency that makes it immediately dangerous to leave the correction of evil counsels to time warrants making any exception to the sweeping command, "Congress shall make no law abridging the freedom of speech." Of course I am speaking only of expressions of opinion and exhortations, which were all that were uttered here, but I regret that I cannot put into more impressive words my belief that in their conviction upon this indictment the defendants were deprived of their rights under the Constitution of the United States.

WALTER LIPPMANN

The Phantom Public (1925)

Social Contracts

1

It is impossible to imagine in the universe a harmony of all things, each with all the others. The only harmonies we know or can conceive, outside of what Mr. Santayana calls the realm of essences, are partial adjustments which sacrifice to some one end all purposes which conflict with it. That the tree may bear fruit for us, we readily kill the insects that eat the fruit. So the fruit will ripen for us, we take no account of the disharmony we create for innumerable flies.

In the light of eternity it may be wholly unimportant whether the harmonies on this earth are suited to men or to insects. For in the light of eternity and from the point of view of the universe as a whole nothing can be what we call good or bad, better or worse. All ideas of value are measurements of some part of this universe with some other part, and it is no more possible to value the universe as a whole than it is to weigh it as a whole. For all scales of value and of weight are contained within it. To judge the whole universe you must, like a god, be outside of it, a point of view no mortal mind can adopt.

Unfortunately for the fly, therefore, we are bound to judge him by human values. In so far as we have power over him, he must submit to the harmonies we seek to establish. We may as a sporting matter admit his theoretical right to establish his own harmonies against us if he can, and to call them better if he likes, but for us that only is good which is good for man. Our universe consists of all that it contains, not as such, not as the fly knows it, but in its relation to us. From any other point of view but man's, his conception of the universe is askew. It has an emphasis and a perspective, it is shaped to a design which is altogether human. The very forms, colors, odors and sound of things are dependent for their quality upon our sense organs. Their relations are seen and understood against the background of our necessities.

In the realm of man's interests and purposes and desires, the perspectives are even narrower. There is no human point of view here, but only the points of view of men. None is valid for all human beings, none for all of human history, none for all corners of the globe. An opinion of the right and the wrong, the good and the bad, the pleasant and the unpleasant, is dated, is localized, is relative. It applies only to some men at some time in some place under some circumstances.

2

Against this deep pluralism thinkers have argued in vain. They have invented social organisms and national souls, and oversouls, and collective souls; they have gone for hopeful analogies to the beehive and the anthill, to the solar system, to the human body; they have gone to Hegel for higher unities and to Rousseau for a general will in an effort to find some basis of union. For though men do not think alike, nor want the same things, though their private interests are so distinct that they do not merge easily in any common interest, yet men cannot live by themselves, nor realize even their private purposes without taking into account the behavior of other people. We, however, no longer expect to find a unity which absorbs diversity. For us the conflicts and differences are so real that we cannot deny them and instead of looking for identity of purpose we look simply for an accommodation of purposes.

When we speak, then, about the solution of a problem in the Great Society, we may mean little more than that two conflicting interests have found a *modus vivendi*. It may be, of course, that they have really removed all their differences, that one interest has yielded to the other, or both to a third. But the solutions of most social problems are not so neat as this; everything does not fit perfectly as in the solution

of a puzzle. The conflicting interests merely find a way of giving a little and taking a little, and of existing together without too much bad blood.

They still remain separate interests. The men involved still think differently. They have no union of mind or purpose. But they travel their own ways without collision, and even with some reliance at times upon the others' help. They know their rights and their duties, what to expect and what will be expected. Their rights are usually less than they claim, and their duties heavier than they like, yet, because they are in some degree enforced, conduct is rendered intelligible and predictable, and cooperation exists in spite of the conflicting interests of men.

The *modus vivendi* of any particular historical period, the system of rights and duties, has generally acquired some high religious or ideal sanction. The thinkers laureate of the age will generally manage to show that the institutions, the laws, the morality and the custom of that age are divinely inspired. These are tiresome illusions which have been exploded a thousand times. The prevailing system of rights and duties at any time is at bottom a slightly antiquated formulation of the balance of power among the active interests in the community. There is always a certain lag, as Mr. Ogburn calls it, so that the system of rights and duties men are taught is generally a little less contemporary than the system they would find most convenient. But, whether the system is obsolete or not, in its naked origin, a right is a claim somebody was able to assert, and a duty is an obligation somebody was able to impose.

3

The prevailing system of rights and duties is designed to regulate the conflicting purposes of men. An established right is a promise that a certain kind of behavior will be backed by the organized force of the state or at least by the sentiment of the community; a duty is a promise that failure to respect the rights of others in a certain way will be punished. The punishment may be death, imprisonment, loss of property, the nullification of a right, the expression of disapproval. In short, the system of rights and duties is the whole system of promises which the courts and public sentiment will support. It is not a fixed system. It varies from place to place, and from time to time, and with the character of the tribunals and the community. But none the less it makes the conduct of men somewhat rational, and establishes a kind of union in diversity by limiting and defining the freedom with which conflicting purposes can be pursued.

Sometimes the promises are embodied in coercive law: Thou shalt, on penalty of this, do that; thou shalt not do so and so. Sometimes the promise is based on a contract between two parties: there is no obligation to make the contract, but, once made, it must be executed or a certain penalty paid. Sometimes the promise is based on an ecclesiastical code: it must be followed or the wages of sin will be visited either in fact or in anticipation upon the sinner. Sometimes the promise is based on custom: it must be respected or the price of nonconformity, whatever it may happen to be, must be paid. Sometimes the promise is based on habit: it must be executed or the disturbance faced which men feel when they break with their habits.

The question of whether any particular right or duty shall be enforced, the question of how it shall be enforced, whether by the police, by public criticism or private conscience, will not be answered by reasoning *a priori*. It will be answered by the dominant interests in society, each imposing to the limit of its powers the system of rights and duties which most nearly approximates the kind of social harmony it finds convenient and desirable. The system will be a reflection of the power that each interest is able to exert. The interests which find the rule good will defend it; the interests which find it bad will attack it. Their arguments will be weapons of defense and offense; even the most objective appeal to reason will turn out to be an appeal to desert one cause and enlist in another.

4

In the controversies between interests the question will be raised as to the merits of a particular rule; the argument will turn on whether the rule is good, on whether it should be enforced with this penalty or that. And out of those arguments, by persuasion or coercion, the specific rules of society are made enforced and revised.

It is the thesis of this book that the members of the public, who are the spectators of action, cannot successfully intervene in a controversy on the merits of the case. They must judge externally, and they can act only by supporting one of the interests directly involved. It follows that the public interest in a controversy cannot turn upon the specific issue. On what, then, does it turn? In what phase of the controversy can the public successfully interest itself?

Only when somebody objects does the public know there is a problem; when nobody any longer objects there is a solution. For the public, then, any rule is right which is agreeable to all concerned. It follows that the public interest in a problem is limited to this: that there shall be rules, which means that the rules which prevail shall be enforced, and that the unenforceable rules shall be changed according to a settled rule. The public's opinion that John Smith should or should not do this or that is immaterial; the public does not know John Smith's motives and needs, and is not concerned with them. But that John Smith shall do what he has promised to do is a matter of public concern, for unless the social contracts of men are made, enforced and revised according to a settled rule, social organization is impossible. Their conflicting purposes will engender unending problems unless they are regulated by some system of rights and duties.

The interest of the public is not in the rules and contracts and customs themselves but in the maintenance of a régime of rule, contract and custom. The public is interested in law, not in the laws; in the method of law, not in the substance; in the sanctity of contract, not in a particular contract; in understanding based on custom, not in this custom or that. It is concerned in these things to the end that men in their active affairs shall find a *modus vivendi*; its interest is in the workable rule which will define and predict the behavior of men so that they can make their adjustments. The pressure which the public is able to apply through praise and blame, through votes, strikes, boycotts or support can yield results only if it reinforces the men who enforce an old rule or sponsor a new one that is needed.

The public in this theory is not the dispenser of law or morals, but, at best, a reserve force that may be mobilized on behalf of the method and spirit of law and morals. In denying that the public can lay down the rules I have not said that it should abandon any function which the public now exercises. I have merely said that it should abandon a pretense. When the public attempts to deal with the substance it merely becomes the dupe or unconscious ally of a special interest. For there is only one common interest: that all special interests shall act according to settled rule. The moment you ask what rule you invade the realm of competing interests of special points of view, of personal, and class, and sectional, and national bias. The public should not ask what rule because it cannot answer the question. It will contribute its part to the solution of social problems if it recognizes that some system of rights and duties is necessary, but that no particular system is peculiarly sacred. [. . .]

Criteria of Reform

1

The random collections of bystanders who constitute a public could not, even if they had a mind to, intervene in all the problems of the day. They can and must play a part occasionally, I believe, but they cannot take an interest in, they cannot make even the coarsest judgments about, and they will not act even in the most grossly partisan way on, all the questions arising daily in a complex and changing society. Normally they leave their proxies to a kind of professional public consisting of more or less eminent persons. Most issues are never carried beyond this ruling group; the lay publics catch only echoes of the debate.

If, by the push and pull of interested parties and public personages, settlements are made more or less continually the party in power has the confidence of the country. In effect, the outsiders are arrayed behind the dominant insiders. But if the interested parties cannot be made to agree, if, as a result, there is disturbance and chronic crisis, then the opposition among the insiders may come to be considered the hope of the country, and be able to entice the bystanders to its side.

To support the Ins when things are going well; to support the Outs when they seem to be going badly, this, in spite of all that has been said about tweedledum and tweedledee, is the essence of popular government. Even the most intelligent large public of which we have any experience must determine finally who shall wield the organized power of the state, its army and its police, by a choice between the Ins and Outs. A community where there is no choice does not have popular government. It is subject to some form of dictatorship or it is ruled by the intrigues of the politicians in the lobbies.

Although it is the custom of partisans to speak as if there were radical differences between the Ins and the Outs, it could be demonstrated, I believe, that in stable and mature societies the differences are necessarily not profound. If they were profound, the defeated minority would be constantly on the verge of rebellion. An election would be catastrophic, whereas the assumption in every election is that the victors will do nothing to make life intolerable to the vanquished. and that the vanquished will endure with good humor policies which they do not approve.

In the United States, Great Britain, Canada, Australia and in certain of the Continental countries an election rarely means even a fraction of what the campaigners said it would mean. It means some new faces and perhaps a slightly different general tendency in the management of affairs. The Ins may have had a bias toward collectivism; the Outs will lean toward individualism. The Ins may have been suspicious and non-coöperative in foreign affairs; the Outs will perhaps be more trusting or entertain another set of suspicions. The Ins may have favored certain manufacturing interests; the Outs may favor agricultural interests. But even these differing tendencies are very small as compared with the immense area of agreement, established habit and unavoidable necessity. In fact, one might say that a nation is politically stable when nothing of radical consequence is determined by its elections.

There is, therefore, a certain mock seriousness about the campaigning for votes in well-established communities. Much of the excitement is not about the fate of the nation but simply about the outcome of the game. Some of the excitement is sincere, like any fervor of intoxication. And much of it is deliberately stoked up by the expenditure of money to overcome the inertia of the mass of the voters. For the most part the real difference between the Ins and the Outs is no more than this: the Ins, after a term of power, become so committed to policies and so entangled with particular interests that they lose their neutral freedom of decision. They cannot then intervene to check the arbitrary movement of the interests with which they have become aligned. Then it is time for the Outs to take power and restore a balance. The virtue of the Outs in this transaction is that they are not committed to those particular policies and those particular interests which have become overweighted.

The test of whether the Ins are handling affairs effectively is the presence or absence of disturbing problems. The need of reform is recognizable, as I pointed out in the chapter before this one, by the test of assent and the test of conformity. But it is my opinion that for the most part the general public cannot back each reformer on each issue. It must choose between the Ins and Outs on the basis of a cumulative judgment as to whether problems are being solved or aggravated. The particular reformers must look for their support normally to the ruling insiders.

If, however, there is to be any refinement of public opinion it must come from the breaking up of these wholesale judgments into somewhat more retail judgments on the major spectacular issues of the day. Not all of the issues which interest the public are within the scope of politics and reachable through the party system. It seems worth while, therefore, to see whether any canons of judgment can be formulated which could guide the bystanders in particular controversies.

The problem is to locate by clear and coarse objective tests the actor in a controversy who is most worthy of public support.

2

When the rule is plain, its validity unchallenged, the breach clear and the aggressor plainly located, the question does not arise. The public supports the agents of the law, though when the law is working well the support or the public is like the gold reserve of a good bank: it is known to be there and need not be drawn upon. But in many fields of controversy the rule is not plain, or its validity is challenged; each party calls the other aggressor, each claims to be acting for the highest ideals of mankind. In disputes between nations, between sectional interests, between classes, between town and country, between churches, the rules of adjustment are lacking and the argument about them is lost in a fog of propaganda.

Yet it is controversies of this kind, the hardest controversies to disentangle, that the public is called in to judge. Where the facts are most obscure, where precedents are lacking, where novelty and confusion pervade everything, the public in all its unfitness is compelled to make its most important decisions. The hardest problems are those which institutions cannot handle. They are the public's problems.

The one test which the members of a public can apply in these circumstances is to note which party to the dispute is least willing to submit its whole claim to inquiry and to abide by the result. This does not mean that experts are always expert or impartial tribunals really impartial. It means simply that where the public is forced to intervene in a strange and complex affair, the test of public inquiry is the surest clue to the sincerity of the claimant, to his confidence in his ability to stand the ordeal of examination, to his willingness to accept risks for the sake of his faith in the possibility of rational human adjustments. He may impugn a particular tribunal. But he must at least propose another. The test is whether, in the absence of an established rule, he is willing to act according to the forms of law and by a process through which law may be made.

Of all the tests which public opinion can employ, the test of inquiry is the most generally useful. If the parties are willing to accept it, there is at once an atmosphere of reason. There is prospect of a settlement. Failing that there is at least a delay of summary action and an opportunity for the clarification of issues. And failing that there is a high probability that the most arbitrary of the disputants will be isolated and clearly identified. It is no wonder that this is the principle invoked for the so-called nonjusticiable questions in all the recent experiments under the covenant of the League of Nations[1] and the Protocol for the Pacific Settlement of International Disputes.[2] For in applying this test of inquiry, what we affirm is this: That there is a dispute. That the merits are not clear. That the policy which ought to be applied is not established. That, nevertheless, we of the public outside say that those who are quarreling must act as

---

1. Articles XIII, XV.
2. Articles 4, 5, 6, 7, 8, 10.

if there were law to cover the case. That, even if the material for a reasoned conclusion is lacking, we demand the method and spirit of reason. That we demand any sacrifice that may be necessary, the postponment of satisfaction of their just needs, the risk that one of them will be defeated and that an injustice will be done. These things we affirm because we are maintaining a society based on the principle that all controversies are soluble by peaceable agreement.

They may not be. But on that dogma our society is founded. And that dogma we are compelled to defend. We can defend it, too, with a good enough conscience, however disconcerting some of its immediate consequences may be. For, by insisting in all disputes upon the spirit of reason, we shall tend in the long run to confirm the habit of reason. And where that habit prevails no point of view can seem absolute to him who holds it, and no problem between men so difficult that there is not at least a *modus vivendi*. [. . .]

This is as far as I know how at present to work out an answer to the question which we inherit from Aristotle: can simple criteria be formulated which will show the bystander where to align himself in complex affairs?

I have suggested that the main value of debate is not that it reveals the truth about the controversy to the audience but that it may identify the partisans. I have suggested further that a problem exists where a rule of action is defective, and that its defectiveness can best be judged by the public through the test of assent and the test of conformity. For remedies I have assumed that normally the public must turn to the Outs as against the Ins, although these wholesale judgments may be refined by more analytical tests for specific issues. As samples of these more analytical tests I have suggested the test of inquiry for confused controversies, and for reforms the test of interpretation, of amendment and of due notice.

These criteria are neither exhaustive nor definitive. Yet, however much tests of this character are improved by practice and reflection, it seems to me there always must remain many public affairs to which they cannot be applied. I do not believe that the public can intervene successfully in all public questions. Many problems cannot be advanced by that obtuse partisanship which is fundamentally all that the public can bring to bear upon them. There

is no reason to be surprised, therefore, if the tests I have outlined, or any others that are a vast improvement upon them, are not readily applicable to all questions that are raised in the discussions of the day.

I should simply maintain that where the members of a public cannot use tests of this sort as a guide to action, the wisest course for them is not to act at all. They had better be neutral, if they can restrain themselves, than blindly partisan. For where events are so confused or so subtly balanced or so hard to understand that they do not yield to judgments of the kind I have been outlining here, the probabilities are very great that the public can produce only muddle if it meddles. For not all problems are soluble in the present state of human knowledge. Many which may be soluble are not soluble with any force the public can exert. Some time alone will cure, and some are the fate of man. It is not essential, therefore, always to do something.

It follows that the proper limits of intervention by the public in affairs are determined by its capacity to make judgments. These limits may be extended as new and better criteria are formulated, or as men become more expert through practice. But where there are no tests, where such tests as these cannot be used, where, in other words, only an opinion on the actual merits of the dispute itself would be of any use, any positive action the bystanders are likely to take is almost certain to be more of a nuisance than a benefit. Their duty is to keep an open mind and wait to see. The existence of a usable test is itself the test of whether the public ought to intervene. [. . .]

Absentee Rulers

1

The practical effect of the monistic theories of society has been to rationalize that vast concentrating of political and economic power in the midst of which we live. Since society was supposed to have organic purposes of its own, it came to seem quite reasonable that these purposes should be made manifest to a people by laws and decisions from a central point. Somebody had to have a purpose revealed to him which could be treated as the common purpose; if it was to be accepted it had to be enforced by command;

if it was really to look like the national purpose, it had to be handed down as a rule binding upon all. Thus men could say with Goethe:

"And then a mighty work completed stands,
One mind suffices for a thousand hands."[3]

In this fashion the eulogies of the Great Society have been made. Two thousand years ago it was possible for whole civilizations as mature as the Chinese and the Greco-Roman to coexist in total indifference to one another. Today the food supplies, the raw materials, the manufactures, the communications and the peace of the world constitute one great system which cannot be thrown severely out of balance in any part without disturbing the whole.

Looked at from the top, the system in its far-flung and intricate adjustments has a certain grandeur. It might, as some hopeful persons think, even ultimately mean the brotherhood of man since all men living in advanced communities are now in quite obvious fashion dependent upon one another. But the individual man cannot look at the system steadily from the top or see it in its ultimate speculative possibilities. For him it means in practice, along with the rise in certain of his material standards of life, a nerve-wracking increase of the incalculable forces that bear upon his fate. My neighbor in the country who borrowed money to raise potatoes which he cannot sell for cash looks at the bills from the village store asking for immediate cash payments, and does not share the philosophic hopeful view of the interdependence of the world. When unseen commission merchants in New York City refuse his potatoes, the calamity is as dumfounding as a drought or a plague of locusts.

The harvest in September of the planting in May is now determined not only by wind and weather, which his religion has from time immemorial justified, but by a tangle of distant human arrangements of which only loose threads are in his hands. He may live more richly than his ancestors; he may be wealthier and healthier and, for all he knows, even happier. But he gambles with the behavior of unseen men in a bewildering way. His relations with invisibly managed markets are decisively important for him; his own foresight is not dependable. He is a link in a chain that stretches beyond his horizon. [. . .]

Under these conditions neither the discipline of the craftsman who controls his process from beginning to end nor the virtues of thrift, economy and work are a complete guide to a successful career. Defoe in his *Complete English Tradesman*[4] could say that "trade is not a ball where people appear in masque and act a part to make sport . . . but is a plain, visible scene of honest life . . . supported by prudence and frugality" . . . and so "prudent management and frugality will increase any fortune to any degree." Benjamin Franklin might opine that "he that gets all he can honestly, and saves all he gets (necessary expenses excepted) will certainly become rich, if that Being who governs the world, to whom all should look for a blessing on their honest endeavors, doth not in His wise providence, otherwise determine." Young men were until quite recently exhorted in the very words of Defoe and Franklin, though Franklin's rather canny allowance for the whims of the Almighty was not always included. But of late the gospel of success contains less about frugality and more about visions and the message of business. This new gospel, beneath all its highfalutin cant, points dimly though excitedly to the truth that for business success a man must project his mind over an invisible environment.

This need has bred an imperious tendency to organization on a large scale. To defend themselves against the economic powers of darkness, against great monopolies or a devastating competition, the farmers set up great centralized selling agencies. Business men form great trade associations. Everybody organizes, until the number of committees and their paid secretaries cannot be computed. The tendency is pervasive. We have had, if I remember correctly, National Smile Week. At any rate we have had Nebraska which discovered that if you wish to prohibit liquor in Nebraska you must prohibit it everywhere. Nebraska cannot live by itself alone, being too

---

3. *Faust*, Part II, Act v, scene 3.

4. *Cf.* Werner Lombart, *The Quintessence of Capitalism*, Chapter VII.

weak to control an international traffic. We have had the socialist who was convinced that socialism can maintain itself only on a socialist planet. We have had Secretary Hughes who was convinced that capitalism could exist only on a capitalist planet. We have had all the imperialists who could not live unless they advanced the backward races. And we have had the Ku Klux Klansmen who were persuaded that if you organized and sold hate on a country-wide scale there would be lots more hate than there was before. We have had the Germans before 1914 who were told they had to choose between "world power or downfall," and the French for some years after 1919 who could not be "secure" in Europe unless every one else was insecure. We have had all conceivable manifestations of the impulse to seek stability in an incalculable environment by standardizing for one's own apparent convenience all those who form the context of one's activity.

It has entailed perpetual effort to bring more and more men under the same law and custom, and then, of course, to assume control of the lawmaking and law-enforcing machinery in this larger area. The effect has been to concentrate decision in central governments, in distant executive offices, in caucuses and in steering committees. Whether this concentration of power is good or bad, permanent or passing, this at least is certain. The men who make the decisions at these central points are remote from the men they govern and the facts with which they deal. Even if they conscientiously regard themselves as agents or trustees, it is a pure fiction to say that they are carrying out the will of the people. They may govern the people wisely. They are not governing with the active consultation of the people. They can at best lay down policy wholesale in response to electorates which judge and act upon only a detail of the result. For the governors see a kind of whole which obscures the infinite varieties of particular interests; their vices are abstraction and generalization which appear in politics as legalism and bureaucracy. The governed, on the contrary, see vivid aspects of a whole which they can rarely imagine, and their prevailing vice is to mistake a local prejudice for a universal truth.

The widening distance between the centers where decisions are taken and the places where the main work of the world is done has undermined the discipline of public opinion upon which all the earlier theorists relied.[5] A century ago the model of popular government was the self-sufficing township in which the voters' opinions were formed and corrected by talk with their neighbors. They might entertain queer opinions about witches and spirits and foreign peoples and other worlds. But about the village itself the facts were not radically in dispute, and nothing was likely to happen that the elders could not with a little ingenuity bring under a well-known precedent of their common law.

But under absentee government these checks upon opinion are lacking. The consequences are often so remote and long delayed that error is not promptly disclosed. The conditioning factors are distant; they do not count vividly in our judgments. The reality is inaccessible; the bounds of subjective opinion are wide. In the interdependent world, desire, rather than custom or objective law, tends to become the criterion of men's conduct. They formulate their demands at large for "security" at the expense of every one else's safety, for "morality" at the expense of other men's tastes and comfort, for the fulfillment of a national destiny that consists in taking what you want when you want it. The lengthening of the interval between conduct and experience, between cause and effect, has nurtured a cult of self-expression in which each thinker thinks about his own thoughts and has subtle feelings about his feelings. That he does not in consequence deeply affect the course of affairs is not surprising.

2

The centralizing tendencies of the Great Society have not been accepted without protest, and the case against them has been stated again and again.[6] Without local institutions, said de Tocqueville, a nation may give itself a free government, but it does not possess the spirit of liberty. To concentrate power at one point is to facilitate the seizure of power. "What are

---

5. *Cf.* my *Public Opinion*, Chapters XVI and XVII.

6. In a convenient form by J. Charles Brun, *Le Régionalisme*, pp.13 *et seq.* Cf. also Walter Thompson, *Federal Centralization*, Chapter XIX.

you going to do?" Arthur Young asked some provincials at the time of the French Revolution. "We do not know," they replied; "we must see what Paris is going to do." Local interests handled from a distant central point are roughly handled by busy and inattentive men. And in the meantime the local training and the local winnowing of political talent are neglected. The overburdened central authority expands into a vast hierarchy of bureaucrats and clerks manipulating immense stacks of paper, always dealing with symbols on paper, rarely with things or with people. The genius of centralization reached its climax in the famous boast of a French minister of education, who said: It is three o'clock; all the pupils in the third grade throughout France are now composing a Latin verse.

There is no need to labor the point. The more centralization the less can the people concerned be consulted and give conscious assent. The more extensive the rule laid down the less account it can take of fact and special circumstance. The more it conflicts with local experience, the more distant its source and wholesale its character, the less easily enforceable it is. General rules will tend to violate particular needs. Distantly imposed rules usually lack the sanction of consent. Being less suited to the needs of men, and more external to their minds, they rest on force rather than on custom and on reason.

A centralized society dominated by the fiction that the governors are the spokesmen of a common will tends not only to degrade initiative in the individual but to reduce to insignificance the play of public opinion. For when the action of a whole people is concentrated, the public is so vast that even the crude objective judgments it might make on specific issues cease to be practicable. The tests indicated in preceding chapters by which a public might judge the workability of a rule or the soundness of a new proposal have little value when the public runs into millions and the issues are hopelessly entangled with each other. It is idle under such circumstances to talk about democracy, or about the refinement of public opinion. With such monstrous complications the public can do little more than at intervals to align itself heavily for or against the régime in power, and for the rest to bear with its works, obeying meekly or evading, as seems most convenient. For, in practice, the organic theory of society means a concentration of power; that is, the way the notion of one purpose is actually embodied in affairs. And this in turn means that men must either accept frustration of their own purposes or contrive somehow to frustrate that declared purpose of that central power which pretends it is the purpose of all.

The Realms of Disorder

Yet the practice of centralization and the philosophy which personifies society have acquired a great hold upon men. The dangers are well known. If, nevertheless, the practice and the theory persist, it cannot be merely because men have been led astray by false doctrine.

If you examine the difficulties enumerated by the sponsors of great centralizing measures, such as national prohibition, the national child labor amendment, federal control of education or the nationalization of railroads, they are reducible, I think, to one dominating idea: that it is necessary to extend the area of control over all the factors in a problem or the problem will be insoluble anywhere. [. . .]

For the democracies are haunted by this dilemma: they are frustrated unless in the laying down of rules there is a large measure of assent; yet they seem unable to find solutions of their greatest problems except through centralized governing by means of extensive rules which necessarily ignore the principle of assent. The problems that vex democracy seem to be unmanageable by democratic methods.

In supreme crises the dilemma is presented absolutely. Possibly a war can be fought for democracy; it cannot be fought democratically. Possibly a sudden revolution may be made to advance democracy; but the revolution itself will be conducted by a dictatorship. Democracy may be defended against its enemies but it will be defended by a committee of safety. The history of the wars and revolutions since 1914 is ample evidence on this point. In the presence of danger, where swift and concerted action is required, the methods of democracy cannot be employed.

That is understandable enough. But how is it that the democratic method should be abandoned so commonly in more leisurely and less catastrophic times? Why in time of peace should people provoke that centralization of power which deprives them of control over the use of that power? Is it not a probable answer to say that in the presence of certain issues, even in time of peace, the dangers have seemed sufficiently menacing to cause people to seek remedies, regardless of method, by the shortest and easiest way at hand?

It could be demonstrated, I think, that the issues which have seemed so overwhelming were of two kinds: those which turned on the national defense or the public safety and those which turned on the power of modern capitalism. Where the relations of a people to armed enemies are in question or where the relations of employee, customer or farmer to large industry are in question the need for solutions has outweighed all interest in the democratic method.

In the issues engendered by the rise of the national state and the development of large scale industries are to be found the essentially new problems of the modern world. For the solution of these problems there are few precedents. There is no established body of custom and law. The field of international affairs and the field of industrial relations are the two great centers of anarchy in society. It is a pervasive anarchy. Out of the national state with its terrifying military force, and out of great industry with all its elaborate economic compulsion, the threat against personal security always rises. To offset it somehow, to check it and thwart it, seemed more important than any finical regard for the principle of assent.

And so to meet the menace of the national state, its neighbors sought to form themselves into more powerful national states; to tame the power of capitalism they supported the growth of vast bureaucracies. Against powers that were dangerous and uncontrolled they set up powers, nominally their own, which were just as vast and just as uncontrolled.

3

But only for precarious intervals has security been attained by these vast balances of power. From 1870 to 1914 the world was held in equilibrium. It was upset, and the world has not yet found a new order. The balances of power within the nations are no less unsteady. For neither in industry nor in international affairs has it yet been possible to hold any balance long enough to fix it by rule and give it an institutional form. Power has been checked by power here and there and now and then but power has not been adjusted to power and the terms of the adjustment settled and accepted.

The attempt to bring power under control by offsetting it with power was sound enough in intention. The conflicting purposes of men cannot be held under pacific control unless the tendency of all power to become arbitrary is checked by other force. All the machinery of conference, of peaceful negotiation, of law and the rule of reason is workable in large affairs only where the power of the negotiators is neutralized one against the other. It may be neutralized because the parties are in fact equally powerful. It may be neutralized because the weaker has invisible allies among the other powers of the world, or in domestic affairs among other interests in society. But before there can be law there must be order, and an order is an arrangement of power.

The worst that can be said of the nationalists and collectivists is that they attempted to establish balances of power which could not endure. The pluralist at least would say that the end they sought must be attained differently, that in place of vast wholesale balances of power it is necessary to create many detailed balances of power. The people as a whole supporting a centralized government cannot tame capitalism as a whole. For the powers which are summed up in the term capitalism are many. They bear separately upon different groups of people. The nation as a unit does not encounter them all, and cannot deal with them all. It is to the different groups of people concerned that we must look for the power which shall offset the arbitrary power that bears upon them. The reduction of capitalism to workable law is no matter of striking at it wholesale by general enactments. It is a matter of defeating its arbitrary power in detail, in every factory, in every office, in every market, and of turning the whole network of relations under which industry operates from the dominion of arbitrary forces into those of settled rules.

And so it is in the anarchy among nations. If all the acts of a citizen are to be treated as organically the actions of that nation, a stable balance of power is impossible. Here also it is necessary to break down the fiction of identity, to insist that the quarrel of one business man with another is their quarrel, and not the nation's, a quarrel in which each is entitled to a vindication of his right to fair adjudication but not to patriotic advocacy of his cause. It is only by this dissociation of private interests that the mass of disputes across frontiers can gradually be brought under an orderly process. For a large part, perhaps the greatest part, of the disputes between nations is an accumulated mass of undetermined disputes between their nationals. If these essentially private disputes could be handled, without patriotic fervor and without confusing an oil prospector with the nation as a whole, with governments acting as friends of the court and not as advocates for a client, the balance of power between governments would be easier to maintain. It would not be subject to constant assault from within each nation by an everlasting propaganda of suspicion by private interests seeking national support. And if only the balance of power between governments could be stabilized long enough to establish a line of precedents for international conference, a longer peace might result.

These in roughest outline are some of the conclusions, as they appear to me, of the attempt to bring the theory of democracy into somewhat truer alignment with the nature of public opinion. I have conceived public opinion to be, not the voice of God, nor the voice of society, but the voice of the interested spectators of action. I have, therefore, supposed that the opinions of the spectators must be essentially different from those of the actors, and that the kind of action they were capable of taking was essentially different too. It has seemed to me that the public had a function and must have methods of its own in controversies, qualitatively different from those of the executive men; that it was a dangerous confusion to believe that private purposes were a mere emanation of some common purpose.

This conception of society seems to me truer and more workable than that which endows public opinion with pantheistic powers. It does not assume that men in action have universal purposes; they are denied the fraudulent support of the fiction that they are the agents of a common purpose. They are regarded as the agents of special purposes, without pretense and without embarrassment. They must live in a world with men who have other special purposes. The adjustments which must be made are society, and the best society is the one in which men

have purposes which they can realize with the least frustration. When men take a position in respect to the purposes of others they are acting as a public. And the end of their acting in this role is to promote the conditions under which special purposes can be composed.

It is a theory which puts its trust chiefly in the individuals directly concerned. They initiate, they administer, they settle. It would subject them to the least possible interference from ignorant and meddlesome outsiders, for in this theory the public intervenes only when there is a crisis of maladjustment, and then not to deal with the substance of the problem but to neutralize the arbitrary force which prevents adjustment. It is a theory which economizes the attention of men as members of the public, and asks them to do as little as possible in matters where they can do nothing very well. It confines the effort of men, when they are a public, to a part they might fulfill, to a part which corresponds to their own greatest interest in any social disturbance; that is, to an intervention which may help to allay the disturbance, and thus allow them to return to their own affairs.

For it is the pursuit of their special affairs that they are most interested in. It is by the private labors of individuals that life is enhanced. I set no great store on what can be done by public opinion and the action of masses. [. . .]

5

I have no legislative program to offer, no new institutions to propose. There are, I believe, immense confusions in the current theory of democracy which frustrate and pervert its action. I have attacked certain of the confusions with no conviction except that a false philosophy tends to stereotype thought against the lessons of experience. I do not know what the lessons will be when we have learned to think of public opinion as it is, and not as the fictitious power we have assumed it to be. It is enough if with Bentham we know that "the perplexity of ambiguous discourse . . . distracts and eludes the apprehension, stimulates and inflames the passions."

Oliver Wendell Holmes

Natural Law (1918)

It is not enough for the knight of romance that you agree that his lady is a very nice girl—if you do not admit that she is the best that God ever made or will make, you must fight. There is in all men a demand for the superlative, so much so that the poor devil who has no other way of reaching it attains it by getting drunk. It seems to me that this demand is at the bottom of the philosopher's effort to prove that truth is absolute and of the jurist's search for criteria of universal validity which he collects under the head of natural law.

I used to say, when I was young, that truth was the majority vote of that nation that could lick all others. Certainly we may expect that the received opinion about the present war will depend a good deal upon which side wins, (I hope with all my soul it will be mine), and I think that the statement was correct in so far as it implied that our test of truth is a reference to either a present or an imagined future majority in favor of our view. If, as I have suggested elsewhere, the truth may be defined as the system of my (intellectual) limitations, what gives it objectivity is the fact that I find my fellow man to a greater or less extent (never wholly) subject to the same *Can't Helps*. If I think that I am sitting at a table I find that the other persons present agree with me; so if I say that the sum of the angles of a triangle is equal to two right angles. If I am in a minority of one they send for a doctor or lock me up; and I am so far able to transcend the to me convincing testimony of my senses or my reason as to recognize that if I am alone probably something is wrong with my works.

Certitude is not the test of certainty. We have been cock-sure of many things that were not so. If I may quote myself again, property, friendship, and truth have a common root in time. One can not be wrenched from the rocky crevices into which one has grown for many years without feeling that one is attacked in one's life. What we most love and revere generally is determined by early associations. I love granite rocks and barberry bushes, no doubt because

with them were my earliest joys that reach back through the past eternity of my life. But while one's experience thus makes certain preferences dogmatic for oneself, recognition of how they came to be so leaves one able to see that others, poor souls, may be equally dogmatic about something else. And this again means scepticism. Not that one's belief or love does not remain. Not that we would not fight and die for it if important—we all, whether we know it or not, are fighting to make the kind of a world that we should like—but that we have learned to recognize that others will fight and die to make a different world, with equal sincerity or belief. Deep-seated preferences can not be argued about—you can not argue a man into liking a glass of beer—and therefore, when differences are sufficiently far reaching, we try to kill the other man rather than let him have his way. But that is perfectly consistent with admitting that, so far as appears, his grounds are just as good as ours.

The jurists who believe in natural law seem to me to be in that naïve state of mind that accepts what has been familiar and accepted by them and their neighbors as something that must be accepted by all men everywhere. No doubt it is true that, so far as we can see ahead, some arrangements and the rudiments of familiar institutions seem to be necessary elements in any society that may spring from our own and that would seem to us to be civilized—some form of permanent association between the sexes—some residue of property individually owned—some mode of binding oneself to specified future conduct—at the bottom of all, some protection for the person. But without speculating whether a group is imaginable in which all but the last of these might disappear and the last be subject to qualifications that most of us would abhor, the question remains as to the *Ought* of natural law.

It is true that beliefs and wishes have a transcendental basis in the sense that their foundation is arbitrary. You can not help entertaining and feeling them, and there is an end of it. As an arbitrary fact people wish to live, and we say with various degrees of certainty that they can do so only on certain conditions. To do it they must eat and drink. That necessity is absolute. It is a necessity of less degree but practically general that they should live in society. If they live in society, so far as we can see, there are further conditions. Reason working on experience does tell us, no doubt, that if our wish to live continues, we can do it only on those terms. But that seems to me the whole of the matter. I see no *a priori* duty to live with others and in that way, but simply a statement of what I must do if I wish to remain alive. If I do live with others they tell me that I must do and abstain from doing various things or they will put the screws on to me. I believe that they will, and being of the same mind as to their conduct I not only accept the rules but come in time to accept them with sympathy and emotional affirmation and begin to talk about duties and rights. But for legal purposes a right is only the hypostasis of a prophecy—the imagination of a substance supporting the fact that the public force will be brought to bear upon those who do things said to contravene it—just as we talk of the force of gravitation accounting for the conduct of bodies in space. One phrase adds no more than the other to what we know without it. No doubt behind these legal rights is the fighting will of the subject to maintain them, and the spread of his emotions to the general rules by which they are maintained; but that does not seem to me the same thing as the supposed *a priori* discernment of a duty or the assertion of a preëxisting right. A dog will fight for his bone.

The most fundamental of the supposed preëxisting rights—the right to life—is sacrificed without a scruple not only in war, but whenever the interest of society, that is, of the predominant power in the community, is thought to demand it. Whether that interest is the interest of mankind in the long run no one can tell, and as, in any event, to those who do not think with Kant and Hegel it is only an interest, the sanctity disappears. I remember a very tender-hearted judge being of opinion that closing a hatch to stop a fire and the destruction of a cargo was justified even if it was known that doing so would stifle a man below. It is idle to illustrate further, because to those who agree with me I am uttering commonplaces and to those who disagree I am ignoring the necessary

foundations of thought. The *a priori* men generally call the dissentients superficial. But I do agree with them in believing that one's attitude on these matters is closely connected with one's general attitude toward the universe. Proximately, as has been suggested, it is determined largely by early associations and temperament, coupled with the desire to have an absolute guide. Men to a great extent believe what they want to—although I see in that no basis for a philosophy that tells us what we should want to want.

Now when we come to our attitude toward the universe I do not see any rational ground for demanding the superlative—for being dissatisfied unless we are assured that our truth is cosmic truth, if there is such a thing—that the ultimates of a little creature on this little earth are the last word of the unimaginable whole. If a man sees no reason for believing that significance, consciousness and ideals are more than marks of the finite, that does not justify what has been familiar in French sceptics; getting upon a pedestal and professing to look with haughty scorn upon a world in ruins. The real conclusion is that the part can not swallow the whole—that our categories are not, or may not be, adequate to formulate what we can not know. If we believe that we come out of the universe, not it out of us, we must admit that we do not know what we are talking about when we speak of brute matter. We do know that a certain complex of energies can wag its tail and another can make syllogisms. These are among the powers of the unknown, and if, as maybe, it has still greater powers that we can not understand, as Fabre in his studies of instinct would have us believe, studies that gave Bergson one of the strongest strands for his philosophy and enabled Maeterlinck to make us fancy for a moment that we heard a clang from behind phenomena—if this be true, why should we not be content? Why should we employ the energy that is furnished to us by the cosmos to defy it and shake our fist at the sky? It seems to me silly.

That the universe has in it more than we understand, that the private soldiers have not been told the plan of campaign, or even that there is one, rather than some vaster unthinkable to which every predicate is an impertinence, has no bearing upon our conduct. We still shall fight—all of us because we want to live, some, at least, because we want to realize our spontaneity and prove our powers, for the joy of it, and we may leave to the unknown the supposed final valuation of that which in any event has value to us. It is enough for us that the universe has produced us and has within it, as less than it, all that we believe and love. If we think of our existence not as that of a little god outside, but as that of a ganglion within, we have the infinite behind us. It gives us our only but our adequate significance. A grain of sand has the same, but what competent person supposes that he understands a grain of sand? That is as much beyond our grasp as man. If our imagination is strong enough to accept the vision of ourselves as parts inseverable from the rest, and to extend our final interest beyond the boundary of our skins, it justifies the sacrifice even of our lives for ends outside of ourselves. The motive, to be sure, is the common wants and ideals that we find in man. Philosophy does not furnish motives, but it shows men that they are not fools for doing what they already want to do. It opens to the forlorn hopes on which we throw ourselves away, the vista of the farthest stretch of human thought, the chords of a harmony that breathes from the unknown.

Buck v. Bell (1927)

Mr. Justice HOLMES delivered the opinion of the Court.

This is a writ of error to review a judgment of the Supreme Court of Appeals of the State of Virginia affirming a judgment of the Circuit Court of Amherst County by which the defendant in error, the superintendent of the State Colony for Epileptics and Feeble Minded, was ordered to perform the operation of salpingectomy upon Carrie Buck, the plaintiff in error, for the purpose of making her sterile. 143 Va. 310. The case comes here upon the contention that the statute authorizing the judgment is void under the Fourteenth Amendment as denying to the plaintiff in error due process of law and the equal protection of the laws.

Carrie Buck is a feeble minded white woman who was committed to the State Colony above mentioned in due form. She is the daughter of a feeble minded mother in the same institution, and the mother of an illegitimate feeble minded child. She was eighteen years old at the time of the trial of her case in the Circuit Court, in the latter part of 1924. An Act of Virginia, approved March 20, 1924, recites that the health of the patient and the welfare of society may be promoted in certain cases by the sterilization of mental defectives, under careful safeguard, etc.; that the sterilization may be effected in males by vasectomy and in females by salpingectomy, without serious pain or substantial danger to life; that the Commonwealth is supporting in various institutions many defective persons who, if now discharged, would become a menace but if incapable of procreating, might be discharged with safety and become self-supporting with benefit to themselves and to society; and that experience has shown that heredity plays an important part in the transmission of insanity, imbecility, etc. The statute then enacts that, whenever the superintendent of certain institutions, including the above named State Colony, shall be of opinion that it is for the best interests of the patients and of society that an inmate under his care should be sexually sterilized, he may have the operation performed upon any patient afflicted with hereditary forms of insanity, imbecility, etc., on complying with the very careful provisions by which the act protects the patients from possible abuse.

The superintendent first presents a petition to the special board of directors of his hospital or colony, stating the facts and the grounds for his opinion, verified by affidavit. Notice of the petition and of the time and place of the hearing in the institution is to be served upon the inmate, and also upon his guardian, and if there is no guardian the superintendent is to apply to the Circuit Court of the County to appoint one. If the inmate is a minor, notice also is to be given to his parents, if any, with a copy of the petition. The board is to see to it that the inmate may attend the hearings if desired by him or his guardian. The evidence is all to be reduced to writing, and, after the board has made its order for or against the operation, the superintendent, or the inmate, or his guardian, may appeal to the Circuit Court of the County. The Circuit Court may consider the record of the board and the evidence before it and such other admissible evidence as may be offered, and may affirm, revise, or reverse the order of the board and enter such order as it deems just. Finally any party may apply to the Supreme Court of Appeals, which, if it grants the appeal, is to hear the case upon the record of the trial in the Circuit Court, and may enter such order as it thinks the Circuit Court should have entered. There can be no doubt that so far as procedure is concerned the rights of the patient are most carefully considered, and as every step in this case was taken in scrupulous compliance with the statute and after months of observation, there is no doubt that in that respect, the plaintiff in error has had due process of law.

The attack is not upon the procedure, but upon the substantive law. It seems to be contended that in no circumstances could such an order be justified. It certainly is contended that the order cannot be justified upon the existing grounds. The judgment finds the facts that have been recited, and that Carrie Buck "is the probable potential parent of socially inadequate offspring, likewise afflicted, that she may be sexually sterilized without detriment to her general health, and that her welfare and that of society will be promoted by her sterilization," and thereupon makes the order. In view of the general declarations of the legislature and the specific findings of the Court, obviously we cannot say as matter of law that the grounds do not exist, and if they exist they justify the result. We have seen more than once that the public welfare may call upon the best citizens for their lives. It would be strange if it could not call upon those who already sap the strength of the State for these lesser sacrifices, often not felt to be such by those concerned, in order to prevent our being swamped with incompetence. It is better for all the world if, instead of waiting to execute degenerate offspring for crime or to let them starve for their imbecility, society can prevent those who are manifestly unfit from continuing their kind. The principle that sustains compulsory vaccination is broad enough to cover cutting the Fallopian tubes. *Jacobson v. Massachusetts*, 197 U.S. 11. Three generations of imbeciles are enough.

But, it is said, however it might be if this reasoning were applied generally, it fails when it is confined to the small number who are in the institutions named and is not applied to the multitudes outside. It is the usual last resort of constitutional arguments to point out shortcomings of this sort. But the answer is that the law does all that is needed when it does all that it can, indicates a policy, applies it to all within the lines, and seeks to bring within the lines all similarly situated so far and so fast as its means allow. Of course, so far as the operations enable those who otherwise must be kept confined to be returned to the world, and thus open the asylum to others, the equality aimed at will be more nearly reached.

Judgment affirmed.

HERBERT HOOVER

Speech on Rugged Individualism (1928)

This campaign now draws near to a close. The platforms of the two parties defining principles and offering solutions of various national problems have been presented and are being earnestly considered by our people.

After four months' debate it is not the Republican Party which finds reason for abandonment of any of the principles it has laid down or of the views it has expressed for solution of the problems before the country. The principles to which it adheres are rooted deeply in the foundations of our national life and the solutions which it proposed are based on experience with government and a consciousness that it may have the responsibility for placing those solutions into action.

In my acceptance speech I endeavored to outline the spirit and ideals with which I would propose to carry that platform into administration. Tonight, I will not deal with the multitude of issues which have been already well canvassed, I propose rather to discuss some of those more fundamental principles and ideals upon which I believe the Government of the United States should be conducted.

Before I enter upon that discussion of principles I wish to lay before you the proof of progress under Republican rule. In doing this I do not need to review its seventy years of constructive history. That history shows that the Republican party has ever been a party of progress. It has reflected the spirit of the American people. We are a progressive people. Our history of 150 years [is] the greatest epic of human progress. Tonight to demonstrate the constructive character of our Party, I need only briefly picture the advance of fundamental progress during the past seven and a half years since we took over the Government amidst the ruin of war.

First of all, let me deal with the material side. I do this because upon the well-being, comfort and security of the American home do we build up the moral and spiritual virtues as well as the finer flowers of civilization and the wider satisfactions of life.

As a nation we came out of the war with great losses. We made no profits from it. The apparent increases in wages were fictitious. We were poorer as a nation when we emerged from it. Yet during these last eight years we have recovered from these losses and increased our national income by over one-third even if we discount the inflation of the dollar. While some individuals have grown rich, yet that there has been a wide diffusion of our gain in wealth and income is marked by a hundred proofs. I know of no better test of the improved conditions of the average family than the combined increase of life and industrial insurance, building and loan assets, and savings deposits. These are the financial agents of the average man. These alone have in seven years increased by nearly 100 per cent to the gigantic sum of over 50 billions of dollars, or nearly one-six of our whole

national wealth. In addition to these evidences of larger savings our people are steadily increasing their spending for higher standards of living. Today there are almost 9 automobiles for each 10 families, where seven and a half years ago only enough automobiles were running to average less than 4 for each 10 families. The slogan of progress is changing from the full dinner pail to the full garage. Our people have more to eat, better things to wear, and better homes. We have even gained in elbow room in our homes, for the increase of residential floor space is over 25 per cent with less than 10 per cent increase in our number of people. We have increased the security of his job to every man and woman. We have decreased the fear of old age, the fear of poverty, the fear of unemployment and these are fears which have always been amongst the greatest calamities of human kind.

All this progress means far more than greater creature comforts. It finds a thousand interpretations into a greater and fuller life. In all this we have steadily reduced the sweat in human labor. A score of new helps save the drudgery of the home. In seven years we have added 25 per cent more electric power to the elbow of every worker, and farther promoted him from a carrier of burdens to a director of machines. Our hours of labor are lessened; our leisure has increased. We have expanded our parks and playgrounds. We have nearly doubled our attendance at games. We pour into outdoor recreation in every direction. The visitors at our national parks have trebled and we have so increased the number of sportsmen fishing in our streams and lakes that the longer time between bites is becoming a political issue. In these seven and one-half years the radio has brought music and laughter, education and political discussion to almost every fireside.

Springing from our prosperity with its greater freedom, its vast endowment of scientific research and the greater resources with which to care for public health, we have according to our insurance actuaries during this short period since the war lengthened the span of life by nearly eight years. We have reduced infant mortality, we have vastly decreased the days of illness and suffering in the life of every man and woman. We have improved the facilities for the care of the crippled and helpless and deranged.

From our increasing resources we have expanded our educational system in eight years from an outlay of 1,200 millions to 2,700 millions of dollars. The education of our youth has become almost the largest and certainly our most important activity. From our ability to free youth from toil we have increased the attendance in our grade schools by 14 per cent, in our high schools by 80 per cent, and in institutions of higher learning by 95 per cent. Today we have more youth in these institutions of higher learning twice over than all the rest of the world put together. We have made progress in literature, art and in public taste.

I do not need to recite more figures and more evidence. There is not a person within the sound of my voice that does not know the profound progress which our country has made in this period. Every man and woman knows that their comfort, their hopes and their confidence for the future are higher this day than they were seven and one-half years ago.

Your city has been an outstanding beneficiary of this great progress. With its suburbs it has, during the last seven and a half years grown by over a million and a half of people, until it has become the largest metropolitan district of all the world. Here you have made abundant opportunity not only for the youth of the land but for the immigrant from foreign shores. This city is the commercial center of the United States. It is the commercial agent of the American people. It is a great organism of specialized skill and leadership in finance, industry and commerce, which reaches every spot in our country. Its progress and its beauty are the pride of the whole American people. It leads our nation in the largest size of its benevolences, in art, in music, literature and drama. It has come to have a greater voice, than any other city in the United States.

But when all is said and done the very life, progress and prosperity of this city is wholly dependent on the prosperity of the 110,000,000 people who dwell in our mountains and valleys across the 3,000 miles to the Pacific Ocean. Every activity of this city is sensitive to every evil and every favorable tide that sweeps this great nation of ours. Be there a slackening of industry in any part of the country it affects New York far more than the rest of the country. In a time of depression one-quarter of all the unemployed in the United States can be numbered in this city. In a time of prosperity the citizens of the great interior of our country pour into your city for business and entertainment at the rate of 200,000 a day. In fact so much is this city the reflex of the varied interests of our country that the concern of every one of your citizens for national stability, for national prosperity and for national progress is far greater than any other single part of our country.

Contributions to Progress

It detracts nothing from the character and energy of the American people, it minimizes in no degree the quality of their accomplishments to say that the policies of the Republican Party have played a large part in the building of this progress of these last seven and one-half years. I can say with emphasis that without the wise policies which the Republican Party has brought into action in this period, no such progress would have been possible.

The first responsibility of the Republican Administration was to renew the march of progress from its collapse by the war. That task involved the restoration of confidence in the future and the liberation and stimulation of the constructive energies of our people. It is not my purpose to enter upon a detailed recitation of the history of the great constructive measures of the past seven and a half years.

It is sufficient to remind you of the restoration of employment to the millions who walked your streets in idleness to remind you of the creation of the budget system; the reduction of six billions of national debt which gave the impulse of that vast sum returned to industry and commerce; the four sequent reductions of taxes and thereby the lift to the living of every family; the enactment of an adequate protective tariff and immigration laws which have raised and safeguarded our wages from floods of goods or labor from foreign countries; the creation of credit facilities and many aids to agriculture; the building up of foreign trade; the care of veterans, the development of aviation, of radio, of our inland waterways, our highways; the expansion of scientific research, of welfare activities, safer highways, safer mines, outdoor recreation, in better homes, in public health and the care of children. Nor do I need remind you that Government today deals with an economic and social system vastly more intricate and delicately adjusted than ever before. It now must be kept in perfect tune if we would not, through dislocation, have a breakdown in employment and in standards of living of our people. The Government has come to more and more touch this delicate web at a thousand points. Yearly the relations of Government to national prosperity becomes more and more intimate. It has only by keen large vision and cooperation by the Government that stability in business and stability in employment has been maintained during this past seven and a half years. Never has there been a period when the Federal Government has given such aid and impulse to the progress of our people, not alone to economic progress but to development of those agencies which make for moral and spiritual progress.

But in addition to this great record of contributions of the Republican Party to progress, there has been a further fundamental contribution—a contribution perhaps more important than all the others—and that is the resistance of the Republican Party to every attempt to inject the Government into business in competition with its citizens.

After the war, when the Republican Party assumed administration of the country, we were faced with the problem of determination of the very nature of our national life. Over 150 years we have builded up a form of self-government and we had builded up a social system which is peculiarly our own. It differs fundamentally from all others in the world. It is the American system. It is just as definite and positive a political and social system as has ever been developed on earth. It is founded upon the conception that self-government can be preserved only by decentralization of Government in the State and by fixing local responsibility; but further than this, it is founded upon the social conception that only through ordered liberty, freedom and equal opportunity to the individual will his initiative and enterprise drive the march of progress.

During the war we necessarily turned to the Government to solve every difficult economic problem—the Government having absorbed every energy of our people to war there was no other solution. For the preservation of the State the Government became a centralized despotism which undertook responsibilities, assumed powers, exercised rights, and took over the business of citizens. To large degree we regimented our whole people temporarily into a socialistic state. However justified it was in time of war if continued in peace time it would destroy not only our system but progress and freedom in our own country and throughout the world. When the war closed the most vital of all issues was whether Governments should continue war ownership and operation of many instrumentalities of production and distribution. We were challenged with the choice of the American system of "rugged individualism" or the choice of a European system of diametrically opposed doctrines—doctrines of paternalism and state socialism. The acceptance of these ideas meant the destruction of self-government through centralization of government; it meant the undermining of initiative and enterprise upon which our people have grown to unparalleled greatness.

The Democratic administration cooperated with the Republican Party to demobilize many of her activities and the Republican Party from the beginning of its period of power resolutely turned its face away from these ideas and these war practices, back to our fundamental conception of the state and the rights and responsibilities of the individual. Thereby it restored confidence and hope in the American people, it freed and stimulated enterprise, it restored the Government to its position as an umpire instead of a player in the economic game. For these reasons the American people have gone forward in progress while the rest of the world is halting and some countries have even gone backwards. If anyone will study the causes which retarded recuperation of Europe, he will find much of it due to the stifling of private initiative on one hand, and overloading of the Government with business on the other.

I regret, however, to say that there has been revived in this campaign a proposal which would be a long step to the abandonment of our American system, to turn to the idea of government in business. Because we are faced with difficulty and doubt over certain national problems which we are faced—that is prohibition, farm relief and electrical power—our opponents propose that we must to some degree thrust government into these businesses and in effect adopt state socialism as a solution.

There is, therefore submitted to the American people the question—Shall we depart from the American system and start upon a new road? And I wish to emphasize this question on this occasion. I wish to make clear my position on the principles involved for they go to the very roots of American life in every act of our Government. I should like to state to you the effect of the extension of government into business upon our system of self government and our economic system. But even more important is the effect upon the average man. That is the effect on the very basis of liberty and freedom not only to those left outside the fold of expanded bureaucracy but to those embraced within it.

When the Federal Government undertakes a business, the state governments are at once deprived of control and taxation of that business; when the state government undertakes a business it at once deprived the municipalities of taxation and control of that business. Business requires centralization; self government requires decentralization. Our government to succeed in business must become in effect a despotism. There is thus at once an insidious destruction of self government.

Moreover there is a limit to human capacity in administration. Particularly is there a limit to the capacity of legislative bodies to supervise governmental activities. Every time the Federal Government goes into business 530 Senators and Congressmen become the Board of Directors of that business. Every time a state government goes into business 100 or 200 state senators and assemblymen become directors of that business. Even if they were supermen, no bodies of such numbers can competently direct that type of human activities which requires instant decision and action. No such body can deal adequately with all sections of the country. And yet if we would preserve government by the people we must preserve the authority of our legislators over the activities of our Government. We have trouble enough with log rolling in legislative bodies today. It originates naturally from desires of citizens to advance their particular section or to secure some necessary service. It would be multiplied a thousandfold were the Federal and state governments in these businesses. The effect upon our economic progress would be even worse. Business progressiveness is dependent on competition. New methods and new ideas are the outgrowth of the spirit of adventure of individual initiative and of individual enterprise. Without adventure there is no progress. No government administration can rightly speculate and take

risks with taxpayers' money. But even more important than this—leadership in business must be through the sheer rise of ability and character. That rise can take place only in the free atmosphere of competition. Competition is closed by bureaucracy. Certainly political choice is a feeble basis for choice of leaders to conduct a business.

There is no better example of the practical incompetence of government to conduct business than the history of our railways. Our railways in the year before being freed from Government operation were not able to meet the demands for transportation. Eight years later we find them under private enterprise, transporting 15 per cent more goods and meeting every demand for service. Rates have been reduced by 15 per cent and net earnings increased from less than 1 per cent on their valuation to about 5 per cent. Wages of employees have improved by 13 per cent. The wages of railway employees are 2 per cent above pre-war. The wages of Government employees are today . . . will check their figure definitely tomorrow but probably about 70 per cent above pre-war. That should be a sufficient sermon upon the efficiency of Government operation.

But we can examine this question from the point of view of the person who gets a Government job and is admitted into the new bureaucracy. Upon that subject let me quote from a speech of that great leader of labor, Samuel Gompers, delivered in Montreal in 1920, a few years before his death. He said:

"I believe there is no man to whom I would take second position in my loyalty to the Republic of the United States, and yet I would not give it more power over the individual citizenship of our country. . . .

"It is a question of whether it shall be Government ownership or private ownership under control. . . . If I were in the minority of one in this convention, I would want to cast my vote so that the men of labor shall not willingly enslave themselves to Government authority in their industrial effort for freedom. . . .

"Let the future tell the story of who is right or who is wrong; who has stood for freedom and who has been willing to submit their fate industrially to the Government."

I would amplify Mr. Gompers' statement. These great bodies of Government employees would either comprise political machines at the disposal of the party in power, or alternatively to prevent this the

Government by stringent civil-service rules must debar its employees from their full rights as free men. If it would keep employees out of politics, its rules must strip them of all right to expression of opinion. It is easy to conceive that they might become so large a body as by their votes to dictate to the Government and their political rights need be further reduced. It must strip them of the liberty to bargain for their own wages, for no Government employee can strike against his Government and thus the whole people. It makes a legislative body with all its political currents their final employer. That bargaining does not rest upon economic need or economic strength but on political potency.

But what of those who are outside the bureaucracy? What is the effect upon their lives of the Government on business and these hundreds of thousands more officials?

At once their opportunities in life are limited because a large area of activities are removed from their participation. Further the Government does not tolerate amongst its customers the freedom of competitive reprisals to which private corporations are subject. Bureaucracy does not spread the spirit of independence; it spreads the spirit of submission into our daily life, penetrates the temper of our people; not with the habit of powerful resistance to wrong, but with the habit of timid acceptance of the irresistible might.

Bureaucracy is ever desirous of spreading its influence and its power. You cannot give to a government the mastery of the daily working life of a people without at the same time giving it mastery of the peoples' souls and thoughts. Every expansion of government means that government in order to protect itself from political consequences of its errors and wrongs is driven onward and onward without peace to greater and greater control of the country's press and platform. Free speech does not live many hours after free industry and free commerce die.

It is false liberalism that interprets itself into the Government operation of business. The bureaucratization of our country would poison the very roots of liberalism that is free speech, free assembly, free press, political equality and equality of opportunity. It is the road, not to more liberty, but to less liberty. Liberalism should be found not striving to spread bureaucracy, but striving to set bounds to it. True liberalism seeks freedom first in the confident belief that without freedom the pursuit of all other blessings and benefits is vain. That belief is the foundation of all American progress, political as well as economic.

Liberalism is a force truly of the spirit, a force proceeding from the deep realization that economic freedom cannot be sacrificed if political freedom is to be preserved. Even if governmental conduct of business could give us more efficiency instead of giving us decreased efficiency, the fundamental objection to it would remain unaltered and unabated. It would destroy political equality. It would cramp and cripple mental and spiritual energies of our people. It would dry up the spirit of liberty and progress. It would extinguish equality of opportunity, and for these reasons fundamentally and primarily it must be resisted. For a hundred and fifty years liberalism has found its true spirit in the American system, not in the European systems.

I do not wish to be misunderstood in this statement. I am defining a general policy! It does not mean that our government is to part with one iota of its national resources without complete protection to the public interest. I have already stated that where the government is engaged in public works for purposes of flood control, of navigation, of irrigation, of scientific research or national defense that, or in pioneering a new art, it will at times necessarily produce power or commodities as a by-product. But they must be by-products, not the major purpose.

Nor do I wish to be misinterpreted as believing that the United States is free-for-all and the devil-take-the-hindmost. The very essence of equality of opportunity is that there shall be no domination by any group or trust or combination in this republic, whether it be business or political. It demands economic justice as well as political and social justice. It is no system to laissez faire.

There is but one consideration in testing these proposals—that is public interest. I do not doubt the sincerity of those who advocate these methods of solving our problems. I believe they will give equal credit to our honesty. If I believed that the adoption of such proposals would decrease taxes, cure abuses or corruption, would produce better service, decrease rates or benefit employees; if I believed they would bring economic equality, would stimulate endeavor, would encourage invention and support individual initiative, would provide equality of opportunity; If I believed that these proposals would not wreck our democracy but would strengthen the foundations of social and spiritual progress in America—or if they would do a few of these things—then I would not hesitate to accept these proposals, stupendous as they are, even though such acceptance would result in the governmental operation of all our power and the buying and selling of the products of our farms or any other product. But it is not true that such benefits would result to the public. The contrary would be true.

I feel deeply on this subject because during the war I had some practical experience with governmental operation and control. I have witnessed not only at home but abroad the many failures of government in business. I have seen its tyrannies, its injustices, its undermining of the very instincts which carry our people forward to progress. I have witnessed the lack of advance, the lowered standards of living, the depressed spirits of people working under such a system. My objection is based not upon theory or upon a failure to recognize wrong or abuse but because I know that the adoption of such methods would strike at the very roots of American life and would destroy the very basis of American progress.

Our people have the right to know whether we can continue to solve our great problems without abandonment of our American system. I know we can. We have demonstrated that our system is responsive enough to meet any new and intricate development in our economic and business life. We have demonstrated that we can maintain our democracy as master in its own house and that we can preserve equality of opportunity and individual freedom.

In the last fifty years we have discovered that mass production will produce articles for us at half the cost that obtained previously. We have seen the resultant growth of large units of production and distribution. This is big business. Business must be bigger for our tools are bigger, our country is bigger. We build a single dynamo of a hundred thousand horsepower. Even fifteen years ago that would have been a big business all by itself. Yet today advance in production requires that we set ten of these units together.

Our great problem is to make certain that while we maintain the fullest use of the large units of business yet that they shall be held subordinate to the public interest. The American people from bitter experience have a rightful fear that these great units might be used to dominate our industrial life and by illegal and unethical practices destroy equality of opportunity. Years ago the Republican Administration established the principle that such evils could be corrected by regulation. It developed methods by which abuses could be prevented and yet the full value of economic advance retained for the public. It insisted that when great public utilities were clothed with the security of part monopoly, whether it be railways, power plants, telephones or what not, then there must be the fullest and most complete control of rates, services, and finances by governmental agencies. These businesses must be conducted with glass pockets. In the development of our great production industry, the Republican Party insisted upon the enactment of a law that not only would maintain competition but would destroy conspiracies to dominate and limit the equality of opportunity amongst our people.

One of the great problems of government is to determine to what extent the Government itself shall interfere with commerce and industry and how much it shall leave to individual exertion. It is just as important that business keep out of government as that government keep out of business. No system is perfect. We have had abuses in the conduct of business that every good citizen resents. But I insist that the results show our system better than any other and retains the essentials of freedom.

As a result of our distinctly American system our country has become the land of opportunity to those born without inheritance not merely because of the wealth of its resources and industry but because of this freedom of initiative and enterprise. Russia has natural resources equal to ours. Her people are equally industrious but she has not had the blessings of 150 years of our form of government and of our social system. The wisdom of our forefathers in their conception that progress must be the sum of the progress of free individuals has been reenforced by all of the great leaders of the country since that day. Jackson, Lincoln, Cleveland, McKinley, Roosevelt, Wilson, and Coolidge have stood unalterably for these principles. By adherence to the principles of decentralization, self-government, ordered liberty, and opportunity and freedom to the individual our American experiment has yielded a degree of well-being unparalleled in all the world. It has come nearer to the abolition of poverty, to the abolition of fear of want that humanity has ever reached before. Progress of the past seven years is the proof of it. It furnishes an answer to those who would ask us to abandon the system by which this has been accomplished.

There is a still further road to progress which is consonant with our American system—a method that reinforces our individualism by reducing, not increasing, Government interference in business.

In this country we have developed a higher sense of cooperation than has ever been known before. This has come partly as the result of stimulation during the war, partly from the impulses of industry itself. We have ten thousand examples of this cooperative tendency in the enormous growth of the associational activities during recent years. Chambers of commerce, trade associations, professional associations, labor unions, trade councils, civic associations, farm cooperatives—these are all so embracing that there is scarcely an individual in our country who does not belong to one or more of them. They represent every phase of our national life both on the economic and the welfare side. They represent a vast ferment toward conscious cooperation. While some of them are selfish and narrow, the majority of them recognize a responsibility to the public as well as to their own interest.

The government in its obligation to the public can through skilled specialists cooperate with these various associations for the accomplishment of high public purposes. And this cooperation can take two distinct directions. The first is in the promotion of constructive projects of public interest, such as the elimination of waste in industry, the stabilization of business and development of scientific research. It can contribute to reducing unemployment and seasonal employment. It can by organized cooperation assist and promote great movements for better homes, for child welfare and for recreation.

The second form that this cooperation can take is in the cure of abuses and the establishment of a higher code of ethics and a more strict standard in its conduct of business. One test of our economic and social system is its capacity to cure its own abuses. New abuses and new relationships to the public interest will occur as long as we continue to progress. If we are to be wholly dependent upon government

to cure every evil we shall by this very method have created an enlarged and deadening abuse through the extension of bureaucracy and the clumsy and incapable handling of delicate economic forces. And much abuse has been and can be cured by inspiration and cooperation, rather than by regulation of the government.

Nor is this any idealistic proposal. For the last seven years the Department of Commerce has carried this into practice in hundreds of directions and every single accomplishment of this character minimizes the necessity for government interference with business.

All this is possible because of the cooperative spirit and ability at team play in the American people. There is here a fundamental relief from the necessity of extension of the government into every avenue of business and welfare and therefore a powerful implement for the promotion of progress.

I wish to say something more on what I believe is the outstanding ideal in our whole political, economic and social system—that is equality of opportunity. We have carried this ideal farther into our life than has any other nation in the world. Equality of opportunity is the right of every American, rich or poor, foreign or native born, without respect to race or faith or color, to attain that position in life to which his ability and character entitle him. We must carry this ideal further than to economic and political fields alone. The first steps to equality of opportunity are that there should be no child in America that has not been born and does not live under sound conditions of health, that does not have full opportunity for education from the beginning to the end of our institutions, that is not free from injurious labor, that does not have stimulation to accomplish to the fullest of its capacities.

It is a matter for concern to our Government that we shall strengthen the safeguards to health, that we shall strengthen the bureaus given to research, that we shall strengthen our educational system at every point, that we shall develop cooperation by our Federal Government with state governments and with the voluntary bodies of the country that we may bring not only better understanding but action in these matters.

Furthermore, equality of opportunity in my vision requires an equal opportunity to the people in every section of our country. In these past few years some groups in our country have lagged behind others in the march of progress. They have not had the same opportunity. I refer more particularly to those engaged in the textile, coal and in the agricultural industries. We can assist in solving these problems by cooperation of our Government. To the agricultural industry we shall need advance initial capital to assist them, to stabilize and conduct their own industry. But this proposal is that they shall conduct it themselves, not by the Government. It is in the interest of our cities that we shall bring agriculture into full stability and prosperity. I know you will cooperate gladly in the faith that in the common prosperity of our country lies its future.

Franklin D. Roosevelt

Commonwealth Club Address (1932)

My friends:

I count it a privilege to be invited to address the Commonwealth Club. It has stood in the life of this city and State, and it is perhaps accurate to add, the Nation, as a group of citizen leaders interested in fundamental problems of Government, and chiefly concerned with achievement of progress in Government through non-partisan means. The privilege of addressing you, therefore, in the heat of a political campaign, is great. I want to respond to your courtesy in terms consistent with your policy.

I want to speak not of politics but of Government. I want to speak not of parties, but of universal principles. They are not political, except in that larger sense in which, a great American once expressed a definition of politics, that nothing in all of human life is foreign to the science of politics. [. . .]

Sometimes, my friends, particularly in years such as these, the hand of discouragement falls upon us. It seems that things are in a rut, fixed, settled, that the world has grown old and tired and very much out of joint. This is the mood of depression, of dire and weary depression.

But then we look around us in America, and everything tells us that we are wrong. America is new. It is in the process of change and development. It has the great potentialities of youth, and particularly is this true of the great West, and of this coast, and of California.

I would not have you feel that I regard this as in any sense a new community. I have traveled in many parts of the world, but never have I felt the arresting thought of the change and development more than here, where the old, mystic East would seem to be near to us, where the currents of life and thought and commerce of the whole world meet us. This factor alone is sufficient to cause man to stop and think of the deeper meaning of things, when he stands in this community.

But more than that, I appreciate that the membership of this club consists of men who are thinking in terms beyond the immediate present, beyond their own immediate tasks, beyond their own individual interests. I want to invite you, therefore, to consider with me in the large, some of the relationships of Government and economic life that go deeply into our daily lives, our happiness, our future and our security.

The issue of Government has always been whether individual men and women will have to serve some system of Government of economics, or whether a system of Government and economics exists to serve individual men and women. This question has persistently dominated the discussion of Government for many generations. On questions relating to these things men have differed, and for time immemorial it is probable that honest men will continue to differ.

The final word belongs to no man; yet we can still believe in change and in progress. Democracy, as a dear old friend of mine in Indian, Meredith Nicholson, has called it, is a quest, a never-ending seeking for better things, and in the seeking for these things and the striving for better things, and in the seeking for these things and the striving for them, there are many roads to follow. But, if we map the course of these roads, we find that there are only two general directions.

When we look about us, we are likely to forget how hard people have worked to win the privilege of Government. The growth of the national Governments of Europe was a struggle for the development of a centralized force in the Nation, strong enough to impose peace upon ruling barons. In many instances the victory of the central Government, the creation of a strong central Government, was a haven of refuge to the individual. The people preferred the master far away to the exploitation and cruelty of the smaller master near at hand.

But the creators of national Government were perforce ruthless men. They were often cruel in their methods, but they did strive steadily toward something that society needed and very much wanted, a strong central State, able to keep the peace, to stamp out civil war, to put the unruly nobleman in his place, and to permit the bulk of individuals to live safely. The man of ruthless force had his place in developing a pioneer country, just as he did in fixing the power of the central Government in the development of Nations. Society paid him well for his services and its development. When the development among the Nations of Europe, however, has been completed, ambition, and ruthlessness, having served its term tended to overstep its mark.

There came a growing feeling that Government was conducted for the benefit of a few who thrived unduly at the expense of all. The people sought a balancing—a limiting force. There came gradually, through town councils, trade guilds, national parliaments, by constitution and by popular participation and control, limitations on arbitrary power.

Another factor that tended to limit the power of those who ruled, was the rise of the ethical conception that a ruler bore a responsibility for the welfare of his subjects.

The American colonies were born in this struggle. The American Revolution was a turning point in it. After the Revolution the struggle continued and shaped itself in the public life of the country. There were those who because they had seen the confusion which attended the years of war for American independence surrendered to the belief that popular Government was essentially dangerous and essentially unworkable. They were honest people, my friends, and we cannot deny that their experience had warranted some measure of fear. The most brilliant, honest and able exponent of this point of view was Hamilton. He was too impatient of slow moving methods. Fundamentally he believed that the safety of the republic lay in the autocratic strength of its Government, that the destiny of individuals was to serve that Government, and that fundamentally a great and strong group of central institutions, guided by a small group of able and public spirited citizens could best direct all Government.

But Mr. Jefferson, in the summer of 1776, after drafting the Declaration of Independence turned his mind to the same problem and took a different view. He did not deceive himself with outward forms. Government to him was a means to an end, not an end in itself; it might be either a refuge and a help or a threat and a danger, depending on the circumstances. We find him carefully analyzing the society for which he was to organize a Government. "We have no paupers. The great mass of our population is of laborers, our rich who cannot live without labor, either manual or professional, being few and of moderate wealth. Most of the laboring class possess property, cultivate their own lands, have families and from the demand for their labor, are enabled to exact from the rich and the competent such prices as enable them to feed abundantly, clothe above mere decency, to labor moderately and raise their families."

These people, he considered, had two sets of rights, those of "personal competency" and those involved in acquiring and possessing property. By "personal competency" he meant the right of free thinking, freedom of forming and expressing opinions, and freedom of personal living each man according to his own lights. To insure the first set of rights, a Government must so order its functions as not to interfere with the individual. But even Jefferson realized that the exercise of the property rights might so interfere with the rights of the individual that the Government, without whose assistance the property rights could not exist, must intervene, not to destroy individualism but to protect it.

You are familiar with the great political duel which followed, and how Hamilton, and his friends, building towards a dominant centralized power were at length defeated in the great election of 1800, by Mr. Jefferson's party. Out of that duel came the two parties, Republican and Democratic, as we know them today.

So began, in American political life, the new day, the day of the individual against the system, the day in which individualism was made the great watchword of American life. The happiest of economic conditions made that day long and splendid. On the Western frontier, land was substantially free. No one, who did not shirk the task of earning a living, was entirely without opportunity to do so. Depressions could, and did, come and go; but they could not alter the fundamental fact that most of the people lived partly by selling their labor and partly by extracting their livelihood from the soil, so that starvation and dislocation were practically impossible. At the very worst there was always the possibility of climbing into a covered wagon and moving west where the untilled prairies afforded a haven for men to whom the East did not provide a place. So great were our natural resources that we could offer this relief not only to our own people, but to the distressed of all the world; we could invite immigration from Europe, and welcome it with open arms. Traditionally, when a depression came, a new section of land was opened in the West; and even our temporary misfortune served our manifest destiny.

It was the middle of the 19th century that a new force was released and a new dream created. The force was what is called the industrial revolution, the advance of steam and machinery and the rise of the forerunners of the modern industrial plant. The dream was the dream of an economic machine, able to raise the standard of living for everyone; to bring luxury within the reach of the humblest; to annihilate distance by steam power and later by electricity, and to release everyone from the drudgery of the heaviest manual toil. It was to be expected that this would necessarily affect Government. Heretofore, Government had merely been called upon to produce conditions within which people could live happily, labor peacefully, and rest secure. Now it was called upon to aid in the consummation of this new dream. There was, however, a shadow over the dream. To be made real, it required use of the talents of men of tremendous will, and tremendous ambition, since by no other force could the problems of financing and engineering and new developments be brought to a consummation.

So manifest were the advantages of the machine age, however, that the United States fearlessly, cheerfully, and, I think, rightly, accepted the bitter with the sweet. It was thought that no price was too high to pay for the advantages which we could draw from a finished industrial system. The history of the last half century is accordingly in large measure a history of a group of financial Titans, whose methods were not scrutinized with too much care, and who were honored in proportion as they produced the results, irrespective of the means they used. The financiers who pushed the railroads to the Pacific were always ruthless, we have them today. It has been estimated that the American investor paid for the American railway system more than three times over in the process; but despite that fact the net advantage was to the United States. As long as we had free land; as long as population was growing by leaps and bounds; as long as our industrial plants were insufficient to supply our needs, society chose to give the ambitious man free play and unlimited reward provided only that he produced the economic plant so much desired.

During this period of expansion, there was equal opportunity for all and the business of Government was not to interfere but to assist in the development of industry. This was done at the request of businessmen themselves. The tariff was originally imposed for the purpose of "fostering our infant industry," a phrase I think the older among you will remember as a political issue not so long ago. The railroads were subsidized, sometimes by grants of money, oftener by grants of land; some of the most valuable oil lands in the United States were granted to assist the financing of the railroad which pushed through the Southwest. A nascent merchant marine was assisted by grants of money, or by mail subsidies, so that our steam shipping might ply the seven seas. Some of my friends tell me that they do not want the Government in business. With this I agree; but I wonder whether they realize the implications of the past. For while it has been American doctrine that the Government must not go into business in competition with private enterprises, still it has been traditional particularly in Republican administrations for business urgently to ask the Government to put at private disposal all kinds of Government assistance. The same man who tells you that he does not want to see the Government interfere in business—and he means it, and has plenty of good reasons for saying so—is the first to go to Washington and ask the Government for a prohibitory tariff on his product. When things get just bad enough—as they did two years ago—he will go with equal speed to the United States Government and ask for a loan; and the Reconstruction Finance Corporation is the outcome of it. Each group has sought protection from the Government for its own special interest, without realizing that the function of Government must be to favor no small group at the expense of its duty to protect the rights of personal freedom and of private property of all its citizens.

In retrospect we can now see that the turn of the tide came with the turn of the century. We were reaching our last frontier; there was no more free land and our industrial combinations had become great uncontrolled and irresponsible units of power within the State. Clear-sighted men saw with fear the danger that opportunity would no longer be equal; that the growing corporation, like the feudal baron of old, might threaten the economic freedom of individuals to earn a living. In that hour, our antitrust laws were born. The cry was raised against the great corporations. Theodore Roosevelt, the first great Republican Progressive, fought a Presidential campaign on the issue of "trust busting" and talked freely about malefactors of great wealth. If the Government had a policy it was rather to turn the clock back, to destroy the large combinations and to return to the time when every man owned his individual small business.

This was impossible; Theodore Roosevelt, abandoning the idea of "trust busting," was forced to work out a difference between "good" trusts and "bad" trusts. The Supreme Court set forth the famous "rule of reason" by which it seems to have meant that a concentration of industrial power was permissible if the method by which it got its power, and the use it made of that power, was reasonable.

Woodrow Wilson, elected in 1912, saw the situation more clearly. Where Jefferson had feared the encroachment of political power on the lives of individuals, Wilson knew that the new power was financial. He saw, in the highly centralized economic system, the depot of the twentieth century, on whom great masses of individuals relied for their safety and their livelihood, and whose irresponsibility and greed (if it were not controlled) would reduce them to starvation and penury. The concentration of financial power had not proceeded so far in 1912 as it has today; but it had grown far enough for Mr. Wilson to realize fully its implications. It is interesting, now, to read his speeches. What is called "radical" today (and I have reason to know whereof I speak) is mild compared to the campaign of Mr. Wilson. "No man can deny," he said, "that the lines of endeavor have more and more narrowed and stiffened; no man who knows anything about the development of industry in this country can have failed to observe that the larger kinds of credit are more and more difficult to obtain unless you obtain them upon terms of uniting your efforts with those who already control the industry of the country, and nobody can fail to observe that every man who tries to set himself up in competition with any process of manufacture which has taken place under the control of large combinations of capital will presently find himself either squeezed out or obliged to sell and allow himself to be absorbed." Had there been no World War—had Mr. Wilson been able to devote eight years to domestic instead of to international affairs—we might have had a wholly different situation at the present time. However, the then distant roar of European cannon, growing ever louder, forced him to abandon the study of this issue. The problem he saw so clearly is left with us as a legacy; and no one of us on either side of the political controversy can deny that it is a matter of grave concern to the Government.

A glance at the situation today only too clearly indicates that equality of opportunity as we have known it no longer exists. Our industrial plant is built; the problem just now is whether under existing conditions it is not overbuilt. Our last frontier has long since been reached, and there is practically no more free land. More than half of our people do not live on the farms or on lands and cannot derive a living by cultivating their own property. There is no safety valve in the form of a Western prairie to which those thrown out of work by the Eastern economic machines can go for a new start. We are not able to invite the immigration from Europe to share our endless plenty. We are now providing a drab living for our own people.

Our system of constantly rising tariffs has at last reacted against us to the point of closing our Canadian frontier on the north, our European markets on the east, many of our Latin American markets to the south, and a goodly proportion of our Pacific markets on the west, through the retaliatory tariffs of those countries. It has forced many of our great industrial institutions who exported their surplus production to such countries, to establish plants in such countries within the tariff walls. This has resulted in the reduction of the operation of their American plants, and opportunity for employment.   *Section*

Just as freedom to farm has ceased, so also the opportunity in business has narrowed. It still is true that men can start small enterprises, trusting to native shrewdness and ability to keep abreast of competitors; but area after area has been preempted altogether by the great corporations, and even in the fields which still have no great concerns, the small man starts with a handicap. The unfeeling statistics of the past three decades show that the independent business man is running a losing race. Perhaps he is forced to the wall; perhaps he cannot command credit; perhaps he is "squeezed out," in Mr. Wilson's words, by highly organized corporate competitors, as your corner grocery man can tell you. Recently a careful study was made of the concentration of business in the United States. It showed that our economic life was dominated by some six hundred odd corporations who controlled two-thirds of American industry. Ten million small business men divided the other third. More striking still, it appeared that if the process of concentration goes on at the same rate, at the end of another century we shall have all American industry controlled by a dozen corporations, and run by perhaps a hundred men. Put plainly, we are steering a steady course toward economic oligarchy, if we are not there already.

Clearly, all this calls for a reappraisal of values. A mere builder of more industrial plants, a creator of more railroad systems, and organizer of more corporations, is as likely to be a danger as a help. The day of the great promoter or the financial Titan, to whom we granted anything if only he would build, or

develop, is over. Our task now is not discovery or exploitation of natural resources, or necessarily producing more goods. It is the soberer, less dramatic business of administering resources and plants already in hand, of seeking to reestablish foreign markets for our surplus production, of meeting the problem of under consumption, of adjusting production to consumption, of distributing wealth and products more equitably, of adapting existing economic organizations to the service of the people. The day of enlightened administration has come.

Just as in older times the central Government was first a haven of refuge, and then a threat, so now in a closer economic system the central and ambitious financial unit is no longer a servant of national desire, but a danger. I would draw the parallel one step farther. We did not think because national Government had become a threat in the 18th century that therefore we should abandon the principle of national Government. Nor today should we abandon the principle of strong economic units called corporations, merely because their power is susceptible of easy abuse. In other times we dealt with the problem of an unduly ambitious central Government by modifying it gradually into a constitutional democratic Government. So today we are modifying and controlling our economic units.

As I see it, the task of Government in its relation to business is to assist the development of an economic declaration of rights, an economic constitutional order. This is the common task of statesman and business man. It is the minimum requirement of a more permanently safe order of things.

Happily, the times indicate that to create such an order not only is the proper policy of Government, but is the only line of safety for our economic structures as well. We know, now, that these economic units cannot exist unless prosperity is uniform, that is, unless purchasing power is well distributed throughout every group in the Nation. That is why even the most selfish of corporations for its own interest would be glad to see wages restored and unemployment ended and to bring the Western farmer back to his accustomed level of prosperity and to assure a permanent safety to both groups. That is why some enlightened industries themselves endeavor to limit the freedom of action of each man and business group within the industry in the common interest of all; why business men everywhere are asking a form of organization which will bring the scheme of things into balance, even though it may in some measure qualify the freedom of action of individual units within the business.

The exposition need not further be elaborated. It is brief and incomplete, but you will be able to expand it in terms of your own business or occupation without difficulty. I think everyone who has actually entered the economic struggle—which means everyone who was not born to safe wealth—knows in his own experience and his own life that we have now to apply the earlier concepts of American Government to the conditions of today.

The Declaration of Independence discusses the problem of Government in terms of a contract. Government is a relation of give and take, a contract, perforce, if we would follow the thinking out of which it grew. Under such a contract rulers were accorded power, and the people consented to that power on consideration that they be accorded certain rights. The task of statesmanship has always been the redefinition of these rights in terms of a changing and growing social order. New conditions impose new requirements upon Government and those who conduct Government.

I held, for example, in proceedings before me as Governor, the purpose of which was the removal of the Sheriff of New York, that under modern conditions it was not enough for a public official merely to evade the legal terms of official wrongdoing. He owed a positive duty as well. I said in substance that if he had acquired large sums of money, he was when accused required to explain the sources of such wealth. To that extent this wealth was colored with a public interest. I said that in financial matters, public servants should, even beyond private citizens, be held to a stern and uncompromising rectitude.

I feel that we are coming to a view through the drift of our legislation and our public thinking in the past quarter century that private power is, to enlarge an old phrase, a public trust as well. I hold that continued enjoyment of that power by any individual or group must depend upon the fulfillment of that trust. The men who have reached the summit of American business life know this best; happily, many of these urge the binding quality of this greater social contract.

The terms of that contract are as old as the Republic, and as new as the new economic order.

Every man has a right to life; and this means that he has also a right to make a comfortable living. He may by sloth or crime decline to exercise that right; but it may not be denied him. We have no actual famine or death; our industrial and agricultural mechanism can produce enough and to spare. Our Government formal and informal, political and economic, owes to every one an avenue to possess himself of a portion of that plenty sufficient for his needs, through his own work.

Every man has a right to his own property; which means a right to be assured, to the fullest extent attainable, in the safety of his savings. By no other means can men carry the burdens of those parts of life which, in the nature of things afford no chance of labor; childhood, sickness, old age. In all thought of property, this right is paramount; all other property rights must yield to it. If, in accord with this principle, we must restrict the operations of the speculator, the manipulator, even the financier, I believe we must accept the restriction as needful, not to hamper individualism but to protect it.

These two requirements must be satisfied, in the main, by the individuals who claim and hold control of the great industrial and financial combinations which dominate so large a pert of our industrial life. They have undertaken to be, not business men, but princes—princes of property. I am not prepared to say that the system which produces them is wrong. I am very clear that they must fearlessly and competently assume the responsibility which goes with the power. So many enlightened business men know this that the statement would be little more that a platitude, were it not for an added implication.

This implication is, briefly, that the responsible heads of finance and industry instead of acting each for himself, must work together to achieve the common end. They must, where necessary, sacrifice this or that private advantage; and in reciprocal self-denial must seek a general advantage. It is here that formal Government—political Government, if you choose—comes in. Whenever in the pursuit of this objective the lone wolf, the unethical competitor, the reckless promoter, the Ishmael or Insull whose hand is against every man's, declines to join in achieving an end recognized as being for the public welfare, and threatens to drag the industry back to a state of anarchy, the Government may properly be asked to apply restraint. Likewise, should the group ever use its collective power contrary to public welfare, the Government must be swift to enter and protect the public interest.

The Government should assume the function of economic regulation only as a last resort, to be tried only when private initiative, inspired by high responsibility, with such assistance and balance as Government can give, has finally failed. As yet there has been no final failure, because there has been no attempt, and I decline to assume that this Nation is unable to meet the situation.

The final term of the high contract was for liberty and the pursuit of happiness. We have learnt a great deal of both in the past century. We know that individual liberty and individual happiness mean nothing unless both are ordered in the sense that one man's meat is not another man's poison. We know that the old "rights of personal competency"—the right to read, to think, to speak to choose and live a mode of life, must be respected at all hazards. We know that liberty to do anything which deprives others of those elemental rights is outside the protection of any compact; and that Government in this regard is the maintenance of a balance, within which every individual may have a place if he will take it; in which every individual may find safety if he wishes it; in which every individual may attain such power as his ability permits, consistent with his assuming the accompanying responsibility.

All this is a long, slow talk. Nothing is more striking than the simple innocence of the men who insist, whenever an objective is present, on the prompt production of a patent scheme guaranteed to produce a result. Human endeavor is not so simple as that. Government includes the art of formulating a policy, and using the political technique to attain so much of that policy as will receive general support; persuading, leading, sacrificing, teaching always, because the greatest duty of a statesman is to educate. But in the matters of which I have spoken, we are learning rapidly, in a severe school. The lessons so learned must not be forgotten, even in the mental lethargy of a speculative upturn. We must build toward the time when a major depression cannot occur again; and if this means sacrificing the easy profits of inflationist booms, then let them go; and good riddance.

Faith in America, faith in our tradition of personal responsibility, faith in our institutions, faith in ourselves demands that we recognize the new terms of the old social contract. We shall fulfill them, as we fulfilled the obligation of the apparent Utopia which Jefferson imagined for us in 1776, and which Jefferson, Roosevelt and Wilson sought to bring to realization. We must do so, lest a rising tide of misery engendered by our common failure, engulf us all. But failure is not an American habit; and in the strength of great hope we must all shoulder our common load.

First Inaugural Address (1933)

I am certain that my fellow Americans expect that on my induction into the Presidency I will address them with a candor and a decision which the present situation of our Nation impels. This is preeminently the time to speak the truth, the whole truth, frankly and boldly. Nor need we shrink from honestly facing conditions in our country today. This great Nation will endure as it has endured, will revive and will prosper. So, first of all, let me assert my firm belief that the only thing we have to fear is fear itself—nameless, unreasoning, unjustified terror which paralyzes needed efforts to convert retreat into advance. In every dark hour of our national life a leadership of frankness and vigor has met with that understanding and support of the people themselves which is essential to victory. I am convinced that you will again give that support to leadership in these critical days.

In such a spirit on my part and on yours we face our common difficulties. They concern, thank God, only material things. Values have shrunken to fantastic levels; taxes have risen; our ability to pay has fallen; government of all kinds is faced by serious curtailment of income; the means of exchange are frozen in the currents of trade; the withered leaves of industrial enterprise lie on every side; farmers find no markets for their produce; the savings of many years in thousands of families are gone.

More important, a host of unemployed citizens face the grim problem of existence, and an equally great number toil with little return. Only a foolish optimist can deny the dark realities of the moment.

Yet our distress comes from no failure of substance. We are stricken by no plague of locusts. Compared with the perils which our forefathers conquered because they believed and were not afraid, we have still much to be thankful for. Nature still offers her bounty and human efforts have multiplied it. Plenty is at our doorstep, but a generous use of it languishes in the very sight of the supply. Primarily this is because the rulers of the exchange of mankind's goods have failed, through their own stubbornness and their own incompetence, have admitted their failure, and abdicated. Practices of the unscrupulous money changers stand indicted in the court of public opinion, rejected by the hearts and minds of men.

True they have tried, but their efforts have been cast in the pattern of an outworn tradition. Faced by failure of credit they have proposed only the lending of more money. Stripped of the lure of profit by which to induce our people to follow their false leadership, they have resorted to exhortations, pleading tearfully for restored confidence. They know only the rules of a generation of self-seekers. They have no vision, and when there is no vision the people perish.

The money changers have fled from their high seats in the temple of our civilization. We may now restore that temple to the ancient truths. The measure of the restoration lies in the extent to which we apply social values more noble than mere monetary profit.

Happiness lies not in the mere possession of money; it lies in the joy of achievement, in the thrill of creative effort. The joy and moral stimulation of work no longer must be forgotten in the mad chase of evanescent profits. These dark days will be worth all they cost us if they teach us that our true destiny is not to be ministered unto but to minister to ourselves and to our fellow men.

Recognition of the falsity of material wealth as the standard of success goes hand in hand with the abandonment of the false belief that public office and high political position are to be valued only by the standards of pride of place and personal profit; and there must be an end to a conduct in banking and in business which too often has given to a sacred trust the likeness of callous and selfish wrongdoing. Small wonder that confidence languishes, for it thrives only on honesty, on honor, on the sacredness of obligations, on faithful protection, on unselfish performance; without them it cannot live.

Restoration calls, however, not for changes in ethics alone. This Nation asks for action, and action now.

Our greatest primary task is to put people to work. This is no unsolvable problem if we face it wisely and courageously. It can be accomplished in part by direct recruiting by the Government itself, treating the task as we would treat the emergency of a war, but at the same time, through this employment, accomplishing greatly needed projects to stimulate and reorganize the use of our natural resources.

Hand in hand with this we must frankly recognize the overbalance of population in our industrial centers and, by engaging on a national scale in a redistribution, endeavor to provide a better use of the land for those best fitted for the land. The task can be helped by definite efforts to raise the values of agricultural products and with this the power to purchase the output of our cities. It can be helped by preventing realistically the tragedy of the growing loss through foreclosure of our small homes and our farms. It can be helped by insistence that the Federal, State, and local governments act forthwith on the demand that their cost be drastically reduced. It can be helped by the unifying of relief activities which today are often scattered, uneconomical, and unequal. It can be helped by national planning for and supervision of all forms of transportation and of communications and other utilities which have a definitely public character. There are many ways in which it can be helped, but it can never be helped merely by talking about it. We must act and act quickly.

Finally, in our progress toward a resumption of work we require two safeguards against a return of the evils of the old order; there must be a strict supervision of all banking and credits and investments; there must be an end to speculation with other people's money, and there must be provision for an adequate but sound currency.

There are the lines of attack. I shall presently urge upon a new Congress in special session detailed measures for their fulfillment, and I shall seek the immediate assistance of the several States.

Through this program of action we address ourselves to putting our own national house in order and making income balance outgo. Our international trade relations, though vastly important, are in point of time and necessity secondary to the establishment of a sound national economy. I favor as a practical policy the putting of first things first. I shall spare no effort to restore world trade by international economic readjustment, but the emergency at home cannot wait on that accomplishment.

The basic thought that guides these specific means of national recovery is not narrowly nationalistic. It is the insistence, as a first consideration, upon the interdependence of the various elements in all parts of the United States—a recognition of the old and permanently important manifestation of the American spirit of the pioneer. It is the way to recovery. It is the immediate way. It is the strongest assurance that the recovery will endure.

In the field of world policy I would dedicate this Nation to the policy of the good neighbor—the neighbor who resolutely respects himself and, because he does so, respects the rights of others—the neighbor who respects his obligations and respects the sanctity of his agreements in and with a world of neighbors.

If I read the temper of our people correctly, we now realize as we have never realized before our interdependence on each other; that we can not merely take but we must give as well; that if we are to go forward, we must move as a trained and loyal army willing to sacrifice for the good of a common discipline, because without such discipline no progress is made, no leadership becomes effective. We are, I know, ready and willing to submit our lives and property to such discipline, because it makes possible a leadership which aims at a larger good. This I propose to offer, pledging that the larger purposes will bind upon us all as a sacred obligation with a unity of duty hitherto evoked only in time of armed strife.

With this pledge taken, I assume unhesitatingly the leadership of this great army of our people dedicated to a disciplined attack upon our common problems.

Action in this image and to this end is feasible under the form of government which we have inherited from our ancestors. Our Constitution is so simple and practical that it is possible always to meet extraordinary needs by changes in emphasis and arrangement without loss of essential form. That is why our constitutional system has proved itself the most superbly enduring political mechanism the modern world has produced. It has met every stress of vast expansion of territory, of foreign wars, of bitter internal strife, of world relations.

It is to be hoped that the normal balance of executive and legislative authority may be wholly adequate to meet the unprecedented task before us. But it may be that an unprecedented demand and need for undelayed action may call for temporary departure from that normal balance of public procedure.

I am prepared under my constitutional duty to recommend the measures that a stricken nation in the midst of a stricken world may require. These measures, or such other measures as the Congress may build out of its experience and wisdom, I shall seek, within my constitutional authority, to bring to speedy adoption.

But in the event that the Congress shall fail to take one of these two courses, and in the event that the national emergency is still critical, I shall not evade the clear course of duty that will then confront me. I shall ask the Congress for the one remaining instrument to meet the crisis—broad Executive power to wage a war against the emergency, as great as the power that would be given to me if we were in fact invaded by a foreign foe.

For the trust reposed in me I will return the courage and the devotion that befit the time. I can do no less.

We face the arduous days that lie before us in the warm courage of the national unity; with the clear consciousness of seeking old and precious moral values; with the clean satisfaction that comes from the stern performance of duty by old and young alike.

We aim at the assurance of a rounded and permanent national life.

We do not distrust the future of essential democracy. The people of the United States have not failed. In their need they have registered a mandate that they want direct, vigorous action. They have asked for discipline and direction under leadership. They have made me the present instrument of their wishes. In the spirit of the gift I take it.

In this dedication of a Nation we humbly ask the blessing of God. May He protect each and every one of us. May He guide me in the days to come.

State of the Union Message (The "Four Freedoms" Speech) (1941)

Mr. President, Mr. Speaker, Members of the Seventy-seventh Congress:

I address you, the Members of the Seventy-seventh Congress, at a moment unprecedented in the history of the Union. I use the word "unprecedented," because at no previous time has American security been as seriously threatened from without as it is today.

Since the permanent formation of our Government under the Constitution, in 1789, most of the periods of crisis in our history have related to our domestic affairs. Fortunately, only one of these—the four-year War Between the States—ever threatened our national unity. Today, thank God, one hundred and thirty million Americans, in forty-eight States, have forgotten points of the compass in our national unity.

It is true that prior to 1914 the United States often had been disturbed by events in other Continents. We had even engaged in two wars with European nations and in a number of undeclared wars in the West Indies, in the Mediterranean and in the Pacific for the maintenance of American rights and for the principles of peaceful commerce. But in no case had a serious threat been raised against our national safety or our continued independence.

What I seek to convey is the historic truth that the United States as a nation has at all times maintained clear, definite opposition, to any attempt to lock us in behind an ancient Chinese wall while the procession of civilization went past. Today, thinking of our children and of their children, we oppose enforced isolation for ourselves or for any other part of the Americas.

That determination of ours, extending over all these years, was proved, for example, during the quarter century of wars following the French Revolution. While the Napoleonic struggles did threaten interests of the United States because of the French foothold in the West Indies and in Louisiana, and while we engaged in the War of 1812 to vindicate our right to peaceful trade, it is nevertheless clear that neither France nor Great Britain, nor any other nation, was aiming at domination of the whole world.

And in like fashion from 1815 to 1914—ninety-nine years—no single war in Europe or in Asia constituted a real threat against our future or against the future of any other American nation.

Except in the Maximilian interlude in Mexico, no foreign power sought to establish itself in this Hemisphere; and the strength of the British fleet in the Atlantic has been a friendly strength. It is still a friendly strength. Even when the World War broke out in 1914, it seemed to contain only small threat of danger to our own American future. But, as time went on, the American people began to visualize what the downfall of democratic nations might mean to our own democracy.

We need not overemphasize imperfections in the Peace of Versailles. We need not harp on failure of the democracies to deal with problems of world reconstruction. We should remember that the Peace of 1919 was far less unjust than the kind of "pacification" which began even before Munich, and which is being carried on under the new order of tyranny that seeks to spread over every continent today. The American people have unalterably set their faces against that tyranny. I suppose that every realist knows that the democratic way of life is at this moment being directly assailed in every part of the world—assailed either by arms, or by secret spreading of poisonous propaganda by those who seek to destroy unity and promote discord in nations that are still at peace.

During sixteen long months this assault has blotted out the whole pattern of democratic life in an appalling number of independent nations, great and small. The assailants are still on the march, threatening other nations, great and small. Therefore, as your President, performing my constitutional duty to "give to the Congress information of the state of the Union," I find it, unhappily, necessary to report that the future and the safety of our country and of our democracy are overwhelmingly involved in events far beyond our borders.

Armed defense of democratic existence is now being gallantly waged in four continents. If that defense fails, all the population and all the resources of Europe, Asia, Africa and Australasia will be dominated by the conquerors. Let us remember that the total of those populations and their resources in those four continents greatly exceeds the sum total of the population and the resources of the whole of the Western Hemisphere—many times over.

In times like these it is immature—and incidentally, untrue—for anybody to brag that an unprepared America, single-handed, and with one hand tied behind its back, can hold off the whole world. No realistic American can expect from a dictator's peace international generosity, or return of true independence, or world disarmament, or freedom of expression, or freedom of religion—or even good business. Such a peace would bring no security for us or for our neighbors. "Those, who would give up essential liberty to purchase a little temporary safety, deserve neither liberty nor safety."

As a nation, we may take pride in the fact that we are softhearted; but we cannot afford to be softheaded. We must always be wary of those who with sounding brass and a tinkling cymbal preach the "ism" of appeasement. We must especially beware of that small group of selfish men who would clip the wings of the American eagle in order to feather their own nests. I have recently pointed out how quickly the tempo of modern warfare could bring into our very midst the physical attack which we must eventually expect if the dictator nations win this war.

There is much loose talk of our immunity from immediate and direct invasion from across the seas. Obviously, as long as the British Navy retains its power, no such danger exists. Even if there were no British Navy, it is not probable that any enemy would be stupid enough to attack us by landing troops in the United States from across thousands of miles of ocean, until it had acquired strategic bases from which to operate. But we learn much from the lessons of the past years in Europe—particularly the lesson of Norway, whose essential seaports were captured by treachery and surprise built up over a series of years.

The first phase of the invasion of this Hemisphere would not be the landing of regular troops. The necessary strategic points would be occupied by secret agents and their dupes—and great numbers of them are already here, and in Latin America. As long as the aggressor nations maintain the offensive, they—not we—will choose the time and the place and the method of their attack. That is why the future of all the American Republics is today in serious danger. That is why this Annual Message to the Congress is unique in our history. That is why every member of the Executive Branch of the Government and every member of the Congress faces great responsibility and great accountability.

The need of the moment is that our actions and our policy should be devoted primarily—almost exclusively—to meeting this foreign peril. For all our domestic problems are now a part of the great emergency. Just as our national policy in internal affairs has been based upon a decent respect for the rights and the dignity of all our fellow men within our gates, so our national policy in foreign affairs has been based on a decent respect for the rights and dignity of all nations, large and small. And the justice of morality must and will win in the end.

Our national policy is this: First, by an impressive expression of the public will and without regard to partisanship, we are committed to all-inclusive national defense. Second, by an impressive expression of the public will and without regard to partisanship, we are committed to full support of all those resolute peoples, everywhere, who are resisting aggression and are thereby keeping war away from our Hemisphere. By this support, we express our determination that the democratic cause shall prevail; and we strengthen the defense and the security of our own nation.

Third, by an impressive expression of the public will and without regard to partisanship, we are committed to the proposition that principles of morality and considerations for our own security will never permit us to acquiesce in a peace dictated by aggressors and sponsored by appeasers. We know that enduring peace cannot be bought at the cost of other people's freedom. In the recent national election there was no substantial difference between the two great parties in respect to that national policy. No issue was fought out on this line before the American electorate. Today it is abundantly evident that American citizens everywhere are demanding and supporting speedy and complete action in recognition of obvious danger.

Therefore, the immediate need is a swift and driving increase in our armament production. Leaders of industry and labor have responded to our summons. Goals of speed have been set. In some cases these goals are being reached ahead of time; in some cases we are on schedule; in other cases there are slight but not serious delays; and in some cases—and I am sorry to say very important cases—we are all concerned by the slowness of the accomplishment of our plans. The Army and Navy, however, have made substantial progress during the past year. Actual experience is improving and speeding up our methods of production with every passing day. And today's best is not good enough for tomorrow.

I am not satisfied with the progress thus far made. The men in charge of the program represent the best in training, in ability, and in patriotism. They are not satisfied with the progress thus far made. None of us will be satisfied until the job is done. No matter whether the original goal was set too high or too low, our objective is quicker and better results. To give you two illustrations: We are behind schedule in turning out finished airplanes; we are working day and night to solve the innumerable problems and to catch up.

We are ahead of schedule in building warships but we are working to get even further ahead of that schedule. To change a whole nation from a basis of peacetime production of implements of peace to a basis of wartime production of implements of war is no small task. And the greatest difficulty comes at the beginning of the program, when new tools, new plant facilities, new assembly lines, and new ship ways must first be constructed before the actual materiel begins to flow steadily and speedily from them.

The Congress, of course, must rightly keep itself informed at all times of the progress of the program. However, there is certain information, as the Congress itself will readily recognize, which, in the interests of our own security and those of the nations that we are supporting, must of needs be kept in confidence. New circumstances are constantly begetting new needs for our safety. I shall ask this Congress for greatly increased new appropriations and authorizations to carry on what we have begun.

I also ask this Congress for authority and for funds sufficient to manufacture additional munitions and war supplies of many kinds, to be turned over to those nations which are now in actual war with aggressor nations. Our most useful and immediate role is to act as an arsenal for them as well as for ourselves. They do not need man power, but they do need billions of dollars worth of the weapons of defense. The time is near when they will not be able to pay for them all in ready cash. We cannot, and we will not, tell them that they must surrender, merely because of present inability to pay for the weapons which we know they must have.

I do not recommend that we make them a loan of dollars with which to pay for these weapons—a loan to be repaid in dollars. I recommend that we make it possible for those nations to continue to obtain war materials in the United States, fitting their orders into our own program. Nearly all their materiel would, if the time ever came, be useful for our own defense. Taking counsel of expert military and naval authorities, considering what is best for our own security, we are free to decide how much should be kept here and how much should be sent abroad to our friends who by their determined and heroic resistance are giving us time in which to make ready our own defense.

For what we send abroad, we shall be repaid within a reasonable time following the close of hostilities, in similar materials, or, at our option, in other goods of many kinds, which they can produce and which we need. Let us say to the democracies: "We Americans are vitally concerned in your defense of freedom. We are putting forth our energies, our resources and our organizing powers to give you the strength to regain and maintain a free world. We shall send you, in ever-increasing numbers, ships, planes, tanks, guns. This is our purpose and our pledge."

In fulfillment of this purpose we will not be intimidated by the threats of dictators that they will regard as a breach of international law or as an act of war our aid to the democracies which dare to resist their aggression. Such aid is not an act of war, even if a dictator should unilaterally proclaim it so to be.

And when the dictators, if the dictators, are ready to make war upon us, they will not wait for an act of war on our part. They did not wait for Norway or Belgium or the Netherlands to commit an act of war. Their only interest is in a new one-way international law, which lacks mutuality in its observance, and, therefore, becomes an instrument of oppression. The happiness of future generations of Americans may well depend upon how effective and how immediate we can make our aid felt. No one can tell the exact character of the emergency situations that we may be called upon to meet. The Nation's hands must not be tied when the Nation's life is in danger.

Yes, and we must prepare, all of us prepare, to make the sacrifices that the emergency—almost as serious as war itself—demands. Whatever stands in the way of speed and efficiency in defense preparations must give way to the national need. A free nation has the right to expect full cooperation from all groups. A free nation has the right to look to the leaders of business, of labor, and of agriculture to take the lead in stimulating effort, not among other groups but within their own groups.

The best way of dealing with the few slackers or trouble makers in our midst is, first, to shame them by patriotic example, and, if that fails, to use the sovereignty of Government to save Government.

As men do not live by bread alone, they do not fight by armaments alone. Those who man our defenses, and those behind them who build our defenses, must have the stamina and the courage which come from unshakable belief in the manner of life which they are defending. The mighty action that we are calling for cannot be based on a disregard of all things worth fighting for.

The Nation takes great satisfaction and much strength from the things which have been done to make its people conscious of their individual stake in the preservation of democratic life in America. Those things have toughened the fiber of our people, have renewed their faith and strengthened their devotion to the institutions we make ready to protect. Certainly this is no time for any of us to stop thinking about the social and economic problems which are the root cause of the social revolution which is today a supreme factor in the world. For there is nothing mysterious about the foundations of a healthy and strong democracy.

The basic things expected by our people of their political and economic systems are simple. They are:

Equality of opportunity for youth and for others.

Jobs for those who can work.

Security for those who need it.

The ending of special privilege for the few.

The preservation of civil liberties for all.

The enjoyment of the fruits of scientific progress in a wider and constantly rising standard of living.

These are the simple, basic things that must never be lost sight of in the turmoil and unbelievable complexity of our modern world. The inner and abiding strength of our economic and political systems is dependent upon the degree to which they fulfill these expectations. Many subjects connected with our social economy call for immediate improvement. As examples:

We should bring more citizens under the coverage of old-age pensions and unemployment insurance.

We should widen the opportunities for adequate medical care.

We should plan a better system by which persons deserving or needing gainful employment may obtain it.

I have called for personal sacrifice. I am assured of the willingness of almost all Americans to respond to that call. A part of the sacrifice means the payment of more money in taxes. In my Budget Message I shall recommend that a greater portion of this great defense program be paid for from taxation than we are paying today. No person should try, or be allowed, to get rich out of this program; and the principle of tax payments in accordance with ability to pay should be constantly before our eyes to guide our legislation.

If the Congress maintains these principles, the voters, putting patriotism ahead of pocketbooks, will give you their applause.

In the future days, which we seek to make secure, we look forward to a world founded upon four essential human freedoms.

The first is freedom of speech and expression—everywhere in the world.

The second is freedom of every person to worship God in his own way—everywhere in the world.

The third is freedom from want—which, translated into world terms, means economic understandings which will secure to every nation a healthy peacetime life for its inhabitants—everywhere in the world.

The fourth is freedom from fear—which, translated into world terms, means a world-wide reduction of armaments to such a point and in such a thorough fashion that no nation will be in a position to commit an act of physical aggression against any neighbor—anywhere in the world.

[handwritten margin note: against what dictators want — must fight to protect]

That is no vision of a distant millennium. It is a definite basis for a kind of world attainable in our own time and generation. That kind of world is the very antithesis of the so-called new order of tyranny which the dictators seek to create with the crash of a bomb.

To that new order we oppose the greater conception—the moral order. A good society is able to face schemes of world domination and foreign revolutions alike without fear. Since the beginning of our American history, we have been engaged in change—in a perpetual peaceful revolution—a revolution which goes on steadily, quietly adjusting itself to changing conditions—without the concentration camp or the quick-lime in the ditch. The world order which we seek is the cooperation of free countries, working together in a friendly, civilized society.

This nation has placed its destiny in the hands and heads and hearts of its millions of free men and women; and its faith in freedom under the guidance of God. Freedom means the supremacy of human rights everywhere. Our support goes to those who struggle to gain those rights or keep them. Our strength is our unity of purpose. To that high concept there can be no end save victory.

JOHN DEWEY

Liberalism and Social Action (1935)

Renascent Liberalism

Nothing is blinder than the supposition that we live in a society and world so static that either nothing new will happen or else it will happen because of the use of violence. Social change is here as a fact, a fact having multifarious forms and marked in intensity. Changes that are revolutionary in effect are in process in every phase of life. Transformations in the family, the church, the school, in science and art, in economic and political relations, are occurring so swiftly that imagination is baffled in attempt to lay hold of them. Flux does not have to be created. But it does have to be directed. It has to be so controlled that it will move to some end in accordance with the principles of life, since life itself is development. Liberalism is committed to an end that is at once enduring and flexible: the liberation of individuals so that realization of their capacities may be the law of their life. It is committed to the use of freed intelligence as the method of directing change. In any case, civilization is faced with the problem of uniting the changes that are going on into a coherent pattern of social organization. The liberal spirit is marked by its own picture of the pattern that is required: a social organization that will make possible effective liberty and opportunity for personal growth in mind and spirit in all individuals. Its present need is recognition that established material security is a prerequisite of the ends which it cherishes, so that, the basis of life being secure, individuals may actively share in the wealth of cultural resources that now exist and may contribute, each in his own way, to their further enrichment. [. . .]

Let me mention three changes that have taken place in one of the institutions in which immense shifts have occurred, but that are still relatively external—external in the sense that the pattern of intelligent purpose and emotion has not been correspondingly modified. Civilization existed for most of human history in a state of scarcity in the material basis for a humane life. Our ways of thinking, planning and working have been attuned to this fact. Thanks to science and technology we now live in an age of potential plenty. The immediate effect of the emergence of the new possibility was simply to stimulate, to a point of incredible exaggeration, the striving for the material resources, called wealth, opened to men in the new vista. It is a characteristic of all development, physiological and mental, that when a new force and factor appears, it is first pushed to an extreme. Only when its possibilities have been exhausted (at least relatively) does it take its place in the life perspective. The economic-material phase of life, which belongs in the basal ganglia of society, has usurped for more than a century the cortex of the social body. The habits of desire and effort that were bred in the age of scarcity do not readily subordinate themselves and take the place of the matter-of-course routine that becomes appropriate to them when machines and impersonal power have the capacity to liberate man from bondage to the strivings that were once needed to make secure his physical basis. Even now when there is a vision of an age of abundance and when the vision is supported by hard fact, it is material security as an end that appeals to most rather than the way of living which this security makes possible. Men's minds are still pathetically held in the clutch of old habits and haunted by old memories.

For, in the second place, insecurity is the natural child and the foster child, too, of scarcity. Early liberalism emphasized the importance of insecurity as a fundamentally necessary economic motive, holding that without this goad men would not work, abstain or accumulate. Formulation of this conception was new. But the fact that was formulated was nothing new. It was deeply rooted in the habits that were formed in the long struggle against material scarcity. The system that goes by the name of capitalism is a systematic manifestation of desires and purposes built up in an age of ever threatening want and now carried over into a time of ever increasing potential plenty. The conditions that generate insecurity for the many no longer spring from nature. They are found in institutions and arrangements that are within deliberate human control. Surely this change marks one of the greatest revolutions that has taken place in all human history. Because of it, insecurity is not now the motive to work and sacrifice but to despair. It is not an instigation to put forth energy but to an impotency that can be converted from death into endurance only by charity. But the habits of mind and action that modify institutions to make potential abundance an actuality are still so inchoate that most of us discuss labels like individualism, socialism and communism instead of even perceiving the possibility, much less the necessity for realizing what can and should be.

In the third place, the patterns of belief and purpose that still dominate economic institutions were formed when individuals produced with their hands, alone or in small groups. The notion that society in general is served by the unplanned coincidence of the consequences of a vast multitude of efforts put forth by isolated individuals without reference to any social end, was also something new as a formulation. But it also formulated the working principle of an epoch which the advent of new forces of production was to bring to an end. It demands no great power of intelligence to see that under present conditions the isolated individual is well-nigh helpless. Concentration and corporate organization are the rule. But the concentration and corporate organization are still controlled in their operation by ideas that were institutionalized in eons of separate individual effort. The attempts at cooperation for mutual benefit that are put forth are precious as experimental moves. But that society itself should see to it that a cooperative industrial order be instituted, one that is consonant with the realities of production enforced by an era of machinery and power, is so novel an idea to the general mind that its mere suggestion is hailed with abusive epithets—sometimes with imprisonment.

When, then, I say that the first object of a renascent liberalism is education, I mean that its task is to aid in producing the habits of mind and character, the intellectual and moral patterns, that are somewhere near even with the actual movements of events. It is, I repeat, the split between the latter as they have externally occurred and the ways of desiring, thinking, and of putting emotion and purpose into execution that is the basic cause of present confusion in mind and paralysis in action. The educational task cannot be accomplished merely by working upon men's minds, without action that effects actual change in institutions. The idea that dispositions and attitudes can be altered by merely "moral" means conceived of as something that goes on wholly inside of persons is itself one of the old patterns that has to be changed. Thought, desire and purpose exist in a constant give and take of interaction with environing conditions. But resolute thought is the first step in that change of action that will itself carry further the needed change in patterns of mind and character.

In short, liberalism must now become radical, meaning by "radical" perception of the necessity of thoroughgoing changes in the setup of institutions and corresponding activity to bring the changes to pass. For the gulf between what the actual situation makes possible and the actual state itself is so great that it cannot be bridged by piecemeal policies undertaken *ad hoc*. The process of producing the changes will be, in any case, a gradual one. But "reforms" that deal now with this abuse and now with that without having a social goal based upon an inclusive plan, differ entirely from effort at reforming, in its literal sense, the institutional scheme of things. The liberals of more than a century ago were denounced in their time as subversive radicals, and only when the new economic order was established did they become apologists for the *status quo* or else content with social patchwork. If radicalism be defined as perception of need for radical change, then today any liberalism which is not also radicalism is irrelevant and doomed.

But radicalism also means, in the minds of many, both supporters and opponents, dependence upon use of violence as the main method of effecting drastic changes. Here the liberal parts company. For he is committed to the organization of intelligent action as the chief method. Any frank discussion of the issue must recognize the extent to which those who decry the use of any violence are themselves willing to resort to violence and are ready to put their will into operation. Their fundamental objection is to change in the economic institution that now exists, and for its maintenance they resort to the use of the force that is placed in their hands by this very institution. They do not need to advocate the use of force; their only need is to employ it. Force, rather than intelligence, is built into the procedures of the existing social system, regularly as coercion, in times of crisis as overt violence. The legal system, conspicuously in its penal aspect, more subtly in civil practice, rests upon coercion. Wars are the methods recurrently used in settlement of disputes between nations. One school of radicals dwells upon the fact that in the past the transfer of power in one society has either been accomplished by or attended with violence. But what we need to realize is that physical force is used, at least in the form of coercion, in the very set-up of our society. That the competitive system, which was thought of by early liberals as the means by which the latent abilities of individuals were to be evoked and directed into socially useful channels, is now in fact a state of scarcely disguised battle hardly needs to be dwelt upon. That the control of the means of production by the few in legal possession operates as a standing agency of coercion of the many, may need emphasis in statement, but is surely evident to one who is willing to observe and honestly report the existing scene. It is foolish to regard the political state as the only agency now endowed with coercive power. Its exercise of this power is pale in contrast with that exercised by concentrated and organized property interests.

It is not surprising in view of our standing dependence upon the use of coercive force that at every time of crisis coercion breaks out into open violence. In this country, with its tradition of violence fostered by frontier conditions and by the conditions under which immigration went on during the greater part of our history, resort to violence is especially recurrent on the part of those who are in power. In times of imminent change, our verbal and sentimental worship of the Constitution, with its guarantees of civil liberties of expression, publication and assemblage, readily goes overboard. Often the officials of the law are the worst offenders, acting as agents of some power that rules the economic life of a community. What is said about the value of free speech as a safety valve is then forgotten with the utmost of ease: a comment, perhaps, upon the weakness of the defense of freedom of expression that values it simply as a means of blowing-off steam.

It is not pleasant to face the extent to which, as matter of fact, coercive and violent force is relied upon in the present social system as a means of social control. It is much more agreeable to evade the fact. But unless the fact is acknowledged as a fact in its full depth and breadth, the meaning of dependence upon intelligence as the alternative method of social direction will not be grasped. Failure in acknowledgment signifies, among other things, failure to realize that those who propagate the dogma of dependence upon force have the sanction of much that is already entrenched in the existing system. They would but turn the use of it to opposite ends. The assumption that the method of intelligence already rules and that those who urge the use of violence are introducing a new element into the social picture may not be hypocritical but it is unintelligently unaware of what is actually involved in intelligence as an alternative method of social action.

I begin with an example of what is really involved in the issue. Why is it, apart from our tradition of violence, that liberty of expression is tolerated and even lauded when social affairs seem to be going in a quiet fashion, and yet is so readily destroyed whenever matters grow critical? The general answer, of course, is that at bottom social institutions have habituated us to the use of force in some veiled form. But a part of the answer is found in our ingrained habit of regarding intelligence as an individual possession and its exercise as an individual right. It is false that freedom of inquiry and of expression are not modes of action. They are exceedingly potent modes of action. The reactionary grasps this fact, in practice if not in express idea, more quickly than the liberal, who is too much given to holding that this freedom is innocent of consequences, as well as being a merely individual right. The result is that this liberty is tolerated as long as it does not seem to menace in any way the *status quo* of society. When it does, every effort is put

forth to identify the established order with the public good. When this identification is established, it follows that any merely individual right must yield to the general welfare. As long as freedom of thought and speech is claimed as a merely individual right, it will give way, as do other merely personal claims, when it is, or is successfully represented to be, in opposition to the general welfare.

I would not in the least disparage the noble fight waged by early liberals in behalf of individual freedom of thought and expression. We owe more to them than it is possible to record in words. No more eloquent words have ever come from any one than those of Justice Brandeis in the case of a legislative act that in fact restrained freedom of political expression. He said: "Those who won our independence believed that the final end of the State was to make men free to develop their faculties, and that in its government the deliberative forces should prevail over the arbitrary. They valued liberty both as an end and as a means. They believed liberty to be the secret of happiness and courage to be the secret of liberty. They believed that freedom to think as you will and to speak as you think are means indispensable to the discovery and spread of political truth; that without free speech and assembly discussion would be futile; that with them, discussion affords ordinarily adequate protection against the dissemination of noxious doctrines; that the greatest menace to freedom is an inert people; that public discussion is a political duty; and that this should be a fundamental principle of the American Government." This is the creed of a fighting liberalism. But the issue I am raising is connected with the fact that these words are found in a dissenting, a minority opinion of the Supreme Court of the United States. The public function of free individual thought and speech is clearly recognized in the words quoted. But the reception of the truth of the words is met by an obstacle: the old habit of defending liberty of thought and expression as something inhering in individuals apart from and even in opposition to social claims.

Liberalism has to assume the responsibility for making it clear that intelligence is a social asset and is clothed with a function as public as is its origin, in the concrete, in social cooperation. It was Comte who, in reaction against the purely individualistic ideas that seemed to him to underlie the French

Revolution, said that in mathematics, physics and astronomy there is no right of private conscience. If we remove the statement from the context of actual scientific procedure, it is dangerous because it is false. The individual inquirer has not only the right but the duty to criticize the ideas, theories and "laws" that are current in science. But if we take the statement in the context of scientific method, it indicates that he carries on this criticism in virtue of a socially generated body of knowledge and by means of methods that are not of private origin and possession. He uses a method that retains public validity even when innovations are introduced in its use and application.

Henry George, speaking of ships that ply the ocean with a velocity of five or six hundred miles a day, remarked, "There is nothing whatever to show that the men who to-day build and navigate and use such ships are one whit superior in any physical or mental quality to their ancestors, whose best vessel was a coracle of wicker and hide. The enormous improvement which these ships show is not an improvement of human nature; it is an improvement of society—it is due to a wider and fuller union of individual efforts in accomplishment of common ends." This single instance, duly pondered, gives a better idea of the nature of intelligence and its social office than would a volume of abstract dissertation. Consider merely two of the factors that enter in and their social consequences. Consider what is involved in the production of steel, from the first use of fire and then the crude smelting of ore, to the processes that now effect the mass production of steel. Consider also the development of the power of guiding ships across trackless wastes from the day when they hugged the shore, steering by visible sun and stars, to the appliances that now enable a sure course to be taken. It would require a heavy tome to describe the advances in science, in mathematics, astronomy, physics, chemistry, that have made these two things possible. The record would be an account of a vast multitude of cooperative efforts, in which one individual uses the results provided for him by a countless number of other individuals, and uses them so as to add to the common and public store. A survey of such facts brings home the actual social character of intelligence as it actually develops and makes its way. Survey of the consequences upon the ways of living of individuals and upon the terms on which men associate together, due to the new method of transportation would take us to the wheat farmer of the prairies, the cattle raiser of the plains, the cotton grower of the South; into a multitude of mills and factories, and to the counting-room of banks, and what would be seen in this country would be repeated in every country of the globe. [. . .]

Discussion, as the manifestation of intelligence in political life, stimulates publicity; by its means sore spots are brought to light that would otherwise remain hidden. It affords opportunity for promulgation of new ideas. Compared with despotic rule, it is an invitation to individuals to concern themselves with public affairs. But discussion and dialectic, however indispensable they are to the elaboration of ideas and policies after ideas are once put forth, are weak reeds to depend upon for systematic origination of comprehensive plans, the plans that are required if the problem of social organization is to be met. There was a time when discussion, the comparison of ideas already current so as to purify and clarify them, was thought to be sufficient in discovery of the structure and laws of physical nature. In the latter field, the method was displaced by that of experimental observation guided by comprehensive working hypotheses, and using all the resources made available by mathematics.

But we still depend upon the method of discussion, with only incidental scientific control, in politics. Our system of popular suffrage, immensely valuable as it is in comparison with what preceded it, exhibits the idea that intelligence is an individualistic possession, at best enlarged by public discussion. Existing political practice, with its complete ignoring of occupational groups and the organized knowledge and purposes that are involved in the existence of such groups, manifests a dependence upon a summation of individuals quantitatively, similar to Bentham's purely quantitative formula of the greatest sum of pleasures of the greatest possible number. The formation of parties or, as the eighteenth-century writers called them, factions, and the system of party government is the practically necessary counterweight to a numerical and atomistic individualism. The idea that the conflict of parties will, by means of public discussion, bring out necessary public truths is a kind of political watered-down version of the Hegelian dialectic, with its synthesis arrived at by a union of antithetical conceptions. The method has nothing in common with the procedure of organized cooperative inquiry which has won the triumphs of science in the field of physical nature.

Intelligence in politics when it is identified with discussion means reliance upon symbols. The invention of language is probably the greatest single invention achieved by humanity. The development of political forms that promote the use of symbols in place of arbitrary power was another great invention. The nineteenth-century establishment of parliamentary institutions, written constitutions and the suffrage as means of political rule, is a tribute to the power of symbols. But symbols are significant only in connection with realities behind them. No intelligent observer can deny, I think, that they are often used in party politics as a substitute for realities instead of as means of contact with them. Popular literacy, in connection with the telegraph, cheap postage and the printing press, has enormously multiplied the number of those influenced. That which we term education has done a good deal to generate habits that put symbols in the place of realities. The forms of popular government make necessary the elaborate use of words to influence political action. "Propaganda" is the inevitable consequence of the combination of these influences and it extends to every area of life. Words not only take the place of realities but are themselves debauched. Decline in the prestige of suffrage and of parliamentary government are intimately associated with the belief, manifest in practice even if not expressed in words, that intelligence is an individual possession to be reached by means of verbal persuasion.

This fact suggests, by way of contrast, the genuine meaning of intelligence in connection with public opinion, sentiment and action. The crisis in democracy demands the substitution of the intelligence that is exemplified in scientific procedure for the kind of intelligence that is now accepted. The need for this change is not exhausted in the demand for greater honesty and impartiality, even though these qualities be now corrupted by discussion carried on mainly for purposes of party supremacy and for imposition of some special but concealed interest. These qualities need to be restored. But the need goes further. The social use of intelligence would remain deficient even if these moral traits were exalted, and yet intelligence continued to be identified simply with discussion and persuasion, necessary as are these things. Approximation to use of scientific method in investigation and of the engineering mind in the invention and projection of far-reaching social plans is demanded. The habit of considering social realities in terms of cause and effect and social policies in terms of means and consequences is still inchoate. The contrast between the state of intelligence in politics and in the physical control of nature is to be taken literally. What has happened in this latter is the outstanding demonstration of the meaning of organized intelligence. The combined effect of science and technology has released more productive energies in a bare hundred years than stands to the credit of prior human history in its entirety. Productively it has multiplied nine million times in the last generation alone. The prophetic vision of Francis Bacon of subjugation of the energies of nature through change in methods of inquiry has well-nigh been realized. The stationary engine, the locomotive, the dynamo, the motor car, turbine, telegraph, telephone, radio and moving picture are not the products of either isolated individual minds nor of the particular economic régime called capitalism. They are the fruit of methods that first penetrated to the working causalities of nature and then utilized the resulting knowledge in bold imaginative ventures of invention and construction.

We hear a great deal in these days about class conflict. The past history of man is held up to us as almost exclusively a record of struggles between classes, ending in the victory of a class that had been oppressed and the transfer of power to it. It is difficult to avoid reading the past in terms of the contemporary scene. Indeed, fundamentally it is impossible to avoid this course. With a certain proviso, it is highly important that we are compelled to follow this path. For the past as past is gone, save for esthetic enjoyment and refreshment, while the present is with us. Knowledge of the past is significant only as it deepens and extends our understanding of the present. Yet there is a proviso. We must grasp the things that are most important in the present when we turn to the past and not allow ourselves to be misled by secondary phenomena no matter how intense and immediately urgent they are. Viewed from this standpoint, the rise of scientific method and of technology based upon it is the genuinely active force in producing the vast complex of changes the world is now undergoing, not the class struggle whose spirit and method are opposed to science. If we lay hold upon the causal force exercised by this embodiment of intelligence we shall know where to turn for the means of directing further change.

When I say that scientific method and technology have been the active force in producing the revolutionary transformations society is undergoing, I do not imply no other forces have been at work to arrest, deflect and corrupt their operation. Rather this fact is positively implied. At this point, indeed, is located the conflict that underlies the confusions and uncertainties of the present scene. The conflict is between institutions and habits originating in the pre-scientific and pre-technological age and the new forces generated by science and technology. The application of science, to a considerable degree, even its own growth, has been conditioned by the system to which the name of capitalism is given, a rough designation of a complex of political and legal arrangements centering about a particular mode of economic relations. Because of the conditioning of science and technology by this setting, the second and humanly most important part of Bacon's prediction has so far largely missed realization. The conquest of natural energies has not accrued to the betterment of the common human estate in anything like the degree he anticipated.

Because of conditions that were set by the legal institutions and the moral ideas existing when the scientific and industrial revolutions came into being, the chief usufruct of the latter has been appropriated by a relatively small class. Industrial entrepreneurs have reaped out of all proportion to what they sowed. By obtaining private ownership of the means of production and exchange they deflected a considerable share of the results of increased productivity to their private pockets. This appropriation was not the fruit of criminal conspiracy or of sinister intent. It was sanctioned not only by legal institutions of age-long standing but by the entire prevailing moral code. The institution of private property long antedated feudal times. It is the institution with which men have lived, with few exceptions, since the dawn of civilization. Its existence has deeply impressed itself upon mankind's moral conceptions. Moreover, the

new industrial forces tended to break down many of the rigid class barriers that had been in force, and to give to millions a new outlook and inspire a new hope;—especially in this country with no feudal background and no fixed class system.

Since the legal institutions and the patterns of mind characteristic of ages of civilization still endure, there exists the conflict that brings confusion into every phase of present life. The problem of bringing into being a new social orientation and organization is, when reduced to its ultimates, the problem of using the new resources of production, made possible by the advance of physical science, for social ends, for what Bentham called the greatest good of the greatest number. Institutional relationships fixed in the pre-scientific age stand in the way of accomplishing this great transformation. Lag in mental and moral patterns provides the bulwark of the older institutions; in expressing the past they still express present beliefs, outlooks and purposes. Here is the place where the problem of liberalism centres today.

The argument drawn from past history that radical change must be effected by means of class struggle, culminating in open war, fails to discriminate between the two forces, one active, the other resistant and deflecting, that have produced the social scene in which we live. The active force is, as I have said, scientific method and technological application. The opposite force is that of older institutions and the habits that have grown up around them. Instead of discrimination between forces and distribution of their consequences, we find the two things lumped together. The compound is labeled the capitalistic or the bourgeois class, and to this class as a class is imputed all the important features of present industrialized society—much as the defenders of the régime of economic liberty exercised for private property are accustomed to attribute every improvement made in the last century and a half to the same capitalistic régime. Thus in orthodox communist literature, from the *Communist Manifesto* of 1848 to the present day, we are told that the bourgeoisie, the name for a distinctive class, has done this and that. It has, so it is said, given a cosmopolitan character to production and consumption; has destroyed the national basis of industry; has agglomerated population in urban centres; has transferred power from the country to the city, in the process of creating colossal productive force, its chief achievement. In addition, it has created crises of ever renewed intensity; has created imperialism of a new type in frantic effort to control raw materials and markets. Finally, it has created a new class, the proletariat, and has created it as a class having a common interest opposed to that of the bourgeoisie, and is giving an irresistible stimulus to its organization, first as a class and then as a political power. According to the economic version of the Hegelian dialectic, the bourgeois class is thus creating its own complete and polar opposite, and this in time will end the old power and rule. The class struggle of veiled civil war will finally burst into open revolution and the result will be either the common ruin of the contending parties or a revolutionary reconstitution of society at large through a transfer of power from one class to another.

The position thus sketched unites vast sweep with great simplicity. I am concerned with it here only as far as it emphasizes the idea of a struggle between classes, culminating in open and violent warfare as being the method for production of radical social change. For, be it noted, the issue is not whether some amount of violence will accompany the effectuation of radical change of institutions. The question is whether force or intelligence is to be the method upon which we consistently rely and to whose promotion we devote our energies. Insistence that the use of violent force is *inevitable* limits the use of available intelligence, for wherever the inevitable reigns intelligence cannot be used. Commitment to inevitability is always the fruit of dogma; intelligence does not pretend to *know* save as a result of experimentation, the opposite of preconceived dogma. Moreover, acceptance in advance of the inevitability of violence tends to produce the use of violence in cases where peaceful methods might otherwise avail. The curious fact is that while it is generally admitted that this and that particular social problem, say of the family, or railroads or banking, must be solved, if at all, by the method of intelligence, yet there is supposed to be some one all-inclusive social problem which can be solved only by the use of violence. This fact would be inexplicable were it not a conclusion from dogma as its premise.

It is frequently asserted that the method of experimental intelligence can be applied to physical facts because physical nature does not present conflicts of class interests, while it is inapplicable to society because the latter is so deeply marked by incompatible interests. It is then assumed that the "experimentalist" is one who has chosen to ignore the uncomfortable fact of conflicting interests. Of course, there *are* conflicting interests; otherwise there would be no social problems. The problem under discussion is precisely *how* conflicting claims are to be settled in the interest of the widest possible contribution to the interests of all—or at least of the great majority. The method of democracy—inasfar as it is that of organized intelligence—is to bring these conflicts out into the open where their special claims can be seen and appraised, where they can be discussed and judged in the light of more inclusive interests than are represented by either of them separately. There is, for example, a clash of interests between munition manufacturers and most of the rest of the population. The more the respective claims of the two are publicly and scientifically weighed, the more likely it is that the public interest will be disclosed and be made effective. There is an undoubted objective clash of interests between finance-capitalism that controls the means of production and whose profit is served by maintaining relative scarcity, and idle workers and hungry consumers. But what generates violent strife is failure to bring the conflict into the light of intelligence where the conflicting interests can be adjudicated in behalf of the interest of the great majority. Those most committed to the dogma of inevitable force recognize the need for intelligently discovering and expressing the dominant social interest up to a certain point and then draw back. The "experimentalist" is one who would see to it that the method depended upon by all in some degree in every democratic community be followed through to completion.

In spite of the existence of class conflicts, amounting at times to veiled civil war, any one habituated to the use of the method of science will view with considerable suspicion the erection of actual human beings into fixed entities called classes, having no overlapping interests and so internally unified and externally separated that they are made the protagonists of history—itself hypothetical. Such an idea of classes is a survival of a rigid logic that once prevailed in the sciences of nature, but that no longer has any place there. This conversion of abstractions into entities smells more of a dialectic of concepts than of a realistic examination of facts, even though it makes more of an emotional appeal to many than do the results of the latter. To say that all past historic social progress has been the result of cooperation and not of conflict would be also an exaggeration. But exaggeration against exaggeration, it is the more reasonable of the two. And it is no exaggeration to say that the measure of civilization is the degree in which the method of cooperative intelligence replaces the method of brute conflict. [. . .]

The argument, drawn from history, that great social changes have been effected only by violent means, needs considerable qualification, in view of the vast scope of changes that are taking place without the use of violence. But even if it be admitted to hold of the past, the conclusion that violence is the method now to be depended upon does not follow—unless one is committed to a dogmatic philosophy of history. The radical who insists that the future method of change must be like that of the past has much in common with the hide-bound reactionary who holds to the past as an ultimate fact. Both overlook the *fact that history in being a process of change generates change not only in details but also in the method of directing social change.* I recur to what I said at the beginning of this chapter. It is true that the social order is largely conditioned by the use of coercive force, bursting at times into open violence. But what is also true is that mankind now has in its possession a new method, that of cooperative and experimental science which expresses the method of intelligence. I should be meeting dogmatism with dogmatism if I asserted that the existence of this historically new factor completely invalidates all arguments drawn from the effect of force in the past. But it is within the bounds of reason to assert that the presence of this social factor demands that the present situation be analyzed on its own terms, and not be rigidly subsumed under fixed conceptions drawn from the past. [. . .]

The final argument in behalf of the use of intelligence is that as are the means used so are the actual ends achieved—that is, the consequences. I know of no greater fallacy than the claim of those who hold to the dogma of the necessity of brute force that this use will be the method of calling genuine democracy into existence—of which they profess themselves the simon-pure adherents. It requires an unusually credulous faith in the Hegelian dialectic of opposites to think that all of a sudden the use of force by a class will be transmuted into a democratic classless society. Force breeds counterforce; the Newtonian law of action and reaction still holds in physics, and violence is physical. To profess democracy as an ultimate ideal and the suppression of democracy as a means to the ideal may be possible in a country that has never known even rudimentary democracy, but when professed in a country that has anything of a genuine democratic spirit in its traditions, it signifies desire for possession and retention of power by a class, whether that class be called Fascist or Proletarian. In the light of what happens in non-democratic countries, it is pertinent to ask whether the rule of a class signifies the dictatorship of the majority, or dictatorship over the chosen class by a minority party; whether dissenters are allowed even within the class the party claims to represent; and whether the development of literature and the other arts proceeds according to a formula prescribed by a party in conformity with a doctrinaire dogma of history and of infallible leadership, or whether artists are free from regimentation? Until these questions are satisfactorily answered, it is permissible to look with considerable suspicion upon those who assert that suppression of democracy is the road to the adequate establishment of genuine democracy. The one exception—and that apparent rather than real—to dependence upon organized intelligence as the method for directing social change is found when society through an authorized majority has entered upon the path of social experimentation leading to great social change, and a minority refuses by force to permit the method of intelligent action to go into effect. Then force may be intelligently employed to subdue and disarm the recalcitrant minority.

There may be some who think I am unduly dignifying a position held by a comparatively small group by taking their arguments as seriously as I have done. But their position serves to bring into strong relief the alternatives before us. It makes clear the meaning of renascent liberalism. The alternatives are continuation of drift with attendant improvisations to meet special emergencies; dependence upon violence; dependence upon socially organized intelligence. The first two alternatives, however, are not mutually exclusive, for if things are allowed to drift the result may be some sort of social change effected by the use of force, whether so planned or not. Upon the whole, the recent policy of liberalism has been to further "social legislation"; that is, measures which add performance of social services to the older functions of government. The value of this addition is not to be despised. It marks a decided move away from *laissez faire* liberalism, and has considerable importance in educating the public mind to a realization of the possibilities of organized social control. It has helped to develop some of the techniques that in any case will be needed in a socialized economy. But the cause of liberalism will be lost for a considerable period if it is not prepared to go further and socialize the forces of production, now at hand, so that the liberty of individuals will be supported by the very structure of economic organization.

The ultimate place of economic organization in human life is to assure the secure basis for an ordered expression of individual capacity and for the satisfaction of the needs of man in non-economic directions. The effort of mankind in connection with material production belongs, as I said earlier, among interests and activities that are, relatively speaking, routine in character, "routine" being defined as that which, without absorbing attention and energy, provides a constant basis for liberation of the values of intellectual, esthetic and companionship life. Every significant religious and moral teacher and prophet has asserted that the material is instrumental to the good life. Nominally at least, this idea is accepted by every civilized community. The transfer of the burden of material production from human muscles and brain to steam, electricity and chemical processes now makes possible the effective actualization of this ideal. Needs, wants, and desires are always the moving force in generating creative action. When these wants are compelled by force of conditions to be directed for the most part, among the mass of mankind, into obtaining the means of subsistence, what should be a means becomes perforce an end in itself. Up to the present the new mechanical forces of production, which are the means of emancipation from this state of affairs, have been employed to intensify and exaggerate the reversal of the true relation between means and ends. Humanly speaking, I do not see how it would have been possible to avoid

an epoch having this character. But its perpetuation is the cause of the continually growing social chaos and strife. Its termination cannot be effected by preaching to individuals that they should place spiritual ends above material means. It can be brought about by organized social reconstruction that puts the results of the mechanism of abundance at the free disposal of individuals. The actual corrosive "materialism" of our times does not proceed from science. It springs from the notion, sedulously cultivated by the class in power, that the creative capacities of individuals can be evoked and developed only in a struggle for material possessions and material gain. We either should surrender our professed belief in the supremacy of ideal and spiritual values and accommodate our beliefs to the predominant material orientation, or we should through organized endeavor institute the socialized economy of material security and plenty that will release human energy for pursuit of higher values.

Since liberation of the capacities of individuals for free, self-initiated expression is an essential part of the creed of liberalism, liberalism that is sincere must will the means that condition the achieving of its ends. Regimentation of material and mechanical forces is the only way by which the mass of individuals can be released from regimentation and consequent suppression of their cultural possibilities. The eclipse of liberalism is due to the fact that it has not faced the alternatives and adopted the means upon which realization of its professed aims depends. Liberalism can be true to its ideals only as it takes the course that leads to their attainment. The notion that organized social control of economic forces lies outside the historic path of liberalism shows that liberalism is still impeded by remnants of its earlier *laissez faire* phase, with its opposition of society and the individual. The thing which now dampens liberal ardor and paralyzes its efforts is the conception that liberty and development of individuality as ends exclude the use of organized social effort as means. Earlier liberalism regarded the separate and competing economic action of individuals as the means to social well-being as the end. We must reverse the perspective and see that socialized economy is the means of free individual development as the end.

That liberals are divided in outlook and endeavor while reactionaries are held together by community of interests and the ties of custom is well-nigh a commonplace. Organization of standpoint and belief among liberals can be achieved only in and by unity of endeavor. Organized unity of action attended by consensus of beliefs will come about in the degree in which social control of economic forces is made the goal of liberal action. The greatest educational power, the greatest force in shaping the dispositions and attitudes of individuals, is the social medium in which they live. The medium that now lies closest to us is that of unified action for the inclusive end of a socialized economy. The attainment of a state of society in which a basis of material security will release the powers of individuals for cultural expression is not the work of a day. But by concentrating upon the task of securing a socialized economy as the ground and medium for release of the impulses and capacities men agree to call ideal, the now scattered and often conflicting activities of liberals can be brought to effective unity.

It is no part of my task to outline in detail a program for renascent liberalism. But the question of "what is to be done" cannot be ignored. Ideas must be organized, and this organization implies an organization of individuals who hold these ideas and whose faith is ready to translate itself into action. Translation into action signifies that the general creed of liberalism be formulated as a concrete program of action. It is in organization for action that liberals are weak, and without this organization there is danger that democratic ideals may go by default. Democracy has been a fighting faith. When its ideals are reenforced by those of scientific method and experimental intelligence, it cannot be that it is incapable of evoking discipline, ardor and organization. To narrow the issue for the future to a struggle between Fascism and Communism is to invite a catastrophe that may carry civilization down in the struggle. Vital and courageous democratic liberalism is the one force that can surely avoid such a disastrous narrowing of the issue. I for one do not believe that Americans living in the tradition of Jefferson and Lincoln will weaken and give up without a whole-hearted effort to make democracy a living reality. This, I repeat, involves organization.

The question cannot be answered by argument. Experimental method means experiment, and the question can be answered only by trying, by organized effort. The reasons for making the trial are not abstract or recondite. They are found in the confusion, uncertainty and conflict that mark the modern world. The reasons for thinking that the effort if made will be successful are also not abstract and remote. They lie in what the method of experimental and cooperative intelligence has already accomplished in subduing to potential human use the energies of physical nature. In material production, the method of intelligence is now the established rule; to abandon it would be to revert to savagery. The task is to go on, and not backward, until the method of intelligence and experimental control is the rule in social relations and social direction. Either we take this road or we admit that the problem of social organization in behalf of human liberty and the flowering of human capacities is insoluble.

It would be fantastic folly to ignore or to belittle the obstacles that stand in the way. But what has taken place, also against great odds, in the scientific and industrial revolutions, is an accomplished fact; the way is marked out. It may be that the way will remain untrodden. If so, the future holds the menace of confusion moving into chaos, a chaos that will be externally masked for a time by an organization of force, coercive and violent, in which the liberties of men will all but disappear. Even so, the cause of the liberty of the human spirit, the cause of opportunity of human beings for full development of their powers, the cause for which liberalism enduringly stands, is too precious and too ingrained in the human constitution to be forever obscured. Intelligence after millions of years of errancy has found itself as a method, and it will not be lost forever in the blackness of night. The business of liberalism is to bend every energy and exhibit every courage so that these precious goods may not even be temporarily lost but be intensified and expanded here and now.

H. L. Mencken

On Being an American (1922)

1

Apparently there are those who begin to find it disagreeable—nay, impossible. Their anguish fills the Liberal weeklies and every ship that puts out from New York carries a groaning cargo of them, bound for Paris, London, Munich, Rome and way points— anywhere to escape the great curses and atrocities that make life intolerable for them at home. Let me say at once that I find little to cavil at in their basic complaints. In more than one direction, indeed, I probably go a great deal further than even the Young Intellectuals. It is, for example, one of my firmest and most sacred beliefs, reached after an inquiry extending over a score of years and supported by incessant prayer and meditation, that the government of the United States, in both its legislative arm and its executive arm, is ignorant, incompetent, corrupt, and disgusting—and from this judgment I except no more than twenty living lawmakers and no more than twenty executioners of their laws. It is a belief no less piously cherished that the administration of justice in the Republic is stupid, dishonest, and against all reason and equity—and from this judgment I except no more than thirty judges, including two upon the bench of the Supreme Court of the United States. It is another that the foreign policy of the United States—its habitual manner of dealing with other nations, whether friend or foe—is hypocritical, disingenuous, knavish, and dishonorable—and from this judgment I consent to no exceptions whatever, either recent or long past. And it is my fourth (and, to avoid too depressing a bill, final) conviction that the American people, taking one with another, constitute the most timorous, sniveling, poltroonish, ignominious mob of serfs and goose-steppers ever gathered under one flag in Christendom since the end of the Middle Ages, and that they grow more timorous, more sniveling, more poltroonish, more ignominious every day.

So far I go with the fugitive Young Intellectuals— and into the Bad Lands beyond. Such, in brief, are the cardinal articles of my political faith, held passionately since my admission to citizenship and now growing stronger and stronger as I gradually disintegrate into my component carbon, oxygen, hydrogen, phosphorus, calcium, sodium, nitrogen and iron. This is what I believe and preach, *in nomine Domini*, Amen. Yet I remain on the dock, wrapped in the flag, when the Young Intellectuals set sail. Yet here I stand, unshaken and undespairing, a loyal and devoted Americano, even a chauvinist, paying taxes without complaint, obeying all laws that are physiologically obeyable, accepting all the searching duties and responsibilities of citizenship unprotestingly, investing the sparse usufructs of my miserable toil in the obligations of the nation, avoiding all commerce with men sworn to overthrow the government, contributing my mite toward the glory of the national arts and sciences, enriching and embellishing the native language, spurning all lures (and even all invitations) to get out and stay out—here am I, a bachelor of easy means, forty-two years old, unhampered by debts or issue, able to go wherever I please and to stay as long as I please—here am I, contentedly and even smugly basking beneath the Stars and Stripes, a better citizen, I daresay, and certainly a less murmurous and exigent one, than thousands who put the Hon. Warren Gamaliel Harding beside Friedrich Barbarossa and Charlemagne, and hold the Supreme Court to be directly inspired by the Holy Spirit, and belong ardently to every Rotary Club, Ku Klux Klan, and Anti-Saloon League, and choke with emotion when the band plays "The Star-Spangled Banner," and believe with the faith of little children that one of Our Boys, taken at random, could dispose in a fair fight of ten Englishmen, twenty Germans, thirty Frogs, forty Wops, fifty Japs, or a hundred Bolsheviki.

Well, then, why am I still here? Why am I so complacent (perhaps even to the point of offensiveness), so free from bile, so little fretting and indignant, so curiously happy? Why did I answer only with a few academic "Hear, Hears" when Henry James, Ezra Pound, Harold Stearns and the *émigrés* of Greenwich Village issued their successive calls to the corn-fed *intelligentsia* to flee the shambles, escape to fairer lands, throw off the curse forever? The answer, of course, is to be sought in the nature of happiness, which tempts to metaphysics. But let me keep upon the ground. To me, at least (and I can only follow my own nose), happiness presents itself in an aspect that is tripartite. To be happy (reducing the thing to its elementals) I must be:

a. Well-fed, unhounded by sordid cares, at ease in Zion.
b. Full of a comfortable feeling of superiority to the masses of my fellow-men.
c. Delicately and unceasingly amused according to my taste.

It is my contention that, if this definition be accepted, there is no country on the face of the earth wherein a man roughly constituted as I am—a man of my general weaknesses, vanities, appetites, prejudices, and aversions—can be so happy, or even one-half so happy, as he can be in these free and independent states. Going further, I lay down the proposition that it is a sheer physical impossibility for such a man to live in These States and *not* be happy—that it is as impossible to him as it would be to a schoolboy to weep over the burning down of his schoolhouse. If he says that he isn't happy here, then he either lies or is insane. Here the business of getting a living, particularly since the war brought the loot of all Europe to the national strong-box, is enormously easier than it is in any other Christian land— so easy, in fact, that an educated and forehanded man who fails at it must actually make deliberate efforts to that end. Here the general average of intelligence, of knowledge, of competence, of integrity, of self-respect, of honor is so low that any man who knows his trade, does not fear ghosts, has read fifty good books, and practices the common decencies stands out as brilliantly as a wart on a bald head, and is thrown willy-nilly into a meager and exclusive aristocracy. And here, more than anywhere else that I know of or have heard of, the daily panorama of human existence, of private and communal folly— the unending procession of governmental extortions and chicaneries, of commercial brigandages and throat-slittings, of theological buffooneries, of aesthetic ribaldries, of legal swindles and harlotries, of miscellaneous rogueries, villainies, imbecilities, grotesqueries, and extravagances—is so inordinately gross and preposterous, so perfectly brought up to the highest conceivable amperage, so steadily enriched with an almost fabulous daring and originality, that only the man who was born with a petrified diaphragm can fail to laugh himself to sleep every night, and to awake every morning with all the eager, unflagging expectation of a Sunday-school superintendent touring the Paris peep-shows. [. . .]

Here in the United States we have no jobs for grand dukes, and none for *Wirkliche Geheimräte*, and none for palace eunuchs, and none for masters of the buck-hounds, and none (any more) for brewery *Todsäufer*—and very few for oboe-players, metaphysicians, astrophysicists, assyriologists, watercolorists, stylites and epic poets. There was a time when the *Todsäufer* served a public need and got an adequate reward, but it is no more. There may come a time when the composer of string quartettes is paid as much as a railway conductor, but it is not yet. Then why practice such trades—that is, as trades? The man of independent means may venture into them prudently; when he does so, he is seldom molested; it may even be argued that he performs a public service by adopting them. But the man who has a living to make is simply silly if he goes into them; he is like a soldier going over the top with a coffin strapped to his back. Let him abandon such puerile vanities, and take to the uplift instead, as, indeed, thousands of other victims of the industrial system have already done. Let him bear in mind that, whatever its neglect of the humanities and their monks, the Republic has never got half enough bond salesmen, quack doctors, ward leaders, phrenologists, Methodist evangelists, circus clowns, magicians, soldiers, farmers, popular song writers, moonshine distillers, forgers of gin labels, mine guards, detectives, spies, snoopers, and *agents provocateurs*. The rules are set by Omnipotence; the discreet man observes them. Observing them, he is safe beneath the starry bed-tick, in fair weather or foul. The *boobus Americanus* is a bird that knows no closed season—and if he won't come down to Texas oil stock, or one-night cancer cures, or building lots in Swampshurst, he will always come down to Inspiration and Optimism, whether political, theological, pedagogical, literary, or economic. [. . .]

And if a lining for the purse is thus facilely obtainable, given a reasonable prudence and resourcefulness, then balm for the ego is just as unlaboriously got, given ordinary dignity and decency. Simply to exist, indeed, on the plane of a civilized man is to attain, in the Republic, to a distinction that should be enough for all save the most vain; it is even likely to be too much, as the frequent challenges of the Ku Klux Klan, the American Legion, the Anti-Saloon League, and other such vigilance committees of the majority testify. Here is a country in which all political thought and activity are concentrated upon the scramble for jobs—in which the normal politician, whether he be a President or a village road supervisor, is willing to renounce any principle, however precious to him, and to adopt any lunacy, however offensive to him, in order to keep his place at the trough. Go into politics, then, without seeking or wanting office, and at once you are as conspicuous as a red-haired blackamoor—in fact, a great deal more conspicuous, for red-haired blackamoors have been seen, but who has ever seen or heard of an American politician, Democrat or Republican, Socialist or Liberal, Whig or Tory, who did not itch for a job? Again, here is a country in which it is an axiom that a business man shall be a member of a Chamber of Commerce, an admirer of Charles M. Schwab, a reader of the *Saturday Evening* Post, a golfer—in brief, a vegetable. Spend your hours of escape from *Geschäft* reading Remy de Gourmont or practicing the violoncello, and the local Sunday newspaper will infallibly find you out and hymn the marvel—nay, your banker will summon you to discuss your notes, and your rivals will spread the report (probably truthful) that you were pro-German during the war. Yet again, here is a land in which women rule and men are slaves. Train your women to get your slippers for you, and your ill fame will match Galileo's or Darwin's. Once more, here is the Paradise of back-slappers, of democrats, of mixers, of go-getters. Maintain ordinary reserve, and you will arrest instant attention—and have your hand kissed by multitudes who, despite democracy, have all the inferior man's unquenchable desire to grovel and admire. [. . .]

2

All of which may be boiled down to this: that the United States is essentially a commonwealth of third-rate men—that distinction is easy here because the general level of culture, of information, of taste and judgment, of ordinary competence is so low. No sane man, employing an American plumber to repair a leaky drain, would expect him to do it at the first trial, and in precisely the same way no sane man, observing an American Secretary of State in negotiation with Englishmen and Japs, would expect him to come off better than second best. Third-rate men, of course, exist in all countries, but it is only here that they are in full control of the state, and with it of all the national standards. The land was peopled, not by the hardy adventurers of legend, but simply by incompetents who could not get on at home, and the lavishness of nature that they found here, the vast ease with which they could get things, confirmed and augmented their native incompetence. No American colonist, even in the worst days of the Indian wars, ever had to face such hardships as ground down the peasants of Central Europe during the Hundred Years War, nor even such hardships as oppressed the English lower classes during the century before the Reform Bill of 1832. In most of the colonies, indeed, he seldom saw any Indians at all: the one thing that made life difficult for him was his congenital dunderheadedness. The winning of the West, so rhetorically celebrated in American romance, cost the lives of fewer men than the single battle of Tannenberg, and the victory was much easier and surer. The immigrants who have come in since those early days have been, if anything, of even lower grade than their forerunners. The old notion that the United States is peopled by the offspring of brave, idealistic and liberty-loving minorities, who revolted against injustice, bigotry and medievalism at home—this notion is fast succumbing to the alarmed study that has been given of late to the immigration of recent years. The truth is that the majority of non-Anglo-Saxon immigrants since the Revolution, like the majority of Anglo-Saxon immigrants before the Revolution, have been, not the superior men of their native lands, but the botched and unfit. [. . .] Here and there among the immigrants, of course, there may be a bravo, or even a superman—*e.g.*, the ancestors of Volstead, Ponzi, Jack Dempsey, Schwab, Daugherty, Debs, Pershing—but the average newcomer is, and always has been simply a poor fish.

Nor is there much soundness in the common assumption, so beloved of professional idealists and wind-machines, that the people of America constitute "the youngest of the great peoples." The phrase turns up endlessly; the average newspaper editorial writer would be hamstrung if the post office suddenly interdicted it, as it interdicted "the right to rebel" during the war. What gives it a certain specious plausibility is the fact that the American Republic, compared to a few other existing governments, is relatively young. But the American Republic is not necessarily identical with the American people; they might overturn it tomorrow and set up a monarchy, and still remain the same people. The truth is that, as a distinct nation, they go back fully three hundred years, and that even their government is older than that of most other nations, *e.g.*, France, Italy, Germany, Russia. Moreover, it is absurd to say that there is anything properly describable as youthfulness in the American outlook. It is not that of young men, but that of old men. All the characteristics of senescence are in it: a great distrust of ideas, an habitual timorousness, a harsh fidelity to a few fixed beliefs, a touch of mysticism. The average American is a prude and a Methodist under his skin, and the fact is never more evident than when he is trying to disprove it. His vices are not those of a healthy boy, but those of an ancient paralytic escaped from the *Greisenheim*. If you would penetrate to the causes thereof, simply go down to Ellis Island and look at the next shipload of immigrants. You will not find the spring of youth in their step; you will find the shuffling of exhausted men. From such exhausted men the American stock has sprung. It was easier for them to survive here than it was where they came from, but that ease, though it made them feel stronger, did not actually strengthen them. It left them what they were when they came: weary peasants, eager only for the comfortable security of a pig in a sty. Out of that eagerness has issued many of the noblest manifestations of American *Kultur*: the national hatred of war, the pervasive suspicion of the aims and intents of all other nations, the short way with heretics and disturbers of the peace, the unshakable belief in devils, the implacable hostility to every novel idea and point of view.

All these ways of thinking are the marks of the peasant—more, of the peasant long ground into the mud of his wallow, and determined at last to stay there—the peasant who has definitely renounced any lewd desire he may have ever had to gape at the stars. The habits of mind of this dull, sempiternal *fellah*—the oldest man in Christendom—are, with a few modifications, the habits of mind of the American people. The peasant has a great practical cunning, but he is unable to see any further than the next farm. He likes money and knows how to amass property, but his cultural development is but little above that of the domestic animals. He is intensely and cocksurely moral, but his morality and his self-interest are crudely identical. He is emotional and easy to scare, but his imagination cannot grasp an abstraction. He is a violent nationalist and patriot, but he admires rogues in office and always beats the tax-collector if he can. He has immovable opinions about all the great affairs of state, but nine-tenths of them are sheer imbecilities. He is violently jealous of what he conceives to be his rights, but brutally disregardful of the other fellow's. He is religious, but his religion is wholly devoid of beauty and dignity. This man, whether city or country bred, is the normal Americano—the 100 per cent Methodist, Odd Fellow, Ku Kluxer, and Know-Nothing. He exists in all countries, but here alone he rules—here alone his anthropoid fears and rages are accepted gravely as logical ideas, and dissent from them is punished as a sort of public offense. Around every one of his principal delusions—of the sacredness of democracy, of the feasibility of sumptuary law, of the incurable sinfulness of all other-peoples, of the menace of ideas, of the corruption lying in all the arts—there is thrown a barrier of taboos, and woe to the anarchist who seeks to break it down!

The multiplication of such taboos is obviously not characteristic of culture that is moving from a lower plane to a higher—that is, of a culture still in the full glow of its youth. It is a sign, rather, of a culture that is slipping downhill—one that is reverting to the most primitive standards and ways of thought. The taboo, indeed, is the trade-mark of the savage, and wherever it exists it is a relentless and effective enemy of civilized enlightenment. The savage is the most meticulously moral of men; there is scarcely an act of his daily life that is not conditioned by unyielding prohibitions and obligations, most of them logically unintelligible. The mob-man, a savage set amid civilization, cherishes a code of the same draconian kind. He believes firmly that right and wrong are immovable things—that they have an actual and unchangeable existence, and that any challenge of them, by word or act, is a crime against society. And with the concept of wrongness, of course, he always confuses the concept of mere differentness—to him the two are indistinguishable. Anything strange is to be combatted; it is of the Devil. The mob-man cannot grasp ideas in their native nakedness. They must be dramatized and personalized for him, and provided with either white wings or forked tails. All discussion of them, to interest him, must take the form of a pursuit and scotching of demons. He cannot think of a heresy without thinking of a heretic to be caught, condemned, and burned.

The Fathers of the Republic, I am convinced, had a great deal more prevision than even their most romantic worshipers give them credit for. They not only sought to create a governmental machine that would be safe from attack without; they also sought to create one that would be safe from attack within. They invented very ingenious devices for holding the mob in check, for protecting the national polity against its transient and illogical rages, for securing the determination of all the larger matters of state to a concealed but none the less real aristocracy. Nothing could have been further from the intent of Washington, Hamilton and even Jefferson than that the official doctrines of the nation, in the year 1922, should be identical with the nonsense heard in the chautauqua, from the evangelical pulpit, and on the stump. But Jackson and his merry men broke through the barbed wires thus so carefully strung, and ever since 1825 *vox populi* has been the true voice of the nation. Today there is no longer any question of statesmanship, in any real sense, in our politics. The only way to success in American public life lies in flattering and kowtowing to the mob. A candidate for office, even the highest, must either adopt its current manias *en bloc,* or convince it hypocritically that he has done so, while cherishing reservations *in petto.* The result is that only two sorts of men stand any chance whatever of getting into actual control of affairs—first, glorified mob-men who genuinely believe what the mob believes, and

secondly, shrewd fellows who are willing to make any sacrifice of conviction and self-respect in order to hold their jobs. One finds perfect examples of the first class in Jackson and Bryan. One finds hundreds of specimens of the second among the politicians who got themselves so affectingly converted to Prohibition, and who voted and blubbered for it with flasks in their pockets. Even on the highest planes our politics seems to be incurably mountebankish. The same Senators who raised such raucous alarms against the League of Nations voted for the Disarmament Treaty—a far more obvious surrender to English hegemony. And the same Senators who pleaded for the League on the ground that its failure would break the heart of the world were eloquently against the treaty. The few men who maintained a consistent course in both cases, voting either for or against both League and treaty, were denounced by the newspapers as deliberate marplots, and found their constituents rising against them. To such an extent had the public become accustomed to buncombe that simple honesty was incomprehensible to it, and hence abhorrent!

As I have pointed out in a previous work, this dominance of mob ways of thinking, this pollution of the whole intellectual life of the country by the prejudices and emotions of the rabble, goes unchallenged because the old landed aristocracy of the colonial era has been engulfed and almost obliterated by the rise of the industrial system, and no new aristocracy has arisen to take its place, and discharge its highly necessary functions. An upper class, of course, exists, and of late it has tended to increase in power, but it is culturally almost indistinguishable from the mob: it lacks absolutely anything even remotely resembling an aristocratic point of view. One searches in vain for any sign of the true *Junker* spirit in the Vanderbilts, Astors, Morgans, Garys, and other such earls and dukes of the plutocracy; their culture, like their aspiration, remains that of the pawnshop. One searches in vain, too, for the aloof air of the don in the official *intelligentsia* of the American universities; they are timorous and orthodox, and constitute a reptile Congregatio de Propaganda Fide to match Bismarck's *Reptilienpresse.* Everywhere else on earth, despite the rise of democracy, an organized minority of aristocrats survives from a more spacious day, and if its personnel has degenerated and its legal powers have decayed it has at least maintained some vestige of its old independence of Spirit, and jealously guarded its old right to be heard without risk of penalty. [. . .] But in the United States it was paralyzed by Jackson and got its death blow from Grant, and since then no successor to it has been evolved. Thus there is no organized force to oppose the irrational vagaries of the mob. The legislative and executive arms of the government yield to them without resistance; the judicial arm has begun to yield almost as supinely, particularly when they take the form of witch-hunts; outside the official circle there is no opposition that is even dependably articulate. The worst excesses go almost without challenge. Discussion, when it is heard at all, is feeble and superficial, and girt about by the taboos that I have mentioned. The clatter about the so-called Ku Klux Klan, two or three years ago, was typical. The astounding program of this organization was discussed in the newspapers for months on end, and a committee of Congress sat in solemn state to investigate it, and yet not a single newspaper or Congressman, so far as I am aware, so much as mentioned the most patent and important fact about it, to wit, that the Ku Klux was, to all intents and purposes, simply the secular arm of the Methodist Church, and that its methods were no more than physical projections of the familiar extravagances of the Anti-Saloon League. The intimate relations between church and Klan, amounting almost to identity, must have been plain to every intelligent American, and yet the taboo upon the realistic consideration of ecclesiastical matters was sufficient to make every public soothsayer disregard it completely. [. . .]

3

Coming down to the time of the world war, one finds precious few signs that the American people, facing an antagonist of equal strength and with both hands free, could be relied upon to give a creditable account of themselves. The American share in that great struggle, in fact, was marked by poltroonery almost as conspicuously as it was marked by knavery. Let us consider briefly what the nation did. For a few months it viewed the struggle idly and unintelligently, as a yokel might stare at a sword-swallower at a county fair. Then, seeing a chance to profit, it undertook with sudden alacrity the ghoulish office of *Kriegslieferant*. One of the contestants being debarred, by the chances of war, from buying, it devoted its whole energies, for two years, to purveying to the other. Meanwhile, it made every effort to aid its customer by lending him the cloak of its neutrality—that is, by demanding all the privileges of a neutral and yet carrying on a stupendous wholesale effort to promote the war. On the official side, this neutrality was fraudulent from the start, as the revelations of Mr. Tumulty have since demonstrated; popularly it became more and more fraudulent as the debts of the customer contestant piled up, and it became more and more apparent—a fact diligently made known by his partisans—that they would be worthless if he failed to win. Then, in the end, covert aid was transformed into overt aid. And under what gallant conditions! In brief, there stood a nation of 65,000,000 people, which, without effective allies, had just closed two and a half years of homeric conflict by completely defeating an enemy state of 135,000,000 and two lesser ones of more than 10,000,000 together, and now stood at bay before a combination of at least 140,000,000. Upon this battle-scarred and war-weary foe the Republic of 100,000,000 freemen now flung itself, so lifting the odds to 4 to 1. And after a year and a half more of struggle it emerged triumphant—a knightly victor surely!

There is no need to rehearse the astounding and unprecedented swinishness that accompanied this glorious business—the colossal waste of public money, the savage persecution of all opponents and critics of the war, the open bribery of labor, the half-insane reviling of the enemy, the manufacture of false news, the knavish robbery of enemy civilians, the incessant spy hunts, the floating of public loans by a process of blackmail, the degradation of the Red Cross to partisan uses, the complete abandonment of all decency, decorum and self-respect. The facts must be remembered with shame by every civilized American; lest they be forgotten by the generations of the future I am even now engaged with collaborators upon an exhaustive record of them, in twenty volumes folio. More important to the present purpose are two things that are apt to be overlooked, the first of which is the capital fact that the war was "sold" to the American people, as the phrase has it, not by appealing to their courage but by appealing to their cowardice—in brief, by adopting the assumption that they were not warlike at all, and certainly not gallant and chivalrous, but merely craven and fearful. The first selling point of the proponents of American participation was the contention that the Germans, with gigantic wars still raging on both fronts, were preparing to invade the United States, burn down all the towns, murder all the men, and carry off all the women—that their victory would bring staggering and irresistible reprisals for the American violation of the duties of a neutral. The second selling point was that the entrance of the United States would end the war almost instantly—that the Germans would be so overwhelmingly outnumbered, in men and guns, that it would be impossible for them to make any effective defense—above all, that it would be impossible for them to inflict any serious damage upon their new foes. Neither argument, it must be plain, showed the slightest belief in the warlike skill and courage of the American people. Both were grounded upon the frank theory that the only way to make the mob fight was to scare it half to death, and then show it a way to fight without risk, to stab a helpless antagonist in the back. And both were mellowed and reenforced by the hint that such a noble assault, beside being safe, would also be extremely profitable—that it would convert very dubious debts into very good debts, and dispose forever of a diligent and dangerous competitor for trade, especially in Latin America. All the idealist nonsense emitted by Dr. Wilson and company was simply icing on the cake. Most of it was abandoned as soon as the bullets began to fly, and the rest consisted simply of meaningless words—the idiotic babbling of a Presbyterian evangelist turned prophet and seer.

The other thing that needs to be remembered is the permanent effect of so dishonest and cowardly a business upon the national character, already far too much inclined toward easy ventures and long odds. Somewhere in his diaries Wilfrid Scawen Blunt speaks of the marked debasement that showed itself in the English spirit after the brutal robbery and assassination of the South African Republics. The heroes that the mob followed after Mafeking Day were far inferior to the heroes that it had followed in the days before the war. The English gentleman began to disappear from public life, and in his place appeared a rabble-rousing bounder obviously almost identical with the American professional politician—the Lloyd George, Chamberlain, F. E. Smith, Isaacs-Reading, Churchill, Bottomley, Northcliffe type. Worse, old ideals went with old heroes. Personal freedom and strict legality, says Blunt, vanished from the English tables of the law, and there was a shift of the social and political center of gravity to a lower plane. Precisely the same effect is now visible in the United States. The overwhelming majority of conscripts went into the army unwillingly, and once there they were debauched by the twin forces of the official propaganda that I have mentioned and a harsh, unintelligent discipline. The first made them almost incapable of soldierly thought and conduct; the second converted them into cringing goose-steppers. The consequences display themselves in the amazing activities of the American Legion, and in the rise of such correlative organizations as the Ku Klux Klan. It is impossible to fit any reasonable concept of the soldierly into the familiar proceedings of the Legion. Its members conduct themselves like a gang of Methodist vice-crusaders on the loose, or a Southern lynching party. They are forever discovering preposterous burglars under the national bed, and they advance to the attack, not gallantly and at fair odds, but cravenly and in overwhelming force. Some of their enterprises, to be set forth at length in the record I have mentioned, have been of almost unbelievable baseness—the mobbing of harmless Socialists, the prohibition of concerts by musicians of enemy nationality, the mutilation of cows designed for shipment abroad to feed starving children, the roughing of women, service as strike-breakers, the persecution of helpless foreigners, regardless of nationality.

During the last few months of the war, when stories of the tyrannical ill-usage of conscripts began to filter back to the United States, it was predicted that they would demand the punishment of the guilty when they got home, and that if it was not promptly forthcoming they would take it into their own hands. It was predicted, too, that they would array themselves against the excesses of Palmer, Burleson and company, and insist upon a restoration of that democratic freedom for which they had theoretically fought. But they actually did none of these things. So far as I know, not a single martinet of a lieutenant or captain has been manhandled by his late victims; the most they have done has been to appeal to Congress for revenge and damages. Nor have they thrown their influence against the medieval despotism which grew up at home during the war; on the contrary, they have supported it actively, and if it has lessened since 1919 the change has been wrought without their aid and in spite of their opposition. In sum, they show all the stigmata of inferior men whose natural inferiority has been made worse by oppression. [. . .]

The typical American of today has lost all the love of liberty that his forefathers had, and all their distrust of emotion, and pride in self-reliance. He is led no longer by Davy Crocketts; he is led by cheer leaders, press agents, word-mongers, up-lifters. I do not believe that such a faint-hearted and inflammatory fellow, shoved into a war demanding every resource of courage, ingenuity and pertinacity, would give a good account of himself. He is fit for lynching-bees and heretic-hunts, but he is not fit for tight corners and desperate odds.

Nevertheless, his docility and pusillanimity may be overestimated, and sometimes I think that they *are* overestimated by his present masters. They assume that there is absolutely no limit to his capacity for being put on and knocked about—that he will submit to any invasion of his freedom and dignity, however outrageous, so long as it is depicted in melodious terms. He permitted the late war to be "sold" to him by the methods of the grind-shop auctioneer. He submitted to conscription without any of the resistance shown by his brother democrats of Canada and Australia. He got no further than academic protests against the brutal usage he had to face in the army. He came home and found Prohibition foisted on him, and contented himself with a few feeble objurgations. He is a pliant slave of capitalism, and ever ready to help it put down fellow-slaves who venture to revolt. But this very weakness, this very credulity and poverty of spirit, on some easily conceivable tomorrow, may convert him into a rebel of a peculiarly insane kind, and so beset the Republic from within with difficulties quite as formidable as those which threaten to afflict it from without. What Mr. James N. Wood calls the corsair of democracy—that is, the professional mob-master, the merchant of delusions, the pumper-up of popular fears and rages—is still content to work for capitalism, and

capitalism knows how to reward him to his taste. He is the eloquent statesman, the patriotic editor, the fount of inspiration, the prancing milch-cow of optimism. He becomes public leader, Governor, Senator, President. He is Billy Sunday, Cyrus K. Curtis, Dr. Frank Crane, Charles E. Hughes, Taft, Wilson, Cal Coolidge, General Wood, Harding. His, perhaps, is the best of trades under democracy—but it has its temptations! Let us try to picture a master corsair, thoroughly adept at pulling the mob nose, who suddenly bethought himself of that Pepin the Short who found himself mayor of the palace and made himself King of the Franks. There were lightnings along that horizon in the days of Roosevelt; there were thunder growls when Bryan emerged from the Nebraska steppes. On some great day of fate, as yet unrevealed by the gods, such a professor of the central democratic science may throw off his employers and set up a business for himself. When that day comes there will be plenty of excuse for black type on the front pages of the newspapers.

I incline to think that military disaster will give him his inspiration and his opportunity—that he will take the form, so dear to democracies, of a man on horseback. The chances are bad today simply because the mob is relatively comfortable—because capitalism has been able to give it relative ease and plenty of food in return for its docility. Genuine poverty is very rare in the United States, and actual hardship is almost unknown. There are times when the proletariat is short of phonograph records, silk shirts and movie tickets, but there are very few times when it is short of nourishment. Even during the most severe business depression, with hundreds of thousands out of work, most of these apparent sufferers, if they are willing, are able to get livings outside their trades. The cities may be choked with idle men, but the country is nearly always short of labor. And if all other resources fail, there are always public agencies to feed the hungry: capitalism is careful to keep them from despair. No American knows what it means to live as millions of Europeans lived during the war and have lived, in some places, since: with the loaves of the baker reduced to half size and no meat at all in the meat-shop. But the time may come and it may not be far off. A national military disaster would disorganize all industry in the United States, already sufficiently wasteful and chaotic, and introduce the American people, for the first time in their history, to genuine want—and capital would be unable to relieve them. The day of such disaster will bring the savior foreordained. The slaves will follow him, their eyes fixed ecstatically upon the newest New Jerusalem. Men bred to respond automatically to shibboleths will respond to this worst and most insane one. Bolshevism, said General Foch, is a disease of defeated nations.

But do not misunderstand me: I predict no revolution in the grand manner, no melodramatic collapse of capitalism, no repetition of what has gone on in Russia. The American proletarian is not brave and romantic enough for that; to do him simple justice, he is not silly enough. Capitalism, in the long run, will win in the United States, if only for the reason that every American hopes to be a capitalist before he dies. Its roots go down to the deepest, darkest levels of the national soil; in all its characters, and particularly in its antipathy to the dreams of man, it is thoroughly American. [. . .]

4

All the while I have been forgetting the third of my reasons for remaining so faithful a citizen of the Federation, despite all the lascivious inducements from expatriates to follow them beyond the seas, and all the surly suggestions from patriots that I succumb. It is the reason which grows out of my medieval but unashamed taste for the bizarre and indelicate, my congenital weakness for comedy of the grosser varieties. The United States, to my eye, is incomparably the greatest show on earth. It is a show which avoids diligently all the kinds of clowning which tire me most quickly—for example, royal ceremonials, the tedious hocus-pocus of *haute politique*, the taking of politics seriously—and lays chief stress upon the kinds which delight me unceasingly—for example, the ribald combats of demagogues, the exquisitely ingenious operations of master rogues, the pursuit of witches and heretics, the desperate struggles of inferior men to claw their way into Heaven. We have clowns in constant practice among us who are as far above the clowns of any great state as a Jack Dempsey is above a paralytic—and not a few dozen or score of them, but whole droves and herds. Human enterprises

which, in all other Christian countries, are resigned despairingly to an incurable dullness—things that seem devoid of exhilarating amusement by their very nature—are here lifted to such vast heights of buffoonery that contemplating them strains the midriff almost to breaking. I cite an example: the worship of God. Everywhere else on earth it is carried on in a solemn and dispiriting manner; in England, of course, the bishops are obscene, but the average man seldom gets a fair chance to laugh at them and enjoy them. Now come home. Here we not only have bishops who are enormously more obscene then even the most gifted of the English bishops; we have also a huge force of lesser specialists in ecclesiastical mountebankery—tin-horn Loyolas, Savonarolas and Xaviers of a hundred fantastic rites, each performing untiringly and each full of a grotesque and illimitable whimsicality. Every American town, however small, has one of its own: a holy clerk with so fine a talent for introducing the arts of jazz into the salvation of the damned that his performance takes on all the gaudiness of a four-ring circus, and the bald announcement that he will raid Hell on such and such a night is enough to empty all the town blind-pigs and bordellos and pack his sanctuary to the doors. And to aid him and inspire him there are traveling experts to whom he stands in the relation of a wart to the Matterhorn—stupendous masters of theological imbecility, contrivers of doctrines utterly preposterous, heirs to the Joseph Smith, Mother Eddy and John Alexander Dowie tradition—Bryan, Sunday, and their like. These are the eminences of the American Sacred College. I delight in them. Their proceedings make me a happier American.

Turn, now, to politics. Consider, for example, a campaign for the Presidency. Would it be possible to imagine anything more uproariously idiotic—a deafening, nerve-wracking battle to the death between Tweedledum and Tweedledee, Harlequin and Sganarelle, Gobbo and Dr. Cook—the unspeakable, with fearful snorts, gradually swallowing the inconceivable? I defy any one to match it elsewhere on this earth. In other lands, at worst, there are at least intelligible issues, coherent ideas, salient personalities. Somebody says something, and somebody replies. But what did Harding say in 1920, and what did Cox reply? Who was Harding, anyhow, and who was Cox? Here, having perfected democracy, we lift the whole combat to symbolism, to transcendentalism, to metaphysics. Here we load a pair of palpably tin cannon with blank cartridges charged with talcum powder, and so let fly. Here one may howl over the show without any uneasy reminder that it is serious, and that some one may be hurt. I hold that this elevation of politics to the plane of undiluted comedy is peculiarly American, that nowhere else on this disreputable ball has the art of the sham-battle been developed to such fineness. Two experiences are in point. During the Harding-Cox combat of bladders an article of mine, dealing with some of its more melodramatic phases, was translated into German and reprinted by a Berlin paper. At the head of it the editor was careful to insert a preface explaining to his readers, but recently delivered to democracy, that such contests were not taken seriously by intelligent Americans, and warning them solemnly against getting into sweats over politics. At about the same time I had dinner with an Englishman. From cocktails to Bromo-Seltzer he bewailed the political lassitude of the English populace—its growing indifference to the whole partisan harlequinade. Here were two typical foreign attitudes: the Germans were in danger of making politics too harsh and implacable, and the English were in danger of forgetting politics altogether. Both attitudes, it must be plain, make for bad shows. Observing a German campaign, one is uncomfortably harassed and stirred up; observing an English campaign (at least in times of peace), one falls asleep. In the United States the thing is done better. Here politics is purged of all menace, all sinister quality, all genuine significance, and stuffed with such gorgeous humors, such inordinate farce that one comes to the end of a campaign with one's ribs loose, and ready for "King Lear," or a hanging, or a course of medical journals.

But feeling better for the laugh. *Ridi si sapis*, said Martial. Mirth is necessary to wisdom, to comfort, above all, to happiness. Well, here is the land of mirth, as Germany is the land of metaphysics and France is the land of fornication. Here the buffoonery never stops. What could be more delightful than the endless struggle of the Puritan to make the joy of the minority unlawful and impossible? The effort is itself a greater joy to one standing on the sidelines than any or all of the carnal joys that it combats. Always, when I contemplate an uplifter at his hopeless business, I recall a scene in an old-time burlesque show, witnessed for hire in my days as a dramatic critic. A chorus girl executed a fall upon the stage, and Rudolph Krausemeyer, the Swiss comedian, rushed to her aid. As he stooped painfully to succor her, Irving Rabinovitz, the Zionist comedian, fetched him a fearful clout across the cofferdam with a slap-stick. So the uplifter, the soul-saver, the Americanizer, striving to make the Republic fit for the Y. M. C. A. secretaries. He is the eternal American, ever moved by the best of intentions, ever running *à la* Krausemeyer to the rescue of virtue, and ever getting his pantaloons fanned by the Devil. I am naturally sinful, and such spectacles caress me. If the slap-stick were a sash-weight the show would be cruel, and I'd probably complain to the *Polizei*. As it is, I know that the uplifter is not really hurt, but simply shocked. The blow, in fact, does him good, for it helps to get him into Heaven, as exegetes prove from Matthew v, 11: *Heureux serez-vous, lorsqu'on vous outragera, qu'on vous persécutera*, and so on. As for me, it makes me a more contented man, and hence a better citizen. One man prefers the Republic because it pays better wages than Bulgaria. Another because it has laws to keep him sober and his daughter chaste. Another because the Woolworth Building is higher than the cathedral at Chartres. Another because, living here, he can read the New York *Evening Journal*. Another because there is a warrant out for him somewhere else. Me, I like it because it amuses me to my taste. I never get tired of the show. It is worth every cent it costs. [. . .]

PLATFORMS OF THE DEMOCRATIC AND REPUBLICAN PARTIES (1936)

Democratic Party

We hold this truth to be self-evident—that the test of a representative government is its ability to promote the safety and happiness of the people.

We hold this truth to be self-evident—that 12 years of Republican leadership left our Nation sorely stricken in body, mind, and spirit; and that three years of Democratic leadership have put it back on the road to restored health and prosperity.

We hold this truth to be self-evident—that 12 years of Republican surrender to the dictatorship of a privileged few have been supplanted by a Democratic leadership which has returned the people themselves to the places of authority, and has revived in them new faith and restored the hope which they had almost lost.

We hold this truth to be self-evident—that this three-year recovery in all the basic values of life and the reestablishment of the American way of living has been brought about by humanizing the policies of the Federal Government as they affect the personal, financial, industrial, and agricultural well-being of the American people.

We hold this truth to be self-evident—that government in a modern civilization has certain inescapable obligations to its citizens, among which are:

(1) Protection of the family and the home.

(2) Establishment of a democracy of opportunity for all the people.

(3) Aid to those overtaken by disaster. These obligations, neglected through 12 years of the old leadership, have once more been recognized by American Government. Under the new leadership they will never be neglected.

For the Protection of the Family and the Home

(1) We have begun and shall continue the successful drive to rid our land of kidnappers and bandits. We shall continue to use the powers of government to end the activities of the malefactors of great wealth who defraud and exploit the people.

Savings and Investment

(2) We have safeguarded the thrift of our citizens by restraining those who would gamble with other peoples savings, by requiring truth in the sale of securities; by putting the brakes upon the use of credit for speculation; by outlawing the manipulation of prices in stock and commodity markets; by curbing the overweening power and unholy practices of utility holding companies; by insuring fifty million bank accounts.

Old Age and Social Security

(3) We have built foundations for the security of those who are faced with the hazards of unemployment and old age; for the orphaned, the crippled, and the blind. On the foundation of the Social Security Act we are determined to erect a structure of economic security for all our people, making sure that this benefit shall keep step with the ever-increasing capacity of America to provide a high standard of living for all its citizens.

Consumer

(4) We will act to secure to the consumer fair value, honest sales and a decreased spread between the price he pays and the price the producer receives.

Rural Electrification

(5) This administration has fostered power rate yardsticks in the Tennessee Valley and in several other parts of the Nation. As a result, electricity has been made available to the people at a lower rate. We will continue to promote plans for rural electrification and for cheap power by means of the yardstick method.

Housing

(6) We maintain that our people are entitled to decent, adequate housing at a price which they can afford. In the last three years, the Federal Government, having saved more than two million homes from foreclosure, has taken the first steps in our history to provide decent housing for people of meagre incomes. We believe every encouragement should be given to the building of new homes by private enterprise; and that the Government should steadily extend its housing program toward the goal of adequate housing for those forced through economic necessities to live in unhealthy and slum conditions.

Veterans

(7) We shall continue just treatment of our war veterans and their dependents.

For the Establishment of a Democracy of Opportunity

Agriculture

We have taken the farmers off the road to ruin. We have kept our pledge to agriculture to use all available means to raise farm income toward its pre-war purchasing power. The farmer is no longer suffering from 15-cent corn, 3-cent hogs, 2 1/2-cent beef at the farm, 5-cent wool, 30-cent wheat, 5-cent cotton, and 8-cent sugar.

By Federal legislation, we have reduced the farmer's indebtedness and doubled his net income. In cooperation with the States and through the farmers' own committees, we are restoring the fertility of his land and checking the erosion of his soil. We are bringing electricity and good roads to his home.

We will continue to improve the soil conservation and domestic allotment program with payments to farmers.

We will continue a fair-minded administration of agricultural laws, quick to recognize and meet new problems and conditions. We recognize the gravity of the evils of farm tenancy, and we pledge the full cooperation of the Government in the refinancing of farm indebtedness at the lowest possible rates of interest and over a long term of years.

We favor the production of all the market will absorb, both at home and abroad, plus a reserve supply sufficient to insure fair prices to consumers; we favor judicious commodity loans on seasonal surpluses; and we favor assistance within Federal authority to enable farmers to adjust and balance production with demand, at a fair profit to the farmers.

We favor encouragement of sound, practical farm co-operatives.

By the purchase and retirement of ten million acres of sub-marginal land, and assistance to those attempting to eke out an existence upon it, we have made a good beginning toward proper land use and rural rehabilitation.

The farmer has been returned to the road to freedom and prosperity. We will keep him on that road.

Labor

We have given the army of America's industrial workers something more substantial than the Republicans' dinner pail full of promises. We have increased the worker's pay and shortened his hours; we have undertaken to put an end to the sweated labor of his wife and children; we have written into the law of the land his right to collective bargaining and self-organization free from the interference of employers; we have provided Federal machinery for the peaceful settlement of labor disputes.

We will continue to protect the worker and we will guard his rights, both as wage-earner and consumer, in the production and consumption of all commodities, including coal and water power and other natural resource products.

The worker has been returned to the road to freedom and prosperity. We will keep him on that road.

Business

We have taken the American business man out of the red. We have saved his bank and given it a sounder foundation; we have extended credit; we have lowered interest rates; we have undertaken to free him from the ravages of cutthroat competition.

The American business man has been returned to the road to freedom and prosperity. We will keep him on that road.

Youth

We have aided youth to stay in school; given them constructive occupation; opened the door to opportunity which 12 years of Republican neglect had closed.

Our youth have been returned to the road to freedom and prosperity. We will keep them on that road.

Monopoly and Concentration of Economic Power

Monopolies and the concentration of economic power, the creation of Republican rule and privilege, continue to be the master of the producer, the exploiter of the consumer, and the enemy of the independent operator. This is a problem challenging the unceasing effort of untrammeled public officials in every branch of the Government. We pledge vigorously and fearlessly to enforce the criminal and civil provisions of the existing anti-trust laws, and to the extent that their effectiveness has been weakened by new corporate devices or judicial construction, we propose by law to restore their efficacy in stamping out monopolistic practice and the concentration of economic power.

Aid to Those Overtaken by Disaster

We have aided and will continue to aid those who have been visited by widespread drought and floods, and have adopted a Nation-wide flood-control policy.

Unemployment

We believe that unemployment is a national problem, and that it is an inescapable obligation of our Government to meet it in a national way.

Due to our stimulation of private business, more than five million people have been reemployed; and we shall continue to maintain that the first objective of a program of economic security is maximum employment in private industry at adequate wages. Where business fails to supply such employment, we believe that work at prevailing wages should be provided in cooperation with State and local governments on useful public projects, to the end that the national wealth may be increased, the skill and energy of the worker may be utilized, his morale maintained and the unemployed assured the opportunity to earn the necessities of life.

The Constitution

The Republican platform proposes to meet many pressing national problems solely by action of the separate States. We know that drought, dust storms, floods, minimum wages, maximum hours, child labor, and working conditions in industry, monopolistic and unfair business practices cannot be adequately handled exclusively by 48 separate State legislatures, 48 separate State administrations, and 48 separate State courts. Transactions and activities which inevitably overflow State boundaries call for both State and Federal treatment.

We have sought and will continue to seek to meet these problems through legislation within the Constitution.

If these problems cannot be effectively solved by legislation within the Constitution, we shall seek such clarifying amendment as will assure to the legislatures of the several States and to the Congress of the United States, each within its proper jurisdiction, the power to enact those laws which the State and Federal legislatures, within their respective spheres, shall find necessary, in order adequately to regulate commerce, protect public health and safety and safeguard economic security. Thus we propose to maintain the letter and spirit of the Constitution.

The Merit System in Government

For the protection of government itself and promotion of its efficiency, we pledge the immediate extension of the merit system through the classified civil service—which was first established and fostered under Democratic auspices—to all non-policy-making positions in the Federal service.

We shall subject to the civil service law all continuing positions which, because of the emergency, have been exempt from its operation.

Civil Liberties

We shall continue to guard the freedom of speech, press, radio, religion and assembly which our Constitution guarantees; with equal rights to all and special privileges to none.

Government Finance

The Administration has stopped deflation, restored values and enabled business to go ahead with confidence.

When national income shrinks, government income is imperilled. In reviving national income, we have fortified government finance. We have raised the public credit to a position of unsurpassed security. The interest rate on Government bonds has been reduced to the lowest point in twenty-eight years. The same Government bonds which in 1932 sold under 83 are now selling over 104.

We approve the objective of a permanently sound currency so stabilized as to prevent the former wide fluctuations in value which injured in turn producers, debtors, and property owners on the one hand, and wage-earners and creditors on the other, a currency which will permit full utilization of the country's resources. We assert that today we have the soundest currency in the world.

We are determined to reduce the expenses of government. We are being aided therein by the recession in unemployment. As the requirements of relief decline and national income advances, an increasing percentage of Federal expenditures can and will be met from current revenues, secured from taxes levied in accordance with ability to pay. Our retrenchment, tax and recovery programs thus reflect our firm determination to achieve a balanced budget and the reduction of the national debt at the earliest possible moment.

Foreign Policy

In our relationship with other nations, this Government will continue to extend the policy of the Good Neighbor. We reaffirm our opposition to war as an instrument of potential policy and declare that disputes between nations should be settled by peaceful means. We shall continue to observe a true neutrality in the disputes of others; to be prepared, resolutely to resist aggression against ourselves; to work for peace and to take the profits out of war; to guard against being drawn, by political commitments, international banking or private trading, into any war which may develop anywhere.

We shall continue to foster the increase in our foreign trade which has been achieved by this administration; to seek by mutual agreement the lowering of those tariff barriers, quotas and embargoes which have been raised against our exports of agricultural and industrial products; but continue as in the past to give adequate protection to our farmers and manufacturers against unfair competition or the dumping on our shores of commodities and goods produced abroad by cheap labor or subsidized by foreign governments.

The Issue

The issue in this election is plain. The American people are called upon to choose between a Republican administration that has and would again regiment them in the service of privileged groups and a Democratic administration dedicated to the establishment of equal economic opportunity for all our people.

We have faith in the destiny of our nation. We are sufficiently endowed with natural resources and with productive capacity to provide for all a quality of life that meets the standards of real Americanism.

Dedicated to a government of liberal American principles, we are determined to oppose equally, the despotism of Communism and the menace of concealed Fascism.

We hold this final truth to be self-evident — that the interests, the security and the happiness of the people of the United States of America can be perpetuated only under democratic government as conceived by the founders of our nation

Republican Party

America is in peril. The welfare of American men and women and the future of our youth are at stake. We dedicate ourselves to the preservation of their political liberty, their individual opportunity and their character as free citizens, which today for the first time are threatened by Government itself.

For three long years the New Deal Administration has dishonored American traditions and flagrantly betrayed the pledges upon which the Democratic Party sought and received public support.

The powers of Congress have been usurped by the President.

The integrity and authority of the Supreme Court have been flouted.

The rights and liberties of American citizens have been violated.

Regulated monopoly has displaced free enterprise.

The New Deal Administration constantly seeks to usurp the rights reserved to the States and to the people.

It has insisted on the passage of laws contrary to the Constitution.

It has intimidated witnesses and interfered with the right of petition.

It has dishonored our country by repudiating its most sacred obligations.

It has been guilty of frightful waste and extravagance, using public funds for partisan political purposes.

It has promoted investigations to harass and intimidate American citizens, at the same time denying investigations into its own improper expenditures.

It has created a vast multitude of new offices, filled them with its favorites, set up a centralized bureaucracy, and sent out swarms of inspectors to harass our people.

It has bred fear and hesitation in commerce and industry, thus discouraging new enterprises, preventing employment and prolonging the depression.

It secretly has made tariff agreements with our foreign competitors, flooding our markets with foreign commodities.

It has coerced and intimidated voters by withholding relief to those opposing its tyrannical policies.

It has destroyed the morale of our people and made them dependent upon government.

Appeals to passion and class prejudice have replaced reason and tolerance.

To a free people, these actions are insufferable. This campaign cannot be waged on the traditional differences between the Republican and Democratic parties. The responsibility of this election transcends all previous political divisions. We invite all Americans, irrespective of party, to join us in defense of American institutions.

Constitutional Government and Free Enterprise

We pledge ourselves:

1. To maintain the American system of Constitutional and local self government, and to resist all attempts to impair the authority of the Supreme Court of the United States, the final protector of the rights of our citizens against the arbitrary encroachments of the legislative and executive branches of government. There can be no individual liberty without an independent judiciary.

2. To preserve the American system of free enterprise, private competition, and equality of opportunity, and to seek its constant betterment in the interests of all.

Reemployment

The only permanent solution of the unemployment problem is the absorption of the unemployed by industry and agriculture. To that end, we advocate:

Removal of restrictions on production. Abandonment of all New Deal policies that raise production costs, increase the cost of living, and thereby restrict buying, reduce volume and prevent reemployment.

Encouragement instead of hindrance to legitimate business.

Withdrawal of government from competition with private payrolls.

Elimination of unnecessary and hampering regulations.

Adoption of such other policies as will furnish a chance for individual enterprise, industrial expansion, and the restoration of jobs.

Relief

The necessities of life must be provided for the needy, and hope must be restored pending recovery. The administration of relief is a major failing of the New Deal. It has been faithless to those who must deserve our sympathy. To end confusion, partisanship, waste and incompetence, we pledge:

1. The return of responsibility for relief administration to non-political local agencies familiar with community problems.
2. Federal grants-in-aid to the States and territories while the need exists, upon compliance with these conditions: (a) a fair proportion of the total relief burden to be provided from the revenues of States and local governments; (b) all engaged in relief administration to be selected on the basis of merit and fitness; (c) adequate provision to be made for the encouragement of those persons who are trying to become self-supporting.
3. Undertaking of Federal public works only on their merits and separate from the administration of relief.
4. A prompt determination of the facts concerning relief and unemployment.

Security

Real security will be possible only when our productive capacity is sufficient to furnish a decent standard of living for all American families and to provide a surplus for future needs and contingencies. For the attainment of that ultimate objective, we look to the energy, self-reliance and character of our people, and to our system of free enterprise.

Society has an obligation to promote the security of the people, by affording some measure of protection against involuntary unemployment and dependency in old age. The New Deal policies, while purporting to provide social security, have, in fact, endangered it.

We propose a system of old age security, based upon the following principles:

1. We approve a pay-as-you-go policy, which requires of each generation the support of the aged and the determination of what is just and adequate.
2. Every American citizen over sixty-five should receive the supplementary payment necessary to provide a minimum income sufficient to protect him or her from want.
3. Each state and territory, upon complying with simple and general minimum standards, should receive from the federal government a graduated contribution in proportion to its own, up to a fixed maximum.
4. To make this program consistent with sound fiscal policy the Federal revenues for this purpose must be provided from the proceeds of a direct tax widely distributed. All will be benefited and all should contribute.

We propose to encourage adoption by the states and territories of honest and practical measures for meeting the problems of unemployment insurance.

The unemployment insurance and old age annuity sections of the present Social Security Act are unworkable and deny benefits to about two-thirds of our adult population, including professional men and woman and all those engaged in agricultrure and domestic service, and the self employed while imposing heavy tax burdens upon all. The so-called reserve fund estimated at forty-seven billion dollars for old age insurance is no reserve at all, because the fund will contain nothing but the Government's promise to pay, while the taxes collected in the guise of premiums will be wasted by the Government in reckless and extravagant political schemes.

Labor

The welfare of labor rests upon increased production and the prevention of exploitation. We pledge ourselves to:

Protect the right of labor to organize and to bargain collectively through representatives of its own choosing without interference from any source.
Prevent governmental job holders from exercising autocratic powers over labor.
Support the adoption of state laws and interstate compacts to abolish sweatshops and child labor, and to protect women and children with respect to maximum hours, minimum wages and working

conditions. We believe that this can be done within the Constitution as it now stands.

Agriculture

The farm problem is an economic and social, not a partisan problem, and we propose to treat it accordingly. Following the wreck of the restrictive and coercive A.A.A., the New Deal Administration has taken to itself the principles of the Republican Policy of soil conservation and land retirement. This action opens the way for a non-political and permanent solution. Such a solution cannot be had under a New Deal Administration which misuses the program to serve partisan ends, to promote scarcity and to limit by coercive methods the farmer's control over his own farm.

Our paramount object is to protect and foster the family type of farm, traditional in American life, and to promote policies which will bring about an adjustment of agriculture to meet the needs of domestic and foreign markets. As an emergency measure, during the agricultural depression, federal benefits payments or grants-in-aid when administered within the means of the Federal government are consistent with a balanced budget.

We propose:

1. To facilitate economical production and increased consumption on a basis of abundance instead of scarcity.
2. A national land-use program, including the acquisition of abandoned and non-productive farm lands by voluntary sale or lease, subject to approval of the legislative and executive branches of the States concerned, and the devotion of such land to appropriate public use, such as watershed protection and flood prevention, reforestation, recreation, and conservation of wild life.
3. That an agricultural policy be pursued for the protection and restoration of the land resources, designed to bring about such a balance between soil-building and soil-depleting crops as will permanently insure productivity, with reasonable benefits to cooperating farmer's on family-type farms, but so regulated as to eliminate the New Deal's destructive policy towards the dairy and live-stock industries.
4. To extend experimental aid to farmers developing new crops suited to our soil and climate.
5. To promote the industrial use of farm products by applied science.
6. To protect the American farmer against the importation of all live stock, dairy, and agricultural products, substitutes thereof, and derivatives therefrom, which will depress American farm prices.
7. To provide effective quarantine against imported live-stock, dairy and other farm products from countries which do not impose health and sanitary regulations fully equal to those required of our own producers.
8. To provide for ample farm credit at rates as low as those enjoyed by other industries, including commodity and live-stock loans, and preference in land loans to the farmer acquiring or refinancing a farm as a home.
9. To provide for decentralized, non-partisan control of the Farm Credit Administration and the election by National Farm Loan Associations of at least one-half of each Board of Directors of the Federal Land Banks, and thereby remove these institutions from politics.
10. To provide in the case of agricultural products of which there are exportable surpluses, the payment of reasonable benefits upon the domestically consumed portion of such crops in order to make the tariff effective. These payments are to be limited to the production level of the family type farm.
11. To encourage and further develop co-operative marketing.
12. To furnish Government assistance in disposing of surpluses in foreign trade by bargaining for foreign markets selectively by countries both as to exports and imports. We strenuously oppose so called reciprocal treaties which trade off the American farmer.

13. To give every reasonable assistance to producers in areas suffering from temporary disaster, so that they may regain and maintain a self-supporting status.

Tariff

Nearly sixty percent of all imports into the United States are now free of duty. The other forty percent of imports compete directly with the product of our industry. We would keep on the free list all products not grown or produced in the United States in commercial quantities. As to all commodities that commercially compete with our farms, our forests, our mines, our fisheries, our oil wells, our labor and our industries, sufficient protection should be maintained at all times to defend the American farmer and the American wage earner from the destructive competition emanating from the subsidies of foreign governments and the imports from low-wage and depreciated-currency countries.

We will repeal the present Reciprocal Trade Agreement Law. It is futile and dangerous. Its effect on agriculture and industry has been destructive. Its continuation would work to the detriment of the wage earner and the farmer.

We will restore the principle of the flexible tariff in order to meet changing economic conditions here and abroad and broaden by careful definition the powers of the Tariff Commission in order to extend this policy along non-partisan lines.

We will adjust tariffs with a view to promoting international trade, the stabilization of currencies, and the attainment of a proper balance between agriculture and industry.

We condemn the secret negotiations of reciprocal trade treaties without public hearing or legislative approval.

Monopolies

A private monopoly is indefensible and intolerable. It menaces and, if continued, will utterly destroy constitutional government and the liberty of the citizen.

We favor the vigorous enforcement of the criminal laws, as well as the civil laws, against monopolies and trusts and their officials, and we demand the enactment of such additional legislation as is necessary to make it impressible for private monopoly to exist in the United States.

We will employ the full powers of the government to the end that monopoly shall be eliminated and that free enterprise shall be fully restored and maintained.

Regulation of Business

We recognize the existence of a field within which governmental regulation is desirable and salutary. The authority to regulate should be vested in an independent tribunal acting under clear and specific laws establishing definite standards. Their determinations on law and facts should be subject to review by the Courts. We favor Federal regulation, within the Constitution, of the marketing of securities to protect investors. We favor also Federal regulation of the interstate activities of public utilities.

Civil Service

Under the New Deal, official authority has been given to inexperienced and incompetent persons. The Civil Service has been sacrificed to create a national political machine. As a result the Federal Government has never presented such a picture of confusion and inefficiency.

We pledge ourselves to the merit system, virtually destroyed by New Deal spoilsmen. It should be restored, improved and extended.

We will provide such conditions as offer an attractive permanent career in government service to young men and women of ability, irrespective of party affiliations.

Government Finance

The New Deal Administration has been characterized by shameful waste, and general financial irresponsibility. It has piled deficit upon deficit. It threatens national bankruptcy and the destruction through inflation of insurance policies and savings bank deposits. We pledge ourselves to:

Stop the folly of uncontrolled spending. Balance the budget—not by increasing taxes but by cutting expenditures, drastically and immediately.

Revise the federal tax system and coordinate it with state and local tax systems.

Use the taxing power for raising revenue and not for punitive or political purposes.

Money and Banking

We advocate a sound currency to be preserved at all hazards.

The first requisite to a sound and stable currency is a balanced budget.

We oppose further devaluation of the dollar. We will restore to the Congress the authority lodged with it by the Constitution to coin money and regulate the value thereof by repealing all the laws delegating this authority to the Executive.

We will cooperate with other countries toward stabilization of currencies as soon as we can do so with due regard for our National interests and as soon as other nations have sufficient stability to justify such action.

Foreign Affairs

We pledge ourselves to promote and maintain peace by all honorable means not leading to foreign alliances or political commitments.

Obedient to the traditional foreign policy of America and to the repeatedly expressed will of the American people, we pledge that America shall not become a member of the League of Nations nor of the World Court nor shall America take on any entangling alliances in foreign affairs.

We shall promote, as the best means of securing and maintaining peace by the pacific settlement of disputes, the great cause of international arbitration through the establishment of free, independent tribunals, which shall determine such disputes in accordance with law, equity and justice.

National Defense

We favor an army and navy, including air forces, adequate for our National Defense.

We will cooperate with other nations in the limitation of armaments and control of traffic in arms.

Bill of Rights

We pledge ourselves to preserve, protect and defend, against all intimidation and threat, freedom of religion, speech, press and radio; and the right of assembly and petition and immunity from unreasonable searches and seizures.

We offer the abiding security of a government of laws as against the autocratic perils of a government of men.

Furthermore

1. We favor the construction by the Federal Government of head-water storage basins to prevent floods, subject to the approval of the legislative and executive branches of the government of the States whose lands are concerned.

2. We favor equal opportunity for our colored citizens. We pledge our protection of their economic status and personal safety. We will do our best to further their employment in the gainfully occupied life of America, particularly in private industry, agriculture, emergency agencies and the Civil Service.

   We condemn the present New Deal policies which would regiment and ultimately eliminate the colored citizen from the country's productive life, and make him solely a ward of the federal government.

3. To our Indian population we pledge every effort on the part of the national government to ameliorate living conditions for them.

4. We pledge continuation of the Republican policy of adequate compensation and care for veterans disabled in the service of our country and for their widows, orphans and dependents.

5. We shall use every effort to collect the war debt due us from foreign countries, amounting to $12,000,000—one-third of

our national debt. No effort has been made by the present administration even to re-open negotiations.

6. We are opposed to legislation which discriminates against women in Federal and State employment.

Conclusion

We assume the obligations and duties imposed upon Government by modern conditions. We affirm our unalterable conviction that, in the future as in the past, the fate of the nation will depend, not so much on the wisdom and power of government, as on the character and virtue, self-reliance, industry and thrift of the people and on their willingness to meet the responsibilities essential to the preservation of a free society.

Finally, as our party affirmed in its first Platform in 1856: "Believing that the spirit of our institutions as well as the Constitution of our country guarantees liberty of conscience and equality of rights among our citizens we oppose all legislation tending to impair them," and "we invite the affiliation and cooperation of the men of all parties, however differing from us in other respects, in support of the principles herein declared."

The acceptance of the nomination tendered by the Convention carries with it, as a matter of private honor and public faith, an undertaking by each candidate to be true to the principles and program herein set forth.

A. PHILIP RANDOLPH

The Crisis of the Negro and the Constitution (1937)

In this hour of crisis in the nation, in the whole wide world, in governments, in industry, in trade union movements and among oppressed minorities everywhere, the Second National Negro Congress, representing hundreds of thousands of Negroes in America, hails the Constitution on its 150th birthday. We hail it as a Magna Charta of human rights. The Negro people, oppressed and persecuted, especially look to the Constitution as an impregnable citadel of their liberties.

Caught between the powerful forces of the southern plantation economy, on the one hand, and the rising financial and industrial power of the north, on the other, the Constitution was a compromise on the question of slavery, but the 13th, 14th, and 15th Amendments sought to chart and establish the guarantees of their full citizenship rights of the Negro people.

Sinister tendencies toward the re-enslavement of the Freedmen manifested themselves soon after the Civil War had ended, and the uncompromising Sumner, and the valiant band of Abolitionists had lost their memorable fight to protect the newly emancipated slaves with federal troops in the south. This unhappy chapter in American history tells of the tragic loss of the liberty of an entire race following the breakdown of the great and inspiring experiment of Reconstruction, rendering the bourbon plantation owners and the former slave-masters free to use the shotgun, the tissue ballot and the Ku Klux Klan terror, to drive the Negro back into a semi-caste status. Indeed, the conditions calculated to achieve the full citizenship for the former slaves were never fulfilled by the Civil War, though the beginning was challenging. Verily, the Constitution, without the force of enlightened public opinion back of it, could not itself effect what a bourgeois revolution did not accomplish.

While the new South with its lumber, turpentine and cotton magnates, went out for cheap labor as its major interest, to pile up high profits, it also attacked the civil rights of the Negro with a view to breaking his hope and faith in the inner redemptive forces of the race so that they would undervalue their human worth and economic role in Southern industry and planting. This created the need and demand for the 14th and 15th Amendments to the Constitution. They were passed. But the due process clause has been employed more as a weapon for defending corporate wealth rather than the human rights of the Negro people.

Now, it has become a common-place that Black America is not only concerned with the 13th, 14th, and 15th Amendments that grew out of the Civil War and the Reconstruction period, a period which though maligned, condemned and misrepresented by historians, with more of the Nordic bias than of the scientific spirit, will ever live as a glorious record of the capacity and genius of the Negro people for orderly, enlightened and the constructive administration of government, but Afro-Americans are, too, interested in the Bill of Rights of the Constitution which provides the framework and basis of civil and political liberties within and upon which alone as free people or rather may seek to secure and maintain their freedom, and build those institutions that help preserve freedom.

It is well nigh a truism that without the freedom of speech, of habeas corpus, of the freedom of worship, of the right to vote and be voted for, the basic institutions of modern society, such as the home, family, church, school, press, free business enterprise, trade union movements and associations seeking the liberation of all oppressed minority groups, could hardly exist and enjoy a healthy growth and development.

The Constitution stands as an imposing bulwark of these rights. But the Constitution is not an end in itself. Nor is it a perfect document. It possesses many grave limitations, and needs some fundamental and permanent change so as to make possible reforms for the protection and advancement of the workers. This worthy objective is now courageously sought by President Roosevelt, without the method of constitutional change, in his Supreme Court reorganization plan. Any such change through the method of legislation only, though desirable and timely, may not be so enduring as if wrought through change of the Constitution itself. But let us back the President's fight for judicial justice.

In very truth, the Constitution is a means to an end. The end is the attainment of an enlightened and humane government, and an economic order that will invest the people with the right and the power to live the good life, the more abundant life.

And today, in a world of storm and stress, of confusion and uncertainty, of arrogant cynicism and deadly pessimism, of war and Fascism, the American Constitution proudly reveals its deeper moorings of stability, assurance and hope for democracy.

While the Negro people, under the Constitution, because of nullification by the spirit of the Lost Cause, are still without the full measure of citizenship in the former Confederate States, the Constitution, at least, vouchsafes complete citizenship rights and provides the grounds of principle and promises to secure it.

Albeit, it is more and more becoming correctly understood that the task of realizing full citizenship for the Negro people is largely in the hands of the Negro people themselves. Assuring full citizenship rights to [the] Afro-American is the duty and responsibility of the State, but securing them is the task of the Negro; it is the task of Labor and the progressive and liberal forces of the nation. Freedom is never given; it is won. And the Negro people must win their freedom. They must achieve justice. This involves struggle, continuous struggle.

True liberation can be acquired and maintained only when the Negro people possess power; and power is the product and flower of organization— organization of the masses, the masses in the mills and mines, on the farms, in the factories, in churches, in fraternal organizations, in homes, colleges, women's clubs, student groups, trade unions, tenants' leagues, in cooperative guilds, political organizations and civil rights associations.

Organization is the purpose and aim of the Second National Negro Conference. While it does not seek, as its primary program, to organize the Negro People into trade unions and civil rights' movements, it does plan to integrate and coordinate the existing Negro organizations into one federated and collective agency so as to develop greater and more effective power. The Congress does not stress or espouse any political faith or religious creed, but seeks to formulate a minimum political, economic and social program which all Negro groups can endorse and for which they can work and fight.

The Congress supports the fight of the National Association for the Advancement of Colored People for a federal anti-lynching bill, for around this issue there is no basic difference of opinion among Negroes. All Negro people desire and seek fair opportunities for work and the right to join trade unions. No one can object to a proposal for more and better jobs, the abolition of Jim-crow labor unions, and for equal educational chances in public schools and universities.

It may not be amiss to add also, in this connection, that the Congress is not Communist or Republican, Democratic or Socialist. It is not Methodist, Baptist or Christian Scientist. It avoids control by any single religion or political party. It shuns the Scylla and Charybdis of the extreme left and the extreme right. But, in the true spirit of the united front, and in the pattern and purpose of integration and coordination, for mass strength, [it] embraces all sections of opinion among the Negro people. It does not seek to impose any issue of philosophy upon any organization or group, but rather to unite varying and various organizations, with various and varying philosophies, left, center, and right among the Negro people upon a simple, minimum program so as to mobilize and rally power and mass support behind vital issues affecting the life and destiny of the race.

Be it also known that the Congress does not seek to change the American form of government, but rather to implement it with new and rugged morals and spiritual sinews to make its democratic traditions, forms and ideals more permanent and abiding and a living force.

Startling changes, economic, political and social, have come upon the world. The empire of the Kaiser, apparently rock-ribbed and as steadfast as the sun, has been replaced by the totalitarian Third Reich. The Italian democratic state has given way to a corporate, fascist system. And of the Czar, of all the Russias, has been relegated to oblivion by the Soviets of the workers.

And even if the honored democracies of the United States, England and France, have not succumbed and capitulated to the drastic and dangerous pattern of the dictator, they are under constant, menacing stress and strain of tendencies toward the rule of fascist force. Deadlocked, withal, in a mighty struggle for supremacy are the governments by the rule of "The man on horseback" and governments by rule of a free people.

Add to our existing political disorder reflected in the amazing and rapid transformation of the structure and direction of modern governments, economic maladjustments as seen in world-wide chronic and permanent unemployment, monetary fluctuations and industrial instability, the ever rising threat of a widening sweep of the wave of war, then optimism and hope are shattered and replaced by pessimism and fear.

Already, large areas of the world are in the flames of war. The "little brown men" of militaristic Nippon are raining fire and destruction upon the land of Confucius, but the Chinese people, proud in their noble heritage, are defending their country with matchless courage and resolve, yielding no single inch of territory except under the imperative of superior force.

And when we turn our eyes to the West, to the Mediterranean, we witness the vile and vicious efforts of Mussolini and Hitler, in accordance with the terms of a Berlin-Rome axis seeking to encompass by open murder the destruction of democracy. Lulled and solaced in conscience by the non-intervention sham, the democratic nations, England, France and the United States, are observing defenseless women and children of the legitimate Loyalists government of Spain massacred in shocking barbarism by the hoards of Franco, backed by the money and men in Italy and Germany. Whither doth it lead, comes the query?

It is well nigh accepted quite generally by the thoughtful peoples everywhere that if the dykes of democracy break in the land of the little Iberian peninsula, a world flood of fascism may not be far behind, and imperil free peoples everywhere.

This may be the tragic price that mankind must pay for its complacent and timid spirit before the brutal and ruthless aggression by Japan upon China in creating the puppet kingdom of Manchukuo, and the cruel and savage invasion of the ancient kingdom of Ethiopia by the fascist legions of Italy. The independence of Ethiopia has been sold down the river by the League of Nations, while winked at by England and France.

And when we return to our shores, we find closer at home that all is not well. Despite signs of some recovery from the depression, unemployment trenches hard upon eight million. Unemployment has taken on the picture of permanency. Production in certain industries increases while the workers decrease. The development of the machine, the refinements in management and the concentration and centralization of economic power in trusts and holding companies make this possible. With grave warning, President Roosevelt has declared that one-third of the population is in ill health, underfed, underhoused and underclothed. Relief needs have not appreciably lessened, for jobs are still scarce for the workers.

Civil rights, in industrial areas, where conflict between labor and capital is on, are arrogantly disregarded and broken down by pliant municipal representatives, and extra-governmental organizations such as the Ku Klux Klan, the Black Legion and other vigilante movements.

But not only are the rights of the workers assailed by vigilante mobs at the behest of the Liberty League and the organized open-shop business interests of America, but in State Legislatures and Congress, diehard tories, such as Senator Vandenberg and others, are seeking to enact legislation, forcing upon trade unions and corporations, compulsory arbitration and the elimination of strikes.

And as we look to Labor we find its house divided. Thus it is obvious that the great problems of the workers in America today is the problem of unity. [. . .] Craft and industrial unionism can and must go side by side in the struggle of the workers for industrial democracy. These forms of organization must develop and function in one house of labor. Now, what of the Negro in relation to these problems?

The Negro people are an integral part of the American commonwealth. They, like our white brothers, bleed and die in war. They suffer and hunger in depression. Thus, theirs is the task of consolidating their interests with the interest of the progressive forces of the nation. Collective bargaining brings power to black as well as to white workers. The abolition of the company union frees the Negro workers from economic bondage and enables them to express their voice in the determination of wage rates, hours and working conditions the same as it does for white workers. Thus, the strengthening of the labor movement, the improvement of labor standards, brings comfort, health and decency to black as well as to white workers.

But there are other problems that the Negro people face. In the South there is a blight of Jim-crowism, segregation, disfranchisement through grandfather clauses and lily white primaries and the terror of the Ku Klux Klan.

Peonage, a form of involuntary servitude, in utter nullification of the 13th Amendment, holds the Negro in many Southern states in a condition of virtual slavery. Negro tenant farmers are browbeaten, persecuted and driven, when they evince any semblance of independence [,] out of their miserable and squalid shacks onto the highway. Civil and political rights for them are virtually unknown. Differentials in wages and hours of work are a common practice. Relief, though given by the Federal Government is administered by whim of Southern prejudice in the mood of arrogant superiority. What can be done about this? The answer is:

Let us build a united front of all Negro organizations, of varying strata, purpose and outlook. Let us build a united front in cooperation with the progressive and liberal agencies of the nation whose interests are common with Black America.

With the spirit and strategy of the United Front, the five remaining Scottsboro Boys can be released from their dark dungeon in Alabama. With it peonage in the South can be wiped out and the share cropper and tenant farmers, black and white, can organize and improve their economic status through collective bargaining. With it the horror of lynching in America may be eliminated and mob terror: relegated to oblivion.

Thus, on the occasion of the 150th Anniversary of the American Constitution, and the Second Anniversary of the National Negro Congress, the Negro peoples face the future, with heads erect and souls uncurbed, resolved to march forward in the van of progress, with hope and faith in the creation of a new and better world. And the Congress shall help to guide them, to lead them on!

What now of the stewardship of the Congress since its memorable bow to black and white America?

Can more be said than that it has fought a good fight? It has kept the faith. It has worked and not grown weary for a happier humanity.

On the far-flung battle lines of steel, it marshalled militant black men to march in the van with the C.I.O. to chalk up an enviable record in bringing workers into the field of industrial organization. And it has worked with the American Federation of Labor. Our men did not fail or faint before blood or bullets — in South Chicago, Detroit, Michigan, Ohio and Pennsylvania.

The Congress has brought eager and aggressive black youth to grapple with the problem of the organization of the tobacco workers in Virginia. And these youth are winning their spurs.

To the laundry workers in Washington, D.C., the Congress is carrying the message of trade union organization. And it enlisted Negro organizers to join C.I.O. forces to organize the automobile industry.

On the civil and political rights' fronts, the Congress joined the fighting forces of the National Association for the Advancement of Colored People, to battle for the Wagner-Gavagan federal antilynching bill.

And to the rescue of Herndon and the Scottsboro Boys, the Congress has carried its unflagging fighting spirit.

But not only has it fought in the front for the defense of the rights of the Negro People, the Congress has also thrown its might with the progressive forces in the land to aid in the cause of Spanish Democracy, the independence of China from the domination of Japan, and the restoration of Hailie Selassie to an independent Kingdom of Ethiopia.

Yes it has joined the great demonstration of the nation against war and fascism. And, too, it is stirring the women and youth of the Negro people to join and struggle with the national and world agencies of their groups for a better world.

Therefore, with humble pride we cry out of the depths of our souls to mankind everywhere. Forward with the destruction of the imperialist domination and oppression of the great peoples of Africa! Forward to the abolition of the fascist rule of Italy over the noble independent, and unconquerable men of Ethiopia! Forward to the creation of a united, free and independent China! Forward to victory of the valiant loyalist armies over the fascist brigands of Franco! Long live the cause of World peace! Long live the spirit of world democracy! Long live the memory and love of the Black Revolution of the 18th Century, led by Denmark Vesey, Nat Turner, Gabriel, Harriet Tubman, Sojourner Truth, and Frederick Douglass! Long live the valor of those black regiments of slaves and freedmen whose blood and courage made . . . Lincoln's Emancipation Proclamation a living reality!

Forward to the unity of the workers! Forward to democracy and freedom, progress and plenty! Forward with the torch of Education, the instrument of agitation, the weapon of organization to a day of peace on earth and toward men, good will!

GEORGE SUTHERLAND

Powell v. Alabama (1932)

Mr. Justice SUTHERLAND delivered the opinion of the Court.

These cases were argued together and submitted for decision as one case.

The petitioners, hereinafter referred to as defendants, are negroes charged with the crime of rape, committed upon the persons of two white girls. The crime is said to have been committed on March 25, 1931. The indictment was returned in a state court of first instance on March 31, and the record recites that on the same day the defendants were arraigned and entered pleas of not guilty. There is a further recital to the effect that upon the arraignment they were represented by counsel. But no counsel had been employed, and aside from a statement made by the trial judge several days later during a colloquy immediately preceding the trial, the record does not disclose when, or under what circumstances, an appointment of counsel was made, or who was appointed. During the colloquy referred to, the trial judge, in response to a question, said that he had appointed all the members of the bar for the purpose of arraigning the defendants and then of course anticipated that the members of the bar would continue to help the defendants if no counsel appeared. Upon the argument here both sides accepted that as a correct statement of the facts concerning the matter.

There was a severance upon the request of the state, and the defendants were tried in three several groups, as indicated above. As each of the three cases was called for trial, each defendant was arraigned, and, having the indictment read to him, entered a plea of not guilty. Whether the original arraignment and pleas were regarded as ineffective is not shown. Each of the three trials was completed within a single day. Under the Alabama statute the punishment for rape is to be fixed by the jury, and in its discretion may be from ten years imprisonment to death. The juries found defendants guilty and imposed the death penalty upon all. The trial court overruled motions for new trials and sentenced the defendants in accordance with the verdicts. Chief Justice Anderson thought the defendants had not been accorded a fair trial and strongly dissented.

In this court the judgments are assailed upon the grounds that the defendants, and each of them, were denied due process of law and the equal protection of the laws, in contravention of the Fourteenth Amendment, specifically as follows: (1) They were not given a fair, impartial, and deliberate trial; (2) they were denied the right of counsel, with the accustomed incidents of consultation and opportunity of preparation for trial; and (3) they were tried before juries from which qualified members of their own race were systematically excluded. These questions were properly raised and saved in the courts below.

The only one of the assignments which we shall consider is the second, in respect of the denial of counsel; and it becomes unnecessary to discuss the facts of the case or the circumstances surrounding the prosecution except in so far as they reflect light upon that question.

The record shows that on the day when the offense is said to have been committed, these defendants, together with a number of other negroes, were upon a freight train on its way through Alabama. On the same train were seven white boys and the two white girls. A fight took place between the negroes and the white boys, in the course of which the white boys, with the exception of one named Gilley, were thrown off the train. A message was sent ahead, reporting the fight and asking that every negro be gotten off the train. The participants in the fight, and the two girls, were in an open gondola car. The two girls testified that each of them was assaulted by six different negroes in turn, and they identified the seven defendants as having been among the number. None of the white boys was called to testify, with the exception of Gilley, who was called in rebuttal.

Before the train reached Scottsboro, Ala., a sheriff's posse seized the defendants and two other negroes. Both girls and the negroes then were taken to Scottsboro, the county seat. Word of their coming and of the alleged assault had preceded them, and they were met at Scottsboro by a large crowd. It does not sufficiently appear that the defendants were seriously threatened with, or that they were actually in danger of, mob violence; but it does appear that the attitude of the community was one of great hostility. The sheriff thought it necessary to call for the militia to assist in safeguarding the prisoners. Chief Justice Anderson pointed out in his opinion that every step taken from the arrest and arraignment to the sentence was accompanied by the military. Soldiers took the defendants to Gadsden for safe-keeping, brought them back to Scottsboro for arraignment, returned them to Gadsden for safe-keeping while awaiting trial, escorted them to Scottsboro for trial a few days later, and guarded the courthouse and grounds at every stage of the proceedings. It is perfectly apparent that the proceedings, from beginning to end, took place in an atmosphere of tense, hostile, and excited public sentiment. During the entire time, the defendants were closely confined or were under military guard. The record does not disclose their ages, except that one of them was nineteen; but the record clearly indicates that most, if not all, of them were youthful, and they are constantly referred to as "the boys." They were ignorant and illiterate. All of them were residents of other states, where alone members of their families or friends resided.

However guilty defendants, upon due inquiry, might prove to have been, they were, until convicted, presumed to be innocent. It was the duty of the court having their cases in charge to see that they were denied no necessary incident of a fair trial. With any error of the state court involving alleged contravention of the state statutes or Constitution we, of course, have nothing to do. The sole inquiry which we are permitted to make is whether the federal Constitution was contravened; and as to that, we confine ourselves, as already suggested, to the inquiry whether the defendants were in substance denied the right of counsel, and if so, whether such denial infringes the due process clause of the Fourteenth Amendment.

First. The record shows that immediately upon the return of the indictment defendants were arraigned and pleaded not guilty. Apparently they were not asked whether they had, or were able to employ, counsel, or wished to have counsel appointed; or whether they had friends or relatives who might assist in that regard if communicated with. That it would not have been an idle ceremony to have given the defendants reasonable opportunity to communicate with their families and endeavor to obtain counsel is demonstrated by the fact that very soon after conviction, able counsel appeared in their behalf. This was pointed out by Chief Justice Anderson in the course of his dissenting opinion. "They were nonresidents," he said, "and had little time or opportunity to get in touch with their families and friends who were scattered throughout two other states, and time has demonstrated that they could or would have been represented by able counsel had a better opportunity been given by a reasonable delay in the trial of the cases judging from the number and activity of counsel that appeared immediately or shortly after their conviction."

It is hardly necessary to say that the right to counsel being conceded, a defendant should be afforded a fair opportunity to secure counsel of his own choice. Not only was that not done here, but such designation of counsel as was attempted was either so indefinite or so close upon the trial as to amount to a denial of effective and substantial aid in that regard.

April 6, six days after indictment, the trials began. When the first case was called, the court inquired whether the parties were ready for trial. The state's attorney replied that he was ready to proceed. No one answered for the defendants or appeared to represent or defend them. Mr. Roddy, a Tennessee lawyer not

a member of the local bar, addressed the court, saying that he had not been employed, but that people who were interested had spoken to him about the case. He was asked by the court whether he intended to appear for the defendants, and answered that he would like to appear along with counsel that the court might appoint. [. . .]

[U]ntil the very morning of the trial no lawyer had been named or definitely designated to represent the defendants. Prior to that time, the trial judge had "appointed all the members of the bar" for the limited "purpose of arraigning the defendants." Whether they would represent the defendants thereafter, if no counsel appeared in their behalf, was a matter of speculation only, or, as the judge indicated, of mere anticipation on the part of the court. Such a designation, even if made for all purposes, would, in our opinion, have fallen far short of meeting, in any proper sense, a requirement for the appointment of counsel. How many lawyers were members of the bar does not appear; but, in the very nature of things, whether many or few, they would not, thus collectively named, have been given that clear appreciation of responsibility or impressed with that individual sense of duty which should and naturally would accompany the appointment of a selected member of the bar, specifically named and assigned.

That this action of the trial judge in respect of appointment of counsel was little more than an expansive gesture, imposing no substantial or definite obligation upon any one, is borne out by the fact that prior to the calling of the case for trial on April 6, a leading member of the local bar accepted employment on the side of the prosecution and actively participated in the trial. It is true that he said that before doing so he had understood Mr. Roddy would be employed as counsel for the defendants. This the lawyer in question, of his own accord, frankly stated to the court; and no doubt he acted with the utmost good faith. Probably other members of the bar had a like understanding. In any event, the circumstance lends emphasis to the conclusion that during perhaps the most critical period of the proceedings against these defendants, that is to say, from the time of their arraignment until the beginning of their trial, when consultation, thorough-going investigation and preparation were vitally important, the defendants did not have the aid of counsel in any real sense, although they were as much entitled to such aid during that period as at the trial itself. [. . .]

The defendants, young, ignorant, illiterate, surrounded by hostile sentiment, hauled back and forth under guard of soldiers, charged with an atrocious crime regarded with especial horror in the community where they were to be tried, were thus put in peril of their lives within a few moments after counsel for the first time charged with any degree of responsibility began to represent them.

It is not enough to assume that counsel thus precipitated into the case thought there was no defense, and exercised their best judgment in proceeding to trial without preparation. Neither they nor the court could say what a prompt and thorough-going investigation might disclose as to the facts. No attempt was made to investigate. No opportunity to do so was given. Defendants were immediately hurried to trial. Chief Justice Anderson, after disclaiming any intention to criticize harshly counsel who attempted to represent defendants at the trials, said: ". . . The record indicates that the appearance was rather pro forma than zealous and active. . . ." Under the circumstances disclosed, we hold that defendants were not accorded the right of counsel in any substantial sense. To decide otherwise, would simply be to ignore actualities. [. . .]

It is true that great and inexcusable delay in the enforcement of our criminal law is one of the grave evils of our time. Continuances are frequently granted for unnecessarily long periods of time, and delays incident to the disposition of motions for new trial and hearings upon appeal have come in many cases to be a distinct reproach to the administration of justice. The prompt disposition of criminal cases is to be commended and encouraged. But in reaching that result a defendant, charged with a serious crime, must not be stripped of his right to have sufficient time to advise with counsel and prepare his defense. To do that is not to proceed promptly in the claim spirit of regulated justice but to go forward with the haste of the mob. [. . .]

Second. The Constitution of Alabama provides that in all criminal prosecutions the accused shall enjoy the right to have the assistance of counsel; and a state statute requires the court in a capital case, where the defendant is unable to employ counsel, to appoint counsel for him. The state Supreme Court held that

these provisions had not been infringed, and with that holding we are powerless to interfere. The question, however, which it is our duty, and within our power, to decide, is whether the denial of the assistance of counsel contravenes the due process clause of the Fourteenth Amendment to the Federal Constitution.

If recognition of the right of a defendant charged with a felony to have the aid of counsel depended upon the existence of a similar right at common law as it existed in England when our Constitution was adopted, there would be great difficulty in maintaining it as necessary to due process. Originally, in England, a person charged with treason or felony was denied the aid of counsel, except in respect of legal questions which the accused himself might suggest. At the same time parties in civil cases and persons accused of misdemeanors were entitled to the full assistance of counsel. After the revolution of 1688, the rule was abolished as to treason, but was otherwise steadily adhered to until 1836, when by act of Parliament the full right was granted in respect of felonies generally.

An affirmation of the right to the aid of counsel in petty offenses, and its denial in the case of crimes of the gravest character, where such aid is most needed, is so outrageous and so obviously a perversion of all sense of proportion that the rule was constantly, vigorously and sometimes passionately assailed by English statesmen and lawyers. As early as 1758, Blackstone, although recognizing that the rule was settled at common law, denounced it as not in keeping with the rest of the humane treatment of prisoners by the English law. "For upon what face of reason," he says "can that assistance be denied to save the life of a man, which yet is allowed him in prosecutions for every petty trespass?" 4 Blackstone, 355. One of the grounds upon which Lord Coke defended the rule was that in felonies the court itself was counsel for the prisoner. 1 Cooley's Constitutional Limitations, supra. But how can a judge, whose functions are purely judicial, effectively discharge the obligations of counsel for the accused? He can and should see to it that in the proceedings before the court the accused shall be dealt with justly and fairly. He cannot investigate the facts, advise and direct the defense, or participate in those necessary conferences between counsel and accused which sometimes partake of the inviolable character of the confessional.

The rule was rejected by the colonies. Before the adoption of the Federal Constitution, the Constitution of Maryland had declared "That, in all criminal prosecutions, every man hath a right . . . to be allowed counsel. . . ." Article 19, Constitution of 1776. The Constitution of Massachusetts, adopted in 1780 (part the first, art. 12), the Constitution of New Hampshire, adopted in 1784 (part 1, art. 15), the Constitution of New York of 1777 (article 34), and the Constitution of Pennsylvania of 1776 (Declaration of Rights, art. 9), had also declared to the same effect. And in the case of Pennsylvania, as early as 1701, the Penn Charter (article 5) declared that "all Criminals shall have the same Privileges of Witnesses and Council as their Prosecutors." [. . .]

It thus appears that in at least twelve of the thirteen colonies the rule of the English common law, in the respect now under consideration, had been definitely rejected and the right to counsel fully recognized in all criminal prosecutions, save that in one or two instances the right was limited to capital offenses or to the more serious crimes; and this court seems to have been of the opinion that this was true in all the colonies. [. . .]

We do not overlook the case of *Hurtado v. California* [1884], where this court determined that due process of law does not require an indictment by a grand jury as a prerequisite to prosecution by a state for murder. In support of that conclusion the court referred to the fact that the Fifth Amendment, in addition to containing the due process of law clause, provides in explicit terms that "no person shall be held to answer for a capital, or otherwise infamous crime, unless on a presentment or indictment of a Grand Jury," and said that since no part of this important amendment could be regarded as superfluous, the obvious inference is that in the sense of the Constitution due process of law was not intended to include, *ex vi termini*, the institution and procedure of a grand jury in any case; and that the same phrase, employed in the Fourteenth Amendment to restrain the action of the states, was to be interpreted as having been used in the same sense and with no greater extent; and that if it had been the purpose of that Amendment to perpetuate the institution of the grand jury in the states, it would have embodied, as did the Fifth Amendment, an express declaration to that effect.

The Sixth Amendment, in terms, provides that in all criminal prosecutions the accused shall enjoy the right "to have the Assistance of Counsel for his defence." In the face of the reasoning of the *Hurtado* case, if it stood alone, it would be difficult to justify the conclusion that the right to counsel, being thus specifically granted by the Sixth Amendment, was also within the [intent] of the due process of law clause. But the *Hurtado* case does not stand alone. [. . .] [T]his court has considered that freedom of speech and of the press are rights protected by the due process clause of the Fourteenth Amendment, although in the First Amendment, Congress is prohibited in specific terms from abridging the right. *Gitlow v. People of State of New York* [1925]; *Stromberg v. California* [1931]; *Near v. Minnesota* [1930].

These later cases establish that notwithstanding the sweeping character of the language in the *Hurtado* case, the rule laid down is not without exceptions. The rule is an aid to construction, and in some instances may be conclusive; but it must yield to more compelling considerations whenever such considerations exist. The fact that the right involved is of such a character that it cannot be denied without violating those "fundamental principles of liberty and justice which lie at the base of all our civil and political institutions" is obviously one of those compelling considerations which must prevail in determining whether it is embraced within the due process clause of the Fourteenth Amendment, although it be specifically dealt with in another part of the Federal Constitution. Evidently this court, in the later cases enumerated, regarded the rights there under consideration as of this fundamental character. That some such distinction must be observed is foreshadowed in *Twining v. New Jersey* [1908], where Mr. Justice Moody, speaking for the court, said that: ". . . It is possible that some of the personal rights safeguarded by the first eight Amendments against national action may also be safeguarded against state action, because a denial of them would be a denial of due process of law. If this is so, it is not because those rights are enumerated in the first eight Amendments, but because they are of such a nature that they are included in the conception of due process of law." While the question has never been categorically determined by this court, a consideration of the nature of the right and a review of the expressions of this and other courts makes it clear that the right to the aid of counsel is of this fundamental character.

It never has been doubted by this court, or any other so far as we know, that notice and hearing are preliminary steps essential to the passing of an enforceable judgment, and that they, together with a legally competent tribunal having jurisdiction of the case, constitute basic elements of the constitutional requirement of due process of law. The words of Webster, so often quoted, that by "the law of the land" is intended "a law which hears before it condemns," have been repeated in varying forms of expression in a multitude of decisions. [. . .]

What, then, does a hearing include? Historically and in practice, in our own country at least, it has always included the right to the aid of counsel when desired and provided by the party asserting the right. The right to be heard would be, in many cases, of little avail if it did not comprehend the right to be heard by counsel. Even the intelligent and educated layman has small and sometimes no skill in the science of law. If charged with crime, he is incapable, generally, of determining for himself whether the indictment is good or bad. He is unfamiliar with the rules of evidence. Left without the aid of counsel he may be put on trial without a proper charge, and convicted upon incompetent evidence, or evidence irrelevant to the issue or otherwise inadmissible. He lacks both the skill and knowledge adequately to prepare his defense, even though he have a perfect one. He requires the guiding hand of counsel at every step in the proceedings against him. Without it, though he be not guilty, he faces the danger of conviction because he does not know how to establish his innocence. If that be true of men of intelligence, how much more true is it of the ignorant and illiterate, or those of feeble intellect. If in any case, civil of criminal, a state or federal court were arbitrarily to refuse to hear a party by counsel, employed by and appearing for him, it reasonably may not be doubted that such a refusal would be a denial of a hearing, and, therefore, of due process in the constitutional sense. [. . .]

In the light of the facts outlined in the forepart of this opinion—the ignorance and illiteracy of the defendants, their youth, the circumstances of public hostility, the imprisonment and the close surveillance of the defendants by the military forces, the fact that their friends and families were all in other states and communication with them necessarily difficult, and above all that they stood in deadly peril of their lives—we think the failure of the trial court to give them reasonable time and opportunity to secure counsel was a clear denial of due process.

But passing that, and assuming their inability, even if opportunity had been given, to employ counsel, as the trial court evidently did assume, we are of opinion that, under the circumstances just stated, the necessity of counsel was so vital and imperative that the failure of the trial court to make an effective appointment of counsel was likewise a denial of due process within the meaning of the Fourteenth Amendment. Whether this would be so in other criminal prosecutions, or under other circumstances, we need not determine. All that it is necessary now to decide, as we do decide, is that in a capital case, where the defendant is unable to employ counsel, and is incapable adequately of making his own defense because of ignorance, feeble-mindedness, illiteracy, or the like, it is the duty of the court, whether requested or not, to assign counsel for him as a necessary requisite of due process of law; and that duty is not discharged by an assignment at such a time or under such circumstances as to preclude the giving of effective aid in the preparation and trial of the case. To hold otherwise would be to ignore the fundamental postulate, already adverted to, "that there are certain immutable principles of justice which inhere in the very idea of free government which no member of the Union may disregard." [. . .]

The United States by statute and every state in the Union by express provision of law, or by the determination of its courts, make it the duty of the trial judge, where the accused is unable to employ counsel, to appoint counsel for him. In most states the rule applies broadly to all criminal prosecutions, in others it is limited to the more serious crimes, and in a very limited number, to capital cases. A rule adopted with such unanimous accord reflects, if it does not establish the inherent right to have counsel appointed at least in cases like the present, and lends convincing support to the conclusion we have reached as to the fundamental nature of that right.

The judgments must be reversed and the causes remanded for further proceedings not inconsistent with this opinion.

Judgments reversed.

CHARLES EVANS HUGHES

West Coast Hotel Co. v. Parrish (1937)

Mr. Chief Justice HUGHES delivered the opinion of the Court.

This case presents the question of the constitutional validity of the minimum wage law of the state of Washington. [. . .]

The appellant conducts a hotel. The appellee Elsie Parrish was employed as a chambermaid and (with her husband) brought this suit to recover the difference between the wages paid her and the minimum wage fixed pursuant to the state law. The minimum wage was $14.50 per week of 48 hours. The appellant challenged the act as repugnant to the due process clause of the Fourteenth Amendment of the Constitution of the United States. The Supreme Court of the state, reversing the trial court, sustained the statute and directed judgment for the plaintiffs. *Parrish v. West Coast Hotel Co.* [1936]. The case is here on appeal.

The appellant relies upon the decision of this Court in *Adkins v. Children's Hospital* [1923], which held invalid the District of Columbia Minimum Wage Act (40 Stat. 960) which was attacked under the due process clause of the Fifth Amendment. [. . .]

The Supreme Court of Washington has upheld the minimum wage statute of that state. It has decided that the statute is a reasonable exercise of the police power of the state. In reaching that conclusion, the state court has invoked principles long established by this Court in the application of the Fourteenth Amendment. The state court has refused to regard the decision in the *Adkins* Case as determinative and has pointed to our decisions both before and since that case as justifying its position. We are of the opinion that this ruling of the state court demands on our part a re-examination of the *Adkins* Case. The importance of the question, in which many states having similar laws are concerned, the close division by which the decision in the *Adkins* Case was reached, and the economic conditions which have supervened, and in the light of which the reasonableness of the exercise of the protective power of the state must be considered, make it not only appropriate, but we think imperative, that in deciding the present case the subject should receive fresh consideration. [. . .]

The principle which must control our decision is not in doubt. The constitutional provision invoked is the due process clause of the Fourteenth Amendment governing the states, as the due process clause invoked in the *Adkins* Case governed Congress. In each case the violation alleged by those attacking minimum wage regulation for women is deprivation of freedom of contract. What is this freedom? The Constitution does not speak of freedom of contract. It speaks of liberty and prohibits the deprivation of liberty without due process of law. In prohibiting that deprivation, the Constitution does not recognize an absolute and uncontrollable liberty. Liberty in each of its phases has its history and connotation. But the liberty safeguarded is liberty in a social organization which requires the protection of law against the evils which menace the health, safety, morals, and welfare of the people. Liberty under the Constitution is thus necessarily subject to the restraints of due process, and regulation which is reasonable in relation to its subject and is adopted in the interests of the community is due process. This essential limitation of liberty in general governs freedom of contract in particular. More than twenty-five years ago we set forth the applicable principle in these words, after referring to the cases where the liberty guaranteed by the Fourteenth Amendment had been broadly described.

But it was recognized in the cases cited, as in many others, that freedom of contract is a qualified, and not an absolute, right. There is no absolute freedom to do as one wills or to contract as one chooses. The guaranty of liberty does not withdraw from legislative supervision that wide department of activity which consists of the making of contracts, or deny to government the power to provide restrictive safeguards. Liberty implies the absence of arbitrary restraint, not immunity from reasonable regulations and prohibitions imposed in the interests of the community. *Chicago, Burlington & Quincy R. Co. v. McGuire* [1911].

This power under the Constitution to restrict freedom of contract has had many illustrations. That it may be exercised in the public interest with respect to contracts between employer and employee is undeniable. Thus statutes have been sustained limiting employment in underground mines and smelters to eight hours a day (*Holden v. Hardy* [1898]); in requiring redemption in cash of store orders or other evidences of indebtedness issued in the payment of wages (*Knoxville Iron Co. v. Harbison*, [1901]); in forbidding the payment of seamen's wages in advance (*Patterson v. The Bark Eudora* [1903]); in making it unlawful to contract to pay miners employed at quantity rates upon the basis of screened coal instead of the weight of the coal as originally produced in the mine (*McLean v. Arkansas* [1909]); in prohibiting contracts limiting liability for injuries to employees (*Chicago, Burlington & Quincy R. Co. v. McGuire, supra*); in limiting hours of work of employees in manufacturing establishments (*Bunting v. Oregon* [1917]); and in maintaining workmen's compensation laws (*New York Central R. Co. v. White* [1917]). In dealing with the relation of employer and employed, the Legislature has necessarily a wide field of discretion in order that there may be suitable protection of health and safety, and that peace and good order may be promoted through regulations designed to insure wholesome conditions of work and freedom from oppression.

The point that has been strongly stressed that adult employees should be deemed competent to make their own contracts was decisively met nearly forty years ago in *Holden v. Hardy, supra*, where we pointed out the inequality in the footing of the parties. We said:

The legislature has also recognized the fact, which the experience of legislators in many states has corroborated, that the proprietors of these establishments and their operatives do not stand upon an equality, and that their interests are, to a certain extent, conflicting. The former naturally desire to obtain as much labor as possible from their employees, while the latter are often induced by the fear of discharge to conform to regulations which their judgment, fairly exercised, would pronounce to be detrimental to their health or strength. In other words, the proprietors lay down the rules, and the laborers are practically constrained to obey them. In such cases self-interest is often an unsafe guide, and the legislature may properly interpose its authority.

And we added that the fact "that both parties are of full age, and competent to contract, does not necessarily deprive the state of the power to interfere, where the parties do not stand upon an equality, or where the public heath demands that one party to the contract shall be protected against himself." "The state still retains an interest in his welfare, however reckless he may be. The whole is no greater than the sum of all the parts, and when the individual health, safety, and welfare are sacrificed or neglected, the state must suffer."

It is manifest that this established principle is peculiarly applicable in relation to the employment of women in whose protection the state has a special interest. That phase of the subject received elaborate consideration in *Muller v. Oregon* [1908], where the constitutional authority of the state to limit the working hours of women was sustained. [. . .]

This array of precedents and the principles they applied were thought by the dissenting Justices in the *Adkins* Case to demand that the minimum wage statute be sustained. The validity of the distinction made by the Court between a minimum wage and a maximum of hours in limiting liberty of contract was especially challenged. That challenge persists and is without any satisfactory answer. [. . .]

We think that the views thus expressed are sound and that the decision in the *Adkins* Case was a departure from the true application of the principles governing the regulation by the state of the relation of employer and employed. [. . .]

With full recognition of the earnestness and vigor which characterize the prevailing opinion in the *Adkins* Case, we find it impossible to reconcile that ruling with these well-considered declarations. What can be closer to the public interest than the health of women and their protection from unscrupulous and overreaching employers? And if the protection of women is a legitimate end of the exercise of state power, how can it be said that the requirement of the payment of a minimum wage fairly fixed in order to meet the very necessities of existence is not an admissible means to that end? The Legislature of the state was clearly entitled to consider the situation of women in employment, the fact that they are in the class receiving the least pay, that their bargaining power is relatively weak, and that they are the ready victims of those who would take advantage of their necessitous circumstances. The Legislature was entitled to adopt measures to reduce the evils of the "sweating system," the exploiting of workers at wages so low as to be insufficient to meet the bare cost of living, thus making their very helplessness the occasion of a most injurious competition. The Legislature had the right to consider that its minimum wage requirements would be an important aid in carrying out its policy of protection. The adoption of similar requirements by many states evidences a deep-seated conviction both as to the presence of the evil and as to the means adapted to check it. Legislative response to that conviction cannot be regarded as arbitrary or capricious and that is all we have to decide. Even if the wisdom of the policy be regarded as debatable and its effects uncertain, still the Legislature is entitled to its judgment.

There is an additional and compelling consideration which recent economic experience has brought into a strong light. The exploitation of a class of workers who are in an unequal position with respect to bargaining power and are thus relatively defenseless against the denial of a living wage is not only detrimental to their health and well being, but casts a direct burden for their support upon the community. What these workers lose in wages the taxpayers are called upon to pay. The bare cost of living must be met. We may take judicial notice of the unparalleled demands for relief which arose during the recent period of depression and still continue to an alarming extent despite the degree of economic recovery which has been achieved. It is unnecessary to cite official statistics to establish what is of common knowledge through the length and breadth of the land. While in the instant case no factual brief has been presented, there is no reason to doubt that the state of Washington has encountered the same social problem that is present elsewhere. The community is not bound to provide what is in effect a subsidy for unconscionable employers. The community may direct its law-making power to correct the abuse which springs from their selfish disregard of the public interest. [. . .]

Our conclusion is that the case of *Adkins v. Children's Hospital*, *supra*, should be, and it is, overruled. The judgment of the Supreme Court of the state of Washington is affirmed.

Affirmed.

BENJAMIN CARDOZO

Palko v. State of Connecticut (1937)

Mr. Justice CARDOZO delivered the opinion of the Court.

A statute of Connecticut permitting appeals in criminal cases to be taken by the state is challenged by appellant as an infringement of the Fourteenth Amendment of the Constitution of the United States. Whether the challenge should be upheld is now to be determined.

Appellant was indicted in Fairfield County, Conn., for the crime of murder in the first degree. A jury found him guilty of murder in the second degree, and he was sentenced to confinement in the state prison for life. Thereafter the State of Connecticut, with the permission of the judge presiding at the trial, gave notice of appeal to the Supreme Court of Errors. This it did pursuant to an act adopted in 1886. [. . .]

Upon such appeal, the Supreme Court of Errors reversed the judgment and ordered a new trial. It found that there had been error of law to the prejudice of the state (1) in excluding testimony as to a confession by defendant; (2) in excluding testimony upon cross-examination of defendant to impeach his credibility; and (3) in the instructions to the jury as to the difference between first and second degree murder.

Pursuant to the mandate of the Supreme Court of Errors, defendant was brought to trial again. Before a jury was impaneled, and also at later stages of the case, he made the objection that the effect of the new trial was to place him twice in jeopardy for the same offense, and in so doing to violate the Fourteenth Amendment of the Constitution of the United States. Upon the overruling of the objection the trial proceeded. The jury returned a verdict of murder in the first degree, and the court sentenced the defendant to the punishment of death. The Supreme Court of Errors affirmed the judgment of conviction. [. . .] The case is here upon appeal. [. . .]

The argument for appellant is that whatever is forbidden by the Fifth Amendment is forbidden by the Fourteenth also. The Fifth Amendment, which is not directed to the States, but solely to the federal government, creates immunity from double jeopardy. No person shall be "subject for the same offense to be twice put in jeopardy of life or limb." The Fourteenth Amendment ordains, "nor shall any State deprive any person of life, liberty, or property, without due process of law." To retry a defendant, though under one indictment and only one, subjects him, it is said, to double jeopardy in violation of the Fifth Amendment, if the prosecution is one on behalf of the United States. From this the consequence is said to follow that there is a denial of life or liberty without due process of law, if the prosecution is one on behalf of the people of a state. [. . .]

We have said that in appellant's view the Fourteenth Amendment is to be taken as embodying the prohibitions of the Fifth. His thesis is even broader. Whatever would be a violation of the original bill of rights (Amendments 1 to 8) if done by the federal government is now equally unlawful by force of the Fourteenth Amendment if done by a state. There is no such general rule.

The Fifth Amendment provides, among other things, that no person shall be held to answer for a capital or otherwise infamous crime unless on presentment or indictment of a grand jury. This court has held that, in prosecutions by a state, presentment or indictment by a grand jury may give way to informations at the instance of a public officer. *Hurtado v. California* [1884]. The Fifth Amendment provides also that no person shall be compelled in any criminal case to be a witness against himself. This court has said that, in prosecutions by a state, the exemption will fail if the state elects to end it. *Twining v. New Jersey* [1908]. The Sixth Amendment calls for a jury trial in criminal cases and the Seventh for a jury trial in civil cases at common law where the value in controversy shall exceed $20. This court has ruled that consistently with those amendments trial by jury may be modified by a state or abolished altogether. [. . .]

On the other hand, the due process clause of the Fourteenth Amendment may make it unlawful for a state to abridge by its statutes the freedom of speech which the First Amendment safeguards against encroachment by the Congress (*De Jonge v. Oregon* [1937]), or the like freedom of the press (*Near v. Minnesota* [1931]), or the free exercise of religion (*Hamilton v. Regents of University* [1934]), or the right of peaceable assembly, without which speech would be unduly trammeled (*De Jonge v. Oregon, supra*), or the right of one accused of crime to the benefit of counsel (*Powell v. Alabama* [1932]). In these and other situations immunities that are valid as against the federal government by force of the specific pledges of particular amendments have been found to be implicit in the concept of ordered liberty, and thus, through the Fourteenth Amendment, become valid as against the states.

The line of division may seem to be wavering and broken if there is a hasty catalogue of the cases on the one side and the other. Reflection and analysis will induce a different view. There emerges the perception of a rationalizing principle which gives to discrete instances a proper order and coherence. The right to trial by jury and the immunity from prosecution except as the result of an indictment may have value and importance. Even so, they are not of the very essence of a scheme of ordered liberty. To abolish them is not to violate a "principle of justice so rooted in the traditions and conscience of our people as to be ranked as fundamental." Few would be so narrow or provincial as to maintain that a fair and enlightened system of justice would be impossible without them. What is true of jury trials and indictments is true also, as the cases show, of the immunity from compulsory self-incrimination. *Twining v. New Jersey, supra*. This too might be lost, and justice still be done. Indeed, today as in the past there are students of our penal system who look upon the immunity as a mischief rather than a benefit, and who would limit its scope, or destroy it altogether. No doubt there would remain the need to give protection against torture, physical or mental. Justice, however, would not perish if the accused were subject to a duty to respond to orderly inquiry. The exclusion of these immunities and privileges from the privileges and immunities protected against the action of the States has not been arbitrary or casual. It has been dictated by a study and appreciation of the meaning, the essential implications, of liberty itself.

We reach a different plane of social and moral values when we pass to the privileges and immunities that have been taken over from the earlier articles of the Federal Bill of Rights and brought within the Fourteenth Amendment by a process of absorption. These in their origin were effective against the federal government alone. If the Fourteenth Amendment has absorbed them, the process of absorption has had its source in the belief that neither liberty nor justice would exist if they were sacrificed. *Twining v. New Jersey, supra*. This is true, for illustration, of freedom of thought and speech. Of that freedom one may say that it is the matrix, the indispensable condition, of nearly every other form of freedom. With rare aberrations a pervasive recognition of that truth can be traced in our history, political and legal. So it has come about that the domain of liberty, withdrawn by the Fourteenth Amendment from encroachment by the states, has been enlarged by latter-day judgments to include liberty of the mind as well as liberty of action. The extension became, indeed, a logical imperative when once it was recognized, as long ago it was, that liberty is something more than exemption from physical restraint, and that even in the field of substantive rights and duties the legislative judgment, if oppressive and arbitrary, may be overridden by the courts. Fundamental too in the concept of due process, and so in that of liberty, is the thought

that condemnation shall be rendered only after trial. The hearing, moreover, must be a real one, not a sham or a pretense. For that reason, ignorant defendants in a capital case were held to have been condemned unlawfully when in truth, though not in form, they were refused the aid of counsel. *Powell v. Alabama, supra*. The decision did not turn upon the fact that the benefit of counsel would have been guaranteed to the defendants by the provisions of the Sixth Amendment if they had been prosecuted in a federal court. The decision turned upon the fact that in the particular situation laid before us in the evidence the benefit of counsel was essential to the substance of a hearing.

Our survey of the cases serves, we think, to justify the statement that the dividing line between them, if not unfaltering throughout its course, has been true for the most part to a unifying principle. On which side of the line the case made out by the appellant has appropriate location must be the next inquiry and the final one. Is that kind of double jeopardy to which the statute has subjected him a hardship so acute and shocking that our policy will not endure it? Does it violate those "fundamental principles of liberty and justice which lie at the base of all our civil and political institutions"? The answer surely must be "no." What the answer would have to be if the state were permitted after a trial free from error to try the accused over again or to bring another case against him, we have no occasion to consider. We deal with the statute before us and no other. The state is not attempting to wear the accused out by a multitude of cases with accumulated trials. It asks no more than this, that the case against him shall go on until there shall be a trial free from the corrosion of substantial legal error. This is not cruelty at all, nor even vexation in any immoderate degree. If the trial had been infected with error adverse to the accused, there might have been review at his instance, and as often as necessary to purge the vicious taint. A reciprocal privilege, subject at all times to the discretion of the presiding judge, has now been granted to the state. There is here no seismic innovation. The edifice of justice stands, its symmetry, to many, greater than before. [. . .]

The judgment is affirmed.

WOODY GUTHRIE

God Blessed America
(This Land Was Made For You and Me) (1940)

This land is your land, this land is my land
From California to the [Staten] New York Island,
From the Redwood Forest, to the Gulf stream
    waters,
God blessed America for me.[1]

As I went walking that ribbon of highway
And saw above me that endless skyway,
And saw below me the golden valley, I said:
God blessed America for me.

I roamed and rambled and followed my footsteps
To the sparkling sands of her diamond deserts,
And all around me, a voice was sounding:
God blessed America for me.

Was a high wall there that tried to stop me
A sign was painted said: Private Property,
But on the back side it didn't say nothing—
God blessed America for me.

When the sun come shining, then I was strolling
In wheat fields waving and dust clouds rolling;
The voice was chanting as the fog was lifting:
God blessed America for me.

One bright sunny morning in the shadow of the
    steeple
By the Relief Office I saw my people—
As they stood hungry, I stood there wondering if
God blessed America for me.

E. B. WHITE

Freedom (1940)

I have often noticed on my trips up to the city that people have recut their clothes to follow the fashion. On my last trip, however, it seemed to me that people had remodeled their ideas too—taken in their convictions a little at the waist, shortened the sleeves of their resolve, and fitted themselves out in a new intellectual ensemble copied from a smart design out of the very latest page of history. It seemed to me they had strung along with Paris a little too long.

I confess to a disturbed stomach. I feel sick when I find anyone adjusting his mind to the new tyranny which is succeeding abroad. Because of its fundamental strictures, fascism does not seem to me to admit of any compromise or any rationalization, and I resent the patronizing air of persons who find in my plain belief in freedom a sign of immaturity. If it is boyish to believe; that a human being should live free, then I'll gladly arrest my development and let the rest of the world grow up.

I shall report some of the strange remarks I heard in New York. One man told me that he thought perhaps the Nazi ideal was a sounder ideal than our constitutional system "because have you ever noticed what fine alert young faces the young German soldiers have in the newsreel?" He added: "Our American youngsters spend all their time at the

---

1. [Later versions present this line as "This land was made for you and me."]

movies—they're a mess." That was his summation of the case, his interpretation of the new Europe. Such a remark leaves me pale and shaken. If it represents the peak of our intelligence, then the steady march of despotism will not receive any considerable setback at our shores.

Another man informed me that our democratic notion of popular government was decadent and not worth bothering about—"because England is really rotten and the industrial towns there are a disgrace." That was the only reason he gave for the hopelessness of democracy; and he seemed mightily pleased with himself, as though he were more familiar than most with the anatomy of decadence, and had detected subtler aspects of the situation than were discernible to the rest of us.

Another man assured me that anyone who took *any* kind of government seriously was a gullible fool. You could be sure, he said, that there is nothing but corruption "of the way Clemenceau acted at Versailles." He said it didn't make any difference really about this war. It was just another war. Having relieved himself of this majestic bit of reasoning, he subsided.

Another individual, discovering signs of zeal creeping into my blood, berated me for having lost my detachment, my pure skeptical point of view. He announced that he wasn't going to be swept away by all this nonsense, but would prefer to remain in the role of innocent bystander, which he said was the duty of any intelligent person. (I noticed, however, that he phoned later to qualify his remark, as though he had lost some of his innocence in the cab on the way home.)

Those are just a few samples of the sort of talk that seemed to be going round—talk which was full of defeatism and disillusion and sometimes of a too studied innocence. Men are not merely annihilating themselves at a great rate these days, but they are telling one another enormous lies, grandiose fibs. Such remarks as I heard are fearfully disturbing in their cumulative effect. They are more destructive than dive bombers and mine fields, for they challenge not merely one's immediate position but one's main defenses. They seemed to me to issue either from persons who could never have really come to grips with freedom, so as to understand her, or from renegades. Where I expected to find indignation, I found paralysis, or a sort of dim acquiescence, as in a child who is dully swallowing a distasteful pill. I was advised of the growing anti-Jewish sentiment by a man who seemed to be watching the phenomenon of intolerance not through tears of shame but with a clear intellectual gaze, as through a well-ground lens.

The least a man can do at such a time is to declare himself and tell where he stands. I believe in freedom with the same burning delight, the same faith, the same intense abandon which attended its birth on this continent more than a century and a half ago. I am writing my declaration rapidly, much as though I were shaving to catch a train. Events abroad give a man a feeling of being pressed for time. Actually I do not believe I am pressed for time, and I apologize to the reader for a false impression that may be created. I just want to tell, before I get slowed down, that I am in love with freedom and that it is an affair of long standing and that it is a fine state to be in, and that I am deeply suspicious of people who are beginning to adjust to fascism and dictators merely because they are succeeding in war. From such adaptable natures a smell rises. I pinch my nose.

For as long as I can remember I have had a sense of living somewhat freely in a natural world. I don't mean I enjoyed freedom of action, but my existence seemed to have the quality of free-ness. I traveled with secret papers pertaining to a divine conspiracy. Intuitively I've always been aware of the vitally important pact which a man has with himself, to be all things to himself, and to be identified with all things, to stand self-reliant, taking advantage of his haphazard connection with a planet, riding his luck, and following his bent with the tenacity of a hound. My first and greatest love affair was with this thing we call freedom, this lady of infinite allure, this dangerous and beautiful and sublime being who restores and supplies us all.

It began with the haunting intimation (which I presume every child receives) of his mystical inner life; of God in man; of nature publishing herself through the "I." This elusive sensation is moving and memorable. It comes early in life: a boy, we'll say, sitting on the front steps on a summer night, thinking of nothing in particular, suddenly hearing as with a new perception and as though for the first time the pulsing sound of crickets, overwhelmed with the novel sense of identification with the natural company of insects and grass and night, conscious of a faint answering cry to the universal perplexing question: "What is 'I'?" Or a little girl, returning from the grave of a pet bird, leaning with her elbows on the windowsill, inhaling the unfamiliar draught of death, suddenly seeing herself as part of the complete story. Or to an older youth, encountering for the first time a great teacher who by some chance word or mood awakens something and the youth beginning to breathe as an individual and conscious of strength in his vitals. I think the sensation must develop in many men as a feeling of identity with God—an eruption of the spirit caused by allergies and the sense of divine existence as distinct from mere animal existence. This is the beginning of the affair with freedom.

But a man's free condition is of two parts: the instinctive free-ness he experiences as an animal dweller on a planet, and the practical liberties he enjoys as a privileged member of human society. The latter is, of the two, more generally understood, more widely admired, more violently challenged and discussed. It is the practical and apparent side of freedom. The United States, almost alone to-day, offers the liberties and the privileges and the tools of freedom. In this land the citizens are still invited to write their plays and books, to paint their pictures, to meet for discussion, to dissent as well as to agree, to mount soapboxes in the public square, to enjoy education in all subjects without censorship, to hold court and judge one another, to compose music, to talk politics with their neighbors without wondering whether the secret police are listening, to exchange ideas as well as goods, to kid the government when it needs kidding, and to read real news of real events instead of phony news manufactured by a paid agent of the state. This is a fact and should give every person pause.

To be free, in a planetary sense, is to feel that you belong to earth. To be free, in a social sense, is to feel at home in a democratic framework. In Adolf Hitler, although he is a freely flowering individual, we do not detect either type of sensibility. From reading his book I gather that his feeling for earth is not a sense of communion but a driving urge to prevail. His feeling for men is not that they co-exist, but that they are capable of being arranged and standardized by a superior intellect—that their existence suggests not a fulfillment of their personalities but a submersion of their personalities in the common racial destiny. His very great absorption in the destiny of the German

people somehow loses some of its effect when you discover, from his writings, in what vast contempt he holds *all* people. "I learned," he wrote, ". . . to gain an insight into the unbelievably primitive opinions and arguments of the people." To him the ordinary man is a primitive, capable only of being used and led. He speaks continually of people as sheep, halfwits, and impudent fools—the same people from whom he asks the utmost in loyalty, and to whom he promises the ultimate in prizes.

Here in America, where our society is based on belief in the individual, not contempt for him, the free principle of life has a chance of surviving. I believe that it must and will survive. To understand freedom is an accomplishment which all men may acquire who set their minds in that direction; and to love freedom is a tendency which many Americans are born with. To live in the same room with freedom, or in the same hemisphere, is still a profoundly shaking experience for me.

One of the earliest truths (and to him most valuable) that the author of *Mein Kampf* discovered was that it is not the written word, but the spoken word, which in heated moments moves great masses of people to noble or ignoble action. The written word, unlike the spoken word, is something which every person examines privately and judges calmly by his own intellectual standards, not by what the man standing next to him thinks. "I know," wrote Hitler, "that one is able to win people far more by the spoken than by the written word. . . . " Later he adds contemptuously: "For let it be said to all knights of the pen and to all the political dandies, especially of to-day: the greatest changes in this world have never yet been brought about by a goose quill! No, the pen has always been reserved to motivate these changes theoretically."

Luckily I am not out to change the world—that's being done for me, and at a great clip. But I know that the free spirit of man is persistent in nature; it recurs, and has never successfully been wiped out, by fire or flood. I set down the above remarks merely (in the words of Mr. Hitler) to motivate that spirit, theoretically. Being myself a knight of the goose quill, I am under no misapprehension about "winning people" but I am inordinately proud these days of the quill, for it has shown itself, historically, to be the hypodermic which inoculates men and keeps the germ of freedom always in circulation, so that there are individuals in every time in every land who are the carriers, the Typhoid Mary's, capable of infecting others by mere contact and example. These persons are feared by every tyrant—who shows his fear by burning the books and destroying the individuals. A writer goes about his task to-day with the extra satisfaction which comes from knowing that he will be the first to have his head lopped off—even before the political dandies. In my own case this is a double satisfaction, for if freedom were denied me by force of earthly circumstance, I am the same as dead and would infinitely prefer to go into fascism without my head than with it, having no use for it any more and not wishing to be saddled with so heavy an encumbrance.

HARLAN FISKE STONE

United States v. Darby Lumber Company (1941)

Mr. Justice STONE delivered the opinion of the Court.

The two principal questions raised by the record in this case are, first, whether Congress has constitutional power to prohibit the shipment in interstate commerce of lumber manufactured by employees whose wages are less than a prescribed minimum or whose weekly hours of labor at that wage are greater than a prescribed maximum, and, second, whether it has power to prohibit the employment of workmen in the production of goods "for interstate commerce" at other than prescribed wages and hours. A subsidiary question is whether in connection with such prohibitions Congress can require the employer subject to them to keep records showing the hours worked each day and week by each of his employees including those engaged "in the production and manufacture of goods to wit, lumber, for 'interstate commerce.'" [. . .]

The Fair Labor Standards Act set up a comprehensive legislative scheme for preventing the shipment in interstate commerce of certain products and commodities produced in the United States under labor conditions as respects wages and hours which fail to conform to standards set up by the Act. Its purpose [. . .] is to exclude from interstate commerce goods produced for the commerce and to prevent their production for interstate commerce, under conditions detrimental to the maintenance of the minimum standards of living necessary for health and general well-being; and to prevent the use of interstate commerce as the means of competition in the distribution of goods so produced, and as the means of spreading and perpetuating such substandard labor conditions among the workers of the several states. [. . .]

Section 15 of the statute prohibits certain specified acts and 16(a) punishes willful violation of it by a fine of not more than $10,000 and punishes each conviction after the first by imprisonment of not more than six months or by the specified fine or both. Section 15(a)(1) makes unlawful the shipment in interstate commerce of any goods "in the production of which any employee was employed in violation of section 6(206) or section 7(207)," which provide, among other things, that during the first year of operation of the Act a minimum wage of 25 cents per hour shall be paid to employees "engaged in (interstate) commerce or in the production of goods for (interstate) commerce," and that the maximum hours of employment for employees "engaged in commerce or in the production of goods for commerce" without increased compensation for overtime, shall be forty-four hours a week.

Section 15(a)(2) makes it unlawful to violate the provisions of 6 and 7 including the minimum wage and maximum hour requirements just mentioned for employees engaged in production of goods for commerce. Section 15(a)(5) makes it unlawful for an employer subject to the Act to violate 11(c) which requires him to keep such records of the persons employed by him and of their wages and hours of employment as the administrator shall prescribe by regulation or order. The indictment charges that appellee is engaged, in the state of Georgia, in the business of acquiring raw materials, which he manufactures into finished lumber with the intent, when manufactured, to ship it in interstate commerce to customers outside the state, and that he does in fact so ship a large part of the lumber so produced. There are numerous counts charging appellee with the shipment in interstate commerce from Georgia to points outside the state of lumber in the production of which, for interstate commerce, appellee has employed workmen at less than the prescribed minimum wage or more than the prescribed maximum hours without payment to them of any wage for overtime. Other counts charge the employment by appellee of workmen in the production of lumber for interstate commerce at wages of less than 25 cents an hour or for more than the maximum hours per week without payment to them of the prescribed overtime wage. Still another count charges appellee with failure to keep records showing the hours worked each day a week by each of his employees as required by 11(c) and the regulation of the administrator, and also that appellee unlawfully failed to keep such records of employees engaged "in the production and manufacture of goods, to-wit lumber, for interstate commerce."

The district court quashed the indictment in its entirety upon the broad grounds that the Act, which it interpreted as a regulation of manufacture within the states, is unconstitutional. It declared that manufacture is not interstate commerce and that the regulation by the Fair Labor Standards Act of wages and hours of employment of those engaged in the manufacture of goods which it is intended at the time of production "may or will be" after production "sold in interstate commerce in part or in whole" is not within the congressional power to regulate interstate commerce. [. . .]

While manufacture is not of itself interstate commerce the shipment of manufactured goods interstate is such commerce and the prohibition of such shipment by Congress is indubitably a regulation of the commerce. The power to regulate commerce is

the power "to prescribe the rule by which commerce is to be governed." *Gibbons v. Ogden* [1824]. It extends not only to those regulations which aid, foster and protect the commerce, but embraces those which prohibit it. It is conceded that the power of Congress to prohibit transportation in interstate commerce includes noxious articles, stolen articles, kidnapped persons, and articles such as intoxicating liquor or convict made goods, traffic in which is forbidden or restricted by the laws of the state of destination. [. . .]

But it is said that the present prohibition falls within the scope of none of these categories; that while the prohibition is nominally a regulation of the commerce its motive or purpose is regulation of wages and hours of persons engaged in manufacture, the control of which has been reserved to the states and upon which Georgia and some of the states of destination have placed no restriction; that the effect of the present statute is not to exclude the prescribed articles from interstate commerce in aid of state regulation as in *Kentucky Whip & Collar Co. v. Illinois Central R. Co.* [1937], but instead, under the guise of a regulation of interstate commerce, it undertakes to regulate wages and hours within the state contrary to the policy of the state which has elected to leave them unregulated.

The power of Congress over interstate commerce "is complete in itself, may be exercised to its utmost extent, and acknowledges no limitations, other than are prescribed by the Constitution." *Gibbons v. Ogden, supra.* That power can neither be enlarged nor diminished by the exercise or non-exercise of state power. Congress, following its own conception of public policy concerning the restrictions which may appropriately be imposed on interstate commerce, is free to exclude from the commerce articles whose use in the states for which they are destined it may conceive to be injurious to the public health, morals or welfare, even though the state has not sought to regulate their use.

Such regulation is not a forbidden invasion of state power merely because either its motive or its consequence is to restrict the use of articles of commerce within the states of destination and is not prohibited unless by other constitutional provisions. It is no objection to the assertion of the power to regulate interstate commerce that its exercise is attended by the same incidents which attend the exercise of the police power of the states. [. . .]

The motive and purpose of the present regulation are plainly to make effective the congressional conception of public policy that interstate commerce should not be made the instrument of competition in the distribution of goods produced under substandard labor conditions, which competition is injurious to the commerce and to the states from and to which the commerce flows. The motive and purpose of a regulation of interstate commerce are matters for the legislative judgment upon the exercise of which the Constitution places no restriction and over which the courts are given no control. [. . .]

Whatever their motive and purpose, regulations of commerce which do not infringe some constitutional prohibition are within the plenary power conferred on Congress by the Commerce Clause. Subject only to that limitation, presently to be considered, we conclude that the prohibition of the shipment interstate of goods produced under the forbidden substandard labor conditions is within the constitutional authority of Congress.

In the more than a century which has elapsed since the decision of *Gibbons v. Ogden*, these principles of constitutional interpretation have been so long and repeatedly recognized by this Court as applicable to the Commerce Clause, that there would be little occasion for repeating them now were it not for the decision of this Court twenty-two years ago in *Hammer v. Dagenhart* [1918]. In that case it was held by a bare majority of the Court over the powerful and now classic dissent of Mr. Justice Holmes setting forth the fundamental issues involved, that Congress was without power to exclude the products of child labor from interstate commerce. The reasoning and conclusion of the Court's opinion there cannot be reconciled with the conclusion which we have reached, that the power of Congress under the Commerce Clause is plenary to exclude any article from interstate commerce subject only to the specific prohibitions of the Constitution.

Hammer v. Dagenhart has not been followed. The distinction on which the decision was rested that congressional power to prohibit interstate commerce is limited to articles which in themselves have some harmful or deleterious property—a distinction which was novel when made and unsupported by any provision of the Constitution—has long since been abandoned. The thesis of the opinion that the motive of the prohibition or its effect to control in some measure the use or production within the states of the article thus excluded from the commerce can operate to deprive the regulation of its constitutional authority has long since ceased to have force. [. . .]

The conclusion is inescapable that *Hammer v. Dagenhart*, was a departure from the principles which have prevailed in the interpretation of the commerce clause both before and since the decision and that such vitality, as a precedent, as it then had has long since been exhausted. It should be and now is overruled.

Validity of the wage and hour requirements.
Section 15(a)(2) and 6 and 7 require employers to conform to the wage and hour provisions with respect to all employees engaged in the production of goods for interstate commerce. As appellee's employees are not alleged to be "engaged in interstate commerce" the validity of the prohibition turns on the question whether the employment, under other than the prescribed labor standards, of employees engaged in the production of goods for interstate commerce is so related to the commerce and so affects it as to be within the reach of the power of Congress to regulate it. [. . .]

[W]e think the acts alleged in the indictment are within the sweep of the statute. The obvious purpose of the Act was not only to prevent the interstate transportation of the proscribed product, but to stop the initial step toward transportation, production with the purpose of so transporting it. Congress was not unaware that most manufacturing businesses shipping their product in interstate commerce make it in their shops without reference to its ultimate destination and then after manufacture select some of it for shipment interstate and some intrastate according to the daily demands of their business, and that it would be practically impossible, without disrupting manufacturing businesses, to restrict the prohibited kind of production to the particular pieces of lumber, cloth, furniture or the like which later move in interstate rather than intrastate commerce.

There remains the question whether such restriction on the production of goods for commerce is a permissible exercise of the commerce power. The power of Congress over interstate commerce is not confined to the regulation of commerce among the states. It extends to those activities intrastate which so affect interstate commerce or the exercise of the power of Congress over it as to make regulation of them appropriate means to the attainment of a legitimate end, the exercise of the granted power of Congress to regulate interstate commerce. See *McCulloch v. Maryland* [1819].

While this Court has many times found state regulation of interstate commerce, when uniformity of its regulation is of national concern, to be incompatible with the Commerce Clause even though Congress has not legislated on the subject, the Court has never implied such restraint on state control over matters intrastate not deemed to be regulations of interstate commerce or its instrumentalities even though they affect the commerce. [. . .]

But it does not follow that Congress may not by appropriate legislation regulate intrastate activities where they have a substantial effect on interstate commerce. A recent example is the National Labor Relations Act, for the regulation of employer and employee relations in industries in which strikes, induced by unfair labor practices named in the Act, tend to disturb or obstruct interstate commerce. But long before the adoption of the National Labor Relations Act, this Court had many times held that the power of Congress to regulate interstate commerce extends to the regulation through legislative action of activities intrastate which have a substantial effect on the commerce or the exercise of the congressional power over it.

In such legislation Congress has sometimes left it to the courts to determine whether the intrastate activities have the prohibited effect on the commerce, as in the Sherman Act. It has sometimes left it to an administrative board or agency to determine whether the activities sought to be regulated or prohibited have such effect, as in the case of the Interstate Commerce Act, and the National Labor Relations Act or whether they come within the statutory definition of the prohibited Act as in the Federal Trade Commission Act. And sometimes Congress itself has said that a particular activity affects the commerce as it did in the present act, the Safety Appliance Act, and the Railway Labor Act. In passing on the validity of legislation of the class last mentioned the only function of courts is to determine whether the particular activity regulated or prohibited is within the reach of the federal power.

Congress, having by the present Act adopted the policy of excluding from interstate commerce all goods produced for the commerce which do not conform to the specified labor standards, it may choose the means reasonably adapted to the attainment of the permitted end, even though they involve control of intrastate activities. Such legislation has often been sustained with respect to powers, other than the commerce power granted to the national government, when the means chosen, although not themselves within the granted power, were nevertheless deemed appropriate aids to the accomplishment of some purpose within an admitted power of the national government. [. . .] A familiar like exercise of power is the regulation of intrastate transactions which are so commingled with or related to interstate commerce that all must be regulated if the interstate commerce is to be effectively controlled. *Shreveport Case* [1914].

Similarly Congress may require inspection and preventive treatment of all cattle in a disease infected area in order to prevent shipment in interstate commerce of some of the cattle without the treatment. It may prohibit the removal, at destination, of labels required by the Pure Food & Drugs Act, to be affixed to articles transported in interstate commerce. And we have recently held that Congress in the exercise of its power to require inspection and grading of tobacco shipped in interstate commerce may compel such inspection and grading of all tobacco sold at local auction rooms from which a substantial part but not all of the tobacco sold is shipped in interstate commerce.

We think also that 15[a], now under consideration, is sustainable independently of 15(a)(1), which prohibits shipment or transportation of the proscribed goods. As we have said the evils aimed at by the Act are the spread of substandard labor conditions through the use of the facilities of interstate commerce for competition by the goods so produced with those produced under the prescribed or better labor conditions; and the consequent dislocation of the commerce itself caused by the impairment or destruction of local businesses by competition made effective through interstate commerce. The Act is thus directed at the suppression of a method or kind of competition in interstate commerce which it has in effect condemned as "unfair," as the Clayton Act, 38 Stat. 730, has condemned other "unfair methods of competition" made effective through interstate commerce. [. . .]

The means adopted by 15(a)(2) for the protection of interstate commerce by the suppression of the production of the condemned goods for interstate commerce is so related to the commerce and so affects it as to be within the reach of the commerce power. [. . .]

Our conclusion is unaffected by the Tenth Amendment which provides: "The powers not delegated to the United States by the Constitution, nor prohibited by it to the States, are reserved to the States respectively, or to the people." The amendment states but a truism that all is retained which has not been surrendered. There is nothing in the history of its adoption to suggest that it was more than declaratory of the relationship between the national and state governments as it had been established by the Constitution before the amendment or that its purpose was other than to allay fears that the new national government might seek to exercise powers not granted, and that the states might not be able to exercise fully their reserved powers. [. . .]

Validity of the requirement of records of wages and hours. 15(a)(5) and 11(c). These requirements are incidental to those for the prescribed wages and hours, and hence validity of the former turns on

validity of the latter. Since, as we have held, Congress may require production for interstate Commerce to conform to those conditions, it may require the employer, as a means of enforcing the valid law, to keep a record showing whether he has in fact complied with it. The requirement for records even of the intrastate transaction is an appropriate means to the legitimate end.

Validity of the wage and hour provisions under the Fifth Amendment. Both provisions are minimum wage requirements compelling the payment of a minimum standard wage with a prescribed increased wage for overtime of "not less than one and one-half times the regular rate" at which the worker is employed. Since our decision in *West Coast Hotel Co. v. Parrish* [1937], it is no longer open to question that the fixing of a minimum wage is within the legislative power and that the bare fact of its exercise is not a denial of due process under the Fifth more than under the Fourteenth Amendment. Nor is it any longer open to question that it is within the legislative power to fix maximum hours. [. . .]

The Act is sufficiently definite to meet constitutional demands. One who employs persons, without conforming to the prescribed wage and hour conditions, to work on goods which he ships or expects to ship across state lines, is warned that he may be subject to the criminal penalties of the Act. No more is required.

Reversed.

ROBERT H. JACKSON

West Virginia State Board of Education v. Barnette (1943)

Mr. Justice JACKSON delivered the opinion of the Court.

The Board of Education on January 9, 1942, adopted a resolution containing recitals taken largely from the Court's [*Minersville School District v.*] *Gobitis* [1940] opinion and ordering that the salute to the flag become "a regular part of the program of

activities in the public schools," that all teachers and pupils "shall be required to participate in the salute honoring the Nation represented by the Flag; provided, however, that refusal to salute the Flag be regarded as an Act of insubordination, and shall be dealt with accordingly." The resolution originally required the "commonly accepted salute to the Flag" which it defined. Objections to the salute as "being too much like Hitler's" were raised by the Parent and Teachers Association, the Boy and Girl Scouts, the Red Cross, and the Federation of Women's Clubs. Some modification appears to have been made in deference to these objections, but no concession was made to Jehovah's Witnesses. What is now required is the "stiff-arm" salute, the saluter to keep the right hand raised with palm turned up while the following is repeated: "I pledge allegiance to the Flag of the United States of America and to the Republic for which it stands; one Nation, indivisible, with liberty and justice for all."

Failure to conform is "insubordination" dealt with by expulsion. Readmission is denied by statute until compliance. Meanwhile the expelled child is "unlawfully absent" and may be proceeded against as a delinquent. His parents or guardians are liable to prosecution, and if convicted are subject to fine not exceeding $50 and jail term not exceeding thirty days.

Appellees, citizens of the United States and of West Virginia, brought suit in the United States District Court for themselves and others similarly situated asking its injunction to restrain enforcement of these laws and regulations against Jehovah's Witnesses. The Witnesses are an unincorporated body teaching that the obligation imposed by law of God is superior to that of laws enacted by temporal government. Their religious beliefs include a literal version of Exodus, Chapter 20, verses 4 and 5, which says: "Thou shalt not make unto thee any graven image, or any likeness of anything that is in heaven above, or that is in the earth beneath, or that is in the water under the earth; thou shalt not bow down thyself to them nor serve them." They consider that the flag is an "image" within this command. For this reason they refuse to salute it. Children of this faith have been expelled from school and are threatened with exclusion for no other cause. Officials threaten to send them to reformatories maintained for criminally inclined juveniles. Parents of such children have been prosecuted and are threatened with prosecutions for causing delinquency. [. . .]

The freedom asserted by these appellees does not bring them into collision with rights asserted by any other individual. It is such conflicts which most frequently require intervention of the State to determine where the rights of one end and those of another begin. But the refusal of these persons to participate in the ceremony does not interfere with or deny rights of others to do so. Nor is there any question in this case that their behavior is peaceable and orderly. The sole conflict is between authority and rights of the individual. The State asserts power to condition access to public education on making a prescribed sign and profession and at the same time to coerce attendance by punishing both parent and child. The latter stand on a right of self-determination in matters that touch individual opinion and personal attitude.

As the present Chief Justice said in dissent in the *Gobitis* case, the State may "require teaching by instruction and study of all in our history and in the structure and organization of our government, including the guaranties of civil liberty which tend to inspire patriotism and love of country." Here, however, we are dealing with a compulsion of students to declare a belief. They are not merely made acquainted with the flag salute so that they may be informed as to what it is or even what it means. The issue here is whether this slow and easily neglected route to aroused loyalties constitutionally may be short-cut by substituting a compulsory salute and slogan. [. . .]

There is no doubt that, in connection with the pledges, the flag salute is a form of utterance. Symbolism is a primitive but effective way of communicating ideas. The use of an emblem or flag to symbolize some system, idea, institution, or personality, is a short cut from mind to mind. Causes and nations, political parties, lodges and ecclesiastical groups seek to knit the loyalty of their followings to a flag or banner, a color or design. The State announces rank, function, and authority through crowns and maces, uniforms and black robes; the church speaks through the Cross, the Crucifix, the altar and shrine, and clerical reiment. Symbols of State often convey political ideas just as religious symbols come to convey theological ones. Associated with many of these symbols are appropriate gestures of acceptance or respect: a salute, a bowed or bared head, a bended knee. A person gets from a symbol the meaning he puts into it, and what is one man's comfort and inspiration is another's jest and scorn.

Over a decade ago Chief Justice Hughes led this Court in holding that the display of a red flag as a symbol of opposition by peaceful and legal means to organized government was protected by the free speech guaranties of the Constitution. *Stromberg v. California* [1931]. Here it is the State that employs a flag as a symbol of adherence to government as presently organized. It requires the individual to communicate by word and sign his acceptance of the political ideas it thus bespeaks. Objection to this form of communication when coerced is an old one, well known to the framers of the Bill of Rights.

It is also to be noted that the compulsory flag salute and pledge requires affirmation of a belief and an attitude of mind. It is not clear whether the regulation contemplates that pupils forego any contrary convictions of their own and become unwilling converts to the prescribed ceremony or whether it will be acceptable if they simulate assent by words without belief and by a gesture barren of meaning. It is now a commonplace that censorship or suppression of expression of opinion is tolerated by our Constitution only when the expression presents a clear and present danger of action of a kind the State is empowered to prevent and punish. It would seem that involuntary affirmation could be commanded only on even more immediate and urgent grounds than silence. But here the power of compulsion is invoked without any allegation that remaining passive during a flag salute ritual creates a clear and present danger that would justify an effort even to muffle expression. To sustain the compulsory flag salute we are required to say that a Bill of Rights which guards the individual's right to speak his own mind, left it open to public authorities to compel him to utter what is not in his mind.

Whether the First Amendment to the Constitution will permit officials to order observance of ritual of this nature does not depend upon whether as a voluntary exercise we would think it to be good, bad or merely innocuous. Any credo of nationalism is likely to include what some disapprove or to omit what others think essential, and to give off different overtones as it takes on different accents or interpretations. If official power exists to coerce acceptance of any patriotic creed, what it shall contain cannot be decided by courts, but must be largely discretionary with the ordaining authority, whose power to prescribe would no doubt include power to amend. Hence validity of the asserted power to force an American citizen publicly to profess any statement of belief or to engage in any ceremony of assent to one

presents questions of power that must be considered independently of any idea we may have as to the utility of the ceremony in question.

Nor does the issue as we see it turn on one's possession of particular religious views or the sincerity with which they are held. While religion supplies appellees' motive for enduring the discomforts of making the issue in this case, many citizens who do not share these religious views hold such a compulsory rite to infringe constitutional liberty of the individual. It is not necessary to inquire whether non-conformist beliefs will exempt from the duty to salute unless we first find power to make the salute a legal duty.

The *Gobitis* decision, however, assumed, as did the argument in that case and in this, that power exists in the State to impose the flag salute discipline upon school children in general. The Court only examined and rejected a claim based on religious beliefs of immunity from an unquestioned general rule. The question which underlies the flag salute controversy is whether such a ceremony so touching matters of opinion and political attitude may be imposed upon the individual by official authority under powers committed to any political organization under our Constitution. We examine rather than assume existence of this power and, against this broader definition of issues in this case, re-examine specific grounds assigned for the *Gobitis* decision.

1. It was said that the flag-salute controversy confronted the Court with "the problem which Lincoln cast in memorable dilemma: 'Must a government of necessity be too strong for the liberties of its people, or too weak to maintain its own existence?' and that the answer must be in favor of strength."

We think these issues may be examined free of pressure or restraint growing out of such considerations.

It may be doubted whether Mr. Lincoln would have thought that the strength of government to maintain itself would be impressively vindicated by our confirming power of the state to expel a handful of children from school. Such oversimplification, so handy in political debate, often lacks the precision necessary to postulates of judicial reasoning. If validly applied to this problem, the utterance cited would resolve every issue of power in favor of those in authority and would require us to override every liberty thought to weaken or delay execution of their policies.

Government of limited power need not be anemic government. Assurance that rights are secure tends to diminish fear and jealousy of strong government, and by making us feel safe to live under it makes for its better support. Without promise of a limiting Bill of Rights it is doubtful if our Constitution could have mustered enough strength to enable its ratification. To enforce those rights today is not to choose weak government over strong government. It is only to adhere as a means of strength to individual freedom of mind in preference to officially disciplined uniformity for which history indicates a disappointing and disastrous end.

The subject now before us exemplifies this principle. Free public education, if faithful to the ideal of secular instruction and political neutrality, will not be partisan or enemy of any class, creed, party, or faction. If it is to impose any ideological discipline, however, each party or denomination must seek to control, or failing that, to weaken the influence of the educational system. Observance of the limitations of the Constitution will not weaken government in the field appropriate for its exercise.

2. It was also considered in the *Gobitis* case that functions of educational officers in states, counties and school districts were such that to interfere with their authority "would in effect make us the school board for the country."

The Fourteenth Amendment, as now applied to the States, protects the citizen against the State itself and all of its creatures—Boards of Education not excepted. These have, of course, important, delicate, and highly discretionary functions, but none that they may not perform within the limits of the Bill of Rights. That they are educating the young for citizenship is reason for scrupulous protection of constitutional freedoms of the individual, if we are not to strangle the free mind at its source and teach youth to discount important principles of our government as mere platitudes. [. . .]

3. The *Gobitis* opinion reasoned that this is a field "where courts possess no marked and certainly no controlling competence," that it is committed to the legislatures as well as the courts to guard cherished liberties and that it is constitutionally appropriate to "fight out the wise use of legislative authority in the forum of public opinion and before legislative assemblies rather than to transfer such a contest to

the judicial arena," since all the "effective means of inducing political changes are left free."

The very purpose of a Bill of Rights was to withdraw certain subjects from the vicissitudes of political controversy, to place them beyond the reach of majorities and officials and to establish them as legal principles to be applied by the courts. One's right to life, liberty, and property, to free speech, a free press, freedom of worship and assembly, and other fundamental rights may not be submitted to vote; they depend on the outcome of no elections. [. . .]

Nor does our duty to apply the Bill of Rights to assertions of official authority depend upon our possession of marked competence in the field where the invasion of rights occurs. True, the task of translating the majestic generalities of the Bill of Rights, conceived as part of the pattern of liberal government in the eighteenth century, into concrete restraints on officials dealing with the problems of the twentieth century, is one to disturb self-confidence. These principles grew in soil which also produced a philosophy that the individual was the center of society, that his liberty was attainable through mere absence of governmental restraints, and that government should be entrusted with few controls and only the mildest supervision over men's affairs. We must transplant these rights to a soil in which the laissez-faire concept or principle of non-interference has withered at least as to economic affairs, and social advancements are increasingly sought through closer integration of society and through expanded and strengthened governmental controls. [. . .]

4. Lastly, and this is the very heart of the *Gobitis* opinion, it reasons that "National unity is the basis of national security," that the authorities have "the right to select appropriate means for its attainment," and hence reaches the conclusion that such compulsory measures toward "national unity" are constitutional. Upon the verity of this assumption depends our answer in this case. [. . .]

Struggles to coerce uniformity of sentiment in support of some end thought essential to their time and country have been waged by many good as well as by evil men. Nationalism is a relatively recent phenomenon but at other times and places the ends have been racial or territorial security, support of a dynasty or regime, and particular plans for saving souls. As first and moderate methods to attain unity have failed, those bent on its accomplishment must resort to an ever-increasing severity. As governmental pressure toward unity becomes greater, so strife becomes more bitter as to whose unity it shall be. Probably no deeper division of our people could proceed from any provocation than from finding it necessary to choose what doctrine and whose program public educational officials shall compel youth to unite in embracing. Ultimate futility of such attempts to compel coherence is the lesson of every such effort from the Roman drive to stamp out Christianity as a disturber of its pagan unity, the Inquisition, as a means to religious and dynastic unity, the Siberian exiles as a means to Russian unity, down to the fast failing efforts of our present totalitarian enemies. Those who begin coercive elimination of dissent soon find themselves exterminating dissenters. Compulsory unification of opinion achieves only the unanimity of the graveyard.

It seems trite but necessary to say that the First Amendment to our Constitution was designed to avoid these ends by avoiding these beginnings. There is no mysticism in the American concept of the State or of the nature or origin of its authority. We set up government by consent of the governed, and the Bill of Rights denies those in power any legal opportunity to coerce that consent. Authority here is to be controlled by public opinion, not public opinion by authority.

The case is made difficult not because the principles of its decision are obscure but because the flag involved is our own. Nevertheless, we apply the limitations of the Constitution with no fear that freedom to be intellectually and spiritually diverse or even contrary will disintegrate the social organization. To believe that patriotism will not flourish if patriotic ceremonies are voluntary and spontaneous instead of a compulsory routine is to make an unflattering estimate of the appeal of our institutions to free minds. We can have intellectual individualism and the rich cultural diversities that we owe to exceptional minds only at the price of occasional eccentricity and abnormal attitudes. When they are so harmless to others or to the State as those we deal with here, the price is not too great. But freedom to differ is not limited to things that do not matter much. That would be a mere shadow of freedom. The test of its substance is the right to differ as to things that touch the heart of the existing order.

If there is any fixed star in our constitutional constellation, it is that no official, high or petty, can prescribe what shall be orthodox in politics, nationalism, religion, or other matters of opinion or force citizens to confess by word or act their faith therein. If there are any circumstances which permit an exception, they do not now occur to us.

We think the action of the local authorities in compelling the flag salute and pledge transcends constitutional limitations on their power and invades the sphere of intellect and spirit which it is the purpose of the First Amendment to our Constitution to reserve from all official control.

The decision of this Court in *Minersville School District v. Gobitis* and the holdings of those few per curiam decisions which preceded and foreshadowed it are overruled, and the judgment enjoining enforcement of the West Virginia Regulation is affirmed.

FELIX FRANKFURTER

West Virginia State Board of Education v. Barnette, Dissent (1943)

Mr. Justice FRANKFURTER, dissenting.

One who belongs to the most vilified and persecuted minority in history is not likely to be insensible to the freedoms guaranteed by our Constitution. Were my purely personal attitude relevant I should whole-heartedly associate myself with the general libertarian views in the Court's opinion, representing as they do the thought and action of a lifetime. But as judges we are neither Jew nor Gentile, neither Catholic nor agnostic. We owe equal attachment to the Constitution and are equally bound by our judicial obligations whether we derive our citizenship from the earliest or the latest immigrants to these shores. As a member of this Court I am not justified in writing my private notions of policy into the Constitution, no matter how deeply I may cherish them or how mischievous I may deem their disregard. The duty of a judge who must decide which of two claims before the Court shall prevail, that of a State to enact and enforce laws within its general competence or that of an individual to refuse obedience because of the demands of his conscience, is not that of the ordinary person. It can never be emphasized too much that one's own opinion about the wisdom or evil of a law should be excluded altogether when one is doing one's duty on the bench. The only opinion of our own even looking in that direction that is material is our opinion whether legislators could in reason have enacted such a law. In the light of all the circumstances, including the history of this question in this Court, it would require more daring than I possess to deny that reasonable legislators could have taken the action which is before us for review. Most unwillingly, therefore, I must differ from my brethren with regard to legislation like this. I cannot bring my mind to believe that the "liberty" secured by the Due Process Clause gives this Court authority to deny to the State of West Virginia the attainment of that which we all recognize as a legitimate legislative end, namely, the promotion of good citizenship, by employment of the means here chosen.

Not so long ago we were admonished that "the only check upon our own exercise of power is our own sense of self-restraint. For the removal of unwise laws from the statute books appeal lies, not to the courts, but to the ballot and to the processes of democratic government." [. . .]

The admonition that judicial self-restraint alone limits arbitrary exercise of our authority is relevant every time we are asked to nullify legislation. The Constitution does not give us greater veto power when dealing with one phase of "liberty" than with another, or when dealing with grade school regulations than with college regulations that offend conscience, as

was the case in *Hamilton v. Regents* [1934]. In neither situation is our function comparable to that of a legislature or are we free to act as though we were a super-legislature. Judicial self-restraint is equally necessary whenever an exercise of political or legislative power is challenged. There is no warrant in the constitutional basis of this Court's authority for attributing different roles to it depending upon the nature of the challenge to the legislation. Our power does not vary according to the particular provision of the Bill of Rights which is invoked. The right not to have property taken without just compensation has, so far as the scope of judicial power is concerned, the same constitutional dignity as the right to be protected against unreasonable searches and seizures, and the latter has no less claim than freedom of the press or freedom of speech or religious freedom. In no instance is this Court the primary protector of the particular liberty that is invoked. [. . .]

When Mr. Justice Holmes, speaking for this Court, wrote that "it must be remembered that legislatures are ultimate guardians of the liberties and welfare of the people in quite as great a degree as the courts," *Missouri, Kansas & Texas R. Co. v. May* [1904], he went to the very essence of our constitutional system and the democratic conception of our society. He did not mean that for only some phases of civil government this Court was not to supplant legislatures and sit in judgment upon the right or wrong of a challenged measure. He was stating the comprehensive judicial duty and role of this Court in our constitutional scheme whenever legislation is sought to be nullified on any ground, namely, that responsibility for legislation lies with legislatures, answerable as they are directly to the people, and this Court's only and very narrow function is to determine whether within the broad grant of authority vested in legislatures they have exercised a judgment for which reasonable justification can be offered.

The framers of the federal Constitution might have chosen to assign an active share in the process of legislation to this Court. They had before them the well-known example of New York's Council of Revision, which had been functioning since 1777. After stating that "laws inconsistent with the spirit of this constitution, or with the public good, may be hastily and unadvisedly passed," the state constitution made the judges of New York part of the legislative process by providing that "all bills which have passed the senate and assembly shall, before they become laws," be presented to a Council of which the judges constituted a majority, "for their revisal and consideration." Art. III, New York Constitution of 1777. Judges exercised this legislative function in New York for nearly fifty years. But the framers of the Constitution denied such legislative powers to the federal judiciary. They chose instead to insulate the judiciary from the legislative function. They did not grant to this Court supervision over legislation.

The reason why from the beginning even the narrow judicial authority to nullify legislation has been viewed with a jealous eye is that it serves to prevent the full play of the democratic process. The fact that it may be an undemocratic aspect of our scheme of government does not call for its rejection or its disuse. But it is the best of reasons, as this Court has frequently recognized, for the greatest caution in its use.

The precise scope of the question before us defines the limits of the constitutional power that is in issue. The State of West Virginia requires all pupils to share in the salute to the flag as part of school training in citizenship. The present action is one to enjoin the enforcement of this requirement by those in school attendance. We have not before us any attempt by the State to punish disobedient children or visit penal consequences on their parents. All that is in question is the right of the state to compel participation in this exercise by those who choose to attend the public schools.

We are not reviewing merely the action of a local school board. The flag salute requirement in this case comes before us with the full authority of the State of West Virginia. We are in fact passing judgment on "the power of the State as a whole." Practically we are passing upon the political power of each of the forty-eight states. Moreover, since the First Amendment has been read into the Fourteenth, our problem is precisely the same is it would be if we had before us an Act of Congress for the District of Columbia. To suggest that we are here concerned with the heedless action of some village tyrants is to distort the augustness of the constitutional issue and the reach of the consequences of our decision.

Under our constitutional system the legislature is charged solely with civil concerns of society. If the avowed or intrinsic legislative purpose is either to promote or to discourage some religious community or creed, it is clearly within the constitutional restrictions imposed on legislatures and cannot stand. But it by no means follows that legislative power is wanting whenever a general non-discriminatory civil regulation in fact touches conscientious scruples or religious beliefs of an individual or a group. Regard for such scruples or beliefs undoubtedly presents one of the most reasonable claims for the exertion of legislative accommodation. It is, of course, beyond our power to rewrite the state's requirement, by providing exemptions for those who do not wish to participate in the flag salute or by making some other accommodations to meet their scruples. That wisdom might suggest the making of such accommodations and that school administration would not find it too difficult to make them and yet maintain the ceremony for those not refusing to conform, is outside our province to suggest. Tact, respect, and generosity toward variant views will always commend themselves to those charged with the duties of legislation so as to achieve a maximum of good will and to require a minimum of unwilling submission to a general law. But the real question is, who is to make such accommodations, the courts or the legislature?

This is no dry, technical matter. It cuts deep into one's conception of the democratic process—it concerns no less the practical differences between the means for making these accommodations that are open to courts and to legislatures. A court can only strike down. It can only say "This or that law is void." It cannot modify or qualify, it cannot make exceptions to a general requirement. And it strikes down not merely for a day. At least the finding of unconstitutionality ought not to have ephemeral significance unless the Constitution is to be reduced to the fugitive importance of mere legislation. [. . .] If the function of this Court is to be essentially no different from that of a legislature, if the considerations governing constitutional construction are to be substantially those that underlie legislation, then indeed judges should not have life tenure and they should be made directly responsible to the electorate. [. . .]

Conscientious scruples, all would admit, cannot stand against every legislative compulsion to do positive acts in conflict with such scruples. We have been told that such compulsions override religious scruples only as to major concerns of the state. But the determination of what is major and what is minor itself raises questions of policy. For the way in which men equally guided by reason appraise importance goes to the very heart of policy. Judges should be very diffident in setting their judgment against that of a state in determining what is and what is not a major concern, what means are appropriate to proper ends, and what is the total social cost in striking the balance of imponderables.

What one can say with assurance is that the history out of which grew constitutional provisions for religious equality and the writings of the great exponents of religious freedom—Jefferson, Madison, John Adams, Benjamin Franklin—are totally wanting in justification for a claim by dissidents of exceptional immunity from civic measures of general applicability, measures not in fact disguised assaults upon such dissident views. The great leaders of the American Revolution were determined to remove political support from every religious establishment. They put on an equality the different religious sects—Episcopalians, Presbyterians, Catholics, Baptists, Methodists, Quakers, Huguenots—which, as dissenters, had been under the heel of the various orthodoxies that prevailed in different colonies. So far as the state was concerned, there was to be neither orthodoxy nor heterodoxy. And so Jefferson and those who followed him wrote guaranties of religious freedom into our constitutions. Religious minorities as well as religious majorities were to be equal in the eyes of the political state. But Jefferson and the others also knew that minorities may disrupt society. It never would have occurred to them to write into the Constitution the subordination of the general civil authority of the state to sectarian scruples.

The constitutional protection of religious freedom terminated disabilities, it did not create new privileges. It gave religious equality, not civil immunity. Its essence is freedom from conformity to religious dogma, not freedom from conformity to law because of religious dogma. Religious loyalties may be exercised without hindrance from the state, not the state may not exercise that which except by leave of religious loyalties is within the domain of temporal power. Otherwise each individual could set up his own censor against obedience to laws conscientiously deemed for the public good by those whose business it is to make laws.

The prohibition against any religious establishment by the government placed denominations on an equal footing—it assured freedom from support by the government to any mode of worship and the freedom of individuals to support any mode of worship. Any person may therefore believe or disbelieve what he pleases. He may practice what he will in his own house of worship or publicly within the limits of public order. But the lawmaking authority is not circumscribed by the variety of religious beliefs, otherwise the constitutional guaranty would be not a protection of the free exercise of religion but a denial of the exercise of legislation.

The essence of the religious freedom guaranteed by our Constitution is therefore this: no religion shall either receive the state's support or incur its hostility. Religion is outside the sphere of political government. This does not mean that all matters on which religious organizations or beliefs may pronounce are outside the sphere of government. Were this so, instead of the separation of church and state, there would be the subordination of the state on any matter deemed within the sovereignty of the religious conscience. Much that is the concern of temporal authority affects the spiritual interests of men. But it is not enough to strike down a non-discriminatory law that it may hurt or offend some dissident view. It would be too easy to cite numerous prohibitions and injunctions to which laws run counter if the variant interpretations of the Bible were made the tests of obedience to law. The validity of secular laws cannot be measured by their conformity to religious doctrines. It is only in a theocratic state that ecclesiastical doctrines measure legal right or wrong. [. . .]

The subjection of dissidents to the general requirement of saluting the flag, as a measure conducive to the training of children in good citizenship, is very far from being the first instance of exacting obedience to general laws that have offended deep religious scruples. Compulsory vaccination, food inspection regulations, the obligation to bear arms, testimonial duties, compulsory medical treatment—these are but illustrations of conduct that has often been compelled in the enforcement of legislation of general applicability even though the religious consciences of particular individuals rebelled at the exaction.

Law is concerned with external behavior and not with the inner life of man. It rests in large measure upon compulsion. Socrates lives in history partly because he gave his life for the conviction that duty of obedience to secular law does not presuppose consent to its enactment or belief in its virtue. The consent upon which free government rests is the consent that comes from sharing in the process of making and unmaking laws. The state is not shut out from a domain because the individual conscience may deny the state's claim. The individual conscience may profess what faith it chooses. It may affirm and promote that faith—in the language of the Constitution, it may "exercise" it freely—but it cannot thereby restrict community action through political organs in matters of community concern, so long as the action is not asserted in a discriminatory way either openly or by stealth. One may have the right to practice one's religion and at the same time owe the duty of formal obedience to laws that run counter to one's beliefs. Compelling belief implies denial of opportunity to combat it and to assert dissident views. Such compulsion is one thing. Quite another matter is submission to conformity of action while denying its wisdom or virtue and with ample opportunity for seeking its change or abrogation. [. . .]

We are told that a flag salute is a doubtful substitute for adequate understanding of our institutions. The states that require such a school exercise do not have to justify it as the only means for promoting good citizenship in children, but merely as one of diverse means for accomplishing a worthy end. We may deem it a foolish measure, but the point is that this Court is not the organ of government to resolve doubts as to whether it will fulfill its purpose. Only if there be no doubt that any reasonable mind could entertain can we deny to the states the right to resolve doubts their way and not ours. [. . .]

We are told that symbolism is a dramatic but primitive way of communicating ideas. Symbolism is inescapable. Even the most sophisticated live by symbols. But it is not for this Court to make psychological judgments as to the effectiveness of a particular symbol in inculcating concededly indispensable feelings, particularly if the state happens to see fit to utilize the symbol that represents our heritage and our hopes. And surely only flippancy could be responsible for the suggestion that constitutional validity of a requirement to salute our flag implies equal validity of a requirement to salute a dictator. The significance

of a symbol lies in what it represents. To reject the swastika does not imply rejection of the Cross. And so it bears repetition to say that it mocks reason and denies our whole history to find in the allowance of a requirement to salute our flag on fitting occasions the seeds of sanction for obeisance to a leader. To deny the power to employ educational symbols is to say that the state's educational system may not stimulate the imagination because this may lead to unwise stimulation. [. . .]

The flag salute exercise has no kinship whatever to the oath tests so odious in history. For the oath test was one of the instruments for suppressing heretical beliefs. [319 U. S. 624, 664] Saluting the flag suppresses no belief not curbs it. Children and their parents may believe what they please, avow their belief and practice it. It is not even remotely suggested that the requirement for saluting the flag involves the slightest restriction against the fullest opportunity on the part both of the children and of their parents to disavow as publicly as they choose to do so the meaning that others attach to the gesture of salute. All channels of affirmative free expression are open to both children and parents. Had we before us any act of the state putting the slightest curbs upon such free expression, I should not lag behind any member of this Court in striking down such an invasion of the right to freedom of thought and freedom of speech protected by the Constitution. [. . .]

One's conception of the Constitution cannot be severed from one's conception of a judge's function in applying it. The Court has no reason for existence if it merely reflects the pressures of the day. Our system is built on the faith that men set apart for this special function, freed from the influences of immediacy and form the deflections of worldly ambition, will become able to take a view of longer range than the period of responsibility entrusted to Congress and legislatures. We are dealing with matters as to which legislators and voters have conflicting views. Are we as judges to impose our strong convictions on where wisdom lies? That which three years ago had seemed to five successive Courts to lie within permissible areas of legislation is now outlawed by the deciding shift of opinion of two Justice. What reason is there to believe that they or their successors may not have another view a few years hence? Is that which was deemed to be of so fundamental a nature as to be written into the Constitution to endure for all times to be the sport of shifting winds of doctrine? Of course, judicial opinions, even as to questions of constitutionality, are not immutable. As has been true in the past, the Court will from time to time reverse its position. But I believe that never before these Jehovah's Witnesses cases (except for minor deviations subsequently retraced) has this Court overruled decisions so as to restrict the powers of democratic government. Always heretofore, it has withdrawn narrow views of legislative authority so as to authorize what formerly it had denied.

In view of this history it must be plain that what thirteen Justices found to be within the constitutional authority of a state, legislators can not be deemed unreasonable in enacting. Therefore, in denying to the states what heretofore has received such impressive judicial sanction, some other tests of unconstitutionality must surely be guiding the Court than the absence of a rational justification for the legislation. But I know of no other test which this Court is authorized to apply in nullifying legislation.

In the past this Court has from time to time set its views of policy against that embodied in legislation by finding laws in conflict with what was called the "spirit of the Constitution." Such undefined destructive power was not conferred on this Court by the Constitution. Before a duly enacted law can be judicially nullified, it must be forbidden by some explicit restriction upon political authority in the Constitution. Equally inadmissible is the claim to strike down legislation because to us as individuals it seems opposed to the "plan and purpose" of the Constitution. That is too tempting a basis for finding in one's personal views the purposes of the Founders.

The uncontrollable power wielded by this Court brings it very close to the most sensitive areas of public affairs. As appeal from legislation to adjudication becomes more frequent, and its consequences more far-reaching, judicial self-restraint becomes more and not less important, lest we unwarrantably enter social and political domains wholly outside our concern. I think I appreciate fully the objections to the law before us. But to deny that it presents a question upon which men might reasonably differ appears to me to be intolerance. And since men may so reasonably differ, I deem it beyond my constitutional power to assert my view of the wisdom of this law against the view of the State of West Virginia.

Jefferson's opposition to judicial review has not been accepted by history, but it still serves as an admonition against confusion between judicial and political functions. As a rule of judicial self-restraint, it is still as valid as Lincoln's admonition. For those who pass laws not only are under duty to pass laws. They are also under duty to observe the Constitution. And even though legislation relates to civil liberties, our duty of deference to those who have the responsibility for making the laws is no less relevant or less exacting. And this is so especially when we consider the accidental contingencies by which one man may determine constitutionality and thereby confine the political power of the Congress of the United States and the legislatures of forty-eight states. The attitude of judicial humility which these considerations enjoin is not an abdication of the judicial function. It is a due observance of its limits. Moreover, it is to be borne in mind that in a question like this we are not passing on the proper distribution of political power as between the states and the central government. We are not discharging the basic function of this Court as the mediator of powers within the federal system. To strike down a law like this is to deny a power to all government. [. . .]

Of course patriotism cannot be enforced by the flag salute. But neither can the liberal spirit be enforced by judicial invalidation of illiberal legislation. Our constant preoccupation with the constitutionality of legislation rather than with its wisdom tends to preoccupation of the American mind with a false value. The tendency of focusing attention on constitutionality is to make constitutionality synonymous with wisdom, to regard a law as all right if it is constitutional. Such an attitude is a great enemy of liberalism. Particularly in legislation affecting freedom of thought and freedom of speech much which should offend a free-spirited society is constitutional. Reliance for the most precious interests of civilization, therefore, must be found outside of their vindication in courts of law. Only a persistent positive translation of the faith of a free society into the convictions and habits and actions of a community is the ultimate reliance against unabated temptations to fetter the human spirit.

Learned Hand

Central Park Address (1944)

We have gathered here to affirm a faith, a faith in a common purpose, a common conviction, a common devotion. Some of us have chosen America as the land of our adoption; the rest have come from those who did the same. For this reason we have some right to consider ourselves a picked group, a group of those who had the courage to break from the past and brave the dangers and the loneliness of a strange land. What was the object that nerved us, or those who went before us, to this choice? We sought liberty; freedom from oppression, freedom from want, freedom to be ourselves. This we then sought; this we now believe that we are by way of winning. What do we mean when we say that first of all we seek liberty? I often wonder whether we do not rest our hopes too much upon constitutions, upon laws and upon courts. These are false hopes; believe me, these are false hopes. Liberty lies in the hearts of men and women; when it dies there, no constitution, no law, no court can even do much to help it. While it lies there it needs no constitution, no law, no court to save it. And what is this liberty which must lie in the hearts of men and women? It is not the ruthless, the unbridled will; it is not freedom to do as one likes. That is the denial of liberty, and leads straight to its overthrow. A society in which men recognize no check upon their freedom soon becomes a society where freedom is the possession of only a savage few; as we have learned to our sorrow.

What then is the spirit of liberty? I cannot define it; I can only tell you my own faith. The spirit of liberty is the spirit which is not too sure that it is right; the spirit of liberty is the spirit which seeks to understand the mind of other men and women; the spirit of liberty is the spirit which weighs their interests alongside its own without bias; the spirit of liberty remembers that not even a sparrow falls to earth unheeded; the spirit of liberty is the spirit of Him who, near two thousand years ago, taught mankind that lesson it has never learned but never quite forgotten; that there may be a kingdom where the least shall be heard and considered side by side with the greatest. And now in that spirit, that spirit of an America which has never been, and which may never be; nay, which never will be except as the conscience and courage of Americans create it; yet in the spirit of that America which lies hidden in some form in the aspirations of us all; in the spirit of that America for which our young men are at this moment fighting and dying; in that spirit of liberty and of America I ask you to rise and with me pledge our faith in the glorious destiny of our beloved country.

Felix Frankfurter

Adamson v. California, Concurrence (1947)

Mr. Justice Frankfurter (concurring).

For historical reasons a limited immunity from the common duty to testify was written into the Federal Bill of Rights, and I am prepared to agree that, as part of that immunity, comment on the failure of an accused to take the witness stand is forbidden in federal prosecutions. It is so, of course, by explicit act of Congress. 20 Stat. 30, 28 U.S.C.A. 632. But to suggest that such a limitation can be drawn out of "due process" in its protection of ultimate decency in a civilized society is to suggest that the Due Process Clause fastened fetters of unreason upon the States. [. . .]

Between the incorporation of the Fourteenth Amendment into the Constitution and the beginning of the present membership of the Court—a period of 70 years—the scope of that Amendment was passed upon by 43 judges. Of all these judges, only one, who may respectfully be called an eccentric exception, ever indicated the belief that the Fourteenth Amendment was a shorthand summary of the first eight Amendments theretofore limiting only the Federal Government, and that due process incorporated those eight Amendments as restrictions upon the powers of the States. Among these judges were not only those who would have to be included among the greatest in the history of the Court, but—it is especially relevant to note—they included those whose services in the cause of human rights and the spirit of freedom are the most conspicuous in our history. It is not invidious to single out Miller, Davis, Bradley, Waite, Matthews, Gray, Fuller, Holmes, Brandeis, Stone and Cardozo (to speak only of the dead) as judges who were alert in safeguarding and promoting the interests of liberty and human dignity through law. But they were also judges mindful of the relation of our federal system to a progressively democratic society and therefore duly regardful of the scope of authority that was left to the States even after the Civil War. And so they did not find that the Fourteenth Amendment, concerned as it was with matters fundamental to the pursuit of justice, fastened upon the States procedural arrangements which, in the language of Mr. Justice Cardozo, only those who are "narrow or provincial" would deem essential to "a fair and enlightened system of justice." *Palko v. Connecticut* [1937]. To suggest that it is inconsistent with a truly free society to begin prosecutions without an indictment, to try petty civil cases without the paraphernalia of a common law jury, to take into consideration that one who has full opportunity to make a defense remains silent is, in de Tocqueville's phrase, to confound the familiar with the necessary.

The short answer to the suggestion that the provision of the Fourteenth Amendment, which ordains "nor shall any State deprive any person of life, liberty,

or property, without due process of law," was a way of saying that every State must thereafter initiate prosecutions through indictment by a grand jury, must have a trial by a jury of 12 in criminal cases, and must have trial by such a jury in common law suits where the amount in controversy exceeds $20, is that it is a strange way of saying it. It would be extraordinarily strange for a constitution to convey such specific commands in such a roundabout and inexplicit way. After all, an amendment to the Constitution should be read in a "sense most obvious to the common understanding at the time of its adoption. For it was for public adoption that it was proposed." See Mr. Justice Holmes in *Eisner v. Macomber* [1920]. Those reading the English language with the meaning which it ordinarily conveys, those conversant with the political and legal history of the concept of due process, those sensitive to the relations of the States to the central government as well as the relation of some of the provisions of the Bill of Rights to the process of justice, would hardly recognize the Fourteenth Amendment as a cover for the various explicit provisions of the first eight Amendments. Some of these are enduring reflections of experience with human nature, while some express the restricted views of Eighteenth-Century England regarding the best methods for the ascertainment of facts. The notion that the Fourteenth Amendment was a covert way of imposing upon the States all the rules which it seemed important to Eighteenth Century statesmen to write into the Federal Amendments, was rejected by judges who were themselves witnesses of the process by which the Fourteenth Amendment became part of the Constitution. Arguments that may now be adduced to prove that the first eight Amendments were concealed within the historic phrasing of the Fourteenth Amendment were not unknown at the time of its adoption. A surer estimate of their bearing was possible for judges at the time than distorting distance is likely to vouchsafe. Any evidence of design or purpose not contemporaneously known could hardly have influenced those who ratified the Amendment. Remarks of a particular proponent of the Amendment, no matter how influential, are not to be deemed part of the Amendment. What was submitted for ratification was his proposal, not his speech. Thus, at the time of the ratification of the Fourteenth Amendment the constitutions of nearly half of the ratifying States did not have the rigorous requirements of the Fifth Amendment for instituting criminal proceedings through a grand jury. It could hardly have occurred to these States that by ratifying the Amendment they uprooted their established methods for prosecuting crime and fastened upon themselves a new prosecutorial system.

Indeed, the suggestion that the Fourteenth Amendment incorporates the first eight Amendments as such is not unambiguously urged. Even the boldest innovator would shrink from suggesting to more than half the States that they may no longer initiate prosecutions without indictment by grand jury, or that thereafter all the States of the Union must furnish a jury of 12 for every case involving a claim above $20. There is suggested merely a selective incorporation of the first eight Amendments into the Fourteenth Amendment. Some are in and some are out, but we are left in the dark as to which are in and which are out. Nor are we given the calculus for determining which go in and which stay out. If the basis of selection is merely that those provisions of the first eight Amendments are incorporated which commend themselves to individual justices as indispensable to the dignity and happiness of a free man, we are thrown back to a merely subjective test. The protection against unreasonable search and seizure might have primacy for one judge, while trial by a jury of 12 for every claim above $20 might appear to another as an ultimate need in a free society. In the history of thought "natural law" has a much longer and much better founded meaning and justification than such subjective selection of the first eight Amendments for incorporation into the Fourteenth. If all that is meant is that due process contains within itself certain minimal standards which are "of the very essence of a scheme of ordered liberty," *Palko v. Connecticut*, putting upon this Court the duty of applying these standards from time to time, then we have merely arrived at the insight which our predecessors long ago expressed. [. . .] This guidance bids us to be duly mindful of the heritage of the past, with its great lessons of how liberties are won and how they are lost. As judges charged with the delicate task of subjecting the government of a continent to the Rule of Law we must be particularly mindful that it is "a constitution we are expounding," so that it should not be imprisoned in what are merely legal forms even though they have the sanction of the Eighteenth Century.

It may not be amiss to restate the pervasive function of the Fourteenth Amendment in exacting from the States observance of basic liberties. The Amendment neither comprehends the specific provisions by which the founders deemed it appropriate to restrict the federal government nor is it confined to them. The Due Process Clause of the Fourteenth Amendment has an independent potency, precisely as does the Due Process Clause of the Fifth Amendment in relation to the Federal Government. It ought not to require argument to reject the notion that due process of law meant one thing in the Fifth Amendment and another in the Fourteenth. The Fifth Amendment specifically prohibits prosecution of an "infamous crime" except upon indictment; it forbids double jeopardy; it bars compelling a person to be a witness against himself in any criminal case; it precludes deprivation of "life, liberty, or property, without due process of law." Are Madison and his contemporaries in the framing of the Bill of Rights to be charged with writing into it a meaningless clause? To consider "due process of law" as merely a shorthand statement of other specific clauses in the same amendment is to attribute to the authors and proponents of this Amendment ignorance of, or indifference to, a historic conception which was one of the great instruments in the arsenal of constitutional freedom which the Bill of Rights was to protect and strengthen. A construction which gives to due process no independent function but turns it into a summary of the specific provisions of the Bill of Rights would, as has been noted, tear up by the roots much of the fabric of law in the several States, and would deprive the States of opportunity for reforms in legal process designed for extending the area of freedom. It would assume that no other abuses would reveal themselves in the course of time than those which had become manifest in 1791. Such a view not only disregards the historic meaning of "due process." It leads inevitably to a warped construction of specific provisions of the Bill of Rights to bring within their scope conduct clearly condemned by due process but not easily fitting into the pigeon-holes of the specific provisions. It seems pretty late in the day to suggest that a phrase so laden with historic meaning should be given an improvised content consisting of some but not all of the provisions of the first eight Amendments, selected on an undefined basis, with improvisation of content for the provisions so selected.

And so, when, as in a case like the present, a conviction in a State court is here for review under a claim that a right protected by the Due Process Clause of the Fourteenth Amendment has been denied, the issue is not whether an infraction of one of the specific provisions of the first eight Amendments is disclosed by the record. The relevant question is whether the criminal proceedings which resulted in conviction deprived the accused of the due process of law to which the United States Constitution entitled him. Judicial review of that guaranty of the Fourteenth Amendment inescapably imposes upon this Court an exercise of judgment upon the whole course of the proceedings in order to ascertain whether they offend those canons of decency and fairness which express the notions of justice of English-speaking peoples even toward those charged with the most heinous offenses. These standards of justice are not authoritatively formulated anywhere as though they were prescriptions in a pharmacopoeia. But neither does the application of the Due Process Clause imply that judges are wholly at large. The judicial judgment in applying the Due Process Clause must move within the limits of accepted notions of justice and is not to be based upon the idiosyncrasies of a merely personal judgment. The fact that judges among themselves may differ whether in a particular case a trial offends accepted notions of justice is not disproof that general rather than idiosyncratic standards are applied. An important safeguard against such merely individual judgment is an alert deference to the judgment of the State court under review.

Hugo Black

Adamson v. California, Dissent (1947)

Mr. Justice Black, dissenting.

The appellant was tried for murder in a California state court. He did not take the stand as a witness in his own behalf. The prosecuting attorney, under purported authority of a California statute, argued to the jury that an inference of guilt could be drawn because of appellant's failure to deny evidence offered against him. The appellant's contention in the state court and here has been that the statute denies him a right guaranteed by the Federal Constitution. The argument is that (1) permitting comment upon his failure to testify has the effect of compelling him to testify so as to violate that provision of the Bill of Rights contained in the Fifth Amendment that "No person shall be compelled in any criminal case to be a witness against himself"; and (2) although this provision of the Fifth Amendment originally applied only as a restraint upon federal courts, *Barron v. Baltimore* [1833], the Fourteenth Amendment was intended to, and did make the prohibition against compelled testimony applicable to trials in state courts. The Court refuses to meet and decide the appellant's first contention. But while the Court's opinion, as I read it, strongly implies that the Fifth Amendment does not, of itself, bar comment upon failure to testify in federal courts, the Court nevertheless assumes that it does in order to reach the second constitutional question involved in appellant's case. I must consider the case on the same assumption that the Court does. For the discussion of the second contention turns out to be a decision which reaches far beyond the relatively narrow issues on which this case might have turned.

This decision reasserts a constitutional theory spelled out in *Twining v. New Jersey* [1908], that this Court is endowed by the Constitution with boundless power under "natural law" periodically to expand and contract constitutional standards to conform to the Court's conception of what at a particular time constitutes "civilized decency" and "fundamental principles of liberty and justice." Invoking this *Twining* rule, the Court concludes that although comment upon testimony in a federal court would violate the Fifth Amendment, identical comment in a state court does not violate today's fashion in civilized decency and fundamentals and is therefore not prohibited by the Federal Constitution as amended.

The *Twining* case was the first, as it is the only decision of this Court, which has squarely held that states were free, notwithstanding to Fifth and Fourteenth Amendments, to extort evidence from one accused of crime. I agree that if *Twining* be reaffirmed, the result reached might appropriately follow. But I would not reaffirm the *Twining* decision. I think that decision and the "natural law" theory of the Constitution upon which it relies, degrade the constitutional safeguards of the Bill of Rights and simultaneously appropriate for this Court a broad power which we are not authorized by the Constitution to exercise. Furthermore, the *Twining* decision rested on previous cases and broad hypotheses which have been undercut by intervening decisions of this Court. [. . .]

The first 10 amendments were proposed and adopted largely because of fear that Government might unduly interfere with prized individual liberties. The people wanted and demanded a Bill of Rights written into their Constitution. The amendments embodying the Bill of Rights were intended to curb all branches of the Federal Government in the fields touched by the amendments—Legislative, Executive, and Judicial. The Fifth, Sixth, and Eighth Amendments were pointedly aimed at confining exercise of power by courts and judges within precise boundaries, particularly in the procedure used for the trial of criminal cases. Past history provided strong reasons for the apprehensions which brought these procedural amendments into being and attest the wisdom of their adoption. For the fears of arbitrary court action sprang largely from the past use of courts in the imposition of criminal punishments to suppress speech, press, and religion. Hence the constitutional limitations of courts' powers were, in the view of the Founders, essential supplements to the First Amendment, which was itself designed to protect the widest scope for all people to believe and to express the most divergent political, religious, and other views.

But these limitations were not expressly imposed upon state court action. In 1833, *Barron v. Baltimore* was decided by this Court. It specifically held inapplicable to the states that provision of the Fifth Amendment which declares: "nor shall private property be taken for public use, without just compensation." In deciding the particular point raised, the Court there said that it could not hold that the first eight amendments applied to the states. This was the controlling constitutional rule when the Fourteenth Amendment was proposed in 1866.

My study of the historical events that culminated in the Fourteenth Amendment, and the expressions of those who sponsored and favored, as well as those who opposed its submission and passage, persuades me that one of the chief objects that the provisions of the Amendment's first section, separately, and as a whole, were intended to accomplish was to make the Bill of Rights, applicable to the states. With full knowledge of the import of the *Barron* decision, the framers and backers of the Fourteenth Amendment proclaimed its purpose to be to overturn the constitutional rule that case had announced. This historical purpose has never received full consideration or exposition in any opinion of this Court interpreting the Amendment. [. . .]

For this reason, I am attaching to this dissent, an appendix which contains a resume, by no means complete, of the Amendment's history. In my judgment that history conclusively demonstrates that the language of the first section of the Fourteenth Amendment, taken as a whole, was thought by those responsible for its submission to the people, and by those who opposed its submission, sufficiently explicit to guarantee that thereafter no state could deprive its citizens of the privileges and protections of the Bill of Rights. Whether this Court ever will, or whether it now should, in the light of past decisions, give full effect to what the Amendment was intended to accomplish is not necessarily essential to a decision here. However that may be, our prior decisions, including *Twining*, do not prevent our carrying out that purpose, at least to the extent of making applicable to the states, not a mere part, as the Court has, but the full protection of the Fifth Amendment's provision against compelling evidence from an accused to convict him of crime. And I further contend that the "natural law" formula which the Court uses to reach its conclusion in this case should be abandoned as an incongruous excrescence on our Constitution. I believe that formula to be itself a violation of our Constitution, in that it subtly conveys to courts, at the expense of legislatures, ultimate power over public policies in fields where no specific provision of the Constitution limits legislative power. And my belief seems to be in accord with the views expressed by this Court, at least for the first two decades after the Fourteenth Amendment was adopted.

In 1872, four years after the Amendment was adopted, the *Slaughter-House Cases* came to this Court. The Court was not presented in that case with the evidence which showed that the special sponsors of the Amendment in the House and Senate had expressly explained one of its principal purposes to be to change the Constitution as construed in *Barron v. Baltimore,* and make the Bill of Rights applicable to the states. Nor was there reason to do so. For the state law under consideration in the *Slaughter-House Cases* was only challenged as one which authorized a monopoly, and the brief for the challenger properly conceded that there was "no direct constitutional provision against a monopoly." The argument did not invoke any specific provision of the Bill of Rights, but urged that the state monopoly statute violated "the natural right of a person" to do business and engage in his trade or vocation. On this basis, it was contended that "bulwarks that have been erected around the investments of capital are impregnable against state legislation." These natural law arguments, so suggestive of the premises on which the present due process formula rest, were flatly rejected by a majority of the Court in the *Slaughter-House Cases.* What the Court did hold was that the privileges and immunities clause of the Fourteenth Amendment only protected from state invasion such rights as a person has because he is a citizen of the United States. The Court enumerated some, but refused to enumerate all of these national rights. The majority of the Court emphatically declined the invitation of counsel to hold that the Fourteenth Amendment subjected all state regulatory legislation to continuous censorship by this Court in order for it to determine whether it collided with this Court's opinion of "natural" right and justice. In effect, the *Slaughter-House Cases*

rejected the very natural justice formula the Court today embraces. The Court did not meet the question of whether the safeguards of the Bill of Rights were protected against state invasion by the Fourteenth Amendment. And it specifically did not say as the Court now does, that particular provisions of the Bill of Rights could be breached by states in part, but not breached in other respects, according to this Court's notions of "civilized standards," "canons of decency," and "fundamental justice."

Later, but prior to the *Twining* case, this Court decided that the following were not "privileges or immunities" of national citizenship, so as to make them immune against state invasion: the Eighth Amendment's prohibition against cruel and unusual punishment; the Seventh Amendment's guarantee of a jury trial in civil cases; the Second Amendment's "right of the people to keep and bear arms; the Fifth and Sixth Amendments" requirements for indictment in capital or other infamous crimes, and for trial by jury in criminal prosecutions. While it can be argued that these cases implied that no one of the provisions of the Bill of Rights was made applicable to the states as attributes of national citizenship, no one of them expressly so decided. [. . .]

After the *Slaughter-House* decision, the Court also said that states could, despite the "due process" clause of the Fourteenth Amendment, take private property without just compensation; abridge the freedom of assembly guaranteed by the First Amendment; prosecute for crime by information rather than indictment; regulate the price for storage of grain in warehouses and elevators, *Munn v. Illinois* [1876]. But this Court also held in a number of cases that colored people must, because of the Fourteenth Amendment, be accorded equal protection of the laws. See, e.g., *Strauder v. West Virginia* [1879]; *Virginia v. Rives* [1879].

Thus, up to and for some years after 1873, when *Munn v. Illinois, supra,* was decided, this Court steadfastly declined to invalidate states' legislative regulation of property rights or business practices under the Fourteenth Amendment unless there were racial discrimination involved in the state law challenged. The first significant breach in this policy came in 1889, in *Chicago, M. & St. P.R. Co. v. Minnesota.* A state's railroad rate regulatory statute was there stricken as violative of the Due Process Clause of the Fourteenth Amendment. This was accomplished by reference to a due process formula which did not necessarily operate so as to protect the Bill of Rights' personal liberty safeguards, but which gave a new and hitherto undiscovered scope for the Court's use of the Due Process Clause to protect property rights under natural law concepts. And in 1896, in *Chicago, B. & Q.R. Co. v. Chicago*, this Court, in effect, overruled *Davidson v. New Orleans* [1877], by holding, under the new due process-natural law formula, that the Fourteenth Amendment forbade a state from taking private property for public use without payment of just compensation.

Following the pattern of the new doctrine formalized in the foregoing decisions, the Court in 1896 applied the Due Process Clause to strike down a state statute which had forbidden certain types of contracts. *Allgeyer v. Louisiana*. In doing so, it substantially adopted the rejected argument of counsel in the *Slaughter-House Cases*, that the Fourteenth Amendment guarantees the liberty of all persons under "natural law" to engage in their chosen business or vocation. In the *Allgeyer* opinion, the Court quoted with approval the concurring opinion of Mr. Justice Bradley in a second *Slaughter-House Case*; *Butchers' Unions Co. v. Crescent City Co.* [1884], which closely followed one phase of the argument of his dissent in the original *Slaughter-House Cases*— not that phase which argued that the Bill of Rights was applicable to the States. And in 1905, three years before the *Twining* case, *Lochner v. New York*, followed the argument used in *Allgeyer* to hold that the Due Process Clause was violated by a state statute which limited the employment of bakery workers to 60 hours per week and 10 hours per day.

The foregoing constitutional doctrine, judicially created and adopted by expanding the previously accepted meaning of "due process," marked a complete departure from the *Slaughter-House* philosophy of judicial tolerance of state regulation of business activities. Conversely, the new formula contracted the effectiveness of the Fourteenth Amendment as a protection from state infringement of individual liberties enumerated in the Bill of Rights. Thus the Court's second-thought interpretation of the Amendment was an about face from the *Slaughter-House* interpretation and represented a failure to carry out the avowed purpose of the Amendment's sponsors.

This reversal is dramatized by the fact that the *Hurtado* case, which had rejected the Due Process Clause as an instrument for preserving Bill of Rights liberties and privileges, was cited as authority for expanding the scope of that clause so as to permit this Court to invalidate all state regulatory legislation it believed to be contrary to "fundamental" principles.

The *Twining* decision, rejecting the compelled testimony clause of the Fifth Amendment, and indeed rejecting all the Bill of Rights, is the end product of one phase of this philosophy. At the same time, that decision consolidated the power of the Court assumed in past cases by laying broader foundations for the Court to invalidate state and even federal regulatory legislation. For the *Twining* decision, giving separate consideration to "due process" and "privileges or immunities," went all the way to say that the "privileges or immunities" clause of the Fourteenth Amendment "did not forbid the states to abridge the personal rights enumerated in the first eight Amendments." And in order to be certain, so far as possible, to leave this Court wholly free to reject all the Bill of Rights as specific restraints upon state actions, the decision declared that even if this Court should decide that the Due Process Clause forbids the states to infringe personal liberties guaranteed by the Bill of Rights, it would do so, not "because those rights are enumerated in the first eight Amendments, but because they are of such a nature that they are included in the conception of due process of law." [. . .]

At the same time that the *Twining* decision held that the states need not conform to the specific provisions of the Bill of Rights, it consolidated the power that the Court had assumed under the Due Process Clause by laying even broader foundations for the Court to invalidate state and even federal regulatory legislation. For under the *Twining* formula, which includes nonregard for the first eight amendments, what are "fundamental rights" and in accord with "canons of decency," as the Court said in *Twining*, and today reaffirms, is to be independently "ascertained from time to time by judicial action." Thus the power of legislatures became what this Court would declare it to be at a particular time independently of the specific guarantees of the Bill of Rights such as the right to freedom of speech, religion and assembly, the right to just compensation for property taken for a public purpose, the right to jury trial or the right to be secure against unreasonable searches and seizures. Neither the contraction of the Bill of Rights safeguards nor the invalidation of regulatory laws by this Court's appraisal of "circumstances" would readily be classified as the most satisfactory contribution of this Court to the nation. [. . .]

In *Palko v. Connecticut*, a case which involved former jeopardy only, this Court re-examined the path it had traveled in interpreting the Fourteenth Amendment since the *Twining* opinion was written. In *Twining* the Court had declared that none of the rights enumerated in the first eight amendments were protected against state invasion because they were incorporated in the Bill of Rights. But the Court in *Palko*, answered a contention that all eight applied with the more guarded statement, [. . .] that "there is no such general rule." Implicit in this statement, and in the cases decided in the interim between *Twining* and *Palko* and since, is the understanding that some of the eight amendments do apply by their very terms. Thus the Court said in the *Palko* case that the Fourteenth Amendment may make it unlawful for a state to abridge by its statutes the "freedom of speech which the First Amendment safeguards against encroachment by the Congress or the like freedom of the press or the free exercise of religion, or the right of peaceable assembly or the right of one accused of crime to the benefit of counsel. In these and other situations immunities that are valid as against the federal government by force of the specific pledges of particular amendments have been found to be implicit in the concept of ordered liberty, and thus, through the Fourteenth Amendment, become valid as against the states." [. . .] In the *Twining* case fundamental liberties were things apart from the Bill of Rights. Now it appears that at least some of the provisions of the Bill of Rights in their very terms satisfy the Court as sound and meaningful expressions of fundamental liberty. If the Fifth Amendment's protection against self-incrimination be such an expression of fundamental liberty, I ask, and have not found a satisfactory answer, why the Court today should consider that it should be "absorbed" in part but not in full? Nothing in the *Palko* opinion requires that when the Court decides that a Bill of Rights' provision is to be applied to the States, it is to be applied piecemeal. Nothing in the *Palko*

opinion recommends that the Court apply part of an amendment's established meaning and discard that part which does not suit the current style of fundamentals.

The Court's opinion in *Twining*, and the dissent in that case, made it clear that the Court intended to leave the states wholly free to compel confessions, so far as the Federal Constitution is concerned. Yet in a series of cases since *Twining* this Court has held that the Fourteenth Amendment does bar all American courts, state or federal, from convicting people of crime on coerced confessions. Federal courts cannot do so because of the Fifth Amendment. And state courts cannot do so because the principles of the Fifth Amendment are made applicable to the States through the Fourteenth by one formula or another. And taking note of these cases, the Court is careful to point out in its decision today that coerced confessions violate the Federal Constitution if secured "by fear of hurt, torture or exhaustion." Nor can a state, according to today's decision, constitutionally compel an accused to testify against himself by "any other type of coercion that falls within the scope of due process." Thus the Court itself destroys or at least drastically curtails the very *Twining* decision it purports to reaffirm. It repudiates the foundation of that opinion, which presented much argument to show that compelling a man to testify against himself does not "violate" a "fundamental" right or privilege.

It seems rather plain to me why the Court today does not attempt to justify all of the broad *Twining* discussion. That opinion carries its own refutation on what may be called the factual issue the Court resolved. The opinion itself shows, without resort to the powerful argument in the dissent of Mr. Justice Harlan, that outside of Star Chamber practices and influences, the "English-speaking" peoples have for centuries abhorred and feared the practice of compelling people to convict themselves of crime. I shall not attempt to narrate the reasons. They are well known. [. . .] Nor does the history of the practice of compelling testimony in this country, relied on in the *Twining* opinion support the degraded rank which that opinion gave the Fifth Amendment's privilege against compulsory self-incrimination. I think the history there recited by the Court belies its conclusion. The Court in *Twining* evidently was forced to resort for its degradation of the privilege to the fact that Governor Winthrop in trying Mrs. Ann Hutchison in 1637 was evidently "not aware of any privilege against self-incrimination or conscious of any duty to respect it." Of course not. Mrs. Hutchison was tried, if trial it can be called, for holding unorthodox religious views. People with a consuming belief that their religious convictions must be forced on others rarely ever believe that the unorthodox have any rights which should or can be rightfully respected. As a result of her trial and compelled admissions, Mrs. Hutchison was found guilty of unorthodoxy and banished from Massachusetts. The lamentable experience of Mrs. Hutchison and others, contributed to the overwhelming sentiment that demanded adoption of a constitutional Bill of Rights. The founders of this Government wanted no more such "trials" and punishments as Mrs. Hutchison had to undergo. They wanted to erect barriers that would bar legislators from passing laws that encroached on the domain of belief, and that would, among other things, strip courts and all public officers of a power to compel people to testify against themselves.

I cannot consider the Bill of Rights to be an outworn 18th Century "strait jacket" as the *Twining* opinion did. Its provisions may be thought outdated abstractions by some. And it is true that they were designed to meet ancient evils. But they are the same kind of human evils that have emerged from century to century wherever excessive power is sought by the few at the expense of the many. In my judgment the people of no nation can lose their liberty so long as a Bill of Rights like ours survives and its basic purposes are conscientiously interpreted, enforced and respected so as to afford continuous protection against old, as well as new, devices and practices which might thwart those purposes. I fear to see the consequences of the Court's practice of substituting its own concepts of decency and fundamental justice for the language of the Bill of Rights as its point of departure in interpreting and enforcing that Bill of Rights. If the choice must be between the selective process of the *Palko* decision applying some of the Bill of Rights to the States, or the *Twining* rule applying none of them, I would choose the *Palko* selective process. But rather than accept either of these choices. I would follow what I believe was the original purpose of the Fourteenth Amendment—to extend to all the people of the nation the complete protection of the Bill of Rights. To hold that this Court can determine what, if any, provisions of the Bill of Rights will be enforced, and if so to what degree, is to frustrate the great design of a written Constitution. Conceding the possibility that this Court is now wise enough to improve on the Bill of Rights by substituting natural law concepts for the Bill of Rights. I think the possibility is entirely too speculative to agree to take that course. I would therefore hold in this case that the full protection of the Fifth Amendment's proscription against compelled testimony must be afforded by California. This I would do because of reliance upon the original purpose of the Fourteenth Amendment.

BERNARD BARUCH

Address before the United Nations (1946)

We are here to make a choice between the quick and the dead.

That is our business.

Behind the black portent of the new atomic age lies a hope which, seized upon with faith, can work our salvation. If we fail, then we have damned every man to be the slave of fear. Let us not deceive ourselves: We must elect world peace or world destruction.

Science has torn from nature a secret so vast in its potentialities that our minds cower from the terror it creates. Yet terror is not enough to inhibit the use of the atomic bomb. The terror created by weapons has never stopped man from employing them. For each new weapon a defense has been produced, in time. But now we face a condition in which adequate defense does not exist.

Science, which gave us this dread power, shows that it can be made a giant help to humanity, but science does not show us how to prevent its baleful use. So we have been appointed to obviate that peril by finding a meeting of the minds and the hearts of our peoples. Only in the will of mankind lies the answer.

In this crisis we represent not only our governments but, in a larger way, we represent the peoples of the world. We must remember that the peoples do not belong to the governments, but that the governments belong to the peoples. We must answer their demands; we must answer the world's longing for peace and security.

In that desire the United States shares ardently and hopefully. The search of science for the absolute weapon has reached fruition in this country. But she stands ready to proscribe and destroy this instrument—to lift its use from death to life—if the world will join in a pact to that end.

In our success lies the promise of a new life, freed from the heart-stopping fears that now beset the world. The beginning of victory for the great ideals for which millions have bled and died lies in building a workable plan. Now we approach the fulfillment of the aspirations of mankind. At the end of the road lies the fairer, better, surer life we crave and mean to have.

Only by a lasting peace are liberties and democracies strengthened and depended. War is their enemy. And it will not do to believe that any of us can escape war's devastation. Victor, vanquished and neutrals alike are affected physically, economically and morally.

Against the degradation of war we can erect a safeguard. That is the *guerdon* for which we reach. Within the scope of the formula we outline here, there will be found, to those who seek it, the essential elements of our purpose. Others will see only emptiness. Each of us carries his own mirror in which is reflected hope—or determined desperation—courage or cowardice.

There is famine throughout the world today. It starves men's bodies. But there is a greater famine—the hunger of men's spirit. That starvation can be cured by the conquest of fear, and the substitution of hope, from which springs faith—faith in each other; faith that we want to work together toward salvation; and determination that those who threaten the peace and safety shall be punished.

The peoples of these democracies gathered here have a particular concern with our answer, for their peoples hate war. They will have a heavy exaction to make of those who fail to provide an escape. They are not afraid of an internationalism that protects; they are unwilling to be fobbed off by mouthings about narrow sovereignty, which its today's phrase for yesterday's isolationism.

The basis of a sound foreign policy, in this new age, for all the nations here gathered, is that: anything that happens, no matter where or how, which menaces the peace of the world, or the economic stability, concerns each and all of us.

That, roughly, may be said to be the central theme of the United Nations. It is with that thought we gain consideration of the most important subject that can engage mankind—life itself.

Now, if ever, is the time to act for the common good. Public opinion supports a world movement toward security. If I read the signs aright, the peoples want a program, not composed merely of pious thoughts, but of enforceable sanctions—an international law with teeth in it.

We, of this nation, desirous of helping to bring peace to the world and realizing the heavy obligations upon us, arising from our possession of the means for producing the bomb and from the fact that it is part of our armament, are prepared to make our full contribution toward effective control of atomic energy.

But before a country is ready to relinquish any winning weapons, it must have more than words to reassure it. It must have a guarantee of safety, not only against the offenders in the atomic area, but against the illegal users of other weapons—bacteriological, biological, gas—perhaps—why not?—against war itself.

In the elimination of war lies our solution, for only then will nations cease to compete with one another in the production and use of dread "secret" weapons which are evaluated soley by their capacity to kill. This devilish program takes us back not merely to the Dark Ages, but from cosmos to chaos. If we succeed in finding a suitable way to control atomic weapons adaptable to mass destruction: when a man learns to say "A" he can, if he chooses, learn the rest of the alphabet too.

Let this be anchored in our minds:

Peace is never long preserved by weight of metal or by an armament race. Peace can be made tranquil and secure only by understanding and agreement fortified by sanctions. We must embrace international cooperation or international disintegration.

Science has taught us how to put the atom to work. But to make it work for good instead of for evil lies in the domain dealing with the principles of human duty. We are now facing a problem more of ethics than physics.

The solution will require apparent sacrifice in pride and in position, but better pain as the price of peace than death as the price of war. [. . .]

ELEANOR ROOSEVELT

The Struggle for Human Rights (1948)

I have come this evening to talk with you on one of the greatest issues of our time—that is the preservation of human freedom. I have chosen to discuss it here in France, at the Sorbonne, because here in this soil the roots of human freedom have long ago struck deep and here they have been richly nourished. It was here the Declaration of the Rights of Man was proclaimed, and the great slogans of the French Revolution—liberty, equality, fraternity—fired the imagination of men. I have chosen to discuss this issue in Europe because this has been the scene of the greatest historic battles between freedom and tyranny. I have chosen to discuss it in the early days of the General Assembly because the issue of human liberty is decisive for the settlement of outstanding political differences and for the future of the United Nations.

The decisive importance of this issue was fully recognized by the founders of the United Nations at San Francisco. Concern for the preservation and promotion of human rights and fundamental freedoms stands at the heart of the United Nations. Its Charter is distinguished by its preoccupation with the rights and welfare of individual men and women. The United Nations has made it clear that it intends to uphold human rights and to protect the dignity of the human personality. In the preamble to the Charter the keynote is set when it declares: "We the people of

the United Nations determined . . . to reaffirm faith in fundamental human rights, in the dignity and worth of the human person, in the equal rights of men and women and of nations large and small, and . . . to promote social progress and better standards of life in larger freedom." This reflects the basic premise of the Charter that the peace and security of mankind are dependent on mutual respect for the rights and freedoms of all.

One of the purposes of the United Nations is declared in article 1 to be: "to achieve international cooperation in solving international problems of an economic, social, cultural, or humanitarian character, and in promoting and encouraging respect for human rights and for fundamental freedoms for all without distinction as to race, sex, language, or religion."

This thought is repeated at several points and notably in articles 55 and 56 the Members pledge themselves to take joint and separate action in cooperation with the United Nations for the promotion of "universal respect for, and observance of, human rights and fundamental freedoms for all without distinction as to race, sex, language, or religion."

The Human Rights Commission was given as its first and most important task the preparation of an International Bill of Rights. The General Assembly, which opened its third session here in Paris a few days ago, will have before it the first fruit of the Commission's labors in this task, that is the International Declaration of Human Rights.

The Declaration was finally completed after much work during the last session of the Human Rights Commission in New York in the spring of 1948. The Economic and Social Council has sent it without recommendation to the General Assembly, together with other documents transmitted by the Human Rights Commission.

It was decided in our Commission that a Bill of Rights should contain two parts:

1. A Declaration which could be approved through action of the Member States of the United Nations in the General Assembly. This declaration would have great moral force, and would say to the peoples of the world "this is what we hope human rights may mean to all people in the years to come." We have put down here the rights that we consider basic for individual human beings the world over to have. Without them, we feel that the full development of individual personality is impossible.

2. The second part of the bill, which the Human Rights Commission has not yet completed because of the lack of time, is a covenant which would be in the form of a treaty to be presented to the nations of the world. Each nation, as it is prepared to do so, would ratify this covenant and the covenant would then become binding on the nations which adhere to it. Each nation ratifying would then be obligated to change its laws wherever they did not conform to the points contained in the covenant.

This covenant, of course, would have to be a simpler document. It could not state aspirations, which we feel to be permissible in the Declaration. It could only state rights which could be assured by law and it must contain methods of implementation, and no state ratifying the covenant could be allowed to disregard it. The methods of implementation have not yet been agreed upon, nor have they been given adequate consideration by the Commission at any of its meetings. There certainly should be discussion on the entire question of this world Bill of Human Rights and there may be acceptance by this Assembly of the Declaration if they come to agreement on it. The acceptance of the Declaration, I think, should encourage every nation in the coming months to discuss its meaning with its people so that they will be better prepared to accept the covenant with a deeper understanding of the problems involved when that is presented, we hope, a year from now and, we hope, accepted.

The Declaration has come from the Human Rights Commission with unanimous acceptance except for four abstentions—the U.S.S.R., Yugoslavia, Ukraine, and Byelorussia. The reason for this is a fundamental difference in the conception of human rights as they exist in these states and in certain other Member States in the United Nations.

In the discussion before the Assembly, I think it should be made crystal clear what these differences are and tonight I want to spend a little time making them clear to you. It seems to me there is a valid reason for taking the time today to think carefully and clearly on the subject of human rights, because in the acceptance and observance of these rights lies the root, I believe, of our chance of peace in the future, and for the strengthening of the United Nations organization to the point where it can maintain peace in the future.

We must not be confused about what freedom is. Basic human rights are simple and easily understood: freedom of speech and a free press; freedom of religion and worship; freedom of assembly and the right of petition; the right of men to be secure in their homes and free from unreasonable search and seizure and from arbitrary arrest and punishment.

We must not be deluded by the efforts of the forces of reaction to prostitute the great words of our free tradition and thereby to confuse the struggle. Democracy, freedom, human rights have come to have a definite meaning to the people of the world which we must not allow any nation to so change that they are made synonymous with suppression and dictatorship.

There are basic differences that show up even in the use of words between a democratic and a totalitarian country. For instance "democracy" means one thing to the U.S.S.R. and another the U.S.A. and, I know, in France. I have served since the first meeting of the nuclear commission on the Human Rights Commission, and I think this point stands out clearly.

The U.S.S.R. representatives assert that they already have achieved many things which we, in what they call the "bourgeois democracies" cannot achieve because their government controls the accomplishment of these things. Our government seems powerless to them because, in the last analysis, it is controlled by the people. They would not put it that way—they would say that the people in the U.S.S.R. control their government by allowing their government to have certain absolute rights. We, on the other hand, feel that certain rights can never be granted to the government, but must be kept in the hands of the people.

For instance, the U.S.S.R. will assert that their press is free because the state makes it free by providing the machinery, the paper, and even the money for salaries for the people who work on the paper. They state that there is no control over what is printed in the various papers that they subsidize in this manner, such, for instance, as a trade-union paper. But what would happen if a paper were to print ideas which were critical of the basic policies and beliefs of the Communist government? I am sure some good reason would be found for abolishing the paper.

It is true that they have been many cases where newspapers in the U.S.S.R. have criticized officials and their actions and have been responsible for the removal of those officials, but in doing so they did not criticize anything which was fundamental to Communist beliefs. They simply criticized methods of doing things, so one must differentiate between things which are permissible, such as criticism of any individual or of the manner of doing things, and the criticism of a belief which would be considered vital to the acceptance of Communism.

What are the differences, for instance, between trade-unions in the totalitarian states and in the democracies? In the totalitarian state a trade-union is an instrument used by the government to enforce duties, not to assert rights. Propaganda material which the government desires the workers to have is furnished by the trade-unions to be circulated to their members.

Our trade-unions, on the other hand, are solely the instrument of the workers themselves. They represent the workers in their relations with the government and with management and they are free to develop their own opinions without government help or interference. The concepts of our trade-unions and those in totalitarian countries are drastically different. There is little mutual understanding.

I think the best example one can give of this basic difference of the use of terms is "the right to work." The Soviet Union insists that this is a basic right which it alone can guarantee because it alone provides full employment by the government. But the right to work in the Soviet Union means the assignment of workers to do whatever task is given to them by the government without an opportunity for the people to participate in the decision that the government should do this. A society in which everyone works is not necessarily a free society and may indeed be a slave society; on the other hand, a society in which there is widespread economic insecurity can turn freedom into a barren and vapid right for millions of people.

We in the United States have come to realize it means freedom to choose one's job, to work or not to work as one desires. We, in the United States, have come to realize, however, that people have a right to demand that their government will not allow them to starve because as individuals they cannot find work of the kind they are accustomed to doing and this is a decision brought about by public opinion which came as a result of the great depression in which many people were out of work, but we would not consider in the United States that we had gained any freedom if we were compelled to follow a dictatorial assignment to work where and when we were told. The right of choice would seem to us an important, fundamental freedom.

I have great sympathy with the Russian people. They love their country and have always defended it valiantly against invaders. They have been through a period of revolution, as a result of which they were for a time cut off from outside contact. They have not lost their resulting suspicion of other countries and the great difficulty is today that their government encourages this suspicion and seems to believe that force alone will bring them respect.

We, in the democracies, believe in a kind of international respect and action which is reciprocal. We do not think others should treat us differently from the way they wish to be treated. It is interference in other countries that especially stirs up antagonism against the Soviet Government. If it wishes to feel secure in developing its economic and political theories within its territory, then it should grant to others that same security. We believe in the freedom of people to make their own mistakes. We do not interfere with them and they should not interfere with others.

The basic problem confronting the world today, as I said in the beginning, is the preservation of human freedom for the individual and consequently for the society of which he is a part. We are fighting this battle again today as it was fought at the time of the French Revolution and as the time of the American Revolution. The issue of human liberty is as decisive now as it was then. I want to give you my conception of what is meant in my country by freedom of the individual.

Long ago in London during a discussion with Mr. Vyshinsky, he told me there was no such things as freedom for the individual in the world. All freedom of the individual was conditioned by the rights of other individuals. That of course, I granted. I said: "We approach the question from a different point of view/ we here in the United Nations are trying to develop ideals which will be broader in outlook, which will consider first the rights of man, which will consider what makes man more free; not governments, but man."

The totalitarian state typically places the will of the people second to decrees promulgated by a few men at the top.

Naturally there must always be consideration of the rights of others; but in a democracy this is not a restriction. Indeed, in our democracies we make our freedoms secure because each of us is expected to respect the rights of others and we are free to make our own laws. Freedom for our peoples is not only a right, but also a tool. Freedom of speech, freedom of the press, freedom of information, freedom of assembly—these are not just abstract ideals to us; they are tools with which we create a way of life, a way of life in which we can enjoy freedom.

Sometimes the processes of democracy are slow, and I have known some of our leaders to say that a benevolent dictatorship would accomplish the ends desired in a much shorter time than it takes to go through the democratic processes of discussion and the slow formation of public opinion. But there is no way of insuring that a dictatorship will remain benevolent or that power once in the hands of a few will be returned to the people without struggle or revolution. This we have learned by experience and we accept the slow processes of democracy because we know that shortcuts compromise principles on which no compromise is possible.

The final expression of the opinion of the people with us is through free and honest elections, with valid choices on basic issues and candidates. The secret ballot is an essential to free elections but you must have a choice before you. I have heard my husband say many times that a people need never lose their freedom if they kept their right to a secret ballot and if they used that secret ballot to the full. Basic decisions of our society are made through the expressed will of the people. That is why when we see these liberties threatened, instead of falling apart, our nation becomes unified and our democracies come together as a unified group in spite of our varied backgrounds and many racial strains.

In the United States we have a capitalistic economy. That is because public opinion favors that type of economy under the conditions in which we live. But we have imposed certain restraints; for instance, we have antitrust laws. These are the legal evidence of the determination of the American people to maintain an economy of free competition and not to allow monopolies to take away the people's freedom.

Our trade-unions grow stronger because the people come to believe that this is the proper way to guarantee the rights of the workers and that the right to organize and to bargain collectively keeps the balance between the actual producer and the investor of money and the manager in industry who watches over the man who works with this hands and who produces the materials which are out tangible wealth.

In the United States we are old enough not to claim perfection. We recognize that we have some problems of discrimination but we find steady progress being made in the solution of these problems. Through normal democratic processes we are coming to understand our needs and how we can attain full equality for all our people. Free discussion on the subject is permitted. Our Supreme Court has recently rendered decisions to clarify a number of our laws to guarantee the rights of all.

The U.S.S.R. claims it has reached a point where all races within her borders are officially considered equal and have equal rights and they insist that they have no discrimination where minorities are concerned.

This is a laudable objective but there are other aspects of the development of freedom for the individual which are essential before the mere absence of discrimination is worth much, and these are lacking in the Soviet Union. Unless they are being denied freedoms which they want and which they see other people have, people do not usually complain of discrimination. It is these other freedoms—the basic freedoms of speech, of the press, of religion and conscience, of assembly, of fair trial and freedom from arbitrary arrest and punishment, which a totalitarian government cannot safely give its people and which give meaning to freedom from discrimination.

It is my belief, and I am sure it is also yours, that the struggle for democracy and freedom is a critical struggle, for their preservation is essential to the great objective of the United Nations to maintain international peace and security. Among free men the end cannot justify the means. We know the patterns of totalitarianism—the single political party, the control of schools, press, radio, the arts, the sciences, and the church to support autocratic authority; these are the age-old patterns against which men have struggled for three thousand years. These are the signs of reaction, retreat, and retrogression. The United Nations must hold fast to the heritage of freedom won by the struggle of its people; it must help us to pass it on to generations to come.

The development of the ideal of freedom and its translation into the everyday life of the people in great areas of the earth is the product of the efforts of many peoples. It is the fruit of a long tradition of vigorous thinking and courageous action. No one race and no one people can claim to have done all the work to achieve greater dignity for human beings and great freedom to develop human personality. In each generation and in each country there must be a continuation of the struggle and new steps forward must be taken since this is preeminently a field in which to stand still its to retreat.

The field of human rights is not one in which compromise on fundamental principles are possible. The work of the Commission on Human Rights is illustrative. The Declaration of Human Rights provides: "Everyone has the right to leave any country, including his own." The Soviet Representative said he would agree to this right if a single phrase was added to it—"in accordance with the procedure laid down in the laws of that country." It is obvious that to accept this would be not only to compromise but to nullify the right stated. This case forcefully illustrates the importance of the proposition that we must ever be alert not to compromise fundamental human rights merely for the sake of reaching unanimity and thus lose them.

As I see it, it is not going to be easy to attain unanimity with respect to our different concepts of government and human rights. The struggle is bound to be difficult and one in which we must be firm but patient. If we adhere faithfully to our principles I think it is possible for us to maintain freedom and to do so peacefully and without recourse to force.

The future must see the broadening of human rights throughout the world. People who have glimpsed freedom will never be content until they have secured it for themselves. In a truest sense, human rights are a fundamental object of law and government in a just society. Human rights exist to the degree that they are respected by people in relations with each other and by governments in relations with their citizens.

The world at large is aware of the tragic consequences for human beings ruled by totalitarian systems. If we examine Hitler's rise to power, we see how the chains are forged which keep the individual a slave and we can see many similarities in the way things are accomplished in other countries. Politically men must be free to discuss and to arrive at as many facts as possible and there must be at least a two-party system in a country because when there is only one political party, too many things can be subordinated to the interests of that one party and it becomes a tyrant and not an instrument of democratic government.

The propaganda we have witnessed in the recent past, like that we perceive in these days, seeks to impugn, to undermine, and to destroy the liberty and independence of peoples. Such propaganda poses to all peoples the issue whether to doubt their heritage of rights and therefore to compromise the principles by which they live, or try to accept the challenge, redouble their vigilance, and stand steadfast in the struggle to maintain and enlarge human freedoms.

People who continue to be denied the respect to which they are entitled as human beings will not acquiesce forever in such denial.

The Charter of the United Nations is a guiding beacon along the way to the achievement of human rights and fundamental freedoms throughout the world. The immediate test is not only to the extent to which human rights and freedoms have already been achieved, but the direction in which the world is moving. Is there a faithful compliance with the objectives of the Charter if some countries continue to curtail human rights and freedoms instead of to promote the universal respect for an observance of human rights and freedoms for all as called for by the Charter?

The place to discuss the issue of human rights is in the forum of the United Nations. The United Nations has been set up as the common meeting ground for nations, where we can consider together our mutual problems and take advantage of our differences in experience. It is inherent in our firm attachment to democracy and freedom that we stand always ready to use the fundamental democratic procedures of honest discussion and negotiation. It is now as always our hope that despite the wide differences in approach we face in the world today, we can with mutual good faith in the principles of the united Nations Charter, arrive at a common basis of understanding.

We are here to join the meetings of this great international Assembly which meets in your beautiful capital of Paris. Freedom for the individual is an inseparable part of the cherished traditions of France. As one of the Delegates from the United States I pray Almighty God that we may win another victory here for the rights and freedoms of all men.

5

The Cold War and the Limits of Dissent

Perhaps more than any other decade in American history, the 1950s is striking for its two dominant and diametrically opposed political and cultural orientations. On the one hand, the decade was characterized by ideological consensus, a consensus represented and disseminated through the influential and increasingly pervasive medium of television. Popular TV shows like *Father Knows Best*, *The Adventures of Ozzie and Harriet*, and *Leave It to Beaver* portrayed an ideal and idyllic America—white, middle-class, and suburban. On the other hand, the decade was marked by trenchant critiques of that contrived consensus. "Let America be America again" the great poet Langston Hughes appealed, but to "bring back our mighty dream" was in fact to realize it for the first time, for America was the "land that never has been yet." America the dream was a place of inclusion, equality, and freedom. America the reality was a place of exclusion, inequality, mob hysteria, and oppression—of unfulfilled promise. Criticism of America found expression in settings as wide ranging as Hughes' poetry, or the untidy, impulsive creativity of the Beat poets; as Rosa Parks' arrest and the subsequent bus boycott in Birmingham, Alabama; as the 1957 musical *West Side Story* (and its 1961 film version); and television shows such as *The Twilight Zone's* "The Monsters Are Due on Maple Street," which aired March 4, 1960.

Anxiety and paranoia defined the age. The threat of communist expansion, not only in Europe but also in Indochina, Africa, and elsewhere, and the constant threat of nuclear war produced a political and cultural environment of suspicion and legal and social restrictiveness. The anxiety over impending nuclear Armageddon was evident in the Federal Civil Defense Administration's *Duck and Cover* film that instructed children how to respond to nuclear attack and in popular science fiction films. The ideological threat perceived in communism evoked cultural and political reactions at home, including Vice President Richard Nixon's "kitchen debate" with Soviet Premier Nikita Khrushchev comparing the achievements of American industry and technology to those of the Soviet Union, in the addition of "under God" to the Pledge of Allegiance in 1954, and in scores of anticommunist films, such as *Big Jim McClain*, starring John Wayne.

For most Americans in the 1950s, conformity was the rule. "A hard and indelible fact of freedom is that a conformity of sorts is always dominant," conservative icon William F. Buckley would write in 1954. As long as conformity promoted the values of Western liberty, he argued, pressure to conform was not out of bounds. It bears remembering, too, that the threats that fostered a culture of conformity were genuine. Stalin was a ruthless tyrant, and Soviet expansionist aims were real. It was Soviet action in Eastern Europe at the end of World War II that spurred the now famous "Long Telegram" by George Kennan ("X"). Kennan represented the thinking of American leadership in the early years of the Cold War and provided a coherent point of departure for the American response to Soviet ambitions. Kennan's influence throughout the four decades of the Cold War cannot be overstated. It is from this document that the policy of containment and deterrence to the expanding reach of the Soviet bloc emerged.

Moreover, the fear of Soviet espionage in the United States also had a basis in reality. For example, KGB files do implicate Julius Rosenberg—convicted in 1951 of passing nuclear secrets to the Russians—as a Soviet operative. Likewise, the guilt of Alger Hiss, accused of giving classified documents to the Russians and convicted of perjury in 1950, seems more certain as a result of Soviet documents made public in 1995. These and other events, including the U-2 spy plane affair, helped produce a political environ-ment in which mainstream American opinion increasingly viewed dissent as disloyal and as legitimately subject to political, social, and legal action. In 1951 the Supreme Court upheld the conviction of Eugene Dennis, who had been found in violation of the Smith Act for engaging in a conspiracy to organ-ize the Communist Party and "to teach and advocate the overthrow and destruction of the Government of the United States by force and violence." What's notable about the case is the Court's application of the "clear and present danger" test, for the Court interpreted the rule in a way that blurred the distinc-tion between the constitutionally protected discussion of ideas and actual conspiracy against the govern-ment. Loyalty oaths for government employees, including university professors, became the norm.

It bears remembering that the Court's ruling came during a time of intense cultural paranoia about the domestic communist threat. And while that threat was legitimate, the domestic response was arguably disproportionate. In 1947 the House Un-American Activities Committee (HUAC) launched a crusade against Hollywood writers and producers perceived to be procommunist and who might use the medium of film to surreptitiously indoctrinate Americans. Perhaps more devastating to a culture of freedom was Senator Joseph McCarthy's campaign against alleged communists within the State Department, military, and other areas of government. Relying heavily on innuendo, false or undocumented accusations, and guilt by association, McCarthy helped blacklist thousands of citizens socially, politically, and economi-cally. Typical of this witch hunt attitude was the case of reserve Air Force weather officer Milo Radulovich, who was dismissed from the military because his father and sister were accused of being communist sympathizers. Radulovich fought the dismissal, and the profoundly effective criticism of his case aired on Edward R. Murrow's television show *See It Now*. A few months later Murrow challenged McCarthy directly, and successfully, helping turn public opinion against such witch hunts and effec-tively ending the senator's political career.

The 1950s were also a decade of considerable material prosperity. The U.S. economy grew steadily throughout the decade, stimulated in part by the 1944 G.I. Bill of Rights, which encouraged university education and home ownership. Well-paying blue-collar jobs, and millions of new white-collar jobs, increased disposable income, which Americans spent on new devices and products that promised a lifestyle of convenience and comfort. The automobile, guaranteed mortgages, and a new assembly-line method of building affordable houses quickly and cheaply—a method begun by William Levitt— encouraged people to move out of cities and into the suburbs. Needless to say, this material abundance was not enjoyed equally by all segments of American society, especially African Americans. But prosper-ity there was, and more broadly enjoyed than at anytime during the century, though primarily by the white middle class. (Nixon linked this vision of prosperity to freedom in his 1959 kitchen debate with Khrushchev.)

It was also this vision against which social critics increasingly declaimed. The 1950s Beat poets, including Lawrence Ferlinghetti, Allen Ginsberg, and Jack Kerouac, criticized their compatriots for being overly materialistic. "I am the young man," Langston Hughes wrote, "full of strength and hope, / Tangled in that ancient endless chain / Of profit, power, gain, of grab the land! / Of grab the gold!" More-over, in works like *The Lonely Crowd*, *The Organization Man*, and *The Man in the Grey Flannel Suit*, critics decried the middle-class "organization man" who conformed to a routine, soulless, bureaucratic life. The Beats called for liberation from this materialism and ennui. Such materialism, commentators such as Reinhold Niebuhr warned, had a price because "a culture which makes 'living standards' the final norm of the good life" was bound to be one that soon lost its moral compass. And C. Wright Mills, in his classic *The Power Elite*, warned against the corruption and eventual dissolution of democracy through the replacement of public life with a mass society managed by an increasingly detached elite.

Even though the possibility of thermonuclear war remained a constant throughout the 1940s and 1950s, positive social and political change did occur. The ongoing threat that "cold war" could easily become "hot," bringing with it the prospect of universal nuclear destruction, did not squelch demands for America to live up to the ideals of the nation's great founding documents. Indeed, the battle against and victory over fascism abroad brought into stark relief the gulf between American principles and political reality, and spurred calls, such as the one made by Hubert Humphrey on July 14, 1948, that "the time has arrived in America for the Democratic Party to get out of the shadow of states' rights and walk forthrightly into the bright sunshine of human rights!" Twelve days later President Harry Truman issued Executive Order 9981, desegregating the armed forces. In 1954 the Court ruled unanimously in *Brown et al. v. Board of Education of Topeka, Kansas* (Chapter 6) to overturn the shameful legal sanction it had given to segregation in 1896. Soon, Rosa Parks, Jackie Robinson, Thurgood Marshall, A. Philip Randolph, Martin Luther King, Jr., Little Rock, and Montgomery would become household names, symbolic of a burgeoning and irrepressible civil rights movement.

Langston Hughes

Selected Poems (1921–1957)

I, Too, Sing America

I, too, sing America.

I am the darker brother.
They send me to eat in the kitchen
When company comes,
But I laugh,
And eat well,
And grow strong.

Tomorrow,
I'll be at the table
When company comes.
Nobody'll dare
Say to me,
"Eat in the kitchen,"
Then.

Besides,
They'll see how beautiful I am
And be ashamed—

I, too, am America.

Dream Deferred

What happens to a dream deferred?

Does it dry up
like a raisin in the sun?

Or fester like a sore—
and then run?

Does it stink like rotten meat?
Or crust and sugar over—
like a syrupy sweet?

Maybe it just sags
like a heavy load

Or does it just explode?

Let America Be America Again

Let America be America again.
Let it be the dream it used to be.
Let it be the pioneer on the plain
Seeking a home where he himself is free.

(America never was America to me.)

Let America be the dream the dreamers dreamed—
Let it be that great strong land of love
Where never kings connive nor tyrants scheme
That any man be crushed by one above.

(It never was America to me.)

O, let my land be a land where Liberty
Is crowned with no false patriotic wreath,
But opportunity is real, and life is free,
Equality is in the air we breathe.

(There's never been equality for me,
Nor freedom in this "homeland of the free.")

Say, who are you that mumbles in the dark?
And who are you that draws your veil across the stars?

I am the poor white, fooled and pushed apart,
I am the Negro bearing slavery's scars.
I am the red man driven from the land,
I am the immigrant clutching the hope I seek—
And finding only the same old stupid plan
Of dog eat dog, of mighty crush the weak.

I am the young man, full of strength and hope,
Tangled in that ancient endless chain
Of profit, power, gain, of grab the land!
Of grab the gold! Of grab the ways of satisfying need!
Of work the men! Of take the pay!
Of owning everything for one's own greed!

I am the farmer, bondsman to the soil.
I am the worker sold to the machine.
I am the Negro, servant to you all.
I am the people, humble, hungry, mean—

Hungry yet today despite the dream.
Beaten yet today—O, Pioneers!
I am the man who never got ahead,
The poorest worker bartered through the years.

Yet I'm the one who dreamt our basic dream
In the Old World while still a serf of kings,
Who dreamt a dream so strong, so brave, so true,
That even yet its mighty daring sings
In every brick and stone, in every furrow turned
That's made America the land it has become.
O, I'm the man who sailed those early seas
In search of what I meant to be my home—
For I'm the one who left dark Ireland's shore,
And Poland's plain, and England's grassy lea,
And torn from Black Africa's strand I came
To build a "homeland of the free."

The free?

Who said the free? Not me?
Surely not me? The millions on relief today?
The millions shot down when we strike?
The millions who have nothing for our pay?
For all the dreams we've dreamed
And all the songs we've sung
And all the hopes we've held
And all the flags we've hung,
The millions who have nothing for our pay—
Except the dream that's almost dead today.

O, let America be America again—
The land that never has been yet—
And yet must be—the land where *every* man is free.
The land that's mine—the poor man's, Indian's,
    Negro's, ME—
Who made America,
Whose sweat and blood, whose faith and pain,
Whose hand at the foundry, whose plow in the rain,
Must bring back our mighty dream again.

Sure, call me any ugly name you choose—
The steel of freedom does not stain.
From those who live like leeches on the people's
    lives,
We must take back our land again,
America!

O, yes,
I say it plain,
America never was America to me,
And yet I swear this oath—
America will be!

Out of the rack and ruin of our gangster death,
The rape and rot of graft, and stealth, and lies,
We, the people, must redeem
The land, the mines, the plants, the rivers.
The mountains and the endless plain—
All, all the stretch of these great green states—
And make America again!

GEORGE KENNAN ("X")

The Sources of Soviet Conduct (July 1947)

I

The political personality of Soviet power as we know it today is the product of ideology and circumstances: ideology inherited by the present Soviet leaders from the movement in which they had their political origin, and circumstances of the power which they now have exercised for nearly three decades in Russia.

There can be few tasks of psychological analysis more difficult than to try to trace the interaction of these two forces and the relative role of each in the determination of official Soviet conduct. Yet the attempt must be made if that conduct is to be understood and effectively countered.

It is difficult to summarize the set of ideological concepts with which the Soviet leaders came into power. Marxian ideology, in its Russian-Communist projection, has always been in process of subtle evolution. The materials on which it bases itself are extensive and complex. But the outstanding features of Communist thought as it existed in 1916 may perhaps be summarized as follows: (a) that the central factor in the life of man, the factor which determines the character of public life and the "physiognomy of society," is the system by which material goods are produced and exchanged; (b) that the capitalist system of production is a nefarious one which inevitable leads to the exploitation of the working class by the capital-owning class and is incapable of developing adequately the economic resources of society or of distributing fairly the material good produced by human labor; (c) that capitalism contains the seeds of its own destruction and must, in view of the inability of the capital-owning class to adjust itself to economic change, result eventually and inescapably in a revolutionary transfer of power to the working class; and (d) that imperialism, the final phase of capitalism, leads directly to war and revolution.

The rest may be outlined in Lenin's own words: "Unevenness of economic and political development is the inflexible law of capitalism. It follows from this that the victory of Socialism may come originally in a few capitalist countries or even in a single capitalist country. The victorious proletariat of that country, having expropriated the capitalists and having organized Socialist production at home, would rise against the remaining capitalist world, drawing to itself in the process the oppressed classes of other countries." [Kennan's footnote: "Concerning the Slogans of the United States of Europe," August 1915, official Soviet edition of Lenin's works.] It must be noted that there was no assumption that capitalism would perish without proletarian revolution. A final push was needed from a revolutionary proletariat movement in order to tip over the tottering structure. But it was regarded as inevitable that sooner or later that push be given.

For 50 years prior to the outbreak of the Revolution, this pattern of thought had exercised great fascination for the members of the Russian revolutionary movement. Frustrated, discontented, hopeless of finding self-expression—or too impatient to seek it—in the confining limits of the Tsarist political system, yet lacking wide popular support or their choice of bloody revolution as a means of social betterment, these revolutionists found in Marxist theory a highly convenient rationalization for their own instinctive desires. It afforded pseudo-scientific justification for their impatience, for their categoric denial of all value in the Tsarist system, for their yearning for power and revenge and for their inclination to cut corners in the pursuit of it. It is therefore no wonder that they had come to believe implicitly in the truth and soundness of the Marxist-Leninist teachings, so congenial to their own impulses and emotions. Their sincerity need not be impugned. This is a phenomenon as old as human nature itself. It is has never been more aptly described than by Edward Gibbon, who wrote in *The Decline and Fall of the Roman Empire*: "From enthusiasm to imposture the step is perilous and slippery; the demon of Socrates affords a memorable instance of how a wise man may deceive himself, how a good man may deceive others, how the conscience may slumber in a mixed and middle state between self-illusion and voluntary fraud." And it was with this set of conceptions that the members of the Bolshevik Party entered into power.

Now it must be noted that through all the years of preparation for revolution, the attention of these men, as indeed of Marx himself, had been centered less on the future form which socialism would take than on the necessary overthrow of rival power which, in their view, had to precede the introduction of socialism. [Kennan's footnote: Here and elsewhere in this paper "socialism" refers to Marxist or Leninist communism, not to liberal socialism of the Second International variety.] Their views, therefore, on the positive program to be put into effect, once power was attained, were for the most part nebulous, visionary and impractical beyond the nationalization of industry and the expropriation of large private capital holdings there was no agreed program. The treatment of the peasantry, which, according to the Marxist formulation was not of the proletariat, had always been a vague spot in the pattern of Communist thought: and it remained an object of controversy and vacillation for the first ten years of Communist power.

The circumstances of the immediate post-revolution period—the existence in Russia of civil war and foreign intervention, together with the obvious fact that the Communists represented only a tiny minority of the Russian people—made the establishment of dictatorial power a necessity. The experiment with war Communism" and the abrupt attempt to eliminate private production and trade had unfortunate economic consequences and caused further bitterness against the new revolutionary regime. While the temporary relaxation of the effort to communize Russia, represented by the New Economic Policy, alleviated some of this economic distress and thereby served its purpose, it also made it evident that the "capitalistic sector of society" was still prepared to profit at once from any relaxation of governmental pressure, and would, if permitted to continue to exist, always constitute a powerful opposing element to the Soviet regime and a serious rival for influence in the country. Somewhat the same situation prevailed with respect to the individual peasant who, in his own small way, was also a private producer.

Lenin, had he lived, might have proved a great enough man to reconcile these conflicting forces to the ultimate benefit of Russian society, though this is questionable. But be that as it may, Stalin, and those whom he led in the struggle for succession to Lenin's position of leadership, were not the men to tolerate rival political forces in the sphere of power which they coveted. Their sense of insecurity was too great. Their particular brand of fanaticism, unmodified by any of the Anglo-Saxon traditions of compromise, was too fierce and too jealous to envisage any permanent sharing of power. From the Russian-Asiatic world out of which they had emerged they carried with them a skepticism as to the possibilities of permanent and peaceful coexistence of rival forces. Easily persuaded of their own doctrinaire "rightness," they insisted on the submission or destruction of all competing power. Outside the Communist Party, Russian society was to have no rigidity. There were to be no forms of collective human activity or association which would not be dominated by the Party. No other force in Russian society was to be permitted to achieve vitality or integrity. Only the Party was to have structure. All else was to be an amorphous mass.

And within the Party the same principle was to apply. The mass of Party members might go through the motions of election, deliberation, decision and action; but in these motions they were to be animated not by their own individual wills but by the awesome breath of the Party leadership and the overbrooding presence of "the word."

Let it be stressed again that subjectively these men probably did not seek absolutism for its own sake. They doubtless believed—and found it easy to believe—that they alone knew what was good for society and that they would accomplish that good once their power was secure and unchallengeable. But in seeking that security of their own rule they were prepared to recognize no restrictions, either of God or man, on the character of their methods. And until such time as that security might be achieved, they placed far down on their scale of operational priorities the comforts and happiness of the peoples entrusted to their care.

Now the outstanding circumstance concerning the Soviet regime is that down to the present day this process of political consolidation has never been completed and the men in the Kremlin have continued to be predominantly absorbed with the struggle to secure and make absolute the power which they seized in November 1917. They have endeavored to secure it primarily against forces at home, within Soviet society itself. But they have also endeavored to secure it against the outside world. For ideology, as we have seen, taught them that the outside world was hostile and that it was their duty eventually to overthrow the political forces beyond their borders. Then powerful hands of Russian history and tradition reached up to sustain them in this feeling. Finally, their own aggressive intransigence with respect to the outside world began to find its own reaction; and they were soon forced, to use another Gibbonesque phrase, "to chastise the contumacy" which they themselves had provoked. It is an undeniable privilege of every man to prove himself right in the thesis that the world is his enemy; for if he reiterates it frequently enough and makes it the background of his conduct he is bound eventually to be right.

Now it lies in the nature of the mental world of the Soviet leaders, as well as in the character of their ideology, that no opposition to them can be officially recognized as having any merit or justification whatsoever. Such opposition can flow, in theory, only from the hostile and incorrigible forces of dying capitalism. As long as remnants of capitalism were officially recognized as existing in Russia, it was possible to place on them, as an internal element, part of the blame for the maintenance of a dictatorial form of society. But as these remnants were liquidated, little by little, this justification fell away, and when it was indicated officially that they had been finally destroyed, it disappeared altogether. And this fact created one of the most basic of the compulsions which came to act upon the Soviet regime: since capitalism no longer existed in Russia and since it could not be admitted that there could be serious or widespread opposition to the Kremlin springing spontaneously from the liberated masses under its authority, it became necessary to justify the retention of the dictatorship by stressing the menace of capitalism abroad.

This began at an early date. In 1924 Stalin specifically defended the retention of the "organs of suppression," meaning, among others, the army and the secret police, on the ground that "as long as there is a capitalistic encirclement there will be danger of intervention with all the consequences that flow from that danger." In accordance with that theory, and from that time on, all internal opposition forces in Russia have consistently been portrayed as the agents of foreign forces of reaction antagonistic to Soviet power.

By the same token, tremendous emphasis has been placed on the original Communist thesis of a basic antagonism between the capitalist and Socialist worlds. It is clear, from many indications, that this emphasis is not founded in reality. The real facts concerning it have been confused by the existence abroad of genuine resentment provoked by Soviet philosophy and tactics and occasionally by the existence of great centers of military power, notably the Nazi regime in Germany and the Japanese Government of the late 1930s, which indeed have aggressive designs against the Soviet Union. But there is ample evidence that the stress laid in Moscow on the menace confronting Soviet society from the world outside its borders is founded not in the realities of foreign antagonism but in the necessity of explaining away the maintenance of dictatorial authority at home.

Now the maintenance of this pattern of Soviet power, namely, the pursuit of unlimited authority domestically, accompanied by the cultivation of the semi-myth of implacable foreign hostility, has gone far to shape the actual machinery of Soviet power as we know it today. Internal organs of administration which did not serve this purpose withered on the vine. Organs which did serve this purpose became vastly swollen. The security of Soviet power came to rest on the iron discipline of the Party, on the severity and ubiquity of the secret police, and on the uncompromising economic monopolism of the state. The "organs of suppression," in which the Soviet leaders had sought security from rival forces, became in large measures the masters of those whom they were designed to serve. Today the major part of the structure of Soviet power is committed to the perfection of the dictatorship and to the maintenance of the concept of Russia as in a state of siege, with the enemy lowering beyond the walls. And the millions of human beings who form that part of the structure of power must defend at all costs this concept of Russia's position, for without it they are themselves superfluous.

As things stand today, the rulers can no longer dream of parting with these organs of suppression. The quest for absolute power, pursued now for nearly three decades with a ruthlessness unparalleled (in scope at least) in modern times, has again produced internally, as it did externally, its own reaction. The excesses of the police apparatus have fanned the potential opposition to the regime into something far greater and more dangerous than it could have been before those excesses began.

But least of all can the rulers dispense with the fiction by which the maintenance of dictatorial power has been defended. For this fiction has been canonized in Soviet philosophy by the excesses already committed in its name; and it is now anchored in the Soviet structure of thought by bonds far greater than those of mere ideology.

II

So much for the historical background. What does it spell in terms of the political personality of Soviet power as we know it today?

Of the original ideology, nothing has been officially junked. Belief is maintained in the basic badness of capitalism, in the inevitability of its destruction, in the obligation of the proletariat to assist in that destruction and to take power into its own hands. But stress has come to be laid primarily on those concepts which relate most specifically to the Soviet regime itself: to its position as the sole truly Socialist regime in a dark and misguided world, and to the relationships of power within it.

The first of these concepts is that of the innate antagonism between capitalism and Socialism. We have seen how deeply that concept has become imbedded in foundations of Soviet power. It has profound implications for Russia's conduct as a member of international society. It means that there can never be on Moscow's side an sincere assumption of a community of aims between the Soviet Union and powers which are regarded as capitalist. It must inevitably be assumed in Moscow that the aims of the capitalist world are antagonistic to the Soviet regime, and therefore to the interests of the peoples it controls. If the Soviet government occasionally sets it[s] signature to documents which would indicate the contrary, this is to regarded as a tactical maneuver permissible in dealing with the enemy (who is without honor) and should be taken in the spirit of caveat emptor. Basically, the antagonism remains. It is postulated. And from it flow many of the phenomena which we find disturbing in the Kremlin's conduct of foreign policy: the secretiveness, the lack of frankness, the duplicity, the wary suspiciousness, and the basic unfriendliness of purpose. These phenomena are there to stay, for the foreseeable future. There can be variations of degree and of emphasis. When there is something the Russians want from us, one or the other of these features of their policy may be thrust temporarily into the background; and when that happens there will always be Americans who will leap forward with gleeful announcements that "the Russians have changed," and some who will even try to take credit for having brought about such "changes." But we should not be misled by tactical maneuvers. These characteristics of Soviet policy, like the postulate from which they flow, are basic to the internal nature of Soviet power, and will be with us, whether in the foreground or the background, until the internal nature of Soviet power is changed.

This means we are going to continue for long time to find the Russians difficult to deal with. It does not mean that they should be considered as embarked upon a do-or-die program to overthrow our society by a given date. The theory of the inevitability of the eventual fall of capitalism has the fortunate connotation that there is no hurry about it. The forces of progress can take their time in preparing the final coup de grâce. meanwhile, what is vital is that the "Socialist fatherland"—that oasis of power

which has already been won for Socialism in the person of the Soviet Union—should be cherished and defended by all good Communists at home and abroad, its fortunes promoted, its enemies badgered and confounded. The promotion of premature, "adventuristic" revolutionary projects abroad which might embarrass Soviet power in any way would be an inexcusable, even a counter-revolutionary act. The cause of Socialism is the support and promotion of Soviet power, as defined in Moscow.

This brings us to the second of the concepts important to contemporary Soviet outlook. That is the infallibility of the Kremlin. The Soviet concept of power, which permits no focal points of organization outside the Party itself, requires that the Party leadership remain in theory the sole repository of truth. For if truth were to be found elsewhere, there would be justification for its expression in organized activity. But it is precisely that which the Kremlin cannot and will not permit.

The leadership of the Communist Party is therefore always right, and has been always right ever since in 1929 Stalin formalized his personal power by announcing that decisions of the Politburo were being taken unanimously.

On the principle of infallibility there rests the iron discipline of the Communist Party. In fact, the two concepts are mutually self-supporting. Perfect discipline requires recognition of infallibility. Infallibility requires the observance of discipline. And the two go far to determine the behaviorism of the entire Soviet apparatus of power. But their effect cannot be understood unless a third factor be taken into account: namely, the fact that the leadership is at liberty to put forward for tactical purposes any particular thesis which it finds useful to the cause at any particular moment and to require the faithful and unquestioning acceptance of that thesis by the members of the movement as a whole. This means that truth is not a constant but is actually created, for all intents and purposes, by the Soviet leaders themselves. It may vary from week to week, from month to month. It is nothing absolute and immutable—nothing which flows from objective reality. It is only the most recent manifestation of the wisdom of those in whom the ultimate wisdom is supposed to reside, because they represent the logic of history. The accumulative effect of these factors is to give to the whole subordinate apparatus of Soviet power an unshakable stubbornness and steadfastness in its orientation. This orientation can be changed at will by the Kremlin but by no other power. Once a given party line has been laid down on a given issue of current policy, the whole Soviet governmental machine, including the mechanism of diplomacy, moves inexorably along the prescribed path, like a persistent toy automobile wound up and headed in a given direction, stopping only when it meets with some unanswerable force. The individuals who are the components of this machine are unamenable to argument or reason, which comes to them from outside sources. Their whole training has taught them to mistrust and discount the glib persuasiveness of the outside world. Like the white dog before the phonograph, they hear only the "master's voice." And if they are to be called off from the purposes last dictated to them, it is the master who must call them off. Thus the foreign representative cannot hope that his words will make any impression on them. The most that he can hope is that they will be transmitted to those at the top, who are capable of changing the party line. But even those are not likely to be swayed by any normal logic in the words of the bourgeois representative. Since there can be no appeal to common purposes, there can be no appeal to common mental approaches. For this reason, facts speak louder than words to the ears of the Kremlin; and words carry the greatest weight when they have the ring of reflecting, or being backed up by, facts of unchallengeable validity.

But we have seen that the Kremlin is under no ideological compulsion to accomplish its purposes in a hurry. Like the Church, it is dealing in ideological concepts which are of long-term validity, and it can afford to be patient. It has no right to risk the existing achievements of the revolution for the sake of vain baubles of the future. The very teachings of Lenin himself require great caution and flexibility in the pursuit of Communist purposes. Again, these precepts are fortified by the lessons of Russian history: of centuries of obscure battles between nomadic forces over the stretches of a vast unfortified plain. Here caution, circumspection, flexibility and deception are the valuable qualities; and their value finds a natural appreciation in the Russian or the oriental mind. Thus the Kremlin has no compunction about retreating in the face of superior forces. And being under

the compulsion of no timetable, it does not get panicky under the necessity for such retreat. Its political action is a fluid stream which moves constantly, wherever it is permitted to move, toward a given goal. Its main concern is to make sure that it has filled every nook and cranny available to it in the basin of world power. But if it finds unassailable barriers in its path, it accepts these philosophically and accommodates itself to them. The main thing is that there should always be pressure, unceasing constant pressure, toward the desired goal. There is no trace of any feeling in Soviet psychology that that goal must be reached at any given time.

These considerations make Soviet diplomacy at once easier and more difficult to deal with than the diplomacy of individual aggressive leaders like Napoleon and Hitler. On the one hand it is more sensitive to contrary force, more ready to yield on individual sectors of the diplomatic front when that force is felt to be too strong, and thus more rational in the logic and rhetoric of power. On the other hand it cannot be easily defeated or discouraged by a single victory on the part of its opponents. And the patient persistence by which it is animated means that it can be effectively countered not by sporadic acts which represent the momentary whims of democratic opinion but only be intelligent long-range policies on the part of Russia's adversaries—policies no less steady in their purpose, and no less variegated and resourceful in their application, than those of the Soviet Union itself.

In these circumstances it is clear that the main element of any United States policy toward the Soviet Union must be that of long-term, patient but firm and vigilant containment of Russian expansive tendencies. It is important to note, however, that such a policy has nothing to do with outward histrionics: with threats or blustering or superfluous gestures of outward "toughness." While the Kremlin is basically flexible in its reaction to political realities, it is by no means unamenable to considerations of prestige. Like almost any other government, it can be placed by tactless and threatening gestures in a position where it cannot afford to yield even though this might be dictated by its sense of realism. The Russian leaders are keen judges of human psychology, and as such they are highly conscious that loss of temper and of self-control is never a source of strength in political affairs. They are quick to exploit such evidences of weakness. For these reasons it is a sine qua non of successful dealing with Russia that the foreign government in question should remain at all times cool and collected and that its demands on Russian policy should be put forward in such a manner as to leave the way open for a compliance not too detrimental to Russian prestige.

III

In the light of the above, it will be clearly seen that the Soviet pressure against the free institutions of the western world is something that can be contained by the adroit and vigilant application of counter-force at a series of constantly shifting geographical and political points, corresponding to the shifts and maneuvers of Soviet policy, but which cannot be charmed or talked out of existence. The Russians look forward to a duel of infinite duration, and they see that already they have scored great successes. It must be borne in mind that there was a time when the Communist Party represented far more of a minority in the sphere of Russian national life than Soviet power today represents in the world community.

But if the ideology convinces the rulers of Russia that truth is on their side and that they can therefore afford to wait, those of us on whom that ideology has no claim are free to examine objectively the validity of that premise. The Soviet thesis not only implies complete lack of control by the west over its own economic destiny, it likewise assumes Russian unity, discipline and patience over an infinite period. Let us bring this apocalyptic vision down to earth, and suppose that the western world finds the strength and resourcefulness to contain Soviet power over a period of ten to fifteen years. What does that spell for Russia itself?

The Soviet leaders, taking advantage of the contributions of modern techniques to the arts of despotism, have solved the question of obedience within the confines of their power. Few challenge their authority; and even those who do are unable to make that challenge valid as against the organs of suppression of the state.

The Kremlin has also proved able to accomplish its purpose of building up Russia, regardless of the interests of the inhabitants, and industrial foundation of heavy metallurgy, which is, to be sure, not yet complete but which is nevertheless continuing to grow and is approaching those of the other major industrial countries. All of this, however, both the maintenance of internal political security and the building of heavy industry, has been carried out at a terrible cost in human life and in human hopes and energies. It has necessitated the use of forced labor on a scale unprecedented in modern times under conditions of peace. It has involved the neglect or abuse of other phases of Soviet economic life, particularly agriculture, consumers' goods production, housing and transportation.

To all that, the war has added its tremendous toll of destruction, death and human exhaustion. In consequence of this, we have in Russia today a population which is physically and spiritually tired. The mass of the people are disillusioned, skeptical and no longer as accessible as they once were to the magical attraction which Soviet power still radiates to its followers abroad. The avidity with which people seized upon the slight respite accorded to the Church for tactical reasons during the war was eloquent testimony to the fact that their capacity for faith and devotion found little expression in the purposes of the regime.

In these circumstances, there are limits to the physical and nervous strength of people themselves. These limits are absolute ones, and are binding even for the cruelest dictatorship, because beyond them people cannot be driven. The forced labor camps and the other agencies of constraint provide temporary means of compelling people to work longer hours than their own volition or mere economic pressure would dictate; but if people survive them at all they become old before their time and must be considered as human casualties to the demands of dictatorship. In either case their best powers are no longer available to society and can no longer be enlisted in the service of the state.

Here only the younger generations can help. The younger generation, despite all vicissitudes and sufferings, is numerous and vigorous; and the Russians are a talented people. But it still remains to be seen what will be the effects on mature performance of the abnormal emotional strains of childhood which Soviet dictatorship created and which were enormously increased by the war. Such things as normal security and placidity of home environment have practically ceased to exist in the Soviet Union outside of the most remote farms and villages. And observers are not yet sure whether that is not going to leave its mark on the over-all capacity of the generation now coming into maturity.

In addition to this, we have the fact that Soviet economic development, while it can list certain formidable achievements, has been precariously spotty and uneven. Russian Communists who speak of the "uneven development of capitalism" should blush at the contemplation of their own national economy. Here certain branches of economic life, such as the metallurgical and machine industries, have been pushed out of all proportion to other sectors of economy. Here is a nation striving to become in a short period one of the great industrial nations of the world while it still has no highway network worthy of the name and only a relatively primitive network of railways. Much has been done to increase efficiency of labor and to teach primitive peasants something about the operation of machines. But maintenance is still a crying deficiency of all Soviet economy. Construction is hasty and poor in quality. Depreciation must be enormous. And in vast sectors of economic life it has not yet been possible to instill into labor anything like that general culture of production and technical self-respect which characterizes the skilled worker of the west.

It is difficult to see how these deficiencies can be corrected at an early date by a tired and dispirited population working largely under the shadow of fear and compulsion. And as long as they are not overcome, Russia will remain economically as vulnerable, and in a certain sense an impotent, nation, capable of exporting its enthusiasms and of radiating the strange charm of its primitive political vitality but unable to back up those articles of export by the real evidences of material power and prosperity.

Meanwhile, a great uncertainty hangs over the political life of the Soviet Union. That is the uncertainty involved in the transfer of power from one individual or group of individuals to others.

This is, of course, outstandingly the problem of the personal position of Stalin. We must remember that his succession to Lenin's pinnacle of pre-eminence in the Communist movement was the only such transfer of individual authority which the Soviet Union has experienced. That transfer took 12 years to consolidate. It cost the lives of millions of people and shook the state to its foundations. The attendant tremors were felt all through the international revolutionary movement, to the disadvantage of the Kremlin itself.

It is always possible that another transfer of pre-eminent power may take place quietly and inconspicuously, with no repercussions anywhere. But again, it is possible that the questions involved may unleash, to use some of Lenin's words, one of those "incredibly swift transitions" from "delicate deceit" to "wild violence" which characterize Russian history, and may shake Soviet power to its foundations.

But this is not only a question of Stalin himself. There has been, since 1938, a dangerous congealment of political life in the higher circles of Soviet power. The All-Union Congress of Soviets, in theory the supreme body of the Party, is supposed to meet not less often than once in three years. It will soon be eight full years since its last meeting. During this period membership in the Party has numerically doubled. Party mortality during the war was enormous; and today well over half of the Party members are persons who have entered since the last Party congress was held. Meanwhile, the same small group of men has carried on at the top through an amazing series of national vicissitudes. Surely there is some reason why the experiences of the war brought basic political changes to every one of the great governments of the west. Surely the causes of that phenomenon are basic enough to be present somewhere in the obscurity of Soviet political life, as well. And yet no recognition has been given to these causes in Russia.

It must be surmised from this that even within so highly disciplined an organization as the Communist Party there must be a growing divergence in age, outlook and interest between the great mass of Party members, only so recently recruited into the movement, and the little self-perpetuating clique of men at the top, whom most of these Party members have never met, with whom they have never conversed, and with whom they can have no political intimacy.

Who can say whether, in these circumstances, the eventual rejuvenation of the higher spheres of authority (which can only be a matter of time) can take place smoothly and peacefully, or whether rivals in the quest for higher power will not eventually reach down into these politically immature and inexperienced masses in order to find support for their respective claims? If this were ever to happen, strange consequences could flow for the Communist Party: for the membership at large has been exercised only in the practices of iron discipline and obedience and not in the arts of compromise and accommodation. And if disunity were ever to seize and paralyze the Party, the chaos and weakness of Russian society would be revealed in forms beyond description. For we have seen that Soviet power is only concealing an amorphous mass of human beings among whom no independent organizational structure is tolerated. In Russia there is not even such a thing as local government. The present generation of Russians have never known spontaneity of collective action. If, consequently, anything were ever to occur to disrupt the unity and efficacy of the Party as a political instrument, Soviet Russia might be changed overnight from one of the strongest to one of the weakest and most pitiable of national societies.

Thus the future of Soviet power may not be by any means as secure as Russian capacity for self-delusion would make it appear to the men of the Kremlin. That they can quietly and easily turn it over to others remains to be proved. Meanwhile, the hardships of their rule and the vicissitudes of international life have taken a heavy toll of the strength and hopes of the great people on whom their power rests. It is curious to note that the ideological power of Soviet authority is strongest today in areas beyond the frontiers of Russia, beyond the reach of its police power. This phenomenon brings to mind a comparison used by Thomas Mann in his great novel *Buddenbrooks*. Observing that human institutions often show the greatest outward brilliance at a moment when inner decay is in reality farthest advanced, he compared one of those stars whose light shines most brightly on this world when in reality it has long since ceased to exist. And who can say with assurance that the strong light still cast by the Kremlin on the dissatisfied peoples of the western world is not the powerful afterglow of a constellation which is in actuality on the wane? This cannot be proved. And it cannot be disproved. But the possibility remains (and in the opinion of this writer it is a strong one) that Soviet power, like the capitalist world of its conception, bears within it the seeds of its own decay, and that the sprouting of these seeds is well advanced.

IV

It is clear that the United States cannot expect in the foreseeable future to enjoy political intimacy with the Soviet regime. It must continue to regard the Soviet Union as a rival, not a partner, in the political arena. It must continue to expect that Soviet policies will reflect no abstract love of peace and stability, no real faith in the possibility of a permanent happy coexistence of the Socialist and capitalist worlds, but rather a cautious, persistent pressure toward the disruption and, weakening of all rival influence and rival power.

Balanced against this are the facts that Russia, as opposed to the western world in general, is still by far the weaker party, that Soviet policy is highly flexible, and that Soviet society may well contain deficiencies which will eventually weaken its own total potential. This would of itself warrant the United States entering with reasonable confidence upon a policy of firm containment, designed to confront the Russians with unalterable counter-force at every point where they show signs of encroaching upon the interests of a peaceful and stable world.

But in actuality the possibilities for American policy are by no means limited to holding the line and hoping for the best. It is entirely possible for the United States to influence by its actions the internal developments, both within Russia and throughout the international Communist movement, by which Russian policy is largely determined. This is not only a question of the modest measure of informational activity which this government can conduct in the Soviet Union and elsewhere, although that, too, is important. It is rather a question of the degree to which the United States can create among the peoples of the world generally the impression of a country which knows what it wants, which is coping successfully with the problem of its internal life and with the responsibilities of a World Power, and which has a spiritual vitality capable of holding its own among the major ideological currents of the time. To the extent that such an impression can be created and maintained, the aims of Russian Communism must appear sterile and quixotic, the hopes and enthusiasm of Moscow's supporters must wane, and added strain must be imposed on the Kremlin's foreign policies. For the palsied decrepitude of the capitalist world is the keystone of Communist philosophy. Even the failure of the United States to experience the early economic depression which the ravens of the Red Square have been predicting with such complacent confidence since hostilities ceased would have deep and important repercussions throughout the Communist world.

By the same token, exhibitions of indecision, disunity and internal disintegration within this country have an exhilarating effect on the whole Communist movement. At each evidence of these tendencies, a thrill of hope and excitement goes through the Communist world; a new jauntiness can be noted in the Moscow tread; new groups of foreign supporters climb on to what they can only view as the band wagon of international politics; and Russian pressure increases all along the line in international affairs.

It would be an exaggeration to say that American behavior unassisted and alone could exercise a power of life and death over the Communist movement and bring about the early fall of Soviet power in Russia. But the United States has it in its power to increase enormously the strains under which Soviet policy must operate, to force upon the Kremlin a far greater degree of moderation and circumspection than it has had to observe in recent years, and in this way to promote tendencies which must eventually find their outlet in either the breakup or the gradual mellowing of Soviet power. For no mystical, Messianic movement—and particularly not that of the Kremlin—can face frustration indefinitely without eventually adjusting itself in one way or another to the logic of that state of affairs.

Thus the decision will really fall in large measure in this country itself. The issue of Soviet-American relations is in essence a test of the overall worth of the United States as a nation among nations. To avoid destruction the United States need only measure up to its own best traditions and prove itself worthy of preservation as a great nation.

Surely, there was never a fairer test of national quality than this. In the light of these circumstances, the thoughtful observer of Russian-American relations will find no cause for complaint in the Kremlin's challenge to American society. He will rather experience a certain gratitude to a Providence which, by providing the American people with this implacable challenge, has made their entire security as a nation dependent on their pulling themselves together and accepting the responsibilities of moral and political leadership that history plainly intended them to bear.

HUBERT H. HUMPHREY

Address at the Democratic National Convention (1948)

Fellow Democrats, fellow Americans:

I realize that in speaking in behalf of the minority report on civil rights as presented by Congressman DeMiller of Wisconsin that I am dealing with a charged issue—with an issue which has been confused by emotionalism on all sides of the fence. I realize that there are here today friends and colleagues of mine, many of them, who feel just as deeply and keenly as I do about this issue and who are yet in complete disagreement with me.

My respect and admiration for these men and their views was great when I came to this convention. It is now far greater because of the sincerity, the courtesy, and the forthrightness with which many of them have argued in our prolonged discussions in the platform committee.

Because of this very great respect—and because of my profound belief that we have a challenging task to do here—because good conscience, decent morality, demands it—I feel I must rise at this time to support a report—the minority report—a report that spells out our democracy, a report that the people of this country can and will understand, and a report that they will enthusiastically acclaim on the great issue of civil rights!

Now let me say at the outset that this proposal is made with no single region. Our proposal is made for no single class, for no single racial or religious groups in mind.

All of the regions of this country, all of the states have shared in the precious heritage of American freedom. All the states and all the regions have seen at least some infringements of that freedom—all people—get this—all people, white and black, all groups, all racial groups have been the victims at times in this nation of—let me say—vicious discrimination.

The masterly statement of our keynote speaker, the distinguished United States Senator from Kentucky, Alben Barkley, made that point with great force. Speaking of the founder of our party, Thomas Jefferson, he said this, and I quote from Alben Barkley:

> He did not proclaim that all the white, or the black, or the red, or the yellow men are equal; that all Christian or Jewish men are equal; that all Protestant and all Catholic men are equal; that all rich or poor men are equal; that all good and bad men are equal. What he declared was that all men are equal; and the equality which he proclaimed was the equality in the right to enjoy the blessings of free government in which they may participate and to which they have given their support.

Now these words of Senator Barkley's are appropriate to this convention—appropriate to this convention of the oldest, the most truly progressive political party in America. From the time of Thomas Jefferson, the time of that immortal American doctrine of individual rights, under just and fairly administered laws, the Democratic party has tried hard to secure expanding freedoms for all citizens. Oh, yes, I know, other political parties may have talked more about civil rights, but the Democratic party has securely done more civil rights.

We have made progress; we have made great progress in every part of this country. We've made great progress in the South; we've made it in the West, in the North, and in the East, but we must now focus the direction of that progress toward the realization of a full program of civil rights for all. This convention must set out more specifically the direction in which our party efforts are to go.

We can be proud that we can be guided by the courageous trail blazing of two great Democratic presidents. We can be proud of the fact that our great and beloved immortal leader Franklin Roosevelt gave us guidance. And we be proud of the fact—we can be proud of the fact—that Harry Truman has had the courage to give to the people of America the new emancipation proclamation!

It seems to me, it seems to me, that the Democratic party needs to make definite pledges of the kinds suggested in the confidence placed in it by the people of all races and all sections of this country.

Sure, we're here as Democrats. But my good friends, we're here as Americans; we're here as the believers in the principal and the ideology of democracy, and I firmly believe that as men concerned with our country's future, we must specify in our platform guarantees which we have mentioned in the minority report.

Yes, this is far more than a party matter. Every citizen has a stake in the emergence of the United States as a leader in a free world. That world is being challenged by the world of slavery. For us to play our part effectively, we must be in a morally sound position.

We can't use a double standard—there's no room for double standards in American politics—for measuring our own and other people's policies. Our demands for democratic practices in other lands will be no more effective than the guarantees of those practiced in our own country.

Friends, delegates, I do not believe that there can be any compromise on the guarantee of civil rights which I have mentioned in the minority report.

In spite of my desire for unanimous agreement on the entire platform, in spite of my desire to see everybody here in honest and unanimous agreement, there are some matters which I think must be stated clearly and without qualification. There can be no hedging—the newspaper headlines are wrong! There will be no hedging, and there will be no watering down—if you please—of the instruments and the principals of the civil-rights program!

To those who say, my friends, to those who say, that we are rushing this issue of civil rights, I say to them we are 172 years late! To those who say, to those who say this civil-rights program is an infringement on states' rights, I say this: the time has arrived in America for the Democratic party to get out of the shadow of states' rights and walk forthrightly into the bright sunshine of human rights!

People, people—human beings—this is the issue of the 20th century. People of all kinds—all sorts of people—and these people are looking to America for leadership, and they're looking to America for precept and example.

My good friends—my fellow Democrats—I ask you for calm consideration of our historic opportunity.

Let us not forget—let us do forget—the evil passions, the blindness of the past. In these times of world economic, political, and spiritual crisis, we cannot—we must not—turn from the path so plainly before us. That path has already lead us through many valleys of the shadow of death. Now is the time to recall those who were left on that path of American freedom.

For all of us here, for the millions who have sent us, for the whole two-billion members of the human family, our land is now, more than ever before, the last best hope on earth. I know that we can—I know that we shall—begging here the fuller and richer realization of that hope—[have] that promise of a land where all men are truly free and equal, and each man uses his freedom and equality wisely and well.

My good friends, I ask my party, I ask the Democratic party, to march down the high road of progressive democracy. I ask this convention, I ask this convention, to say in unmistakable terms that we proudly hail, and we courageously support, our President and leader Harry Truman in his great fight for civil rights in America!

REINHOLD NIEBUHR

The Irony of American History (1952)

The Ironic Element in the American Situation

Everybody understands the obvious meaning of the world struggle in which we are engaged. We are defending freedom against tyranny and are trying to preserve justice against a system which has, demonically, distilled injustice and cruelty out of its original promise of a higher justice. The obvious meaning is analyzed for us in every daily journal; and the various facets of this meaning are illumined for us in every banquet and commencement-day speech. The obvious meaning is not less true for having become trite. Nevertheless it is not the whole meaning.

We also have some awareness of an element of tragedy in this struggle, which does not fit into the obvious pattern. Could there be a clearer tragic dilemma than that which faces our civilization?

Though confident of its virtue, it must yet hold atomic bombs ready for use so as to prevent a possible world conflagration. It may actually make the conflict the more inevitable by this threat; and yet it cannot abandon the threat. Furthermore, if the conflict should break out, the non-communist world would be in danger of destroying itself as a moral culture in the process of defending itself physically. For no one can be sure that a war won by the use of the modern means of mass destruction would leave enough physical and social substance to rebuild a civilization among either victors or vanquished. The victors would also face the "imperial" problem of using power in global terms but from one particular center of authority, so preponderant and unchallenged that its world rule would almost certainly violate basic standards of justice.

Such a tragic dilemma is an impressive aspect of our contemporary situation. But tragic elements in present history are not as significant as the ironic ones. Pure tragedy elicits tears of admiration and pity for the hero who is willing to brave death or incur guilt for the sake of some great good. Irony however prompts some laughter and a nod of comprehension beyond the laughter; for irony involves comic absurdities which cease to be altogether absurd when fully understood. Our age is involved in irony because so many dreams of our nation have been so cruelly refuted by history. Our dreams of a pure virtue are dissolved in a situation in which it is possible to exercise the virtue of responsibility toward a community of nations only by courting the prospective guilt of the atomic bomb. And the irony is increased by the frantic efforts of some of our idealists to escape this hard reality by dreaming up schemes of an ideal world order which have no relevance to either our present dangers or our urgent duties.

Our dreams of bringing the whole of human history under the control of the human will are ironically, refuted by the fact that no group of idealists can easily move the pattern of history toward the desired goal of peace and justice. The recalcitrant forces in the historical drama have a power and persistence beyond our reckoning. Our own nation, always a vivid symbol of the most characteristic attitudes of a bourgeois culture, is less potent to do what it wants in the hour of its greatest strength than it was in the days of its infancy. The infant, is more secure in his world than the mature man is in his wider world. The pattern of the historical drama grows more quickly than the strength of even the most powerful man or nation.

Our situation of historic frustration becomes doubly ironic through the fact that the power of recalcitrance against our fondest hopes is furnished by a demonic religio-political creed which had even simpler notions than we of finding an escape from the ambiguity of man's strength and weakness. For communism believes that it is possible for man, at a particular moment in history, to take "the leap from the realm of necessity to the realm of freedom." The cruelty of communism is partly derived from the absurd pretension that the communist movement stands on the other side of this leap and has the whole of history in its grasp. Its cruelty is partly due to the frustration of the communist overlords of history when they discover that the "logic" of history does not conform to their delineation of it. One has an uneasy feeling that some of our dreams of managing history might have resulted in similar cruelties if they had flowered into action. But there was fortunately no program to endow our elite of prospective philosopher-scientist-kings with actual political power.

Modern man's confidence in his power over historical destiny prompted the rejection of every older conception of an overruling providence in history. Modern man's confidence in his virtue caused an equally unequivocal rejection of the Christian idea of the ambiguity of human virtue. In the liberal world the evils in human nature and history were ascribed to social institutions or to ignorance or to some other manageable defect in human nature or environment. Again the communist doctrine is more explicit and therefore more dangerous. It ascribes the origin of evil to the institution of property. The abolition of this institution by communism therefore prompts the ridiculous claim of innocency for one of the vastest concentrations of power in human history. This distillation of evil from the claims of innocency is ironic enough. But the irony is increased by the fact that the so-called free world must cover itself with guilt in order to ward off the peril of communism. The final height of irony is reached by the fact that the most powerful nation in the alliance of free peoples is the United States. For every illusion of a liberal culture has achieved a special emphasis in the United States, even while its power grew to phenominal proportions. [. . .]

The question of "materialism" leads to equally ironic consequences in our debate and contest with communism. The communists are consistent philosophical materialists who believe that mind is the fruit of matter; and that culture is the product of economic forces. Perhaps the communists are not as consistently materialistic in the philosophical sense as they pretend to be. For they are too Hegelian to be mechanistic materialists. They have the idea of a "dialectic" or "logic" running through both nature and history which means that a rational structure of meaning runs through the whole of reality. Despite the constant emphasis upon the "dignity of man" in our own liberal culture, its predominant naturalistic bias frequently results in views of human nature in which the dignity of man is not very clear.

It is frequently assumed that human nature can be manipulated by methods analogous to those used in physical nature. Furthermore it is generally taken for granted that the highest ends of life can be fulfilled in man's historic existence. This confidence makes for utopian visions of historical possibilities on the one hand and for rather materialistic conceptions of human ends on the other. All concepts of immortality are dismissed as the fruit of wishful thinking. This dismissal usually involves indifference toward the tension in human existence, created by the fact that "our reach is beyond our grasp," and that every sensitive individual has a relation to a structure of meaning which is never fulfilled in the vicissitudes of actual history.

The crowning irony in this debate about materialism lies in the tremendous preoccupation of our own technical culture with the problem of gaining physical security against the hazards of nature. Since our nation has carried this preoccupation to a higher degree of consistency than any other we are naturally more deeply involved in the irony. Our orators profess abhorrence of the communist creed of "materialism" but we are rather more successful practitioners of materialism as a working creed than the communists, who have failed so dismally in raising the general standards of well-being.

Meanwhile we are drawn into an historic situation in which the paradise of our domestic security is suspended in a hell of global insecurity; and the conviction of the perfect compatibility of virtue and prosperity which we have inherited from both our Calvinist and our Jeffersonian ancestors is challenged by the cruel facts of history. For our sense of responsibility to a world community beyond our own borders is a virtue, even though it is partly derived from the prudent understanding of our own interests. But this virtue does not guarantee our ease, comfort, or prosperity. We are the poorer for the global responsibilities which we bear. And the fulfillments of our desires are mixed with frustrations and vexations.

Sometimes the irony in our historic situation is derived from the extravagant emphasis in our culture upon the value and dignity of the individual and upon individual liberty as the final value of life. Our cherished values of individualism are real enough; and we are right in preferring death to their annulment. But our exaltation of the individual involves us in some very ironic contradictions. On the one hand, our culture does not really value the individual as much as it pretends; on the other hand, if justice is to

be maintained and our survival assured, we cannot make individual liberty as unqualifiedly the end of life as our ideology asserts.

A culture which is so strongly influenced by both scientific concepts and technocratic illusions is constantly tempted to annul or to obscure the unique individual. Schemes for the management of human nature usually involve denials of the "dignity of man" by their neglect of the chief source of man's dignity, namely, his essential freedom and capacity for self-determination. This denial is the more inevitable because scientific analyses of human actions and events are bound to be preoccupied with the relations of previous causes to subsequent events. Every human action ostensibly can be explained by some efficient cause or complex of causes. The realm of freedom which allows the individual to make his decision within, above and beyond the pressure of causal sequences is beyond the realm of scientific analysis. Furthermore the acknowledgment of its reality introduces an unpredictable and incalculable element into the causal sequence. It is therefore embarrassing to any scientific scheme. Hence scientific cultures are bound to incline to determinism. The various sociological determinisms are reinforced by the general report which the psychologists make of the human psyche. For they bear witness to the fact that their scientific instruments are unable to discover that integral, self-transcendent center of personality, which is in and yet above the stream of nature and time and which religion and poetry take for granted.[1]

---

1. In his comprehensive empirical study of human personality Gardner Murphy nicely suggests the limits of empiricism in dealing with the self. He declares: "We do not wish to deny the possibility suggested by James Ward that all awareness is colored by selfhood. . . . Least of all do we wish to attempt to set aside the still unsolved philosophical question whether the process of experiencing necessitates the existence of a non-empirical experiencer. . . . Nothing could be gained by a Gordian-knot solution of such a tangled problem. We are concerned solely with the immediate question: Should the student of personality at the present stage of research postulate a non-empirical entity distinct from the organism and its perceptual responses? . . . To this limited question a negative answer seems advisable." Gardner Murphy, *Personality*, p. 491. There can of course be no "non-empirical entity." But there may be an entity which cannot be isolated by scientific techniques.

Furthermore it is difficult for a discipline, whether philosophical or scientific, operating, as it must, with general concepts, to do justice to the tang and flavor of individual uniqueness. The unique and irreplaceable individual, with his

> Thoughts hardly to be packed
> Into a narrow act,
> Fancies that broke through language and escaped.
> (BROWNING)

with his private history and his own peculiar mixture of hopes and fears, may be delineated by the poet. The artist-novelist may show that his personality is not only unique but subject to infinite variation in his various encounters with other individuals; but all this has no place in a strictly scientific account of human affairs. In such accounts the individual is an embarrassment. [. . .]

Prosperity and Virtue

[. . .] If it is not possible for modern man to hold by faith that there is a larger meaning in the intricate patterns of history than those which his own virtues or skills supply, he would do well to emphasize fortune and caprice in his calculations. On the other hand, a simple belief in providence also does not rescue us from these perils of a false estimate of our own contributions. Of this, the course of Puritanism in our history is proof. [. . .]

In ascribing preoccupation with the material basis of life to democracy De Toqueville may not do justice to all aspects of the issue, but he does place his finger upon an unsolved problem of our democracy. For it is certainly the character of our particular democracy, founded on a vast continent, expanding as a culture with its expanding frontier and creating new frontiers of opportunity when the old geographic frontiers were ended, that every ethical and social problem of a just distribution of the privileges of life is solved by so enlarging the privileges that either an equitable distribution is made easier, or a lack of equity is rendered less noticeable. For in this abundance the least privileged members of the community are still privileged, compared with less favored communities. No democratic community has followed this technique of social adjustment more consistently than we. No other community had the resources to do so. It would be quite unjust to make a purely cynical estimate of this achievement. For the achievement includes recognition by American capitalists (what French capitalists, for instance, have not learned) that high wages for workers make mass production efficiency possible. Perhaps it ought to be added that this insight was not a purely rational achievement. It was forced upon the industrialists by the pressure of organized labor; but they learned to accept the policy of high wages as not detrimental to their own interests somewhat in the same fashion as monarchists learned the value of constitutional monarchy, after historic pressures had destroyed the institution of monarchy in its old form.

Yet the price which American culture has paid for this amelioration of social tensions through constantly expanding production has been considerable. It has created moral illusions about the ease with which the adjustment of interests to interests can be made in human society. These have imparted a quality of sentimentality to both our religious and our secular, social and political theories. It has also created a culture which makes "living standards" the final norm of the good life and which regards the perfection of techniques as the guarantor of every cultural as well as of every social-moral value.

The progress of American culture toward hegemony in the world community as well as toward the ultimate in standards of living has brought us everywhere to limits where our ideals and norms are brought under ironic indictment. Our confidence in the simple compatibility between prosperity and virtue is challenged particularly in our relations with Asia; for the Asians, barely emerging from the desperate poverty of an agrarian economy, are inclined to regard our prosperity as evidence of our injustice. Our confidence in the compatibility between our technical efficiency and our culture is challenged, particularly in our relations with Europe. For the European nations, France especially, find our culture "vulgar," and pretend to be imperiled by the inroads of an American synthetic drink upon the popularity of their celebrated wines. The French protest against "Cocacolonialism" expresses this ironic conflict in a nutshell. Our confidence in happiness as the end of life, and in prosperity as the basis of happiness is challenged by every duty and sacrifice, every wound and anxiety which our world-wide responsibilities bring upon us.

The cultural aversion of France toward us expresses explicitly what most of Europe seems to feel. In its most pessimistic moods European neutralism charges, in the words of *Le Monde*, that we are a "technocracy" not too sharply distinguished from the Russian attempt to bring all of life under technical control. It is doubly ironic that this charge should be made against us by France. Europe accuses us of errors of which the whole of modern bourgeois society is guilty and which we merely developed more consistently than European nations; for the cult of technical efficiency was elaborated among us without the checks which the ethos of a traditional aristocratic culture provided in Europe. On the other hand, there is a measure of truth in the charge of similarity between our culture and that of the pure Marxists because both are offshoots of the ethos which had its rise, significantly, in the same France which is now our principal critic in Europe. Marxism transmutes every illusion of a technical society into an obvious corruption by giving a monopoly of power to an elite, who desires to remold life within terms of the simple limits which it has set for life's meaning. Against such corruptions our democratic society offers guarantees, and prevents the consistent application of standards of technical efficiency to all the ends and purposes of life.

But it cannot be denied that a bourgeois society is in the process of experiencing the law of diminishing returns in the relation of technics and efficiency to the cultural life. The pursuit of culture requires certain margins of physical security and comfort; but the extension of the margins does not guarantee the further development of cultural values. It may lead to a preoccupation with the margins and obsession with the creature comforts. The elaboration of technics is basic to the advancement of culture. The inventions of writing and printing represent two of the most important chapters in the history of culture. But the further elaboration of communications in the arts of mass communication have led to the vulgarization of culture as well as to the dissemination of its richest prizes among the general public. Television may represent a threat to our culture analogous to the threat of atomic weapons to our

civilization: America is the home of Hollywood in the imagination of Europe; though Europe hardly makes a fair appraisal of the relative involvement of producer and consumer in the purveyance of vulgar or sentimental art, holding us responsible for the production of what its millions avidly consume. In this, as in other respects, we must discount some of the European criticisms. Europe's belief that a nation as fortunate as our own could not possibly also possess and appreciate the nobler values of life may sometimes hide frustrated desire.

Yet we cannot deny the indictment that we seek a solution for practically every problem of life in quantitative terms; and are not fully aware of the limits of this approach. The constant multiplication of our high school and college enrollments has not had the effect of making us the most "intelligent" nation, whether we measure intelligence in terms of social wisdom, æsthetic discrimination, spiritual serenity or any other basic human achievement. It may have made us technically the most proficient nation, thereby proving that technical efficiency is more easily achieved in purely quantitative terms than any other value of culture.

Our preoccupation with technics has had an obviously deleterious effect upon at least one specific sector of our classical cultural inheritance. No national culture has been as assiduous as our own in trying to press the wisdom of the social and political sciences, indeed of all the humanities, into the limits of the natural sciences. The consequence of this effort must be analyzed more carefully in another context. It is worth noting here that, when political science is severed from its ancient rootage in the humanities and "enriched" by the wisdom of sociologists, psychologists and anthropologists, the result is frequently a preoccupation with minutiae which obscures the grand and tragic outlines of contemporary history, and offers vapid solutions for profound problems. Who can deny the irony of the contrast between the careful study of human "aggressiveness" in our socio-psychological sciences, and our encounter with a form of aggressiveness in actual life which is informed by such manias, illusions, historic aberrations and confusions, as could not possibly come under the microscope of the scientific procedures used in some of these studies? [. . .]

The Master of Destiny

[T]he idea of the abolition of the institution of monarchy as the most important strategy for the redemption of mankind was as characteristic of the peculiar prejudices of middle-class life as the idea of the abolition of the institution of property was of the unique viewpoint of propertyless proletarians. In each case they identified all evil with the type of power from which they suffered and which they did not control; and they regarded particular sources of particular social evils as the final source of all evil in history. Neither Condorcet, nor Comte in his subsequent elaborations of similar hopes, placed all their trust in this single strategy. The liberal world has always oscillated between the hope of creating perfect men by eliminating the social sources of evil and the hope of so purifying human "reason" by educational techniques that all social institutions would gradually become the bearers of a universal human will, informed by a universal human mind. These ambiguities, which have saved the Messianic dreams of the liberal culture from breeding the cruelties of communism, must be considered more fully presently. At the moment it is worth recording that the Frenchman, Condorcet, envisaged the French and the "Anglo-Americans" as the Messianic nations. Here we have in embryo what has become the ironic situation of our own day. The French Enlightenment consistently saw the American Revolution and the founding of the new American nation as a harbinger of the perfect world which was in the making. Though Comte, almost a century later, rigorously clung to the idea of French hegemony in the coming utopia and fondly hoped that French would be its universal language, France has fallen by the wayside as a nation with a Messianic consciousness, its present mood being characterized by extreme skepticism rather than apocalyptic hopes.

This leaves America as the prime bearer of this hope and dream. From the earliest days of its history to the present moment, there is a deep layer of Messianic consciousness in the mind of America. We never dreamed that we would have as much political power as we possess today; nor for that matter did we anticipate that the most powerful nation on earth would suffer such an ironic refutation of its dreams of mastering history. For our increased power related our will and purpose to a vaster and vaster entanglement with other wills and purposes, which made it impossible for any single will to prevail or any specific human goal of history easily to become the goal of all mankind.

We were, as a matter of fact, always vague, as the whole liberal culture is fortunately vague, about how power is to be related to the allegedly universal values which we hold in trust for mankind. We were, of course, not immune to the temptation of believing that the universal validity of what we held in trust justified our use of power to establish it. Thus in the debate on the annexation of Oregon, in which the imperial impulse of a youthful nation expressed itself, a Congressman could thunder: "If ours is to be the home of the oppressed, we must extend our territory in latitude and longitude to the demand of the millions which are to follow us; as well for our own posterity as for those who are invited to our peaceful shores to partake in our republican institutions."

Generally, however, the legitimization of power was not the purpose of our Messianic consciousness. We felt that by example and by unexplained forces in history our dream would become the regnant reality of history.

We have noted in another connection that in both the Calvinist and the Jeffersonian concept of our national destiny the emphasis lay at the beginning upon providence rather than human power. Jefferson had proposed for the seal of the United States a picture of "the children of Israel, led by a cloud by day and a pillar of fire by night." Washington declared in his first inaugural that "the preservation of the sacred fire of liberty and the destiny of the republican model of government are justly considered, perhaps as deeply, as finally staked on the experiment intrusted to the hands of the American people." Most significant was the assurance that we were acting as surrogates, as trustees for mankind. As Dr. Priestley put it in 1802: "It is impossible not to be sensible that we are acting for all mankind."

This concept of America as the darling of divine providence did not of course exclude the idea of fulfilling its destiny by actions which would help in the universal realization of the democratic ideal of society. The Puritans, as we have seen, gradually shifted from their emphasis upon a divine favor to the nation, to an emphasis upon the virtue which the nation had acquired by divine favor. Even a very early Puritan was certain that "God had sifted a whole nation that he might send choice grain into the wilderness" (William Stoughton, 1668).

President Johnson in his message to Congress in 1868 expressed the most popular form of our Messianic dream. "The conviction is rapidly growing ground in the American mind," he declared, "that with increased facilities for inter-communication between all portions of the earth the principles of free government as embraced in our constitution . . . would prove sufficient strength and breadth to comprehend within their sphere and influence the civilized nations of the world." Except in moments of aberration we do not think of ourselves as the potential masters, but as tutors of mankind in its pilgrimage to perfection.

Such Messianic dreams, though fortunately not corrupted by the lust of power, are of course not free of the moral pride which creates a hazard to their realization. "God has not been preparing the English-speaking and Teutonic peoples," declared Senator Beveridge of Indiana, "for a thousand years for nothing but vain and idle self-contemplation and self-admiration. He has made us the master organizers of the world to establish system where chaos reigns. . . . He has made us adept in government that we may administer government among savage and senile peoples. Were it not for such a force this world would relapse into barbarism and night. And of all our race he has marked the American people as his chosen nation to finally lead in the regeneration of the world." The concept of administering "government among savage and senile peoples" does of course have power implications. But the legitimization of power is generally subordinate in the American dream to the fact that the concept that a divine favor upon the nation implies a commitment "to lead in the regeneration of mankind." Among us, as well as among communists, an excessive voluntarism which finally brings human history under the control of the human will is in tentative, but not in final, contradiction to a determinism which finds historical destiny favorable at some particular point to man's assumption of mastery over that destiny. The American dream is not particularly unique. Almost every nation has had a version of it.[2]

But the American experience represents a particularly unique and ironic refutation of the illusion in all such dreams. The illusions about the possibility of managing historical destiny from any particular standpoint in history, always involve, as already noted, miscalculations about both the power and the wisdom of the managers and of the weakness and the manageability of the historical "stuff" which is to be managed. [. . .]

Consistent with the general liberal hope of redeeming history, the American Messianic dream is vague about the political or other power which would be required to subject all recalcitrant wills to the one will which is informed by the true vision. [. . .] American government is regarded as the final and universally valid form of political organization. But, on the whole, it is expected to gain its ends by moral attraction and imitation. Only occasionally does an hysterical statesman suggest that we must increase our power and use it in order to gain the ideal ends, of which providence has made us the trustees.

The first element of irony lies in the fact that our nation has, without particularly seeking it, acquired a greater degree of power than any other nation of history. The same technics, proficiency in the use of which lies at the foundation of American power, have created a "global" political situation in which the responsible use of this power has become a condition of survival of the free world. It is not surprising that the communist elite should be filled with fury when they behold the unfolding of this power, marked by their "logic" for self-destruction through its "inner contradictions."

---

2. See Lionel Curtis' *Civitas Dei* for the British version. Fichte had a vision of the German nation becoming a *Menschheitsnation*. Mazzini artfully combined national pride with the hope of Italy's peculiar contribution to the development of mankind. Russia has always been filled with Messianic illusions. In Nicholas Berdyaev's posthumously published *The Russian Idea*, he analyzes these Messianic illusions humorously and comes to the conclusion that the Soviet messianism is not an ideal but yet a tolerable culmination of all these Messianic dreams.

But, the second element of irony lies in the fact that a strong America is less completely master of its own destiny than was a comparatively weak America, rocking in the cradle of its continental security and serene in its infant innocence. The same strength which has extended our power beyond a continent has also interwoven our destiny with the destiny of many peoples and brought us into a vast web of history in which other wills, running in oblique or contrasting directions to our own, inevitably hinder or contradict what we most fervently desire. We cannot simply have our way, not even when we believe our way to have the "happiness of mankind" as its promise. Even in the greatness of our power we are thwarted by a ruthless foe, who is ironically the more recalcitrant and ruthless because his will is informed by an impossible dream of bringing happiness to all men if only he can eliminate our recalcitrance.

But we are thwarted by friends and allies as well as by foes. Our dream of the universal good is sufficiently valid to bring us in voluntary alliance with many peoples, who have similar conceptions of the good life. But neither their conceptions of the good, nor their interests, which are always compounded with ideals, are identical with our own. In this situation it is natural that many of our people should fail to perceive that historical destiny may be beguiled, deflected and transfigured by human policy, but that it cannot be coerced. They become impatient and want to use the atomic bomb (symbol of the technical efficiency upon which our world authority rests) not only to put an end to the recalcitrance of our foes but to eliminate the equivocal attitudes of the Asian and other peoples, who are not as clearly our allies as we should like them to be. Yet on the whole, we have as a nation learned the lesson of history tolerably well. We have heeded the warning "let not the wise man glory in his wisdom, let not the mighty man glory in his strength." Though we are not without vainglorious delusions in regard to our power, we are saved by a certain grace inherent in common sense rather than in abstract theories from attempting to cut through the vast ambiguities of our historic situation and thereby bringing our destiny to a tragic conclusion by seeking to bring it to a neat and logical one.

Significantly the elements in our population which are most prone to defy the limits of power, possessed by any particular agent in history, and to seek a resolution of our difficulties by a sheer display of military power, are frequently drawn from a bourgeois-liberal tradition which was, until recently, unconscious of the factor of power in political life. It is the nature of a business community that it deals with the covert forms of power in economic life and to be insensible to significance and the complexity of more overt forms of power, even as it is insensible to the motive of the lust for power as an element in human nature. It is quite conscious of the force of self-interest in life; but it imagines that this force is nicely checked and contained by prudence on the one hand and by the balance of competing interests on the other. The realm of the political with its vast imponderables of power is a *terra incognita* to it. When experience suddenly thrusts the facts and perils of this world upon it, it is inclined to exchange the sentimentalities and pretensions of yesterday, which obscured the power element in life, for the cynicism of today. This is the greater temptation for elements in the American business community because American world authority rests so directly upon our military power; and this in turn is drawn so immediately from our economic strength. We have had so little experience in managing or participating in the conscious and quasi-conscious power struggles of life and in fathoming the endlessly complex compounds of ethnic loyalties, historic traditions, military strength and ideological hopes which constitute historic forms of power, that we would fain move with one direct leap from the use of economic to the use of military power. These are the political and moral hazards of a great commercial nation, moving directly and precipitately into the baffling currents of world politics. Despite the hazards, we have managed to achieve some patience and shrewdness and have avoided the ultimate error of trying to bring the historic process to what would seem to us to be its ultimate conclusion. [. . .]

Today the success of America in world politics depends upon its ability to establish community with many nations, despite the hazards created by pride of power on the one hand and the envy of the weak on the other. This success requires a modest awareness of the contingent elements in the values and ideals of our devotion, even when they appear to us to be universally valid; and a generous appreciation of the valid elements in the practices and institutions of other nations though they deviate from our own. In other words, our success in world politics necessitates a disavowal of the pretentious elements in our original dream, and a recognition of the values and virtues which enter into history in unpredictable ways and which defy the logic which either liberal or Marxist planners had conceived for it. [. . .]

J. Edgar Hoover

Testimony before the House Un-American Activities Committee (1947)

My feelings concerning the Communist Party of the United States are well known. I have not hesitated over the years to express my concern and apprehension. As a consequence its professional smear brigades have conducted a relentless assault against the FBI. You who have been members of this committee also know the fury with which the party, its sympathizers and fellow travelers can launch an assault. I do not mind such attacks. What has been disillusioning is the manner in which they have been able to enlist support often from apparently well-meaning but thoroughly duped persons. [. . .]

The communist movement in the United States began to manifest itself in 1919. Since then it has changed its name and its party line whenever expedient and tactical. But always it comes back to fundamentals and bills itself as the party of Marxism-Leninism. As such, it stands for the destruction of our American form of government; it stands for the destruction of American democracy; it stands for the destruction of free enterprise; and it stands for the creation of a "Soviet of the United States" and ultimate world revolution. [. . .]

The communist, once he is fully trained and indoctrinated, realizes that he can create his order in the United States only by "bloody revolution." Their chief textbook, "The History of the Communist Party of the Soviet Union," is used as a basis for planning their revolution. Their tactics require that to be successful they must have:

1. The will and sympathy of the people.
2. Military aid and assistance.
3. Plenty of guns and ammunition.
4. A program for extermination of the police as they are the most important enemy and are termed "trained fascists."
5. Seizure of all communications, buses, railroads, radio stations, and other forms of communications and transportation. [. . .]

One thing is certain. The American progress which all good citizens seek, such as old-age security, houses for veterans, child assistance, and a host of others, is being adopted as window dressing by the communists to conceal their true aims and entrap gullible followers. [. . .]

The mad march of Red fascism is a cause for concern in America. But the deceit, the trickery, and the lies of the American communists are catching up with them. Whenever the spotlight of truth is focused upon them they cry, "Red-baiting." Now that their aims and objectives are being exposed, they are creating a Committee for the Constitutional Rights of Communists, and are feverishly working to build up what they term a quarter-million-dollar defense fund to place ads in papers, to publish pamphlets, to buy radio time. They know that their backs will soon be to the wall. [. . .]

What is important is the claim of the communists themselves that for every party member there are 10 others ready, willing and able to do the party's work. Herein lies the greatest menace of communism. For these are the people who infiltrate and corrupt various spheres of American life. So rather than the size of the Communist Party, the way to weigh its true importance is by testing its influence, its ability to infiltrate. [. . .]

The communists have developed one of the greatest propaganda machines the world has ever known. They have been able to penetrate and infiltrate many respectable public opinion mediums. They capitalize upon ill-founded charges associating known honest progressive liberals with left-wing causes. I have always entertained the view that there are few appellations more degrading than "communist" and hence it should be reserved for those justly deserving the degradation.

The communist propaganda technique is designed to promote emotional response with the hope that the victim will be attracted by what he is told the communist way of life holds in store for him. The objective, of course, is to develop discontent and hasten the day when the communists can gather sufficient support and following to overthrow the American way of life. [. . .]

Communists and their followers are prolific letter writers, and some of the more energetic ones follow the practice of directing numerous letters of protest to editors but signing a different name to each. Members of Congress are well aware of communists starting their pressure campaigns by an avalanche of mail which follows the party line. [. . .]

The American communists launched a furtive attack on Hollywood in 1935 by the issuance of a directive calling for a concentration in Hollywood. The orders called for action on two fronts: One, an effort to infiltrate the labor unions; two, infiltrate the so-called intellectual and creative fields.

In movie circles, communists developed an effective defense a few years ago in meeting criticism. They would counter with the question "After all, what is the matter with communism?" It was effective because many persons did not possess adequate knowledge of the subject to give an intelligent answer. [. . .]

I feel that this committee could render a great service to the nation through its power of exposure in quickly spotlighting existing front organizations and those which will be created in the future. There are easy tests to establish the real character of such organizations:

1. Does the group espouse the cause of Americanism or the cause of Soviet Russia?
2. Does the organization feature as speakers at its meeting known communists, sympathizers, or fellow travelers?
3. Does the organization shift when the party line shifts?
4. Does the organization sponsor causes, campaigns, literature, petitions, or other activities sponsored by the party or other front organizations?
5. Is the organization used as a sounding board by or is it endorsed by communist-controlled labor unions?
6. Does its literature follow the communist line or is it printed by the communist press?
7. Does the organization receive consistent favorable mention in the communist publications?
8. Does the organization present itself to be nonpartisan yet engage in political activities and consistently advocate causes favored by the communists?
9. Does the organization denounce American and British foreign policy while always lauding Soviet policy?
10. Does the organization utilize communist "double-talk" by referring to Soviet dominated countries as democracies, complaining that the United States is imperialistic and constantly denouncing monopoly-capital?
11. Have outstanding leaders in public life openly renounced affiliation with the organization?
12. Does the organization, if espousing liberal progressive causes, attract well-known honest patriotic liberals or does it denounce well-known liberals?
13. Does the organization have a consistent record of supporting the American viewpoint over the years?
14. Does the organization consider matters now directly related to its avowed purposes and objectives?

The Communist Party of the United States is a fifth column if there ever was one. It is far better organized than were the Nazis in occupied countries prior to their capitulation. They are seeking to weaken America just as they did in their era of obstruction when they were aligned with the Nazis. Their goal is the overthrow of our government. There is no doubt as to where a real communist's loyalty rests. Their allegiance is to Russia, not the United States. [. . .]

What can we do? And what should be our course of action? The best antidote to communism is vigorous, intelligent, old-fashioned Americanism, with eternal vigilance. I do not favor any course of action which would give the communists cause to portray and pity themselves as martyrs. I do favor unrelenting prosecution wherever they are found to be violating our country's laws.

As Americans, our most effective defense is a workable democracy that guarantees and preserves our cherished freedoms.

I would have no fears if more Americans possessed the zeal, the fervor, the persistence and the industry to learn about this menace of Red fascism. I do fear for the liberal and progressive who has been hoodwinked and duped into joining hands with the communists. I confess to a real apprehension so long as communists are able to secure ministers of the gospel to promote their evil work and espouse a cause that is alien to the religion of Christ and Judaism. I do fear so long as school boards and parents tolerate conditions whereby communists and fellow travelers, under the guise of academic freedom, can teach our youth a way of life that eventually will destroy the sanctity of the home, that undermines faith in God, that causes them to scorn respect for constituted authority and sabotage our revered Constitution.

I do fear so long as American labor groups are infiltrated, dominated or saturated with the virus of communism. I do fear the palliation and weasel-worded gestures against communism indulged in by some of our labor leaders who should know better, but who have become pawns in the hands of sinister but astute manipulations for the communist cause.

I fear for ignorance on the part of all our people who may take the poisonous pills of communist propaganda.

JOSEPH MCCARTHY

Speech at Wheeling, West Virginia (1950)

Ladies and Gentlemen:

Tonight as we celebrate the 141st birthday of one of the great men in American history, I would like to be able to talk about what a glorious day today is in the history of the world. As we celebrate the birth of this man, who with his whole heart and soul hated war, I would like to be able to speak of peace in our time, of war being outlawed, and of worldwide disarmament. These would be truly appropriate things to be able to mention as we celebrate the birthday of Abraham Lincoln.

Five years after a world war has been won, men's hearts should anticipate a long peace, and men's minds should be free from the heavy weight that comes with war. But this is not such a period—for this is not a period of peace. This is a time of the Cold War. This is a time when all the world is split into two vast, increasingly hostile armed camps—a time of a great armaments race. Today we can almost physically hear the mutterings and rumblings of an invigorated god of war. You can see it, feel it, and hear it all the way from the hills of Indochina, from the shores of Formosa right over into the very heart of Europe itself. [. . .]

Today we are engaged in a final, all-out battle between communistic atheism and Christianity. The modern champions of communism have selected this as the time. And, ladies and gentlemen, the chips are down—they are truly down.

Lest there be any doubt that the time has been chosen, let us go directly to the leader of communism today—Joseph Stalin. Here is what he said—not back in 1928, not before the war, not during the war—but two years after the last war was ended: "To think that the communist revolution can be carried out peacefully, within the framework of a Christian democracy, means one has either gone out of one's mind and lost all normal understanding, or has grossly and openly repudiated the communist revolution."

And this is what was said by Lenin in 1919, which was also quoted with approval by Stalin in 1947: "We are living," said Lenin, "not merely in a state but in a system of states, and the existence of the Soviet Republic side by side with Christian states for a long time is unthinkable. One or the other must triumph in the end. And before that end supervenes, a series of frightful collisions between the Soviet Republic and the bourgeois states will be inevitable."

Ladies and gentlemen, can there be anyone here tonight who is so blind as to say that the war is not on? Can there be anyone who fails to realize that the communist world has said, "The time is now"—that this is the time for the showdown between the democratic Christian world and the communist atheistic world? Unless we face this fact, we shall pay the price that must be paid by those who wait too long.

Six years ago, at the time of the first conference to map out peace—Dumbarton Oaks—there was within the Soviet orbit 180 million people. Lined up on the anti-totalitarian side there were in the world at that time roughly 1.625 billion people. Today, only six years later, there are 800 million people under the absolute domination of Soviet Russia—an increase of over 400 percent. On our side, the figure has shrunk to around 500 million. In other words, in less than six years the odds have changed from 9 to 1 in our favor to 8 to 5 against us. This indicates the swiftness of the tempo of communist victories and American defeats in the Cold War. As one of our outstanding historical figures once said, "When a great democracy is destroyed, it will not be because of enemies from without but rather because of enemies from within." The truth of this statement is becoming terrifyingly clear as we see this country each day losing on every front.

At war's end we were physically the strongest nation on earth and, at least potentially, the most powerful intellectually and morally. Ours could have been the honor of being a beacon in the desert of destruction, a shining, living proof that civilization was not yet ready to destroy itself. Unfortunately, we have failed miserably and tragically to arise to the opportunity.

The reason why we find ourselves in a position of impotency is not because our only powerful, potential enemy has sent men to invade our shores, but rather because of the traitorous actions of those who have been treated so well by this nation. It has not been the less fortunate members of minority groups who have been selling this nation out, but rather those who have had all the benefits that the wealthiest nation on earth has had to offer—the finest homes, the finest college education, and the finest jobs in government we can give.

This is glaringly true in the State Department. There the bright young men who are born with silver spoons in their mouths are the ones who have been worst.

Now I know it is very easy for anyone to condemn a particular bureau or department in general terms. Therefore, I would like to cite one rather unusual case—the case of a man who has done much to shape our foreign policy.

When Chiang Kai-shek was fighting our war, the State Department had in China a young man named John S. Service. His task, obviously, was not to work for the communization of China. Strangely, however, he sent official reports back to the State Department urging that we torpedo our ally Chiang Kai-shek and stating, in effect, that communism was the best hope of China.

Later, this man—John Service—was picked up by the Federal Bureau of Investigation for turning over to the communists secret State Department information. Strangely, however, he was never prosecuted. However, Joseph Grew, the undersecretary of state, who insisted on his prosecution, was forced to resign. Two days after, Grew's successor, Dean Acheson, took over as undersecretary of state, this man—John Service—who had been picked up by the FBI and who had previously urged that communism was the best hope of China, was not only reinstated in the State Department but promoted; and finally, under

Acheson, placed in charge of all placements and promotions. Today, ladies and gentlemen, this man Service is on his way to represent the State Department and Acheson in Calcutta—by far and away the most important listening post in the Far East.

Now, let's see what happens when individuals with communist connections are forced out of the State Department. Gustave Duran, who was labeled as, I quote, "a notorious international communist," was made assistant secretary of state in charge of Latin American affairs. He was taken into the State Department from his job as a lieutenant colonel in the Communist International Brigade. Finally, after intense congressional pressure and criticism, he resigned in 1946 from the State Department—and, ladies and gentlemen, where do you think he is now? He took over a high-salaried job as chief of Cultural Activities Section in the office of the assistant secretary-general of the United Nations. [. . .]

This, ladies and gentlemen, gives you somewhat of a picture of the type of individuals who have been helping to shape our foreign policy. In my opinion the State Department, which is one of the most important government departments, is thoroughly infested with communists.

I have in my hand 57 cases of individuals who would appear to be either card-carrying members or certainly loyal to the Communist Party, but who nevertheless are still helping to shape our foreign policy. One thing to remember in discussing the communists in our government is that we are not dealing with spies who get 30 pieces of silver to steal the blueprints of new weapons. We are dealing with a far more sinister type of activity because it permits the enemy to guide and shape our policy.

This brings us down to the case of one Alger Hiss, who is important not as an individual anymore but rather because he is so representative of a group in the State Department. It is unnecessary to go over the sordid events showing how he sold out the nation which had given him so much. Those are rather fresh in all of our minds. However, it should be remembered that the facts in regard to his connection with this international communist spy ring were made known to the then-Undersecretary of State Berle three days after Hitler and Stalin signed the Russo-German Alliance Pact. At that time one Whittaker Chambers—who was also part of the spy ring—apparently decided that with Russia on Hitler's side, he could no longer betray our nation to Russia. He gave Undersecretary of State Berle—and this is all a matter of record—practically all, if not more, of the facts upon which Hiss' conviction was based.

Undersecretary Berle promptly contacted Dean Acheson and received word in return that Acheson, and I quote, "could vouch for Hiss absolutely"—at which time the matter was dropped. And this, you understand, was at a time when Russia was an ally of Germany. This condition existed while Russia and Germany were invading and dismembering Poland, and while the communist groups here were screaming "warmonger" at the United States for their support of the Allied nations.

Again in 1943, the FBI had occasion to investigate the facts surrounding Hiss' contacts with the Russian spy ring. But even after that FBI report was submitted, nothing was done.

Then, late in 1948—on August 5—when the Un-American Activities Committee called Alger Hiss to give an accounting, President Truman at once issued a presidential directive ordering all government agencies to refuse to turn over any information whatsoever in regard to the communist activities of any government employee to a congressional committee.

Incidentally, even after Hiss was convicted, it is interesting to note that the president still labeled the expose of Hiss as a "red herring."

If time permitted, it might be well to go into detail about the fact that Hiss was Roosevelt's chief adviser at Yalta when Roosevelt was admittedly in ill health and tired physically and mentally [. . .] and when, according to the secretary of state, Hiss and Gromyko drafted the report on the conference.

According to the then-Secretary of State Stettinius, here are some of the things that Hiss helped to decide at Yalta: (1) the establishment of a European High Commission; (2) the treatment of Germany—this you will recall was the conference at which it was decided that we would occupy Berlin with Russia occupying an area completely encircling the city, which as you know, resulted in the Berlin airlift which cost 31 American lives; (3) the Polish question; (4) the relationship between UNRRA and the Soviet; (5) the rights of Americans on control commissions of Rumania, Bulgaria and Hungary; (6) Iran; (7) China—here's where we gave away Manchuria;

(8) Turkish Straits question; (9) international trusteeships; (10) Korea.

Of the results of this conference, Arthur Bliss Lane of the State Department had this to say: "As I glanced over the document, I could not believe my eyes. To me, almost every line spoke of a surrender to Stalin."

As you hear this story of high treason, I know that you are saying to yourself, "Well, why doesn't the Congress do something about it?" Actually, ladies and gentlemen, one of the important reasons for the graft, the corruption, the dishonesty, the disloyalty, the treason in high government positions—one of the most important reasons why this continues—is a lack of moral uprising on the part of the 140 million American people. In the light of history, however, this is not hard to explain.

It is the result of an emotional hangover and a temporary moral lapse which follows every war. It is the apathy to evil which people who have been subjected to the tremendous evils of war feel. As the people of the world see mass murder, the destruction of defenseless and innocent people, and all of the crime and lack of morals which go with war, they become numb and apathetic. It has always been thus after war. However, the morals of our people have not been destroyed. They still exist. This cloak of numbness and apathy has only needed a spark to rekindle them. Happily, this spark has finally been supplied.

As you know, very recently the secretary of state proclaimed his loyalty to a man guilty of what has always been considered as the most abominable of all crimes—of being a traitor to the people who gave him a position of great trust. The secretary of state, in attempting to justify his continued devotion to the man who sold out the Christian world to the atheistic world, referred to Christ's Sermon on the Mount as a justification and reason therefore, and the reaction of the American people to this would have made the heart of Abraham Lincoln happy. When this pompous diplomat in striped pants, with a phony British accent, proclaimed to the American people that Christ on the Mount endorsed communism, high treason, and betrayal of a sacred trust, the blasphemy was so great that it awakened the dormant indignation of the American people.

He has lighted the spark which is resulting in a moral uprising and will end only when the whole sorry mess of twisted warped thinkers are swept from the national scene so that we may have a new birth of national honesty and decency in government.

Frederick M. Vinson

Dennis v. United States (1951)

Mr. Chief Justice Vinson announced the judgment of the Court and an opinion in which Mr. Justice Reed, Mr. Justice Burton and Mr. Justice Minton join.

Petitioners were indicted in July, 1948, for violation of the conspiracy provisions of the Smith Act, 54 Stat. 671, 18 U.S.C. (1946 ed.) § 11, during the period of April, 1945, to July, 1948. [. . .] A verdict of guilty as to all the petitioners was returned by the jury on October 14, 1949. The Court of Appeals affirmed the convictions. We granted *certiorari*, limited to the following two questions: (1) Whether either § 2 or § 3 of the Smith Act, inherently or as construed and applied in the instant case, violates the First Amendment and other provisions of the Bill of Rights; (2) whether either § 2 or § 3 of the Act, inherently or as construed and applied in the instant case, violates the First and Fifth Amendments because of indefiniteness.

Sections 2 and 3 of the Smith Act provide as follows:

Sec. 2.(a) It shall be unlawful for any person—

(1) to knowingly or willfully advocate, abet, advise, or teach the duty, necessity, desirability, or propriety of overthrowing or destroying any government in the United States by force or violence,

or by the assassination of any officer of any such government;

(2) with intent to cause the overthrow or destruction of any government in the United States, to print, publish, edit, issue, circulate, sell, distribute, or publicly display any written or printed matter advocating, advising, or teaching the duty, necessity, desirability, or propriety of overthrowing or destroying any government in the United States by force or violence;

(3) to organize or help to organize any society, group, or assembly of persons who teach, advocate, or encourage the overthrow or destruction of any government in the United States by force or violence; or to be or become a member of, or affiliate with, any such society, group, or assembly of persons, knowing the purposes thereof.

(b) For the purposes of this section, the term "government in the United States" means the Government of the United States, the government of any State, Territory, or possession of the United States, the government of the District of Columbia, or the government of any political subdivision of any of them.

Sec. 3. It shall be unlawful for any person to attempt to commit, or to conspire to commit, any of the acts prohibited by the provisions of this title.

The indictment charged the petitioners with willfully and knowingly conspiring (1) to organize as the Communist Party of the United States of America a society, group and assembly of persons who teach and advocate the overthrow and destruction of the Government of the United States by force and violence, and (2) knowingly and willfully to advocate and teach the duty and necessity of overthrowing and destroying the Government of the United States by force and violence. [. . .]

The trial of the case extended over nine months, six of which were devoted to the taking of evidence, resulting in a record of 16,000 pages. Our limited grant of the writ of *certiorari* has removed from our consideration any question as to the sufficiency of the evidence to support the jury's determination that petitioners are guilty of the offense charged. Whether, on this record, petitioners did, in fact, advocate the overthrow of the Government by force and violence is not before us, and we must base any discussion of this point upon the conclusions stated

in the opinion of the Court of Appeals, which treated the issue in great detail. That court held that the record in this case amply supports the necessary finding of the jury that petitioners, the leaders of the Communist Party in this country, were unwilling to work within our framework of democracy, but intended to initiate a violent revolution whenever the propitious occasion appeared. Petitioners dispute the meaning to be drawn from the evidence, contending that the Marxist-Leninist doctrine they advocated taught that force and violence to achieve a Communist form of government in an existing democratic state would be necessary only because the ruling classes of that state would never permit the transformation to be accomplished peacefully, but would use force and violence to defeat any peaceful political and economic gain the Communists could achieve. [. . .]

II

The obvious purpose of the statute is to protect existing Government not from change by peaceable, lawful and constitutional means, but from change by violence, revolution and terrorism. That it is within the power of the Congress to protect the Government of the United States from armed rebellion is a proposition which requires little discussion. Whatever theoretical merit there may be to the argument that there is a "right" to rebellion against dictatorial governments is without force where the existing structure of the government provides for peaceful and orderly change. We reject any principle of governmental helplessness in the face of preparation for revolution, which principle, carried to its logical conclusion, must lead to anarchy. No one could conceive that it is not within the power of Congress to prohibit acts intended to overthrow the Government by force and violence. The question with which we are concerned here is not whether Congress has such power, but whether the means which it has employed conflict with the First and Fifth Amendments to the Constitution.

One of the bases for the contention that the means which Congress has employed are invalid takes the form of an attack on the face of the statute on the grounds that, by its terms, it prohibits academic discussion of the merits of Marxism-Leninism, that it stifles ideas and is contrary to all concepts of a free speech and a free press. Although we do not agree that the language itself has that significance, we must bear in mind that it is the duty of the federal courts to interpret federal legislation in a manner not inconsistent with the demands of the Constitution. [. . .]

The very language of the Smith Act negates the interpretation which petitioners would have us impose on that Act. It is directed at advocacy, not discussion. Thus, the trial judge properly charged the jury that they could not convict if they found that petitioners did "no more than pursue peaceful studies and discussions or teaching and advocacy in the realm of ideas." He further charged that it was not unlawful to conduct in an American college or university a course explaining the philosophical theories set forth in the books which have been placed in evidence.

Such a charge is in strict accord with the statutory language, and illustrates the meaning to be placed on those words. Congress did not intend to eradicate the free discussion of political theories, to destroy the traditional rights of Americans to discuss and evaluate ideas without fear of governmental sanction. Rather Congress was concerned with the very kind of activity in which the evidence showed these petitioners engaged.

III

But although the statute is not directed at the hypothetical cases which petitioners have conjured, its application in this case has resulted in convictions for the teaching and advocacy of the overthrow of the Government by force and violence, which, even though coupled with the intent to accomplish that overthrow, contains an element of speech. For this reason, we must pay special heed to the demands of the First Amendment marking out the boundaries of speech. [. . .]

The rule we deduce from these cases is that, where an offense is specified by a statute in nonspeech or nonpress terms, a conviction relying upon speech or press as evidence of violation may be sustained only when the speech or publication created a "clear and present danger" of attempting or accomplishing the prohibited crime, *e.g.*, interference with enlistment. The dissents, we repeat, in emphasizing the value of speech, were addressed to the argument of the sufficiency of the evidence. [. . .]

Although no case subsequent to *Whitney* [*v. California* (1927)] and *Gitlow* [*v. New York* (1925)] has expressly overruled the majority opinions in those cases, there is little doubt that subsequent opinions have inclined toward the Holmes-Brandeis rationale. [. . .] [But] neither Justice Holmes nor Justice Brandeis ever envisioned that a shorthand phrase should be crystallized into a rigid rule to be applied inflexibly without regard to the circumstances of each case. Speech is not an absolute, above and beyond control by the legislature when its judgment, subject to review here, is that certain kinds of speech are so undesirable as to warrant criminal sanction. Nothing is more certain in modern society than the principle that there are no absolutes, that a name, a phrase, a standard has meaning only when associated with the considerations which gave birth to the nomenclature. To those who would paralyze our Government in the face of impending threat by encasing it in a semantic straitjacket we must reply that all concepts are relative.

In this case, we are squarely presented with the application of the "clear and present danger" test, and must decide what that phrase imports. We first note that many of the cases in which this Court has reversed convictions by use of this or similar tests have been based on the fact that the interest which the State was attempting to protect was itself too insubstantial to warrant restriction of speech. In this category we may put such cases as *Schneider v. State* (1939); *Cantwell v. Connecticut* (1940); *Martin v. Struthers* (1943); *West Virginia Board of Education v. Barnette* (1943). [. . .] Overthrow of the Government by force and violence is certainly a substantial enough interest for the Government to limit speech. Indeed, this is the ultimate value of any society, for if a society cannot protect its very structure from armed internal attack, it must follow that no subordinate value can be protected. If, then, this interest may be protected, the literal problem which is presented is what has been meant by the use of the phrase "clear and present danger" of the utterances bringing about the evil within the power of Congress to punish.

Obviously, the words cannot mean that, before the Government may act, it must wait until the *putsch* is about to be executed, the plans have been laid and the signal is awaited. If Government is aware that a group aiming at its overthrow is attempting to indoctrinate its members and to commit them to a course whereby they will strike when the leaders feel the circumstances permit, action by the Government is required. The argument that there is no need for Government to concern itself, for Government is strong, it possesses ample powers to put down a rebellion, it may defeat the revolution with ease needs no answer. For that is not the question. Certainly an attempt to overthrow the Government by force, even though doomed from the outset because of inadequate numbers or power of the revolutionists, is a sufficient evil for Congress to prevent. The damage which such attempts create both physically and politically to a nation makes it impossible to measure the validity in terms of the probability of success, or the immediacy of a successful attempt. In the instant case, the trial judge charged the jury that they could not convict unless they found that petitioners intended to overthrow the Government "as speedily as circumstances would permit." This does not mean, and could not properly mean, that they would not strike until there was certainty of success. What was meant was that the revolutionists would strike when they thought the time was ripe. We must therefore reject the contention that success or probability of success is the criterion.

The situation with which Justices Holmes and Brandeis were concerned in *Gitlow* was a comparatively isolated event, bearing little relation in their minds to any substantial threat to the safety of the community. [. . .] They were not confronted with any situation comparable to the instant one—the development of an apparatus designed and dedicated to the overthrow of the Government, in the context of world crisis after crisis.

Chief Judge Learned Hand, writing for the majority below, interpreted the phrase as follows:

> In each case, [courts] must ask whether the gravity of the "evil," discounted by its improbability, justifies such invasion of free speech as is necessary to avoid the danger.

We adopt this statement of the rule. As articulated by Chief Judge Hand, it is as succinct and inclusive as any other we might devise at this time. It takes into consideration those factors which we deem relevant, and relates their significances. More we cannot expect from words.

Likewise, we are in accord with the court below, which affirmed the trial court's finding that the requisite danger existed. The mere fact that, from the period 1945 to 1948, petitioners' activities did not result in an attempt to overthrow the Government by force and violence is, of course, no answer to the fact that there was a group that was ready to make the attempt. The formation by petitioners of such a highly organized conspiracy, with rigidly disciplined members subject to call when the leaders, these petitioners, felt that the time had come for action, coupled with the inflammable nature of world conditions, similar uprisings in other countries, and the touch-and-go nature of our relations with countries with whom petitioners were in the very least ideologically attuned, convince us that their convictions were justified on this score. And this analysis disposes of the contention that a conspiracy to advocate, as distinguished from the advocacy itself, cannot be constitutionally restrained, because it comprises only the preparation. It is the existence of the conspiracy which creates the danger. If the ingredients of the reaction are present, we cannot bind the Government to wait until the catalyst is added.

IV

When facts are found that establish the violation of a statute, the protection against conviction afforded by the First Amendment is a matter of law. The doctrine that there must be a clear and present danger of a substantive evil that Congress has a right to prevent is a judicial rule to be applied as a matter of law by the courts. The guilt is established by proof of facts. Whether the First Amendment protects the activity which constitutes the violation of the statute must depend upon a judicial determination of the scope of the First Amendment applied to the circumstances of the case. [. . .]

[I]n the very case in which the phrase was born, *Schenck,* this Court itself examined the record to find whether the requisite danger appeared, and the issue was not submitted to a jury. And in every later case in which the Court has measured the validity of a statute by the "clear and present danger" test, that determination has been by the court, the question of the danger not being submitted to the jury.

The question in this case is whether the statute which the legislature has enacted may be constitutionally applied. In other words, the Court must examine judicially the application of the statute to the particular situation, to ascertain if the Constitution prohibits the conviction. We hold that the statute may be applied where there is a "clear and present danger" of the substantive evil which the legislature had the right to prevent. Bearing, as it does, the marks of a "question of law," the issue is properly one for the judge to decide.

V

We hold that §§ 2(a)(1), 2(a)(3) and 3 of the Smith Act do not inherently, or as construed or applied in the instant case, violate the First Amendment and other provisions of the Bill of Rights, or the First and Fifth Amendments because of indefiniteness. Petitioners intended to overthrow the Government of the United States as speedily as the circumstances would permit. Their conspiracy to organize the Communist Party and to teach and advocate the overthrow of the Government of the United States by force and violence created a "clear and present danger" of an attempt to overthrow the Government by force and violence. They were properly and constitutionally convicted for violation of the Smith Act. The judgments of conviction are

Affirmed.

FELIX FRANKFURTER

Dennis v. United States, Concurrence (1951)

Mr. Justice FRANKFURTER, concurring in affirmance of the judgment.

The defendants were convicted under § 3 of the Smith Act for conspiring to violate § 2 of that Act, which makes it unlawful to organize or help to organize any society, group, or assembly of persons who teach, advocate, or encourage the overthrow or destruction of any government in the United States by force or violence. [. . .]

Few questions of comparable import have come before this Court in recent years. The appellants maintain that they have a right to advocate a political theory, so long, at least, as their advocacy does not create an immediate danger of obvious magnitude to the very existence of our present scheme of society. On the other hand, the Government asserts the right to safeguard the security of the Nation by such a measure as the Smith Act. Our judgment is thus

solicited on a conflict of interests of the utmost concern to the wellbeing of the country. This conflict of interests cannot be resolved by a dogmatic preference for one or the other, nor by a sonorous formula which is, in fact, only a euphemistic disguise for an unresolved conflict. If adjudication is to be a rational process, we cannot escape a candid examination of the conflicting claims with full recognition that both are supported by weighty title-deeds.

I

There come occasions in law, as elsewhere, when the familiar needs to be recalled. Our whole history proves even more decisively than the course of decisions in this Court that the United States has the powers inseparable from a sovereign nation.

America has chosen to be, in many respects, and to many purposes, a nation, and for all these purposes, her government is complete; to all these objects, it is competent.

Chief Justice Marshall in *Cohens v. Virginia* [1821]. The right of a government to maintain its existence—self-preservation—is the most pervasive aspect of sovereignty. "Security against foreign danger," wrote Madison, "is one of the primitive objects of civil society." *The Federalist*, No. 41. The constitutional power to act upon this basic principle has been recognized by this Court at different periods and under diverse circumstances.

> To preserve its independence, and give security against foreign aggression and encroachment, is the highest duty of every nation, and to attain these ends nearly all other considerations are to be subordinated. It matters not in what form such aggression and encroachment come. . . . The government, possessing the powers which are to be exercised for protection and security, is clothed with authority to determine the occasion on which the powers shall be called forth. *Chinese Exclusion Case* [1889].

The most tragic experience in our history is a poignant reminder that the Nation's continued existence may be threatened from within. To protect itself from such threats, the Federal Government "is invested with all those inherent and implied powers which, at the time of adopting the Constitution, were generally considered to belong to every government as such, and as being essential to the exercise of its functions." [. . .]

But even the all-embracing power and duty of self-preservation are not absolute. Like the war power, which is indeed an aspect of the power of self-preservation, it is subject to applicable constitutional limitations. Our Constitution has no provision lifting restrictions upon governmental authority during periods of emergency, although the scope of a restriction may depend on the circumstances in which it is invoked.

The First Amendment is such a restriction. It exacts obedience even during periods of war; it is applicable when war clouds are not figments of the imagination no less than when they are. The First Amendment categorically demands that

Congress shall make no law respecting an establishment of religion, or prohibiting the free exercise thereof; or abridging the freedom of speech, or of the press; or the right of the people peaceably to assemble, and to petition the Government for a redress of grievances.

The right of a man to think what he pleases, to write what he thinks, and to have his thoughts made available for others to hear or read has an engaging ring of universality. The Smith Act and this conviction under it no doubt restrict the exercise of free speech and assembly. Does that, without more, dispose of the matter? [. . .]

The language of the First Amendment is to be read not as barren words found in a dictionary but as symbols of historic experience illumined by the presuppositions of those who employed them. Not what words did Madison and Hamilton use, but what was it in their minds which they conveyed? Free speech is subject to prohibition of those abuses of expression which a civilized society may forbid. As in the case of every other provision of the Constitution that is not crystallized by the nature of its technical concepts, the fact that the First Amendment is not self-defining and self-enforcing neither impairs its usefulness nor compels its paralysis as a living instrument. [. . .]

But how are competing interests to be assessed? Since they are not subject to quantitative ascertainment, the issue necessarily resolves itself into asking, who is to make the adjustment?—who is to balance the relevant factors and ascertain which interest is in the circumstances to prevail? Full responsibility for the choice cannot be given to the courts. Courts are not representative bodies. They are not designed to be a good reflex of a democratic society. Their judgment is best informed, and therefore most dependable, within narrow limits. Their essential quality is detachment, founded on independence. History teaches that the independence of the judiciary is jeopardized when courts become embroiled in the passions of the day and assume primary responsibility in choosing between competing political, economic and social pressures.

Primary responsibility for adjusting the interests which compete in the situation before us of necessity belongs to the Congress. The nature of the power to be exercised by this Court has been delineated in decisions not charged with the emotional appeal of situations such as that now before us. We are to set aside the judgment of those whose duty it is to legislate only if there is no reasonable basis for it. [. . .]

"Great cases," it is appropriate to remember, like hard cases, make bad law. For great cases are called great not by reason of their real importance in shaping the law of the future, but because of some accident of immediate overwhelming interest which appeals to the feelings and distorts the judgment. These immediate interests exercise a kind of hydraulic pressure which makes what previously was clear seem doubtful, and before which even well settled principles of law will bend. Mr. Justice Holmes, dissenting in *Northern Securities Co. v. United States* [1904].

This is such a case. Unless we are to compromise judicial impartiality and subject these defendants to the risk of an *ad hoc* judgment influenced by the impregnating atmosphere of the times, the constitutionality of their conviction must be determined by principles established in cases decided in more tranquil periods. [. . .]

II

First.—Free-speech cases are not an exception to the principle that we are not legislators, that direct policymaking is not our province. How best to reconcile competing interests is the business of legislatures, and the balance they strike is a judgment not to be displaced by ours, but to be respected unless outside the pale of fair judgment. [. . .]

Second.—A survey of the relevant decisions indicates that the results which we have reached are on the whole those that would ensue from careful weighing of conflicting interests. The complex issues presented by regulation of speech in public places, by picketing, and by legislation prohibiting advocacy of crime have been resolved by scrutiny of many factors besides the imminence and gravity of the evil threatened. The matter has been well summarized by a reflective student of the Court's work.

> The truth is that the "clear and present danger" test is an oversimplified judgment unless it takes account also of a number of other factors: the relative seriousness of the danger in comparison with the value of the occasion for speech or political activity; the availability of more moderate controls than those which the state has imposed, and perhaps the specific intent with which the speech or activity is launched. No matter how rapidly we utter the phrase "clear and present danger," or how closely we hyphenate the words, they are not a substitute for the weighing of values. They tend to convey a delusion of certitude when what is most certain is the complexity of the strands in the web of freedoms which the judge must dissentangle. Freund, *On Understanding the Supreme Court*, 27–28.

It is a familiar experience in the law that new situations do not fit neatly into legal conceptions that arose under different circumstances to satisfy different needs. So it was when the injunction was tortured into an instrument of oppression against labor in industrial conflicts. So it is with the attempt to use the direction of thought lying behind the criterion of "clear and present danger" wholly out of the context in which it originated, and to make of it an absolute dogma and definitive measuring rod for the power of Congress to deal with assaults against security through devices other than overt physical attempts.

Bearing in mind that Mr. Justice Holmes regarded questions under the First Amendment as questions of "proximity and degree," *Schenck v. United States*, it would be a distortion, indeed a mockery, of his reasoning to compare the "puny anonymities," to which he was addressing himself in the *Abrams* case in 1919 or the publication that was "futile and too remote from possible consequences," in the *Gitlow* case in 1925 with the setting of events in this case in 1950.

It does an ill service to the author of the most quoted judicial phrases regarding freedom of speech, to make him the victim of a tendency which he fought all his life, whereby phrases are made to do service for critical analysis by being turned into dogma.

It is one of the misfortunes of the law that ideas become encysted in phrases, and thereafter for a long time cease to provoke further analysis.

Holmes, J., dissenting, in *Hyde v. United States* [1912]. The phrase "clear and present danger," in its origin, served to indicate the importance of freedom of speech to a free society, but also to emphasize that its exercise must be compatible with the preservation of other freedoms essential to a democracy and guaranteed by our Constitution.

Pennekamp v. Florida [1946] (concurring). It were far better that the phrase be abandoned than that it be sounded once more to hide from the believers in an absolute right of free speech the plain fact that the interest in speech, profoundly important as it is, is no more conclusive in judicial review than other attributes of democracy or than a determination of the people's representatives that a measure is necessary to assure the safety of government itself.

Third.—Not every type of speech occupies the same position on the scale of values. There is no substantial public interest in permitting certain kinds of utterances:

> the lewd and obscene, the profane, the libelous, and the insulting or "fighting" words—those which, by their very utterance, inflict injury or tend to incite an immediate breach of the peace.

Chaplinsky v. New Hampshire [1942]. We have frequently indicated that the interest in protecting speech depends on the circumstances of the occasion. It is pertinent to the decision before us to consider where on the scale of values we have in the past placed the type of speech now claiming constitutional immunity.

The defendants have been convicted of conspiring to organize a party of persons who advocate the overthrow of the Government by force and violence. The jury has found that the object of the conspiracy is advocacy as "a rule or principle of action," "by language reasonably and ordinarily calculated to incite persons to such action," and with the intent to cause the overthrow "as speedily as circumstances would permit."

On any scale of values which we have hitherto recognized, speech of this sort ranks low. [. . .]

But there is underlying validity in the distinction between advocacy and the interchange of ideas, and we do not discard a useful tool because it may be misused. That such a distinction could be used unreasonably by those in power against hostile or unorthodox views does not negate the fact that it may be used reasonably against an organization wielding the power of the centrally controlled international Communist movement. The object of the conspiracy

before us is so clear that the chance of error in saying that the defendants conspired to advocate, rather than to express ideas is slight. Mr. Justice Douglas quite properly points out that the conspiracy before us is not a conspiracy to overthrow the Government. But it would be equally wrong to treat it as a seminar in political theory.

III

These general considerations underlie decision of the case before us.

On the one hand is the interest in security. The Communist Party was not designed by these defendants as an ordinary political party. For the circumstances of its organization, its aims and methods, and the relation of the defendants to its organization and aims, we are concluded by the jury's verdict. The jury found that the Party rejects the basic premise of our political system—that change is to be brought about by nonviolent constitutional process. The jury found that the Party advocates the theory that there is a duty and necessity to overthrow the Government by force and violence. It found that the Party entertains and promotes this view not as a prophetic insight or as a bit of unworldly speculation, but as a program for winning adherents and as a policy to be translated into action. [. . .]

On the other hand is the interest in free speech. The right to exert all governmental powers in aid of maintaining our institutions and resisting their physical overthrow does not include intolerance of opinions and speech that cannot do harm although opposed and perhaps alien to dominant, traditional opinion. The treatment of its minorities, especially their legal position, is among the most searching tests of the level of civilization attained by a society. It is better for those who have almost unlimited power of government in their hands to err on the side of freedom. We have enjoyed so much freedom for so long that we are perhaps in danger of forgetting how much blood it cost to establish the Bill of Rights.

Of course, no government can recognize a "right" of revolution, or a "right" to incite revolution if the incitement has no other purpose or effect. But speech is seldom restricted to a single purpose, and its effects may be manifold. A public interest is not wanting in granting freedom to speak their minds even to those who advocate the overthrow of the Government by force. For, as the evidence in this case abundantly illustrates, coupled with such advocacy is criticism of defects in our society. Criticism is the spur to reform, and Burke's admonition that a healthy society must reform in order to conserve has not lost its force. Astute observers have remarked that one of the characteristics of the American Republic is indifference to fundamental criticism. Bryce, *The American Commonwealth*, c. 84. It is a commonplace that there may be a grain of truth in the most uncouth doctrine, however false and repellent the balance may be. Suppressing advocates of overthrow inevitably will also silence critics who do not advocate overthrow but fear that their criticism may be so construed. No matter how clear we may be that the defendants now before us are preparing to overthrow our Government at the propitious moment, it is self-delusion to think that we can punish them for their advocacy without adding to the risks run by loyal citizens who honestly believe in some of the reforms these defendants advance. It is a sobering fact that, in sustaining the convictions before us, we can hardly escape restriction on the interchange of ideas.

We must not overlook the value of that interchange. Freedom of expression is the well spring of our civilization—the civilization we seek to maintain and further by recognizing the right of Congress to put some limitation upon expression. Such are the paradoxes of life. For social development of trial and error, the fullest possible opportunity for the free play of the human mind is an indispensable prerequisite. The history of civilization is in considerable measure the displacement of error which once held sway as official truth by beliefs which in turn have yielded to other truths. Therefore, the liberty of man to search for truth ought not to be fettered, no matter what orthodoxies he may challenge. Liberty of thought soon shrivels without freedom of expression. Nor can truth be pursued in an atmosphere hostile to the endeavor or under dangers which are hazarded only by heroes. [. . .]

It is not for us to decide how we would adjust the clash of interests which this case presents were the primary responsibility for reconciling it ours. Congress has determined that the danger created by advocacy of overthrow justifies the ensuing restriction on freedom of speech. The determination was made after due deliberation, and the seriousness of the congressional purpose is attested by the volume of legislation passed to effectuate the same ends. [. . .]

To make validity of legislation depend on judicial reading of events still in the womb of time a forecast, that is, of the outcome of forces, at best, appreciated only with knowledge of the topmost secrets of nations—is to charge the judiciary with duties beyond its equipment. We do not expect courts to pronounce historic verdicts on bygone events. Even historians have conflicting views to this day on the origins and conduct of the French Revolution, or, for that matter, varying interpretations of "the glorious Revolution" of 1688. It is as absurd to be confident that we can measure the present clash of forces and their outcome as to ask us to read history still enveloped in clouds of controversy.

In the light of their experience, the Framers of the Constitution chose to keep the judiciary dissociated from direct participation in the legislative process. In asserting the power to pass on the constitutionality of legislation, Marshall and his Court expressed the purposes of the Founders. See Charles A. Beard, *The Supreme Court and the Constitution*. But the extent to which the exercise of this power would interpenetrate matters of policy could hardly have been foreseen by the most prescient. The distinction which the Founders drew between the Court's duty to pass on the power of Congress and its complementary duty not to enter directly the domain of policy is fundamental. But, in its actual operation, it is rather subtle, certainly to the common understanding. Our duty to abstain from confounding policy with constitutionality demands perceptive humility as well as self-restraint in not declaring unconstitutional what in a judge's private judgment is deemed unwise and even dangerous. [. . .]

William O. Douglas

Dennis v. United States, Dissent (1951)

Mr. Justice Douglas, dissenting.

If this were a case where those who claimed protection under the First Amendment were teaching the techniques of sabotage, the assassination of the President, the filching of documents from public files, the planting of bombs, the art of street warfare, and the like, I would have no doubts. The freedom to speak is not absolute; the teaching of methods of terror and other seditious conduct should be beyond the pale along with obscenity and immorality. This case was argued as if those were the facts. The argument imported much seditious conduct into the record. That is easy, and it has popular appeal, for the activities of Communists in plotting and scheming against the free world are common knowledge. But the fact is that no such evidence was introduced at the trial. There is a statute which makes a seditious conspiracy unlawful. Petitioners, however, were not charged with a "conspiracy to overthrow" the Government. They were charged with a conspiracy to form a party and groups and assemblies of people who teach and advocate the overthrow of our Government by force or violence and with a conspiracy to advocate and teach its overthrow by force and violence. It may well be that indoctrination in the techniques of terror to destroy the Government would be indictable under either statute. But the teaching which is condemned here is of a different character.

So far as the present record is concerned, what petitioners did was to organize people to teach and themselves teach the Marxist-Leninist doctrine contained chiefly in four books: Stalin, *Foundations of Leninism* (1924); Marx and Engels, *Manifesto of the Communist Party* (1848); Lenin, *The State and Revolution* (1917); *History of the Communist Party of the Soviet Union* (1939).

Those books are to Soviet Communism what *Mein Kampf* was to Nazism. If they are understood, the ugliness of Communism is revealed, its deceit and cunning are exposed, the nature of its activities becomes apparent, and the chances of its success less likely. That is not, of course, the reason why petitioners chose these books for their classrooms. They are fervent Communists to whom these volumes are gospel. They preached the creed with the hope that some day it would be acted upon.

The opinion of the Court does not outlaw these texts nor condemn them to the fire, as the Communists do literature offensive to their creed. But if the books themselves are not outlawed, if they can lawfully remain on library shelves, by what reasoning does their use in a classroom become a crime? It would not be a crime under the Act to introduce these books to a class, though that would be teaching what the creed of violent overthrow of the Government is. The Act, as construed, requires the element of intent—that those who teach the creed believe in it. The crime then depends not on what is taught, but on who the teacher is. That is to make freedom of speech turn not on *what is said*, but on the intent with which it is said. Once we start down that road, we enter territory dangerous to the liberties of every citizen.

There was a time in England when the concept of constructive treason flourished. Men were punished not for raising a hand against the king, but for thinking murderous thoughts about him. The Framers of the Constitution were alive to that abuse, and took steps to see that the practice would not flourish here. Treason was defined to require overt acts—the evolution of a plot against the country into an actual project. The present case is not one of treason. But the analogy is close when the illegality is made to turn on intent, not on the nature of the act. We then start probing men's minds for motive and purpose; they become entangled in the law not for what they did, but *for what they thought*; they get convicted not for what they said, but for the purpose with which they said it.

Intent, of course, often makes the difference in the law. An act otherwise excusable or carrying minor penalties may grow to an abhorrent thing if the evil intent is present. We deal here, however, not with ordinary acts, but with speech, to which the Constitution has given a special sanction.

The vice of treating speech as the equivalent of overt acts of a treasonable or seditious character is emphasized by a concurring opinion, which, by invoking the law of conspiracy, makes speech do service for deeds which are dangerous to society. The doctrine of conspiracy has served divers and oppressive purposes, and, in its broad reach, can be made to do great evil. But never until today has anyone seriously thought that the ancient law of conspiracy could constitutionally be used to turn speech into seditious conduct. Yet that is precisely what is suggested. I repeat that we deal here with speech alone, not with speech plus acts of sabotage or unlawful conduct. Not a single seditious act is charged in the indictment. To make a lawful speech unlawful because two men conceive it is to raise the law of conspiracy to appalling proportions. That course is to make a radical break with the past and to violate one of the cardinal principles of our constitutional scheme.

Free speech has occupied an exalted position because of the high service it has given our society. Its protection is essential to the very existence of a democracy. The airing of ideas releases pressures which otherwise might become destructive. When ideas compete in the market for acceptance, full and free discussion exposes the false, and they gain few adherents. Full and free discussion even of ideas we hate encourages the testing of our own prejudices and preconceptions. Full and free discussion keeps a society from becoming stagnant and unprepared for the stresses and strains that work to tear all civilizations apart.

Full and free discussion has indeed been the first article of our faith. We have founded our political system on it. It has been the safeguard of every religious, political, philosophical, economic, and racial group amongst us. We have counted on it to keep us from embracing what is cheap and false; we have trusted the common sense of our people to choose the doctrine true to our genius and to reject the rest. This has been the one single outstanding tenet that has made our institutions the symbol of freedom and equality. We have deemed it more costly to liberty to suppress a despised minority than to let them vent their spleen. We have above all else feared the political censor. We have wanted a land where our people can be exposed to all the diverse creeds and cultures of the world.

There comes a time when even speech loses its constitutional immunity. Speech innocuous one year may at another time fan such destructive flames that it must be halted in the interests of the safety of the Republic. That is the meaning of the clear and present danger test. When conditions are so critical that there will be no time to avoid the evil that the speech threatens, it is time to call a halt. Otherwise, free speech which is the strength of the Nation will be the cause of its destruction.

Yet free speech is the rule, not the exception. The restraint to be constitutional must be based on more than fear, on more than passionate opposition against the speech, on more than a revolted dislike for its contents. There must be some immediate injury to society that is likely if speech is allowed. The classic statement of these conditions was made by Mr. Justice Brandeis in his concurring opinion in *Whitney v. California* [1927].

> Fear of serious injury cannot alone justify suppression of free speech and assembly. Men feared witches and burnt women. It is the function of speech to free men from the bondage of irrational fears. To justify suppression of free speech, there must be reasonable ground to fear that serious evil will result if free speech is practiced. There must be reasonable ground to believe that the danger apprehended is imminent. There must be reasonable ground to believe that the evil to be prevented is a serious one. Every denunciation of existing law tends in some measure to increase the probability that there will be violation of it. Condonation of a breach enhances the probability. Expressions of approval add to the probability. Propagation of the criminal state of mind by teaching syndicalism increases it. Advocacy of law-breaking heightens it still further. But even advocacy of violation, however reprehensible morally, is not a justification for denying free speech where the advocacy falls short of incitement and there is nothing to indicate that the advocacy would be immediately acted on. The wide difference between advocacy and incitement, between preparation and attempt, between assembling and conspiracy, must be borne in

mind. In order to support a finding of clear and present danger, it must be shown either that immediate serious violence was to be expected or was advocated, or that the past conduct furnished reason to believe that such advocacy was then contemplated. [. . .]

The nature of Communism as a force on the world scene would, of course, be relevant to the issue of clear and present danger of petitioners' advocacy within the United States. But the primary consideration is the strength and tactical position of petitioners and their converts in this country. On that, there is no evidence in the record. If we are to take judicial notice of the threat of Communists within the nation, it should not be difficult to conclude that, as a political party, they are of little consequence. Communists in this country have never made a respectable or serious showing in any election. I would doubt that there is a village, let alone a city or county or state, which the Communists could carry. Communism in the world scene is no bogeyman; but Communism as a political faction or party in this country plainly is. Communism has been so thoroughly exposed in this country that it has been crippled as a political force. Free speech has destroyed it as an effective political party. It is inconceivable that those who went up and down this country preaching the doctrine of revolution which petitioners espouse would have any success. In days of trouble and confusion, when bread lines were long, when the unemployed walked the streets, when people were starving, the advocates of a short-cut by revolution might have a chance to gain adherents. But today there are no such conditions. The country is not in despair; the people know Soviet Communism; the doctrine of Soviet revolution is exposed in all of its ugliness, and the American people want none of it. [. . .]

How it can be said that there is a clear and present danger that this advocacy will succeed is, therefore, a mystery. Some nations less resilient than the United States, where illiteracy is high and where democratic traditions are only budding, might have to take drastic steps and jail these men for merely speaking their creed. But in America, they are miserable merchants of unwanted ideas; their wares remain unsold. The fact that their ideas are abhorrent does not make them powerful. [. . .]

The First Amendment provides that "Congress shall make no law . . . abridging the freedom of speech." The Constitution provides no exception. This does not mean, however, that the Nation need hold its hand until it is in such weakened condition that there is no time to protect itself from incitement to revolution. Seditious conduct can always be punished. But the command of the First Amendment is so clear that we should not allow Congress to call a halt to free speech except in the extreme case of peril from the speech itself. The First Amendment makes confidence in the common sense of our people and in their maturity of judgment the great postulate of our democracy. Its philosophy is that violence is rarely, if ever, stopped by denying civil liberties to those advocating resort to force. The First Amendment reflects the philosophy of Jefferson "that it is time enough for the rightful purposes of civil government for its officers to interfere when principles break out into overt acts against peace and good order." The political censor has no place in our public debates. Unless and until extreme and necessitous circumstances are shown, our aim should be to keep speech unfettered and to allow the processes of law to be invoked only when the provocateurs among us move from speech to action.

Vishinsky wrote in 1938 in *The Law of the Soviet State,* "In our state, naturally, there is and can be no place for freedom of speech, press, and so on for the foes of socialism."

Our concern should be that we accept no such standard for the United States. Our faith should be that our people will never give support to these advocates of revolution, so long as we remain loyal to the purposes for which our Nation was founded.

HUGO BLACK

Youngstown Co. v. Sawyer (1952)

Mr. Justice BLACK delivered the opinion of the Court.

We are asked to decide whether the President was acting within his constitutional power when he issued an order directing the Secretary of Commerce to take possession of and operate most of the Nation's steel mills. The mill owners argue that the President's order amounts to lawmaking, a legislative function which the Constitution has expressly confided to the Congress and not to the President. The Government's position is that the order was made on findings of the President that his action was necessary to avert a national catastrophe which would inevitably result from a stoppage of steel production, and that in meeting this grave emergency the President was acting within the aggregate of his constitutional powers as the Nation's Chief Executive and the Commander in Chief of the Armed Forces of the United States. The issue emerges here from the following series of events:

In the latter part of 1951, a dispute arose between the steel companies and their employees over terms and conditions that should be included in new collective bargaining agreements. Long-continued conferences failed to resolve the dispute. On December 18, 1951, the employees' representative, United Steelworkers of America, C.I.O., gave notice of an intention to strike when the existing bargaining agreements expired on December 31. The Federal Mediation and Conciliation Service then intervened in an effort to get labor and management to agree. This failing, the President on December 22, 1951, referred the dispute to the Federal Wage Stabilization Board to investigate and make recommendations for fair and equitable terms of settlement. This Board's report resulted in no settlement. On April 4, 1952, the Union gave notice of a nation-wide strike called to begin at 12:01 a.m. April 9. The indispensability of steel as a component of substantially all weapons and other war materials led the President to believe that the proposed work stoppage would immediately jeopardize our national defense and that governmental seizure of the steel mills was necessary in order to assure the continued availability of steel. Reciting these considerations for his action, the President, a few hours before the strike was to begin, issued Executive Order 10340. [. . .] The order directed the Secretary of Commerce to take possession of most of the steel mills and keep them running. The Secretary immediately issued his own possessory orders, calling upon the presidents of the various seized companies to serve as operating managers for the United States. They were directed to carry on their activities in accordance with regulations and directions of the Secretary. The next morning the President sent a message to Congress reporting his action. Twelve days later he sent a second message. Congress has taken no action.

Obeying the Secretary's orders under protest, the companies brought proceedings against him in the District Court. Their complaints charged that the seizure was not authorized by an act of Congress or by any constitutional provisions. The District Court was asked to declare the orders of the President and the Secretary invalid and to issue preliminary and permanent injunctions restraining their enforcement. Opposing the motion for preliminary injunction, the United States asserted that a strike disrupting steel production for even a brief period would so endanger the well-being and safety of the Nation that the President had "inherent power" to do what he had done—power "supported by the Constitution, by historical precedent, and by court decisions." [. . .] Holding against the Government on all points, the District Court on April 30 issued a preliminary injunction restraining the Secretary from "continuing the seizure and possession of the plants . . . and from acting under the purported authority of Executive Order No. 10340." On the same day the Court of Appeals stayed the District Court's injunction. Deeming it best that the issues raised be promptly decided by this Court, we granted certiorari on May 3 and set the cause for argument on May 12. [. . .]

The President's power, if any, to issue the order must stem either from an act of Congress or from the Constitution itself. There is no statute that expressly authorizes the President to take possession of property as he did here. Nor is there any act of Congress to which our attention has been directed from which such a power can fairly be implied. Indeed, we do not understand the Government to rely on statutory authorization for this seizure. There are two statutes which do authorize the President to take both personal and real property under certain conditions. However, the Government admits that these conditions were not met and that the President's order was not rooted in either of the statutes. The Government refers to the seizure provisions of one of these statutes (201 (b) of the Defense Production Act) as "much too cumbersome, involved, and time-consuming for the crisis which was at hand."

Moreover, the use of the seizure technique to solve labor disputes in order to prevent work stoppages was not only unauthorized by any congressional enactment; prior to this controversy, Congress had refused to adopt that method of settling labor disputes. When the Taft-Hartley Act was under consideration in 1947, Congress rejected an amendment which would have authorized such governmental seizures in cases of emergency. Apparently it was thought that the technique of seizure, like that of compulsory arbitration, would interfere with the process of collective bargaining. Consequently, the plan Congress adopted in that Act did not provide for seizure under any circumstances. Instead, the plan sought to bring about settlements by use of the customary devices of mediation, conciliation, investigation by boards of inquiry, and public reports. In some instances temporary injunctions were authorized to provide cooling-off periods. All this failing, unions were left free to strike after a secret vote by employees as to whether they wished to accept their employers' final settlement offer.

It is clear that if the President had authority to issue the order he did, it must be found in some provision of the Constitution. And it is not claimed that express constitutional language grants this power to the President. The contention is that presidential power should be implied from the aggregate of his powers under the Constitution. Particular reliance is placed on provisions in Article II which say that "The

executive Power shall be vested in a President . . ."; that "he shall take Care that the Laws be faithfully executed"; and that he "shall be Commander in Chief of the Army and Navy of the United States."

The order cannot properly be sustained as an exercise of the President's military power as Commander in Chief of the Armed Forces. The Government attempts to do so by citing a number of cases upholding broad powers in military commanders engaged in day-to-day fighting in a theater of war. Such cases need not concern us here. Even though "theater of war" be an expanding concept, we cannot with faithfulness to our constitutional system hold that the Commander in Chief of the Armed Forces has the ultimate power as such to take possession of private property in order to keep labor disputes from stopping production. This is a job for the Nation's lawmakers, not for its military authorities.

Nor can the seizure order be sustained because of the several constitutional provisions that grant executive power to the President. In the framework of our Constitution, the President's power to see that the laws are faithfully executed refutes the idea that he is to be a lawmaker. The Constitution limits his functions in the lawmaking process to the recommending of laws he thinks wise and the vetoing of laws he thinks bad. And the Constitution is neither silent nor equivocal about who shall make laws which the President is to execute. The first section of the first article says that "All legislative Powers herein granted shall be vested in a Congress of the United States. . . ." After granting many powers to the Congress, Article I goes on to provide that Congress may "make all Laws which shall be necessary and proper for carrying into Execution the foregoing Powers, and all other Powers vested by this Constitution in the Government of the United States, or in any Department or Officer thereof."

The President's order does not direct that a congressional policy be executed in a manner prescribed by Congress—it directs that a presidential policy be executed in a manner prescribed by the President. The preamble of the order itself, like that of many statutes, sets out reasons why the President believes certain policies should be adopted, proclaims these policies as rules of conduct to be followed, and again, like a statute, authorizes a government official to promulgate additional rules and regulations consistent with the policy proclaimed and needed to carry that policy into execution. The power of Congress to adopt such public policies as those proclaimed by the order is beyond question. It can authorize the taking of private property for public use. It can make laws regulating the relationships between employers and employees, prescribing rules designed to settle labor disputes, and fixing wages and working conditions in certain fields of our economy. The Constitution does not subject this lawmaking power of Congress to presidential or military supervision or control.

It is said that other Presidents without congressional authority have taken possession of private business enterprises in order to settle labor disputes. But even if this be true, Congress has not thereby lost its exclusive constitutional authority to make laws necessary and proper to carry out the powers vested by the Constitution "in the Government of the United States, or any Department or Officer thereof."

The Founders of this Nation entrusted the lawmaking power to the Congress alone in both good and bad times. It would do no good to recall the historical events, the fears of power and the hopes for freedom that lay behind their choice. Such a review would but confirm our holding that this seizure order cannot stand.

The judgment of the District Court is Affirmed.

ROBERT JACKSON

Youngstown Co. v. Sawyer, Concurrence (1952)

Mr. Justice JACKSON, concurring in the judgment and opinion of the Court.

That comprehensive and undefined presidential powers hold both practical advantages and grave dangers for the country will impress anyone who has served as legal adviser to a President in time of transition and public anxiety. While an interval of detached reflection may temper teachings of that experience, they probably are a more realistic influence on my views than the conventional materials of judicial decision which seem unduly to accentuate doctrine and legal fiction. But as we approach the question of presidential power, we half overcome mental hazards by recognizing them. The opinions of judges, no less than executives and publicists, often suffer the infirmity of confusing the issue of a power's validity with the cause it is invoked to promote, of confounding the permanent executive office with its temporary occupant. The tendency is strong to emphasize transient results upon policies—such as wages or stabilization—and lose sight of enduring consequences upon the balanced power structure of our Republic.

A judge, like an executive adviser, may be surprised at the poverty of really useful and unambiguous authority applicable to concrete problems of executive power as they actually present themselves. Just what our forefathers did envision, or would have envisioned had they foreseen modern conditions, must be divined from materials almost as enigmatic as the dreams Joseph was called upon to interpret for Pharaoh. A century and a half of partisan debate and scholarly speculation yields no net result but only supplies more or less apt quotations from respected sources on each side of any question. They largely cancel each other. And court decisions are indecisive because of the judicial practice of dealing with the largest questions in the most narrow way.

The actual art of governing under our Constitution does not and cannot conform to judicial definitions of the power of any of its branches based on isolated clauses or even single Articles torn from context. While the Constitution diffuses power the better to secure liberty, it also contemplates that practice will integrate the dispersed powers into a workable government. It enjoins upon its branches separateness but interdependence, autonomy but reciprocity. Presidential powers are not fixed but fluctuate, depending upon their disjunction or conjunction with those of Congress. We may well begin by a somewhat over-simplified grouping of practical situations in which a President may doubt, or others may challenge, his powers, and by distinguishing roughly the legal consequences of this factor of relativity.

1. When the President acts pursuant to an express or implied authorization of Congress, his authority is at its maximum, for it includes all that he possesses in his own right plus all that Congress can delegate. In these circumstances, and in these only, may he be said (for what it may be worth) to personify the federal sovereignty. If his act is held unconstitutional under these circumstances, it usually means that the Federal Government as an undivided whole lacks power. A seizure executed by the President pursuant to an Act of Congress would be supported by the strongest of presumptions and the widest latitude of judicial interpretation, and the burden of persuasion would rest heavily upon any who might attack it.

2. When the President acts in absence of either a congressional grant or denial of authority, he can only rely upon his own independent powers, but there is a zone of twilight in which he and Congress may have concurrent authority, or in which its distribution is uncertain. Therefore, congressional inertia, indifference or quiescence may sometimes, at least as a practical matter, enable, if not invite, measures on independent presidential responsibility. In this area, any actual test of power is likely to depend on the imperatives of events and contemporary imponderables rather than on abstract theories of law.

3. When the President takes measures incompatible with the expressed or implied will of Congress, his power is at its lowest ebb, for then he can rely only upon his own constitutional powers minus any constitutional powers of Congress over the matter. Courts can sustain exclusive presidential control in such a case only by disabling the Congress from acting upon the subject. Presidential claim to a power at once so conclusive and preclusive must be scrutinized with caution, for what is at stake is the equilibrium established by our constitutional system.

Into which of these classifications does this executive seizure of the steel industry fit? It is eliminated from the first by admission, for it is conceded that no congressional authorization exists for this seizure. That takes away also the support of the many precedents and declarations which were made in relation, and must be confined, to this category.

Can it then be defended under flexible tests available to the second category? It seems clearly eliminated from that class because Congress has not left seizure of private property an open field but has covered it by three statutory policies inconsistent with this seizure. In cases where the purpose is to supply needs of the Government itself, two courses are provided: one, seizure of a plant which fails to comply with obligatory orders placed by the Government; another, condemnation of facilities, including temporary use under the power of eminent domain. The third is applicable where it is the general economy of the country that is to be protected rather than exclusive governmental interests. None of these were invoked. In choosing a different and inconsistent way of his own, the President cannot claim that it is necessitated or invited by failure of Congress to legislate upon the occasions, grounds and methods for seizure of industrial properties.

This leaves the current seizure to be justified only by the severe tests under the third grouping, where it can be supported only by any remainder of executive power after subtraction of such powers as Congress may have over the subject. In short, we can sustain the President only by holding that seizure of such strike-bound industries is within his domain and beyond control by Congress. Thus, this Court's first review of such seizures occurs under circumstances which leave presidential power most vulnerable to attack and in the least favorable of possible constitutional postures.

I did not suppose, and I am not persuaded, that history leaves it open to question, at least in the courts, that the executive branch, like the Federal Government as a whole, possesses only delegated powers. The purpose of the Constitution was not only to grant power, but to keep it from getting out of hand. However, because the President does not enjoy unmentioned powers does not mean that the mentioned ones should be narrowed by a niggardly construction. Some clauses could be made almost unworkable, as well as immutable, by refusal to indulge some latitude of interpretation for changing times. I have heretofore, and do now, give to the enumerated powers the scope and elasticity afforded by what seem to be reasonable, practical implications instead of the rigidity dictated by a doctrinaire textualism. [. . .]

The clause on which the Government next relies [to defend the Presidential order] is that "The President shall be Commander in Chief of the Army and Navy of the United States. . . ." These cryptic words have given rise to some of the most persistent controversies in our constitutional history. Of course, they imply something more than an empty title. But just what authority goes with the name has plagued presidential advisers who would not waive or narrow it by nonassertion yet cannot say where it begins or ends. It undoubtedly puts the Nation's armed forces under presidential command. Hence, this loose appellation is sometimes advanced as support for any presidential action, internal or external, involving use of force, the idea being that it vests power to do anything, anywhere, that can be done with an army or navy.

That seems to be the logic of an argument tendered at our bar—that the President having, on his own responsibility, sent American troops abroad derives from that act "affirmative power" to seize the means of producing a supply of steel for them. To quote, "Perhaps the most forceful illustration of the scope of Presidential power in this connection is the fact that American troops in Korea, whose safety and effectiveness are so directly involved here, were sent to the field by an exercise of the President's constitutional powers." Thus, it is said, he has invested himself with "war powers."

I cannot foresee all that it might entail if the Court should indorse this argument. Nothing in our Constitution is plainer than that declaration of a war is entrusted only to Congress. Of course, a state of war may in fact exist without a formal declaration. But no doctrine that the Court could promulgate would seem to me more sinister and alarming than that a President whose conduct of foreign affairs is so largely uncontrolled, and often even is unknown, can vastly enlarge his mastery over the internal affairs of the country by his own commitment of the Nation's armed forces to some foreign venture. [. . .]

Assuming that we are in a war de facto, whether it is or is not a war de jure, does that empower the Commander in Chief to seize industries he thinks necessary to supply our army? The Constitution expressly places in Congress power "to raise and support Armies" and "to provide and maintain a Navy." This certainly lays upon Congress primary responsibility for supplying the armed forces. Congress alone controls the raising of revenues and their appropriation and may determine in what manner and by what means they shall be spent for military and naval procurement. I suppose no one would doubt that Congress can take over war supply as a Government enterprise. On the other hand, if Congress sees fit to rely on free private enterprise collectively bargaining with free labor for support and maintenance of our armed forces, can the Executive, because of lawful disagreements incidental to that process, seize the facility for operation upon Government-imposed terms?

There are indications that the Constitution did not contemplate that the title Commander in Chief of the Army and Navy will constitute him also Commander in Chief of the country, its industries and its inhabitants. He has no monopoly of "war powers," whatever they are. While Congress cannot deprive the President of the command of the army and navy, only Congress can provide him an army or navy to command. It is also empowered to make rules for the "Government and Regulation of land and naval Forces," by which it may to some unknown extent impinge upon even command functions.

That military powers of the Commander in Chief were not to supersede representative government of internal affairs seems obvious from the Constitution and from elementary American history. Time out of mind, and even now in many parts of the world, a military commander can seize private housing to shelter his troops. Not so, however, in the United States, for the Third Amendment says, "No Soldier shall, in time of peace be quartered in any house, without the consent of the Owner, nor in time of war, but in a manner to be prescribed by law." Thus, even in war time, his seizure of needed military housing must be authorized by Congress. It also was expressly left to Congress to "provide for calling forth the Militia to execute the Laws of the Union, suppress Insurrections and repel Invasions. . . ." Such a limitation on the command power, written at a time when the militia rather than a standing army was contemplated as the military weapon of the Republic, underscores the Constitution's policy that Congress, not the Executive, should control utilization of the war power as an instrument of domestic policy. Congress, fulfilling that function, has authorized the President to use the army to enforce certain civil rights. On the other hand. Congress has forbidden him to use the army for the purpose of executing general laws except when expressly authorized by the Constitution or by Act of Congress. [. . .]

We should not use this occasion to circumscribe, much less to contract, the lawful role of the President as Commander in Chief. I should indulge the widest latitude of interpretation to sustain his exclusive function to command the instruments of national force, at least when turned against the outside world for the security of our society. But, when it is turned inward, not because of rebellion but because of a lawful economic struggle between industry and labor, it should have no such indulgence. His command power is not such an absolute as might be implied from that office in a militaristic system but is subject to limitations consistent with a constitutional Republic whose law and policy-making branch is a representative Congress. The purpose of lodging dual titles in one man was to insure that the civilian would control the military, not to enable the military to subordinate the presidential office. No penance would ever expiate the sin against free government of holding that a President can escape control of executive powers by law through assuming his military role. What the power of command may include I do not try to envision, but I think it is not a military prerogative, without support of law, to seize persons or property because they are important or even essential for the military and naval establishment. [. . .]

The Solicitor General lastly grounds support of the seizure upon nebulous, inherent powers never expressly granted but said to have accrued to the office from the customs and claims of preceding administrations. The plea is for a resulting power to deal with a crisis or an emergency according to the necessities of the case, the unarticulated assumption being that necessity knows no law.

Loose and irresponsible use of adjectives colors all nonlegal and much legal discussion of presidential powers. "Inherent" powers, "implied" powers, "incidental" powers, "plenary" powers, "war" powers and "emergency" powers are used, often interchangeably and without fixed or ascertainable meanings.

The vagueness and generality of the clauses that set forth presidential powers afford a plausible basis for pressures within and without an administration for presidential action beyond that supported by those whose responsibility it is to defend his actions in court. The claim of inherent and unrestricted presidential powers has long been a persuasive dialectical weapon in political controversy. While it is not surprising that counsel should grasp support from such unadjudicated claims of power, a judge cannot accept self-serving press statements of the attorney for one of the interested parties as authority in answering a constitutional question, even if the advocate was himself. But prudence has counseled that actual reliance on such nebulous claims stop short of provoking a judicial test. [. . .]

The appeal [. . .] however, that we declare the existence of inherent powers *ex necessitate* to meet an emergency asks us to do what many think would be wise, although it is something the forefathers omitted. They knew what emergencies were, knew the pressures they engender for authoritative action, knew, too, how they afford a ready pretext for usurpation. We may also suspect that they suspected that emergency powers would tend to kindle emergencies. Aside from suspension of the privilege of the writ of habeas corpus in time of rebellion or invasion, when the public safety may require it, they made no express provision for exercise of extraordinary authority because of a crisis. I do not think we rightfully may so amend their work, and, if we could, I am not convinced it would be wise to do so. . . .

In view of the ease, expedition and safety with which Congress can grant and has granted large emergency powers, certainly ample to embrace this crisis, I am quite unimpressed with the argument that we should affirm possession of them without statute. Such power either has no beginning or it has no end. If it exists, it need submit to no legal restraint. I am not alarmed that it would plunge us straightway into dictatorship, but it is at least a step in that wrong direction.

As to whether there is imperative necessity for such powers, it is relevant to note the gap that exists between the President's paper powers and his real powers. The Constitution does not disclose the measure of the actual controls wielded by the modern presidential office. That instrument must be understood as an Eighteenth-Century sketch of a government hoped for, not as a blueprint of the Government that is. Vast accretions of federal power, eroded from that reserved by the States, have magnified the scope of presidential activity. Subtle shifts take place in the centers of real power that do not show on the face of the Constitution.

Executive power has the advantage of concentration in a single head in whose choice the whole Nation has a part, making him the focus of public hopes and expectations. In drama, magnitude and finality his decisions so far overshadow any others that almost alone he fills the public eye and ear. No other personality in public life can begin to compete with him in access to the public mind through modern methods of communications. By his prestige as head of state and his influence upon public opinion he exerts a leverage upon those who are supposed to check and balance his power which often cancels their effectiveness.

Moreover, rise of the party system has made a significant extraconstitutional supplement to real executive power. No appraisal of his necessities is realistic which overlooks that he heads a political system as well as a legal system. Party loyalties and interests, sometimes more binding than law, extend his effective control into branches of government other than his own and he often may win, as a political leader, what he cannot command under the Constitution. Indeed, Woodrow Wilson, commenting on the President as leader both of his party and of the Nation, observed, "If he rightly interpret the national thought and boldly insist upon it, he is irresistible. [. . .] His office is anything he has the sagacity and force to make it." I cannot be brought to believe that this country will suffer if the Court refuses further to aggrandize the presidential office, already so potent and so relatively immune from judicial review, at the expense of Congress.

But I have no illusion that any decision by this Court can keep power in the hands of Congress if it is not wise and timely in meeting its problems. A crisis that challenges the President equally, or perhaps primarily, challenges Congress. If not good law, there was worldly wisdom in the maxim attributed to Napoleon that "The tools belong to the man who can use them." We may say that power to legislate for emergencies belongs in the hands of Congress, but only Congress itself can prevent power from slipping through its fingers.

The essence of our free Government is "leave to live by no man's leave, underneath the law"—to be governed by those impersonal forces which we call law. Our Government is fashioned to fulfill this concept so far as humanly possible. The Executive, except for recommendation and veto, has no legislative power. The executive action we have here originates in the individual will of the President and represents an exercise of authority without law. No one, perhaps not even the President, knows the limits of the power he may seek to exert in this instance and the parties affected cannot learn the limit of their rights. We do not know today what powers over labor or property would be claimed to flow from Government possession if we should legalize it, what rights to compensation would be claimed or recognized, or on what contingency it would end. With all its defects, delays and inconveniences, men have discovered no technique for long preserving free government except that the Executive be under the law, and that the law be made by parliamentary deliberations.

Such institutions may be destined to pass away. But it is the duty of the Court to be last, not first, to give them up.

Frederick M. Vinson

Youngstown Co. v. Sawyer, Dissent (1952)

Mr. Chief Justice VINSON, with whom Mr. Justice REED and Mr. Justice MINTON join, dissenting.

I

Those who suggest that this is a case involving extraordinary powers should be mindful that these are extraordinary times. A world not yet recovered from the devastation of World War II has been forced to face the threat of another and more terrifying global conflict. [. . .]

Accepting in full measure its responsibility in the world community, the United States was instrumental in securing adoption of the United Nations Charter, approved by the Senate by a vote of 89 to 2. The first purpose of the United Nations is to "maintain international peace and security, and to that end: to take effective collective measures for the prevention and removal of threats to the peace, and for the suppression of acts of aggression or other breaches of the peace, . . ." In 1950, when the United Nations called upon member nations "to render every assistance" to repel aggression in Korea, the United States furnished its vigorous support. For almost two full years, our armed forces have been fighting in Korea, suffering casualties of over 108,000 men. Hostilities have not abated. The "determination of the United Nations to continue its action in Korea to meet the aggression" has been reaffirmed. Congressional support of the action in Korea has been manifested by provisions for increased military manpower and equipment and for economic stabilization described. [. . .]

Further efforts to protect the free world from aggression are found in the congressional enactments of the Truman Plan for assistance to Greece and Turkey and the Marshall Plan for economic aid needed to build up the strength of our friends in Western Europe. In 1949, the Senate approved the North Atlantic Treaty under which each member nation agrees that an armed attack against one is an armed attack against all. [. . .]

Our treaties represent not merely legal obligations but show congressional recognition that mutual security for the free world is the best security against the threat of aggression on a global scale. The need for mutual security is shown by the very size of the armed forces outside the free world. Defendant's brief informs us that the Soviet Union maintains the largest air force in the world and maintains ground forces much larger than those presently available to the United States. [. . .]

One is not here called upon even to consider the possibility of executive seizure of a farm, a corner grocery store or even a single industrial plant. Such considerations arise only when one ignores the central fact of this case—that the Nation's entire basic steel production would have shut down completely if there had been no Government seizure. Even ignoring for the moment whatever confidential information the President may possess as "the Nation's organ for foreign affairs," the uncontroverted affidavits in this record amply support the finding that "a work stoppage would immediately jeopardize and imperil our national defense." [. . .]

Accordingly, if the President has any power under the Constitution to meet a critical situation in the absence of express statutory authorization, there is no basis whatever for criticizing the exercise of such power in this case.

II

Admitting that the Government could seize the mills, plaintiffs claim that the implied power of eminent domain can be exercised only under an Act of Congress; under no circumstances, they say, can that power be exercised by the President unless he can point to an express provision in enabling legislation.

This was the view adopted by the District Judge when he granted the preliminary injunction. Without an answer, without hearing evidence, he determined the issue on the basis of his "fixed conclusion . . . that defendant's acts are illegal" because the President's only course in the face of an emergency is to present the matter to Congress and await the final passage of legislation which will enable the Government to cope with threatened disaster.

Under this view, the President is left powerless at the very moment when the need for action may be most pressing and when no one, other than he, is immediately capable of action. Under this view, he is left powerless because a power not expressly given to Congress is nevertheless found to rest exclusively with Congress.

Consideration of this view of executive impotence calls for further examination of the nature of the separation of powers under our tripartite system of Government.

The Constitution provides [. . .] [that] "The executive Power shall be vested in a President of the United States of America. . . ." [. . .]

The whole of the "executive Power" is vested in the President. Before entering office, the President swears that he "will faithfully execute the Office of President of the United States, and will to the best of [his] Ability, preserve, protect and defend the Constitution of the United States." Art. II, 1.

This comprehensive grant of the executive power to a single person was bestowed soon after the country had thrown the yoke of monarchy. Only by instilling initiative and vigor in all of the three departments of Government, declared Madison, could tyranny in any form be avoided. Hamilton added: "Energy in the Executive is a leading character in the definition of good government. It is essential to the protection of the community against foreign attacks; it is not less essential to the steady administration of the laws; to the protection of property against those irregular and high-handed combinations which sometimes interrupt the ordinary course of justice; to the security of liberty against the enterprises and assaults of ambition, of faction, and of anarchy" [*Federalist* no. 70]. It is thus apparent that the Presidency was deliberately fashioned as an office of power and independence. Of course, the Framers created no autocrat capable of arrogating any power unto himself at any time. But

neither did they create an automaton impotent to exercise the powers of Government at a time when the survival of the Republic itself may be at stake.

In passing upon the grave constitutional question presented in this case, we must never forget, as Chief Justice Marshall admonished, that the Constitution is "intended to endure for ages to come, and, consequently, to be adapted to the various crises of human affairs," and that "[i]ts means are adequate to its ends." Cases do arise presenting questions which could not have been foreseen by the Framers. In such cases, the Constitution has been treated as a living document adaptable to new situations. But we are not called upon today to expand the Constitution to meet a new situation. For, in this case, we need only look to history and time-honored principles of constitutional law—principles that have been applied consistently by all branches of the Government throughout our history. It is those who assert the invalidity of the Executive Order who seek to amend the Constitution in this case.

III

A review of executive action demonstrates that our Presidents have on many occasions exhibited the leadership contemplated by the Framers when they made the President Commander in Chief, and imposed upon him the trust to "take Care that the Laws be faithfully executed." With or without explicit statutory authorization, Presidents have at such times dealt with national emergencies by acting promptly and resolutely to enforce legislative programs, at least to save those programs until Congress could act. Congress and the courts have responded to such executive initiative with consistent approval.

Our first President displayed at once the leadership contemplated by the Framers. When the national revenue laws were openly flouted in some sections of Pennsylvania, President Washington, without waiting for a call from the state government, summoned the militia and took decisive steps to secure the faithful execution of the laws. When international disputes engendered by the French revolution threatened to involve this country in war, and while congressional policy remained uncertain, Washington issued his Proclamation of Neutrality.

Hamilton, whose defense of the Proclamation has endured the test of time, invoked the argument that the Executive has the duty to do that which will preserve peace until Congress acts and, in addition, pointed to the need for keeping the Nation informed of the requirements of existing laws and treaties as part of the faithful execution of the laws. [. . .]

Jefferson's initiative in the Louisiana Purchase, the Monroe Doctrine, and Jackson's removal of Government deposits from the Bank of the United States further serve to demonstrate by deed what the Framers described by word when they vested the whole of the executive power in the President. Without declaration of war, President Lincoln took energetic action with the outbreak of the War Between the States. He summoned troops and paid them out of the Treasury without appropriation therefor. He proclaimed a naval blockade of the Confederacy and seized ships violating that blockade. Congress, far from denying the validity of these acts, gave them express approval. The most striking action of President Lincoln was the Emancipation Proclamation, issued in aid of the successful prosecution of the War Between the States, but wholly without statutory authority.

In an action furnishing a most apt precedent for this case, President Lincoln without statutory authority directed the seizure of rail and telegraph lines leading to Washington. Many months later, Congress recognized and confirmed the power of the President to seize railroads and telegraph lines and provided criminal penalties for interference with Government operation. This Act did not confer on the President any additional powers of seizure. Congress plainly rejected the view that the President's acts had been without legal sanction until ratified by the legislature. Sponsors of the bill declared that its purpose was only to confirm the power which the President already possessed. Opponents insisted a statute authorizing seizure was unnecessary and might even be construed as limiting existing Presidential powers. [. . .]

President Hayes authorized the wide-spread use of federal troops during the Railroad Strike of 1877. President Cleveland also used the troops in the Pullman Strike of 1895 and his action is of special significance. No statute authorized this action. No call for help had issued from the Governor of Illinois; indeed Governor Altgeld disclaimed the need for supplemental forces. But the President's concern was that federal laws relating to the free flow of interstate commerce and the mails be continuously and faithfully executed without interruption. To further this aim his agents sought and obtained the injunction upheld by this Court in *In re Debs* (1895). The Court scrutinized each of the steps taken by the President to insure execution of the "mass of legislation" dealing with commerce and the mails and gave his conduct full approval. Congress likewise took note of this use of Presidential power to forestall apparent obstacles to the faithful execution of the laws. By separate resolutions, both the Senate and the House commended the Executive's action.

President Theodore Roosevelt seriously contemplated seizure of Pennsylvania coal mines if a coal shortage necessitated such action. In his autobiography, President Roosevelt expounded the "Stewardship Theory" of Presidential power, stating that "the executive as subject only to the people, and, under the Constitution, bound to serve the people affirmatively in cases where the Constitution does not explicitly forbid him to render the service." Because the contemplated seizure of the coal mines was based on this theory, then ex-President Taft criticized President Roosevelt in a passage in his book [*Our Chief Magistrate and His Powers* 1916] relied upon by the District Court in this case. [. . .]

Beginning with the Bank Holiday Proclamation and continuing through World War II, executive leadership and initiative were characteristic of President Franklin D. Roosevelt's administration. In 1939, upon the outbreak of war in Europe, the President proclaimed a limited national emergency for the purpose of strengthening our national defense. In May of 1941, the danger from the Axis belligerents having become clear, the President proclaimed "an unlimited national emergency" calling for mobilization of the Nation's defenses to repel aggression. The President took the initiative in strengthening our defenses by acquiring rights from the British Government to establish air bases in exchange for overage destroyers.

In 1941, President Roosevelt acted to protect Iceland from attack by Axis powers, when British forces were withdrawn, by sending our forces to occupy Iceland. Congress was informed of this action on the same day that our forces reached Iceland. The occupation of Iceland was but one of "at least 125 incidents" in our history in which Presidents "without congressional authorization, and in the absence of a declaration of war, [have] ordered the Armed Forces to take action or maintain positions abroad." Some six months before Pearl Harbor, a dispute at a single aviation plant at Inglewood, California, interrupted a segment of the productive of military aircraft. In spite of the comparative insignificance of this work stoppage to total defense production as contrasted with the complete paralysis now threatened by a shutdown of the entire basic steel industry, and even though our armed forces were not then engaged in combat, President Roosevelt ordered the seizure of the plant "pursuant to the powers vested in [him] by the Constitution and laws of the United States, as President of the United States of America and Commander in Chief of the Army and Navy of the United States." The Attorney General (Jackson) vigorously proclaimed that the President had the moral duty to keep this Nation's defense effort a "going concern." His ringing moral justification was coupled with a legal justification equally well stated. [. . .]

> The Constitution lays upon the President the duty "to take care that the laws be faithfully executed." Among the laws which he is required to find means to execute are those which direct him to equip an enlarged army, to provide for a strengthened navy, to protect Government property, to protect those who are engaged in carrying out the business of the Government, and to carry out the provisions of the Lend-Lease Act. For the faithful execution of such laws the President has back of him not only each general law-enforcement power conferred by the various acts of Congress but the aggregate of all such laws plus that wide discretion as to method vested in him by the Constitution for the purpose of executing the laws. [. . .]

More recently, President Truman acted to repel aggression by employing our armed forces in Korea. Upon the intervention of the Chinese Communists, the President proclaimed the existence of an unlimited national emergency requiring the speedy build-up of our defense establishment. Congress responded by providing for increased manpower and weapons for our own armed forces, by increasing military aid under the Mutual Security Program and by enacting economic stabilization measures, as previously described.

This is but a cursory summary of executive leadership. But it amply demonstrates that Presidents have taken prompt action to enforce the laws and protect the country whether or not Congress happened to provide in advance for the particular method of execution. At the minimum, the executive actions reviewed herein sustain the action of the President in this case. And many of the cited examples of Presidential practice go far beyond the extent of power necessary to sustain the President's order to seize the steel mills. The fact that temporary executive seizures of industrial plants to meet an emergency have not been directly tested in this Court furnishes not the slightest suggestion that such actions have been illegal. Rather, the fact that Congress and the courts have consistently recognized and given their support to such executive action indicates that such a power of seizure has been accepted throughout our history. History bears out the genius of the Founding Fathers, who created a Government subject to law but not left subject to inertia when vigor and initiative are required. [. . .]

VI

The diversity of views expressed in the six opinions of the majority, the lack of reference to authoritative precedent, the repeated reliance upon prior dissenting opinions, the complete disregard of the uncontroverted facts showing the gravity of the emergency and the temporary nature of the taking all serve to demonstrate how far afield one must go to affirm the order of the District Court.

The broad executive power granted by Article II to an officer on duty 365 days a year cannot, it is said, be invoked to avert disaster. Instead, the President must confine himself to sending a message to Congress recommending action. Under this messenger-boy concept of the Office, the President cannot even act to preserve legislative programs from destruction so that Congress will have something left to act upon. There is no judicial finding that the executive action was unwarranted because there was in fact no basis for the President's finding of the existence of an emergency for, under this view, the gravity of the emergency and the immediacy of the threatened disaster are considered irrelevant as a matter of law. [. . .]

As the District Judge stated, this is no time for "timorous" judicial action. But neither is this a time for timorous executive action. Faced with the duty of executing the defense programs which Congress had enacted and the disastrous effects that any stoppage in steel production would have on those programs, the President acted to preserve those programs by seizing the steel mills. There is no question that the possession was other than temporary in character and subject to congressional direction—either approving, disapproving or regulating the manner in which the mills were to be administered and returned to the owners. The President immediately informed Congress of his action and clearly stated his intention to abide by the legislative will. No basis for claims of arbitrary action, unlimited powers or dictatorial usurpation of congressional power appears from the facts of this case. On the contrary, judicial, legislative and executive precedents throughout our history demonstrate that in this case the President acted in full conformity with his duties under the Constitution. Accordingly, we would reverse the order of the District Court.

WHITTAKER CHAMBERS

Witness (1952)

Forward in the Form of a Letter to My Children

Beloved Children,

I am sitting in the kitchen of the little house at Medfield, our second farm which is cut off by the ridge and a quarter-mile across the fields from our home place, where you are. I am writing a book. In it I am speaking to you. But I am also speaking to the world. To both I owe an accounting.

It is a terrible book. It is terrible in what it tells about men. If anything, it is more terrible in what it tells about the world in which you live. It is about what the world calls the Hiss-Chambers Case, or even more simply, the Hiss Case. It is about a spy case. All the props of an espionage case are there—foreign agents, household traitors, stolen documents, microfilm, furtive meetings, secret hideaways, phony names, an informer, investigations, trials, official justice.

But if the Hiss Case were only this, it would not be worth my writing about or your reading about. It would be another fat folder in the sad files of the police, another crime drama in which the props would be mistaken for the play (as many people have consistently mistaken them). It would not be what alone gave it meaning, what the mass of men and women instinctively sensed it to be, often without quite knowing why. It would not be what, at the very beginning, I was moved to call it: "a tragedy of history."

For it was more than human tragedy. Much more than Alger Hiss or Whittaker Chambers was on trial in the trials of Alger Hiss. Two faiths were on trial. Human societies, like human beings, live by faith and die when faith dies. At issue in the Hiss Case was the question whether this sick society, which we call Western civilization, could in its extremity still cast up a man whose faith in it was so great that he would voluntarily abandon those things which men hold good, including life, to defend it. At issue was the question whether this man's faith could prevail against a man whose equal faith it was that this society is sick beyond saving, and that mercy itself pleads for its swift extinction and replacement by another. At issue was the question whether, in the desperately divided society, there still remained the will to recognize the issues in time to offset the immense rally of public power to distort and pervert the facts.

At heart, the Great Case was this critical conflict of faiths; that is why it was a great case. On a scale personal enough to be felt by all, but big enough to be symbolic, the two irreconcilable faiths of our time—Communism and Freedom—came to grips in the persons of two conscious and resolute men.

Indeed, it would have been hard, in a world still only dimly aware of what the conflict is about, to find two other men who knew so clearly. Both had been schooled in the same view of history (the Marxist view). Both were trained by the same party in the same selfless, semisoldierly discipline. Neither would nor could yield without betraying, not himself, but his faith; and the different character of these faiths was shown by the different conduct of the two men toward each other throughout the struggle. For, with dark certitude, both knew, almost from the beginning, that the Great Case could end only in the destruction of one or both of the contending figures, just as the history of our times (both men had been taught) can end only in the destruction of one or both of the contending forces.

But this destruction is not the tragedy. The nature of tragedy is itself misunderstood. Part of the world supposes that the tragedy in the Hiss Case lies in the acts of disloyalty revealed. Part believes that the tragedy lies in the fact that an able, intelligent man, Alger Hiss, was cut short in the course of a brilliant public career. Some find it tragic that Whittaker Chambers, of his own will, gave up a $30,000-a-year job and a secure future to haunt for the rest of his days the ruins of his life. These are shocking facts, criminal facts, disturbing facts: they are not tragic.

Crime, violence, infamy are not tragedy. Tragedy occurs when a human soul awakes and seeks, in suffering and pain, to free itself from crime, violence, infamy, even at the cost of life. The struggle is the tragedy—not defeat or death. That is why the spectacle of tragedy has always filled men, not with despair, but with a sense of hope and exaltation. That is why this terrible book is also a book of hope. For it is about the struggle of the human soul—of more than one human soul. It is in this sense that the Hiss Case is a tragedy. This is its meaning beyond the headlines, the revelations, the shame and suffering of the people involved. But this tragedy will have been for nothing unless men understand it rightly, and from it the world takes hope and heart to begin its own tragic struggle with the evil that besets it from within and from without, unless it faces the fact that the world, the whole world, is sick unto death and that, among other things, this Case has turned a finger of fierce light into the suddenly opened and reeking body of our time.

My children, as long as you live, the shadow of the Hiss Case will brush you. In every pair of eyes that rests on you, you will see pass, like a cloud passing behind a woods in winter, the memory of your father—dissembled in friendly eyes, lurking in unfriendly eyes. Sometimes you will wonder which is harder to bear: friendly forgiveness or forthright hate. In time, therefore, when the sum of your experience of life gives you authority, you will ask yourselves the question: What was my father?

I will give you an answer: I was a witness. I do not mean a witness for the Government or against Alger Hiss and the others. Nor do I mean the short, squat, solitary figure, trudging through the impersonal halls of public buildings to testify before Congressional committees, grand juries, loyalty boards, courts of law. A man is not primarily a witness *against* something. That is only incidental to the fact that he is a witness *for* something. A witness, in the sense that I am using the word, is a man whose life and faith are so completely one that when the challenge comes to step out and testify for his faith, he does so, disregarding all risks, accepting all consequences.

One day in the great jury room of the Grand Jury of the Southern District of New York, a juror leaned forward slightly and asked me: "Mr. Chambers, what does it mean to be a Communist?" I hesitated for a moment, trying to find the simplest, most direct way to convey the heart of this complex experience to men and women to whom the very fact of the experience was all but incomprehensible. Then I said:

"When I was a Communist, I had three heroes. One was a Russian. One was a Pole. One was a German Jew.

"The Pole was Felix Djerjinsky. He was ascetic, highly sensitive, intelligent. He was a Communist. After the Russian Revolution, he became head of the Tcheka and organizer of the Red Terror. As a young man, Djerjinsky had been a political prisoner in the Paviak Prison in Warsaw. There he insisted on being given the task of cleaning the latrines of the other prisoners. For he held that the most developed member of any community must take upon himself the lowliest tasks as an example to those who are less developed. That is one thing that it meant to be a Communist.

"The German Jew was Eugen Leviné. He was a Communist. During the Bavarian Soviet Republic in

1919, Leviné was the organizer of the Workers and Soldiers Soviets. When the Bavarian Soviet Republic was crushed, Leviné was captured and court-martialed. The court-martial told him: 'You are under sentence of death.' Leviné answered: 'We Communists are always under sentence of death.' That is another thing that it meant to be a Communist.

"The Russian was not a Communist. He was a pre-Communist revolutionist named Kalyaev. (I should have said Sazonov.) He was arrested for a minor part in the assassination of the Tsarist prime minister, von Plehve. He was sent into Siberian exile to one of the worst prison camps, where the political prisoners were flogged. Kalyaev sought some way to protest this outrage to the world. The means were few, but at last he found a way. In protest against the flogging of other men, Kalyaev drenched himself in kerosene, set himself on fire and burned himself to death. That also is what it meant to be a Communist."

That also is what it means to be a witness.

But a man may also be an involuntary witness. I do not know any way to explain why God's grace touches a man who seems unworthy of it. But neither do I know any other way to explain how a man like myself—tarnished by life, unprepossessing, not brave—could prevail so far against the powers of the world arrayed almost solidly against him, to destroy him and defeat his truth. In this sense, I am an involuntary witness to God's grace and to the fortifying power of faith.

It was my fate to be in turn a witness to each of the two great faiths of our time. And so we come to the terrible word, Communism. My very dear children, nothing in all these pages will be written so much for you, though it is so unlike anything you would want to read. In nothing shall I be so much a witness, in no way am I so much called upon to fulfill my task, as in trying to make clear to you (and to the world) the true nature of Communism and the source of its power, which was the cause of my ordeal as a man, and remains the historic ordeal of the world in the 20th century. For in this century, within the next decades, will be decided for generations whether all mankind is to become Communist, whether the whole world is to become free, or whether, in the struggle, civilization as we know it is to be completely destroyed or completely changed. It is our fate to live upon that turning point in history.

The world has reached that turning point by the steep stages of a crisis mounting for generations. The turning point is the next to the last step. It was reached in blood, sweat, tears, havoc and death in World War II. The chief fruit of the First World War was the Russian Revolution and the rise of Communism as a national power. The chief fruit of the Second World War was our arrival at the next to the last step of the crisis with the rise of Communism as a world power. History is likely to say that these were the only decisive results of the world wars.

The last war simplified the balance of political forces in the world by reducing them to two. For the first time, it made the power of the Communist sector of mankind (embodied in the Soviet Union) roughly equal to the power of the free sector of mankind (embodied in the United States). It made the collision of these powers all but inevitable. For the world wars did not end the crisis. They raised its tensions to a new pitch. They raised the crisis to a new stage. All the politics of our time, including the politics of war, will be the politics of this crisis.

Few men are so dull that they do not know that the crisis exists and that it threatens their lives at every point. It is popular to call it a social crisis. It is in fact a total crisis—religious, moral, intellectual, social, political, economic. It is popular to call it a crisis of the Western world. It is in fact a crisis of the whole world. Communism, which claims to be a solution of the crisis, is itself a symptom and an irritant of the crisis.

In part, the crisis results from the impact of science and technology upon mankind which, neither socially nor morally, has caught up with the problems posed by that impact. In part, it is caused by men's efforts to solve those problems. World wars are the military expression of the crisis. World-wide depressions are its economic expression. Universal desperation is its spiritual climate. This is the climate of Communism. Communism in our time can no more be considered apart from the crisis than a fever can be acted upon apart from an infected body.

I see in Communism the focus of the concentrated evil of our time. You will ask: Why, then, do men become Communists? How did it happen that you, our gentle and loved father, were once a Communist? Were you simply stupid? No, I was not stupid. Were you morally depraved? No, I was not morally depraved. Indeed, educated men become Communists chiefly for moral reasons. Did you not know that the crimes and horrors of Communism are inherent in Communism? Yes, I knew that fact. Then why did you become a Communist? It would help more to ask: How did it happen that this movement, once a mere muttering of political outcasts, became this immense force that now contests the mastery of mankind? Even when all the chances and mistakes of history are allowed for, the answer must be: Communism makes some profound appeal to the human mind. You will not find out what it is by calling Communism names. That will not help much to explain why Communism whose horrors, on a scale unparalleled in history, are now public knowledge, still recruits its thousands and holds its millions — among them some of the best minds alive. Look at Klaus Fuchs, standing in the London dock, quiet, doomed, destroyed, and say whether it is possible to answer in that way the simple question: Why?

First, let me try to say what Communism is not. It is not simply a vicious plot hatched by wicked men in a sub-cellar. It is not just the writings of Marx and Lenin, dialectical materialism, the Politburo, the labor theory of value, the theory of the general strike, the Red Army, secret police, labor camps, underground conspiracy, the dictatorship of the proletariat, the technique of the coup d'état. It is not even those chanting, bannered millions that stream periodically, like disorganized armies, through the heart of the world's capitals: Moscow, New York, Tokyo, Paris, Rome. These are expressions of Communism, but they are not what Communism is about.

In the Hiss trials, where Communism was a haunting specter, but which did little or nothing to explain Communism, Communists were assumed to be criminals, pariahs, clandestine men who lead double lives under false names, travel on false passports, deny traditional religion, morality, the sanctity of oaths, preach violence and practice treason. These things are true about Communists, but they are not what Communism is about.

The revolutionary heart of Communism is not the theatrical appeal: "Workers of the world, unite. You have nothing to lose but your chains. You have a world to gain." It is a simple statement of Karl Marx, further simplified for handy use: Philosophers have explained the world; it is necessary to change the world." Communists are bound together by no secret oath. The tie that binds them across the frontiers of nations, across barriers of language and differences of class and education, in defiance of religion, morality, truth, law, honor, the weaknesses of the body and the irresolutions of the mind, even unto death, is a simple conviction: It is necessary to change the world. Their power, whose nature baffles the rest of the world, because in a large measure the rest of the world has lost that power, is the power to hold convictions and to act on them. It is the same power that moves mountains; it is also an unfailing power to move men. Communists are that part of mankind which has recovered the power to live or die — to bear witness — for its faith. And it is a simple, rational faith that inspires men to live or die for it.

It is not new. It is, in fact, man's second oldest faith. Its promise was whispered in the first days of the Creation under the Tree of the Knowledge of Good and Evil: "Ye shall be as gods." It is the great alternative faith of mankind. Like all great faiths, its force derives from a simple vision. Other ages have had great visions. They have always been different versions of the same vision: the vision of God and man's relationship to God. The Communist vision is the vision of Man without God.

It is the vision of man's mind displacing God as the creative intelligence of the world. It is the vision of man's liberated mind, by the sole force of its rational intelligence, redirecting man's destiny and reorganizing man's life and the world. It is the vision of man, once more the central figure of the Creation, not because God made man in His image, but because man's mind makes him the most intelligent of the animals. Copernicus and his successors displaced man as the central fact of the universe by proving that the earth was not the central star of the universe. Communism restores man to his sovereignty by the simple method of denying God.

The vision is a challenge and implies a threat. It challenges man to prove by his acts that he is the masterwork of the Creation — by making thought and act one. It challenges him to prove it by using the force of his rational mind to end the bloody meaninglessness of man's history — by giving it purpose and a plan. It challenges him to prove it by reducing the meaningless chaos of nature, by imposing on it his rational will to order, abundance, security, peace.

It is the vision of materialism. But it threatens, if man's mind is unequal to the problems of man's progress, that he will sink back into savagery (the A and the H bombs have raised the issue in explosive forms), until nature replaces him with a more intelligent form of life.

It is an intensely practical vision. The tools to turn it into reality are at hand—science and technology, whose traditional method, the rigorous exclusion of all supernatural factors in solving problems, has contributed to the intellectual climate in which the vision flourishes, just as they have contributed to the crisis in which Communism thrives. For the vision is shared by millions who are not Communists (they are part of Communism's secret strength). Its first commandment is found, not in the *Communist Manifesto*, but in the first sentence of the physics primer: "All of the progress of mankind to date results from the making of careful measurements." But Communism, for the first time in history, has made this vision the faith of a great modern political movement.

Hence the Communist Party is quite justified in calling itself the most revolutionary party in history. It has posed in practical form the most revolutionary question in history: God or Man? It has taken the logical next step which three hundred years of rationalism hesitated to take, and said what millions of modern minds think, but do not dare or care to say: If man's mind is the decisive force in the world, what need is there for God? Henceforth man's mind is man's fate.

This vision *is* the Communist revolution, which, like all great revolutions, occurs in man's mind before it takes form in man's acts. Insurrection and conspiracy are merely methods of realizing the vision; they are merely part of the politics of Communism. Without its vision, they, like Communism, would have no meaning and could not rally a parcel of pickpockets. Communism does not summon men to crime or to utopia, as its easy critics like to think. On the plane of faith, it summons mankind to turn its vision into practical reality. On the plane of action, it summons men to struggle against the inertia of the past which, embodied in social, political and economic forms, Communism claims, is blocking the will of mankind to make its next great forward stride. It summons men to overcome the crisis, which, Communism claims, is in effect a crisis of rending frustration, with the world, unable to stand still, but unwilling to go forward along the road that the logic of a technological civilization points out—Communism.

This is Communism's moral sanction, which is twofold. Its vision points the way to the future; its faith labors to turn the future into present reality. It says to every man who joins it: the vision is a practical problem of history; the way to achieve it is a practical problem of politics, which is the present tense of history. Have you the moral strength to take upon yourself the crimes of history so that man at last may close his chronicle of age-old, senseless suffering, and replace it with purpose and a plan? The answer a man makes to this question is the difference between the Communist and those miscellaneous socialists, liberals, fellow travelers, unclassified progressives and men of good will, all of whom share a similar vision, but do not share the faith because they will not take upon themselves the penalties of the faith. The answer is the root of that sense of moral superiority which makes Communists, though caught in crime, berate their opponents with withering self-righteousness.

The Communist vision has a mighty agitator and a mighty propagandist. They are the crisis. The agitator needs no soap box. It speaks insistently to the human mind at the point where desperation works. The propagandist writes no Communist gibberish. It speaks insistently to the human mind at the point where man's hope and man's energy fuse to fierceness.

The vision inspires. The crisis impels. The workingman is chiefly moved by the crisis. The educated man is chiefly moved by the vision. The workingman, living upon a mean margin of life, can afford few visions—even practical visions. An educated man, peering from the Harvard Yard, or any college campus, upon a world in chaos, finds in the vision the two certainties for which the mind of man tirelessly seeks: a reason to live and a reason to die. No other faith of our time presents them with the same practical intensity. That is why Communism is the central experience of the first half of the 20th century, and may be its final experience—will be, unless the free world, in the agony of its struggle with Communism, overcomes its crisis by discovering, in suffering and pain, a power of faith which will provide man's mind, at the same intensity, with the same two certainties: a reason to live and a reason to die. If it fails, this will be the century of the great social wars. If it succeeds, this will be the century of the great wars of faith.

You will ask: Why, then, do men cease to be Communists? One answer is: Very few do. Thirty years after the Russian Revolution, after the known atrocities, the purges, the revelations, the jolting zigzags of Communist politics, there is only a handful of ex-Communists in the whole world. By ex-Communists I do not mean those who break with Communism over differences of strategy and tactics (like Trotsky) or organization (like Tito). Those are merely quarrels over a road map by people all of whom are in a hurry to get to the same place.

Nor, by ex-Communists, do I mean those thousands who continually drift into the Communist Party and out again. The turnover is vast. These are the spiritual vagrants of our time whose traditional faith has been leached out in the bland climate of rationalism. They are looking for an intellectual night's lodging. They lack the character for Communist faith because they lack the character for any faith. So they drop away, though Communism keeps its hold on them.

By an ex-Communist, I mean a man who knew clearly why he became a Communist, who served Communism devotedly and knew why he served it, who broke with Communism unconditionally and knew why he broke with it. Of these there are very few—an index to the power of the vision and the power of the crisis.

History very largely fixes the patterns of force that make men Communists. Hence one Communist conversion sounds much like another—rather impersonal and repetitious, awesome and tiresome, like long lines of similar people all stolidly waiting to get in to see the same movie. A man's break with Communism is intensely personal. Hence the account of no two breaks is likely to be the same. The reasons that made one Communist break may seem without force to another ex-Communist.

It is a fact that a man can join the Communist Party, can be very active in it for years, without completely understanding the nature of Communism or the political methods that follow inevitably from its vision. One day such incomplete Communists discover that the Communist Party is not what they thought it was. They break with it and turn on it with the rage of an honest dupe, a dupe who has given a part of his life to a swindle. Often they forget that it takes two to make a swindle.

Others remain Communists for years, warmed by the light of its vision, firmly closing their eyes to the crimes and horrors inseparable from its practical politics. One day they have to face the facts. They are appalled at what they have abetted. They spend the rest of their days trying to explain, usually without great success, the dark clue to their complicity. As their understanding of Communism was incomplete and led them to a dead end, their understanding of breaking with it is incomplete and leads them to a dead end. It leads to less than Communism, which was a vision and a faith. The world outside Communism, the world in crisis, lacks a vision and a faith. There is before these ex-Communists absolutely nothing. Behind them is a threat. For they have, in fact, broken not with the vision, but with the politics of the vision. In the name of reason and intelligence, the vision keeps them firmly in its grip—self-divided, paralyzed, powerless to act against it.

Hence the most secret fold of their minds is haunted by a terrifying thought: What if we were wrong? What if our inconstancy is our guilt? That is the fate of those who break without knowing clearly that Communism is wrong because something else is right, because to the challenge: *God or Man?*, they continue to give the answer: *Man.* Their pathos is that not even the Communist ordeal could teach them that man without God is just what Communism said he was: the most intelligent of the animals, that man without God is a beast, never more beastly than when he is most intelligent about his beastliness. *"Er nennt's Vernunft,"* says the Devil in Goethe's *Faust, "und braucht's allein, nur tierischer als jedes Tier zu sein"*—Man calls it reason and uses it simply to be more beastly than any beast. Not grasping the source of the evil they sincerely hate, such ex-Communists in general make ineffectual witnesses against it. They are witnesses against something; they have ceased to be witnesses for anything.

Yet there is one experience which most sincere ex-Communists share, whether or not they go only part way to the end of the question it poses. The daughter of a former German diplomat in Moscow was trying to explain to me why her father, who, as an enlightened modern man, had been extremely pro-Communist, had become an implacable anti-Communist. It was hard for her because, as an enlightened modern girl, she shared the Communist vision without being a Communist. But she loved her father and the irrationality of his defection embarrassed her. "He was immensely pro-Soviet," she said, "and then—you will laugh at me—but you must not laugh at my father—and then—one night—in Moscow—he heard screams. That's all. Simply one night he heard screams."

A child of Reason and the 20th century, she knew that there is a logic of the mind. She did not know that the soul has a logic that may be more compelling than the mind's. She did not know at all that she had swept away the logic of the mind, the logic of history, the logic of politics, the myth of the 20th century, with five annihilating words: one night he heard screams.

What Communist has not heard those screams? They come from husbands torn forever from their wives in midnight arrests. They come, muffled, from the execution cellars of the secret police, from the torture chambers of the Lubianka, from all the citadels of terror now stretching from Berlin to Canton. They come from those freight cars loaded with men, women and children, the enemies of the Communist State, locked in, packed in, left on remote sidings to freeze to death at night in the Russian winter. They come from minds driven mad by the horrors of mass starvation ordered and enforced as a policy of the Communist State. They come from the starved skeletons, worked to death, or flogged to death (as an example to others) in the freezing filth of sub-arctic labor camps. They come from children whose parents are suddenly, inexplicably, taken away from them—parents they will never see again.

What Communist has not heard those screams? Execution, says the Communist code, is the highest measure of social protection. What man can call himself a Communist who has not accepted the fact that Terror is an instrument of policy, right if the vision is right, justified by history, enjoined by the balance of forces in the social wars of this century? Those screams have reached every Communist's mind. Usually they stop there. What judge willingly dwells upon the man the laws compel him to condemn to death—the laws of nations or the laws of history?

But one day the Communist really hears those screams. He is going about his routine party tasks. He is lifting a dripping reel of microfilm from a developing tank. He is justifying to a Communist fraction in a trade union an extremely unwelcome directive of the Central Committee. He is receiving from a trusted superior an order to go to another country and, in a designated hotel, at a designated hour, meet a man whose name he will never know, but who will give him a package whose contents he will never learn. Suddenly, there closes around that Communist a separating silence, and in that silence he hears screams. He hears them for the first time. For they do not merely reach his mind. They pierce beyond. They pierce to his soul. He says to himself: "Those are not the screams of man in agony. Those are the screams of a soul in agony." He hears them for the first time because a soul in extremity has communicated with that which alone can hear it—another human soul.

Why does the Communist ever hear them? Because in the end there persists in every man, however he may deny it, a scrap of soul. The Communist who suffers this singular experience then says to himself: "What is happening to me? I must be sick." If he does not instantly stifle that scrap of soul, he is lost. If he admits it for a moment, he has admitted that there is something greater than Reason, greater than the logic of mind, of politics, of history, of economics, which alone justifies the vision. If the party senses his weakness, and the party is peculiarly cunning at sensing such weakness, it will humiliate him, degrade him, condemn him, expel him. If it can, it will destroy him. And the party will be right. For he has betrayed that which alone justifies its faith—the vision of Almighty Man. He has brushed the only vision that has force against the vision of Almighty Mind. He stands before the fact of God.

The Communist Party is familiar with this experience to which its members are sometimes liable in prison, in illness, in indecision. It is recognized frankly as a sickness. There are ways of treating it—if it is confessed. It is when it is not confessed that the party, sensing a subtle crisis, turns upon it savagely. What ex-Communist has not suffered this experience in one form or another, to one degree or another? What he does about it depends on the individual man. That is why no ex-Communist dare answer for his sad fraternity the question: Why do men break with Communism? He can only answer the question: How did you break with Communism? My answer is: Slowly, reluctantly, in agony.

Yet my break began long before I heard those screams. Perhaps it does for everyone. I do not know how far back it began. Avalanches gather force and crash, unheard, in men as in the mountains. But I date my break from a very casual happening. I was sitting in our apartment on St. Paul Street in Baltimore. It was shortly before we moved to Alger Hiss's apartment in Washington. My daughter was in her high chair. I was watching her eat. She was the most miraculous thing that had ever happened in my life. I liked to watch her even when she smeared porridge on her face or dropped it meditatively on the floor. My eye came to rest on the delicate convolutions of her ear—those intricate, perfect ears. The thought passed through my mind: "No, those ears were not created by any chance coming together of atoms in nature (the Communist view). They could have been created only by immense design." The thought was involuntary and unwanted. I crowded it out of my mind. But I never wholly forgot it or the occasion. I had to crowd it out of my mind. If I had completed it, I should have had to say: Design presupposes God. I did not then know that, at that moment, the finger of God was first laid upon my forehead.

One thing most ex-Communists could agree upon: they broke because they wanted to be free. They do not all mean the same thing by "free." Freedom is a need of the soul, and nothing else. It is in striving toward God that the soul strives continually after a condition of freedom. God alone is the inciter and guarantor of freedom. He is the only guarantor. External freedom is only an aspect of interior freedom. Political freedom, as the Western world has known it, is only a political reading of the Bible. Religion and freedom are indivisible. Without freedom the soul dies. Without the soul there is no justification for freedom. Necessity is the only ultimate justification known to the mind. Hence every sincere break with Communism is a religious experience, though the Communist fail to identify its true nature, though he fail to go to the end of the experience. His break is the political expression of the perpetual need of the soul whose first faint stirring he has felt within him, years, months or days before he breaks. A Communist

breaks because he must choose at last between irreconcilable opposites—God or Man, Soul or Mind, Freedom or Communism.

Communism is what happens when, in the name of Mind, men free themselves from God. But its view of God, its knowledge of God, its experience of God, is what alone gives character to a society or a nation, and meaning to its destiny. Its culture, the voice of this character, is merely that view, knowledge, experience, of God, fixed by its most intense spirits in terms intelligible to the mass of men. There has never been a society or a nation without God. But history is cluttered with the wreckage of nations that became indifferent to God, and died.

The crisis of Communism exists to the degree in which it has failed to free the peoples that it rules from God. Nobody knows this better than the Communist Party of the Soviet Union. The crisis of the Western world exists to the degree in which it is indifferent to God. It exists to the degree in which the Western world actually shares Communism's materialist vision, is so dazzled by the logic of the materialist interpretation of history, politics and economics, that it fails to grasp that, for it, the only possible answer to the Communist challenge: Faith in God or Faith in Man? is the challenge: Faith in God.

Economics is not the central problem of this century. It is a relative problem which can be solved in relative ways. Faith is the central problem of this age. The Western world does not know it, but it already possesses the answer to this problem—but only provided that its faith in God and the freedom He enjoins is as great as Communism's faith in Man.

My dear children, before I close this foreword, I want to recall to you briefly the life that we led in the ten years between the time when I broke with Communism and the time when I began to testify—the things we did, worked for, loved, believed in. For it was that happy life, which, on the human side, in part made it possible for me to do later on the things I had to do, or endure the things that happened to me.

Those were the days of the happy little worries, which then seemed so big. We know now that they were the golden days. They will not come again. In those days, our greatest worry was, how to meet the payments on the mortgage, how to get the ploughing done in time, how to get health accreditation for our

herd, how to get the hay in before the rain. I sometimes took my vacation in hay harvest so that I could
help work the load. You two little children used to
trample the load, drive the hay truck in the fields
when you could barely reach the foot pedals, or drive
the tractor that pulled up the loaded harpoons to the
mow. At evening, you would break off to help
Mother milk while I went on haying. For we came of
age on the farm when we decided not to hire barn
help, but to run the herd ourselves as a family.

Often the ovenlike heat in the comb of the barn
and the sweet smell of alfalfa made us sick. Sometimes we fell asleep at the supper table from fatigue.
But the hard work was good for us; and you knew
only the peace of a home governed by a father and
mother whose marriage the years (and an earlier suffering which you could not remember) had deepened into the perfect love that enveloped you.

Mother was a slight, overalled figure forever working for you in the house or beside you in the barns
and gardens. Papa was a squat, overalled figure, fat
but forceful, who taught John, at nine, the man-size
glory of driving the tractor; or sat beside Ellen, at the
wheel of the truck, an embodiment of security and
power, as we drove loads of cattle through the night.
On summer Sundays, you sat between Papa and
Mama in the Quaker meeting house. Through the
open doors, as you tried not to twist and turn in the
long silence, you could see the far, blue Maryland
hills and hear the redbirds and ground robins in the
graveyard behind.

Only Ellen had a vague, troubled recollection of
another time and another image of Papa. Then (it
was during the years 1938 and 1939), if for any reason she pattered down the hall at night, she would
find Papa, with the light on, writing, with a revolver
on the table or a gun against the chair. She knew that
there were people who wanted to kill Papa and who
might try to kidnap her. But a wide sea of sunlight
and of time lay between that puzzling recollection
and the farm.

The farm was your kingdom, and the world lay far
beyond the protecting walls thrown up by work and
love. It is true that comic strips were not encouraged,
comic books were banned, the radio could be turned
on only by permission which was seldom given (or
asked), and you saw few movies. But you grew in the
presence of eternal wonders. There was the birth of
lambs and calves. You remember how once, when I
was away and the veterinarian could not come, you
saw Mother reach in and turn the calf inside the cow
so that it could be born. There was also the death of
animals, sometimes violent, sometimes slow and
painful—nothing is more constant on a farm than
death.

Sometimes, of a spring evening, Papa would hear
that distant honking that always makes his scalp tin-
gle, and we would all rush out to see the wild geese,
in lines of hundreds, steer up from the southwest,
turn over the barn as over a landmark, and head into
the north. Or on autumn nights of sudden cold that
set the ewes breeding in the orchard, Papa would call
you out of the house to stand with him in the now celebrated pumpkin patch and watch the northern lights
flicker in electric clouds on the horizon, mount, die
down, fade and mount again till they filled the whole
northern sky with ghostly light in motion.

Thus, as children, you experienced two of the
most important things men ever know—the wonder
of life and the wonder of the universe, the wonder of
life within the wonder of the universe. More important, you knew them not from books, not from lectures, but simply from living among them. Most
important, you knew them with reverence and awe—
that reverence and awe that has died out of the modern world and been replaced by man's monkeylike
amazement at the cleverness of his own inventive
brain.

I have watched greatness touch you in another
way. I have seen you sit, uninvited and unforced, listening in complete silence to the third movement of
the Ninth Symphony. I thought you understood, as
much as children can, when I told you that that music
was the moment at which Beethoven finally passed
beyond the suffering of his life on earth and reached
for the hand of God, as God reaches for the hand of
Adam in Michelangelo's vision of the Creation.

And once, in place of a bedtime story, I was reading Shakespeare to John—at his own request, for I
never forced such things on you. I came to that passage in which Macbeth, having murdered Duncan,
realizes what he has done to his own soul, and asks if
all the water in the world can ever wash the blood
from his hand, or will it not rather

The multitudinous seas incarnadine?

At that line, John's whole body twitched. I gave great silent thanks to God. For I knew that if, as children, you could thus feel in your souls the reverence and awe for life and the world, which is the ultimate meaning of Beethoven and Shakespeare, as man and woman you could never be satisfied with less. I felt a great faith that sooner or later you would understand what I once told you, not because I expected you to understand it then, but because I hoped that you would remember it later: "True wisdom comes from the overcoming of suffering and sin. All true wisdom is therefore touched with sadness."

If all this sounds unduly solemn, you know that our lives were not; that all of us suffer from an incurable itch to puncture false solemnity. In our daily lives, we were fun-loving and gay. For those who have solemnity in their souls generally have enough of it there, and do not need to force it into their faces.

Then, on August 3, 1948, you learned for the first time that your father had once been a Communist, that he had worked in something called "the underground," that it was shameful, and that for some reason he was in Washington telling the world about it. While he was in the underground, he testified, he had worked with a number of other Communists. One of them was a man with the odd name of Alger Hiss. Later, Alger Hiss denied the allegation. Thus the Great Case began, and with it our lives were changed forever.

Dear children, one autumn twilight, when you were much smaller, I slipped away from you in play and stood for a moment alone in the apple orchard near the barn. Then I heard your two voices, piping together anxiously, calling to me: "Papa! Papa!" from the harvested cornfield. In the years when I was away five days a week in New York, working to pay for the farm, I used to think of you both before I fell asleep at night. And that is how you almost always came to me—voices of beloved children, calling to me from the gathered fields at dusk.

You called to me once again at night in the same orchard. That was a good many years later. A shadow deeper and more chilling than the autumn evening had closed upon us—I mean the Hiss Case. It was the first year of the Case. We had been doing the evening milking together. For us, one of the few happy results of the Case was that at last I could be home with you most of the time (in life these good

things usually come too little or too late). I was washing and disinfecting the cows, and putting on and taking off the milkers. You were stripping after me.

In the quiet, there suddenly swept over my mind a clear realization of our true position—obscure, all but friendless people (some of my great friends had already taken refuge in aloofness; the others I had withdrawn from so as not to involve them in my affairs). Against me was an almost solid line-up of the most powerful groups and men in the country, the bitterly hostile reaction of much of the press, the smiling skepticism of much of the public, the venomous calumnies of the Hiss forces, the all but universal failure to understand the real meaning of the Case or my real purpose. A sense of the enormous futility of my effort, and my own inadequacy, drowned me. I felt a physical cold creep through me, settle around my heart and freeze any pulse of hope. The sight of you children, guiltless and defenseless, was more than I could bear. I was alone against the world; my longing was to be left completely alone, or not to be at all. It was that death of the will which Communism, with great cunning, always tries to induce in its victims.

I waited until the last cow was stripped and the last can lifted into the cooler. Then I stole into the upper barn and out into the apple orchard. It was a very dark night. The stars were large and cold. This cold was one with the coldness in myself. The lights of the barn, the house and the neighbors houses were warm in the windows and on the ground; they were not for me. Then I heard Ellen call me in the barn and John called: "Papa!" Still calling, Ellen went down to the house to see if I were there. I heard John opening gates as he went to the calf barn, and he called me there. With all the longing of my love for you, I wanted to answer. But if I answered, I must come back to the living world. I could not do that.

John began to call me in the cow stable, in the milk house. He went into the dark side of the barn (I heard him slide the door back), into the upper barn, where at night he used to be afraid. He stepped outside in the dark, calling: "Papa! Papa!"—then, frantically, on the verge of tears: "Papa!" I walked over to him. I felt that I was making the most terrible surrender I should have to make on earth. "Papa," he cried and threw his arms around me, "don't ever go away." "No," I said, "no, I won't ever go away." Both, of us knew that the words "go away" stood for something else, and that I had given him my promise not to kill myself. Later on, as you will see, I was tempted, in my wretchedness, to break that promise.

My children, when you were little, we used sometimes to go for walks in our pine woods. In the open fields, you would run along by yourselves. But you used instinctively to give me your hands as we entered those woods, where it was darker, lonelier, and in the stillness our voices sounded loud and frightening. In this book I am again giving you my hands. I am leading you, not through cool pine woods, but up and up a narrow defile between bare and steep rocks from which in shadow things uncoil

and slither away. It will be dark. But, in the end, if I have led you aright, you will make out three crosses, from two of which hang thieves. I will have brought you to Golgotha—the place of skulls. This is the meaning of the journey. Before you understand, I may not be there, my hands may have slipped from yours. It will not matter. For when you understand what you see, you will no longer be children. You will know that life is pain, that each of us hangs always upon the cross of himself. And when you know that this is true of every man, woman and child on earth, you will be wise.

Your Father

Sydney Hook

Political Power and Personal Freedom (1959)

Security and Freedom

The quest for security in human life, like the quest for certainty in human knowledge, has many sources. All are rooted in man's finitude in a complex world of danger and mystery. Of the varied methods man has pursued to reduce the dangers and cope with the mysteries, the way of piecemeal knowledge and continuous experiment has been most fruitful. For it is in the fields in which human knowledge has foresworn the quest for absolute certainty, as in the scientific disciplines, that it has proved both reliable and capable of winning universal agreement. On the other hand, in the fields in which the strongest claims to certainty have been made—politics and philosophy—there is the least agreement.

Because absolute certainty in human affairs is impossible, absolute security is impossible. Unless we are aware of this, the price we pay for straining to achieve an impossible ideal may result in netting us less security than would otherwise be attainable. This is not an unusual phenomenon: it is observable in large things and small. The man who strives for

absolute health may end up a valetudinarian. The man who won't venture on the highways until they are accident-proof may as well not own an automobile; and if he crawls along playing it supersafe, traffic-enforcement authorities tell us he adds to the dangers of the road.

The real problem, then, is not one of absolute security, or security in general. It is always one of achieving more and better security in meeting specific hazards in a particular area of risk and uncertainty—and meeting them in such a way that we do not lose more by the methods we use than by the disasters we would prevent.

As a rule we feel more insecure in our personal relations than we really are. About public affairs, on the other hand, when times are normal, we are apt to feel less insecure, because less interested, than we have reason to be. But we are living in times which are not normal. It is in such times that the expert and the insider, the savior and demagogue, command an audience merely by assuming a posture of authority.

Most political commentators and analysts sustain their reputation, and continue in their vocations only because their audiences have neither memory nor a sense of history. Everyone can and does make errors. One can be wrong and yet, because of the evidence at hand, have a right to be wrong. The man who takes a long chance and wins is lucky, not intelligent. It is because of the grounds on which judgments are made in the light of knowledge of the past and present that we appraise their validity. Subsequent experience tests the reliability of these grounds.

The McCarthy episode in American history was a test of political judgment and political morality. Those who dismissed him as an unimportant phenomenon or extenuated his methods in the light of his goals failed the tests of both judgment and morality. So did those who exaggerated his power, who proclaimed that he had transformed America into a police state, and who fought McCarthy with the weapons of McCarthy instead of the weapons of truth. Even at the height of McCarthy's power a more rational view was not impossible. [. . .]

The American public was not altogether unaware of the effects of McCarthy at home and abroad. Why, then, did it countenance his antics for so long and to the extent it did? What was the source of McCarthy's popular support? The obvious answer is that public concern about the apparent indifference to national security on the part of previous administrations had reached a point where the demagogic methods of McCarthy were waved aside as unessential or dismissed as a small price to pay for a security long delayed. Those who spoke in this fashion, and at one time they were many, were profoundly in error. The methods by which a democracy defends itself are never unessential, and the price of McCarthy's methods, it is now apparent, is much too high to compensate for the dubious securities they have won. It is not necessary to deny that McCarthy uncovered a few Communists in government service and called attention to some administrative bungling. All this was far outweighed by the harm he did in dividing the country more than Henry Wallace ever succeeded in doing, undermining American prestige abroad, and intimidating American officialdom.

Nonetheless, this does not answer the basic question. Why should the public, especially a public liberal enough to have followed Roosevelt and Truman, have been so much concerned with security? For

without this concern McCarthy would never have captured his audience.

I

"Security is like liberty," writes Mr. Justice Jackson in one of his dissenting opinions, "in that many are the crimes that have been committed in its name." Yet he would be the first to admit that this is no more warrant for abandoning the quest for reasonable rules of security than for relinquishing the struggle for a more humane conception of liberty.

Nonetheless, in the past, problems of security were never considered seriously by lovers of freedom except in the guise of *social* securities. In pre-totalitarian days many did not care if these social securities were achieved by undermining to some extent the *political* securities with which special privilege was hedged. After all, "law and order" was the traditional slogan of social reaction; and the social gospel, whether secular or religious, considered itself above the call of patriotism.

Not until a democratic law and a democratic order were firmly established, and not until they were threatened by Fascist and Communist movements, operating in some countries as Fifth Columns of powers bent on world domination, did it dawn on liberal thinkers that without political security the very social securities, so painfully built, might be lost. They had long since understood that the abstractions of *economic* liberalism under modern historical conditions were semantic fetishes. That the same might be true of some of the slogans of *political* liberalism, when used for purposes of conspiratorial evasion by one's own nationals in the service of a foreign power posing as a universal church, was a disturbing thought. The actual facts were not so much a challenge to the principles of political liberalism as to the intelligence of the liberals to apply their principles to the relatively new problems created by conspirators masquerading as heretics.

With some notable exceptions, American liberals were particularly insensitive to the problems of ideologically motivated subversion of democratic institutions and processes. This was in part due to the fact that until the Roosevelt era twentieth-century American liberalism was in the main an opposition movement sympathetic to any group opposed to entrenched political power without paying too much attention to the grounds of its opposition. It was in part due to the absence of a politically mature conservatism which could recognize the abysses that separated the opponents of the status quo from each other. Herbert Hoover characterized socialism as "the weak sister of Bolshevism" at the very time when the socialist movement was more hostile to the Kremlin than the business community. Until surprised by events, the conservatives were no more aware of the problems of ideologically motivated subversion than the liberals. By indiscriminately tagging progressive ideas and the New Deal as "communistic," they had blinded themselves to the genuine article.

After the Seventh Congress of the Communist International, the Communists kidnapped the vocabulary of American liberalism. This "corruption of the word," as I called it then, made it easier for some sentimental liberals to interpret sharp criticisms of Communism as oblique attacks on liberalism, if not a first step towards Fascism. In liberal circles to be an anti-Fascist was always honorable. But to be anti-Communist, especially during the war years, invited distrust. That liberals had a stake in the survival of the democratic system whose defects they could freely criticize under the ground rules of the Bill of Rights was granted, of course. That they therefore also had a stake in preventing the ground rules from being abused, that they had a responsibility to think about the problem, was resolutely ignored. This was something for the state to worry about. To this day most liberals tend to dismiss questions of political security as subjects only police minds are fit to consider. On the Continent even a theoretical discussion of the *principles* of political security is regarded with suspicion as a kind of collaboration with the police. In view of the actual situation in some European countries, this makes as much sense as saying that the discussion of theories of capital punishment is a kind of collaboration with the executioner. There is a certain logic in the refusal to think about problems of political security if one regards the state as nothing but the executive committee of the ruling class. But this dogma of vulgar Marxism is certainly unacceptable to any genuine liberal. It is rejected even by intelligent Marxists.

The preeminent intellectual concern among liberals in the United States was with the question of civil rights which, however justifiable, led to a paradoxical situation: since it went hand in hand with an intellectual taboo against a consideration of the question of political security, the defense against ideologically motivated infiltration, espionage and sabotage came to be entrusted to the police mind. But the police mind is helpless in dealing with it. For the problem is not one primarily of detection and punishment, but of prevention and avoidance. Unless this is understood, nothing is understood about the unprecedented type of ideological espionage organized by the Kremlin, whose operatives are totally dedicated, and because of a large reservoir of replacements, totally expendable. Yet precisely because the professional police mind centers on detection and punishment, it is unable to cope with the complex problems created when Machiavellianism is harnessed to fanaticism. The police mind seems constitutionally incapable of distinguishing between heretics, whose criticism is essential to the health of a democratic community, and conspirators playing outside the rules of the game, sometimes with deadly effect. In this respect, the military mind is hardly different from the police mind. Both can recognize and judge actions which formally violate rules and regulations. Neither is in a position to assess qualifications for employment, especially for employment in which political motivation and political beliefs have a bearing upon security.

The results have been what any politically sophisticated person could have expected. On the one hand, inefficiency in preventing widespread espionage and subversion; and on the other, frenzied efforts either to conceal the situation for narrow political purposes or to retrieve the situation by hasty executive decree. And as usual when confusion rules, individual hardships and injustices result.

This was not helped by ritualistic liberals whose protests against genuine abuses in security programs were coupled with an almost willful ignorance of the facts that make such programs an unpleasant necessity in times of emergency. Instead of offering a viable alternative to eliminate or reduce these injustices, they wrote as if the only problem was to develop more efficient methods of detecting acts of espionage *after* they had been committed. They thereby revealed the extent of their misunderstanding. Not the acts prevented but those which are discovered create public disquietude, because they give the impression that many more remain undiscovered and beyond the reach of prosecution in virtue of the statute of limitations. [. . .]

[. . .] It is the liberal *attitude*, however, which is most crucial in the reasonable administration of a security program. Just as only those who love children can be trusted to discipline them without doing psychological harm, so only those who love freedom can be trusted to devise appropriate safeguards without throttling intellectual independence or smothering all but the mediocre in blankets of regulations. No safeguards are appropriate or even efficient which impose conformity of belief or inhibit intellectual spontaneity. The fresh and unfamiliar solution to difficulties depends on a certain imaginative daring and a receptivity to such solutions by those in a position of authority. A liberal with a sense of history is aware of the possibility that in a specific situation there may be a sharp conflict between the legitimate demands of national security and the freedom of the individual. But on balance, and in perspective, he is convinced that the two are not in opposition. In the very interest of a freely expressed dissent, some security measures are required to protect the institutional processes which, however imperfectly, reflect a freely given consent. At the same time, the faith and practices of freedom, indeed, an almost religious veneration for the *élan* of the free spirit, may generate a sense of security even in the shadows of war.

II

It may seem odd to have to justify the necessity of a security program at the present juncture of world affairs. My experiences, however, in England and western Europe have convinced me that in the eyes of a great many people in those countries it certainly needed justification. Parents who would not entrust the care of their children to anyone without the most painstaking investigation of character references, businessmen most meticulous about whom they would employ even in minor posts of trust, professional men who set absurdly high qualifications for their assistants, scoffed at "all this fuss" about security

in positions assuredly more important to their community than that of nursemaid or cashier or dental aid. [. . .]

Not only did my friends shrug off the question of security in their own countries, they regarded concern about security in the United States as nothing but downright hysteria. But why, I asked, were Americans "hysterical" about Communists and not Nazis? Why did no hysteria develop in the United States toward the Japanese after Pearl Harbor or toward the Germans during World War II? Indeed, I found it possible to present the argument and evidence for the necessity of a security program only in the puzzled silences with which those questions were met.

The argument and evidence can be put briefly. The one unshakeable dogma in the Bolshevik faith is that the Soviet Union is not safe from attack so long as the "capitalistic democracies" of the West—and not only the United States but also countries like Great Britain and France—exist. Let not those who in the past assured us that Hitler's racial myth and ideology of world conquest were "just words" tell us again that ideologies do not count in politics and history. If anything, the Kremlin has gone further than Hitler because it has publicly proclaimed that "encirclement" is a *political*, not a geographical, concept. The Communist parties of the West, affiliated with the Cominform, have as their *first* function the defense of the Soviet Union. Instructions are explicit to all of them to organize secretly (as well as publicly) even in "the freest" and "most democratic" countries and to infiltrate into strategic centers. This type of activity has been extensively carried on for years especially during the days of the popular front struggle against the Nazis. Even during the war which Hitler forced on the Soviets, the Kremlin engaged in the most comprehensive types of espionage against its Allies as part of the underlying struggle which, according to their fanatical conviction, must end either with the victory of the West or the Soviet power.

Because it can count on the devotion *à outrance*[1] of Communist nationals of other countries, many of them highly trained, intelligent and inspired by a misguided idealism which does not see under the

---

1.   [Meaning "to excess, in the extreme."]

flowers of official rhetoric the chains of Soviet control on its own people, the Kremlin possesses an incomparable advantage over the West. For one thing, it is the best informed regime in the world. It knew the date of Pearl Harbor but did not notify the United States government from whom it was receiving generous aid at the time. It was even informed by its agents about the scheduled German invasion of Russia though it gave the reports no credence. It knew that General Clay's proposal to arm military trains and fight his way through to feed Western Berlin in the event of a Soviet blockade had been vetoed by the State Department, so that the blockade could be clamped on the city with absolutely no risk. If the Soviet government did not know that the United States would propose to the United Nations to fight in the event that South Korea were invaded, it was only because the United States government didn't know it either. It is amusing to note Truman's confession of astonishment at Stalin's impassivity when he was informed at Potsdam that the United States had manufactured an atomic bomb. For we know today that at the time Stalin was being kept at least as well informed about some of the details of the progress of American research on atomic weapons as Truman. Although one would hardly suspect it from present attitudes to security in many circles in those countries, it is from Canadian and British sources that we have the most incontrovertible, if not the weightiest evidence, of how Communist Parties are involved in the espionage nets the Soviet Union has spun around the free world.[2]

Since the Kremlin combines this belief in the inevitability of war with a dialectical conception according to which a sudden attack or offense, as in Korea, is the best method of defense and because of the centralized organization of western industrial life, the location of America's undispersed plants, and the evolution of thermonuclear weapons, an attempt at a sudden knockout blow cannot be ruled out as a possibility. Since Bolshevik morality is confessedly subordinate to what will further the victory of the "proletarian dictatorship"—indeed, this is *the whole* of their morality—the possession of information about strategic weakness on the part of the West, or the hope that a sudden blow may prevent instant retaliatory action, may make a decisive difference to the Kremlin in resolving to launch the Blitzkrieg which will end "the final struggle." It does not require many persons to betray the key secrets of the radar defense of a nation.

The consequences of less extreme suppositions may be equally disastrous. The free world cannot deploy its defense forces everywhere. Its decisions where to stand, where to fight, once known to the Kremlin, give the latter a flexibility that it can exploit most skillfully to draw the world bit by bit into its orbit. On the other hand, there is no possibility for the free world to build up a counterweight within the Soviet sphere to redress the balance. No democratic Jeffersonian or Millsian International exists with affiliated parties in the Soviet world. [. . .]

The concern of the American people with the question of Communist penetration, in the light of the evidence, was legitimate enough. Questionable only was the character of the reaction to it on the part of the government. Buffeted by cultural vigilantes on the one side and ritualistic liberals on the other, it swung from one position to another, pleasing no one with its eclecticism. Almost all of the excesses of loyalty and security programs are attributable to the incredible political ignorance and naiveté of the personnel of the Review Boards. It was not the procedures themselves which were at fault, because oddly enough American procedures in crucial respects are fairer than the English. For example, in hearings before English boards, civil servants under investigation are rarely, if ever, told of the evidence against them. They are also denied rights of legal counsel, and even of representation. Nonetheless, American procedures worked hardship and injustices because instead of being administered by knowledgeable men and women with a little common sense who had some political experience, they were entrusted to investment bankers, corporation lawyers, army and navy officers, small town officials, or Republican or Democratic party regulars to whom Communist language was gobbledegook, Communist ideas suspiciously like

2. Cf. *The Report of the Royal Commission to Investigate the Facts Relating to and Circumstances Surrounding the Communication by Public Officials and Other Persons in Positions of Secret and Confidential Information to Agents of a Foreign Power* (Ottawa, 1946); also Alexander Foote's *Handbook for Spies* (London, 1949).

the ideas of socialists, dogooders and even New Dealers, and Communist organizations with the distinctions between member, sympathizer, front, dupe,
innocent, and honest mistaken liberal, as mysterious
as the order of beings in the science of angelology.

In the light of the above, the answer to our final
question regarding the relative unconcern of other
nations to the problem of Communist penetration is
not hard to give. The greatest Soviet effort was
directed against the United States as the Kremlin's
chief and strongest enemy. Since 1939 the United
States has been the center of atomic weapons
research and development. Its policies are more fateful for the U.S.S.R. than those of any other single
nation. To make these policies miscarry, to delay, distort and abort government directives pays rich political dividends. The Kremlin is quite aware of the fact
that a defeat or paralysis of the United States would
mean the end of the independence of Austria,
France and Italy. Further, the Communist movement in the United States is not a mass party and, in
all likelihood, will never become one. But it has a
solid core of some thousands of hardened "professional revolutionists." From the Soviet viewpoint they
are expendable. What is more natural, therefore,
than to employ them for all sorts of conspiratorial
purposes from direct espionage to the capture of
small but key unions, to the seeding of government
services with "sleepers"? A few thousand totally dedicated persons, working underground with the help of
a sympathetic periphery of several times that size, can
cause a great many headaches. Countries like Austria
need not worry about the problem, one is tempted to
observe, because it wouldn't make a difference if they

did. There isn't much the Kremlin can learn from
them and an attempt at a Communist putsch on
Czechoslovakian lines, so long as the United States is
still strong, risks a war for which at the moment the
U.S.S.R. is unready. Countries like France and, Italy,
on the other hand, which have mass Communist parties and where infiltration and underground organization are not inconsiderable can hardly solve the
problem without facing crippling strikes and extensive public disorders. Too weak to act they sometimes
pretend that there is no need for action. *They can live
with the Communist menace only because the United
States is free of it and only so long as the United States
is strong enough to restrain the Soviet Union from
overrunning the free world.*

Only those who are ignorant of the stupendous
extent of Soviet infiltration and espionage over the
years, the complexity of its patterns and its potential
for harm, can sneer at the problems of security in the
free world. It is not enough to shout slogans—
whether of security or freedom. What is required is
creative intelligence to devise just and effective procedures which will protect the free cultures of the
world from their hidden enemies without making
less free those who are not its hidden enemies. These
procedures must be flexible. They cannot be formalized into a code without inviting abuses. They must
be devised and administered by civil libertarians who
are familiar with Communist theory and who have
studied Communist conspiratorial practice. They
must be applied discreetly, without fanfare, without
developing a climate of public concern. And their
primary function must be effective prevention rather
than exemplary punishment.

C. Wright Mills

The Power Elite (1956)

The Higher Circles

The powers of ordinary men are circumscribed by the everyday worlds in which they live, yet even in these rounds of job, family, and neighborhood they often seem driven by forces they can neither understand nor govern. "Great changes" are beyond their control, but affect their conduct and outlook none the less. The very framework of modern society confines them to projects not their own, but from every side, such changes now press upon the men and women of the mass society, who accordingly feel that they are without purpose in an epoch in which they are without power.

But not all men are in this sense ordinary. As the means of information and of power are centralized, some men come to occupy positions in American society from which they can look down upon, so to speak, and by their decisions mightily affect, the everyday worlds of ordinary men and women. They are not made by their jobs; they set up and break down jobs for thousands of others; they are not confined by simple family responsibilities; they can escape. They may live in many hotels and houses, but they are bound by no one community. They need not merely "meet the demands of the day and hour" in some part, they create these demands, and cause others to meet them. Whether or not they profess their power, their technical and political experience of it far transcends that of the underlying population. What Jacob Burckhardt said of "great men," most Americans might well say of their elite: "They are all that we are not."[1]

The power elite is composed of men whose positions enable them to transcend the ordinary environments of ordinary men and women; they are in positions to make decisions having major consequences. Whether they do or do not make such decisions is less important than the fact that they do occupy such pivotal positions: their failure to act, their failure to make decisions, is itself an act that is often of greater consequence than the decisions they do make. For they are in command of the major hierarchies and organizations of modern society. They rule the big corporations. They run the machinery of the state and claim its prerogatives. They direct the military establishment. They occupy the strategic command posts of the social structure, in which are now centered the effective means of the power and the wealth and the celebrity which they enjoy.

The power elite are not solitary rulers. Advisers and consultants, spokesmen and opinion-makers are often the captains of their higher thought and decision. Immediately below the elite are the professional politicians of the middle levels of power, in the Congress and in the pressure groups, as well as among the new and old upper classes of town and city and region. Mingling with them, in curious ways which we shall explore, are those professional celebrities who live by being continually displayed but are never, so long as they remain celebrities, displayed enough. If such celebrities are not at the head of any dominating hierarchy, they do often have the power to distract the attention of the public or afford sensations to the masses, or, more directly, to gain the ear of those who do occupy positions of direct power. More or less unattached, as critics of morality and technicians of power, as spokesmen of God and creators of mass sensibility, such celebrities and consultants are part of the immediate scene in which the drama of the elite is enacted. But that drama itself is centered in the command posts of the major institutional hierarchies.

---

1. Jacob Burckhardt, *Force and Freedom* (New York: Pantheon Books, 1943), pp. 303 ff.

1

The truth about the nature and the power of the elite is not some secret which men of affairs know but will not tell. Such men hold quite various theories about their own roles in the sequence of event and decision. Often they are uncertain about their roles, and even more often they allow their fears and their hopes to affect their assessment of their own power. No matter how great their actual power, they tend to be less acutely aware of it than of the resistances of others to its use. Moreover, most American men of affairs have learned well the rhetoric of public relations, in some cases even to the point of using it when they are alone, and thus coming to believe it. The personal awareness of the actors is only one of the several sources one must examine in order to understand the higher circles. Yet many who believe that there is no elite, or at any rate none of any consequence, rest their argument upon what men of affairs believe about themselves, or at least assert in public.

There is, however, another view: those who feel, even if vaguely, that a compact and powerful elite of great importance does now prevail in America often base that feeling upon the historical trend of our time. They have felt, for example, the domination of the military event, and from this they infer that generals and admirals, as well as other men of decision influenced by them, must be enormously powerful. They hear that the Congress has again abdicated to a handful of men decisions clearly related to the issue of war or peace. They know that the bomb was dropped over Japan in the name of the United States of America, although they were at no time consulted about the matter. They feel that they live in a time of big decisions; they know that they are not making any. Accordingly, as they consider the present as history, they infer that at its center, making decisions or failing to make them, there must be an elite of power.

On the one hand, those who share this feeling about big historical events assume that there is an elite and that its power is great. On the other hand, those who listen carefully to the reports of men apparently involved in the great decisions often do not believe that there is an elite whose powers are of decisive consequence.

Both views must be taken into account, but neither is adequate. The way to understand the power of the American elite lies neither solely in recognizing the historic scale of events nor in accepting the personal awareness reported by men of apparent decision. Behind such men and behind the events of history, linking the two, are the major institutions of modern society. These hierarchies of state and corporation and army constitute the means of power; as such they are now of a consequence not before equaled in human history—and at their summits, there are now those command posts of modern society which offer us the sociological key to an understanding of the role of the higher circles in America.

Within American society, major national power now resides in the economic, the political, and the military domains. Other institutions seem off to the side of modern history, and, on occasion, national affairs as any major corporation; no church is as directly powerful in the external biographies of young men in America today as the military establishment; no college is as powerful in the shaping of momentous events as the National Security Council. Religious, educational, and family institutions are not autonomous centers of national power; on the contrary, these decentralized areas are increasingly shaped by the big three, in which developments of decisive and immediate consequence now occur. [...]

Within each of the big three, the typical institutional unit has become enlarged, has become administrative, and, in the power of its decisions, has become centralized. Behind these developments there is a fabulous technology, for as institutions, they have incorporated this technology and guide it, even as it shapes and paces their developments.

The economy—once a great scatter of small productive units in autonomous balance—has become dominated by two or three hundred giant corporations, administratively and politically interrelated, which together hold the keys to economic decisions.

The political order, once a decentralized set of several dozen states with a weak spinal cord, has become a centralized, executive establishment which has taken up into itself many powers previously scattered, and now enters into each and every crany of the social structure.

The military order, once a slim establishment in a context of distrust fed by state militia, has become the largest and most expensive feature of government, and, although well versed in smiling public relations, now has all the grim and clumsy efficiency of a sprawling bureaucratic domain.

In each of these institutional areas, the means of power at the disposal of decision makers have increased enormously; their central executive powers have been enhanced; within each of them modern administrative routines have been elaborated and tightened up.

As each of these domains becomes enlarged and centralized, the consequences of its activities become greater, and its traffic with the others increases. The decisions of a handful of corporations bear upon military and political as well as upon economic developments around the world. The decisions of the military establishment rest upon and grievously affect political life as well as the very level of economic activity. The decisions made within the political domain determine economic activities and military programs. There is no longer, on the one hand, an economy, and, on the other hand, a political order containing a military establishment unimportant to politics and to money-making. There is a political economy linked, in a thousand ways, with military institutions and decisions. On each side of the world-split running through central Europe and around the Asiatic rimlands, there is an ever-increasing interlocking of economic, military, and political structures. If there is government intervention in the corporate economy, so is there corporate intervention in the governmental process. In the structural sense, this triangle of power is the source of the interlocking directorate that is most important for the historical structure of the present.

The fact of the interlocking is clearly revealed at each of the points of crisis of modern capitalist society—slump, war, and boom. In each, men of decision are led to an awareness of the interdependence of the major institutional orders. In the nineteenth century, when the scale of all institutions was smaller, their liberal integration was achieved in the automatic economy, by an autonomous play of market forces in the automatic political domain, by the bargain and the vote. It was then assumed that out of the imbalance and friction that followed the limited decisions then possible a new equilibrium would in due course emerge. That can no longer be assumed, and it is not assumed by the men at the top of each of the three dominant hierarchies.

For given the scope of their consequences, decisions—and indecisions—in any one of these ramify into the others, and hence top decisions tend either to become co-ordinated or to lead to a commanding indecision. It has not always been like this. When numerous small entrepreneurs made up the economy, for example, many of them could fail and the consequences still remain local; political and military authorities did not intervene. But now, given political expectations and military commitments, can they afford to allow key units of the private corporate economy to break down in slump? Increasingly, they do intervene in economic affairs, and as they do so, the controlling decisions in each order are inspected by agents of the other two, and economic, military, and political structures are interlocked.

At the pinnacle of each of the three enlarged and centralized domains, there have arisen those higher circles which make up the economic, the political, and the military elites. At the top of the economy, among the corporate rich, there are the chief executives; at the top of the political order, the members of the political directorate; at the top of the military establishment, the elite of soldier-statesmen clustered in and around the Joint Chiefs of Staff and the upper echelon. As each of these domains has coincided with the others, as decisions tend to become total in their consequence, the leading men in each of the three domains of power—the warlords, the corporation chieftains, the political directorate—tend to come together, to form the power elite of America. [. . .]

The Power Elite

[. . .] The earlier and middle Roosevelt administrations can best be understood as a desperate search for ways and means, within the existing capitalist system, of reducing the staggering and ominous army of the unemployed. In these years, the New Deal as a system of power was essentially a balance of pressure groups and interest blocs. The political top adjusted many conflicts, gave way to this demand, sidetracked that one, was the unilateral servant of none, and so evened it all out into such going policy line as prevailed from one minor crisis to another. Policies were the result of a political act of balance at the top. Of course, the balancing act that Roosevelt performed did not affect the fundamental institutions of capitalism as a type of economy. By his policies, he subsidized the defaults of the capitalist economy, which had simply broken down; and by his rhetoric, he balanced its political disgrace, putting "economic royalists" in the political doghouse.

The "welfare state," created to sustain the balance and to carry out the subsidy, differed from the "laissez-faire" state: "If the state was believed neutral in the days of T. R. because its leaders claimed to sanction favors for no one," Richard Hofstadter has remarked, "the state under F. D. R. could be called neutral only in the sense that it offered favors to everyone."[2] The new state of the corporate commissars differs from the old welfare state. In fact, the later Roosevelt years—beginning with the entrance of the United States into overt acts of war and preparations for World War II—cannot be understood entirely in terms of an adroit equipoise of political power.

2

We study history, it has been said, to rid ourselves of it, and the history of the power elite is a clear case for which this maxim is correct. Like the tempo of American life in general, the long-term trends of the power structure have been greatly speeded up since World War II, and certain newer trends within and between the dominant institutions have also set the shape of the power elite and given historically specific meaning to its fifth epoch:

I. In so far as the structural clue to the power elite today lies in the political order, that clue is the decline of politics as genuine and public debate of alternative decisions—with nationally responsible and policy-coherent parties and with autonomous organizations connecting the lower and middle levels of power with the top levels of decision. America is now in considerable part more a formal political democracy than a democratic social structure, and even the formal political mechanics are weak.

The long-time tendency of business and government to become more intricately and deeply involved with each other has, in the fifth epoch, reached a new point of explicitness. The two cannot now be seen clearly as two distinct worlds. It is in terms of the executive agencies of the state that the rapprochement has proceeded most decisively. The growth of the executive branch of the government, with its agencies that patrol the complex economy, does not mean merely the "enlargement of government" as some sort of autonomous bureaucracy: it has meant the ascendancy of the corporation's man as a political eminence.

During the New Deal the corporate chieftains joined the political directorate; as of World War II they have come to dominate it. Long interlocked with government, now they have moved into quite full direction of the economy of the war effort and of the postwar era. This shift of the corporation executives into the political directorate has accelerated the long-term relegation of the professional politicians in the Congress to the middle levels of power.

II. In so far as the structural clue to the power elite today lies in the enlarged and military state, that clue becomes evident in the military ascendancy. The warlords have gained decisive political relevance, and the military structure of America is now in considerable part a political structure. The seemingly permanent military threat places a premium on the military and upon their control of men, materiel, money, and power; virtually all political and economic actions are now judged in terms of military definitions of reality: the higher warlords have ascended to a firm position within the power elite of the fifth epoch.

In part at least this has resulted from one simple historical fact, pivotal for the years since 1939: the focus of elite attention has been shifted from domestic problems, centered in the 'thirties around slump, to international problems, centered in the 'forties and 'fifties around war. Since the governing apparatus of the United States has by long historic usage been adapted to and shaped by domestic clash and balance, it has not, from any angle, had suitable agencies and traditions for the handling of international problems. Such formal democratic mechanics as had arisen in the century and a half of national

---

2. Richard Hofstadter, *The Age of Reform* (New York: Knopf, 1955), p.305.

development prior to 1941, had not been extended to the American handling of international affairs. It is, in considerable part, in this vacuum that the power elite has grown.

III. In so far as the structural clue to the power elite today lies in the economic order, that clue is the fact that the economy is a permanent-war economy and a private-corporation economy. American capitalism is now in considerable part a military capitalism, and the most important relation of the big corporation to the state rests on the coincidence of interests between military and corporate needs, as defined by warlords and corporate rich. Within the elite as a whole, this coincidence of interest between the high military and the corporate chieftains strengthens both of them and further subordinates the role of the merely political men. Not politicians, but corporate executives, sit with the military and plan the organization of war effort.

The shape and meaning of the power elite today can be understood only when these three sets of structural trends are seen at their point of coincidence: the military capitalism of private corporations exists in a weakened and formal democratic system containing a military order already quite political in outlook and demeanor. Accordingly, at the top of this structure, the power elite has been shaped by the coincidence of interest between those who control the major means of production and those who control the newly enlarged means of violence; from the decline of the professional politician and the rise to explicit political command of the corporate chieftains and the professional warlords; from the absence of any genuine civil service of skill and integrity, independent of vested interests.

The power elite is composed of political, economic, and military men, but this instituted elite is frequently in some tension: it comes together only on certain coinciding points and only on certain occasions of "crisis." In the long peace of the nineteenth century, the military were not in the high councils of state, not of the political directorate, and neither were the economic men—they made raids upon the state but they did not join its directorate. During the 'thirties, the political man was ascendant. Now the military and the corporate men are in top positions.

Of the three types of circle that compose the power elite today, it is the military that has benefited the most in its enhanced power, although the corporate circles have also become more explicitly intrenched in the more public decision-making circles. It is the professional politician that has lost the most, so much that in examining the events and decisions, one is tempted to speak of a political vacuum in which the corporate rich and the high warlord, in their coinciding interests, rule.

It should not be said that the three "take turns" in carrying the initiative, for the mechanics of the power elite are not often as deliberate as that would imply. At times, of course, it is—as when political men, thinking they can borrow the prestige of generals, find that they must pay for it, or, as when during big slumps, economic men feel the need of a politician at once safe and possessing vote appeal. Today all three are involved in virtually all widely ramifying decisions. Which of the three types seems to lead depends upon "the tasks of the period" as they, the elite, define them. Just now, these tasks center upon "defense" and international affairs. Accordingly, as we have seen, the military are ascendant in two senses: as personnel and as justifying ideology. That is why, just now, we can most easily specify the unity and the shape of the power elite in terms of the military ascendancy.

But we must always be historically specific and open to complexities. The simple Marxian view makes the big economic man the *real* holder of power; the simple liberal view makes the big political man the chief of the power system; and there are some who would view the warlords as virtual dictators. Each of these is an oversimplified view. It is to avoid them that we use the term "power elite" rather than, for example, "ruling class."[3]

---

3. "Ruling class" is a badly loaded phrase. "Class" is an economic term; "rule" a political one. The phrase, "ruling class," thus contains the theory that an economic class rules politically. That short-cut theory may or may not at times be true, but we do not want to carry that one rather simple theory about in the terms that we use to define our problems; we wish to state the theories explicitly, using terms of more precise and unilateral meaning. Specifically,

In so far as the power elite has come to wide public attention, it has done so in terms of the "military clique." The power elite does, in fact, take its current shape from the decisive entrance into it of the military. Their presence and their ideology are its major legitimations, whenever the power elite feels the need to provide any. But what is called the "Washington military clique" is not composed merely of military men, and it does not prevail merely in Washington. Its members exist all over the country, and it is a coalition of generals in the roles of corporation executives, of politicians masquerading as admirals, of corporation executives acting like politicians, of civil servants who become majors, of vice-admirals who are also the assistants to a cabinet officer, who is himself, by the way, really a member of the managerial elite.

Neither the idea of a "ruling class" nor of a simple monolithic rise of "bureaucratic politicians" nor of a "military clique" is adequate. The power elite today involves the often uneasy coincidence of economic, military, and political power. [. . .]

The power elite, as we conceive it, also rests upon the similarity of its personnel, and their personal and official relations with one another, upon their social and psychological affinities. In order to grasp the personal and social basis of the power elite's unity, we have first to remind ourselves of the facts of origin, career, and style of life of each of the types of circle whose members compose the power elite.

The power elite is *not* an aristocracy, which is to say that it is not a political ruling group based upon a

nobility of hereditary origin. It has no compact basis in a small circle of great families whose members can and do consistently occupy the top positions in the several higher circles which overlap as the power elite. But such nobility is only one possible basis of common origin. That it does not exist for the American elite does not mean that members of this elite derive socially from the full range of strata composing American society. They derive in substantial proportions from the upper classes, both new and old, of local society and the metropolitan 400. The bulk of the very rich, the corporate executives, the political outsiders, the high military, derive from, at most, the upper third of the income and occupational pyramids. Their fathers were at least of the professional and business strata, and very frequently higher than that. They are native-born Americans of native parents, primarily from urban areas, and, with the exceptions of the politicians among them, overwhelmingly from the East. They are mainly Protestants, especially Episcopalian or Presbyterian. In general, the higher the position, the greater the proportion of men within it who have derived from and who maintain connections with the upper classes. The generally similar origins of the members of the power elite are underlined and carried further by the fact of their increasingly common educational routine. Overwhelmingly college graduates, substantial proportions have attended Ivy League colleges, although the education of the higher military, of course, differs from that of other members of the power elite. [. . .]

We cannot infer the direction of policy merely from the social origins and careers of the policymakers. The social and economic backgrounds of the men of power do not tell us all that we need to know in order to understand the distribution of social power. For: (1) Men from high places may be ideological representatives of the poor and humble. (2) Men of humble origin, brightly self-made, may energetically serve the most vested and inherited interests. Moreover (3), not all men who effectively represent the interests of a stratum need in any way belong to it or personally benefit by policies that further its interests. Among the politicians, in short, there are sympathetic *agents* of given groups, conscious and unconscious, paid and unpaid. Finally (4), among the top decision-makers we find men who

---

the phrase "ruling class," in its common political connotations, does not allow enough autonomy to the political order and its agents, and it says nothing about the military as such. It should be clear to the reader by now that we do not accept as adequate the simple view that hight economic men unilaterally make all decisions of national consequence. We hold that such a simple view of "economic determinism" must be elaborated by "political determinism" and "military determinism"; that the higher agents of each of these three domains now often have a noticable degree of autonomy; and that only in the often intricate ways of coalition do they make up and carry through the most important decisions. Those are the major reasons we prefer "power elite" to "ruling class" as a characterizing phrase for the higher circles when we consider them in terms of power.

have been chosen for their positions because of their "expert knowledge." These are some of the obvious reasons why the social origins and careers of of the power elite do not enable us to infer the class interests and policy directions of a modern system of power.

Do the high social origin and careers of the top men mean nothing, then, about the distribution of power? By no means. They simply remind us that we must be careful of any simple and direct inference from origin and career to political character and policy, not that we must ignore them in our attempt at political understanding. They simply mean that we must analyze the political psychology and the actual decisions of the political directorate as well as its social composition. And they mean, above all, that we should control, as we have done here, any inference we make from the origin and careers of the political actors by close understanding of the institutional landscape in which they act out their drama. Otherwise we should be guilty of a rather simple-minded biographical theory of society and history.

Just as we cannot rest the notion of the power elite solely upon the institutional mechanics that lead to its formation, so we cannot rest the notion solely upon the facts of the origin and career of its personnel. We need both, and we have both—as well as other bases, among them that of the status intermingling. [. . .]

Despite their social similarity and psychological affinities, the members of the power elite do not constitute a club having a permanent membership with fixed and formal boundaries. It is of the nature of the power elite that within it there is a good deal of shifting about, and that it thus does not consist of one small set of the same men in the same positions in the same hierarchies. Because men know each other personally does not mean that among them there is a unity of policy; and because they do not know each other personally does not mean that among them there is a disunity. The conception of the power elite does not rest, as I have repeatedly said, primarily upon personal friendship.

As the requirements of the top places in each of the major hierarchies become similar; the types of men occupying these roles at the top—by selection and by training in the jobs—become similar, this is no mere deduction from structure and personnel. That it is a fact is revealed by the heavy traffic that has been going on between the three structures, often in very intricate patterns. The chief executives, the warlords, and selected politicians came into contact with one another in an intimate, working way during World War II; after that war ended, they continued their associations, out of common beliefs, social congeniality, and coinciding interests. Noticeable proportions of top men from the military, the economic, and the political worlds have during the last fifteen years occupied positions in one or both of the other worlds: between these higher circles there is an interchangeability of position, based formally upon the supposed transferability of "executive ability," based in substance upon the co-optation by cliques of insiders. As members of a power elite, many of those busy in this traffic have come to look upon "the government" as an umbrella under whose authority they do their work.

As the business between the big three increases in volume and importance, so does the traffic in personnel. The very criteria for selecting men who will rise come to embody this fact. The corporate commissar, dealing with the state and its military, is wiser to choose a young man who has experienced the state and its military than one who has not. The political director, often dependent for his own political success upon corporate decisions and corporations, is also wiser to choose a man with corporate experience. Thus, by virtue of the very criterion of success, the interchange of personnel and the unity of the power elite is increased.

Given the formal similarity of the three hierarchies in which the several members of the elite spend their working lives, given the ramifications of the decisions made in each upon the others, given the coincidence of interest that prevails among them at many points, and given the administrative vacuum of the American civilian state along with its enlargement of tasks—given these trends of structure, and adding to them the psychological affinities we have noted—we should indeed be surprised were we to find that men said to be skilled in administrative contacts and full of organizing ability would fail to do more than get in touch with one another. They have, of course, done much more than that: increasingly, they assume positions in one another's domains.

The unity revealed by the interchangeability of top roles rests upon the parallel development of the top jobs in each of the big three domains. The interchange occurs most frequently at the points of their coinciding interest, as between regulatory agency and the regulated industry; contracting agency and contractor. And, as we shall see, it leads to co-ordinations that are more explicit, and even formal.

The inner core of the power elite consists, first, of those who interchange commanding roles at the top of one dominant institutional order with those in another: the admiral who is also a banker and a lawyer and who heads up an important federal commission; the corporation executive whose company was one of the two or three leading war materiel producers who is now the Secretary of Defense; the wartime general who dons civilian clothes to sit on the political directorate and then becomes a member of the board of directors of a leading economic corporation.

Although the executive who becomes a general, the general who becomes a statesman, the statesman who becomes a banker, see much more than ordinary men in their ordinary environments, still the perspectives of even such men often remain tied to their dominant locales. In their very career, however, they interchange roles within the big three and thus readily transcend the particularity of interest in any one of these institutional milieux. By their very careers and activities, they lace the three types of milieux together. They are, accordingly, the core members of the power elite.

These men are not necessarily familiar with every major arena of power. We refer to one man who moves in and between perhaps two circles—say the industrial and the military—and to another man who moves in the military and the political, and to a third who moves in the political as well as among opinion-makers. These in-between types most closely display our image of the power elite's structure and operation, even of behind-the-scenes operations. To the extent that there is any "invisible elite," these advisory and liaison types are its core. Even if—as I believe to be very likely—many of them are, at least in the first part of their careers, "agents" of the various elites rather than themselves elite, it is they who are most active in organizing the several top milieux into a structure of power and maintaining it.

The inner core of the power elite also includes men of the higher legal and financial type from the great law factories and investment firms, who are almost professional go-betweens of economic, political and military affairs, and who thus act to unify the power elite. The corporation lawyer and the investment banker perform the functions of the "go-between" effectively and powerfully. By the nature of their work, they transcend the narrower milieu of any one industry, and accordingly are in a position to speak and act for the corporate world or at least sizable sectors of it. The corporation lawyer is a key link between the economic and military and political areas; the investment banker is a key organizer and unifier of the corporate world and a person well versed in spending the huge amounts of money the American military establishment now ponders. When you get a lawyer who handles the legal work of investment bankers you get a key member of the power elite. [. . .]

The conception of the power elite and of its unity rests upon the corresponding developments and the coincidence of interests among economic, political, and military organizations. It also rests upon the similarity of origin and outlook, and the social and personal intermingling of the top circles from each of these dominant hierarchies. This conjunction of institutional and psychological forces, in turn, is revealed by the heavy personnel traffic within and between the big three institutional orders, as well as by the rise of go-betweens as in the high-level lobbying. The conception of the power elite, accordingly, does *not* rest upon the assumption that American history since the origins of World War II must be understood as a secret plot, or as a great and co-ordinated conspiracy of the members of this elite. The conception rests upon quite impersonal grounds.

There is, however, little doubt that the American power elite—which contains, we are told, some of "the greatest organizers in the world"—has also planned and has plotted. The rise of the elite, as we have already made clear, was not and could not have been caused by a plot; and the tenability of the conception does not rest upon the existence of any secret or any publicly known organization. But, once the conjunction of structural trend and of the personal will to utilize it gave rise to the power elite, then plans and programs did occur to its members and indeed it is not possible to interpret many events and official policies of the fifth epoch without reference to the power elite. "There is a great difference," Richard Hofstadter has remarked, "between locating conspiracies *in* history and saying that history *is*, in effect, a conspiracy . . ."[4] [. . .]

The idea of the power elite rests upon and enables us to make sense of (1) the decisive institutional trends that characterize the structure of our epoch, in particular, the military ascendancy in a privately incorporated economy, and more broadly, the several coincidences of objective interests between economic, military, and political institutions; (2) the social similarities and the psychological affinities of the men who occupy the command posts of these structures, in particular the increased interchangeability of the top positions in each of them and the increased traffic between these orders in the careers of men of power; (3) the ramifications, to the point of virtual totality, of the kind of decisions that are made at the top, and the rise to power of a set of men who, by training and bent, are professional organizers of considerable force and who are unrestrained by democratic party training.

Negatively, the formation of the power elite rests upon (1) the relegation of the professional party politician to the middle levels of power, (2) the semi-organized stalemate of the interests of sovereign localities into which the legislative function has fallen, (3) the virtually complete absence of a civil service that constitutes a politically neutral, but politically relevant, depository of brainpower and executive skill, and (4) the increased official secrecy behind which great decisions are made without benefit of public or even Congressional debate.

As a result, the political directorate, the corporate rich, and the ascendant military have come together as the power elite, and the expanded and centralized hierarchies which they head have encroached upon the old balances and have now relegated them to the middle levels, of power. Now the balancing society is a conception that pertains accurately to the middle levels, and on that level the balance has become more often an affair of intrenched provincial and nationally irresponsible forces and demands than a center of power and national decision.

But how about the bottom? As all these trends have become visible at the top and on the middle,

what has been happening to the great American public? If the top is unprecedentedly powerful and increasingly unified and willful; if the middle zones are increasingly a semi-organized stalemate — in what shape is the bottom, in what condition is the public at large? The rise of the power elite, we shall now see, rests upon, and in some ways is part of, the transformation of the publics of America into a mass society.

Mass Society

[. . .] From almost any angle of vision that we might assume, when we look upon the public, we realize that we have moved a considerable distance along the road to the mass society. At the end of that road there is totalitarianism, as in Nazi Germany or in Communist Russia. We are not yet at that end. In the United States today, media markets are not entirely ascendant over primary publics. But surely we can see that many aspects of the public life of our times are more the features of a mass society than of a community of publics.

What is happening might again be stated in terms of the historical parallel between the economic market and the public of public opinion. In brief, there is a movement from widely scattered little powers to concentrated powers and the attempt at monopoly control from powerful centers, which, being partially hidden, are centers of manipulation as well as of authority. The small shop serving the neighborhood is replaced by the anonymity of the national corporation: mass advertisement replaces the personal influence of opinion between merchant and customer. The political leader hooks up his speech to a national network and speaks, with appropriate personal touches, to a million people he never saw and never will see. Entire brackets of professions and industries are in the "opinion business," impersonally manipulating the public for hire.

In the primary public the competition of opinions goes on between people holding views in the service of their interests and their reasoning. But in the mass society of media markets, competition, if any, goes on between the manipulators with their mass media on the one hand, and the people receiving their propaganda on the other.

---

4. Richard Hofstadter, op. cit., pp. 71–2.

Under such conditions, it is not surprising that there should arise a conception of public opinion as a mere reaction—we cannot say "response"—to the content of the mass media. In this view, the public is merely the collectivity of individuals each rather passively exposed to the mass media and rather helplessly opened up to the suggestions and manipulations that flow from these media. The fact of manipulation from centralized points of control constitutes, as it were, an expropriation of the old multitude of little opinion producers and consumers operating in a free and balanced market.

In official circles, the very term itself, "the public"—as Walter Lippmann noted thirty years ago—has come to have a phantom meaning, which dramatically reveals its eclipse. From the standpoint of the deciding elite, some of those who clamor publicly can be identified as "Labor," others as "Business," still others as "Farmer." Those who can *not* readily be so identified make up "The Public." In this usage, the public is composed of the unidentified and the non-partisan in a world of defined and partisan interests. It is socially composed of well-educated salaried professionals, especially college professors; of non-unionized employees, especially white-collar people, along with self-employed professionals and small businessmen.

[. . .] [I]n a *mass*, (1) far fewer people express opinions than receive them; for the community of publics becomes an abstract collection of individuals who receive impressions from the mass media. (2) The communications that prevail are so organized that it is difficult or impossible for the individual to answer back immediately or with any effect. (3) The realization of opinion in action is controlled by authorities who organize and control the channels of such action. (4) The mass has no autonomy from institutions; on the contrary, agents of authorized institutions penetrate this mass, reducing any autonomy it may have in the formation of opinion by discussion.

The public and the mass may be most readily distinguished by their dominant modes of communication: in a community of publics, discussion is the ascendant means of communication, and the mass media, if they exist simply enlarge and animate discussion, linking one *primary public* with the discussions of another. In a mass society, the dominant type of communication is the formal media, and the publics become mere *media markets*: all those exposed to the contents of given mass media. [. . .]

In a curious adaptation, "the public" often becomes, in fact, "the unattached expert," who, although well informed, has never taken a clear-cut, public stand on controversial issues which are brought to a focus by organized interests. These are the "public" members of the board, the commission, the committee. What the public stands for, accordingly, is often a vagueness of policy (called open-mindedness), a lack of involvement in public affairs (known as reasonableness), and a professional disinterest (known as tolerance). [. . . .]

All those trends that make for the decline of the politician and of his balancing society bear decisively upon the transformation of public into mass. One of the most important of the structural transformations involved is the decline of the voluntary association as a genuine instrument of the public. As we have already seen, the executive ascendancy in economic, military, and political institutions has lowered the effective use of all those voluntary associations which operate between the state and the economy on the one hand, and the family and the individual in the primary group on the other. It is not only that institutions of power have become large-scale and inaccessibly centralized; they have at the same time become less political and more administrative, and it is within this great change of framework that the organized public has waned.

In terms of *scale*, the transformation of public into mass has been underpinned by the shift from a political public decisively restricted in size (by property and education, as well as by sex and age) to a greatly enlarged mass having only the qualifications of citizenship and age.

In terms of *organization*, the transformation has been underpinned by the shift from the individual and his primary community to the voluntary association and the mass party as the major units of organized power.

Voluntary associations have become larger to the extent that they have become effective; and to just that extent they have become inaccessible to the individual who would shape by discussion the policies of the organization to which he belongs. Accordingly, along with older institutions, these voluntary associations have lost their grip on the individual. As more people are drawn into the political arena, these associations become mass in scale; and as the power of the individual becomes more dependent upon such mass associations, they are less accessible to the individual's influence.

Mass democracy means the struggle of powerful and large-scale interest groups and associations, which stand between the big decisions that are made by state, corporation, army, and the will of the individual citizen as a member of the public. Since these middle-level associations are the citizen's major link with decision, his relation to them is of decisive importance. For it is only through them that he exercises such power as he may have.

The gap between the members and the leaders of the mass association is becoming increasingly wider. As soon as a man gets to be a leader of an association large enough to count he readily becomes lost as an instrument of that association. He does so (1) in the interests of maintaining his leading position in, or rather over, his mass association, and he does (2) because he comes to see himself not as a mere delegate, instructed or not, of the mass association he represents, but as a member of "an elite" composed of such men as himself. These facts, in turn, lead to (3) the big gap between the terms in which issues are debated and resolved among members of this elite, and the terms in which they are presented to the members of the various mass associations. For the decisions that are made must *take into account* those who are important—other elites—but they must be *sold* to the mass memberships. [. . .]

[. . .] [T]he man in the mass does not gain a transcending view from these media; instead he gets his experience stereotyped, and then he gets sunk further by that experience. He cannot detach himself in order to observe, much less to evaluate, what he is experiencing, much less what he is not experiencing. Rather than that internal discussion we call reflection, he is accompanied through his life-experience with a sort of unconscious, echoing monologue. He has no projects of his own: he fulfills the routines that exist. He does not transcend whatever he is at any moment, because he does not, he cannot, transcend his daily milieux. He is not truly aware of his own daily experience and of its actual standards: he drifts, he fulfills habits, his behavior a result of a planless mixture of the confused standards

and the uncriticized expectations that he has taken over from others whom he no longer really knows or trusts, if indeed he ever really did.

He takes things for granted, he makes the best of them, he tries to look ahead—a year or two perhaps, or even longer if he has children or a mortgage—but he does not seriously ask, What do I want? How can I get it? A vague optimism suffuses and sustains him, broken occasionally by little miseries and disappointments that are soon buried. He is smug, from the standpoint of those who think something might be the matter with the mass style of life in the metropolitan frenzy where self-making is an externally busy branch of industry. By what standards does he judge himself and his efforts? What is really important to him? Where are the models of excellence for this man?

He loses his independence, and more importantly, he loses the desire to be independent: in fact, he does not have hold of the idea of being an independent individual with his own mind and his own worked-out way of life. It is not that he likes or does not like this life; it is that the question does not come up sharp and clear so he is not bitter and he is not sweet about conditions and events. He thinks he wants merely to get his share of what is around with as little trouble as he can and with as much fun as possible.

Such order and movement as his life possesses is in conformity with external routines; otherwise his day-to-day experience is a vague chaos—although he often does not know it because, strictly speaking, he does not truly possess or observe his own experience. He does not formulate his desires; they are insinuated into him. And, in the mass, he loses the self-confidence of the human being—if indeed he has ever had it. For life in a society of masses implants insecurity and furthers impotence; it makes men uneasy and vaguely anxious; it isolates the individual from the solid group; it destroys firm group standards. Acting without goals, the man in the mass just feels pointless.

The idea of a mass society suggests the idea of an elite of power. The idea of the public, in contrast, suggests the liberal tradition of a society without any power elite, or at any rate with shifting elites of no sovereign consequence. For, if a genuine public is sovereign, it needs no master; but the masses, in their full development, are sovereign only in some plebiscitarian moment of adulation to an elite as authoritative celebrity. The political structure of a democratic state requires the public; and, the democratic man, in his rhetoric, must assert that this public is the very seat of sovereignty.

But now, given all those forces that have enlarged and centralized the political order and made modern societies less political and more administrative; given the transformation of the old middle classes into something which perhaps should not even be called middle class; given all the mass communications that do not truly communicate; given all the metropolitan segregation that is not community; given the absence of voluntary associations that really connect the public at large with the centers of power—what is happening is the decline of a set of publics that is sovereign only in the most formal and rhetorical sense. Moreover, in many countries the remnants of such publics as remain are now being frightened out of existence. They lose their will for rationally considered decision and action because they do not possess the instruments for such decision and action; they lose their sense of political belonging because they do not belong; they lose their political will because they see no way to realize it.

The top of modern American society is increasingly unified, and often seems willfully co-ordinated: at the top there has emerged an elite of power. The middle levels are a drifting set of stalemated, balancing forces: the middle does not link the bottom with the top. The bottom of this society is politically fragmented, and even as a passive fact, increasingly powerless: at the bottom there is emerging a mass society.

The Higher Immorality

The higher immorality can neither be narrowed to the political sphere nor understood as primarily a matter of corrupt men in fundamentally sound institutions. Political corruption is one aspect of a more general immorality; the level of moral sensibility that now prevails is not merely a matter of corrupt men. The higher immorality is a systematic feature of the American elite; its general acceptance is an essential feature of the mass society.

Of course, there may be corrupt men in sound institutions, but when institutions are corrupting many of the men who live and work in them are necessarily corrupted. In the corporate era, economic relations become impersonal—and the executive feels less personal responsibility. Within the corporate worlds of business, war-making and politics, the private conscience is attenuated—and the higher immorality is institutionalized. It is not merely a question of a corrupt administration in corporation, army, or state; it is a feature of the corporate rich, as a capitalist stratum, deeply intertwined with the politics of the military state. [. . .]

The moral uneasiness of our time results from the fact that older values and codes of uprightness no longer grip the men and women of the corporate era, nor have they been replaced by new values and codes which would lend moral meaning and sanction to the corporate routines they must now follow. It is not that the mass public has explicitly rejected received codes; it is rather that to many of the members these codes have become hollow. No moral terms of acceptance are available, but neither are any moral terms of rejection. As individuals they are morally defenseless; as groups, they are politically indifferent. It is this generalized lack of commitment that is meant when it is said that "the public" is morally confused.

But, of course, not only "the public" is morally confused in this way. "The tragedy of official Washington," James Reston has commented, "is that it is confounded at every turn by the hangover of old political habits and outworn institutions but *is* no longer nourished by the ancient faith on which it was founded. It clings to the bad things and casts away the permanent. It professes belief but does not believe. It knows the old words but has forgotten the melody. It is engaged in an ideological war without being able to define its own ideology. It condemns the materialism of an atheistic enemy, but glorifies its own materialism."[5] [. . .]

The absence of any firm moral order of belief makes men in the mass all the more open to the manipulation and distraction of the world of the

---

5. James Reston, *The New York Times*, 10 April 1955, p. 10E.

celebrities. In due course, such a "turnover" of appeals and codes and values as they are subjected to leads them to distrust and cynicism, to a sort of Machiavellianism-for-the-little-man. Thus they vicariously enjoy the prerogatives of the corporate rich, the nocturnal antics of the celebrity, and the sad-happy life of the very rich.

But with all this, there is still one old American value that has not markedly declined: the value of money and of the things money can buy—these, even in inflated times, seem as solid and enduring as stainless steel. "I've been rich and I've been poor," Sophie Tucker has said, "and believe me, rich is best." As many other values are weakened, the question for Americans becomes not "Is there anything that money, used with intelligence, will not buy?" but, "How many of the things that money will *not* buy are valued and desired more than what money *will* buy?" Money is the one unambiguous criterion of success, and such success is still the sovereign American value. [. . .]

A society that is in its higher circles and on its middle levels widely believed to be a network of smart rackets does not produce men with an inner moral sense; a society that is merely expedient does not produce men of conscience. A society that narrows the meaning of "success" to the big money and in its terms condemns failure as the chief vice, raising money to the plane of absolute value, will produce the sharp operator and the shady deal. Blessed are the cynical, for only they have what it takes to succeed. [. . .]

The democratic man assumes the existence of a public, and in his rhetoric asserts that this public is the very seat of sovereignty. Two things are needed in a democracy: articulate and knowledgeable publics, and political leaders who if not men of reason are at least reasonably responsible to such knowledgeable publics as exist. Only where publics and leaders are responsive and responsible, are human affairs in democratic order, and only when knowledge has public relevance is this order possible. Only when mind has an autonomous basis, independent of power, but powerfully related to it, can mind exert its force in the shaping of human affairs. This is democratically possible only when there exists a free and knowledgeable public, to which men of knowledge may address themselves, and to which men of power

are truly responsible. Such a public and such men—either of power or of knowledge—do not now prevail, and accordingly, knowledge does not now have democratic relevance in America.

The characteristic member of the higher circles today is an intellectual mediocrity, sometimes a conscientious one, but still a mediocrity. His intelligence is revealed only by his occasional realization that he is not up to the decisions he sometimes feels called upon to confront. But usually he keeps such feelings private, his public utterances being pious and sentimental, grim and brave, cheerful and empty in their universal generality. He is open only to abbreviated and vulgarized, predigested and slanted ideas. He is a commander of the age of the phone call, the memo, and the briefing.

By the mindlessness and mediocrity of men of affairs, I do not, of course, mean that these men are not sometimes intelligent—although that is by no means automatically the case. It is not, however, primarily a matter of the distribution of "intelligence"—as if intelligence were a homogeneous something of which there may be more or less. It is rather a matter of the type of intelligence, of the quality of mind that is selected and formed. It is a matter of the evaluation of substantive rationality as the chief value in a man's life and character and conduct. That evaluation is what is lacking in the American power elite. In its place there are "weight" and "judgment" which count for much more in their celebrated success than any subtlety of mind or force of intellect.

All around and just below the weighty man of affairs are his technical lieutenants of power who have been assigned the role of knowledge and even of speech: his public relations men, his ghost, his administrative assistants, his secretaries. And do not forget The Committees. With the increased means of decision, there is a crisis of understanding among the political directorate of the United States, and accordingly, there is often a commanding indecision. [. . .]

In America today, men of affairs are not so much dogmatic as they are mindless. Dogma has usually meant some more or less elaborated justification of ideas and values, and thus has had some features (however inflexible and closed) of mind, of intellect, of reason. Nowadays what we are up against is precisely the absence of mind of any sort as a public force; what we are up against is a disinterest in and a fear of knowledge that might have liberating public relevance. What this makes possible are decisions having no rational justifications which the intellect could confront and engage in debate.

It is not the barbarous irrationality of dour political primitives that is the American danger; it is the respected judgments of Secretaries of State, the earnest platitudes of Presidents, the fearful self-righteousness of sincere young American politicians from sunny California. These men have replaced mind with platitude, and the dogmas by which they are legitimated are so widely accepted that no counter-balance of mind prevails against them. Such men as these are crackpot realists: in the name of realism they have constructed a paranoid reality all their own; in the name of practicality they have projected a utopian image of capitalism. They have replaced the responsible interpretation of events with the disguise of events by a maze of public relations; respect for public debate with unshrewd notions of psychological warfare; intellectual ability with agility of the sound, mediocre judgment; the capacity to elaborate alternatives and gauge their consequences with the executive stance. [. . .]

The higher circles in America today contain, on the one hand, the laughing, erotic, dazzling glamour of the professional celebrity, and, on the other, the prestige aura of power, of authority, of might and wealth. These two pinnacles are not unrelated. The power elite is not so noticeable as the celebrities, and often does not want to be; the "power" of the professional celebrity is the power of distraction. America as a national public is indeed possessed of a strange set of idols. The professionals, in the main, are either glossy little animals or frivolous clowns; the men of power, in the main, rarely seem to be models of representative men.

Such moral uneasiness as prevails among the American elite themselves is accordingly quite understandable. Its existence is amply confirmed by the more serious among those who have come to feel that they represent America abroad. There, the double-faced character of the American celebrity is reflected both by the types of Americans who travel to play or to work, and in the images many literate and articulate Europeans hold of "Americans." Public honor in America tends now to be either frivolous or grim; either altogether trivial or portentous of a greatly tightened-up system of prestige.

The American elite is not composed of representative men whose conduct and character constitute models for American imitation and aspiration. There is no set of men with whom members of the mass public can rightfully and gladly identify. In this fundamental sense, America is indeed without leaders. Yet such is the nature of the mass public's morally cynical and politically unspecified distrust that it is readily drained off without real political effect. That this is so, after the men and events of the last thirty years, is further proof of the extreme difficulty of finding and of using in America today the political means of sanity for morally sane objectives.

America—a conservative country without any conservative ideology—appears now before the world a naked and arbitrary power, as, in the name of realism, its men of decision enforce their often crackpot definitions upon world reality. The second-rate mind is in command of the ponderously spoken platitude. In the liberal rhetoric, vagueness, and in the conservative mood, irrationality, are raised to principle. Public relations and the official secret, the trivializing campaign and the terrible fact clumsily accomplished, are replacing the reasoned debate of political ideas in the privately incorporated economy, the military ascendancy, and the political vacuum of modern America.

The men of the higher circles are not representative men; their high position is not a result of moral virtue; their fabulous success is not firmly connected with meritorious ability. Those who sit in the seats of the high and the mighty are selected and formed by the means of power, the sources of wealth, the mechanics of celebrity, which prevail in their society. They are not men selected and formed by a civil service that is linked with the world of knowledge and sensibility. They are not men shaped by nationally responsible parties that debate openly and clearly the issues this nation now so unintelligently confronts. They are not men held in responsible check by a plurality of voluntary associations which connect debating publics with the pinnacles of decision. Commanders of power unequaled in human history, they have succeeded within the American system of organized irresponsibility.

Dwight D. Eisenhower

Farewell Address (1961)

My fellow Americans:

Three days from now, after half a century in the service of our country, I shall lay down the responsibilities of office as, in traditional and solemn ceremony; the authority of the Presidency is vested in my successor.

This evening I come to you with a message of leave-taking and farewell, and to share a few final thoughts with you, my countrymen.

Like every other citizen, I wish the new President, and all who will labor with him, Godspeed. I pray that the coming years will be blessed with peace and prosperity for all.

Our people expect their President and the Congress to find essential agreement on issues of great moment, the wise resolution of which will better shape the future of the Nation.

My own relations with the Congress, which began on a remote and tenuous basis when, long ago, a member of the Senate appointed me to West Point, have since ranged to the intimate during the war and immediate post-war period, and, finally, to the mutually interdependent during these past eight years.

In this final relationship, the Congress and the Administration have, on most vital issues, cooperated well, to serve the national good rather than mere partisanship, and so have assured that the business of the Nation should go forward. So, my official relationship with the Congress ends in a feeling, on my part, of gratitude that we have been able to do so much together.

II

We now stand ten years past the midpoint of a century that has witnessed four major wars among great nations. Three of these involved our own country. Despite these holocausts America is today the strongest, the most influential and most productive nation in the world. Understandably proud of this pre-eminence, we yet realize that America's leadership and prestige depend, not merely upon our unmatched material progress, riches and military strength, but on how we use our power in the interests of world peace and human betterment.

III

Throughout America's adventure in free government, our basic purposes have been to keep the peace; to foster progress in human achievement, and to enhance liberty, dignity and integrity among people and among nations. To strive for less would be unworthy of a free and religious people. Any failure traceable to arrogance, or our lack of comprehension or readiness to sacrifice would inflict upon us grievous hurt both at home and abroad.

Progress toward these noble goals is persistently threatened by the conflict now engulfing the world. It commands our whole attention, absorbs our very beings. We face a hostile ideology—global in scope, atheistic in character, ruthless in purpose, and insidious in method. Unhappily the danger it poses promises to be of indefinite duration. To meet it successfully, there is called for, not so much the emotional and transitory sacrifices of crisis, but rather those which enable us to carry forward steadily, surely, and without complaint the burdens of a prolonged and complex struggle—with liberty the stake. Only thus shall we remain, despite every provocation, on our charted course toward permanent peace and human betterment.

Crises there will continue to be. In meeting them, whether foreign or domestic, great or small, there is a recurring temptation to feel that some spectacular and costly action could become the miraculous solution to all current difficulties. A huge increase in newer elements of our defense; development of unrealistic programs to cure every ill in agriculture; a dramatic expansion in basic and applied research—these and many other possibilities, each possibly promising in itself, may be suggested as the only way to the road we wish to travel.

But each proposal must be weighed in the light of a broader consideration: the need to maintain balance in and among national programs—balance between the private and the public economy, balance between cost and hoped for advantage—balance between the clearly necessary and the comfortably desirable; balance between our essential requirements as a nation and the duties imposed by the nation upon the individual; balance between actions of the moment and the national welfare of the future. Good judgment seeks balance and progress; lack of it eventually finds imbalance and frustration.

The record of many decades stands as proof that our people and their government have, in the main, understood these truths and have responded to them well, in the face of stress and threat. But threats, new in kind or degree, constantly arise. I mention two only.

IV

A vital element in keeping the peace is our military establishment. Our arms must be mighty, ready for instant action, so that no potential aggressor may be tempted to risk his own destruction.

Our military organization today bears little relation to that known by any of my predecessors in peacetime, or indeed by the fighting men of World War II or Korea.

Until the latest of our world conflicts, the United States had no armaments industry. American makers of plowshares could, with time and as required, make swords as well. But now we can no longer risk emergency improvisation of national defense; we have been compelled to create a permanent armaments industry of vast proportions. Added to this, three and a half million men and women are directly engaged in the defense establishment. We annually spend on military security more than the net income of all United States corporations.

This conjunction of an immense military establishment and a large arms industry is new in the American experience. The total influence—economic, political, even spiritual—is felt in every city, every State house, every office of the Federal government. We recognize the imperative need for this development. Yet we must not fail to comprehend its grave implications. Our toil, resources and livelihood are all involved; so is the very structure of our society.

In the councils of government, we must guard against the acquisition of unwarranted influence, whether sought or unsought, by the military industrial complex. The potential for the disastrous rise of misplaced power exists and will persist.

We must never let the weight of this combination endanger our liberties or democratic processes. We should take nothing for granted. Only an alert and knowledgeable citizenry can compel the proper meshing of the huge industrial and military machinery of defense with our peaceful methods and goals, so that security and liberty may prosper together.

Akin to, and largely responsible for the sweeping changes in our industrial-military posture, has been the technological revolution during recent decades.

In this revolution, research has become central; it also becomes more formalized, complex, and costly. A steadily increasing share is conducted for, by, or at the direction of, the Federal government.

Today, the solitary inventor, tinkering in his shop, has been overshadowed by task forces of scientists in laboratories and testing fields. In the same fashion, the free university, historically the fountainhead of free ideas and scientific discovery, has experienced a revolution in the conduct of research. Partly because of the huge costs involved, a government contract becomes virtually a substitute for intellectual curiosity. For every old blackboard there are now hundreds of new electronic computers.

The prospect of domination of the nation's scholars by Federal employment, project allocations, and the power of money is ever present and is gravely to be regarded.

Yet, in holding scientific research and discovery in respect, as we should, we must also be alert to the equal and opposite danger that public policy could itself become the captive of a scientific technological elite.

It is the task of statesmanship to mold, to balance, and to integrate these and other forces, new and old, within the principles of our democratic system—ever aiming toward the supreme goals of our free society.

V

Another factor in maintaining balance involves the element of time. As we peer into society's future, we—you and I, and our government—must avoid the impulse to live only for today, plundering, for our own ease and convenience, the precious resources of tomorrow. We cannot mortgage the material assets of our grandchildren without risking the loss also of their political and spiritual heritage. We want democracy to survive for all generations to come, not to become the insolvent phantom of tomorrow.

VI

Down the long lane of the history yet to be written America knows that this world of ours, ever growing smaller, must avoid becoming a community of dreadful fear and hate, and be instead, a proud confederation of mutual trust and respect.

Such a confederation must be one of equals. The weakest must come to the conference table with the same confidence as do we, protected as we are by our moral, economic, and military strength. That table, though scarred by many past frustrations, cannot be abandoned for the certain agony of the battlefield.

Disarmament, with mutual honor and confidence, is a continuing imperative. Together we must learn how to compose differences, not with arms, but with intellect and decent purpose. Because this need is so sharp and apparent I confess that I lay down my official responsibilities in this field with a definite sense of disappointment. As one who has witnessed the horror and the lingering sadness of war—as one who knows that another war could utterly destroy this civilization which has been so slowly and painfully built over thousands of years—I wish I could say tonight that a lasting peace is in sight.

Happily, I can say that war has been avoided. Steady progress toward our ultimate goal has been made. But, so much remains to be done. As a private citizen, I shall never cease to do what little I can to help the world advance along that road.

VII

So—in this my last good night to you as your President—I thank you for the many opportunities you have given me for public service in war and peace. I trust that in that service you find some things worthy; as for the rest of it, I know you will find ways to improve performance in the future.

You and I—my fellow citizens—need to be strong in our faith that all nations, under God, will reach the goal of peace with justice. May we be ever unswerving in devotion to principle, confident but humble with power, diligent in pursuit of the Nation's great goals.

To all the peoples of the world, I once more give expression to America's prayerful and continuing aspiration:

We pray that peoples of all faiths, all races, all nations, may have their great human needs satisfied; that those now denied opportunity shall come to enjoy it to the full; that all who yearn for freedom may experience its spiritual blessings; that those who have freedom will understand, also, its heavy responsibilities; that all who are insensitive to the needs of others will learn charity; that the scourges of poverty, disease and ignorance will be made to disappear from the earth, and that, in the goodness of time, all peoples will come to live together in a peace guaranteed by the binding force of mutual respect and love.

John F. Kennedy

Campaign Address to the Greater Houston Ministerial Association (1960)

Reverend Meza, Reverend Reck, I'm grateful for your generous invitation to state my views.

While the so-called religious issue is necessarily and properly the chief topic here tonight, I want to emphasize from the outset that I believe that we have far more critical issues in the 1960 campaign; the spread of Communist influence, until it now festers only 90 miles from the coast of Florida—the humiliating treatment of our President and Vice President by those who no longer respect our power—the hungry children I saw in West Virginia, the old people who cannot pay their doctors bills, the families forced to give up their farms—an America with too many slums, with too few schools, and too late to the moon and outer space. These are the real issues which should decide this campaign. And they are not religious issues—for war and hunger and ignorance and despair know no religious barrier.

But because I am a Catholic, and no Catholic has ever been elected President, the real issues in this campaign have been obscured—perhaps deliberately, in some quarters less responsible than this. So it is apparently necessary for me to state once again— not what kind of church I believe in, for that should be important only to me—but what kind of America I believe in.

I believe in an America where the separation of church and state is absolute; where no Catholic prelate would tell the President—should he be Catholic—how to act, and no Protestant minister would tell his parishioners for whom to vote; where no church or church school is granted any public funds or political preference, and where no man is denied public office merely because his religion differs from the President who might appoint him, or the people who might elect him.

I believe in an America that is officially neither Catholic, Protestant nor Jewish; where no public official either requests or accept instructions on public policy from the Pope, the National Council of Churches or any other ecclesiastical source; where no religious body seeks to impose its will directly or indirectly upon the general populace or the public acts of its officials, and where religious liberty is so indivisible that an act against one church is treated as an act against all.

For while this year it may be a Catholic against whom the finger of suspicion is pointed, in other years it has been—and may someday be again—a Jew, or a Quaker, or a Unitarian, or a Baptist. It was Virginia's harassment of Baptist preachers, for example, that led to Jefferson's statute of religious freedom. Today, I may be the victim, but tomorrow it may be you—until the whole fabric of our harmonious society is ripped apart at a time of great national peril.

Finally, I believe in an America where religious intolerance will someday end—where all men and all churches are treated as equals, where every man has the same right to attend or not to attend the church of his choice, where there is no Catholic vote, no anti-Catholic vote, no bloc voting of any kind, and where Catholics, Protestants, and Jews, at both the lay and the pastoral levels, will refrain from those attitudes of disdain and division which have so often marred their works in the past, and promote instead the American ideal of brotherhood.

That is the kind of America in which I believe. And it represents the kind of Presidency in which I believe, a great office that must be neither humbled by making it the instrument of any religious group nor tarnished by arbitrarily withholding its occupancy from the members of any one religious group. I believe in a President whose views on religion are his own private affair, neither imposed upon him by the nation, nor imposed by the nation upon him [sic] as a condition to holding that office.

I would not look with favor upon a President working to subvert the First Amendment's guarantees of religious liberty. Nor would our system of checks and balances permit him to do so. And neither do I look with favor upon those who would work to subvert Article VI of the Constitution by requiring a religious test, even by indirection. For if they disagree with that safeguard, they should be out openly working to repeal it.

I want a Chief Executive whose public acts are responsible to all and obligated to none, who can attend any ceremony, service, or dinner his office may appropriately require of him to fulfill; and whose fulfillment of his Presidential office is not limited or conditioned by any religious oath, ritual, or obligation.

This is the kind of America I believe in—and this is the kind of America I fought for in the South Pacific, and the kind my brother died for in Europe. No one suggested then that we might have a divided loyalty, that we did not believe in liberty, or that we belonged to a disloyal group that threatened "the freedoms for which our forefathers died."

And in fact this is the kind of America for which our forefathers did when they fled here to escape religious test oaths that denied office to members of less favored churches—when they fought for the Constitution, the Bill of Rights, the Virginia Statute of Religious Freedom—and when they fought at the shrine I visited today, the Alamo. For side by side with Bowie and Crockett died Fuentes, and McCafferty, and Bailey, and Badillo, and Carey—but no one knows whether they were Catholics or not. For there was no religious test there.

I ask you tonight to follow in that tradition—to judge me on the basis of 14 years in the Congress, on my declared stands against an Ambassador to the Vatican, against unconstitutional aid to parochial schools, and against any boycott of the public schools—which I attended myself. And instead of doing this, do not judge me on the basis of these pamphlets and publications we all have seen that carefully select quotations out of context from the statements of Catholic church leaders, usually in other countries, frequently in other centuries, and rarely relevant to any situation here. And always omitting, of course, the statement of the American Bishops in 1948 which strongly endorsed Church-State separation, and which more nearly reflects the views of almost every American Catholic.

I do not consider these other quotations binding upon my public acts. Why should you?

But let me say, with respect to other countries, that I am wholly opposed to the State being used by any religious group, Catholic or Protestant, to compel, prohibit, or prosecute the free exercise of any other religion. And that goes for any persecution, at any time, by anyone, in any country. And I hope that you and I condemn with equal fervor those nations which deny their Presidency to Protestants, and those which deny it to Catholics. And rather than cite the misdeeds of those who differ, I would also cite the record of the Catholic Church in such nations as France and Ireland, and the independence of such statesmen as De Gaulle and Adenauer.

But let me stress again that these are my views.

For contrary to common newspaper usage, I am not the Catholic candidate for President.

I am the Democratic Party's candidate for President who happens also to be a Catholic.

I do not speak for my church on public matters; and the church does not speak for me. Whatever issue may come before me as President, if I should be elected, on birth control, divorce, censorship, gambling or any other subject, I will make my decision in accordance with these views—in accordance with what my conscience tells me to be in the national interest, and without regard to outside religious pressure or dictates. And no power or threat of punishment could cause me to decide otherwise.

But if the time should ever come—and I do not concede any conflict to be remotely possible—when my office would require me to either violate my conscience or violate the national interest, then I would resign the office; and I hope any conscientious public servant would do likewise.

But I do not intend to apologize for these views to my critics of either Catholic or Protestant faith; nor do I intend to disavow either my views or my church in order to win this election.

If I should lose on the real issues, I shall return to my seat in the Senate, satisfied that I'd tried my best and was fairly judged.

But if this election is decided on the basis that 40 million Americans lost their chance of being President on the day they were baptized, then it is the whole nation that will be the loser, in the eyes of Catholics and non-Catholics around the world, in the eyes of history, and in the eyes of our own people.

But if, on the other hand, I should win this election, then I shall devote every effort of mind and spirit to fulfilling the oath of the Presidency—practically identical, I might add, with the oath I have taken for 14 years in the Congress. For without reservation, I can, "solemnly swear that I will faithfully execute the office of President of the United States, and will to the best of my ability preserve, protect, and defend the Constitution—so help me God."

Inaugural Address (1961)

Vice President Johnson, Mr. Speaker, Mr. Chief Justice, President Eisenhower, Vice President Nixon, President Truman, reverend clergy, fellow citizens, we observe today not a victory of party, but a celebration of freedom—symbolizing an end, as well as a beginning—signifying renewal, as well as change. For I have sworn before you and Almighty God the same solemn oath our forebears prescribed nearly a century and three quarters ago.

The world is very different now. For man holds in his mortal hands the power to abolish all forms of human poverty and all forms of human life. And yet the same revolutionary beliefs for which our forebears fought are still at issue around the globe—the belief that the rights of man come not from the generosity of the state, but from the hand of God.

We dare not forget today that we are the heirs of that first revolution. Let the word go forth from this time and place, to friend and foe alike, that the torch has been passed to a new generation of Americans—born in this century, tempered by war, disciplined by a hard and bitter peace, proud of our ancient heritage—and unwilling to witness or permit the slow undoing of those human rights to which this Nation has always been committed, and to which we are committed today at home and around the world.

Let every nation know, whether it wishes us well or ill, that we shall pay any price, bear any burden, meet any hardship, support any friend, oppose any foe, in order to assure the survival and the success of liberty.

This much we pledge—and more.

To those old allies whose cultural and spiritual origins we share, we pledge the loyalty of faithful friends. United, there is little we cannot do in a host of cooperative ventures. Divided, there is little we can do—for we dare not meet a powerful challenge at odds and split asunder.

To those new States whom we welcome to the ranks of the free, we pledge our word that one form of colonial control shall not have passed away merely to be replaced by a far more iron tyranny. We shall not always expect to find them supporting our view. But we shall always hope to find them strongly supporting their own freedom—and to remember that, in the past, those who foolishly sought power by riding the back of the tiger ended up inside.

To those peoples in the huts and villages across the globe struggling to break the bonds of mass misery, we pledge our best efforts to help them help themselves, for whatever period is required—not because the Communists may be doing it, not because we seek their votes, but because it is right. If a free society cannot help the many who are poor, it cannot save the few who are rich.

To our sister republics south of our border, we offer a special pledge—to convert our good words into good deeds—in a new alliance for progress—to assist free men and free governments in casting off the chains of poverty. But this peaceful revolution of hope cannot become the prey of hostile powers. Let all our neighbors know that we shall join with them to oppose aggression or subversion anywhere in the Americas. And let every other power know that this Hemisphere intends to remain the master of its own house.

To that world assembly of sovereign states, the United Nations, our last best hope in an age where the instruments of war have far outpaced the instruments of peace, we renew our pledge of support—to prevent it from becoming merely a forum for invective—to strengthen its shield of the new and the weak—and to enlarge the area in which its writ may run.

Finally, to those nations who would make themselves our adversary, we offer not a pledge but a request: that both sides begin anew the quest for peace, before the dark powers of destruction unleashed by science engulf all humanity in planned or accidental self-destruction.

We dare not tempt them with weakness. For only when our arms are sufficient beyond doubt can we be certain beyond doubt that they will never be employed.

But neither can two great and powerful groups of nations take comfort from our present course—both sides overburdened by the cost of modern weapons, both rightly alarmed by the steady spread of the deadly atom, yet both racing to alter that uncertain balance of terror that stays the hand of mankind's final war.

So let us begin anew—remembering on both sides that civility is not a sign of weakness, and sincerity is always subject to proof. Let us never negotiate out of fear. But let us never fear to negotiate.

Let both sides explore what problems unite us instead of belaboring those problems which divide us.

Let both sides, for the first time, formulate serious and precise proposals for the inspection and control of arms—and bring the absolute power to destroy other nations under the absolute control of all nations.

Let both sides seek to invoke the wonders of science instead of its terrors. Together let us explore the stars, conquer the deserts, eradicate disease, tap the ocean depths, and encourage the arts and commerce.

Let both sides unite to heed in all corners of the earth the command of Isaiah—to "undo the heavy burdens . . . and to let the oppressed go free."

And if a beachhead of cooperation may push back the jungle of suspicion, let both sides join in creating a new endeavor, not a new balance of power, but a new world of law, where the strong are just and the weak secure and the peace preserved.

All this will not be finished in the first 100 days. Nor will it be finished in the first 1,000 days, nor in the life of this Administration, nor even perhaps in our lifetime on this planet. But let us begin.

In your hands, my fellow citizens, more than in mine, will rest the final success or failure of our course. Since this country was founded, each generation of Americans has been summoned to give testimony to its national loyalty. The graves of young Americans who answered the call to service surround the globe.

Now the trumpet summons us again—not as a call to bear arms, though arms we need; not as a call to battle, though embattled we are—but a call to bear the burden of a long twilight struggle, year in and year out, "rejoicing in hope, patient in tribulation"—a struggle against the common enemies of man: tyranny, poverty, disease, and war itself.

Can we forge against these enemies a grand and global alliance, North and South, East and West, that can assure a more fruitful life for all mankind? Will you join in that historic effort?

In the long history of the world, only a few generations have been granted the role of defending freedom in its hour of maximum danger. I do not shrink from this responsibility—I welcome it. I do not believe that any of us would exchange places with any other people or any other generation. The energy, the faith, the devotion which we bring to this endeavor will light our country and all who serve it—and the glow from that fire can truly light the world.

And so, my fellow Americans: ask not what your country can do for you—ask what you can do for your country.

My fellow citizens of the world: ask not what America will do for you, but what together we can do for the freedom of man.

Finally, whether you are citizens of America or citizens of the world, ask of us the same high standards of strength and sacrifice which we ask of you. With a good conscience our only sure reward, with history the final judge of our deeds, let us go forth to lead the land we love, asking His blessing and His help, but knowing that here on earth God's work must truly be our own.

Leo Strauss

City and Man (1964)

Introduction

It is not self-forgetting and pain-loving antiquarianism nor self-forgetting and intoxicating romanticism which induces us to turn with passionate interest, with unqualified willingness to learn, toward the political thought of classical antiquity. We are impelled to do so by the crisis of our time, the crisis of the West.

It is not sufficient for everyone to obey and to listen to the Divine message of the City of Righteousness, the Faithful City. In order to propagate that message among the heathen, nay, in order to understand it as clearly and as fully as is humanly possible, one must also consider to what extent man could discern the outlines of that City if left to himself, to the proper exercise of his own powers. But in our age it is much less urgent to show that political philosophy is the indispensable handmaid of theology than to show that political philosophy is the rightful queen of the social sciences, the sciences of man and of human affairs: even the highest lawcourt in the land is more likely to defer to the contentions of social science than to the Ten Commandments as the words of the living God.

The theme of political philosophy is the City and Man. The City and Man is explicitly the theme of classical political philosophy. Modern political philosophy, while building on classical political philosophy, transforms it and thus no longer deals with that theme in its original terms. But one cannot understand the transformation, however legitimate, if one has not understood the original form.

Modern political philosophy presupposes Nature as understood by modern natural science and History as understood by the modern historical awareness. Eventually these presuppositions prove to be incompatible with modern political philosophy. Thus one seems to be confronted with the choice between abandoning political philosophy altogether and returning to classical political philosophy. Yet such a return seems to be impossible. For what has brought about the collapse of modern political philosophy seems to have buried classical political philosophy which did not even dream of the difficulties caused by what we believe to know of nature and history. Certain it is that a simple continuation of the tradition of classical political philosophy—of a tradition which was hitherto never entirely interrupted—is no longer possible. As regards modern political philosophy, it has been replaced by ideology: what originally was a political philosophy has turned into an ideology. This fact may be said to form the core of the contemporary crisis of the West.

That crisis was diagnosed at the time of World War I by Spengler as the going down (or decline) of the West. Spengler understood by the West one culture among a small number of high cultures. But the West was for him more than one high culture among a number of them. It was for him the comprehensive culture. It is the only culture which has conquered the earth. Above all, it is the only culture which is open to all cultures and which does not reject the other cultures as forms of barbarism or which tolerates them condescendingly as "underdeveloped"; it is the only culture which has acquired full consciousness of culture as such. Whereas "culture" originally and naively meant *the* culture of *the* mind, the derivative and reflective notion of "culture" necessarily implies that there is a variety of equally high cultures. But precisely since the West is the culture in which culture reaches full self-consciousness, it is the final culture: the owl of Minerva begins its flight in the dusk; the decline of the West is identical with the exhaustion of the very possibility of high culture; the highest possibilities of man are exhausted. But man's highest possibilities cannot be exhausted as long as there are still high human tasks—as long as the fundamental riddles which confront man, have not been solved to the extent to which they can be solved. We may therefore say that Spengler's analysis and prediction is wrong: our highest authority, natural science, considers itself susceptible of infinite progress, and this claim does not make sense, it seems, if the fundamental riddles are solved. If science is susceptible of infinite progress, there cannot be a meaningful end or completion of history; there can only be a brutal stopping of man's onward march through natural forces acting, by themselves or directed by human brains and hands.

However this may be, in one sense Spengler has proved to be right; some decline of the West has taken place before our eyes. In 1913 the West—in fact this country together with Great Britain and Germany—could have laid down the law for the rest of the earth without firing a shot. Surely for at least a century the West controlled the whole globe with ease. Today, so far from ruling the globe, the West's very survival is endangered by the East as it has not been since its beginning. From the Communist Manifesto it would appear that the victory of Communism would be the complete victory of the West—of the synthesis, transcending the national boundaries, of British industry, the French Revolution and German philosophy—over the East. We see that the victory of Communism would mean indeed the victory of originally Western natural science but surely at the same time the victory of the most extreme form of Eastern despotism.

However much the power of the West may have declined, however great the dangers to the West may be, that decline, that danger, nay, the defeat, even the destruction of the West would not necessarily prove that the West is in a crisis: the West could go down in honor, certain of its purpose. The crisis of the West consists in the West's having become uncertain of its purpose. The West was once certain of its purpose—of a purpose in which all men could be united, and hence it had a clear vision of its future as the future of mankind. We do no longer have that certainty and that clarity. Some among us even despair of the future, and this despair explains many forms of contemporary Western degradation. The foregoing statements are not meant to imply that no society can be healthy unless it is dedicated to a universal purpose, to a purpose in which all men can be united: a society can be tribal and yet healthy. But a society which was accustomed to understand itself in terms of a universal purpose, cannot lose faith in that purpose

without becoming completely bewildered. We find such a universal purpose expressly stated in our immediate past, for instance in famous official declarations made during the two World Wars. These declarations merely restate the purpose stated originally by the most successful form of modern political philosophy—a kind of that political philosophy which aspired to build on the foundation laid by classical political philosophy but in opposition to the structure erected by classical political philosophy, a society superior in truth and justice to the society toward which the classics aspired. According to the modern project, philosophy or science was no longer to be understood as essentially contemplative and proud but as active and charitable; it was to be in the service of the relief of man's estate; it was to be cultivated for the sake of human power; it was to enable man to become the master and owner of nature through the intellectual conquest of nature. Philosophy or science should make possible progress toward ever greater prosperity; it thus should enable everyone to share in all the advantages of society or life and therewith give full effect to everyone's natural right to comfortable self-preservation and all that that right entails or to everyone's natural right to develop all his faculties fully in concert with everyone else's doing the same. The progress toward ever greater prosperity would thus become, or render possible, the progress toward ever greater freedom and justice. This progress would necessarily be the progress toward a society embracing equally all human beings: a universal league of free and equal nations, each nation consisting of free and equal men and women. For it had come to be believed that the prosperous, free, and just society in a single country or in only a few countries is not possible in the long run: to make the world safe for the Western democracies, one must make the whole globe democratic, each country in itself as well as the society of nations. Good order in one country presupposes good order in all countries and among all countries. The movement toward the universal society or the universal state was thought to be guaranteed not only by the rationality, the universal validity, of the goal but also because the movement towards the goal seemed to be the movement of the large majority of men on behalf of the large majority of men: only small groups of men who, however, hold in thrall many millions of their fellow human beings and who defend their own antiquated interests, resist that movement.

This view of the human situation in general and of the situation in our century in particular retained a certain plausibility, not in spite of Fascism but because of it, until Communism revealed itself even to the meanest capacities as Stalinism and post-Stalinism, for Trotskyism, being a flag without an army and even without a general, is condemned or refuted by its own principle. For some time it appeared to many teachable Westerners—to say nothing of the unteachable ones—that Communism was only a parallel movement to the Western movement—as it were its somewhat impatient, wild, wayward twin who was bound to become mature, patient, and gentle. But except when in mortal danger, Communism responded to the fraternal greetings only with contempt or at most with manifestly dissembled signs of friendship; and when in mortal danger, it was as eager to receive Western help as it was determined to give not even sincere words of thanks in return. It was impossible for the Western movement to understand Communism as merely a new version of that eternal reactionism against which it had been fighting for centuries. It had to admit that the Western project which had provided in its way against all earlier forms of evil could not provide against the new form in speech or in deed. For some time it seemed sufficient to say that while the Western movement agrees with Communism regarding the goal—the universal prosperous society of free and equal men and women—it disagrees with it regarding the means: for Communism, the end, the common good of the whole human race, being the most sacred thing, justifies any means; whatever contributes to the achievement of the most sacred end partakes of its sacredness and is therefore itself sacred; whatever hinders the achievement of that end is devilish. The murder of Lumumba was described by a Communist as a reprehensible murder by which he implied that there can be irreprehensible murders, like the murder of Nagy. It came to be seen then that there is not only a difference of degree but of kind between the Western movement and Communism, and this difference was seen to concern morality, the choice of means. In other words, it became clearer than it had been for some time that no bloody or unbloody change of society can eradicate the evil in man: as long as there will be men, there will be malice, envy and hatred, and hence there cannot be a society which does not have to employ coercive restraint. For the same reason it could no longer be denied that Communism will remain, as long as it lasts in fact and not merely in name, the iron rule of a tyrant which is mitigated or aggravated by his fear of palace revolutions. The only restraint in which the West can put some confidence is the tyrant's fear of the West's immense military power.

The experience of Communism has provided the Western movement with a twofold lesson: a political lesson, a lesson regarding what to expect and what to do in the foreseeable future, and a lesson regarding the principles of politics. For the foreseeable future there cannot be a universal state, unitary or federative. Apart from the fact that there does not exist now a universal federation of nations but only of those nations which are called peace-loving, the federation that exists masks the fundamental cleavage. If that federation is taken too seriously, as a milestone on man's onward march toward the perfect and hence universal society, one is bound to take great risks supported by nothing but an inherited and perhaps antiquated hope, and thus to endanger the very progress one endeavors to bring about. It is imaginable that in the face of the danger of thermonuclear destruction, a federation, however incomplete, of nations outlaws wars, i.e. wars of aggression; but this means that it acts on the assumption that all present boundaries are just, i.e. in accordance with the self-determination of nations; but this assumption is a pious fraud of which the fraudulence is more evident than the piety. In fact, the only changes of present boundaries for which there is any provision are those not disagreeable to the Communists. One must also not forget the glaring disproportion between the legal equality and the factual inequality of the confederates. The factual inequality is recognized in the expression "underdeveloped nations." The expression implies the resolve to develop them fully, i.e. to make them either Communist or Western, and this despite the fact that the West claims to stand for cultural pluralism. Even if one would still contend that the Western purpose is as universal as the Communist, one must rest satisfied for the foreseeable future with a practical particularism. The situation resembles the one which existed during the centuries in which Christianity and Islam each raised its universal claim but had to be satisfied with uneasily coexisting with its antagonist. All this amounts to saying that for the foreseeable future, political society remains what it always has been: a partial or particular society whose most urgent and primary task is its self-reservation and whose highest task is its self-improvement. As for the meaning of self-improvement, we may observe that the same experience which has made the West doubtful of the viability of a world-society has made it doubtful of the belief that affluence is the sufficient and even necessary condition of happiness and justice: affluence does not cure the deepest evils.

The doubt of the modern project is more than merely a strong but vague feeling. It has acquired the status of scientific exactitude. One may wonder whether there is a single social scientist left who would assert that the universal and prosperous society constitutes the rational solution of the human problem. For present-day social science admits and even proclaims its inability to validate any value-judgments proper. The teaching originated by modern political philosophy in favor of the universal and prosperous society has admittedly become an ideology—a teaching not superior in truth and justice to any other among the innumerable ideologies. Social science which studies all ideologies is itself free from all ideological biases. Through this Olympian freedom it overcomes the crisis of our time. That crisis may destroy the conditions of social science: it cannot affect the validity of its findings.

Social science has not always been as skeptical or restrained as it has become during the last two generations. The change in the character of social science is not unconnected with the change in the status of the modern project. The modern project was originated as required by nature (natural right), *i.e.* it was originated by philosophers; the project was meant to satisfy in the most perfect manner the most powerful natural needs of men: nature was to be conquered for the sake of man who himself was supposed to possess a nature, an unchangeable nature; the originators of the project took it for granted that philosophy and science are identical. After some time it appeared that the conquest of nature requires the conquest of human nature and hence in the first place the questioning of the unchangeability of human nature: an unchangeable human nature might set absolute limits to progress. Accordingly, the natural needs of men

could no longer direct the conquest of nature; the direction had to come from reason as distinguished from nature, from the rational Ought as distinguished from the neutral Is. Thus philosophy (logic, ethics, esthetics) as the study of the Ought or the norms became separated from science as the study of the Is. The ensuing depreciation of reason brought it about that while the study of the Is or science succeeded ever more in increasing men's power, one could no longer distinguish between the wise or right and the foolish or wrong use of power. Science cannot teach wisdom. There are still some people who believe that this predicament will disappear when social science and psychology catch up with physics and chemistry. This belief is wholly unreasonable, for social science and psychology, however perfected, being sciences, can only bring about a still further increase of man's power; they will enable men to manipulate man still better than ever before; they will as little teach man how to use his power over man or non-man as physics and chemistry do. The people who indulge this hope have not grasped the bearing of the distinction between facts and values.

The decay of political philosophy into ideology reveals itself most obviously in the fact that in both research and teaching, political philosophy has been replaced by the history of political philosophy. This substitution can be excused as a well-meaning attempt to prevent, or at least to delay, the burial of a great tradition. In fact it is not merely a half measure but an absurdity: to replace political philosophy by the history of political philosophy means to replace a doctrine which claims to be true by a survey of more or less brilliant errors. The discipline which takes the place of political philosophy is the one which shows the impossibility of political philosophy. That discipline is logic. What for the time being is still tolerated under the name of history of political philosophy will find its place within a rational scheme of research and teaching in footnotes to the chapters in logic textbooks which deal with the distinction between factual judgments and value-judgments; those footnotes will supply slow learners with examples of the faulty transition, by which political philosophy stands or falls, from factual judgments to value-judgments.

It would be wrong to believe that in the new dispensation the place once occupied by political philosophy is filled entirely by logic however enlarged. A considerable part of the matter formerly treated by political philosophy is now treated by a non-philosophic political science which forms part of social science. This new political science is concerned with discovering laws of political behavior and ultimately universal laws of political behavior. Lest it mistake the peculiarities of the politics of the time and the places in which social science is at home for the character of all politics, it must study also the politics of other climes and other ages. The new political science thus becomes dependent on a kind of study which belongs to the comprehensive enterprise called universal history. It is controversial whether history can be modelled on the natural science on which the new political science aspires to be modelled. At any rate, the historical studies in which the new political science must engage must become concerned not only with the working of institutions but with the ideologies informing those institutions as well. Within the context of these studies, the meaning of an ideology is primarily the meaning in which its adherents understand it. In some cases the ideologies are known to have been originated by outstanding men. In such cases it becomes necessary to consider whether and how the ideology as conceived by the originator was modified by the adherents. For precisely if only the crude understanding of ideologies can be politically effective, it is necessary to grasp the characteristics of crudity: if the routinization of charisma is a permitted theme, the vulgarization of thought ought to be a permitted theme. One kind of ideology consists of the teachings of the political philosophers. These teachings may have played only a minor political role, but one cannot know this before one knows them solidly. This solid knowledge consists primarily in understanding the teachings of the political philosophers as they themselves meant them. Each of them was undoubtedly mistaken in believing that his teaching is the true and final teaching regarding political things: we know through a reliable tradition that this belief forms part of a rationalization; but the process of rationalization is not so thoroughly understood that it would not be worthwhile to study it in the case of the greatest minds; for all we know there may be various kinds of rationalization. It is then necessary to study the political philosophies as they were understood by their originators in contradistinction to the way in which they were understood by their adherents, and various kinds of their adherents, but also by their adversaries and even by detached or indifferent bystanders or historians. For indifference does not offer a sufficient protection against the danger that one identifies the view of the originator with a compromise between the views of his adherents and those of his adversaries. The genuine understanding of the political philosophies which is then necessary may be said to have been rendered possible by the shaking of all traditions; the crisis of our time may have the accidental advantage of enabling us to understand in an untraditional or fresh manner what was hitherto understood only in a traditional or derivative manner. This may apply especially to classical political philosophy which has been seen for a considerable time only through the lenses of modern political philosophy and its various successors.

Social science will then not live up to its claim if it does not concern itself with a genuine understanding of the political philosophies proper and therewith primarily of classical political philosophy. As has been indicated, such an understanding cannot be presumed to be available. It is frequently asserted today that such an understanding is not possible: all historical understanding is relative to the point of view of the historian, in particular to his country and his time; the historian cannot understand a teaching as it was meant by its originator but he necessarily understands it differently than its originator understood it; ordinarily the historian's understanding is inferior to the originator's understanding; in the best case the understanding will be a creative transformation of the original understanding. Yet it is hard to see how one can speak of a creative transformation of the original teaching if it is not possible to grasp the original teaching as such. Besides, one may grant that the initial point of view of the historian who studies a teaching expounded in the past necessarily differs from that of the originator of the teaching or, in other words, that the question which the historian addresses to his author necessarily differs from the question which his author attempted to answer; yet surely the primary duty of the historian consists in suspending his initial question in favor of the question with which his author is concerned or in learning to look at the subject matter in question from his author's point of view. To the extent to which the social scientist succeeds in this kind of study which is imposed on him by the requirements of social science, he not only enlarges the horizon of present-day social science, he even transcends the limitations of social science, for he learns to look at things in a manner which is as it were forbidden to the social scientist. He will have learned from his logic that his science rests on certain hypotheses, certainties or assumptions. He learns now to suspend these assumptions. He is thus compelled to make these assumptions his theme. Far from being merely one of the innumerable themes of social science, history of political philosophy, and not logic, proves to be the pursuit concerned with the presuppositions of social science.

Those presuppositions prove to be modifications of the principles of modern political philosophy, and these principles in turn prove to be modifications of the principles of classical political philosophy. One cannot understand the presuppositions of present-day social science without a return to classical political philosophy. Social science claims to be decisively superior to classical political philosophy which surely lacked the alleged insight into the radical difference between facts and values. When attempting to understand classical political philosophy on its own terms, the social scientist is compelled to wonder whether the distinction is as necessary or as evident as it seems today. He is compelled to wonder whether not present-day social science but classical political philosophy is the true science of political things. This suggestion is dismissed out of hand because a return to an earlier position is believed to be impossible. But one must realize that this belief is a dogmatic assumption whose hidden basis is the belief in progress or in the rationality of the historical process.

The return to classical political philosophy is both necessary and tentative or experimental. Not in spite but because of its tentative character, it must be carried out seriously, *i.e.* without squinting at our present predicament. There is no danger that we can ever become oblivious of this predicament since it is the incentive to our whole concern with the classics. We cannot reasonably expect that a fresh understanding of classical political philosophy will supply us with recipes for today's use. For the relative success of modern political philosophy has brought into being a kind of society wholly unknown to the classics, a kind of society to which the classical principles as stated and elaborated by the classics are not immediately applicable. Only we living today can possibly find a solution to the problems of today. But an adequate understanding of the principles as elaborated by the classics may be the indispensable starting point for an adequate analysis, to be achieved by us, of present-day society in its peculiar character, and for the wise application, to be achieved by us, of these principles to our tasks.

One can come to doubt the fundamental premise of present-day social science—the distinction between values and facts—by merely considering the reasons advanced in its support as well as the consequences following from it. These considerations lead one to see that the issue concerning that distinction is part of a larger issue. The distinction is alien to that understanding of political things which belongs to political life but it becomes necessary, it seems, when the citizens' understanding of political things is replaced by the scientific understanding. The scientific understanding implies then a break with the pre-scientific understanding, yet at the same time it remains dependent on the pre-scientific understanding. Regardless of whether the superiority of the scientific understanding to the pre-scientific understanding can be demonstrated or not, the scientific understanding is secondary or derivative. Hence, social science cannot reach clarity about its doings if it does not possess a coherent and comprehensive understanding of what is frequently called the common sense view of political things, *i.e.* if it does not primarily understand the political things as they are experienced by the citizen or statesman; only if it possesses such a coherent and comprehensive understanding of its basis or matrix can it possibly show the legitimacy, and make intelligible the character, of that peculiar modification of the primary understanding of political things which is their scientific understanding. We contend that that coherent and comprehensive understanding of political things is available to us in Aristotle's *Politics* precisely because the *Politics* contains the original form of political science: that form in which political science is nothing other than the fully conscious form of the common sense understanding of political things. Classical political philosophy is the primary form of political science because the common sense understanding of political things is primary.

ALLEN GINSBERG

America (1956)

America I've given you all and now I'm nothing.
America two dollars and twenty seven cents January
    17, 1956.
I can't stand my own mind.
America when will we end the human war?
Go fuck yourself with your atom bomb.
I don't feel good don't bother me.
I won't write my poem till I'm in my right mind.
America when will you be angelic?
When will you take off your clothes?
When will you look at yourself through the grave?
When will you be worthy of your million
    Trotskyites?
America why are your libraries full of tears?
America when will you send your eggs to India?
I'm sick of your insane demands.
When can I go into the supermarket and buy what I
    need with my good looks?
America after all it is you and I who are perfect not
    the next world.
Your machinery is too much for me.
You made me want to be a saint.
There must be some other way to settle this
    argument.
Burroughs is in Tangiers I don't think he'll come
    back it's sinister.
Are you being sinister or is this some form of
    practical joke?
I'm trying to come to the point.
I refuse to give up my obsession.
America stop pushing I know what I'm doing.
America the plum blossoms are falling.
I haven't read the newspapers for months, everyday
    somebody goes on trial for murder.
America I feel sentimental about the Wobblies.
America I used to be a communist when I was a
    kid. I'm not sorry.
I smoke marijuana every chance I get.
I sit in my house for days on end and stare at the
    roses in the closet.

When I go to Chinatown I get drunk and never get
    laid.
My mind is made up there's going to be trouble.
You should have seen me reading Marx.
My psychoanalyst thinks I'm perfectly right.
I won't say the Lord's Prayer.
I have mystical visions and cosmic vibrations.
America I still haven't told you what you did to
    Uncle Max after he came over from Russia.

I'm addressing you.
Are you going to let your emotional life be run by
    Time Magazine?
I'm obsessed by Time Magazine.
I read it every week.
Its cover stares at me every time I slink past the
    corner candy store.
I read it in the basement of the Berkeley Public
    Library.
It's always telling me about responsibility.
    Businessmen are serious. Movie producers
    are serious. Everybody's serious but me.
It occurs to me that I am America.
I am talking to myself again.

Asia is rising against me.
I haven't got a chinaman's chance.
I'd better consider my national resources.
My national resources consist of two joints of
    marijuana millions of genitals an unpublishable
    private literature that goes 1400 miles an hour
    and twenty-five-thousand mental institutions.
I say nothing about my prisons nor the millions of
    underprivileged who live in my flowerpots under
    the light of five hundred suns.
I have abolished the whorehouses of France,
    Tangiers is the next to go.
My ambition is to be President despite the fact that
    I'm a Catholic.

America how can I write a holy litany in your silly
    mood?

I will continue like Henry Ford my strophes are as
    individual as his automobiles more so they're all
    different sexes.
America I will sell you strophes $2500 a piece $500
    down on your old strophe.
America free Tom Mooney.
America save the Spanish Loyalists.
America Sacco & Vanzetti must not die.
America I am the Scottsboro boys.
America when I was seven momma took me to
    Communist Cell meetings they sold us
    garbanzos a handful per ticket a ticket costs a
    nickel and the speeches were free everybody was
    angelic and sentimental about the workers it was
    all so sincere you have no idea what a good thing
    the party was in 1835 Scott Nearing was a grand
    old man a real mensch Mother Bloor made me
    cry I once saw Israel Amter plain. Everybody
    must have been a spy.
America you don't really want to go to war.
America it's them bad Russians.
Them Russians them Russians and them
    Chinamen. And them Russians.

The Russia wants to eat us alive. The Russia's power
    mad. She wants to take our cars from out our
    garages.
Her wants to grab Chicago. Her needs a Red
    Readers' Digest. Her wants our auto plants in
    Siberia. Him big bureaucracy running our
    fillingstations.
That no good. Ugh. Him make Indians learn read.
    Him need big black niggers. Hah. Her make us
    all work sixteen hours a day. Help.
America this is quite serious.
America this is the impression I get from looking in
    the television set.
America is this correct?
I'd better get right down to the job.
It's true I don't want to join the Army or turn lathes
    in precision parts factories, I'm nearsighted and
    psychopathic anyway.
America I'm putting my queer shoulder to the
    wheel.

Berkeley, January 17, 1956

LAWRENCE FERLINGHETTI

I Am Waiting (1958)

I am waiting for my case to come up
and I am waiting
for a rebirth of wonder
and I am waiting for someone
to really discover America
and wail
and I am waiting
for the discovery
of a new symbolic western frontier
and I am waiting
for the American Eagle
to really spread its wings
and straighten up and fly right
and I am waiting

for the Age of Anxiety
to drop dead
and I am waiting
for the war to be fought
which will make the world safe
for anarchy
and I am waiting
for the final withering away
of all governments
and I am perpetually awaiting
a rebirth of wonder

I am waiting for the Second Coming
and I am waiting

for a religious revival
to sweep thru the state of Arizona
and I am waiting
for the Grapes of Wrath to be stored
and I am waiting
for them to prove
that God is really American
and I am seriously waiting
for Billy Graham and Elvis Presley
to exchange roles seriously
and I am waiting
to see God on television
piped onto church altars
if only they can find
the right channel
to tune in on
and I am waiting
for the Last Supper to be served again
with a strange new appetizer
and I am perpetually awaiting
a rebirth of wonder

I am waiting for my number to be called
and I am waiting
for the living end
and I am waiting
for dad to come home
his pockets full
of irradiated silver dollars
and I am waiting
for the atomic tests to end
and I am waiting happily
for things to get much worse
before they improve
and I am waiting
for the Salvation Army to take over
and I am waiting
for the human crowd
to wander off a cliff somewhere
clutching its atomic umbrella
and I am waiting
for Ike to act
and I am waiting
for the meek to be blessed
and inherit the earth
without taxes
and I am waiting
for forests and animals

to reclaim the earth as theirs
and I am waiting
for a way to be devised
to destroy all nationalisms
without killing anybody
and I am waiting
for linnets and planets to fall like rain
and I am waiting for lovers and weepers
to lie down together again
in a new rebirth of wonder

I am waiting for the Great Divide to be crossed
and I am anxiously waiting
for the secret of eternal life to be discovered
by an obscure general practitioner
and save me forever from certain death
and I am waiting
for life to begin
and I am waiting
for the storms of life
to be over
and I am waiting
to set sail for happiness
and I am waiting
for a reconstructed Mayflower
to reach America
with its picture story and tv rights
sold in advance to the natives
and I am waiting
for the lost music to sound again
in the Lost Continent
in a new rebirth of wonder

I am waiting for the day
that maketh all things clear
and I am waiting
for Ole Man River
to just stop rolling along
past the country club
and I am waiting
for the deepest South
to just stop Reconstructing itself
in its own image
and I am waiting
for a sweet desegregated chariot
to swing low
and carry me back to Ole Virginie
and I am waiting
for Ole Virginie to discover

just why Darkies are born
and I am waiting
for God to lookout
from Lookout Mountain
and see the *Ode to the Confederate Dead*
as a real farce
and I am awaiting retribution
for what America did
to Tom Sawyer
and I am perpetually awaiting
a rebirth of wonder

I am waiting for Tom Swift to grow up
and I am waiting
for the American Boy
to take off Beauty's clothes
and get on top of her
and I am waiting
for Alice in Wonderland
to retransmit to me
her total dream of innocence
and I am waiting
for Childe Roland to come
to the final darkest tower
and I am waiting
for Aphrodite

to grow live arms
at a final disarmament conference
in a new rebirth of wonder

I am waiting
to get some intimations
of immortality
by recollecting my early childhood
and I am waiting
for the green mornings to come again
youth's dumb green fields come back again
and I am waiting
for some strains of unpremeditated art
to shake my typewriter
and I am waiting to write
the great indelible poem
and I am waiting
for the last long careless rapture
and I am perpetually waiting
for the fleeing lovers on the Grecian Urn
to catch each other up at last
and embrace
and I am awaiting
perpetually and forever
a renaissance of wonder

6

THE GREAT SOCIETY AND ITS CRITICS

Two major issues dominated American political life during the 1960s and early 1970s: the Vietnam War and the civil rights movement. Both were rooted in America's involvement in World War II. The attack on Pearl Harbor and the eventual discovery of the atrocities committed by Germany and its allies helped reverse a generation of isolationism in American foreign policy. The threats to democracy were now global—and ideological—and America, now a world superpower, adopted an aggressive policy to check those threats. American leadership committed to the policy of containment. When a communist threat emerged in Indochina in the 1950s, America responded, first with money and military advisors to aid the French, and soon thereafter, and increasingly, with troops of its own.

The war in Vietnam and other American responses to communist expansion, including the Marshall Plan, the Korean War, and the Bay of Pigs, were all driven by containment policies formed during the Truman administration following the strategies of George Kennan and fueled by the "domino theory." But the Vietnam War proved particularly divisive at home. In 1967 Martin Luther King, Jr., publicly called the United States "the greatest purveyor of violence in the world." The Tet Offensive (January–June) and the My Lai Massacre (March) in 1968 further increased American disillusionment and opposition to American engagement in Vietnam. On March 31, 1968, President Lyndon Johnson announced that he would not seek reelection, a consequence of the political tumult caused by the war— unrest that intensified during the chaos of the 1968 Democratic Convention that summer in Chicago and later in the fatal shooting of antiwar protesters at Kent State and Jackson State in 1970.

Nonetheless, containment remained the policy, having been firmly etched into the American political psyche by President John F. Kennedy, who in 1961 promised that the nation would "bear any burden, meet any hardship, support any friend, [and] oppose any foe in order to assure the survival and success of liberty." That commitment to liberty abroad contrasted sharply with the halting pace of domestic reform, exposing the tepid response to combating racism and oppression at home. In his 1964 acceptance speech at the Republican National Convention, Arizona senator Barry Goldwater, standing firm against communism, declaimed: "I would remind you that extremism in the defense of liberty is no vice. And let me remind you also that moderation in the pursuit of justice is no virtue." But Goldwater was also the first Republican presidential candidate to campaign seriously in the South, advocating "states' rights," a position that militated against rapid and substantive social change. Goldwater's commitment— and after him, that of politicians like Ronald Reagan—to local government was principled, grounded in the Jeffersonian notion that democratic government works best when most accountable to the people, and thus should be as close to the people as possible. But for a generation of Southern politicians committed to "massive resistance," the principle of "states' rights" resonated conveniently with an obstructionist agenda that sought to implement the Supreme Court's *Brown et al. v. Board of Education of Topeka, Kansas* decision as slowly as possible.

Throughout the South, belligerent tactics prevented the mandated desegregation of America's educational system. Indeed, despite the 1954 *Brown* ruling, it was not until 1963 that James Meredith, an African American student, was permitted to enroll at the University of Mississippi. Federal troops were deployed to enforce desegregation in Little Rock, Arkansas. African Americans boycotted buses in

Birmingham, Alabama. Segregated lunch counters became a battleground throughout the South. These and other protests culminated in the historic March on Washington for Jobs and Freedom in August 1963. It was at this gathering on behalf of racial equality and social justice, that Dr. King delivered his brilliant "I Have a Dream" speech, reproving America for defaulting on its promissory note guaranteeing all citizens the rights to "life, liberty, and the pursuit of happiness." While the practice of de jure segregation had been unanimously renounced by the Supreme Court in *Brown*, little had changed. Now, King urged, was the "time to make justice a reality for all of God's children."

The ongoing resistance to social and political change exacerbated already strained racial tensions, particularly in America's inner cities. "What happens to a dream deferred?" the poet Langston Hughes asked, and his suggested answer—that it explodes—proved prescient. In 1965 a major riot broke out in Watts (Los Angeles), and the violence soon spread to cities like Newark, Detroit, and Washington D.C. President Johnson and Congress responded to the growing crisis with ambitious legislation shaped by Johnson's vision for a "Great Society" in which poverty and racial injustice no longer existed, and in which personal freedom and cultural and natural beauty abounded. Following Johnson's leadership, Congress enacted major antipoverty legislation (the 1964 Economic Opportunity Act); the 1965 Elementary and Secondary Education Act, which provided substantial federal dollars to public schools; the Medicare and Medicaid programs in 1965 and 1966, respectively; numerous environmental laws; and a series of consumer protection laws. Congress also approved the 1965 Voting Rights Act and three civil rights acts: the 1964 act, prohibiting job discrimination and segregation in public accommodations; the 1965 Immigration and Nationality Services Act, which eliminated the nationality-origin quotas that had been at the core of U.S. immigration since 1924; and the 1968 act, which banned discrimination in housing.

The administration stirred further controversy when, seeking to alleviate the chronic unemployment that plagued African Americans, it initiated affirmative action policies. A section of the 1964 Civil Rights Act permitted courts to require employers to take "affirmative action" when job applicants were deliberately denied work on the basis of race. The following year, President Johnson issued Executive Order 11246, one of a series of executive orders dating back to the presidency of Franklin Delano Roosevelt that addressed the issue of racial discrimination in employment. Johnson's order prohibited racial discrimination by companies under contract with the federal government and required those companies to take affirmative action in hiring minorities, mandating fair treatment of all employees regardless of "race, creed, color, or national origin." Initially, this policy of affirmative action was color-blind, but subsequent judicial statutory interpretations—and most importantly, the implementation of the race-conscious Philadelphia Plan by Republican President Richard Nixon—attached explicit racial quotas to the policy of affirmative action.

Such reforms notwithstanding, new voices emerged to demand deeper and more rapid change. Organizations like the Student Nonviolent Coordinating Committee (SNCC) depicted Dr. King and the Southern Christian Leadership Conference (SCLC) as too moderate and too dependent on the largesse of white liberals, and challenged King's policy of nonviolent protest. King and the SCLC sought lasting reform through spiritual conversion, calling on white Southerners to "realize that the treatment of Negroes is a basic spiritual problem" while firmly adhering to nonviolent resistance. But the SNCC, the Black Panther Party for Self-Defense, and a new generation of charismatic African American leaders like Malcolm X promoted "black power" and "black nationalism." These groups questioned whether the peaceful methods and integrationist goals of Dr. King were realistic. Instead, they called for greater independence and economic, social, cultural, and political empowerment, emphasizing self-reliance rather than integration for African Americans. Moreover, they now viewed violence as an option in the struggle for justice. "I don't favor violence," Malcolm X said. "If we could bring about recognition and respect of our people by peaceful means, well and good. Everybody would like to reach his objectives peacefully. But I'm also a realist. The only people in this country who are asked to be nonviolent are black people."

Similar criticism was voiced by white liberals on the radical left, such as the Students for a Democratic Society, who charged that the programs of the Great Society and institutional remedies afforded only superficial solutions to America's social ills. The promise of democracy and the transformative hope of social justice could be achieved, they argued, only through a more radical and systematic sociocultural revolution. Pervasive corruption and hypocrisy, along with the effects of centuries of racism, sexism, environmental destruction, and economic exploitation, required a decisive overhaul of American life if true democracy and justice were finally to be delivered.

This cultural emphasis on equality and rights also found voice in the women's movement. Betty Friedan's *The Feminine Mystique*, published in 1963, argued that women were unhappy in conforming to the *Leave It to Beaver* view of the good life. Women were unfulfilled serving merely as homemakers, dependent on men economically and politically. Women insisted on a revolution of their own, one that went beyond race to recognize sex and gender in the pursuit of equality and freedom. Friedan spearheaded the creation of the National Organization for Women (1966), institutionalizing the "sexual revolution." Central to Friedan's argument was the demand for economic, political, legal, and sexual autonomy for women. Birth control (especially the pill) became a key component of liberation for some women and a sign of changing attitudes about family roles, gender relationships, and individual privacy. The personal was becoming political in ways unforeseen by previous generations.

Many of the rulings issued by the Supreme Court in this period, and presented in this chapter, reflected this changing cultural understanding of rights, liberty, and equality. The Court continually spoke of the Constitution as a bulwark for individual dignity and personal privacy, particularly in its "reproductive rights" rulings (*Griswold v. Connecticut* in 1965 and *Roe v. Wade* in 1973), but also in its Fourth, Fifth, and Sixth Amendment jurisprudence. For example, the Court overturned a long-standing precedent in *Katz v. United States* (1967) when it ruled on personal privacy grounds that police must obtain a search warrant prior to wiretapping a public pay phone. Similarly, in *Miranda v. Arizona* (1966), the Court mandated specific guidelines for police when interrogating criminal suspects, finding that the existing "interrogation environment . . . is destructive of human dignity."

These judicial rulings were controversial, as were rulings concerning federalism, libel, obscenity, political speech, and religious liberty. Indeed, critics from the right decried a Court and culture that seemed to be waging war on the nation's social, economic, and political institutions and traditions. For conservative politicians, the threat to liberty did not lie in school prayer, in a robust federalism in which the states exercised autonomy in their police powers, or in a common law rule of decency that maintained decent norms for acceptable speech. Rather, the threat to liberty lurked in the prospect of a centralized, godless, impersonal state, one that unfairly confiscated the wealth of the industrious, and one that failed to confront foreign threats to Western liberty. Only free markets, they held, produce rational, enterprising, and moral citizens. Efforts to guarantee outcomes according to some preconceived notion of equity were at best inefficient and at worst the blueprint for social engineering. Such conceit, the argument held, failed to respect natural differences in human effort and ability, leveling worthwhile achievement in the process. Thus, the tax policies and social programs of FDR's New Deal and Johnson's Great Society failed to respect each person's right as sovereign over his or her own interests, eroding the virtues of self-reliance and personal responsibility.

Philosophers such as John Rawls and Michael Walzer, activists such as Russell Means, and statesmen-scholars such as the young Daniel Patrick Moynihan and Justice Thurgood Marshall offered alternative conceptions and assessments of the just society. Rawls' *Theory of Justice* returned to the social contract tradition to reconsider the just distribution of social goods. For a social arrangement to be just, Rawls concluded, it must be to the clear benefit of the least advantaged. Walzer asserted that a monopoly of advantages in one sphere of society, such as wealth, should never translate into dominance in other spheres, such as education or political empowerment. America appeared to fall short on these criteria. Activist Russell Means dedicated his efforts to the restoration of dignity among Native Americans, while in a controversial and groundbreaking report, Moynihan focused on the unfair burdens on African American families arising from the legacy of slavery and other forms of racial oppression. Finally, in 1987, twenty-two years after the Moynihan report and during the bicentennial of the Constitution, Justice Marshall excoriated the Founders, charging them with failure and hypocrisy in the generation of a document that frustrated the progress of freedom and equality, dooming an entire race to forced subjugation and demoralizing injustice.

James Baldwin

Nobody Knows My Name (1961)

The Discovery of What It Means to Be an American

"It is a complex fate to be an American," Henry James observed, and the principal discovery an American writer makes in Europe is just how complex this fate is. America's history, her aspirations, her peculiar triumphs, her even more peculiar defeats, and her position in the world—yesterday and today—are all so profoundly and stubbornly unique that the very word "America" remains a new, almost completely undefined and extremely controversial proper noun. No one in the world, seems to know exactly what it describes, not even we motley millions who call ourselves Americans.

I left America because I doubted my ability to survive the fury of the color problem here. (Sometimes I still do.) I wanted to prevent myself from becoming *merely* a Negro; or, even, merely a Negro writer. I wanted to find out in what way the *specialness* of my experience could be made to connect me with other people instead of dividing me from them. (I was as isolated from Negroes as I was from whites, which is what happens when a Negro begins, at bottom, to believe what white people say about him.)

In my necessity to find the terms on which my experience could be related to that of others, Negroes and whites, writers and non-writers, I proved, to my astonishment, to be as American as any Texas G.I. And I found my experience was shared by every American writer I knew in Paris. Like me, they had been divorced from their origins, and it turned out to make very little difference that the origins of white Americans were European and mine were African— they were no more at home in Europe than I was.

The fact that I was the son of a slave and they were the sons of free men meant less, by the time we confronted each other on European soil, than the fact that we were both searching for our separate identities. When we had found these, we seemed to

be saying, why, then, we would no longer need to cling to the shame and bitterness which had divided us so long.

It became terribly clear in Europe, as it never had been here, that we knew more about each Other than any European ever could. And, it also became clear that, no matter where our fathers had been born, or what they had endured, the fact of Europe had formed us both, was part of our identity and part of our inheritance.

I had been in Paris a couple of years before any of this became clear to me. When it did, I, like many a writer before me upon the discovery that his props have all been knocked out from under him, suffered a species of breakdown and was carried off to the mountains of Switzerland. There, in that absolutely alabaster landscape, armed with two Bessie Smith records and a typewriter, I began to try to re-create the life that I had fast known as a child and from which I had spent so many years in flight.

It was Bessie Smith, through her tone and her cadence, who helped me to dig back to the way I myself must have spoken when I was a pickaninny, and to remember the things I had heard and seen and felt. I had buried them very deep. I had never listened to Bessie Smith in America (in the same way that, for years, I would not touch watermelon), but in Europe she helped to reconcile me to being a "nigger."

I do not think that I could have made this reconciliation here. Once I was able to accept my role—as distinguished, I must say, from my "place"—in the extraordinary drama which is America, I was released from the illusion that I hated America.

The story of what can happen to an American Negro writer in Europe simply illustrates, in some relief, what can happen to any American writer there. It is not meant, of course, to imply that it happens to them all, for Europe can be very crippling, too; and, anyway, a writer, when he has made his first breakthrough, has simply won a crucial skirmish in a dangerous, unending and unpredictable battle. Still, the breakthrough is important, and the point is that an American writer, in order to achieve it, very often has to leave this country.

The American writer, in Europe, is released, first of all, from the necessity of apologizing for himself. It is not until he *is* released from the habit of flexing his muscles and proving that he is just a "regular guy" that he realizes how crippling this habit has been. It is not necessary for him, there, to pretend to be something he is not, for the artist does not encounter in Europe the same suspicion he encounters here. Whatever the Europeans may actually think of artists, they have killed enough of them off by now to know that they are as real—and as persistent—as rain, snow, taxes or businessmen.

Of course, the reason for Europe's comparative clarity concerning the different functions of men in society is that European society has always been divided into classes in a way that American society never has been. A European writer considers himself to be part of an old and honorable tradition—of intellectual activity, of letters—and his choice of a vocation does not cause him any uneasy wonder as to whether or not it will cost him all his friends. But this tradition does not exist in America.

On the contrary, we have a very deep-seated distrust of real intellectual effort (probably because we suspect that it will destroy, as I hope it does, that myth of America to which we cling so desperately). An American writer fights his way to one of the lowest rungs on the American social ladder by means of pure bull-headedness and an indescribable series of odd jobs. He probably *has* been a "regular fellow" for much of his adult life, and it is not easy for him to step out of that lukewarm bath.

We must, however, consider a rather serious paradox: though American society is more mobile than Europe's, it is easier to cut across social and occupational lines there than it is here. This has something to do, I think, with the problem of status in American life. Where everyone has status, it is also perfectly possible, after all, that no one has. It seems inevitable, in any case, that a man may become uneasy as to just what his status is.

But Europeans have lived with the idea of status for a long time. A man can be as proud of being a good waiter as of being a good actor, and in neither case feel threatened. And this means that the actor and the waiter can have a freer and more genuinely friendly relationship in Europe than they are likely to have here. The waiter does not feel, with obscure resentment, that the actor has "made it," and the actor is not tormented by the fear; that he may find himself, tomorrow, once again a waiter.

This lack of what may roughly be called social paranoia causes the American writer in Europe to feel—almost certainly for the first time in his life—that he can reach out to everyone, that he is accessible to everyone and open to everything. This is an extraordinary feeling. He feels, so to speak, his own weight, his own value.

It is as though he suddenly came out of a dark tunnel and found himself beneath the open sky. And, in fact, in Paris, I began to see the sky for what seemed to be the first time. It was borne in on me—and it did not make me feel melancholy—that this sky had been there before I was born and would be there when I was dead. And it was up to me, therefore, to make of my brief opportunity the most that could be made.

I was born in New York, but have lived only in pockets of it. In Paris, I lived in all parts of the city—on the Right Bank and the Left, among the bourgeoisie and among *les misérables*, and knew all kinds of people, from pimps and prostitutes in Pigalle to Egyptian bankers in Neuilly. This may sound extremely unprincipled or even obscurely immoral: I found it healthy. I love to talk to people, all kinds of people, and almost everyone, as I hope we still know, loves a man who loves to listen.

This perpetual dealing with people very different from myself caused a shattering in me of preconceptions I scarcely knew I held. The writer is meeting in Europe people who are not American, whose sense of reality is entirely different from his own. They may love or hate or admire or fear or envy this country—they see it, in any case, from another point of view, and this forces the writer to reconsider many things he had always taken for granted. This reassessment, which can be very painful, is also very valuable.

This freedom, like all freedom, has its dangers and its responsibilities. One day it begins to be borne in on the writer, and with great force, that he is living in Europe as an American. If he were living there as a European, he would be living on a different and far less attractive continent.

This crucial day may be the day on which an Algerian taxi-driver tells him how it feels to be an Algerian in Paris. It may be the day on which he passes a café terrace and catches a glimpse of the tense, intelligent and troubled face of Albert Camus. Or it may be the day on which someone asks him to explain Little Rock and he begins to feel that it would be simpler—and, corny as the words may sound, more honorable—to go to Little Rock than sit in Europe, on an American passport, trying to explain it.

This is a personal day, a terrible day, the day to which his entire sojourn has been tending. It is the day he realizes that there are no untroubled countries in this fearfully troubled world; that if he has been preparing himself for anything in Europe, he has been preparing himself—for America. In short, the freedom that the American writer finds in Europe brings him, full circle, back to himself, with the responsibility for his development where it always was: in his own hands.

Even the most incorrigible maverick has to be born somewhere. He may leave the group that produced him—he may be forced to—but nothing will efface his origins, the marks of which he carries with him everywhere. I think it is important to know this and even find it a matter for rejoicing, as the strongest people do, regardless of their station. On this acceptance, literally, the life, of a writer depends.

The charge has often been made against American writers that they do not describe society, and have no interest in it. They only describe individuals in opposition to it, or isolated from it. Of course, what the American writer is describing is his own situation. But what is *Anna Karenina* describing if not the tragic fate of the isolated individual, at odds with her time and place?

The real difference is that Tolstoy was describing an old and dense society in which everything seemed—to the people in it, though not to Tolstoy—to be fixed forever. And the book is a masterpiece because Tolstoy was able to fathom, and make us see, the hidden laws which really governed this society and made Anna's doom inevitable.

American writers do not have a fixed society to describe. The only society they know is one in which nothing is fixed and in which the individual must fight for his identity. This is a rich confusion, indeed, and it creates for the American writer unprecedented opportunities.

That the tensions of American life, as well as the possibilities, are tremendous is certainly not even a question. But these are dealt with in contemporary literature mainly compulsively; that is, the book is more likely to be a symptom of our tension than an examination of it. The time has come, God knows, for us to examine ourselves, but we can only do this if we are willing to free ourselves of the myth of America and try to find out what is really happening here.

Every society is really governed by hidden laws, by unspoken but profound assumptions on the part of the people, and ours is no exception. It is up to the American writer to find out what these laws and assumptions are in a society much given to smashing taboos without thereby managing to be liberated from them, it will be no easy matter.

It is no wonder, in the meantime, that the American writer keeps running off to Europe. He needs sustenance for his journey and the best models he can find. Europe has what we do not have yet, a sense of the mysterious and inexorable limits of life, a sense, in a word, of tragedy. And we have what they sorely need: a new sense of life's possibilities.

In this endeavor to wed the vision of the Old World with that of the New, it is the writer, not the statesman, who is our strongest arm. Though we do not wholly believe it yet, the interior life is a real life, and the intangible dreams of people have a tangible effect on the world.

Fifth Avenue, Uptown: A Letter from Harlem

There is a housing project standing now where the house in which we grew up once stood, and one of those stunted city trees is snarling where our doorway used to be. This is on the rehabilitated side of the avenue. The other side of the avenue—for progress takes time—has not been rehabilitated yet, and it looks exactly as it looked in the days when we sat with our noses pressed against the windowpane, longing to be allowed to go "across the street." The grocery store which gave us credit is still there, and there can be no doubt that it is still giving credit. The people in the project certainly need it—far more, indeed, than they ever needed the project. The last time I passed by, the Jewish proprietor was still standing among his shelves, looking sadder and heavier but scarcely any older. Farther down the block stands the shoe-repair store in which our shoes were repaired until reparation became impossible and in which, then, we bought all our "new" ones. The Negro proprietor is still in the window, head down, working at the leather.

These two, I imagine, could tell a long tale if they would (perhaps they would be glad to if they could), having watched so many, for so long, struggling in the fishhooks, the barbed wire, of this avenue.

The avenue is elsewhere the renowned and elegant Fifth. The area I am describing, which, in today's gang parlance, would be called "the turf," is bounded by Lenox Avenue on the west, the Harlem River on the east, 135th Street on the north, and 130th Street on the south. We never lived beyond these boundaries; this is where we grew up. Walking along 145th Street—for example—familiar as it is, and similar, does not have the same impact because I do not know any of the people on the block. But when I turn east on 131st Street and Lenox Avenue, there is first a soda-pop joint, then a shoeshine "parlor," then a grocery store, then a dry cleaner's, then the houses. All along the street there are people who watched me grow up, people who grew up with me, people I watched grow up along with my brothers and sisters; and, sometimes in my arms, sometimes underfoot, sometimes at my shoulder—or on it— their children, a riot, a forest of children, who include my nieces and nephews.

When we reach the end of this long block, we find ourselves on wide, filthy, hostile Fifth Avenue, facing that project which hangs over the avenue like a monument to the folly, and the cowardice, of good intentions. All along the block, for anyone who knows it, are immense human gaps, like craters. These gaps are not created merely by those who have moved away, inevitably into some other ghetto; or by those who have risen, almost always into a greater capacity for self-loathing and self-delusion; or yet by those who, by whatever means—World War II, the Korean war, a policeman's gun or billy, a gang war, a brawl, madness, an overdose of heroin or, simply, unnatural exhaustion—are dead. I am talking about those who are left, and I am talking principally about the young. What are they doing? Well, some, a minority, are fanatical churchgoers members, of the more extreme of the Holy Roller sects. Many, many more are "moslems," by affiliation or sympathy, that is to say that they are united by nothing more—and nothing less—than a hatred of the white world and all its works. They are present, for example, at every Buy Black street-corner meeting—meetings in which the speaker urges his hearers to cease trading with white men and establish a separate economy. Neither the speaker nor his hearers can possibly do this, of course, since Negroes do not own General Motors or RCA or the A&P, nor, indeed, do they own more than a wholly insufficient fraction of anything else in Harlem (those who *do* own anything are more interested in their profits than in their fellows). But these meetings nevertheless keep alive in the participators a certain pride of bitterness without which, however futile this bitterness may be, they could scarcely remain alive at all. Many have given up. They stay home and watch the TV screen, living on the earnings of their parents, cousins, brothers, or uncles; and only leave the house to go to the movies or to the nearest bar. "How're you making it?" one may ask, running into them along the block, or in the bar. "Oh, I'm TV-ing it"; with the saddest, sweetest, most shamefaced of smiles, and from a great distance. This distance one is compelled to respect; anyone who has traveled so far will not easily be dragged again into the world. There are further retreats, of course, than the TV screen or the bar. There are those who are simply sitting on their stoops, "stoned," animated for a moment only, and hideously, by the approach of someone who may lend them the money for a "fix." Or by the approach of someone from whom they can purchase it, one of the shrewd ones, on the way to prison or just coming out.

And the others, who have avoided all of these deaths, get up in the morning and go downtown to meet "the man." They work in the white man's world all day and come home in the evening to this fetid block. They struggle to instill in their children some private sense of honor or dignity which will help the child to survive. This means, of course, that they must struggle, stolidly, incessantly, to keep this sense alive in themselves, in spite of the insults, the indifference, and the cruelty they are certain to encounter in their working day. They patiently browbeat the landlord into fixing the heat, the plaster, the plumbing; this demands prodigious patience, nor is patience usually enough. In trying to make their hovels habitable, they are perpetually throwing good money after bad. Such frustration, so long endured, is driving many strong, admirable men and women whose only crime is color to the very gates of paranoia.

One remembers them from another time—playing handball in the playground, going to church, wondering if they were going to be promoted at school. One remembers them going off to war—gladly, to escape this block. One remembers their return. Perhaps one remembers their wedding day. And one sees where the girl is now—vainly looking for salvation from some other embittered, trussed, and struggling boy—and sees the all-but-abandoned children in the streets.

Now I am perfectly aware that there are other slums in which white men are fighting for their lives, and mainly losing. I know that blood is also flowing through those streets and that the human damage there is incalculable. People are continually pointing out to me the wretchedness of white people in order to console me for the wretchedness of blacks. But an itemized account of the American failure does not console me and it should not console anyone else. That hundreds of thousands of white people are living, in effect, no better than the "niggers" is not a fact to be regarded with complacency. The social and moral bankruptcy suggested by this fact is of the bitterest, most terrifying kind.

The people, however, who believe that this democratic anguish has some consoling value are always pointing out that So-and-So, white, and So-and-So, black, rose from the slums into the big time. The existences—the public existence—of, say, Frank Sinatra and Sammy Davis, Jr. proves to them that America is still the land of opportunity and that inequalities vanish before the determined will. It proves nothing of the sort. The determined will is rare—at the moment, in this country, it is unspeakably rare—and the inequalities suffered by the many are in no way justified by the rise of a few. A few have always risen—in every country, every era, and in the teeth of regimes which can by no stretch of the imagination be thought of as free. Not all of these people, it is worth remembering, left the world better than they found it. The determined will is rare, but it is not invariably

benevolent. Furthermore, the American equation of success with the big time reveals an awful disrespect for human life and human achievement. This equation has placed our cities among the most dangerous in the world and has placed our youth among the most empty and most bewildered. The situation of our youth is not mysterious. Children have never been very good at listening to their elders, but they have never failed to imitate them. They must, they have no other models. That is exactly what our children are doing. They are imitating our immorality, our disrespect for the pain of others.

All other slum dwellers, when the bank account permits it, can move out of the slum and vanish altogether from the eye of persecution. No Negro in this country, has ever made that much money and it will be a long time before any Negro does. The Negroes in Harlem, who have no money, spend what they have on such gimcracks as, they are sold. These include "wider" TV screens, more "faithful" hi-fi sets, more "powerful" cars, all of which, of course, are obsolete long before they are paid for. Anyone who has ever struggled with poverty knows how extremely expensive it is to be poor; and if one is a member of a captive population, economically speaking, one's feet have simply been placed on the treadmill forever. One is victimized, economically, in a thousand ways—rent, for example, or car insurance. Go shopping one day in Harlem—for anything—and compare Harlem prices and quality with those downtown.

The people who have managed to get off this block have only got as far as a more respectable ghetto. This respectable ghetto does not even have the advantages of the disreputable one—friends, neighbors, a familiar church, and friendly tradesmen; and it is not, moreover, in the nature of any ghetto to remain respectable long. Every Sunday, people who have left the block take the lonely ride back, dragging their increasingly discontented children with them. They spend the day talking, not always with words, about the trouble they've seen and the trouble—one must watch their eyes as they watch their children—they are only too likely to see. For children do not like ghettos. It takes them nearly no time to discover exactly why they are there.

The projects in Harlem are hated. They are hated almost as much as policemen, and this is saying a great deal. And they are hated for the same reason:

both reveal, unbearably, the real attitude of the white world, no matter how many liberal speeches are made, no matter how many lofty editorials are written, no matter how many civil-rights commissions are set up.

The projects are hideous, of course, there being a law, apparently respected throughout the world, that popular housing shall be as cheerless as a prison. They are lumped all over Harlem, colorless, bleak, high, and revolting. The wide windows look out on Harlem's invincible and indescribable squalor: the Park Avenue railroad tracks, around which, about forty years ago, the present dark community began; the unrehabilitated houses, bowed down, it would seem, under the great weight of frustration and bitterness they contain; the dark, the ominous schoolhouses from which the child may emerge maimed, blinded, hooked, or enraged for life; and the churches, churches, block upon block of churches, niched in the walls like cannon in the walls of a fortress. Even if the administration of the projects were not so insanely humiliating (for example: one must report raises in salary to the management, which will then eat up the profit by raising one's rent; the management has the right to know who is staying in your apartment; the management can ask you to leave, at their discretion), the projects would still be hated because they are an insult to the meanest intelligence.

Harlem got its first private project, Riverton[1]— which is now, naturally, a slum—about twelve years ago because at that time Negroes were not allowed to live in Stuyvesant Town. Harlem watched Riverton go up, therefore, in the most violent bitterness of spirit,

and hated it long before the builders arrived. They began hating it at about the time people began moving out of their condemned houses to make room for this additional proof of how thoroughly the white world despised them. And they had scarcely moved in, naturally, before they began smashing windows, defacing walls, urinating in the elevators, and fornicating in the playgrounds. Liberals, both white and black, were appalled at the spectacle. I was appalled by the liberal innocence—or cynicism, which comes out in practice as much the same thing. Other people were delighted to be able to point to proof positive that nothing could be done to better the lot of the colored people. They were, and are, right in one respect: that nothing can be done as long as they are treated like colored people. The people in Harlem know they are living there because white people do not think they are good enough to live anywhere else. No amount of "improvement" can sweeten this fact. Whatever money is now being earmarked to improve this, or any other ghetto, might as well be burnt. A ghetto can be improved in one way only: out of existence.

Similarly, the only way to police a ghetto is to be oppressive. None of the Police Commissioner's men, even with the best will in the world, have any way of understanding the lives led by the people they swagger about in twos and threes controlling. Their very presence is an insult, and it would be, even if they spent their entire day feeding gumdrops to children. They represent the force of the white world, and that world's real intentions are, simply, for that world's criminal profit and ease, to keep the black man corraled up here, in his place. The badge, the gun in the holster, and the swinging club make vivid what will happen should his rebellion become overt. Rare, indeed, is the Harlem citizen, from the most circumspect church member to the most shiftless adolescent, who does not have a long tale to tell of police incompetence, injustice, or brutality. I myself have witnessed and endured it more than once. The businessmen and racketeers also have a story. And so do the prostitutes. (And this is not, perhaps, the place to discuss Harlem's very complex attitude toward black policemen, nor the reasons, according to Harlem, that they are nearly all downtown.)

It is hard, on the other hand, to blame the policeman, blank, good-natured, thoughtless, and insuperably innocent, for being such a perfect representative

1. The inhabitants of Riverton were much embittered by this description; they have, apparently, forgotten how their project came into being; and have repeatedly informed me that I cannot possibly be referring to Riverton, but to another housing project which is directly across the street. It is quite clear, I think, that I have no interest in accusing any individuals or families of the depredations herein described, but neither can I deny the evidence of my own eyes. Nor do I blame anyone in Harlem for making the best of a dreadful bargain. But anyone who lives in Harlem and imagines he has **not** struck this bargain, or that what he takes to be his status (in whose eyes?) protects him against the common pain, demoralization, and danger, is simply self deluded.

of the people he serves. He, too, believes in good intentions and is astounded and offended when they are not taken for the deed. He has never, himself, done anything for which to be hated—which of us has?—and yet he is facing, daily and nightly, people who would gladly see him dead, and he knows it. There is no way for him not to know it; there are few things under heaven more unnerving than the silent, accumulating contempt and hatred of a people. He moves through Harlem, therefore, like an occupying soldier in a bitterly hostile country; which is precisely what, and where, he is, and is the reason he walks in twos and threes. And he is not the only one who knows why he is always in company: the people who are watching him know why, too. Any street meeting, sacred or secular, which he and his colleagues uneasily cover has as its explicit or implicit burden the cruelty and injustice of the white domination. And these days, of course, in terms increasingly vivid and jubilant, it speaks of the end of that domination. The white policeman standing on a Harlem street corner finds himself at the very center of the revolution now occurring in the world. He is not prepared for it—naturally, nobody, is—and, what is possibly much more to the point, he is exposed, as few white people are, to the anguish of the black people around him. Even if he is gifted with the merest mustard grain of imagination, something must seep in. He cannot avoid observing that some of the children, in spite of their color, remind him of children he has known and loved, perhaps even of his own children. He knows that he certainly does not want *his* children living this way. He can retreat from his uneasiness in only one direction, into a callousness which very shortly becomes second nature. He becomes more callous, the population becomes more hostile, the situation grows more tense, and the police force is increased. One day, to everyone's astonishment, someone drops a match in the powder keg and everything blows up. Before the dust has settled, or the blood congealed, editorials, speeches, and civil-rights commissions are loud in the land, demanding to know what happened. What happened is that Negroes want to be treated like men.

Negroes want to be treated like men: a perfectly straightforward statement, containing only seven words. People who have mastered Kant, Hegel, Shakespeare, Marx, Freud, and the Bible find this statement utterly impenetrable. The idea seems to threaten profound, barely conscious assumptions. A kind of panic paralyzes their features, as though they found themselves trapped on the edge of a steep place. I once tried to describe to a very well-known American intellectual the conditions among Negroes in the South. My recital disturbed him and made him indignant; and he asked me in perfect innocence, "Why don't all the Negroes in the South move North?" I tried to explain what *has* happened, unfailingly, whenever a significant body of Negroes move North. They do not escape Jim Crow, they merely encounter another, not-less-deadly variety. They do not move to Chicago, they move to the South Side; they do not move to New York, they move to Harlem. The pressure within the ghetto causes the ghetto walls to expand, and this expansion is always violent. White people hold the line as long as they can, and in as many ways as they can, from verbal intimidation to physical violence. But inevitably the border which has divided the ghetto from the rest of the world falls into the hands of the ghetto. The white people fall back bitterly before the black horde; the landlords make a tidy profit by raising the rent, chopping up the rooms, and all but dispensing with the upkeep; and what has once been a neighborhood turns into a "turf." This is precisely what happened when the Puerto Ricans arrived in their thousands—and the bitterness thus caused is, as I write, being fought out all up and down those streets.

Northerners indulge in an extremely dangerous luxury. They seem to feel that because they fought on the right side during the Civil War, and won, they have earned the right merely to deplore what is going on in the South, without taking any responsibility for it; and that they can ignore what is happening in Northern cities because what is happening in Little Rock or Birmingham is worse. Well, in the first place, it is not possible for anyone who has not endured both to know which is "worse." I know Negroes who prefer the South and white Southerners, because "At least there, you haven't got to play any guessing games!" The guessing games referred to have driven more than one Negro into the narcotics ward, the madhouse, or the river. I know another Negro, a man very dear to me, who says, with conviction and with truth, "The spirit of the South is the spirit of America." He was born in the North and did his military training in the South. He did not, as far as I can gather, find the South "worse"; he found it, if anything, all too familiar. In the second place, though, even if Birmingham *is* worse, no doubt Johannesburg, South Africa, beats it by several miles, and Buchenwald was one of the worst things that ever happened in the entire history of the world. The world has never lacked for horrifying examples, but I do not believe that these examples are meant to be used as justification for our own crimes. This perpetual justification empties the heart of all human feeling. The emptier our hearts become, the greater will be our crimes. Thirdly, the South is not merely an embarrassingly backward region, but a part of this country, and what happens there concerns every one of us.

As far as the color problem is concerned, there is but one great difference between the Southern white and the Northerner: the Southerner remembers, historically, and in his own psyche, a kind of Eden in which he loved black people and they loved him. Historically, the flaming sword laid across this Eden is the Civil War. Personally, it is the Southerner's sexual coming of age, when, without any warning, unbreakable taboos are set up between himself and his past. Everything, thereafter, is permitted him except the love he remembers and has never ceased to need. The resulting, indescribable torment affects every Southern mind and is the basis at the Southern hysteria.

None of this is true for the Northerner. Negroes represent nothing to him personally, except, perhaps, the dangers of carnality. He never sees Negroes. Southerners see them all the time. Northerners never think about them whereas Southerners are never really thinking of anything else. Negroes are, therefore, ignored in the North and are under surveillance in the South, and suffer hideously in both places. Neither the Southerner nor the Northerner is able to look on the Negro simply as a man. It seems to be indispensable to the national self-esteem that the Negro be considered either as a kind of ward (in which case we are told how many Negroes, comparatively, bought Cadillacs last year and how few, comparatively, were lynched), or as a victim (in which case we are promised that he will never vote in our assemblies or go to school with our kids). They are two sides of the same coin and the South will not change—*cannot* change—until the North changes. The country will not change until it reexamines itself and discovers what it really means by freedom. In the meantime, generations keep being born, bitterness is increased by incompetence, pride, and folly, and the world shrinks around us.

It is a terrible, an inexorable, law that one cannot deny the humanity of another without diminishing one's own; in the face of one's victim, one sees oneself. Walk through the streets of Harlem and see what we, this nation, have become.

Earl Warren

Brown et al. v. Board of Education of Topeka, Kansas (1954)

Mr. Chief Justice WARREN delivered the opinion of the Court.

These cases come to us from the States of Kansas, South Carolina, Virginia, and Delaware. They are premised on different facts and different local conditions, but a common legal question justifies their consideration together in this consolidated opinion.

In each of the cases, minors of the Negro race, through their legal representatives, seek the aid of the courts in obtaining admission to the public schools of their community on a nonsegregated basis. In each instance, they had been denied admission to schools attended by white children under laws requiring or permitting segregation according to race. This segregation was alleged to deprive the plaintiffs of the equal protection of the laws under the Fourteenth Amendment. In each of the cases other than the Delaware case, a three-judge federal district court denied relief to the plaintiffs on the so-called "separate but equal" doctrine announced by this Court in *Plessy v. Ferguson.* Under that doctrine, equality of treatment is accorded when the races are provided substantially equal facilities, even though these facilities be separate. In the Delaware case, the Supreme Court of Delaware adhered to that doctrine, but ordered that the plaintiffs be admitted to the white schools because of their superiority to the Negro schools.

The plaintiffs contend that segregated public schools are not "equal" and cannot be made "equal," and that hence they are deprived of the equal protection of the laws. Because of the obvious importance of the question presented, the Court took jurisdiction. Argument was heard in the 1952 Term, and reargument was heard this Term on certain questions propounded by the Court.

Reargument was largely devoted to the circumstances surrounding the adoption of the Fourteenth Amendment in 1868. It covered exhaustively consideration of the Amendment in Congress, ratification by the states, then existing practices in racial segregation, and the views of proponents and opponents of the Amendment. This discussion and our own investigation convince us that, although these sources cast some light, it is not enough to resolve the problem with which we are faced. At best, they are inconclusive. The most avid proponents of the post-War Amendments undoubtedly intended them to remove all legal distinctions among "all persons born or naturalized in the United States." Their opponents, just as certainly, were antagonistic to both the letter and the spirit of the Amendments and wished them to have the most limited effect. What others in Congress and the state legislatures had in mind cannot be determined with any degree of certainty.

An additional reason for the inconclusive nature of the Amendment's history, with respect to segregated schools, is the status of public education at that time. In the South, the movement toward free common schools, supported by general taxation, had not yet taken hold. Education of white children was largely in the hands of private groups. Education of Negroes was almost nonexistent, and practically all of the race were illiterate. In fact, any education of Negroes was forbidden by law in some states. Today, in contrast, many Negroes have achieved outstanding success in the arts and sciences as well as in the business and professional world. It is true that public school education at the time of the Amendment had advanced further in the North, but the effect of the Amendment on Northern States was generally ignored in the congressional debates. Even in the North, the conditions of public education did not approximate those existing today. The curriculum was usually rudimentary; ungraded schools were common in rural areas; the school term was but three months a year in many states; and compulsory school attendance was virtually unknown. As a consequence, it is not surprising that there should be so little in the history of the Fourteenth Amendment relating to its intended effect on public education.

In the first cases in this Court construing the Fourteenth Amendment, decided shortly after its adoption, the Court interpreted it as proscribing all state-imposed discriminations against the Negro race. The doctrine of "separate but equal" did not make its appearance in this Court until 1896 in the case of *Plessy v. Ferguson,* involving not education but transportation. American courts have since labored with the doctrine for over half a century. In this Court, there have been six cases involving the "separate but equal" doctrine in the field of public education. In *Cumming v. County Board of Education* [1899], and *Gong Lum v. Rice* [1927], the validity of the doctrine itself was not challenged. In more recent cases, all on the graduate school level, inequality was found in that specific benefits enjoyed by white students were denied to Negro students of the same educational qualifications. *Missouri ex rel. Gaines v. Canada* [1938]; *Sipuel v. Oklahoma* [1948]; *Sweatt v. Painter* [1950]; *McLaurin v. Oklahoma State Regents* [1950]. In none of these cases was it necessary to re-examine the doctrine to grant relief to the Negro plaintiff. And in *Sweatt v. Painter,* the Court expressly reserved decision on the question whether *Plessy v. Ferguson* should be held inapplicable to public education.

In the instant cases, that question is directly presented. Here, unlike *Sweatt v. Painter,* there are findings below that the Negro and white schools involved have been equalized, or are being equalized, with respect to buildings, curricula, qualifications and salaries of teachers, and other "tangible" factors. Our decision, therefore, cannot turn on merely a comparison of these tangible factors in the Negro and white schools involved in each of the cases. We must look instead to the effect of segregation itself on public education.

In approaching this problem, we cannot turn the clock back to 1868 when the Amendment was adopted, or even to 1896 when *Plessy v. Ferguson* was written. We must consider public education in the light of its full development and its present place in American life throughout the Nation. Only in this way can it be determined if segregation in public schools deprives these plaintiffs of the equal protection of the laws.

Today, education is perhaps the most important function of state and local governments. Compulsory school attendance laws and the great expenditures for education both demonstrate our recognition of the importance of education to our democratic society. It is required in the performance of our most basic public responsibilities, even service in the armed forces. It is the very foundation of good citizenship. Today it is a principal instrument in awakening the child to cultural values, in preparing him for later professional training, and in helping him to adjust normally to his environment. In these days, it is doubtful that any child may reasonably be expected to succeed in life if he is denied the opportunity of an education. Such an opportunity, where the state has undertaken to provide it, is a right which must be made available to all on equal terms.

We come then to the question presented: Does segregation of children in public schools solely on the basis of race, even though the physical facilities and other "tangible" factors may be equal, deprive the children of the minority group of equal educational opportunities? We believe that it does.

In *Sweatt v. Painter*, in finding that a segregated law school for Negroes could not provide them equal educational opportunities, this Court relied in large part on "those qualities which are incapable of objective measurement but which make for greatness in a law school." In *McLaurin v. Oklahoma State Regents*, the Court, in requiring that a Negro admitted to a white graduate school be treated like all other students, again resorted to intangible considerations:

". . . his ability to study, to engage in discussions and exchange views with other students, and, in general, to learn his profession." Such considerations apply with added force to children in grade and high schools. To separate them from others of similar age and qualifications solely because of their race generates a feeling of inferiority as to their status in the community that may affect their hearts and minds in a way unlikely ever to be undone. The effect of this separation on their educational opportunities was well stated by a finding in the Kansas case by a court which nevertheless felt compelled to rule against the Negro plaintiffs:

> Segregation of white and colored children in public schools has a detrimental effect upon the colored children. The impact is greater when it has the sanction of the law; for the policy of separating the races is usually interpreted as denoting the inferiority of the negro group. A sense of inferiority affects the motivation of a child to learn. Segregation with the sanction of law, therefore, has a tendency to [retard] the educational and mental development of negro children and to deprive them of some of the benefits they would receive in a racial[ly] integrated school system.

Whatever may have been the extent of psychological knowledge at the time of *Plessy v. Ferguson*, this finding is amply supported by modern authority. Any language in *Plessy v. Ferguson* contrary to this finding is rejected.

We conclude that in the field of public education the doctrine of "separate but equal" has no place. Separate educational facilities are inherently unequal. Therefore, we hold that the plaintiffs and others similarly situated for whom the actions have been brought are, by reason of the segregation complained of, deprived of the equal protection of the laws guaranteed by the Fourteenth Amendment. This disposition makes unnecessary any discussion whether such segregation also violates the Due Process Clause of the Fourteenth Amendment.

Because these are class actions, because of the wide applicability of this decision, and because of the great variety of local conditions, the formulation of decrees in these cases presents problems of considerable complexity. On reargument, the consideration of appropriate relief was necessarily subordinated to the primary question—the constitutionality of segregation in public education. We have now announced that such segregation is a denial of the equal protection of the laws. In order that we may have the full assistance of the parties in formulating decrees, the cases will be restored to the docket, and the parties are requested to present further argument on Questions 4 and 5 previously propounded by the Court for the reargument this Term. The Attorney General of the United States is again invited to participate. The Attorneys General of the states requiring or permitting segregation in public education will also be permitted to appear as amici curiae upon request to do so by September 15, 1954, and submission of briefs by October 1, 1954.

It is so ordered.

HANNAH ARENDT

Reflections on Little Rock[1] (1959)

Preliminary Remarks

This article was written more than a year ago upon the suggestion of one of the editors of Commentary. *It was a topical article whose publication was delayed for months because of the controversial nature of my reflections which, obviously, were at variance with the magazine's stand on matters of discrimination and segregation. Meanwhile, things had quieted down temporarily; I had hopes that my fears concerning the seriousness of the situation might prove exaggerated and no longer wished to publish this article. Recent developments have convinced me that such hopes are futile and that the routine repetition of liberal clichés may be even more dangerous than I thought a year ago. I therefore agreed to let* Dissent *publish the article as it was written—not because I thought that a year-old topical essay could possibly exhaust the subject or even do justice to the many difficult problems involved, but in the hope that even an inadequate attempt might help to break the dangerous routine in which the discussion of these issues is being held from both sides.*

*There are, however, two points which were brought to my attention after I wrote the article which I would like to mention at least. The first concerns my contention that the marriage laws in 29 of the 49 states constitute a much more flagrant breach of letter and spirit of the Constitution than segregation of schools. To this, Sidney Hook (*New Leader, *April 13), replied that Negroes were "profoundly uninterested" in these laws; in their eyes, "the discriminatory ban against intermarriages and miscegenation is last in the order of priorities." I have my doubts about this, especially with respect to the educated strata in the Negro population, but it is of course perfectly true that Negro public opinion and the policies of the NAACP are almost exclusively concerned with discrimination in employment, housing and education. This is understandable; oppressed minorities were never the best judges on the order of priorities in such matters and there are many instances when they preferred to fight for social opportunity rather than for basic human or political rights. But this does not make the marriage laws any more constitutional or any less shameful; the order of priorities in the question of rights is to be determined by the Constitution, and not by public opinion or by majorities.*

The second point was mentioned by a friend who rightly observed that my criticism of the Supreme Court's decision did not take into account the role education plays, and has always played, in the political framework of this country. This criticism is entirely just and I would have tried to insert a discussion of this role

---

1.   [From *Dissent* 6/1 (1959).]

into the article if I had not meanwhile published a few remarks on the wide-spread, uncritical acceptance of a Rousseauian ideal in education in another context, i.e. in an article in the Fall 1958 issue of Partisan Review, *entitled "The Crisis in Education." In order not to repeat myself, I left the article unchanged.*

Finally, I should like to remind the reader that I am writing as an outsider. I have never lived in the South and have even avoided occasional trips to Southern states because they would have brought me into a situation that I personally would find unbearable. Like most people of European origin I have difficulty in understanding, let alone sharing, the common prejudices of Americans in this area. Since what I wrote may shock good people and be misused by bad ones, I should like to make it clear that as a Jew I take my sympathy for the cause of the Negroes as for all oppressed or under-privileged peoples for granted and should appreciate it if the reader did likewise.

It is unfortunate and even unjust (though hardly unjustified) that the events at Little Rock should have had such an enormous echo in public opinion throughout the world and have become a major stumbling block to American foreign policy. For unlike other domestic problems which have beset this country since the end of World War II (a security hysteria, a runaway prosperity, and the concomitant transformation of an economy of abundance into a market where sheer superfluity and nonsense almost wash out the essential and the productive), and unlike such long-range difficulties as the problem of mass culture and mass education—both of which are typical of modern society in general and not only of America—the country's attitude to its Negro population is rooted in American tradition and nothing else. The color question was created by the one great crime in America's history and is soluble only within the political and historical framework of the Republic. The fact that this question has also become a major issue in world affairs is sheer coincidence as far as American history and politics are concerned; for the color problem in world politics grew out of the colonialism and imperialism of European nations—that is, the one great crime in which America was never involved. The tragedy is that the unsolved color problem within the United States may cost her the advantages she otherwise would rightly enjoy as a world power.

For historical and other reasons, we are in the habit of identifying the Negro question with the South, but the unsolved problems connected with Negroes living in our midst concern of course the whole country, not the South alone. Like other race questions, it has a special attraction for the mob and is particularly well fitted to serve as the point around which a mob ideology and a mob organization can crystallize. This aspect may one day even prove more explosive in the big Northern urban centers than in the more tradition-bound South, especially if the number of Negroes in Southern cities continues to decline while the Negro population of non-Southern cities increases at the same rate as in recent years. The United States is not a nation-state in the European sense and never was. The principle of its political structure is, and always has been, independent of a homogeneous population and of a common past. This is somewhat less true of the South whose population is more homogeneous and more rooted in the past than that of any other part of the country. When William Faulkner recently declared that in a conflict between the South and Washington he would ultimately have to act as a citizen of Mississippi, he sounded more like a member of a European nation-state than a citizen of this Republic. But this difference between North and South, though still marked, is bound to disappear with the growing industrialization of Southern states and plays no role in some of them even today. In all parts of the country, in the East and North with its host of nationalities no less than in the more homogeneous South, the Negroes stand out because of their "visibility." They are not the only "visible minority," but they are the most visible one. In this respect, they somewhat resemble new immigrants, who invariably constitute the most "audible" of all minorities and therefore are always the most likely to arouse xenophobic sentiments. But while audibility is a temporary phenomenon, rarely persisting beyond one generation, the Negroes' visibility is unalterable and permanent. This is not a trivial matter. In the public realm, where nothing counts that cannot make itself seen and heard, visibility and audibility are of prime importance. To argue that they are merely exterior appearances is to beg the question. For it is precisely appearances that "appear" in public, and inner qualities, gifts of heart or mind, are political only to the extent that their owner wishes to expose them in public, to place them in the lime-light of the market place.

The American Republic is based on the equality of all citizens, and while equality before the law has become an inalienable principle of all modern constitutional government, equality as such is of greater importance in the political life of a republic than in any other form of government. The point at stake, therefore, is not the well-being of the Negro population alone, but, at least in the long run, the survival of the Republic. Tocqueville saw over a century ago that equality of opportunity and condition, as well as equality of rights, constituted the basic "law" of American democracy, and he predicted that the dilemmas and perplexities inherent in the principle of equality might one day become the most dangerous challenge to the American way of life. In its all-comprehensive, typically American form, equality possesses an enormous power to equalize what by nature and origin is different—and it is only due to this power that the country has been able to retain its fundamental identity against the waves of immigrants who have always flooded its shores. But the principle of equality, even in its American form, is not omnipotent; it cannot equalize natural, physical characteristics. This limit is reached only when inequalities of economic and educational condition have been ironed out, but at that juncture a danger point, well known to students of history, invariably emerges: the more equal people have become in every respect, and the more equality permeates the whole texture of society, the more will differences be resented, the more conspicuous will those become who are visibly and by nature unlike the others.

It is therefore quite possible that the achievement of social, economic, and educational equality for the Negro may sharpen the color problem in this country instead of assuaging it. This, of course, does not have to happen, but it would be only natural if it did, and it would be very surprising if it did not. We have not yet reached the danger point, but we shall reach it in the foreseeable future, and a number of developments have already taken place which clearly point toward it. Awareness of future trouble does not commit one to advocating a reversal of the trend which happily for more than fifteen years now has been greatly in favor of the Negroes. But it does commit one to advocating that government intervention be guided by caution and moderation rather than by impatience and ill-advised measures. Since the Supreme Court decision to enforce desegregation in public schools, the general situation in the South has deteriorated. And while recent events indicate that it will not be possible to avoid Federal enforcement of Negro civil rights in the South altogether, conditions demand that such intervention be restricted to the few instances in which the law of the land and the principle of the Republic are at stake. The question therefore is whether this is the case in general, and whether it is the case in public education in particular.

The administration's Civil Rights program covers two altogether different points. It reaffirms the franchise of the Negro population, a matter of course in the North, but not at all in the South. And it also takes up the issue of segregation, which is a matter of fact in the whole country and a matter of discriminatory legislation only in Southern states. The present massive resistance throughout the South is an outcome of enforced desegregation, and not of legal enforcement of the Negroes' right to vote. The results of a public opinion poll in Virginia showing that 92% of the citizens were totally opposed to school integration, that 65% were willing to forgo public education under these conditions, and that 79% denied any obligation to accept the Supreme Court decision as binding, illustrates how serious the situation is. What is frightening here is not the 92% opposed to integration, for the dividing line in the South was never between those who favored and those who opposed segregation—practically speaking, no such opponents existed—but the proportion of people who prefer mob rule to law-abiding citizenship. The so-called liberals and moderates of the South are simply those who are law-abiding, and they have dwindled to a minority of 21%.

No public opinion poll was necessary to reveal this information. The events in Little Rock were quite sufficiently enlightening; and those who wish to blame the disturbances solely on the extraordinary misbehavior of Governor Faubus can set themselves right by listening to the eloquent silence of Arkansas' two liberal Senators. The sorry fact was that the town's law-abiding citizens left the streets to the mob, that neither white nor black citizens felt it their duty to see the Negro children safely to school. That is, even prior to the arrival of Federal troops, law-abiding Southerners had decided that enforcement of the law against mob rule and protection of children against adult mobsters were none of their business. In other words, the arrival of troops did little more than change passive into massive resistance.

It has been said, I think again by Mr. Faulkner, that enforced integration is no better than enforced segregation, and this is perfectly true. The only reason that the Supreme Court was able to address itself to the matter of desegregation in the first place was that segregation has been a legal, and not just a social, issue in the South for many generations. For the crucial point to remember is that it is not the social custom of segregation that is unconstitutional, but its *legal enforcement*. To abolish this legislation is of great and obvious importance and in the case of that part of the Civil Rights bill regarding the right to vote, no Southern state in fact dared to offer strong opposition. Indeed, with respect to unconstitutional legislation, the Civil Rights bill did not go far enough, for it left untouched the most outrageous law of Southern states—the law which makes mixed marriage a criminal offense. The right to marry whoever one wishes is an elementary human right compared to which "the right to attend an integrated school, the right to sit where one pleases on a bus, the right to go into any hotel or recreation area or place of amusement, regardless of one's skin or color or race" are minor indeed. Even political rights, like the right to vote, and nearly all other rights enumerated in the Constitution, are secondary to the inalienable human rights to "life, liberty and the pursuit of happiness" proclaimed in the Declaration of Independence; and to this category the right to home and marriage unquestionably belongs. It would have been much more important if this violation had been brought to the attention of the Supreme Court; yet had the Court ruled the anti-miscegenation laws unconstitutional, it would hardly have felt compelled to encourage, let alone enforce, mixed marriages.

However, the most startling part of the whole business was the Federal decision to start integration in, of all places, the public schools. It certainly did not require too much imagination to see that this was to burden children, black and white, with the working out of a problem which adults for generations have confessed themselves unable to solve. I think no

one will find it easy to forget the photograph reproduced in newspapers and magazines throughout the country, showing a Negro girl, accompanied by a white friend of her father, walking away from school, persecuted and followed into bodily proximity by a jeering and grimacing mob of youngsters. The girl, obviously, was asked to be a hero—that is, something neither her absent father nor the equally absent representatives of the NAACP felt called upon to be. It will be hard for the white youngsters, or at least those among them who outgrow their present brutality, to live down this photograph which exposes so mercilessly their juvenile delinquency. The picture looked to me like a fantastic caricature of progressive education which, by abolishing the authority of adults, implicitly denies their responsibility for the world into which they have borne their children and refuses the duty of guiding them into it. Have we now come to the point where it is the children who are being asked to change or improve the world? And do we intend to have our political battles fought out in the school yards?

Segregation is discrimination enforced by law, and desegregation can do no more than abolish the laws enforcing discrimination; it cannot abolish discrimination and force equality upon society but it can, and indeed must, enforce equality within the body politic. For equality not only has its origin in the body politic; its validity is clearly restricted to the political realm. Only there are we all equals. Under modern conditions, this equality has its most important embodiment in the right to vote, according to which the judgment and opinion of the most exalted citizen are on a par with the judgment and opinion of the hardly literate. Eligibility, the right to be voted into office, is also an inalienable right of every citizen; but here equality is already restricted, and though the necessity for personal distinction in an election arises out of the numerical equality, in which everybody is literally reduced to being one, it is distinction and qualities which count in the winning of votes and not sheer equality.

Yet unlike other differences (for example, professional specialization, occupational qualification, or social and intellectual distinction) the political qualities needed for winning office are so closely connected with being an equal among equals, that one may say that, far from being specialties, they are precisely those distinctions to which all voters equally aspire—not necessarily as human beings, but as citizens and political beings. Thus the qualities of officials in a democracy always depend upon the qualities of the electorate. Eligibility, therefore, is a necessary corollary of the right to vote; it means that everyone is given the opportunity to distinguish himself in those things in which all are equals to begin with. Strictly speaking, the franchise and eligibility for office are the only political rights, and they constitute in a modern democracy the very quintessence of citizenship. In contrast to all other rights, civil or human, they cannot be granted to resident aliens.

What equality is to the body politic—its innermost principle—discrimination is to society. Society is that curious, somewhat hybrid realm between the political and the private in which, since the beginning of the modern age, most men have spent the greater part of their lives. For each time we leave the protective four walls of our private homes and cross over the threshold into the public world, we enter first, not the political realm of equality, but the social sphere. We are driven into this sphere by the need to earn a living or attracted by the desire to follow our vocation or enticed by the pleasure of company, and once we have entered it, we become subject to the old adage of "like attracts like" which controls the whole realm of society in the innumerable variety of its groups and associations. What matters here is not personal distinction but the differences by which people belong to certain groups whose very identifiability demands that they discriminate against other groups in the same domain. In American society, people group together, and therefore discriminate against each other, along lines of profession, income, and ethnic origin, while in Europe the lines run along class origin, education, and manners. From the viewpoint of the human person, none of these discriminatory practices makes sense; but then it is doubtful whether the human person as such ever appears in the social realm. At any rate, without discrimination of some sort, society would simply cease to exist and very important possibilities of free association and group formation would disappear.

Mass society—which blurs lines of discrimination and levels group distinctions—is a danger to society as such, rather than to the integrity of the person, for personal identity has its source beyond the social realm. Conformism, however, is not a characteristic of mass society alone, but of every society insofar as only those are admitted to a given social group who conform to the general traits of difference which keep the group together. The danger of conformism in this country—a danger almost as old as the Republic—is that, because of the extraordinary heterogeneity of its population, social conformism tends to become an absolute and a substitute for national homogeneity. In any event, discrimination is as indispensable a social right as equality is a political right. The question is not how to abolish discrimination, but how to keep it confined within the social sphere, where it is legitimate, and prevent its trespassing on the political and the personal sphere, where it is destructive.

In order to illustrate this distinction between the political and the social, I shall give two examples of discrimination, one in my opinion entirely justified and outside the scope of government intervention, the other scandalously unjustified and positively harmful to the political realm.

It is common knowledge that vacation resorts in this country are frequently "restricted" according to ethnic origin. There are many people who object to this practice; nevertheless it is only an extension of the right to free association. If as a Jew I wish to spend my vacations only in the company of Jews, I cannot see how anyone can reasonably prevent my doing so; just as I see no reason why other resorts should not cater to a clientele that wishes not to see Jews while on a holiday. There cannot be a "right to go into any hotel or recreation area or place of amusement," because many of these are in the realm of the purely social where the right to free association and therefore to discrimination, has greater validity than the principle of equality. (This does not apply to theaters and museums, where people obviously do not congregate for the purpose of associating with each other.) The fact that the "right" to enter social places is silently granted in most countries and has become highly controversial only in American democracy is due not to the greater tolerance of other countries but in part to the homogeneity of their population and in part to their class system, which operates socially even when its economic foundations have disappeared. Homogeneity and class working together assure a "likeness" of clientele in any given place that even restriction and discrimination cannot achieve in America.

It is, however, another matter altogether when we come to "the right to sit where one pleases in a bus" or a railroad car or station, as well as the right to enter hotels and restaurants in business districts—in short, when we are dealing with services which, whether privately or publicly owned, are in fact public services that everyone needs in order to pursue his business and lead his life. Though not strictly in the political realm, such services are clearly in the public domain where all men are equal; and discrimination in Southern railroads and buses is as scandalous as discrimination in hotels and restaurants throughout the country. Obviously the situation is far worse in the South because segregation in public services is enforced by law and plainly visible to all. It is unfortunate indeed that the first steps toward clearing up the segregation situation in the South after so many decades of complete neglect did not begin with its most inhuman and its most conspicuous aspects.

The third realm, finally, in which we move and live together with other people—the realm of privacy—is ruled neither by equality nor by discrimination, but by exclusiveness. Here we choose those with whom, we wish to spend our lives, personal friends and those we love; and our choice is guided not by likeness or qualities shared by a group of people—it is not guided, indeed, by any objective standards or rules—but strikes, inexplicably and unerringly, at one person in his uniqueness, his unlikeness to all other people we know. The rules of uniqueness and exclusiveness are, and always will be, in conflict with the standards of society precisely because social discrimination violates the principle, and lacks validity for the conduct, of private life. Thus every mixed marriage constitutes a challenge to society and means that the partners to such a marriage have so far preferred personal happiness to social adjustment that they are willing to bear the burden of discrimination. This is and must remain their private business. The scandal begins only when their challenge to society and prevailing customs, to which every citizen has a right, is interpreted as a criminal offense so that by stepping outside the social realm they find themselves in conflict with the law as well. Social standards are not legal standards and if legislature follows social prejudice, society has become tyrannical.

For reasons too complicated to discuss here, the power of society in our time is greater than it ever was before, and not many people are left who know the rules of and live a private life. But this provides the body politic with no excuse for forgetting the rights of privacy, for failing to understand that the rights of privacy are grossly violated whenever legislation begins to enforce social discrimination. While the government has no right to interfere with the prejudices and discriminatory practices of society, it has not only the right but the duty to make sure that these practices are not legally enforced.

Just as the government has to ensure that social discrimination never curtails political equality, it must also safeguard the rights of every person to do as he pleases within the four walls of his own home. The moment social discrimination is legally enforced it becomes persecution, and of this crime many Southern states have been guilty. The moment social discrimination is legally abolished, the freedom of society is violated, and the danger is that thoughtless handling of the civil rights issue by the Federal government will result in such a violation. The government can legitimately take no steps against social discrimination because government can act only in the name of equality—a principle which does not obtain in the social sphere. The only public force that can fight social prejudice is the churches, and they can do so in the name of the uniqueness of the person, for it is on the principle of the uniqueness of souls that religion (and especially the Christian faith) is based. The churches are indeed the only communal and public place where appearances do not count, and if discrimination creeps into the houses of worship, this is an infallible sign of their religious failing. They then have become social and are no longer religious institutions.

Another issue involved in the present conflict between Washington and the South is the matter of states' rights. For some time it has been customary among liberals to maintain that no such issue exists at all but is only a ready-made subterfuge of Southern reactionaries who have nothing in their hands except "abstruse arguments and constitutional history." In my opinion, this is a dangerous error. In contradistinction to the classical principle of the European nation-state that power, like sovereignty, is indivisible, the power structure of this country rests on the principle of division of power and on the conviction that the body politic as a whole is strengthened by the division of power. To be sure, this principle is embodied in the system of checks and balances between the three branches of government; but it is no less rooted in the government's Federal structure which demands that there also be a balance and a mutual check between Federal power and the powers of the forty-eight states. If it is true (and I am convinced it is) that unlike force, power generates more power when it is divided, then it follows that every attempt of the Federal government to deprive the states of some of their legislative sovereignty can be justified only on grounds of legal argument and constitutional history. Such arguments are not abstruse; they are based on a principle which indeed was uppermost in the minds of the founders of the Republic.

All this has nothing to do with being a liberal or a conservative, although it may be that where the nature of power is at stake, liberal judgment with its long and honorable history of deep distrust of power in any form can be less trusted than on other questions. Liberals fail to understand that the nature of power is such that the power potential of the Union as a whole will suffer if the regional foundations on which this power rests are undermined. The point is that force can, indeed must, be centralized in order to be effective, but power cannot and must not. If the various sources from which it springs are dried up, the whole structure becomes impotent. And states' rights in this country are among the most authentic sources of power, not only for the promotion of regional interests and diversity, but for the Republic as a whole.

The trouble with the decision to force the issue of desegregation in the field of public education rather than in some other field in the campaign for Negro rights has been that this decision unwittingly touched upon an area in which every one of the different rights and principles we have discussed is involved. It is perfectly true, as Southerners have repeatedly pointed out, that the Constitution is silent on education and that legally as well as traditionally, public education lies in the domain of state legislation. The counter-argument that all public schools today are Federally supported is weak, for Federal subvention is intended in these instances to match and supplement local contributions and does not transform the schools into Federal institutions, like the Federal District courts. It would be very unwise indeed if the Federal government—which now must come to the assistance of more and more enterprises that once were the sole responsibility of the states—were to use its financial support as a means of whipping the states into agreement with positions they would otherwise be slow or altogether unwilling to adopt.

The same overlapping of rights and interests becomes apparent when we examine the issue of education in the light of the three realms of human life—the political, the social, and the private. Children are first of all part of family and home, and this means that they are, or should be, brought up in that atmosphere of idiosyncratic exclusiveness which alone makes a home a home, strong and secure enough to shield its young against the demands of the social and the responsibilities of the political realm. The right of parents to bring up their children as they see fit is a right of privacy, belonging to home and family. Ever since the introduction of compulsory education, this right has been challenged and restricted, but not abolished, by the right of the body politic to prepare children to fulfill their future duties as citizens. The stake of the government in the matter is undeniable—as is the right of the parents. The possibility of private education provides no way out of the dilemma, because it would make the safeguarding of certain private rights dependent upon economic status and consequently underprivilege those who are forced to send their children to public schools.

Parents' rights over their children are legally restricted by compulsory education and nothing else. The state has the unchallengeable right to prescribe minimum requirements for future citizenship and beyond that to further and support the teaching of subjects and professions which are felt to be desirable and necessary to the nation as a whole. All this involves, however, only the content of the child's education, not the context of association and social life which invariably develops out of his attendance at school; otherwise one would have to challenge the right of private schools to exist. For the child himself, school is the first place away from home where he establishes contact with the public world that surrounds him and his family. This public world is not political but social, and the school is to the child what a job is to an adult. The only difference is that the element of free choice which, in a free society, exists at least in principle in the choosing of jobs and the associations connected with them, is not yet at the disposal of the child but rests with his parents.

To force parents to send their children to an integrated school against their will means to deprive them of rights which clearly belong to them in all free societies—the private right over their children and the social rights to free association. As for the children, forced integration means a very serious conflict between home and school, between their private and their social life, and while such conflicts are common in adult life, children cannot be expected to handle them and therefore should not be exposed to them. It has often been remarked that man is never so much of a conformer—that is, a purely social being—as in childhood. The reason is that every child instinctively seeks authorities to guide it into the world in which he is still a stranger, in which he cannot orient himself by his own judgment. To the extent that parents and teachers fail him as authorities, the child will conform more strongly to his own group, and under certain conditions the peer group will become his supreme authority. The result can only be a rise of mob and gang rule, as the news photograph we mentioned above so eloquently demonstrates. The conflict between a segregated home and a desegregated school, between family prejudice and school demands, abolishes at one stroke both the teachers' and the parents' authority, replacing it with the rule of public opinion among children who have neither the ability nor the right to establish a public opinion of their own.

Because the many different factors involved in public education can quickly be set to work at cross purposes, government intervention, even at its best, will always be rather controversial. Hence it seems highly questionable whether it was wise to begin enforcement of civil rights in a domain where no basic human and no basic political right is at stake, and where other rights—social and private—whose protection is no less vital, can so easily be hurt.

HUGO BLACK

Engel et al. v. Vitale et al. (1962)

Mr. Justice BLACK delivered the opinion of the Court.

The respondent Board of Education of Union Free School District No. 9, New Hyde Park, New York, acting in its official capacity under state law, directed the School District's principal to cause the following prayer to be said aloud by each class in the presence of a teacher at the beginning of each school day:

Almighty God, we acknowledge our dependence upon Thee, and we beg Thy blessings upon us, our parents, our teachers and our Country.

This daily procedure was adopted on the recommendation of the State Board of Regents, a governmental agency created by the State Constitution to which the New York Legislature has granted broad supervisory, executive, and legislative powers over the State's public school system. These state officials composed the prayer which they recommended and published as a part of their "Statement on Moral and Spiritual Training in the Schools." [. . .]

Shortly after the practice of reciting the Regents' prayer was adopted by the School District, the parents of ten pupils brought this action in a New York

State Court insisting that use of this official prayer in the public schools was contrary to the beliefs, religions, or religious practices of both themselves and their children. Among other things, these parents challenged the constitutionality of both the state law authorizing the School District to direct the use of prayer in public schools and the School District's regulation ordering the recitation of this particular prayer on the ground that these actions of official governmental agencies violate that part of the First Amendment of the Federal Constitution which commands that "Congress shall make no law respecting an establishment of religion"—a command which was "made applicable to the State of New York by the Fourteenth Amendment of the said Constitution." The New York Court of Appeals, over the dissents of Judges Dye and Fuld, sustained an order of the lower state courts which had upheld the power of New York to use the Regents' prayer as a part of the daily procedures of its public schools so long as the schools did not compel any pupil to join in the prayer over his or his parents' objection. We granted certiorari to review this important decision involving rights protected by the First and Fourteenth Amendments.

We think that by using its public school system to encourage recitation of the Regents' prayer, the State of New York has adopted a practice wholly inconsistent with the Establishment Clause. There can, of course, be no doubt that New York's program of daily classroom invocation of God's blessings as prescribed in the Regents' prayer is a religious activity. It is a solemn avowal of divine faith and supplication for the blessings of the Almighty. The nature of such a prayer has always been religious, none of the respondents has denied this. [. . .]

The petitioners contend among other things that the state laws requiring or permitting use of the Regents' prayer must be struck down as a violation of the Establishment Clause because that prayer was composed by governmental officials as a part of a governmental program to further religious beliefs. For this reason, petitioners argue, the State's use of the Regents' prayer in its public school system breaches the constitutional wall of separation between Church and State. We agree with that contention since we think that the constitutional prohibition against laws respecting an establishment of religion must at least mean that in this country it is no part of the business of government to compose official prayers for any group of the American people to recite as a part of a religious program carried on by government.

It is a matter of history that this very practice of establishing governmentally composed prayers for religious services was one of the reasons which caused many of our early colonists to leave England and seek religious freedom in America. The Book of Common Prayer, which was created under governmental direction and which was approved by Acts of Parliament in 1548 and 1549, set out in minute detail the accepted form and content of prayer and other religious ceremonies to be used in the established, tax-supported Church of England. The controversies over the Book and what should be its content repeatedly threatened to disrupt the peace of that country as the accepted forms of prayer in the established church changed with the views of the particular ruler that happened to be in control at the time. Powerful groups representing some of the varying religious views of the people struggled among themselves to impress their particular views upon the Government and obtain amendments of the Book more suitable to their respective notions of how religious services should be conducted in order that the official religious establishment would advance their particular religious beliefs. Other groups, lacking the necessary political power to influence the Government on the matter, decided to leave England and its established church and seek freedom in America from England's governmentally ordained and supported religion.

It is an unfortunate fact of history that when some of the very groups which had most strenuously opposed the established Church of England found themselves sufficiently in control of colonial governments in this country to write their own prayers into law, they passed laws making their own religion the official religion of their respective colonies. Indeed, as late as the time of the Revolutionary War, there were established churches in at least eight of the thirteen former colonies and established religions in at least four of the other five. But the successful Revolution against English political domination was shortly followed by intense opposition to the practice of establishing religion by law. This opposition crystallized rapidly into an effective political force in Virginia where the minority religious groups such as

Presbyterians, Lutherans, Quakers and Baptists had gained such strength that the adherents to the established Episcopal Church were actually a minority themselves. In 1785–1786, those opposed to the established Church, led by James Madison and Thomas Jefferson, who, though themselves not members of any of these dissenting religious groups, opposed all religious establishments by law on grounds of principle, obtained the enactment of the famous "Virginia Bill for Religious Liberty" by which all religious groups were placed on an equal footing so far as the State was concerned. Similar though less far-reaching legislation was being considered and passed in other States.

By the time of the adoption of the Constitution, our history shows that there was a widespread awareness among many Americans of the dangers of a union of Church and State. These people knew, some of them from bitter personal experience, that one of the greatest dangers to the freedom of the individual to worship in his own way lay in the Government's placing its official stamp of approval upon one particular kind of prayer or one particular form of religious services. They knew the anguish, hardship and bitter strife that could come when zealous religious groups struggled with one another to obtain the Government's stamp of approval from each King, Queen, or Protector that came to temporary power. The Constitution was intended to avert a part of this danger by leaving the government of this country in the hands of the people rather than in the hands of any monarch. But this safeguard was not enough. Our Founders were no more willing to let the content of their prayers and their privilege of praying whenever they pleased be influenced by the ballot box than they were to let these vital matters of personal conscience depend upon the succession of monarchs. The First Amendment was added to the Constitution to stand as a guarantee that neither the power nor the prestige of the Federal Government would be used to control, support or influence the kinds of prayer the American people can say—that the people's religions must not be subjected to the pressures of government for change each time a new political administration is elected to office. Under that Amendment's prohibition against governmental establishment of religion, as reinforced by the provisions of the Fourteenth Amendment, government in this country, be it state

or federal, is without power to prescribe by law any particular form of prayer which is to be used as an official prayer in carrying on any program of governmentally sponsored religious activity.

There can be no doubt that New York's state prayer program officially establishes the religious beliefs embodied in the Regents' prayer. The respondents' argument to the contrary, which is largely based upon the contention that the Regents' prayer is "non-denominational" and the fact that the program, as modified and approved by state courts, does not require all pupils to recite the prayer but permits those who wish to do so to remain silent or be excused from the room, ignores the essential nature of the program's constitutional defects. Neither the fact that the prayer may be denominationally neutral nor the fact that its observance on the part of the students is voluntary can serve to free it from the limitations of the Establishment Clause. [. . .] The Establishment Clause [. . .] does not depend upon any showing of direct governmental compulsion and is violated by the enactment of laws which establish an official religion whether those laws operate directly to coerce nonobserving individuals or not. This is not to say, of course, that laws officially prescribing a particular form of religious worship do not involve coercion of such individuals. When the power, prestige and financial support of government is placed behind a particular religious belief, the indirect coercive pressure upon religious minorities to conform to the prevailing officially approved religion is plain. But the purposes underlying the Establishment Clause go much further than that. Its first and most immediate purpose rested on the belief that a union of government and religion tends to destroy government and to degrade religion. The history of governmentally established religion, both in England and in this country, showed that whenever government had allied itself with one particular form of religion, the inevitable result had been that it had incurred the hatred, disrespect and even contempt of those who held contrary beliefs. That same history showed that many people had lost their respect for any religion that had relied upon the support of government to spread its faith. The Establishment Clause thus stands as an expression of principle on the part of the Founders of our Constitution that religion is too personal, too sacred, too holy, to permit its "unhallowed perversion" by a civil magistrate. Another purpose of the Establishment Clause rested upon an awareness of the historical fact that governmentally established religions and religious persecutions go hand in hand. The Founders knew that only a few years after the Book of Common Prayer became the only accepted form of religious services in the established Church of England, an Act of Uniformity was passed to compel all Englishmen to attend those services and to make it a criminal offense to conduct or attend religious gatherings of any other kind—a law which was consistently flouted by dissenting religious groups in England and which contributed to widespread persecutions of people like John Bunyan who persisted in holding "unlawful [religious] meetings [. . .] to the great disturbance and distraction of the good subjects of this kingdom. . . ." And they knew that similar persecutions had received the sanction of law in several of the colonies in this country soon after the establishment of official religions in those colonies. It was in large part to get completely away from this sort of systematic religious persecution that the Founders brought into being our Nation, our Constitution, and our Bill of Rights with its prohibition against any governmental establishment of religion. The New York laws officially prescribing the Regents' prayer are inconsistent both with the purposes of the Establishment Clause and with the Establishment Clause itself.

It has been argued that to apply the Constitution in such a way as to prohibit state laws respecting an establishment of religious services in public schools is to indicate a hostility toward religion or toward prayer. Nothing, of course, could be more wrong. The history of man is inseparable from the history of religion. And perhaps it is not too much to say that since the beginning of that history many people have devoutly believed that "More things are wrought by prayer than this world dreams of." It was doubtless largely due to men who believed this that there grew up a sentiment that caused men to leave the cross-currents of officially established state religions and religious persecution in Europe and come to this country filled with the hope that they could find a place in which they could pray when they pleased to the God of their faith in the language they chose. And there were men of this same faith in the power of prayer who led the fight for adoption of our Constitution and also for our Bill of Rights with the very guarantees of religious freedom that forbid the sort of governmental activity which New York has attempted here. These men knew that the First Amendment, which tried to put an end to governmental control of religion and of prayer, was not written to destroy either. They knew rather that it was written to quiet well-justified fears which nearly all of them felt arising out of an awareness that governments of the past had shackled men's tongues to make them speak only the religious thoughts that government wanted them to speak and to pray only to the God that government wanted them to pray to. It is neither sacrilegious nor antireligious to say that each separate government in this country should stay out of the business of writing or sanctioning official prayers and leave that purely religious function to the people themselves and to those the people choose to look to for religious guidance.

It is true that New York's establishment of its Regents' prayer as an officially approved religious doctrine of that State does not amount to a total establishment of one particular religious sect to the exclusion of all others—that, indeed, the governmental endorsement of that prayer seems relatively insignificant when compared to the governmental encroachments upon religion which were commonplace 200 years ago. To those who may subscribe to the view that because the Regents' official prayer is so brief and general there can be no danger to religious freedom in its governmental establishment, however, it may be appropriate to say in the words of James Madison, the author of the First Amendment:

> [I]t is proper to take alarm at the first experiment on our liberties. . . . Who does not see that the same authority which can establish Christianity, in exclusion of all other Religions, may establish with the same ease any particular sect of Christians, in exclusion of all other Sects? That the same authority which can force a citizen to contribute three pence only of his property for the support of any one establishment, may force him to conform to any other establishment in all cases whatsoever?

The judgment of the Court of Appeals of New York is reversed and the cause remanded for further proceedings not inconsistent with this opinion.

POTTER STEWART

Engel et al., v. Vitale, et al., Dissent (1962)

Mr. Justice STEWART dissenting.

A local school board in New York has provided that those pupils who wish to do so may join in a brief prayer at the beginning of each school day, acknowledging their dependence upon God and asking His blessing upon them and upon their parents, their teachers, and their country. The Court today decides that in permitting this brief nondenominational prayer the school board has violated the Constitution of the United States. I think this decision is wrong.

The Court does not hold, nor could it, that New York has interfered with the free exercise of anybody's religion. For the state courts have made clear that those who object to reciting the prayer must be entirely free of any compulsion to do so, including any "embarrassments and pressures." But the Court says that in permitting school children to say this simple prayer, the New York authorities have established "an official religion."

With all respect, I think the Court has misapplied a great constitutional principle. I cannot see how an "official religion" is established by letting those who want to say a prayer say it. On the contrary, I think that to deny the wish of these school children to join in reciting this prayer is to deny them the opportunity of sharing in the spiritual heritage of our Nation.

The Court's historical review of the quarrels over the Book of Common Prayer in England throws no light for me on the issue before us in this case. England had then and has now an established church. Equally unenlightening, I think, is the history of the early establishment and later rejection of an official church in our own States. For we deal here not with the establishment of a state church, which would, of course, be constitutionally impermissible, but with whether school children who want to begin their day by joining in prayer must be prohibited from doing so. Moreover, I think that the Court's task, in this as in all areas of constitutional adjudication, is not responsibly aided by the uncritical invocation of metaphors like the "wall of separation," a phrase nowhere to be found in the Constitution. What is relevant to the issue here is not the history of an established church in sixteenth century England or in eighteenth century America, but the history of the religious traditions of our people, reflected in countless practices of the institutions and officials of our government.

At the opening of each day's Session of this Court we stand, while one of our officials invokes the protection of God. Since the days of John Marshall our Crier has said, "God save the United States and this Honorable Court." Both the Senate and the House of Representatives open their daily Sessions with prayer. Each of our Presidents, from George Washington to John F. Kennedy, has upon assuming his Office asked the protection and help of God.

The Court today says that the state and federal governments are without constitutional power to prescribe any particular form of words to be recited by any group of the American people on any subject touching religion. One of the stanzas of "The Star-Spangled Banner," made our National Anthem by Act of Congress in 1931, contains these verses:

Blest with victory and peace, may the heav'n rescued land
Praise the Pow'r that hath made and preserved us a nation!
Then conquer we must, when our cause it is just,
And this be our motto "In God is our Trust."

In 1954 Congress added a phrase to the Pledge of Allegiance to the Flag so that it now contains the words "one Nation under God, indivisible, with liberty and justice for all." In 1952 Congress enacted legislation calling upon the President each year to proclaim a National Day of Prayer. Since 1865 the words "IN GOD WE TRUST" have been impressed on our coins.

Countless similar examples could be listed, but there is no need to belabor the obvious. It was all summed up by this Court just ten years ago in a single sentence: "We are a religious people whose institutions presuppose a Supreme Being." *Zorach v. Clauson* (1952).

I do not believe that this Court, or the Congress, or the President has by the actions and practices I have mentioned established an "official religion" in violation of the Constitution. And I do not believe

the State of New York has done so in this case. What each has done has been to recognize and to follow the deeply entrenched and highly cherished spiritual traditions of our Nation—traditions which come down to us from those who almost two hundred years ago avowed their "firm Reliance on the Protection of divine Providence" when they proclaimed the freedom and independence of this brave new world.

I dissent.

TOM C. CLARK

School District of Abington Township, Pennsylvania v. Schempp (1963)

Mr. Justice CLARK delivered the opinion of the Court.

Once again we are called upon to consider the scope of the provision of the First Amendment to the United States Constitution which declares that "Congress shall make no law respecting an establishment of religion, or prohibiting the free exercise thereof. . . ." These companion cases present the issues in the context of state action requiring that schools begin each day with readings from the Bible. . . . In light of the history of the First Amendment and of our cases interpreting and applying its requirements, we hold that the practices at issue and the laws requiring them are unconstitutional under the Establishment Clause, as applied to the States through the Fourteenth Amendment.

I

The facts in each case: No. 142. The Commonwealth of Pennsylvania by law requires that "At least ten verses from the Holy Bible shall be read, without comment, at the opening of each public school on each school day. Any child shall be excused from such Bible reading, or attending such Bible reading,

upon the written request of his parent or guardian." The Schempp family, husband and wife and two of their three children, brought suit to enjoin enforcement of the statute, contending that their rights under the Fourteenth Amendment to the Constitution of the United States are, have been, and will continue to be violated unless this statute be declared unconstitutional as violative of these provisions of the First Amendment. They sought to enjoin the appellant school district, wherein the Schempp children attend school, and its officers and the Superintendent of Public Instruction of the Commonwealth from continuing to conduct such readings and recitation of the Lord's Prayer in the public schools of the district pursuant to the statute. A three-judge statutory District Court for the Eastern District of Pennsylvania held that the statute is violative of the Establishment Clause of the First Amendment as applied to the States by the Due Process Clause of the Fourteenth Amendment and directed that appropriate injunctive relief issue. [. . .]

The appellees Edward Lewis Schempp, his wife Sidney, and their children, Roger and Donna, are of the Unitarian faith and are members of the Unitarian church in Germantown, Philadelphia, Pennsylvania, where they, as well as another son, Ellory, regularly attend religious services. The latter was originally a party but having graduated from the school system *pendente lite* was voluntarily dismissed from the action. The other children attend the Abington Senior High School, which is a public school operated by appellant district.

On each school day at the Abington Senior High School between 8:15 and 8:30 a.m., while the pupils are attending their home rooms or advisory sections, opening exercises are conducted pursuant to the statute. The exercises are broadcast into each room in the school building through an intercommunications system and are conducted under the supervision of a teacher by students attending the school's radio and television workshop. Selected students from this course gather each morning in the school's workshop studio for the exercises, which include readings by one of the students of 10 verses of the Holy Bible, broadcast to each room in the building. This is followed by the recitation of the Lord's Prayer, likewise over the intercommunications system, but also by the students in the various classrooms, who are asked to stand and join in repeating the prayer in unison. The exercises are closed with the flag salute and such pertinent announcements as are of interest to the students. Participation in the opening exercises, as directed by the statute, is voluntary. The student reading the verses from the Bible may select the passages and read from any version he chooses, although the only copies furnished by the school are the King James version, copies of which were circulated to each teacher by the school district. During the period in which the exercises have been conducted the King James, the Douay and the Revised Standard versions of the Bible have been used, as well as the Jewish Holy Scriptures. There are no prefatory statements, no questions asked or solicited, no comments or explanations made and no interpretations given at or during the exercises. The students and parents are advised that the student may absent himself from the classroom or, should he elect to remain, not participate in the exercises.

It appears from the record that in schools not having an intercommunications system the Bible reading and the recitation of the Lord's Prayer were conducted by the home-room teacher, who chose the text of the verses and read them herself or had

students read them in rotation or by volunteers. This was followed by a standing recitation of the Lord's Prayer, together with the Pledge of Allegiance to the Flag by the class in unison and a closing announcement of routine school items of interest.

At the first trial Edward Schempp and the children testified as to specific religious doctrines purveyed by a literal reading of the Bible "which were contrary to the religious beliefs which they held and to their familial teaching." The children testified that all of the doctrines to which they referred were read to them at various times as part of the exercises. Edward Schempp testified at the second trial that he had considered having Roger and Donna excused from attendance at the exercises but decided against it for several reasons, including his belief that the children's relationships with their teachers and classmates would be adversely affected.

Expert testimony was introduced by both appellants and appellees at the first trial, which testimony was summarized by the trial court as follows:

> Dr. Solomon Grayzel testified that there were marked differences between the Jewish Holy Scriptures and the Christian Holy Bible, the most obvious of which was the absence of the New Testament in the Jewish Holy Scriptures. Dr. Grayzel testified that portions of the New Testament were offensive to Jewish tradition and that, from the standpoint of Jewish faith, the concept of Jesus Christ as the Son of God was "practically blasphemous." He cited instances in the New Testament which, assertedly, were not only sectarian in nature but tended to bring the Jews into ridicule or scorn. Dr. Grayzel gave as his expert opinion that such material from the New Testament could be explained to Jewish children in such a way as to do no harm to them. But if portions of the New Testament were read without explanation, they could be, and in his specific experience with children Dr. Grayzel observed, had been, psychologically harmful to the child and had caused a divisive force within the social media of the school.
>
> Dr. Grayzel also testified that there was significant difference in attitude with regard to the respective Books of the Jewish and Christian Religions in that Judaism attaches no special significance to the reading of the Bible per se and that the Jewish Holy Scriptures are source materials to

be studied. But Dr. Grayzel did state that many portions of the New, as well as of the Old, Testament contained passages of great literary and moral value. [. . .]

No. 119. In 1905 the Board of School Commissioners of Baltimore City adopted a rule pursuant to Art. 77, 202 of the Annotated Code of Maryland. The rule provided for the holding of opening exercises in the schools of the city, consisting primarily of the "reading, without comment, of a chapter in the Holy Bible and/or the use of the Lord's Prayer." The petitioners, Mrs. Madalyn Murray and her son, William J. Murray III, are both professed atheists. Following unsuccessful attempts to have the respondent school board rescind the rule, this suit was filed for mandamus to compel its rescission and cancellation. It was alleged that William was a student in a public school of the city and Mrs. Murray, his mother, was a taxpayer therein; that it was the practice under the rule to have a reading on each school morning from the King James version of the Bible; that at petitioners' insistence the rule was amended to permit children to be excused from the exercise on request of the parent and that William had been excused pursuant thereto; that nevertheless the rule as amended was in violation of the petitioners' rights "to freedom of religion under the First and Fourteenth Amendments" and in violation of "the principle of separation between church and state, contained therein. . . ." The petition particularized the petitioners' atheistic beliefs and stated that the rule, as practiced, violated their rights

> in that it threatens their religious liberty by placing a premium on belief as against non-belief and subjects their freedom of conscience to the rule of the majority; it pronounces belief in God as the source of all moral and spiritual values, equating these values with religious values, and thereby renders sinister, alien and suspect the beliefs and ideals of your Petitioners, promoting doubt and question of their morality, good citizenship and good faith.

The respondents demurred and the trial court, recognizing that the demurrer admitted all facts well pleaded, sustained it without leave to amend. The Maryland Court of Appeals affirmed, the majority of four justices holding the exercise not in violation of the First and Fourteenth Amendments, with three justices dissenting.

II

It is true that religion has been closely identified with our history and government. As we said in *Engel v. Vitale* (1962), "The history of man is inseparable from the history of religion. And . . . since the beginning of that history many people have devoutly believed that 'More things are wrought by prayer than this world dreams of.'" In *Zorach v. Clauson* (1952), we gave specific recognition to the proposition that "[w]e are a religious people whose institutions presuppose a Supreme Being." The fact that the Founding Fathers believed devotedly that there was a God and that the unalienable rights of man were rooted in Him is clearly evidenced in their writings, from the Mayflower Compact to the Constitution itself. This background is evidenced today in our public life through the continuance in our oaths of office from the Presidency to the Alderman of the final supplication, "So help me God." Likewise each House of the Congress provides through its Chaplain an opening prayer, and the sessions of this Court are declared open by the crier in a short ceremony, the final phrase of which invokes the grace of God. Again, there are such manifestations in our military forces, where those of our citizens who are under the restrictions of military service wish to engage in voluntary worship. Indeed, only last year an official survey of the country indicated that 64% of our people have church membership, while less than 30% profess no religion whatever. It can be truly said, therefore, that today, as in the beginning, our national life reflects a religious people who, in the words of Madison, are "earnestly praying, as . . . in duty bound, that the Supreme Lawgiver of the Universe . . . guide them into every measure which may be worthy of his [blessing. . . .]" *Memorial and Remonstrance Against Religious Assessments.*

This is not to say, however, that religion has been so identified with our history and government that religious freedom is not likewise as strongly imbedded in our public and private life. Nothing but the most telling of personal experiences in religious persecution suffered by our forebears, could have planted our belief in liberty of religious opinion any more deeply in our heritage. It is true that this liberty frequently was not realized by the colonists, but this is readily accountable by their close ties to the Mother Country. However, the views of Madison and Jefferson, preceded by Roger Williams, came to be incorporated not only in the Federal Constitution but likewise in those of most of our States. This freedom to worship was indispensable in a country whose people came from the four quarters of the earth and brought with them a diversity of religious opinion. Today authorities list 83 separate religious bodies, each with membership exceeding 50,000, existing among our people, as well as innumerable smaller groups. [. . .]

III

[T]his Court has rejected unequivocally the contention that the Establishment Clause forbids only governmental preference of one religion over another. Almost 20 years ago in *Everson* [*v. Board of Education* (1947)], the Court said that "[n]either a state nor the Federal Government can set up a church. Neither can pass laws which aid one religion, aid all religions, or prefer one religion over another." [. . .]

Further, Mr. Justice Rutledge, joined by Justices Frankfurter, Jackson and Burton, declared:

> The [First] Amendment's purpose was not to strike merely at the official establishment of a single sect, creed or religion, outlawing only a formal relation such as had prevailed in England and some of the colonies. Necessarily it was to uproot all such relationships. But the object was broader than separating church and state in this narrow sense. It was to create a complete and permanent separation of the spheres of religious activity and civil authority by comprehensively forbidding every form of public aid or support for religion. [. . .]

IV

Only one year later the Court was asked to reconsider and repudiate the doctrine of [*Everson*] in *McCollum*

v. Board of Education (1948). It was argued that "historically the First Amendment was intended to forbid only government preference of one religion over another. . . . In addition they ask that we distinguish or overrule our holding in the *Everson* case that the Fourteenth Amendment made the 'establishment of religion' clause of the First Amendment applicable as a prohibition against the States." The Court, with Mr. Justice Reed alone dissenting, was unable to "accept either of these contentions." Mr. Justice Frankfurter, joined by Justices Jackson, Rutledge and Burton, wrote a very comprehensive and scholarly concurrence in which he said that "[s]eparation is a requirement to abstain from fusing functions of Government and of religious sects, not merely to treat them all equally." Continuing, he stated that:

> the Constitution . . . prohibited the Government common to all from becoming embroiled, however innocently, in the destructive religious conflicts of which the history of even this country records some dark pages. [. . .]

[T]hen in 1961 [. . .] Chief Justice Warren in *McGowan* [*v. Maryland*], for a unanimous Court [. . .] said:

> [T]he First Amendment, in its final form, did not simply bar a congressional enactment establishing a church; it forbade all laws respecting an establishment of religion. Thus, this Court has given the Amendment a "broad interpretation [. . .] in the light of its history and the evils it was designed forever to suppress. . . ."

And Mr. Justice Black for the Court in *Torcaso* [*v. Watkins* 1961], without dissent but with Justices Frankfurter and Harlan concurring in the result, used this language:

> We repeat and again reaffirm that neither a State nor the Federal Government can constitutionally force a person "to profess a belief or disbelief in any religion." Neither can constitutionally pass laws or impose requirements which aid all religions as against non-believers, and neither can aid those religions based on a belief in the existence of God as against those religions founded on different beliefs.

Finally, in *Engel v. Vitale*, only last year, these principles were so universally recognized that the Court, without the citation of a single case and over the sole dissent of Mr. Justice Stewart, reaffirmed them. [. . .]

V

The wholesome "neutrality" of which this Court's cases speak thus stems from a recognition of the teachings of history that powerful sects or groups might bring about a fusion of governmental and religious functions or a concert or dependency of one upon the other to the end that official support of the State or Federal Government would be placed behind the tenets of one or of all orthodoxies. This the Establishment Clause prohibits. And a further reason for neutrality is found in the Free Exercise Clause, which recognizes the value of religious training, teaching and observance and, more particularly, the right of every person to freely choose his own course with reference thereto, free of any compulsion from the state. This the Free Exercise Clause guarantees. Thus, as we have seen, the two clauses may overlap. As we have indicated, the Establishment Clause has been directly considered by this Court eight times in the past score of years and, with only one Justice dissenting on the point, it has consistently held that the clause withdrew all legislative power respecting religious belief or the expression thereof. The test may be stated as follows: what are the purpose and the primary effect of the enactment? If either is the advancement or inhibition of religion then the enactment exceeds the scope of legislative power as circumscribed by the Constitution. That is to say that to withstand the strictures of the Establishment Clause there must be a secular legislative purpose and a primary effect that neither advances nor inhibits religion. The Free Exercise Clause, likewise considered many times here, withdraws from legislative power, state and federal, the exertion of any restraint on the free exercise of religion. Its purpose is to secure religious liberty in the individual by prohibiting any invasions thereof by civil authority. Hence it is necessary in a free exercise case for one to show the coercive effect of the enactment as it operates against him in the practice of his religion. The distinction between the two clauses is apparent—a violation of the Free Exercise Clause is predicated on coercion while the Establishment Clause violation need not be so attended.

Applying the Establishment Clause principles to the cases at bar we find that the States are requiring the selection and reading at the opening of the school day of verses from the Holy Bible and the recitation of the Lord's Prayer by the students in unison. These exercises are prescribed as part of the curricular activities of students who are required by law to attend school. They are held in the school buildings under the supervision and with the participation of teachers employed in those schools. [. . .] The trial court in No. 142 has found that such an opening exercise is a religious ceremony and was intended by the State to be so. We agree with the trial court's finding as to the religious character of the exercises. Given that finding, the exercises and the law requiring them are in violation of the Establishment Clause.

There is no such specific finding as to the religious character of the exercises in No. 119, and the State contends (as does the State in No. 142) that the program is an effort to extend its benefits to all public school children without regard to their religious belief. Included within its secular purposes, it says, are the promotion of moral values, the contradiction to the materialistic trends of our times, the perpetuation of our institutions and the teaching of literature. The case came up on demurrer, of course, to a petition which alleged that the uniform practice under the rule had been to read from the King James version of the Bible and that the exercise was sectarian. The short answer, therefore, is that the religious character of the exercise was admitted by the State. But even if its purpose is not strictly religious, it is sought to be accomplished through readings, without comment, from the Bible. Surely the place of the Bible as an instrument of religion cannot be gainsaid, and the State's recognition of the pervading religious character of the ceremony is evident from the rule's specific permission of the alternative use of the Catholic Douay version as well as the recent amendment permitting nonattendance at the exercises. None of these factors is consistent with the contention that the Bible is here used either as an instrument for nonreligious moral inspiration or as a reference for the teaching of secular subjects.

The conclusion follows that in both cases the laws require religious exercises and such exercises are being conducted in direct violation of the rights of the appellees and petitioners. Nor are these required exercises mitigated by the fact that individual students may absent themselves upon parental request, for that fact furnishes no defense to a claim of unconstitutionality under the Establishment Clause. Further, it is no defense to urge that the religious practices here may be relatively minor encroachments on the First Amendment. The breach of neutrality that is today a trickling stream may all too soon become a raging torrent and, in the words of Madison, "it is proper to take alarm at the first experiment on our liberties."

It is insisted that unless these religious exercises are permitted a "religion of secularism" is established in the schools. We agree of course that the State may not establish a "religion of secularism" in the sense of affirmatively opposing or showing hostility to religion, thus "preferring those who believe in no religion over those who do believe." We do not agree, however, that this decision in any sense has that effect. In addition, it might well be said that one's education is not complete without a study of comparative religion or the history of religion and its relationship to the advancement of civilization. It certainly may be said that the Bible is worthy of study for its literary and historic qualities. Nothing we have said here indicates that such study of the Bible or of religion, when presented objectively as part of a secular program of education, may not be effected consistently with the First Amendment. But the exercises here do not fall into those categories. They are religious exercises, required by the States in violation of the command of the First Amendment that the Government maintain strict neutrality, neither aiding nor opposing religion.

Finally, we cannot accept that the concept of neutrality, which does not permit a State to require a religious exercise even with the consent of the majority of those affected, collides with the majority's right to free exercise of religion. While the Free Exercise Clause clearly prohibits the use of state action to deny the rights of free exercise to anyone, it has never meant that a majority could use the machinery of the State to practice its beliefs. Such a contention was effectively answered by Mr. Justice Jackson for the Court in *West Virginia Board of Education v. Barnette* (1943):

> The very purpose of a Bill of Rights was to withdraw certain subjects from the vicissitudes of political controversy, to place them beyond the reach of majorities and officials and to establish them as legal principles to be applied by the courts. One's right to . . . freedom of worship . . . and other fundamental rights may not be submitted to vote; they depend on the outcome of no elections.

The place of religion in our society is an exalted one, achieved through a long tradition of reliance on the home, the church and the inviolable citadel of the individual heart and mind. We have come to recognize through bitter experience that it is not within the power of government to invade that citadel, whether its purpose or effect be to aid or oppose, to advance or retard. In the relationship between man and religion, the State is firmly committed to a position of neutrality. Though the application of that rule requires interpretation of a delicate sort, the rule itself is clearly and concisely stated in the words of the First Amendment. Applying that rule to the facts of these cases, we affirm the judgment in No. 142. In No. 119, the judgment is reversed and the cause remanded to the Maryland Court of Appeals for further proceedings consistent with this opinion.

Heart of Atlanta Motel, Inc. v. United States (1964)

Mr. Justice CLARK delivered the opinion of the Court.

This is a declaratory judgment action, attacking the constitutionality of Title II of the Civil Rights Act of 1964. [. . .]

1. The Factual Background and Contentions of the Parties

The case comes here on admissions and stipulated facts. Appellant owns and operates the Heart of Atlanta Motel which has 216 rooms available to transient guests. The motel is located on Courtland Street, two blocks from downtown Peachtree Street. It is readily accessible to interstate highways 75 and 85 and state highways 23 and 41. Appellant solicits patronage from outside the State of Georgia through various national advertising media, including magazines of national circulation; it maintains over 50 billboards and highway signs within the State, soliciting patronage for the motel; it accepts convention trade from outside Georgia and approximately 75% of its registered guests are from out of State. Prior to passage of the Act the motel had followed a practice of refusing to rent rooms to Negroes, and it alleged that it intended to continue to do so. In an effort to perpetuate that policy this suit was filed. [. . .]

3. Title II of the Act

This Title is divided into seven sections beginning with 201(a) which provides that:

> All persons shall be entitled to the full and equal enjoyment of the goods, services, facilities, privileges, advantages, and accommodations of any place of public accommodation, as defined in this section, without discrimination or segregation on the ground of race, color, religion, or national origin.

There are listed in 201(b) four classes of business establishments, each of which "serves the public" and "is a place of public accommodation" within the meaning of 201(a) "if its operations affect commerce, or if discrimination or segregation by it is supported by State action." The covered establishments are:

> (1) any inn, hotel, motel, or other establishment which provides lodging to transient guests, other than an establishment located within a building which contains not more than five rooms for rent or hire and which is actually occupied by the proprietor of such establishment as his residence. [. . .]

Section 201(c) defines the phrase "affect commerce" as applied to the above establishments. It first declares that "any inn, hotel, motel, or other establishment which provides lodging to transient guests" affects commerce *per se.*" [. . .]

4. Application of Title II to Heart of Atlanta Motel

It is admitted that the operation of the motel brings it within the provisions of 201(a) of the Act and that appellant refused to provide lodging for transient Negroes because of their race or color and that it intends to continue that policy unless restrained.

The sole question posed is, therefore, the constitutionality of the Civil Rights Act of 1964 as applied to these facts. The legislative history of the Act indicates that Congress based the Act on 5 and the Equal Protection Clause of the Fourteenth Amendment as well as its power to regulate interstate commerce under Art. I, 8, cl. 3, of the Constitution.

The Senate Commerce Committee made it quite clear that the fundamental object of Title II was to vindicate "the deprivation of personal dignity that surely accompanies denials of equal access to public establishments." At the same time, however, it noted that such an objective has been and could be readily achieved "by congressional action based on the commerce power of the Constitution." Our study of the legislative record, made in the light of prior cases, has brought us to the conclusion that Congress possessed ample power in this regard, and we have therefore not considered the other grounds relied upon. This is not to say that the remaining authority upon which it acted was not adequate, a question upon which we do not pass, but merely that since the commerce power is sufficient for our decision here we have considered it alone. [. . .]

5. *The Civil Rights Cases (1883)*
and Their Application

In light of our ground for decision, it might be well at the outset to discuss the *Civil Rights Cases* which declared provisions of the Civil Rights Act of 1875 unconstitutional. We think that decision inapposite, and without precedential value in determining the constitutionality of the present Act. Unlike Title II of the present legislation, the 1875 Act broadly proscribed discrimination in "inns, public conveyances on land or water, theaters, and other places of public amusement," without limiting the categories of affected businesses to those impinging upon interstate commerce. In contrast, the applicability of Title II is carefully limited to enterprises having a direct and substantial relation to the interstate flow of goods and people, except where state action is involved. Further, the fact that certain kinds of businesses may not in 1875 have been sufficiently involved in interstate commerce to warrant bringing them within the ambit of the commerce power is not necessarily dispositive of the same question today. Our populace had not reached its present mobility, nor were facilities, goods and services circulating as readily in interstate commerce as they are today. Although the principles which we apply today are those first formulated by Chief Justice Marshall in *Gibbons v. Ogden* (1824), the conditions of transportation and commerce have changed dramatically, and we must apply those principles to the present state of commerce. The sheer increase in volume of interstate traffic alone would give discriminatory practices which inhibit travel a far larger impact upon the Nation's commerce than such practices had on the economy of another day. Finally, there is language in the Civil Rights Cases which indicates that the Court did not fully consider whether the 1875 Act could be sustained as an exercise of the commerce power. [. . .]

Since the commerce power was not relied on by the Government and was without support in the record it is understandable that the Court narrowed

its inquiry and excluded the Commerce Clause as a possible source of power. In any event, it is clear that such a limitation renders the opinion devoid of authority for the proposition that the Commerce Clause gives no power to Congress to regulate discriminatory practices now found substantially to affect interstate commerce. We, therefore, conclude that the *Civil Rights Cases* have no relevance to the basis of decision here where the Act explicitly relies upon the commerce power, and where the record is filled with testimony of obstructions and restraints resulting from the discriminations found to be existing. We now pass to that phase of the case.

6. *The Basis of Congressional Action*

While the Act as adopted carried no congressional findings the record of its passage through each house is replete with evidence of the burdens that discrimination by race or color places upon interstate commerce. This testimony included the fact that our people have become increasingly mobile with millions of people of all races traveling from State to State; that Negroes in particular have been the subject of discrimination in transient accommodations, having to travel great distances to secure the same; that often they have been unable to obtain accommodations and have had to call upon friends to put them up overnight, and that these conditions had become so acute as to require the listing of available lodging for Negroes in a special guidebook which was itself "dramatic testimony to the difficulties" Negroes encounter in travel. These exclusionary practices were found to be nationwide, the Under Secretary of Commerce testifying that there is "no question that this discrimination in the North still exists to a large degree" and in the West and Midwest as well. This testimony indicated a qualitative as well as quantitative effect on interstate travel by Negroes. The former was the obvious impairment of the Negro traveler's pleasure and convenience that resulted when he continually was uncertain of finding lodging. As for the latter, there was evidence that this uncertainty stemming from racial discrimination had the effect of discouraging travel on the part of a substantial portion of the Negro community. This was the conclusion not only of the Under Secretary of Commerce but also of the Administrator of the

Federal Aviation Agency who wrote the Chairman of the Senate Commerce Committee that it was his "belief that air commerce is adversely affected by the denial to a substantial segment of the traveling public of adequate and desegregated public accommodations." We shall not burden this opinion with further details since the voluminous testimony presents overwhelming evidence that discrimination by hotels and motels impedes interstate travel.

7. *The Power of Congress over Interstate Travel*

The power of Congress to deal with these obstructions depends on the meaning of the Commerce Clause. Its meaning was first enunciated 140 years ago by the great Chief Justice John Marshall in *Gibbons v. Ogden* (1824), in these words: [. . .]

> It is the power to regulate; that is, to prescribe the rule by which commerce is to be governed. This power, like all others vested in Congress, is complete in itself, may be exercised to its utmost extent, and acknowledges no limitations, other than are prescribed in the Constitution. . . . If, as has always been understood, the sovereignty of Congress . . . is plenary as to those objects [specified in the Constitution], the power over commerce . . . is vested in Congress as absolutely as it would be in a single government, having in its constitution the same restrictions on the exercise of the power as are found in the Constitution of the United States. The wisdom and the discretion of Congress, their identity with the people, and the influence which their constituents possess at elections, are, in this, as in many other instances, as that, for example, of declaring war, the sole restraints on which they have relied, to secure them from its abuse. They are the restraints on which the people must often rely solely, in all representative governments.

In short, the determinative test of the exercise of power by the Congress under the Commerce Clause is simply whether the activity sought to be regulated is "commerce which concerns more States than one" and has a real and substantial relation to the national interest. Let us now turn to this facet of the problem.

That the "intercourse" of which the Chief Justice spoke included the movement of persons through more States than one was settled as early as 1849, in the *Passenger Cases*, where Mr. Justice McLean stated: "That the transportation of passengers is a part of commerce is not now an open question." [. . .]

The same interest in protecting interstate commerce which led Congress to deal with segregation in interstate carriers and the white-slave traffic has prompted it to extend the exercise of its power to gambling, *Lottery Case* (1903); to criminal enterprises, *Brooks v. United States* (1925); to deceptive practices in the sale of products, *Federal Trade Comm'n v. Mandel Bros., Inc.* (1959); to fraudulent security transactions, *Securities & Exchange Comm'n v. Ralston Purina Co.* (1953); to misbranding of drugs, *Weeks v. United States* (1918); to wages and hours, *United States, v. Darby* (1941); to members of labor unions, *Labor Board v. Jones & Laughlin Steel Corp.* (1937); to crop control, *Wickard v. Filburn* (1942); to discrimination against shippers, *United States v. Baltimore & Ohio R. Co.* (1948); to the protection of small business from injurious price cutting, *Moore v. Mead's Fine Bread Co.* (1954); to resale price maintenance, *Hudson Distributors, Inc. v. Eli Lilly & Co.* (1964); to professional football, *Radovich v. National Football League* (1957); and to racial discrimination by owners and managers of terminal restaurants, *Boynton v. Virginia* (1960).

That Congress was legislating against moral wrongs in many of these areas rendered its enactments no less valid. In framing Title II of this Act Congress was also dealing with what it considered a moral problem. But that fact does not detract from the overwhelming evidence of the disruptive effect that racial discrimination has had on commercial intercourse. It was this burden which empowered Congress to enact appropriate legislation, and, given this basis for the exercise of its power, Congress was not restricted by the fact that the particular obstruction to interstate commerce with which it was dealing was also deemed a moral and social wrong.

It is said that the operation of the motel here is of a purely local character. But, assuming this to be true, "[i]f it is interstate commerce that feels the pinch, it does not matter how local the operation which applies the squeeze." *United States v. Women's Sportswear Mfrs. Assn.* (1949). As Chief Justice Stone put it in *United States v. Darby,*

The power of Congress over interstate commerce is not confined to the regulation of commerce among the states. It extends to those activities intrastate which so affect interstate commerce or the exercise of the power of Congress over it as to make regulation of them appropriate means to the attainment of a legitimate end, the exercise of the granted power of Congress to regulate interstate commerce.

Thus the power of Congress to promote interstate commerce also includes the power to regulate the local incidents thereof, including local activities in both the States of origin and destination, which might have a substantial and harmful effect upon that commerce. One need only examine the evidence which we have discussed above to see that Congress may—as it has—prohibit racial discrimination by motels serving travelers, however "local" their operations may appear.

Nor does the Act deprive appellant of liberty or property under the Fifth Amendment. The commerce power invoked here by the Congress is a specific and plenary one authorized by the Constitution itself. The only questions are: (1) whether Congress had a rational basis for finding that racial discrimination by motels affected commerce, and (2) if it had such a basis, whether the means it selected to eliminate that evil are reasonable and appropriate. If they are, appellant has no "right" to select its guests as it sees fit, free from governmental regulation. [. . .]

We [. . .] conclude that the action of the Congress in the adoption of the Act as applied here to a motel which concededly serves interstate travelers is within the power granted it by the Commerce Clause of the Constitution, as interpreted by this Court for 140 years. It may be argued that Congress could have pursued other methods to eliminate the obstructions it found in interstate commerce caused by racial discrimination. But this is a matter of policy that rests entirely with the Congress not with the courts. How obstructions in commerce may be removed—what means are to be employed—is within the sound and exclusive discretion of the Congress. It is subject only to one caveat—that the means chosen by it must be reasonably adapted to the end permitted by the Constitution. We cannot say that its choice here was not so adapted. The Constitution requires no more.

Katzenbach, Acting Attorney General, et al. v. McClung et al. (1964)

Mr. Justice CLARK delivered the opinion of the Court.

This case was argued with No. 515, *Heart of Atlanta Motel v. United States*, decided this date, in which we upheld the constitutional validity of Title II of the Civil Rights Act of 1964 against an attack by hotels, motels, and like establishments. This complaint for injunctive relief against appellants attacks the constitutionality of the Act as applied to a restaurant. The case was heard by a three-judge United States District Court and an injunction was issued restraining appellants from enforcing the Act against the restaurant. [. . .]

2. The Facts

Ollie's Barbecue is a family-owned restaurant in Birmingham, Alabama, specializing in barbecued meats and homemade pies, with a seating capacity of 220 customers. It is located on a state highway 11 blocks from [. . .] interstate one and a somewhat greater distance from railroad and bus stations. The restaurant caters to a family and white-collar trade with a take-out service for Negroes. It employs 36 persons, two-thirds of whom are Negroes.

In the 12 months preceding the passage of the Act, the restaurant purchased locally approximately $150,000 worth of food, $69,683 or 46% of which was meat that it bought from a local supplier who had procured it from outside the State. The District Court expressly found that a substantial portion of the food served in the restaurant had moved in interstate commerce. The restaurant has refused to serve Negroes in its dining accommodations since its original opening in 1927, and since July 2, 1964, it has been operating in violation of the Act. The court below concluded that if it were required to serve Negroes it would lose a substantial amount of business. [. . .]

The basic holding in *Heart of Atlanta Motel,* answers many of the contentions made by the appellees. There we outlined the overall purpose and operational plan of Title II and found it a valid exercise of the power to regulate interstate commerce insofar as it requires hotels and motels to serve transients without regard to their race or color. In this case we consider its application to restaurants which serve food a substantial portion of which has moved in commerce. [. . .]

3. *The Act as Applied*

Sections 201 (b) (2) and (c) place any "restaurant . . . principally engaged in selling food for consumption on the premises" under the Act "if . . . it serves or offers to serve interstate travelers or a substantial portion of the food which it serves . . . has moved in commerce."

Ollie's Barbecue admits that it is covered by these provisions of the Act. The Government makes no contention that the discrimination at the restaurant was supported by the State of Alabama. There is no claim that interstate travelers frequented the restaurant. The sole question, therefore, narrows down to whether Title II, as applied to a restaurant annually receiving about $70,000 worth of food which has moved in commerce, is a valid exercise of the power of Congress. The Government has contended that Congress had ample basis upon which to find that racial discrimination at restaurants which receive from out of state a substantial portion of the food served does, in fact, impose commercial burdens of national magnitude upon interstate commerce. The appellees' major argument is directed to this premise. They urge that no such basis existed. It is to that question that we now turn.

4. *The Congressional Hearings*

As we noted in *Heart of Atlanta Motel* both Houses of Congress conducted prolonged hearings on the Act. And, as we said there, while no formal findings were made, which of course are not necessary, it is well that we make mention of the testimony at these hearings the better to understand the problem before Congress and determine whether the Act is a reasonable and appropriate means toward its solution. The record is replete with testimony of the burdens placed on interstate commerce by racial discrimination in restaurants. A comparison of per capita spending by Negroes in restaurants, theaters, and like establishments indicated less spending, after discounting income differences, in areas where discrimination is widely practiced. This condition, which was especially aggravated in the South, was attributed in the testimony of the Under Secretary of Commerce to racial segregation. This diminutive spending springing from a refusal to serve Negroes and their total loss as customers has, regardless of the absence of direct evidence, a close connection to interstate commerce. The fewer customers a restaurant enjoys the less food it sells and consequently the less it buys. In addition, the Attorney General testified that this type of discrimination imposed "an artificial restriction on the market" and interfered with the flow of merchandise. In addition, there were many references to discriminatory situations causing wide unrest and having a depressant effect on general business conditions in the respective communities.

Moreover there was an impressive array of testimony that discrimination in restaurants had a direct and highly restrictive effect upon interstate travel by Negroes. This resulted, it was said, because discriminatory practices prevent Negroes from buying prepared food served on the premises while on a trip, except in isolated and unkempt restaurants and under most unsatisfactory and often unpleasant conditions. This obviously discourages travel and obstructs interstate commerce for one can hardly travel without eating. Likewise, it was said, that discrimination deterred professional, as well as skilled, people from moving into areas where such practices occurred and thereby caused industry to be reluctant to establish there.

We believe that this testimony afforded ample basis for the conclusion that established restaurants in such areas sold less interstate goods because of the discrimination, that interstate travel was obstructed directly by it, that business in general suffered and that many new businesses refrained from establishing there as a result of it. Hence the District Court was in error in concluding that there was no connection between discrimination and the movement of interstate commerce. The court's conclusion that such a connection is outside "common experience" flies in the face of stubborn fact.

It goes without saying that, viewed in isolation, the volume of food purchased by Ollie's Barbecue from sources supplied from out of state was insignificant when compared with the total foodstuffs moving in commerce. But, as our late Brother Jackson said for the Court in *Wickard v. Filburn* (1942):

> That appellee's own contribution to the demand for wheat may be trivial by itself is not enough to remove him from the scope of federal regulation where, as here, his contribution, taken together with that of many others similarly situated, is far from trivial.

We noted in *Heart of Atlanta Motel* that a number of witnesses attested to the fact that racial discrimination was not merely a state or regional problem but was one of nationwide scope. Against this background, we must conclude that while the focus of the legislation was on the individual restaurant's relation to interstate commerce, Congress appropriately considered the importance of that connection with the knowledge that the discrimination was but "representative of many others throughout the country, the total incidence of which if left unchecked may well become far-reaching in its harm to commerce." *Polish Alliance v. Labor Board* (1944). [. . .]

5. The Power of Congress to Regulate Local Activities

Article I, 8, cl. 3, confers upon Congress the power "[t]o regulate Commerce . . . among the several States" and Clause 18 of the same Article grants it the power "[t]o make all Laws which shall be necessary and proper for carrying into Execution the foregoing Powers. . . ." This grant, as we have pointed out in *Heart of Atlanta Motel* "extends to those activities intrastate which so affect interstate commerce, or the exertion of the power of Congress over it, as to make regulation of them appropriate means to the attainment of a legitimate end, the effective execution of the granted power to regulate interstate commerce." Much is said about a restaurant business being local but "even if appellee's activity be local and though it may not be

regarded as commerce, it may still, whatever its nature, be reached by Congress if it exerts a substantial economic effect on interstate commerce. . . ." *Wickard v. Filburn*. The activities that are beyond the reach of Congress are "those which are completely within a particular State, which do not affect other States, and with which it is not necessary to interfere, for the purpose of executing some of the general powers of the government." *Gibbons v. Ogden* (1824). This rule is as good today as it was when Chief Justice Marshall laid it down almost a century and a half ago.

This Court has held time and again that this power extends to activities of retail establishments, including restaurants, which directly or indirectly burden or obstruct interstate commerce. We have detailed the cases in *Heart of Atlanta Motel*, and will not repeat them here. [. . .]

The appellees contend that Congress has arbitrarily created a conclusive presumption that all restaurants meeting the criteria set out in the Act "affect commerce." Stated another way, they object to the omission of a provision for a case-by-case determination—judicial or administrative—that racial discrimination in a particular restaurant affects commerce.

But Congress' action in framing this Act was not unprecedented. In *United States v. Darby* (1941), this Court held constitutional the Fair Labor Standards Act of 1938. There Congress determined that the payment of substandard wages to employees engaged in the production of goods for commerce, while not itself commerce, so inhibited it as to be subject to federal regulation. The appellees in that case argued, as do the appellees here, that the Act was invalid because it included no provision for an independent inquiry regarding the effect on commerce of substandard wages in a particular business. But the Court rejected the argument, observing that:

> [S]ometimes Congress itself has said that a particular activity affects the commerce, as it did in the present Act, the Safety Appliance Act and the Railway Labor Act. In passing on the validity of legislation of the class last mentioned the only function of courts is to determine whether the particular activity regulated or prohibited is within the reach of the federal power.

Here, as there, Congress has determined for itself that refusals of service to Negroes have imposed burdens both upon the interstate flow of food and upon the movement of products generally. Of course, the mere fact that Congress has said when particular activity shall be deemed to affect commerce does not preclude further examination by this Court. But where we find that the legislators, in light of the facts and testimony before them, have a rational basis for finding a chosen regulatory scheme necessary to the protection of commerce, our investigation is at an end. The only remaining question— one answered in the affirmative by the court below—is whether the particular restaurant either serves or offers to serve interstate travelers or serves food a substantial portion of which has moved in interstate commerce. [. . .]

Confronted as we are with the facts laid before Congress, we must conclude that it had a rational basis for finding that racial discrimination in restaurants had a direct and adverse effect on the free flow of interstate commerce. Insofar as the sections of the Act here relevant are concerned, 201(b) (2) and (c), Congress prohibited discrimination only in those establishments having a close tie to interstate commerce, i.e., those, like the McClungs', serving food

that has come from out of the State. We think in so doing that Congress acted well within its power to protect and foster commerce in extending the coverage of Title II only to those restaurants offering to serve interstate travelers or serving food, a substantial portion of which has moved in interstate commerce.

The absence of direct evidence connecting discriminatory restaurant service with the flow of interstate food, a factor on which the appellees place much reliance, is not, given the evidence as to the effect of such practices on other aspects of commerce, a crucial matter.

The power of Congress in this field is broad and sweeping; where it keeps within its sphere and violates no express constitutional limitation it has been the rule of this Court, going back almost to the founding days of the Republic, not to interfere. The Civil Rights Act of 1964, as here applied, we find to be plainly appropriate in the resolution of what the Congress found to be a national commercial problem of the first magnitude. We find it in no violation of any express limitations of the Constitution and we therefore declare it valid.

The judgment is therefore Reversed.

STUDENTS FOR A DEMOCRATIC SOCIETY

Port Huron Statement (1962)

Introduction:
Agenda for a Generation

We are people of this generation, bred in at least modest comfort, housed now in universities, looking uncomfortably to the world we inherit.

When we were kids the United States was the wealthiest and strongest country in the world: the only one with the atom bomb, the least scarred by modern war, an initiator of the United Nations that we thought would distribute Western influence throughout the world. Freedom and equality for each

individual, government of, by, and for the people— these American values we found good, principles by which we could live as men. Many of us began maturing in complacency.

As we grew, however, our comfort was penetrated by events too troubling to dismiss. First, the permeating and victimizing fact of human degradation, symbolized by the Southern struggle against racial bigotry, compelled most of us from silence to activism. Second, the enclosing fact of the Cold War, symbolized by the presence of the Bomb, brought awareness that we ourselves, and our friends, and millions of abstract "others" we knew more directly because of our common peril, might die at any time. We might deliberately ignore, or avoid, or fail to feel all other human problems, but not these two, for these were too immediate and crushing in their impact, too challenging in the demand that we as individuals take the responsibility for encounter and resolution.

While these and other problems either directly oppressed us or rankled our consciences and became our own subjective concerns, we began to see complicated and disturbing paradoxes in our surrounding America. The declaration "all men are created equal . . ." rang hollow before the facts of Negro life in the South and the big cities of the North. The proclaimed peaceful intentions of the United States contradicted its economic and military investments in the Cold War status quo.

We witnessed, and continue to witness, other paradoxes. With nuclear energy whole cities can easily be powered, yet the dominant nation-states seem more likely to unleash destruction greater than that incurred in all wars of human history. Although our own technology is destroying old and creating new forms of social organization, men still tolerate meaningless work and idleness. While two-thirds of mankind suffers undernourishment, our own upper classes revel amidst superfluous abundance. Although world population is expected to double in forty years, the nations still tolerate anarchy as a major principle of international conduct and uncontrolled exploitation governs the sapping of the earth's physical resources. Although mankind desperately needs revolutionary leadership, America rests in national stalemate, its goals ambiguous and tradition-bound instead of informed and clear, its democratic system apathetic and manipulated rather than "of, by, and for the people."

Not only did tarnish appear on our image of American virtue, not only did disillusion occur when the hypocrisy of American ideals was discovered, but we began to sense that what we had originally seen as the American Golden Age was actually the decline of an era. The worldwide outbreak of revolution against colonialism and imperialism, the entrenchment of totalitarian states, the menace of war, overpopulation, international disorder, supertechnology—these trends were testing the tenacity of our own commitment to democracy and freedom and our abilities to visualize their application to a world in upheaval.

Our work is guided by the sense that we may be the last generation in the experiment with living. But we are a minority—the vast majority of our people regard the temporary equilibriums of our society and world as eternally-functional parts. In this is perhaps the outstanding paradox: we ourselves are imbued with urgency, yet the message of our society is that there is no viable alternative to the present. Beneath the reassuring tones of the politicians, beneath the common opinion that America will "muddle through," beneath the stagnation of those who have closed their minds to the future, is the pervading feeling that there simply are no alternatives, that our times have witnessed the exhaustion not only of Utopias, but of any new departures as well. Feeling the press of complexity upon the emptiness of life, people are fearful of the thought that at any moment things might thrust out of control. They fear change itself, since change might smash whatever invisible framework seems to hold back chaos for them now. For most Americans, all crusades are suspect, threatening. The fact that each individual sees apathy in his fellows perpetuates the common reluctance to organize for change. The dominant institutions are complex enough to blunt the minds of their potential critics, and entrenched enough to swiftly dissipate or entirely repel the energies of protest and reform, thus limiting human expectancies. Then, too, we are a materially improved society, and by our own improvements we seem to have weakened the case for further change.

Some would have us believe that Americans feel contentment amidst prosperity—but might it not better be called a glaze above deeply felt anxieties about their role in the new world? And if these anxieties produce a developed indifference to human affairs, do they not as well produce a yearning to believe there is an alternative to the present, that something can be done to change circumstances in the school, the workplaces, the bureaucracies, the government? It is to this latter yearning, at once the spark and engine of change, that we direct our present appeal. The search for truly democratic alternatives to the present, and a commitment to social experimentation with them, is a worthy and fulfilling human enterprise, one which moves us and, we hope, others today. On such a basis do we offer this document of our convictions and analysis: as an effort in understanding and changing the conditions of humanity in the late twentieth century, an effort rooted in the ancient, still unfulfilled conception of man attaining determining influence over his circumstances of life. [. . .]

We regard men as infinitely precious and possessed of unfulfilled capacities for reason, freedom, and love. In affirming these principles we are aware of countering perhaps the dominant conceptions of man in the twentieth century: that he is a thing to be manipulated, and that he is inherently incapable of directing his own affairs. We oppose the depersonalization that reduces human beings to the status of things—if anything, the brutalities of the twentieth century teach that means and ends are intimately related, that vague appeals to "posterity" cannot justify the mutilations of the present. We oppose, too, the doctrine of human incompetence because it rests essentially on the modern fact that men have been "competently" manipulated into incompetence—we see little reason why men cannot meet with increasing skill the complexities and responsibilities of their situation, if society is organized not for minority, but for majority, participation in decision-making.

Men have unrealized potential for self-cultivation, self-direction, self-understanding, and creativity. It is this potential that we regard as crucial and to which we appeal, not to the human potentiality for violence, unreason, and submission to authority. The goal of man and society should be human independence: a concern not with image of popularity but with finding a meaning in life that is personally authentic: a quality of mind not compulsively driven by a sense of powerlessness, nor one which unthinkingly adopts status values, nor one which represses all threats to its habits, but one which has full, spontaneous access to present and past experiences, one which easily unites the fragmented parts of personal history, one which openly faces problems which are troubling and unresolved: one with an intuitive awareness of possibilities, an active sense of curiosity, an ability and willingness to learn.

This kind of independence does not mean egoistic individualism—the object is not to have one's way so much as it is to have a way that is one's own. Nor do we deify man—we merely have faith in his potential.

Human relationships should involve fraternity and honesty. Human interdependence is contemporary fact; human brotherhood must be willed however, as a condition of future survival and as the most appropriate form of social relations. Personal links between man and man are needed, especially to go beyond the partial and fragmentary bonds of function that bind men only as worker to worker, employer to employee, teacher to student, American to Russian.

Loneliness, estrangement, isolation describe the vast distance between man and man today. These dominant tendencies cannot be overcome by better personnel management, nor by improved gadgets, but only when a love of man overcomes the idolatrous worship of things by man.

As the individualism we affirm is not egoism, the selflessness we affirm is not self-elimination. On the contrary, we believe in generosity of a kind that imprints one's unique individual qualities in the relation to other men, and to all human activity. Further, to dislike isolation is not to favor the abolition of privacy; the latter differs from isolation in that it occurs or is abolished according to individual will. Finally, we would replace power and personal uniqueness rooted in possession, privilege, or circumstance by power and uniqueness rooted in love, reflectiveness, reason, and creativity.

As a social system we seek the establishment of a democracy of individual participation, governed by two central aims: that the individual share in those social decisions determining the quality and direction of his life; that society be organized to encourage independence in men and provide the media for their common participation.

In a participatory democracy, the political life would be based in several root principles:

- that decision-making of basic social consequence be carried on by public groupings;
- that politics be seen positively, as the art of collectively creating an acceptable pattern of social relations;
- that politics has the function of bringing people out of isolation and into community, thus being a necessary, though not sufficient, means of finding meaning in personal life;
- that the political order should serve to clarify problems in a way instrumental to their solution; it should provide outlets for the expression of personal grievance and

aspiration; opposing views should be organized so as to illuminate choices and facilities the attainment of goals; channels should be commonly available to related men to knowledge and to power so that private problems—from bad recreation facilities to personal alienation—are formulated as general issues.

The economic sphere would have as its basis the principles:

- that work should involve incentives worthier than money or survival. It should be educative, not stultifying; creative, not mechanical; self-directed, not manipulated, encouraging independence; a respect for others, a sense of dignity and a willingness to accept social responsibility, since it is this experience that has crucial influence on habits, perceptions and individual ethics;
- that the economic experience is so personally decisive that the individual must share in its full determination;
- that the economy itself is of such social importance that its major resources and means of production should be open to democratic participation and subject to democratic social regulation.

Like the political and economic ones, major social institutions—cultural, education, rehabilitative, and others—should be generally organized with the well-being and dignity of man as the essential measure of success.

In social change or interchange, we find violence to be abhorrent because it requires generally the transformation of the target, be it a human being or a community of people, into a depersonalized object of hate. It is imperative that the means of violence be abolished and the institutions—local, national, international—that encourage nonviolence as a condition of conflict be developed.

These are our central values, in skeletal form. It remains vital to understand their denial or attainment in the context of the modern world.

The Students

In the last few years, thousands of American students demonstrated that they at least felt the urgency of the times. They moved actively and directly against racial injustices, the threat of war, violations of individual rights of conscience and, less frequently, against economic manipulation. They succeeded in restoring a small measure of controversy to the campuses after the stillness of the McCarthy period. They succeeded, too, in gaining some concessions from the people and institutions they opposed, especially in the fight against racial bigotry.

The significance of these scattered movements lies not in their success or failure in gaining objectives—at least not yet. Nor does the significance lie in the intellectual "competence" or "maturity" of the students involved—as some pedantic elders allege. The significance is in the fact the students are breaking the crust of apathy and overcoming the inner alienation that remain the defining characteristics of American college life.

If student movements for change are rarities still on the campus scene, what is commonplace there? The real campus, the familiar campus, is a place of private people, engaged in their notorious "inner emigration." It is a place of commitment to business-as-usual, getting ahead, playing it cool. It is a place of mass affirmation of the Twist, but mass reluctance toward the controversial public stance. Rules are accepted as "inevitable," bureaucracy as "just circumstances," irrelevance as "scholarship," selflessness as "martyrdom," politics as "just another way to make people, and an unprofitable one, too."

Almost no students value activity as a citizen. Passive in public, they are hardly more idealistic in arranging their private lives: Gallup concludes they will settle for "low success, and won't risk high failure." There is not much willingness to take risks (not even in business), no setting of dangerous goals, no real conception of personal identity except one manufactured in the image of others, no real urge for personal fulfillment except to be almost as successful as the very successful people. Attention is being paid to social status (the quality of shirt collars, meeting people, getting wives or husbands, making solid contacts for later on); much too, is paid to academic status (grades, honors, the med school rat-race). But neglected generally is real intellectual status, the personal cultivation of the mind.

"Students don't even give a damn about the apathy," one has said. Apathy toward apathy begets a privately-constructed universe, a place of systematic study schedules, two nights each week for beer, a girl or two, and early marriage; a framework infused with personality, warmth, and under control, no matter how unsatisfying otherwise.

Under these conditions university life loses all relevance to some. Four hundred thousand of our classmates leave college every year.

But apathy is not simply an attitude; it is a product of social institutions, and of the structure and organization of higher education itself. The extracurricular life is ordered according to in loco parentis theory, which ratifies the Administration as the moral guardian of the young. The accompanying "let's pretend" theory of student extracurricular affairs validates student government as a training center for those who want to spend their lives in political pretense, and discourages initiative from more articulate, honest, and sensitive students. The bounds and style of controversy are delimited before controversy begins. The university "prepares" the student for "citizenship" through perpetual rehearsals and, usually, through emasculation of what creative spirit there is in the individual.

The academic life contains reinforcing counterparts to the way in which extracurricular life is organized. The academic world is founded in a teacher-student relation analogous to the parent-child relation which characterizes in loco parentis. Further, academia includes a radical separation of student from the material of study. That which is studied, the social reality, is "objectified" to sterility, dividing the student from life—just as he is restrained in active involvement by the deans controlling student government. The specialization of function and knowledge, admittedly necessary to our complex technological and social structure, has produced and exaggerated compartmentalization of study and understanding. This has contributed to: an overly parochial view, by faculty, of the role of its research and scholarship; a discontinuous and truncated understanding, by students, of the surrounding social order; a loss of personal attachment, by nearly all, to the worth of study as a humanistic enterprise.

There is, finally, the cumbersome academic bureaucracy extending throughout the academic as well as extracurricular structures, contributing to the sense of outer complexity and inner powerlessness that transforms so many students from honest searching to ratification of convention and, worse, to a numbness of present and future catastrophes. The size and financing systems of the university enhance the permanent trusteeship of the administrative bureaucracy, their power leading to a shift to the value standards of business and administrative mentality within the university. Huge foundations and other private financial interests shape under-financed colleges and universities, not only making them more commercial, but less disposed to diagnose society critically, less open to dissent. Many social and physical scientists, neglecting the liberating heritage of higher learning, develop "human relations" or "morale-producing" techniques for the corporate economy, while others exercise their intellectual skills to accelerate the arms race.

Tragically, the university could serve as a significant source of social criticism and an initiator of new modes and molders of attitudes. But the actual intellectual effect of the college experience is hardly distinguishable from that of any other communications channel—say, a television set—passing on the stock truths of the day. Students leave college somewhat more "tolerant" than when they arrived, but basically unchallenged in their values and political orientations. With administrators ordering the institutions, and faculty the curriculum, the student learns by his isolation to accept elite rule within the university, which prepares him to accept later forms of minority control. The real function of the educational system—as opposed to its more rhetorical function of "searching for truth"—is to impart the key information and styles that will help the student get by, modestly but comfortably, in the big society beyond. [. . .]

Politics without Publics

The American political system is not the democratic model of which its glorifiers speak. In actuality it frustrates democracy by confusing the individual citizen, paralyzing policy discussion, and consolidating the irresponsible power of military and business interests.

A crucial feature of the political apparatus in America is that greater differences are harbored within each major party than the differences existing between them. Instead of two parties presenting distinctive and significant differences of approach, what dominates the system if a natural interlocking of Democrats from Southern states with the more conservative elements of the Republican party. This arrangement of forces is blessed by the seniority system of Congress which guarantees congressional committee domination by conservatives—ten of 17 committees in the Senate and 13 of 21 in House of Representatives are chaired currently by Dixiecrats.

The party overlap, however, is not the only structural antagonist of democracy in politics. First, the localized nature of the party system does not encourage discussion of national and international issues: thus problems are not raised by and for people, and political representatives usually are unfettered from any responsibilities to the general public except those regarding parochial matters. Second, whole constituencies are divested of the full political power they might have: many Negroes in the South are prevented from voting, migrant workers are disenfranchised by various residence requirements, some urban and suburban dwellers are victimized by gerrymandering, and poor people are too often without the power to obtain political representation. Third, the focus of political attention is significantly distorted by the enormous lobby force, composed predominantly of business interests, spending hundreds of millions each year in an attempt to conform facts about productivity, agriculture, defense, and social services, to the wants of private economic groupings.

What emerges from the party contradictions and insulation of privately held power is the organized political stalemate: calcification dominates flexibility as the principle of parliamentary organization, frustration is the expectancy of legislators intending liberal reform, and Congress becomes less and less central to national decision-making, especially in the area of foreign policy. In this context, confusion and blurring is built into the formulation of issues, long-range priorities are not discussed in the rational manner needed for policymaking, the politics of personality and "image" become a more important mechanism than the construction of issues in a way that affords each voter a challenging and real option.

The American voter is buffeted from all directions by pseudo-problems, by the structurally-initiated sense that nothing political is subject to human mastery. Worried by his mundane problems which never get solved, but constrained by the common belief that politics is an agonizingly slow accommodation of views, he quits all pretense of bothering.

A most alarming fact is that few, if any, politicians are calling for changes in these conditions. Only a handful even are calling on the President to "live up to" platform pledges; no one is demanding structural changes, such as the shuttling of Southern Democrats out of the Democratic Party. Rather than protesting the state of politics, most politicians are reinforcing and aggravating that state. While in practice they rig public opinion to suit their own interests, in word and ritual they enshrine "the sovereign public" and call for more and more letters. Their speeches and campaign actions are banal, based on a degrading conception of what people want to hear. They respond not to dialogue, but to pressure: and knowing this, the ordinary citizen sees even greater inclination to shun the political sphere. The politicians is usually a trumpeter to "citizenship" and "service to the nation," but since he is unwilling to seriously rearrange power relationships, his trumpetings only increase apathy by creating no outlets. Much of the time the call to "service" is justified not in idealistic terms, but in the crasser terms of "defending the free world from communism"—thus making future idealistic impulses harder to justify in anything but Cold War terms.

In such a setting of status quo politics, where most if not all government activity is rationalized in Cold War anti-communist terms, it is somewhat natural that discontented, super-patriotic groups would emerge through political channels and explain their ultra-conservatism as the best means of Victory over Communism. They have become a politically influential force within the Republican Party, at a national level through Senator Goldwater, and at a local level through their important social and economic roles. Their political views are defined generally as the opposite of the supposed views of communists: complete individual freedom in the economic sphere, non-participation by the government in the machinery of production. But actually "anticommunism" becomes an umbrella by which to protest liberalism, internationalism, welfarism, the active civil rights and labor movements. It is to the disgrace of the United States that such a movement should become a prominent kind of public participation in the modem world—but, ironically, it is somewhat to the interests of the United States that such a movement should be a public constituency pointed toward realignment of the political parties, demanding a conservative Republican Party in the South and an exclusion of the "leftist" elements of the national GOP.

The Economy

American capitalism today advertises itself as the Welfare State. Many of us comfortably expect pensions, medical care, unemployment compensation, and other social services in our lifetimes. Even with one-fourth of our productive capacity unused, the majority of Americans are living in relative comfort—although their nagging incentive to "keep up" makes them continually dissatisfied with their possessions. In many places, unrestrained bosses, uncontrolled machines, and sweatshop conditions have been reformed or abolished and suffering tremendously relieved. But in spite of the benign yet obscuring effects of the New Deal reforms and the reassuring phrases of government economists and politicians, the paradoxes and myths of the economy are sufficient to irritate our complacency and reveal to us some essential causes of the American malaise.

We live amidst a national celebration of economic prosperity while poverty and deprivation remain an unbreakable way of life for millions in the "affluent society," including many of our own generation. We hear glib reference to the "welfare state," "free enterprise," and "shareholder's democracy" while military defense is the main item of "public" spending and obvious oligopoly and other forms of minority rule defy real individual initiative or popular control. Work, too, is often unfulfilling and victimizing, accepted as a channel to status or plenty, if not a way to pay the bills, rarely as a means of understanding and controlling self and events. In work and leisure the individual is regulated as part of the system, a consuming unit, bombarded by hardsell softsell, lies and semi-true appeals and his basest drives.

He is always told what he is supposed to enjoy while being told, too, that he is a "free" man because of "free enterprise."

The Remote Control Economy.   We are subject to a remote control economy, which excludes the mass of individual "units"—the people—from basic decisions affecting the nature and organization of work, rewards, and opportunities. The modem concentration of wealth is fantastic. The wealthiest one percent of Americans own more than 80 percent of all personal shares of stock. From World War II until the mid-Fifties, the 50 biggest corporations increased their manufacturing production from 17 to 23 percent of the national total, and the share of the largest 200 companies rose from 30 to 37 percent. To regard the various decisions of these elites as purely economic is short-sighted: their decisions affect in a momentous way the entire fabric of social life in America. Foreign investments influence political policies in under-developed areas—and our efforts to build a "profitable" capitalist world blind our foreign policy to mankind's needs and destiny. The drive for sales spurs phenomenal advertising efforts; the ethical drug industry, for instance, spent more than $750 million on promotions in 1960, nearly for times the amount available to all American medical schools for their educational programs. The arts, too, are organized substantially according to their commercial appeal aesthetic values are subordinated to exchange values, and writers swiftly learn to consider the commercial market as much as the humanistic marketplace of ideas. The tendency to over-production, to gluts of surplus commodities, encourages "market research" techniques to deliberately create pseudo-needs in consumers—we learn to buy "smart" things, regardless of their utility—and introduces wasteful "planned obsolescence" as a permanent feature of business strategy. While real social needs accumulate as rapidly as profits, it becomes evident that Money, instead of dignity of character, remains a pivotal American value and Profitability, instead of social use, a pivotal standard in determining priorities of resource allocation.

Within existing arrangements, the American business community cannot be said to encourage a democratic process nationally. Economic minorities not responsible to a public in any democratic fashion make decisions of a more profound importance than even those made by Congress. Such a claim is usually dismissed by respectful and knowing citations of the ways in which government asserts itself as keeper of the public interest at times of business irresponsibility. But the real, as opposed to the mythical, range of government "control" of the economy includes only:

1. some limited "regulatory" powers—which usually just ratify industry policies or serve as palliatives at the margins of significant business activity;

2. a fiscal policy built upon defense expenditures as pump-priming "public works"—without a significant emphasis on "peaceful public works" to meet social priorities and alleviate personal hardships;

3. limited fiscal and monetary weapons which are rigid and have only minor effects, and are greatly limited by corporate veto: tax cuts and reforms; interest rate control (used generally to tug on investment by hurting the little investor most); tariffs which protect noncompetitive industries with political power and which keep less-favored nations out of the large trade mainstream, as the removal of barriers reciprocally with the Common Market may do disastrously to emerging countries outside of Europe; wage arbitration, the use of government coercion in the name of "public interest" to hide the tensions between workers and business production controllers; price controls, which further maintains the status quo of big ownership and flushes out little investors for me sake of "stability";

4. very limited "poverty-solving" which is designed for the organized working class but not the shut-out, poverty-stricken migrants, farm workers, the indigent unaware of medical care or the lower-middle class person riddled with medical bills, the "unhireables" of minority groups or workers over 45 years of age, etc.

5. regional development programs—such as the Area Redevelopment Act

- which have been only "trickle down" welfare programs without broad authority for regional planning and development and public works spending. The federal highway program has been more significant than the "depressed areas" program in meeting the needs of people, but is generally too remote and does not reach the vicious circle of poverty itself.

In short, the theory of government "countervailing" business neglects the extent to which government influence is marginal to the basic production decisions, the basic decision-making environment of society, the basic structure or distribution and allocation which is still determined by major corporations with power and wealth concentrated among the few. A conscious conspiracy—as in the case of price rigging in the electrical industry—is by no means generally or continuously operative but power undeniably does rest in comparative insulation from the public and its political representatives.

The Military-Industrial Complex.   The most spectacular and important creation of the authoritarian and oligopolistic structure of economic decision-making in America is the institution called "the military industrial complex" by former President Eisenhower, the powerful congruence of interest and structure among military and business elites which affects so much of our development and destiny. Not only is ours the first generation to live with the possibility of world-wide cataclysm—it is the first to experience the actual social preparation for cataclysm, the general militarization of American society. In 1948 Congress established Universal Military Training, the first peacetime conscription. The military became a permanent institution. Four years earlier, General Motor's Charles E. Wilson had heralded the creation of what he called the "permanent war economy," the continuous use of military spending as a solution to economic problems unsolved before the post-war boom, most notably the problem of the seventeen million jobless after eight years of the New Deal. This has left a "hidden crisis" in the allocation of resources by the American economy. [. . .]

The Individual
in the Warfare State

Business and politics, when significantly militarized, affect the whole living condition of each American citizen. Worker and family depend on the Cold War for life. Half of all research and development is concentrated on military ends. The press mimics conventional cold war opinion in its editorials. In less than a full generation, most Americans accept the military-industrial structure as "the way things are." War is still pictured as one more kind of diplomacy, perhaps a gloriously satisfying kind. Our saturation and atomic bombings of Germany and Japan are little more than memories of past "policy necessities" that preceded the wonderful economic boom of 1946. The facts that our once-revolutionary 20,000 ton Hiroshima Bomb is now paled by 50 megaton weapons, that our lifetime has included the creation of intercontinental ballistic missiles, that "greater" weapons are to follow, that weapons refinement is more rapid than the development of weapons of defense, that soon a dozen or more nations will have the Bomb, that one simple miscalculation could incinerate mankind: these orienting facts are but remotely felt. A shell of moral callousness separates the citizen from sensitivity of the common peril: this is the result of a lifetime saturation with horror. After all, some ask, where could we begin, even if we wanted to? After all, others declare, we can only assume things are in the best of hands. A coed at the University of Kentucky says, "we regard peace and war as fairy tales." And a child has asked in helplessness, perhaps for us all, "Daddy, why is there a cold war?"

Past senselessness permits present brutality; present brutality is prelude to future deeds of still greater inhumanity; that is the moral history of the twentieth century, from the First World War to the present. A half-century of accelerating destruction has flattened out the individual's ability to make moral distinction, it has made people understandably give up, it has forced private worry and public silence.

To a decisive extent, the means of defense, the military technology itself, determines the political and social character of the state being defended — that is, defense mechanism themselves in the nuclear age alter the character of the system that creates them

for protection. So it has been with America, as her democratic institutions and habits have shriveled in almost direct proportion to the growth of her armaments. Decisions about military strategy, including the monstrous decision to go to war, are more and more the property of the military and the industrial arms race machine, with the politicians assuming a ratifying role instead of a determining one. This is increasingly a fact not just because of the installation of the permanent military, but because of constant revolutions in military technology. The new technologies allegedly require military expertise, scientific comprehension, and the mantle of secrecy. As Congress relies more and more on the Joint Chiefs of Staff, the existing chasm between people and decision-makers becomes irreconcilably wide, and more alienating in its effects. [. . .]

Deterrence Policy

The accumulation of nuclear arsenals, the threat of accidental war, the possibility of limited war becoming illimitable holocaust, the impossibility of achieving final arms superiority or invulnerability, the approaching nativity of a cluster of infant atomic powers; all of these events are tending to undermine traditional concepts of power relations among nations. War can no longer be considered as an effective instrument of foreign policy, a means of strengthening alliances, adjusting the balance of power, maintaining national sovereignty, or preserving human values. War is no longer simply a forceful extension of foreign policy; it can obtain no constructive ends in the modem world. Soviet or American "megatonnage" is sufficient to destroy all existing social structures as well as value systems. Missiles have (figuratively) thumbed their nose cones at national boundaries. But America, like other countries, still operates by means of national defense and deterrence systems. These are seen to be useful so long as they are never fully used: unless we as a national entity can convince Russia that we are willing to commit the most heinous action in human history, we will be forced to commit it. [. . .]

All the deterrence theories suffer in several common ways. They allow insufficient attention to preserving, extending, and enriching democratic values, such matters being subordinate rather than governing in the process of conducting foreign policy. Second, they inadequately realize the inherent instabilities of the continuing arms race and balance of fear. Third, they operationally tend to eclipse interest and action towards disarmament by solidifying economic, political and even moral investments in continuation of tensions. Fourth, they offer a disinterested and even patriotic rationale for the boondoggling, belligerence, and privilege of military and economic elites. Finally, deterrence stratagems invariably understate or dismiss the relatedness of various dangers; they inevitably lend tolerability to the idea of war by neglecting the dynamic interaction of problems—such as the menace of accidental war, the probable future tensions surrounding the emergence of ex-colonial nations, the imminence of several new nations joining the "Nuclear Club," the destabilizing potential of technological breakthrough by either arms race contestant, the threat of Chinese atomic might, the fact that "recovery" after World War III would involve not only human survivors but, as well, a huge and fragile social structure and culture which would be decimated perhaps irreparably by total war.

Such a harsh critique of what we are doing as a nation by no means implies that sole blame for the Cold War rests on the United States. Both sides have behaved irresponsibly—the Russians by an exaggerated lack of trust, and by much dependence on aggressive military strategists rather than on proponents of nonviolent conflict and coexistence. But we do contend, as Americans concerned with the conduct of our representative institutions, that our government has blamed the Cold War stalemate on nearly everything but its own hesitations, its own anachronistic dependence on weapons. To be sure, there is more to disarmament than wishing for it. There are inadequacies in international rule-making institutions—which could be corrected. There are faulty inspection mechanisms—which could be perfected by disinterested scientists. There is Russian intransigency and evasiveness—which do not erase the fact that the Soviet Union, because of a strained economy, an expectant population, fears of Chinese potential, and interest in the colonial revolution, is increasingly disposed to real disarmament with real controls. But there is, too, our own reluctance to face the uncertain world beyond the Cold War, our own

shocking assumption that the risks of the present are fewer than the risks of a policy re-orientation to disarmament, our own unwillingness to face the implementation of our rhetorical commitments to peace and freedom. [. . .]

The Industrialization of the World

Many Americans are prone to think of the industrialization of the newly developed countries as a modern form of American noblesse, undertaken sacrificially for the benefit of others. On the contrary, the task of world industrialization, of eliminating the disparity between have and have-not nations, is as important as any issue facing America. The colonial revolution signals the end of an era for the old Western powers and a time of new beginnings for most of the people of the earth. In the course of these upheavals, many problems will emerge: American policies must be revised or accelerated in several ways.

1. The United States' principal goal should be creating a world where hunger, poverty, disease, ignorance, violence, and exploitation are replaced as central features by abundance, reason, love, and international cooperation. To many this will seem the product of juvenile hallucination: but we insist it is a more realistic goal than is a world of nuclear stalemate. Some will say this is a hope beyond all bounds: but is far better to us to have positive vision than a "hard headed" resignation. Some will sympathize, but claim it is impossible: if so, then, we, not Fate, are the responsible ones, for we have the means at our disposal. We should not give up the attempt for fear of failure.

2. We should undertake here and now a fifty-year effort to prepare for all nations the conditions of industrialization. Even with far more capital and skill than we now import to emerging areas, serious prophets expect that two generations will pass before accelerating industrialism is a worldwide act. The needs are numerous: every nation must build an adequate infrastructure (transportation, communication, land resources, waterways) for future industrial growth; there must be industries suited to the rapid development of differing raw materials and other resources; education must begin on a continuing basis for everyone in the society, especially including engineering and technical training; technical

assistance from outside sources must be adequate to meet present and long-term needs; atomic power plants must spring up to make electrical energy available. With America's idle productive capacity, it is possible to begin this process immediately without changing our military allocations. This might catalyze a "peace race" since it would demand a response of such magnitude from the Soviet Union that arms spending and "coexistence" spending would become strenuous, perhaps impossible, for the Soviets to carry on simultaneously.

3. We should not depend significantly on private enterprise to do the job. Many important projects will not be profitable enough to entice the investment of private capital. The total amount required is far beyond the resources of corporate and philanthropic concerns. The new nations are suspicious, legitimately, of foreign enterprises dominating their national life. World industrialization is too huge an undertaking to be formulated or carried out by private interests. Foreign economic assistance is a national problem, requiring long range planning, integration with other domestic and foreign policies, and considerable public debate and analysis. Therefore the Federal government should have primary responsibility in this area.

4. We should not lock the development process into the Cold War: we should view it as a way of ending that conflict. When President Kennedy declared that we must aid those who need aid because it is right, he was unimpeachably correct—now principle must become practice. We should reverse the trend of aiding corrupt anti-communist regimes. To support dictators like Diem while trying to destroy ones like Castro will only enforce international cynicism about American "principle," and is bound to lead to even more authoritarian revolutions, especially in Latin America where we did not even consider foreign aid until Castro had challenged the status quo. We should end the distinction between communist hunger and anti-communist hunger. To feed only anticommunists is to directly fatten men like Boun Oum, to incur the wrath of real democrats, and to distort our own sense of human values. We must cease seeing development in terms of communism and capitalism. To fight communism by capitalism in the newly-developing areas is to fundamentally misunderstand the international hatred of imperialism and colonialism and to confuse the needs of 19th century industrial America with those of contemporary nations.

Quite fortunately, we are edging away from the Dullesian "either-or" foreign policy ultimatum towards an uneasy acceptance of neutralism and nonalignment. If we really desire the end of the Cold War, we should now welcome nonalignment—that is, the creation of whole blocs of nations concerned with growth and with independently trying to break out of the Cold War apparatus.

Finally, while seeking disarmament as the genuine deterrent, we should shift from financial support of military regimes to support of national development. Real security cannot be gained by propping up military defenses, but only through the hastening of political stability, economic growth, greater social welfare, improved education. Military aid is temporary in nature, a "shoring up" measure that only postpones crisis. In addition, it tends to divert the allocations of the nation being defended to supplementary military spending (Pakistan's budget is 70% oriented to defense measures). Sometimes it actually creates crisis situations, as in Latin America where we have contributed to the growth of national armies which are opposed generally to sweeping democratization. Finally, if we are really generous, it is harder for corrupt governments to exploit unfairly economic aid—especially if it is to plentiful that rulers cannot blame the absence of real reforms on anything but their own power lusts.

5. America should show its commitment to democratic institutions not by withdrawing support from undemocratic regimes, but by making domestic democracy exemplary. Worldwide amusement, cynicism and hatred toward the United States as a democracy is not simply a communist propaganda trick, but an objectively justifiable phenomenon. If respect for democracy is to be international, then the significance of democracy must emanate from America shores, not from the "soft sell" of the United States Information Agency. [. . .]

Towards American Democracy

Every effort to end the Cold War and expand the process of world industrialization is an effort hostile to people and institutions whose interests lie in perpetuation of the East-West military threat and the postponement of change in the "have not" nations of the world. Every such effort, too, is bound to establish greater democracy in America. The major goals of a domestic effort would be:

1. America must abolish its political party stalemate. Two genuine parties, centered around issues and essential values, demanding allegiance to party principles shall supplant the current system of organized stalemate which is seriously inadequate to a world in flux. It has long been argued that the very overlapping of American parties guarantees that issues will be considered responsibly, that progress will be gradual instead of intemperate, and that therefore America will remain stable instead of torn by class strife. On the contrary: the enormous party overlap itself confuses issues and makes responsible presentation of choice to the electorate impossible, that guarantees Congressional listlessness and the drift of power to military and economic bureaucracies, that directs attention away from the more fundamental causes of social stability, such as a huge middle class, Keynesian economic techniques and Madison Avenue advertising. The ideals of political democracy, then, the imperative need for flexible decision-making apparatus makes a real two-party system an immediate social necessity. What is desirable is sufficient party disagreement to dramatize major issues, yet sufficient party overlap to guarantee stable transitions from administration to administration.

Every time the President criticizes a recalcitrant Congress, we must ask that he no longer tolerate the Southern conservatives in the Democratic Party. Every time [a] liberal representative complains that "we can't expect everything at once" we must ask if we received much of anything from Congress in the last generation. Every time he refers to "circumstances beyond control" we must ask why he fraternizes with racist scoundrels. Every time he speaks of the "unpleasantness of personal and party fighting" we should insist that pleasantry with Dixiecrats is inexcusable when the dark peoples of the world call for American support.

2. Mechanisms of voluntary association must be created through which political information can be imparted and political participation encouraged. Political parties, even if realigned, would not provide adequate outlets for popular involvement. Institutions should be created that engage people with issues and express political preference, not as now with huge business lobbies which exercise undemocratic power, but which carry political influence (appropriate to private, rather than public, groupings) in national decision-making enterprise. Private in nature, these should be organized around single issues (medical care, transportation systems reform, etc.), concrete interest (labor and minority group organizations), multiple issues or general issues. These do not exist in America in quantity today. If they did exist, they would be a significant politicizing and educative force bringing people into touch with public life and affording them means of expression and action. Today, giant lobby representatives of business interests are dominant, but not educative. The Federal government itself should counter the latter forces whose intent is often public deceit for private gain, by subsidizing the preparation and decentralized distribution of objective materials on all public issues facing government.

3. Institutions and practices which stifle dissent should be abolished, and the promotion of peaceful dissent should be actively promoted. The first Amendment freedoms of speech, assembly, thought, religion and press should be seen as guarantees, not threats, to national security. While society has the right to prevent active subversion of its laws and institutions, it has the duty as well to promote open discussion of all issues—otherwise it will be in fact promoting real subversion as the only means to implementing ideas. To eliminate the fears and apathy from national life it is necessary that the institutions bred by fear and apathy be rooted out: the House Un-American Activities Committee, the Senate Internal Security Committee, the loyalty oaths on Federal loans, the Attorney General's list of subversive organizations, the Smith and McCarren Acts. The process of eliminating these blighting institutions is the process of restoring democratic participation. Their existence is a sign of the decomposition and atrophy of the participation.

4. Corporations must be made publicly responsible. It is not possible to believe that true democracy can exist where a minority utterly controls enormous wealth and power. The influence of corporate elites on foreign policy is neither reliable nor democratic;

a way must be found to [. . .] subordinate private American foreign investment to a democratically-constructed foreign policy. The influence of the same giants on domestic life is intolerable as well; a way must be found to direct our economic resources to genuine human needs, not the private needs of corporations nor the rigged needs of maneuvered citizenry.

We can no longer rely on competition of the many to insure that business enterprise is responsive to social needs. The many have become the few. Nor can we trust the corporate bureaucracy to be socially responsible or to develop a "corporate conscience" that is democratic. The community of interest of corporations, the anarchic actions of industrial leaders, should become structurally responsible to the people—and truly to the people rather than to an ill-defined and questionable "national interest." Labor and government as presently constituted are not sufficient to "regulate" corporations. A new re-ordering, a new calling of responsibility is necessary: more than changing "work rules" we must consider changes in the rules of society by challenging the unchallenged politics of American corporations. Before the government can really begin to control business in a "public interest," the public must gain more substantial control of government: this demands a movement for political as well as economic realignments. We are aware that simple government "regulation," if achieved, would be inadequate without increased worker participation in management decision-making, strengthened and independent regulatory power, balances of partial and/or complete public ownership, various means of humanizing the conditions and types of work itself, sweeping welfare programs and regional public government authorities. These are examples of measures to re-balance the economy toward public—and individual—control. [. . .]

5. America should concentrate on its genuine social priorities: abolish squalor, terminate neglect, and establish an environment for people to live in with dignity and creativeness.

6. A program against poverty must be just as sweeping as the nature of poverty itself. It must not be just palliative, but directed to the abolition of the structural circumstances of poverty. At a bare minimum it should include a housing act far larger than the one supported by the Kennedy Administration, but one that is geared more to low- and middle-income needs than to the windfall aspirations of small and large private entrepreneurs, one that is more sympathetic to the quality of communal life than to the efficiency of city-split highways. Second, medical care must become recognized as a lifetime human right just as vital as food, shelter and clothing—the Federal government should guarantee health insurance as a basic social service turning medical treatment into a social habit, not just an occasion of crisis, fighting sickness among the aged, not just by making medical care financially feasible but by reducing sickness among children and younger people. Third, existing institutions should be expanded so the Welfare State cares for everyone's welfare according to read. Social security payments should be extended to everyone and should be proportionately greater for the poorest. A minimum wage of at least $1.50 should be extended to all workers (including the 16 million currently not covered at all). Equal education opportunity is an important part of the battle against poverty. [. . .]

The fight for peace is one for a stable and racially integrated world; for an end to the inherently volatile exploitation of most of mankind by irresponsible elites; and for freedom of economic, political and cultural organization. The fight for civil rights is also one for social welfare for all Americans; for free speech and the right to protest; for the shield of economic independence and bargaining power; for a reduction of the arms race which takes national attention and resources away from the problems of domestic injustice. Labor's fight for jobs and wages is also for the right to petition and strike; for world industrialization; for the stability of a peacetime economy instead of the insecurity of the war economy; for expansion of the Welfare State. The fight for a liberal Congress is a fight for a platform from which these concerns can issue. And the fight for students, for internal democracy in the university, is a fight to gain a forum for the issues.

But these scattered movements have more in common: a need for their concerns to be expressed by a political party responsible to their interests. That they have no political expression, no political channels, can be traced in large measure to the existence of a Democratic Party which tolerates the perverse unity of liberalism and racism, prevents the social change wanted by Negroes, peace protesters, labor unions, students, reform Democrats, and other liberals. Worse, the party stalemate prevents even the raising of controversy—a full Congressional assault on racial discrimination, disengagement in Central Europe, sweeping urban reform, disarmament and inspection, public regulation of major industries; these and other issues are never heard in the body that is supposed to represent the best thoughts and interests of all Americans.

An imperative task for these publicly disinherited groups, then, is to demand a Democratic Party responsible to their interests. They must support Southern voter registration and Negro political candidates and demand that Democratic Party liberals do the same (in the last Congress, Dixiecrats split with Northern Democrats on 119 of 300 roll-calls, mostly on civil rights, area redevelopment and foreign aid bills; and breach was much larger than in the previous several sessions). Labor should begin a major drive in the South. In the North reform clubs (either independent or Democratic) should be formed to run against big city regimes on such issues as peace, civil rights, and urban needs. Demonstrations should be held at every Congressional or convention seating of Dixiecrats. A massive research and publicity campaign should be initiated, showing to every housewife, doctor, professor, and worker the damage done to their interests every day a racist occupies a place in the Democratic Party. Where possible, the peace movement should challenge the "peace credentials" of the otherwise-liberals by threatening or actually running candidates against them.

The University and Social Change.   There is perhaps little reason to be optimistic about the above analysis. True, the Dixiecrat-GOP coalition is the weakest point in the dominating complex of corporate, military and political power. But the civil rights and peace and student movements are too poor and socially slighted, and the labor movement too quiescent, to be counted with enthusiasm. From where else can power and vision be summoned? We believe that the universities are an overlooked seat of influence.

First, the university is located in a permanent position of social influence. Its educational function makes it indispensable and automatically makes it a crucial institution in the formation of social attitudes.

Second, in an unbelievably complicated world, it is the central institution for organizing, evaluating, and transmitting knowledge. Third, the extent to which academic resources presently [are] used to buttress immoral social practice is revealed first, by the extent to which defense contracts make the universities engineers of the arms race. Too, the use of modern social science as a manipulative tool reveals itself in the "human relations" consultants to the modem corporation, who introduce trivial sops to give laborers feelings of "participation" or "belonging," while actually deluding them in order to further exploit their labor. And, of course, the use of motivational research is already infamous as a manipulative aspect of American politics. But these social uses of the universities' resources also demonstrate the unchangeable reliance by men of power on the men and storehouses of knowledge: this makes the university functionally tied to society in new ways, revealing new potentialities, new levers for change. Fourth, the university is the only mainstream institution that is open to participation by individuals of nearly any viewpoint.

These, at least, are facts, no matter how dull the teaching, how paternalistic the rules, how irrelevant the research that goes on. Social relevance, the accessibility to knowledge, and internal openness; these together make the university a potential base and agency in a movement of social change.

1. Any new left in America must be, in large measure, a left with real intellectual skills, committed to deliberativeness, honesty, reflection as working tools. The university permits the political life to be an adjunct to the academic one, and action to be informed by reason.

2. A new left must be distributed in significant social roles throughout the country. The universities are distributed in such a manner.

3. A new left must consist of younger people who matured in the postwar world, and partially directed to the recruitment of younger people. The university is an obvious beginning point.

4. A new left must include liberals and socialists, the former for their relevance, the latter for their sense of thoroughgoing reforms in the system. The university is a more sensible place than a political party for these two traditions to begin to discuss their differences and look for political synthesis.

5. A new left must start controversy across the land, if national policies and national apathy are to be reversed. The ideal university is a community of controversy, within itself and in its effects on communities beyond.

6. A new left must transform modern complexity into issues that can be understood and felt close-up by every human being. It must give form to the feelings of helplessness and indifference, so that people may see the political, social and economic sources of their private troubles and organize to change society. In a time of supposed prosperity, moral complacency and political manipulation, a new left cannot rely on only aching stomachs to be the engine force of social reform. The case for change, for alternatives that will involve uncomfortable personal efforts, must be argued as never before. The university is a relevant place for all of these activities.

But we need not indulge in illusions: the university system cannot complete a movement of ordinary people making demands for a better life. From its schools and colleges across the nation, a militant left might awaken its allies, and by beginning the process towards peace, civil rights, and labor struggles, reinsert theory and idealism where too often reign confusion and political barter. The power of students and faculty united is not only potential; it has shown its actuality in the South, and in the reform movements of the North.

The bridge to political power, though, will be built through genuine cooperation, locally, nationally, and internationally, between a new left of young people, and an awakening community of allies. In each community we must look within the university and act with confidence that we can be powerful, but we must look outwards to the less exotic but more lasting struggles for justice.

To turn these possibilities into realities will involve national efforts at university reform by an alliance of students and faculty. They must wrest control of the educational process from the administrative bureaucracy. They must make fraternal and functional contact with allies in labor, civil rights, and other liberal forces outside the campus. They must import major public issues into the curriculum—research and teaching on problems of war and peace is an outstanding example. They must make debate and controversy, not dull pedantic cant, the common style for educational life. They must consciously build a base for their assault upon the loci of power.

As students, for a democratic society, we are committed to stimulating this kind of social movement, this kind of vision and program is campus and community across the country. If we appear to seek the unattainable, it has been said, then let it be known that we do so to avoid the unimaginable.

JOHN F. KENNEDY

Civil Rights Address (1963)

Good evening, my fellow citizens.

This afternoon, following a series of threats and defiant statements, the presence of Alabama National Guardsmen was required on the University of Alabama to carry out the final and unequivocal order of the United States District Court of the Northern District of Alabama. That order called for

the admission of two clearly qualified young Alabama residents who happened to have been born Negro.

That they were admitted peacefully on the campus is due in good measure to the conduct of the students of the University of Alabama, who met their responsibilities in a constructive way.

I hope that every American, regardless of where he lives, will stop and examine his conscience about this and other related incidents. This Nation was founded by men of many nations, and backgrounds. It was founded on the principle that all men are created equal, and that the rights of every man are diminished when the rights of one man are threatened.

Today we are committed to a worldwide struggle to promote and protect the rights of all who wish to be free. And when Americans are sent to Viet-Nam or West Berlin, we do not ask for whites only. It ought to be possible, therefore, for American students of any color to attend any public institution they select without having to be backed up by troops.

It ought to be possible for American consumers of any color to receive equal service in places of public accommodation, such as hotels and restaurants and theaters and retail stores, without being forced to resort to demonstrations in the street, and it ought to be possible for American citizens of any color to register and to vote in a free election without interference or fear of reprisal.

It ought to be possible, in short, for every American to enjoy the privileges of being American without regard to his race or his color. In short, every American ought to have the right to be treated as he would wish to be treated, as one would wish his children to be treated. But this is not the case.

The Negro baby born in America today, regardless of the section of the Nation in which he is born, has about one-half as much chance of completing a high school as a white baby born in the same place on the same day, one-third as much chance of completing college, one-third as much chance of becoming a professional man, twice as much chance of becoming unemployed, about one-seventh as much chance of earning $10,000 a year, a life expectancy which is 7 years shorter, and the prospects of earning only half as much.

This is not a sectional issue. Difficulties over segregation and discrimination exist in every city, in every State of the Union, producing in many cities a rising tide of discontent that threatens the public safety. Nor is this a partisan issue. In a time of domestic crisis men of good will and generosity should be able to unite regardless of party or politics. This is not even a legal or legislative issue alone. It is better to settle these matters in the courts than on the streets, and new laws are needed at every level, but law alone cannot make men see right.

We are confronted primarily with a moral issue. It is as old as the scriptures and is as clear as the American Constitution.

The heart of the question is whether all Americans are to be afforded equal rights and equal opportunities, whether we are going to treat our fellow Americans as we want to be treated. If an American, because his skin is dark, cannot eat lunch in a restaurant open to the public, if he cannot send his children to the best public school available, if he cannot vote for the public officials who represent him, if, in short, he cannot enjoy the full and free life which all of us want, then who among us would be content to have the color of his skin changed and stand in his place? Who among us would then be content with the counsels of patience and delay?

One hundred years of delay have passed since President Lincoln freed the slaves, yet their heirs, their grandsons, are not fully free. They are not yet freed from the bonds of injustice. They are not yet freed from social and economic oppression. And this Nation, for all its hopes and all its boasts, will not be fully free until all its citizens are free.

We preach freedom around the world, and we mean it, and we cherish our freedom here at home, but are we to say to the world, and much more importantly, to each other that this is a land of the free except for the Negroes; that we have no second-class citizens except Negroes; that we have no class or caste system, no ghettoes, no master race except with respect to Negroes?

Now the time has come for this Nation to fulfill its promise. The events in Birmingham and elsewhere have so increased the cries for equality that no city or State or legislative body can prudently choose to ignore them.

The fires of frustration and discord are burning in every city, North and South, where legal remedies are not at hand. Redress is sought in the streets, in demonstrations, parades, and protests which create tensions and threaten violence and threaten lives.

We face, therefore, a moral crisis as a country and as a people. It cannot be met by repressive police action. It cannot be left to increased demonstrations in the streets. It cannot be quieted by token moves or talk. It is a time to act in the Congress, in your State and local legislative body and, above all, in all of our daily lives.

It is not enough to pin the blame on others, to say this is a problem of one section of the country or another, or deplore the fact that we face. A great change is at hand, and our task, our obligation, is to make that revolution, that change, peaceful and constructive for all.

Those who do nothing are inviting shame as well as violence. Those who act boldly are recognizing right as well as reality.

Next week I shall ask the Congress of the United States to act, to make a commitment it has not fully made in this century to the proposition that race has no place in American life or law. The Federal judiciary has upheld that proposition in a series of forthright cases. The executive branch has adopted that proposition in the conduct of its affairs, including the employment of Federal personnel, the use of Federal facilities, and the sale of federally financed housing.

But there are other necessary measures which only the Congress can provide, and they must be provided at this session. The old code of equity law under which we live commands for every wrong a remedy, but in too many communities, in too many parts of the country, wrongs are inflicted on Negro citizens and there are no remedies at law. Unless the Congress acts, their only remedy is in the street.

I am, therefore, asking the Congress to enact legislation giving all Americans the right to be served in facilities which are open to the public — hotels, restaurants, theaters, retail stores, and similar establishments.

This seems to me to be an elementary right. Its denial is an arbitrary indignity that no American in 1963 should have to endure, but many do.

I have recently met with scores of business leaders urging them to take voluntary action to end this discrimination and I have been encouraged by their response, and in the last two weeks over 75 cities have seen progress made in desegregating these kinds of facilities. But many are unwilling to act alone, and for this reason, nationwide legislation is needed if we are to move this problem from the streets to the courts.

I am also asking Congress to authorize the Federal Government to participate more fully in lawsuits designed to end segregation in public education. We have succeeded in persuading many districts to desegregate voluntarily. Dozens have admitted Negroes without violence. Today a Negro is attending a State-supported institution in every one of our 50 States, but the pace is very slow.

Too many Negro children entering segregated grade schools at the time of the Supreme Court's decision 9 years ago will enter segregated high schools this fall, having suffered a loss which can never be restored. The lack of an adequate education denies the Negro a chance to get a decent job.

The orderly implementation of the Supreme Court decision, therefore, cannot be left solely to those who may not have the economic resources to carry the legal action or who may be subject to harassment.

Other features will be also requested, including greater protection for the right to vote. But legislation, I repeat, cannot solve this problem alone. It must be solved in the homes of every American in every community across our country.

In this respect, I want to pay tribute to those citizens North and South who have been working in their communities to make life better for all. They are acting not out of a sense of legal duty but out of a sense of human decency.

Like our soldiers and sailors in all parts of the world they are meeting freedom's challenge on the firing line, and I salute them for their honor and their courage.

My fellow Americans, this is a problem which faces us all — in every city of the North as well as the South. Today there are Negroes unemployed, two or three times as many compared to whites, inadequate in education, moving into the large cities, unable to find work, young people particularly out of work without hope, denied equal rights, denied the opportunity to eat at a restaurant or lunch counter or go to a movie theater, denied the right to a decent education, denied almost today the right to attend a State university even though qualified. It seems to me that these are matters which concern us all, not merely Presidents or Congressmen or Governors, but every citizen of the United States.

This is one country. It has become one country because all of us and all the people who came here had an equal chance to develop their talents.

We cannot say to 10 percent of the population that you can't have that right; that your children can't have the chance to develop whatever talents they have; that the only way that they are going to get their rights is to go into the streets and demonstrate. I think we owe them and we owe ourselves a better country than that.

Therefore, I am asking for your help in making it easier for us to move ahead and to provide the kind of equality of treatment which we would want ourselves; to give a chance for every child to be educated to the limit of his talents.

As I have said before, not every child has an equal talent or an equal ability or an equal motivation, but they should have the equal right to develop their talent and their ability and their motivation, to make something of themselves.

We have a right to expect that the Negro community will be responsible, will uphold the law, but they have a right to expect that the law will be fair, that the Constitution will be color blind, as Justice Harlan said at the turn of the century.

This is what we are talking about and this is a matter which concerns this country and what it stands for, and in meeting it I ask the support of all our citizens.

Thank you very much.

Richard Russell

Response to President Kennedy (1963)

The President's speech appealed eloquently to the emotions but completely disregarded reason, human experience and true equality under the Constitution.

The fact that every citizen has the same right to own and operate a swimming pool or dining hall constitutes equality. The use of federal power to force the owner of a dining hall or swimming pool to unwillingly accept those of a different race as guests creates a new and special right for Negroes in derogation of the property rights of all of our people to own and control the fruits of their labor and ingenuity.

The outstanding distinction between a government of free men and a socialistic or communistic state is the fact that free men can own and control property, whereas statism denies property rights.

"From each according to his ability and to each according to his need" may have greater emotional appeal than "work hard to acquire property and the law will protect you in its enjoyment." However, Marxism has not worked and can never work because it does not take human nature into account. To rebut the emotional appeal, we have the hard, undeniable fact that in our free-enterprise system we have plenty, whereas the Marxists—though they have never been able to apply literally their avowed creed—all suffer from scarcity and privation.

Our American system has always rejected the idea that one group of citizens may deprive another of legal rights in property by process of agitation, demonstration, intimidation, law defiance and civil disobedience.

I do not believe that the American people will be easily frightened into discarding our system for adventures into socialism that have been discredited wherever tried.

The highest office of the land should symbolize respect for law, whether it be legally enacted ordinances of the meanest hamlet in the land or the written word of our national charter—the Constitution.

I was, therefore, shocked to hear the President justify, if not encourage, the present wave of mass demonstrations, accompanied by the practices of sitting or lying in public streets and blocking traffic; forming human walls before the doors of legal businesses and assaulting with deadly weapons officers of the law whose only offense was undertaking to maintain order and protect private property.

The South has its shortcomings as well as other areas. But a calculated campaign waged by the metropolitan press, television and radio has magnified the unfortunate occurrences in the South while crimes of violence in other areas have been minimized. This has generated bitterness and hatred against the white people of the Southern States almost amounting to a national disease. It is also encouraging a condition bordering on anarchy in many communities. These terrible conditions are sure to further deteriorate with increasing disorder unless the President of the United States desists from using threats of mass violence to rush his social equality legislation through the Congress.

No American citizen has the right to select the laws he will obey and those he will disobey.

The President of the United States has a higher call to leadership than to use threats of mass violence and disregard of reasonable local laws as a means of securing action in the courts and Congress, however desirable he may regard it to be.

The Congress of the United States, by an enactment of March 1, 1875, declared that all persons were entitled "to the full and equal enjoyment of the accommodations, advantages, facilities and privileges of inns, public conveyances on land or water, theaters and other places of public amusement." The Supreme Court of the United States on Oct. 15, 1883, declared this federal restriction upon the use and control of private property to be unconstitutional. In accordance with the contentions of those who would use federal power to mix the races socially, this has been the "law of the land" from that date and still applies today.

The President and the Attorney General now say that they will predicate this new thrust for race mixing on the already tortured commerce clause of the Constitution. If the commerce clause will sustain an act to compel the white owner of a dining hall to accept a Negro against his wishes, it can be used to sustain the validity of legislation that will compel his admittance into the living room or bedroom of any citizen.

I believe in equality before the law for every American. In equal measure, I reject the idea that federal power may be invoked to compel the mingling of the races in social activities to achieve the nebulous aim of social equality.

Every Negro citizen possesses every legal right that is possessed by any white citizen, but there is nothing in either the Constitution or Judaeo-Christian principles or common sense and reason which would compel one citizen to share his rights with one of another race at the same place and at the same time. Such compulsion would amount to a complete denial of the inalienable rights of the individual to choose or select his associates.

I hope that the American people will not be swept further down the road to socialism by the present unprecedented wave of propaganda. To me, the President's legislative proposals are clearly destructive of the American system and the constitutional rights of American citizens. I shall oppose them with every means and resource at my command. I do not believe a majority of the Congress will be frightened by thinly veiled threats of violence.

MARTIN LUTHER KING, JR.

Stride toward Freedom (1958)

Pilgrimage to Nonviolence

Often the question has arisen concerning my own intellectual pilgrimage to nonviolence. In order to get at this question it is necessary to go back to my early teens in Atlanta. I had grown up abhorring not only segregation but also the oppressive and barbarous acts that grew out of it. I had passed spots where Negroes had been savagely lynched, and had watched the Ku Klux Klan on its rides at night. I had seen police brutality with my own eyes, and watched Negroes receive the most tragic injustice in the courts.

All of these things had done something to my growing personality. I had come perilously close to resenting all white people.

I had also learned that the inseparable twin of racial injustice was economic injustice. Although I came from a home of economic security and relative comfort, I could never get out of my mind the economic insecurity of many of my playmates and the tragic poverty of those living around me. During my late teens I worked two summers, against my father's wishes—he never wanted my brother and me to work around white people because of the oppressive conditions—in a plant that hired both Negroes and whites. Here I saw economic injustice firsthand, and realized that the poor white was exploited just as much as the Negro. Through these early experiences I grew up deeply conscious of the varieties of injustice in our society.

So when I went to Atlanta's Morehouse College as a freshman in 1944 my concern for racial and economic justice was already substantial. During my student days at Morehouse I read Thoreau's *Essay on Civil Disobedience* for the first time. Fascinated by the idea of refusing to cooperate with an evil system, I was so deeply moved that I reread the work several times. This was my first intellectual contact with the theory of nonviolent resistance.

Not until I entered Crozer Theological Seminary in 1948, however, did I begin a serious intellectual quest for a method to eliminate social evil. Although my major interest was in the fields of theology and philosophy, I spent a great deal of time reading the works of the great social philosophers. I came early to Walter Rauschenbusch's *Christianity and the Social Crisis*, which left an indelible imprint on my thinking by giving me a theological basis for the social concern which had already grown up in me as a result of my early experiences. Of course there were points at which I differed with Rauschenbusch. I felt that he had fallen victim to the nineteenth-century "cult of inevitable progress" which led him to a superficial optimism concerning man's nature. Moreover, he came perilously close to identifying the Kingdom of God with a particular social and economic system—a tendency which should never befall the Church. But in spite of these shortcomings Rauschenbusch had done a great service for the Christian Church by insisting that the gospel deals with the whole man,

not only his soul but his body; not only his spiritual well-being but his material well-being. It has been my conviction ever since reading Rauschenbusch that any religion which professes to be concerned about the souls of men and is not concerned about the social and economic conditions that scar the soul, is a spiritually moribund religion only waiting for the day to be buried. It well has been said: "A religion that ends with the individual, ends." [. . .]

[O]ne Sunday afternoon I traveled to Philadelphia to hear a sermon by Dr. Mordecai Johnson, president of Howard University. He was there to preach for the Fellowship House of Philadelphia. Dr. Johnson had just returned from a trip to India, and, to my great interest, he spoke of the life and teachings of Mahatma Gandhi. His message was so profound and electrifying that I left the meeting and bought a half-dozen books on Gandhi's life and works.

Like most people, I had heard of Gandhi, but I had never studied him seriously. As I read I became deeply fascinated by his campaigns of nonviolent resistance. I was particularly moved by the Salt March to the Sea and his numerous fasts. The whole concept of "Satyagraha" (*Satya* is truth which equals love, and *agraha* is force; "Satyagraha," therefore, means truth-force or love force) was profoundly significant to me. As I delved deeper into the philosophy of Gandhi my skepticism concerning the power of love gradually diminished, and I came to see for the first time its potency in the area of social reform. Prior to reading Gandhi, I had about concluded that the ethics of Jesus were only effective in individual relationship. The "turn the other cheek" philosophy and the "love your enemies" philosophy were only valid, I felt, when individuals were in conflict with other individuals; when racial groups and nations were in conflict a more realistic approach seemed necessary. But after reading Gandhi, I saw how utterly mistaken I was.

Gandhi was probably the first person in history to lift the love ethic of Jesus above mere interaction between individuals to a powerful and effective social force on a large scale. Love for Gandhi was a potent instrument for social and collective transformation. It was in this Gandhian emphasis on love and nonviolence that I discovered the method for social reform that I had been seeking for so many months. The intellectual and moral satisfaction that I failed to gain from the utilitarianism of Bentham and Mill, the revolutionary methods of Marx and Lenin, the social-contracts theory of Hobbes, the "back to nature" optimism of Rousseau, and the superman philosophy of Nietzsche, I found in the nonviolent resistance philosophy of Gandhi. I came to feel that this was the only morally and practically sound method open to oppressed people in their struggle for freedom. [. . .]

When I went to Montgomery as a pastor, I had not the slightest idea that I would later become involved in a crisis in which nonviolent resistance would be applicable. I neither started the protest nor suggested it. I simply responded to the call of the people for a spokesman. When the protest began, my mind, consciously or unconsciously, was driven back to the Sermon on the Mount, with its sublime teachings on love, and the Gandhian method of nonviolent resistance. As the days unfolded, I came to see the power of nonviolence more and more. Living through the actual experience of the protest, nonviolence became more than a method to which I gave intellectual assent; it became a commitment to a way of life. Many of the things that I had not cleared up intellectually concerning nonviolence were now solved in the sphere of practical action.

Since the philosophy of nonviolence played such a positive role in the Montgomery Movement, it may be wise to turn to a brief discussion of some basic aspects of this philosophy.

First, it must be emphasized that nonviolent resistance is not a method for cowards; it does resist. If one uses this method because he is afraid or merely because he lacks the instruments of violence, he is not truly nonviolent. This is why Gandhi often said that if cowardice is the only alternative to violence, it is better to fight. He made this statement conscious of the fact that there is always another alternative: no individual or group need submit to any wrong, nor need they use violence to right the wrong; there is the way of nonviolence resistance. This is ultimately the way of the strong man. It is not a method of stagnant passivity. The phrase "passive resistance" often gives the false impression that this is a sort of "do-nothing method" in which the resister quietly and passively accepts evil. But nothing is further from the truth. For while the nonviolent resister is passive in the sense that he is not physically aggressive toward his opponent, his mind and emotions are always active, constantly seeking to persuade his opponent that he is wrong. The method is passive physically, but strongly active spiritually. It is not passive nonresistance to evil, it is active nonviolent resistance to evil.

A second basic fact that characterizes nonviolence is that it does not seek to defeat or humiliate the opponent, but to win his friendship and understanding. The nonviolent resister must often express his protest through noncooperation or boycotts, but he realizes that these are not ends themselves; they are merely means to awaken a sense of moral shame in the opponent. The end is redemption and reconciliation. The aftermath of nonviolence is the creation of the beloved community, while the aftermath of violence is tragic bitterness.

A third characteristic of this method is that the attack is directed against forces of evil rather than against persons who happen to be doing the evil. It is evil that the nonviolent resister seeks to defeat, not the persons victimized by evil. If he is opposing racial injustice, the nonviolent resister has the vision to see that the basic tension is not between races. As I like to say to the people in Montgomery: "The tension in this city is not between white people and Negro people. The tension is, at bottom, between justice and injustice, between the forces of light and the forces of darkness. And if there is a victory, it will be a victory not merely for fifty thousand Negroes, but a victory for justice and the forces of fight. We are out to defeat injustice and not white persons who may be unjust."

A fourth point that characterizes nonviolent resistance is a willingness to accept suffering without retaliation, to accept blows from the opponent without striking back. "Rivers of blood may have to flow before we gain our freedom, but it must be our blood," Gandhi said to his countrymen. The nonviolent resister is willing to accept violence if necessary, but never to inflict it. He does not seek to dodge jail. If going to jail is necessary, he enters it "as a bridegroom enters the bride's chamber."

One may well ask: "What is the nonviolent resister's justification for this ordeal to which he invites men, for this mass political application of the ancient doctrine of turning the other cheek?" The answer is found in the realization that unearned suffering is redemptive. Suffering, the nonviolent resister realizes, has tremendous educational and transforming possibilities. "Things of fundamental importance to people are not secured by reason alone, but have to be purchased with their suffering," said Gandhi. He continues: "Suffering is infinitely more powerful than the law of the jungle for converting the opponent and opening his ears which are otherwise shut to the voice of reason."

A fifth point concerning nonviolent resistance is that it avoids not only external physical violence but also internal violence of spirit. The nonviolent resister not only refuses to shoot his opponent but he also refuses to hate him. At the center of nonviolence stands the principle of love. The nonviolent resister would contend that in the struggle for human dignity, the oppressed people of the world must not succumb to the temptation of becoming bitter or indulging in hate campaigns. To retaliate in kind would do nothing but intensify the existence of hate in the universe. Along the way of life, someone must have sense enough and morality enough to cut off the chain of hate. This can only be done by projecting the ethic of love to the center of our lives.

In speaking of love at this point, we are not referring to some sentimental or affectionate emotion. It would be nonsense to urge men to love their oppressors in an affectionate sense. Love in this connection means understanding, redemptive good will. Here the Greek language comes to our aid. There are three words for love in the Greek New Testament. First, there is *eros*. In Platonic philosophy *eros* meant the yearning of the soul for the realm of the divine. It has come now to mean a sort of aesthetic or romantic love. Second, there is *philia* which means intimate affection between personal friends. *Philia* denotes a sort of reciprocal love; the person loves because he is loved. When we speak of loving those who oppose us, we refer to neither *eros* nor *philia*; we speak of a love which is expressed in the Greek word *agape*. *Agape* means understanding, redeeming good will for all men. It is an overflowing love which is purely spontaneous, unmotivated, groundless, and creative. It is not set in motion by any quality or function of its object. It is the love of God operating in the human heart.

Agape is disinterested love. It is a love in which the individual seeks not his own good, but the good of his neighbor (I Cor. 10:24). *Agape* does not begin by discriminating between worthy and unworthy people, or any qualities people possess. It begins by loving others *for their sakes*. It is an entirely "neighbor-regarding concern for others," which discovers the neighbor in every man it meets. Therefore, *agape* makes no distinction between friend and enemy; it is directed toward both. If one loves an individual merely on account of his friendliness, he loves him for the sake of the benefits to be gained from the friendship, rather than for the friend's own sake. Consequently the best way to assure oneself that Love is disinterested is to have love for the enemy-neighbor from whom you can expect no good in return, but only hostility and persecution.

Another basic point about *agape* is that it springs from the *need* of the other person—his need for belonging to the best in the human family. The Samaritan who helped the Jew on the Jericho Road was "good" because he responded to the human need that he was presented with. God's love is eternal and fails not because man needs his love. St. Paul assures us that the loving act of redemption was done "while we were yet sinners"—that is, at the point of our greatest need for love. Since the white man's personality is greatly distorted by segregation, and his soul is greatly scarred, he needs the love of the Negro. The Negro must love the white man, because the white man needs his love to remove his tensions, insecurities, and fears.

Agape is not a weak, passive love. It is love in action. *Agape* is love seeking to preserve and create community. It is insistence on community even when one seeks to break it. *Agape* is a willingness to sacrifice in the interest of mutuality. *Agape* is a willingness to go to any length to restore community. It doesn't stop at the first mile, but it goes the second mile to restore community. It is a willingness to forgive, not seven times, but seventy times seven to restore community. The cross is the eternal expression of the length to which God will go in order to restore broken community. The resurrection is a symbol of God's triumph over all the forces that seek to block community. The Holy Spirit is the continuing community creating reality that moves through history. He who works against community is working against the whole of creation. Therefore, if I respond to hate with a reciprocal hate I do nothing but intensify the cleavage in broken community. I can only close the gap in broken community by meeting hate with love. If I meet hate with hate, I become depersonalized, because creation is so designed that my personality can only be fulfilled in the context of community. Booker T. Washington was right: "Let no man pull you so low as to make you hate him." When he pulls you that low he brings you to the point of working against community; he drags you to the point of defying creation, and thereby becoming depersonalized.

In the final analysis, *agape* means a recognition of the fact that all life is interrelated. All humanity is involved in a single process, and all men are brothers. To the degree that I harm my brother, no matter what he is doing to me, to that extent I am harming myself. For example, white men often refuse federal aid to education in order to avoid giving the Negro his rights; but because all men are brothers they cannot deny Negro children without harming their own. They end, all efforts to the contrary, by hurting themselves. Why is this? Because men are brothers. If you harm me, you harm yourself.

Love, *agape*, is the only cement that can hold this broken community together. When I am commanded to love, I am commanded to restore community, to resist injustice, and to meet the needs of my brothers.

A sixth basic fact about nonviolent resistance is that it is based on the conviction that the universe is on the side of justice. Consequently, the believer in nonviolence has deep faith in the future. This faith is another reason why the nonviolent resister can accept suffering without retaliation. For he knows that in his struggle for justice he has cosmic companionship. It is true that there are devout believers in nonviolence who find it difficult to believe in a personal God. But even these persons believe in the existence of some creative force that works for universal wholeness. Whether we call it an unconscious process, an impersonal Brahman, or a Personal Being of matchless power and infinite love, there is a creative force in this universe that works to bring the disconnected aspects of reality into a harmonious whole.

Where Do We Go from Here?

It is becoming clear that the Negro is in for a season of suffering. As victories for civil rights mount in the federal courts, angry passions and deep prejudices are further aroused. The mountain of state and local segregation laws still stands. Negro leaders continue to be arrested and harassed under city ordinances, and their homes continue to be bombed. State laws continue to be enacted to circumvent integration. I pray that, recognizing the necessity of suffering, the Negro will make of it a virtue. To suffer in a righteous cause is to grow to our humanity's full stature. If only to save himself from bitterness, the Negro needs the vision to see the ordeals of this generation as the opportunity to transfigure himself and American society. If he has to go to jail for the cause of freedom, let him enter it in the fashion Gandhi urged his countrymen, "as the bridegroom enters the bride's chamber"—that is, with a little trepidation but with a great expectation.

Nonviolence is a way of humility and self-restraint. We Negroes talk a great deal about our rights, and rightly so. We proudly proclaim that three-fourths of the people of the world are colored. We have the privilege of watching in our generation the great drama of freedom and independence as it unfolds in Asia and Africa. All of these things are in line with the work of providence. We must be sure, however, that we accept them in the right spirit. In an effort to achieve freedom in America, Asia, and Africa we must not try to leap from a position of disadvantage to one of advantage, thus subverting justice. We must seek democracy and not the substitution of one tyranny for another. Our aim must never be to defeat or humiliate the white man. We must not become victimized with a philosophy of black supremacy. God is not interested merely in the freedom of black men, and brown men, and yellow men; God is interested in the freedom of the whole human race.

The nonviolent approach provides an answer to the long debated question of gradualism *versus* immediacy. On the one hand it prevents one from falling into the sort of patience which is an excuse for do-nothingism and escapism, ending up in standstillism. On the other hand it saves one from the irresponsible words which estrange without reconciling and the hasty judgment which is blind to the necessities of social process. It recognizes the need for moving toward the goal of justice with wise restraint and calm reasonableness. But it also recognizes the immorality of slowing up in the move toward justice and capitulating to the guardians of an unjust status quo. It recognizes that social change cannot come overnight. But it causes one to work as if it were a possibility the next morning.

Through nonviolence we avoid the temptation of taking on the psychology of victors. Thanks largely to the noble and invaluable work of the NAACP, we have won great victories in the federal courts. But we must not be self-satisfied. We must respond to every decision with an understanding of those who have opposed us and with acceptance of the new adjustments that the court orders pose for them. We must act in such a way that our victories will be triumphs for good will in all men, white and Negro.

Nonviolence is essentially a positive concept. Its corollary must always be growth. On the one hand nonviolence requires noncooperation with evil; on the other hand it requires cooperation with the constructive forces of good. Without this constructive aspect noncooperation ends where it begins. Therefore, the Negro must get to work on a program with a broad range of positive goals.

This then must be our present program: Nonviolent resistance to all forms of racial injustice, including state and local laws and practices, even when this means going to jail; and imaginative, bold, constructive action to end the demoralization caused by the legacy of slavery and segregation, inferior schools, slums, and second-class citizenship. The nonviolent struggle, if conducted with the dignity and courage already shown by the people of Montgomery and the children of Little Rock, will in itself help end the demoralization; but a new frontal assault on the poverty, disease, and ignorance of a people too long ignored by America's conscience will make victory more certain.

In short, we must work on two fronts. On the one hand, we must continue to resist the system of segregation which is the basic cause of our lagging standards; on the other hand we must work constructively to improve the standards themselves. There must be a rhythmic alternation between attacking the causes and healing the effects.

This is a great hour for the Negro. The challenge is here. To become the instruments of a great idea is a privilege that history gives only occasionally. Arnold Toynbee says in *A Study of History* that it may be the Negro who will give the new spiritual dynamic to Western civilization that it so desperately needs to survive. I hope this is possible. The spiritual power that the Negro can radiate to the world comes from love, understanding, good will, and nonviolence. It may even be possible for the Negro, through adherence to nonviolence, so to challenge the nations of the world that they will seriously seek an alternative to war and destruction. In a day when Sputniks and Explorers dash through outer space and guided ballistic missiles are carving highways of death through the stratosphere, nobody can win a war. Today the choice is no longer between violence and nonviolence. It is either nonviolence or nonexistence. The Negro may be God's appeal to this age—an age drifting rapidly to its doom. The eternal appeal takes the form of a warning: "All who take the sword will perish by the sword."

Letter from a Birmingham Jail (1963)

My Dear Fellow Clergymen:

While confined here in the Birmingham city jail, I came across your recent statement calling present activities "unwise and untimely." Seldom do I pause to answer criticism of my work and ideas. If I sought to answer all the criticisms that cross my desk, my secretaries would have little time for anything other than such correspondence in the course of the day, and I would have no time for constructive work. But since I feel that you are men of genuine good will and that your criticisms are sincerely set forth, I want to try to answer your statement in what I hope will be patient and reasonable terms.

I think I should indicate why I am here in Birmingham, since you have been influenced by the view which argues against "outsiders coming in." I have the honor of serving as President of the Southern Christian Leadership Conference, an organization operating in every southern state, with headquarters in Atlanta, Georgia. We have some eighty-five affiliated organizations across the South, and one of them is the Alabama Christian Movement for Human Rights. Frequently we share staff, educational and financial resources with our affiliates. Several months ago the affiliate here in Birmingham asked us to be on call to engage in a nonviolent direct-action program if such were deemed necessary. We readily consented, and when the hour came we lived up to our promise. So I, along with several members of my staff, am here because I was invited here. I am here because I have organizational ties here.

But more basically, I am in Birmingham because injustice is here. Just as the prophets of the eighth century B.C. left their villages and carried their "thus saith the Lord" far beyond the boundaries of their home towns, and just as the Apostle Paul left his village of Tarsus and carried the gospel of Jesus Christ to the far corners of the Greco-Roman world, so am I compelled to carry the gospel of freedom beyond my own home town. Like Paul, I must constantly respond to the Macedonian call for aid.

Moreover, I am cognizant of the interrelatedness of all communities and states. I cannot sit idly in Atlanta and not be concerned about what happens in Birmingham. Injustice anywhere is a threat to justice everywhere. We are caught in an inescapable network of mutuality, tied in a single garment of destiny. Whatever affects one directly, affects all indirectly. Never again can we afford to live with the narrow, provincial "outside agitator" idea. Anyone who lives inside the United States can never be considered an outsider anywhere within its bounds.

You deplore the demonstrations taking place in Birmingham. But your statement, I am sorry to say, fails so express a similar concern for the conditions that brought about the demonstrations. I am sure that none of you would want to rest content with the superficial kind of social analysis that deals merely with effects and does not grapple with underlying causes. It is unfortunate that demonstrations are taking place in Birmingham, but it is even more unfortunate that the city's white power structure left the Negro community with no alternative.

In any nonviolent campaign there are four basic steps: collection of the facts to determine whether injustices exist; negotiation; self-purification; and direct action. We have gone through all these steps in Birmingham. There can be no gain saying the fact that racial injustice engulfs this community. Birmingham is probably the most thoroughly segregated city in the United States. Its ugly record of brutality is widely known. Negroes have experienced grossly unjust treatment in the courts. There have been more unsolved bombings of Negro homes and churches in Birmingham that in any other city in the nation. These are the hard, brutal facts of the case. On the basis of these conditions, Negro leaders sought to negotiate with the city fathers. But the latter consistently refused to engage in good-faith negotiation.

Then, last September, came the opportunity to talk with leaders of Birmingham's economic community. In the course of the negotiations, certain promises were made by the merchants—for example, to remove the stores' humiliating racial signs. On the basis of these promises, the Reverend Fred Shuttlesworth and the leaders of the Alabama Christian Movement for Human Rights agreed to a moratorium on all demonstrations. As the weeks and months went by, we realized that we were the victims of a broken promise. A few signs, briefly removed, returned; the others remained.

As in so many past experiences, our hopes had been blasted, and the shadow of deep disappointment settled upon us. We had no alternative except to prepare for direct action, whereby we would present our very bodies as a means of laying our case before the conscience of the local and the national community. Mindful of the difficulties involved, we decided to undertake a process of self-purification. We began a series of workshops on nonviolence, and we repeatedly asked ourselves: "Are you able to accept blows without retaliation?" "Are you able to endure the ordeal of jail?" We decided to schedule our direct-action program for the Easter season, realizing that except for Christmas, this is the main shopping period of the year. Knowing that a strong economic withdrawal program would be the by-product of direct action, we felt that this would be the best time to bring pressure to bear on the merchants for the needed change.

Then it occurred to us that Birmingham's mayoralty election was coming up in March, and we speedily decided to postpone action until after election day. When we discovered that the Commissioner of Public Safety, Eugene "Bull" Connor, had piled up enough votes to be in the run-off, we decided again to postpone action until the day after the run-off so that the demonstrations could not be used to cloud the issues. Like many others, we waited to see Mr. Connor defeated, and to this end we endured postponement after postponement. Having aided in this community need, we felt that our direct-action program could be delayed no longer.

You may well ask: "Why direct action? Why sit-ins, marches, and so forth? Isn't negotiation a better path?" You are quite right in calling for negotiation. Indeed, this is the very purpose of direct action. Nonviolent direct action seeks to create such a crisis and foster such a tension that a community which has constantly refused to negotiate is forced to confront the issue. It seeks so to dramatize the issue that it can no longer be ignored. My citing the creation of tension as part of the work of the nonviolent-resister may sound rather shocking. But I must confess that I am not afraid of the word "tension." I have earnestly opposed violent tension, but there is a type of constructive, nonviolent tension which is necessary for growth. Just as Socrates felt that it was necessary to create a tension in the mind so that individuals could rise from the bondage of myths and half-truths to the unfettered realm of creative analysis and objective appraisal, so must we see the need for nonviolent gadflies to create the kind of tension in society that will help men rise from the dark depths of prejudice and racism to the majestic heights of understanding and brotherhood.

The purpose of our direct-action program is to create a situation so crisis-packed that it will inevitably open the door to negotiation. I therefore concur with you in your call for negotiation. Too long has our beloved Southland been bogged down in a tragic effort to live in monologue rather than dialogue.

One of the basic points in your statement is that the action that I and my associates have taken in Birmingham is untimely. Some have asked: "Why didn't you give the new city administration time to act?" The only answer that I can give to this query is that the new Birmingham administration must be prodded about as much as the outgoing one, before it will act. We are sadly mistaken if we feel that the election of Albert Boutwell as mayor will bring the millennium to Birmingham. While Mr. Boutwell is a much more gentle person than Mr. Connor, they are both segregationists, dedicated to maintenance of the status quo. I have hoped that Mr. Boutwell will be reasonable enough to see the futility of massive resistance to desegregation. But he will not see this without pressure from devotees of civil rights. My friends, I must say to you that we have not made a single gain in civil rights without determined legal and nonviolent pressure. Lamentably, it is an historical fact that privileged groups seldom give up their privileges voluntarily. Individuals may see the moral light and voluntarily give up their unjust posture; but as Reinhold Niebuhr has reminded us, groups tend to be more immoral than individuals.

We know through painful experience that freedom is never voluntarily given by the oppressor, it must be demanded by the oppressed. Frankly, I have yet to engage in a direct-action campaign that was "well timed" in view of those who have not suffered unduly from the disease of segregation. For years now I have heard the word "wait!" It rings in the ear of every Negro with piercing familiarity. This "Wait" has almost always meant "Never." We must come to see, with one of our distinguished jurists, that "justice too long delayed is justice denied."

We have waited for more that 340 years for our constitutional and God-given rights. The nations of Asia and Africa are moving with jet-like speed toward gaining political independence, but we still creep at horse-and-buggy pace toward gaining a cup of coffee at a lunch counter. Perhaps it is easy for those who have never felt the stinging darts of segregation to say, "Wait." But when you have seen vicious mobs lynch your mothers and fathers at will and drown your sisters and brothers at whim; when you have seen hate-filled policemen curse, kick, and even kill your black brothers and sisters; when you see the vast majority of your twenty million Negro brothers smothering in an airtight cage of poverty in the midst of an affluent society; when you suddenly find your tongue twisted and your speech stammering as you seek to explain to your six-year-old daughter why she can't go to the public amusement park that has just been advertised on television, and see tears welling up in her eyes when she is told that Funtown is closed to colored children, and see ominous clouds of inferiority beginning to form in her little mental sky, and see her beginning to distort her personality by developing an unconscious bitterness toward white people; when you have to concoct an answer for a five-year-old son who is asking, "Daddy, why do white people treat colored people so mean?"; when you take a cross-country drive and find it necessary to sleep night after night in the uncomfortable corners of your automobile because no motel will accept you; when you are humiliated day in and day out by nagging signs reading "white" and "colored" when your first name becomes "Nigger," your middle name becomes "boy" (however old you are) and your last name becomes "John," and your wife and mother are never given the respected title "Mrs."; when your are harried by day and haunted by night by the fact that you are a Negro, living constantly at tiptoe stance, never quite knowing what to expect next, and are plagued with inner fears and outer resentments; when you are forever fighting a degenerating sense of "nobodiness" then you will understand why we find it difficult to wait. There comes a time when the cup of endurance runs over, and men are no longer willing to be plunged into the abyss of despair. I hope, sirs, you can understand our legitimate and unavoidable impatience.

You express a great deal of anxiety over our willingness to break laws. This is certainly a legitimate concern. Since we so diligently urge people to obey the Supreme Court's decision of 1954 outlawing segregation in the public schools, at first glance it may seem rather paradoxical for us consciously to break laws. One may ask: "How can you advocate breaking some laws and obeying others?" The answer lies in the fact that there are two types of laws: just and unjust. I would be the first to advocate obeying just laws. One has not only a legal but a moral responsibility to obey just laws. Conversely, one has a moral responsibility to disobey unjust laws. I would agree with St. Augustine that "an unjust law is no law at all."

Now, what is the difference between the two? How does one determine whether a law is just or unjust? A just law is a man-made code that squares with the moral law or the law of God. An unjust law is a code that is out of Harmony with the moral law. To put it in the terms of St. Thomas Aquinas: An unjust law is a human law that is not rooted in eternal law and natural law. Any law that uplifts human personality is just. Any law that degrades human personality is unjust. All segregation statutes are unjust because segregation distorts the soul and damages the personality. It gives the segregator a false sense of superiority and the segregated a false sense of inferiority. Segregation, to use the terminology of the Jewish philosopher Martin Buber, substitutes an "I-it" relationship for an "I-thou" relationship and ends up relegating persons to the status of things. Hence segregation is not only politically, economically and sociologically unsound, it is morally wrong and sinful. Paul Tillich has said that sin is separation. Is not segregation an existential expression of man's tragic separation, his awful estrangement, his terrible sinfulness? Thus is it that I can urge men to obey the 1954 decision of the Supreme Court, for it is morally right; and I can urge them to disobey segregation ordinances, for they are morally wrong.

Let us consider a more concrete example of just and unjust laws. An unjust law is a code that a numerical or power majority group compels a minority group to obey but does not make binding on itself. This is difference made legal. By the same token, a just law is a code that a majority compels a minority to follow and that it is willing to follow itself. This is sameness made legal.

Let me give another explanation. A law is unjust if it is inflicted on a minority that, as a result of being denied the right to vote, had no part in enacting or devising the law. Who can say that the legislature of Alabama which set up that state's segregation laws was democratically elected? Throughout Alabama all sorts of devious methods are used to prevent Negroes from becoming registered voters, and there are some counties in which, even though Negroes constitute a majority of the population, not a single Negro is registered. Can any law enacted under such circumstances be considered democratically structured?

Sometimes a law is just on its face and unjust in it's application. For instance, I have been arrested on a charge of parading without a permit. Now, there is nothing wrong in having an ordinance which requires a permit for a parade. But such an ordinance becomes unjust when it is used to maintain segregation and to deny citizens the First-Amendment privilege of peaceful assembly and protest.

I hope you are able to see the distinction I am trying to point out. In no sense do I advocate evading or defying the law, as would the rabid segregationist. That would lead to anarchy. One who breaks an unjust law must do so openly, lovingly, and with a willingness to accept the penalty. I submit that an individual who breaks a law that conscience tells him is unjust, and who willingly accepts the penalty of imprisonment in order to arouse the conscience of the community over its injustice, is in reality expressing the highest respect for law.

Of course, there is nothing new about this kind of civil disobedience. It was evidenced sublimely in the refusal of Shadrach, Meshach, and Abednego to obey the laws of Nebuchadnezzar, on the ground that a higher moral law was at stake. It was practiced superbly by the early Christians, who were willing to face hungry lions and the excruciating pain of chopping blocks rather than submit to certain unjust laws of the Roman Empire. To a degree, academic freedom is a reality today because Socrates practiced civil disobedience. In our own nation, the Boston Tea Party represented a massive act of civil disobedience.

We should never forget that everything Adolf Hitler did in Germany was "legal" and everything the Hungarian freedom fighters did in Hungary was "illegal." It was "illegal" to aid and comfort a Jew in Hitler's Germany. Even so, I am sure that, had I lived in Germany at the time, I would have aided and comforted my Jewish brothers. If today I lived in a Communist country where certain principles dear to the Christian faith are suppressed, I would openly advocate disobeying that country's anti-religious laws.

I must make two honest confessions to you, my Christian and Jewish brothers. First, I must confess that over the past few years I have been gravely disappointed with the white moderate. I have almost reached the regrettable conclusion that the Negro's great stumbling block in his stride toward freedom is not the White Citizen's Councilor or the Ku Klux Klanner, but the white moderate, who is more devoted to "order" than to justice; who prefers a negative peace which is the absence of tension to a positive peace which is the presence of justice; who constantly says, "I agree with you in the goal you seek, but I cannot agree with your methods of direct action"; who paternalistically believes he can set the timetable for another man's freedom; who lives by a mythical concept of time and who constantly advises the Negro the wait for a "more convenient season." Shallow understanding from people of good will is more frustrating than absolute misunderstanding from people of ill will. Lukewarm acceptance is much more bewildering than outright rejection.

I had hoped that the white moderate would understand that law and order exist for the purpose of establishing justice and that when they fail in this purpose they become the dangerously structured dams that block the flow of social progress. I had hoped that the white moderate would understand that the present tension in the South is a necessary phase of the transition from an obnoxious negative peace, in which the Negro passively accepted his unjust plight, to a substantive and positive peace, in which all men will respect the dignity and worth of human personality. Actually, we who engage in nonviolent direct action are not the creators of tension. We merely bring to the surface the hidden tension that is already alive. We bring it out in the open, where it can be seen and dealt with. Like a boil that can never be cured so long as it is covered up but must be opened with all it ugliness to the natural medicines of air and light injustice must be exposed with all the tension its exposure creates, to the light of human conscience and the air of national opinion, before it can be cured.

In your statement you assert that our actions, even though peaceful, must be condemned because they precipitate violence. But is this a logical assertion? Isn't this like condemning a robbed man because his possession of money precipitated the evil act of robbery? Isn't this like condemning Socrates because his unswerving commitment to truth and his philosophical inquiries precipitated the act by the misguided populace in which they made him drink hemlock? Isn't this like condemning Jesus because his unique God-consciousness and never-ceasing devotion to God's will precipitated the evil act of crucifixion? We must come to see that, as the federal courts have consistently affirmed, it is wrong to urge an individual to cease his efforts to gain his basic constitutional rights because the quest may precipitate violence. Society must protect the robbed and punish the robber.

I had also hoped that the white moderate would reject the myth concerning time in relations to the struggle for freedom. I have just received a letter from a white brother in Texas. He writes: "All Christians know that the colored people will receive equal rights eventually, but it is possible that you are in too great a religious hurry. It has taken Christianity almost two thousand years to accomplish what it has. The teachings of Christ take time to come to earth." Such an attitude stems from a tragic misconception of time, from the strangely irrational notion that there is something in the very flow of time that will inevitably cure all ills. Actually, time itself is neutral; it can be used either destructively or constructively. More and more I feel that the people of ill will have used time much more effectively than have the people of good will. We will have to repent in this generation not merely for the hateful words and actions of the bad people, but for the appalling silence of the good people. Human progress never rolls in on wheels of inevitability; it comes through the tireless efforts of men willing to be co-workers with God, and without this hard work, time itself becomes an ally of the forces of stagnation. We must use time creatively, in the knowledge that the time is always ripe to do right. Now is the time to make real the promise of democracy and transform our pending national elegy into a creative psalm of brotherhood. Now is the time to lift our national policy from the quicksand of racial injustice to the solid rock of human dignity.

You speak of our activity in Birmingham as extreme. At first I was rather disappointed that fellow clergyman would see my nonviolent efforts as those of an extremist. I began thinking about the fact that I stand in the middle of two opposing forces in the Negro community. One is a force of complacency, made up in part of Negroes who, as a result of long years of oppression, are so drained of self-respect and a sense of "somebodiness" that they have adjusted to segregation; and in part of a few middle-class Negroes who, because of a degree of academic and economic security and because in some ways they profit by segregation, have become insensitive to the problems of the masses. The other force is one of bitterness and hatred, and it comes perilously closed on advocating violence. It is expressed in the various black nationalist groups that are springing up across the nation, the largest and best-known being Elijah Muhammad's Muslim movement. Nourished by the Negro's frustration over the continued existence of racial discrimination, this movement is made up of

people who have lost faith in America, who have absolutely repudiated Christianity, and who have concluded that the white man is an incorrigible "devil."

I have tried to stand between these two forces, saying that we need emulate neither the "do-nothingism" of the complacent nor the hatred and despair of the black nationalist. For there is the more excellent way of love and nonviolent protest. I am grateful to God that, through the influence of the Negro church, the way of nonviolence became an integral part of our struggle.

If this philosophy had not emerged, by now many streets of the South would, I am convinced, be flowing with blood. And I am further convinced that if our white brothers dismiss as "rabble-rousers" and "outside agitators" those of us who employ nonviolent direct action, and if they refuse to support our nonviolent efforts, millions of Negroes will, out of frustration and despair, seek solace and security in black nationalist ideologies—a development that would inevitably lead to a frightening racial nightmare.

Oppressed people cannot remain oppressed forever. The yearning for freedom eventually manifests itself, and that is what has happened to the American Negro. Something within has reminded him of his birthright of freedom, and something without has reminded him that it can be gained. Consciously or unconsciously, he has been caught up by the Zeitgeist, and with his black brothers of Africa and his brown and yellow brothers of Asia, South America, and the Caribbean, the United States Negro is moving with a sense of great urgency toward the promised land of racial justice. If one recognizes this vital urge that has engulfed the Negro community, one should readily understand why public demonstrations are taking place. The Negro has many pent-up resentments and latent frustrations, and he must release them. So let him march; let him make prayer pilgrimages to the city hall; let him go on freedom rides—and try to understand why he must do so. If his repressed emotions are not released in nonviolent ways, they will seek expression through violence; this is not a threat but a fact of history. So I have not said to my people, "Get rid of your discontent." Rather, I have tried to say that this normal and healthy discontent can be channeled into the creative outlet of nonviolent direct action. And now this approach is being termed extremist.

But though I was initially disappointed at being categorized as an extremist, as I continued to think about the matter I gradually gained a measure of satisfaction from the label. Was not Jesus and extremist for love: "Love your enemies, bless them that curse you, do good to them that hate you, and pray for them which despitefully use you, and persecute you." Was not Amos an extremist for justice: "Let justice roll down like waters and righteousness like am ever-flowing stream." Was not Paul an extremist for the Christian gospel: "I bear in my body the marks of the Lord Jesus." Was not Martin Luther an extremist: "Here I stand; I cannot do otherwise, so help me God." And John Bunyan: "I will stay in jail to the end of my days before I make a butchery of my conscience." And Abraham Lincoln: "This nation cannot survive half slave and half free." And Thomas Jefferson: "We hold these truths to be self-evident, that all men are created equal. . . ." So the question is not whether we will be extremists, but what kind of extremists we will be. Will we be extremists for hate or for love? Will we be extremists for the preservation of injustice or for the extension of justice? In that dramatic scene on Calvery's hill three men were crucified. We must never forget that all three were crucified for the same crime—the crime of extremism. Two were extremists for immorality, and thus fell below their environment. The other, Jesus Christ, was an extremist for love, truth, and goodness, and thereby rose above his environment. Perhaps the South, the nation, and the world are in dire need of creative extremists.

I had hoped that the white moderate would see this need. Perhaps I was too optimistic; perhaps I expected too much. I suppose I should have realized that few members of the oppressor race can understand the deep groans and passionate yearnings of the oppressed race, and still fewer have the vision to see that injustice must be rooted out by strong, persistent, and determined action. I am thankful, however, that some of our white brothers in the South have grasped the meaning of this social revolution and committed themselves to it. They are still all too few in quantity, but they are big in quality. Some—such as Ralph McGill, Lillian Smith, Harry Golden, James McBride Dabbs, Ann Braden, and Sarah Patton Boyle—have written about our struggle in eloquent and prophetic terms. Others have marched with us down nameless streets of the South. They have languished in filthy, roach-infested jails, suffering the abuse and brutality of policemen who view them as "dirty nigger-lovers." Unlike so many of their moderate brothers and sisters, they have recognized the urgency of the moment and sensed the need for powerful "action" antidotes to combat the disease of segregation.

Let me take note of my other major disappointment. I have been so greatly disappointed with the white church and its leadership. Of course, there are some notable exceptions. I am not unmindful of the fact that each of you has taken some significant stands on this issue. I commend you, Reverend Stallings, for your Christian stand on this past Sunday, in welcoming Negroes to your worship service on a nonsegregated basis. I commend the Catholic leaders of this state for integrating Spring Hill College several years ago.

But despite these notable exceptions, I must honestly reiterate that I have been disappointed with the church. I do not say this as one of those negative critics who can always find something wrong with the church. I say this as a minister of the gospel, who loves the church; who was nurtured in its bosom; who has been sustained by its spiritual blessings and who will remain true to it as long as the cord of life shall lengthen.

When I was suddenly catapulted into the leadership of the bus protest in Montgomery, Alabama, a few years ago, I felt we would be supported by the white church. I felt that the ministers, priests, and rabbis of the South would be among our strongest allies. Instead, some have been outright opponents, refusing to understand the freedom movement and misrepresenting its leaders; all too many others have been more cautious than courageous and have remained silent behind the anesthetizing security of stained-glass windows.

In spite of my shattered dreams, I came to Birmingham with the hope that the white religious leadership of this community would see the justice of our cause and, with deep moral concern, would serve as the channel through which our just grievances could reach the power structure. I had hoped that each of you would understand. But again I have been disappointed.

I have heard numerous southern religious leaders admonish their worshipers to comply with a desegregation decision because it is the law, but I have longed to hear white ministers declare: "Follow this decree because integration is morally right and because the Negro is your brother." In the midst of blatant injustices inflicted upon the Negro, I have watched white churchmen stand on the sideline and mouth pious irrelevancies and sanctimonious trivialities. In the midst of a mighty struggle to rid our nation of racial and economic injustice, I have heard many ministers say: "Those are social issues, with which the gospel has no real concern." And I have watched many churches commit themselves to a completely otherworldly religion which makes a strange, un-Biblical distinction between body and soul, between the sacred and the secular.

I have traveled the length and breadth of Alabama, Mississippi, and all the other southern states. On sweltering summer days and crisp autumn mornings I have looked at the South's beautiful churches with their lofty spires pointing heavenward. I have beheld the impressive outlines of her massive religious-education buildings. Over and over I have found myself asking: "What kind of people worship here? Who is their God? Where were their voices when the lips for Governor Barnett dripped with words of interposition and nullification? Where were they when Governor Wallace gave a clarion call of defiance and hatred? Where were their voices of support when bruised and weary Negro men and women decided to rise from the dark dungeons of complacency to the bright hills of creative protest?"

Yes, these questions are still in my mind. In deep disappointment I have wept over the laxity of the church. But be assured that my tears have been tears of love. Yes, I love the church. How could I do otherwise? I am in the rather unique position of being the son, the grandson, and the great-grandson of preachers. Yes, I see the church as the body of Christ. But, oh! How we have blemished and scarred that body through social neglect and through fear of being nonconformists.

There was a time when the church was very powerful—in the time when the early Christians rejoiced at being deemed worthy to suffer for what they believed. In those days the church was not merely a thermometer that recorded the ideas and principles of popular opinion; it was a thermostat that transformed the mores of society. Whenever the early Christians entered a town, the people in power became disturbed and immediately sought to convict the Christians for being "disturbers of the peace" and "outside agitators." But the Christians pressed on, in the conviction that they were "a colony of heaven," called to obey God rather than man. Small in number, they were big in commitment. They were too God-intoxicated to be "astronomically intimidated." By their effort and example they brought an end to such ancient evils as infanticide and gladiatorial contests.

Things are different now. So often the contemporary church is a weak, ineffectual voice with an uncertain sound. So often it is an arch-defender of the status quo. Far from being disturbed by the presence of the church, the power structure of the average community is consoled by the church's silent—and often even vocal—sanction of things as they are. But the judgment of God is upon the church as never before. If today's church does not recapture the sacrificial spirit of the early church, it will lose its authenticity, forfeit the loyalty of millions, and be dismissed as an irrelevant social club with no meaning for the twentieth century. Every day I meet young people whose disappointment with the church has turned into outright disgust.

Perhaps I have once again been too optimistic. Is organized religion to inextricably bound to the status quo to save our nation and the world? Perhaps I must turn my faith to the inner spiritual church, the church within the church, as the true ekklesia and the hope of the world. But again I am thankful to God that some noble souls from the ranks of organized religion have broken loose from the paralyzing chains of conformity and joined us as active partners in the struggle for freedom. They have left their secure congregations and walked the streets of Albany, Georgia, with us. They have gone down the highways of the South on tortuous rides for freedom. Yes, they have gone to jail with us. Some have been dismissed from their churches, have lost the support of their bishops and fellow ministers. But they have acted in the faith that right defeated is stronger than evil triumphant. Their witness has been the spiritual salt that has preserved the true meaning of the gospel in these troubled times. They have carved a tunnel of hope through the dark mountain of disappointment.

I hope the church as a whole will meet the challenge of this decisive hour. But even if the church does not come to the aid of justice, I have no despair about the future. I have no fear about the outcome of our struggle in Birmingham, even if our motives are at present misunderstood. We will reach the goal of freedom in Birmingham and all over the nation, because the goal of America is freedom. Abused and scorned though we may be, our destiny is tied up with America's destiny. Before the pilgrims landed at Plymouth, we were here. For more than two centuries our forebears labored in this country without wages; they made cotton king; they built the homes of their masters while suffering gross injustice and shameful humiliation—and yet out of bottomless vitality they continued to thrive and develop. If the inexpressible cruelties of slavery could not stop us, the opposition we not face will surely fail. We will win our freedom because the sacred heritage of our nation and the eternal will of God are embodied in our echoing demands.

Before closing I feel impelled to mention one other point in your statement that has troubled me profoundly. You warmly commended the Birmingham police force for keeping "order" and "preventing violence." I doubt that you would so quickly commend the policemen if you were to observe their ugly and inhumane treatment of Negroes here in the city jail; if you were to watch them push and curse old Negro women and young Negro girls; if you were to see them slap and kick Negro men and young boys; if you were to observe them, as they did on two occasions, refuse to give us food because we wanted to sing our grace together. I cannot join you in your praise of the Birmingham police department.

It is true that the police have exercised a degree of discipline in handling the demonstrations. In this sense they have conducted themselves rather "nonviolently" in public. But for what purpose? To preserve the evil system of segregation. Over the past few years I have consistently preached that nonviolence demands that the means we use must be as pure as the ends we seek. I have tried to make clear that it is wrong to use immoral means to attain moral ends. But now I must affirm that it is just as wrong, or perhaps even more so, to use moral means to preserve immoral ends. Perhaps Mr. Connor and his policemen have been rather nonviolent in public, as was Chief Pritchett in Albany, Georgia, but they have used the moral means of nonviolence to maintain the immoral end or racial injustice. As T. S. Eliot has said, "The last temptation is the greatest treason: To do the right deed for the wrong reason."

I wish you had commended the Negro sit-inners and demonstrators of Birmingham for their sublime courage, their willingness to suffer, and their amazing discipline in the midst of great provocation. One day the South will recognize its real heroes. They will be the James Merediths, with the noble sense of purpose that enables them to face jeering and hostile mobs, and with the agonizing loneliness that characterizes the life of the pioneer. They will be old, oppressed, battered Negro women, symbolized in a seventy-two-year-old woman in Montgomery, Alabama, who rose up with a sense of dignity and when her people decided not to ride segregated buses, and who responded with ungrammatical profundity to one who inquired about her weariness: "My feets is tired, but my soul is at rest." They will be the young high school and college students, the young ministers of the gospel and a host of their elders, courageously and nonviolently sitting in at lunch counters and willingly going to jail for conscience' sake. One day the South will know that when these disinherited children of God sat down at lunch counters, they were in reality standing up for what is best in the American dream and for the most sacred values in our Judaeo-Christian heritage, thereby bringing our nation back to those great wells of democracy which were dug deep by the founding fathers in their formulation of the Constitution and the Declaration of Independence.

Never before have I written so long a letter. I'm afraid it is much too long to take your precious time. I can assure you that it would have been much shorter if I had been writing from a comfortable desk, but what else can one do when he is alone in a narrow jail cell, other than write long letters, think long thoughts, and pray long prayers?

If I have said anything in this letter that overstates the truth and indicates an unreasonable impatience, I beg you to forgive me. If I have said anything that understates the truth and indicates my having a patience that allows me to settle for anything less than brotherhood, I beg God to forgive me.

I hope this letter finds you strong in the faith. I also hope that circumstances will soon make it possible for me to meet each of you, not as an integrationist or a civil-rights leader but as a fellow clergyman and a Christian brother. Let us all hope that the dark clouds of racial prejudice will soon pass away and the deep fog of misunderstanding will be lifted from our fear-drenched communities, and in some not too distant tomorrow the radiant stars of love and brotherhood will shine over our great nation with all their scintillating beauty.

Yours for the cause of
Peace and Brotherhood,

Martin Luther King, Jr.

Lincoln Memorial Address ("I Have a Dream") (1963)

I am happy to join with you today in what will go down in history as the greatest demonstration for freedom in the history of our nation.

Five score years ago, a great American, in whose symbolic shadow we stand today, signed the Emancipation Proclamation. This momentous decree came as a great beacon light of hope to millions of Negro slaves who had been seared in the flames of withering injustice. It came as a joyous daybreak to end the long night of their captivity.

But one hundred years later, the Negro still is not free. One hundred years later, the life of the Negro is still sadly crippled by the manacles of segregation and the chains of discrimination. One hundred years later, the Negro lives on a lonely island of poverty in the midst of a vast ocean of material prosperity. One hundred years later, the Negro is still languishing in the corners of American society and finds himself an exile in his own land. So we have come here today to dramatize a shameful condition.

In a sense we have come to our nation's capital to cash a check. When the architects of our republic wrote the magnificent words of the Constitution and the Declaration of Independence, they were signing a promissory note to which every American was to fall heir. This note was a promise that all men, yes, black men as well as white men, would be guaranteed the unalienable rights of life, liberty, and the pursuit of happiness.

It is obvious today that America has defaulted on this promissory note insofar as her citizens of color are concerned. Instead of honoring this sacred obligation, America has given the Negro people a bad check, a check which has come back marked "insufficient funds." But we refuse to believe that the bank of justice is bankrupt. We refuse to believe that there are insufficient funds in the great vaults of opportunity of this nation. So we have come to cash this check—a check that will give us upon demand the riches of freedom and the security of justice. We have also come to this hallowed spot to remind America of the fierce urgency of now. This is no time to engage in the luxury of cooling off or to take the tranquilizing drug of gradualism. Now is the time to make real the promises of democracy. Now is the time to rise from the dark and desolate valley of segregation to the sunlit path of racial justice. Now is the time to lift our nation from the quick sands of racial injustice to the solid rock of brotherhood. Now is the time to make justice a reality for all of God's children.

It would be fatal for the nation to overlook the urgency of the moment. This sweltering summer of the Negro's legitimate discontent will not pass until there is an invigorating autumn of freedom and equality. Nineteen sixty-three is not an end, but a beginning. Those who hope that the Negro needed to blow off steam and will now be content will have a rude awakening if the nation returns to business as usual. There will be neither rest nor tranquility in America until the Negro is granted his citizenship rights. The whirlwinds of revolt will continue to shake the foundations of our nation until the bright day of justice emerges.

But there is something that I must say to my people who stand on the warm threshold which leads into the palace of justice. In the process of gaining our rightful place we must not be guilty of wrongful deeds. Let us not seek to satisfy our thirst for freedom by drinking from the cup of bitterness and hatred.

We must forever conduct our struggle on the high plane of dignity and discipline. We must not allow our creative protest to degenerate into physical violence. Again and again we must rise to the majestic heights of meeting physical force with soul force. The marvelous new militancy which has engulfed the Negro community must not lead us to distrust of all white people, for many of our white brothers, as evidenced by their presence here today, have come to realize that their destiny is tied up with our destiny and their freedom is inextricably bound to our freedom. We cannot walk alone.

As we walk, we must make the pledge that we shall march ahead. We cannot turn back. There are those who are asking the devotees of civil rights, "When will you be satisfied?" We can never be satisfied as long as the Negro is the victim of the unspeakable horrors of police brutality. We can never be satisfied, as long as our bodies, heavy with the fatigue of travel, cannot gain lodging in the motels of the highways and the hotels of the cities. We can never be satisfied as long as a Negro in Mississippi cannot vote and a Negro in New York believes he has nothing for which to vote. No, no, we are not satisfied, and we will not be satisfied until justice rolls down like waters and righteousness like a mighty stream.

I am not unmindful that some of you have come here out of great trials and tribulations. Some of you have come fresh from narrow jail cells. Some of you have come from areas where your quest for freedom left you battered by the storms of persecution and staggered by the winds of police brutality. You have been the veterans of creative suffering. Continue to work with the faith that unearned suffering is redemptive.

Go back to Mississippi, go back to Alabama, go back to South Carolina, go back to Georgia, go back to Louisiana, go back to the slums and ghettos of our northern cities, knowing that somehow this situation can and will be changed. Let us not wallow in the valley of despair.

I say to you today, my friends, so even though we face the difficulties of today and tomorrow, I still have a dream. It is a dream deeply rooted in the American dream.

I have a dream that one day this nation will rise up and live out the true meaning of its creed: "We hold these truths to be self-evident: that all men are created equal."

I have a dream that one day on the red hills of Georgia the sons of former slaves and the sons of former slave owners will be able to sit down together at the table of brotherhood.

I have a dream that one day even the state of Mississippi, a state sweltering with the heat of injustice, sweltering with the heat of oppression, will be transformed into an oasis of freedom and justice.

I have a dream that my four little children will one day live in a nation where they will not be judged by the color of their skin but by the content of their character.

I have a dream today.

I have a dream that one day, down in Alabama, with its vicious racists, with its governor having his lips dripping with the words of interposition and nullification; one day right there in Alabama, little black boys and black girls will be able to join hands with little white boys and white girls as sisters and brothers.

I have a dream today.

I have a dream that one day every valley shall be exalted, every hill and mountain shall be made low, the rough places will be made plain, and the crooked places will be made straight, and the glory of the Lord shall be revealed, and all flesh shall see it together.

This is our hope. This is the faith that I go back to the South with. With this faith we will be able to hew out of the mountain of despair a stone of hope. With this faith we will be able to transform the jangling discords of our nation into a beautiful symphony of brotherhood. With this faith we will be able to work together, to pray together, to struggle together, to go to jail together, to stand up for freedom together, knowing that we will be free one day.

This will be the day when all of God's children will be able to sing with a new meaning, "My country, 'tis of thee, sweet land of liberty, of thee I sing. Land where my fathers died, land of the pilgrim's pride, from every mountainside, let freedom ring."

And if America is to be a great nation this must become true. So let freedom ring from the prodigious hilltops of New Hampshire. Let freedom ring from the mighty mountains of New York. Let freedom ring from the heightening Alleghenies of Pennsylvania!

Let freedom ring from the snowcapped Rockies of Colorado!

Let freedom ring from the curvaceous slopes of California!

But not only that; let freedom ring from Stone Mountain of Georgia!

Let freedom ring from Lookout Mountain of Tennessee!

Let freedom ring from every hill and molehill of Mississippi. From every mountainside, let freedom ring.

And when this happens, when we allow freedom to ring, when we let it ring from every village and every hamlet, from every state and every city, we will be able to speed up that day when all of God's children, black men and white men, Jews and Gentiles, Protestants and Catholics, will be able to join hands and sing in the words of the old Negro spiritual, "Free at last! free at last! thank God Almighty, we are free at last!"

MALCOLM X

The Ballot or the Bullet (1964)

Mr. Moderator, Brother Lomax, brothers and sisters, friends and enemies; I just can't believe everyone in here is a friend and I don't want to leave anybody out. The question tonight, as I understand it, is "The Negro Revolt, and Where Do We Go From Here?" or "What Next?" In my little humble way of understanding it, it points toward either the ballot or the bullet.

Before we try and explain what is meant by the ballot or the bullet, I would like to clarify something concerning myself. I'm still a Muslim, my religion is still Islam. That's my personal belief. Just as Adam Clayton Powell is a Christian minister who heads the Abyssinian Baptist Church in New York, but at the same time takes part in the political struggles to try and bring about rights to the black people in this country; and Dr. Martin Luther King is a Christian minister down in Atlanta, Georgia, who heads another organization fighting for the civil rights of black people in this country; and Rev. Galamison, I guess you've heard of him, is another Christian minister in New York who has been deeply involved in the school boycotts to eliminate segregated education; well, I myself am a minister, not a Christian minister, but a Muslim minister; and I believe in action on all fronts by whatever means necessary.

Although I'm still a Muslim, I'm not here tonight to discuss my religion. I'm not here to try and change your religion. I'm not here to argue or discuss anything that we differ about, because it's time for us to submerge our differences and realize that it is best for us to first see that we have the same problem, a common problem—a problem that will make you catch hell whether you're a Baptist, or a Methodist, or a Muslim, or a nationalist. Whether you're educated or illiterate, whether you live on the boulevard or in the alley, you're going to catch hell just like I am. We're all in the same boat and we all are going to catch hell from the same man. He just happens to be a white man. All of us have suffered here, in this country, political oppression at the hands of the white man, economic exploitation at the hands of the white man, and social degradation at the hands of the white man.

Now in speaking like this, it doesn't mean that we're anti-white, but it does mean we're anti-exploitation, we're anti-degradation, we're anti-oppression. And if the white man doesn't want us to be anti-him, let him stop oppressing and exploiting and degrading us. Whether we are Christians or Muslims or nationalists or agnostics or atheists, we must first learn to forget our differences. If we have differences, let us differ in the closet; when we come out in front, let us not have anything to argue about until we get finished arguing with the man. If the late President Kennedy could get together with

Khrushchev and exchange some wheat, we certainly have more in common with each other than Kennedy and Khrushchev had with each other.

If we don't do something real soon, I think you'll have to agree that we're going to be forced either to use the ballot or the bullet. It's one or the other in 1964. It isn't that time is running out—time has run out! 1964 threatens to be the most explosive year America has ever witnessed. The most explosive year. Why? It's also a political year. It's the year when all of the white politicians will be back in the so-called Negro community jiving you and me for some votes. The year when all the white political crooks will be right back in your and my community with their false promises, building up our hopes for a letdown, with their trickery and their treachery, with their false promises which they don't intend to keep. As they nourish these dissatisfactions, it can only lead to one thing, an explosion; and we have the type of black man on the scene in America today—I'm sorry, Brother Lomax—who just doesn't intend to turn the other cheek any longer.

Don't let anybody tell you anything about the odds that are against you. If they draft you, they send you to Korea or South Vietnam and make you face 800 million Chinese. If you can be brave over there, you can be brave right here. These odds aren't as great as those odds. And if you fight here, you will at least know what you're fighting for.

I'm not a politician, not even a student of politics; in fact, I'm not a student of much anything. I'm not a Democrat, I'm not a Republican, and I don't even consider myself an American. If you and I were Americans, there'd be no problem. Those Honkies that just got off the boat, they're already Americans; Polacks are already Americans; the Italian refugees are already Americans. Everything that came out of Europe, every blue-eyed thing, is already an American. And as long as you and I have been over here, we aren't Americans yet.

Well, I am one who doesn't believe in deluding myself. I'm not going to sit at your table and watch you eat, with nothing on my plate, and call myself a diner. Sitting at the table doesn't make you a diner, unless you eat some of what's on that plate. Being here in America doesn't make you an American. Why, if birth made you American, you wouldn't need any legislation, you wouldn't need any amendments to the Constitution, you wouldn't be faced with civil-rights filibustering in Washington, D.C., right now. They don't have to pass civil rights legislation to make a Polack an American.

No, I'm not an American. I'm one of the 22 million black people who are the victims of Americanism. One of the 22 million black people who are the victims of democracy, nothing but disguised hypocrisy. So, I'm not standing here speaking to you as an American, or a patriot, or a flag-saluter, or a flag waver—no, not I. I'm speaking as a victim of this American system. And I see America through the eyes of the victim. I don't see any American dream; I see an American nightmare.

These 22 million victims are waking up. Their eyes are coming open. They're beginning to see what they used to only look at. They're becoming politically mature. They are realizing that there are new political trends from coast to coast. As they see these new political trends, it's possible for them to see that every time there's an election the races are so close that they have a recount. They had to recount in Massachusetts to see who was going to be governor, it was so close. It was the same way in Rhode Island, in Minnesota, and in many other parts of the country. And the same with Kennedy and Nixon when they ran for president. It was so close they had to count all over again. Well, what does this mean? It means that when white people are evenly divided, and black people have a bloc of votes of their own, it is left up to them to determine who's going to sit in the White House and who's going to be in the dog house.

It was the black man's vote that put the present administration in Washington, D.C. Your vote, your dumb vote, your ignorant vote, your wasted vote put in an administration in Washington, D.C. that has seen fit to pass every kind of legislation imaginable, saving you until last, then filibustering on top of that. And your and my leaders have the audacity to run around clapping their hands and talk about how much progress we're making. And what a good president we have. If he wasn't good in Texas, he sure can't be good in Washington, D.C. because Texas is a lynch state. It is in the same breath as Mississippi, no different; only they lynch you in Texas with a Texas accent. And these Negro leaders have the audacity to go and have some coffee in the White House with a Texan, a Southern cracker—that's all he is—and then come out and tell you and me that he's going to be better for us because, since he's from the South, he knows how to deal with the Southerners. What kind of logic is that? Let Eastland be president, he's from the South too. He should be better able to deal with them than Johnson.

In this present administration they have in the House of Representatives 257 Democrats to only 177 Republicans. They control two-thirds of the House vote. Why can't they pass something that will help you and me? In the Senate, there are 67 senators who are of the Democratic Party. Only 33 are Republicans. Why, the Democrats have got the government sewed up, and you're the one who sewed it up for them. And what have they given you for it? Four years in office, and just now getting around to some civil-rights legislation. Just now, after everything else is done, out of the way, they're going to sit down now and play with you all summer long—the same old giant con game that they call filibuster. All those are in cahoots together. Don't you ever think they're not in cahoots together, for the man that is heading the civil-rights filibuster is a man from Georgia named Richard Russell. When Johnson became president, the first man he asked for when he got back to Washington, D.C., was "Dicky"—that's how tight they are. That's his boy, that's his pal, that's his buddy. But they're playing that old con game. One of them makes believe he's for you, and he's got it fixed where the other one is so tight against you, he never has to keep his promise.

So it's time in 1964 to wake up. And when you see them coming up with that kind of conspiracy, let them know your eyes are open. And let them know you got something else that's wide open too. It's got to be the ballot or the bullet. If you're afraid to use an expression like that, you should get on out of the country, you should get back in the cotton patch, you should get back in the alley. They get all the Negro vote, and after they get it, the Negro gets nothing in return. All they did when they got to Washington was give a few big Negroes big jobs. Those big Negroes didn't need big jobs, they already had jobs. That's camouflage, that's trickery, that's treachery, window-dressing. I'm not trying to knock out the Democrats for the Republicans, we'll get to them in a minute. But it is true—you put the Democrats first and the Democrats put you last.

Look at it the way it is. What alibis do they use, since they control Congress and the Senate? What alibi do they use when you and I ask, "Well, when are you going to keep your promise?" They blame the Dixiecrats. What is a Dixiecrat? A Democrat. A Dixiecrat is nothing but a Democrat in disguise. The titular head of the Democrats is also the head of the Democratic Party. The Democrats have never kicked the Dixiecrats out of the party. The Dixiecrats bolted themselves once, but the Democrats didn't put them out. Imagine these lowdown Southern segregationists put the Northern Democrats down. Now, look at that thing the way it is. They have got a con game going on, a political con game, and you and I are in the middle. It's time for you and me to wake up and start looking at it like it is, and trying to understand it like it is; and then we can deal with it like it is.

The Dixiecrats in Washington, D.C. control the key committees that run the government. The only reason the Dixiecrats control these committees is because they have seniority. The only reason they have seniority is because they come from states where Negroes can't vote. This is not even a government that's based on democracy. It is not a government that is made up of representatives of the people. Half of the people in the South can't even vote. Eastland is not even supposed to be in Washington. Half of the senators and congressmen who occupy these key positions in Washington, D.C., are there illegally, are there unconstitutionally.

I was in Washington, D.C. a week ago Thursday, when they were debating whether or not they should let the bill come onto the floor. And in the back of the room where the Senate meets, there's a huge map of the United States, and on that map it shows the location of Negroes throughout the country, the states that are most heavily concentrated with Negroes, are the ones that have senators and congressmen standing up filibustering and doing all other kinds of trickery to keep the Negro from being able to vote. This is pitiful. But it's not pitiful for us any longer, it's actually pitiful for the white man, because soon now, as the Negro awakens a little more and sees the vise that he's in, see the bag that he's in, sees the real game that he's in, then the Negro's going to develop a new tactic.

These senators and congressmen actually violate the constitutional amendments that guarantee the people of that particular state or county the right to vote. And the Constitution itself has within it the machinery to expel any representative from a state where the voting rights of the people are violated. You don't even need new legislation. Any person in Congress right now, who is there from a state or a district where the voting rights of the people are violated, that particular person should be expelled from Congress. And when you expel him, you've removed one of the obstacles in the path of any real meaningful legislation in this country. In fact, when you expel them, you don't need new legislation, because they will be replaced by black representatives from counties and districts where the black man is in the majority, not in the minority.

If the black man in these Southern states had his full voting rights, the key Dixiecrats in Washington, D.C., which means the key Democrats in Washington, D.C., would lose their seats. The Democratic Party itself would lose its power. It would cease to be powerful as a party. When you see the amount of power that would be lost by the Democratic Party if it were to lose the Dixiecrat wing, or branch, or element, you can see where it's against the interest of the Democrats to give voting rights to Negroes and authority ever since the Civil War. You just can't belong to that party without analyzing it.

I say again, I'm not anti-Democrat, I'm not anti-Republican, I'm not anti-anything. I'm just questioning their sincerity, and some of the strategy that they've been using on our people by promising them promises that they don't intend to keep. When you keep the Democrats in power, you're keeping the Dixiecrats in power. I doubt that my good Brother Lomax will deny that. A vote for a Democrat is a vote for a Dixiecrat. That's why, in 1964, it's time now for you and me to become more politically mature and realize what the ballot is for; what we're supposed to get when we cast a ballot; and that if we don't cast a ballot, it's going to end up in a situation where we're going to have to cast a bullet. It's either a ballot or a bullet.

In the North, they do it a different way. They have a system that's known as gerrymandering, whatever that means. It means when Negroes become too heavily concentrated in a certain area, and begin to gain too much political power, the white man comes along and changes the district lines. You may say,

"Why do you keep saying the white man?" Because it's the white man who does it. I haven't ever seen any Negro changing any lines. They don't let him get near the line. It's the white man who grins at you the most, and pats you on the back, and is supposed to be your friend. He may be friendly, but he's not your friend. So, what I'm trying to impress upon you, in essence, is this: You and I in American are faced not with a segregationist conspiracy, we're faced with a government conspiracy. Everyone who's filibustering is a senator—that's the government. Everyone who's finagling in Washington, D.C., is a congressman—that's the government. You don't have anybody putting blocks in your path but people who are a part of the government. The same government that you go abroad to fight for and die for is the government that is in a conspiracy to deprive you of your voting rights, deprive you of your economic opportunities, deprive you of decent housing, deprive you of decent education. You don't need to go to the employer alone, it is the government itself, the government of America, that is responsible for the oppression and exploitation and degradation of black people in this country. And you should drop it in their lap. This government has failed the Negro. This so-called democracy has failed the Negro. And all these white liberals have definitely failed the Negro.

So, where do we go from here? First, we need some friends. We need some new allies. The entire civil-rights struggle needs a new interpretation, a broader interpretation. We need to look at this civil-rights thing from another angle—from the inside as well as from the outside. To those of us whose philosophy is black nationalism, the only way you can get involved in the civil-rights struggle is give it a new interpretation. That old interpretation excluded us. It kept us out. So, we're giving a new interpretation to the civil-rights struggle, an interpretation that will enable us to come into it, take part in it. And these handkerchief-heads who have been dillydallying and pussyfooting and compromising—we don't intend to let them pussyfoot and dillydally and compromise any longer.

How can you thank a man for giving you what's already yours? How then can you thank him for giving you only part of what's already yours? You haven't even made progress, if what's being given to you, you should already have had already. That's not progress.

And I love my Brother Lomax, the way he pointed out we're right back where we were in 1954. We're not even as far up as we were in 1954. We're behind where we were in 1954. There's more segregation now than there was in 1954. There's more racial animosity, more racial hatred, more racial violence today in 1964, than there was in 1954. Where is the progress?

And now you're facing a situation where the young Negro's coming up. They don't want to hear that "turn-the-other-cheek" stuff, no. In Jacksonville, those were teenagers, they were throwing Molotov cocktails. Negroes have never done that before. But it shows you there's a new deal coming in. There's new thinking coming in. There's new strategy coming in. It'll be Molotov cocktails this month, hand grenades next month, and something else next month. It'll be ballots, or it'll be bullets. It'll be liberty, or it will be death. The only difference about this kind of death—it'll be reciprocal. You know what is meant by "reciprocal"? That's one of Brother Lomax's words, I stole it from him. I don't usually deal with those big words because I don't usually deal with big people. I deal with small people. I find you can get a whole lot of small people and whip hell out of a whole lot of big people. They haven't got anything to lose, and they've got everything to gain. And they'll let you know in a minute: "It takes two to tango; when I go, you go."

The black nationalists, those whose philosophy is black nationalism, in bringing about this new interpretation of the entire meaning of civil rights, look upon it as a mean, as Brother Lomax has pointed out, to equality of opportunity. Well, we're justified in seeking civil rights, if it means equality of opportunity, because all we're doing there is trying to collect for our investment. Our mothers and fathers invested sweat and blood. Three hundred and ten years we worked in this country without a dime in return—I mean without a dime in return. You let the white man walk around here talking about how rich this country is, but you never stop to think how it got rich so quick. It got rich because you made it rich.

You take the people who are in this audience right now. They're poor, we're all poor as individuals. Our weekly salary individually amounts to hardly anything. But if you take the salary of everyone in here collectively it'll fill up a whole lot of baskets. It's a lot of wealth. If you can collect the wages of just these people right here for a year, you'll be rich—richer than rich. When you look at it like that, think how rich Uncle Sam had to become, not with this handful, but millions of black people. Your and my mother and father, who didn't work an eight-hour shift, but worked from "can't see" in the morning until "can't see" at night, and worked for nothing, making the white man rich, making Uncle Sam rich.

This is our investment. This is our contribution—our blood. Not only did we give of our free labor, we gave of our blood. Every time he had a call to arms, we were the first ones in uniform. We died on every battlefield the white man had. We have made a greater sacrifice than anybody who's standing up in America today. We have made a greater contribution and have collected less. Civil rights, for those of us whose philosophy is black nationalism, means: "Give it to us now. Don't wait for next year. Give it to us yesterday, and that's not fast enough."

I might stop right here to point out one thing. Whenever you're going after something that belongs to you, anyone who's depriving you of the right to have it is a criminal. Understand that. Whenever you are going after something that is yours, you are within your legal rights to lay claim to it. And anyone who puts forth any effort to deprive you of that which is yours, is breaking the law, is a criminal. And this was pointed out by the Supreme Court decision. It outlawed segregation. Which means segregation is against the law. Which means a segregationist is breaking the law. A segregationist is a criminal. You can't label him as anything other than that. And when you demonstrate against segregation, the law is on your side. The Supreme Court is on your side.

Now, who is that opposes you in carrying out the law? The police department itself. With police dogs and clubs. Whenever you demonstrate against segregation, whether it is segregated education, segregated housing, or anything else, the law is on your side, and anyone who stands in the way is not the law any longer. They are breaking the law, they are not representatives of the law. Any time you demonstrate against segregation and a man has the audacity to put a police dog on you, kill that dog, kill him, I'm telling you, kill that dog. I say it, if they put me in jail tomorrow, kill—that—dog. Then you'll put a stop to it. Now, if these white people in here don't want to see that kind of action, get down and tell the mayor to tell the police department to pull the dogs in. That's all you have to do. If you don't do it, someone else will.

If you don't take this kind of stand, your little children will grow up and look at you and think "shame." If you don't take an uncompromising stand—I don't mean go out and get violent; but at the same time you should never be nonviolent unless you run into some nonviolence. I'm nonviolent with those who are nonviolent with me. But when you drop that violence on me, then you've made me go insane, and I'm not responsible for what I do. And that's the way every Negro should get. Any time you know you're within the law, within your legal rights, within your moral rights, in accord with justice, then die for what you believe in. But don't die alone. Let your dying be reciprocal. This is what is meant by equality. What's good for the goose is good for the gander.

When we begin to get in this area, we need new friends, we need new allies. We need to expand the civil-rights struggle to a higher level—to the level of human rights. Whenever you are in a civil-rights struggle, whether you know it or not, you are confining yourself to the jurisdiction of Uncle Sam. No one from the outside world can speak out in your behalf as long as your struggle is a civil-rights struggle. Civil rights comes within the domestic affairs of this country. All of our African brothers and our Asian brothers and our Latin-American brothers cannot open their mouths and interfere in the domestic affairs of the United States. And as long as it's civil rights, this comes under the jurisdiction of Uncle Sam.

But the United Nations has what's known as the charter of human rights, it has a committee that deals in human rights. You may wonder why all of the atrocities that have been committed in Africa and in Hungary and in Asia and in Latin America are brought before the UN, and the Negro problem is never brought before the UN. This is part of the conspiracy. This old, tricky, blue-eyed liberal who is supposed to be your and my friend, supposed to be in our corner, supposed to be subsidizing our struggle, and supposed to be acting in the capacity of an adviser never tells you anything about human rights. They keep you wrapped up in civil rights. And you spend so much time barking up the civil-rights tree, you don't even know there's a human-rights tree on the same floor.

When you expand the civil-rights struggle to the level of human rights, you can then take the case of the black man in this country before the nations in the UN. You can take it before the General Assembly. You can take Uncle Sam before a world court. But the only level you can do it on is the level of human rights. Civil rights keeps you under his restrictions, under his jurisdiction. Civil rights keeps you in his pocket. Civil rights means you're asking Uncle Sam to treat you right. Human rights are your God-given rights. Human rights are the rights that are recognized by all nations of this earth. And any time any one violates your human rights, you can take them to the world court. Uncle Sam's hands are dripping with blood, dripping with the blood of the black man in this country. He's the earth's number-one hypocrite. He has the audacity—yes, he has—imagine him posing as the leader of the free world. The free world!—and you over here singing "We Shall Overcome." Expand the civil-rights struggle to the level of human rights, take it into the United Nations, where our African brothers can throw their weight on our side, where our Asian brothers can throw their weight on our side, where our Latin-American brothers can throw their weight on our side, and where 800 million Chinamen are sitting there waiting to throw their weight on our side.

Let the world know how bloody his hands are. Let the world know the hypocrisy that's practiced over here. Let it be the ballot or the bullet. Let him know that it must be the ballot or the bullet.

When you take your case to Washington, D.C., you're taking it to the criminal who's responsible; it's like running from the wolf to the fox. They're all in cahoots together. They all work political chicanery and make you look like a chump before the eyes of the world. Here you are walking around in America, getting ready to be drafted and sent abroad, like a tin soldier, and when you get over there, people ask you what are you fighting for, and you have to stick your tongue in your cheek. No, take Uncle Sam to court, take him before the world.

By ballot I only mean freedom. Don't you know—I disagree with Lomax on this issue—that the ballot is much more important than the dollar? Can I prove it? Yes. Look in the UN. There are poor nations in the UN; yet those poor nations can get together with their voting power and keep the rich nations from making a move. They have one nation—one vote, everyone has an equal vote. And when those brothers from Asia, and Africa and the darker parts of this earth get together, their voting power is sufficient to hold Sam in check. Or Russia in check. Or some other section of the earth in check. So the ballot is most important.

Right now, in this country, if you and I, 22 million African-Americans—that's what we are—Africans who are in America. You're nothing but Africans. Nothing but Africans. In fact, you'd get farther calling yourself African instead of Negro. Africans don't catch hell. You're the only one catching hell. They don't have to pass civil-rights bills for Africans. An African can go anywhere he wants right now. All you've got to do is tie your head up. That's right, go anywhere you want. Just stop being a Negro. Change your name to Hoogagagobba. That'll show you how silly the white man is. You're dealing with a silly man. A friend of mine who's very dark put a turban on his head and went into a restaurant in Atlanta before they called themselves desegregated. He went into a white restaurant, he sat down, they served him, and he said, "What would happen if a Negro came in here?" And there he's sitting, black as night, but because he had his head wrapped up the waitress looked back at him and says, "Why, there wouldn't no nigger dare come in here."

So, you're dallying with a man whose bias and prejudice are making him lose his mind, his intelligence, every day. He's frightened. He looks around and sees what's taking place on this earth, and he sees that the people are waking up. They're losing their fear of the white man. No place where he's fighting right now is he winning. Everywhere he's fighting, he's fighting someone [of] your and my complexion. And they're beating him. He can't win any more. He's won his last battle. He failed to win the Korean War. He couldn't win it. He had to sign a truce. That's a loss. Any time Uncle Sam, with all his machinery for warfare, is held to a draw by some rice-eaters, he's lost the battle. He had to sign a truce. America's not supposed to sign a truce. She's supposed to be bad. But she's not bad any more. She's bad as long as she can use her hydrogen bomb, but she can't use hers for fear Russia might use hers. Russia can't use hers, for fear that Sam might use his. So, both of them are weaponless. They can't use the weapon because each's weapon nullifies the other's. So the only place where action can take place is on the ground. And the white man can't win another war fighting on the ground. Those days are over. The black man knows it, the brown man knows it, the red man knows it, and the yellow man knows it. So they engage him in guerrilla warfare. That's not his style. You've got to have heart to be a guerrilla warrior, and he hasn't got any heart I'm telling you now.

I just want to give you a little briefing on guerrilla warfare because, before you know it, before you know it—it takes heart to be a guerrilla warrior because you're on your own. In conventional warfare you have tanks and a whole lot of other people with you to back you up, planes over your head and all that kind of stuff. But a guerilla is on his own. All you have is a rifle, some sneakers and a bowl of rice, and that's all you need—and a lot of heart. The Japanese on some of those islands in the Pacific, when the American soldiers landed, one Japanese sometimes could hold the whole army off. He'd just wait until the sun went down, and when the sun went down they were all equal. He would take his little blade and slip from bush to bush, and from American to American. The white soldiers couldn't cope with that. Whenever you see a white soldier that fought in the Pacific, he has the shakes, he has a nervous condition, because they scared him to death.

The same thing happened to the French up in French Indochina. People who just a few years previously were rice farmers got together and ran the heavily mechanized French army out of Indochina. You don't need it—modern warfare today won't work. This is the day of the guerrilla. They did the same thing in Algeria. Algerians, who were nothing but Bedouins, took a rifle and sneaked off to the hills, and de Gaulle and all of his highfalutin' war machinery couldn't defeat those guerrillas. Nowhere on this earth does the white man win in guerrilla warfare. It's not his speed. Just as guerrilla warfare is prevailing in Asia and in parts of Africa and in parts of Latin America you've got to be mighty naïve, or you've got to play the black man cheap, if you don't think some day he's going to wake up and find that it's got to be the ballot or the bullet.

I would like to say, in closing, a few things concerning the Muslim Mosque, Inc., which we established recently in New York City. It's true we're

Muslims and our religion is Islam, but we don't mix our religion with our politics and our economics and our social and civil activities—not any more. We keep our religion in our mosque. After our religious services are over, then as Muslims we become involved with anybody, anywhere, any time and in any manner that's designed to eliminate the evils, the political, economic and social evils that are afflicting the people of our community.

The political philosophy of black nationalism means that the black man should control the politics and the politicians in his own community. The black man in the black community has to be re-educated into the science of politics so he will know what politics is supposed to bring him in return. Don't be throwing out any ballots. A ballot is like a bullet. You don't throw your ballots until you see a target, and if that target is not within your reach, keep your ballot in your pocket. The political philosophy of black nationalism is being taught in the Christian church. It's being taught in the NAACP. It's being taught in CORE meetings. It's being taught in SNCC meetings. It's being taught in Muslim meetings. It's being taught where nothing but atheists and agnostics come together. It's being taught everywhere. Black people are fed up with the dillydallying, pussyfooting, compromising approach that we've been using toward getting our freedom. We want freedom *now*, but we're not going to get it saying "We Shall Overcome." We've got to fight until we overcome.

The economic philosophy of black nationalism is pure and simple. It only means that we should control the economy of our community. Why should white people be running all the stores in our community? Why should white people be running the banks of our community? Why should the economy of our community be in the hands of the white man? Why? If a black man can't move his store into a white community, you tell me why a white man should move his store into a black community. The philosophy of black nationalism involves a re-education program in the black community in regards to economics. Our people have to be made to see that any time you take your dollars out of your community and spend it in a community where you don't live, the community where you live will get poorer and poorer, and the community where you spend your money will get richer and richer. Then you wonder why where you live is always a ghetto or a slum area. And where you and I are concerned, not only do we lose it when we spend it out of the community, but the white man has got all our stores in the community, at sundown the man who runs the store takes it over across town somewhere. He's got us in a vise.

So the economic philosophy of black nationalism means in every church, in every civic organization, in every fraternal order, it's time now for our people to become conscious of the importance of controlling the economy of our community. If we own the store, if we operate the businesses, if we try and establish some industry in our own community, then we're developing to the position where we are creating employment for our own kind. Once you gain control of the economy of your own community, then you don't have to picket and boycott and beg some cracker downtown for a job in his business.

The social philosophy of black nationalism only means that we have to get together and remove the evils, the vices, alcoholism, drug addiction, and other evils that are destroying the moral fiber of our community. We ourselves have to lift the level of our community, the standard of our community to a higher level, make our own society beautiful so that we will be satisfied in our own social circles and won't be running around here trying to knock our way into a social circle where we're not wanted.

So, I say, in spreading a gospel such as black nationalism, it is not designed to make the black man re-evaluate the white man—you know him already—but to make the black man re-evaluate himself. Don't change the white man's mind—you can't change his mind, and that whole thing about appealing to the moral conscience of America—America's conscience is bankrupt. She lost all conscience a long time ago. Uncle Sam has no conscience. They don't know what morals are. They don't try and eliminate an evil because it's evil, or because it's illegal, or because it's immoral; they eliminate it only when it threatens their existence. So you're wasting your time appealing to the moral conscience of a bankrupt man like Uncle Sam. If he had a conscience, he'd straighten this thing out with no more pressure being put upon him. So it is not necessary to change the white man's mind. We have to change our own mind. You can't change his mind about us. We've got to change our own minds about each other. We have to see each other with new eyes. We have to see each other as brothers and sisters. We have to come together with warmth so we can develop unity and harmony that's necessary to get this problem solved ourselves. How can we do this? How can we avoid jealousy? How can we avoid the suspicion and the division that exist in the community? I'll tell you how.

I have watched how Billy Graham comes into a city, spreading what he calls the gospel of Christ, which is only white nationalism. That's what he is. Billy Graham is a white nationalist; I'm a black nationalist. But since it's the natural tendency for leaders to be jealous and look upon a powerful figure like Graham with suspicion and envy, how is it possible for him to come into a city and get all the cooperation of the church leaders? Don't think because they're church leaders that they don't have weaknesses that make them—envious and jealous—no, everybody's got it. It's not an accident that when they want to choose a Pope over there in Rome, they get in a closet so you can't hear them cussing and fighting and carrying on.

Billy Graham comes in preaching the gospel of Christ, he evangelizes the gospel, he stirs everybody up, but he never tries to start a church. If he came in trying to start a church, all the churches would be against him. So, he just comes in talking about Christ and tells everybody who gets Christ to go to any church where Christ is; and in this way the church cooperates with him. So we're going to take a page from his book.

Our gospel is black nationalism. We're not trying to threaten the existence of any organization, but we're spreading the gospel of black nationalism. Anywhere there's a church that is also preaching and practicing the gospel of black nationalism, join that church. If the NAACP is preaching and practicing the gospel of black nationalism, join the NAACP. If CORE is spreading and practicing the gospel of black nationalism, join CORE. Join any organization that has a gospel that's for the uplift of the black man. And when you get into it and see them pussyfooting or compromising, pull out of it because that's not black nationalism. We'll find another one.

And in this manner, the organizations will increase in number and in quantity and in quality, and by August, it is then our intention to have a black nationalist convention which will consist of delegates from all over the country who are interested in the political, economic and social philosophy of black nationalism. After these delegates convene, we will hold a seminar, we will hold discussions, we will listen to everyone. We want to hear new ideas and new solutions and new answers. And at that time, if we see then to form a black nationalist party, we'll form a black nationalist party, we'll form a black nationalist party. If it's necessary to form a black nationalist army, we'll form a black nationalist army. It'll be the ballot or the bullet. It'll be liberty or it'll be death.

It's time for you and me to stop sitting in this country, letting some cracker senators, Northern crackers and Southern crackers, sit there in Washington, D.C., and come to a conclusion in their mind that you and I are supposed to have civil rights. There's no white man going to tell me anything about *my* rights. Brothers and sisters, always remember, if it doesn't take senators and congressmen and presidential proclamations to give freedom to the white man, it is not necessary for legislation or proclamation or Supreme Court decisions to give freedom to the black man. You let that white man know, if this is a country of freedom, let it be a country of freedom; and if it's not a country of freedom, change it.

We will work with anybody, anywhere, at any time, who is genuinely interested in tackling the problem head-on as long as the enemy is nonviolent, but violent when the enemy gets violent. We'll work with you on the voter-registration drive, we'll work with you on school boycotts—I don't believe in any kind of integration; I'm not even worried about it because I know you're not going to get it anyway; you're not going to get it because you're afraid to die; you've got to be ready to die if you try and force yourself on the white man, because he'll get just as violent as those crackers in Mississippi, right here in Detroit. But we will still work with you on the school boycotts because we're against a segregated school system. A segregated school system produces children who, when they graduate, graduate with crippled minds. But this does not mean that a school is segregated because it's all black. A segregated school means a school that is controlled by people who have no real interest in it whatsoever.

Let me explain what I mean. A segregated district or community is a community in which people live, but outsiders control the politics and the economy of that community. They never refer to the white section as segregated community. It's the all-Negro section that's a segregated community. Why? The white man controls his own school, his own bank, his own economy, his own politics, his own everything, his own community—but he also controls yours. When you're under someone else's control, you're segregated. They'll always give you the lowest or the worst that there is to offer, but it doesn't mean you're segregated just because you have your own. You've got to control your own. Just like the white man has control of his, you need to control yours.

You know the best way to get rid of segregation? The white man is more afraid of separation than he is of integration. Segregation means that he puts you away from him, but not far enough for you to be out of his jurisdiction; separation means you're gone. And the white man will integrate faster than he'll let you separate. So we will work with you against the segregation school system because it's criminal, because it is absolutely destructive, in every way imaginable, to the minds of the children who have to be exposed to that type of crippling education.

Last but not least, I must say this concerning the great controversy over rifles and shotguns. The only thing that I've ever said is that in areas where the government has proven itself either unwilling or unable to defend the lives and the property of Negroes, it's time for Negroes to defend themselves. Article number two of the constitutional amendments provides you and me the right to own a rifle and form battalions and go out looking for white folks, although you'd be within your rights—I mean, you'd be justified; but that would be illegal and we don't do anything illegal. If the white man doesn't want the black man buying rifles and shotguns, then let the government do its job. That's all. And don't let the white man come to you and ask you what you think about what Malcolm says—why, you old Uncle Tom. He would never ask you if he thought you were going to say, "Amen!" No, he is making a Tom out of you.

So, this doesn't mean forming rifle clubs and going out looking for people, but it is time, in 1964, if you are a man, to let that man know. If he's not going to do his job in running the government and providing you and me with the protection that our taxes are supposed to be for, since he spends all those billions for his defense budget, he certainly can't begrudge you and me spending $12 or $15 for a single-shot, or double-action. I hope you understand. Don't go out shooting people, but any time, brothers and sisters, and especially the men in this audience—wearing Congressional Medals of Honor, with shoulders this wide chests this big, muscles that big—any time you and I sit around and read where they bomb a church and murder in cold blood, not some grownups, but four little girls while they were praying to the same god the white man taught them to pray to, and you and I see the government go down and can't find who did it.

Why, this man—he can find Eichmann hiding down in Argentina somewhere. Let two or three American soldiers, who are minding somebody else's business way over in South Vietnam, get killed, and he'll send battleships, sticking his nose in their business. He wanted to send troops down to Cuba and make them have what he calls free elections—this old cracker who doesn't have free elections in his own country. No, if you never see me another time in your life, if I die in the morning, I'll die saying one thing: the ballot or the bullet, the ballot or the bullet.

If a Negro in 1964 has to sit around and wait for some cracker senator to filibuster when it comes to the rights of black people, why, you and I should hang our heads in shame. You talk about a march on Washington in 1963, you haven't seen anything. There's some more going down in 1964. And this time they're not going like they went last year. They're not going singing "We Shall Overcome." They're not going with white friends. They're not going with placards already painted for them. They're not going with round-trip tickets. They're going with one way tickets.

And if they don't want that non-nonviolent army going down there, tell them to bring the filibuster to a halt. The black nationalists aren't going to wait. Lyndon B. Johnson is the head of the Democratic Party. If he's for civil rights, let him go into the Senate next week and declare himself. Let him go in there right now and declare himself. Let him go in there and denounce the Southern branch of his party. Let him go in there right now and take a moral stand—right now, not later. Tell him, don't wait until election time. If he waits too long, brothers and sisters, he will be responsible for letting a condition develop in this country which will create a climate that will bring seeds up out of the ground with vegetation on the end of them looking like something these people never dreamed of. In 1964, it's the ballot or the bullet. Thank you.

RONALD REAGAN

A Time for Choosing (1964)

Thank you very much. Thank you and good evening. The sponsor has been identified, but unlike most television programs, the performer hasn't been provided with a script. As a matter of fact, I have been permitted to choose my own ideas regarding the choice that we face in the next few weeks.

I have spent most of my life as a Democrat. I recently have seen fit to follow another course. I believe that the issues confronting us cross party lines. Now, one side in this campaign has been telling us that the issues of this election are the maintenance of peace and prosperity. The line has been used "We've never had it so good."

But I have an uncomfortable feeling that this prosperity isn't something on which we can base our hopes for the future. No nation in history has ever survived a tax burden that reached a third of its national income. Today, 37 cents of every dollar earned in this country is the tax collector's share, and yet our government continues to spend $17 million a day more than the government takes in. We haven't balanced our budget 28 out of the last 34 years. We have raised our debt limit three times in the last twelve months, and now our national debt is one and a half times bigger than all the combined debts of all the nations in the world. We have $15 billion in gold in our treasury—we don't own an ounce. Foreign dollar claims are $27.3 billion, and we have just had announced that the dollar of 1939 will now purchase 45 cents in its total value.

As for the peace that we would preserve, I wonder who among us would like to approach the wife or mother whose husband or son has died in South Vietnam and ask them if they think this is a peace that should be maintained indefinitely. Do they mean peace, or do they mean we just want to be left in peace? There can be no real peace while one American is dying some place in the world for the rest of us. We are at war with the most dangerous enemy that has ever faced mankind in his long climb from the swamp to the stars, and it has been said if we lose that war, and in doing so lose this way of freedom of ours, history will record with the greatest astonishment that those who had the most to lose did the least to prevent its happening. Well, I think it's time we ask ourselves if we still know the freedoms that were intended for us by the Founding Fathers.

Not too long ago two friends of mine were talking to a Cuban refugee, a businessman who had escaped from Castro, and in the midst of his story one of my friends turned to the other and said, "We don't know how lucky we are." And the Cuban stopped and said, "How lucky you are! I had someplace to escape to." In that sentence he told us the entire story. If we lose freedom here, there is no place to escape to. This is the last stand on Earth. And this idea that government is beholden to the people, that it has no other source of power except to sovereign people, is still the newest and most unique idea in all the long history of man's relation to man. This is the issue of this election. Whether we believe in our capacity for self-government or whether we abandon the American revolution and confess that a little intellectual elite in a far-distant capital can plan our lives for us better than we can plan them ourselves.

You and I are told increasingly that we have to choose between a left or right, but I would like to suggest that there is no such thing as a left or right. There is only an up or down—up to a man's age-old dream, the ultimate in individual freedom consistent with law and order—or down to the ant heap totalitarianism, and regardless of their sincerity, their humanitarian motives, those who would trade our freedom for security have embarked on this downward course.

In this vote-harvesting time, they use terms like the "Great Society," or as we were told a few days ago by the President, we must accept a "greater government activity in the affairs of the people." But they have been a little more explicit in the past and among themselves—and all of the things that I now will quote have appeared in print. These are not Republican accusations. For example, they have voices that say "the cold war will end through acceptance of a not undemocratic socialism." Another voice says that the profit motive has become outmoded, it must be replaced by the incentives of the welfare state; or our traditional system of individual freedom is incapable of solving the complex problems of the 20th century. Senator Fullbright has said at Stanford University that the Constitution is outmoded. He referred to the president as our moral teacher and our leader, and he said he is hobbled in his task by the restrictions in power imposed on him by this antiquated document. He must be freed so that he can do for us what he knows is best. And Senator Clark of Pennsylvania, another articulate spokesman, defines liberalism as "meeting the material needs of the masses through the full power of centralized government." Well, I for one resent it when a representative of the people refers to you and me—the free man and woman of this country—as "the masses." This is a term we haven't applied to ourselves in America. But beyond that, "the full power of centralized government"—this was the very thing the Founding Fathers sought to minimize. They knew that governments don't control things. A government can't control the economy without controlling people. And they know when a government sets out to do that, it must use force and coercion to achieve its purpose. They also knew, those Founding Fathers, that outside of its legitimate functions, government does nothing as well or as economically as the private sector of the economy.

Now, we have no better example of this than the government's involvement in the farm economy over the last 30 years. Since 1955, the cost of this program has nearly doubled. One-fourth of farming in America is responsible for 85% of the farm surplus. Three-fourths of farming is out on the free market and has known a 21% increase in the per capita consumption of all its produce. You see, that one-fourth of farming is regulated and controlled by the federal government. In the last three years we have spent $43 in feed grain program for every bushel of corn we don't grow.

Senator Humphrey last week charged that Barry Goldwater as President would seek to eliminate farmers. He should do his homework a little better, because he will find out that we have had a decline of 5 million in the farm population under these government programs. He will also find that the Democratic administration has sought to get from Congress an extension of the farm program to include that three-fourths that is now free. He will find that they have also asked for the right to imprison farmers who wouldn't keep books as prescribed by the federal government. The Secretary of Agriculture asked for the right to seize farms through condemnation and resell them to other individuals. And contained in that same program was a provision that would have allowed the federal government to remove 2 million farmers from the soil.

At the same time, there has been an increase in the Department of Agriculture employees. There is now one for every 30 farms in the United States, and still they can't tell us how 66 shiploads of grain headed for Austria disappeared without a trace and Billie Sol Estes never left shore.

Every responsible farmer and farm organization has repeatedly asked the government to free the farm economy, but who are farmers to know what is best for them? The wheat farmers voted against a wheat program. The government passed it anyway. Now the price of bread goes up; the price of wheat to the farmer goes down.

Meanwhile, back in the city, under urban renewal the assault on freedom carries on. Private property rights are so diluted that public interest is almost anything that a few government planners decide it should be. In a program that takes for the needy and gives to the greedy, we see such spectacles as in Cleveland, Ohio, a million-and-a-half-dollar building completed only three years ago must be destroyed to make way for what government officials call a "more compatible use of the land." The President tells us he is now going to start building public housing units in the thousands where heretofore we have only built them in the hundreds. But FHA and the Veterans Administration tell us that they have 120,000 housing units they've taken back through mortgage foreclosures. For three decades, we have sought to solve the problems of unemployment through government planning, and the more the plans fail, the more the planners plan. The latest is the Area Redevelopment Agency. They have just declared Rice County, Kansas, a depressed area. Rice County, Kansas, has two hundred oil wells, and the 14,000 people there have over $30 million on deposit in personal savings in their banks. When the government tells you you're depressed, lie down and be depressed.

We have so many people who can't see a fat man standing beside a thin one without coming to the conclusion that the fat man got that way by taking advantage of the thin one. So they are going to solve all the problems of human misery through government and government planning. Well, now, if government planning and welfare had the answer and they've had almost 30 years of it, shouldn't we expect government to almost read the score to us once in a while? Shouldn't they be telling us about the decline each year in the number of people needing help? The reduction in the need for public housing?

But the reverse is true. Each year the need grows greater, the program grows greater. We were told four years ago that 17 million people went to bed hungry each night. Well, that was probably true. They were all on a diet. But now we are told that 9.3 million families in this country are poverty-stricken on the basis of earning less than $3,000 a year. Welfare spending is 10 times greater than in the dark depths of the Depression. We are spending $45 billion on welfare. Now do a little arithmetic, and you will find that if we divided the $45 billion up equally among those 9 million poor families, we would be able to give each family $4,600 a year, and this added to their present income should eliminate poverty! Direct aid to the poor, however, is running only

about $600 per family. It would seem that someplace there must be some overhead.

So now we declare "war on poverty," or "you, too, can be a Bobby Baker!" Now, do they honestly expect us to believe that if we add $1 billion to the $45 million we are spending . . . one more program to the 30-odd we have—and remember, this new program doesn't replace any, it just duplicates existing programs—do they believe that poverty is suddenly going to disappear by magic? Well, in all fairness I should explain that there is one part of the new program that isn't duplicated. This is the youth feature. We are now going to solve the dropout problem, juvenile delinquency, by reinstituting something like the old CCC camps, and we are going to put our young people in camps, but again we do some arithmetic, and we find that we are going to spend each year just on room and board for each young person that we help $4,700 a year! We can send them to Harvard for $2,700! Don't get me wrong. I'm not suggesting that Harvard is the answer to juvenile delinquency.

But seriously, what are we doing to those we seek to help? Not too long ago, a judge called me here in Los Angeles. He told me of a young woman who had come before him for a divorce. She had six children, was pregnant with her seventh. Under his questioning, she revealed her husband was a laborer earning $250 a month. She wanted a divorce so that she could get an $80 raise. She is eligible for $330 a month in the Aid to Dependent Children Program. She got the idea from two women in her neighborhood who had already done that very thing.

Yet anytime you and I question the schemes of the do-gooders, we are denounced as being against their humanitarian goals. They say we are always "against" things, never "for" anything. Well, the trouble with our liberal friends is not that they are ignorant, but that they know so much that isn't so. We are for a provision that destitution should not follow unemployment by reason of old age, and to that end we have accepted Social Security as a step toward meeting the problem.

But we are against those entrusted with this program when they practice deception regarding its fiscal shortcomings, when they charge that any criticism of the program means that we want to end payments to those who depend on them for livelihood. They have called it insurance to us in a hundred million pieces of literature. But then they appeared before the Supreme Court and they testified that it was a welfare program. They only use the term "insurance" to sell it to the people. And they said Social Security dues are a tax for the general use of the government, and the government has used that tax. There is no fund, because Robert Byers, the actuarial head, appeared before a congressional committee and admitted that Social Security as of this moment is $298 billion in the hole. But he said there should be no cause for worry because as long as they have the power to tax, they could always take away from the people whatever they needed to bail them out of trouble! And they are doing just that.

A young man, 21 years of age, working at an average salary . . . his Social Security contribution would, in the open market, buy him an insurance policy that would guarantee $220 a month at age 65. The government promises $127. He could live it up until he is 31 and then take out a policy that would pay more than Social Security. Now, are we so lacking in business sense that we can't put this program on a sound basis so that people who do require those payments will find that they can get them when they are due . . . that the cupboard isn't bare? Barry Goldwater thinks we can.

At the same time, can't we introduce voluntary features that would permit a citizen who can do better on his own to be excused upon presentation of evidence that he had made provisions for the non-earning years? Should we allow a widow with children to work, and not lose the benefits supposedly paid for by her deceased husband? Shouldn't you and I be allowed to declare who our beneficiaries will be under these programs, which we cannot do? I think we are for telling our senior citizens that no one in this country should be denied medical care because of a lack of funds. But I think we are against forcing all citizens, regardless of need, into a compulsory government program, especially when we have such examples, as announced last week, when France admitted that their Medicare program was now bankrupt. They've come to the end of the road.

In addition, was Barry Goldwater so irresponsible when he suggested that our government give up its program of deliberate planned inflation so that when you do get your Social Security pension, a dollar will buy a dollar's worth, and not 45 cents' worth?

I think we are for an international organization, where the nations of the world can seek peace. But I think we are against subordinating American interests to an organization that has become so structurally unsound that today you can muster a two-thirds vote on the floor of the General Assembly among the nations that represent less than 10 percent of the world's population. I think we are against the hypocrisy of assailing our allies because here and there they cling to a colony, while we engage in a conspiracy of silence and never open our mouths about the millions of people enslaved in Soviet colonies in the satellite nation.

I think we are for aiding our allies by sharing of our material blessings with those nations which share in our fundamental beliefs, but we are against doling out money government to government, creating bureaucracy, if not socialism, all over the world. We set out to help 19 countries. We are helping 107. We spent $146 billion. With that money, we bought a $2 million yacht for Haile Selassie. We bought dress suits for Greek undertakers, extra wives for Kenyan government officials. We bought a thousand TV sets for a place where they have no electricity. In the last six years, 52 nations have bought $7 billion worth of our gold, and all 52 are receiving foreign aid from this country.

No government ever voluntarily reduces itself in size. Government programs, once launched, never disappear. Actually, a government bureau is the nearest thing to eternal life we'll ever see on this Earth. Federal employees number 2.5 million, and federal, state, and local, one out of six of the nation's work force is employed by the government. These proliferating bureaus with their thousands of regulations have cost us many of our constitutional safeguards. How many of us realize that today federal agents can invade a man's property without a warrant? They can impose a fine without a formal hearing, let alone a trial by jury, and they can seize and sell his property in auction to enforce the payment of that fine. In Chico County, Arkansas, James Wier overplanted his rice allotment. The government obtained a $17,000 judgment, and a U.S. marshal sold his 950-acre farm at auction. The government said it was necessary as a warning to others to make the system work. Last February 19 at the University of Minnesota, Norman Thomas, six-time candidate for President on the

Socialist Party ticket, said, "If Barry Goldwater became President, he would stop the advance of socialism in the United States." I think that's exactly what he will do.

As a former Democrat, I can tell you Norman Thomas isn't the only man who has drawn this parallel to socialism with the present administration. Back in 1936, Mr. Democrat himself, Al Smith, the great American, came before the American people and charged that the leadership of his party was taking the party of Jefferson, Jackson, and Cleveland down the road under the banners of Marx, Lenin, and Stalin. And he walked away from his party, and he never returned to the day he died, because to this day, the leadership of that party has been taking that party, that honorable party, down the road in the image of the labor socialist party of England. Now it doesn't require expropriation or confiscation of private property or business to impose socialism on a people. What does it mean whether you hold the deed or the title to your business or property if the government holds the power of life and death over that business or property? Such machinery already exists. The government can find some charge to bring against any concern it chooses to prosecute. Every businessman has his own tale of harassment. Somewhere a perversion has taken place. Our natural, inalienable rights are now considered to be a dispensation of government, and freedom has never been so fragile, so close to slipping from our grasp as it is at this moment. Our Democratic opponents seem unwilling to debate these issues. They want to make you and I believe that this is a contest between two men . . . that we are to choose just between two personalities.

Well, what of this man that they would destroy? And in destroying, they would destroy that which he represents, the ideas that you and I hold dear. Is he the brash and shallow and trigger-happy man they say he is? Well, I have been privileged to know him "when." I knew him long before he ever dreamed of trying for high office, and I can tell you personally I have never known a man in my life I believe so incapable of doing a dishonest or dishonorable thing.

This is a man who in his own business, before he entered politics, instituted a profit-sharing plan, before unions had ever thought of it. He put in health and medical insurance for all his employees.

He took 50 percent of the profits before taxes and set up a retirement program, a pension plan for all his employees. He sent checks for life to an employee who was ill and couldn't work. He provided nursing care for the children of mothers who work in the stores. When Mexico was ravaged by floods from the Rio Grande, he climbed in his airplane and flew medicine and supplies down there.

An ex-GI told me how he met him. It was the week before Christmas during the Korean War, and he was at the Los Angeles airport trying to get a ride home to Arizona for Christmas, and he said that there were a lot of servicemen there and no seats available on the planes. Then a voice came over the loudspeaker and said, "Any men in uniform wanting a ride to Arizona, go to runway such-and-such," and they went down there, and there was this fellow named Barry Goldwater sitting in his plane. Every day in the weeks before Christmas, all day long, he would load up the plane, fly to Arizona, fly them to their homes, then fly back over to get another load.

During the hectic split-second timing of a campaign, this is a man who took time out to sit beside an old friend who was dying of cancer. His campaign managers were understandably impatient, but he said, "There aren't many left who care what happens to her. I'd like her to know I care." This is a man who said to his 19-year-old son, "There is no foundation like the rock of honesty and fairness, and when you begin to build your life upon that rock, with the cement of the faith in God that you have, then you have a real start." This is not a man who could carelessly send other people's sons to war. And that is the issue of this campaign that makes all of the other problems I have discussed academic, unless we realize that we are in a war that must be won.

Those who would trade our freedom for the soup kitchen of the welfare state have told us that they have a utopian solution of peace without victory. They call their policy "accommodation." And they say if we only avoid any direct confrontation with the enemy, he will forget his evil ways and learn to love us. All who oppose them are indicted as warmongers. They say we offer simple answers to complex problems. Well, perhaps there is a simple answer—not an easy answer—but simple.

If you and I have the courage to tell our elected officials that we want our national policy based upon what we know in our hearts is morally right. We cannot buy our security, our freedom from the threat of the bomb by committing an immorality so great as saying to a billion now in slavery behind the Iron Curtain, "Give up your dreams of freedom because to save our own skin, we are willing to make a deal with your slave masters." Alexander Hamilton said, "A nation which can prefer disgrace to danger is prepared for a master, and deserves one." Let's set the record straight. There is no argument over the choice between peace and war, but there is only one guaranteed way you can have peace—and you can have it in the next second—surrender.

Admittedly there is a risk in any course we follow other than this, but every lesson in history tells us that the greater risk lies in appeasement, and this is the specter our well-meaning liberal friends refuse to face—that their policy of accommodation is appeasement, and it gives no choice between peace and war, only between fight and surrender. If we continue to accommodate, continue to back and retreat, eventually we have to face the final demand—the ultimatum. And what then? When Nikita Khrushchev has told his people he knows what our answer will be? He has told them that we are retreating under the pressure of the Cold War, and someday when the time comes to deliver the ultimatum, our surrender will be voluntary because by that time we will have weakened from within spiritually, morally, and economically. He believes this because from our side he has heard voices pleading for "peace at any price" or "better Red than dead," or as one commentator put it, he would rather "live on his knees than die on his feet." And therein lies the road to war, because those voices don't speak for the rest of us. You and I know and do not believe that life is so dear and peace so sweet as to be purchased at the price of chains and slavery. If nothing in life is worth dying for, when did this begin—just in the face of this enemy? Or should Moses have told the children of Israel to live in slavery under the pharaohs? Should Christ have refused the cross? Should the patriots at Concord Bridge have thrown down their guns and refused to fire the shot heard "round the world"? The martyrs of history were not fools, and our honored dead who gave their lives to stop the advance of the Nazis didn't die in vain. Where, then, is the road to peace? Well, it's a simple answer after all.

You and I have the courage to say to our enemies, "There is a price we will not pay." There is a point beyond which they must not advance. This is the meaning in the phrase of Barry Goldwater's "peace through strength." Winston Churchill said that "the destiny of man is not measured by material computation. When great forces are on the move in the world, we learn we are spirits—not animals." And he said, "There is something going on in time and space, and beyond time and space, which, whether we like it or not, spells duty."

You and I have a rendezvous with destiny. We will preserve for our children this, the last best hope of man on Earth, or we will sentence them to take the last step into a thousand years of darkness.

We will keep in mind and remember that Barry Goldwater has faith in us. He has faith that you and I have the ability and the dignity and the right to make our own decisions and determine our own destiny.

Thank you very much.

LYNDON BAINES JOHNSON

Commencement Address at Howard University (1965)

Dr. Nabrit, my fellow Americans:

I am delighted at the chance to speak at this important and this historic institution. Howard has long been an outstanding center for the education of Negro Americans. Its students are of every race and color and they come from many countries of the world. It is truly a working example of democratic excellence.

Our earth is the home of revolution. In every corner of every continent men charged with hope contend with ancient ways in the pursuit of justice. They reach for the newest of weapons to realize the oldest of dreams, that each may walk in freedom and pride, stretching his talents, enjoying the fruits of the earth.

Our enemies may occasionally seize the day of change, but it is the banner of our revolution they take. And our own future is linked to this process of swift and turbulent change in many lands in the world. But nothing in any country touches us more profoundly, and nothing is more freighted with meaning for our own destiny than the revolution of the Negro American.

In far too many ways American Negroes have been another nation: deprived of freedom, crippled by hatred, the doors of opportunity closed to hope.

In our time change has come to this Nation, too. The American Negro, acting with impressive restraint, has peacefully protested and marched, entered the courtrooms and the seats of government, demanding a justice that has long been denied. The voice of the Negro was the call to action. But it is a tribute to America that, once aroused, the courts and the Congress, the President and most of the people, have been the allies of progress.

Legal Protection for Human Rights

Thus we have seen the high court of the country declare that discrimination based on race was repugnant to the Constitution, and therefore void. We have seen in 1957, and 1960, and again in 1964, the first civil rights legislation in this Nation in almost an entire century.

As majority leader of the United States Senate, I helped to guide two of these bills through the Senate. And, as your President, I was proud to sign the third. And now very soon we will have the fourth—a new law guaranteeing every American the right to vote.

No act of my entire administration will give me greater satisfaction than the day when my signature makes this bill, too, the law of this land.

The voting rights bill will be the latest, and among the most important, in a long series of victories. But this victory—as Winston Churchill said of another triumph for freedom—"is not the end. It is not even the beginning of the end. But it is, perhaps, the end of the beginning."

That beginning is freedom; and the barriers to that freedom are tumbling down. Freedom is the right to share, share fully and equally, in American society—to vote, to hold a job, to enter a public place, to go to school. It is the right to be treated in every part of our national life as a person equal in dignity and promise to all others.

Freedom Is Not Enough

But freedom is not enough. You do not wipe away the scars of centuries by saying: Now you are free to go where you want, and do as you desire, and choose the leaders you please.

You do not take a person who, for years, has been hobbled by chains and liberate him, bring him up to the starting line of a race and then say, "you are free to compete with all the others," and still justly believe that you have been completely fair.

Thus it is not enought just to open the gates of opportunity. All our citizens must have the ability to walk through those gates.

This is the next and the more profound stage of the battle for civil rights. We seek not just freedom but opportunity. We seek not just legal equity but human ability, not just equality as a right and a theory but equality as a fact and equality as a result.

For the task is to give 20 million Negroes the same chance as every other American to learn and grow, to work and share in society, to develop their abilities—physical, mental and spiritual, and to pursue their individual happiness.

To this end equal opportunity is essential, but not enough, not enough. Men and women of all races are born with the same range of abilities. But ability is not just the product of birth. Ability is stretched or stunted by the family that you live with, and the neighborhood you live in—by the school you go to and the poverty or the richness of your surroundings. It is the product of a hundred unseen forces playing upon the little infant, the child, and finally the man.

Progress for Some

This graduating class at Howard University is witness to the indomitable determination of the Negro American to win his way in American life.

The number of Negroes in schools of higher learning has almost doubled in 15 years. The number of nonwhite professional workers has more than doubled in 10 years. The median income of Negro college women tonight exceeds that of white college women. And there are also the enormous accomplishments of distinguished individual Negroes—many of them graduates of this institution, and one of them the first lady ambassador in the history of the United States.

These are proud and impressive achievements. But they tell only the story of a growing middle class minority, steadily narrowing the gap between them and their white counterparts.

A Widening Gulf

But for the great majority of Negro Americans—the poor, the unemployed, the uprooted, and the dispossessed—there is a much grimmer story. They still, as we meet here tonight, are another nation. Despite the court orders and the laws, despite the legislative victories and the speeches, for them the walls are rising and the gulf is widening.

Here are some of the facts of this American failure.

Thirty-five years ago the rate of unemployment for Negroes and whites was about the same. Tonight the Negro rate is twice as high.

In 1948 the 8 percent unemployment rate for Negro teenage boys was actually less than that of whites. By last year that rate had grown to 23 percent, as against 13 percent for whites unemployed.

Between 1949 and 1959, the income of Negro men relative to white men declined in every section of this country. From 1952 to 1963 the median income of Negro families compared to white actually dropped from 57 percent to 53 percent.

In the years 1955 through 1957, 22 percent of experienced Negro workers were out of work at some time during the year. In 1961 through 1963 that proportion had soared to 29 percent.

Since 1947 the number of white families living in poverty has decreased 27 percent while the number of poorer nonwhite families decreased only 3 percent.

The infant mortality of nonwhites in 1940 was 70 percent greater than whites. Twenty-two years later it was 90 percent greater.

Moreover, the isolation of Negro from white communities is increasing, rather than decreasing as Negroes crowd into the central cities and become a city within a city.

Of course Negro Americans as well as white Americans have shared in our rising national abundance. But the harsh fact of the matter is that in the battle for true equality too many—far too many—are losing ground every day.

The Causes of Inequality

We are not completely sure why this is. We know the causes are complex and subtle. But we do know the two broad basic reasons. And we do know that we have to act.

First, Negroes are trapped—as many whites are trapped—in inherited, gateless poverty. They lack training and skills. They are shut in, in slums, without decent medical care. Private and public poverty combine to cripple their capacities.

We are trying to attack these evils through our poverty program, through our education program, through our medical care and our other health programs, and a dozen more of the Great Society programs that are aimed at the root causes of this poverty.

We will increase, and we will accelerate, and we will broaden this attack in years to come until this most enduring of foes finally yields to our unyielding will.

But there is a second cause—much more difficult to explain, more deeply grounded, more desperate in its force. It is the devastating heritage of long years of slavery; and a century of oppression, hatred, and injustice.

Special Nature of Negro Poverty

For Negro poverty is not white poverty. Many of its causes and many of its cures are the same. But there are differences—deep, corrosive, obstinate differences—radiating painful roots into the community, and into the family, and the nature of the individual.

These differences are not racial differences. They are solely and simply the consequence of ancient brutality, past injustice, and present prejudice. They are anguishing to observe. For the Negro they are a constant reminder of oppression. For the white they are a constant reminder of guilt. But they must be faced and they must be dealt with and they must be overcome, if we are ever to reach the time when the only difference between Negroes and whites is the color of their skin.

Nor can we find a complete answer in the experience of other American minorities. They made a valiant and a largely successful effort to emerge from poverty and prejudice.

The Negro, like these others, will have to rely mostly upon his own efforts. But he just can not do it alone. For they did not have the heritage of centuries to overcome, and they did not have a cultural tradition which had been twisted and battered by endless years of hatred and hopelessness, nor were they excluded—these others—because of race or color— a feeling whose dark intensity is matched by no other prejudice in our society.

Nor can these differences be understood as isolated infirmities. They are a seamless web. They cause

each other. They result from each other. They reinforce each other.

Much of the Negro community is buried under a blanket of history and circumstance. It is not a lasting solution to lift just one corner of that blanket. We must stand on all sides and we must raise the entire cover if we are to liberate our fellow citizens.

The Roots of Injustice

One of the differences is the increased concentration of Negroes in our cities. More than 73 percent of all Negroes live in urban areas compared with less than 70 percent of the whites. Most of these Negroes live in slums. Most of these Negroes live together—a separated people.

Men are shaped by their world. When it is a world of decay, ringed by an invisible wall, when escape is arduous and uncertain, and the saving pressures of a more hopeful society are unknown, it can cripple the youth and it can desolate the men.

There is also the burden that a dark skin can add to the search for a productive place in our society. Unemployment strikes most swiftly and broadly at the Negro, and this burden erodes hope. Blighted hope breeds despair. Despair brings indifferences to the learning which offers a way out. And despair, coupled with indifferences, is often the source of destructive rebellion against the fabric of society.

There is also the lacerating hurt of early collision with white hatred or prejudice, distaste or condescension. Other groups have felt similar intolerance. But success and achievement could wipe it away. They do not change the color of a man's skin. I have seen this uncomprehending pain in the eyes of the little, young Mexican-American schoolchildren that I taught many years ago. But it can be overcome. But, for many, the wounds are always open.

Family Breakdown

Perhaps most important—its influence radiating to every part of life—is the breakdown of the Negro family structure. For this, most of all, white America must accept responsibility. It flows from centuries of oppression and persecution of the Negro man. It flows from the long years of degradation and discrimination, which have attacked his dignity and assaulted his ability to produce for his family.

This, too, is not pleasant to look upon. But it must be faced by those whose serious intent is to improve the life of all Americans.

Only a minority—less than half—of all Negro children reach the age of 18 having lived all their lives with both of their parents. At this moment, tonight, little less than two-thirds are at home with both of their parents. Probably a majority of all Negro children receive federally-aided public assistance sometime during their childhood.

The family is the cornerstone of our society. More than any other force it shapes the attitude, the hopes, the ambitions, and the values of the child. And when the family collapses it is the children that are usually damaged. When it happens on a massive scale the community itself is crippled.

So, unless we work to strengthen the family, to create conditions under which most parents will stay together—all the rest: schools, and playgrounds, and public assistance, and private concern, will never be enough to cut completely the circle of despair and deprivation.

To Fulfill These Rights

There is no single easy answer to all of these problems.

Jobs are part of the answer. They bring the income which permits a man to provide for his family.

Decent homes in decent surroundings and a chance to learn—an equal chance to learn—are part of the answer.

Welfare and social programs better designed to hold families together are part of the answer.

Care for the sick is part of the answer.

An understanding heart by all Americans is another big part of the answer.

And to all of these fronts—and a dozen more—I will dedicate the expanding efforts of the Johnson administration.

But there are other answers that are still to be found. Nor do we fully understand even all of the problems. Therefore, I want to announce tonight that this fall I intend to call a White House conference of scholars, and experts, and outstanding Negro leaders—men of both races—and officials of Government at every level.

This White House conference's theme and title will be "To Fulfill These Rights."

Its object will be to help the American Negro fulfill the rights which, after the long time of injustice, he is finally about to secure.

To move beyond opportunity to achievement.

To shatter forever not only the barriers of law and public practice, but the walls which bound the condition of many by the color of his skin.

To dissolve, as best we can, the antique enmities of the heart which diminish the holder, divide the great democracy, and do wrong—great wrong—to the children of God.

And I pledge you tonight that this will be a chief goal of my administration, and of my program next year, and in the years to come. And I hope, and I pray, and I believe, it will be a part of the program of all America.

What Is Justice

For what is justice?

It is to fulfill the fair expectations of man.

Thus, American justice is a very special thing. For, from the first, this has been a land of towering expectations. It was to be a nation where each man could be ruled by the common consent of all—enshrined in law, given life by institutions, guided by men themselves subject to its rule. And all—all of every station and origin—would be touched equally in obligation and in liberty.

Beyond the law lay the land. It was a rich land, glowing with more abundant promise than man had ever seen. Here, unlike any place yet known, all were to share the harvest.

And beyond this was the dignity of man. Each could become whatever his qualities of mind and spirit would permit—to strive, to seek, and, if he could, to find his happiness.

This is American justice. We have pursued it faithfully to the edge of our imperfections, and we have failed to find it for the American Negro.

So, it is the glorious opportunity of this generation to end the one huge wrong of the American Nation and, in so doing, to find America for ourselves, with the same immense thrill of discovery which gripped those who first began to realize that here, at last, was a home for freedom.

All it will take is for all of us to understand what this country is and what this country must become.

The Scripture promises: "I shall light a candle of understanding in thine heart, which shall not be put out."

Together, and with millions more, we can light that candle of understanding in the heart of all America. And, once lit, it will never again go out.

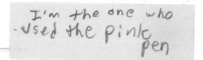

I'm the one who used the pink pen

JAMES BALDWIN AND WILLIAM F. BUCKLEY

Debate at Cambridge University (1965)

Resolved: The American Dream Is at the Expense of the American Negro

James Baldwin:

I find myself, not for the first time, in the position of a kind of Jeremiah. It would seem to me that the question before the house is a proposition horribly loaded, that one's response to that question depends on where you find yourself in the world, what your sense of reality is. That is, it depends on assumptions we hold so deeply as to be scarcely aware of them.

The white South African or Mississippi sharecropper or Alabama sheriff has at bottom a system of reality which compels them really to believe when they face the Negro that this woman, this man, this child must be insane to attack the system to which he owes his entire identity. For such a person, the proposition which we are trying to discuss here does not exist.

On the other hand, I have to speak as one of the people who have been most attacked by the Western system of reality. It comes from Europe. That is how it got to America. It raises the question of whether or not civilizations can be considered equal, or whether one civilization has a right to subjugate—in fact, to destroy—another.

Now, leaving aside all the physical factors one can quote—leaving aside the rape or murder, leaving aside the bloody catalogue of oppression which we are too familiar with anyway—what the system does to the subjugated is to destroy his sense of reality. It destroys his father's authority over him. His father can no longer tell him anything because his past has disappeared.

In the case of the American Negro, from the moment you are born every stick and stone, every face, is white. Since you have not yet seen a mirror, you suppose you are, too. It comes as a great shock around the age of 5, 6 or 7 to discover that the flag to which you have pledged allegiance, along with everybody else, has not pledged allegiance to you. It comes as a great shock to see Gary Cooper killing off the Indians and, although you are rooting for Gary Cooper, that the Indians are you.

It comes as a great shock to discover that the country which is your birthplace and to which you owe your life and identity has not, in its whole system of reality, evolved any place for you. The disaffection and the gap between people, only on the basis of their skins, begins there and accelerates throughout your whole lifetime. You realize that you are 30 and you are having a terrible time. You have been through a certain kind of mill and the most serious effect is again not the catalogue of disaster—the policeman, the taxi driver, the waiters, the landlady, the banks, the insurance companies, the millions of details 24 hours of every day which spell out to you that you are a worthless human being. It is not that. By that time you have begun to see it happening in your daughter, your son or your niece or your nephew. You are 30 by now and nothing you have done has helped you to escape the trap. But what is worse is that nothing you have done, and as far as you can tell nothing you *can* do, will save your son or your daughter from having the same disaster and from coming to the same end.

We speak about expense. There are several ways of addressing oneself to some attempt to find out what that word means here. From a very literal point of view, the harbors and the ports and the railroads of the country—the economy, especially in the South—could not conceivably be what they are if it had not been (and this is still so) for cheap labor. I am speaking very seriously, and this is not an over-statement: I picked cotton, I carried it to the market, I built the railroads under someone else's whip for nothing. For nothing.

The Southern oligarchy which has still today so very much power in Washington, and therefore some power in the world, was created by my labor and my sweat and the violation of my women and the murder of my children. This in the land of the free, the home of the brave. None can challenge that statement. It is a matter of historical record.

In the Deep South you are dealing with a sheriff or a landlord or a landlady or the girl at the Western Union desk. She doesn't know quite whom she is dealing with—by which I mean, if you are not part of a town and if you are a Northern nigger, it shows in millions of ways. She simply knows that it is an unknown quantity and she wants to have nothing to do with it. You have to wait a while to get your telegram. We have all been through it. By the time you get to be a man it is fairly easy to deal with.

But what happens to the poor white man's, the poor white woman's, mind? It is this: they have been raised to believe, and by now they helplessly believe, that no matter how terrible some of their lives may be and no matter what disaster overtakes them, there is one consolation like a heavenly revelation—at least they are not black. I suggest that of all the terrible things that could happen to a human being that is one of the worst. I suggest that what has happened to the white Southerner is in some ways much worse than what has happened to the Negroes there.

Sheriff Clark in Selma, Ala., cannot be dismissed as a total monster; I am sure he loves his wife and children and likes to get drunk. One has to assume that he is a man like me. But he does not know what drives him to use the club, to menace with the gun and to use the cattle prod. Something awful must have happened to a human being to be able to put a cattle prod against a woman's breasts. What happens to the woman is ghastly. What happens to the man who does it is in some ways much, much worse. Their moral lives have been destroyed by the plague called color.

This is not being done 100 years ago, but in 1965 and in a country which is pleased with what we call prosperity, with a certain amount of social coherence, which calls itself a civilized nation and which espouses the notion of freedom in the world. If it were white people being murdered, the Government would find some way of doing something about it. We have a civil rights bill now. We had the 15th Amendment nearly 100 years ago. If it was not honored then, I have no reason to believe that the civil rights bill will be honored now.

The American soil is full of the corpses of my ancestors, through 400 years and at least three wars. Why is my freedom, my citizenship, in question now? What one begs the American people to do, for all our sakes, is simply to accept our history.

It seems to me when I watch Americans in Europe that what they don't know about Europeans is what they don't know about me. They were not trying to be nasty to the French girl, rude to the French waiter. They did not know that they hurt their feelings; they didn't have any sense that this particular man and woman were human beings. They walked over them with the same sort of bland ignorance and condescension, the charm and cheerfulness, with which they had patted me on the head and which made them upset when I was upset.

When I was brought up I was taught in American history books that Africa had no history and that neither had I. I was a savage about whom the least said the better, who had been saved by Europe and who had been brought to America. Of course, I believed it. I didn't have much choice. These were the only books there were. Everyone else seemed to agree. If you went out of Harlem the whole world agreed. What you saw was much bigger, whiter, cleaner, safer. The garbage was collected, the children were happy. You would go back home and it would seem, of course, that this was an act of God. You belonged where white people put you.

It is only since World War II that there has been a counter-image in the world. That image has not come about because of any legislation by any American Government, but because Africa was suddenly on the stage of the world and Africans had to be dealt with in a way they had never been dealt with before. This gave the American Negro, for the first time, a sense of himself not as a savage. It has created and will create a great many conundrums.

One of the things the white world does not know, but I think I know, is that black people are just like everybody else. We are also mercenaries, dictators, murderers, liars. We are human, too. Unless we can establish some kind of dialogue between those people who enjoy the American dream and those other people who have not achieved it, we will be in terrible trouble. This is what concerns me most. We are sitting in this room and we are all civilized; we can talk to each other, at least on certain levels, so that we can walk out of here assuming that the measure of our politeness has some effect on the world.

I remember when the ex-Attorney General, Mr. Robert Kennedy, said it was conceivable that in 40 years in America we might have a Negro President. That sounded like a very emancipated statement to white people. They were not in Harlem when this statement was first heard. They did not hear the laughter and bitterness and scorn with which this statement was greeted. From the point of view of the man in the Harlem barber shop, Bobby Kennedy only got here yesterday and now he is already on his way to the Presidency. We were here for 400 years and now he tells us that maybe in 40 years, if you are good, we may let you become President.

Perhaps I can be reasoned with, but I don't know—neither does Martin Luther King—none of us knows how to deal with people whom the white world has so long ignored, who don't believe anything the white world says and don't entirely believe anything I or Martin say. You can't blame them.

It seems to me that the City of New York has had, for example, Negroes in it for a very long time. The City of New York was able in the last 15 years to reconstruct itself, to tear down buildings and raise great new ones and has done nothing whatever except build housing projects, mainly in the ghettoes, for the Negroes. And of course the Negroes hate it. The children can't bear it. They want to move out of the ghettoes. If American pretensions were based on more honest assessments of life, it would not mean for Negroes that when someone says "urban renewal" some Negroes are going to be thrown out into the streets, which is what it means now.

It is a terrible thing for an entire people to surrender to the notion that one-ninth of its population is beneath them. Until the moment comes when we, the Americans, are able to accept the fact that my ancestors are both black and white, that on that continent we are trying to forge a new identity, that we need each other, that I am not a ward of America, I am not an object of missionary charity, I am one of the people who built the country—until this moment comes there is scarcely any hope for the American dream. If the people are denied participation in it, by their very presence they will wreck it. And if that happens it is a very grave moment for the West.

William Buckley:

It seems to me that of all the indictments Mr. Baldwin has made of America here tonight, and in his copious literature of protest, the one that is most striking involves, in effect, the refusal of the American community to treat him other than as a Negro. The American community has refused to do this. The American community, almost everywhere he goes, treats him with the kind of unction, with the kind of satisfaction that a posturing hero gets for his flagellations of our civilization, so that he quite properly commands the contempt he so eloquently showers upon us.

It is quite impossible in my judgment to deal with the indictments of Mr. Baldwin unless one is prepared to deal with him as a white man, unless one is prepared to say to him that the fact that your skin is black is utterly irrelevant to the arguments you raise. The fact that you sit here, carrying the entire weight of the Negro ordeal on your own shoulders, is irrelevant to the argument we are here to discuss.

I am treating you as a fellow American, as a man whose indictments of our civilization are unjustified, as an American who—if his counsels were listened to—would be cursed by all his grandchildren's grandchildren.

About 125 years ago this house was bitterly divided over the question of whether or not some people in England who practiced the faith of Erasmus, your most distinguished lecturer, should be allowed to vote. By a slim margin it was decided that they ought to be allowed to do so. We know that there was more blood shed trying to emancipate the Irish here in the British Isles than has been shed by 10 times the number of people who have been lynched as a result of the delirium of race consciousness, race supremacy, in the United States. Shall we devote the night to these luridities? Shall we devote the evening to examining the sociological facts of human nature? Shall we discuss these class antagonisms in terms of race, in terms of economic standing? Shall we discuss the existential dilemma of humankind?

It is a fact that the position in America is as it is, that the situation in Africa is as it is. The question before the house is not whether we should have purchased slaves generations ago, or ought the blacks to have sold us those slaves. The question, rather, is this: Is there anything in the American dream which intrinsically argues against some kind of deliverance from the system that we all recognize as evil? What shall we do about it? What shall we in America do to eliminate these psychic humiliations which I join Mr. Baldwin in believing are the very worst aspects of this discrimination?

It is the case that seven-tenths of the average white's income in the United States is equal to the entire income of the average Negro. But my great-grandparents worked hard. I do not know of anything which has ever been created without the expense of something. We have a dastardly situation. But I am going to ask you not to make politics as the crow flies.

What is it that we Americans ought to do? I wonder. What is it we should do, for instance, to avoid the humiliations mentioned by Mr. Baldwin as having been part of his own experiences? At the age of 12 he trespassed outside the ghetto of Harlem and was taken by the scruff of his neck by a policeman on 42d Street and Madison Avenue and told, "Here, you nigger, go back to where you belong." Fifteen to 20 years later he asks for a Scotch whisky in Chicago and is told by the white barman that he is obviously under age and under the circumstances cannot be served. I know from your faces that you share with me a feeling of compassion and a feeling of outrage that this kind of thing should have happened. How are we going to avoid the kind of humiliations which are visited perpetually upon members of the minority race?

Obviously, the first element is concern. We have got to care that it happens. We have got to do what

we can to change the warp and woof of moral feelings and society to make it happen less and less.

The proposition before us tonight as elaborated by Mr. Baldwin is that we ought precisely to recognize that the American civilization, and indeed the Western civilization, has failed him and his people, that we ought to throw it over. He tells us that our civilization rests on the rantings of the Hebrew, sunbaked fanatic called Jesus—not, says he, truly the founder of the Christian religion. The founder of the Christian religion was actually Paul, whom he describes as a merciless fanatic.[1] And as a result of these teachings of Jesus and Paul, we have Dachau.

If we assume that Dachau was the natural consequence of the teachings of St. Paul and Jesus, what shall we do with the library around here? Shall we descend on it and uproot all the literature that depends in any way on the teachings of Plato and Aristotle because they justified slavery? The primary question before the house is whether or not our civilization has shown itself so flawed as the result of the failure of its response to the Negro problem of the United States that it ought to be jettisoned. *abandoned*

Now I suggest that anyone who argued that English civilization ought to have been jettisoned because Catholics were not allowed to vote in England as late as 1829 and Jews not until 1832 should consider the other possibility. Precisely the reason they *did* get the vote was because English civilization was not jettisoned. The whole point of our philosophical concern ought never to make that terrible fault made so frequently by the positivists, that we should rush forward and overthrow our civilization because we don't live up to our high ideals.

It may be that there has been some sort of sunburst of moral enlightenment that has hit this community so as to make it predictable that if you were the governors of the United States the situation would change overnight. The engines of concern in the United States are working. The presence of Mr. Baldwin here is, in part, a reflection of that concern.

---

1. [Buckley refers to a passage in Baldwin's *The Fire Next Time*, viz. "The real architect of the Christian church was not the disreputable sunbaked Hebrew (Jesus Christ) who gave it its name but rather the mercilessly fanatical and self-righteous Paul."]

You cannot go to any university in the United States in which practically every other problem of public policy is not pre-empted by the primary concern for the Negro. I challenge you to name me another civilization in the history of the world in which the problems of the minority, which have been showing considerable material and political advancement, are as much a subject of dramatic concern as in the United States.

Americans are not willing, as a result of Mr. Baldwin's aspirations, to say that the whole American proposition was an unfortunate experiment. They are not willing to say that because we have not accelerated Negro progress faster, we are going to desert the constitutional system, the idea of the rule of law, the idea of the individual rights of the American citizen, that we are going to burn all the Bibles, burn our books, that we want to reject our entire Judeo-Christian civilization because of the continued persistence of the kind of evil that has been so eloquently described by Mr. Baldwin.

There is no instant cure for the race problem in America. Anyone who tells you that there is a quick solution is a charlatan and ultimately a boring man— a boring man because he is then speaking in the kind of abstractions which do not relate to human experience. The Negro problem is a very complicated one. I urge those of you who have an actual interest in the problem to read "Beyond the Melting Pot," by Nathan Glazer and Daniel Moynihan. They say that in 1900 there were 3,500 Negro doctors in America. In 1960, there were 3,900, an increase of 400. Is this because there were no opportunities? No, they say. There are a great many medical schools which by no means practice discrimination. It is because the Negro's particular energy is not directed toward that goal.

What should James Baldwin be doing other than telling us to renounce our civilization? He should be addressing his own people and urging them to take advantage of those opportunities which do exist. And urging us to make those opportunities wider.

Where Negroes are concerned, the danger, as far as I can see at this moment, is that they will seek to reach out for some sort of radical solutions, on the basis of which the true problem is obscured. They have done a great deal to focus on the facts of white discrimination against Negroes. They have done a great deal to agitate a moral concern. But where in

fact do they go now? They seem to be slipping into some sort of Procrustean formulation which ends up by urging the advancement of the Negro less than the regression of white people.

[Interjection from an American undergraduate: "Mr. Buckley, one thing you can do is to let them vote in Mississippi."]

[Buckley: "I agree. Except, lest I appear too ingratiating, I think actually what is wrong in Mississippi is not that not enough Negroes have the vote but that too many white people are voting."]

What we need is a considerable amount of frankness that acknowledges there are two sets of difficulties. We must recognize the difficulty that brown people, white people, black people have all over the world to protect their own vested interests. They suffer from a kind of racial narcissism which tends always to convert every contingency in such a way as to maximize their own power. We must acknowledge that problem, but we must also reach through to the Negro people and tell them that their best chances are in a mobile society and the most mobile society in the world today is in the United States.

It is precisely that mobility which can give opportunities to the Negroes, which they must be encouraged to take. But they must not be encouraged to adopt the kind of cynicism, the kind of despair, the kind of iconoclasm that is urged by Mr. Baldwin.

For one thing I believe—that the fundamental trend in the United States is to the good nature, the generosity and good wishes, the decency that do lie in the spirit of the American people. These qualities must not be laughed at, and under no circumstances must America be told that the only alternative is the overthrow of that civilization which we consider to be the faith of our fathers, the faith of your fathers.

If it finally does come to a confrontation between giving up the best features of the American way of life and fighting for them, then we will fight the issue. We will fight the issue not only in the Cambridge Union, but we will fight as you were once asked to fight—on the beaches, in the hills, in the mountains. And just as you waged war to save civilization, you also waged war for the benefit of the Germans, your enemies. We, too, are convinced that if it should ever come to that kind of confrontation, then our determination will be to wage war not only for the whites, but also for the Negroes.

Daniel Patrick Moynihan

The Negro Family: The Case for National Action (The Moynihan Report) (1965)

Two hundred years ago, in 1765, nine assembled colonies first joined together to demand freedom from arbitrary power.

For the first century we struggled to hold together the first continental union of democracy in the history of man. One hundred years ago, in 1865, following a terrible test of blood and fire, the compact of union was finally sealed.

For a second century we labored to establish a unity of purpose and interest among the many groups which make up the American community.

That struggle has often brought pain and violence. It is not yet over.

> *State of the Union Message of President Lyndon B. Johnson, January 4, 1965.*

The United States is approaching a new crisis in race relations.

In the decade that began with the school desegregation decision of the Supreme Court, and ended with the passage of the Civil Rights Act of 1964, the demand of Negro Americans for full recognition of their civil rights was finally met.

The effort, no matter how savage and brutal, of some State and local governments to thwart the exercise of those rights is doomed. The nation will not put up with it—least of all the Negroes. The present moment will pass. In the meantime, a new period is beginning.

In this new period the expectations of the Negro Americans will go beyond civil rights. Being Americans, they will now expect that in the near future equal opportunities for them as a group will produce roughly equal results, as compared with other groups. This is not going to happen. Nor will it happen for generations to come unless a new and special effort is made.

There are two reasons. First, the racist virus in the American blood stream still afflicts us: Negroes will encounter serious personal prejudice for at least another generation. Second, three centuries of sometimes unimaginable mistreatment have taken their toll on the Negro people. The harsh fact is that as a group, at the present time, in terms of ability to win out in the competitions of American life, they are not equal to most of those groups with which they will be competing. Individually, Negro Americans reach the highest peaks of achievement. But collectively, in the spectrum of American ethnic and religious and regional groups, where some get plenty and some get none, where some send eighty percent of their children to college and others pull them out of school at the 8th grade, Negroes are among the weakest.

The most difficult fact for white Americans to understand is that in these terms the circumstances of the Negro American community in recent years has probably been getting *worse, not better.*

Indices of dollars of income, standards of living, and years of education deceive. The gap between the Negro and most other groups in American society is widening.

The fundamental problem, in which this is most clearly the case, is that of family structure. The evidence—not final, but powerfully persuasive—is that the Negro family in the urban ghettos is crumbling. A middle-class group has managed to save itself, but for vast numbers of the unskilled, poorly educated city working class the fabric of conventional social relationships has all but disintegrated. There are indications that the situation may have been arrested in the past few years, but the general post-war trend is unmistakable. So long as this situation persists, the cycle of poverty and disadvantage will continue to repeat itself.

The thesis of this paper is that these events, in combination, confront the nation with a new kind of problem. Measures that have worked in the past, or would work for most groups in the present, will not work here. A national effort is required that will give a unity of purpose to the many activities of the Federal government in this area, directed to a new kind of national goal: the establishment of a stable Negro family structure.

This would be a new departure for Federal policy. And a difficult one. But it almost certainly offers the only possibility of resolving in our time what is, after all, the nation's oldest, and most intransigent, and now its most dangerous social problem. What Gunnar Myrdal said in *An American Dilemma* remains true today: *"America is free to choose whether the Negro shall remain her liability or become her opportunity."*

Chapter I
The Negro American Revolution

The Negro American revolution is rightly regarded as the most important domestic event of the postwar period in the United States.

Nothing like it has occurred since the upheavals of the 1930s which led to the organization of the great industrial trade unions, and which in turn profoundly altered both the economy and the political scene. There have been few other events in our history—the American Revolution itself, the surge of Jacksonian Democracy in the 1830s, the Abolitionist movement, and the Populist movement of the late 19th century—comparable to the current Negro movement.

There has been none more important. The Negro American revolution holds forth the prospect that the American Republic, which at birth was flawed by the institution of Negro slavery, and which throughout its history has been marred by the unequal treatment of Negro citizens, will at last redeem the full promise of the Declaration of Independence.

Although the Negro leadership has conducted itself with the strictest propriety, acting always and only as American citizens asserting their rights within the framework of the American political system, it is no less clear that the movement has profound international implications.

It was in no way a matter of chance that the nonviolent tactics and philosophy of the movement, as it began in the South, were consciously adapted from the techniques by which the Congress Party

undertook to free the Indian nation from British colonial rule. It was not a matter of chance that the Negro movement caught fire in America at just that moment when the nations of Africa were gaining their freedom. Nor is it merely incidental that the world should have fastened its attention on events in the United States at a time when the possibility that the nations of the world will divide along color lines seems suddenly not only possible, but even imminent.

(Such racist views have made progress within the Negro American community itself—which can hardly be expected to be immune to a virus that is endemic in the white community. The Black Muslim doctrines, based on total alienation from the white world, exert a powerful influence. On the far left, the attraction of Chinese Communism can no longer be ignored.)

It is clear that what happens in America is being taken as a sign of what can, or must, happen in the world at large. The course of world events will be profoundly affected by the success or failure of the Negro American revolution in seeking the peaceful assimilation of the races in the United States. The award of the Nobel Peace Prize to Dr. Martin Luther King was as much an expression of the hope for the future, as it was recognition for past achievement.

It is no less clear that carrying this revolution forward to a successful conclusion is a first priority confronting the Great Society.

The End of the Beginning

The major events of the onset of the Negro revolution are now behind us.

The *political events* were three: First, the Negroes themselves organized as a mass movement. Their organizations have been in some ways better disciplined and better led than any in our history. They have established an unprecedented alliance with religious groups throughout the nation and have maintained close ties with both political parties and with most segments of the trade union movement. Second, the Kennedy-Johnson Administration committed the Federal government to the cause of Negro equality. This had never happened before. Third, the 1964 Presidential election was practically a referendum on this commitment: if these were terms made by the opposition, they were in effect accepted by the President.

The overwhelming victory of President Johnson must be taken as emphatic popular endorsement of the unmistakable, and openly avowed course which the Federal government has pursued under his leadership.

The *administrative events* were threefold as well: First, beginning with the establishment of the President's Committee on Equal Employment Opportunity and on to the enactment of the Manpower Development and Training Act of 1962, the Federal government has launched a major national effort to redress the profound imbalance between the economic position of the Negro citizens and the rest of the nation that derives primarily from their unequal position in the labor market. Second, the Economic Opportunity Act of 1964 began a major national effort to abolish poverty, a condition in which almost half of Negro families are living. Third, the Civil Rights Act of 1964 marked the end of the era of legal and formal discrimination against Negroes and created important new machinery for combating covert discrimination and unequal treatment. (The Act does not guarantee an end to harassment in matters such as voter registration, but does make it more or less incumbent upon government to take further steps to thwart such efforts when they do occur.)

The *legal events* were no less specific. Beginning with *Brown v. Board of Education* in 1954, through the decade that culminated in the recent decisions upholding Title II of the Civil Rights Act, the Federal judiciary, led by the Supreme Court, has used every opportunity to combat unequal treatment of Negro citizens. It may be put as a general proposition that the laws of the United States now look upon any such treatment as obnoxious, and that the courts will strike it down wherever it appears.

The Demand for Equality

With these events behind us, the nation now faces a different set of challenges, which may prove more difficult to meet, if only because they cannot be cast as concrete propositions of right and wrong.

The fundamental problem here is that the Negro revolution, like the industrial upheaval of the 1930s, is a movement for equality as well as for liberty.

Liberty and Equality are the twin ideals of American democracy. But they are not the same thing. Nor, most importantly, are they equally attractive to all groups at any given time nor yet are they always compatible, one with the other.

Many persons who would gladly die for liberty are appalled by equality. Many who are devoted to equality are puzzled and even troubled by liberty. Much of the political history of the American nation can be seen as a competition between these two ideals, as for example, the unending troubles between capital and labor.

By and large, liberty has been the ideal with the higher social prestige in America. It has been the middle class aspiration, par excellence. (Note the assertions of the conservative right that ours is a republic, not a democracy.) Equality, on the other hand, has enjoyed tolerance more than acceptance. Yet it has roots deep in Western civilization and "is at least coeval with, if not prior to, liberty in the history of Western political thought."[1]

American democracy has not always been successful in maintaining a balance between these two ideals, and notably so where the Negro American is concerned. "Lincoln freed the slaves," but they were given liberty, not equality. It was therefore possible in the century that followed to deprive their descendants of much of their liberty as well.

The ideal of equality does not ordain that all persons end up, as well as start out equal. In traditional terms, as put by Faulkner, "there is no such thing as equality *per se*, but only equality *to*: equal right and opportunity to make the best one can of one's life within one's capability, without fear of injustice or oppression or threat of violence."[2] But the evolution of American politics, with the distinct persistence of ethnic and religious groups, has added a profoundly significant new dimension to that egalitarian ideal. It is increasingly demanded that the distribution of success and failure within one group be roughly comparable

1. Robert Harris, *The Quest for Equality* (Baton Rouge, Louisiana State University Press, 1960), p. 4.

2. William Faulkner, in a speech before the Southern Historical Society in November, 1955, quoted in *Mississippi: The Closed Society*, by James W. Silver (New York, Harcourt, Brace and World, Inc., 1964), p. xiii.

to that within other groups. It is not enough that all individuals start out on even terms, if the members of one group almost invariably end up well to the fore, and those of another far to the rear. This is what ethnic politics are all about in America, and in the main the Negro American demands are being put forth in this now traditional and established framework.[3]

Here a point of semantics must be grasped. The demand for Equality of Opportunity has been generally perceived by white Americans as a demand for liberty, a demand not to be excluded from the competitions of life—at the polling place, in the scholarship examinations, at the personnel office, on the housing market. Liberty does, of course, demand that everyone be free to try his luck, or test his skill in such matters. But these opportunities do not necessarily produce equality: on the contrary, to the extent that winners imply losers, equality of opportunity almost insures inequality of results.

The point of semantics is that equality of opportunity now has a different meaning for Negroes than it has for whites. It is not (or at least no longer) a demand for liberty alone, but also for equality—in terms of group results. In Bayard Rustin's terms, "It is now concerned not merely with removing the barriers to full *opportunity* but with achieving the fact of *equality*."[4] By equality Rustin means a distribution of achievements among Negroes roughly comparable to that among whites. [. . .]

Chapter II
The Negro American Family

At the heart of the deterioration of the fabric of Negro society is the deterioration of the Negro family.

It is the fundamental source of the weakness of the Negro community at the present time.

---

3.   For a view that present Negro demands go beyond this traditional position see Nathan Glazer, "Negroes and Jews: The Challenge to Pluralism," *Commentary*, December 1964, pp. 29–34.

4.   Bayard Rustin, "From Protest to Politics: The Future of the Civil Rights Movement," *Commentary*, February 1965, p. 27.

There is probably no single fact of Negro American life so little understood by whites. The Negro situation is commonly perceived by whites in terms of the visible manifestation of discrimination and poverty, in part because Negro protest is directed against such obstacles, and in part, no doubt, because these are facts which involve the actions and attitudes of the white community as well. It is more difficult, however, for whites to perceive the effect that three centuries of exploitation have had on the fabric of Negro society itself. Here the consequences of the historic injustices done to Negro Americans are silent and hidden from view. But here is where the true injury has occurred: unless this damage is repaired, all the effort to end discrimination and poverty and injustice will come to little.

The role of the family in shaping character and ability is so pervasive as to be easily overlooked. The family is the basic social unit of American life; it is the basic socializing unit. By and large, adult conduct in society is learned as a child.

A fundamental insight of psychoanalytic theory, for example, is that the child learns a way of looking at life in his early years through which all later experience is viewed and which profoundly shapes his adult conduct.

It may be hazarded that the reason family structure does not loom larger in public discussion of social issues is that people tend to assume that the nature of family life is about the same throughout American society. The mass media and the development of suburbia have created an image of the American family as a highly standardized phenomenon. It is therefore easy to assume that whatever it is that makes for differences among individuals or groups of individuals, it is not a different family structure.

There is much truth to this; as with any other nation, Americans are producing a recognizable family system. But that process is not completed by any means. There are still, for example, important differences in family patterns surviving from the age of the great European migration to the United States, and these variations account for notable differences in the progress and assimilation of various ethnic and religious groups.[5] A number of immigrant groups

---

5.   Nathan Glazer and Daniel Patrick Moynihan, *Beyond*

were characterized by unusually strong family bonds; these groups have characteristically progressed more rapidly than others.

But there is one truly great discontinuity in family structure in the United States at the present time: that between the white world in general and that of the Negro American.

The white family has achieved a high degree of stability and is maintaining that stability.

By contrast, the family structure of lower class Negroes is highly unstable, and in many urban centers is approaching complete breakdown.

(N.B. There is considerable evidence that the Negro community is in fact dividing between a stable middle-class group that is steadily growing stronger and more successful, and an increasingly disorganized and disadvantaged lower-class group. There are indications, for example, that the middle-class Negro family puts a higher premium on family stability and the conserving of family resources than does the white middle-class family.[6]) [. . .]

There are two points to be noted in this context.

First, the emergence and increasing visibility of a Negro middle-class may beguile the nation into supposing that the circumstances of the remainder of the Negro community are equally prosperous, whereas just the opposite is true at present, and is likely to continue so.

Second, the lumping of all Negroes together in one statistical measurement very probably conceals the extent of the disorganization among the lower-class group. If conditions are improving for one and deteriorating for the other, the resultant statistical averages might show no change. Further, the statistics on the Negro family and most other subjects treated in this paper refer only to a specific point in time. They are a vertical measure of the situation at a given movement. They do not measure the experience of individuals over time. Thus the average monthly unemployment rate for Negro males for 1964 is recorded as 9 percent. But *during* 1964, some 29 percent of Negro males were unemployed at one time or another. Similarly, for example, if 36 percent of Negro children are living in broken homes *at any specific moment*, it is likely that a far higher proportion of Negro children find themselves in that situation *at one time or another* in their lives.

Nearly a Quarter of Urban Negro Marriages Are Dissolved

Nearly a quarter of Negro women living in cities who have ever married are divorced, separated, or are living apart from their husbands.

The rates are highest in the urban Northeast where 26 percent of Negro women ever married are either divorced, separated, or have their husbands absent.

On the urban frontier, the proportion of husbands absent is even higher. In New York City in 1960, it was 30.2 percent, *not* including divorces.

Among ever-married nonwhite women in the nation, the proportion with husbands present *declined* in *every* age group over the decade 1950–60. [. . .][7]

Although similar declines occurred among white females, the proportion of white husbands present never dropped below 90 percent except for the first and last age group.[8]

Nearly One-Quarter of Negro Births Are Now Illegitimate

Both white and Negro illegitimacy rates have been increasing, although from dramatically different bases. The white rate was 2 percent in 1940; it was 3.07 percent in 1963. In that period, the Negro rate went from 16.8 percent to 23.6 percent.

The number of illegitimate children per 1,000 live births increased by 11 among whites in the period 1940–63, but by 68 among nonwhites. There are, of course, limits to the dependability of these statistics. There are almost certainly a considerable number of Negro children who, although technically illegitimate, are in fact the offspring of stable unions. On the other hand, it may be assumed that many births that are in fact illegitimate are recorded

---

the Melting Pot (MIT Press and Harvard University Press, Cambridge, 1963), pp. 290–291.

6.   E. Franklin Frazier, *Black Bourgeoisie* (New York, Collier Books, 1962).

---

7.   [A chart with supporting data is not reproduced here.]

8.   Furnished by Dr. Margaret Bright, in a communication on January 20, 1965.

otherwise. Probably the two opposite effects cancel each other out.

On the urban frontier, the nonwhite illegitimacy rates are usually higher than the national average, and the increase of late has been drastic.

In the District of Columbia, the illegitimacy rate for nonwhites grew from 21.8 percent in 1950, to 29.5 percent in 1964.

A similar picture of disintegrating Negro marriages emerges from the divorce statistics. Divorces have increased of late for both whites and nonwhites, but at a much greater rate for the latter. In 1940 both groups had a divorce rate of 2.2 percent. By 1964 the white rate had risen to 3.6 percent, but the nonwhite rate had reached 5.1 percent—40 percent greater than the formerly equal white rate.

Almost One-Fourth of Negro Families Are Headed by Females

As a direct result of this high rate of divorce, separation, and desertion, a very large percent of Negro families are headed by females. While the percentage of such families among whites has been dropping since 1940, it has been rising among Negroes.

The percent of nonwhite families headed by a female is more than double the percent for whites. Fatherless nonwhite families increased by a sixth between 1950 and 1960, but held constant for white families.

It has been estimated that only a minority of Negro children reach the age of 18 having lived all their lives with both of their parents.

Once again, this measure of family disorganization is found to be diminishing among white families and increasing among Negro families.

The Breakdown of the Negro Family Has Led to a Startling Increase in Welfare Dependency

The majority of Negro children receive public assistance under the AFDC program at one point or another in their childhood.

At present, 14 percent of Negro children are receiving AFDC assistance, as against 2 percent of white children. Eight percent of white children receive such assistance at some time, as against 56 percent of nonwhites, according to an extrapolation based on HEW data. (Let it be noted, however, that out of a total of 1.8 million nonwhite illegitimate children in the nation in 1961, 1.3 million were *not* receiving aid under the AFDC program, although a substantial number have, or will, receive aid at some time in their lives.)

Again, the situation may be said to be worsening. The AFDC program, deriving from the long established Mothers' Aid programs, was established in 1935 principally to care for widows and orphans, although the legislation covered all children in homes deprived of parental support because one or both of their parents are absent or incapacitated.

In the beginning, the number of AFDC families in which the father was absent because of desertion was less than a third of the total. Today it is two-thirds. HEW estimates "that between two-thirds and three-fourths of the 50 percent increase from 1948 to 1955 in the number of absent-father families receiving ADC may be explained by an increase in broken homes in the population."[9] [. . .]

Chapter III
The Roots of the Problem

Slavery

The most perplexing question about American slavery, which has never been altogether explained, and which indeed most Americans hardly know exists, has been stated by Nathan Glazer as follows: "Why was American slavery the most awful the world has ever known?"[10] The only thing that can be said with certainty is that this is true: it was.

American slavery was profoundly different from, and in its lasting effects on individuals and their children, indescribably worse than, any recorded servitude, ancient or modern. The peculiar nature of

---

9. Maurine McKeany, *The Absent Father and Public Policy in the Program of Aid to Dependent Children* (Berkeley, University of California Press, 1960), p. 3.

10. Nathan Glazer, "Introduction," *Slavery*, Stanley M. Elkins (New York, Grosset and Dunlap, 1963), p. ix.

American slavery was noted by Alexis de Tocqueville and others, but it was not until 1948 that Frank Tannenbaum, a South American specialist, pointed to the striking differences between Brazilian and American slavery. The feudal, Catholic society of Brazil had a legal and religious tradition which accorded the slave a place as a human being in the hierarchy of society—a luckless, miserable place, to be sure, but a place withal. In contrast, there was nothing in the tradition of English law or Protestant theology which could accommodate to the fact of human bondage—the slaves were therefore reduced to the status of chattels—often, no doubt, well cared for, even privileged chattels, but chattels nevertheless.

Glazer, also focusing on the Brazil-United States comparison, continues.

In Brazil, the slave had many more rights than in the United States: he could legally marry, he could, indeed had to, be baptized and become a member of the Catholic Church, his family could not be broken up for sale, and he had many days on which he could either rest or earn money to buy his freedom. The Government encouraged manumission, and the freedom of infants could often be purchased for a small sum at the baptismal font. In short: the Brazilian slave knew he was a man, and that he differed in degree, not in kind, from his master.[11]

[In the United States,] the slave was totally removed from the protection of organized society (compare the elaborate provisions for the protection of slaves in the Bible), his existence as a human being was given no recognition by any religious or secular agency, he was totally ignorant of and completely cut off from his past, and he was offered absolutely no hope for the future. His children could be sold, his marriage was not recognized, his wife could be violated or sold (there was something comic about calling the woman with whom the master permitted him to live a "wife"), and he could also be subject, without redress, to frightful barbarities—there were presumably as many sadists among slave-owners, men and women, as there are in other groups. The slave could not, by law, be taught to read or write; he could not practice any religion without

the permission of his master, and could never meet with his fellows, for religious or any other purposes, except in the presence of a white; and finally, if a master wished to free him, every legal obstacle was used to thwart such action. This was not what slavery meant in the ancient world, in medieval and early modern Europe, or in Brazil and the West Indies.

More important, American slavery was also awful in its effects. If we compared the present situation of the American Negro with that of, let us say, Brazilian Negroes (who were slaves 20 years longer), we begin to suspect that the differences are the result of very different patterns of slavery. Today the Brazilian Negroes are Brazilians; though most are poor and do the hard and dirty work of the country, as Negroes do in the United States, they are not cut off from society. They reach into its highest strata, merging there—in smaller and smaller numbers, it is true, but with complete acceptance—with other Brazilians of all kinds. The relations between Negroes and whites in Brazil show nothing of the mass irrationality that prevails in this country.[12]

Stanley M. Elkins, drawing on the aberrant behavior of the prisoners in Nazi concentration camps, drew an elaborate parallel between the two institutions. This thesis has been summarized as follows by Thomas Pettigrew:

Both were closed systems, with little chance of manumission, emphasis on survival, and a single, omnipresent authority. The profound personality change created by Nazi internment, as independently reported by a number of psychologists and psychiatrists who survived, was toward childishness and total acceptance of the SS guards as father-figures—a syndrome strikingly similar to the "Sambo" caricature of the Southern slave. Nineteenth-century racists readily believed that the "Sambo" personality was simply an inborn racial type. Yet no African anthropological data have ever shown any personality type resembling Sambo; and the concentration camps molded the equivalent personality pattern in a wide variety of Caucasian prisoners. Nor was Sambo merely a product of "slavery" in the abstract, for the less

---

11. Ibid., pp. xi–xii.

12. Ibid., pp. ix–x.

devastating Latin American system never developed such a type.

Extending this line of reasoning, psychologists point out that slavery in all its forms sharply lowered the need for achievement in slaves. . . . Negroes in bondage, stripped of their African heritage, were placed in a completely dependent role. All of their rewards came, not from individual initiative and enterprise, but from absolute obedience—a situation that severely depresses the need for achievement among all peoples. Most important of all, slavery vitiated family life. . . . Since many slave-owners neither fostered Christian marriage among their slave couples nor hesitated to separate them on the auction block, the slave household often developed a fatherless matrifocal (mother-centered) pattern.[13]

The Reconstruction

With the emancipation of the slaves, the Negro American family began to form in the United States on a widespread scale. But it did so in an atmosphere markedly different from that which has produced the white American family.

The Negro was given liberty, but not equality. Life remained hazardous and marginal. Of the greatest importance, the Negro male, particularly in the South, became an object of intense hostility, an attitude unquestionably based in some measure of fear.

When Jim Crow made its appearance towards the end of the 19th century, it may be speculated that it was the Negro male who was most humiliated thereby; the male was more likely to use public facilities, which rapidly became segregated once the process began, and just as important, segregation, and the submissiveness it exacts, is surely more destructive to the male than to the female personality. Keeping the Negro "in his place" can be translated as keeping the Negro male in his place: the female was not a threat to anyone.

Unquestionably, these events worked against the emergence of a strong father figure. The very essence of the male animal, from the bantam rooster to the four-star general, is to strut. Indeed, in 19th century America, a particular type of exaggerated male boastfulness became almost a national style. Not for the Negro male. The "sassy nigger [sic]" was lynched.

In this situation, the Negro family made but little progress toward the middle-class pattern of the present time. Margaret Mead has pointed out that while "In every known human society, everywhere in the world, the young male learns that when he grows up one of the things which he must do in order to be a full member of society is to provide food for some female and her young."[14] This pattern is not immutable, however: it can be broken, even though it has always eventually reasserted itself.

> Within the family, each new generation of young males learn the appropriate nurturing behavior and superimpose upon their biologically given maleness this learned parental role. When the family breaks down—as it does under slavery, under certain forms of indentured labor and serfdom, in periods of extreme social unrest during wars, revolutions, famines, and epidemics, or in periods of abrupt transition from one type of economy to another—this delicate line of transmission is broken. Men may founder badly in these periods, during which the primary unit may again become mother and child, the biologically given, and the special conditions under which man has held his social traditions in trust are violated and distorted.[15]

E. Franklin Frazier makes clear that at the time of emancipation Negro women were already "accustomed to playing the dominant role in family and marriage relations" and that this role persisted in the decades of rural life that followed.

Urbanization

Country life and city life are profoundly different. The gradual shift of American society from a rural to an urban basis over the past century and a half has caused abundant strains, many of which are still

---

13. Thomas F. Pettigrew, *A Profile of the Negro American* (Princeton, New Jersey, D. Van Nostrand Company, Inc., 1964), pp. 13–14.

14. Margaret Mead, *Male and Female* (New York, New American Library, 1962), p. 146.

15. Ibid., p. 148.

much in evidence. When this shift occurs suddenly, drastically, in one or two generations, the effect is immensely disruptive of traditional social patterns.

It was this abrupt transition that produced the wild Irish slums of the 19th century Northeast. Drunkenness, crime, corruption, discrimination, family disorganization, juvenile delinquency were the routine of that era. In our own time, the same sudden transition has produced the Negro slum—different from, but hardly better than its predecessors, and fundamentally the result of the same process.

Negroes are now more urbanized than whites.

Negro families in the cities are more frequently headed by a woman than those in the country. The difference between the white and Negro proportions of families headed by a woman is greater in the city than in the country.

The promise of the city has so far been denied the majority of Negro migrants, and most particularly the Negro family.

In 1939, E. Franklin Frazier described its plight movingly in that part of *The Negro Family* entitled "In the City of Destruction":

> The impact of hundreds of thousands of rural southern Negroes upon northern metropolitan communities presents a bewildering spectacle. Striking contrasts in levels of civilization and economic well-being among these newcomers to modern civilization seem to baffle any attempt to discover order and direction in their mode of life.[16]

> In many cases, of course, the dissolution of the simple family organization has begun before the family reaches the northern city. But, if these families have managed to preserve their integrity until they reach the northern city, poverty, ignorance, and color force them to seek homes in deteriorated slum areas from which practically all institutional life has disappeared. Hence, at the same time that these simple rural families are losing their internal cohesion, they are being freed from the controlling force of public opinion and communal institutions. Family desertion among Negroes in cities appears, then, to be one of the inevitable consequences of the impact of urban life on the simple family organization and folk culture which the Negro has evolved in the rural South. The distribution of desertions in relation to the general economic and cultural organization of Negro communities that have grown up in our American cities shows in a striking manner the influence of selective factors in the process of adjustment to the urban environment.[17]

Frazier concluded his classic study, *The Negro Family*, with the prophesy that the "travail of civilization is not yet ended."

> First, it appears that the family which evolved within the isolated world of the Negro folk will become increasingly disorganized. Modern means of communication will break down the isolation of the world of the black folk, and, as long as the bankrupt system of southern agriculture exists, Negro families will continue to seek a living in the towns and cities of the country. They will crowd the slum areas of southern cities or make their way to northern cities where their family life will become disrupted and their poverty will force them to depend upon charity.[18]

In every index of family pathology—divorce, separation, and desertion, female family head, children in broken homes, and illegitimacy—the contrast between the urban and rural environment for Negro families is unmistakable. [. . .]

Unemployment and Poverty

The impact of unemployment on the Negro family, and particularly on the Negro male, is the least understood of all the developments that have contributed to the present crisis. There is little analysis because there has been almost no inquiry. Unemployment, for whites and nonwhites alike, has on the whole been treated as an economic phenomenon, with almost no attention paid for at least a quarter-century to social and personal consequences.

---

16. E. Franklin Frazier, *The Negro Family in the United States* (Chicago, The University of Chicago Press, 1939), p. 298.

17. Ibid., pp. 340–341.
18. Ibid., p. 487.

In 1940, Edward Wight Bakke described the effects of unemployment on family structure in terms of six stages of adjustment.[19] Although the families studied were white, the pattern would clearly seem to be a general one, and apply to Negro families as well.

The first two stages end with the exhaustion of credit and the entry of the wife into the labor force. The father is no longer the provider and the elder children become resentful.

The third stage is the critical one of commencing a new day-to-day existence. At this point two women are in charge:

> Consider the fact that relief investigators or case workers are normally women and deal with the housewife. Already suffering a loss in prestige and authority in the family because of his failure to be the chief bread winner, the male head of the family feels deeply this obvious transfer of planning for the family's well-being to two women, one of them an outsider. His role is reduced to that of errand boy to and from the relief office.[20]

If the family makes it through this stage Bakke finds that it is likely to survive, and the rest of the process is one of adjustment. *The critical element of adjustment was not welfare payments, but work.*

> Having observed our families under conditions of unemployment with no public help, or with that help coming from direct [sic] and from work relief, we are convinced that after the exhaustion of self-produced resources, work relief is the only type of assistance which can restore the strained bonds of family relationship in a way which promises the continued functioning of that family in meeting the responsibilities imposed upon it by our culture.[21]

The fundamental, overwhelming fact is that *Negro unemployment*, with the exception of a few years during World War II and the Korean War, *has continued at disaster levels for 35 years.* [. . .]

---

19. Edward Wight Bakke, *Citizens Without Work* (New Haven, Yale University Press, 1940).

20. Ibid., p. 212.

21. Ibid., p. 224.

The impact of poverty on Negro family structure is no less obvious, although again it may not be widely acknowledged. There would seem to be an American tradition, agrarian in its origins but reinforced by attitudes of urban immigrant groups, to the effect that family morality and stability decline as income and social position rise. Over the years this may have provided some consolation to the poor, but there is little evidence that it is true. On the contrary, higher family incomes are unmistakably associated with greater family stability—which comes first may be a matter for conjecture, but the conjunction of the two characteristics is unmistakable.

The Negro family is no exception. In the District of Columbia, for example, census tracts with median incomes over $8,000 had an illegitimacy rate one-third that of tracts in the category under $4,000. [. . .]

Chapter IV
The Tangle of Pathology

That the Negro American has survived at all is extraordinary—a lesser people might simply have died out, as indeed others have. That the Negro community has not only survived, but in this political generation has entered national affairs as a moderate, humane, and constructive national force is the highest testament to the healing powers of the democratic ideal and the creative vitality of the Negro people.

But it may not be supposed that the Negro American community has not paid a fearful price for the incredible mistreatment to which it has been subjected over the past three centuries.

In essence, the Negro community has been forced into a matriarchal structure which, because it is to out of line with the rest of the American society, seriously retards the progress of the group as a whole, and imposes a crushing burden on the Negro male and, in consequence, on a great many Negro women as well.

There is, presumably, no special reason why a society in which males are dominant in family relationships is to be preferred to a matriarchal arrangement. However, it is clearly a disadvantage for a minority group to be operating on one principle, while the great majority of the population, and the one with the most advantages to begin with, is operating on another. This is the present situation of the Negro. Ours is a society which presumes male leadership in private and public affairs. The arrangements of society facilitate such leadership and reward it. A subculture, such as that of the Negro American, in which this is not the pattern, is placed at a distinct disadvantage.

Here an earlier word of caution should be repeated. There is much evidence that a considerable number of Negro families have managed to break out of the tangle of pathology and to establish themselves as stable, effective units, living according to patterns of American society in general. E. Franklin Frazier has suggested that the middle-class Negro American family is, if anything, more patriarchal and protective of its children than the general run of such families.[22] Given equal opportunities, the children of these families will perform as well or better than their white peers. They need no help from anyone, and ask none.

While this phenomenon is not easily measured, one index is that middle-class Negroes have even fewer children than middle-class whites, indicating a desire to conserve the advances they have made and to insure that their children do as well or better. Negro women who marry early to uneducated laborers have more children than white women in the same situation; Negro women who marry at the common age for the middle class to educated men doing technical or professional work have only four-fifths as many children as their white counterparts.

It might be estimated that as much as half of the Negro community falls into the middle class. However, the remaining half is in desperate and deteriorating circumstances. Moreover, because of housing segregation it is immensely difficult for the stable half to escape from the cultural influences of the unstable one. The children of middle-class Negroes often as not must grow up in, or next to the slums, an experience almost unknown to white middle-class children. They are therefore constantly exposed to the pathology of the disturbed group and constantly in danger of being drawn into it. It is for this reason that the propositions put forth in this study may be thought of as having a more or less general application.

In a word, most Negro youth are in *danger* of being caught up in the tangle of pathology that affects their world, and probably a majority are so entrapped. Many of those who escape do so for one generation only: as things now are, their children may have to run the gauntlet all over again. That is not the least vicious aspect of the world that white America has made for the Negro.

Obviously, not every instance of social pathology afflicting the Negro community can be traced to the weakness of family structure. If, for example, organized crime in the Negro community were not largely controlled by whites, there would be more capital accumulation among Negroes, and therefore probably more Negro business enterprises. If it were not for the hostility and fear many whites exhibit toward Negroes, they in turn would be less afflicted by hostility and fear and so on. There is no one Negro community. There is no one Negro problem. There is no one solution. Nonetheless, at the center of the tangle of pathology is the weakness of the family structure. Once or twice removed, it will be found to be the principal source of most of the aberrant, inadequate, or antisocial behavior that did not establish, but now serves to perpetuate the cycle of poverty and deprivation.

It was by destroying the Negro family under slavery that white America broke the will of the Negro people. Although that will has reasserted itself in our time, it is a resurgence doomed to frustration unless the viability of the Negro family is restored.

Matriarchy

A fundamental fact of Negro American family life is the often reversed roles of husband and wife.

Robert O. Blood, Jr. and Donald M. Wolfe, in a study of Detroit families, note that "Negro husbands have unusually low power,"[23] and while this is characteristic of all low income families, the pattern pervades the Negro social structure: "the cumulative result of discrimination in jobs . . . , the segregated housing, and the poor schooling of Negro men."[24] In

---

22. E. Franklin Frazier, *Black Bourgeoisie* (New York, Collier Books, 1962).

23. Robert O. Blood, Jr. and Donald M. Wolfe, *Husbands and Wives: The Dynamics of Married Living* (Illinois, The Free Press of Glencoe, 1960), p. 34.

24. Ibid., p. 35.

44 percent of the Negro families studied, the wife was dominant, as against 20 percent of white wives. "Whereas the majority of white families are equalitarian, the largest percentage of Negro families are dominated by the wife."[25]

The matriarchal pattern of so many Negro families reinforces itself over the generations. This process begins with education. Although the gap appears to be closing at the moment, for a long while, Negro females were better educated than Negro males, and this remains true today for the Negro population as a whole.

The difference in educational attainment between nonwhite men and women in the labor force is even greater; men lag 1.1 years behind women.

The disparity in educational attainment of male and female youth 16 to 21 who were out of school in February 1963, is striking. Among the nonwhite males, 66.3 percent were not high school graduates, compared with 55.0 percent of the females. A similar difference existed at the college level, with 4.5 percent of the males having completed 1 to 3 years of college compared with 7.3 percent of the females. [. . .]

Inevitably, these disparities have carried over to the area of employment and income. [. . .]

[. . .] [I]t is clear that Negro females have established a strong position for themselves in white collar and professional employment, precisely the areas of the economy which are growing most rapidly, and to which the highest prestige is accorded.

The President's Committee on Equal Employment Opportunity, making a preliminary report on employment in 1964 of over 16,000 companies with nearly 5 million employees, revealed this pattern with dramatic emphasis.

> In this work force, Negro males outnumber Negro females by a ratio of 4 to 1. Yet Negro males represent only 1.2 percent of all males in white collar occupations, while Negro females represent 3.1 percent of the total female white collar work force. Negro males represent 1.1 percent of all male professionals, whereas Negro females represent roughly 6 percent of all female professionals. Again, in technician occupations,

Negro males represent 2.1 percent of all male technicians while Negro females represent roughly 10 percent of all female technicians. It would appear therefore that there are proportionately 4 times as many Negro females in significant white collar jobs than Negro males.

Although it is evident that office and clerical jobs account for approximately 50 percent of all Negro female white collar workers, it is significant that 6 out of every 100 Negro females are in professional jobs. This is substantially similar to the rate of all females in such jobs. Approximately 7 out of every 100 Negro females are in technician jobs. This exceeds the proportion of all females in technician jobs—approximately 5 out of every 100.

Negro females in skilled jobs are almost the same as that of all females in such jobs. Nine out of every 100 Negro males are in skilled occupations while 21 out of 100 of all males are in such jobs.[26] [. . .]

The Failure of Youth

[. . .] White children without fathers at least perceive all about them the pattern of men working.

Negro children without fathers flounder—and fail.

Not always, to be sure. The Negro community produces its share, very possibly more than its share, of young people who have the something extra that carries them over the worst obstacles. But such persons are always a minority. The common run of young people in a group facing serious obstacles to success do not succeed.

A prime index of the disadvantage of Negro youth in the United States is their consistently poor performance on the mental tests that are a standard means of measuring ability and performance in the present generation.

There is absolutely no question of any genetic differential: Intelligence potential is distributed among Negro infants in the same proportion as among Icelanders or Chinese or any other group. American society, however, impairs the Negro potential. The

---

25. Ibid.

26. Based on a preliminary draft of a report by the President's Committee on Equal Employment Opportunity.

statement of the HARYOU report that "there is no basic disagreement over the fact that central Harlem students are performing poorly in school"[27] may be taken as true of Negro slum children throughout the United States.

Eighth grade children in central Harlem have a median IQ of 87.7, which means that perhaps a third of the children are scoring at levels perilously near to those of retardation. IQ *declines* in the first decade of life, rising only slightly thereafter.

The effect of broken families on the performance of Negro youth has not been extensively measured, but studies that have been made show an unmistakable influence. [. . .]

Alienation

The term "alienation" may by now have been used in too many ways to retain a clear meaning, but it will serve to sum up the equally numerous ways in which large numbers of Negro youth appear to be withdrawing from American society.

One startling way in which this occurs is that the men are just not there when the Census enumerator comes around.

According to Bureau of Census population estimates for 1963, there are only 87 nonwhite males for every 100 females in the 30-to-34-year age group. The ratio does not exceed 90 to 100 throughout the 25-to-44-year age bracket. In the urban Northeast, there are only 76 males per 100 females 20-to-24-years of age, and males as a percent of females are below 90 percent throughout all ages after 14.

There are not really fewer men than women in the 20-to-40 age bracket. What obviously in involved is an error in counting: the surveyors simply do not find the Negro man. Donald J. Bogue and his associates, who have studied the Federal count of the Negro man, place the error as high as 19.8 percent at age 28; a typical error of around 15 percent is estimated from age 19 through 43.[28] Preliminary research in the

Bureau of the Census on the 1960 enumeration has resulted in similar conclusions, although not necessarily the same estimates of the extent of the error. The Negro male *can* be found at age 17 and 18. On the basis of birth records and mortality records, the conclusion must be that he is there at age 19 as well.

When the enumerators do find him, his answers to the standard questions asked in the monthly unemployment survey often result in counting him as "not in the labor force." In other words, Negro male unemployment may in truth be somewhat greater than reported. [. . .]

Understated or not, the official unemployment rates for Negroes are almost unbelievable.

The unemployment statistics for Negro teenagers — 29 percent in January 1965 — reflect lack of training and opportunity in the greatest measure, but it may not be doubted that they also reflect a certain failure of nerve.

"Are you looking for a job?" Secretary of Labor Wirtz asked a young man on a Harlem street corner. "Why?" was the reply. [. . .]

Narcotic addiction is a characteristic form of withdrawal. In 1963, Negroes made up 54 percent of the addict population of the United States. Although the Federal Bureau of Narcotics reports a decline in the Negro proportion of new addicts, HARYOU reports the addiction rate in central Harlem rose from 22.1 per 10,000 in 1955 to 40.4 in 1961.[29]

There is a larger fact about the alienation of Negro youth than the tangle of pathology described by these statistics. It is a fact particularly difficult to grasp by white persons who have in recent years shown increasing awareness of Negro problems.

The present generation of Negro youth growing up in the urban ghettos has probably less personal contact with the white world than any generation in the history of the Negro American.[30]

Until World War II it could be said that in general the Negro and white worlds live, if not together, at least side by side. Certainly they did, and do, in the South.

27. *Youth in the Ghetto* (Harlem Youth Opportunities Unlimited, Inc., New York, 1964), p. 195.

28. Donald J. Bogue, Bhaskar D. Misra, and D. P. Dandekar, "A New Estimate of the Negro Population and

Negro Vital Rates in the United States, 1930–1960," *Demography*, Vol. 1, No. 1, 1964, p. 350.

29. *Youth in the Ghetto*, p. 144.

30. Nathan Glazer and Daniel Patrick Moynihan, op. cit.

Since World War II, however, the two worlds have drawn physically apart. The symbol of this development was the construction in the 1940s and 1950s of the vast white, middle- and lower-middle class suburbs around all the Nation's cities. Increasingly the inner cities have been left to Negroes—who now share almost no community life with whites.

In turn, because of this new housing pattern—most of which has been financially assisted by the Federal government—it is probable that the American school system has become *more*, rather than less segregated in the past two decades.

School integration has not occurred in the South, where a decade after *Brown v. Board of Education* only 1 Negro in 9 is attending school with white children.

And in the North, despite strenuous official efforts, neighborhoods and therefore schools are becoming more and more of one class and one color.

In New York City, in the school year 1957–58 there were 64 schools that were 90 percent of [*sic*] more Negro or Puerto Rican. Six years later there were 134 such schools.

Along with the diminution of white middle-class contacts for a large percentage of Negroes, observers report that the Negro churches have all but lost contact with men in the Northern cities as well. This may be a normal condition of urban life, but it is probably a changed condition for the Negro American and cannot be a socially desirable development.

The only religious movement that appears to have enlisted a considerable number of lower class Negro males in Northern cities of late is that of the Black Muslims: a movement based on total rejection of white society, even though it emulates whites more.

In a word: the tangle of pathology is tightening.

Chapter V
The Case for National Action

[. . .] What then is that problem? We feel the answer is clear enough. Three centuries of injustice have brought about deep-seated structural distortions in the life of the Negro American. At this point, the present tangle of pathology is capable of perpetuating itself without assistance from the white world. The cycle can be broken only if these distortions are set right.

In a word, a national effort towards the problems of Negro Americans must be directed towards the question of family structure. The object should be to strengthen the Negro family so as to enable it to raise and support its members as do other families. After that, how this group of Americans chooses to run its affairs, take advantage of its opportunities, or fail to do so, is none of the nation's business.

The fundamental importance and urgency of restoring the Negro American Family structure has been evident for some time. E. Franklin Frazier put it most succinctly in 1950:

> As the result of family disorganization a large proportion of Negro children and youth have not undergone the socialization which only the family can provide. The disorganized families have failed to provide for their emotional needs and have not provided the discipline and habits which are necessary for personality development. Because the disorganized family has failed in its function as a socializing agency, it has handicapped the children in their relations to the institutions in the community. Moreover, family disorganization has been partially responsible for a large amount of juvenile delinquency and adult crime among Negroes. Since the widespread family disorganization among Negroes has resulted from the failure of the father to play the role in family life required by American society, the mitigation of this problem must await those changes in the Negro and American society which will enable the Negro father to play the role required of him.[31]

Nothing was done in response to Frazier's argument. Matters were left to take care of themselves, and as matters will, grew worse not better. The problem is now more serious, the obstacles greater. There is, however, a profound change for the better in one respect. The President has committed the nation to an all out effort to eliminate poverty wherever it exists, among whites or Negroes, and a militant,

---

31. E. Franklin Frazier, "Problems and Needs of Negro Children and Youth Resulting from Family Disorganization," *Journal of Negro Education*, Summer 1960, pp. 276–277.

organized, and responsible Negro movement exists to join in that effort.

Such a national effort could be stated thus:

The policy of the United States is to bring the Negro American to full and equal sharing in the *responsibilities and rewards of citizenship. To this end, the programs of the Federal government bearing on this objective shall be designed to have the effect, directly or indirectly, of enhancing the stability and resources of the Negro American family.*

STOKELY CARMICHAEL

What We Want (1966)

One of the tragedies of the struggle against racism is that up to now there has been no national organization that could speak to the growing militancy of young black people in the urban ghetto. There has been only a civil rights movement, whose tone of voice was adapted to an audience of liberal whites. It served as a sort of buffer zone between them and angry young blacks. None of its so-called leaders could go into a rioting community and be listened to. In a sense, I blame ourselves—together with the mass media—for what has happened in Watts, Harlem, Chicago, Cleveland, and Omaha. Each time the people in those cities saw Martin Luther King get slapped, they became angry; when they saw four little black girls bombed to death, they were angrier; and when nothing happened, they were steaming. We had nothing to offer that they could see, except to go out and be beaten again. We helped to build their frustration.

For too many years, black Americans marched and had their heads broken and got shot. They were saying to the country, "Look, you guys are supposed to be nice guys and we are only going to do what we are supposed to do—why do you beat us up, why don't you give us what we ask, why don't you straighten yourself out?" After years of this, we are at almost the same point—because we demonstrated from a position of weakness. We cannot be expected any longer to march and have our heads broken in order to say to whites: Come on, you're nice guys. For you are not nice guys. We have found you out.

An organization which claims to speak for the needs of a community—as does the Student Nonviolent Coordinating Committee—must speak in the tone of that community, not as somebody else's buffer zone. This is the significance of Black Power as a slogan. For once, black people are going to use the words they want to use—not just the words whites want to hear. And they will do this no matter how often the press tries to stop the use of the slogan by equating it with racism or separatism.

An organization which claims to be working for the needs of a community—as SNCC does—must work to provide that community with a position of strength from which to make its voice heard. This is the significance of Black Power beyond the slogan.

Black Power can be clearly defined for those who do not attach the fears of white America to their questions about it. We should begin with the basic fact that black Americans have two problems: they are poor and they are black. All other problems arise from this two-sided reality: lack of education, the so-called apathy of black men. Any program to end racism must address itself to that double reality.

Almost from its beginning, SNCC sought to address itself to both conditions with a program aimed at winning political power for impoverished Southern blacks. We had to begin with politics because black Americans are a propertyless people in a country where property is valued above all. We had to work for power, because this country does not function by morality, love, and nonviolence, but by power. Thus we determined to win political power, with the idea of moving on from there into activity that would have economic effects. With power, the masses could *make or participate in making* the decisions which govern their destinies, and thus create basic change in their day-to-day lives.

But if political power seemed to be the key to self-determination, it was also obvious that the key had been thrown down a deep well many years earlier. Disenfranchisement, maintained by racist terror, made it impossible to talk about organizing for political power in 1960. The right to vote had to be won, and SNCC workers devoted their energies to this from 1961 to 1965. They set up voter registration drives in the Deep South. They created pressure for the vote by holding mock elections in Mississippi in 1963 and by helping to establish the Mississippi Freedom Democratic Party (MFDP) in 1964. That struggle was eased, though not won, with the passage of the 1965 Voting Rights Act. SNCC workers could then address themselves to the question: Who can we vote for, to have our needs met—how do we make our vote meaningful?

SNCC had already gone to Atlantic City for recognition of the Mississippi Freedom Democratic Party by the Democratic convention and been rejected; it had gone with the MFDP to Washington for recognition by Congress and been rejected. In Arkansas, SNCC helped thirty Negroes to run for school board elections; all but one were defeated, and there was evidence of fraud and intimidation sufficient to cause their defeat. In Atlanta, Julian Bond ran for the state legislature and was elected—twice—and unseated—twice. In several states, black farmers ran in elections for agricultural committees which make crucial decisions concerning land use, loans, etc. Although they won places on a number of committees, they never gained the majorities needed to control them.

All of the efforts were attempts to win Black Power. Then, in Alabama, the opportunity came to see how blacks could be organized on an independent party basis. An unusual Alabama law provides that any group of citizens can nominate candidates for county office, and if they win 20 per cent of the vote, may be recognized as a county political party. The same then applies on a state level. SNCC went to organize in several counties, such as Lowndes,

where black people—who form 80 per cent of the population and have an average annual income of $943—felt they could accomplish nothing within the framework of the Alabama Democratic Party because of its racism and because the qualifying fee for the 1966 elections was raised from $50 to $500 in order to prevent most Negroes from becoming candidates. On May 3, 1966, five new county "freedom organizations" convened and nominated candidates for the offices of sheriff, tax assessor, members of the school boards.[1] Their ballot symbol was the black panther: a bold, beautiful animal, representing the strength and dignity of black demands today. A man needs a black panther on his side when he and his family must endure—as hundreds of Alabamans have endured—loss of job, eviction, starvation, and sometimes death for political activity. He may also need a gun, and SNCC reaffirms the right of black men everywhere to defend themselves when threatened or attacked. As for initiating the use of violence, we hope that such programs as ours will make that unnecessary; but it is not for us to tell black communities whether they can or cannot use any particular form of action to resolve their problems. Responsibility for the use of violence by black men, whether in self-defense or initiated by them, lies with the white community.

This is the specific historical experience from which SNCC's call for Black Power emerged on the Mississippi march in July 1966. But the concept of Black Power is not a recent or isolated phenomenon: it has grown out of the ferment of agitation and activity by different people and organizations in many black communities over the years. Our last year of work in Alabama added a new concrete possibility. In Lowndes County, for example, Black Power will mean that if a Negro is elected sheriff, he can end police brutality. If a black man is elected tax assessor, he can collect and channel funds for the building of better roads and schools serving black people—thus advancing the move from political power into the

---

1.   The Lowndes County Freedom Organization slate lost that election by a narrow margin amid much violence on election day. They received enough votes, however, to qualify as an official party in Alabama, and are now called the Lowndes County Freedom Party.

economic arena. In such areas as Lowndes, where black men have a majority, they will attempt to use it to exercise control. This is what they seek: control. Where Negroes lack a majority, Black Power means proper representation and sharing of control. It means the creation of power bases from which black people can work to change statewide or nationwide patterns of oppression through pressure from strength—instead of weakness. Politically, Black Power means what it has always meant to SNCC: the coming-together of black people to elect representatives and *to force those representatives to speak to their needs.* It does not mean merely putting black faces into office. A man or woman who is black and from the slums cannot be automatically expected to speak to the needs of black people. Most of the black politicians we see around the country today are not what SNCC means by Black Power. The power must be that of a community, and emanate from there.

SNCC today is working in both North and South on programs of voter registration and independent political organizing. In some places, such as Alabama, Los Angeles, New York, Philadelphia, and New Jersey, independent organizing under the black panther symbol is in progress. The creation of a national "black panther party" must come about; it will take time to build, and it is much too early to predict its success. We have no infallible master plan and we make no claim to exclusive knowledge of how to end racism; different groups will work in their own different ways. SNCC cannot spell out the full logistics of self-determination, but it can address itself to the problem by helping black communities define their needs, realize their strength, and go into action along a variety of lines which they must choose for themselves. Without knowing all the answers, it can address itself to the basic problem of poverty, to the fact that in Lowndes County 86 white families own 90 per cent of the land. What are black people in that county going to do for jobs; where are they going to get money? There must be reallocation of land, of money.

Ultimately, the economic foundations of this country must be shaken if black people are to control their lives. The colonies of the United States—and this includes the black ghettos within its borders, North and South—must be liberated. For a century, this nation has been like an octopus of exploitation, its tentacles stretching from Mississippi and Harlem to South America, the Middle East, southern Africa, and Vietnam; the form of exploitation varies from area to area but the essential result has been the same—a powerful few have been maintained and enriched at the expense of the poor and voiceless colored masses. This pattern must be broken. As its grip loosens here and there around the world, the hopes of black Americans become more realistic. For racism to die, a totally different America must be born.

This is what the white society does not wish to face; this is why that society prefers to talk about integration. But integration speaks not at all to the problem of poverty—only to the problem of blackness. Integration today means the man who "makes it," leaving his black brothers behind in the ghetto. It has no relevance to the Harlem wino or to the cotton-picker making three dollars a day.

Integration, moreover, speaks to the problem of blackness in a despicable way. As a goal, it has been based on complete acceptance of the fact that in order to have a decent house or education, blacks must move into a white neighborhood or send their children to a white school. This reinforces, among both black and white, the idea that "white" is automatically better and "black" is by definition inferior. This is why integration is a subterfuge for the maintenance of white supremacy. It allows the nation to focus on a handful of Southern children who get into white schools, at great price, and to ignore the 94 per cent who are left behind in unimproved all-black schools. Such situations will not change until black people have power—to control their own school boards, in this case. Then Negroes become equal in a way that means something, and integration ceases to be a one-way street. Then integration doesn't mean draining skills and energies from the ghetto into white neighborhoods; then it can mean white people moving from Beverly Hills into Watts, white people joining the Lowndes County Freedom Organization. Then integration becomes relevant.

In April 1966, before the furor over Black Power, Christopher Jencks wrote in a *New Republic* article on white Mississippi's manipulation of the anti-poverty program:

The war on poverty has been predicated on the notion that there is such a thing as *a community* which can be defined geographically and mobilized for a collective effort to help the poor. This theory has no relationship to reality in the Deep South. In every Mississippi county there are *two* communities. Despite all the pious platitudes of the moderates on both sides, these two communities habitually see their interests in terms of conflict rather than cooperation. Only when the Negro community can muster enough political, economic and professional strength to compete on somewhat equal terms, will Negroes believe in the possibility of true cooperation and whites accept its necessity. En route to integration, the Negro community needs to develop greater independence—a chance to run its own affairs and not cave in whenever "the man" barks . . . Or so it seems to me, and to most of the knowledgeable people with whom I talked in Mississippi. To OEO, this judgment may sound like black nationalism . . .

Mr. Jencks, a white reporter, perceived the reason why America's anti-poverty program has been a sick farce in both North and South. In the South, it is clearly racism which prevents the poor from running their own programs; in the North, it more often seems to be politicking and bureaucracy. But the results are not so different: in the North, non-whites make up 42 per cent of all families in metropolitan "poverty areas" and only 6 per cent of families in areas classified as not poor. SNCC has been working with local residents in Arkansas, Alabama, and Mississippi to achieve control by the poor of the program and its funds; it has also been working with groups in the North, and the struggle is no less difficult. Behind it all is a federal government which cares far more about winning the war on the Vietnamese than the war on poverty; which has put the poverty program in the hands of self-serving politicians and bureaucrats rather than the poor themselves; which is unwilling to curb the misuse of white power but quick to condemn Black Power.

To most whites, Black Power seems to mean that the Mau Mau are coming to the suburbs at night. The Mau Mau are coming, and whites must stop them. Articles appear about plots to "get Whitey," creating an atmosphere in which "law and order must be maintained." Once again, responsibility is shifted from the oppressor to the oppressed. Other whites chide, "Don't forget—you're only 10 per cent of the population; if you get too smart, we'll wipe you out." If they are liberals, they complain, "What about me—don't you want my help any more?" These are people supposedly concerned about black Americans, but today they think first of themselves, of their feelings of rejection. Or they admonish, "You can't get anywhere without coalitions," when there is in fact no group at present with whom to form a coalition in which blacks will not be absorbed and betrayed. Or they accuse us of "polarizing the races" by our calls for black unity, when the true responsibility for polarization lies with whites who will not accept their responsibility as the majority power for making the democratic process work.

White America will not face the problem of color, the reality of it. The well-intended say: "We're all human, everybody is really decent, we must forget color." But color cannot be "forgotten" until its weight is recognized and dealt with. White America will not acknowledge that the ways in which this country sees itself are contradicted by being black— and always have been. Whereas most of the people who settled this country came here for freedom or for economic opportunity, blacks were brought here to be slaves. When the Lowndes County Freedom Organization chose the black panther as its symbol, it was christened by the press "the Black Panther Party"—but the Alabama Democratic Party, whose symbol is a rooster, has never been called the White Cock Party. No one ever talked about "white power" because power in this country *is* white. All this adds up to more than merely identifying a group phenomenon by some catchy name or adjective. The furor over that black panther reveals the problems that white America has with color and sex; the furor over Black Power reveals how deep racism runs and the great fear which is attached to it.

Whites will not see that I, for example, as a person oppressed because of my blackness, have common cause with other blacks who are oppressed because of blackness. This is not to say that there are no white people who see things as I do, but that it is black people I must speak to first. It must be the oppressed to whom SNCC addresses itself primarily, not to friends from the oppressing group.

From birth, black people are told a set of lies about themselves. We are told that we are lazy—yet I drive through the Delta area of Mississippi and watch black people picking cotton in the hot sun for fourteen hours. We are told, "If you work hard, you'll succeed"—but if that were true, black people would own this country. We are oppressed because we are black—not because we are ignorant, not because we are lazy, not because we're stupid (and got good rhythm), but because we're black.

I remember that when I was a boy I used to go to see Tarzan movies on Saturday. White Tarzan used to beat up the black natives. I would sit there yelling, "Kill the beasts, kill the savages, kill 'em!" I was saying: Kill *me*. It was as if a Jewish boy watched Nazis taking Jews off to concentration camps and cheered them on. Today, I want the chief to beat hell out of Tarzan and send him back to Europe. But it takes time to become free of the lies and their shaming effect on black minds. It takes time to reject the most important lie: that black people inherently can't do the same things white people can do, unless white people help them.

The need for psychological equality is the reason why SNCC today believes that blacks must organize in the black community. Only black people can convey the revolutionary idea that black people are able to do things themselves. Only they can help create in the community an aroused and continuing black consciousness that will provide the basis for political strength. In the past, white allies have furthered white supremacy without the whites involved realizing it—or wanting it, I think. Black people must do things for themselves; they must get poverty money they will control and spend themselves, they must conduct tutorial programs themselves so that black children can identify with black people. This is one reason Africa has such importance: the reality of black men ruling their own nations gives blacks elsewhere a sense of possibility, of power, which they do not now have.

This does not mean we don't welcome help, or friends. But we want the right to decide whether anyone is, in fact, our friend. In the past, black Americans have been almost the only people whom everybody and his momma could jump up and call their friends. We have been tokens, symbols, objects—as I was in high school to many young whites, who liked having "a Negro friend." We want to decide who is our friend, and we will not accept someone who comes to us and says: "If you do X, Y, and Z, then I'll help you." We will not be told whom we should choose as allies. We will not be isolated from any group or nation except by our own choice. We cannot have the oppressors telling the oppressed how to rid themselves of the oppressor.

I have said that most liberal whites react to Black Power with the question, "What about me?" rather than saying: "Tell me what you want me to do and I'll see if I can do it." There are answers to the right question. One of the most disturbing things about almost all white supporters of the movement has been that they are afraid to go into their own communities—which is where the racism exists—and work to get rid of it. They want to run from Berkeley to tell us what to do in Mississippi; let them look instead at Berkeley. They admonish blacks to be nonviolent; let them preach nonviolence in the white community. They come to teach me Negro history; let them go to the suburbs and open up freedom schools for whites. Let them work to stop America's racist foreign policy; let them press this government to cease supporting the economy of South Africa.

There is a vital job to be done among poor whites. We hope to see, eventually, a coalition between poor blacks and poor whites. That is the only coalition which seems acceptable to us, and we see such a coalition as the major internal instrument of change in American society. SNCC has tried several times to organize poor whites; we are trying again now, with an initial training program in Tennessee. It is purely academic today to talk about bringing poor blacks and whites together, but the job of creating a poor-white power bloc must be attempted. The main responsibility for it falls upon whites. Black and white can work together in the white community where possible; it is not possible, however, to go into a poor Southern town and talk about integration. Poor whites everywhere are becoming more hostile—not less—partly because they see the nation's attention focused on black poverty and nobody coming to them. Too many young middle-class Americans, like some sort of Pepsi generation, have wanted to come alive through the black community; they've wanted to be where the action is—and the action has been in the black community.

Black people do not want to "take over" this country. They don't want to "get Whitey"; they just want to get him off their backs, as the saying goes. It was, for example, the exploitation by Jewish landlords and merchants which first created black resentment toward Jews—not Judaism. The white man is irrelevant to blacks, except as an oppressive force. Blacks want to be in his place, yes, but not in order to terrorize and lynch and starve him. They want to be in his place because that is where a decent life can be had.

But our vision is not merely of a society in which all black men have enough to buy the good things of life. When we urge that black money go into black pockets, we mean the communal pocket. We want to see money go back into the community and used to benefit it. We want to see the cooperative concept applied in business and banking. We want to see black ghetto residents demand that an exploiting landlord or storekeeper sell them, at minimal cost, a building or a shop that they will own and improve cooperatively; they can back their demand with a rent strike, or a boycott, and a community so unified behind them that no one else will move into the building or buy at the store. The society we seek to build among black people, then, is not a capitalist one. It is a society in which the spirit of community and humanistic love prevail. The word "love" is suspect; black expectations of what it might produce have been betrayed too often. But those were expectations of a response from the white community, which failed us. The love we seek to encourage is within the black community, the only American community where men call each other "brother" when they meet. We can build a community of love only where we have the ability and power to do so: among blacks.

As for white America, perhaps it can stop crying out against "black supremacy," "black nationalism," "racism in reverse," and begin facing reality. The reality is that this nation is racist; that racism is not primarily a problem of "human relations" but of an exploitation maintained—either actively or through silence—by the society as a whole. Can whites, particularly liberal whites, condemn themselves? Can they stop blaming us, and blame their own system? Are they capable of the shame which might become a revolutionary emotion?

We have found that they usually cannot condemn themselves, and so we have done it. But the rebuilding of this society, if at all possible, is basically the responsibility of whites—not blacks. We won't fight to save the present society, in Vietnam or anywhere else. We are just going to work, in the way *we* see fit, and on goals *we* define, not for civil rights but for all our human rights.

ROY WILKINS

Address before the NAACP Convention (1966)

All about us are alarums and confusions as well as great and challenging developments. Differences of opinion are sharper. For the first time since several organizations began to function where only two had functioned before, there emerges what seems to be a difference in goals.

Heretofore there were some differences in methods and emphasis but none in ultimate goals. The end was always to be the inclusion of the American Negro, without racial discrimination, as a full-fledged equal in all phases of American citizenship.

There has now emerged, first a strident and threatening challenge to a strategy widely employed by civil rights groups, namely non-violence. One organization which has been meeting in Baltimore has passed a resolution declaring for defense of themselves by Negro citizens if they are attacked.

This position is not new as far as the NAACP is concerned. Historically, our Association has defended in court those persons who have defended themselves and their homes with firearms.

But neither have we couched a policy of manly

resistance in such a way that our members and supporters felt compelled to maintain themselves in an armed state, ready to retaliate instantly and in kind whenever attacked.

We venture the observation that such a published posture could serve to stir counterplanning, counteraction and possible conflict. If carried out literally as instant retaliation, in cases adjudged by aggrieved persons to have been grossly unjust, this policy could produce—in extreme situations—lynchings, or, in better-sounding phraseology, private vigilante vengeance.

Moreover, in attempting to substitute for derelict enforcement machinery, the policy entails the risk of a broader, more indiscriminate crack-down by law officers under the ready-made excuse of restoring law and order.

It seems reasonable to assume that proclaimed protective violence is as likely to encourage counterviolence as it is to discourage violent persecution.

But the more serious division in the civil rights movement is the one posed by a word formulation that implies clearly a difference in goals.

No matter how endlessly they try to explain it, the term "black power" means anti-white power. In a racially pluralistic society, the concept, the formation and the exercise of an ethnically tagged power means opposition to other ethnic powers, just as the term "white supremacy" means subjection of all non-white peoples. In the black-white relationship, it has to mean that every other ethnic power is the rival and the antagonist of "black power." It has to mean "going it alone." It has to mean separatism.

Now, separatism, whether on the rarefied debate level of "black power" or on the wishful level of a secessionist Freedom City in Watts, offers a disadvantaged minority little except to shrivel and die.

The only possible dividend of "black power" is embodied in its offer to millions of frustrated and deprived and persecuted black people of a solace, a tremendous psychological lift, quite apart from its political and economic implications.

Ideologically it dictates "up with black and down with white" in precisely the same manner that South Africa reverses that slogan.

It is a reverse Mississippi, a reverse Hitler, a reverse Ku Klux Klan.

If these were evil in our judgment, what virtue can we claim for black over white? If, as some proponents claim, this concept instills pride of race, cannot this pride be taught without preaching hatred or supremacy based on race?

Though it be clarified and clarified again, "black power" in the quick, uncritical and highly emotional adoption it has received from segments of a beleaguered people can mean in the end only black death. Even if, through some miracle, it should be enthroned briefly, the human spirit, which knows no color or geography or time, would die a little, leaving for wiser and stronger and more compassionate men the painful beating back to the upper trail.

We of the NAACP will have none of this. We have fought it too long. It is the ranging of race against race on the irrelevant basis of skin color. It is the father of hatred and the mother of violence.

It is the wicked fanaticism which has swelled our tears, broken our bodies, squeezed our hearts and taken the blood of our black and white loved ones. It shall not now poison our forward march.

We seek, therefore, as we have sought these many years, for the inclusion of Negro Americans in the nation's life, not their exclusion. This is our land, as much as it is any American's—every square foot of every city and town and village. The task of winning our share is not the easy one of disengagement and flight, but the hard one of work, of short as well as long jumps, of disappointments and of sweet success.

Caesar Chavez

Delano Statement (1968)

I have asked the Rev. James Drake to read this statement to you because my heart is so full and my body too weak to be able to say what I feel.

My warm thanks to all of you for coming today. Many of you have been here before, during the Fast. Some have sent beautiful cards and telegrams and made offerings at the Mass. All of these expressions of your love have strengthened me and I am grateful.

We should all express our thanks to Senator Kennedy for his constant work on behalf of the poor, for his personal encouragement to me, and for taking the time to break bread with us today. I do not want any of you to [be] deceived about the Fast. The strict Fast of water only which I undertook on February 15 ended after the 21st day because of the advice of our doctor, James McKnight, and other physicians. Since that time I have been taking liquids in order to prevent serious damage to my kidneys.

We are gathered here today not so much to observe the end of the Fast but because we are a family bound together in a common struggle for justice. We are a Union family celebrating our unity and the non-violent nature of our movement. Perhaps in the future we will come together at other times and places to break bread and to renew our courage and to celebrate important victories.

The Fast has had different meanings for different people. Some of you may still wonder about its meaning and importance. It was not intended as a pressure against any growers. For that reason we have suspended negotiations and arbitration proceedings and relaxed the militant picketing and boycotting of the strike during this period. I undertook this Fast because my heart was filled with grief and pain for the sufferings of farm workers. The Fast was first for me and then for all of us in this Union. It was a Fast for non-violence and a call to sacrifice.

Our struggle is not easy. Those who oppose our cause are rich and powerful and they have many allies in high places. We are poor. Our allies are few. But we have something the rich do not own. We have our own bodies and spirits and the justice of our cause as our weapons.

When we are really honest with ourselves we must admit that our lives are all that really belong to us. So, it is how we use our lives that determines what kind of men we are. It is my deepest belief that only by giving our lives do we find life. I am convinced that the truest act of courage, the strongest act of manliness is to sacrifice ourselves for others in a totally non-violent struggle for justice.

To be a man is to suffer for others. God help us to be men!

Delano Plan (1968)

PLAN for the liberation of the Farm Workers associated with the Delano Grape Strike in the State of California, seeking social justice in farm labor with those reforms that they believe necessary for their well-being as workers in the United States.

We, the undersigned, gathered in Pilgrimage to the capital of the State in Sacramento in penance for all the failings of Farm Workers as free and sovereign men, do solemnly declare before the civilized world which judges our actions, and before the nation to which we belong, the propositions we have formulated to end the injustice that oppresses us.

We are conscious of the historical significance of our Pilgrimage. It is clearly evident that our path travels through a valley well known to all Mexican farm workers. We know all of these towns of Delano, Madera, Fresno, Modesto, Stockton, and Sacramento, because along this very same road, in this very same valley, the Mexican race has sacrificed itself for the last hundred years. Our sweat and our blood have fallen on this land to make other men rich. The pilgrimage is a witness to the suffering we have seen for generations.

The penance we accept symbolizes the suffering we shall have in order to bring justice to these same towns, to this same valley. The pilgrimage we make symbolizes the long historical road we have traveled in this valley alone, and the long road we have yet to travel, with much penance, in order to bring about the revolution we need, and for which we present the propositions in the following PLAN:

1. This is the beginning of a social movement in fact and not in pronouncements. We seek our basic, God-given rights as human beings. Because we have suffered—and are not afraid to suffer in order to survive, we are ready to give up everything, even our lives, in our flight for social justice. We shall do it without violence because that is our destiny. To the ranchers, and to all those who oppose, we say, in the words of Benito Juarez, "EL RESPETO AL DERECHO AJENO ES LA PAZ."

2. We seek the support of all political groups and protection of the government, which is also our government, in our struggle. For too many years we have been treated like the lowest of the low. Our wages and working conditions have been determined from above, because irresponsible legislators who could have helped us, have supported the rancher's argument that the plight of the Farm Worker was a "special case." They saw the obvious effects of an unjust system, starvation wages, contractors, day hauls, forced migration, sickness, illiteracy, camps and subhuman living conditions, and acted as if they were irremediable causes. The farm worker has been abandoned to his own fate—without representation, without powers—subject to mercy and caprice of the rancher. We are tired of words, of betrayals, of indifference. To the politicians we say that the years are

gone when the farm worker said nothing and did nothing to help himself. From this movement shall spring leaders who shall understand us, lead us, be faithful to us, and we shall elect them to represent us. WE SHALL BE HEARD.

3. We seek, and have, the support of the Church in what we do. At the head of the pilgrimage we carry LA VIRGEN DE LA GUADALUPE because she is ours, all ours, Patroness of the Mexican people. We also carry the Sacred Cross and the Star of David because we are not sectarians, and because we ask the help and prayers of all religions. All men are brothers, sons of the same God; that is why we say to all of good will, in the words of Pope Leo XIII, "everyone's first duty is protect the workers from the greed of speculators who use human beings as instruments to provide themselves with money. It is neither just nor human to oppress men with excessive work to the point where their minds become enfeebled and their bodies worn out." GOD SHALL NOT ABANDON US.

4. We are suffering. We have suffered, and we are not afraid to suffer in order to win our cause. We have suffered unnumbered ills and crimes in the name of the Law of the Land. Our men, women, and children have suffered not only the basic brutality of stoop labor, and the most obvious injustices of the system; they have also suffered the desperation of knowing that the system caters to the greed of callous men and not to our needs. Now we will suffer for the purpose of ending the poverty, the misery, and the injustice, with the hope that our children will not be exploited as we have been. They have imposed hunger on us, and now we hunger for justice. We draw our strength from the very despair in which we have been forced to live. WE SHALL ENDURE.

5. We shall unite. We have learned the meaning of unity. We know why these are just that—united. The strength of the poor is also in union. We know that the poverty of the Mexican or Filipino worker in California is the same as that of all farm workers across the country, the Negroes and poor whites, the Puerto Ricans, Japanese, and Arabians; in short, all of the races that comprise the oppressed minorities of the United States. The majority of the people on our Pilgrimage are of Mexican decent, but the triumph of our race depends on a national association of all farm workers. The ranchers want to keep us divided in order to keep us weak. Many of us have signed

individual "work contracts" with the ranchers or contractors, contracts in which they had all power. These contracts were farces, one more cynical joke at our impotence. That is why we must get together and bargain collectively. We must use the only strength that we have, the force of our numbers. The ranchers are few; we are many. UNITED WE SHALL STAND.

6. We shall Strike. We shall pursue the REVOLUTION we have proposed. We are sons of the Mexican Revolution, a revolution of the poor seeking, bread and justice. Our revolution will not be armed, but we want the existing social order to dissolve, we want a new social order. We are poor, we are humble, and our only choices is to Strike in those ranches where we are not treated with the respect we deserve as working men, where our rights as free and sovereign men are not recognized. We do not want the paternalism of the rancher, we do not want the contractor; we do not want charity at the price of our dignity. We want to be equal with all the working men in the nation; we want just wages, better working conditions, a decent future for our children. To those who oppose us, be they ranchers, police, politicians, or speculators, we say that we are going to continue fighting until we die, or we win. WE SHALL OVERCOME. Across the San Joaquin Valley, across California, across the entire Southwest of the United States, wherever there are Mexican people, wherever there are farm workers, our movement is spreading like flames across a dry plain. Our PILGRIMAGE is the MATCH that will light our cause for all farm workers to see what is happening here, so that they may do as we have done. The time has come for the liberation of the poor farm worker.

History is on our side.

MAY THE STRIKE GO ON! VIVA LA CAUSA!

Interview with *The Observer* (1970)

OBSERVER: [. . .] *Why do you insist on non-violent means in this struggle?*

CHAVEZ: Our conviction is that human life and limb are a very special possession given by God to man and that no one has the right to take that away, in any cause, however just. We also find that violence is contagious; it is uncontrollable. If we use it, then the opposition is going to respond in kind and it is going to be escalated.

Also we are convinced that non-violence is more powerful than violence. We are convinced that non-violence supports you if you have a just and moral cause. Non-violence gives the opportunity to stay on the offensive, which is of vital importance to win any contest. Suppose we are striking and the opponent appears to be getting the best of us and we resort to violence. Then he will bring in other forces and one of two things happens: violence has to be escalated, or there is total demoralization of the workers. Non-violence works in exactly the opposite manner: when for every violent action committed against us, we respond with non-violence, we tend to attract people's support; we have a chance of attracting other people who are not involved because they are workers, but are involved because they have a conscience and because they would rather see a non-violent solution to things.

OBSERVER: *So it is a good strategy.*

CHAVEZ: Yes, but that alone is not reason enough. If you have no basis for non-violence other than a strategy, a tactic, then when it fails your only alternative is completely the reverse and that's violence. So you have to balance the strategy with a clear understanding of what you are doing. However important the struggle is and however much misery and poverty and degradation exist, we know that it cannot be more important than one human life. That's basic. Second, we operate on the theory that men who are involved and truly concerned about people are not by nature violent. If they were violent they couldn't have that love and that concern for people. That sort of man becomes violent when that deep concern he has for people is frustrated, when he's faced with overwhelming odds against what he is trying to do.

Then sometimes he feels that violence is really a short-cut or a sort of miracle to end everything and bring about a solution. We don't want to get into that trap.

OBSERVER: *What if violence is a short-cut?*

CHAVEZ: It isn't. It has never been proved in the history of mankind that it is a short-cut.

OBSERVER: *You're using a very broad perspective.*

CHAVEZ: Well, let me tell you—if I were to tell the workers: "All right, we're going to be violent; we're going to burn the sheds and we're going to dynamite the grower's homes and we're going to burn the vineyards," provided we could get away with it, the growers would sign a contract. But you see that that victory came at the expense of violence; it came at the expense of injuring. I think that once that happens it would have a tremendous impact on us. We would lose our perspective and we would lose the regard we have for human beings—and then the struggle would become a mechanical thing.

OBSERVER: *If you lose a sense of justice in your cause, you lose a lot of strength . . .*

CHAVEZ: Nothing can replace that strength. And the victory is not total. If you use violence, you have to sell part of yourself for that violence, either because of your own self-guilt or because you have to incorporate people who are extremists and violent or whatever it might be. Then you are no longer the master of your own struggle, and the important thing is that for poor people to be able to get a clean victory is something you don't often see. If we get it through violence, then the employers will just wait long enough until they can get even with you—and then the workers will respond, and then. [. . .]

OBSERVER: *So a violent resolution to a problem is never a resolution, just a cessation?*

CHAVEZ: Let me give you an example: the armed revolutions we have. What happens? Once you set up an army or militia to gain independence you have to maintain that army. You know against whom? Against your own people.

OBSERVER: *All violence is necessarily an oppression then?*

CHAVEZ: That's right. If we were to become violent and we won the strike, as an example, then what would prevent us from turning violence against opponents in the movement who wanted to displace us? Say they felt they had more leadership and they wanted to be the leaders. What would prevent us

from turning violence against them? Nothing. Because we had already experienced that violence awarded us victory. If we are concerned about human beings and if we are concerned about respecting man, then we have to be concerned about the consequences.

Another thing is that people think non-violence is really weak and non-militant. These are misconceptions that people have because they don't understand what non-violence means. Non-violence takes more guts, if I can put it bluntly, than violence. Most violent acts are accomplished by getting the opponent off guard, and it doesn't take that much character, I think, if one wants to do it. I am confronted frequently by people who say, "So-and-so tried non-violence and it didn't work." That's not really so. Non-violence is very weak in the theoretical sense; it cannot defend itself. But it is most powerful in the action situation where people are using non-violence because they want desperately to bring about some change. Non-violence in action is a very potent force and it can't be stopped. The people who are struggling have the complete say-so. No man-made law, no human ruler, no army can destroy this. There is no way it can be destroyed, except by those within the non-violent struggle. And so, if we have the capacity to endure, if we have the patience, things will change.

OBSERVER: *What do you say to the honest activist who feels that so many of the channels to change in this society are closed that he has no choice but to take up arms? I'm thinking of people like Camillo Torres in Columbia.*

CHAVEZ: There is no question that they have tremendous love for people and they want to bring about change. In the case of Torres, we see very clearly how he went from a life of priesthood to the extreme of using violence. And I'm sure he felt he had no other way of doing it. But I'm sure that if we examine the development of this man, and if we examine the reasons for which he worked, we would find that he probably was a failure as an organizer, an an organizer of masses of people. [. . .]

OBSERVER: *Then for you non-violence is a universal approach regardless of the degree of oppression?*

CHAVEZ: The greater the oppression, the more leverage you have. What I'm trying to say is violence didn't work and it's not going to work, and if it works it replaces, as in Latin America, one violent government with another mat is more violent. People are abused with violence. In Latin America, who gets killed in case of a revolution? The poor people, the workers.

Who gets nothing but crumbs when another force comes into power? Take the Mexican revolution, take any revolution—the people of the land are the ones who give their bodies, who get killed, and they really don't gain that much from it. I think it's too big a price to pay for not getting anything. They are being exploited as much by the ones who "help" them as by the others. To call men to arms with a lot of promises and to ask them to give their lives for a cause, and then not produce for them afterward is the most vicious sort of oppression. And we've seen it happen.

OBSERVER: *Has Christianity affected your philosophy of non-violence?*

CHAVEZ: Very definitely. Christianity is not the only religion, but it is the one that I am a believer in. It has taught us the message of Christ with regard to loving our neighbor and with regard to respecting one another and exhorting us to be able to forgive. Now these are very difficult things and, of course, we are not even approaching that. But we have seen very little action in a dramatic form by Christians in our world. There is a lot of good will, and they talk a lot about that—but people sacrificing themselves—very little.

Gandhi is an example. He was not a Christian but in my estimation he probably personifies a Christian more than most men. He showed us not by talking, not by what he wrote as much as by his actions, his own willingness to live by truth and by respect for mankind and accepting the sacrifices, you see non-violence exacts a very high price from one who practices it. But once you are able to meet that demand then you can do most tilings, provided you have the time. Gandhi showed how a whole nation could be liberated without an army. This is the first time in the history of the world when a huge nation, occupied for over a century, achieved independence by non-violence. It was a long struggle and it takes time.

OBSERVER: *You speak of patience and determination as a necessary part of non-violent politics. The grape workers' strike is one of the longest in American history. What keeps you going?*

CHAVEZ: I think that it is a conviction in what we are doing—that we are involved in a just cause. We know that most likely we are not going to do anything else in the rest of our life except this. We know that if we weren't doing this we wouldn't be doing anything we would like to do more than this. We know really there is nowhere else to go and although we would like to see victory come soon we are willing to wait. Non-violence calls for hard-nosed organizing, for a minimum of dramatics and a great deal of understanding of what the situation is—being able to assess the opposition, being able to win by winning small victories constantly, and by not letting yourself be locked into a position where you can't move because you're cornered.

OBSERVER: *Do you see your struggle as having historical significance?*

CHAVEZ: All successful struggles tend to set precedents, but I think more important than that, perhaps for the first time in the history of the richest nation in the world, it would give those people who work at producing food some food for themselves. [. . .] And also it would point out very concretely that this came about because of the determination of the people in the struggle, and more important because of the way the people conducted themselves through the struggle.

Betty Friedan

Our Revolution Is Unique (NOW Report) (1968)

We new feminists have begun to define ourselves— existentially—through action. We have learned that while we had much to learn from the black civil rights movement and their revolution against economic and racial oppression, our own revolution is unique: it must define its own ideology.

We can cut no corners; we are, in effect, where the black revolution was perhaps fifty years ago; but the speed with which our revolution is moving now is our unearned historical benefit from what has happened in that revolution. Yet there can be no illusion on our part that a separatist ideology copied from black power will work for us. Our tactics and strategy and, above all, our ideology must be firmly based in the historical, biological, economic, and psychological reality of our two-sexed world, which is not the same as the black reality and different also from the reality of the first feminist wave.

Thanks to the early feminists, we who have mounted this second stage of the feminist revolution have grown up with the right to vote, little as we may have used it for our own purposes. We have grown up with the right to higher education and to employment, and with some, not all, of the legal rights of equality. Insofar as we have moved on the periphery of the mainstream of society, with the skills and the knowledge to command its paychecks, even if insufficient; and to make decisions, even if not consulted beyond housework; we begin to have a self-respecting image of ourselves, as women, not just in sexual relation to men, but as full human beings in society. We are able, at least some of us, to see men, in general or in particular, without blind rancor or hostility, and to face oppression as it reveals itself in our concrete experience with politicians, bosses, priests, or husbands. We do not need to suppress our just grievances. We now have enough courage to express them. And yet we are able to conceive the possibility of full affirmation for man. Man is not the enemy, but the fellow victim of the present half-equality. As we speak, act, demonstrate, testify, and appear on television on matters such as sex discrimination in employment, public accommodations, education, divorce-marriage reform, or abortion repeal, we hear from men who feel they can be freed to greater self-fulfillment to the degree that women are released from the binds that now constrain them.

This sense of freeing men as the other half of freeing women has always been there, even in the early writings of Mary Wollstonecraft, Elizabeth Stanton, and the rest; our action-created new awareness has confirmed this. [. . .]

We do not speak for every woman in America, but we speak for the *right* of every woman in America to become all she is capable of becoming—on her own and/or in partnership with a man. And we already know that we speak not for a few, not for hundreds, not for thousands, but for millions—especially for millions in the younger generation who have tasted more equality than their elders. We know this simply from the resonance, if you will, that our actions have aroused in society. [. . .]

As an example of the new feminism in action, consider the matter of abortion law repeal. NOW was the first organization to speak on the basic rights of women on the question of abortion. We said that it is the inalienable human right of every woman to control her own reproductive process. To establish that right would require that all laws penalizing abortion be repealed, removed from the penal code; the state would not be empowered either to force or prevent a woman from having an abortion. Now many groups are working on abortion law repeal, while at the same time California and Washington, D.C., court decisions have spelled out the right of a woman to control her own reproduction.

What right has any man to say to any woman, "You must bear this child"? What right has any state to say it? The child-bearing decision is a woman's right and not a technical question needing the sanction of the state, nor should the state control access to birth control devices.

This question can only really be confronted in terms of the basic personhood and dignity of woman, which is violated forever if she does not have the right to control her own reproductive process. And the heart of this idea goes far beyond abortion and birth control.

Women, almost too visible as sex objects in this country today, are at the same time invisible people. As the Negro was the invisible man, so women are the invisible people in America today. To be taken seriously as people, women have to share in the decisions of government, of politics, of the church—not just to cook the church supper, but to preach the sermon; not just to look up the zip codes and address the envelopes, but to make the political decisions; not just to do the housework of industry, but to make some of the executive decisions. Women, above all, want to say what their own lives are going to be, what their own personalities are going to be, not permitting male experts to define what is "feminine" or isn't or should be.

The essence of the denigration of women is their definition as sex objects. And to confront our inequality, we must confront our own self-denigration and our denigration by society in these terms. [. . .]

Perhaps the least understood fact of American political life is the enormous buried violence of women in this country today. Like all oppressed people, women have been taking their violence out on their own bodies, in all the maladies with which they plague the doctors' offices and the psychoanalysts. They have been taking out their violence inadvertently and in subtle and in insidious ways on their children and on their husbands. And sometimes, they are not so subtle, for the battered child syndrome that we are hearing more and more about in our hospitals is almost always to be found in the instance of unwanted children, and women are doing the battering, as much or more than men.

Man, we have said, is not the enemy. Men will only be truly liberated, to love women and to be fully themselves, when women are liberated to be full people. Until that happens, men are going to bear the burden and the guilt of the destiny they have forced upon women, the suppressed resentment of that passive stage—the sterility of love, when love is not between two fully active, fully participant, fully joyous people, but has in it the element of

exploitation. And men will also not be fully free to be all they can be as long as they must live up to an image of masculinity that denies to a man all the tenderness and sensitivity that might be considered feminine. Men have in them enormous capacities that they have to repress and fear in themselves, in living up to this obsolete and brutal man-eating, lion-killing, Ernest Hemingway image of masculinity—the image of all-powerful masculine superiority. All the burdens and responsibilities that men are supposed to shoulder alone, make them, I think, resent women's pedestal, while the burden to women is enforced passivity.

So the real sexual revolution is not the cheap headlines in the papers—at what age boys and girls go to bed with each other and whether they do it with or without the benefit of marriage. That's the least of it. The real sexual revolution is the emergence of women from passivity, from thingness, to full self-determination, to full dignity. And insofar as they can do this, men are also emerging from the stage of identification with brutality and masters to full and sensitive complete humanity.

A revolutionary theory that's adequate to the current demand of the sexual revolution must also address itself to the concrete realities of our society. We can only transcend the reality of the institutions that oppress us by confronting them in our actions now; confronting reality, we change it; we begin to create alternatives, not in abstract discussion, but here and now.

Some women who call themselves revolutionaries get into abstractions. They say, "What's really wrong is marriage altogether. What's wrong is having babies altogether; let's have them in test tubes. Man is the oppressor, and women are enslaved. We don't want jobs because who wants to be equal to men who aren't free. All jobs today are just a rat race anyway."

Now we are rationalizing in radical terms of the extremists of the women's liberation ideology. This is a rationalization for inaction, because in the end we're going to weep and go home and yell at our husbands and make life miserable for a while, but we'll eventually conclude that it's hopeless that nothing can be done.

If we are going to address ourselves to the need for changing the social institutions that will permit women to be free and equal individuals, participating actively in their society and changing that society—with men—then we must talk in terms of what is possible, and not accept what is as what must be. In other words, don't talk to me about test tubes because I am interested in leading a revolution for the foreseeable future of my society. And I have a certain sense of optimism that things can be changed. [. . .]

I don't happen to think that women and men are so completely different that it is impossible for us to see each other as human beings. I think that it is as possible for men to put themselves finally in woman's place by an act of empathy or by guilt or by awareness of human rights as it has been possible for some whites to do for blacks. But it's perhaps not much more possible than that, although there are more bonds between men and women, and really men's stake in this revolution is greater, because a woman can make a man's life hell if it isn't solved. But I think it would be as much of a mistake to expect men to hand this to women as to consider all men as the enemy, all men as oppressors. This revolution can have the support of men, but women must take the lead in fighting it as any other oppressed group has had to.

I think that it is possible in education to create and disseminate the radical ideology that is needed to influence the great change in expectations and institutions for the revolution of women. In the education of women, I think it is nonsense to keep talking about optional life styles and the freedom of choice that American women have. They do not have them, and we should face this right away. [. . .]

It is a perversion of the new feminism for some to exhort those who would join this revolution to cleanse themselves of sex and the need for love or to refuse to have children. This not only means a revolution with very few followers—but is a cop-out from the problem of moving in society for the *majority* of women, who do want love and children. To enable *all* women, not just the exceptional few, to participate in society we must confront the fact of life—as a temporary fact of most women's lives today—that women do give birth to children. But we must challenge the idea that a woman is primarily responsible

for raising children. Man and society have to be educated to accept their responsibility for that role as well. And this is first of all a challenge to education.

In Sweden I was impressed that these expectations are considered absolutely normal. The need for child-care centers is accepted as so important by all the fathers as well as the mothers of the younger generation that every major young politician has it high on his agenda. The equivalent of the Sunday editor of *New York Times* in Sweden, or a rising state senator, would each tell me how both he and his wife have part-time schedules so that they can both go on with their professions, and how this is fine but they realize it's only makeshift because what's really needed is more child-care centers. And the editor would pick up the baby and say proudly that she relates to him more than to his wife. And in the Volvo factory, even the public relations man with a crewcut says the same thing.

I couldn't believe it! I asked, "How do you explain this? Why do so many have these attitudes?" And they said, "Education." Eight years ago they decided that they were going to have absolute equality, and the only way to achieve this was to challenge the sex-role idea. The sex-role debate is not considered a woman question, not even an individual woman question or a societal woman question, but a question for men and women alike. [. . .]

We must overcome our diversity of varied political beliefs. Our common commitment is to equality for women. And we are not single-issue people; we want a voice for all women, to raise our voices in decision making on all matters from war and peace to the kinds of cities we're going to inhabit. Many large issues concern all of us; on these things we may differ. We will surmount this. Political power is necessary to change the situation of the oppressed 51 percent, to realize the power potential in the fact that women *are* 51 percent. [. . .]

We must begin to use the power of our actions: to make women finally *visible* as people in America, as conscious political and social power; to change our society *now*, so all women can move freely, as people, in it.

Kurt Vonnegut

Harrison Bergeron (1968)

The year was 2081, and everybody was finally equal. They weren't only equal before God and the law. They were equal every which way. Nobody was smarter than anybody else. Nobody was better looking than anybody else. Nobody was stronger or quicker than anybody else. All this equality was due to the 211th, 212th, and 213th Amendments to the Constitution, and to the unceasing vigilance of agents of the United States Handicapper General.

Some things about living still weren't quite right, though. April, for instance, still drove people crazy by not being springtime. And it was in that clammy month that the H-G men took George and Hazel Bergeron's fourteen-year-old son, Harrison, away.

It was tragic, all right, but George and Hazel couldn't think about it very hard. Hazel had a perfectly average intelligence, which meant she couldn't think about anything except in short bursts. And George, while his intelligence was way above normal, had a little mental handicap radio in his ear. He was required by law to wear it at all times. It was tuned to a government transmitter. Every twenty seconds or so, the transmitter would send out some sharp noise to keep people like George from taking unfair advantage of their brains.

George and Hazel were watching television. There were tears on Hazel's cheeks, but she'd forgotten for the moment what they were about.

On the television screen were ballerinas.

A buzzer sounded in George's head. His thoughts fled in panic, like bandits from a burglar alarm.

"That was a real pretty dance, that dance they just did," said Hazel.

"Huh?" said George.

"That dance—it was nice," said Hazel.

"Yup," said George. He tried to think a little about the ballerinas. They weren't really very good—no better than anybody else would have been, anyway. They were burdened with sashweights and bags of birdshot, and their faces were masked, so that no one, seeing a free and graceful gesture or a pretty face, would feel like something the cat drug in. George was toying with the vague notion that maybe dancers shouldn't be handicapped. But he didn't get very far with it before another noise in his ear radio scattered his thoughts.

George winced. So did two out of the eight ballerinas.

Hazel saw him wince. Having no mental handicap herself, she had to ask George what the latest sound had been.

"Sounded like somebody hitting a milk bottle with a ball peen hammer," said George.

"I'd think it would be real interesting, hearing all the different sounds," said Hazel, a little envious. "All the things they think up."

"Um," said George.

"Only, if I was Handicapper General, you know what I would do?" said Hazel. Hazel, as a matter of fact, bore a strong resemblance to the Handicapper General, a woman named Diana Moon Glampers. "If I was Diana Moon Glampers," said Hazel, "I'd have chimes on Sunday—just chimes. Kind of in honor of religion."

"I could think, if it was just chimes," said George.

"Well—maybe make 'em real loud," said Hazel. "I think I'd make a good Handicapper General."

"Good as anybody else," said George.

"Who knows better'n I do what normal is?" said Hazel.

"Right," said George. He began to think glimmeringly about his abnormal son who was now in jail, about Harrison, but a twenty-one gun salute in his head stopped that.

"Boy!" said Hazel, "that was a doozy, wasn't it?"

It was such a doozy that George was white and trembling, and tears stood on the rims of his red eyes. Two of the eight ballerinas had collapsed to the studio floor, were holding their temples.

"All of a sudden you look so tired," said Hazel. "Why don't you stretch out on the sofa, so's you can rest your handicap bag on the pillows, honeybunch."

She was referring to the forty-seven pounds of bird-shot in a canvas bag, which was padlocked around George's neck. "Go on and rest the bag for a little while," she said. "I don't care if you're not equal to me for a while."

George weighed the bag with his hands. "I don't mind it," he said. "I don't notice it any more. It's just a part of me."

"You been so tired lately—kind of wore out," said Hazel. "If there was just some way we could make a little hole in the bottom of the bag, and just take out a few of them lead balls. just a few."

"Two years in prison and two thousand dollars fine for every ball I took out," said George. "I don't call that a bargain."

"If you could just take a few out when you came home from work," said Hazel. "I mean—you don't compete with anybody around here. You just set around."

"If I tried to get away with it," said George, "then other people'd get away with it—and pretty soon we'd be right back to the dark ages again, with everybody competing against everybody else. You wouldn't like that, would you?"

"I'd hate it," said Hazel.

"There you are," said George. "The minute people start cheating on laws, what do you think happens to society?"

If Hazel hadn't been able to come up with an answer to this question, George couldn't have supplied one. A siren was going off in his head.

"Reckon it'd fall all apart," said Hazel.

"What would?" said George blankly.

"Society," said Hazel uncertainly. "Wasn't that what you just said?"

"Who knows?" said George.

The television program was suddenly interrupted for a news bulletin. It wasn't clear at first as to what the bulletin was about, since the announcer, like all announcers, had a serious speech impediment. For about half a minute, and in a state of high excitement, the announcer tried to say, "Ladies and gentlemen—"

He finally gave up, handed the bulletin to a ballerina to read.

"That's all right—" Hazel said to the announcer, "he tried. That's the big thing. He tried to do the best he could with what God gave him. He should get a nice raise for trying so hard."

"Ladies and gentlemen—" said the ballerina, reading the bulletin. She must have been extraordinarily beautiful, because the mask she wore was hideous. And it was easy to see that she was the strongest and most graceful of all the dancers, for her handicap bags were as big as those worn by two-hundred-pound men.

And she had to apologize at once for her voice, which was a very unfair voice for a woman to use. Her voice was a warm, luminous, timeless, melody. "Excuse me—" she said, and she began again, making her voice absolutely uncompetitive.

"Harrison Bergeron, age fourteen," she said in a grackle squawk, "has just escaped from jail, where he was held on suspicion of plotting to overthrow the government. He is a genius and an athlete, is under-handicapped, and should be regarded as extremely dangerous."

A police photograph of Harrison Bergeron was flashed on the screen—upside down, then sideways, upside down again, then right side up. The picture showed the full length of Harrison against a background calibrated in feet and inches. He was exactly seven feet tall.

The rest of Harrison's appearance was Halloween and hardware. Nobody had ever borne heavier handicaps. He had outgrown hindrances faster than the H-G men could think them up. Instead of a little ear radio for a mental handicap, he wore a tremendous pair of earphones and spectacles with thick wavy lenses. The spectacles were intended to make him not only half blind, but to give him whanging headaches besides.

Scrap metal was hung all over him. Ordinarily, there was a certain symmetry, a military neatness to the handicaps issued to strong people, but Harrison looked like a walking junkyard. In the race of life, Harrison carried three hundred pounds.

And to offset his good looks, the H-G men required that he wear at all times a red rubber ball for a nose, keep his eyebrows shaved off, and cover his even white teeth with black caps at snaggle-tooth random.

"If you see this boy," said the ballerina, "do not—I repeat, do not—try to reason with him."

There was the shriek of a door being torn from its hinges.

Screams and barking cries of consternation came from the television set. The photograph of Harrison

Bergeron on the screen jumped again and again, as though dancing to the tune of an earthquake.

George Bergeron correctly identified the earthquake, and well he might have—for many was the time his own home had danced to the same crashing tune. "My God—" said George, "that must be Harrison!"

The realization was blasted from his mind instantly by the sound of an automobile collision in his head.

When George could open his eyes again, the photograph of Harrison was gone. A living, breathing Harrison filled the screen.

Clanking, clownish, and huge, Harrison stood in the center of the studio. The knob of the uprooted studio door was still in his hand. Ballerinas, technicians, musicians, and announcers cowered on their knees before him, expecting to die.

"I am the Emperor!" cried Harrison. "Do you hear? I am the Emperor! Everybody must do what I say at once!" He stamped his foot and the studio shook.

"Even as I stand here—" he bellowed, "crippled, hobbled, sickened—I am a greater ruler than any man who ever lived! Now watch me become what I *can* become!"

Harrison tore the straps of his handicap harness like wet tissue paper, tore straps guaranteed to support five thousand pounds.

Harrison's scrap-iron handicaps crashed to the floor.

Harrison thrust his thumbs under the bar of the padlock that secured his head harness. The bar snapped like celery. Harrison smashed his headphones and spectacles against the wall.

He flung away his rubber-ball nose, revealed a man that would have awed Thor, the god of thunder.

"I shall now select my Empress!" he said, looking down on the cowering people. "Let the first woman who dares rise to her feet claim her mate and her throne!"

A moment passed, and then a ballerina rose, swaying like a willow.

Harrison plucked the mental handicap from her ear, snapped off her physical handicaps with marvelous delicacy. Last of all, he removed her mask.

She was blindingly beautiful.

"Now—" said Harrison, taking her hand, "shall we show the people the meaning of the word dance? Music!" he commanded.

The musicians scrambled back into their chairs, and Harrison stripped them of their handicaps, too. "Play your best," he told them, "and I'll make you barons and dukes and earls."

The music began. It was normal at first—cheap, silly, false, but Harrison snatched two musicians from their chairs, waved them like batons as he sang the music as he wanted it played. He slammed them back into their chairs.

The music began again and was much improved.

Harrison and his Empress merely listened to the music for a while—listened gravely, as though synchronizing their heartbeats with it.

They shifted their weights to their toes.

Harrison placed his big hands on the girl's tiny waist, letting her sense the weightlessness that would soon be hers.

And then, in an explosion of joy and grace, into the air they sprang!

Not only were the laws of the land abandoned, but the law of gravity and the laws of motion as well.

They reeled, whirled, swiveled, flounced, capered, gamboled, and spun.

They leaped like deer on the moon.

The studio ceiling was thirty feet high, but each leap brought the dancers nearer to it.

It became their obvious intention to kiss the ceiling. They kissed it.

And then, neutralizing gravity with love and pure will, they remained suspended in air inches below the ceiling, and they kissed each other for a long, long time.

It was then that Diana Moon Glampers, the Handicapper General came into the studio with a double-barreled ten-gauge shotgun. She fired twice, and the Emperor and Empress were dead before they hit the floor.

Diana Moon Glampers loaded the gun again. She aimed it at the musicians and told them they had ten seconds to get their handicaps back on.

It was then that the Bergerons' television tube burned out.

Hazel turned to comment about the blackout to George. But George had gone out into the kitchen for a can of beer.

George came back in with the beer, paused while a handicap signal shook him up. And then he sat down again. "You've been crying?" he said to Hazel.

"Yup," she said.

"What about?" he said.

"I forget," she said. "Something real sad on television."

"What was it?" he said.

"It's all kind of mixed up in my mind," said Hazel.

"Forget sad things," said George.

"I always do," said Hazel.

"That's my girl," said George. He winced. There was the sound of a rivetting gun in his head.

"Gee—I could tell that one was a doozy," said Hazel.

"You can say that again," said George.

"Gee—" said Hazel, "I could tell that one was a doozy."

EARL WARREN

Miranda v. Arizona (1966)

Mr. Chief Justice WARREN delivered the opinion of the Court.

The cases before us raise questions which go to the roots of our concepts of American criminal jurisprudence: the restraints society must observe consistent with the Federal Constitution in prosecuting individuals for crime. More specifically, we deal with the admissibility of statements obtained from an individual who is subjected to custodial police interrogation and the necessity for procedures which assure that the individual is accorded his privilege under the Fifth Amendment to the Constitution not to be compelled to incriminate himself.

We dealt with certain phases of this problem recently in *Escobedo v. Illinois* (1964). There, as in the four cases before us, law enforcement officials took the defendant into custody and interrogated him in a police station for the purpose of obtaining a confession. The police did not effectively advise him of his right to remain silent or of his right to consult with his attorney. Rather, they confronted him with an alleged accomplice who accused him of having perpetrated a murder. When the defendant denied the accusation and said "I didn't shoot Manuel, you did it," they handcuffed him and took him to an interrogation room. There, while handcuffed and standing, he was questioned for four hours until he confessed. During this interrogation, the police denied his request to speak to his attorney, and they prevented his retained attorney, who had come to the police station, from consulting with him. At his trial, the State, over his objection, introduced the confession against him. We held that the statements thus made were constitutionally inadmissible.

This case has been the subject of judicial interpretation and spirited legal debate since it was decided two years ago. [. . .] We granted certiorari in these cases in order further to explore some facets of the problems, thus exposed, of applying the privilege against self-incrimination to in-custody interrogation, and to give concrete constitutional guidelines for law enforcement agencies and courts to follow.

We start here, as we did in *Escobedo*, with the premise that our holding is not an innovation in our jurisprudence, but is an application of principles long recognized and applied in other settings. We have undertaken a thorough re-examination of the *Escobedo* decision and the principles it announced, and we reaffirm it. That case was but an explication of basic rights that are enshrined in our Constitution— that "No person . . . shall be compelled in any criminal case to be a witness against himself," and that "the accused shall . . . have the Assistance of Counsel"— rights which were put in jeopardy in that case through official overbearing. These precious rights were fixed in our Constitution only after centuries of persecution and struggle. [. . .]

Our holding will be spelled out with some specificity in the pages which follow but briefly stated it is this: the prosecution may not use statements, whether exculpatory or inculpatory, stemming from custodial interrogation of the defendant unless it demonstrates the use of procedural safeguards effective to secure the privilege against self-incrimination. By custodial interrogation, we mean questioning initiated by law enforcement officers after a person has been taken into custody or otherwise deprived of his freedom of action in any significant way. As for the procedural safeguards to be employed, unless other fully effective means are devised to inform accused persons of their right of silence and to assure a continuous opportunity to exercise it, the following measures are required. Prior to any questioning, the person must be warned that he has a right to remain silent, that any statement he does make may be used as evidence against him, and that he has a right to the presence of an attorney, either retained or appointed. The defendant may waive effectuation of these rights, provided the waiver is made voluntarily, knowingly and intelligently. If, however, he indicates in any manner and at any stage of the process that he wishes to consult with an attorney before speaking there can be no questioning. Likewise, if the individual is alone and indicates in any manner that he does not wish to be interrogated, the police may not question him. The mere fact that he may have answered some questions or volunteered some statements on his own does not deprive him of the right to refrain from answering any further inquiries until he has consulted with an attorney and thereafter consents to be questioned.

I

The constitutional issue we decide in each of these cases is the admissibility of statements obtained from a defendant questioned while in custody or otherwise deprived of his freedom of action in any significant way. In each, the defendant was questioned by police officers, detectives, or a prosecuting attorney in a room in which he was cut off from the outside world. In none of these cases was the defendant given a full and effective warning of his rights at the outset of the interrogation process. In all the cases, the questioning elicited oral admissions, and in three of them, signed statements as well which were admitted at their trials. They all thus share salient features— incommunicado interrogation of individuals in a police-dominated atmosphere, resulting in self-incriminating statements without full warnings of constitutional rights.

An understanding of the nature and setting of this in-custody interrogation is essential to our decisions today. The difficulty in depicting what transpires at such interrogations stems from the fact that in this country they have largely taken place incommunicado. From extensive factual studies undertaken in the early 1930's, including the famous Wickersham Report to Congress by a Presidential Commission, it is clear that police violence and the "third degree" flourished at that time. In a series of cases decided by this Court long after these studies, the police resorted to physical brutality—beating, hanging, whipping— and to sustained and protracted questioning incommunicado in order to extort confessions. The Commission on Civil Rights in 1961 found much evidence to indicate that "some policemen still resort to physical force to obtain confessions." The use of physical brutality and violence is not, unfortunately, relegated to the past or to any part of the country. Only recently in Kings County, New York, the police brutally beat, kicked and placed lighted cigarette butts on the back of a potential witness under interrogation for the purpose of securing a statement incriminating a third party.

The examples given above are undoubtedly the exception now, but they are sufficiently widespread to be the object of concern. Unless a proper limitation upon custodial interrogation is achieved—such as these decisions will advance—there can be no assurance that practices of this nature will be eradicated in the foreseeable future. [. . .]

[W]e stress that the modern practice of in-custody interrogation is psychologically rather than physically oriented. As we have stated before, "Since *Chambers v. Florida* [1940], this Court has recognized that coercion can be mental as well as physical, and that the blood of the accused is not the only hallmark of an unconstitutional inquisition." *Blackburn v. Alabama* (1960). Interrogation still takes place in privacy. Privacy results in secrecy and this in turn results in a gap in our knowledge as to what in fact goes on in the interrogation rooms. A valuable source of information about present police practices, however, may be found in various police manuals and texts which document procedures employed with success in the past, and which recommend various other effective tactics. These texts are used by law enforcement agencies themselves as guides. It should be noted that these texts professedly present the most enlightened and effective means presently used to obtain statements through custodial interrogation. By considering these texts and other data, it is possible to describe procedures observed and noted around the country.

The officers are told by the manuals that the "principal psychological factor contributing to a successful interrogation is privacy—being alone with the person under interrogation." The efficacy of this tactic has been explained as follows:

> If at all practicable, the interrogation should take place in the investigator's office or at least in a room of his own choice. The subject should be deprived of every psychological advantage. In his own home he may be confident, indignant, or recalcitrant. He is more keenly aware of his rights and more reluctant to tell of his indiscretions or criminal behavior within the walls of his home. Moreover his family and other friends are nearby, their presence lending moral support. In his own office, the investigator possesses all the advantages. The atmosphere suggests the invincibility of the forces of the law. [O'Hara, *Fundamentals of Criminal Investigation* (1956)]

To highlight the isolation and unfamiliar surroundings, the manuals instruct the police to display an air of confidence in the suspect's guilt and from outward appearance to maintain only an interest in confirming certain details. The guilt of the subject is to be posited as a fact. The interrogator should direct his comments toward the reasons why the subject committed the act, rather than court failure by asking the subject whether he did it. Like other men, perhaps the subject has had a bad family life, had an unhappy childhood, had too much to drink, had an unrequited desire for women. The officers are instructed to minimize the moral seriousness of the offense, to cast blame on the victim or on society. These tactics are designed to put the subject in a psychological state where his story is but an elaboration of what the police purport to know already—that he is guilty. Explanations to the contrary are dismissed and discouraged. [. . .]

The manuals suggest that the suspect be offered legal excuses for his actions in order to obtain an initial admission of guilt. Where there is a suspected revenge-killing, for example, the interrogator may say:

> Joe, you probably didn't go out looking for this fellow with the purpose of shooting him. My guess is, however, that you expected something from him and that's why you carried a gun—for your own protection. You knew him for what he was, no good. Then when you met him he probably started using foul, abusive language and he gave some indication that he was about to pull a gun on you, and that's when you had to act to save your own life. That's about it, isn't it, Joe?

Having then obtained the admission of shooting, the interrogator is advised to refer to circumstantial evidence which negates the self-defense explanation. This should enable him to secure the entire story. One text notes that "Even if he fails to do so, the inconsistency between the subject's original denial of the shooting and his present admission of at least doing the shooting will serve to deprive him of a self-defense 'out' at the time of trial."

When the techniques described above prove unavailing, the texts recommend they be alternated with a show of some hostility. One ploy often used has been termed the "friendly-unfriendly" or the "Mutt and Jeff" act:

> . . . In this technique, two agents are employed. Mutt, the relentless investigator, who knows the subject is guilty and is not going to waste any time. He's sent a dozen men away for this crime and he's going to send the subject away for the full term. Jeff, on the other hand, is obviously a kindhearted man. He has a family himself. He has a brother who was involved in a little scrape like this. He disapproves of Mutt and his tactics and will arrange to get him off the case if the subject will cooperate. He can't hold Mutt off for very long. The subject would be wise to make a quick decision. The technique is applied by having both investigators present while Mutt acts out

his role. Jeff may stand by quietly and demur at some of Mutt's tactics. When Jeff makes his plea for cooperation, Mutt is not present in the room.

The interrogators sometimes are instructed to induce a confession out of trickery. The technique here is quite effective in crimes which require identification or which run in series. In the identification situation, the interrogator may take a break in his questioning to place the subject among a group of men in a line-up. "The witness or complainant (previously coached, if necessary) studies the line-up and confidently points out the subject as the guilty party." Then the questioning resumes "as though there were now no doubt about the guilt of the subject." A variation on this technique is called the "reverse line-up":

> The accused is placed in a line-up, but this time he is identified by several fictitious witnesses or victims who associated him with different offenses. It is expected that the subject will become desperate and confess to the offense under investigation in order to escape from the false accusations.

The manuals also contain instructions for police on how to handle the individual who refuses to discuss the matter entirely, or who asks for an attorney or relatives. The examiner is to concede him the right to remain silent. "This usually has a very undermining effect. First of all, he is disappointed in his expectation of an unfavorable reaction on the part of the interrogator. Secondly, a concession of this right to remain silent impresses the subject with the apparent fairness of his interrogator." After this psychological conditioning, however, the officer is told to point out the incriminating significance of the suspect's refusal to talk:

> Joe, you have a right to remain silent. That's your privilege and I'm the last person in the world who'll try to take it away from you. If that's the way you want to leave this, O.K. But let me ask you this. Suppose you were in my shoes and I were in yours and you called me in to ask me about this and I told you, "I don't want to answer any of your questions." You'd think I had something to hide, and you'd probably be right in thinking that. That's exactly what I'll have to

think about you, and so will everybody else. So let's sit here and talk this whole thing over.

Few will persist in their initial refusal to talk, it is said, if this monologue is employed correctly.

In the event that the subject wishes to speak to a relative or an attorney, the following advice is tendered:

> [T]he interrogator should respond by suggesting that the subject first tell the truth to the interrogator himself rather than get anyone else involved in the matter. If the request is for an attorney, the interrogator may suggest that the subject save himself or his family the expense of any such professional service, particularly if he is innocent of the offense under investigation. The interrogator may also add, "Joe, I'm only looking for the truth, and if you're telling the truth, that's it. You can handle this by yourself."

From these representative samples of interrogation techniques, the setting prescribed by the manuals and observed in practice becomes clear. In essence, it is this: To be alone with the subject is essential to prevent distraction and to deprive him of any outside support. The aura of confidence in his guilt undermines his will to resist. He merely confirms the preconceived story the police seek to have him describe. Patience and persistence, at times relentless questioning, are employed. To obtain a confession, the interrogator must "patiently maneuver himself or his quarry into a position from which the desired objective may be attained." When normal procedures fail to produce the needed result, the police may resort to deceptive stratagems such as giving false legal advice. It is important to keep the subject off balance, for example, by trading on his insecurity about himself or his surroundings. The police then persuade, trick, or cajole him out of exercising his constitutional rights.

Even without employing brutality, the "third degree" or the specific stratagems described above, the very fact of custodial interrogation exacts a heavy toll on individual liberty and trades on the weakness of individuals. [. . .]

The potentiality for compulsion is forcefully apparent, for example, in *Miranda*, where the indigent Mexican defendant was a seriously disturbed individual with pronounced sexual fantasies. [. . .] To be sure, the records do not evince overt physical coercion or patent psychological ploys. The fact remains that in none of these cases did the officers undertake to afford appropriate safeguards at the outset of the interrogation to insure that the statements were truly the product of free choice.

It is obvious that such an interrogation environment is created for no purpose other than to subjugate the individual to the will of his examiner. This atmosphere carries its own badge of intimidation. To be sure, this is not physical intimidation, but it is equally destructive of human dignity. The current practice of incommunicado interrogation is at odds with one of our Nation's most cherished principles — that the individual may not be compelled to incriminate himself. Unless adequate protective devices are employed to dispel the compulsion inherent in custodial surroundings, no statement obtained from the defendant can truly be the product of his free choice.

From the foregoing, we can readily perceive an intimate connection between the privilege against self-incrimination and police custodial questioning. [. . .]

II

[T]he constitutional foundation underlying the privilege is the respect a government — state or federal — must accord to the dignity and integrity of its citizens. To maintain a "fair state-individual balance," to require the government "to shoulder the entire load," to respect the inviolability of the human personality, our accusatory system of criminal justice demands that the government seeking to punish an individual produce the evidence against him by its own independent labors, rather than by the cruel, simple expedient of compelling it from his own mouth. In sum, the privilege is fulfilled only when the person is guaranteed the right "to remain silent unless he chooses to speak in the unfettered exercise of his own will." *Malloy v. Hogan* (1964).

The question in these cases is whether the privilege is fully applicable during a period of custodial interrogation. In this Court, the privilege has consistently been accorded a liberal construction. We are satisfied that all the principles embodied in the privilege apply to informal compulsion exerted by law-enforcement officers during in-custody questioning. An individual swept from familiar surroundings into police custody, surrounded by antagonistic forces, and subjected to the techniques of persuasion described above cannot be otherwise than under compulsion to speak. As a practical matter, the compulsion to speak in the isolated setting of the police station may well be greater than in courts or other official investigations, where there are often impartial observers to guard against intimidation or trickery. [. . .]

III

Today, then, there can be no doubt that the Fifth Amendment privilege is available outside of criminal court proceedings and serves to protect persons in all settings in which their freedom of action is curtailed in any significant way from being compelled to incriminate themselves. We have concluded that without proper safeguards the process of in-custody interrogation of persons suspected or accused of crime contains inherently compelling pressures which work to undermine the individual's will to resist and to compel him to speak where he would not otherwise do so freely. In order to combat these pressures and to permit a full opportunity to exercise the privilege against self-incrimination, the accused must be adequately and effectively apprised of his rights and the exercise of those rights must be fully honored.

It is impossible for us to foresee the potential alternatives for protecting the privilege which might be devised by Congress or the States in the exercise of their creative rule-making capacities. Therefore we cannot say that the Constitution necessarily requires adherence to any particular solution for the inherent compulsions of the interrogation process as it is presently conducted. Our decision in no way creates a constitutional straitjacket which will handicap sound efforts at reform, nor is it intended to have this effect. We encourage Congress and the States to continue their laudable search for increasingly effective ways of protecting the rights of the individual while promoting efficient enforcement of our criminal laws. However, unless we are shown other procedures which are at least as effective in apprising accused persons of their right of silence and in assuring a continuous opportunity to exercise it, the following safeguards must be observed.

At the outset, if a person in custody is to be subjected to interrogation, he must first be informed in clear and unequivocal terms that he has the right to remain silent. For those unaware of the privilege, the warning is needed simply to make them aware of it— the threshold requirement for an intelligent decision as to its exercise. More important, such a warning is an absolute prerequisite in overcoming the inherent pressures of the interrogation atmosphere. It is not just the subnormal or woefully ignorant who succumb to an interrogator's imprecations, whether implied or expressly stated, that the interrogation will continue until a confession is obtained or that silence in the face of accusation is itself damning and will bode ill when presented to a jury. Further, the warning will show the individual that his interrogators are prepared to recognize his privilege should he choose to exercise it.

The Fifth Amendment privilege is so fundamental to our system of constitutional rule and the expedient of giving an adequate warning as to the availability of the privilege so simple, we will not pause to inquire in individual cases whether the defendant was aware of his rights without a warning being given. Assessments of the knowledge the defendant possessed, based on information as to his age, education, intelligence, or prior contact with authorities, can never be more than speculation; a warning is a clear-cut fact. More important, whatever the background of the person interrogated, a warning at the time of the interrogation is indispensable to overcome its pressures and to insure that the individual knows he is free to exercise the privilege at that point in time.

The warning of the right to remain silent must be accompanied by the explanation that anything said can and will be used against the individual in court. This warning is needed in order to make him aware not only of the privilege, but also of the consequences of forgoing it. It is only through an awareness of these consequences that there can be any assurance of real understanding and intelligent exercise of the privilege. Moreover, this warning may serve to make the individual more acutely aware that he is faced with a phase of the adversary system—that he is not in the presence of persons acting solely in his interest.

The circumstances surrounding in-custody interrogation can operate very quickly to overbear the will of one merely made aware of his privilege by his interrogators. Therefore, the right to have counsel present at the interrogation is indispensable to the protection of the Fifth Amendment privilege under the system we delineate today. Our aim is to assure that the individual's right to choose between silence and speech remains unfettered throughout the interrogation process. A once-stated warning, delivered by those who will conduct the interrogation, cannot itself suffice to that end among those who most require knowledge of their rights. A mere warning given by the interrogators is not alone sufficient to accomplish that end. Prosecutors themselves claim that the admonishment of the right to remain silent without more "will benefit only the recidivist and the professional." Even preliminary advice given to the accused by his own attorney can be swiftly overcome by the secret interrogation process. Thus, the need for counsel to protect the Fifth Amendment privilege comprehends not merely a right to consult with counsel prior to questioning, but also to have counsel present during any questioning if the defendant so desires.

The presence of counsel at the interrogation may serve several significant subsidiary functions as well. If the accused decides to talk to his interrogators, the assistance of counsel can mitigate the dangers of untrustworthiness. With a lawyer present the likelihood that the police will practice coercion is reduced, and if coercion is nevertheless exercised the lawyer can testify to it in court. The presence of a lawyer can also help to guarantee that the accused gives a fully accurate statement to the police and that the statement is rightly reported by the prosecution at trial.

An individual need not make a pre-interrogation request for a lawyer. While such request affirmatively secures his right to have one, his failure to ask for a lawyer does not constitute a waiver. No effective waiver of the right to counsel during interrogation can be recognized unless specifically made after the warnings we here delineate have been given. The accused who does not know his rights and therefore does not make a request may be the person who most needs counsel. [. . .]

Accordingly we hold that an individual held for interrogation must be clearly informed that he has the right to consult with a lawyer and to have the lawyer with him during interrogation under the system for protecting the privilege we delineate today. As with the warnings of the right to remain silent and that anything stated can be used in evidence against him, this warning is an absolute prerequisite to interrogation. No amount of circumstantial evidence that the person may have been aware of this right will suffice to stand in its stead: Only through such a warning is there ascertainable assurance that the accused was aware of this right.

If an individual indicates that he wishes the assistance of counsel before any interrogation occurs, the authorities cannot rationally ignore or deny his request on the basis that the individual does not have or cannot afford a retained attorney. The financial ability of the individual has no relationship to the scope of the rights involved here. The privilege against self-incrimination secured by the Constitution applies to all individuals. [. . .] The cases before us as well as the vast majority of confession cases with which we have dealt in the past involve those unable to retain counsel. While authorities are not required to relieve the accused of his poverty, they have the obligation not to take advantage of indigence in the administration of justice. [. . .]

In order fully to apprise a person interrogated of the extent of his rights under this system then, it is necessary to warn him not only that he has the right to consult with an attorney, but also that if he is indigent a lawyer will be appointed to represent him. Without this additional warning, the admonition of the right to consult with counsel would often be understood as meaning only that he can consult with a lawyer if he has one or has the funds to obtain one. The warning of a right to counsel would be hollow if not couched in terms that would convey to the indigent—the person most often subjected to interrogation—the knowledge that he too has a right to have counsel present. As with the warnings of the right to remain silent and of the general right to counsel, only by effective and express explanation to the indigent of this right can there be assurance that he was truly in a position to exercise it.

Once warnings have been given, the subsequent procedure is clear. If the individual indicates in any manner, at any time prior to or during questioning, that he wishes to remain silent, the interrogation must cease. At this point he has shown that he intends to exercise his Fifth Amendment privilege; any statement taken after the person invokes his privilege cannot be other than the product of compulsion, subtle or otherwise. Without the right to cut off questioning, the setting of in-custody interrogation operates on the individual to overcome free choice in producing a statement after the privilege has been once invoked. If the individual states that he wants an attorney, the interrogation must cease until an attorney is present. At that time, the individual must have an opportunity to confer with the attorney and to have him present during any subsequent questioning. If the individual cannot obtain an attorney and he indicates that he wants one before speaking to police, they must respect his decision to remain silent. [. . .]

If the interrogation continues without the presence of an attorney and a statement is taken, a heavy burden rests on the government to demonstrate that the defendant knowingly and intelligently waived his privilege against self-incrimination and his right to retained or appointed counsel. This Court has always set high standards of proof for the waiver of constitutional rights, and we re-assert these standards as applied to in-custody interrogation. [. . .]

An express statement that the individual is willing to make a statement and does not want an attorney followed closely by a statement could constitute a waiver. But a valid waiver will not be presumed simply from the silence of the accused after warnings are given or simply from the fact that a confession was in fact eventually obtained. [. . .] Moreover, where in-custody interrogation is involved, there is no room for the contention that the privilege is waived if the individual answers some questions or gives some information on his own prior to invoking his right to remain silent when interrogated.

Whatever the testimony of the authorities as to waiver of rights by an accused, the fact of lengthy interrogation or incommunicado incarceration before a statement is made is strong evidence that the accused did not validly waive his rights. In these circumstances the fact that the individual eventually made a statement is consistent with the conclusion that the compelling influence of the interrogation finally forced him to do so. It is inconsistent with any notion of a voluntary relinquishment of the privilege. Moreover, any evidence that the accused was threatened, tricked, or cajoled into a waiver will, of course, show that the defendant did not voluntarily waive his privilege. The requirement of warnings and waiver of rights is a fundamental with respect to the Fifth Amendment privilege and not simply a preliminary ritual to existing methods of interrogation.

The warnings required and the waiver necessary in accordance with our opinion today are, in the absence of a fully effective equivalent, prerequisites to the admissibility of any statement made by a defendant. [. . .]

The principles announced today deal with the protection which must be given to the privilege against self-incrimination when the individual is first subjected to police interrogation while in custody at the station or otherwise deprived of his freedom of action in any significant way. It is at this point that our adversary system of criminal proceedings commences, distinguishing itself at the outset from the inquisitorial system recognized in some countries. Under the system of warnings we delineate today or under any other system which may be devised and found effective, the safeguards to be erected about the privilege must come into play at this point.

Our decision is not intended to hamper the traditional function of police officers in investigating crime. When an individual is in custody on probable cause, the police may, of course, seek out evidence in the field to be used at trial against him. Such investigation may include inquiry of persons not under restraint. General on-the-scene questioning as to facts surrounding a crime or other general questioning of citizens in the fact-finding process is not affected by our holding. It is an act of responsible citizenship for individuals to give whatever information they may have to aid in law enforcement. In such situations the compelling atmosphere inherent in the process of in-custody interrogation is not necessarily present.

In dealing with statements obtained through interrogation, we do not purport to find all confessions inadmissible. Confessions remain a proper element in law enforcement. Any statement given freely and voluntarily without any compelling influences is, of course, admissible in evidence. The fundamental import of the privilege while an individual is in custody is not whether he is allowed to talk to the police without the benefit of warnings and counsel, but whether he can be interrogated. There is no requirement that police stop a person who enters a police station and states that he wishes to confess to a crime, or a person who calls the police to offer a confession or any other statement he desires to make. Volunteered statements of any kind are not barred by the Fifth Amendment and their admissibility is not affected by our holding today.

To summarize, we hold that when an individual is taken into custody or otherwise deprived of his freedom by the authorities in any significant way and is subjected to questioning, the privilege against self-incrimination is jeopardized. Procedural safeguards must be employed to protect the privilege, and unless other fully effective means are adopted to notify the person of his right of silence and to assure that the exercise of the right will be scrupulously honored, the following measures are required. He must be warned prior to any questioning that he has the right to remain silent, that anything he says can be used against him in a court of law, that he has the right to the presence of an attorney, and that if he cannot afford an attorney one will be appointed for him prior to any questioning if he so desires. Opportunity to exercise these rights must be afforded to him throughout the interrogation. After such warnings have been given, and such opportunity afforded him, the individual may knowingly and intelligently waive these rights and agree to answer questions or make a statement. But unless and until such warnings and waiver are demonstrated by the prosecution at trial, no evidence obtained as a result of interrogation can be used against him. [. . .]

POTTER STEWART

Katz v. United States (1967)

Mr. Justice STEWART delivered the opinion of the Court.

The petitioner was convicted in the District Court for the Southern District of California under an eight-count indictment charging him with transmitting wagering information by telephone from Los Angeles to Miami and Boston, in violation of a federal statute. At trial the Government was permitted, over the petitioner's objection, to introduce evidence of the petitioner's end of telephone conversations, overheard by FBI agents who had attached an electronic listening and recording device to the outside of the public telephone booth from which he had placed his calls. In affirming his conviction, the Court of Appeals rejected the contention that the recordings had been obtained in violation of the Fourth Amendment, because "[t]here was no physical entrance into the area occupied by [the petitioner]." We granted certiorari in order to consider the constitutional questions thus presented.

The petitioner has phrased those questions as follows:

A. Whether a public telephone booth is a constitutionally protected area so that evidence obtained by attaching an electronic listening recording device to the top of such a booth is obtained in violation of the right to privacy of the user of the booth.

B. Whether physical penetration of a constitutionally protected area is necessary before a search and seizure can be said to be violative of the Fourth Amendment to the United States Constitution. [. . .]

Because of the misleading way the issues have been formulated, the parties have attached great significance to the characterization of the telephone booth from which the petitioner placed his calls. The petitioner has strenuously argued that the booth was a "constitutionally protected area." The Government has maintained with equal vigor that it was not. But this effort to decide whether or not a given "area," viewed in the abstract, is "constitutionally protected" deflects attention from the problem presented by this case. For the Fourth Amendment protects people, not places. What a person knowingly exposes to the public, even in his own home or office, is not a subject of Fourth Amendment protection. But what he seeks to preserve as private, even in an area accessible to the public, may be constitutionally protected.

The Government stresses the fact that the telephone booth from which the petitioner made his calls was constructed partly of glass, so that he was as visible after he entered it as he would have been if he had remained outside. But what he sought to exclude when he entered the booth was not the intruding eye—it was the uninvited ear. He did not shed his right to do so simply because he made his calls from a place where he might be seen. No less than an individual in a business office, in a friend's apartment, or in a taxicab, a person in a telephone booth may rely upon the protection of the Fourth Amendment. One who occupies it, shuts the door behind him, and pays the toll that permits him to place a call is surely entitled to assume that the words he utters into the mouthpiece will not be broadcast to the world. To read the Constitution more narrowly is to ignore the vital role that the public telephone has come to play in private communication.

The Government contends, however, that the activities of its agents in this case should not be tested by Fourth Amendment requirements, for the surveillance technique they employed involved no physical penetration of the telephone booth from which the petitioner placed his calls. It is true that the absence of such penetration was at one time thought to foreclose further Fourth Amendment inquiry, *Olmstead v. United States* (1928), for that Amendment was thought to limit only searches and seizures of tangible property. [. . .] [But] although a closely divided

Court supposed in *Olmstead* that surveillance without any trespass and without the seizure of any material object fell outside the ambit of the Constitution, we have since departed from the narrow view on which that decision rested. Indeed, we have expressly held that the Fourth Amendment governs not only the seizure of tangible items, but extends as well to the recording of oral statements, over-heard without any "technical trespass under . . . local property law." Once this much is acknowledged, and once it is recognized that the Fourth Amendment protects people—and not simply "areas"—against unreasonable searches and seizures, it becomes clear that the reach of that Amendment cannot turn upon the presence or absence of a physical intrusion into any given enclosure.

We conclude that the underpinnings of *Olmstead* [. . .] have been so eroded by our subsequent decisions that the "trespass" doctrine there enunciated can no longer be regarded as controlling. The Government's activities in electronically listening to and recording the petitioner's words violated the privacy upon which he justifiably relied while using the telephone booth and thus constituted a "search and seizure" within the meaning of the Fourth Amendment. The fact that the electronic device employed to achieve that end did not happen to penetrate the wall of the booth can have no constitutional significance.

The question remaining for decision, then, is whether the search and seizure conducted in this case complied with constitutional standards. [. . .]

The Government urges that, because its agents relied upon the [decision] in *Olmstead* [. . .] , and because they did no more here than they might properly have done with prior judicial sanction, we should retroactively validate their conduct. That we cannot do. It is apparent that the agents in this case acted with restraint. Yet the inescapable fact is that this restraint was imposed by the agents themselves, not by a judicial officer. They were not required,

before commencing the search, to present their estimate of probable cause for detached scrutiny by a neutral magistrate. They were not compelled, during the conduct of the search itself, to observe precise limits established in advance by a specific court order. Nor were they directed, after the search had been completed, to notify the authorizing magistrate in detail of all that had been seized. In the absence of such safeguards, this Court has never sustained a search upon the sole ground that officers reasonably expected to find evidence of a particular crime and voluntarily confined their activities to the least intrusive means consistent with that end. Searches conducted without warrants have been held unlawful "notwithstanding facts unquestionably showing probable cause," for the Constitution requires "that the deliberate, impartial judgment of a judicial officer . . . be interposed between the citizen and the police. . . ." "Over and again this Court has emphasized that the mandate of the [Fourth] Amendment requires adherence to judicial processes," and that searches conducted outside the judicial process, without prior approval by judge or magistrate, are per se unreasonable under the Fourth Amendment—subject only to a few specifically established and well-delineated exceptions. [. . .]

These considerations do not vanish when the search in question is transferred from the setting of a home, an office, or a hotel room to that of a telephone booth. Wherever a man may be, he is entitled to know that he will remain free from unreasonable searches and seizures. The government agents here ignored "the procedure of antecedent justification . . . that is central to the Fourth Amendment," a procedure that we hold to be a constitutional precondition of the kind of electronic surveillance involved in this case. Because the surveillance here failed to meet that condition, and because it led to the petitioner's conviction, the judgment must be reversed.

It is so ordered.

John Marshall Harlan II

Katz v. United States, Concurrence (1967)

Mr. Justice HARLAN, concurring.

I join the opinion of the Court, which I read to hold only (a) that an enclosed telephone booth is an area where, like a home, and unlike a field, a person has a constitutionally protected reasonable expectation of privacy; (b) that electronic as well as physical intrusion into a place that is in this sense private may constitute a violation of the Fourth Amendment; and (c) that the invasion of a constitutionally protected area by federal authorities is, as the Court has long held, presumptively unreasonable in the absence of a search warrant.

As the Court's opinion states, "the Fourth Amendment protects people, not places." The question, however, is what protection it affords to those people. Generally, as here, the answer to that question requires reference to a "place." My understanding of the rule that has emerged from prior decisions is that there is a twofold requirement, first that a person have exhibited an actual (subjective) expectation of privacy and, second, that the expectation be one that society is prepared to recognize as "reasonable." Thus a man's home is, for most purposes, a place where he expects privacy, but objects, activities, or statements that he exposes to the "plain view" of outsiders are not "protected" because no intention to keep them to himself has been exhibited. On the other hand, conversations in the open would not be protected against being overheard, for the expectation of privacy under the circumstances would be unreasonable.

The critical fact in this case is that "[o]ne who occupies [a telephone booth] shuts the door behind him, and pays the toll that permits him to place a call is surely entitled to assume" that his conversation is not being intercepted. The point is not that the booth is "accessible to the public" at other times, but that it is a temporarily private place whose momentary occupants' expectations of freedom from intrusion are recognized as reasonable. [. . .]

Hugo Black

Katz v. United States, Dissent (1967)

Mr. Justice BLACK, dissenting.

If I could agree with the Court that eavesdropping carried on by electronic means (equivalent to wiretapping) constitutes a "search" or "seizure," I would be happy to join the Court's opinion. [. . .]

My basic objection is twofold: (1) I do not believe that the words of the Amendment will bear the meaning given them by today's decision, and (2) I do not believe that it is the proper role of this Court to rewrite the Amendment in order "to bring it into harmony with the times" and thus reach a result that many people believe to be desirable.

While I realize that an argument based on the meaning of words lacks the scope, and no doubt the appeal, of broad policy discussions and philosophical discourses on such nebulous subjects as privacy, for me the language of the Amendment is the crucial place to look in construing a written document such as our Constitution. The Fourth Amendment says that

The right of the people to be secure in their persons, houses, papers, and effects, against unreasonable searches and seizures, shall not be violated, and no Warrants shall issue, but upon probable cause, supported by Oath or affirmation, and particularly describing the place to be searched, and the persons or things to be seized.

The first clause protects "persons, houses, papers, and effects, against unreasonable searches and seizures. . . ." These words connote the idea of tangible things with size, form, and weight, things capable of being searched, seized, or both. The second clause of the Amendment still further establishes its Framers' purpose to limit its protection to tangible things by providing that no warrants shall issue but those "particularly describing the place to be searched, and the persons or things to be seized." A conversation overheard by eavesdropping, whether by plain snooping or wiretapping, is not tangible and, under the normally accepted meanings of the words, can neither be searched nor seized. In addition the language of the second clause indicates that the Amendment refers not only to something tangible so it can be seized but to something already in existence so it can be described. Yet the Court's interpretation would have the Amendment apply to overhearing future conversations which by their very nature are nonexistent until they take place. How can one "describe" a future conversation, and, if one cannot, how can a magistrate issue a warrant to eavesdrop one in the future? It is argued that information showing what is expected to be said is sufficient to limit the boundaries of what later can be admitted into evidence; but does such general information really meet the specific language of the Amendment which says "particularly describing"? Rather than using language in a completely artificial way, I must conclude that the Fourth Amendment simply does not apply to eavesdropping.

Tapping telephone wires, of course, was an unknown possibility at the time the Fourth Amendment was adopted. But eavesdropping (and wiretapping is nothing more than eavesdropping by telephone) was, as even the majority opinion in *Berger* [*v. New York* (1967)], recognized, "an ancient practice which at common law was condemned as a nuisance. Blackstone, *Commentaries.* In those days

the eavesdropper listened by naked ear under the eaves of houses or their windows, or beyond their walls seeking out private discourse." There can be no doubt that the Framers were aware of this practice, and if they had desired to outlaw or restrict the use of evidence obtained by eavesdropping, I believe that they would have used the appropriate language to do so in the Fourth Amendment. They certainly would not have left such a task to the ingenuity of language-stretching judges. No one, it seems to me, can read the debates on the Bill of Rights without reaching the conclusion that its Framers and critics well knew the meaning of the words they used, what they would be understood to mean by others, their scope and their limitations. Under these circumstances it strikes me as a charge against their scholarship, their common sense and their candor to give to the Fourth Amendment's language the eavesdropping meaning the Court imputes to it today.

I do not deny that common sense requires and that this Court often has said that the Bill of Rights' safeguards should be given a liberal construction. This principle, however, does not justify construing the search and seizure amendment as applying to eavesdropping or the "seizure" of conversations. The Fourth Amendment was aimed directly at the abhorred practice of breaking in, ransacking and searching homes and other buildings and seizing people's personal belongings without warrants issued by magistrates. The Amendment deserves, and this Court has given it, a liberal construction in order to protect against warrantless searches of buildings and seizures of tangible personal effects. But until today this Court has refused to say that eavesdropping comes within the ambit of Fourth Amendment restrictions. [. . .]

Since I see no way in which the words of the Fourth Amendment can be construed to apply to eavesdropping, that closes the matter for me. In interpreting the Bill of Rights, I willingly go as far as a liberal construction of the language takes me, but I simply cannot in good conscience give a meaning to words which they have never before been thought to have and which they certainly do not have in common ordinary usage. I will not distort the words of the Amendment in order to "keep the Constitution up to date" or "to bring it into harmony with the times." It was never meant that this Court have such power, which in effect would make us a continuously functioning constitutional convention.

With this decision the Court has completed, I hope, its rewriting of the Fourth Amendment, which started only recently when the Court began referring incessantly to the Fourth Amendment not so much as a law against unreasonable searches and seizures as one to protect an individual's privacy. By clever word juggling the Court finds it plausible to argue that language aimed specifically at searches and seizures of things that can be searched and seized may, to protect privacy, be applied to eavesdropped evidence of conversations that can neither be searched nor seized. Few things happen to an individual that do not affect his privacy in one way or another. Thus, by arbitrarily substituting the Court's language, designed to protect privacy, for the Constitution's language, designed to protect against unreasonable searches and seizures, the Court has made the Fourth Amendment its vehicle for holding all laws violative of the Constitution which offend the Court's broadest concept of privacy. As I said in *Griswold v. Connecticut*

(1965), "The Court talks about a constitutional 'right of privacy' as though there is some constitutional provision or provisions forbidding any law ever to be passed which might abridge the 'privacy' of individuals. But there is not." I made clear in that dissent my fear of the dangers involved when this Court uses the "broad, abstract and ambiguous concept" of "privacy" as a "comprehensive substitute for the Fourth Amendment's guarantee against 'unreasonable searches and seizures.'"

The Fourth Amendment protects privacy only to the extent that it prohibits unreasonable searches and seizures of "persons, houses, papers, and effects." No general right is created by the Amendment so as to give this Court the unlimited power to hold unconstitutional everything which affects privacy. Certainly the Framers, well acquainted as they were with the excesses of governmental power, did not intend to grant this Court such omnipotent lawmaking authority as that. The history of governments proves that it is dangerous to freedom to repose such powers in courts.

For these reasons I respectfully dissent.

WILLIAM O. DOUGLAS

Brandenburg v. Ohio, Concurrence (1969)

Mr. Justice DOUGLAS, concurring.

While I join the opinion of the Court, I desire to enter a caveat.

The "clear and present danger" test was adumbrated by Mr. Justice Holmes in a case arising during World War I. [. . .] The case was *Schenck v. United States* [1919], where the defendant was charged with attempts to cause insubordination in the military and obstruction of enlistment. The pamphlets that were distributed urged resistance to the draft, denounced conscription, and impugned the motives of those backing the war effort. The First Amendment was tendered as a defense. Mr. Justice Holmes in rejecting that defense said:

The question in every case is whether the words used are used in such circumstances and are of such a nature as to create a clear and present danger that they will bring about the substantive evils that Congress has a right to prevent. It is a question of proximity and degree.

Frohwerk v. United States [. . .] involved prosecution and punishment for publication of articles very critical of the war effort in World War I. [. . .] [T]he conviction in *Frohwerk* was sustained because "the circulation of the paper was in quarters where a little breath would be enough to kindle a flame."

Debs v. United States was the third of the trilogy of the 1918 Term. Debs was convicted of speaking in opposition to the war where his "opposition was so expressed that its natural and intended effect would be to obstruct recruiting." [. . .]

In the 1919 Term, the Court applied the *Schenck* doctrine to affirm the convictions of other dissidents in World War I. *Abrams v. United States* was one instance. Mr. Justice Holmes, with whom Mr. Justice Brandeis concurred, dissented. While adhering to *Schenck*, he did not think that on the facts a case for overriding the First Amendment had been made out:

> It is only the present danger of immediate evil or an intent to bring it about that warrants Congress in setting a limit to the expression of opinion where private rights are not concerned. Congress certainly cannot forbid all effort to change the mind of the country.

Another instance was *Schaefer v. United States* in which Mr. Justice Brandeis, joined by Mr. Justice Holmes, dissented. A third was *Pierce v. United States* in which again Mr. Justice Brandeis, joined by Mr. Justice Holmes, dissented.

Those, then, were the World War I cases that put the gloss of "clear and present danger" on the First Amendment. Whether the war power—the greatest leveler of them all—is adequate to sustain that doctrine is debatable. The dissents in *Abrams, Schaefer*, and *Pierce* show how easily "clear and present danger" is manipulated to crush what Brandeis called "[t]he fundamental right of free men to strive for better conditions through new legislation and new institutions" by argument and discourse even in time of war. Though I doubt if the "clear and present danger" test is congenial to the First Amendment in time of a declared war, I am certain it is not reconcilable with the First Amendment in days of peace. [. . .]

Mr. Justice Holmes, though never formally abandoning the "clear and present danger" test, moved closer to the First Amendment ideal when he said in dissent in *Gitlow v. New York* [1925]:

> Every idea is an incitement. It offers itself for belief and if believed it is acted on unless some other belief outweighs it or some failure of energy stifles the movement at its birth. The only difference between the expression of an opinion and an incitement in the narrower sense is the speaker's enthusiasm for the result. Eloquence

may set fire to reason. But whatever may be thought of the redundant discourse before us it had no chance of starting a present conflagration. If in the long run the beliefs expressed in proletarian dictatorship are destined to be accepted by the dominant forces of the community, the only meaning of free speech is that they should be given their chance and have their way.

We have never been faithful to the philosophy of that dissent. [. . .]

[I]n *Dennis v. United States* (1951) we opened wide the door, distorting the "clear and present danger" test beyond recognition. In that case the prosecution dubbed an agreement to teach the Marxist creed a "conspiracy." The case was submitted to a jury on a charge that the jury could not convict unless it found that the defendants "intended to overthrow the Government 'as speedily as circumstances would permit'." The Court sustained convictions under that charge, construing it to mean a determination of "whether the gravity of the 'evil,' discounted by its improbability, justifies such invasion of free speech as is necessary to avoid the danger."

Out of the "clear and present danger" test came other offspring. Advocacy and teaching of forcible overthrow of government as an abstract principle is immune from prosecution. *Yates v. United States* (1957). But an "active" member, who has a guilty knowledge and intent of the aim to overthrow the Government by violence, *Noto v. United States* (1961), may be prosecuted. And the power to investigate, backed by the powerful sanction of contempt, includes the power to determine which of the two categories fits the particular witness. *Barenblatt v. United States* (1959). And so the investigator roams at will through all of the beliefs of the witness, ransacking his conscience and his innermost thoughts. [. . .]

My own view is quite different. I see no place in the regime of the First Amendment for any "clear and present danger" test, whether strict and tight as some would make it, or free-wheeling as the Court in *Dennis* rephrased it.

When one reads the opinions closely and sees when and how the "clear and present danger" test has been applied, great misgivings are aroused. First, the threats were often loud but always puny and made serious only by judges so wedded to the status quo that critical analysis made them nervous.

Second, the test was so twisted and perverted in *Dennis* as to make the trial of those teachers of Marxism an all-out political trial which was part and parcel of the cold war that has eroded substantial parts of the First Amendment.

Action is often a method of expression and within the protection of the First Amendment.

Suppose one tears up his own copy of the Constitution in eloquent protest to a decision of this Court. May he be indicted? [. . .]

Last Term the Court held in *United States v. O'Brien* (1968) that a registrant under Selective Service who burned his draft card in protest of the war in Vietnam could be prosecuted. The First Amendment was tendered as a defense and rejected, the Court saying:

> The issuance of certificates indicating the registration and eligibility classification of individuals is a legitimate and substantial administrative aid in the functioning of this system. And legislation to insure the continuing availability of issued certificates serves a legitimate and substantial purpose in the system's administration.

But O'Brien was not prosecuted for not having his draft card available when asked for by a federal agent. He was indicted, tried, and convicted for burning the card. And this Court's affirmance of that conviction was not, with all respect, consistent with the First Amendment. [. . .]

One's beliefs have long been thought to be sanctuaries which government could not invade. *Barenblatt* is one example of the ease with which that sanctuary can be violated. The lines drawn by the Court between the criminal act of being an "active" Communist and the innocent act of being a nominal or inactive Communist mark the difference only between deep and abiding belief and casual or uncertain belief. But I think that all matters of belief are beyond the reach of subpoenas or the probings of investigators. That is why the invasions of privacy made by investigating committees were notoriously unconstitutional. That is the deep-seated fault in the infamous loyalty-security hearings which, since 1947 when President Truman launched them, have processed 20,000,000 men and women. Those hearings were primarily concerned with one's thoughts, ideas, beliefs, and convictions. They were the most blatant violations of the First Amendment we have ever known.

The line between what is permissible and not subject to control and what may be made impermissible and subject to regulation is the line between ideas and overt acts.

The example usually given by those who would punish speech is the case of one who falsely shouts fire in a crowded theatre.

This is, however, a classic case where speech is brigaded with action. They are indeed inseparable and a prosecution can be launched for the overt acts actually caused. Apart from rare instances of that kind, speech is, I think, immune from prosecution. Certainly there is no constitutional line between advocacy of abstract ideas as in *Yates* and advocacy of political action as in *Scales*. The quality of advocacy turns on the depth of the conviction; and government has no power to invade that sanctuary of belief and conscience.

ABE FORTAS

Tinker v. Des Moines School District (1969)

Mr. Justice FORTAS delivered the opinion of the Court.

Petitioner John F. Tinker, 15 years old, and petitioner Christopher Eckhardt, 16 years old, attended high schools in Des Moines, Iowa. Petitioner Mary Beth Tinker, John's sister, was a 13-year-old student in junior high school.

In December 1965, a group of adults and students in Des Moines held a meeting at the Eckhardt home. The group determined to publicize their objections to the hostilities in Vietnam and their support for a truce by wearing black armbands during the holiday season and by fasting on December 16 and New Year's Eve. Petitioners and their parents had previously engaged in similar activities, and they decided to participate in the program.

The principals of the Des Moines schools became aware of the plan to wear armbands. On December 14, 1965, they met and adopted a policy that any student wearing an armband to school would be asked to remove it, and if he refused he would be suspended until he returned without the armband. Petitioners were aware of the regulation that the school authorities adopted.

On December 16, Mary Beth and Christopher wore black armbands to their schools. John Tinker wore his armband the next day. They were all sent home and suspended from school until they would come back without their armbands. They did not return to school until after the planned period for wearing armbands had expired—that is, until after New Year's Day.

This complaint was filed in the United States District Court by petitioners, through their fathers, under 1983 of Title 42 of the United States Code. It prayed for an injunction restraining the respondent school officials and the respondent members of the board of directors of the school district from disciplining the petitioners, and it sought nominal damages. After an evidentiary hearing the District Court dismissed the complaint. It upheld the constitutionality of the school authorities' action on the ground that it was reasonable in order to prevent disturbance of school discipline. [. . .]

On appeal, the Court of Appeals for the Eighth Circuit considered the case *en banc*. The court was equally divided, and the District Court's decision was accordingly affirmed, without opinion.

I

The District Court recognized that the wearing of an armband for the purpose of expressing certain views is the type of symbolic act that is within the Free Speech Clause of the First Amendment. As we shall discuss, the wearing of armbands in the circumstances of this case was entirely divorced from actually or potentially disruptive conduct by those participating in it. It was closely akin to "pure speech" which, we have repeatedly held, is entitled to comprehensive protection under the First Amendment.

First Amendment rights, applied in light of the special characteristics of the school environment, are available to teachers and students. It can hardly be argued that either students or teachers shed their constitutional rights to freedom of speech or expression at the schoolhouse gate. This has been the unmistakable holding of this Court for almost 50 years. In *Meyer v. Nebraska* (1923), and *Bartels v. Iowa* (1923), this Court, in opinions by Mr. Justice McReynolds, held that the Due Process Clause of the Fourteenth Amendment prevents States from forbidding the teaching of a foreign language to young students. Statutes to this effect, the Court held, unconstitutionally interfere with the liberty of teacher, student, and parent.

In *West Virginia v. Barnette* (1943), this Court held that under the First Amendment, the student in public school may not be compelled to salute the flag. [. . .]

On the other hand, the Court has repeatedly emphasized the need for affirming the comprehensive authority of the States and of school officials, consistent with fundamental constitutional safeguards, to prescribe and control conduct in the schools. Our problem lies in the area where students in the exercise of First Amendment rights collide with the rules of the school authorities.

II

The problem posed by the present case does not relate to regulation of the length of skirts or the type of clothing, to hair style, or deportment. It does not concern aggressive, disruptive action or even group demonstrations. Our problem involves direct, primary First Amendment rights akin to "pure speech."

The school officials banned and sought to punish petitioners for a silent, passive expression of opinion, unaccompanied by any disorder or disturbance on the part of petitioners. There is here no evidence whatever of petitioners' interference, actual or nascent, with the schools' work or of collision with the rights of other students to be secure and to be let alone. Accordingly, this case does not concern speech or action that intrudes upon the work of the schools or the rights of other students.

Only a few of the 18,000 students in the school system wore the black armbands. Only five students were suspended for wearing them. There is no indication that the work of the schools or any class was disrupted. Outside the classrooms, a few students made hostile remarks to the children wearing armbands, but there were no threats or acts of violence on school premises.

The District Court concluded that the action of the school authorities was reasonable because it was based upon their fear of a disturbance from the wearing of the armbands. But, in our system, undifferentiated fear or apprehension of disturbance is not enough to overcome the right to freedom of expression. Any departure from absolute regimentation may cause trouble. Any variation from the majority's opinion may inspire fear. Any word spoken, in class, in the lunchroom, or on the campus, that deviates from the views of another person may start an argument or cause a disturbance. But our Constitution says we must take this risk, and our history says that it is this sort of hazardous freedom—this kind of openness—that is the basis of our national strength and of the independence and vigor of Americans who grow up and live in this relatively permissive, often disputatious, society.

In order for the State in the person of school officials to justify prohibition of a particular expression of opinion, it must be able to show that its action was caused by something more than a mere desire to avoid the discomfort and unpleasantness that always accompany an unpopular viewpoint. Certainly where there is no finding and no showing that engaging in the forbidden conduct would "materially and substantially interfere with the requirements of appropriate discipline in the operation of the school," the prohibition cannot be sustained.

In the present case, the District Court made no such finding, and our independent examination of the record fails to yield evidence that the school authorities had reason to anticipate that the wearing of the armbands would substantially interfere with the work of the school or impinge upon the rights of other students. Even an official memorandum prepared after the suspension that listed the reasons for the ban on wearing the armbands made no reference to the anticipation of such disruption.

On the contrary, the action of the school authorities appears to have been based upon an urgent wish to avoid the controversy which might result from the expression, even by the silent symbol of armbands, of opposition to this Nation's part in the conflagration in Vietnam. It is revealing, in this respect, that the meeting at which the school principals decided to issue the contested regulation was called in response to a student's statement to the journalism teacher in one of the schools that he wanted to write an article on Vietnam and have it published in the school paper. (The student was dissuaded.)

It is also relevant that the school authorities did not purport to prohibit the wearing of all symbols of political or controversial significance. The record shows that students in some of the schools wore buttons relating to national political campaigns, and some even wore the Iron Cross, traditionally a symbol of Nazism. The order prohibiting the wearing of armbands did not extend to these. Instead, a particular symbol—black armbands worn to exhibit opposition to this Nation's involvement in Vietnam—was singled out for prohibition. Clearly, the prohibition of expression of one particular opinion, at least without evidence that it is necessary to avoid material and substantial interference with schoolwork or discipline, is not constitutionally permissible.

In our system, state-operated schools may not be enclaves of totalitarianism. School officials do not possess absolute authority over their students. Students in school as well as out of school are "persons" under our Constitution. They are possessed of fundamental rights which the State must respect, just as they themselves must respect their obligations to the State. In our system, students may not be regarded as closed-circuit recipients of only that which the State chooses to communicate. They may not be confined to the expression of those sentiments that are officially approved. In the absence of a specific showing of constitutionally valid reasons to regulate their speech, students are entitled to freedom of expression of their views. As Judge Gewin, speaking for the Fifth Circuit, said, school officials cannot suppress "expressions of feelings with which they do not wish to contend." [. . .]

This principle has been repeated by this Court on numerous occasions during the intervening years. In *Keyishian v. Board of Regents* [1967], Mr. Justice Brennan, speaking for the Court, said:

> "The vigilant protection of constitutional freedoms is nowhere more vital than in the community of American schools." The classroom is peculiarly the "marketplace of ideas." The Nation's future depends upon leaders trained through wide exposure to that robust exchange of ideas which discovers truth "out of a multitude of tongues, [rather] than through any kind of authoritative selection."

The principle of these cases is not confined to the supervised and ordained discussion which takes place in the classroom. The principal use to which the schools are dedicated is to accommodate students during prescribed hours for the purpose of certain types of activities. Among those activities is personal intercommunication among the students. This is not only an inevitable part of the process of attending school; it is also an important part of the educational process. A student's rights, therefore, do not embrace merely the classroom hours. When he is in the cafeteria, or on the playing field, or on the campus during the authorized hours, he may express his opinions, even on controversial subjects like the conflict in Vietnam, if he does so without "materially and substantially interfer[ing] with the requirements of appropriate discipline in the operation of the school" and without colliding with the rights of others. But conduct by the student, in class or out of it, which for any reason—whether it stems from time, place, or type of behavior—materially disrupts classwork or involves substantial disorder or invasion of the rights of others is, of course, not immunized by the constitutional guarantee of freedom of speech.

Under our Constitution, free speech is not a right that is given only to be so circumscribed that it exists in principle but not in fact. Freedom of expression would not truly exist if the right could be exercised only in an area that a benevolent government has provided as a safe haven for crackpots. The Constitution says that Congress (and the States) may not abridge the right to free speech. This provision means what it says. We properly read it to permit reasonable regulation of speech-connected activities in carefully restricted circumstances. But we do not confine the permissible exercise of First Amendment rights to a telephone booth or the four corners of a pamphlet, or to supervised and ordained discussion in a school classroom.

If a regulation were adopted by school officials forbidding discussion of the Vietnam conflict, or the expression by any student of opposition to it anywhere on school property except as part of a prescribed classroom exercise, it would be obvious that the regulation would violate the constitutional rights of students, at least if it could not be justified by a showing that the students' activities would materially and substantially disrupt the work and discipline of the school. In the circumstances of the present case, the prohibition of the silent, passive "witness of the armbands," as one of the children called it, is no less offensive to the Constitution's guarantees.

As we have discussed, the record does not demonstrate any facts which might reasonably have led school authorities to forecast substantial disruption of or material interference with school activities, and no disturbances or disorders on the school premises in fact occurred. These petitioners merely went about their ordained rounds in school. Their deviation consisted only in wearing on their sleeve a band of black cloth, not more than two inches wide. They wore it to exhibit their disapproval of the Vietnam hostilities and their advocacy of a truce, to make their views known, and, by their example, to influence others to adopt them. They neither interrupted school activities nor sought to intrude in the school affairs or the lives of others. They caused discussion outside of the classrooms, but no interference with work and no disorder. In the circumstances, our Constitution does not permit officials of the State to deny their form of expression. [. . .]

William O. Douglas

Griswold v. Connecticut (1965)

Mr. Justice DOUGLAS delivered the opinion of the Court.

Coming to the merits, we are met with a wide range of questions that implicate the Due Process Clause of the Fourteenth Amendment. Overtones of some arguments suggest that *Lochner v. New York* [1905], should be our guide. But we decline that invitation as we did in *West Coast Hotel Co. v. Parrish* [1937]. [. . .] We do not sit as a super-legislature to determine the wisdom, need, and propriety of laws that touch economic problems, business affairs, or social conditions. This law, however, operates directly on an intimate relation of husband and wife and their physician's role in one aspect of that relation.

The association of people is not mentioned in the Constitution nor in the Bill of Rights. The right to educate a child in a school of the parents' choice— whether public or private or parochial—is also not mentioned. Nor is the right to study any particular subject or any foreign language. Yet the First Amendment has been construed to include certain of those rights.

By *Pierce v. Society of Sisters* [1925], the right to educate one's children as one chooses is made applicable to the States by the force of the First and Fourteenth Amendments. By *Meyer v. Nebraska* [1923], the same dignity is given the right to study the German language in a private school. In other words, the State may not, consistently with the spirit of the First Amendment, contract the spectrum of available knowledge. The right of freedom of speech and press includes not only the right to utter or to print, but the right to distribute, the right to receive, the right to read; and freedom of inquiry, freedom of thought, and freedom to teach—indeed the freedom of the entire university community. *Sweezy v. New Hampshire* [1958]. Without those peripheral rights the specific rights would be less secure. And so we reaffirm the principle of the Pierce and the Meyer cases.

In *NAACP v. Alabama* [1958], we protected the "freedom to associate and privacy in one's associations," noting that freedom of association was a peripheral First Amendment right. Disclosure of membership lists of a constitutionally valid association, we held, was invalid "as entailing the likelihood of a substantial restraint upon the exercise by petitioner's members of their right to freedom of association." Ibid. In other words, the First Amendment has a penumbra where privacy is protected from governmental intrusion. In like context, we have protected forms of "association" that are not political in the customary sense but pertain to the social, legal, and economic benefit of the members. [. . .]

Those cases involved more than the "right of assembly"—a right that extends to all irrespective of their race or ideology. The right of "association," like the right of belief (*West Virginia State Board of Education v. Barnette* [1943]), is more than the right to attend a meeting; it includes the right to express one's attitudes or philosophies by membership in a group or by affiliation with it or by other lawful means. Association in that context is a form of expression of opinion; and while it is not expressly included in the First Amendment its existence is necessary in making the express guarantees fully meaningful.

The foregoing cases suggest that specific guarantees in the Bill of Rights have penumbras, formed by emanations from those guarantees that help give them life and substance. See *Poe v. Ullman* [1961] (dissenting opinion). Various guarantees create zones of privacy. The right of association contained in the penumbra of the First Amendment is one, as we have seen. The Third Amendment in its prohibition against the quartering of soldiers "in any house" in time of peace without the consent of the owner is another facet of that privacy. The Fourth Amendment explicitly affirms the "right of the people to be secure in their persons, houses, papers, and effects, against unreasonable searches and seizures." The Fifth Amendment in its Self-Incrimination Clause enables the citizen to create a zone of privacy which government may not force him to surrender to his detriment. The Ninth Amendment provides: "The enumeration in the Constitution, of certain rights, shall not be construed to deny or disparage others retained by the people."

The Fourth and Fifth Amendments were described in *Boyd v. United States* [1886], as protection against all governmental invasions "of the sanctity of a man's home and the privacies of life."

We recently referred in *Mapp v. Ohio* [1961], to the Fourth Amendment as creating a "right to privacy, no less important than any other right carefully and particularly reserved to the people." [. . .]

We have had many controversies over these penumbral rights of "privacy and repose." These cases bear witness that the right of privacy which presses for recognition here is a legitimate one.

The present case, then, concerns a relationship lying within the zone of privacy created by several fundamental constitutional guarantees. And it concerns a law which, in forbidding the use of contraceptives rather than regulating their manufacture or sale, seeks to achieve its goals by means having a maximum destructive impact upon that relationship. Such a law cannot stand in light of the familiar principle, so often applied by this Court, that a "governmental purpose to control or prevent activities constitutionally subject to state regulation may not be achieved by means which sweep unnecessarily broadly and thereby invade the area of protected freedoms." *NAACP v. Alabama.* Would we allow the police to search the sacred precincts of marital bedrooms for telltale signs of the use of contraceptives? The very idea is repulsive to the notions of privacy surrounding the marriage relationship.

We deal with a right of privacy older than the Bill of Rights—older than our political parties, older than our school system. Marriage is a coming together for better or for worse, hopefully enduring, and intimate to the degree of being sacred. It is an association that promotes a way of life, not causes; a harmony in living, not political faiths; a bilateral loyalty, not commercial or social projects. Yet it is an association for as noble a purpose as any involved in our prior decisions.

Reversed.

ARTHUR GOLDBERG

Griswold v. Connecticut, Concurrence (1965)

Mr. Justice GOLDBERG, whom the Chief Justice and Mr. Justice BRENNAN join, concurring.

I agree with the Court that Connecticut's birth-control law unconstitutionally intrudes upon the right of marital privacy, and I join in its opinion and judgment. Although I have not accepted the view that "due process" as used in the Fourteenth Amendment incorporates all of the first eight Amendments (see my concurring opinion in *Pointer v. Texas* [1965], and the dissenting opinion of Mr. Justice Brennan in *Cohen v. Hurley* [1961]), I do agree that the concept of liberty protects those personal rights that are fundamental, and is not confined to the specific terms of the Bill of Rights. My conclusion that the concept of liberty is not so restricted and that it embraces the right of marital privacy though that right is not mentioned explicitly in the Constitution is supported both by numerous decisions of this Court, referred to in the Court's opinion, and by the language and history of the Ninth Amendment. In reaching the conclusion that the right of marital privacy is protected, as being within the protected penumbra of specific guarantees of the Bill of Rights, the Court refers to the Ninth Amendment. I add these words to emphasize the relevance of that Amendment to the Court's holding. [. . .]

The language and history of the Ninth Amendment reveal that the Framers of the Constitution believed that there are additional fundamental rights, protected from governmental infringement, which exist alongside those fundamental rights specifically mentioned in the first eight constitutional amendments.

The Ninth Amendment reads, "The enumeration in the Constitution, of certain rights, shall not be construed to deny or disparage others retained by the people." The Amendment is almost entirely the work of James Madison. It was introduced in Congress by him and passed the House and Senate with little or no debate and virtually no change in language. It was proffered to quiet expressed fears that a bill of specifically enumerated rights could not be sufficiently broad to cover all essential rights and that the specific mention of certain rights would be interpreted as a denial that others were protected.

In presenting the proposed Amendment, Madison said:

It has been objected also against a bill of rights, that, by enumerating particular exceptions to the grant of power, it would disparage those rights which were not placed in that enumeration; and it might follow by implication, that those rights which were not singled out, were intended to be assigned into the hands of the General Government, and were consequently insecure. This is one of the most plausible arguments I have ever heard urged against the admission of a bill of rights into this system; but, I conceive, that it may be guarded against. I have attempted it, as gentlemen may see by turning to the [381 U.S. 479, 490] last clause of the fourth resolution [the Ninth Amendment]. I *Annals of Congress* 439 (Gales and Seaton ed. 1834).

Mr. Justice Story wrote of this argument against a bill of rights and the meaning of the Ninth Amendment:

In regard to . . . [a] suggestion, that the affirmance of certain rights might disparage others, or might lead to argumentative implications in favor of other powers, it might be sufficient to say that such a course of reasoning could never be sustained upon any solid basis. . . . But a conclusive answer is, that such an attempt may be interdicted (as it has been) by a positive declaration in such a bill of rights that the enumeration of certain rights shall not be construed to deny or disparage others retained by the people. II Story,

Commentaries on the Constitution of the United States 626–627 (5th ed. 1891).

He further stated, referring to the Ninth Amendment:

This clause was manifestly introduced to prevent any perverse or ingenious misapplication of the well-known maxim, that an affirmation in particular cases implies a negation in all others; and, *e converso*, that a negation in particular cases implies an affirmation in all others. Id., at 651.

These statements of Madison and Story make clear that the Framers did not intend that the first eight amendments be construed to exhaust the basic and fundamental rights which the Constitution guaranteed to the people.

While this Court has had little occasion to interpret the Ninth Amendment, "[i]t cannot be presumed that any clause in the Constitution is intended to be without effect." *Marbury v. Madison* [1803]. In interpreting the Constitution, "real effect should be given to all the words it uses." *Myers v. United States* [1926]. The Ninth Amendment to the Constitution may be regarded by some as a recent discovery and may be forgotten by others, but since 1791 it has been a basic part of the Constitution which we are sworn to uphold. To hold that a right so basic and fundamental and so deep-rooted in our society as the right of privacy in marriage may be infringed because that right is not guaranteed in so many words by the first eight amendments to the Constitution is to ignore the Ninth Amendment and to give it no effect whatsoever.

Moreover, a judicial construction that this fundamental right is not protected by the Constitution because it is not mentioned in explicit terms by one of the first eight amendments or elsewhere in the Constitution would violate the Ninth Amendment, which specifically states that "[t]he enumeration in the Constitution, of certain rights, shall not be *construed* to deny or disparage others retained by the people." (Emphasis added.)

A dissenting opinion suggests that my interpretation of the Ninth Amendment somehow "broaden[s] the powers of this Court." Post, at 520. With all due respect, I believe that it misses the import of what I am saying. I do not take the position of my Brother

Black in his dissent in *Adamson v. California* [1947], that the entire Bill of Rights is incorporated in the Fourteenth Amendment, and I do not mean to imply that the Ninth Amendment is applied against the States by the Fourteenth. Nor do I mean to state that the Ninth Amendment constitutes an independent source of rights protected from infringement by either the States or the Federal Government. Rather, the Ninth Amendment shows a belief of the Constitution's authors that fundamental rights exist that are not expressly enumerated in the first eight amendments and an intent that the list of rights included there not be deemed exhaustive. As any student of this Court's opinions knows, this Court has held, often unanimously, that the Fifth and Fourteenth Amendments protect certain fundamental personal liberties from abridgment by the Federal Government or the States. The Ninth Amendment simply shows the intent of the Constitution's authors that other fundamental personal rights should not be denied such protection or disparaged in any other way simply because they are not specifically listed in the first eight constitutional amendments. I do not see how this broadens the authority of the Court; rather it serves to support what this Court has been doing in protecting fundamental rights.

Nor am I turning somersaults with history in arguing that the Ninth Amendment is relevant in a case dealing with a State's infringement of a fundamental right. While the Ninth Amendment—and indeed the entire Bill of Rights—originally concerned restrictions upon federal power, the subsequently enacted Fourteenth Amendment prohibits the States as well from abridging fundamental personal liberties. And, the Ninth Amendment, in indicating that not all such liberties are specifically mentioned in the first eight amendments, is surely relevant in showing the existence of other fundamental personal rights, now protected from state, as well as federal, infringement. In sum, the Ninth Amendment simply lends strong support to the view that the "liberty" protected by the Fifth and Fourteenth Amendments from infringement by the Federal Government or the States is not restricted to rights specifically mentioned in the first eight amendments.

In determining which rights are fundamental, judges are not left at large to decide cases in light of their personal and private notions. Rather, they must look to the "traditions and [collective] conscience of our people" to determine whether a principle is "so rooted [there] . . . as to be ranked as fundamental." *Snyder v. Massachusetts* [1934]. The inquiry is whether a right involved "is of such a character that it cannot be denied without violating those 'fundamental principles of liberty and justice which lie at the base of all our civil and political institutions.' . . ." *Powell v. Alabama* [1932]. [. . .]

The entire fabric of the Constitution and the purposes that clearly underlie its specific guarantees demonstrate that the rights to marital privacy and to marry and raise a family are of similar order and magnitude as the fundamental rights specifically protected.

Although the Constitution does not speak in so many words of the right of privacy in marriage, I cannot believe that it offers these fundamental rights no protection. The fact that no particular provision of the Constitution explicitly forbids the State from disrupting the traditional relation of the family—a relation as old and as fundamental as our entire civilization—surely does not show that the Government was meant to have the power to do so. Rather, as the Ninth Amendment expressly recognizes, there are fundamental personal rights such as this one, which are protected from abridgment by the Government though not specifically mentioned in the Constitution. [. . .]

The logic of the dissents would sanction federal or state legislation that seems to me even more plainly unconstitutional than the statute before us. Surely the Government, absent a showing of a compelling subordinating state interest, could not decree that all husbands and wives must be sterilized after two children have been born to them. Yet by their reasoning such an invasion of marital privacy would not be subject to constitutional challenge because, while it might be "silly," no provision of the Constitution specifically prevents the Government from curtailing the marital right to bear children and raise a family. While it may shock some of my Brethren that the Court today holds that the Constitution protects the right of marital privacy, in my view it is far more shocking to believe that the personal liberty guaranteed by the Constitution does not include protection against such totalitarian limitation of family size, which is at complete variance with our constitutional concepts. Yet, if upon a showing of a slender basis of rationality, a law outlawing voluntary birth control by married persons is valid, then, by the same reasoning, a law requiring compulsory birth control also would seem to be valid. In my view, however, both types of law would unjustifiably intrude upon rights of marital privacy which are constitutionally protected.

In a long series of cases this Court has held that where fundamental personal liberties are involved, they may not be abridged by the States simply on a showing that a regulatory statute has some rational relationship to the effectuation of a proper state purpose. "Where there is a significant encroachment upon personal liberty, the State may prevail only upon showing a subordinating interest which is compelling," *Bates v. Little Rock* [1960]. [. . .]

Although the Connecticut birth-control law obviously encroaches upon a fundamental personal liberty, the State does not show that the law serves any "subordinating [state] interest which is compelling" or that it is "necessary . . . to the accomplishment of a permissible state policy." The State, at most, argues that there is some rational relation between this statute and what is admittedly a legitimate subject of state concern—the discouraging of extra-marital relations. It says that preventing the use of birth-control devices by married persons helps prevent the indulgence by some in such extramarital relations. The rationality of this justification is dubious, particularly in light of the admitted widespread availability to all persons in the State of Connecticut, unmarried as well as married, of birth-control devices for the prevention of disease, as distinguished from the prevention of conception. But, in any event, it is clear that the state interest in safeguarding marital fidelity can be served by a more discriminately tailored statute, which does not, like the present one, sweep unnecessarily broadly, reaching far beyond the evil sought to be dealt with and intruding upon the privacy of all married couples. [. . .]

In sum, I believe that the right of privacy in the marital relation is fundamental and basic—a personal right "retained by the people" within the meaning of the Ninth Amendment. Connecticut cannot constitutionally abridge this fundamental right, which is protected by the Fourteenth Amendment from infringement by the States. I agree with the Court that petitioners' convictions must therefore be reversed.

John Marshall Harlan II

Griswold v. Connecticut, Concurrence (1965)

Mr. Justice HARLAN, concurring in the judgment.

I fully agree with the judgment of reversal, but find myself unable to join the Court's opinion. The reason is that it seems to me to evince an approach to this case very much like that taken by my Brothers Black and Stewart in dissent, namely: the Due Process Clause of the Fourteenth Amendment does not touch this Connecticut statute unless the enactment is found to violate some right assured by the letter or penumbra of the Bill of Rights.

In other words, what I find implicit in the Court's opinion is that the "incorporation" doctrine may be used to restrict the reach of Fourteenth Amendment Due Process. For me, this is just as unacceptable constitutional doctrine as is the use of the "incorporation" approach to impose upon the States all the requirements of the Bill of Rights as found in the provisions of the first eight amendments and in the decisions of this Court interpreting them.

In my view, the proper constitutional inquiry in this case is whether this Connecticut statute infringes the Due Process Clause of the Fourteenth Amendment because the enactment violates basic values "implicit in the concept of ordered liberty," *Palko v. Connecticut* [1937]. For reasons stated at length in my dissenting opinion in *Poe v. Ullman* [1961], I believe that it does. While the relevant inquiry may be aided by resort to one or more of the provisions of the Bill of Rights, it is not dependent on them or any of their radiations. The Due Process Clause of the Fourteenth Amendment stands, in my opinion, on its own bottom.

A further observation seems in order respecting the justification of my Brothers Black and Stewart for their "incorporation" approach to this case. Their approach does not rest on historical reasons, which are, of course, wholly lacking [. . .] but on the thesis that, by limiting the content of the Due Process Clause of the Fourteenth Amendment to the protection of rights which can be found elsewhere in the Constitution, in this instance, in the Bill of Rights, judges will thus be confined to "interpretation" of specific constitutional provisions, and will thereby be restrained from introducing their own notions of constitutional right and wrong into the "vague contours of the Due Process Clause." *Rochin v. California* [1952]. While I could not more heartily agree that judicial "self-restraint" is an indispensable ingredient of sound constitutional adjudication, I do submit that the formula suggested for achieving it is more hollow than real. "Specific" provisions of the Constitution, no less than "due process," lend themselves as readily to "personal" interpretations by judges whose constitutional outlook is simply to keep the Constitution in supposed "tune with the times." Need one go further

than to recall last Term's reapportionment cases, *Wesberry v. Sanders* [1964], and *Reynolds v. Sims* [1964], where a majority of the Court "interpreted" "by the People" (Art. I, § 2) and "equal protection" (Amdt. 14) to command "one person, one vote," an interpretation that was made in the face of irrefutable and still unanswered history to the contrary? *See* my dissenting opinions in those cases.

Judicial self-restraint will not, I suggest, be brought about in the "due process" area by the historically unfounded incorporation formula long advanced by my Brother Black, and now in part espoused by my Brother Stewart. It will be achieved in this area, as in other constitutional areas, only by continual insistence upon respect for the teachings of history, solid recognition of the basic values that underlie our society, and wise appreciation of the great roles that the doctrines of federalism and separation of powers have played in establishing and preserving American freedoms. *See Adamson v. California* [1947] (Mr. Justice Frankfurter, concurring). Adherence to these principles will not, of course, obviate all constitutional differences of opinion among judges, nor should it. Their continued recognition will, however, go farther toward keeping most judges from roaming at large in the constitutional field than will the interpolation into the Constitution of an artificial and largely illusory restriction on the content of the Due Process Clause.

HUGO BLACK

Griswold v. Connecticut, Dissent (1965)

Mr. Justice BLACK, with whom Mr. Justice Stewart joins, dissenting.

I agree with my Brother Stewart's dissenting opinion. And, like him, I do not to any extent whatever base my view that this Connecticut law is constitutional on a belief that the law is wise, or that its policy is a good one. In order that there may be no room at all to doubt why I vote as I do, I feel constrained to

add that the law is every bit as offensive to me as it is to my Brethren of the majority and my Brothers Harlan, White and Goldberg, who, reciting reasons why it is offensive to them, hold it unconstitutional. There is no single one of the graphic and eloquent strictures and criticisms fired at the policy of this Connecticut law either by the Court's opinion or by those of my concurring Brethren to which I cannot subscribe—except their conclusion that the evil qualities they see in the law make it unconstitutional. [. . .]

The Court talks about a constitutional "right of privacy" as though there is some constitutional provision or provisions forbidding any law ever to be passed which might abridge the "privacy" of individuals. But there is not. There are, of course, guarantees in certain specific constitutional provisions which are designed in part to protect privacy at certain times and places with respect to certain activities. Such, for example, is the Fourth Amendment's guarantee against "unreasonable searches and seizures." But I think it belittles that Amendment to talk about it as though it protects nothing but "privacy." To treat it that way is to give it a niggardly interpretation, not the kind of liberal reading I think any Bill of Rights provision should be given. The average man would very likely not have his feelings soothed any more by having his property seized openly than by having it seized privately and by stealth. He simply wants his property left alone. And a person can be just as much, if not more, irritated, annoyed and injured by an unceremonious public arrest by a policeman as he is by a seizure in the privacy of his office or home.

One of the most effective ways of diluting or expanding a constitutionally guaranteed right is to substitute for the crucial word or words of a constitutional guarantee another word or words, more or less flexible and more or less restricted in meaning. This fact is well illustrated by the use of the term "right of privacy" as a comprehensive substitute for the Fourth Amendment's guarantee against "unreasonable searches and seizures." "Privacy" is a broad, abstract and ambiguous concept which can easily be shrunken in meaning but which can also, on the other hand, easily be interpreted as a constitutional ban against many things other than searches and seizures. I have expressed the view many times that First Amendment freedoms, for example, have suffered from a failure of the courts to stick to the simple language of the First Amendment in construing it, instead of invoking multitudes of words substituted for those the Framers used. *See, e.g., New York Times Co. v. Sullivan* [1964], (concurring opinion). For these reasons, I get nowhere in this case by talk about a constitutional "right of privacy" as an emanation from one or more constitutional provisions. I like my

privacy as well as the next one, but I am nevertheless compelled to admit that government has a right to invade it unless prohibited by some specific constitutional provision. For these reasons, I cannot agree with the Court's judgment and the reasons it gives for holding this Connecticut law unconstitutional.

This brings me to the arguments made by my Brothers Harlan, White and Goldberg for invalidating the Connecticut law. Brothers Harlan and White would invalidate it by reliance on the Due Process Clause of the Fourteenth Amendment, but Brother Goldberg, while agreeing with Brother Harlan, relies also on the Ninth Amendment. I have no doubt that the Connecticut law could be applied in such a way as to abridge freedom of speech and press, and therefore violate the First and Fourteenth Amendments. My disagreement with the Court's opinion holding that there is such a violation here is a narrow one, relating to the application of the First Amendment to the facts and circumstances of this particular case. But my disagreement with Brothers Harlan, White and Goldberg is more basic. I think that, if properly construed, neither the Due Process Clause nor the Ninth Amendment, nor both together, could under any circumstances be a proper basis for invalidating the Connecticut law. I discuss the due process and Ninth Amendment arguments together because, on analysis, they turn out to be the same thing—merely using different words to claim for this Court and the federal judiciary power to invalidate any legislative act which the judges find irrational, unreasonable or offensive.

The due process argument which my Brothers Harlan and White adopt here is based, as their opinions indicate, on the premise that this Court is vested with power to invalidate all state laws that it considers to be arbitrary, capricious, unreasonable, or oppressive, or on this Court's belief that a particular state law under scrutiny has no "rational or justifying" purpose, or is offensive to a "sense of fairness and justice." If these formulas based on "natural justice," or others which mean the same thing, are to prevail, they require judges to determine what is or is not constitutional on the basis of their own appraisal of what laws are unwise or unnecessary. The power to make such decisions is, of course, that of a legislative body. Surely it has to be admitted that no provision of the Constitution specifically gives such blanket power to courts to exercise such a supervisory veto over the wisdom and value of legislative policies and to hold unconstitutional those laws which they believe unwise or dangerous. I readily admit that no legislative body, state or national, should pass laws that can justly be given any of the invidious labels invoked as constitutional excuses to strike down state laws. But perhaps it is not too much to say that no legislative body ever does pass laws without believing that they will accomplish a sane, rational, wise and justifiable purpose. While I completely subscribe to the holding of *Marbury v. Madison* [1803], and subsequent cases, that our Court has constitutional power to strike down statutes, state or federal, that violate commands of the Federal Constitution, I do not believe that we are granted power by the Due Process Clause or any other constitutional provision or provisions to measure constitutionality by our belief that legislation is arbitrary, capricious or unreasonable, or accomplishes no justifiable purpose, or is offensive to our own notions of "civilized standards of conduct." Such an appraisal of the wisdom of legislation is an attribute of the power to make laws, not of the power to interpret them. The use by federal courts of such a formula or doctrine or whatnot to veto federal or state laws simply takes away from Congress and States the power to make laws based on their own judgment of fairness and wisdom, and transfers that power to this Court for ultimate determination—a power which was specifically denied to federal courts by the convention that framed the Constitution. [. . .]

My Brother Goldberg has adopted the recent discovery that the Ninth Amendment as well as the Due Process Clause can be used by this Court as authority to strike down all state legislation which this Court thinks violates "fundamental principles of liberty and justice," or is contrary to the "traditions and [collective] conscience of our people." He also states, without proof satisfactory to me, that, in making decisions on this basis, judges will not consider "their personal and private notions." One may ask how they can avoid considering them. Our Court certainly has no machinery with which to take a Gallup Poll. And the scientific miracles of this age have not yet produced a gadget which the Court can use to determine what traditions are rooted in the "[collective] conscience of our people." Moreover, one would certainly have

to look far beyond the language of the Ninth Amendment to find that the Framers vested in this Court any such awesome veto powers over lawmaking, either by the States or by the Congress. Nor does anything in the history of the Amendment offer any support for such a shocking doctrine. The whole history of the adoption of the Constitution and Bill of Rights points the other way, and the very material quoted by my Brother Goldberg shows that the Ninth Amendment was intended to protect against the idea that, "by enumerating particular exceptions to the grant of power" to the Federal Government, "those rights which were not singled out were intended to be assigned into the hands of the General Government [the United States], and were consequently insecure." That Amendment was passed not to broaden the powers of this Court or any other department of "the General Government," but, as every student of history knows, to assure the people that the Constitution in all its provisions was intended to limit the Federal Government to the powers granted expressly or by necessary implication. If any broad, unlimited power to hold laws unconstitutional because they offend what this Court conceives to be the "[collective] conscience of our people" is vested in this Court by the Ninth Amendment, the Fourteenth Amendment, or any other provision of the Constitution, it was not given by the Framers, but rather has been bestowed on the Court by the Court. [. . .]

I repeat, so as not to be misunderstood, that this Court does have power, which it should exercise, to hold laws unconstitutional where they are forbidden by the Federal Constitution. My point is that there is no provision of the Constitution which either expressly or impliedly vests power in this Court to sit as a supervisory agency over acts of duly constituted legislative bodies and set aside their laws because of the Court's belief that the legislative policies adopted are unreasonable, unwise, arbitrary, capricious or irrational. The adoption of such a loose flexible. uncontrolled standard for holding laws unconstitutional, if ever it is finally achieved, will amount to a great unconstitutional shift of power to the courts which I believe and am constrained to say will be bad for the courts, and worse for the country. Subjecting federal and state laws to such an unrestrained and unrestrainable judicial control as to the wisdom of legislative enactments would, I fear, jeopardize the separation of governmental powers that the Framers set up, and, at the same time, threaten to take away much of the power of States to govern themselves which the Constitution plainly intended them to have.

I realize that many good and able men have eloquently spoken and written, sometimes in rhapsodical strains, about the duty of this Court to keep the Constitution in tune with the times. The idea is that the Constitution must be changed from time to time, and that this Court is charged with a duty to make those changes. For myself, I must, with all deference, reject that philosophy. The Constitution makers knew the need for change, and provided for it. Amendments suggested by the people's elected representatives can be submitted to the people or their selected agents for ratification. That method of change was good for our Fathers, and, being somewhat old-fashioned, I must add it is good enough for me. And so I cannot rely on the Due Process Clause or the Ninth Amendment or any mysterious and uncertain natural law concept as a reason for striking down this state law. The Due Process Clause, with an "arbitrary and capricious" or "shocking to the conscience" formula, was liberally used by this Court to strike down economic legislation in the early decades of this century, threatening, many people thought, the tranquility and stability of the Nation. See, e.g., *Lochner v. New York* [1905]. That formula, based on subjective considerations of "natural justice," is no less dangerous when used to enforce this Court's views about personal rights than those about economic rights. [. . .]

The doctrine that prevailed in *Lochner*, *Coppage*, *Adkins*, *Burns*, and like cases—that due process authorizes courts to hold laws unconstitutional when they believe the legislature has acted unwisely—has long since been discarded. We have returned to the original constitutional proposition that courts do not substitute their social and economic beliefs for the judgment of legislative bodies, who are elected to pass laws. [. . .]

In 1798, when this Court was asked to hold another Connecticut law unconstitutional, Justice Iredell said:

[I]t has been the policy of all the American states which have individually framed their state constitutions since the revolution, and of the people of

the United States when they framed the Federal Constitution, to define with precision the objects of the legislative power, and to restrain its exercise within marked and settled boundaries. If any act of Congress, or of the Legislature of a state, violates those constitutional provisions, it is unquestionably void, though I admit that, as the authority to declare it void is of a delicate and awful nature, the Court will never resort to that authority but in a clear and urgent case. If, on the other hand, the Legislature of the Union, or the Legislature of any member of the Union, shall pass a law within the general scope of their constitutional power, the Court cannot pronounce it to be void, merely because it is, in their judgment, contrary to the principles of natural justice. The ideas of natural justice are regulated by no fixed standard: the ablest and the purest men have differed upon the subject, and all that the Court could properly say in such an event would be that the Legislature (possessed of an equal right of opinion) had passed an act which, in the opinion of the judges, was inconsistent with the abstract principles of natural justice. *Calder v. Bull* (emphasis in original).

I would adhere to that constitutional philosophy in passing on this Connecticut law today. I am not persuaded to deviate from the view which I stated in 1947 in *Adamson v. California* (dissenting opinion).

Since *Marbury v. Madison* was decided, the practice has been firmly established, for better or worse, that courts can strike down legislative enactments which violate the Constitution. This process, of course, involves interpretation, and since words can have many meanings, interpretation obviously may result in contraction or extension of the original purpose of a constitutional provision, thereby affecting policy. But to pass upon the constitutionality of statutes by looking to the particular standards enumerated in the Bill of Rights and other parts of the Constitution is one thing; to invalidate statutes because of application of "natural law" deemed to be above and undefined by the Constitution is another.

In the one instance, courts, proceeding within clearly marked constitutional boundaries, seek to execute policies written into the Constitution; in the other, they roam at will in the limitless area of their own beliefs as to reasonableness, and actually select policies, a responsibility which the Constitution entrusts to the legislative representatives of the people.

The late Judge Learned Hand, after emphasizing his view that judges should not use the due process formula suggested in the concurring opinions today or any other formula like it to invalidate legislation offensive to their "personal preferences," made the statement, with which I fully agree, that:

For myself, it would be most irksome to be ruled by a bevy of Platonic Guardians, even if I knew how to choose them, which I assuredly do not.

So far as I am concerned, Connecticut's law, as applied here, is not forbidden by any provision of the Federal Constitution as that Constitution was written, and I would therefore affirm.

HARRY A. BLACKMUN

Roe v. Wade (1973)

Mr. Justice BLACKMUN delivered the opinion of the Court.

This Texas federal appeal [. . .] and its Georgia companion, *Doe v. Bolton*, present constitutional challenges to state criminal abortion legislation. The Texas statutes under attack here are typical of those that have been in effect in many States for approximately a century. The Georgia statutes, in contrast, have a modern cast, and are a legislative product that, to an extent at least, obviously reflects the influences of recent attitudinal change, of advancing medical knowledge and techniques, and of new thinking about an old issue.

We forthwith acknowledge our awareness of the sensitive and emotional nature of the abortion controversy, of the vigorous opposing views, even among physicians, and of the deep and seemingly absolute convictions that the subject inspires. One's philosophy, one's experiences, one's exposure to the raw edges of human existence, one's religious training, one's attitudes toward life and family and their values, and the moral standards one establishes and seeks to observe, are all likely to influence and to color one's thinking and conclusions about abortion. [. . .]

Our task, of course, is to resolve the issue by constitutional measurement, free of emotion and of predilection. We seek earnestly to do this, and, because we do, we have inquired into, and in this opinion place some emphasis upon, medical and

medical-legal history and what that history reveals about man's attitudes toward the abortion procedure over the centuries. [. . .]

[The Constitution] is made for people of fundamentally differing views, and the accident of our finding certain opinions natural and familiar or novel and even shocking ought not to conclude our judgment upon the question whether statutes embodying them conflict with the Constitution of the United States.

I

The Texas statutes that concern us here make it a crime to "procure an abortion," as therein defined, or to attempt one, except with respect to "an abortion procured or attempted by medical advice for the purpose of saving the life of the mother." Similar statutes are in existence in a majority of the States. [. . .]

V

The principal thrust of appellant's attack on the Texas statutes is that they improperly invade a right, said to be possessed by the pregnant woman, to choose to terminate her pregnancy. Appellant would discover this right in the concept of personal "liberty" embodied in the Fourteenth Amendment's Due Process Clause; or in personal, marital, familial, and sexual privacy said to be protected by the Bill of Rights or its penumbras, *see Griswold v. Connecticut* (1965); *Eisenstadt v. Baird* (1972); or among those rights reserved to the people by the Ninth Amendment, *Griswold v. Connecticut* (Goldberg, J., concurring). Before addressing this claim, we feel it desirable briefly to survey, in several aspects, the history of abortion, for such insight as that history may afford us, and then to examine the state purposes and interests behind the criminal abortion laws.

VI

It perhaps is not generally appreciated that the restrictive criminal abortion laws in effect in a majority of States today are of relatively recent vintage. Those laws, generally proscribing abortion or its attempt at any time during pregnancy except when necessary to preserve the pregnant woman's life, are not of ancient or even of common law origin. Instead, they derive from statutory changes effected, for the most part, in the latter half of the 19th century.

   1. Ancient attitudes.   These are not capable of precise determination. We are told that, at the time of the Persian Empire, abortifacients were known, and that criminal abortions were severely punished. We are also told, however, that abortion was practiced in Greek times as well as in the Roman Era, and that "it was resorted to without scruple." The Ephesian, Soranos, often described as the greatest of the ancient gynecologists, appears to have been generally opposed to Rome's prevailing free-abortion practices. He found it necessary to think first of the life of the mother, and he resorted to abortion when, upon this standard, he felt the procedure advisable. Greek and Roman law afforded little protection to the unborn. If abortion was prosecuted in some places, it seems to have been based on a concept of a violation of the father's right to his offspring. Ancient religion did not bar abortion.

   2. The Hippocratic Oath.   What then of the famous Oath that has stood so long as the ethical guide of the medical profession and that bears the name of the great Greek (460(?)–377(?) B.C.), who has been described as the Father of Medicine, the

"wisest and the greatest practitioner of his art," and the "most important and most complete medical personality of antiquity," who dominated the medical schools of his time, and who typified the sum of the medical knowledge of the past? The Oath varies somewhat according to the particular translation, but in any translation the content is clear:

> I will give no deadly medicine to anyone if asked, nor suggest any such counsel; and in like manner, I will not give to a woman a pessary to produce abortion,

or

> I will neither give a deadly drug to anybody if asked for it, nor will I make a suggestion to this effect. Similarly, I will not give to a woman an abortive remedy.

   Although the Oath is not mentioned in any of the principal briefs in this case or in *Doe v. Bolton*, it represents the apex of the development of strict ethical concepts in medicine, and its influence endures to this day. Why did not the authority of Hippocrates dissuade abortion practice in his time and that of Rome? The late Dr. Edelstein provides us with a theory: The Oath was not uncontested even in Hippocrates' day; only the Pythagorean school of philosophers frowned upon the related act of suicide. Most Greek thinkers, on the other hand, commended abortion, at least prior to viability. See Plato, *Republic*, V, 461; Aristotle, *Politics*, VII, 1335b25. For the Pythagoreans, however, it was a matter of dogma. For them, the embryo was animate from the moment of conception, and abortion meant destruction of a living being. The abortion clause of the Oath, therefore, "echoes Pythagorean doctrines," and "[i]n no other stratum of Greek opinion were such views held or proposed in the same spirit of uncompromising austerity."

   Dr. Edelstein then concludes that the Oath originated in a group representing only a small segment of Greek opinion, and that it certainly was not accepted by all ancient physicians. He points out that medical writings down to Galen (A.D. 130–200) "give evidence of the violation of almost every one of its injunctions." But with the end of antiquity, a decided change took place. Resistance against suicide and against abortion became common. The Oath came to be popular. The emerging teachings of Christianity were in agreement with the Pythagorean ethic. The Oath "became the nucleus of all medical ethics," and "was applauded as the embodiment of truth." Thus, suggests Dr. Edelstein, it is "a Pythagorean manifesto, and not the expression of an absolute standard of medical conduct."

This, it seems to us, is a satisfactory and acceptable explanation of the Hippocratic Oath's apparent rigidity. It enables us to understand, in historical context, a long-accepted and revered statement of medical ethics.

3. *The common law.*   It is undisputed that, at common law, abortion performed before "quickening"—the first recognizable movement of the fetus in utero, appearing usually from the 16th to the 18th week of pregnancy—was not an indictable offense. The absence of a common law crime for pre-quickening abortion appears to have developed from a confluence of earlier philosophical, theological, and civil and canon law concepts of when life begins. These disciplines variously approached the question in terms of the point at which the embryo or fetus became "formed" or recognizably human, or in terms of when a "person" came into being, that is, infused with a "soul" or "animated." A loose consensus evolved in early English law that these events occurred at some point between conception and live birth. This was "mediate animation." Although Christian theology and the canon law came to fix the point of animation at 40 days for a male and 80 days for a female, a view that persisted until the 19th century, there was otherwise little agreement about the precise time of formation or animation. There was agreement, however, that, prior to this point, the fetus was to be regarded as part of the mother, and its destruction, therefore, was not homicide. Due to continued uncertainty about the precise time when animation occurred, to the lack of any empirical basis for the 40-80-day view, and perhaps to Aquinas' definition of movement as one of the two first principles of life, Bracton focused upon quickening as the critical point. The significance of quickening was echoed by later common law scholars, and found its way into the received common law in this country.

Whether abortion of a quick fetus was a felony at common law, or even a lesser crime, is still disputed.

Bracton, writing early in the 13th century, thought it homicide. But the later and predominant view, following the great common law scholars, has been that it was, at most, a lesser offense. In a frequently cited passage, Coke took the position that abortion of a woman "quick with childe" is "a great misprision, and no murder." Blackstone followed, saying that, while abortion after quickening had once been considered manslaughter (though not murder), "modern law" took a less severe view. A recent review of the common law precedents argues, however, that those precedents contradict Coke, and that even post-quickening abortion was never established as a common law crime. This is of some importance, because, while most American courts ruled, in holding or dictum, that abortion of an unquickened fetus was not criminal under their received common law, others followed Coke in stating that abortion of a quick fetus was a "misprision," a term they translated to mean "misdemeanor." That their reliance on Coke on this aspect of the law was uncritical and, apparently in all the reported cases, dictum (due probably to the paucity of common law prosecutions for post-quickening abortion), makes it now appear doubtful that abortion was ever firmly established as a common law crime even with respect to the destruction of a quick fetus. [. . .]

5. *The American law.*   In this country, the law in effect in all but a few States until mid-19th century was the preexisting English common law. Connecticut, the first State to enact abortion legislation, adopted in 1821 that part of Lord Ellenborough's Act that related to a woman "quick with child." The death penalty was not imposed. Abortion before quickening was made a crime in that State only in 1860. In 1828, New York enacted legislation that, in two respects, was to serve as a model for early anti-abortion statutes. First, while barring destruction of an unquickened fetus as well as a quick fetus, it made the former only a misdemeanor, but the latter second-degree manslaughter. Second, it incorporated a concept of therapeutic abortion by providing that an abortion was excused if it shall have been necessary to preserve the life of such mother, or shall have been advised by two physicians to be necessary for such purpose. By 1840, when Texas had received the common law, only eight American States had statutes dealing with abortion. It was not until after the War

Between the States that legislation began generally to replace the common law. Most of these initial statutes dealt severely with abortion after quickening, but were lenient with it before quickening. Most punished attempts equally with completed abortions. While many statutes included the exception for an abortion thought by one or more physicians to be necessary to save the mother's life, that provision soon disappeared, and the typical law required that the procedure actually be necessary for that purpose.

Gradually, in the middle and late 19th century, the quickening distinction disappeared from the statutory law of most States and the degree of the offense and the penalties were increased. By the end of the 1950's, a large majority of the jurisdictions banned abortion, however and whenever performed, unless done to save or preserve the life of the mother. The exceptions, Alabama and the District of Columbia, permitted abortion to preserve the mother's health. Three States permitted abortions that were not "unlawfully" performed or that were not "without lawful justification," leaving interpretation of those standards to the courts. In the past several years, however, a trend toward liberalization of abortion statutes has resulted in adoption, by about one-third of the States, of less stringent laws. [. . .]

It is thus apparent that, at common law, at the time of the adoption of our Constitution, and throughout the major portion of the 19th century, abortion was viewed with less disfavor than under most American statutes currently in effect. Phrasing it another way, a woman enjoyed a substantially broader right to terminate a pregnancy than she does in most States today. At least with respect to the early stage of pregnancy, and very possibly without such a limitation, the opportunity to make this choice was present in this country well into the 19th century. Even later, the law continued for some time to treat less punitively an abortion procured in early pregnancy. [. . .]

VII

Three reasons have been advanced to explain historically the enactment of criminal abortion laws in the 19th century and to justify their continued existence.

It has been argued occasionally that these laws were the product of a Victorian social concern to discourage illicit sexual conduct. Texas, however, does not advance this justification in the present case, and it appears that no court or commentator has taken the argument seriously. The appellants and *amici* contend, moreover, that this is not a proper state purpose, at all and suggest that, if it were, the Texas statutes are overbroad in protecting it, since the law fails to distinguish between married and unwed mothers.

A second reason is concerned with abortion as a medical procedure. When most criminal abortion laws were first enacted, the procedure was a hazardous one for the woman. This was particularly true prior to the development of antisepsis. Antiseptic techniques, of course, were based on discoveries by Lister, Pasteur, and others first announced in 1867, but were not generally accepted and employed until about the turn of the century. Abortion mortality was high. Even after 1900, and perhaps until as late as the development of antibiotics in the 1940's, standard modern techniques such as dilation and curettage were not nearly so safe as they are today. Thus, it has been argued that a State's real concern in enacting a criminal abortion law was to protect the pregnant woman, that is, to restrain her from submitting to a procedure that placed her life in serious jeopardy.

Modern medical techniques have altered this situation. Appellants and various *amici* refer to medical data indicating that abortion in early pregnancy, that is, prior to the end of the first trimester, although not without its risk, is now relatively safe. Mortality rates for women undergoing early abortions, where the procedure is legal, appear to be as low as or lower than the rates for normal childbirth. Consequently, any interest of the State in protecting the woman from an inherently hazardous procedure, except when it would be equally dangerous for her to forgo it, has largely disappeared. Of course, important state interests in the areas of health and medical standards do remain. The State has a legitimate interest in seeing to it that abortion, like any other medical procedure, is performed under circumstances that insure maximum safety for the patient. This interest obviously extends at least to the performing physician and his staff, to the facilities involved, to the availability of after-care, and to adequate provision for any complication or emergency that might arise. The prevalence of high mortality rates at illegal "abortion mills" strengthens, rather than weakens, the State's interest in regulating the conditions under which abortions are performed. Moreover, the risk to the woman increases as her pregnancy continues. Thus, the State retains a definite interest in protecting the woman's own health and safety when an abortion is proposed at a late stage of pregnancy.

The third reason is the State's interest—some phrase it in terms of duty—in protecting prenatal life. Some of the argument for this justification rests on the theory that a new human life is present from the moment of conception. The State's interest and general obligation to protect life then extends, it is argued, to prenatal life. Only when the life of the pregnant mother herself is at stake, balanced against the life she carries within her, should the interest of the embryo or fetus not prevail. Logically, of course, a legitimate state interest in this area need not stand or fall on acceptance of the belief that life begins at conception or at some other point prior to live birth. In assessing the State's interest, recognition may be given to the less rigid claim that as long as at least *potential* life is involved, the State may assert interests beyond the protection of the pregnant woman alone.

Parties challenging state abortion laws have sharply disputed in some courts the contention that a purpose of these laws, when enacted, was to protect prenatal life. Pointing to the absence of legislative history to support the contention, they claim that most state laws were designed solely to protect the woman. Because medical advances have lessened this concern, at least with respect to abortion in early pregnancy, they argue that with respect to such abortions the laws can no longer be justified by any state interest. There is some scholarly support for this view of original purpose. The few state courts called upon to interpret their laws in the late 19th and early 20th centuries did focus on the State's interest in protecting the woman's health, rather than in preserving the embryo and fetus. Proponents of this view point out that in many States, including Texas, by statute or judicial interpretation, the pregnant woman herself could not be prosecuted for self-abortion or for cooperating in an abortion performed upon her by another. They claim that adoption of the "quickening" distinction through received common law and state statutes tacitly recognizes the greater health

hazards inherent in late abortion and impliedly repudiates the theory that life begins at conception.

It is with these interests, and the eight to be attached to them, that this case is concerned.

VIII

The Constitution does not explicitly mention any right of privacy. In a line of decisions, however, going back perhaps as far as *Union Pacific R. Co. v. Botsford* (1891), the Court has recognized that a right of personal privacy, or a guarantee of certain areas or zones of privacy, does exist under the Constitution. In varying contexts, the Court or individual Justices have, indeed, found at least the roots of that right in the First Amendment, *Stanley v. Georgia* (1969); in the Fourth and Fifth Amendments, *Terry v. Ohio* (1968), *Katz v. United States* (1967), *Boyd v. United States* (1886), see *Olmstead v. United States* (1928) (Brandeis, J., dissenting); in the penumbras of the Bill of Rights, *Griswold v. Connecticut*; in the Ninth Amendment, *id.* (Goldberg, J., concurring); or in the concept of liberty guaranteed by the first section of the Fourteenth Amendment, see *Meyer v. Nebraska* (1923). These decisions make it clear that only personal rights that can be deemed "fundamental" or "implicit in the concept of ordered liberty," *Palko v. Connecticut* (1937), are included in this guarantee of personal privacy. They also make it clear that the right has some extension to activities relating to marriage, *Loving v. Virginia* (1967); procreation, *Skinner v. Oklahoma* (1942); contraception, *Eisenstadt v. Baird* [1972]; *Prince v. Massachusetts* (1944); and childrearing and education, *Pierce v. Society of Sisters* (1925).

This right of privacy, whether it be founded in the Fourteenth Amendment's concept of personal liberty and restrictions upon state action, as we feel it is, or, as the District Court determined, in the Ninth Amendment's reservation of rights to the people, is broad enough to encompass a woman's decision whether or not to terminate her pregnancy. The detriment that the State would impose upon the pregnant woman by denying this choice altogether is apparent. Specific and direct harm medically diagnosable even in early pregnancy may be involved. Maternity, or additional offspring, may force upon the woman a distressful life and future. Psychological harm may be imminent. Mental and physical health may be taxed by child care. There is also the distress, for all concerned, associated with the unwanted child, and there is the problem of bringing a child into a family already unable, psychologically and otherwise, to care for it. In other cases, as in this one, the additional difficulties and continuing stigma of unwed motherhood may be involved. All these are factors the woman and her responsible physician necessarily will consider in consultation.

On the basis of elements such as these, appellant and some *amici* argue that the woman's right is absolute and that she is entitled to terminate her pregnancy at whatever time, in whatever way, and for whatever reason she alone chooses. With this we do not agree. Appellant's arguments that Texas either has no valid interest at all in regulating the abortion decision, or no interest strong enough to support any limitation upon the woman's sole determination, are unpersuasive. The Court's decisions recognizing a right of privacy also acknowledge that some state regulation in areas protected by that right is appropriate. As noted above, a State may properly assert important interests in safeguarding health, in maintaining medical standards, and in protecting potential life. At some point in pregnancy, these respective interests become sufficiently compelling to sustain regulation of the factors that govern the abortion decision. The privacy right involved, therefore, cannot be said to be absolute. In fact, it is not clear to us that the claim asserted by some *amici* that one has an unlimited right to do with one's body as one pleases bears a close relationship to the right of privacy previously articulated in the Court's decisions. [. . .]

We, therefore, conclude that the right of personal privacy includes the abortion decision, but that this right is not unqualified, and must be considered against important state interests in regulation. [. . .]

Where certain "fundamental rights" are involved, the Court has held that regulation limiting these rights may be justified only by a "compelling state interest," and that legislative enactments must be narrowly drawn to express only the legitimate state interests at stake.

In the recent abortion cases cited above, courts have recognized these principles. Those striking down state laws have generally scrutinized the State's interests in protecting health and potential life, and have concluded that neither interest justified broad limitations on the reasons for which a physician and his pregnant patient might decide that she should have an abortion in the early stages of pregnancy. Courts sustaining state laws have held that the State's determinations to protect health or prenatal life are dominant and constitutionally justifiable.

IX

The District Court held that the appellee failed to meet his burden of demonstrating that the Texas statute's infringement upon Roe's rights was necessary to support a compelling state interest, and that, although the appellee presented "several compelling justifications for state presence in the area of abortions," the statutes outstripped these justifications and swept "far beyond any areas of compelling state interest." Appellant and appellee both contest that holding. Appellant, as has been indicated, claims an absolute right that bars any state imposition of criminal penalties in the area. Appellee argues that the State's determination to recognize and protect prenatal life from and after conception constitutes a compelling state interest. As noted above, we do not agree fully with either formulation.

A. The appellee and certain *amici* argue that the fetus is a "person" within the language and meaning of the Fourteenth Amendment. In support of this, they outline at length and in detail the well known facts of fetal development. If this suggestion of personhood is established, the appellant's case, of course, collapses, for the fetus' right to life would then be guaranteed specifically by the Amendment. The appellant conceded as much on reargument. On the other hand, the appellee conceded on reargument that no case could be cited that holds that a fetus is a person within the meaning of the Fourteenth Amendment.

The Constitution does not define "person" in so many words. Section 1 of the Fourteenth Amendment contains three references to "person." The first, in defining "citizens," speaks of "persons born or naturalized in the United States." The word also appears both in the Due Process Clause and in the Equal Protection Clause. "Person" is used in other places in the Constitution: in the listing of qualifications for Representatives and Senators, Art. I, § 2, cl. 2, and § 3, cl. 3; in the Apportionment Clause, Art. I, § 2, cl. 3; in the Migration and Importation provision, Art. I, § 9, cl. 1; in the Emolument Clause, Art. I, § 9, cl. 8; in the Electors provisions, Art. II, § 1, cl. 2, and the superseded cl. 3; in the provision outlining qualifications for the office of President, Art. II, § 1, cl. 5; in the Extradition provisions, Art. IV, § 2, cl. 2, and the superseded Fugitive Slave Clause 3; and in the Fifth, Twelfth, and Twenty-second Amendments, as well as in §§ 2 and 3 of the Fourteenth Amendment. But in nearly all these instances, the use of the word is such that it has application only post-natally. None indicates, with any assurance, that it has any possible prenatal application.

All this, together with our observation, *supra*, that, throughout the major portion of the 19th century, prevailing legal abortion practices were far freer than they are today, persuades us that the word "person," as used in the Fourteenth Amendment, does not include the unborn. [. . .]

This conclusion, however, does not of itself fully answer the contentions raised by Texas, and we pass on to other considerations.

B. The pregnant woman cannot be isolated in her privacy. She carries an embryo and, later, a fetus, if one accepts the medical definitions of the developing young in the human uterus. The situation therefore is inherently different from marital intimacy, or bedroom possession of obscene material, or marriage, or procreation, or education, with which *Eisenstadt* and *Griswold, Stanley, Loving, Skinner,* and *Pierce* and *Meyer* were respectively concerned. As we have intimated above, it is reasonable and appropriate for a State to decide that, at some point in time another interest, that of health of the mother or that of potential human life, becomes significantly involved. The woman's privacy is no longer sole and any right of privacy she possesses must be measured accordingly.

Texas urges that, apart from the Fourteenth Amendment, life begins at conception and is present throughout pregnancy, and that, therefore, the State has a compelling interest in protecting that life from and after conception. We need not resolve the difficult question of when life begins. When those trained in the respective disciplines of medicine, philosophy, and theology are unable to arrive at any consensus, the judiciary, at this point in the development of man's knowledge, is not in a position to speculate as to the answer.

It should be sufficient to note briefly the wide divergence of thinking on this most sensitive and difficult question. There has always been strong support for the view that life does not begin until live birth. This was the belief of the Stoics. It appears to be the predominant, though not the unanimous, attitude of the Jewish faith. It may be taken to represent also the position of a large segment of the Protestant community, insofar as that can be ascertained; organized groups that have taken a formal position on the abortion issue have generally regarded abortion as a matter for the conscience of the individual and her family. As we have noted, the common law found greater significance in quickening. Physician and their scientific colleagues have regarded that event with less interest and have tended to focus either upon conception, upon live birth, or upon the interim point at which the fetus becomes "viable," that is, potentially able to live outside the mother's womb, albeit with artificial aid. Viability is usually placed at about seven months (28 weeks) but may occur earlier, even at 24 weeks. The Aristotelian theory of "mediate animation," that held sway throughout the Middle Ages and the Renaissance in Europe, continued to be official Roman Catholic dogma until the 19th century, despite opposition to this "ensoulment" theory from those in the Church who would recognize the existence of life from the moment of conception. The latter is now, of course, the official belief of the Catholic Church. As one brief *amicus* discloses, this is a view strongly held by many non-Catholics as well, and by many physicians. Substantial problems for precise definition of this view are posed, however, by new embryological data that purport to indicate that conception is a "process" over time, rather than an event, and by new medical techniques such as menstrual extraction, the "morning-after" pill, implantation of embryos, artificial insemination, and even artificial wombs.

In areas other than criminal abortion, the law has been reluctant to endorse any theory that life, as we recognize it, begins before live birth, or to accord legal rights to the unborn except in narrowly defined situations and except when the rights are contingent upon live birth. [. . .]

X

In view of all this, we do not agree that, by adopting one theory of life, Texas may override the rights of the pregnant woman that are at stake. We repeat, however, that the State does have an important and legitimate interest in preserving and protecting the health of the pregnant woman, whether she be a resident of the State or a nonresident who seeks medical consultation and treatment there, and that it has still *another* important and legitimate interest in protecting the potentiality of human life. These interests are separate and distinct. Each grows in substantiality as the woman approaches term and, at a point during pregnancy, each becomes "compelling."

With respect to the State's important and legitimate interest in the health of the mother, the "compelling" point, in the light of present medical knowledge, is at approximately the end of the first trimester. This is so because of the now-established medical fact, referred to above at 149, that, until the end of the first trimester mortality in abortion may be less than mortality in normal childbirth. It follows that, from and after this point, a State may regulate the abortion procedure to the extent that the regulation reasonably relates to the preservation and protection of maternal health. Examples of permissible state regulation in this area are requirements as to the qualifications of the person who is to perform the abortion; as to the licensure of that person; as to the facility in which the procedure is to be performed, that is, whether it must be a hospital or may be a clinic or some other place of less-than-hospital status; as to the licensing of the facility; and the like.

This means, on the other hand, that, for the period of pregnancy prior to this "compelling" point, the attending physician, in consultation with his patient, is free to determine, without regulation by the State, that, in his medical judgment, the patient's pregnancy should be terminated. If that decision is reached, the judgment may be effectuated by an abortion free of interference by the State.

With respect to the State's important and legitimate interest in potential life, the "compelling" point is at viability. This is so because the fetus then presumably has the capability of meaningful life outside the mother's womb. State regulation protective of fetal life after viability thus has both logical and biological justifications. If the State is interested in protecting fetal life after viability, it may go so far as to proscribe abortion during that period, except when it is necessary to preserve the life or health of the mother.

Measured against these standards, Art. 1196 of the Texas Penal Code, in restricting legal abortions to those "procured or attempted by medical advice for the purpose of saving the life of the mother," sweeps too broadly. The statute makes no distinction between abortions performed early in pregnancy and those performed later, and it limits to a single reason, "saving" the mother's life, the legal justification for the procedure. The statute, therefore, cannot survive the constitutional attack made upon it here. [. . .]

XI

To summarize and to repeat:

1. A state criminal abortion statute of the current Texas type, that excepts from criminality only a *life-saving* procedure on behalf of the mother, without regard to pregnancy stage and without recognition of the other interests involved, is violative of the Due Process Clause of the Fourteenth Amendment.

(a) For the stage prior to approximately the end of the first trimester, the abortion decision and its effectuation must be left to the medical judgment of the pregnant woman's attending physician.

(b) For the stage subsequent to approximately the end of the first trimester, the State, in promoting its interest in the health of the mother, may, if it chooses, regulate the abortion procedure in ways that are reasonably related to maternal health.

(c) For the stage subsequent to viability, the State in promoting its interest in the potentiality of human life may, if it chooses, regulate, and even proscribe, abortion except where it is necessary, in appropriate medical judgment, for the preservation of the life or health of the mother. [. . .]

This holding, we feel, is consistent with the relative weights of the respective interests involved, with the lessons and examples of medical and legal history, with the lenity of the common law, and with the demands of the profound problems of the present day. The decision leaves the State free to place increasing restrictions on abortion as the period of pregnancy lengthens, so long as those restrictions are tailored to the recognized state interests. The decision vindicates the right of the physician to administer medical treatment according to his professional judgment up to the points where important state interests provide compelling justifications for intervention. Up to those points, the abortion decision in all its aspects is inherently, and primarily, a medical decision, and basic responsibility for it must rest with the physician. If an individual practitioner abuses the privilege of exercising proper medical judgment, the usual remedies, judicial and intra-professional, are available.

WILLIAM REHNQUIST

Roe v. Wade, Dissent (1973)

Mr. Justice REHNQUIST, dissenting.

The Court's opinion brings to the decision of this troubling question both extensive historical fact and a wealth of legal scholarship. While the opinion thus commands my respect, I find myself nonetheless in fundamental disagreement with those parts of it that invalidate the Texas statute in question, and therefore dissent. [. . .]

I have difficulty in concluding, as the Court does, that the right of "privacy" is involved in this case. Texas, by the statute here challenged, bars the performance of a medical abortion by a licensed physician on a plaintiff such as Roe. A transaction resulting in an operation such as this is not "private" in the ordinary usage of that word. Nor is the "privacy" that the Court finds here even a distant relative of the freedom from searches and seizures protected by the Fourth Amendment to the Constitution, which the Court has referred to as embodying a right to privacy. *Katz v. United States* (1967).

If the Court means by the term "privacy" no more than that the claim of a person to be free from unwanted state regulation of consensual transactions may be a form of "liberty" protected by the Fourteenth Amendment, there is no doubt that similar claims have been upheld in our earlier decisions on the basis of that liberty. I agree with the statement of Mr. Justice Stewart in his concurring opinion that the "liberty," against deprivation of which without due process the Fourteenth Amendment protects, embraces more than the rights found in the Bill of Rights. But that liberty is not guaranteed absolutely against deprivation, only against deprivation without due process of law. The test traditionally applied in the area of social and economic legislation is whether or not a law such as that challenged has a rational relation to a valid state objective. *Williamson v. Lee Optical Co.* (1955). The Due Process Clause of the Fourteenth Amendment undoubtedly does place a limit, albeit a broad one, on legislative power to enact laws such as this. If the Texas statute were to prohibit an abortion even where the mother's life is in jeopardy, I have little doubt that such a statute would lack a rational relation to a valid state objective under the test stated in Williamson, supra. But the Court's sweeping invalidation of any restrictions on abortion during the first trimester is impossible to justify under that standard, and the conscious weighing of competing factors that the Court's opinion apparently substitutes for the established test is far more appropriate to a legislative judgment than to a judicial one. [. . .]

While the Court's opinion quotes from the dissent of Mr. Justice Holmes in *Lochner v. New York* (1905), the result it reaches is more closely attuned to the majority opinion of Mr. Justice Peckham in that case. As in *Lochner* and similar cases applying substantive due process standards to economic and social welfare legislation, the adoption of the compelling state interest standard will inevitably require this Court to examine the legislative policies and pass on the wisdom of these policies in the very process of deciding whether a particular state interest put forward may or may not be "compelling." The decision here to break pregnancy into three distinct terms and to outline the permissible restrictions the State may impose in each one, for example, partakes more of judicial legislation than it does of a determination of the intent of the drafters of the Fourteenth Amendment.

The fact that a majority of the States reflecting, after all, the majority sentiment in those States, have had restrictions on abortions for at least a century is a strong indication, it seems to me, that the asserted right to an abortion is not "so rooted in the traditions and conscience of our people as to be ranked as fundamental," *Snyder v. Massachusetts* (1934). Even today, when society's views on abortion are changing, the very existence of the debate is evidence that the "right" to an abortion is not so universally accepted as the appellant would have us believe.

To reach its result, the Court necessarily has had to find within the scope of the Fourteenth Amendment a right that was apparently completely unknown to the drafters of the Amendment. As early as 1821, the first state law dealing directly with abortion was enacted by the Connecticut Legislature. By the time of the adoption of the Fourteenth Amendment in 1868, there were at least 36 laws enacted by state or territorial legislatures limiting abortion. While many States have amended or updated their laws, 21 of the laws on the books in 1868 remain in effect today. Indeed, the Texas statute struck down today was, as the majority notes, first enacted in 1857 and "has remained substantially unchanged to the present time."

There apparently was no question concerning the validity of this provision or of any of the other state statutes when the Fourteenth Amendment was adopted. The only conclusion possible from this history is that the drafters did not intend to have the Fourteenth Amendment withdraw from the States the power to legislate with respect to this matter.

III

Even if one were to agree that the case that the Court decides were here, and that the enunciation of the substantive constitutional law in the Court's opinion were proper, the actual disposition of the case by the Court is still difficult to justify. The Texas statute is struck down *in toto*, even though the Court apparently concedes that at later periods of pregnancy Texas might impose these selfsame statutory limitations on abortion. My understanding of past practice is that a statute found to be invalid as applied to a particular plaintiff, but not unconstitutional as a whole, is not simply "struck down" but is, instead, declared unconstitutional as applied to the fact situation before the Court.

For all of the foregoing reasons, I respectfully dissent.

Byron White

Roe v. Wade, Dissent (1973)

Mr. Justice WHITE, with whom Justice Rehnquist joins, dissenting.

At the heart of the controversy in these cases are those recurring pregnancies that pose no danger whatsoever to the life or health of the mother but are, nevertheless, unwanted for any one or more of a variety of reasons—convenience, family planning, economics, dislike of children, the embarrassment of illegitimacy, etc. The common claim before us is that, for any one of such reasons, or for no reason at all, and without asserting or claiming any threat to life or health, any woman is entitled to an abortion at her request if she is able to find a medical advisor willing to undertake the procedure.

The Court, for the most part, sustains this position: during the period prior to the time the fetus becomes viable, the Constitution of the United States values the convenience, whim, or caprice of the putative mother more than the life or potential life of the fetus; the Constitution, therefore, guarantees the right to an abortion as against any state law or policy seeking to protect the fetus from an abortion not prompted by more compelling reasons of the mother.

With all due respect, I dissent. I find nothing in the language or history of the Constitution to support the Court's judgment. The Court simply fashions and announces a new constitutional right for pregnant mothers and, with scarcely any reason or authority for its action, invests that right with sufficient substance to override most existing state abortion statutes. The upshot is that the people and the legislatures of the 50 States are constitutionally disentitled to weigh the relative importance of the continued existence and development of the fetus, on the one hand, against a spectrum of possible impacts on the mother, on the other hand. As an exercise of raw judicial power, the Court perhaps has authority to do what it does today; but, in my view, its judgment is an improvident and extravagant exercise of the power of judicial review that the Constitution extends to this Court.

The Court apparently values the convenience of the pregnant mother more than the continued existence and development of the life or potential life that she carries. Whether or not I might agree with that marshaling of values, I can in no event join the Court's judgment because I find no constitutional warrant for imposing such an order of priorities on the people and legislatures of the States. In a sensitive area such as this, involving as it does issues over which reasonable men may easily and heatedly differ, I cannot accept the Court's exercise of its clear power of choice by interposing a constitutional barrier to state efforts to protect human life and by investing mothers and doctors with the constitutionally protected right to exterminate it. This issue, for the most part, should be left with the people and to the political processes the people have devised to govern their affairs.

It is my view, therefore, that the Texas statute is not constitutionally infirm because it denies abortions to those who seek to serve only their convenience, rather than to protect their life or health. Nor is this plaintiff, who claims no threat to her mental or physical health, entitled to assert the possible rights of those women whose pregnancy assertedly implicates their health. [. . .]

IRVING KRISTOL

"When Virtue Loses All Her Loveliness" — Some Reflections on Capitalism and "The Free Society" (1970)

When we lack the will to see things as they really are, there is nothing so mystifying as the obvious. This is the case, I think, with the new upsurge of radicalism that is now shaking much of Western society to its foundations. We have constructed the most ingenious sociological and psychological theories—as well as a few disingenuously naive ones—to explain this phenomenon. But there is in truth no mystery here. Our youthful rebels are anything but inarticulate; and though they utter a great deal of nonsense, the import of what they are saying is clear enough. What they are saying is that they dislike—to put it mildly—the liberal, individualist, capitalist civilization that stands ready to receive them as citizens. They are rejecting this offer of citizenship and are declaring their desire to see some other kind of civilization replace it.

That most of them do not always put the matter as explicitly or as candidly as this is beside the point.

Some of them do, of course; we try to dismiss them as "the lunatic fringe." But the mass of dissident young are not, after all, sufficiently educated to understand the implications of everything they say. Besides, it is so much easier for the less bold among them to insist that what they find outrageous are the defects and shortcomings of the present system. Such shortcomings undeniably exist and are easy polemical marks. And, at the other end, it is so much easier for the adult generations to accept such polemics as representing the sum and substance of their dissatisfaction. It is consoling to think that the turmoil among them is provoked by the extent to which our society falls short of realizing its ideals. But the plain truth is that it is these ideals themselves that are being rejected. Our young radicals are far less dismayed at America's failure to become what it ought to be than they are contemptuous of what it thinks it ought to be. For them, as for Oscar Wilde, it is not the average American who is disgusting; it is the ideal American.

This is why one can make so little impression on them with arguments about how much progress has been made in the past decades, or is being made today, toward racial equality, or abolishing poverty, or fighting pollution, or whatever it is that we conventionally take as a sign of "progress." The obstinacy with which they remain deaf to such "liberal" arguments is not all perverse or irrational, as some would like to think. It arises, rather, out of a perfectly sincere, if often inchoate, animus against the American system itself. This animus stands for a commitment— *to* what, remains to be seen, but *against* what is already only too evident.

Capitalism's Three Promises

Dissatisfaction with the liberal-capitalist ideal, as distinct from indignation at failures to realize this ideal, are coterminous with the history of capitalism itself. Indeed, the cultural history of the capitalist epoch is not much more than a record of the varying ways such dissatisfaction could be expressed—in poetry, in the novel, in the drama, in painting, and today even in the movies. Nor, again, is there any great mystery why, from the first stirrings of the romantic movement, poets and philosophers have never had much regard for the capitalist civilization in which they lived and worked. But to understand this fully, one must be able to step outside the "progressive" ideology which makes us assume that liberal capitalism is the "natural" state of man toward which humanity has always aspired. There is nothing more natural about capitalist civilization than about many others that have had, or will have, their day. Capitalism represents a sum of human choices about the good life and the good society. These choices inevitably have their associated costs, and after two hundred years the conviction seems to be spreading that the costs have got out of line.

What did capitalism promise? First of all, it promised continued improvement in the material conditions of all its citizens, a promise without precedent in human history. Secondly, it promised an equally unprecedented measure of individual freedom for all of these same citizens. And lastly, it held out the promise that, amidst this prosperity and liberty, the individual could satisfy his instinct for self-perfection—for leading a virtuous life that satisfied the demands of his spirit (or, as one used to say, his soul)—and that the free exercise of such individual virtue would aggregate into a just society.

Now, it is important to realize that, though these aims were in one sense more ambitious than any previously set forth by a political ideology, in another sense they were far more modest. Whereas, as Joseph Cropsey has pointed out, Adam Smith defined "prudence" democratically as "the care of the health, of the fortune, of the rank of the individual," Aristotle had defined that term aristocratically, to mean "the quality of mind concerned with things just and noble and good for man." By this standard, all pre-capitalist systems had been, to one degree or another, Aristotelian: they were interested in creating a high and memorable civilization even if this were shared only by a tiny minority. In contrast, capitalism lowered its sights, but offered its shares in bourgeois civilization to the entire citizenry. Tocqueville, as usual, astutely caught this difference between the aristocratic civilizations of the past and the new liberal capitalism he saw emerging in the United States:

> In aristocratic societies the class that gives the tone to opinion and has the guidance of affairs, being permanently and hereditarily placed above the multitude, naturally conceives a lofty idea of

itself and man. It loves to invent for him noble pleasures, to carve out splendid objects for his ambition. Aristocracies often commit very tyrannical and inhuman actions, but they rarely entertain groveling thoughts. . . .

[In democracies, in contrast] there is little energy of character but customs are mild and laws humane. If there are few instances of exalted heroism or of virtues of the highest, brightest, and purest temper, men's habits are regular, violence is rare, and cruelty almost unknown. . . . Genius becomes rare, information more diffused. . . . There is less perfection, but more abundance, in all the productions of the arts.

It is because "high culture" inevitably has an aristocratic bias—it would not be "high" if it did not—that, from the beginnings of the capitalist era, it has always felt contempt for the bourgeois mode of existence. That mode of existence purposively depreciated the very issues that were its *raison d'être*. It did so by making them, as no society had ever dared or desired to do, matters of personal taste, according to the prescription of Adam Smith in his *Theory of Moral Sentiments*:

Though you despise that picture, or that poem, or even that system of philosophy, which I admire, there is little danger of our quarreling upon that account. Neither of us can reasonably be much interested about them. They ought all of them to be matters of great indifference to us both; so that, though our opinions may be opposite, our affections shall be very nearly the same.

In short, an amiable philistinism was inherent in bourgeois society, and this was bound to place its artists and intellectuals in an antagonistic posture toward it. This antagonism was irrepressible—the bourgeois world could not suppress it without violating its own liberal creed; the artists could not refrain from expressing their hostility without denying their most authentic selves. But the conflict could, and was, contained so long as capitalist civilization delivered on its three basic promises. It was only when the third promise, of a virtuous life and a just society, was subverted by the dynamics of capitalism itself, as it strove to fulfill the other two—affluence and liberty—that the bourgeois order came, in the minds of the young especially, to possess a questionable legitimacy.

From Bourgeois Society to a "Free Society"

I can think of no better way of indicating the distance that capitalism has travelled from its original ideological origins than by contrasting the most intelligent defender of capitalism today with his predecessors. I refer to Friederich von Hayek, who has as fine and as powerful a mind as is to be found anywhere, and whose *Constitution of Liberty* is one of the most thoughtful works of the last decades. In that book, he offers the following argument against viewing capitalism as a system that incarnates any idea of justice:

Most people will object not to the bare fact of inequality but to the fact that the differences in reward do not correspond to any recognizable differences in the merit of those who receive them. The answer commonly given to this is that a free society on the whole achieves this kind of justice. This, however, is an indefensible contention if by justice is meant proportionality of reward to moral merit. Any attempt to found the case for freedom on this argument is very damaging to it, since it concedes that material rewards ought to be made to correspond to recognizable merit and then opposes the conclusion that most people will draw from this by an assertion which is untrue. The proper answer is that in a free society it is neither desirable nor practicable that material rewards should be made generally to correspond to what men recognize as merit and that it is an essential characteristic of a free society that an individual's position should not necessarily depend on the views that his fellows hold about the merit he has acquired. . . . A society in which the position of the individual was made to correspond to human ideas of moral merit would therefore be the exact opposite of a free society. It would be a society in which people were rewarded for duty performed instead of for success. . . . But if nobody's knowledge is sufficient to guide all human action, there is also no human being who is competent to reward all efforts according to merit.

This argument is admirable both for its utter candor and for its firm opposition to all those modern authoritarian ideologies, whether rationalist or irrationalist, which give a self-selected elite the right to shape men's lives and fix their destinies according to its preconceived notions of good and evil, merit and demerit. But it is interesting to note what Hayek is doing: he is opposing a *free* society to a *just* society—because, he says, while we know what freedom is, we have no generally accepted knowledge of what justice is. Elsewhere he writes:

> Since they [i.e., differentials in wealth and income] are not the effect of anyone's design or intentions, it is meaningless to describe the manner in which the market distributed the good things of this world among particular people as just or unjust. . . . No test or criteria have been found or can be found by which such rules of "social justice" can be assessed. . . . They would have to be determined by the arbitrary will of the holders of power.

Now, it may be that this is the best possible defense that can be made of a free society. But if this is the case, one can fairly say that "capitalism" is (or was) one thing, and a "free society" another. For capitalism, during the first hundred years or so of its existence, did lay claim to being a just social order, in the meaning later given to that concept by Paul Elmer More: "Such a distribution of power and privilege, and of property as the symbol and instrument of these, as at once will satisfy the distinctions of reason among the superior, and will not outrage the feelings of the inferior." As a matter of fact, capitalism at its apogee saw itself as the most just social order the world has ever witnessed, because it replaced all arbitrary (e.g., inherited) distributions of power, privilege, and property with a distribution that was directly and intimately linked to personal merit—this latter term being inclusive of both personal abilities and personal virtues.

Writing shortly before the Civil War, George Fitzhugh, the most gifted of Southern apologists for slavery, attacked the capitalist North in these terms:

> In a free society none but the selfish virtues are in repute, because none other help a man in the race of competition. In such a society virtue loses all her loveliness, because of her selfish aims. Good men and bad men have the same end in view—self-promotion and self-elevation.

At the time, this accusation was a half-truth. The North was not yet "a free society," in Hayek's sense or Fitzhugh's. It was still in good measure a bourgeois society in which the capitalist mode of existence involved moral self-discipline and had a visible aura of spiritual grace. It was a society in which "success" was indeed seen as having what Hayek has said it ought never to have: a firm connection with "duty performed." It was a society in which Theodore Parker could write of a leading merchant: "He had no uncommon culture of the understanding or the imagination, and of the higher reason still less. But in respect of the *greater faculties*—in respect of conscience, affection, the religious element—he was well born, well bred." In short, it was a society still permeated by the Puritan ethic, the Protestant ethic, the capitalist ethic—call it what you will. It was a society in which it was agreed that there was a strong correlation between certain personal virtues—frugality, industry, sobriety, reliability, piety—and the way in which power, privilege, and property were distributed. And this correlation was taken to be the sign of a just society, not merely of a free one. Samuel Smiles or Horatio Alger would have regarded Professor Hayek's writings as slanderous of his fellow Christians, blasphemous of God, and ultimately subversive of the social order. I am not sure about the first two of these accusations, but I am fairly certain of the validity of the last.

This is not the place to recount the history and eventual degradation of the capitalist ethic in America. Suffice it to say that, with every passing decade, Fitzhugh's charge, that "virtue loses all her loveliness, because of her selfish aims," became more valid. From having been a *capitalist, republican community*, with shared values and a quite unambiguous claim to the title of a just order, the United States became a *free, democratic society* where the will to success and privilege was severed from its moral moorings.

Three Current Apologia

But can men live in a free society if they have no reason to believe it is also a just society? I do not think so. My reading of history is that, in the same way as men cannot for long tolerate a sense of spiritual meaninglessness in their individual lives, so they cannot for long accept a society in which power, privilege, and property are not distributed according to some morally meaningful criteria. Nor is equality itself any more acceptable than inequality—neither is more "natural" than the other—if equality is merely a brute fact rather than a consequence of an ideology or social philosophy. This explains what otherwise seems paradoxical that small inequalities in capitalist countries can become the source of intense controversy while relatively larger inequalities in socialist or communist countries are blandly overlooked. Thus, those same young radicals who are infuriated by trivial inequalities in the American economic system are quite blind to grosser inequalities in the Cuban system. This is usually taken as evidence of hypocrisy or self-deception. I would say it shows, rather, that people's notions of equality or inequality have extraordinarily little to do with arithmetic and almost everything to do with political philosophy.

I believe that what holds for equality also holds for liberty. People feel free when they subscribe to a prevailing social philosophy; they feel unfree when the prevailing social philosophy is unpersuasive; and the existence of constitutions or laws or judiciaries have precious little to do with these basic feelings. The average working man in nineteenth-century America had far fewer "rights" than his counterpart today; but he was far more likely to boast about his being a free man.

So I conclude, despite Professor Hayek's ingenious analysis, that men cannot accept the historical accidents of the marketplace—seen merely as accidents—as the basis for an enduring and legitimate entitlement to power, privilege, and property. And, in actual fact, Professor Hayek's rationale for modern capitalism is never used outside a small academic enclave; I even suspect it cannot be believed except by those whose minds have been shaped by overlong exposure to scholasticism. Instead, the arguments offered to justify the social structure of capitalism now fall into three main categories:

1) **The Protestant Ethic.**   This, however, is now reserved for the lower socioeconomic levels. It is still believed, and it is still reasonable to believe that worldly success among the working class, lower-middle class, and even middle class has a definite connection with personal virtues such as diligence,

rectitude, sobriety, honest ambition, etc., etc. And so far as I can see the connection is not only credible but demonstrable. It does seem that the traditional bourgeois virtues are efficacious among these classes—at least it is rare to find successful men emerging from these classes who do not to a significant degree exemplify them. But no one seriously claims that these traditional virtues will open the corridors of corporate power to anyone, or that the men who now occupy the executive suites are—or even aspire to be—models of bourgeois virtue.

2) **The Darwinian Ethic.**   This is to be found mainly among small businessmen who are fond of thinking that their "making it" is to be explained as "the survival of the fittest." They are frequently quite right, of course, in believing the metaphor appropriate to their condition and to the ways in which they achieved it. But it is preposterous to think that the mass of men will ever accept as legitimate a social order formed in accordance with the laws of the jungle. Men may be animals, but they are political animals—and, what comes to not such a different thing, moral animals too. The fact that for several decades after the Civil War, the Darwinian ethic, as popularized by Herbert Spencer, could be taken seriously by so many social theorists represents one of the most bizarre and sordid episodes in American intellectual history. It could not last; and did not.

3) **The Technocratic Ethic.**   This is the most prevalent justification of corporate capitalism today and finds expression in an insistence on "performance." Those who occupy the seats of corporate power, and enjoy the prerogatives and privileges thereof, are said to acquire legitimacy by their superior ability to achieve superior "performance"—in economic growth, managerial efficiency, technological innovation. In a sense, what is claimed is that these men are accomplishing social tasks, and fulfilling social responsibilities, in an especially efficacious way.

There are, however, two fatal flaws in this argument. First, if one defines "performance" in a strictly limited and measurable sense, then one is applying a test that any ruling class is bound, on fairly frequent occasions, to fail. Life has its ups and downs; so do history and economics; and men who can only claim legitimacy *via* performance are going to have to spend an awful lot of time and energy explaining why things are not going as well as they ought to. Such repeated, defensive apologias, in the end, will be hollow and unconvincing. Indeed, the very concept of "legitimacy," in its historical usages, is supposed to take account of and make allowances for all those rough passages a society will have to navigate. If the landed gentry of Britain during those centuries of its dominance, or the business class in the United States during the first century and a half of our national history, had insisted that it be judged by performance alone, it would have flunked out of history. So would every other ruling class that ever existed.

Secondly, if one tries to avoid this dilemma by giving the term "performance" a broader and larger meaning, then one inevitably finds oneself passing beyond the boundaries of bourgeois propriety. It is one thing to say with Samuel Johnson that men honestly engaged in business are doing the least mischief that men are capable of; it is quite another thing to assert that they are doing the greatest good—this is only too patently untrue. For the achievement of the greatest good, more than successful performance in business is necessary. Witness how vulnerable our corporate managers are to accusations that they are befouling our environment. What these accusations really add up to is the statement that the business system in the United States does not create a beautiful, refined, gracious, and tranquil civilization. To which our corporate leaders are replying: "Oh, we can perform that mission too—just give us time." But there is no good reason to think they can accomplish this noncapitalist mission; nor is there any reason to believe that they have any proper entitlement even to try.

"Participation" or Leadership?

It is, I think, because of the decline of the bourgeois ethic, and the consequent drainage of legitimacy out of the business system, that the issue of "participation" has emerged with such urgency during these past years. It is a common error to take this word at its face value—to assume that, in our organized and bureaucratized society, the average person is more isolated, alienated, or powerless than ever before, and that the proper remedy is to open new avenues of "participation." We are then perplexed when, the avenues having been open, we find so little traffic

passing through. We give college students the right to representation on all sorts of committees—and then discover they never bother to come to meetings. We create new popularly elected "community" organizations in the ghettos—and then discover that ghetto residents won't come out to vote. We decentralize New York City's school system—only to discover that the populace is singularly uninterested in local school board elections.

I doubt very much that the average American is actually more isolated or powerless today than in the past. The few serious studies that have been made on this subject indicate that we have highly romanticized notions of the past—of the degree to which ordinary people were ever involved in community activities—and highly apocalyptic notions of the present. If one takes membership in civic-minded organizations as a criterion, people are unquestionably more "involved" today than ever before in our history. Maybe that's not such a good criterion; but it is a revealing aspect of this whole problem that those who make large statements on this matter rarely give us any workable or testable criteria at all.

But I would not deny that more people, even if more specifically "involved" than ever before, also feel more "alienated" in a general way. And this, I would suggest, is because the institutions of our society have lost their vital connection with the values which are supposed to govern the private lives of our citizenry. They no longer exemplify these values; they no longer magnify them; they no longer reassuringly sustain them. When it is said that the institutions of our society have become appallingly "impersonal," I take this to mean that they have lost any shape that is congruent with the private moral codes which presumably govern individual life. (That presumption, of course, may be factually weak; but it is nonetheless efficacious so long as people hold it.) The "outside" of our social life has ceased being harmonious with the "inside"—the mode of distribution of power, privilege, and property, and hence the very principle of authority, no longer "makes sense" to the bewildered citizen. And when institutions cease to "make sense" in this way, all the familiar criteria of success or failure become utterly irrelevant.

As I see it, then, the demand for "participation" is best appreciated as a demand for authority—for leadership that holds the promise of reconciling the inner and outer worlds of the citizen. So far from its being a hopeful reawakening of the democratic spirit, it signifies a hunger for authority that leads toward some kind of plebiscitary democracy at best, and is in any case not easy to reconcile with liberal democracy as we traditionally have known it. I find it instructive that such old-fashioned populists as Hubert Humphrey and Edmund Muskie, whose notions of "participation" are both liberal and traditional, fail to catch the imagination of our dissidents in the way that Robert Kennedy did. The late Senator Kennedy was very much a leader—one can imagine Humphrey or Muskie participating in an old-fashioned town meeting, one can only envision Kennedy dominating a town rally. One can also envision those who "participated" in such a rally feeling that they had achieved a kind of "representation" previously denied them.

A Case of Regression

For a system of liberal, representative government to work, free elections are not enough. The results of the political process and of the exercise of individual freedom—the distribution of power, privilege, and property—must also be seen as in some profound sense expressive of the values that govern the lives of individuals. An idea of self-government, if it is to be viable, must encompass both the private and the public sectors. If it does not—if the principles that organize public life seem to have little relation to those that shape private lives—you have "alienation" and anomie, and a melting away of established principles of authority.

Milton Friedman, arguing in favor of Hayek's extreme libertarian position, has written that the free man "recognizes no national purpose except as it is the consensus of the purposes for which the citizens severally strive." If he is using the term "consensus" seriously, then he must be assuming that there is a strong homogeneity of values among the citizenry, and that these values give a certain corresponding shape to the various institutions of society, political and economic. Were that the case, then it is indeed true that a "national purpose" arises automatically and organically out of the social order itself. Something like this did happen when liberal capitalism

was in its prime, vigorous and self-confident. But is that our condition today? I think not—just as I think Mr. Friedman doesn't really mean "consensus" but rather the mere aggregation of selfish aims. In such a blind and accidental arithmetic, the sum floats free from the addenda, and its legitimacy is infinitely questionable.

The inner spiritual chaos of the times, so powerfully created by the dynamics of capitalism itself, is such as to make nihilism an easy temptation. A "free society" in Hayek's sense gives birth in massive numbers to "free spirits"—emptied of moral substance but still driven by primordial moral aspirations. Such people are capable of the most irrational actions. Indeed, it is my impression that, under the strain of modern life, whole classes of our population—and the educated classes most of all—are entering what can only be called, in the strictly clinical sense, a phase of infantile regression. With every passing year, public discourse becomes sillier and more petulant, while human emotions become, apparently, more ungovernable. Some of our most intelligent university professors are now loudly saying things that, had they been uttered by one of their students twenty years ago, would have called forth gentle and urbane reproof.

The Reforming Spirit and the Conservative Ideal

And yet, if the situation of liberal capitalism today seems so precarious, it is likely nevertheless to survive for a long while, if only because the modern era has failed to come up with any plausible alternatives. Socialism, communism, and fascism have all turned out to be either utopian illusions or sordid frauds. So we shall have time—though not an endless amount of it, for we have already wasted a great deal. We are today in a situation not very different from that described by Herbert Croly in *The Promise of American Life* (1912):

The substance of our national Promise has consisted . . . of an improving popular economic condition, guaranteed by democratic political institutions, and resulting in moral and social amelioration. These manifold benefits were to be obtained merely by liberating the enlightened self-enterprise of the American people. . . . The fulfillment of the American Promise was considered inevitable because it was based upon a combination of self-interest and the natural goodness of human nature. On the other hand, if the fulfillment of our national Promise can no longer be considered inevitable, if it must be considered as equivalent to a conscious national purpose instead of an inexorable national destiny, the implication necessarily is that the trust reposed in individual self-interest has been in some measure betrayed. No pre-established harmony can then exist between the free and abundant satisfaction of private needs and the accomplishment of a morally and socially desirable result.

Croly is not much read these days. He was a liberal reformer with essentially conservative goals. So was Matthew Arnold, fifty years earlier—and he isn't much read these days, either. Neither of them can pass into the conventional anthologies of liberal or conservative thought. I think this is a sad commentary on the ideological barrenness of the liberal and conservative creeds. I also think it is a great pity. For if our private and public worlds are ever again, in our lifetimes, to have a congenial relationship—if virtue is to regain her lost loveliness—then some such combination of the reforming spirit with the conservative ideal seems to me to be what is most desperately wanted.

I use the word "conservative" advisedly. Though the discontents of our civilization express themselves in the rhetoric of "liberation" and "equality," one can detect beneath the surface an acute yearning for order and stability—but a legitimate order, of course, and a legitimized stability. In this connection, I find the increasing skepticism as to the benefits of economic growth and technological innovation most suggestive. Such skepticism has been characteristic of conservative critics of liberal capitalism since the beginning of the nineteenth century. One finds it in Coleridge, Carlyle, and Newman—in all those who found it impossible to acquiesce in a "progressive" notion of human history or social evolution. Our dissidents today may think they are exceedingly progressive; but no one who puts greater emphasis on "the quality of life" than on "mere" material enrichment can properly be placed in that category. For the idea of progress in the modern era has always signified that the quality of life would inevitably be improved by material enrichment. To doubt this is to doubt the political metaphysics of modernity and to start the long trek back to premodern political philosophy—Plato, Aristotle, Thomas Aquinas, Hooker, Calvin, etc. It seems to me that this trip is quite necessary. Perhaps there we shall discover some of those elements that are most desperately needed by the spiritually impoverished civilization that we have constructed on what once seemed to be sturdy bourgeois foundations.

Saul Alinksy

Rules for Radicals (1971)

Prologue

The revolutionary force today has two targets, moral as well as material. Its young protagonists are one moment reminiscent of the idealistic early Christians, yet they also urge violence and cry, "Burn the system down!" They have no illusions about the system, but plenty of illusions about the way to change our world. It is to this point that I have written this book. These words are written in desperation, partly because it is what they do and will do that will give meaning to what I and the radicals of my generation have done with our lives.

They are now the vanguard, and they had to start almost from scratch. Few of us survived the Joe McCarthy holocaust of the early 1950s and of those there were even fewer whose understanding and insights had developed beyond the dialectical materialism of orthodox Marxism. My fellow radicals who were supposed to pass on the torch of experience and insights to a new generation just were not there. As the young looked at the society around them, it was all, in their words, "materialistic, decadent, bourgeois in its values, bankrupt and violent." Is it any wonder that they rejected us in toto.

Today's generation is desperately trying to make some sense out of their lives and out of the world. Most of them are products of the middle class. They have rejected their materialistic backgrounds, the goal of a well-paid job, suburban home, automobile, country club membership, first-class travel, status, security, and everything that meant success to their parents. They have had it. They watched it lead their parents to tranquilizers, alcohol, long-term-endurance marriages, or divorces, high blood pressure, ulcers, frustration, and the disillusionment of "the good life." They have seen the almost unbelievable idiocy of our political leadership—in the past political leaders, ranging from the mayors to governors to the White House, were regarded with respect and almost reverence; today they are viewed with contempt. This negativism now extends to all institutions, from the police and the courts to "the system" itself. We are living in a world of mass media which daily exposes society's innate hypocrisy, its contradictions and the apparent failure of almost every facet of our social and political life. The young have seen their "activist" participatory democracy turn into its antithesis—nihilistic bombing and murder. The political panaceas of the past, such as the revolutions in Russia and China, have become the same old stuff under a different name. The search for freedom does not seem to have any road or destination. The young are inundated with a barrage of information and facts so overwhelming that the world has come to seem an utter bedlam, which has them spinning in a frenzy, looking for what man has always looked for from the beginning of time, a way of life that has some meaning or sense. A way of life means a certain degree of order where things have some relationship and can be pieced together into a system that at least provides

some clues to what life is about. Men have always yearned for and sought direction by setting up religions, inventing political philosophies, creating scientific systems like Newton's, or formulating ideologies of various kinds. This is what is behind the common cliché, "getting it all together"—despite the realization that all values and factors are relative, fluid, and changing, and that it will be possible to "get it all together" only relatively. The elements will shift and move together just like the changing pattern in a turning kaleidoscope.

In the past the "world," whether in its physical or intellectual terms, was much smaller, simpler, and more orderly. It inspired credibility. Today everything is so complex as to be incomprehensible. What sense does it make for men to walk on the moon while other men are waiting on welfare lines, or in Vietnam killing and dying for a corrupt dictatorship in the name of freedom? These are the days when man has his hands on the sublime while he is up to his hips in the muck of madness. The establishment in many ways is as suicidal as some of the far left, except that they are infinitely more destructive than the far left can ever be. The outcome of the hopelessness and despair is morbidity. There is a feeling of death hanging over the nation.

Today's generation faces all this and says, "I don't want to spend my life the way my family and their friends have. I want to do something, to create, to be me, to 'do my own thing,' to live. The older generation doesn't understand and worse doesn't want to. I don't want to be just a piece of data to be fed into a computer or a statistic in a public opinion poll, just a voter carrying a credit card." To the young the world seems insane and falling apart.

On the other side is the older generation, whose members are no less confused. If they are not as vocal or conscious, it may be because they can escape to a past when the world was simpler. They can still cling to the old values in the simple hope that everything will work out somehow, some way. That the younger generation will "straighten out" with the passing of time. Unable to come to grips with the world as it is, they retreat in any confrontation with the younger generation with that infuriating cliché, *"when you get older you'll understand."* One wonders at their reaction if some youngster were to reply, *"When you get younger* which will never be *then you'll understand,* so of course you'll never understand." Those of the older generation who claim a desire to understand say, "When I talk to my kids or their friends I'll say to them, 'Look, I believe what you have to tell me is important and I respect it. You call me a square and say that 'I'm not with it' or 'I don't know where it's at' or 'I don't know where the scene is' and all of the rest of the words you use. Well, I'm going to agree with you. So suppose you tell me. What do you want? What do you mean when you say 'I want to do my thing.' What the hell is your thing? You say you want a better world. Like what? And don't tell me a world of peace and love and all the rest of that stuff because people are people, as you will find out when you get older—I'm sorry, I didn't mean to say anything about 'when you get older.' I really do respect what you have to say. Now why don't you answer me? Do you know what you want? Do you know what you're talking about? Why can't we get together?'"

And that is what we call the generation gap.

What the present generation wants is what all generations have always wanted—a meaning, a sense of what the world and life are—a chance to strive for some sort of order.

If the young were now writing our Declaration of Independence they would begin, "When in the course of inhuman events . . ." and their bill of particulars would range from Vietnam to our black, Chicano, and Puerto Rican ghettos, to the migrant workers, to Appalachia, to the hate, ignorance, disease, and starvation in the world. Such a bill of particulars would emphasize the absurdity of human affairs and the forlornness and emptiness, the fearful loneliness that comes from not knowing if there is any meaning to our lives.

When they talk of values they're asking for a reason. They are searching for an answer, at least for a time, to man's greatest question, "Why am I here?" [. . .]

For the real radical, doing "his thing" is to do the social thing, for and with people. In a world where everything is so interrelated that one feels helpless to know where or how to grab hold and act, defeat sets in; for years there have been people who've found society too overwhelming and have withdrawn, concentrated on "doing their own thing." Generally we have put them into mental hospitals and diagnosed them as schizophrenics. If the real radical finds that having long hair sets up psychological barriers to communication and organization, he cuts his hair. If I were organizing in an orthodox Jewish community I would not walk in there eating a ham sandwich, unless I wanted to be rejected so I could have an excuse to cop out. My "thing," if I want to organize, is solid communication with the people in the community. Lacking communication I am in reality silent; throughout history silence has been regarded as assent—in this case assent to the system.

As an organizer I start from where the world is, as it is, not as I would like it to be. That we accept the world as it is does not in any sense weaken our desire to change it into what we believe it should be—it is necessary to begin where the world is if we are going to change it to what we think it should be. That means working in the system.

There's another reason for working inside the system. Dostoevski said that taking a new step is what people fear most. Any revolutionary change must be preceded by a passive, affirmative, non-challenging attitude toward change among the mass of our people. They must feel so frustrated, so defeated, so lost, so futureless in the prevailing system that they are willing to let go of the past and chance the future. This acceptance is the reformation essential to any revolution. [. . .]

Our youth are impatient with the preliminaries that are essential to purposeful action. Effective organization is thwarted by the desire for instant and dramatic change, or as I have phrased it elsewhere the demand for revelation rather than revolution. It's the kind of thing we see in play writing; the first act introduces the characters and the plot, in the second act the plot and characters are developed as the play strives to hold the audience's attention. In the final act good and evil have their dramatic confrontation and resolution. The present generation wants to go right into the third act, skipping the first two, in which case there is no play, nothing but confrontation for confrontation's sake—a flare-up and back to darkness. To build a powerful organization takes time. It is tedious, but that's the way the game is played—if you want to play and not just yell, "Kill the umpire."

What is the alternative to working "inside" the system? A mess of rhetorical garbage about "Burn the system down!" Yippie yells of "Do it!" or "Do your thing." What else? Bombs? Sniping? Silence when police are killed and screams of "murdering fascist pigs" when others are killed? Attacking and baiting the police? Public suicide? "Power comes out of the barrel of a gun!" is an absurd rallying cry when the other side has all the guns. Lenin was a pragmatist; when he returned to what was then Petrograd from exile, he said that the Bolsheviks stood for getting power through the ballot but would reconsider after they got the guns! Militant mouthings? Spouting quotes from Mao, Castro, and Che Guevara, which are as germane to our highly technological, computerized, cybernetic, nuclear-powered, mass media society as a stagecoach on a jet runway at Kennedy airport?

Let us in the name of radical pragmatism not forget that in our system with all its repressions we can still speak out and denounce the administration, attack its policies, work to build an opposition political base. True, there is government harassment, but there still is that relative freedom to fight. I can attack my government, try to organize to change it. That's more than I can do in Moscow, Peking, or Havana. Remember the reaction of the Red Guard to the "cultural revolution" and the fate of the Chinese college students. Just a few of the violent episodes of bombings or a courtroom shootout that we have experienced here would have resulted in a sweeping purge and mass executions in Russia, China, or Cuba. Let's keep some perspective. [. . .]

In the midst of the gassing and violence by the Chicago Police and National Guard during the 1968 Democratic Convention many students asked me, "Do you still believe we should try to work inside our system?" [. . .]

It hurt me to see the American army with drawn bayonets advancing on American boys and girls. But the answer I gave the young radicals seemed to me the only realistic one: "Do one of three things. One, go find a wailing wall and feel sorry for yourselves. Two, go psycho and start bombing—but this will only swing people to the right. Three, learn a lesson. Go home, organize, build power and at the next convention, *you be the delegates*."

Remember: once you organize people around something as commonly agreed upon as pollution, then an organized people is on the move. From there it's a short and natural step to political pollution, to Pentagon pollution.

It is not enough just to elect your candidates. You must keep the pressure on. Radicals should keep in mind Franklin D. Roosevelt's response to a reform delegation, "Okay, you've convinced me. Now go on out and bring pressure on me!" Action comes from keeping the heat on. No politician can sit on a hot issue if you make it hot enough.

As for Vietnam, I would like to see our nation be the first in the history of man to publicly say, "We were wrong! What we did was horrible. We got in and kept getting in deeper and deeper and at every step we invented new reasons for staying. We have paid part of the price in 44,000 dead Americans. There is nothing we can ever do to make it up to the people of Indo-China—or to our own people—but we will try. We believe that our world has come of age so that it is no longer a sign of weakness or defeat to abandon a childish pride and vanity, to admit we were wrong." Such an admission would shake up the foreign policy concepts of all nations and open the door to a new international order. This is our alternative to Vietnam—anything else is the old makeshift patchwork. If this were to happen, Vietnam may even have been somewhat worth it.

A final word on our system. The democratic ideal springs from the ideas of liberty, equality, majority rule through free elections, protection of the rights of minorities, and freedom to subscribe to multiple loyalties in matters of religion, economics, and politics rather than to a total loyalty to the state. The spirit of democracy is the idea of importance and worth in the individual, and faith in the kind of world where the individual can achieve as much of his potential as possible.

Great dangers always accompany great opportunities. The possibility of destruction is always implicit in the act of creation. Thus the greatest enemy of individual freedom is the individual himself.

From the beginning the weakness as well as the strength of the democratic ideal has been the people. People cannot be free unless they are willing to sacrifice some of their interests to guarantee the freedom of others. The price of democracy is the ongoing pursuit of the common good by *all* of the people. One hundred and thirty-five years ago Tocqueville[1] gravely

---

1. "It must not be forgotten that it is especially dangerous to enslave men in the minor details of life. For my own part, I should be inclined to think freedom less necessary in

warned that unless individual citizens were regularly involved in the action of governing themselves, self-government would pass from the scene. Citizen participation is the animating spirit and force in a society predicated on voluntarism.

We are not here concerned with people who profess the democratic faith but yearn for the dark security of dependency where they can be spared the burden of decisions. Reluctant to grow up, or incapable of doing so, they want to remain children and be cared for by others. Those who can, should be encouraged to grow; for the others, the fault lies not in the system but in themselves.

Here we are desperately concerned with the vast mass of our people who, thwarted through lack of interest or opportunity, or both, do not participate in the endless responsibilities of citizenship and are resigned to lives determined by others. To lose your "identity" as a citizen of democracy is but a step from losing your identity as a person. People react to this frustration by not acting at all. The separation of the people from the routine daily functions of citizenship is heartbreak in a democracy.

It is a grave situation when a people resign their citizenship or when a resident of a great city, though he may desire to take a hand, lacks the means to participate. That citizen sinks further into apathy, anonymity, and depersonalization. The result is that he comes to depend on public authority and a state of civic-sclerosis sets in.

From time to time there have been external enemies at our gates; there has always been the enemy within, the hidden and malignant inertia that foreshadows more certain destruction to our life and future than any nuclear warhead. There can be no darker or more devastating tragedy than the death of man's faith in himself and in his power to direct his future.

I salute the present generation. Hang on to one of your most precious parts of youth, laughter—don't lose it as many of you seem to have done, you need it. Together we may find some of what we're looking for—laughter, beauty, love, and the chance to create.

A Word about Words

The passions of mankind have boiled over into all areas of political life, including its vocabulary. The words most common in politics have become stained with human hurts, hopes, and frustrations. All of them are loaded with popular opprobrium, and their use results in a conditioned, negative, emotional response. Even the word *politics* itself, which Webster says is "the science and art of government," is generally viewed in a context of corruption. Ironically, the dictionary synonyms are "discreet; provident, diplomatic, wise."

Power

The question may legitimately be raised, why not use other words—words that mean the same but are peaceful, and do not result in such negative emotional reactions? There are a number of fundamental reasons for rejecting such substitution. First, by using combinations of words such as "harnessing the energy" instead of the single word "power," we begin to dilute the meaning; and as we use purifying synonyms, we dissolve the bitterness, the anguish, the hate and love, the agony and the triumph attached to these words, leaving an aseptic imitation of life. In the politics of life we are concerned with the slaves and the Caesars, not the vestal virgins. It is not just that, in communication as in thought, we must ever strive

---

great things than in little ones, if it were possible to be secure of the one without possessing the other.

"Subjection in minor affairs breaks out every day, and is felt by the whole community indiscriminately. It does not drive men to resistance, but it crosses them at every turn, till they are led to surrender the exercise of their will. Thus their spirit is gradually broken and their character enervated; whereas that obedience, which is exacted on a few but rare occasions, only exhibits servitude at certain intervals, and throws the burden of it upon a small number of men. It is vain to summon a people, which has been rendered so dependant on the central power, to choose from time to time the representatives of that power; this rare and brief exercise of their free choice, however, important it may be, will not prevent them from gradually losing the faculties of thinking, feeling, and acting for themselves, and thus gradually falling below the level of humanity."

—Alexis de Tocqueville, *Democracy in America*

toward simplicity. (The masterpieces of philosophic or scientific statement are frequently no longer than a few words, for example, "E = mc^2.") It is more than that: it is a determination not to detour around reality.

To use any other word but power is to change the meaning of everything we are talking about. As Mark Twain once put it, "The difference between the right word and the almost-right word is the difference between lightning and the lightning bug."

Power is the right word just as self-interest, compromise, and the other simple political words are, for they were conceived in and have become part of politics from the beginning of time. To pander to those who have no stomach for straight language, and insist upon bland, noncontroversial sauces, is a waste of time. They cannot or deliberately will not understand what we are discussing here. I agree with Nietzsche's statement in *The Genealogy of Morals* on this point;

> Why stroke the hypersensitive ears of our modern weaklings? Why yield even a single step . . . to the Tartuffery of words? For us psychologists that would involve a Tartuffery of *action* . . . For a psychologist today shows his good taste (others may say his integrity) in this, if in anything, that he resists the shamefully *moralized* manner of speaking which makes all modern judgments about men and things slimy.

We approach a critical point when our tongues trap our minds. I do not propose to be trapped by tact at the expense of truth. Striving to avoid the force, vigor, and simplicity of the word "power," we soon become averse to thinking in vigorous, simple, honest terms. We strive to invent sterilized synonyms, cleansed of the opprobrium of the word *power*—but the new words mean something different, so that they tranquilize us, begin to shepherd our mental processes off the main, conflict-ridden, grimy, and realistic power-paved highway of life. To travel down the sweeter-smelling, peaceful, more socially acceptable, more respectable, indefinite byways, ends in a failure to achieve an honest understanding of the issues that we must come to grips with if we are to do the job.

Let us look at the word *power*. Power, meaning "ability, whether physical, mental, or moral, to act," has become an evil word, with overtones and undertones that suggest the sinister, the unhealthy, the Machiavellian. It suggests a phantasmagoria of the nether regions. The moment the word *power* is mentioned it is as though hell had been opened, exuding the stench of the devil's cesspool of corruption. It evokes images of cruelty, dishonesty, selfishness, arrogance, dictatorship, and abject suffering. The word *power* is associated with conflict; it is unacceptable in our present Madison Avenue deodorized hygiene, where controversy is blasphemous and the value is being liked and not offending others. Power, in our minds, has become almost synonymous with corruption and immorality.

Whenever the word *power* is mentioned, somebody sooner or later will refer to the classical statement of Lord Acton and cite it as follows: "Power corrupts, and absolute power corrupts absolutely." In fact the correct quotation is: "Power *tends* to corrupt, and absolute power corrupts absolutely." We can't even read Acton's statement accurately, our minds are so confused by our conditioning.

The corruption of power is not in power, but in ourselves. And yet, what is this power which men live by and to a significant degree live for? Power is the very essence, the dynamo of life. It is the power of the heart pumping blood and sustaining life in the body. It is the power of active citizen participation pulsing upward, providing a unified strength for a common purpose. Power is an essential life force always in operation, either changing the world or opposing change. Power, or organized energy, may be a man-killing explosive or a life-saving drug. The power of a gun may be used to enforce slavery, or to achieve freedom.

The power of the human brain can create man's most glorious achievements, and develop perspectives and insights into the nature of life-opening horizons previously beyond the imagination. The power of the human mind can also devise philosophies and ways of life that are most destructive for the future of mankind. Either way, power is the dynamo of life.

Alexander Hamilton, in *The Federalist Papers*, put it this way: "What is a power, but the ability or faculty of doing a thing? What is the ability to do a thing, but the power of employing the *means* necessary to its execution?" Pascal, who was definitely not a cynic, observed that: "Justice without power is impotent; power without justice is tyranny." St. Ignatius, the founder of the Jesuit order, did not shrink from the recognition of power when he issued his dictum: "To do a thing well a man needs power and competence." We could call the roll of all who have played their parts in history and find the word *power*, not a substitute word, used in their speech and writings.

It is impossible to conceive of a world devoid of power; the only choice of concepts is between organized and unorganized power. Mankind has progressed only through learning how to develop and organize instruments of power in order to achieve order, security, morality, and civilized life itself, instead of a sheer struggle for physical survival. Every organization known to man, from government down, has had only one reason for being—that is, organization for power in order to put into practice or promote its common purpose.

When we talk about a person's "lifting himself by his own bootstraps" we are talking about power. Power must be understood for what it is, for the part it plays in every area of our life, if we are to understand it and thereby grasp the essentials of relationships and functions between groups and organizations, particularly in a pluralistic society. *To know power and not fear it is essential to its constructive use and control.* In short, life without power is death; a world without power would be a ghostly wasteland, a dead planet!

Self-Interest

Self-interest, like *power*, wears the black shroud of negativism and suspicion. To many the synonym for self-interest is selfishness. The word is associated with a repugnant conglomeration of vices such as narrowness, self-seeking, and self-centeredness, everything that is opposite to the virtues of altruism and selflessness. This common definition is contrary, of course, to our everyday experiences, as well as to the observations of all great students of politics and life. The myth of altruism as a motivating factor in our behavior could arise and survive only in a society bundled in the sterile gauze of New England puritanism and Protestant morality and tied together with the ribbons of Madison Avenue public relations. It is one of the classic American fairy tales.

From the great teachers of Judaeo-Christian morality and the philosophers, to the economists, and to the wise observers of the politics of man, there has always been universal agreement on the part that self-interest plays as a prime moving force in man's behavior. The importance of self-interest has never been challenged; it has been accepted as an inevitable fact of life. In the words of Christ, "Greater love has no man than this, that a man lay down his life for his friends." Aristotle said, in *Politics*, "Everyone thinks chiefly of his own, hardly ever of the public interest." Adam Smith, in *The Wealth of Nations*, noted that "It is not from the benevolence of the butcher, the brewer, or the baker that we expect our dinner, but from their regard of their own interest. We address ourselves not to their humanity, but to their self-love, and never talk to them of our own necessities, but of their advantage." In all the reasoning found in *The Federalist Papers*, no point is so central and agreed upon as "Rich and poor alike are prone to act upon impulse rather than pure reason and to narrow conceptions of self-interest. . . . " To question the force of self-interest that pervades all areas of political life is to refuse to see man as he is, to see him only as we would like him to be.

And yet, next to this acceptance of self-interest, there are certain observations I would like to make. Machiavelli, with whom the idea of self-interest seems to have gained its greatest notoriety, at least among those who are unaware of the tradition, said:

> This is to be asserted in general of men, that they are ungrateful, fickle, fake, cowardly, covetous, as long as you succeed they are yours entirely; they will offer you their blood, property, life, and children when the need is far distant; but when it approaches they turn against you.

But Machiavelli makes a mortal mistake when he rules out the "moral" factors of politics and holds purely to self-interest as he defines it. This mistake can only be accounted for on the basis that Machiavelli's experience as an active politician was not too great, for otherwise he could not have overlooked the obvious fluidity of every man's self-interest. The overall case must be of larger dimensions than that of self-interest narrowly defined; it must be large enough to include and provide for the shifting dimensions of self-interest. You may appeal to one self-interest to get me to the battlefront to fight; but once I am there, my prime self-interest becomes to stay alive, and if we are victorious my self-interest may, and usually does, dictate entirely unexpected goals rather than those I had before the war. For example, the United States in World War II fervently allied with Russia against Germany, Japan, and Italy, and shortly after victory fervently allied with its former enemies—Germany, Japan, and Italy—against its former ally, the U.S.S.R.

These drastic shifts of self-interest can be rationalized only under a huge, limitless umbrella of general "moral" principles such as liberty, justice, freedom, a law higher than man-made law, and so on. Morality, so-called, becomes the continuum as self-interests shift.

Within this morality there appears to be a tearing conflict, probably due to the layers of inhibition in our kind of moralistic civilization—it appears shameful to admit that we operate on the basis of naked self-interest, so we desperately try to reconcile every shift of circumstances that is to our self-interest in terms of a broad moral justification or rationalization. With one breath we point out that we are utterly opposed to communism, but that we love the Russian people (loving people is in keeping with the tenets of our civilization). What we hate is the atheism and the suppression of the individual that we attribute as characteristics substantiating the "immorality" of communism. On this we base our powerful opposition. We do not admit the actual fact: our own self-interest.

We proclaimed all of these negative, diabolical Russian characteristics just prior to the Nazi invasion of Russia. The Soviets were then the cynical despots who connived in the non-aggression pact with Hitler, the ruthless invaders who brought disaster to the Poles and the Finns. They were a people in chains and in misery, held in slavery by a dictator's might; they were a people whose rulers so distrusted them that the Red Army was not permitted to have live ammunition because they might turn their guns against the Kremlin. All this was our image. But within minutes of the invasion of Russia by the Nazis, when self-interest dictated that the defeat of Russia would be disastrous to our interest, then—suddenly—they became the gallant, great, warm, loving Russian people; the dictator became the benevolent and loving Uncle Joe; the Red Army soon was filled with trust and devotion to its government, fighting with an unparalleled bravery and employing a scorched-earth policy against the enemy. The Russian allies certainly had God on their side—after all, He was on ours. Our June, 1941,

shift was more dramatic and sudden than our shift against the Russians shortly after the defeat of our common enemy. In both cases our self-interest was disguised, as the banners of freedom, liberty, and decency were unveiled—first against the Nazis, and six years later against the Russians.

In our present relationship with Tito and the Yugoslavian communists, then, the issue is not that Tito represents communism, but that he is not part of the Russian power alignment. Here we take the position we took after the Nazi invasion, where suddenly communism became, "Well, after all, it's their way of life and we believe in the right of self-determination and it's up to the Russians to have the government they like," *as long as they are on our side and do not threaten our self-interest.* Too, there is no question that, with all our denunciation of the Red Chinese, if they announced that they were no longer a part of the world communist conspiracy or alignment of forces, they would be overnight acceptable to us, acclaimed by us, and provided with all kinds of aid, just so long as they were on our side. In essence, what we are saying is that we do not care what kind of a communist you are *so long as you do not threaten our self-interest.* Too, there is no question that, with all our denunciation of the Red Chinese, if they announced that they were no longer a part of the world communist conspiracy or alignment of forces, they would be overnight acceptable to us, acclaimed by us, and provided with all kinds of aid, just so long as they were on our side. In essence, what we are saying is that we do not care what kind of communist you are so long as you do not threaten our self interest [. . .]

Compromise

Compromise is another word that carries shades of weakness, vacillation, betrayal of ideals, surrender of moral principles. In the old culture, when virginity was a virtue, one referred to a woman's being "compromised." The word is generally regarded as ethically unsavory and ugly.

But to the organizer, compromise is a key and beautiful word. It is always present in the pragmatics of operation. It is making the deal, getting that vital breather, usually the victory. If you start with nothing, demand 100 per cent, then compromise for 30 per cent, you're 30 per cent ahead.

A free and open society is an on-going conflict, interrupted periodically by compromises—which then become the start for the continuation of conflict, compromise, and on ad infinitum. Control of power is based on compromise in our Congress and among the executive, legislative, and judicial branches. A society devoid of compromise is totalitarian. If I had to define a free and open society in one word, the word would be "compromise." [. . .]

Conflict

Conflict is another bad word in the general opinion. This is a consequence of two influences in our society: one influence is organized religion, which has espoused a rhetoric of "turning the other cheek" and has quoted the Scriptures as the devil never would have dared because of their major previous function of supporting the Establishment. The second influence is probably the most subversive and insidious one, and it has permeated the American scene in the last generation: that is Madison Avenue public relations, middle-class moral hygiene, which has made of conflict or controversy something negative and undesirable. This has all been part of an Advertising Culture that emphasizes getting along with people and avoiding friction. If you look at our television commercials you get the picture that American society is largely devoted to ensuring that no odors come from our mouths or armpits. Consensus is a keynote—one must not offend one's fellow man; and so today we find that people in the mass media are fired for expressing their opinions or being "controversial"; in the churches they are fired for the same reason but the words used there are "lacking in prudence"; and on university campuses, faculty members are fired for the same reason, but the words used there are "personality difficulties."

Conflict is the essential core of a free and open society. If one were to project the democratic way of life in the form of a musical score, its major theme would be the harmony of dissonance.

RUSSELL MEANS

Speech during the Wounded Knee Occupation (1973)

The white man says that the 1890 massacre was the end of the wars with the Indian, that it was the end of the Indian, the end of the Ghost Dance. Yet here we are at war, we're still Indians, and we're Ghost Dancing again. And the spirits of Big Foot and his people are all around us. They suffered through here once before, in the snow and the cold, and they were hungry, they were surrounded at that time with the finest weapons the United States had available to them, brand new machine guns and cannons.

What came to me was that Big Foot and his band were like a grandfather. It was time for them to go to sleep, but they had a child that was just born. And this child had to grow and learn all kinds of new things before it once again could return here to Wounded Knee. World War I came along, and the United States asked the American Indian if they would fight their war for them. So we went out and saw around the world what was happening, and we came back. Then another war happened. This time they not only took Indians into the army, but into the defense plants all across America, and into the big cities. And we learned the ways of the white man, right here in this country, found out about the white man to bring that knowledge back for the use of our people. But we still had patience, and all this time we had been watching the white man.

When armed white men were fighting in the labor movement, riots and armed clashes with the pigs, we watched that. And in the '50s when the Communist scare was going throughout the country. And white man was fighting white man, arresting him and putting him in jail. And in the '60s, we watched the black man, that black cloud that Black-Elk prophesied would cover this country. Then the 1970s came. And as a people we are beginning to see. [. . .]

Human Rights Commission Address (1977)

We are people who live in the belly of the monster. The monster being the U.S.A. Every country in the Western Hemisphere follows the lead of the monster. I come not to turn the other cheek. We have turned it now for almost five hundred years, and we realize that here in Geneva, this is our first small step into the international community. [. . .] The President of the U.S.—to show you what a racist he is—[talks] about human rights while my people are suffering genocide. Not only in the U.S. but in the entire Hemisphere—planned genocide by governments. We have brought documents to Geneva that support this charge.

We are approaching the international community this first time for support and assistance to stop not only this rape of our sacred mother earth, but also to stop the genocide of a whole people. A people with

international rights backed up especially in North America by treaties between the U.S. and Indian Nations. The U.S., the monster, and its multinational corporations have dictated foreign policy in this world. They no longer care about the future as witnessed by the Dene [Navajo], by my people, by Central and South America. [. . .]

You see, there is only one color of mankind that is not allowed to participate in the international community, and that color is red. The black, the white, the brown, the yellow—all participate in one form or another. We no longer, until this day, have had a voice within the international community.

Someone once said you can tell the power of a country by the oppressive nature of its military. No longer will we tolerate the monster.

JOHN RAWLS

Theory of Justice (1971)

My aim is to present a conception of justice which generalizes and carries to a higher level of abstraction the familiar theory of the social contract as found, say, in Locke, Rousseau, and Kant.[1] In order to do

this we are not to think of the original contract as one to enter a particular society or to set up a particular form of government. Rather, the guiding idea is that the principles of justice for the basic structure of

---

1. As the text suggests, I shall regard Locke's *Second Treatise of Government*, Rousseau's *The Social Contract* and Kant's ethical works beginning with *The Foundations of the*

Metaphysics of Morals as definitive of the contract tradition. For all of its greatness, Hobbes's *Leviathan* raises special problems. A general historical survey is provided by J.

society are the object of the original agreement. They are the principles that free and rational persons concerned to further their own interests would accept in an initial position of equality as defining the fundamental terms of their association. These principles are to regulate all further agreements; they specify the kinds of social cooperation that can be entered into and the forms of government that can be established. This way of regarding the principles of justice I shall call justice as fairness.

Thus we are to imagine that those who engage in social cooperation choose together, in one joint act, the principles which are to assign basic rights and duties and to determine the division of social benefits. Men are to decide in advance how they are to regulate their claims against one another and what is to be the foundation charter of their society. Just as each person must decide by rational reflection what constitutes his good, that is, the system of ends which it is rational for him to pursue, so a group of persons must decide once and for all what is to count among them as just and unjust. The choice which rational men would make in this hypothetical situation of equal liberty, assuming for the present that this choice problem has a solution, determines the principles of justice.

In justice as fairness the original position of equality corresponds to the state of nature in the traditional theory of the social contract. This original position is not, of course, thought of as an actual historical state of affairs, much less as a primitive condition of culture. It is understood as a purely hypothetical situation characterized so as to lead to a certain conception of justice.[2] Among the essential features of this situation is that no one knows his place in society, his class position or social status, nor does any one know his fortune in the distribution of natural assets and abilities, his intelligence, strength, and the like. I shall even assume that the parties do not know their conceptions of the good or their special psychological propensities. The principles of justice are chosen behind a veil of ignorance. This ensures that no one is advantaged or disadvantaged in the choice of principles by the outcome of natural chance or the contingency of social circumstances. Since all are similarly situated and no one is able to design principles to favor his particular condition, the principles of justice are the result of a fair agreement or bargain. For given the circumstances of the original position, the symmetry of everyone's relations to each other, this initial situation is fair between individuals as moral persons, that is, as rational beings with their own ends and capable, I shall assume, of a sense of justice. The original position is, one might say, the appropriate initial status quo, and thus the fundamental agreements reached in it are fair. This explains the propriety of the name "justice as fairness": it conveys the idea that the principles of justice are agreed to in an initial situation that is fair. The name does not mean that the concepts of justice and fairness are the same, any more than the phrase "poetry as metaphor" means that the concepts of poetry and metaphor are the same.

Justice as fairness begins, as I have said, with one of the most general of all choices which persons might make together, namely, with the choice of the first principles of a conception of justice which is to regulate all subsequent criticism and reform of institutions. Then, having chosen a conception of justice, we can suppose that they are to choose a constitution and a legislature to enact laws, and so on, all in accordance with the principles of justice initially agreed

---

W. Gough, *The Social Contract*, 2nd ed. (Oxford, The Clarendon Press, 1957), and Otto Gierke, *Natural Law and the Theory of Society*, trans. with an introduction by Ernest Barker (Cambridge, The University Press, 1934). A presentation of the contract view as primarily an ethical theory is to be found to G. R. Grice, *The Grounds of Moral Judgment* (Cambridge, The University Press, 1967). See also §19, note 30.

2.   Kant is clear that the original agreement is hypothetical. See *The Metaphysics of Morals* pt. I (*Rechtslehre*),

especially §§47, 52; and pt. II of the essay "Concerning the Common Saying: This May Be True in Theory but It Does Not Apply in Practice," in *Kant's Political Writings*, ed. Hans Reiss and trans. by H. B. Nisbet (Cambridge, The University Press, 1970), pp. 73–87. See Georges Vlachos, *La Pensée politique de Kant* (Paris, Presses Universitaires de France, 1962), pp. 326–335; and J. G. Murphy, *Kant: The Philosophy of Right* (London, Macmillan, 1970), pp. 109–112, 133–136, for a further discussion.

upon. Our social situation is just if it is such that by this sequence of hypothetical agreements we would have contracted into the general system of rules which defines it. Moreover, assuming that the original position does determine a set of principles (that is, that a particular conception of justice would be chosen), it will then be true that whenever social institutions satisfy these principles those engaged in them can say to one another that they are cooperating on terms to which they would agree if they were free and equal persons whose relations with respect to one another were fair. They could all view their arrangements as meeting the stipulations which they would acknowledge in an initial situation that embodies widely accepted and reasonable constraints on the choice of principles. The general recognition of this fact would provide the basis for a public acceptance of the corresponding principles of justice. No society can, of course, be a scheme of cooperation which men enter voluntarily in a literal sense; each person finds himself placed at birth in some particular position in some particular society, and the nature of this position materially affects his life prospects. Yet a society satisfying the principles of justice as fairness comes as close as a society can to being a voluntary scheme, for it meets the principles which free and equal persons would assent to under circumstances that are fair. In this sense its members are autonomous and the obligations they recognize self-imposed.

One feature of justice as fairness is to think of the parties in the initial situation as rational and mutually disinterested. This does not mean that the parties are egoists, that is, individuals with only certain kinds of interests, say in wealth, prestige, and domination. But they are conceived as not taking an interest in one another's interests. They are to presume that even their spiritual aims may be opposed, in the way that the aims of those of different religions may be opposed. Moreover, the concept of rationality must be interpreted as far as possible in the narrow sense, standard in economic theory, of taking the most effective means to given ends. I shall modify this concept to some extent, as explained later (§ 25), but one must try to avoid introducing into it any controversial ethical elements. The initial situation must be characterized by stipulations that are widely accepted.

In working out the conception of justice as fairness one main task clearly is to determine which principles of justice would be chosen in the original position. To do this we must describe this situation in some detail and formulate with care the problem of choice which it presents. These matters I shall take up in the immediately succeeding chapters. It may be observed, however, that once the principles of justice are thought of as arising from an original agreement in a situation of equality, it is an open question whether the principle of utility would be acknowledged. Offhand it hardly seems likely that persons who view themselves as equals, entitled to press their claims upon one another, would agree to a principle which may require lesser life prospects for some simply for the sake of a greater sum of advantages enjoyed by others. Since each desires to protect his interests, his capacity to advance his conception of the good, no one has a reason to acquiesce in an enduring loss for himself in order to bring about a greater net balance of satisfaction. In the absence of strong and lasting benevolent impulses, a rational man would not accept a basic structure merely because it maximized the algebraic sum of advantages irrespective of its permanent effects on his own basic rights and interests. Thus it seems that the principle of utility is incompatible with the conception of social cooperation among equals for mutual advantage. It appears to be inconsistent with the idea of reciprocity implicit in the notion of a well-ordered society. Or, at any rate, so I shall argue.

I shall maintain instead that the persons in the initial situation would choose two rather different principles: the first requires equality in the assignment of basic rights and duties, while the second holds that social and economic inequalities, for example inequalities of wealth and authority, are just only if they result in compensating benefits for everyone, and in particular for the least advantaged members of society. These principles rule out justifying institutions on the grounds that the hardships of some are offset by a greater good in the aggregate. It may be expedient but it is not just that some should have less in order that others may prosper. But there is no injustice in the greater benefits earned by a few provided that the situation of persons not so fortunate is thereby improved. The intuitive idea is that since everyone's well-being depends upon a scheme of cooperation without which no one could have a satisfactory life, the division of advantages should be such as to draw forth the willing cooperation of everyone taking part in it, including those less well situated. The two principles mentioned seem to be a fair basis on which those better endowed, or more fortunate in their social position, neither of which we can be said to deserve, could expect the willing cooperation of others when some workable scheme is a necessary condition of the welfare of all.[3] Once we decide to look for a conception of justice that prevents the use of the accidents of natural endowment and the contingencies of social circumstance as counters in a quest for political and economic advantage, we are led to these principles. They express the result of leaving aside those aspects of the social world that seem arbitrary from a moral point of view.

The problem of the choice of principles, however, is extremely difficult. I do not expect the answer I shall suggest to be convincing to everyone. It is, therefore, worth noting from the outset that justice as fairness, like other contract views, consists of two parts: (1) an interpretation of the initial situation and of the problem of choice posed there, and (2) a set of principles which, it is argued, would be agreed to. One may accept the first part of the theory (or some variant thereof), but not the other, and conversely. The concept of the initial contractual situation may seem reasonable although the particular principles proposed are rejected. To be sure, I want to maintain that the most appropriate conception of this situation does lead to principles of justice contrary to utilitarianism and perfectionism, and therefore that the contract doctrine provides an alternative to these views. Still, one may dispute this contention even though one grants that the contractarian method is a useful way of studying ethical theories and of setting forth their underlying assumptions.

Justice as fairness is an example of what I have called a contract theory. Now there may be an objection to the term "contract" and related expressions, but I think it will serve reasonably well. Many words have misleading connotations which at first are likely to confuse. The terms "utility" and "utilitarianism" are surely no exception. They too have unfortunate suggestions which hostile critics have been willing to exploit; yet they are clear enough for those prepared to study utilitarian doctrine. The same should be true of the term "contract" applied to moral theories. As I have mentioned, to understand it one has to keep in mind that it implies a certain level of abstraction. In particular, the content of the relevant agreement is not to enter a given society or to adopt a given form of government, but to accept certain moral principles. Moreover, the undertakings referred to are purely hypothetical: a contract view holds that certain principles would be accepted in a well-defined initial situation.

The merit of the contract terminology is that it conveys the idea that principles of justice may be conceived as principles that would be chosen by rational persons, and that in this way conceptions of justice may be explained and justified. The theory of justice is a part, perhaps the most significant part, of the theory of rational choice. Furthermore, principles of justice deal with conflicting claims upon the advantages won by social cooperation; they apply to the relations among several persons or groups. The word "contract" suggests this plurality as well as the condition that the appropriate division of advantages must be in accordance with principles acceptable to all parties. The condition of publicity for principles of justice is also connoted by the contract phraseology. Thus, if these principles are the outcome of an agreement, citizens have a knowledge of the principles that others follow. It is characteristic of contract theories to stress the public nature of political principles. Finally there is the long tradition of the contract doctrine. Expressing the tie with this line of thought helps to define ideas and accords with natural piety. There are then several advantages in the use of the term "contract." With due precautions taken, it should not be misleading.

A final remark. Justice as fairness is not a complete contract theory. For it is clear that the contractarian idea can be extended to the choice of more or less an entire ethical system, that is, to a system including principles for all the virtues and not only for justice. Now for the most part I shall consider only principles of justice and others closely related to them; I make no attempt to discuss the virtues in a systematic way. Obviously if justice as fairness succeeds reasonably well, a next step would be to study the more general view suggested by the

---

3. For the formulation of this intuitive idea I am indebted to Allan Gibbard.

name "rightness as fairness." But even this wider theory fails to embrace all moral relationships, since it would seem to include only our relations with other persons and to leave out of account how we are to conduct ourselves toward animals and the rest of nature. I do not contend that the contract notion offers a way to approach these questions which are certainly of the first importance; and I shall have to put them aside. We must recognize the limited scope of justice as fairness and of the general type of view that it exemplifies. How far its conclusions must be revised once these other matters are understood cannot be decided in advance. [. . .]

I shall now state in a provisional form the two principles of justice that I believe would be agreed to in the original position. The first formulation of these principles is tentative. As we go on I shall consider several formulations and approximate step by step the final statement to be given much later. I believe that doing this allows the exposition to proceed in a natural way.

The first statement of the two principles reads as follows.

First: each person is to have an equal right to the most extensive scheme of equal basic liberties compatible with a similar scheme of liberties for others.

Second: social and economic inequalities are to be arranged so that they are both (a) reasonably expected to be to everyone's advantage, and (b) attached to positions and offices open to all.

There are two ambiguous phrases in the second principle, namely "everyone's advantage" and "open to all." Determining their sense more exactly will lead to a second formulation of the principle in §13. The final version of the two principles is given in §46; §39 considers the rendering of the first principle.

These principles primarily apply, as I have said, to the basic structure of society and govern the assignment of rights and duties and regulate the distribution of social and economic advantages. Their formulation presupposes that, for the purposes of a theory of justice, the social structure may be viewed as having two more or less distinct parts, the first principle applying to the one, the second principle to the other. Thus we distinguish between the aspects of the social system that define and secure the equal basic liberties and the aspects that specify and establish social and economic inequalities. Now it is essential to observe that the basic liberties are given by a list of such liberties. Important among these are political liberty (the right to vote and to hold public office) and freedom of speech and assembly; liberty of conscience and freedom of thought; freedom of the person, which includes freedom from psychological oppression and physical assault and dismemberment (integrity of the person); the right to hold personal property and freedom from arbitrary arrest and seizure as defined by the concept of the rule of law. These liberties are to be equal by the first principle.

The second principle applies, in the first approximation, to the distribution of income and wealth and to the design of organizations that make use of differences in authority and responsibility. While the distribution of wealth and income need not be equal, it must be to everyone's advantage, and at the same time, positions of authority and responsibility must be accessible to all. One applies the second principle by holding positions open, and then, subject to this constraint, arranges social and economic inequalities so that everyone benefits.

These principles are to be arranged in a serial order with the first principle prior to the second. This ordering means that infringements of the basic equal liberties protected by the first principle cannot be justified, or compensated for, by greater social and economic advantages. These liberties have a central range of application within which they can be limited and compromised only when they conflict with other basic liberties. Since they may be limited when they clash with one another, none of these liberties is absolute; but however they are adjusted to form one system, this system is to be the same for all. It is difficult, and perhaps impossible, to give a complete specification of these liberties independently from the particular circumstances—social, economic, and technological—of a given society. The hypothesis is that the general form of such a list could be devised with sufficient exactness to sustain this conception of justice. Of course, liberties not on the list, for example, the right to own certain kinds of property (e.g., means of production) and freedom of contract as understood by the doctrine of laissez-faire are not basic; and so they are not protected by the priority of the first principle. Finally, in regard to the second principle, the distribution of wealth and income, and positions of authority and responsibility, are to be consistent with both the basic liberties and equality of opportunity.

The two principles are rather specific in their content, and their acceptance rests on certain assumptions that I must eventually try to explain and justify. For the present, it should be observed that these principles are a special case of a more general conception of justice that can be expressed as follows.

> All social values—liberty and opportunity, income and wealth, and the social bases of self-respect—are to be distributed equally unless an unequal distribution of any, or all, of these values is to everyone's advantage.

Injustice, then, is simply inequalities that are not to the benefit of all. Of course, this conception is extremely vague and requires interpretation.

As a first step, suppose that the basic structure of society distributes certain primary goods, that is, things that every rational man is presumed to want. These goods normally have a use whatever a person's rational plan of life. For simplicity, assume that the chief primary goods at the disposition of society are rights, liberties, and opportunities, and income and wealth. [. . .]

These are the social primary goods. Other primary goods such as health and vigor, intelligence and imagination, are natural goods; although their possession is influenced by the basic structure, they are not so directly under its control. Imagine, then, a hypothetical initial arrangement in which all the social primary goods are equally distributed: everyone has similar rights and duties, and income and wealth are evenly shared. This state of affairs provides a benchmark for judging improvements. If certain inequalities of wealth and differences in authority would make everyone better off than in this hypothetical starting situation, then they accord with the general conception.

Now it is possible, at least theoretically, that by giving up some of their fundamental liberties men are sufficiently compensated by the resulting social and economic gains. The general conception of justice imposes no restrictions on what sort of inequalities are permissible; it only requires that everyone's position be improved. We need not suppose anything so drastic as consenting to a condition of slavery. Imagine instead that people seem willing to forego

certain political rights when the economic returns are significant. It is this kind of exchange which the two principles rule out; being arranged in serial order they do not permit exchanges between basic liberties and economic and social gains except under extenuating circumstances. [. . .]

The fact that the two principles apply to institutions has certain consequences. First of all, the rights and basic liberties referred to by these principles are those which are defined by the public rules of the basic structure. Whether men are free is determined by the rights and duties established by the major institutions of society. Liberty is a certain pattern of social forms. The first principle simply requires that certain sorts of rules, those defining basic liberties, apply to everyone equally and that they allow the most extensive liberty compatible with a like liberty for all. The only reason for circumscribing basic liberties and making them less extensive is that otherwise they would interfere with one another. [. . .]

Now the second principle insists that each person benefit from permissible inequalities in the basic structure. This means that it must be reasonable for each relevant representative man defined by this structure, when he views it as a going concern, to prefer his prospects with the inequality to his prospects without it. One is not allowed to justify differences in income or in positions of authority and responsibility on the ground that the disadvantages of those in one position are outweighed by the greater advantages of those in another. Much less can infringements of liberty be counterbalanced in this way. It is obvious, however, that there are indefinitely many ways in which all may be advantaged when the initial arrangement of equality is taken as a benchmark. How then are we to choose among these possibilities? The principles must be specified so that they yield a determinate conclusion. [. . .]

I now wish to give the final statement of the two principles of justice for institutions. For the sake of completeness, I shall give a full statement including earlier formulations.

First Principle

Each person is to have an equal right to the most extensive total system of equal basic liberties compatible with a similar system of liberty for all.

Second Principle

Social and economic inequalities are to be arranged so that they are both:

(a) to the greatest benefit of the least advantaged, consistent with the just savings principle, and
(b) attached to offices and positions open to all under conditions of fair equality of opportunity.

First Priority Rule (The Priority of Liberty)

The principles of justice are to be ranked in lexical order and therefore the basic liberties can be restricted only for the sake of liberty. There are two cases:

(a) a less extensive liberty must strengthen the total system of liberties shared by all;
(b) a less than equal liberty must be acceptable to those with the lesser liberty.

Second Priority Rule (The Priority of Justice over Efficiency and Welfare)

The second principle of justice is lexically prior to the principle of efficiency and to that of maximizing the sum of advantages; and fair opportunity is prior to the difference principle. There are two cases:

(a) an inequality of opportunity must enhance the opportunities of those with the lesser opportunity;
(b) an excessive rate of saving must on balance mitigate the burden of those bearing this hardship.

By way of comment, these principles and priority rules are no doubt incomplete. Other modifications will surely have to be made, but I shall not further complicate the statement of the principles. It suffices to observe that when we come to nonideal theory, the lexical ordering of the two principles, and the valuations that this ordering implies, suggest priority rules which seem to be reasonable enough in many cases. By various examples I have tried to illustrate how these rules can be used and to indicate their plausibility. Thus the ranking of the principles of justice in ideal theory reflects back and guides the application of these principles to nonideal situations. It identifies which limitations need to be dealt with first. In the more extreme and tangled instances of nonideal theory this priority of rules will no doubt fail; and indeed, we may be able to find no satisfactory answer at all. But we must try to postpone the day of reckoning as long as possible, and try to arrange society so that it never comes.

Robert Nozick

Anarchy, State, and Utopia (1974)

Preface

Individuals have rights, and there are things no person or group may do to them (without violating their rights). So strong and far-reaching are these rights that they raise the question of what, if anything, the state and its officials may do. How much room do individual rights leave for the state? The nature of the state, its legitimate functions and its justifications, if any, is the central concern of this book; a wide and diverse variety of topics intertwine in the course of our investigation.

Our main conclusions about the state are that a minimal state, limited to the narrow functions of protection against force, theft, fraud, enforcement of contracts, and so on, is justified; that any more extensive state will violate persons' rights not to be forced to do certain things, and is unjustified; and that the minimal state is inspiring as well as right. Two noteworthy implications are that the state may not use its coercive apparatus for the purpose of getting some citizens to aid others, or in order to prohibit activities to people for their *own* good or protection.

Despite the fact that it is only coercive routes toward these goals that are excluded, while voluntary ones remain, many persons will reject our conclusions instantly, knowing they don't *want* to believe anything so apparently callous toward the needs and suffering of others. I know that reaction; it was mine when I first began to consider such views. With reluctance, I found myself becoming convinced of (as they are now often called) libertarian views, due to various considerations and arguments. This book contains little evidence of my earlier reluctance. Instead, it contains many of the considerations and arguments, which I present as forcefully as I can. Thereby, I run the risk of offending doubly: for the position expounded, and for the fact that I produce reasons to support this position. [. . .]

Chapter Seven: Distributive Justice

The minimal state is the most extensive state that can be justified. Any state more extensive violates people's rights. Yet many persons have put forth reasons purporting to justify a more extensive state. It is impossible within the compass of this book to examine all the reasons that have been put forth. Therefore, I shall focus upon those generally acknowledged to be most weighty and influential, to see precisely wherein they fail. In this chapter we consider the claim that a more extensive state is justified, because necessary (or the best instrument) to achieve distributive justice; in the next chapter we shall take up diverse other claims.

The term "distributive justice" is not a neutral one. Hearing the term "distribution," most people presume that some thing or mechanism uses some principle or criterion to give out a supply of things. Into this process of distributing shares some error may have crept. So it is an open question, at least, whether redistribution should take place; whether we

should do again what has already been done once, though poorly. However, we are not in the position of children who have been given portions of pie by someone who now makes last minute adjustments to rectify careless cutting. There is no *central* distribution, no person or group entitled to control all the resources, jointly deciding how they are to be doled out. What each person gets, he gets from others who give to him in exchange for something, or as a gift. In a free society, diverse persons control different resources, and new holdings arise out of the voluntary exchanges and actions of persons. There is no more a distributing or distribution of shares than there is a distributing of mates in a society in which persons choose whom they shall marry. The total result is the product of many individual decisions which the different individuals involved are entitled to make. Some uses of the term "distribution," it is true, do not imply a previous distributing appropriately judged by some criterion (for example, "probability distribution"); nevertheless, despite the title of this chapter, it would be best to use a terminology that clearly is neutral. We shall speak of people's holdings; a principle of justice in holdings describes (part of) what justice tells us (requires) about holdings. [. . .]

Entitlement Theory

If the world were wholly just, the following inductive definition would exhaustively cover the subject of justice in holdings.

1. A person who acquires a holding in accordance with the principle of justice in acquisition is entitled to that holding.
2. A person who acquires a holding in accordance with the principle of justice in transfer, from someone else entitled to the holding, is entitled to the holding.
3. No one is entitled to a holding except by (repeated) applications of 1 and 2.

The complete principle of distributive justice would say simply that a distribution is just if everyone is entitled to the holdings they possess under the distribution.

A distribution is just if it arises from another just distribution by legitimate means. The legitimate means of moving from one distribution to another are specified by the principle of justice in transfer. The legitimate first "moves" are specified by the principle of justice in acquisition.[1] Whatever arises from a just situation by just steps is itself just. The means of change specified by the principle of justice in transfer preserve justice. [. . .]

Patterning

Let us call a principle of distribution *patterned* if it specifies that a distribution is to vary along with some natural dimension, weighted sum of natural dimensions, or lexicographic ordering of natural dimensions. And let us say a distribution is patterned if it accords with some patterned principle. (I speak of natural dimensions, admittedly without a general criterion for them, because for any set of holdings some artificial dimensions can be gimmicked up to vary along with the distribution of the set.) The principle of distribution in accordance with moral merit is a patterned historical principle, which specifies a patterned distribution. "Distribute according to I.Q." is a patterned principle that looks to information not contained in distributional matrices. It is not historical, however, in that it does not look to any past actions creating differential entitlements to evaluate a distribution; it requires only distributional matrices whose columns are labeled by I.Q. scores. The distribution in a society, however, may be composed of such simple patterned distributions, without itself being simply patterned. Different sectors may operate different patterns, or some combination of patterns may operate in different proportions across a society. A distribution composed in this manner, from a small number of patterned distributions, we also shall term "patterned." And we extend the use of "pattern" to include the overall designs put forth by combinations of end-state principles.

Almost every suggested principle of distributive justice is patterned: to each according to his moral merit, or needs, or marginal product, or how hard he tries, or the weighted sum of the foregoing, and so on. [. . .]

Will people tolerate for long a system yielding distributions that they believe are unpatterned? No doubt people will not long accept a distribution they believe is *unjust*. People want their society to be and to look just. But must the look of justice reside in a resulting pattern rather than in the underlying generating principles? We are in no position to conclude that the inhabitants of a society embodying an entitlement conception of justice in holdings will find it unacceptable. Still, it must be granted that were people's reasons for transferring some of their holdings to others always irrational or arbitrary, we would find this disturbing. (Suppose people always determined what holdings they would transfer, and to whom, by using a random device.) We feel more comfortable upholding the justice of an entitlement system if most of the transfers under it are done for reasons. This does not mean necessarily that all deserve what holdings they receive. It means only that there is a purpose or point to someone's transferring a holding to one person rather than to another; that usually we can see what the transferrer thinks he's gaining, what cause he thinks he's serving, what goals he thinks he's helping to achieve, and so forth. [. . .]

To think that the task of a theory of distributive justice is to fill in the blank in "to each according to his _____" is to be predisposed to search for a pattern; and the separate treatment of "from each according to his _____" treats production and distribution as two separate and independent issues. On an entitlement view these are *not* two separate questions. Whoever makes something, having bought or contracted for all other held resources used in the process (transferring some of his holdings for these cooperating factors), is entitled to it. The situation is *not* one of something's getting made, and there being an open question of who is to get it. Things come into the world already attached to people having entitlements over them. From the point of view of the historical entitlement conception of justice in holdings, those who start afresh to complete "to each according to his _____" treat objects as if they appeared from nowhere, out of nothing. A complete theory of justice might cover this limit case as well; perhaps here is a use for the usual conceptions of distributive justice.

---

1. Applications of the principle of justice in acquisition may also occur as part of the move from one distribution to another. You may find an unheld thing now and appropriate it. Acquisitions also are to be understood as included when, to simplify, I speak only of transitions by transfers.

So entrenched are maxims of the usual form that perhaps we should present the entitlement conception as a competitor. Ignoring acquisition and rectification, we might say:

> From each according to what he chooses to do, to each according to what he makes for himself (perhaps with the contracted aid of others) and what others choose to do for him and choose to give him of what they've been given previously (under this maxim) and haven't yet expended or transferred.

This, the discerning reader will have noticed, has its defects as a slogan. So as a summary and great simplification (and not as a maxim with any independent meaning) we have:

> *From each as they choose, to each as they are chosen.*

How Liberty Upsets Patterns

It is not clear how those holding alternative conceptions of distributive justice can reject the entitlement conception of justice in holdings. For suppose a distribution favored by one of these nonentitlement conceptions is realized. Let us suppose it is your favorite one and let us call this distribution D_1, perhaps everyone has an equal share, perhaps shares vary in accordance with some dimension you treasure. Now suppose that Wilt Chamberlain is greatly in demand by basketball teams, being a great gate attraction. (Also suppose contracts run only for a year, with players being free agents.) He signs the following sort of contract with a team: In each home game, twenty-five cents from the price of each ticket of admission goes to him. (We ignore the question of whether he is "gouging" the owners, letting them look out for themselves.) The season starts, and people cheerfully attend his team's games; they buy their tickets, each time dropping a separate twenty-five cents of their admission price into a special box with Chamberlain's name on it. They are excited about seeing him play; it is worth the total admission price to them. Let us suppose that in one season one million persons attend his home games, and Wilt Chamberlain winds up with $250,000, a much larger sum than the average income and larger even than anyone else has. Is he entitled to this income? Is this new distribution D_2, unjust? If so, why? There is *no* question about whether each of the people was entitled to the control over the resources they held in D_1; because that was the distribution (your favorite) that (for the purposes of argument) we assumed was acceptable. Each of these persons *chose* to give twenty-five cents of their money to Chamberlain. They could have spent it on going to the movies, or on candy bars, or on copies of *Dissent* magazine, or of *Montly Review.* But they all, at least one million of them, converged on giving it to Wilt Chamberlain in exchange for watching him play basketball. If D_1 was a just distribution, and people voluntarily moved from it to D_2, transferring parts of their shares they were given under D_1 (what was it for if not to do something with?), isn't D_2 also just? If the people were entitled to dispose of the resources to which they were entitled (under D_1), didn't this include their being entitled to give it to, or exchange it with, Wilt Chamberlain? Can anyone else complain on grounds of justice? Each other person already has his legitimate share under D_1. Under D_1, there is nothing that anyone has that anyone else has a claim of justice against. After someone transfers something to Wilt Chamberlain, third parties *still* have their legitimate shares; *their* shares are not changed. By what process could such a transfer among two persons give rise to a legitimate claim of distributive justice on a portion of what was transferred, by a third party who had no claim of justice on any holding of the others *before* the transfer?[2] To cut off objections irrelevant here, we might imagine the exchanges occurring in a socialist society, after hours. After playing whatever

---

2. Might not a transfer have instrumental effects on a third party, changing his feasible options? (But what if the two parties to the transfer independently had used their holdings in this fashion?) I discuss this question below, but note here that this question concedes the point for distributions of ultimate intrinsic noninstrumental goods (pure utility experiences, so to speak) that are transferrable. It also might be objected that the transfer might make a third party more envious because it worsens his position relative to someone else. I find it incomprehensible how this can be thought to involve a claim of justice. [. . .]

Here and elsewhere in this chapter, a theory which incorporates elements of pure procedural justice might find what I say acceptable, *if* kept in its proper place; that

basketball he does in his daily work, or doing whatever other daily work he does, Wilt Chamberlain decides to put in *overtime* to earn additional money. (First his work quota is set; he works time over that.) Or imagine it is a skilled juggler people like to see, who puts on shows after hours.

Why might someone work overtime in a society in which it is assumed their needs are satisfied? Perhaps because they care about things other than needs. I like to write in books that I read, and to have easy access to books for browsing at odd hours. It would be very pleasant and convenient to have the resources of Widener Library in my back yard. No society, I assume, will provide such resources close to each person who would like them as part of his regular allotment (under D_1). Thus, persons either must do without some extra things that they want, or be allowed to do something extra to get some of these things. On what basis could the inequalities that would eventuate be forbidden? Notice also that small factories would spring up in a socialist society, unless forbidden. I melt down some of my personal possessions (under D_1) and build a machine out of the material. I offer you, and others, a philosophy lecture once a week in exchange for your cranking the handle on my machine, whose products I exchange for yet other things, and so on. (The raw materials used by the machine are given to me by others who possess them under D_1, in exchange for hearing lectures.) Each person might participate to gain things over and above their allotment under D_1. Some persons even might want to leave their job in socialist industry and work full time in this private sector. I shall say something more about these issues in the next chapter. Here I wish merely to note how private property even in means of production would occur in a socialist society that did not forbid people to use as they wished

some of the resources they are given under the socialist distribution D_1. The socialist society would have to forbid capitalist acts between consenting adults.

The general point illustrated by the Wilt Chamberlain example and the example of the entrepreneur in a socialist society is that no end-state principle or distributional patterned principle of justice can be continuously realized without continuous interference with people's lives. Any favored pattern would be transformed into one unfavored by the principle, by people choosing to act in various ways; for example, by people exchanging goods and services with other people, or giving things to other people, things the transferrers are entitled to under the favored distributional pattern. To maintain a pattern one must either continually interfere to stop people from transferring resources as they wish to, or continually (or periodically) interfere to take from some persons resources that others for some reason chose to transfer to them. (But if some time limit is to be set on how long people may keep resources others voluntarily transfer to them, why let them keep these resources for *any* period of time? Why not have immediate confiscation?) It might be objected that all persons voluntarily will choose to refrain from actions which would upset the pattern. This presupposes unrealistically (1) that all will most want to maintain the pattern (are those who don't, to be "reeducated" or forced to undergo "self-criticism"?), (2) that each can gather enough information about his own actions and the ongoing activities of others to discover which of his actions will upset the pattern, and (3) that diverse and far-flung persons can coordinate their actions to dovetail into the pattern. Compare the manner in which the market is neutral among persons' desires, as it reflects and transmits widely scattered information via prices, and coordinates persons' activities.

It puts things perhaps a bit too strongly to say that every patterned (or end-state) principle is liable to be thwarted by the voluntary actions of the individual parties transferring some of their shares they receive under the principle. For perhaps some *very* weak patterns are not so thwarted.[3] Any distributional pattern

---

is, if background institutions exist to ensure the satisfaction of certain conditions on distributive shares. But if these institutions are not themselves the sum or invisible-hand result of people's voluntary (nonaggressive) actions, the constraints they impose require justification. At no point does *our* argument assume any background institutions more extensive than those of the minimal night-watchman state, a state limited to protecting persons against murder, assault, theft, fraud, and so forth.

---

3. Is the patterned principle stable that requires merely that a distribution be Pareto-optimal? One person might

with any egalitarian component is overturnable by the voluntary actions of individual persons over time; as is every patterned condition with sufficient content so as actually to have been proposed as presenting the central core of distributive justice. Still, given the possibility that some weak conditions or patterns may not be unstable in this way, it would be better to formulate an explicit description of the kind of interesting and contentful patterns under discussion, and to prove a theorem about their instability. Since the weaker the patterning, the more likely it is that the entitlement system itself satisfies it, a plausible conjecture is that any patterning either is unstable or is satisfied by the entitlement system.

Michael Walzer

Spheres of Justice (1983)

Complex Equality

Pluralism

In the matter of distributive justice, history displays a great variety of arrangements and ideologies. But the first impulse of the philosopher is to resist the displays of history, the world of appearances, and to search for some underlying unity: a short list of basic goods, quickly abstracted to a single good; a single distributive criterion or an interconnected set; and the philosopher himself standing, symbolically at least, at a single decision point. I shall argue that to search for unity is to misunderstand the subject matter of distributive justice. Nevertheless, in some sense the philosophical impulse is unavoidable. Even if we choose pluralism, as I shall do, that choice still requires a coherent defense. There must be principles that justify the choice and set limits to it, for pluralism does not require us to endorse every proposed distributive criteria or to accept every would be agent. Conceivably, there is a single principle and a single legitimate kind of pluralism. But this would still be a pluralism that encompassed a wide range of distributions. By contrast, the deepest assumption of most of the philosophers who have written about justice, from Plato onward, is that there is one, and only one, distributive system that philosophy can rightly encompass.

Today this system is commonly described as the one that ideally rational men and women would choose if they were forced to choose impartially, knowing nothing of their own situation, barred from making particularist claims, confronting an abstract

---

give another a gift or bequest that the second could exchange with a third to their mutual benefit. Before the second makes this exchange, there is not Pareto-optimality. Is a stable pattern presented by a principle choosing that among the Pareto-optimal positions that satisfies some further condition C? It may seem that there cannot be a counterexample, for won't any voluntary exchange made away from a situation show that the first situation wasn't Pareto-optimal? (Ignore the implausibility of this last claim for the case of bequests.) But principles are to be satisfied over time, during which new possibilities arise. A distribution that at one time satisfies the criterion of Pareto-optimality might not do so when some new possibilities arise (Wilt Chamberlain grows up and starts playing basketball); and though people's activities will tend to move them to a new Pareto-optimal position, *this* new one need not satisfy the contentful condition C. Continual interference will be needed to insure the continual satisfaction of C. (The theoretical possiblity of a pattern's being maintained by some invisible-hand process that brings it back to an equilibrium that fits the pattern when deviations occur should be investigated.)

set of goods.[1] If these constraints on knowing and claiming are suitably shaped, and if the goods are suitably defined, it is probably true that a singular conclusion can be produced. Rational men and women, constrained this way or that, will choose one, and only one, distributive system. But the force of that singular conclusion is not easy to measure. It is surely doubtful that those same men and women, if they were transformed into ordinary people, with a firm sense of their own identity, with their own goods in their hands, caught up in everyday troubles, would reiterate their hypothetical choice or even recognize it as their own. The problem is not, most importantly, with the particularism of interest, which philosophers have always assumed they could safely—that is, uncontroversially—set aside. Ordinary people can do that too, for the sake, say, of the public interest. The greater problem is with the particularism of history, culture, and membership. Even if they are committed to impartiality, the question most likely to arise in the minds of the members of a political community is not, What would rational individuals choose under universalizing conditions of such-and-such a sort? But rather, What would individuals like us choose, who are situated as we are, who share a culture and are determined to go on sharing it? And this is a question that is readily transformed into, What choices have we already made in the course of our common life? What understandings do we (really) share?

Justice is a human construction, and it is doubtful that it can be made in only one way. At any rate, I shall begin by doubting, and more than doubting, this standard philosophical assumption. The questions posed by the theory of distributive justice admit of a range of answers, and there is room within the range for cultural diversity and political choice. It's not only a matter of implementing some singular principle or set of principles in different historical settings. No one would deny that there is a range of morally permissible implementations. I want to argue for more than this: that the principles of justice are themselves pluralistic in form; that different social goods ought to be distributed for different reasons, in accordance with different procedures, by different agents; and these differences derive from different understandings of the social goods themselves—the inevitable product of historical and cultural particularism.

Theory of Goods

Theories of distributive justice focus on a social process commonly described as if it had this form:

People distribute goods to (other) people.

Here, "distribute" means give, allocate, exchange, and so on, and the focus is on the individuals who stand at either end of these actions: not on producers and consumers, but on distributive agents and recipients of goods. We are as always interested in ourselves, but, in this case, in a special and limited version of ourselves, as people who give and take. What is our nature? What are our rights? What do we need, want, deserve? What are we entitled to? What would we accept under ideal conditions? Answers to these questions are turned into distributive principles, which are supposed to control the movement of goods. The goods, defined by abstraction, are taken to be movable in any direction.

But this is too simple an understanding of what actually happens, and it forces us too quickly to make large assertions about human nature and moral agency—assertions unlikely, ever, to command general agreement. I want to propose a more precise and complex description of the central process:

People conceive and create goods, which they then distribute among themselves.

Here, the conception and creation precede and control the distribution. Goods don't just appear in the hands of distributive agents who do with them as they like or give them out in accordance with some general principle.[2] Rather, goods with their

---

1. See John Rawls, *A Theory of Justice* (Cambridge, Mass., 1971); Jürgen Habermas, *Legitimation Crisis*, trans. Thomas McCarthy (Boston, 1975), esp. p. 113; Bruce Ackerman, *Social Justice in the Liberal State* (New Haven, 1980).

2. Robert Nozick makes a similar argument in *Anarchy, State, and Utopia* (New York, 1974), pp. 149–50, but with radically individualistic conclusions that seem to me to miss the social character of production.

meanings—because of their meanings—are the crucial medium of social relations; they come into people's minds before they come into their hands; distributions are patterned in accordance with shared conceptions of what the goods are and what they are for. Distributive agents are constrained by the goods they hold; one might almost say that goods distribute themselves among people.

> Things are in the saddle
> And ride mankind.[3]

But these are always particular things and particular groups of men and women. And, of course, we make the things—even the saddle. I don't want to deny the importance of human agency, only to shift our attention from distribution itself to conception and creation: the naming of the goods, and the giving of meaning, and the collective making. What we need to explain and limit the pluralism of distributive possibilities is a theory of goods. For our immediate purposes, that theory can be summed up in six propositions.

1. All the goods with which distributive justice is concerned are social goods. They are not and they cannot be idiosyncratically valued. I am not sure that there are any other kinds of goods; I mean to leave the question open. Some domestic objects are cherished for private and sentimental reasons, but only in cultures where sentiment regularly attaches to such objects. A beautiful sunset, the smell of new-mown hay, the excitement of an urban vista: these perhaps are privately valued goods, though they are also, and more obviously, the objects of cultural assessment. Even new inventions are not valued in accordance with the ideas of their inventors; they are subject to a wider process of conception and creation. God's goods, to be sure, are exempt from this rule—as in the first chapter of Genesis: "and God saw every thing that He had made, and, behold, it was very good" (1:31). That evaluation doesn't require the agreement of mankind (who might be doubtful), or of a majority of men and women, or of any group of men and women meeting under ideal conditions (though Adam and Eve in Eden would probably endorse it). But I can't think of any other exemptions. Goods in the world have shared meanings because conception and creation are social processes. For the same reason, goods have different meanings in different societies. The same "thing" is valued for different reasons, or it is valued here and disvalued there. John Stuart Mill once complained that "people like in crowds," but I know of no other way to like or to dislike social goods.[4] A solitary person could hardly understand the meaning of the goods or figure out the reasons for taking them as likable or dislikable. Once people like in crowds, it becomes possible for individuals to break away, pointing to latent or subversive meanings, aiming at alternative values—including the values, for example, of notoriety and eccentricity. An easy eccentricity has sometimes been one of the privileges of the aristocracy: it is a social good like any other.

2. Men and women take on concrete identities because of the way they conceive and create, and then possess and employ social goods. "The line between what is me and mine," wrote William James, "is very hard to draw."[5] Distributions cannot be understood as the acts of men and women who do not yet have particular goods in their minds or in their hands. In fact, people already stand in a relation to a set of goods; they have a history of transactions, not only with one another but also with the moral and material world in which they live. Without such a history, which begins at birth, they wouldn't be men and women in any recognizable sense, and they wouldn't have the first notion of how to go about the business of giving, allocating, and exchanging goods.

3. There is no single set of primary or basic goods conceivable across all moral and material worlds— or, any such set would have to be conceived in terms

---

3. Ralph Waldo Emerson, "Ode," in *The Complete Essays and Other Writings*, ed. Brooks Atkinson (New York, 1940), p. 770.

4. John Stuart Mill, *On Liberty* in *The Philosophy of John Stuart Mill*, ed. Marshall Cohen (New York, 1961), p. 255. For an anthropological account of liking and not liking social goods, see Mary Douglas and Baron Isherwood, *The World of Goods* (New York, 1979).

5. William James, quoted in C. R. Snyder and Howard Fromkin, *Uniqueness: The Human Pursuit of Difference* (New York, 1980), p. 108.

so abstract that they would be of little use in thinking about particular distributions. Even the range of necessities, if we take into account moral as well as physical necessities, is very wide, and the rank orderings are very different. A single necessary good, and one that is always necessary—food, for example—carries different meanings in different places. Bread is the staff of life, the body of Christ, the symbol of the Sabbath, the means of hospitality, and so on. Conceivably, there is a limited sense in which the first of these is primary, so that if there were twenty people in the world and just enough bread to feed the twenty, the primacy of bread-as-staff-of-life would yield a sufficient distributive principle. But that is the only circumstance in which it would do so; and even there, we can't be sure. If the religious uses of bread were to conflict with its nutritional uses—if the gods demanded that bread be baked and burned rather than eaten—it is by no means clear which use would be primary. How, then, is bread to be incorporated into the universal list? The question is even harder to answer, the conventional answers less plausible, as we pass from necessities to opportunities, powers, reputations, and so on. These can be incorporated only if they are abstracted from every particular meaning—hence, for all practical purposes, rendered meaningless.

4. But it is the meaning of goods that determines their movement. Distributive criteria and arrangements are intrinsic not to the good-in-itself but to the social good. If we understand what it is, what it means to those for whom it is a good, we understand how, by whom, and for what reasons it ought to be distributed. All distributions are just or unjust relative to the social meanings of the goods at stake. This is in obvious ways a principle of legitimation, but it is also a critical principle. When medieval Christians, for example, condemned the sin of simony, they were claiming that the meaning of a particular social good, ecclesiastical office, excluded its sale and purchase. Given the Christian understanding of office, it followed—I am inclined to say, it necessarily followed—that office holders should be chosen for their knowledge and piety and not for their wealth. There are presumably things that money can buy, but not this thing. Similarly, the words *prostitution* and *bribery*, like *simony*, describe the sale and purchase of goods that, given certain understandings of their meanings, ought never to be sold or purchased.

5. Social meanings are historical in character; and so distributions, and just and unjust distributions, change over time. To be sure, certain key goods have what we might think of as characteristic normative structures, reiterated across the lines (but not all the lines) of time and space. It is because of this reiteration that the British philosopher Bernard Williams is able to argue that goods should always be distributed for "relevant reasons"—where relevance seems to connect to essential rather than to social meanings.[6] The idea that offices, for example, should go to qualified candidates—though not the only idea that has been held about offices—is plainly visible in very different societies where simony and nepotism, under different names, have similarly been thought sinful or unjust. (But there has been a wide divergence of views about what sorts of position and place are properly called "offices.") Again, punishment has been widely understood as a negative good that ought to go to people who are judged to deserve it on the basis of a verdict, not of a political decision. (But what constitutes a verdict? Who is to deliver it? How, in short, is justice to be done to accused men and women? About these questions there has been significant disagreement.) These examples invite empirical investigation. There is no merely intuitive or speculative procedure for seizing upon relevant reasons.

6. When meanings are distinct, distributions must be autonomous. Every social good or set of goods constitutes, as it were, a distributive sphere within which only certain criteria and arrangements are appropriate. Money is inappropriate in the sphere of ecclesiastical office; it is an intrusion from another sphere. And piety should make for no advantage in the marketplace, as the marketplace has commonly been understood. Whatever can rightly be sold ought to be sold to pious men and women and also to profane, heretical, and sinful men and women (else no one would do much business). The market is open to

---

6.   Bernard Williams, *Problems of the Self: Philosophical Papers, 1956–1972* (Cambridge, England, 1973), pp. 230–49 ("The Idea of Equality"). This essay is one of the starting points of my own thinking about distributive justice. See also the critique of William's argument (and of an earlier essay of my own) in Amy Gutmann, *Liberal Equality* (Cambridge, England, 1980), chap. 4.

all comers; the church is not. In no society, of course, are social meanings entirely distinct. What happens in one distributive sphere affects what happens in the others; we can look, at most, for relative autonomy. But relative autonomy, like social meaning, is a critical principle—indeed, as I shall be arguing throughout this book, a radical principle. It is radical even though it doesn't point to a single standard against which all distributions are to be measured. There is no single standard. But there are standards (roughly knowable even when they are also controversial) for every social good and every distributive sphere in every particular society; and these standards are often violated, the goods usurped, the spheres invaded, by powerful men and women.

Dominance and Monopoly

In fact, the violations are systematic. Autonomy is a matter of social meaning and shared values, but it is more likely to make for occasional reformation and rebellion than for everyday enforcement. For all the complexity of their distributive arrangements, most societies are organized on what we might think of as a social version of the gold standard: one good or one set of goods is dominant and determinative of value in all the spheres of distribution. And that good or set of goods is commonly monopolized, its value upheld by the strength and cohesion of its owners. I call a good dominant if the individuals who have it, because they have it, can command a wide range of other goods. It is monopolized whenever a single man or woman, a monarch in the world of value—or a group of men and women, oligarchs—successfully hold it against all rivals. Dominance describes a way of using social goods that isn't limited by their intrinsic meanings or that shapes those meanings in its own image. Monopoly describes a way of owning or controlling social goods in order to exploit their dominance. When goods are scarce and widely needed, like water in the desert, monopoly itself will make them dominant. Mostly, however, dominance is a more elaborate social creation, the work of many hands, mixing reality and symbol. Physical strength, familial reputation, religious or political office, landed wealth, capital, technical knowledge: each of these, in different historical periods, has been dominant; and each of them has been monopolized by

some group of men and women. And then all good things come to those who have the one best thing. Possess that one, and the others come in train. Or, to change the metaphor, a dominant good is converted into another good, into many others, in accordance with what often appears to be a natural process but is in fact magical, a kind of social alchemy.

No social good ever entirely dominates the range of goods; no monopoly is ever perfect. I mean to describe tendencies only, but crucial tendencies. For we can characterize whole societies in terms of the patterns of conversion that are established within them. Some characterizations are simple: in a capitalist society, capital is dominant and readily converted into prestige and power; in a technocracy, technical knowledge plays the same part. But it isn't difficult to imagine, or to find, more complex social arrangements. Indeed, capitalism and technocracy are more complex than their names imply, even if the names do convey real information about the most important forms of sharing, dividing, and exchanging. Monopolistic control of a dominant good makes a ruling class, whose members stand atop the distributive system—much as philosophers, claiming to have the wisdom they love, might like to do. But since dominance is always incomplete and monopoly imperfect, the rule of every ruling class is unstable. It is continually challenged by other groups in the name of alternative patterns of conversion. [. . .]

History reveals no single dominant good and no naturally dominant good, but only different kinds of magic and competing bands of magicians.

The claim to monopolize a dominant good—when worked up for public purposes—constitutes an ideology. Its standard form is to connect legitimate possession with some set of personal qualities through the medium of a philosophical principle. [. . .]

One group wins, and then a different one; or coalitions are worked out, and supremacy is uneasily shared. There is no final victory, nor should there be. But that is not to say that the claims of the different groups are necessarily wrong, or that the principles they invoke are of no value as distributive criteria; the principles are often exactly right within the limits of a particular sphere. Ideologies are readily corrupted, but their corruption is not the most interesting thing about them. [. . .]

Some group of men and women—class, caste, strata, estate, alliance, or social formation—comes to enjoy a monopoly or a near monopoly of some dominant good; or, a coalition of groups comes to enjoy, and so on. This dominant good is more or less systematically converted into all sorts of other things—opportunities, powers, and reputations. So wealth is seized by the strong, honor by the wellborn, office by the well educated. Perhaps the ideology that justifies the seizure is widely believed to be true. But resentment and resistance are (almost) as pervasive as belief. There are always some people, and after a time there are a great many, who think the seizure is not justice but usurpation. The ruling group does not possess, or does not uniquely possess, the qualities it claims; the conversion process violates the common understanding of the goods at stake. Social conflict is intermittent, or it is endemic; at some point, counterclaims are put forward. Though these are of many different sorts, three general sorts are especially important:

1. The claim that the dominant good, whatever it is, should be redistributed so that it can be equally or at least more widely shared: this amounts to saying that monopoly is unjust.
2. The claim that the way should be opened for the autonomous distribution of all social goods: this amounts to saying that dominance is unjust.
3. The claim that some new good, monopolized by some new group, should replace the currently dominant good: this amounts to saying that the existing pattern of dominance and monopoly is unjust. [. . .]

Simple Equality

It is with the first two claims that I shall be concerned, and ultimately with the second alone, for that one seems to me to capture best the plurality of social meanings and the real complexity of distributive systems. But the first is the more common among philosophers; it matches their own search for unity and singularity; and I shall need to explain its difficulties at some length.

Men and women who make the first claim challenge the monopoly but not the dominance of a particular social good. This is also a challenge to monopoly in general; for if wealth, for example, is dominant and widely shared, no other good can possibly be monopolized. Imagine a society in which everything is up for sale and every citizen has as much money as every other. I shall call this the "regime of simple equality." Equality is multiplied through the conversion process, until it extends across the full range of social goods. The regime of simple equality won't last for long, because the further progress of conversion, free exchange in the market, is certain to bring inequalities in its train. If one wanted to sustain simple equality over time, one would require a "monetary law" like the agrarian laws of ancient times or the Hebrew sabbatical, providing for a periodic return to the original condition. Only a centralized and activist state would be strong enough to force such a return; and it isn't clear that state officials would actually be able or willing to do that, if money were the dominant good. In any case, the original condition is unstable in another way. It's not only that monopoly will reappear, but also that dominance will disappear.

In practice, breaking the monopoly of money neutralizes its dominance. Other goods come into play, and inequality takes on new forms. Consider again the regime of simple equality. Everything is up for sale, and everyone has the same amount of money. So everyone has, say, an equal ability to buy an education for his children. Some do that, and others don't. It turns out to be a good investment: other social goods are, increasingly, offered for sale only to people with educational certificates. Soon everyone invests in education; or, more likely, the purchase is universalized through the tax system. But then the school is turned into a competitive world within which money is no longer dominant. Natural talent or family upbringing or skill in writing examinations is dominant instead, and educational success and certification are monopolized by some new group. Let's call them (what they call themselves) the "group of the talented." Eventually the members of this group claim that the good they control should be dominant outside the school: offices, titles, prerogatives, wealth too, should all be possessed by themselves. This is the career open to talents, equal opportunity, and so on. This is what fairness requires; talent will out; and in any case, talented men and women will enlarge the resources available to everyone else. [. . .]

Simple equality would require continual state intervention to break up or constrain incipient monopolies and to repress new forms of dominance. But then state power itself will become the central object of competitive struggles. Groups of men and women will seek to monopolize and then to use the state in order to consolidate their control of other social goods. Or, the state will be monopolized by its own agents in accordance with the iron law of oligarchy. Politics is always the most direct path to dominance, and political power (rather than the means of production) is probably the most important, and certainly the most dangerous, good in human history. Hence the need to constrain the agents of constraint, to establish constitutional checks and balances. These are limits imposed on political monopoly, and they are all the more important once the various social and economic monopolies have been broken.

One way of limiting political power is to distribute it widely. This may not work, given the well-canvassed dangers of majority tyranny; but these dangers are probably less acute than they are often made out to be. The greater danger of democratic government is that it will be weak to cope with re-emerging monopolies in society at large, with the social strength of plutocrats, bureaucrats, technocrats, meritocrats, and so on. In theory, political power is the dominant good in a democracy, and it is convertible in any way the citizens choose. But in practice, again, breaking the monopoly of power neutralizes its dominance. Political power cannot be widely shared without being subjected to the pull of all the other goods that the citizens already have or hope to have. Hence democracy is, as Marx recognized, essentially a reflective system, mirroring the prevailing and emerging distribution of social goods.[7] Democratic decision making will be shaped by the cultural conceptions that determine or underwrite the new monopolies. To prevail against these monopolies, power will have to be centralized, perhaps itself monopolized. Once again, the state must be very powerful if it is to fulfill the purposes assigned to it by the difference principle or by any similarly interventionist rule.

Still, the regime of simple equality might work. One can imagine a more or less stable tension between emerging monopolies and political constraints, between the claim to privilege put forward by the talented, say, and the enforcement of the difference principle, and then between the agents of enforcement and the democratic constitution. But I suspect that difficulties will recur, and that at many points in time the only remedy for private privilege will be statism, and the only escape from statism will be private privilege. We will mobilize power to check monopoly, then look for some way of checking the power we have mobilized. But there is no way that doesn't open opportunities for strategically placed men and women to seize and exploit important social goods.

These problems derive from treating monopoly, and not dominance, as the central issue in distributive justice. It is not difficult, of course, to understand why philosophers (and political activists, too) have focused on monopoly. The distributive struggles of the modern age begin with a war against the aristocracy's singular hold on land, office, and honor. This seems an especially pernicious monopoly because it rests upon birth and blood, with which the individual has nothing to do, rather than upon wealth, or power, or education, all of which—at least in principle—can be earned. And when every man and woman becomes, as it were, a smallholder in the sphere of birth and blood, an important victory is indeed won. Birthright ceases to be a dominant good; henceforth, it purchases very little; wealth, power, and education come to the fore. With regard to these latter goods, however, simple equality cannot be sustained at all, or it can only be sustained subject to the vicissitudes I have just described. Within their own spheres, as they are currently understood, these three tend to generate natural monopolies that can be repressed only if state power is itself dominant and if it is monopolized by officials committed to the repres-

7.   See Marx's comment, in his "Critique of the Gotha Program," that the domocratic republic is the "form of state" within which the class struggle will be fought to a conclusion: the struggle is immediately and without distortion reflected in political life (Marx and Engels, *Selected Works* [Moscow, 1951], vol. II, p. 31).

sion. But there is, I think, another path to another kind of equality.

Tyranny and Complex Equality

I want to argue that we should focus on the reduction of dominance—not, or not primarily, on the break-up or the constraint of monopoly. We should consider what it might mean to narrow the range within which particular goods are convertible and to vindicate the autonomy of distributive spheres. But this line of argument, though it is not uncommon historically, has never fully emerged in philosophical writing. Philosophers have tended to criticize (or to justify) existing or emerging monopolies of wealth, power, and education. Or, they have criticized (or justified) particular conversions—of wealth into education or of office into wealth. And all this, most often, in the nature of some radically simplified distributive system. The critique of dominance will suggest instead a way of reshaping and then living with the actual complexity of distributions.

Imagine now a society in which different social goods are monopolistically held—as they are in fact and always will be, barring continual state intervention—but in which no particular good is generally convertible. As I go along, I shall try to define the precise limits on convertibility, but for now the general description will suffice. This is a complex egalitarian society. Though there will be many small inequalities, inequality will not be multiplied through the conversion process. Nor will it be summed across different goods, because the autonomy of distributions will tend to produce a variety of local monopolies, held by different groups of men and women. I don't want to claim that complex equality would necessarily be more stable than simple equality, but I am inclined to think that it would open the way for more diffused and particularized forms of social conflict. And the resistance to convertibility would be maintained, in large degree, by ordinary men and women within their own spheres of competence and control, without large-scale state action.

This is, I think, an attractive picture, but I have not yet explained just why it is attractive. The argument for complex equality begins from our understanding—I mean, our actual, concrete, positive, and particular understanding—of the various social goods. And then it moves on to an account of the way we relate to one another through those goods. Simple equality is a simple distributive condition, so that if I have fourteen hats and you have fourteen hats, we are equal. And it is all to the good if hats are dominant, for then our equality is extended through all the spheres of social life. On the view that I shall take here, however, we simply have the same number of hats, and it is unlikely that hats will be dominant for long. Equality is a complex relation of persons, mediated by the goods we make, share, and divide among ourselves; it is not an identity of possessions. It requires then, a diversity of distributive criteria that mirrors the diversity of social goods.

The argument for complex equality has been beautifully put by Pascal in one of his *Pensées*.

> The nature of tyranny is to desire power over the whole world and outside its own sphere.
>
> There are different companies—the strong, the handsome, the intelligent, the devout—and each man reigns in his own, not elsewhere. But sometimes they meet, and the strong and the handsome fight for mastery—foolishly, for their mastery is of different kinds. They misunderstand one another, and make the mistake of each aiming at universal dominion. Nothing can win this, not even strength, for it is powerless in the kingdom of the wise. . . .
>
> *Tyranny.* The following statements, therefore, are false and tyrannical: "Because I am handsome, so I should command respect." "I am strong, therefore men should love me. . . ." "I am . . . et cetera."
>
> Tyranny is the wish to obtain by one means what can only be had by another. We owe different duties to different qualities: love is the proper response to charm, fear to strength, and belief to learning.[8]

Marx made a similar argument in his early manuscripts; perhaps he had this *pensée* in mind:

> Let us assume man to be man, and his relation to the world to be a human one. Then love can only

---

8. Blaise Pascal, *The Pensées*, trans. J. M. Cohen (Hammondsworth, England, 1961), p. 96 (no. 244).

be exchanged for love, trust for trust, etc. If you wish to enjoy art you must be an artistically cultivated person; if you wish to influence other people, you must be a person who really has a stimulating and encouraging effect upon others. . . . If you love without evoking love in return, i.e., if you are not able, by the manifestation of yourself as a loving person, to make yourself a beloved person—then your love is impotent and a misfortune.[9]

These are not easy arguments, and most of my book is simply an exposition of their meaning. But here I shall attempt something more simple and schematic: a translation of the arguments into the terms I have already been using.

The first claim of Pascal and Marx is that personal qualities and social goods have their own spheres of operation, where they work their effects freely, spontaneously, and legitimately. There are ready or natural conversions that follow from, and are intuitively plausible because of, the social meaning of particular goods. The appeal is to our ordinary understanding and, at the same time, against our common acquiescence in illegitimate conversion patterns. Or, it is an appeal from our acquiescence to our resentment. There is something wrong, Pascal suggests, with the conversion of strength into belief. In political terms, Pascal means that no ruler can rightly command my opinions merely because of the power he wields. Nor can he, Marx adds, rightly claim to influence my actions: if a ruler wants to do that, he must be persuasive, helpful, encouraging, and so on. These arguments depend for their force on some shared understanding of knowledge, influence, and power. Social goods have social meaning, and we find our way to distributive justice through an interpretation of those meanings. We search for principles internal to each distributive sphere.

The second claim is that the disregard of these principles is tyranny. To convert one good into another, when there is no intrinsic connection between the two, is to invade the sphere where another company of men and women properly rules. Monopoly is not inappropriate within the spheres. There is nothing wrong, for example, with the grip that persuasive and helpful men and women (politicians) establish on political power. But the use of political power to gain access to other goods is a tyrannical use. Thus, an old description of tyranny is generalized: princes become tyrants, according to medieval writers, when they seize the property or invade the family of their subjects.[10] In political life—but more widely, too—the dominance of goods makes for the domination of people.

The regime of complex equality is the opposite of tyranny. It establishes a set of relationships such that domination is impossible. In formal terms, complex equality means that no citizen's standing in one sphere or with regard to one social good can be undercut by his standing in some other sphere, with regard to some other good. Thus, citizen X may be chosen over citizen Y for political office, and then the two of them will be unequal in the sphere of politics. But they will not be unequal generally so long as X's office gives him no advantages over Y in any other sphere—superior medical care, access to better schools for his children, entrepreneurial opportunities, and so on. So long as office is not a dominant good, is not generally convertible, office holders will stand, or at least can stand, in a relation of equality to the men and women they govern.

But what if dominance were eliminated, the autonomy of the spheres established—and the same people were successful in one sphere after another, triumphant in every company, piling up goods without the need for illegitimate conversions? This would certainly make for an inegalitarian society, but it would also suggest in the strongest way that a society of equals was not a lively possibility. I doubt that any egalitarian argument could survive in the face of such evidence. Here is a person whom we have freely

9. Karl Marx, *Economic and Philosophical Manuscripts*, in *Early Writings*, ed. T. B. Bottomore (London, 1963), pp. 193–94. It is interesting to note an earlier echo of Pascal's argument in Adam Smith's *Theory of Moral Sentiment* (Edinburgh, 1813), vol. I, pp. 378–79; but Smith seems to have believed that distribution in his own society actually conformed to this view of appropriateness—a mistake neither Pascal nor Marx ever made.

10. See the summary account in Jean Bodin, *Six Books of a Commonweale*, ed. Kenneth Douglas McRae (Cambridge, Mass., 1962), pp. 210–18.

chosen (without reference to his family ties or personal wealth) as our political representative. He is also a bold and inventive entrepreneur. When he was younger, he studied science, scored amazingly high grades in every exam, and made important discoveries. In war, he is surpassingly brave and wins the highest honors. Himself compassionate and compelling, he is loved by all who know him. Are there such people? Maybe so, but I have my doubts. We tell stories like the one I have just told, but the stories are fiction, the conversion of power or money or academic talent into legendary fame. In any case, there aren't enough such people to constitute a ruling class and dominate the rest of us. Nor can they be successful in every distributive sphere, for there are some spheres to which the idea of success doesn't pertain. Nor are their children likely, under conditions of complex equality, to inherit their success. By and large, the most accomplished politicians, entrepreneurs, scientists, soldiers, and lovers will be different people; and so long as the goods they possess don't bring other goods in train, we have no reason to fear their accomplishments.

The critique of dominance and domination points toward an open-ended distributive principle. *No social good x should be distributed to men and women who possess some other good y merely because they possess y and without regard to the meaning of x.* This is a principle that has probably been reiterated, at one time or another, for every y that has ever been dominant. But it has not often been stated in general terms. Pascal and Marx have suggested the application of the principle against all possible y's, and I shall attempt to work out that application. I shall be looking, then, not at the members of Pascal's companies—the strong or the weak, the handsome or the plain—but at the goods they share and divide. The purpose of the principle is to focus our attention; it doesn't determine the shares or the division. The principle directs us to study the meaning of social goods, to examine the different distributive spheres from the inside.

MICHAEL SANDEL

The Procedural Republic and the Unencumbered Self (1984)

Political philosophy seems often to reside at a distance from the world. Principles are one thing, politics another, and even our best efforts to "live up" to our ideals typically founder on the gap between theory and practice.[1]

But if political philosophy is unrealizable in one sense, it is unavoidable in another. This is the sense in which philosophy inhabits the world from the start; our practices and institutions are embodiments of theory. To engage in a political practice is already to stand in relation to theory.[2] For all our uncertainties

Author's Note: An earlier version of this article was presented to the Political Philosophy Colloquium at Princeton University, and to the Legal Theory Workshop at Columbia Law School. I am grateful to the participants, and also to the editor, William Connolly, for helpful comments and criticisms. I would also like to thank the Ford Foundation for support of a larger project of which this essay is a first installment.

1. An excellent example of this view can be found in Samuel Huntington, *American Politics: The Promise of Disharmony* (Cambridge: Harvard University Press, 1981).

See especially his discussion of the "ideals versus institutions" gap, pp. 10–12, 39–41, 61–84, 221–262.

2. See, for example, the conceptions of a "practice" advanced by Alasdair MacIntyre and Charles Taylor. MacIntyre, *After Virtue* (Notre Dame: University of Notre Dame Press, 1981), pp. 175–209. Taylor, "Interpretation and the Sciences of Man," *Review of Metaphysics* 25, (1971), pp. 3–51.

about ultimate questions of political philosophy—of justice and value and the nature of the good life—the one thing we know is that we live *some* answer all the time.

In this essay I will try to explore the answer we live now, in contemporary America. What is the political philosophy implicit in our practices and institutions? How does it stand, as philosophy? And how do tensions in the philosophy find expression in our present political condition?

It may be objected that it is a mistake to look for a single philosophy, that we live no "answer," only answers. But a plurality of answers is itself a kind of answer. And the political theory that affirms this plurality is the theory I propose to explore.

The Right and the Good

We might begin by considering a certain moral and political vision. It is a liberal vision, and like most liberal visions gives pride of place to justice, fairness, and individual rights. Its core thesis is this: a just society seeks not to promote any particular ends, but enables its citizens to pursue their own ends, consistent with a similar liberty for all; it therefore must govern by principles that do not presuppose any particular conception of the good. What justifies these regulative principles above all is not that they maximize the general welfare, or cultivate virtue, or otherwise promote the good, but rather that they conform to the concept of *right*, a moral category given prior to the good, and independent of it.

This liberalism says, in other words, that what makes the just society just is not the *telos* or purpose or end at which it aims, but precisely its refusal to choose in advance among competing purposes and ends. In its constitution and its laws, the just society seeks to provide a framework within which its citizens can pursue their own values and ends, consistent with a similar liberty for others.

The ideal I've described might be summed up in the claim that the right is prior to the good, and in two senses: The priority of the right means first, that individual rights cannot be sacrificed for the sake of the general good (in this it opposes utilitarianism), and second, that the principles of justice that specify these rights cannot be premised on any particular

vision of the good life. (In this it opposes teleological conceptions in general.)

This is the liberalism of much contemporary moral and political philosophy, most fully elaborated by Rawls, and indebted to Kant for its philosophical foundations.[3] But I am concerned here less with the lineage of this vision than with what seem to me three striking facts about it.

First, it has a deep and powerful philosophical appeal. Second, despite its philosophical force, the claim for the priority of the right over the good ultimately fails. And third, despite its philosophical failure, this liberal vision is the one by which we live. For us in late twentieth century America, it is our vision, the theory most thoroughly embodied in the practices and institutions most central to our public life. And seeing how it goes wrong as philosophy may help us to diagnose our present political condition. So first, its philosophical power, second, its philosophical failure; and third, however briefly, its uneasy embodiment in the world.

But before taking up these three claims, it is worth pointing out a central theme that connects them. And that is a certain conception of the person, of what it is to be a moral agent. Like all political theories, the liberal theory I have described is something more than a set of regulative principles. It is also a view about the way the world is, and the way we move within it. At the heart of this ethic lies a vision of the person that both inspires and undoes it. As I

---

3. John Rawls, *A Theory of Justice* (Oxford: Oxford University Press, 1971). Immanuel Kant, *Groundwork of the Metaphysics of Morals*, trans. H. J. Paton (1785; New York: Harper and Row, 1956). Kant, *Critique of Pure Reason*, trans. Norman Kemp Smith (1781, 1787; London: Macmillan, 1929). Kant, *Critique of Practical Reason*, trans. L. W. Beck (1788; Indianapolis: Bobbs-Merrill, 1956). Kant, "On the Common Saying: 'This May Be True in Theory, But It Does Not Apply in Practice,'" in Hans Reiss. ed., *Kant's Political Writings* (1793; Cambridge: Cambridge University Press, 1970). Other recent versions of the claim for the priority of the right over good can be found in Robert Nozick, *Anarchy, State, and Utopia* (New York: Basic Books, 1974); Ronald Dworkin, *Taking Rights Seriously* (London: Duckworth, 1977); Bruce Ackerman, *Social Justice in the Liberal State* (New Haven: Yale University Press, 1980).

will try to argue now, what make this ethic so compelling, but also, finally, vulnerable, are the promise and the failure of the unencumbered self.

Kantian Foundations

The liberal ethic asserts the priority of right, and seeks principles of justice that do not presuppose any particular conception of the good.[4] This is what Kant means by the supremacy of the moral law, and what Rawls means when he writes that "justice is the first virtue of social institutions."[5] Justice is more than just another value. It provides the framework that *regulates* the play of competing values and ends; it must therefore have a sanction independent of those ends. But it is not obvious where such a sanction could be found.

Theories of justice, and for that matter, ethics, have typically founded their claims on one or another conception of human purposes and ends. Thus Aristotle said the measure of a *polis* is the good at which it aims, and even J. S. Mill, who in the nineteenth century called "justice the chief part, and incomparably the most binding part of all morality," made justice an instrument of utilitarian ends.[6]

This is the solution Kant's ethic rejects. Different persons typically have different desires and ends, and so any principle derived from them can only be contingent. But the moral law needs a *categorical* foundation, not a contingent one. Even so universal a desire as happiness will not do. People still differ in what happiness consists of, and to install any particular conception as regulative would impose on some the conceptions of others, and so deny at least to some the freedom to choose their *own* conceptions. In any case, to govern ourselves in conformity with desires and inclinations, given as they are by nature or circumstance, is not really to be *self*-governing at all. It is rather a refusal of freedom, a capitulation to determinations given outside us.

According to Kant, the right is "derived entirely from the concept of freedom in the external relationships of human beings, and has nothing to do with the end which all men have by nature [i.e., the aim of achieving happiness] or with the recognized means of attaining this end."[7] As such, it must have a basis prior to all empirical ends. Only when I am governed by principles that do not presuppose any particular ends am I free to pursue my own ends consistent with a similar freedom for all.

But this still leaves the question of what the basis of the right could possibly be. If it must be a basis prior to all purposes and ends, unconditioned even by what Kant calls "the special circumstances of human nature,"[8] where could such a basis conceivably be found? Given the stringent demands of the Kantian ethic, the moral law would seem almost to require a foundation in nothing, for any empirical precondition would undermine its priority. "Duty" asks Kant at his most lyrical, "What origin is there worthy of thee, and where is to be found the root of thy noble descent which proudly rejects all kinship with the inclinations?"[9]

His answer is that the basis of the moral law is to be found in the *subject* not the object of practical reason, a subject capable of an autonomous will. No empirical end, but rather "a subject of ends, namely a rational being himself, must be made the ground for all maxims of action."[10] Nothing other than what Kant calls "the subject of all possible ends himself" can give rise to the right, for only this subject is also the subject of an autonomous will. Only this subject could be that "something which elevates man above himself as part of the world of sense" and enables him to participate in an ideal, unconditioned realm wholly independent of our social and psychological inclinations. And only this thoroughgoing independence

---

4.   This section, and the two that follow, summarize arguments developed more fully in Michael Sandel, *Liberalism and the Limits of Justice* (Cambridge: Cambridge University Press, 1982).

5.   Rawls (1971), p. 3.

6.   John Stuart Mill, *Utilitarianism*, in *The Utilitarians* (1893; Garden City: Doubleday, 1973), p. 465. Mill, *On Liberty*, in *The Utilitarians*, p. 485 (Originally published 1849).

7.   Kant (1793), p. 73.

8.   Kant (1785), p. 92.

9.   Kant (1788), p. 89.

10.   Kant (1785). p. 105.

can afford us the detachment we need if we are ever freely to choose for ourselves, unconditioned by the vagaries of circumstance.[11]

Who or what exactly *is* this subject? It is, in a certain sense, *us*. The moral law, after all, is a law we give *ourselves*; we don't *find* it, we *will* it. That is how it (and we) escape the reign of nature and circumstance and merely empirical ends. But what is important to see is that the "we" who do the willing are not "we" qua particular persons, you and me, each for ourselves—the moral law is not up to us as individuals—but "we" qua participants in what Kant calls "pure practical reason," "we" qua participants in a transcendental subject.

Now what is to guarantee that I *am* a subject of this kind, capable of exercising pure practical reason? Well, strictly speaking, there is no guarantee; the transcendental subject is only a possibility. But it is a possibility I must *presuppose* if I am to think of myself as a free moral agent. Were I wholly an empirical being, I would not be capable of freedom, for every exercise of will would be conditioned by the desire for some object. All choice would be heteronomous choice, governed by the pursuit of some end. My will could never be a first cause, only the effect of some prior cause, the instrument of one or another impulse or inclination. "When we think of ourselves as free," writes Kant, "we transfer ourselves into the intelligible world as members and recognize the autonomy of the will."[12] And so the notion of a subject prior to and independent of experience, such as the Kantian ethic requires, appears not only possible but indispensible, a necessary presupposition of the possibility of freedom.

How does all of this come back to politics? As the subject is prior to its ends, so the right is prior to the good. Society is best arranged when it is governed by principles that do not presuppose any particular conception of the good, for any other arrangement would fail to respect persons as being capable of choice; it would treat them as objects rather than subjects, as means rather than ends in themselves.

We can see in this way how Kant's notion of the subject is bound up with the claim for the priority of right. But for those in the Anglo-American tradition, the transcendental subject will seem a strange foundation for a familiar ethic. Surely, one may think, we can take rights seriously and affirm the primacy of justice without embracing the *Critique of Pure Reason*. This, in any case, is the project of Rawls.

He wants to save the priority of right from the obscurity of the transcendental subject. Kant's idealist metaphysic, for all its moral and political advantage, cedes too much to the transcendent, and wins for justice its primacy only by denying it its human situation. "To develop a viable Kantian conception of justice," Rawls writes, "the force and content of Kant's doctrine must be detached from its background in transcendental idealism" and recast within the "canons of a reasonable empiricism."[13] And so Rawls' project is to preserve Kant's moral and political teaching by replacing Germanic obscurities with a domesticated metaphysic more congenial to the Anglo-American temper. This is the role of the original position.

From Transcendental Subject to Unencumbered Self

The original position tries to provide what Kant's transcendental argument cannot—a foundation for the right that is prior to the good, but still situated in the world. Sparing all but essentials, the original position works like this: It invites us to imagine the principles we would choose to govern our society if we were to choose them in advance, before we knew the particular persons we would be—whether rich or poor, strong or weak, lucky or unlucky—before we knew even our interests or aims or conceptions of the good. These principles—the ones we would choose in that imaginary situation—are the principles of justice. What is more, if it works, they are principles that do not presuppose any particular ends.

What they *do* presuppose is a certain picture of the person, of the way we must be if we are beings for whom justice is the first virtue. This is the picture of

---

11. Kant (1788), p. 89.
12. Kant (1785), p. 121.

13. Rawls. "The Basic Structure as Subject," *American Philosophical Quarterly* (1977), p. 165.

the unencumbered self, a self understood as prior to and independent of purposes and ends.

Now the unencumbered self describes first of all the way we stand toward the things we have, or want, or seek. It means there is always a distinction between the values I *have* and the person I *am*. To identify any characteristics as *my* aims, ambitions, desires, and so on, is always to imply some subject "me" standing behind them, at a certain distance, and the shape of this "me" must be given prior to any of the aims or attributes I bear. One consequences of this distance is to put the self *itself* beyond the reach of its experience, to secure its identity once and for all. Or to put the point another way, it rules out the possibility of what we might call *constitutive* ends. No role or commitment could define me so completely that I could not understand myself without it. No project could be so essentail that turning away from it would call into question the person I am.

For the unencumbered self, what matters above all, what is most essential to our personhood, are not the ends we choose but our capacity to choose them. The original position sums up this central claim about us. "It is not our aims that primarily reveal our nature," writes Rawls, "but rather the principles that we would acknowledge to govern the background conditions under which these aims are to be formed. . . . We should therefore reverse the relation between the right and the good proposed by teleological doctrines and view the right as prior."[14]

Only if the self is prior to its ends can the right be prior to the good. Only if my identity is never tied to the aims and interests I may have at any moment can I think of myself as a free and independent agent, capable of choice.

This notion of independence carries consequences for the kind of community of which we are capable. Understood as unencumbered selves, we are of course free to join in voluntary association with others, and so are capable of community in the cooperative sense. What is denied to the unencumbered self is the possibility of membership in any community bound by moral lies antecedent to choice; he cannot belong to any community where the *itself* could be at stake. Such a community—call it constitutive as against merely cooperative—would engage the identity as well as the interests of the participants, and so implicate its members in a citizenship more thoroughgoing than the unencumbered self can know.

For justice to be primary, then, we must be creatures of a certain kind, related to human circumstance in a certain way We must stand to our circumstance always at a certain distance, whether as transcendental subject in the case of Kant, or as unencumbered selves in the case of Rawls. Only in this way can we view ourselves as subjects as well as objects of experience, as agents and not just instruments of the purposes we pursue.

The unencumbered self and the ethic it inspires, taken together, hold out a liberating vision. Freed from the dicates of nature and the sanction of social roles, the human subject is installed as sovereign, cast as the author of the only moral meanings there are. As participants in pure practical reason, or as parties to the original position, we are free to construct principles of justice unconstrained by an order of value antecedently given. And as actual, individual selves, we are free to choose our purposes and ends unbound by such an order, or by custom or tradition or inherited status. So long as they are not unjust, our conceptions of the good carry weight, whatever they are, simply in virtue of our having chosen them. We are, in Rawls' words, "self-originating sources of valid claims."[15]

This is an exhilarating promise, and the liberalism it animates is perhaps the fullest expression of the Enlightenment's quest for the self-defining subject. But is it true? Can we make sense of our moral and political life by the light of the self-image it requires? I do not think we can, and I will try to show why not by arguing first within the liberal project, then beyond it.

Justice and Community

We have focused so far on the foundations of the liberal vision, on the way it derives the principles it defends. Let us turn briefly now to the substance of

---

14. Rawls (1971), p. 560.

15. Rawls. "Kantian Constructivism in Moral Theory," *Journal of Philosophy* 77 (1980), p. 543.

those principles, using Rawls as our example. Sparing all but essentials once again, Rawls' two principles of justice are these: first, equal basic liberties for all, and second, only those social and economic inequalities that benefit the least-advantaged members of society (the difference principle).

In arguing for these principles, Rawls argues against two familiar alternatives—utilitarianism and libertarianism. He argues against utilitarianism that it fails to take seriously the distinction between persons. In seeking to maximize the general welfare, the utilitarian treats society as whole as if it were a single person; it conflates our many, diverse desires into a single system of desires, and tries to maximize. It is indifferent to the distribution of satisfactions among persons, except insofar as this may affect the overall sum. But this fails to respect our plurality and distinctness. It uses some as means to the happiness of all, and so fails to respect each as an end in himself. While utilitarians may sometimes defend individual rights, their defense must rest on the calculation that respecting those rights will serve utility in the long run. But this calculation is contingent and uncertain. So long as utility is what Mill said it is, "the ultimate appeal on all ethical questions,"[16] individual rights can never be secure. To avoid the danger that their life prospects might one day be sacrificed for the greater good of others, the parties to the original position therefore insist on certain basic liberties for all, and make those liberties prior.

If utilitarians fail to take seriously the distinctness of persons, libertarians go wrong by failing to acknowledge the arbitrariness of fortune. They define as just whatever distribution results from an efficient market economy, and oppose all redistribution on the grounds that people are entitled to whatever they get, so long as they do not cheat or steal or otherwise violate someone's rights in getting it. Rawls opposes this principle on the ground that the distribution of talents and assets and even efforts by which some get more and others get less is arbitrary from a moral point of view, a matter of good luck. To distribute the good things in life on the basis of these differences is not to do justice, but simply to carry over into human arrangements the arbitrariness of social

and natural contingency We deserve, as individuals, neither the talents our good fortune may have brought, nor the benefits that flow from them. We should therefore regard these talents as common assets, and regard one another as common beneficiaries of the rewards they bring. "Those who have been favored by nature, whoever they are, may gain from their good fortune only on terms that improve the situation of those who have lost out. . . . Injustice as fairness, men agree to share one another's fate."[17]

This is the reasoning that leads to the difference principle. Notice how it reveals, in yet another guise, the logic of the unencumbered self. I cannot be said to deserve the benefits that flow from, say, my fine physique and good looks, because they are only accidental, not essential facts about me. They describe attributes I *have*, not the person I *am*, and so cannot give rise to a claim of desert. Being an unencumbered self, this is true of *everything* about me. And so I cannot, as an individual, deserve anything at all.

However jarring to our ordinary understandings this argument may be, the picture so far remains intact; the priority of right, the denial of desert, and the unencumbered self all hang impressively together.

But the difference principle requires more, and it is here that the argument comes undone. The difference principle begins with the thought, congenial to the unencumbered self, that the assets I have are only accidentally mine. But it ends by assuming that these assets are therefore *common* assets and that society has a prior claim on the fruits of their exercise. But this assumption is without warrant. Simply because I, as an individual, do not have a privileged claim on the assets accidentally residing "here," it does not follow that everyone in the world collectively does. For there is no reason to think that their location in society's province or, for that matter, within the province of humankind, is any *less* arbitrary from a moral point of view. And if their arbitrariness within *me* makes them ineligible to serve *my* ends, there seems no obvious reason why their arbitrariness within any particular society should not make them ineligible to serve that society's ends as well.

To put the point another way, the difference principle, like utilitarianism, is a principle of sharing. As

---

16. Mill (1849), p. 485.

17. Rawls (1971), pp. 101–102.

such, it must presuppose some prior moral tie among those whose assets it would deploy and whose efforts it would enlist in a common endeavor. Otherwise, it is simply a formula for using some as means to others ends, a formula this liberalism is committed to reject.

But on the cooperative vision of community alone, it is unclear what the moral basis for this sharing could be. Short of the constitutive conception, deploying an individual's assets for the sake of the common good would seem an offense against the "plurality and distinctness" of individuals this liberalism seeks above all to secure.

If those whose fate I am required to share really are, morally speaking, *others*, rather than fellow participants in a way of life with which my identity is bound, the difference principle falls prey to the same objections as utilitarianism. Its claim on me is not the claim of a constitutive community whose attachments I acknowledge, but rather the claim of a concatenated collectivity whose entanglements I confront.

What the difference principle requires, but cannot provide, is some way of identifying those *among* whom the assets I bear are properly regarded as common, some way of seeing ourselves as mutually indebted and morally engaged to begin with. But as we have seen, the constitutive aims and attachments that would save and situate the difference principle are precisely the ones denied to the liberal self; the moral encumbrances and antecedent obligations they imply would undercut the priority of right.

What, then, of those encumbrances? The point so far is that we cannot be persons for whom justice is primary, and also be persons for whom the difference principle is a principle of justice. But which must give way? Can we view ourselves as independent selves, independent in the sense that our identity is never tied to our aims and attachments?

I do not think we can, at least not without cost to those loyalties and convictions whose moral force consists partly in the fact that living by them is inseparable from understanding ourselves as the particular persons we are—as members of this family or community or nation or people, as bearers of that history, as citizens of this republic. Allegiances such as these are more than values I happen to have, and to hold, at a certain distance. They go beyond the obligations I voluntarily incur and the "natural duties" I owe to human beings as such. They allow that to some I owe more than justice requires or even permits, not by reason of agreements I have made but instead in virtue of those more or less enduring attachments and commitments that, taken together, partly define the person I am.

To imagine a person incapable of constitutive attachments such as these is not to conceive an ideally free and rational agent, but to imagine a person wholly without character, without moral depth. For to have character is to know that I move in a history I neither summon nor command, which carries consequences nonetheless for my choices and conduct. It draws me closer to some and more distant from others; it makes some aims more appropriate, others less so. As a self-interpreting being, I am able to reflect on my history and in this sense to distance myself from it, but the distance is always precarious and provisional, the point of reflection never finally secured outside the history itself. But the liberal ethic puts the self beyond the reach of its experience, beyond deliberation and reflection. Denied the expansive self-understandings that could shape a common life, the liberal self is left to lurch between detachment on the one hand, and entanglement on the other. Such is the fate of the unencumbered self, and its liberating promise.

The Procedural Republic

But before my case can be complete, I need to consider one powerful reply. While it comes from a liberal direction, its spirit is more practical than philosophical. It says, in short, that I am asking too much. It is one thing to seek constitutive attachments in our private lives; among families and friends, and certain lightly knit groups, there may be found a common good that makes justice and rights less pressing. But with public life—at least today, and probably always—it is different. So long as the nation-state is the primary form of political association, talk of constitutive community too easily suggests a darker politics rather than a brighter one; amid echoes of the moral majority, the priority of right, for all its philosophical faults, still seems the safer hope.

This is a challenging rejoinder, and no account of political community in the twentieth century can fail to lake it seriously.[18] It is challenging not least because it calls into question the status of political philosophy and its relation to the world. For if my argument is correct, if the liberal vision we have considered is not morally self-sufficient but parasitic on a notion of community it officially rejects, then we should expect to find that the political practice that embodies this vision is not *practically* self-sufficient either—that it must draw on a sense of community it cannot supply and may even undermine. But is that so far from the circumstance we face today? Could it be that through the original position darkly, on the far side of the veil of ignorance, we may glimpse an intimation of our predicament, a refracted vision of ourselves?

How does the liberal vision—and its failure—help us make sense of our public life and its predicament? Consider, to begin, the following paradox in the citizen's relation to the modern welfare state. In many ways, we in the 1980s stand near the completion of a liberal project that has run its course from the New Deal through the Great Society and into the present. But notwithstanding the extension of the franchise and the expansion on individual rights and entitlements in recent decades, there is a widespread sense that, individually and collectively, our control over the forces that govern our lives is receding rather than increasing. This sense is deepened by what appear simultaneously as the power and the powerlessness of the nation-state. One the one hand, increasing numbers of citizens view the state as an overly intrusive presence, more likely to frustrate their purposes than advance them. And yet, despite its unprecedented role in the economy and society, the modern state seems itself disempowered, unable effectively to control the domestic economy, to respond to persisting social ills, or to work America's will in the world.

This is a paradox that has fed the appeals of recent politicians (including Carter and Reagan), even as it has frustrated their attempts to govern. To sort it out, we need to identify the public philosophy implicit in our political practice, and to reconstruct us arrival.

We need to trace the advent of the procedural republic, by which I mean a public life presented by the liberal vision and self-image we've considered.

The story of the procedural republic goes back in some ways to the founding of the republic, but is central drama begins to unfold around the turn of the century. As national markets and large-scale enterprise displaced a decentralized economy, the decentralized political forms of the early republic became outmoded as well. If democracy was to survive, the concentration of economic power would have to be met by a similar concentration of political power. But the Progressives understood, or some of them did, that the success of democracy required more than the centralization of government; it also required the nationalization of politics. The primary form of political community had to be a recast on a national scale. For Herbert Croly, writing in 1909, the "nationalizing of American political, economic, and social life" was "an essentially formative and enlightening political transformation." We would become more of a democracy only as we became "more of a nation . . . in ideas, in institutions, and in spirit."[19]

This nationalizing project would be consummated in the New Deal, but for the democratic tradition in America, the embrace of the nation was a decisive departure. From Jefferson to the populists, the party of democracy in American political debate had been, roughly speaking, the party of the provinces, of decentralized power, of small-town and small-scale America. And against them had stood the party of the nation—first Federalists, then Whigs, then the Republicans of Lincoln—a party that spoke for the consolidation of the union. It was thus the historic achievement of the New Deal to unite, in a single party and political program, what Samuel Beer has called "liberalism and the national idea."[20]

What matters for our purpose is that, in the twentieth century, liberalism made us peace with concentrated power. But it was understood at the start that the terms of this peace required a strong sense of national community, morally and politically to

---

18. The account that follows is a tentative formulation of themes requiring more detailed elaboration and support.

19. Croly, *The Promise of American Life* (Indianapolis: Bobbs-Merrill, 1965), pp. 270–273.

20. Beer, "Liberalism and the National Idea," *The Public Interest*, Fall (1966), pp. 70–82.

underwrite the extended involvements of a modern industrial order. If a virtuous republic of small-scale, democratic communities was no longer a possibility, a national republic seemed democracy's next best hope. This was still, in principle at least, a politics of the common good. It looked to the nation, not as a neutral framework for the play of competing interests, but rather as a formative community, concerned to shape a common life suited to the scale of modern social and economic forms.

But this project failed. By the mid- or late twentieth century, the national republic had run its course. Except for extraordinary moments, such as war, the nation proved too vast a scale across which to cultivate the shared self-understandings necessary to community in the formative, or constitutive sense. And so the gradual shift, in our practices and institutions, from a public philosophy of common purposes to one of fair procedures, from a politics of good to a politics of right, from the national republic to the procedural republic.

Our Present Predicament

A full account of this transition would take a detailed look at the changing shape of political institutions, constitutional interpretation, and the terms of political discourse in the broadest sense. But I suspect we would find in the *practice* of the procedural republic two broad tendencies foreshadowed by its philosophy: first, a tendency to crowd out democratic possibilities; second, a tendency to undercut the kind of community on which it nonetheless depends.

Where liberty in the early republic was understood as a function of democratic institutions and dispersed power,[21] liberty in the procedural republic is defined in opposition to democracy, as an individual's guarantee against what the majority might will. I am free insofar as I am the bearer of rights, where rights are trumps.[22] Unlike the liberty of the early

republic, the modern version permits—in fact even requires—concentrated power. This has to do with the universalizing logic of rights. Insofar as I have a right, whether to free speech or a minimum income, its provision cannot be left to the vagaries of local preferences but must be assured at the most comprehensive level of political association. It cannot be one thing in New York and another in Alabama. As rights and entitlements expand, politics is therefore displaced from smaller forms of association and relocated at the most universal form—in our case, the nation. And even as politics flows to the nation, power shifts away from democratic institutions (such as legislatures and political parties) and toward institutions designed to be insulated from democratic pressures, and hence better equipped to dispense and defend individual rights (notably the judiciary and bureaucracy).

These institutional developments may begin to account for the sense of powerlessness that the welfare state fails to address and in some ways doubtless deepens. But it seems to me a further clue to our condition and the predicament of the unencumbered self—lurching, as we left it, between detachment on the one hand, the entanglement on the other. For it is a striking feature of the welfare state that it offers a powerful promise of individual rights, and also demands of its citizens a high measure of mutual engagement. But the self-image that attends the rights cannot sustain the engagement.

As bearers of rights, where rights are trumps, we think of ourselves as freely choosing, individual selves, unbound by obligations antecedent to rights, or to the agreements we make. And yet, as citizens of the procedural republic that secures these rights, we find ourselves implicated willy-nilly in a formidable array of dependencies and expectations we did not choose and increasingly reject.

In our public life, we are more entangled, but less attached, than ever before. It is as though the unencumbered self presupposed by the liberal ethic had begun to come true—less liberated than disempowered, entangled in a network of obligations and involvements unassociated with any act of will, and yet unmediated by those common identifications or expansive self-definitions that would make them tolerable. As the scale of social and political organization has become more comprehensive, the terms of

---

21. See, for example, Laurence Tribe, *American Constitutional Law* (Mineola: The Foundation Press, 1978), pp. 2–3.

22. See Ronald Dworkin, "Liberalism," in Stuart Hampshire, ed., *Public and Private Morality* (Cambridge: Cambridge University Press, 1978), p. 136.

our collective identity have become more fragmented, and the forms of political life have outrun the common purpose needed to sustain them.

Something like this, it seems to me, has been unfolding in America for the past half-century or so. I hope I have said at least enough to suggest the shape a fuller story might take. And I hope in any case to have conveyed a certain view about politics and philosophy and the relation between them—that our practices and institutions arc themselves embodiments of theory, and to unravel their predicament is, at least in part, to seek after the self-image of the age.

Barbara Jordan

Address before the Democratic National Convention (1976)

Thank you ladies and gentlemen for a very warm reception.

It was one hundred and forty-four years ago that members of the Democratic Party first met in convention to select a Presidential candidate. Since that time, Democrats have continued to convene once every four years and draft a party platform and nominate a Presidential candidate. And our meeting this week is a continuation of that tradition. But there is something different about tonight. There is something special about tonight. What is different? What is special?

I, Barbara Jordan, am a keynote speaker.

A lot of years passed since 1832, and during that time it would have been most unusual for any national political party to ask that a Barbara Jordan deliver a keynote address. But tonight here I am. And I feel that notwithstanding the past that my presence here is one additional bit of evidence that the American Dream need not forever be deferred.

Now that I have this grand distinction what in the world am I supposed to say? I could easily spend this time praising the accomplishments of this party and attacking the Republicans—but I don't choose to do that. I could list the many problems which Americans have. I could list the problems which cause people to feel cynical, angry, frustrated: problems which include lack of integrity in government; the feeling that the individual no longer counts; the reality of material and spiritual poverty; the feeling that the grand American experiment is failing or has failed. I could recite these problems, and then I could sit down and offer no solutions. But I don't choose to do that either. The citizens of America expect more. They deserve and they want more than a recital of problems.

We are a people in a quandary about the present. We are a people in search of our future. We are a people in search of a national community. We are a people trying not only to solve the problems of the present, unemployment, inflation, but we are attempting on a larger scale to fulfill the promise of America. We are attempting to fulfill our national purpose, to create and sustain a society in which all of us are equal.

Throughout our history, when people have looked for new ways to solve their problems, and to uphold the principles of this nation, many times they have turned to political parties. They have often turned to the Democratic Party. What is it? What is it about the Democratic Party that makes it the instrument the people use when they search for ways to shape their future? Well I believe the answer to that question lies in our concept of governing. Our concept of governing is derived from our view of people. It is a concept deeply rooted in a set of beliefs firmly etched in the national conscience of all of us.

Now what are these beliefs? First, we believe in equality for all and privileges for none. This is a belief that each American regardless of background has equal standing in the public forum—all of us. Because we believe this idea so firmly, we are an inclusive rather than an exclusive party. Let everybody come! I think it no accident that most of those emigrating to America in the 19th century identified with the Democratic Party. We are a heterogeneous party made up of Americans of diverse backgrounds. We believe that the people are the source of all governmental power; that the authority of the people is to be extended, not restricted.

This can be accomplished only by providing each citizen with every opportunity to participate in the management of the government. They must have that, we believe. We believe that the government which represents the authority of all the people, not just one interest group, but all the people, has an obligation to actively—underscore actively—seek to remove those obstacles which would block individual achievement—obstacles emanating from race, sex, economic condition. The government must remove them, seek to remove them.

We are a party of innovation. We do not reject our traditions, but we are willing to adapt to changing circumstances, when change we must. We are willing to suffer the discomfort of change in order to achieve a better future. We have a positive vision of the future founded on the belief that the gap between the promise and reality of America can one day be finally closed.

We believe that.

This, my friends, is the bedrock of our concept of governing. This is a part of the reason why Americans have turned to the Democratic Party. These are the foundations upon which a national community can be built. Let's all understand that these guiding principles cannot be discarded for short-term political gains. They represent what this country is all about. They are indigenous to the American idea. And these are principles which are not negotiable.

In other times, I could stand here and give this kind of exposition on the beliefs of the Democratic Party and that would be enough. But today that is not enough. People want more. That is not sufficient reason for the majority of the people of this country to vote Democratic. We have made mistakes. We realize that. In our haste to do all things for all people, we did not foresee the full consequences of our actions. And when the people raised their voices, we didn't hear. But our deafness was only a temporary condition, and not an irreversible condition.

Even as I stand here and admit that we have made mistakes, I still believe that as the people of America sit in judgment on each party, they will recognize that our mistakes were mistakes of the heart. They'll recognize that.

And now we must look to the future. Let us heed the voice of the people and recognize their common sense. If we do not, we not only blaspheme our political heritage, we ignore the common ties that bind all Americans. Many fear the future. Many are distrustful of their leaders, and believe that their voices are never heard. Many seek only to satisfy their private work wants. To satisfy their private interests. But this is the great danger America faces. That we will cease to be one nation and become instead a collection of interest groups: city against suburb, region against region, individual against individual. Each seeking to satisfy private wants. If that happens, who then will speak for America? Who then will speak for the common good?

This is the question which must be answered in 1976.

Are we to be one people bound together by common spirit, sharing in a common endeavor; or will we become a divided nation? For all of its uncertainty, we cannot flee the future. We must not become the new Puritans and reject our society. We must address and master the future together. It can be done if we restore the belief that we share a sense of national community, that we share a common national endeavor. It can be done.

There is no executive order; there is no law that can require the American people to form a national community. This we must do as individuals, and if we do it as individuals, there is no President of the United States who can veto that decision.

As a first step, we must restore our belief in ourselves. We are a generous people so why can't we be generous with each other? We need to take to heart the words spoken by Thomas Jefferson:

Let us restore to social intercourse that harmony
and affection without which liberty and even life
are but dreary things.

A nation is formed by the willingness of each of us to share in the responsibility for upholding the common good. A government is invigorated when each of us is willing to participate in shaping the future of this nation. In this election year we must define the common good and begin again to shape a common future. Let each person do his or her part. If one citizen is unwilling to participate, all of us are going to suffer. For the American idea, though it is shared by all of us, is realized in each one of us.

And now, what are those of us who are elected public officials supposed to do? We call ourselves public servants but I'll tell you this: We as public servants must set an example for the rest of the nation. It is hypocritical for the public official to admonish and exhort the people to uphold the common good if we are derelict in upholding the common good. More is required of public officials than slogans and handshakes and press releases. More is required. We must hold ourselves strictly accountable. We must provide the people with a vision of the future.

If we promise as public officials, we must deliver. If we as public officials propose, we must produce. If we say to the American people it is time for you to be sacrificial; sacrifice. If the public official says that, we [public officials] must be the first to give. We must be. And again, if we make mistakes, we must be willing to admit them. We have to do that. What we have to do is strike a balance between the idea that government should do everything and that idea, the belief, that government ought to do nothing. Strike a balance. Let there be no illusions about the difficulty of forming this kind of a national community. It's tough, difficult, not easy. But a spirit of harmony will survive in America only if each of us remembers that we share a common destiny. If each of us remembers when self-interest and bitterness seem to prevail that we share a common destiny.

I have confidence that we can form this kind of national community.

I have confidence that the Democratic Party can lead the way.

I have that confidence.

We cannot improve on the system of government handed down to us by the founders of the Republic. There is no way to improve upon that. But what we can do is to find new ways to implement that system and realize our destiny.

Now, I began this speech by commenting to you on the uniqueness of a Barbara Jordan making a keynote address. Well I am going to close my speech by quoting a Republican President and I ask you that as you listen to these words of Abraham Lincoln, relate them to the concept of a national community in which every last one of us participates:

> "As I would not be a slave, so I would not be a master. This expresses my idea of Democracy. Whatever differs from this, to the extent of the difference, is no Democracy."

Thank you.

Jeane Kirkpatrick

Dictatorships and Double Standards (1979)

The failure of the Carter administration's foreign policy is now clear to everyone except its architects, and even they must entertain private doubts, from time to time, about a policy whose crowning achievement has been to lay the groundwork for a transfer of the Panama Canal from the United States to a swaggering Latin dictator of Castroite bent. In the thirty-odd months since the inauguration of Jimmy Carter as President there has occurred a dramatic Soviet military buildup, matched by the stagnation of American armed forces, and a dramatic extension of Soviet influence in the Horn of Africa, Afghanistan, Southern Africa, and the Caribbean, matched by a declining American position in all these areas. The United

States has never tried so hard and failed so utterly to make and keep friends in the Third World.

As if this were not bad enough, in the current year the United States has suffered two other major blows—in Iran and Nicaragua—of large and strategic significance. In each country, the Carter administration not only failed to prevent the undesired outcome; it actively collaborated in the replacement of moderate autocrats friendly to American interests with less friendly autocrats of extremist persuasion. It is too soon to be certain about what kind of regime will ultimately emerge in either Iran or Nicaragua, but accumulating evidence suggests that things are as likely to get worse as to get better in both countries. The Sandinistas in Nicaragua appear to be as skillful in consolidating power as the Ayatollah Khomeini is inept, and leaders of both revolutions display an intolerance and arrogance that do not bode well for the peaceful sharing of power or the establishment of constitutional governments, especially since those leaders have made clear that they have no intention of seeking either.

It is at least possible that the SALT debate may stimulate new scrutiny of the nation's strategic position and defense policy, but there are no signs that anyone is giving serious attention to this nation's role in Iranian and Nicaraguan developments—despite clear warnings that the United States is confronted with similar situations and options in El Salvador, Guatemala, Morocco, Zaire, and elsewhere. Yet no problem of American foreign policy is more urgent than that of formulating a morally and strategically acceptable, and politically realistic, program for dealing with nondemocratic governments who are threatened by Soviet-sponsored subversion. In the absence of such a policy, we can expect that the same reflexes that guided Washington in Iran and Nicaragua will be permitted to determine American actions from Korea to Mexico—with the same disastrous effects on the U.S. strategic position. (That the administration has not called its policies in Iran and Nicaragua a failure—and probably does not consider them such—complicates the problem without changing its nature.)

There were, of course, significant differences in the relations between the United States and each of these countries during the past two or three decades. Oil, size, and proximity to the Soviet Union gave Iran greater economic and strategic import than any Central American "republic," and closer relations were cultivated with the Shah, his counselors, and family than with President Somoza, his advisers, and family. Relations with the Shah were probably also enhanced by our approval of his manifest determination to modernize Iran regardless of the effects of modernization on traditional social and cultural patterns (including those which enhanced his own authority and legitimacy). And, of course, the Shah was much better looking and altogether more dashing than Somoza; his private life was much more romantic, more interesting to the media, popular and otherwise. Therefore, more Americans were more aware of the Shah than of the equally tenacious Somoza.

But even though Iran was rich, blessed with a product the United States and its allies needed badly, and led by a handsome king, while Nicaragua was poor and rocked along under a long-tenure president of less striking aspect, there were many similarities between the two countries and our relations with them. Both these small nations were led by men who had not been selected by free elections, who recognized no duty to submit themselves to searching tests of popular acceptability. Both did tolerate limited opposition, including opposition newspapers and political parties, but both were also confronted by radical, violent opponents bent on social and political revolution. Both rulers, therefore, sometimes invoked martial law to arrest, imprison, exile, and occasionally, it was alleged, torture their opponents. Both relied for public order on police forces whose personnel were said to be too harsh, too arbitrary, and too powerful. Each had what the American press termed "private armies," which is to say, armies pledging their allegiance to the ruler rather than the "constitution" or the "nation" or some other impersonal entity.

In short, both Somoza and the Shah were, in central ways, traditional rulers of semitraditional societies. Although the Shah very badly wanted to create a technologically modern and powerful nation and Somoza tried hard to introduce modern agricultural methods, neither sought to reform his society in the light of any abstract idea of social justice or political virtue. Neither attempted to alter significantly the distribution of goods, status, or power (though the democratization of education and skills that accompanied modernization in Iran did result in some redistribution of money and power there).

Both Somoza and the Shah enjoyed long tenure, large personal fortunes (much of which were no doubt appropriated from general revenues), and good relations with the United States. The Shah and Somoza were not only anticommunist; they were positively friendly to the United States, sending their sons and others to be educated in our universities, voting with us in the United Nations, and regularly supporting American interests and positions even when these entailed personal and political cost. The embassies of both governments were active in Washington social life, and were frequented by powerful Americans who occupied major roles in this nation's diplomatic, military, and political life. And the Shah and Somoza themselves were both welcome in Washington, and had many American friends.

Though each of the rulers was from time to time criticized by American officials for violating civil and human rights, the fact that the people of Iran and Nicaragua only intermittently enjoyed the rights accorded to citizens in the Western democracies did not prevent successive administrations from granting—with the necessary approval of successive Congresses—both military and economic aid. In the case of both Iran and Nicaragua, tangible and intangible tokens of U.S. support continued until the regime became the object of a major attack by forces explicitly hostile to the United States.

But once an attack was launched by opponents bent on destruction, everything changed. The rise of serious, violent opposition in Iran and Nicaragua set in motion a succession of events which bore a suggestive resemblance to one another and a suggestive similarity to our behavior in China before the fall of Chiang Kaishek, in Cuba before the triumph of Castro, in certain crucial periods of the Vietnamese war, and, more recently, in Angola. In each of these countries, the American effort to impose liberalization and democratization on a government confronted with violent internal opposition not only failed, but actually assisted the coming to power of new regimes in which ordinary people enjoy fewer freedoms and less personal security than under the previous autocracy—regimes, moreover, hostile to American interests and policies.

The pattern is familiar enough: an established autocracy with a record of friendship with the United States is attacked by insurgents, some of whose leaders have long ties to the Communist movement, and most of whose arms are of Soviet, Chinese, or Czechoslovak origin. The "Marxist" presence is ignored and/or minimized by American officials and by the elite media on the ground that U.S. support for the dictator gives the rebels little choice but to seek aid "elsewhere." Violence spreads and American officials wonder aloud about the viability of a regime that "lacks the support of its own people." The absence of an opposition party is deplored and civil-right violations are reviewed. Liberal columnists question the morality of continuing to aid a "rightist dictatorship" and provide assurances concerning the essential moderation of some insurgent leaders who "hope" for some sign that the United States will remember its own revolutionary origins. Requests for help from the beleaguered autocrat go unheeded, and the argument is increasingly voiced that ties should be established with rebel leaders "before it is too late." The President, delaying U.S. aid, appoints a special emissary who confirms the deterioration of the government position and its diminished capacity to control the situation and recommends various measures for "strengthening" and "liberalizing" the regime, all of which involve diluting its power.

The emissary's recommendations are presented in the context of a growing clamor for American disengagement on grounds that continued involvement confirms our status as an agent of imperialism, racism, and reaction; is inconsistent with support for human rights; alienates us from the "forces of democracy" and threatens to put the United States once more on the side of history's "losers." This chorus is supplemented daily by interviews with returning missionaries and "reasonable" rebels.

As the situation worsens, the President assures the world that the United States desires only that the "people choose their own form of government"; he blocks delivery of all arms to the government and undertakes negotiations to establish a "broadly based" coalition headed by a "moderate" critic of the regime who, once elevated, will move quickly to seek a "political" settlement to the conflict. Should the incumbent autocrat prove resistant to American demands that he step aside, he will be readily overwhelmed by the military strength of his opponents, whose patrons will have continued to provide sophisticated arms and advisers at the same time the United States cuts off military sales. Should the incumbent be so demoralized as to agree to yield power, he will be replaced by a "moderate" of American selection. Only after the insurgents have refused the proffered political solution and anarchy has spread throughout the nation will it be noticed that the new head of government has no significant following, no experience at governing, and no talent for leadership. By then, military commanders, no longer bound by loyalty to the chief of state, will depose the faltering "moderate" in favor of a fanatic of their own choosing.

In either case, the United States will have been led by its own misunderstanding of the situation to assist actively in deposing an erstwhile friend and ally and installing a government hostile to American interests and policies in the world. At best we will have lost access to friendly territory. At worst the Soviets will have gained a new base. And everywhere our friends will have noted that the United States cannot be counted on in times of difficulty and our enemies will have observed that American support provides no security against the forward march of history. [. . .]

Although most governments in the world are, as they always have been, autocracies of one kind or another, no idea holds greater sway in the mind of educated Americans than the belief that it is possible to democratize governments, anytime, anywhere, under any circumstances. This notion is belied by an enormous body of evidence based on the experience of dozens of countries which have attempted with more or less (usually less) success to move from autocratic to democratic government. Many of the wisest political scientists of this and previous centuries agree that democratic institutions are especially difficult to establish and maintain—because they make heavy demands on all portions of a population and because they depend on complex social, cultural, and economic conditions.

Two or three decades ago, when Marxism enjoyed its greatest prestige among American intellectuals, it was the economic prerequisites of democracy that were emphasized by social scientists. Democracy, they argued, could function only in relatively rich societies with an advanced economy, a substantial middle class, and a literate population, but it could be expected to emerge more or less automatically whenever these conditions prevailed. Today, this picture seems grossly oversimplified. While it surely helps to have an economy strong enough to provide decent levels of well-being for all, and "open" enough to provide mobility and encourage achievement, a pluralistic society and the right kind of political culture—and time—are even more essential.

In his essay on *Representative Government,* John Stuart Mill indentified three fundamental conditions which the Carter administration would do well to ponder. These are "One, that the people should be willing to receive it [representative government]; two, that they should be willing and able to do what is necessary for its preservation; three, that they should be willing and able to fulfill the duties and discharge the functions which it imposes on them."

Fulfilling the duties and discharging the functions of representative government make heavy demands on leaders and citizens, demands for participation and restraint, for consensus and compromise. It is not necessary for all citizens to be avidly interested in politics or well-informed about public affairs—although far more widespread interest and mobilization are needed than in autocracies. What is necessary is that a substantial number of citizens think of themselves as participants in society's decision-making and not simply as subjects bound by its laws. Moreover, leaders of all major sectors of the society must agree to pursue power only by legal means, must eschew (at least in principle) violence, theft, and fraud, and must accept defeat when necessary. They must also be skilled at finding and creating common ground among diverse points of view and interests, and correlatively willing to compromise on all but the most basic values.

In addition to an appropriate political culture, democratic government requires institutions strong enough to channel and contain conflict. Voluntary, nonofficial institutions are needed to articulate and aggregate diverse interests and opinions present in the society. Otherwise, the formal governmental institutions will not be able to translate popular demands into public policy.

In the relatively few places where they exist, democratic governments have come into being slowly, after extended prior experience with more limited forms of participation during which leaders have reluctantly grown accustomed to tolerating dissent and opposition, opponents have accepted the notion that they may defeat but not destroy incumbents, and people have become aware of government's effects on their lives and of their own possible effects on government. Decades, if not centuries, are normally required for people to acquire the necessary disciplines and habits. In Britain, the road from the Magna Carta to the Act of Settlement, to the great Reform Bills of 1832, 1867, and 1885, took seven centuries to traverse. American history gives no better grounds for believing that democracy comes easily, quickly, or for the asking. A war of independence, an unsuccessful constitution, a civil war, a long process of gradual enfranchisement marked our progress toward constitutional democratic government. The French path was still more difficult. Terror, dictatorship, monarchy, instability, and incompetence followed on the revolution that was to usher in a millennium of brotherhood. Only in the twentieth century did the democratic principle finally gain wide acceptance in France and not until after World War II were the principles of order and democracy, popular sovereignty and authority, finally reconciled in institutions strong enough to contain conflicting currents of public opinion.

Although there is no instance of a revolutionary "socialist" or Communist society being democratized, right-wing autocracies do sometimes evolve into democracies—given time, propitious economic, social, and political circumstances, talented leaders, and a strong indigenous demand for representative government. Something of the kind is in progress on the Iberian peninsula and the first steps have been taken in Brazil. Something similar could conceivably have also occurred in Iran and Nicaragua if contestation and participation had been more gradually expanded.

But it seems clear that the architects of contemporary American foreign policy have little idea of how to go about encouraging the liberalization of an autocracy. In neither Nicaragua nor Iran did they realize that the only likely result of an effort to replace an incumbent autocrat with one of his moderate critics or a "broad-based coalition" would be to sap the foundations of the existing regime without moving the nation any closer to democracy. Yet this outcome was entirely predictable. Authority in traditional autocracies is transmitted through personal relations: from the ruler to his close associates (relatives, household members, personal friends) and

from them to people to whom the associates are related by personal ties resembling their own relation to the ruler. The fabric of authority unravels quickly when the power and status of the man at the top are undermined or eliminated. The longer the autocrat has held power, and the more dependant a nation's institutions will be on his influence, the more dependent a nation's institutions will be on him. Without him, the organized life of society will collapse, like an arch from which the keystone has been removed. The blend of qualities that bound the Iranian army to the Shah or the national guard to Somoza is typical of the relationships—personal, hierarchical, nontransferable—that support a traditional autocracy. The speed with which armies collapse, bureaucracies abdicate, and social structures dissolve once the autocrat is removed frequently surprises American policy makers and journalists accustomed to public institutions based on universalistic norms rather than particularistic relations.

The failure to understand these relations is one source of the failure of U.S. policy in this and previous administrations. There are others. In Iran and Nicaragua (as previously in Vietnam, Cuba, and China) Washington overestimated the political diversity of the opposition—especially the strength of "moderates" and "democrats" in the opposition movement; underestimated the strength and intransigence of radicals in the movement; and misestimated the nature and extent of American influence on both the government and the opposition.

Confusion concerning the character of the opposition, especially its intransigence and will to power, leads regularly to downplaying the amount of force required to counteract its violence. In neither Iran nor Nicaragua did the United States adequately appreciate the government's problem in maintaining order in a society confronted with an ideologically extreme opposition. Yet the presence of such groups was well known. The State Department's 1977 report on human rights described an Iran confronted

> with a small number of extreme rightist and leftist terrorists operating within the country. There is evidence that they have received substantial foreign support and training . . . [and] have been responsible for the murder of Iranian government officials and Americans.

The same report characterized Somoza's opponents in the following terms:

> A guerrilla organization known as the Sandinista National Liberation Front (FSLN) seeks the violent overthrow of the government, and has received limited support from Cuba. The FSLN carried out an operation in Managua in December 1974, killing four people, taking several officials hostage, . . . since then, it continues to challenge civil authority in certain isolated regions.

In 1978, the State Department's report said that Sandinista violence was continuing—after the state of siege had been lifted by the Somoza government.

When U.S. policy makers and large portions of the Liberal press interpret insurgency as evidence of widespread popular discontent and a will to democracy, the scene is set for disaster. For if civil strife reflects a popular demand for democracy, it follows that a "liberalized" government will be more acceptable to "public opinion."

Thus, in the hope of strengthening a government, U.S. policy makers are led, mistake after mistake, to impose measures almost certain to weaken its authority. Hurried efforts to force complex and unfamiliar political practices on societies lacking the requisite political culture, tradition, and social structures not only fail to produce desired outcomes; if they are undertaken at a time when the traditional regime is under attack, they actually facilitate the job of the insurgents.

Vietnam presumably taught us that the United States could not serve as the world's policeman; it should also have taught us the dangers of trying to be the world's midwife to democracy when the birth is scheduled to take place under conditions of guerrilla war.

If the administration's actions in Iran and Nicaragua reflect the pervasive and equally flawed belief that change per se in such autocracies is inevitable, desirable, and in the American interest. It is this belief which induces the Carter administration to participate actively in the toppling of noncommunist autocracies while remaining passive in the face of communist expansion.

At the time the Carter administration came into office it was widely reported that the President had assembled a team who shared a new approach to foreign policy and a new conception of the national interest. The principal elements of this new approach were said to be two: the conviction that the cold war was over, and the conviction that, this being the case, the United States should give priority to North-South problems and help less developed nations achieve their own destiny.

More is involved in these changes than originally meets the eye. For, unlikely as it may seem, the foreign policy of the Carter administration is guided by a relatively full-blown philosophy of history which includes, as philosophies of history always do, a theory of social change, or, as it is currently called, a doctrine of modernization. Like most other philosophies of history that have appeared in the West since the eighteenth century, the Carter administration's doctrine predicts progress (in the form of modernization for all societies) and a happy ending (in the form of a world community of developed, autonomous nations).

The administration's approach to foreign affairs was clearly foreshadowed in Zbigniew Brzezinski's 1970 book on the U.S. role in the "technetronic era," *Between Two Ages*. In that book, Brzezinski showed that he had the imagination to look beyond the cold war to a brave new world of global politics and interdependence. To deal with that new world a new approach was said to be "evolving," which Brzezinski designated "rational humanism." In the new approach, the "preoccupation" with "national supremacy" would give way to "global" perspectives, and international problems would be viewed as "human issues" rather than as "political confrontations." The traditional intellectual framework for dealing with foreign policy would have to be scrapped:

> Today, the old framework of international politics . . . with their spheres of influence, military alliances between nation states, the fiction of sovereignty, doctrinal conflicts arising from 19th-century crisis—is clearly no longer compatible with reality.[1]

---

1. Concerning Latin America, Brzezinski observed: "Latin American nationalism, more and more radical as it widens its popular base, will be directed with increasing animosity against the United States unless the United

Only the "delayed development" of the Soviet Union, "an archaic religious community that experiences modernity existentially but not quite yet normatively," prevented wider realization of the fact that the end of ideology was already here. For the United States, Brzezinski recommended "a great deal of patience," a more detached attitude toward world revolutionary processes, and a less anxious preoccupation with the Soviet Union. Instead of engaging in ancient diplomatic pastimes, we should make "a broader effort to contain the global tendencies toward chaos," while assisting the processes of change that will move the world toward the "community of developed nations."

The central concern of Brzezinski's book, as of the Carter administration's foreign policy, is with the modernization of the Third World. From the beginning, the administration has manifested a special, intense interest in the problems of the so-called Third World. But instead of viewing international developments in terms of the American national interest, as national interest is historically conceived, the architects of administration policy have viewed them in terms of a contemporary version of the same idea of progress that has traumatized Western imaginations since the Enlightenment.

In its current form, the concept of modernization involves more than industrialization, more than "political development" (whatever that is). It is used instead to designate "the process through which a traditional or pretechnological society passes as it is transformed into a society characterized by machine technology, rational and secular attitudes, and highly differentiated social structures." Condorcet, Comte, Hegel, Marx, and Weber are all present in this view of history as the working out of the idea of modernity.

States rapidly shifts its own posture. Accordingly, it would be wise for the United States to make an explicit move to abandon the Monroe Doctrine and to concede that in the new global age geographic or hemispheric contiguity no longer need be politically decisive. Nothing could be healthier for Pan-American relations than for the United States to place them on the same level as its relations with the rest of the world, confining itself to emphasis on cultural-political affinities (as it does with Western Europe) and economic-social obligations (as it does with less developed countries)."

The crucial elements of the modernization concept have been clearly explicated by Samuel P. Huntington (who, despite a period at the National Security Council, was assuredly not the architect of the administration's policy). The modernization paradigm, Huntington has observed, postulates an ongoing process of change: complex, because it involves all dimensions of human life in society; systemic, because its elements interact in predictable, necessary ways; global, because all societies will, necessarily, pass through the transition from traditional to modern; lengthy, because time is required to modernize economic and social organization, character, and culture; phased, because each modernizing society must pass through essentially the same stages; homogenizing, because it tends toward the convergence and interdependence of societies; irreversible, because the direction of change is "given" in the relation of the elements of the process; progressive, in the sense that it is desirable, and in the long run provides significant benefits to the affiliated people.

Although the modernization paradigm has proved a sometimes useful as well as influential tool in social science, it has become the object of searching critiques that have challenged one after another of its central assumptions. Its shortcomings as an analytical tool pale, however, when compared to its inadequacies as a framework for thinking about foreign policy, where its principal effects are to encourage the view that events are manifestations of deep historical forces which cannot be controlled and that the best any government can do is to serve as a "midwife" to history, helping events to move where they are already headed.

This perspective on contemporary events is optimistic in the sense that it foresees continuing human progress; deterministic in the sense that it perceives events as fixed by processes over which persons and policies can have but little influence; moralistic in the sense that it perceives history and U.S. policy as having moral ends; cosmopolitan in the sense that it attempts to view the world not from the perspective of American interests or intentions but from the perspective of the modernizing nation and the "end" of history. It identifies modernization with both revolution and morality, and U.S. policy with all three.

The idea that it is "forces" rather than people which shape events recurs each time an administration spokesman articulates or explains policy. The President, for example, assured us in February of this year:

> The revolution in Iran is a product of deep social, political, religious, and economic factors growing out of the history of Iran itself.

And of Asia he said:

> At this moment there is turmoil or change in various countries from one end of the Indian Ocean to the other; some turmoil as in Indochina is the product of age-old enmities, inflamed by rivalries for influence by conflicting forces. Stability in some other countries is being shaken by the process of modernization, the search for national significance, or the desire to fulfill legitimate human hopes and human aspirations.

Harold Saunders, Assistant Secretary for Near Eastern and South Asian Affairs, commenting on "instability" in Iran and the Horn of Africa, states:

> "We, of course, recognize that fundamental changes are taking place across this area of western Asia and northeastern Africa—economic modernization, social change, a revival of religion, resurgent nationalism, demands for broader popular participation in the political process. These changes are generated by forces within each country.

Or here is Anthony Lake, chief of the State Department's Policy Planning staff, on South Africa:

> Change will come in South Africa. The welfare of the people there, and American interests, will be profoundly affected by the way in which it comes. The question is whether it will be peaceful or not.

Brzezinski makes the point still clearer. Speaking as chief of the National Security Council, he has assured us that the struggles for power in Asia and Africa are really only incidents along the route to modernization:

> all the developing countries in the arc from northeast Asia to southern Africa continue to search for viable forms of government capable of managing the process of modernization.

No matter that the invasions, coups, civil wars, and political struggles of less violent kinds that one sees all around do not seem to be incidents in a global personnel search for someone to manage the modernization process. Neither Brzezinski nor anyone else seems bothered by the fact that the political participants in that arc from northeast Asia to southern Africa do not *know* that they are "searching for viable forms of government capable of managing the process of modernization." The motives and intentions of real persons are no more relevant to the modernization paradigm than they are to the Marxist view of history. Viewed from this level of abstraction, it is the "forces" rather than the people that count.

So what if the "deep historical forces" at work in such diverse places as Iran, the Horn of Africa, Southeast Asia, Central America, and the United Nations look a lot like Russians or Cubans? Having moved past what the President calls our "inordinate fear of Communism," identified by him with the cold war, we should, we are told, now be capable of distinguishing Soviet and Cuban "machinations," which anyway exist mainly in the minds of cold warriors and others guilty of oversimplifying the world, from evolutionary changes, which seem to be the only kind that actually occur.

What can a U.S. President faced with such complicated, inexorable, impersonal processes *do?* The answer, offered again and again by the President and his top officials, is, not much. Since events are not caused by human decisions, they cannot be stopped or altered by them. Brzezinski, for example, has said: "We recognize that the world is changing under the influence of forces no government can control." And Cyrus Vance has cautioned: "The fact is that we can no more stop change than Canute could still the waters."

The Carter administration's essentially deterministic and apolitical view of contemporary events discourages an active American response and encourages passivity. The American inability to influence events in Iran became the President's theme song:

> Those who argue that the U.S. should *or could* intervene directly to thwart [the revolution in Iran] are wrong about the realities of Iran. . . . We have encouraged *to the limited extent of our own ability* the public support for the Bakhtiar government. . . . How long [the Shah] will be out of

Iran, we have no way to determine. Future events and his own desires will determine that. . . . It is impossible for anyone to anticipate all future political events. . . . Even if we had been able to anticipate events that were going to take place in Iran or in other countries, obviously our ability to determine those events is very limited. (Emphasis added.)

Vance made the same point:

In Iran our policy throughout the current crisis has been based on the fact that only Iranians can resolve the fundamental political issues which they now confront.

Where once upon a time an American President might have sent Marines to assure the protection of American strategic interests, there is no room for force in this world of progress and self-determination. Force, the President told us at Notre Dame, does not work; that is the lesson he extracted from Vietnam. It offers only "superficial" solutions. Concerning Iran, he said:

Certainly we have no desire or ability to intrude massive forces into Iran or any other country to determine the outcome of domestic political issues. This is something that we have no intention of ever doing in another country. We've tried this once in Vietnam. It didn't work, as you well know.

There was nothing unique about Iran. In Nicaragua, the climate and language were different but the "historical forces" and the U.S. response were the same. Military intervention was out of the question. Assistant Secretary of State Viron Vaky described as "unthinkable" the "use of U.S. military power to intervene in the internal affairs of another American republic." Vance provided parallel assurances for Africa, asserting that we would not try to match Cuban and Soviet activities there.

What *is* the function of foreign policy under these conditions? It is to understand the processes of change and then, like Marxists, to align ourselves with history, hoping to contribute a bit of stability along the way. And this, administration spokesmen assure us, is precisely what we are doing. The Carter administration has defined the U.S. national interest in the Third World as identical with the putative end of the modernization process. Vance put this with

characteristic candor in a recent statement when he explained that U.S. policy vis-à-vis the Third World is "grounded in the conviction that we best serve our interest there by supporting the efforts of developing nations to advance their economic well-being and preserve their political independence." Our "commitment to the promotion of constructive change worldwide" (Brzezinski's words) has been vouchsafed in every conceivable context.

But there is a problem. The conceivable contexts turn out to be mainly those in which noncommunist autocracies are under pressure from revolutionary guerrillas. Since Moscow is the aggressive, expansionist power today, it is more often than not insurgents, encouraged and armed by the Soviet Union, who challenge the status quo. The American commitment to "change" in the abstract ends up by aligning us tacitly with Soviet clients and irresponsible extremists like the Ayatollah Khomeini or, in the end, Yasir Arafat.

So far, assisting "change" has not led the Carter administration to undertake the destabilization of a *Communist* country. The principles of self-determination and nonintervention are thus both selectively applied. We seem to accept the status quo in Communist nations (in the name of "diversity" and national autonomy), but not in nations ruled by "right wing" dictators or white oligarchies. Concerning China, for example, Brzezinski has observed: "We recognize that the PRC and we have different ideologies and economic and political systems. . . . We harbor neither the hope nor the desire that through extensive contacts with China we can remake that nation into the American image. Indeed, we accept our differences." Of Southeast Asia, the President noted in February:

Our interest is to promote peace and the withdrawal of outside forces and not to become embroiled in the conflict among Asian nations. And, in general, our interest is to promote the health and the development of individual societies, not to a pattern cut exactly like ours in the United States but tailored rather to the hopes and the needs and desires of the peoples involved.

But the administration's position shifts sharply when South Africa is discussed. For example, Anthony Lake asserted in late 1978:

We have indicated to South Africa the fact that if it does not make significant progress toward racial equality, its relations with the international community, including the United States, are bound to deteriorate.

Over the years, we have tried through a series of progressive steps to demonstrate that the U.S. cannot and will not be associated with the continued practice of apartheid.

As to Nicaragua, Hodding Carter III said in February 1979:

The unwillingness of the Nicaraguan government to accept the [OAS] group's proposal, the resulting prospects for renewal and polarization, and the human-rights situation in Nicaragua . . . unavoidably affect the kind of relationships we can maintain with that government.

And Carter commented on Latin American autocracies:

My government will not be deterred from protecting human rights, including economic and social rights, in whatever ways we can. We prefer to take actions that are positive, but where nations persist in serious violations of human rights, we will continue to demonstrate that there are costs to the flagrant disregard of international standards.

Something very odd is going on here. How does an administration that desires to let people work out their own destinies get involved in determined efforts at reform in South Africa, Zaire, Nicaragua, El Salvador, and elsewhere? How can an administration committed to nonintervention in Cambodia and Vietnam announce that it "will not be deterred" from righting wrongs in South Africa? What should be made of an administration that sees the U.S. interest as identical with economic modernization and political independence and yet heedlessly endangers the political independence of Taiwan, a country whose success in economic modernization and egalitarian distribution of wealth is unequaled in Asia? The contrast is as striking as that between the administration's frenzied speed in recognizing the new dictatorship in Nicaragua and its continuing refusal to recognize the elected government of Zimbabwe Rhodesia, or its refusal to maintain any presence in Zimbabwe Rhodesia while staffing a U.S. Information Office in Cuba. Not only are there ideology and a double standard at work here; the ideology neither fits nor explains reality, and the double standard involves the administration in the wholesale contradiction of its own principles.

Inconsistencies are a familiar part of politics in most societies. Usually, however, governments behave hypocritically when their principles conflict with the national interest. What makes the inconsistencies of the Carter administration noteworthy are, first, the administration's moralism—which renders it especially vulnerable to charges of hypocrisy; and, second, the administration's predilection for policies that violate the strategic and economic interests of the United States. The administration's conception of national interest borders on doublethink: it finds friendly powers to be guilty representatives of the status quo and views the triumph of unfriendly groups as beneficial to America's "true interests."

This logic is quite obviously reinforced by the prejudices and preferences of many administration officials. Traditional autocracies are, in general and in their very nature, deeply offensive to modern American sensibilities. The notion that public affairs should be ordered on the basis of kinship, friendship, and other personal relations rather than on the basis of objective "rational" standards violates our conception of justice and efficiency. The preference for stability rather than change is also disturbing to Americans whose whole national experience rests on the principles of change, growth, and progress. The extremes of wealth and poverty characteristic of traditional societies also offend us, the more so since the poor are usually *very* poor and bound to their squalor by a hereditary allocation of role. Moreover, the relative lack of concern of rich, comfortable rulers for the poverty, ignorance, and disease of "their" people is likely to be interpreted by Americans as moral dereliction pure and simple. The truth is that Americans can hardly bear such societies and such rulers. Confronted with them, our vaunted cultural relativism evaporates and we become as censorious as Cotton Mather confronting sin in New England.

But if the politics of traditional and semitraditional autocracy is nearly antithetical to our own—at both the symbolic and the operational level—the rhetoric of progressive revolutionaries sounds much better to us; their symbols are much more acceptable. One reason that some modern Americans prefer "socialist" to traditional autocracies is that the former have embraced modernity and have adopted modern modes and perspectives, including an instrumental, manipulative, functional orientation toward most social, cultural, and personal affairs; a profession of universalistic norms; an emphasis on reason, science, education, and progress; a de-emphasis of the sacred; and "rational," bureaucratic organizations. They speak our language.

Because socialism of the Soviet/Chinese/Cuban variety is an ideology rooted in a version of the same values that sparked the Enlightenment and the democratic revolutions of the eighteenth century; because it is modern and not traditional; because it postulates goals that appeal to Christian as well as secular values (brotherhood of man, elimination of power as a mode of human relations), it is highly congenial to many Americans at the symbolic level. Marxist revolutionaries speak the language of a hopeful future while traditional autocrats speak the language of an unattractive past. Because left-wing revolutionaries invoke the symbols and values of democracy—emphasizing eglitarianism rather than hierarchy and privilege, liberty rather than order, activity rather than passivity—they are again and again accepted as partisans in the cause of freedom and democracy.

Nowhere is the affinity of liberalism, Christianity, and Marxist socialism more apparent than among liberals who are "duped" time after time into supporting "liberators" who turn out to be totalitarians, and among Left-leaning clerics whose attraction to a secular style of "redemptive community" is stronger than their outrage at the hostility of socialist regimes to religion. In Jimmy Carter—egalitarian, optimist, liberal, Christian—the tendency to be repelled by frankly nondemocratic rulers and hierarchical societies is almost as strong as the tendency to be attracted to the idea of popular revolution, liberation, and progress. Carter is, *par excellence*, the kind of liberal most likely to confound revolution with idealism, change with progress, optimism with virtue.

Where concern about "socialist encirclement," Soviet expansion, and traditional conceptions of the national interest inoculated his predecessors against

such easy equations, Carter's doctrine of national interest and modernization encourages support for all change that takes place in the name of "the people," regardless of its "superficial" Marxist or anti-American content. Any lingering doubt about whether the United States should, in case of conflict, support a "tested friend" such as the Shah or a friendly power such as Zimbabwe Rhodesia against an opponent who despises us is resolved by reference to our "true," our "long-range" interests.

Stephen Rosenfeld of the *Washington Post* described the commitment of the Carter administration to this sort of "progressive liberalism":

> The Carter administration came to power, after all, committed precisely to reducing the centrality of strategic competition with Moscow in American foreign policy, and to extending the United States' association with what it was prepared to accept as legitimate wave-of-the-future popular movements around the world—first of all with the victorious movement in Vietnam. . . .
>
> Indochina was supposed to be the state on which Americans could demonstrate their "post-Vietnam" intent to come to terms with the progressive popular element that Kissinger, the villain, had denied.

In other words, the Carter administration, Rosenfeld tells us, came to power resolved not to assess international developments in the light of "cold war" perspectives but to accept at face value the claim of revolutionary groups to represent "popular" aspirations and "progressive" forces—regardless of the ties of these revolutionaries to the Soviet Union. To this end, overtures were made looking to the "normalization" of relations with Vietnam, Cuba, and the Chinese People's Republic, and steps were taken to cool relations with South Korea, South Africa, Nicaragua, the Philippines, and others. These moves followed naturally from the conviction that the United States had, as our enemies said, been on the wrong side of history in supporting the status quo and opposing revolution.

One might have thought that this perspective would have been undermined by events in Southeast Asia since the triumph of "progressive" forces there over the "agents of reaction." To cite Rosenfeld again:

In this administration's time, Vietnam has been transformed for much of American public opinion, from a country wronged by the U.S. to one revealing a brutal essence of its own.

This has been quiet but major trauma to the Carter people (as to all liberals) scarring their self-confidence and their claim on public trust alike.

Presumably, however, the barbarity of the "progressive" governments in Cambodia and Vietnam has been less traumatic for the President and his chief advisers than for Rosenfeld, since there is little evidence of changed predispositions at crucial levels of the White House and the State Department. The President continues to behave as before—not like a man who abhors autocrats but like one who abhors only right-wing autocrats. [. . .]

The foreign policy of the Carter administration fails not for lack of good intentions but for lack of realism about the nature of traditional versus revolutionary autocracies and the relation of each to the American national interest. Only intellectual fashion and the tyranny of Right/Left thinking prevent intelligent men of good will from perceiving the *facts* that traditional authoritarian governments are less repressive than revolutionary autocracies, that they are more susceptible of liberalization, and that they are more compatible with U.S. interests. The evidence on all these points is clear enough.

Surely it is now beyond reasonable doubt that the present governments of Vietnam, Cambodia, Laos are much more repressive than those of the despised previous rulers; that the government of the People's Republic of China is more repressive than that of Taiwan, that North Korea is more repressive than South Korea, and so forth. This is the most important lesson of Vietnam and Cambodia. It is not new but it is a gruesome reminder of harsh facts.

From time to time a truly bestial ruler can come to power in either type of autocracy—Idi Amin, Papa Doc Duvalier, Joseph Stalin, Pol Pot are examples—but neither type regularly produces such moral monsters (though democracy regularly prevents their accession to power). There are, however, *systemic* differences between traditional and revolutionary autocracies that have a predictable effect on their degree of repressiveness. Generally speaking, traditional autocrats tolerate social inequities, brutality, and poverty while revolutionary autocracies create them.

Traditional autocrats leave in place existing allocations of wealth, power, status, and other resources which in most traditional societies favor an affluent few and maintain masses in poverty. But they worship traditional gods and observe traditional taboos. They do not disturb the habitual rhythms of work and leisure, habitual places of residence, habitual patterns of family and personal relations. Because the miseries of traditional life are familiar, they are bearable to ordinary people who, growing up in the society, learn to cope, as children born to untouchables in India acquire the skills and attitudes necessary for survival in the miserable roles they are destined to fill. Such societies create no refugees.

Precisely the opposite is true of revolutionary Communist regimes. They create refugees by the million because they claim jurisdiction over the whole life of the society and make demands for change that so violate internalized values and habits that inhabitants flee by the tens of thousands in the remarkable expectation that their attitudes, values, and goals will "fit" better in a foreign country than in their native land.

The former deputy chairman of Vietnam's National Assembly from 1976 to his defection early in August 1979, Hoang Van Hoan, described recently the impact of Vietnam's ongoing revolution on that country's more than one million Chinese inhabitants:

> They have been expelled from places they have lived in for generations. They have been dispossessed of virtually all possessions—their lands, their houses. They have been driven into areas called new economic zones, but they have not been given any aid.
>
> How can they eke out a living in such conditions reclaiming new land? They gradually die for a number of reasons—diseases, the hard life. They also die of humiliation.

It is not only the Chinese who have suffered in Southeast Asia since the "liberation," and it is not only in Vietnam that the Chinese suffer. By the end of 1978 more than six million refugees had fled countries ruled by Marxist governments. In spite of walls, fences, guns, and sharks, the steady stream of people fleeing revolutionary utopias continues. [. . .]

A realistic policy which aims at protecting our own interest and assisting the capacities for self-determination of less developed nations will need to face the unpleasant fact that, if victorious, violent insurgency headed by Marxist revolutionaries is unlikely to lead to anything but totalitarian tyranny. Armed intellectuals citing Marx and supported by Soviet-bloc arms and advisers will almost surely not turn out to be agrarian reformers, or simple nationalists, or democratic socialists. However incomprehensible it may be to some, Marxist revolutionaries are not contemporary embodiments of the Americans who wrote the Declaration of Independence, and they will not be content with establishing a broad-based coalition in which they have only one voice among many.

It may not always be easy to distinguish between democratic and totalitarian agents of change, but it is also not too difficult. Authentic democratic revolutionaries aim at securing governments based on the consent of the governed and believe that ordinary men are capable of using freedom, knowing their own interest, choosing rulers. They do not, like the current leaders in Nicaragua, assume that it will be necessary to postpone elections for three to five years during which time they can "cure" the false consciousness of almost everyone.

If, moreover, revolutionary leaders describe the United States as the scourge of the twentieth century,
the enemy of freedom-loving people, the perpetrator of imperialism, racism, colonialism, genocide, war, then they are not authentic democrats or, to put it mildly, friends. Groups which define themselves as enemies should be treated as enemies. The United States is not in fact a racist, colonial power, it does not practice genocide, it does not threaten world peace with expansionist activities. In the last decade especially we have practiced remarkable forbearance everywhere and undertaken the "unilateral restraints on defense spending" recommended by Brzezinski as appropriate for the technetronic era. We have also moved further, faster, in eliminating domestic racism than any multiracial society in the world or in history.

For these reasons and more, a posture of continuous self-abasement and apology vis-à-vis the Third World is neither morally necessary nor politically appropriate. No more is it necessary or appropriate to support vocal enemies of the United States because they invoke the rhetoric of popular liberation. It is not even necessary or appropriate for our leaders to forswear unilaterally the use of military force to counter military force. Liberal idealism need not be identical with masochism, and need not be incompatible with the defense of freedom and the national interest.

Ronald Reagan

Address before the Conservative Political Action Committee ("City upon a Hill" Speech) (1974)

There are three men here tonight I am very proud to introduce. It was a year ago this coming February when this country had its spirits lifted as they have never been lifted in many years. This happened when planes began landing on American soil and in the Philippines, bringing back men who had lived with honor for many miserable years in North Vietnam prisons. Three of those men are here tonight,
John McCain, Bill Lawrence, and Ed Martin. It is an honor to be here tonight. I am proud that you asked me and I feel more than a little humble in the presence of this distinguished company.

There are men here tonight who, through their wisdom, their foresight and their courage, have earned the right to be regarded as prophets of our philosophy. Indeed they are prophets of our times. In years past when others were silent or too blind to the facts, they spoke up forcefully and fearlessly for what they believed to be right. A decade has passed since Barry Goldwater walked a lonely path across this land reminding us that even a land as rich as ours can't go on forever borrowing against the future, leaving a legacy of debt for another generation and causing a runaway inflation to erode the savings and reduce the standard of living. Voices have been raised trying to rekindle in our country all of the great ideas and principles which set this nation apart from all the others that preceded it, but louder and more strident voices utter easily sold clichés.

Cartoonists with acid-tipped pens portray some of the reminders of our heritage and our destiny as old-fashioned. They say that we are trying to retreat into a past that actually never existed. Looking to the past in an effort to keep our country from repeating the errors of history is termed by them as "taking the country back to McKinley." Of course I never found that was so bad—under McKinley we freed Cuba. On the span of history, we are still thought of as a young upstart country celebrating soon only our second century as a nation, and yet we are the oldest continuing republic in the world.

I thought that tonight, rather than talking on the subjects you are discussing, or trying to find something new to say, it might be appropriate to reflect a bit on our heritage.

You can call it mysticism if you want to, but I have always believed that there was some divine plan that placed this great continent between two oceans to be sought out by those who were possessed of an abiding love of freedom and a special kind of courage.

This was true of those who pioneered the great wilderness in the beginning of this country, as it is also true of those later immigrants who were willing to leave the land of their birth and come to a land where even the language was unknown to them. Call it chauvinistic, but our heritage does set us apart. Some years ago a writer, who happened to be an avid student of history, told me a story about that day in the little hall in Philadelphia where honorable men, hard-pressed by a King who was flouting the very law they were willing to obey, debated whether they should take the fateful step of declaring their independence from that king. I was told by this man that the story could be found in the writings of Jefferson.

Founding

I confess, I never researched or made an effort to verify it. Perhaps it is only legend. But story, or legend, he described the atmosphere, the strain, the debate, and that as men for the first time faced the consequences of such an irretrievable act, the walls resounded with the dread word of treason and its price—the gallows and the headman's axe. As the day wore on the issue hung in the balance, and then, according to the story, a man rose in the small gallery. He was not a young man and was obviously calling on all the energy he could muster. Citing the grievances that had brought them to this moment he said, "Sign that parchment. They may turn every tree into a gallows, every home into a grave and yet the words of that parchment can never die. For the mechanic in his workshop, they will be words of hope, to the slave in the mines—freedom." And he added, "If my hands were freezing in death, I would sign that parchment with my last ounce of strength. Sign, sign if the next moment the noose is around your neck, sign even if the hall is ringing with the sound of headman's axe, for that parchment will be the textbook of freedom, the bible of the rights of man forever." And then it is said he fell back exhausted. But 56 delegates, swept by his eloquence, signed the Declaration of Independence, a document destined to be as immortal as any work of man can be. And according to the story, when they turned to thank him for his timely oratory, he could not be found nor were there any who knew who he was or how he had come in or gone out through the locked and guarded doors.

Well, as I say, whether story or legend, the signing of the document that day in Independence Hall was miracle enough. Fifty-six men, a little band so unique—we have never seen their like since—pledged their lives, their fortunes and their sacred honor. Sixteen gave their lives, most gave their fortunes and all of them preserved their sacred honor. What manner of men were they? Certainly they were not an unwashed, revolutionary rebel, nor were then adventurers in a heroic mood. Twenty-four were lawyers and jurists, 11 were merchants and tradesmen, nine were farmers. They were men who would achieve security but valued freedom more.

And what price did they pay? John Hart was driven from the side of his desperately ill wife. After more than a year of living almost as an animal in the forest and in caves, he returned to find his wife had died and his children had vanished. He never saw them again, his property was destroyed and he died of a broken heart—but with no regret, only pride in the part he had played that day in Independence Hall. Carter Braxton of Virginia lost all his ships—they were sold to pay his debts. He died in rags. So it was with Ellery, Clymer, Hall, Walton, Gwinnett, Rutledge, Morris, Livingston, and Middleton. Nelson, learning that Cornwallis was using his home for a headquarters, personally begged Washington to fire on him and destroy his home—he died bankrupt. It has never been reported that any of these men ever expressed bitterness or renounced their action as not worth the price. Fifty-six rank-and-file, ordinary citizens had founded a nation that grew from sea to shining sea, five million farms, quiet villages, cities that never sleep—all done without an area re-development plan, urban renewal or a rural legal assistance program.

Now we are a nation of 211 million people with a pedigree that includes blood lines from every corner of the world. We have shed that American-melting-pot blood in every corner of the world, usually in defense of someone's freedom. Those who remained of that remarkable band we call our Founding Fathers tied up some of the loose ends about a dozen years after the Revolution. It had been the first revolution in all man's history that did not just exchange one set of rulers for another. This had been a philosophical revolution. The culmination of men's dreams for 6,000 years were formalized with the Constitution, probably the most unique document ever drawn in the long history of man's relation to man. I know there have been other constitutions, new ones are being drawn today by newly emerging nations. Most of them, even the one of the Soviet Union, contains many of the same guarantees as our own Constitution, and still there is a difference. The difference is so subtle that we often overlook it, but it is so great that it tells the whole story. Those other constitutions say, "Government grants you these rights" and ours says, "You are born with these rights, they are yours by the grace of God, and no government on earth can take them from you."

Lord Acton of England, who once said, "Power corrupts, and absolute power corrupts absolutely," would say of that document, "They had solved with astonishing ease and unduplicated success two problems which had heretofore baffled the capacity of the most enlightened nations. They had contrived a system of federal government which prodigiously increased national power and yet respected local liberties and authorities, and they had founded it on a principle of equality without surrendering the securities of property or freedom." Never in any society has the preeminence of the individual been so firmly established and given such a priority.

In less than twenty years we would go to war because the God-given rights of the American sailors, as defined in the Constitution, were being violated by a foreign power. We served notice then on the world that all of us together would act collectively to safeguard the rights of even the least among us. But still, in an older, cynical world, they were not convinced. The great powers of Europe still had the idea that one day this great continent would be open again to colonizing and they would come over and divide us up.

In the meantime, men who yearned to breathe free were making their way to our shores. Among them was a young refugee from the Austro-Hungarian Empire. He had been a leader in an attempt to free Hungary from Austrian rule. The attempt had failed and he fled to escape execution. In America, this young Hungarian, Koscha by name, became an importer by trade and took out his first citizenship papers. One day, business took him to a Mediterranean port. There was a large Austrian warship under the command of an admiral in the harbor. He had a manservant with him. He had described to this manservant what the flag of his new country looked like. Word was passed to the Austrian warship that this revolutionary was there and in the night he was kidnapped and taken aboard that large ship. This man's servant, desperate, walking up and down the harbor, suddenly spied a flag that resembled the description he had heard. It was a small American war sloop. He went aboard and told Captain Ingraham, of that war sloop, his story. Captain Ingraham went to the American Consul. When the American Consul learned that Koscha had only taken out his first citizenship papers, the consul washed his hands of the incident. Captain Ingraham said, "I am the senior officer in this port and I believe, under my oath of my office, that I owe this man the protection of our flag."

He went aboard the Austrian warship and demanded to see their prisoner, our citizen. The Admiral was amused, but they brought the man on deck. He was in chains and had been badly beaten. Captain Ingraham said, "I can hear him better without those chains," and the chains were removed. He walked over and said to Koscha, "I will ask you one question; consider your answer carefully. Do you ask the protection of the American flag?" Koscha nodded dumbly "Yes," and the Captain said, "You shall have it." He went back and told the frightened consul what he had done. Later in the day three more Austrian ships sailed into harbor. It looked as though the four were getting ready to leave. Captain Ingraham sent a junior officer over to the Austrian flag ship to tell the Admiral that any attempt to leave that harbor with our citizen aboard would be resisted with appropriate force. He said that he would expect a satisfactory answer by four o'clock that afternoon. As the hour neared they looked at each other through the glasses. As it struck four he had them roll the cannons into the ports and had then light the tapers with which they would set off the cannons—one little sloop. Suddenly the lookout tower called out and said, "They are lowering a boat," and they rowed Koscha over to the little American ship.

Captain Ingraham then went below and wrote his letter of resignation to the United States Navy. In it he said, "I did what I thought my oath of office required, but if I have embarrassed my country in any way, I resign." His resignation was refused in the United States Senate with these words: "This battle that was never fought may turn out to be the most important battle in our Nation's history." Incidentally, there is to this day, and I hope there always will be, a USS Ingraham in the United States Navy.

I did not tell that story out of any desire to be narrowly chauvinistic or to glorify aggressive militarism, but it is an example of government meeting its highest responsibility.

In recent years we have been treated to a rash of noble-sounding phrases. Some of them sound good, but they don't hold up under close analysis. Take for instance the slogan so frequently uttered by the young senator from Massachusetts, "The greatest good for the greatest number." Certainly under that slogan, no modern day Captain Ingraham would risk even the smallest craft and crew for a single citizen. Every dictator who ever lived has justified the enslavement of his people on the theory of what was good for the majority.

We are not a warlike people. Nor is our history filled with tales of aggressive adventures and imperialism, which might come as a shock to some of the placard painters in our modern demonstrations. The lesson of Vietnam, I think, should be that never again will young Americans be asked to fight and possibly die for a cause unless that cause is so meaningful that we, as a nation, pledge our full resources to achieve victory as quickly as possible.

I realize that such a pronouncement, of course, would possibly be laying one open to the charge of warmongering—but that would also be ridiculous. My generation has paid a higher price and has fought harder for freedom that any generation that had ever lived. We have known four wars in a single lifetime. All were horrible, all could have been avoided if at a particular moment in time we had made it plain that we subscribed to the words of John Stuart Mill when he said that "war is an ugly thing, but not the ugliest of things."

The decayed and degraded state of moral and patriotic feeling which thinks nothing is worth a war is worse. The man who has nothing which he cares about more than his personal safety is a miserable creature and has no chance of being free unless made and kept so by the exertions of better men than himself.

The widespread disaffection with things military is only a part of the philosophical division in our land today. I must say to you who have recently, or presently are still receiving an education, I am awed by your powers of resistance. I have some knowledge of the attempts that have been made in many classrooms and lecture halls to persuade you that there is little to admire in America. For the second time in this century, capitalism and the free enterprise are under assault. Privately owned business is blamed for spoiling the environment, exploiting the worker and seducing, if not outright raping, the customer. Those who make the charge have the solution, of course—government regulation and control. We may never get around to explaining how citizens who are so gullible that they can be suckered into buying cereal or soap that they don't need and would not be good for them, can at the same time be astute enough to choose representatives in government to which they would entrust the running of their lives.

Not too long ago, a poll was taken on 2,500 college campuses in this country. Thousands and thousands of responses were obtained. Overwhelmingly, 65, 70, and 75 percent of the students found business responsible, as I have said before, for the things that were wrong in this country. That same number said that government was the solution and should take over the management and the control of private business. Eighty percent of the respondents said they wanted government to keep its paws out of their private lives.

We are told every day that the assembly-line worker is becoming a dull-witted robot and that mass production results in standardization. Well, there isn't a socialist country in the world that would not give its copy of Karl Marx for our standardization.

Standardization means production for the masses and the assembly line means more leisure for the worker—freedom from backbreaking and mind-dulling drudgery that man had known for centuries past. Karl Marx did not abolish child labor or free the women from working in the coal mines in England—the steam engine and modern machinery did that.

Unfortunately, the disciples of the new order have had a hand in determining too much policy in recent decades. Government has grown in size and power and cost through the New Deal, the Fair Deal, the New Frontier and the Great Society. It costs more for government today than a family pays for food, shelter and clothing combined. Not even the Office of Management and Budget knows how many boards, commissions, bureaus and agencies there are in the federal government, but the federal registry, listing their regulations, is just a few pages short of being as big as the Encyclopedia Britannica.

During the Great Society we saw the greatest growth of this government. There were eight cabinet departments and 12 independent agencies to administer the federal health program. There were 35 housing programs and 20 transportation projects. Public utilities had to cope with 27 different agencies on just routine business. There were 192 installations and nine departments with 1,000 projects having to do with the field of pollution.

One Congressman found the federal government was spending 4 billion dollars on research in its own laboratories but did not know where they were, how many people were working in them, or what they were doing. One of the research projects was "The Demography of Happiness," and for 249,000 dollars we found that "people who make more money are happier than people who make less, young people are happier than old people, and people who are healthier are happier than people who are sick." For 15 cents they could have bought an Almanac and read the old bromide, "It's better to be rich, young and healthy, than poor, old and sick."

The course that you have chosen is far more in tune with the hopes and aspirations of our people than are those who would sacrifice freedom for some fancied security.

Standing on the tiny deck of the Arabella in 1630 off the Massachusetts coast, John Winthrop said, "We will be as a city upon a hill. The eyes of all people are upon us, so that if we deal falsely with our God in this work we have undertaken and so cause Him to withdraw His present help from us, we shall be made a story and a byword throughout the world." Well, we have not dealt falsely with our God, even if He is temporarily suspended from the classroom.

When I was born my life expectancy was 10 years less than I have already lived—that's a cause of regret for some people in California, I know. Ninety percent of Americans at that time lived beneath what is considered the poverty line today, three-quarters lived in what is considered substandard housing. Today each of those figures is less than 10 percent. We have increased our life expectancy by wiping out, almost totally, diseases that still ravage mankind in other parts of the world. I doubt if the young people here tonight know the names of some of the diseases that were commonplace when we were growing up. We have more doctors per thousand people than any nation in the world. We have more hospitals that any nation in the world.

When I was your age, believe it or not, none of us knew that we even had a racial problem. When I graduated from college and became a radio sport announcer, broadcasting major league baseball, I didn't have a Hank Aaron or a Willie Mays to talk about. The *Spaulding Guide* said baseball was a game for Caucasian gentlemen. Some of us then began editorializing and campaigning against this.

Gradually we campaigned against all those other areas where the constitutional rights of a large segment of our citizenry were being denied. We have not finished the job. We still have a long way to go, but we have made more progress in a few years than we have made in more than a century.

One-third of all the students in the world who are pursuing higher education are doing so in the United States. The percentage of our young Negro community that is going to college is greater than the percentage of whites in any other country in the world.

One-half of all the economic activity in the entire history of man has taken place in this republic. We have distributed our wealth more widely among our people than any society known to man. Americans work less hours for a higher standard of living than any other people. Ninety-five percent of all our families have an adequate daily intake of nutrients—and a part of the five percent that don't are trying to lose weight! Ninety-nine percent have gas or electric refrigeration, 92 percent have televisions, and an equal number have telephones. There are 120 million cars on our streets and highways—and all of them are on the street at once when you are trying to get home at night. But isn't this just proof of our materialism—the very thing that we are charged with? Well, we also have more churches, more libraries, we support voluntarily more symphony orchestras, and opera companies, non-profit theaters, and publish more books than all the other nations of the world put together.

Somehow America has bred a kindliness into our people unmatched anywhere, as has been pointed out in that best-selling record by a Canadian journalist. We are not a sick society. A sick society could not produce the men that set foot on the moon, or who are now circling the earth above us in the Skylab. A sick society bereft of morality and courage did not produce the men who went through those year of torture and captivity in Vietnam. Where did we find such men? They are typical of this land as the Founding Fathers were typical. We found them in our streets, in the offices, the shops and the working places of our country and on the farms.

We cannot escape our destiny, nor should we try to do so. The leadership of the free world was thrust upon us two centuries ago in that little hall of Philadelphia. In the days following World War II, when the economic strength and power of America was all that stood between the world and the return to the dark ages, Pope Pius XII said, "The American people have a great genius for splendid and unselfish actions. Into the hands of America God has placed the destinies of an afflicted mankind."

We are indeed, and we are today, the last best hope of man on earth.

First Inaugural Address (1981)

Senator Hatfield, Mr. Chief Justice, Mr. President, Vice President Bush, Vice President Mondale, Senator Baker, Speaker O'Neill, Reverend Moomaw, and my fellow citizens: To a few of us here today, this is a solemn and most momentous occasion; and yet, in the history of our Nation, it is a commonplace occurrence. The orderly transfer of authority as called for in the Constitution routinely takes place as it has for almost two centuries and few of us stop to think how unique we really are. In the eyes of many in the world, this every-4-year ceremony we accept as normal is nothing less than a miracle.

Mr. President, I want our fellow citizens to know how much you did to carry on this tradition. By your gracious cooperation in the transition process, you have shown a watching world that we are a united people pledged to maintaining a political system which guarantees individual liberty to a greater degree than any other, and I thank you and your people for all your help in maintaining the continuity which is the bulwark of our Republic.

The business of our nation goes forward. These United States are confronted with an economic affliction of great proportions. We suffer from the longest and one of the worst sustained inflations in our national history. It distorts our economic decisions, penalizes thrift, and crushes the struggling young and the fixed-income elderly alike. It threatens to shatter the lives of millions of our people.

Idle industries have cast workers into unemployment, causing human misery and personal indignity. Those who do work are denied a fair return for their labor by a tax system which penalizes successful achievement and keeps us from maintaining full productivity.

But great as our tax burden is, it has not kept pace with public spending. For decades, we have piled deficit upon deficit, mortgaging our future and our children's future for the temporary convenience of the present. To continue this long trend is to guarantee tremendous social, cultural, political, and economic upheavals.

You and I, as individuals, can, by borrowing, live beyond our means, but for only a limited period of time. Why, then, should we think that collectively, as a nation, we are not bound by that same limitation? We must act today in order to preserve tomorrow. And let there be no misunderstanding—we are going to begin to act, beginning today.

The economic ills we suffer have come upon us over several decades. They will not go away in days, weeks, or months, but they will go away. They will go away because we, as Americans, have the capacity now, as we have had in the past, to do whatever needs to be done to preserve this last and greatest bastion of freedom.

In this present crisis, government is not the solution to our problem.

From time to time, we have been tempted to believe that society has become too complex to be managed by self-rule, that government by an elite group is superior to government for, by, and of the people. But if no one among us is capable of governing himself, then who among us has the capacity to govern someone else? All of us together, in and out of government, must bear the burden. The solutions we seek must be equitable, with no one group singled out to pay a higher price.

We hear much of special interest groups. Our concern must be for a special interest group that has been too long neglected. It knows no sectional boundaries or ethnic and racial divisions, and it crosses political party lines. It is made up of men and women who raise our food, patrol our streets, man our mines and our factories, teach our children, keep our homes, and heal us when we are sick—professionals, industrialists, shopkeepers, clerks, cabbies, and truck drivers. They are, in short, "We the people," this breed called Americans.

Well, this administration's objective will be a healthy, vigorous, growing economy that provides equal opportunity for all Americans, with no barriers born of bigotry or discrimination. Putting America back to work means putting all Americans back to work. Ending inflation means freeing all Americans from the terror of runaway living costs. All must share in the productive work of this "new beginning" and all must share in the bounty of a revived economy. With the idealism and fair play which are the core of our system and our strength, we can have a strong and prosperous America at peace with itself and the world.

So, as we begin, let us take inventory. We are a nation that has a government—not the other way around. And this makes us special among the nations of the Earth. Our Government has no power except that granted it by the people. It is time to check and reverse the growth of government which shows signs of having grown beyond the consent of the governed.

It is my intention to curb the size and influence of the Federal establishment and to demand recognition of the distinction between the powers granted to the Federal Government and those reserved to the States or to the people. All of us need to be reminded that the Federal Government did not create the States; the States created the Federal Government.

Now, so there will be no misunderstanding, it is not my intention to do away with government. It is, rather, to make it work—work with us, not over us; to stand by our side, not ride on our back. Government can and must provide opportunity, not smother it; foster productivity, not stifle it.

If we look to the answer as to why, for so many years, we achieved so much, prospered as no other people on Earth, it was because here, in this land, we unleashed the energy and individual genius of man to a greater extent than has ever been done before. Freedom and the dignity of the individual have been more available and assured here than in any other place on Earth. The price for this freedom at times

Freedom

has been high, but we have never been unwilling to pay that price.

It is no coincidence that our present troubles parallel and are proportionate to the intervention and intrusion in our lives that result from unnecessary and excessive growth of government. It is time for us to realize that we are too great a nation to limit ourselves to small dreams. We are not, as some would have us believe, loomed to an inevitable decline. I do not believe in a fate that will fall on us no matter what we do. I do believe in a fate that will fall on us if we do nothing. So, with all the creative energy at our command, let us begin an era of national renewal. Let us renew our determination, our courage, and our strength. And let us renew our faith and our hope.

We have every right to dream heroic dreams. Those who say that we are in a time when there are no heroes just don't know where to look. You can see heroes every day going in and out of factory gates. Others, a handful in number, produce enough food to feed all of us and then the world beyond. You meet heroes across a counter—and they are on both sides of that counter. There are entrepreneurs with faith in themselves and faith in an idea who create new jobs, new wealth and opportunity. They are individuals and families whose taxes support the Government and whose voluntary gifts support church, charity, culture, art, and education. Their patriotism is quiet but deep. Their values sustain our national life.

I have used the words "they" and "their" in speaking of these heroes. I could say "you" and "your" because I am addressing the heroes of whom I speak—you, the citizens of this blessed land. Your dreams, your hopes, your goals are going to be the dreams, the hopes, and the goals of this administration, so help me God.

We shall reflect the compassion that is so much a part of your makeup. How can we love our country and not love our countrymen, and loving them, reach out a hand when they fall, heal them when they are sick, and provide opportunities to make them self-sufficient so they will be equal in fact and not just in theory?

Can we solve the problems confronting us? Well, the answer is an unequivocal and emphatic "yes." To paraphrase Winston Churchill, I did not take the oath I have just taken with the intention of presiding over the dissolution of the world's strongest economy.

In the days ahead I will propose removing the roadblocks that have slowed our economy and reduced productivity. Steps will be taken aimed at restoring the balance between the various levels of government. Progress may be slow—measured in inches and feet, not miles—but we will progress. Is it time to reawaken this industrial giant, to get government back within its means, and to lighten our punitive tax burden. And these will be our first priorities, and on these principles, there will be no compromise.

On the eve of our struggle for independence a man who might have been one of the greatest among the Founding Fathers, Dr. Joseph Warren, President of the Massachusetts Congress, said to his fellow Americans, "Our country is in danger, but not to be despaired of. . . . On you depend the fortunes of America. You are to decide the important questions upon which rests the happiness and the liberty of millions yet unborn. Act worthy of yourselves."

Well, I believe we, the Americans of today, are ready to act worthy of ourselves, ready to do what must be done to ensure happiness and liberty for ourselves, our children and our children's children.

And as we renew ourselves here in our own land, we will be seen as having greater strength throughout the world. We will again be the exemplar of freedom and a beacon of hope for those who do not now have freedom.

To those neighbors and allies who share our freedom, we will strengthen our historic ties and assure them of our support and firm commitment. We will match loyalty with loyalty. We will strive for mutually beneficial relations. We will not use our friendship to impose on their sovereignty, for or own sovereignty is not for sale.

As for the enemies of freedom, those who are potential adversaries, they will be reminded that peace is the highest aspiration of the American people. We will negotiate for it, sacrifice for it; we will not surrender for it—now or ever.

Our forbearance should never be misunderstood. Our reluctance for conflict should not be misjudged as a failure of will. When action is required to preserve our national security, we will act. We will maintain sufficient strength to prevail if need be, knowing that if we do so we have the best chance of never having to use that strength.

Above all, we must realize that no arsenal, or no weapon in the arsenals of the world, is so formidable as the will and moral courage of free men and women. It is a weapon our adversaries in today's world do not have. It is a weapon that we as Americans do have. Let that be understood by those who practice terrorism and prey upon their neighbors.

I am told that tens of thousands of prayer meetings are being held on this day, and for that I am deeply grateful. We are a nation under God, and I believe God intended for us to be free. It would be fitting and good, I think, if on each Inauguration Day in future years it should be declared a day of prayer.

This is the first time in history that this ceremony has been held, as you have been told, on this West Front of the Capitol. Standing here, one faces a magnificent vista, opening up on this city's special beauty and history. At the end of this open mall are those shrines to the giants on whose shoulders we stand.

Directly in front of me, the monument to a monumental man: George Washington, Father of our country. A man of humility who came to greatness reluctantly. He led America out of revolutionary victory into infant nationhood. Off to one side, the stately memorial to Thomas Jefferson. The Declaration of Independence flames with his eloquence.

And then beyond the Reflecting Pool the dignified columns of the Lincoln Memorial. Whoever would understand in his heart the meaning of America will find it in the life of Abraham Lincoln.

Beyond those monuments to heroism is the Potomac River, and on the far shore the sloping hills of Arlington National Cemetery with its row on row of simple white markers bearing crosses or Stars of David. They add up to only a tiny fraction of the price that has been paid for our freedom.

Each one of those markers is a monument to the kinds of hero I spoke of earlier. Their lives ended in places called Belleau Wood, the Argonne, Omaha Beach, Salerno and halfway around the world on Guadalcanal, Tarawa, Pork Chop Hill, the Chosin Reservoir, and in a hundred rice paddies and jungles of a place called Vietnam.

Under one such marker lies a young man—Martin Treptow—who left his job in a small town barber shop in 1917 to go to France with the famed Rainbow Division. There, on the western front, he was killed trying to carry a message between battalions under heavy artillery fire.

We are told that on his body was found a diary. On the flyleaf under the heading, "My Pledge," he had written these words: "America must win this war. Therefore, I will work, I will save, I will sacrifice, I will endure, I will fight cheerfully and do my utmost, as if the issue of the whole struggle depended on me alone."

The crisis we are facing today does not require of us the kind of sacrifice that Martin Treptow and so many thousands of others were called upon to make. It does require, however, our best effort, and our willingness to believe in ourselves and to believe in our capacity to perform great deeds; to believe that together, with God's help, we can and will resolve the problems which now confront us.

And, after all, why shouldn't we believe that? We are Americans. God bless you, and thank you.

Address before the National Association of Evangelists (1983)

Reverend Clergy all, Senator Hawkins, distinguished members of the Florida congressional delegation, and all of you:

I can't tell you how you have warmed my heart with your welcome. I'm delighted to be here today.

Those of you in the National Association of Evangelicals are known for you spiritual and humanitarian work. And I would be especially remiss if I didn't discharge right now one personal debt of gratitude. Thank you for your prayers. Nancy and I have felt their presence many times in many years. And believe me, for us they've made all the difference.

The other day in the East Room of the White House at a meeting there, someone asked me whether I was aware of all the people out there who were praying for the President. And I had to say, "Yes, I am. I've felt it. I believe in intercessionary prayer." But I couldn't help but say to that questioner after he'd asked the question that—or at least say to them that if sometimes when he was praying he got a busy signal, it was just me in there ahead of him. I think I understand how Abraham Lincoln felt when he said, "I have been driven many times to my knees by the overwhelming conviction that I had nowhere else to go." From the joy and the good feeling of this conference, I go to a political reception. Now, I don't know why, but that bit of scheduling reminds me of a story—which I'll share with you.

An evangelical minister and a politician arrived at Heaven's gate one day together. And St. Peter, after doing all the necessary formalities, took them in hand to show them where their quarters would be. And he took them to a small, single room with a bed, a chair, and a table and said this was for the clergyman. And the politician was a little worried about what might be in store for him. And he couldn't believe it then when St. Peter stopped in front of a beautiful mansion with lovely grounds, many servants, and told him that these would be his quarters.

And he couldn't help but ask, he said, "But wait, now—there's something wrong—how do I get this mansion while that good and holy man only gets a single room?" And St. Peter said, "You have to understand how things are up here. We've got thousands and thousands of clergy. You're the first politician who ever made it."

But I don't want to contribute to a stereotype. So I tell you there are a great many God-fearing, dedicated, noble men and women in public life, present company included. And yes, we need your help to keep us ever mindful of the ideas and the principles that brought us into the public arena in the first place. The basis of those ideals and principles is a commitment to freedom and personal liberty that, itself, is grounded in the much deeper realization that freedom prospers only where the blessings of God are avidly sought and humbly accepted.

The American experiment in democracy rests on this insight. Its discovery was the great triumph of our Founding Fathers, voiced by William Penn when he said: "If we will not be governed by God, we must be governed by tyrants." Explaining the inalienable rights of men, Jefferson said, "The God who gave us

life, gave us liberty at the same time." And it was George Washington who said that "of all the disposition and habits which lead to political prosperity, religion and morality are indispensable supporters."

And finally, that shrewdest of all observers of American democracy, Alexis de Tocqueville, put it eloquently after he had gone on a search for the secret of America's greatness and genius—and he said: "Not until I went into the churches of America and heard her pulpits aflame with righteousness did I understand the greatness and the genius of America . . . America is good. And if America ever ceases to be good, America will cease to be great."

Well, I'm pleased to be here today with you who are keeping America great by keeping her good. Only through your work and prayers and those of millions of others cans we hope to survive this perilous century and keep alive this experiment in liberty, this last, best hope of man.

I want you to know that this administration is motivated by a political philosophy that sees the greatness of America in you, here people, and in your families, churches, neighborhoods, communities— the institutions that foster and nourish values like concern for others and respect for the rule of law under God.

Now, I don't have to tell you that this puts us in opposition to, or at least out of step with, a prevailing attitude of many who have turned to a modern-day secularism, discarding the tried and time-tested values upon which our very civilization is based. No matter how well intentioned, their value system is radically different from that of most Americans. And while they proclaim that they're freeing us from superstitions of the past, they've taken upon themselves the job of superintending us by government rule and regulation. Sometimes their voices are louder than ours, but they are not yet a majority.

An example of that vocal superiority is evident in a controversy now going on in Washington. And since I'm involved I've been waiting to hear from the parents of young America. How far are they willing to go in giving to government their prerogatives as parents?

Let me state the case as briefly and simply as I can. An organization of citizens, sincerely motivated and deeply concerned about the increase in illegitimate births and abortions involving girls well below the age of consent, some time ago established a nationwide network of clinics to offer help to these girls and, hopefully, alleviate this situation. Now, again, let me say, I do not fault their intent. However, in their well-intentioned effort, these clinics have decided to provide advice and birth control drugs and devices to underage girls without the knowledge of their parents.

For some years now, the federal government has helped with funds to subsidize these clinics. In providing for this, the Congress decreed that every effort would be made to maximize parental participation. Nevertheless, the drugs and devices are prescribed without getting parental consent or giving notification after they've done so. Girls termed "sexually active"—and that has replaced the word "promiscuous"—are given this help in order to prevent illegitimate birth or abortion.

Well, we have ordered clinics receiving federal funds to notify the parents such help has been given. One of the nation's leading newspapers has created the term "squeal rule" in editorializing against us for doing this, and we're being criticized for violating the privacy of young people. A judge has recently granted an injunction against an enforcement of our rule. I've watched TV panel shows discuss the issue, seen columnists pontificating on our error, but no one seems to mention morality as playing a part in the subject of sex.

Is all of Judeo-Christian tradition wrong? Are we to believe that something so sacred can be looked upon as a purely physical thing with no potential for emotional and psychological harm? And isn't it the parents' right to give counsel and advice to keep their children from making mistakes that may affect their entire lives?

Many of us in government would like to know what parents think about this intrusion in their family by government. We're going to fight in the courts. The right of parents and the rights of family take precedence over those of Washington-based bureaucrats and social engineers.

But the fight against parental notification is really only one example of many attempts to water down traditional values and even abrogate the original terms of American democracy. Freedom prospers when religion is vibrant and the rule of law under God is acknowledged. When our Founding Fathers passed the First Amendment, they sought to protect churches from government interference. They never intended to construct a wall of hostility between government and the concept of religious belief itself.

The evidence of this permeates our history and our government. The Declaration of Independence mentions the Supreme Being no less than four times. "In God We Trust" is engraved on our coinage. The Supreme Court opens its proceedings with a religious invocation. And the members of Congress open their sessions with a prayer. I just happen to believe the schoolchildren of the United States are entitled to the same privileges as Supreme Court justices and congressmen.

Last year, I sent the Congress a constitutional amendment to restore prayer to public schools. Already this session, there's growing bipartisan support for the amendment, and I am calling on the Congress to act speedily to pass it and to let our children pray.

Perhaps some of you read recently about the Lubbock school case, where a judge actually ruled that it was unconstitutional for a school district to give equal treatment to religious and nonreligious student groups, even when the group meetings were being held during the students' own time. The First Amendment never intended to require government to discriminate against religious speech.

Senators Denton and Hatfield have proposed legislation in the Congress on the whole question of prohibiting discrimination against religious forms of student speech. Such legislation could go far to restore freedom of religious speech for public school students. And I hope the Congress considers these bills quickly. And with your help, I think it's possible we could also get the constitutional amendment through the Congress this year.

More than a decade ago, a Supreme Court decision literally wiped off the books of fifty states statutes protecting the rights of unborn children. Abortion on demand now takes the lives of up to one and a half million unborn children a year. Human life legislation ending this tragedy will someday pass the Congress, and you and I must never rest until it does. Unless and until it can be proven that the unborn child is not a living entity, then its right to life, liberty, and the pursuit of happiness must be protected.

You may remember that when abortion on demand began, many, and indeed, I'm sure many of you, warned that the practice would lead to a decline in respect for human life, that the philosophical premises used to justify abortion on demand would ultimately be used to justify other attacks on the sacredness of human life—infanticide or mercy killing. Tragically enough, those warnings proved all too true. Only last year a court permitted the death by starvation of a handicapped infant.

I have directed the Health and Human Services Department to make clear to every health care facility in the United States that the Rehabilitation Act of 1973 protects all handicapped persons against discrimination based on handicaps, including infants. And we have taken the further step of requiring that each and every recipient of federal funds who provides health care services to infants must post and keep posted in a conspicuous place a notice stating that "discriminatory failure to feed and care for handicapped infants in this facility is prohibited by federal law." It also lists a twenty-four-hour, toll-free number so that nurses and others may report violations in time to save the infant's life.

In addition, recent legislation introduced in the Congress by Representative Henry Hyde of Illinois not only increases restrictions on publicly financed abortions, it also addresses this whole problem of infanticide. I urge the Congress to begin hearings and to adopt legislation that will protect the right of life to all children, including the disabled or handicapped.

Now, I'm sure that you must get discouraged at times, but you've done better than you know, perhaps. There's a great spiritual awakening in America, a renewal of the traditional values that have been the bedrock of America's goodness and greatness.

One recent survey by a Washington-based research council concluded that Americans were far more religious than the people of other nations; 95 percent of those surveyed expressed a belief in God and a huge majority believed the Ten Commandments had real meaning in their lives. And another study has found that an overwhelming majority of Americans disapprove of adultery, teenage sex, pornography, abortion, and hard drugs. And this same study showed a deep reverence for the importance of family ties and religious belief.

I think the items that we've discussed here today must be a key part of the nation's political agenda. For the first time the Congress is openly and seriously debating and dealing with the prayer and abortion issues—and that's enormous progress right there. I repeat: America is in the midst of a spiritual awakening and a moral renewal. And with your biblical keynote, I say today, "Yes, let justice roll on like a river, righteousness like a never-failing stream."

Now, obviously, much of this new political and social consensus I've talked about is based on a positive view of American history, one that takes pride in our country's accomplishments and record. But we must never forget that no government schemes are going to perfect man. We know that living in this world means dealing with what philosophers would call the phenomenology of evil or, as theologians would put it, the doctrine of sin.

There is sin and evil in the world, and we're enjoined by Scripture and the Lord Jesus to oppose it with all our might. Our nation, too, has a legacy of evil with which it must deal. The glory of this land has been its capacity for transcending the moral evils of our past. For example, the long struggle of minority citizens for equal rights, once a source of disunity and civil war, is now a point of pride for all Americans. We must never go back. There is no room for racism, anti-Semitism, or other forms of ethnic and racial hatred in this country.

I know that you've been horrified, as have I, by the resurgence of some hate groups preaching bigotry and prejudice. Use the mighty voice of your pulpits and the powerful standing of your churches to denounce and isolate these hate groups in our midst. The commandment given us is clear and simple: "Thou shalt love thy neighbor as thyself."

But whatever sad episodes exist in our past, any objective observer must hold a positive view of American history, a history that has been the story of hopes fulfilled and dreams made into reality. Especially in this century, America has kept alight the torch of freedom, but not just for ourselves but for millions of others around the world.

And this brings me to my final point today. During my first press conference as president, in answer to a direct question, I pointed out that, as good Marxist-Leninists, the Soviet leaders have openly and publicly declared that the only morality they recognize is that which will further their cause, which is world revolution. I think I should point out I was only quoting Lenin, their guiding spirit, who said in 1920 that they repudiate all morality that proceeds from super-natural ideas—that's their name for religion—or ideas that are outside class conceptions. Morality is entirely subordinate to the interests of class war. And everything is moral that is necessary for the annihilation of the old, exploiting social order and for uniting the proletariat.

Well, I think the refusal of many influential people to accept this elementary fact of Soviet doctrine illustrates a historical reluctance to see totalitarian powers for what they are. We saw this phenomenon in the 1930s. We see it too often today.

This doesn't mean we should isolate ourselves and refuse to seek an understanding with them. I intend to do everything I can to persuade them of our peaceful intent, to remind them that it was the West that refused to use its nuclear monopoly in the forties and fifties for territorial gain and which now proposes a 50-percent cut in strategic ballistic missiles and the elimination of an entire class of land-based, intermediate-range nuclear missiles.

At the same time, however, they must be made to understand we will never compromise our principles and standards. We will never give away our freedom. We will never abandon our belief in God. And we will never stop searching for a genuine peace. But we can assure none of these things America stands for through the so-called nuclear freeze solutions proposed by some.

The truth is that a freeze now would be a very dangerous fraud, for that is merely the illusion of peace. The reality is that we must find peace through strength.

I would agree to freeze if only we could freeze the Soviets' global desires. A freeze at current levels of weapons would remove any incentive for the Soviets to negotiate seriously in Geneva and virtually end our chances to achieve the major arms reductions which we have proposed. Instead, they would achieve their objectives through the freeze.

A freeze would reward the Soviet Union for its enormous and unparalleled military buildup. It would prevent the essential and long overdue modernization of United States and allied defenses and would leave our aging forces increasingly vulnerable. And an honest freeze would require extensive prior negotiations on the systems and numbers to be limited and on the measures to ensure effective verification and compliance. And the kind of a freeze that has been suggested would be virtually impossible to verify. Such a major effort would divert us completely from our current negotiations on achieving substantial reductions.

A number of years ago, I heard a young father, a very prominent young man in the entertainment world, addressing a tremendous gathering in California. It was during the time of the cold war, and communism and our own way of life were very much on people's minds. And he was speaking to that subject. And suddenly, though, I heard him saying, "I love my little girls more than anything—" And I said to myself, "Oh, no, don't. You can't—don't say that." But I had underestimated him. He went on: "I would rather see my little girls die now, still believing in God, than have them grow up under communism and one day die no longer believing in God."

There were thousands of young people in that audience. They came to their feet with shouts of joy. They had instantly recognized the profound truth in what he had said, with regard to the physical and the soul and what was truly important.

Yes, let us pray for the salvation of all of those who live in that totalitarian darkness—pray they will discover the joy of knowing God. But until they do, let us be aware that while they preach the supremacy of the state, declare its omnipotence over individual man, and predict its eventual domination of all peoples on the earth, they are the focus of evil in the modern world.

It was C. S. Lewis who, in his unforgettable *Screwtape Letters*, wrote: "The greatest evil is not done now in those sordid 'dens of crime' that Dickens loved to paint. It is not even done in concentration camps and labor camps. In those we see its final result. But it is conceived and ordered (moved, seconded, carried and minuted) in clean, carpeted, warmed, and well-lighted offices, by quiet men with white collars and cut fingernails and smooth-shaven cheeks who do not need to raise their voice."

Well, because these "quiet men" do not "raise their voices," because they sometimes speak in soothing tones of brotherhood and peace, because, like other dictators before them, they're always making "their final territorial demand," some would have us accept them at their word and accommodate ourselves to their aggressive impulses. But if history teaches anything, it teaches that simpleminded appeasement or wishful thinking about our adversaries is folly. It means the betrayal of our past, the squandering of our freedom.

So, I urge you to speak out against those who would place the United States in a position of military and moral inferiority. You know, I've always believed that old Screwtape reserved his best efforts for those of you in the church. So, in your discussions of the nuclear freeze proposals, I urge you to beware the temptation of pride—the temptation of blithely declaring yourselves above it all and label both sides equally at fault, to ignore the facts of history and the aggressive impulses of an evil empire, to simply call the arms race a giant misunderstanding and thereby remove yourself from the struggle between right and wrong and good and evil.

I ask you to resist the attempts of those who would have you withhold your support for our efforts, this administration's efforts, to keep America strong and free, while we negotiate real and verifiable reductions in the world's nuclear arsenals and one day, with God's help, their total elimination.

While America's military strength is important, let me add here that I've always maintained that the struggle now going on for the world will never be decided by bombs or rockets, by armies or military might. The real crisis we face today is a spiritual one; at root, it is a test of moral will and faith.

Whittaker Chambers, the man whose own religious conversion made him a witness to one of the terrible traumas of our time, the Hiss-Chambers case, wrote that the crisis of the Western world exists to the degree in which the West is indifferent to God, the degree to which it collaborates in communism's attempt to make man stand alone without God. And then he said, for Marxism-Leninism is actually the second-oldest faith, first proclaimed in the Garden of Eden with the words of temptation, "Ye shall be as gods."

The Western world can answer this challenge, he wrote, "but only provided that its faith in God and the freedom He enjoins is as great as communism's faith in Man."

I believe we shall rise to the challenge. I believe that communism is another sad, bizarre chapter in human history whose last pages even now are being written. I believe this because the source of our strength in the quest for human freedom is not material, but spiritual. And because it knows no limitation, it must terrify and ultimately triumph over those who would enslave their fellow man. For in the words of Isaiah: "He giveth power to the faint; and to them that have no might He increased strength . . . But they that wait upon the Lord shall renew their strength; they shall mount up with wings as eagles; they shall run, and not be weary . . ."

Yes, change your world. One of our Founding Fathers, Thomas Paine, said, "We have it within our power to begin the world over again." We can do it, doing together what no one church could do by itself.

God bless you, and thank you very much.

URSULA K. LE GUIN

A Left-Handed Commencement Address (1983)

I want to thank the Mills College Class of '83 for offering me a rare chance: to speak aloud in public in the language of women.

I know there are men graduating, and I don't mean to exclude them, far from it. There is a Greek tragedy where the Greek says to the foreigner, "If you don't understand Greek, please signify by nodding." Anyhow, commencements are usually operated under the unspoken agreement that everybody graduating is either male or ought to be. That's why we are all wearing these twelfth-century dresses that look so great on men and make women look either like a mushroom or a pregnant stork. Intellectual tradition is male. Public speaking is done in the public tongue, the national or tribal language; and the language of our tribe is the men's language. Of course women learn it. We're not dumb. If you can tell Margaret Thatcher from Ronald Reagan, or Indira Gandhi from General Somoza, by anything they say, tell me how. This is a man's world, so it talks a man's language. The words are all words of power. You've come a long way, baby, but no way is long enough. You can't even get there by selling yourself out: because there is theirs, not yours.

Maybe we've had enough words of power and talk about the battle of life. Maybe we need some words of weakness. Instead of saying now that I hope you will all go forth from this ivory tower of college into the Real World and forge a triumphant career or at least help your husband to and keep our country strong and be a success in everything—instead of talking about power, what if I talked like a woman right here in public? It won't sound right. It's going to sound terrible. What if I said what I hope for you is first, if— only if—you want kids, I hope you have them. Not hordes of them. A couple, enough. I hope they're beautiful. I hope you and they have enough to eat, and a place to be warm and clean in, and friends, and work you like doing. Well, is that what you went to college for? Is that all? What about success?

Success is somebody else's failure. Success is the American Dream we can keep dreaming because most people in most places, including thirty million of ourselves, live wide awake in the terrible reality of poverty. No, I do not wish you success. I don't even want to talk about it. I want to talk about failure.

Because you are human beings you are going to meet failure. You are going to meet disappointment, injustice, betrayal, and irreparable loss. You will find you're weak where you thought yourself strong. You'll work for possessions and then find they possess you. You will find yourself—as I know you already have— in dark places, alone, and afraid.

What I hope for you, for all my sisters and daughters, brothers and sons, is that you will be able to live there, in the dark place. To live in the place that our rationalizing culture of success denies, calling it a place of exile, uninhabitable, foreign.

Well, we're already foreigners. Women as women are largely excluded from, alien to, the self-declared male norms of this society, where human beings are called Man, the only respectable god is male, the the only direction is up. So that's their country; let's explore our own. I'm not talking about sex; that's a whole other universe, where every man and woman is on their own. I'm talking about society, the so-called man's world of institutionalized competition, aggression, violence, authority, and power. If we want to live as women, some separatism is forced upon us: Mills College is a wise embodiment of that separatism. The war-games world wasn't made by us or for us; we can't even breathe the air there without masks. And if you put the mask on you'll have a hard time getting it off. So how about going on doing things our own way, as to some extent you did here at Mills? Not *for* men and the male power hierarchy—that's their game. Not *against* men, either—that's still playing by their rules. But *with* any men who are with us: that's our game. Why should a free woman with a college education either fight Machoman or serve him? Why should she live her life on his terms?

Machoman is afraid of our terms, which are not all rational, positive, competitive, etc. And so he has taught us to despise and deny them. In our society, women have lived, and have been despised for living, the whole side of life that includes and takes responsibility for helplessness, weakness, and illness, for the irrational and the irreparable, for all that is obscure, passive, uncontrolled, animal, unclean—the valley of the shadow, the deep, the depths of life. All that the Warrior denies and refuses is left to us and the men who share it with us and therefore, like us, can't play doctor, only nurse, can't be warriors, only civilians, can't be chiefs, only indians. Well, so that is our country. The night side of our country. If there is a day side to it, high sierras, prairies of bright grass, we only know pioneers' tales about it, we haven't got there yet. We're never going to get there by imitating Machoman. We are only going to get there by going our own way, by living there, by living through the night in our own country.

So what I hope for you is that you live there not as prisoners, ashamed of being women, consenting captives of a psychopathic social system, but as natives. That you will be at home there, keep house there, be your own mistress, with a room of your own. That you will do your work there, whatever you're good at, art or science or tech or running a company or sweeping under the beds, and when they tell you that it's second-class work because a woman is doing it, I hope you tell them to go to hell and while they're going to give you equal pay for equal time. I hope you live without the need to dominate, and without the need to be dominated. I hope you are never victims, but I hope you have no power over other people. And when you fail, and are defeated, and in pain, and in the dark, then I hope you will remember that darkness is your country, where you live, where no wars are fought and no wars are won, but where the future is. Our roots are in the dark; the earth is our country. Why did we look up for blessing—instead of around, and down? What hope we have lies there. Not in the sky full of orbiting spy-eyes and weaponry, but in the earth we have looked down upon. Not from above, but from below. Not in the light that blinds, but in the dark that nourishes, where human beings grow human souls.

These have nothing to do with the readings, I was just bored.

THURGOOD MARSHALL

Remarks on the Bicentennial of the Constitution (1987)

1987 marks the 200th anniversary of the United States Constitution. A Commission has been established to coordinate the celebration. The official meetings, essay contests, and festivities have begun.

The planned commemoration will span three years, and I am told that 1987 is "dedicated to the memory of the Founders and the document they drafted in Philadelphia." We are to "recall the achievements of our Founders and the knowledge and experience that inspired them, the nature of the government they established, its origins, its character, and its ends, and the rights and privileges of citizenship, as well as its attendant responsibilities."

Like many anniversary celebrations, the plan for 1987 take particular events and holds them up as the source of all the very best that has followed. Patriotic feelings will surely swell, prompting proud proclamations of the wisdom, foresight and sense of justice shared by the Framers and reflected in a written document now yellowed with age. This is unfortunate not in the patriotism itself, but the tendency for the celebration to oversimplify, and overlook the many other events that have been instrumental to our achievements as a nation. The focus of this celebration invites a complacent belief that the vision of those who debated and compromised in Philadelphia yielded the "more perfect Union" it is said we now enjoy.

I cannot accept this invitation, for I do not believe that the meaning of the Constitution was forever "fixed" at the Philadelphia Convention. Nor do I find the wisdom, foresight, and sense of justice exhibited by the Framers particularly profound. To the contrary, the government they devised was defective from the start, requiring several amendments, a civil war, and momentous social transformation to attain the system of constitutional government, and its respect for the individual freedoms and human rights, we hold as fundamental today. When contemporary American cite "The Constitution," they invoke a concept that is vastly different from what the Framers barely began to construct two centuries ago.

For a sense of the evolving nature of the Constitution we need look no further than the first three words of the document's preamble: "We the People." When the Founding Fathers used this phrase in 1787, they did not have in mind the majority of America's citizens. "We the People" included, in the words of the Framers, "the whole number of free Persons." On a matter so basic as the right to vote, for example, Negro slaves were excluded, although they were counted for representational purposes at three-fifths each. Women did not gain the right to vote for over a hundred and thirty years.

These omissions were intentional. The record of the Framers' debates on the slave question is especially clear: the Southern States acceded to the demands of the New England States for giving Congress broad power to regulate commerce, in exchange for the right to continue the slave trade. The economic interests of the regions coalesced: New Englanders engaged in the "carrying trade" would profit from transporting slaves from Africa as well as good produced in America by slave labor. The perpetuation of slavery ensured the primary source of wealth in the Southern States.

Despite this clear understanding of the role slavery would play in the new republic, use of the words "slaves" and "slavery" was carefully avoided in the original document. Political representation in the lower House of Congress was to be based on the population of "free Persons" in each State, plus three-fifths of all "other Persons." Moral principles against slavery, for those who had them, were compromised, with no explanation of the conflicting principles for which the American Revolutionary War had ostensibly been fought: the self-evident truths "that all men are created equal, that they are endowed by their Creator with certain unalienable Rights, that among these are Life, Liberty and the pursuit of Happiness."

It was not the first such compromise. Even these ringing phrases from the Declaration of Independence are filled with irony, for an early draft of what later became that Declaration assailed the King of England for suppressing legislative attempts to end the slave trade and for encouraging slave rebellions. The final draft adopted in 1776 did not contain this criticism. And so again at the Constitutional Convention eloquent objections to the institution of slavery went unheeded, and its opponents eventually consented to a document which laid a foundation for the tragic events that were to follow.

Pennsylvania's Governor Morris provides an example. He opposed slavery and the counting of slaves in determining the bases for representation in Congress. At the convention he objected that

> the inhabitant of Georgia or South Carolina who goes to the coast of Africa, and in defiance of the most sacred laws of humanity tears away his fellow

creatures from their dearest connections and damns them to the most cruel bondage, shall have more votes in a Government instituted for protection of the rights of mankind, than the Citizen of Pennsylvania or New Jersey who views with a laudable horror, so nefarious a practice.

And yet Governor Morris eventually accepted the three-fifths accommodation. In fact, he wrote the final draft of the Constitution, the very document the bicentennial will commemorate.

As a result of compromise, the right of the southern States to continue importing slaves was extended, officially, at least until 1808. We know that it actually lasted a good deal longer, as the Framers possessed no monopoly on the ability to trade moral principles for self-interest. But they nevertheless set an unfortunate example. Slaves could be imported, if the commercial interests of the North were protected. To make the compromise even more palatable, customs duties would be imposed at up to ten dollars per slave as a means of raising public revenues.

No doubt it will be said, when the unpleasant truth of the history of slavery in America is mentioned during this bicentennial year, that the Constitution was a product of its times, and embodied a compromise which, under other circumstances, would not have been made. But the effects of the Framers' compromise have remained for generations. They arose from the contradiction between guaranteeing liberty and justice to all, and denying both to Negroes.

The original intent of the phrase, "We the People," was far too clear for any ameliorating construction. Writing for the Supreme Court in 1857, Chief Justice Taney penned the following passage in the Dred Scott case, on the issue whether, in the eyes of the Framers, slaves were "constituent member of the sovereignty," and were to be included among "We the People":

> We think they are not, and that they are not included, and were not intended to be included. They had for more than a century before been regarded as beings of an inferior order, and altogether unfit to associate with the white race; and so far inferior, that they had no rights which the white man was bound to respect; and that the Negro might justly and lawfully be reduced to

slavery for his benefit. Accordingly, a Negro of the Africa race was regarded as an article of property, and held, and brought and sold as such. No one seems to have doubted the correctness of the prevailing opinion of the time.

And so, nearly seven decades after the Constitutional Convention, the Supreme Court reaffirmed the prevailing opinion of the Framers regarding the rights of Negroes in America. It took a bloody civil war before the 13th Amendment could be adopted to abolish slavery, though not the consequences slavery would have for future Americans.

While the Union survived the civil war, the Constitution did not. In its place arose a new, more promising basis for justice and equality, the 14th Amendment, ensuring protection of the life, liberty, and property of all persons against deprivations without due process, and guaranteeing equal protection of the laws. And yet almost another century would pass before any significant recognition was obtained of the rights of black Americans to share equally even in such basic opportunities as education, housing, and employment, and to have their votes counted, and counted equally. In the meantime, blacks joined America's military to fight its wars and invested untold hours working in its factories and on its farms, contributing to the development of this country's magnificent wealth and waiting to share in its prosperity.

What is striking is the role legal principles have played throughout America's history in determining the condition of Negroes. They were enslaved by law, emancipated by law, disenfranchised and segregated by law; and, finally, they have begun to win equality by law. Along the way, new constitutional principles have emerged to meet the challenges of a changing society. The progress has been dramatic, and it will continue.

The men who gathered in Philadelphia in 1787 could not have envisioned these changes. They could not have imagined, nor would they have accepted, that the document they were drafting would one day be construed by a Supreme Court to which had been appointed a woman and the descendent of an African slave. "We the People" no longer enslaved, but the credit does not belong to the Framers. It belongs to those who refused to acquiesce in outdated notions of "liberty," "justice," and "equality," and who strived to better them.

And so we must be careful, when focusing on the events which took place in Philadelphia two centuries ago, that we not overlook the momentous events which followed, and thereby lose our proper sense of perspective. Otherwise, the odds are that for many Americans the bicentennial celebration will be little more than a blind pilgrimage to the shrine of the original document now stored in a vault in the National Treasury, with its inherent defects, and its promising evolution through 200 years of history, the celebration of the "Miracle at Philadelphia" will, in my view, be a far more meaningful and humbling experience. We will see that the true miracle was not the birth of the Constitution, but its life, a life nurtured through two turbulent centuries of our own making, and a life embodying much good fortune that was not.

Thus, in this bicentennial year, we may not all participate in the festivities with flag waving fervor. Some may more quietly commemorate the suffering, struggle, and sacrifice that has triumphed over much of what was wrong with the original document, and observe the anniversary with hopes not realized and promises not fulfilled. I plan to celebrate the bicentennial of the Constitution as a living document, including the Bill of Rights and the other amendments protecting individual freedoms and human rights.

7

DEMOCRACY'S CHALLENGES
AND THE PRICE OF POWER

During the 1980s, the ideals of free-market liberalism pervaded America's intellectual landscape. The American economy prospered. By 1985, as President Ronald Reagan entered his second term, Soviet leader Mikhail Gorbachev had begun implementing *perestroika*, his design to move Soviet economic and social policy in the direction of free markets and liberal democratic reform. Gorbachev's effort portended an end to the Cold War and the breakup of the Soviet Union, leading scholars of international affairs to declare the ideological battles of the past century over, with capitalism and democracy reigning victorious. Supply-side economic theory, embraced by conservative advocates of free-market capitalism, influenced federal public policy. This theory held that government policies associated with the Great Society discouraged the type of private investment essential to economic growth, and moreover, that such policies were a disincentive to work. "Supply-siders" argued that lower taxes, fewer entitlements for the unemployed and the needy, and less government regulation would encourage hard work, stimulate the economy, and eventually spread new wealth throughout society.

As evident in this chapter's selections, some of America's most prominent intellectuals and scholars reinforced these trends. Gertrude Himmelfarb, for example, reexamined Alexis de Tocqueville's analysis of the English Poor Law and considered seriously the lessons from Victorian England. She maintained, with Tocqueville, that the spirit behind the English Poor Law of the nineteenth century exacerbated poverty by shifting care for the poor from private charity to public relief. In the United States, the same problem resulted from New Deal and Great Society programs. Though well intentioned, public relief laws adversely affected personal virtue, producing a society in which the idea of entitlement was no longer bound to individual character. Such laws thereby corrupted the idea of merit in pursuit of a misguided notion of social justice. What was needed, she concluded, was a return to private charity. Protracted welfare subsidies provided by the political and legal spheres ultimately corroded personal dignity.

Social critics like Himmelfarb and William Kristol extended this argument to the relationship between civic virtue and democratic life. Certainly, they argued, the market is an efficient producer of wealth that justly rewarded merit and hard work, encouraging virtues such as thrift and industry. But democracy requires truly self-regulating individuals extolling virtues beyond those imposed by the market. A "sociology of virtue" was now needed, a return—in Himmelfarb's version of the argument—to Victorian sensibilities and a decorum informed by a sense of shame invoked against unrestrained passions. In extending the argument in this fashion, these critics returned to the republican concerns of many of the Founders, who worried that modes of public life premised on popular sovereignty could be sustained only as long as the people themselves were virtuous.

One important strand of this argument focused on the role of religion in cultivating civic character. Many cultural critics, particularly (but not exclusively) evangelical Protestants, perceived a profound breakdown in personal responsibility since the New Deal, aggravated by what they described as the libertine decay of American culture rooted in the 1960s. Ultimately, they argued, the immorality and personal irresponsibility evident in American culture resulted directly from a sustained assault on religious values, an assault grounded in post-Enlightenment relativism. Such critics thus called for a revival of religion in the public sphere to help govern personal conduct in a manner conducive to a healthy, self-governing society. President George W. Bush's faith-based initiative is an example of the blending of neo-conservative and evangelical thought: it seeks to shift charity from the public sphere to the private, claiming that the private delivery of charity is more efficient and, more importantly, more conducive to the education in virtue needed to foster a responsible citizenry.

The desire to roll back New Deal and Great Society policies, and to reinject religion into the public sphere, continued to resonate politically throughout the 1990s. Conservatives continued to win elections, particularly in the South, which experienced a profound partisan realignment following the 1964 Goldwater presidential campaign. Indeed, in 1994 the Republican Party gained control of Congress for the first time since the Eisenhower administration, and President Bill Clinton—a Democrat—found himself approving historic changes to New Deal social policies like welfare and generally declaring "the era of big government" over.

These battles over elections and control of the policy-making process eventually politicized even judicial nominations. Defenders of welfare programs and the civil liberties rulings of the Supreme Court under Earl Warren sought to block nominees, such as Appellate Judge Robert Bork, whom they believed would overturn precedents supportive of federal social programs and civil and reproductive rights. Critics of political and judicial activism sought to place judges on the bench who would narrowly interpret the Constitution and overturn many of the precedents established by the Warren Court. Indeed, the very nature of constitutional interpretation was under debate, with judicial and political conservatives like Supreme Court Justice Antonin Scalia and former Attorney General Edwin Meese arguing for a "Jurisprudence of Original Intention." This doctrine claims that the Constitution should be interpreted according to the intent of the Framers. In response, critics of this doctrine, like former Justice William Brennan, admonished against becoming captive to "anachronistic views of long-gone generations." According to Brennan and others, there are real theoretical and practical problems with a jurisprudence of original intent. Indeed, for Brennan, the Constitution is deliberately broad in its language and adaptive in its meaning, and is best understood and applied on behalf of the principle of dignity. "If we are to be a shining city upon a hill," Brennan declared, "it will be because of our ceaseless pursuit of the constitutional ideal of human dignity."

Ultimately, the rulings issued by the Supreme Court under William Rehnquist (1986–2005) fell short of conservative expectations, despite the fact that since 1994, seven of the Court's nine members were Republican nominees. The Rehnquist Court reasserted limits to federal power, curtailing Congress' commerce clause power in *United States v. Lopez* (1995) and checking its authority over state governments in *New York v. United States* (1992) and *Printz v. United States* (1997). The Court, however, upheld precedents anathema to many conservatives, including the core rights announced in *Roe v. Wade* (1973) and *Miranda v. Arizona* (1966). Indeed, in some cases the Court issued rulings seemingly reminiscent of the Warren Court, including new restrictions regarding the death penalty, announced in *Roper v. Simmons* (2005), and in its rejection of state laws criminalizing private, consensual sex in *John Geddes Lawrence and Tyron Garner, Petitioners v. Texas* (2003).

Advocates for the humanist traditions grounded in the Enlightenment and in liberal Christianity and Judaism found themselves in the midst of this conservative ascendancy, with their conception of a just society successfully challenged for the first time in a generation. In response, public intellectuals like Daniel Elazar argued for a renewed public commitment to social justice. For Elazar, "it is the task of the individual and the community . . . to strive to be holy by observing not only what are today referred to as prescribed religious rituals, but by doing justice, providing for the poor, maintaining human freedom and dignity, and assuring a basic economic floor for every household." Elazar explains that this is part of the great covenant tradition tracing its roots to ancient Judaism and relevant to a deeper understanding of American democracy. Similarly, the United States Council of Catholic Bishops called for a concerted effort toward "greater economic justice" in line with ethical teachings of the Church. "All members of society," the Council affirmed, have a special obligation to the poor and vulnerable." More than a question of political necessity, this represented a set of moral imperatives generated by Christian ethical principles. But these principles have political implications, for they point toward a conception of liberty requiring the full commitment of public institutions. The policies advocated by the Catholic bishops remind us that despite the recent influence of evangelical Protestants on American politics—typically conservative and Republican—the religious American community does not speak with one mind on issues of social and economic justice.

Other important recent voices defy the easy dichotomies of "liberal" and "conservative" that have shaped American political life over the past half-century. In seeking to renew the American progressive tradition, Cornel West and Roberto Unger evoke the traditions of Ralph Waldo Emerson and John Dewey. They speak with hopefulness of a "religion of possibility" and of an energized, active public that is willing to "submit the country's basic institutions to the experimentalist impulse that is otherwise so strong." While they outline possible alternative institutions, such as a consumption tax, the means are not to be framed within a complex blueprint or single vision for reform, but rather discovered in the spirit of collective cooperation in the experimentalism of democracy. This requires true community, absent the racial, ethnic, and religious divisions that have often prevented the achievement of social and political justice. Notable in their work is the emphasis on possibility, or what Irving Howe, when characterizing Emersonian America, called "the American newness," a frame of mind in which "people start to feel socially invigorated and come to think they can act to determine their fate." Former New York senator Daniel Patrick Moynihan similarly defied the standard liberal and conservative labels in American domestic policy. Long concerned with the state of the American family, Moynihan called for a national family policy, one that transcended conservatives' exclusive emphasis on "values" and liberals' focus on social policy. Moynihan demanded a national commitment to the family, one that fostered a culture of responsibility while providing humane support for those in need.

The deeply contested debate over the power and scope of governmental power has intensified and become more complex since the terrorist attacks of September 11, 2001 (9/11), as the problem of terrorism has thrust itself onto the American political agenda. The threat of terrorism is not new to the United States but in reality has a long pedigree, as the history of lynching African Americans attests. More recently, 9/11 was preceded by an attack on the World Trade Center in 1993, by attacks on U.S. embassies abroad, and by a homegrown attack on the Alfred P. Murrah Federal Building in Oklahoma City. The political responses to 9/11 revived profound questions that have periodically challenged America's commitment to republican principles.[1] The Patriot Act and revelations in 2006 that President Bush ordered the use of secret, warrantless wiretaps of phone conversations involving United States' citizens have renewed tensions between civil liberties and security that Alexander Hamilton foresaw two centuries ago. The president's announcement of a new National Security strategy, the doctrine of preemptive action, along with his assertion of a power to declare even U.S. citizens "enemy combatants"—and on that basis to deny them the rights to habeas corpus and jury trials in civilian courts—represent the return of an enduring problem in republican government: the reconciliation of the necessity of executive power with devotion to the rule of law.

The delicate balance between a commitment to civil liberties and the rule of law, on the one hand, and security on the other, has been challenged by the current president, and the controversial nature of those actions is revealed in the growing dissension among Republicans and conservatives over their political and legal legitimacy. The president's assertion of extensive war powers, including the power to deny

---

1. The word *republican* refers to a type of regime and its supporting principles, not to be confused with the Republican Party.

the right of habeas corpus to U.S. citizens, was rejected by the Court in *Hamdi et al. v. Rumsfeld* (2004), a case in which Justice Scalia delivered a particularly scathing attack against this assertion of presidential power. A disgusted Francis Fukuyama recently declared the era of neoconservatism over, arguing that neoconservatives had lost their way and depicting leading neoconservatives like William Kristol as Leninists obsessed with power alone.

The readings in this chapter, then, remind us that our republican experiment requires an ongoing dedication to core cultural, political, and institutional values, first among them being the commitment to liberty and equality, to the rule of law, to a vibrant marketplace of ideas, and to what James Madison in *Federalist* 51 declared "the end of government": namely, justice.

GARY SNYDER

Before the Stuff Comes Down (1970)

Walking out of the "big E,"
Dope store of the suburb,
        canned music plugging up your ears
        the wide aisles,
        miles of wares
        from nowheres,

Suddenly it's California:
Live oak, brown grasses

Butterflies over the parking lot and the freeway
A Turkey Buzzard power in the blue air.

A while longer,
Still here.

EDWIN MEESE

Address before the American Bar Association (1985)

Welcome to our Federal City. It is an honor to be here today to address the House of Delegates of the American Bar Association. I know the sessions here and those next week in London will be very productive.

It is, of course entirely fitting that we lawyers gather here in this home of our government. We Americans, after all, rightly pride ourselves on having produced the greatest political wonder of the world—a government of laws and not of men. Thomas Paine was right: "America has no monarch: Here the law is king."

Perhaps nothing underscores Paine's assessment quite as much as the eager anticipation with which Americans await the conclusion of the term of the Supreme Court. Lawyers and laymen alike regard the Court not so much with awe as with a healthy respect. The law matters here and the business of our highest court—the subject of my remarks today—is crucially important to our political order.

At this time of year I'm always reminded of how utterly unpredictable the Court can be in rendering its judgments. Several years ago, for example, there was quite a controversial case, *TVA v. Hill.* This dispute involved the EPA and the now-legendary snail darter, a creature of curious purpose and forgotten origins. In any event, when the case was handed down, one publication announced that there was some good news and some bad news. The bad news in their view was that the snail darter had won; the good news was that he didn't use the 14th Amendment.

Once again, the Court has finished a term characterized by a nearly crushing workload. There were

4,935 cases on the docket this year; 179 cases were granted review; 140 cases issued in signed opinions, 11 were per curiam rulings. Such a docket lends credence to Tocqueville's assessment that in America, every political question seems sooner or later to become a legal question. (I won't even mention the statistics of the lower federal courts; let's just say I think we'll all be in business for quite a while.)

In looking back over the work of the Court, I am again struck by how little the statistics tell us about the true role of the Court. In reviewing a term of the Court, it is important to take a moment and reflect upon the proper role of the Supreme Court in our constitutional system.

The intended role of the judiciary generally and the Supreme Court in particular was to serve as the "bulwarks of a limited constitution." The judges, the Founders believed, would not fail to regard the Constitution as "fundamental law" and would "regulate their decisions" by it. As the "faithful guardians of the Constitution," the judges were expected to resist any political effort to depart from the literal provisions of the Constitution. The text of the document and the original intention of those who framed it would be the judicial standard in giving effect to the Constitution.

You will recall that Alexander Hamilton, defending the federal courts to be created by the new Constitution, remarked that the want of a judicial power under the Articles of Confederation had been the crowning defect of that first effort at a national constitution. Ever the consummate lawyer, Hamilton pointed out that "laws are a dead letter without courts to expound and define their true meaning."

The Anti-Federalist Brutus took him to task in the New York press for what the critics of the Constitution considered his naïveté. That prompted Hamilton to write his classic defense of judicial power in *The Federalist*, No. 78.

An independent judiciary under the Constitution, he said, would prove to be the "citadel of public justice and the public security." Courts were "peculiarly essential in a limited constitution." Without them, there would be no security against "the encroachments and oppressions of the representative body," no protection against "unjust and partial" laws.

Hamilton, like his colleague Madison, knew that all political power is "of an encroaching nature." In order to keep the powers created by the Constitution within the boundaries marked out by the Constitution, an independent—but constitutionally bound—Judiciary was essential. The purpose of the Constitution, after all, was the creation of limited but also energetic government, institutions with the power to govern, but also with structures to keep the power in check. As Madison put it, the Constitution enabled the government to control the governed, but also obliged it to control itself.

But even beyond the institutional role, the Court serves the American republic in yet another, more subtle way. The problem of any popular government, of course, is seeing to it that the people obey the laws. There are but two ways: either by physical force or by moral force. In many ways the Court remains the primary moral force in American politics.

Tocqueville put it best:

> The great object of justice is to substitute the idea of right for that of violence, to put intermediaries between the government and the use of its physical force . . .

> It is something astonishing what authority is accorded to the intervention of a court of justice by the general opinion of mankind . . .

> The moral force in which tribunals are clothed makes the use of physical force infinitely rarer, for in most cases it takes its place; and when finally physical force is required, its power is doubled by his moral authority.

By fulfilling its proper function, the Supreme Court contributes both to institutional checks and balances and to the moral undergirding of the entire constitutional edifice. For the Supreme Court is the only national institution that daily grapples with the most fundamental political questions—and defends them with written expositions. Nothing less would serve to perpetuate the sanctity of the rule of law so effectively.

But that is not to suggest that the justices are a body of Platonic guardians. Far from it. The Court is what it was understood to be when the Constitution was framed—a political body. The judicial process is, at its most fundamental level, a political process. While not a partisan political process, it is political in the truest sense of that word. It is a process wherein public deliberations occur over what constitutes the common good under the terms of a written constitution.

As a result, as Benjamin Cardozo pointed out, "the great tides and currents which engulf the rest of men do not turn aside in their course and pass the judges by." Granting that, Tocqueville knew what was required.

As he wrote:

> The federal judges therefore must not only be good citizens and men of education and integrity, . . . (they) must also be statesmen; they must know how to understand the spirit of the age, to confront those obstacles that can be overcome, and to steer out of the current when the tide threatens to carry them away, and with them the sovereignty of the union and obedience to its laws.

On that confident note, let's consider the Court's work this past year.

As has been generally true in recent years, the 1984 term did not yield a coherent set of decisions. Rather, it seemed to produce what one commentator has called a "jurisprudence of idiosyncracy." Taken as a whole, the work of the term defies analysis by any strict standard. It is neither simply liberal nor simply conservative; neither simply activist nor simply restrained; neither simply principled nor simply partisan. The Court this term continued to roam at large in a veritable constitutional forest.

I believe, however, that there are at least three general areas that merit close scrutiny: Federalism, Criminal Law, and Freedom of Religion.

Federalism

In *Garcia v. San Antonio Metropolitan Transit Authority*, the Court displayed what was in the view of this Administration an inaccurate reading of the text of the Constitution and a disregard for the Framers' intention that state and local governments be a buffer against the centralizing tendencies of the national Leviathan. Specifically, five Justices denied that the Tenth Amendment protects states from federal laws regulating the wages and hours of state or local employees. Thus the Court overruled—but barely—a contrary holding in *National League of Cities v. Usery*. We hope

for a day when the Court returns to the basic principles of the Constitution as expressed in *Usery*; such instability in decisions concerning the fundamental principle of federalism does our Constitution no service.

Meanwhile, the constitutional status of the states further suffered as the Court curbed state power to regulate the economy, notably the professions. In *Metropolitan Life Insurance Co. v. Ward*, the Court used the Equal Protection Clause to spear an Alabama insurance tax on gross premiums preferring in-state companies over out-of-state rivals. In *New Hampshire v. Piper*, the Court held that the Privileges and Immunities Clause of Article IV barred New Hampshire from completely excluding a nonresident from admission to its bar. With the apparent policy objective of creating unfettered national markets for occupations before its eyes, the court unleashed Article IV against any state preference for residents involving the professions or service industries. *Hicklin v. Orbeck* and *Baldwin v. Montana Fish and Game Commission* are illustrative.

On the other hand, we gratefully acknowledge the respect shown by the Court for state and local sovereignty in a number of cases, including *Atascadero State Hospital v. Scanlon*.

In *Atascadero*, a case involving violations of § 504 of Rehabilitation Act of 1973, the Court honored the Eleventh Amendment in limiting private damage suits against states. Congress, it said, must express its intent to expose states to liability affirmatively and clearly.

In *Town of Haile v. City of Eau Claire*, the Court found that active state supervision of municipal activity was not required to cloak municipalities with immunity under the Sherman Act.

And, states were judged able to confer Sherman Act immunity upon private parties in *Southern Motor Carrier Rate Conference v. U.S.* They must, said the Court, clearly articulate and affirmatively express a policy to displace competition with compelling anti-competitive action so long as the private action is actively supervised by the state.

And, in *Oklahoma City v. Tuttle*, the Court held that a single incident of unconstitutional and egregious police misconduct is insufficient to support a Section 1983 action against municipalities for allegedly inadequate police training or supervision.

Our view is that federalism is one of the most basic principles of our Constitution. By allowing the states sovereignty sufficient to govern we better secure our ultimate goal of political liberty through decentralized government. We do not advocate states' rights; we advocate states' responsibilities. We need to remember that state and local governments are not inevitably abusive of rights. It was, after all, at the turn of the century the states that were the laboratories of social and economic progress—and the federal courts that blocked their way. We believe that there is a proper constitutional sphere for state governance under our scheme of limited, popular government.

Criminal Law

Recognizing, perhaps, that the nation is in the throes of a drug epidemic which has severely increased the burden borne by law enforcement officers, the Court took a more progressive stance on the Fourth Amendment, undoing some of the damage previously done by its piece-meal incorporation through the Fourteenth Amendment. Advancing from its landmark *Leon* decision in 1984 which created a good-faith exception to the Exclusionary Rule when a flawed warrant is obtained by police, the Court permitted warrantless searches under certain limited circumstances.

The most prominent among these Fourth Amendment cases were:

New Jersey v. T.L.O., which upheld warrantless searches of public school students based or reasonable suspicion that a law or school rule has been violated; this also restored a clear local authority over another problem in our society, school discipline; *California v. Carney* which upheld the warrantless search of a mobile home; *U.S. v. Sharpe*, which approved on-the-spot detention of a suspect for preliminary questioning and investigation; *U.S. v. Johns*, upholding the warrantless search of sealed packages in a car several days after their removal by police who possessed probable cause to believe the vehicle contained contraband; *U.S. v. Hensley*, which permitted a warrantless investigatory stop based on an unsworn flyer from a neighboring police department which possessed reasonable suspicion that the detainee was a felon, *Hayes v. Florida*, which tacitly endorsed warrantless seizures in the field for the purpose of fingerprinting based on reasonable suspicion of

criminal activity; *U.S. v. Hernandez*, which upheld border detentions and warrantless searches by customs officials based on reasonable suspicion of criminal activity.

Similarly, the Court took steps this term to place the *Miranda* ruling in proper perspective stressing its origin in the court rather than in the Constitution. In *Oregon v. Elstad*, the Court held that failure to administer *Miranda* warnings and the consequent receipt of a confession ordinarily will not taint a second confession after *Miranda* warnings are received.

The enforcement of criminal law remains one of our most important efforts. It is crucial that the state and local authorities—from the police to the prosecutors—be able to combat the growing tide of crime effectively. Toward that end we advocate a due regard for the rights of the accused—but also a due regard for the keeping of the public peace and the safety and happiness of the people. We will continue to press for a proper scope for the rules of exclusion, lest truth in the fact-finding process be allowed to suffer.

I have mentioned the areas of Federalism and Criminal Law, now I will turn to the Religion cases.

Religion

Most probably, this term will be best remembered for the decisions concerning the Establishment Clause of the First Amendment. The Court continued to apply its standard three-pronged test. Four cases merit mention.

In the first, *City of Grand Rapids v. Ball*, the Court nullified Shared Time and Community Education programs offered within parochial schools. Although the programs provided instruction in nonsectarian subjects, and were taught by full-time or part-time public school teachers, the Court nonetheless found that they promoted religion in three ways: the state-paid instructors might wittingly or unwittingly indoctrinate students; the symbolic union of church and state interest in state-provided instruction signaled support for religion; and, the programs in effect subsidized the religious functions of parochial schools by relieving them of responsibility for teaching some secular subjects. The symbolism test proposed in *Ball* precludes virtually any state assistance offered to parochial schools.

In *Aguilar v. Felton*, the Court invalidated a program of secular instruction for low-income students in sectarian schools, provided by public school teachers who were supervised to safeguard students against efforts of indoctrination.

With a bewildering Catch-22 logic, the Court declared that the supervisory safeguards at issue in the statute constituted unconstitutional government entanglement: "The religious school, which has as a primary purpose the advancement and preservation of a particular religion, must endure the ongoing presence of state personnel whose primary purpose is to monitor teachers and students in an attempt to guard against the infiltration of religious thought." Secretary of Education William Bennett has suggested such logic may reveal a "disdain" for education as well as religion.

In *Wallace v. Jaffree*, the Court said in essence that states may set aside time in public schools for meditation or reflection so long as the legislation does not stipulate that it be used for voluntary prayer. Of course, what the Court gave with one hand, it took back with the other; the Alabama moment of silence statute failed to pass muster.

In *Thornton v. Caldor*, a 7–2 majority overturned a state law prohibiting private employees from discharging an employee for refusing to work on his Sabbath. We hope that this does not mean that the Court is abandoning last term's first but tentative steps toward state accommodation of religion in the creche case.

In trying to make sense of the religion cases—from whichever side—it is important to remember how this body of tangled case law came about. Most Americans forget that it was not until 1925, in *Gitlow v. New York*, that any provision of the Bill of Rights was applied to the states. Nor was it until 1947 that the Establishment Clause was made applicable to the states through the 14th Amendment. This is striking because the Bill of Rights, as debated, created and ratified, was designed to apply only to the national government.

The Bill of Rights came about largely as the result of the demands of the critics of the new Constitution, the unfortunately misnamed Anti-Federalists. They feared, as George Mason of Virginia put it, that in time the national authority would "devour" the states. Since each state had a bill of rights, it was only

appropriate that so powerful a national government as that created by the Constitution have one as well. Though Hamilton insisted a Bill of Rights was not necessary and even destructive, and Madison (at least at first) thought a Bill of Rights to be but a "parchment barrier" to political power, the Federalists agreed to add a Bill of Rights.

Though the first ten amendments that were ultimately ratified fell far short of what the Anti-Federalists desired, both Federalists and Anti-Federalists agreed that the amendments were a curb on national power.

When this view was questioned before the Supreme Court in *Barron v. Baltimore* (1833), Chief Justice Marshall wholeheartedly agreed. The Constitution said what it meant and meant what it said. Neither political expediency nor judicial desire was sufficient to change the clear import of the language of the Constitution. The Bill of Rights did not apply to the states—and, he said, that was that.

Until 1925, that is.

Since then a good portion of constitutional adjudication has been aimed at extending the scope of the doctrine of incorporation. But the most that can be done is to expand the scope; nothing can be done to shore up the intellectually shaky foundation upon which the doctrine rests. And nowhere else has the principle of federalism been dealt so politically violent and constitutionally suspect a blow as by the theory of incorporation.

In thinking particularly of the use to which the First Amendment has been put in the area of religion, one finds much merit in Justice Rehnquist's recent dissent in *Jaffree*. "It is impossible," Justice Rehnquist argued, "to build sound constitutional doctrine upon a mistaken understanding of constitutional history." His conclusion was bluntly to the point: "If a constitutional theory has no basis in the history of the amendment it seeks to interpret, it is difficult to apply and yields unprincipled results."

The point, of course, is that the Establishment Clause of the First Amendment was designed to prohibit Congress from establishing a national church. The belief was that the Constitution should not allow Congress to designate a particular faith or sect as politically above the rest. But to have argued, as is popular today, that the amendment demands a strict neutrality between religion and irreligion would have struck the founding generation as bizarre. The purpose was to prohibit religious tyranny, not to undermine religion generally.

In considering these areas of adjudication—Federalism, Criminal Law, and Religion—it seems fair to conclude that far too many of the Court's opinions were, on the whole, more policy choices than articulations of constitutional principle. The voting blocs, the arguments, all reveal a greater allegiance to what the Court thinks constitutes sound public policy than a deference to what the Constitution—its text and intention—may demand.

It is also safe to say that until there emerges a coherent jurisprudential stance, the work of the Court will continue in this ad hoc fashion. But that is not to argue for any jurisprudence.

In my opinion a drift back toward the radical egalitarianism and expansive civil libertarianism of the Warren Court would once again be a threat to the notion of limited but energetic government.

What, then, should a constitutional jurisprudence actually be? It should be a Jurisprudence of Original Intention. By seeking to judge policies in light of principles, rather than remold principles in light of policies, the Court could avoid both the charge of incoherence and the charge of being either too conservative or too liberal.

A jurisprudence seriously aimed at the explication of original intention would produce defensible principles of government that would not be tainted by ideological predilection.

This belief in a Jurisprudence of Original Intention also reflects a deeply rooted commitment to the idea of democracy. The Constitution represents the consent of the governed to the structures and powers of the government. The Constitution is the fundamental will of the people; that is why it is the fundamental law. To allow the courts to govern simply by what it views at the time as fair and decent, is a scheme of government no longer popular; the idea of democracy has suffered. The permanence of the Constitution has been weakened. A Constitution that is viewed as only what the judges say it is, is no longer a constitution in the true sense.

Those who framed the Constitution chose their words carefully; they debated at great length the most minute points. The language they chose meant something. It is incumbent upon the Court to determine what that meaning was. This is not a shockingly new theory; nor is it arcane or archaic.

Joseph Story, who was in a way a lawyer's everyman—lawyer, justice, and teacher of law—had a theory of judging that merits reconsideration.

Though speaking specifically of the Constitution, his logic reaches to statutory construction as well.

> In construing the Constitution of the United States, we are in the first instance to consider, what are its nature and objects, its scope and design, as apparent from the structure of the instrument, viewed as a whole and also viewed in its component parts. Where its words are plain, clear and determinate, they require no interpretation. . . . Where the words admit of two senses, each of which is conformable to general usage, that sense is to be adopted, which without departing from the literal import of the words, best harmonizes with the nature and objects, the scope and design of the instrument.

A Jurisprudence of Original Intention would take seriously the admonition of Justice Story's friend and colleague, John Marshall, in *Marbury*, that the Constitution is a limitation on judicial power as well as executive and legislative. That is what Chief Justice Marshall meant in *McCulloch* when he cautioned judges never to forget it is a constitution they are expounding.

It has been and will continue to be the policy of this administration to press for a Jurisprudence of Original Intention. In the cases we file and those we join as amicus, we will endeavor to resurrect the original meaning of constitutional provisions and statutes as the only reliable guide for judgment.

Within this context, let me reaffirm our commitment to pursuing the policies most necessary to public justice. We will continue our vigorous enforcement of civil rights laws; we will not rest till unlawful discrimination ceases. We will continue our all out war on drugs—both supply and demand; both national and international in scope. We intend to bolster public safety by a persistent war on crime. We will endeavor to stem the growing tide of pornography and its attendant costs, sexual and child abuse. We will be battling the heretofore largely ignored legal cancer of white collar crime; and its cousin, defense procurement fraud. And finally, as we still reel as a people, I pledge to you our commitment to fight terrorism here and abroad. For as long as the innocent are fair prey for the barbarians of this world, civilization is not safe.

We will pursue our agenda within the context of our written Constitution of limited yet energetic powers. Our guide in every case will be the sanctity of the rule of law and the proper limits of governmental power.

It is our belief that only "the sense in which the Constitution was accepted and ratified by the nation," and only the sense in which laws were drafted and passed provide a solid foundation for adjudication. Any other standard suffers the defect of pouring new meaning into old words, thus creating new powers and new rights totally at odds with the logic of our Constitution and its commitment to the rule of law.

Thank you.

William J. Brennan, Jr.

Address before the Text and Teaching Symposium, Georgetown University (1985)

I am deeply grateful for the invitation to participate in the "Text and Teaching" symposium. This rare opportunity to explore classic texts with participants of such wisdom, acumen and insight as those who have preceded and will follow me to this podium is indeed exhilarating. But it is also humbling. Even to approximate the standards of excellence of these vigorous and graceful intellects is a daunting task. I am honored that you have afforded me this opportunity to try.

It will perhaps not surprise you that the text I have chosen for exploration is the amended Constitution of the United States, which, of course, entrenches the Bill of Rights and the Civil War amendments, and draws sustenance from the bedrock principles of another great text, the Magna Carta. So fashioned, the Constitution embodies the aspiration to social justice, brotherhood, and human dignity that brought this nation into being. The Declaration of Independence, the Constitution and the Bill of Rights solemnly committed the United States to be a country where the dignity and rights of all persons were equal before all authority. In all candor we must concede that part of this egalitarianism in America has

been more pretension than realized fact. But we are an aspiring people, a people with faith in progress. Our amended Constitution is the lodestar for our aspirations. Like every text worth reading, it is not crystalline. The phrasing is broad and the limitations of its provisions are not clearly marked. Its majestic generalities and ennobling pronouncements are both luminous and obscure. This ambiguity of course calls forth interpretation, the interaction of reader and text. The encounter with the constitutional text has been, in many senses, my life's work.

My approach to this text may differ from the approach of other participants in this symposium to their texts. Yet such differences may themselves stimulate reflection about what it is we do when we "interpret" a text. Thus I will attempt to elucidate my approach to the text as well as my substantive interpretation.

Perhaps the foremost difference is the fact that my encounters with the constitutional text are not purely or even primarily introspective; the Constitution cannot be for me simply a contemplative haven for private moral reflection. My relation to this great text is inescapably public. That is not to say that my reading of the text is not a personal reading, only that the personal reading perforce occurs in a public context, and is open to critical scrutiny from all quarters.

The Constitution is fundamentally a public text—the monumental charter of a government and a people—and a Justice of the Supreme Court must apply it to resolve public controversies. For, from our beginnings, a most important consequence of the constitutionally created separation of powers has been the American habit, extraordinary to other democracies, of casting social, economic, philosophical and political questions in the form of law suits, in an attempt to secure ultimate resolution by the Supreme Court. In this way, important aspects of the most fundamental issues confronting our democracy may finally arrive in the Supreme Court for judicial determination. Not infrequently, these are the issues upon which contemporary society is most deeply divided. They arouse our deepest emotions. The main burden of my twenty-nine terms on the Supreme Court has thus been to wrestle with the Constitution in this heightened public context, to draw meaning from the text in order to resolve public controversies.

Two other aspects of my relation to this text warrant mention. First, constitutional interpretation for a federal judge is, for the most part, obligatory. When litigants approach the bar of court to adjudicate a constitutional dispute, they may justifiably demand an answer. Judges cannot avoid a definitive interpretation because they feel unable to, or would prefer not to, penetrate to the full meaning of the Constitution's provisions. Unlike literary critics, judges cannot merely savor the tensions or revel in the ambiguities inhering in the text—judges must resolve them.

Second, consequences flow from a justice's interpretation in a direct and immediate way. A judicial decision respecting the incompatibility of Jim Crow with a constitutional guarantee of equality is not simply a contemplative exercise in defining the shape of a just society. It is an order—supported by the full coercive power of the State—that the present society change in a fundamental aspect. Under such circumstances the process of deciding can be a lonely, troubling experience for fallible human beings conscious that their best may not be adequate to the challenge. We Justices are certainly aware that we are not final

because we are infallible; we know that we are infallible only because we are. [. . .]

[The] three defining characteristics of my relation to the constitutional text—its public nature, obligatory character, and consequentialist aspect—cannot help but influence the way I read that text. When Justices interpret the Constitution they speak for their community, not for themselves alone. The act of interpretation must be undertaken with full consciousness that it is, in a very real sense, the community's interpretation that is sought. Justices are not platonic guardians appointed to wield authority according to their personal moral predilections. Precisely because coercive force must attend any judicial decision to countermand the will of a contemporary majority, the Justices must render constitutional interpretations that are received as legitimate. The source of legitimacy is, of course, a wellspring of controversy in legal and political circles. At the core of the debate is what the late Yale Law School professor Alexander Bickel labeled "the counter-majoritarian difficulty." Our commitment to self-governance in a representative democracy must be reconciled with vesting in electorally unaccountable Justices the power to invalidate the expressed desires of representative bodies on the ground of inconsistency with higher law. Because judicial power resides in the authority to give meaning to the Constitution, the debate is really a debate about how to read the text, about constraints on what is legitimate interpretation.

There are those who find legitimacy in fidelity to what they call "the intentions of the Framers." In its most doctrinaire incarnation, this view demands that Justices discern exactly what the Framers thought about the question under consideration and simply follow that intention in resolving the case before them. It is a view that feigns self-effacing deference to the specific judgments of those who forged our original social compact. But in truth it is little more than arrogance cloaked as humility. It is arrogant to pretend that from our vantage we can gauge accurately the intent of the Framers on application of principle to specific, contemporary questions. All too often, sources of potential enlightenment such as records of the ratification debates provide sparse or ambiguous evidence of the original intention. Typically, all that can be gleaned is that the Framers themselves did not agree about the application or meaning of particular constitutional provisions, and hid their differences in cloaks of generality. Indeed, it is far from clear whose intention is relevant—that of the drafters, the congressional disputants, or the ratifiers in the states?—or even whether the idea of an original intention is a coherent way of thinking about a jointly drafted document drawing its authority from a general assent of the states. And apart from the problematic nature of the sources, our distance of two centuries cannot but work as a prism refracting all we perceive. One cannot help but speculate that the chorus of lamentations calling for interpretation faithful to "original intention"—and proposing nullification of interpretations that fail this quick litmus test—must inevitably come from persons who have no familiarity with the historical record.

Perhaps most importantly, while proponents of this facile historicism justify it as a depoliticization of the judiciary, the political underpinnings of such a choice should not escape notice. A position that upholds constitutional claims only if they were within the specific contemplation of the Framers in effect establishes a presumption of resolving textual ambiguities against the claim of constitutional right. It is far from clear what justifies such a presumption against claims of right. Nothing intrinsic in the nature of interpretation—if there is such a thing as the "nature" of interpretation—commands such a passive approach to ambiguity. This is a choice no less political than any other; it expresses antipathy to claims of the minority rights against the majority. Those who would restrict claims of right to the values of 1789 specifically articulated in the Constitution turn a blind eye to social progress and eschew adaptation of overarching principles to changes of social circumstance.

Another, perhaps more sophisticated, response to the potential power of judicial interpretation stresses democratic theory: because ours is a government of the people's elected representatives, substantive value choices should by and large be left to them. This view emphasizes not the transcendent historical authority of the framers but the predominant contemporary authority of the elected branches of government. Yet it has similar consequences for the nature of proper judicial interpretation. Faith in the majoritarian process counsels restraint. Even

under more expansive formulations of this approach, judicial review is appropriate only to the extent of ensuring that our democratic process functions smoothly. Thus, for example, we would protect freedom of speech merely to ensure that the people are heard by their representatives, rather than as a separate, substantive value. When, by contrast, society tosses up to the Supreme Court a dispute that would require invalidation of a legislature's substantive policy choice, the Court generally would stay its hand because the Constitution was meant as a plan of government and not as an embodiment of fundamental substantive values.

The view that all matters of substantive policy should be resolved through the majoritarian process has appeal under some circumstances, but I think it ultimately will not do. Unabashed enshrinement of majority will would permit the imposition of a social caste system or wholesale confiscation of property so long as a majority of the authorized legislative body, fairly elected, approved. Our Constitution could not abide such a situation. It is the very purpose of a Constitution—and particularly of the Bill of Rights—to declare certain values transcendent, beyond the reach of temporary political majorities. The majoritarian process cannot be expected to rectify claims of minority right that arise as a response to the outcomes of that very majoritarian process. As James Madison put it:

> The prescriptions in favor of liberty ought to be leveled against that quarter where the greatest danger lies, namely, that which possesses the highest prerogative of power. But this is not found in either the Executive or Legislative departments of Government, but in the body of the people, operating by the majority against the minority. (I Annals 437)

Faith in democracy is one thing, blind faith quite another. Those who drafted our Constitution understood the difference. One cannot read the text without admitting that it embodies substantive value choices; it places certain values beyond the power of any legislature. Obvious are the separation of powers; the privilege of the Writ of Habeas Corpus; prohibition of Bills of Attainder and *ex post facto* laws; prohibition of cruel and unusual punishments; the requirement of just compensation for official taking of property; the prohibition of laws tending to establish religion or enjoining the free exercise of religion; and, since the Civil War, the banishment of slavery and official race discrimination. With respect to at least such principles, we simply have not constituted ourselves as strict utilitarians. While the Constitution may be amended, such amendments require an immense effort by the People as a whole.

To remain faithful to the content of the Constitution, therefore, an approach to interpreting the text must account for the existence of these substantive value choices, and must accept the ambiguity inherent in the effort to apply them to modern circumstances. The Framers discerned fundamental principles through struggles against particular malefactions of the Crown; the struggle shapes the particular contours of the articulated principles. But our acceptance of the fundamental principles has not and should not bind us to those precise, at times anachronistic, contours. Successive generations of Americans have continued to respect these fundamental choices and adopt them as their own guide to evaluating quite different historical practices. Each generation has the choice to overrule or add to the fundamental principles enunciated by the Framers; the Constitution can be amended or it can be ignored. Yet with respect to its fundamental principles, the text has suffered neither fate. Thus, if I may borrow the words of an esteemed predecessor, Justice Robert Jackson, the burden of judicial interpretation is to translate "the majestic generalities of the Bill of Rights, conceived as part of the pattern of liberal government in the eighteenth century, into concrete restraints on officials dealing with the problems of the twentieth century." *Board of Education v. Barnette* [319 U.S. 624, 639, (1943)]

We current Justices read the Constitution in the only way that we can: as Twentieth Century Americans. We look to the history of the time of framing and to the intervening history of interpretation. But the ultimate question must be, what do the words of the text mean in our time. For the genius of the Constitution rests not in any static meaning it might have had in a world that is dead and gone, but in the adaptability of its great principles to cope with current problems and current needs. What the constitutional fundamentals meant to the wisdom of other times cannot be their measure to the vision of our

time. Similarly, what those fundamentals mean for us, our descendants will learn, cannot be the measure to the vision of their time. This realization is not, I assure you, a novel one of my own creation. Permit me to quote from one of the opinions of our Court, *Weems v. United States* [217 U.S. 349 (1910)] written nearly a century ago:

> Time works changes, brings into existence new conditions and purposes. Therefore, a principle to be vital must be capable of wider application than the mischief which gave it birth. This is peculiarly true of constitutions. They are not ephemeral enactments, designed to meet passing occasions. They are, to use the words of Chief Justice John Marshall, "designed to approach immortality as nearly as human institutions can approach it." The future is their care and provision or events of good and bad tendencies of which no prophesy can be made. In the application of a constitution, therefore, our contemplation cannot be only of what has been, but of what may be.

Interpretation must account for the transformative purpose of the text. Our Constitution was not intended to preserve a preexisting society but to make a new one, to put in place new principles that the prior political community had not sufficiently recognized. Thus, for example, when we interpret the Civil War Amendments to the charter—abolishing slavery, guaranteeing blacks equality under law, and guaranteeing blacks the right to vote—we must remember that those who put them in place had no desire to enshrine the status quo. Their goal was to make over their world, to eliminate all vestige of slave caste.

Having discussed at some length how I, as a Supreme Court Justice, interact with this text, I think it time to turn to the fruits of this discourse. For the Constitution is a sublime oration on the dignity of man, a bold commitment by a people to the ideal of libertarian dignity protected through law. Some reflection is perhaps required before this can be seen.

The Constitution on its face is, in large measure, a structuring text, a blueprint for government. And when the text is not prescribing the form of government it is limiting the powers of that government. The original document, before addition of any of the amendments, does not speak primarily of the rights of man, but of the abilities and disabilities of government. When one reflects upon the text's preoccupation with the scope of government as well as its shape, however, one comes to understand that what this text is about is the relationship of the individual and the state. The text marks the metes and bounds of official authority and individual autonomy. When one studies the boundary that the text marks out, one gets a sense of the vision of the individual embodied in the Constitution.

As augmented by the Bill of Rights and the Civil War Amendments, this text is a sparkling vision of the supremacy of the human dignity of every individual. This vision is reflected in the very choice of democratic self-governance: the supreme value of a democracy is the presumed worth of each individual. And this vision manifests itself most dramatically in the specific prohibitions of the Bill of Rights, a term which I henceforth will apply to describe not only the original first eight amendments, but the Civil War amendments as well. It is a vision that has guided us as a people throughout our history, although the precise rules by which we have protected fundamental human dignity have been transformed over time in response to both transformations of social condition and evolution of our concepts of human dignity.

Until the end of the nineteenth century, freedom and dignity in our country found meaningful protection in the institution of real property. In a society still largely agricultural, a piece of land provided men not just with sustenance but with the means of economic independence, a necessary precondition of political independence and expression. Not surprisingly, property relationships formed the heart of litigation and of legal practice, and lawyers and judges tended to think stable property relationships the highest aim of the law.

But the days when common law property relationships dominated litigation and legal practice are past. To a growing extent economic existence now depends on less certain relationships with government— licenses, employment, contracts, subsidies, unemployment benefits, tax exemptions, welfare and the like. Government participation in the economic existence of individuals is pervasive and deep. Administrative matters and other dealings with government are at the epicenter of the exploding law. We turn to government and to the law for controls which would never have been expected or tolerated before this century, when a man's answer to economic oppression or difficulty was to move two hundred miles west. Now hundreds of thousands of Americans live entire lives without any real prospect of the dignity and autonomy that ownership of real property could confer. Protection of the human dignity of such citizens requires a much modified view of the proper relationship of individual and state.

In general, problems of the relationship of the citizen with government have multiplied and thus have engendered some of the most important constitutional issues of the day. As government acts ever more deeply upon those areas of our lives once marked "private," there is an even greater need to see that individual rights are not curtailed or cheapened in the interest of what may temporarily appear to be the "public good." And as government continues in its role of provider for so many of our disadvantaged citizens, there is an even greater need to ensure that government act with integrity and consistency in its dealings with these citizens. To put this another way, the possibilities for collision between government activity and individual rights will increase as the power and authority of government itself expands, and this growth, in turn, heightens the need for constant vigilance at the collision points. If our free society is to endure, those who govern must recognize human dignity and accept the enforcement of constitutional limitations on their power conceived by the Framers to be necessary to preserve that dignity and the air of freedom which is our proudest heritage. Such recognition will not come from a technical understanding of the organs of government, or the new forms of wealth they administer. It requires something different, something deeper—a personal confrontation with the well-springs of our society. Solutions of constitutional questions from that perspective have become the great challenge of the modern era. All the talk in the last half-decade about shrinking the government does not alter this reality or the challenge it imposes. The modern activist state is a concomitant of the complexity of modern society; it is inevitably with us. We must meet the challenge rather than wish it were not before us.

The challenge is essentially, of course, one to the capacity of our constitutional structure to foster and protect the freedom, the dignity, and the rights of all persons within our borders, which it is the great design of the Constitution to secure. During the time of my public service this challenge has largely taken shape within the confines of the interpretive question whether the specific guarantees of the Bill of Rights operate as restraints on the power of State government. We recognize the Bill of Rights as the primary source of express information as to what is meant by constitutional liberty. The safeguards enshrined in it are deeply etched in the foundation of America's freedoms. Each is a protection with centuries of history behind it, often dearly bought with the blood and lives of people determined to prevent oppression by their rulers. The first eight Amendments, however, were added to the Constitution to operate solely against federal power. It was not until the Thirteenth and Fourteenth Amendments were added, in 1865 and 1868, in response to a demand for national protection against abuses of state power, that the Constitution could be interpreted to require application of the first eight amendments to the states.

It was in particular the Fourteenth Amendment's guarantee that no person be deprived of life, liberty or property without process of law that led us to apply many of the specific guarantees of the Bill of Rights to the States. In my judgment, Justice Cardozo best captured the reasoning that brought us to such decisions when he described what the Court has done as a process by which the guarantees "have been taken over from the earlier articles of the federal bill of rights and brought within the Fourteenth Amendment by a process of absorption . . . [that] has had its source in the belief that neither liberty nor justice would exist if [those guarantees] . . . were sacrificed." *Palko v. Connecticut* [302 U.S. 319, 326 (1937)] But this process of absorption was neither swift nor steady. As late as 1922 only the Fifth Amendment guarantee of just compensation for official taking of property had been given force against the states. Between then and 1956 only the First Amendment guarantees of speech and conscience and the Fourth Amendment ban of unreasonable searches and seizures had been incorporated—the latter, however, without the exclusionary rule to give it force. As late as 1961, I could stand before a distinguished assemblage of the bar at New York University's James Madison Lecture and list the following as guarantees that

had not been thought to be sufficiently fundamental to the protection of human dignity so as to be enforced against the states: the prohibition of cruel and unusual punishments, the right against self-incrimination, the right to assistance of counsel in a criminal trial, the right to confront witnesses, the right to compulsory process, the right not to be placed in jeopardy of life or limb more than once upon accusation of a crime, the right not to have illegally obtained evidence introduced at a criminal trial, and the right to a jury of one's peers.

The history of the quarter century following that Madison Lecture need not be told in great detail. Suffice it to say that each of the guarantees listed above has been recognized as a fundamental aspect of ordered liberty. Of course, the above catalogue encompasses only the rights of the criminally accused, those caught, rightly or wrongly, in the maw of the criminal justice system. But it has been well said that there is no better test of a society than how it treats those accused of transgressing against it. Indeed, it is because we recognize that incarceration strips a man of his dignity that we demand strict adherence to fair procedure and proof of guilt beyond a reasonable doubt before taking such a drastic step. These requirements are, as Justice Harlan once said, "bottomed on a fundamental value determination of our society that it is far worse to convict an innocent man than to let a guilty man go free." *In re Winship* [397 U.S. 358, 372, (1970)] (concurring opinion). There is no worse injustice than wrongly to strip a man of his dignity. And our adherence to the constitutional vision of human dignity is so strict that even after convicting a person according to these stringent standards, we demand that his dignity be infringed only to the extent appropriate to the crime and never by means of wanton infliction of pain or deprivation. I interpret the Constitution plainly to embody these fundamental values.

Of course the constitutional vision of human dignity has, in this past quarter century, infused far more than our decisions about the criminal process. Recognition of the principle of "one person, one vote" as a constitutional one redeems the promise of self-governance by affirming the essential dignity of every citizen in the right to equal participation in the democratic process. Recognition of so-called "new property" rights in those receiving government entitlements affirms the essential dignity of the least fortunate among us by demanding that government treat with decency, integrity and consistency those dependent on its benefits for their very survival. After all, a legislative majority initially decides to create governmental entitlements; the Constitution's Due Process Clause merely provides protection for entitlements thought necessary by society as a whole. Such due process rights prohibit government from imposing the devil's bargain of bartering away human dignity in exchange for human sustenance. Likewise, recognition of full equality for women—equal protection of the laws—ensures that gender has no bearing on claims to human dignity.

Recognition of broad and deep rights of expression and of conscience reaffirm the vision of human dignity in many ways. They too redeem the promise of self-governance by facilitating—indeed demanding—robust, uninhibited and wide-open debate on issues of public importance. Such public debate is of course vital to the development and dissemination of political ideas. As importantly, robust public discussion is the crucible in which personal political convictions are forged. In our democracy, such discussion is a political duty, it is the essence of self government. The constitutional vision of human dignity rejects the possibility of political orthodoxy imposed from above; it respects the right of each individual to form and to express political judgments, however far they may deviate from the mainstream and however unsettling they might be to the powerful or the elite. Recognition of these rights of expression and conscience also frees up the private space for both intellectual and spiritual development free of government dominance, either blatant or subtle. Justice Brandeis put it so well sixty years ago when he wrote: "Those who won our independence believed that the final end of the State was to make men free to develop their faculties; and that in its government the deliberative forces should prevail over the arbitrary. They valued liberty both as an end and as a means." *Whitney v. California* [274 U.S. 357, 375 (1927)] (concurring opinion).

I do not mean to suggest that we have in the last quarter century achieved a comprehensive definition of the constitutional ideal of human dignity. We are still striving toward that goal, and doubtless it will be an eternal quest. For if the interaction of this Justice and the constitutional text over the years confirms

any single proposition, it is that the demands of human dignity will never cease to evolve.

Indeed, I cannot in good conscience refrain from mention of one grave and crucial respect in which we continue, in my judgment, to fall short of the constitutional vision of human dignity. It is in our continued tolerance of State-administered execution as a form of punishment. I make it a practice not to comment on the constitutional issues that come before the Court, but my position on this issue, of course, has been for some time fixed and immutable. I think I can venture some thoughts on this particular subject without transgressing my usual guideline too severely.

As I interpret the Constitution, capital punishment is under all circumstances cruel and unusual punishment prohibited by the Eighth and Fourteenth Amendments. This is a position of which I imagine you are not unaware. Much discussion of the merits of capital punishment has in recent years focused on the potential arbitrariness that attends its administration, and I have no doubt that such arbitrariness is a grave wrong. But for me, the wrong of capital punishment transcends such procedural issues. As I have said in my opinions, I view the Eighth Amendment's prohibition of cruel and unusual punishments as embodying to a unique degree moral principles that substantively restrain the punishments our civilized society may impose on those persons who transgress its laws. Foremost among the moral principles recognized in our cases and inherent in the prohibition is the primary principle that the State, even as it punishes, must treat its citizens in a manner consistent with their intrinsic worth as human beings. A punishment must not be so severe as to be utterly and irreversibly degrading to the very essence of human dignity. Death for whatever crime and under all circumstances is a truly awesome punishment. The calculated killing of a human being by the State involves, by its very nature, an absolute denial of the executed person's humanity. The most vile murder does not, in my view, release the State from constitutional restraints on the destruction of human dignity. Yet an executed person has lost the very right to have rights, now or ever. For me, then, the fatal constitutional infirmity of capital punishment is that it treats members of the human race as nonhumans, as objects to be toyed with and discarded. It is, indeed, "cruel and unusual." It is thus inconsistent with the fundamental premise of the Clause that even the most base criminal remains a human being possessed of some potential, at least, for common human dignity.

This is an interpretation to which a majority of my fellow Justices—not to mention, it would seem, a majority of my fellow countrymen—does not subscribe. Perhaps you find my adherence to it, and my recurrent publication of it, simply contrary, tiresome, or quixotic. Or perhaps you see in it a refusal to abide by the judicial principle of *stare decisis,* obedience to precedent. In my judgment, however, the unique interpretive role of the Supreme Court with respect to the Constitution demands some flexibility with respect to the call of *stare decisis.* Because we are the last word on the meaning of the Constitution, our views must be subject to revision over time, or the Constitution falls captive, again, to the anachronistic views of long-gone generations. I mentioned earlier the judge's role in seeking out the community's interpretation of the Constitutional text. Yet, again in my judgment, when a Justice perceives an interpretation of the text to have departed so far from its essential meaning, that Justice is bound, by a larger constitutional duty to the community, to expose the departure and point toward a different path. On this issue, the death penalty, I hope to embody a community striving for human dignity for all, although perhaps not yet arrived.

You have doubtless observed that this description of my personal encounter with the constitutional text has in large portion been a discussion of public developments in constitutional doctrine over the last century. That, as I suggested at the outset, is inevitable because my interpretive career has demanded a public reading of the text. This public encounter with the text, however, has been a profound source of personal inspiration. The vision of human dignity embodied there is deeply moving. It is timeless. It has inspired Americans for two centuries and it will continue to inspire as it continues to evolve. That evolutionary process is inevitable and indeed, it is the true interpretive genius of the text.

If we are to be as a shining city upon a hill, it will be because of our ceaseless pursuit of the constitutional ideal of human dignity. For the political and legal ideals that form the foundation of much that is best in American institutions—ideals jealously preserved and guarded throughout our history—still form the vital force in creative political thought and activity within the nation today. As we adapt our institutions to the ever-changing conditions of national and international life, those ideals of human dignity—liberty and justice for all individuals—will continue to inspire and guide us because they are entrenched in our Constitution. The Constitution with its Bill of Rights thus has a bright future, as well as a glorious past, for its spirit is inherent in the aspirations of our people.

DANIEL PATRICK MOYNIHAN

Family and Nation (1986)

"In the War on Poverty, Poverty Won"

In January 1973, in the Alfred E. Stearns Lecture at Andover Academy, I offered what was then, I believe, a minority view that ours would soon become a more

"conservative" society. My little learning was hardly up to forecasting that in 1984 some 59 percent of voters from ages eighteen to twenty-four would cast their ballot for Ronald Reagan; but it did appear to me that our politics were not at all turning radical, as many seemed to suppose.

The 1960s had been, of course, a time of extraordinary protest, and not less extraordinary pronouncements about the future. A great shift, one heard, was under way. The center, in a phrase that had gained currency at the Democratic National Convention of 1972, was no longer where the center once was. It went without saying, in 1973 that that shift had been to the left.

I thought otherwise, once again turning to demographics to see what the future might hold. James S. Coleman and I had served together on the President's Science Advisory Committee, where Coleman had headed a group searching for some generalization that might be made about the turbulence of the 1960s. The key determinant seemed to be the size of the cohort of persons aged fourteen to twenty-four. These are the people who cause "trouble" to any society; the passage from childhood to adulthood is rarely easy. If sometimes destructive, it is just as often brilliantly creative. So much for the obvious. What was not obvious until Coleman's group asked the right question was that during the 1960s the *size* of this cohort was incomparably greater than it had ever been, or would ever again be (in, say, a half-century span), and in consequence had quite overwhelmed the institutions that are supposed to look after young people and guide them into adulthood. From 1890 to 1960 the total size of this cohort grew by 12.5 million persons. Then in the 1960s it grew by 13.8 million. It would grow by 600,000 in the 1970s and decline in the 1980s.

I reasoned that when the time for locking up the dean or harassing the police passed and these no-longer-young persons turned to matters such as who would become dean or make the list for sergeant, the effect of numbers would be quite different: it would dampen spirits rather than raise them. The lecture was entitled "Peace." I proposed that the campus disorders of the preceding period would now end, but I tried to look further ahead than that. I observed that had I been asked ten years earlier who to read to find out what America was like, or was going to be like, I would unhesitatingly have said, "Read Mark Twain. Twain mostly told the truth, as Huck Finn testified, and perfectly conveyed a sense of the ebullience, the growth, the prospects, the limitless energy and potential, of our great and far, far reaching land." On the other hand, I continued, if asked then about the future, I would have recommended Balzac. "Find out what it's like to live in a society where if you want to be a professor, you wait until the man who is professor dies. Then the fifteen of you who want the job compete. . . . one of you gets it. The rest hope the best for their sons." [. . .]

If we will accept that individuals tend to acquire more or less permanent political attachments in the years between age twenty-five and thirty-four, we see a great cohort of the population acquiring its political orientation during a time of real or at least relative economic distress. It appeared that it might be the first such group of young people in American history which faced the prospect that its standard of living might permanently decline. Levy and Michel note that between 1968 and 1972 the annual American Council on Education survey of the attitudes of college freshmen showed that only about half felt that "being well-off financially" was "essential" or "very important" in their lives. This number jumped in the fall of 1973 as the economy began to turn sour, and reached 69 percent by the end of the decade. Career choices were more and more frequently made with earnings in mind: law, medicine, business. Income could not be taken for granted. "It was this fear— baby boomers' perceptions that they would never live as well as their parents— that lay behind the sense of a 'vanishing middle class.'" Things could look up, of course, and probably will. But for the moment *these* family statistics will have a profound bearing on those outlined in the previous chapter. We have been a generous people, and remain such, but there is not likely to be any widespread renewed interest in the condition of the poor until the prospects of this uncertain, apprehensive middle class are settled, and for the better, and until it gets beyond the seeming selfishness of the moment.

In that sense I probably ought not to have used the term *conservative* to describe the period I anticipated. Conservative should be kept a simple word. Conservatives conserve. Sometimes, as has been written, they conserve liberalism. Indeed, a great development of democracy in the nineteenth century was the pattern that appeared in Britain, whereby a conservative government coming to office left the initiatives of the preceding liberal government pretty much intact. It made for a rhythm of innovation and consolidation; it made elections less fateful affairs, all to the enhancement of stability in a democracy. By the twentieth century this pattern was well established here. The Republican presidents of the 1920s left Wilson's program pretty much intact; Eisenhower even added to the programs of the New Deal and Fair Deal; Nixon both kept the Great Society intact and proposed some singular extensions.

This would not be so of the conservatism I anticipated at Andover. It would be a threatened, not a confident or, if you like, complacent, conservatism. The term *Reagan Revolution* had not yet appeared, but on the other hand *six years* earlier, in 1967, James Q. Wilson's "A Guide to Reagan Country," published in *Commentary*, offered the American public a prescient appreciation of the near future of American politics. Mr. Reagan had then just been elected governor of California, and something new was coming out of the West. It was in some sense "reactionary, seeking to turn back the clock to a day when life was easier, virtues less complicated, and the Ten Commandments a sufficient guide." Yet it was not, Wilson argued, in any sense a movement to return to the life of the small towns and farms that southern California electorate had left behind on the prairies from which they had migrated. It was a movement toward the values and viewpoints that the American electorate overwhelmingly endorsed in the reelection campaign of President Reagan in 1984, an electorate that felt threatened, not least by a reported explosion of social spending.

As a candidate in 1980, Mr. Reagan had quite avoided any specific commitments on social policy. But as a candidate for reelection there was the record of his first term to judge by; and to judge by the reelection returns, the American electorate was prepared to see measures proposed that, if enacted, would indeed constitute something of a revolution.

Thus, in the area of social welfare, in his second year in office President Reagan had proposed that the AFDC program be wholly turned over to the states. The federal government would assume some state medical costs in return, but the issue was one of principle rather than budget: the new administration desired to abolish a central feature of the Social Security Act of 1935. AFDC began as a "mixed" program in which each state set its own level of benefits and shared the costs with the federal government. But almost from the first, which is to say for almost a

half century, the thrust of almost all discussion of the subject was to make the program fully national, with uniform payments and full federal funding. President Eisenhower, much concerned with the growth of federal power, would never have dreamed of making the Reagan proposal to turn responsibility for poor children over entirely to the states. President Nixon had indeed come forward with just the opposite idea: a federally guaranteed income for all. (And in the end, of course, Nixon did obtain a guaranteed income for the poor elderly, blind, and the permanently and totally disabled.) Not President Reagan. He wanted to undo what had been done, *because he was convinced that much that had been done had been harmful.* In a December 1983 radio broadcast he said: "There is no question that many well-intentioned Great Society-type programs contributed to family breakups, welfare dependency, and a large increase in births out of wedlock."

These had been his views, and experience in his new office did not change them, as it is said to do with many Presidents. Somewhat to the contrary, it seems to have confirmed his earlier judgments. In January 1985, three days into his second term, he told the Associated Press, "In the war on poverty, poverty won."

It would be mistaken to see this as merely ideological pessimism, reflecting, say, the biblical passage with which William H. Ayres had opened the Minority questioning on the first day of House committee hearings on the Economic Opportunity Act, back in 1964: "For ye have the poor always with you." True, the President had brought to Washington a disposition against "welfare" that had played well with audiences over many years. [. . .]

Disposition apart, the President was now being told that the *evidence* accumulated in the course of the War on Poverty showed that it *had* failed. Here, for example, is Paul Craig Roberts, the first assistant secretary of the treasury for tax policy in the Reagan administration, testifying in January 1985 before the Senate Finance Committee:

> The growth of government has brought an enormous transformation in the nature of U.S. society. Over most of our country's history, there was neither an income tax nor a welfare system. This was a period during which the economy

simultaneously absorbed millions of penniless immigrants, many of whom could not even speak the language, and rapidly reduced the poverty rate. *Today poverty has been institutionalized by the government's poverty programs, and the poverty rate no longer declines.* In the U.S. today, only the illegal poor—aliens who do not qualify for the government's transfer and welfare programs—are consistently able to work themselves out of poverty. By undermining private property rights, a welfare state restricts opportunities for all on the grounds that otherwise some will succeed more than others. (His emphasis.)

At one level this is so much blather. No one, for example, in or out of the U.S. government has the least bit of information as to whether "only the illegal poor . . . are consistently able to work themselves out of poverty." But it does reflect deeply held beliefs on the part of many who helped fashion Mr. Reagan's economic and social policies. It can be dismissed as social science; not as social theory. Recall that the "inalienable rights" claimed by the Continental Congress when it first assembled in 1774 were "life, liberty, and property." It was Jefferson's felicitous touch in the Declaration of Independence that gave us "the pursuit of Happiness" instead. But the founders of the American political system, working from Locke, clearly regarded respect for the rights of private property as a prime necessity of republican government. To hold that the income tax and the AFDC program undermine those rights is to make no small charge. This charge was routinely made during the first Reagan administration and went all but unanswered. [. . .]

The advent of federal aid to education—after two decades of political struggle and ever-heightening expectations—came just as the scores on standardized achievement tests began a long slide. It doesn't matter that educational psychologists might object to the use of test scores as a measure of system performance; the public will accept them if the case is made. It doesn't matter that any systemwide difference the Great Society education programs might have brought about would surely have required a decade or more to appear; publics rarely think in decades. Similarly, as more federal programs were directed to the problems of dependency, the only seeming result was an increase in dependency.

But there was more. In the 1960s and into the 1970s, there was a great surge of social-science research in areas related to social policy. Much of this was ongoing work that would have taken place regardless of any political cycle. But much also arose from the times themselves. There was a good deal of what Alice M. Rivlin was to call "forensic social science," which is to say work done to develop facts that could then be used to argue a case. The negative income-tax experiments come under this heading. And then, most importantly, there was a tremendous surge of what came to be known as evaluation research. Some of this also partook of advocacy. The early studies of Head Start—not all, but most—were undertaken not only to learn how the program worked but to demonstrate that it did. Show and tell. But it is also the case that the move toward evaluation research reflected a genuine desire to introduce a measure of conceptual discipline into the formulation of social policy. At that time Washington was teeming with persons with fiercely assertive interests in particular interpretations of events.

This view was not without its politics. In the main, if one may speak from personal acquaintance, the principal social scientists involved were more than sympathetic to the general goals of the period but had professional interests also—what worked?—and a prudent concern about a lot of overpromising. Had it not been for the overpromising, the findings when they began coming in would perhaps not have been so devastating. Two asides are in order here. Overpromising is endemic to any period of political vitality and may be necessary. (The claims for Mr. Reagan's economic policies are turning out, if anything, to have been even more wildly exaggerated.) It may further be the case that existing methodologies in the social sciences have a bias toward the null hypothesis, which is to say to find little or no program effect in the short order. But neither of these propositions can be settled, and in any event the findings that came in—came in.

It fell to Peter H. Rossi, among the most sympathetic and innovative persons in his discipline, to break the news. In a review article published in 1978, he announced his "Iron Law."

"If there is any empirical law that is emerging from the past decade of widespread evaluation research activities, it is that the expected value for any measured effect of a social program is zero." More recently (1984), in the *Annual Review of Sociology*, he and James D. Wright have written:

> One of the most important lessons to be taken from all the evaluations of the golden age is that it is extremely difficult to design programs that produce noticeable effects in the desired direction. In retrospect, a reasonable summary of findings is that the expected value for the effect of any program hovers around zero. This finding was devastating to the social reformers who had hoped that the Great Society programs would make appreciable (or at least detectable) gains in bettering the lot of the poor and redressing the ills of society.

Henry Aaron, a Brookings Institution economist who has served in government, does not disagree. In a short paper delivered to a 1981 conference on social experimentation he observed: "Social experiments, like most research on social experiments, have been a force for slowing the adoption of new social policies. . . . Social experiments, like other analysis, show problems to be more complicated and subtle than we had thought and that results are harder to achieve than we had hoped."

As Aaron suggests, the 1960s and 1970s saw not merely an increase in evaluation research but an even more significant increase in experiments seeking to discover the effects on individual and collective behavior of different, controlled experiences. Perhaps this overstates. As Martin Diamond wrote on the occasion of the Bicentennial, the United States began as a conscious experiment in government, and we have been given to experiment in the area of government responsibilities. Recall that Tocqueville and Beaumont came to America to have a look at the New York State Penitentiary in Auburn. But experiments don't always work. Auburn never worked as advertised.

From its own perspective, Aaron suggested, the new administration ought to have been encouraging yet more such research. But in its enthusiasm for domestic budget cutting, it had failed to sense its opportunity. "Mr. Stockman [then the newly appointed director of the Office of Management and Budget] is making a grave mistake in trying to put us all out of work. He has not realized that we are the

instrumentality for inaction. By diverting us to teaching rather than research or even to still more reputable ways of earning a living he will make easier the growth of ideas for activist social change undisturbed by critical analyses when the mood of the country shifts." Granting a measure of irony, the observation even so deserves to be taken seriously and, in my view, to be rejected.

If this is to happen, several things will be required. First of all, we need to recapture the history of the 1960s. For one thing, the Johnson administration was never nearly so carried away by the more bizarre enthusiasm of the period as it sometimes let on. Further, there is something faintly patronizing in the notion that politicians are quite traumatized by the discovery that problems are "complicated and subtle." I have lived among social scientists and also among politicians and would prefer to avoid generalizations about either; but if the issue is that of relative ease in the face of subtlety and complexity, I would be disposed to think politicians at least as well prepared as academics.

Lyndon B. Johnson was fully alive to the complexities of the domestic issues the Great Society was addressing. But in time he realized that the activists of the moment did not want to hear of such matters, and so he made a deliberate decision to conceal his own reservations. He would tell the story about the school teacher who arrived in a town in west Texas during the depression of the 1930s to be interviewed for a job that he needed in the worst way. At one point an old rancher on the school board looked up at him and asked: "Do you teach the world is round or the world is flat?" The teacher looked about for any clue as to the desired answer, found none, and replied: "I can teach it either way." When Johnson found himself surrounded by the equivalent of flat-earth enthusiasts, he thought it over maybe a nanosecond and, not without a measure of contempt, commenced to teach the world was flat.

In this specific context let me offer three propositions on the aftermath of what Rossi and Wright describe as "The Golden Age."

First, there never was a Golden Age. There never is. [. . .]

On a Saturday morning early in the administration of John F. Kennedy, Harlan Cleveland found himself in a sailboat off Hyannisport with the new

President and a few associates, going over some foreign-policy matters. Work done, talk turned to a new volume by Arthur M. Schlesinger, Jr., on the New Deal. The trouble with Arthur, said the new President, was that he made all those White House staff members such as Corcoran and Cohen and Rowe seem like demigods, when for sure they were no different from O'Donnell and Sorensen and Dungan of his own White House. Having known all these men, I can only agree. The President was not denigrating the talents of the New Dealers but merely commenting on the aura that distance lends to men and events.

Almost no social legislation was adopted under Kennedy. Under Johnson, we saw two magnificent civil rights acts, an enduring achievement, but which in truth did little more than enact as statute the constitutional guarantees of the post–Civil War amendments. Medicare and Medicaid were true innovations, but the rest were limited. Lyndon B. Johnson began life as a high school teacher. He wanted to be known as the Education President, but his notion of becoming so was to sign a blizzard of small bills and keep the pens on display.

The Elementary and Secondary School Act was not unimportant—nearly twenty years later the federal government provides 7. 5 percent of all funds for these levels of education. But the proportion has been going down of late. Apart from civil rights and Medicare, his administration had no very large legislative ideas, and he was continuously constrained by fear of being labeled a "big spender." Even with a major war in progress, his annual budget deficits (FYs 1964–69) averaged under $6 billion, and he left a surplus to his successor. It has been observed that in these years there was a division between new men with new enthusiasms—abolishing poverty, organizing communities, pursuing equality—and an older generation of New Dealers, men of the 1930s still pressing to complete a social insurance agenda formed in the early years of the twentieth century. Johnson knew the New Dealers and trusted them. He knew the general outlines of the Medicare and Medicaid proposals from the years they had been bandied about in Senate corridors and committee rooms. These were *not* poverty programs, albeit they would have a huge impact *on* poverty. They were social insurance programs available to all as a matter of entitlement. Johnson made Wilbur J. Cohen, one of the most eminent of the remaining New Dealers, his secretary of health, education and welfare. By contrast, the Office of Economic Opportunity was awarded Sargent Shriver, John F. Kennedy's brother-in-law: not wholly a signal of presidential enthusiasm. OEO survived as a separate agency for about a decade. The Social Security Administration, by contrast, routinely, projects the income and outgo of the Medicare trust fund year by year into the mid-twenty-first century. [. . .]

The Great Society years are remembered as a time of great increases in the size of government and especially in the amount of social spending. This is so only to the extent that the Social Security programs of the 1930s (with Eisenhower's addition of disability benefits) began to mature and pay out large sums from the respective trust funds. But this, in a sense, was an event that had been maturing for years before the Kennedy-Johnson administrations. Much is counterintuitive in our politics. That is part of the art, I suppose. For if you would look for a *true* increase in the size of government—to 24 percent of gross national product—you must await the advent of the Reagan administration.

Second, there were not nearly so many claims made for the Great Society as now are being remembered.

In a 1984 conference on the Great Society—eras end; conferences go on—Richard Nathan, who worked for Nelson A. Rockefeller during much of this period and who, if professionally skeptical, was even so friendly to the effort, described the sometimes unreal expectations concerning social science at that time:

> Social science is *one among many* inputs to social policy. It was never otherwise. Yet there was a period of wistful expectation—a Camelot for social science—when many practitioners believed it could be more than that, a determinant in and of itself of new policy directions, or, if not that, the input with a presumed special claim and higher standing than others in the policy making process. In fact, one of the unspoken assumptions of the Great Society, which crested near the peak of the most influential period for economists in government, was that doing good in substantial measure was an intellectual undertaking, when of course it is, and has always been, a matter of desire, belief, and values.

True, but this was well enough understood. In 1966 I appeared before a subcommittee of the Senate Committee on Government Operations to propose that the Congress establish an Office of Legislative Evaluation "which would have the task of systematically evaluating the results of the social and economic programs enacted by it and paid for out of public monies." It might, I suggested, be established as a separate agency or located in the Library of Congress or the General Accounting Office. But the essential feature" must be that it will be staffed by professional social scientists who will routinely assess the results of government programs in the manner that the GAO routinely audits them." Evaluation was in that sense a development of the auditing process. (Under the leadership of Senator Abraham Ribicoff, this role was eventually assumed by the GAO. By the 1980s, some 45 percent of all GAO projects could be called evaluation research.)

I gave my testimony the title "The Crisis of Confidence" and argued simply that unless the federal government was prepared to track the results of its new programs, and be open with the public about those results, public support would fade.

"The usual whispered argument" was that to be candid about programs that don't seem to produce results is "to give a weapon to the enemies of progress." I offered the thought that the public was more realistic than generally thought and hence more accepting of difficulties, even failure. Peter Rossi had noted that "our" commitment to evaluation research was fundamentally ambivalent, one of attraction and fear, trust and distrust, both because of the possibility of negative or null findings and—more importantly—because in areas of social policy facts are simply not neutral. Social science data were necessarily political. Most social arrangements rested on assumptions about the "facts" of a given situation. To challenge such facts was to challenge those social arrangements, an earlier observation of Louis Wirth's. It was because of this that Walter B. Miller had suggested there was a direct incompatibility between careful evaluation research and the political process.

That I was optimistic even so—pressing for the kind of analysis that in time, and in not far distant time, would prove so devastating itself—is awkwardly revealing. So much of all this strategizing and disputation was an affair of a circumscribed circle of fifty

or so persons who happened to have been in government at the assassination of John F. Kennedy and the sudden release of political energies under his successor. They and five hundred or a thousand assorted academics and administrators and the occasional politician they happened to know or had gotten to know. When I testified to the Senate committee about "our" hopes and "our" aspirations, I was speaking of that small community. The plain fact, the large and indispensable fact, is that the attempt to address the issue of poverty in the whole of the United States came in the first instance from an informal committee of a half-dozen persons thinking up themes for President Kennedy's 1964 reelection campaign. At one point it appeared that the likeliest choice would be the emerging, challenging problems of the suburbs. Poverty held on, however, and it was, as he was reported saying at the time, LBJ's kind of program. But the electorate never asked for it; the *poor* never asked for it. Congress took it on say-so, with no structural commitment. The press was interested at first; but the press is never interested long. As for my family initiative, well, that was an affair of a dozen persons at most. All this in turn accounted for the rhetoric of the time: self-levitation.

Rhetoric *was* a problem. Hannah Arendt once observed that the "superiority" of the totalitarian elites of the 1920s and 1930s in Europe lay in the ability to immediately dissolve every statement of fact into a declaration of purpose. In the spring of 1967 I gave the Clark A. Sanford Lecture at the State University Agricultural and Technical College at Delhi, New York. The lecture series deals with local government and community life, and I described—it was no more than description—the misunderstandings that had arisen in Washington over the purposes of the Community Action programs in the antipoverty effort. There had been three distinct views—in the White House, in the Bureau of the Budget, in the Office of Economic Opportunity—and the simple fact was that the views were incompatible. Not an unheard-of event in public administration. The view inside OEO derived more or less directly from a theory of juvenile delinquency that had been in vogue during the Kennedy administration. This was the so-called opportunity theory in which deviancy was ascribed to efforts to achieve normal goals in situations where there were not enough normal opportunities to do so. Fair enough, but the essential fact was that *"government did not know what it was doing. It had a theory. . . . Nothing more."* (Emphasis in original.) A respectable theory, I insisted, but nothing approaching confident knowledge. One result was that when challenged by stronger bureaucratic competitors, OEO was usually bested, to accompanying protestation. Again, not an unfamiliar event in public administration. But the lecture, when published (1969) as a small volume with the title *Maximum Feasible Misunderstanding*, was reviewed by former Kennedy and Johnson aides with a degree of animus rarely aroused by essays on public administration. Adam Walinsky, who had been Robert F. Kennedy's legislative assistant in the Senate, excoriated the book in the *New York Times:* "Basically anti-intellectual, anti-participatory, quietist, above all flattering . . . [to] political passivity. . . ."

An irony of the 1960s is that in the main the most important social science published in the period described with great clarity and equal calm the *obstacles* to social change. (To insist on difficulty is not necessarily to be daunted by it.) In the field of education, for example, the period began with the publication of Greeley and Rossi's *The Education of Catholic Americans* and was brought to a close with Colemen's *Equality of Educational Opportunity*. Each was a profoundly reserved statement, and this was more widely grasped than might be thought.

It was such research that led President Nixon, in 1970, to propose the creation of a National Institute of Education. Drawing on Coleman's work, the President's message to Congress argued that the emphasis in education had to move from inputs to outputs, which is to say results. An earlier era had assumed an easy, fairly straight-line relationship that research no longer supported; now a more complex problem had to be addressed, with final educational results being the measure of effect. The message reflected Kenneth Boulding's contention that a major obstacle to progress in education was "the absence of any adequate theory regarding the nature and machinery of human learning." It was further to be understood that this learning process would require much more sustained, long-term longitudinal work than had yet been done. We had about exhausted the possibilities of one-time surveys. An institution was needed that

would nourish and protect work that can take twenty and thirty years to complete.

It happens I presented the opening testimony to the House Select Committee on Education at its February 1971 hearings on the National Institute of Education. The chairman was John Brademas of Indiana, now president of New York University. He was for the bill (and in time saw to its passage) but found himself besieged by arguments that the *real* strategy of the White House in proposing "more" educational research was to establish grounds on which to cut aid to education. I did my best to explain that this had become a "predictable" response.

> I would ask this Committee to understand that this is not a pattern of reaction confined to the field of Education. To the contrary, it is almost a standard reflexive response to a plea for more research in the social sciences, or at least it has become so of late. I have elsewhere suggested that there has indeed been something of a change here. For decades, even generations, social science enjoyed a comfortable relationship with what were perceived as progressive social policies. In recent years, this relationship has become troubled. Social science has emerged as a threatening discipline. It tells you a lot of things you thought weren't so, or wished weren't so. This is no way to win support.
>
> Increasingly, the proposal for more research is seen almost as a hostile act.

Herman Badillo, representative from the Bronx, was troubled by this. He responded:

> I am not committed to promoting social unrest, but I can think of no greater formula for doing so than if I were to go tomorrow—as I intend to—to a group of black and Puerto Rican parents in the South Bronx and tell them that they have to show fortitude in the face of disappointment and that it may be 10 years before their children can expect to learn, because the educators really don't know what to do. I would suspect they would say that is not enough; that it is true that the educators don't know how to teach, but they haven't really tried.

In education, to keep with that subject for a moment, inequalities associated with economic status, with race commonly a surrogate term, do respond to effort. The results are relatively weak in large sys-temwide programs, more pronounced in small exper-imental settings, but results withal. There appear to be some systemwide results. In 1982 Nancy W. Bur-ton and Lyle V. Jones reported the findings of the National Assessment of Education Progress, which began conducting surveys in 1969: During the 1970s the discrepancy in average achievement levels between the nation's white and black youth had become smaller in five important learning areas at ages nine and thirteen. Typically, when achievement for white students declined, that for black students declined less; when whites improved, blacks improved more. The difference between the races decreased at both ages in mathematics, science, read-ing, writing, and social studies. In their view, "Pro-grams designed to foster equal educational opportunity may be among the factors that have con-tributed to the reduction in white-black achievement differences."

I was out of government at the time and not much in a mood for this sort of thing. I answered that it would make no difference whatever whether he or his constituents or whosoever thought that what I had said was "not enough." If he wanted my advice, it would be to "go up there and tell the mothers in the Bronx that they are doing damn well with their chil-dren and they ought to be proud of them." Where-upon the questioning concluded: realities were beginning to be understood and accepted.

In sum: *There never was a Golden Age. There were not nearly so many claims made as are now being remembered.*

Finally: *There have been more successes than we seem to want to know.* [. . .]

Common Ground?

In the opening passages of his 1985 State of the Union Address, President Reagan spoke of the achievements of his first term and the promise of his second. The American people, he said, had brought forth "a nation renewed—stronger, freer, and more secure. . . . New freedom in our lives has planted rich seeds for future success." First of all: "For an America of wisdom that honors the family, knowing that as the family goes, so goes our civilization . . ." At the close

of his address he turned to the balcony of the House of Representatives and introduced "an American hero," Mrs. Clara Hale, seated there next to the First Lady, which is to say the honored guest of that state occasion.

The President spoke: "She lives in the inner city where she cares for infants born of mothers who are heroin addicts. The children born in withdrawal are sometimes even dropped on her doorstep. She helps them with love."

The manifest sincerity of the President's belief that "as the family goes, so goes our civilization" seemed, even so, incomplete. Much of his political career had centered on the celebration of family and "traditional values." (Wilson in his 1967 article had focused on that single-family house, however modest, the center and symbol of all in Reagan Country.) None could doubt the President's conviction. Yet clearly it did not occur to him, nor to his speech writers (Mrs. Hale's really quite splendid story had been told in the Sep-tember 1984 issue of *Reader's Digest*), that her work was not wholly reassuring to anyone concerned with the well-being of the American family.

"Go to her home some night," Mr. Reagan said, "and you'll see her silhouette against the window as she walks the floor, talking softly, soothing a child in her arms." There is a problem of detail here. Hale House, at 154 West 122d Street, is a five-story tene-ment. Only with some difficulty will the passerby see through even first-story windows in this burnt-out sec-tion of the city. Not exactly candlelight gleaming through the sycamores on the banks of the Wabash far away. Nor yet a split-level ranch in Orange County.

Nor did the President seem aware that to the degree that he was honoring the work of Hale House, begun in 1969, as well as the character of its founder, he was honoring a government program. In the New York Fiscal Year 1983–84, Hale House received $297,573 from all sources, of which $272,299 came from the federal, New York State, and New York City governments. Far the largest amount came from the foster care, child welfare services, and adoption assis-tance programs of the federal government, for which state and local governments provide matching grants. [. . .]

Nor yet, we may suppose, had anyone told the President that less than a block from Hale House, on Seventh Avenue between 122d and 124th streets, at just about the time lights go on, enabling Mrs. Hale's reassuring silhouette to be observed, a drug exchange opens. Three to four to five hundred men stand about on the sidewalks—much as in the Curb Exchange of nineteenth-century commerce in downtown Manhattan (this is uptown)—and trade narcotics. Here and there a federal agent will be found purchasing drugs to keep up-to-date the government price index for heroin, cocaine, and other assorted substances. No arrests are made. Thus we are at the end point of a sequence of federal crimes—illegal smuggling, illegal possession, illegal sale—that the federal government has quite failed to prevent, much less to punish, with grim consequences for portions of the American population who might otherwise think of themselves as being protected by their government.

A conservative slogan of sorts gained currency in these years. The task of the federal government, it held, was to "deliver the mail and defend the coast." The mail hasn't been getting through to Harlem very well these days, so many of the apartment mailboxes having been jimmied to steal welfare checks with which to purchase drugs that had made their way uptown, in consequence of the manifest failure of government to defend the coast. The President, like his predecessors, had taken an oath to "faithfully execute the office of President of the United States," which office includes the responsibility to enforce the laws of the United States. But to the contrary, the narcotics laws were not being enforced. Mr. Reagan was in a position to celebrate Mrs. Hale as an American hero because the federal government had not seen to the enforcement of its laws, and consequently the environs of Hale House teemed with drug addicts. Is this not curious? [. . .]

In the past, the number of poor had generally decreased when average family income increased. This did not happen in these years, owing partly to a huge increase in the number of female-headed families and of unrelated (largely single) individuals. Their incomes did not rise. Certainly, economic factors—particularly the lingering effects of the 1981–82 recession—contributed to this. Nevertheless, *for the first time since the federal government began keeping track there was a simultaneous increase in wealth and poverty within the population.* Now this is something we heard a lot about in the last century. Half of mankind, or thereabouts, is committed to a

doctrine that insists this is the way capitalist society will go. It isn't. There is no "immiserization" of the proletariat to be seen in these statistics. There is, however, a continuing change in family structure ineluctably associated with poverty. [. . .]

To say yet again, what emerges here is the realization that in the nature of modern industrial society, no government, however firm might be its wish otherwise, can avoid having policies that profoundly influence family relationships. This is not to be avoided. The only option is whether these will be purposeful, intended policies or whether they will be residual, derivative, in a sense concealed ones.

This sensibility does not come readily to American government; and yet it may be rising. Social historians study the diffusion of social issues and responses; there is much trans-Atlantic movement, in the main westward, at least until of late. Consider again President Reagan's State of the Union Address and Mrs. Hale. The family connection was there, in full view of the President and his advisors, yet it was not quite taken in. [. . .]

Americans are *not* against government but do tend to say they are. Robert J. Shapiro, a veteran of Budget and Finance Committee hearings in the Senate, offers the nice insight that while political liberals look to government to subsidize consumption of certain sorts, let us say food stamps, political conservatives are if anything more voracious in their demand for government subsidies for production, as in the farm program. In the first Reagan term, for example, farm subsidies rose from $2 billion (FY 1981) to $9 billion (FY 1984), an astonishing increase that went all but unnoticed, not least because farm subsidies are hidden in "off-budget" loan programs. Industrial subsidies are provided in the tax code under the heading of "Accelerated Cost Recovery System" and other such mysteries, which are, however, perfectly comprehensible to those who make use of them, and, to them, eminently defensible.

To say again, because it must be repeated if it is ever to be understood, the federal government grew larger under Mr. Reagan during his first term. It grew bigger in ways that those in office thought desirable; those who saw their notion of government provision shrink generally tended to accept the view that there was some great battle going on in Washington as to whether government should be reduced in size. Not really. The real conflict was over which aspects of government should grow. [. . .]

The prospect that the needs of families might be the means for bringing liberals and conservatives together on matters of policy is intriguing and real.

I am indebted to Nicholas Eberstat for the observation that "liberals" emphasize social policy but are criticized for ignoring values. "Conservatives" emphasize values in the outcomes for children but seem threatened by the idea of social policy. Surely each group is seeing part of the truth and can find common ground in accepting one another's perceptions. Social policy, through the funding of medical research and the provision of medical care, brought about a one-third decline in neonatal mortality rates in the ten years from 1965 to 1975. Social policy can concern itself with the lives of the children who did not die. Let none suppose this a simple matter. Michael Novak points to a further divergence of liberal and conservative approaches. In matters of social policy, liberals don't mind being coercive about matters that affect large groups and classes, but insist on the fullest possible liberties in private lives. If family policy interferes with that, liberals balk. By contrast, conservatives tend to resent the coercions the liberal agenda imposes on large social groups and classes, while thinking of restrictions on family morality as matters of discipline and virtue rather than coercion.

Even so, the promise of the 1980s, such as it may be, is that conservatives and liberals are encountering one another as equals. The long liberal hegemony in the world of social policy has collapsed. (Does anyone recall that in 1947 Lionel Trilling could call for the creation of an opposition within liberalism, to put some pressure on orthodoxy, given the complete collapse of any conservative opposition?) By mid-decade some conservatives were beginning to assert that "poverty" itself was a misleading term—natural only to 1960s liberals who were transfixed by illusory notions that the state could produce abundance and who were indifferent to the proper duty of the state, which is to require virtue of its citizens. From this point, of course, it is not a great distance to the proposition that the virtuous citizen does not permit himself to become poor or that, alternatively, inasmuch as being poor does not preclude being virtuous, it is a matter of no great consequence. We have this sort of analysis degenerate into a genteel social Darwinism

or rise to a rugged individualism that is part of our cultural tradition as much as any ethic of collective provision. The central conservative truth is that it is culture, not politics, that determines the success of a society. The central liberal truth is that politics can change a culture and save it from itself. Witness the civil rights legislation of the 1960s that conservatives so opposed.

Nothing warrants optimism. If we turn to the great analysts of our age, we encounter something very like despair. Urie Bronfenbrenner took the occasion of the year 1984 to note in *Innovator* (September) that Orwell's vision of a war-ravaged world in which the functions of the family were taken over by child-rearing institutions, with the resulting atrophy of close and intimate enduring personal relations, might well be coming true, but not, as Orwell anticipated, because of government interference. "Rather, these changes are the products of governmental and, especially, public indifference. . . . We Americans didn't need any . . . disasters . . . to transform our family life. We did it all on our own. . . . " History, he notes, records in family patterns. But always "the product of some great cataclysmic event: the Huns had come, earthquakes, epidemics, wars, catastrophic economic depressions, or periods of massive oppression. But we Americans didn't need any such disasters to transform our family life. We did it all on our own. . . . " As a basic social proposition he declares, "A child requires public policies and practices that provide opportunity, status, example, encouragement, stability, and above all, time for parenthood, primarily by parents, but also by all adults in the society. And unless you have those external supports, the internal systems can't work. They fail." And fail they do. Such has been "the erosion of the ecology of family life in the United States."

To James S. Coleman (1982), "it would appear that the process of making human beings human is breaking down in American society." The same forces that break apart the household as a productive unit, in an economic sense, have broken it as a unit of redistribution of income. The elderly are looked after by external institutions; increasingly the young. Could it be, he asks, that ours will be the first species to forget *how* to raise its young? Coleman resists. (Bronfenbrenner resists.) In the Ryerson Lecture at the University of Chicago in 1985 he asserts that "the fundamental assumption on which publicly supported education in the United States is based is wrong for the social structure in which we find ourselves today. Perhaps the school should not be an agent of the state or of the larger society, but an agent of the community of families closest to the child." Diversity attracts him: in "the ghetto and the suburb" schooling should strengthen the norms that those parents hold for their children, "norms that parents often find undercut by intrusions from the larger society." He proposes to reverse the "very" philosophy that now governs our schools, "public and private."

William J. Goode comes closer to an avowed despair than either Bronfenbrenner or Coleman. From Durkheim we have the proposition that no purely contractual society can arise or continue to exist. ("A dust of individuals.") Analysts following Durkheim assert that "a purely individualistic hedonism does not produce enough commitment to the collectivity for many of the needs of society . . . to be met, that the larger system will not work without important inputs from the family, and that if all individuals calculate only what is best for each person personally, then the integration of the society, and even of the economy is likely to falter." Goode has no great expectations: "Although great social events, as well as specific policies, do affect the family, there is no evidence that any serious attempt at manipulating family patterns on a large scale has ever had much success." Indeed there is none. He foresees an enveloping entropy not likely to be reversed.

And the Godkin Lecturer? Well, there is that business about it being darkest before dawn. All he ever hoped was that this matter might rise to the level of public discourse. This seems now to be happening. If it does, the future will be different, at least somewhat different, and possibly better.

A commonplace of political rhetoric has it that the quality of a civilization may be measured by how it cares for its elderly. Just as surely, the future of a society may be forecast by how it cares for its young.

ANTONIN SCALIA

Employment Division, Oregon Department of Human Resources v. Smith (1990)

Justice SCALIA delivered the opinion of the Court.

This case requires us to decide whether the Free Exercise Clause of the First Amendment permits the State of Oregon to include religiously inspired peyote use within the reach of its general criminal prohibition on use of that drug, and thus permits the State to deny unemployment benefits to persons dismissed from their jobs because of such religiously inspired use.

I

Oregon law prohibits the knowing or intentional possession of a "controlled substance" unless the substance has been prescribed by a medical practitioner. The law defines "controlled substance" as a drug classified in Schedules I through V of the Federal Controlled Substances Act, as modified by the State Board of Pharmacy. Persons who violate this provision by possessing a controlled substance listed on Schedule I are "guilty of a Class B felony." As compiled by the State Board of Pharmacy under its statutory authority, Schedule I contains the drug peyote, a hallucinogen derived from the plant Lophophora williamsii Lemaire.

Respondents Alfred Smith and Galen Black (hereinafter respondents) were fired from their jobs with a private drug rehabilitation organization because they ingested peyote for sacramental purposes at a ceremony of the Native American Church, of which both are members. When respondents applied to petitioner Employment Division (hereinafter petitioner) for unemployment compensation, they were determined to be ineligible for benefits because they had been discharged for work-related "misconduct." The Oregon Court of Appeals reversed that determination, holding that the denial of benefits violated respondents' free exercise rights under the First Amendment. [. . .]

[T]he Oregon Supreme Court held that respondents' religiously inspired use of peyote fell within the prohibition of the Oregon statute, which "makes no exception for the sacramental use" of the drug. It then considered whether that prohibition was valid under the Free Exercise Clause, and concluded that it was not. [. . .]

II

A

The Free Exercise Clause [. . .] provides that "Congress shall make no law respecting an establishment of religion, or *prohibiting the free exercise thereof. . . .*" U.S. Const., Amdt. 1 (emphasis added). The free exercise of religion means, first and foremost, the right to believe and profess whatever religious doctrine one desires. Thus, the First Amendment obviously excludes all "governmental regulation of religious beliefs as such." *Sherbert v. Verner* (1963). The government may not compel affirmation of religious belief, punish the expression of religious doctrines it believes to be false, impose special disabilities on the basis of religious views or religious status, or lend its power to one or the other side in controversies over religious authority or dogma.

But the "exercise of religion" often involves not only belief and profession but the performance of (or abstention from) physical acts: assembling with others for a worship service, participating in sacramental use of bread and wine, proselytizing, abstaining from certain foods or certain modes of transportation. It would be true, we think (though no case of ours has involved the point), that a State would be "prohibiting the free exercise [of religion]" if it sought to ban such acts or abstentions only when they are engaged

in for religious reasons, or only because of the religious belief that they display. It would doubtless be unconstitutional, for example, to ban the casting of "statues that are to be used for worship purposes," or to prohibit bowing down before a golden calf.

Respondents in the present case, however, seek to carry the meaning of "prohibiting the free exercise [of religion]" one large step further. They contend that their religious motivation for using peyote places them beyond the reach of a criminal law that is not specifically directed at their religious practice, and that is concededly constitutional as applied to those who use the drug for other reasons. They assert, in other words, that "prohibiting the free exercise [of religion]" includes requiring any individual to observe a generally applicable law that requires (or forbids) the performance of an act that his religious belief forbids (or requires). As a textual matter, we do not think the words must be given that meaning. It is no more necessary to regard the collection of a general tax, for example, as "prohibiting the free exercise [of religion]" by those citizens who believe support of organized government to be sinful, than it is to regard the same tax as "abridging the freedom . . . of the press" of those publishing companies that must pay the tax as a condition of staying in business. It is a permissible reading of the text, in the one case as in the other, to say that if prohibiting the exercise of religion (or burdening the activity of printing) is not the object of the tax but merely the incidental effect of a generally applicable and otherwise valid provision, the First Amendment has not been offended.

Our decisions reveal that the latter reading is the correct one. We have never held that an individual's religious beliefs excuse him from compliance with an otherwise valid law prohibiting conduct that the State is free to regulate. On the contrary, the record of more than a century of our free exercise jurisprudence contradicts that proposition. As described succinctly by Justice Frankfurter in *Minersville School Dist. Bd. of Ed. v. Gobitis* (1940): "Conscientious scruples have not, in the course of the long struggle for religious toleration, relieved the individual from obedience to a general law not aimed at the promotion or restriction of religious beliefs. The mere possession of religious convictions which contradict the relevant concerns of a political society does not relieve the citizen from the discharge of political responsibilities." We first had occasion to assert that principle in *Reynolds v. United States* (1879), where we rejected the claim that criminal laws against polygamy could not be constitutionally applied to those whose religion commanded the practice. "Laws," we said, "are made for the government of actions, and while they cannot interfere with mere religious belief and opinions, they may with practices. . . . Can a man excuse his practices to the contrary because of his religious belief? To permit this would be to make the professed doctrines of religious belief superior to the law of the land, and in effect to permit every citizen to become a law unto himself." [. . .]

Our most recent decision involving a neutral, generally applicable regulatory law that compelled activity forbidden by an individual's religion was *United States v. Lee* (1982). There, an Amish employer, on behalf of himself and his employees, sought exemption from collection and payment of Social Security taxes on the ground that the Amish faith prohibited participation in governmental support programs. We rejected the claim that an exemption was constitutionally required. There would be no way, we observed, to distinguish the Amish believer's objection to Social Security taxes from the religious objections that others might have to the collection or use of other taxes. [. . .]

The only decisions in which we have held that the First Amendment bars application of a neutral, generally applicable law to religiously motivated action have involved not the Free Exercise Clause alone, but the Free Exercise Clause in conjunction with other constitutional protections, such as freedom of speech and of the press. . . . Some of our cases prohibiting compelled expression, decided exclusively upon free speech grounds, have also involved freedom of religion. . . . And it is easy to envision a case in which a challenge on freedom of association grounds would likewise be reinforced by Free Exercise Clause concerns. [. . .]

The present case does not present such a hybrid situation, but a free exercise claim unconnected with any communicative activity or parental right. Respondents urge us to hold, quite simply, that when otherwise prohibitable conduct is accompanied by religious convictions, not only the convictions but the conduct itself must be free from governmental regulation. We have never held that, and decline to do so now. There being no contention that Oregon's drug law represents an attempt to regulate religious beliefs, the communication of religious beliefs, or the raising of one's children in those beliefs, the rule to which we have adhered ever since *Reynolds* plainly controls. [. . .]

B

Respondents argue that even though exemption from generally applicable criminal laws need not automatically be extended to religiously motivated actors, at least the claim for a religious exemption must be evaluated under the balancing test set forth in *Sherbert v. Verner* (1963). Under the *Sherbert* test, governmental actions that substantially burden a religious practice must be justified by a compelling governmental interest. Applying that test we have, on three occasions, invalidated state unemployment compensation rules that conditioned the availability of benefits upon an applicant's willingness to work under conditions forbidden by his religion. We have never invalidated any governmental action on the basis of the *Sherbert* test except the denial of unemployment compensation. Although we have sometimes purported to apply the *Sherbert* test in contexts other than that, we have always found the test satisfied. In recent years we have abstained from applying the *Sherbert* test (outside the unemployment compensation field) at all. [. . .]

Even if we were inclined to breathe into *Sherbert* some life beyond the unemployment compensation field, we would not apply it to require exemptions from a generally applicable criminal law. [. . .]

To make an individual's obligation to obey such a law contingent upon the law's coincidence with his religious beliefs, except where the State's interest is "compelling"—permitting him, by virtue of his beliefs, "to become a law unto himself," contradicts both constitutional tradition and common sense.

The "compelling government interest" requirement seems benign, because it is familiar from other fields. But using it as the standard that must be met before the government may accord different treatment on the basis of race, or before the government may regulate the content of speech, is not remotely comparable to using it for the purpose asserted here. What it produces in those other fields—equality of treatment and an unrestricted flow of contending speech—are constitutional norms; what it would produce here—a private right to ignore generally applicable laws—is a constitutional anomaly.

Nor is it possible to limit the impact of respondents' proposal by requiring a "compelling state interest" only when the conduct prohibited is "central" to the individual's religion. It is no more appropriate for judges to determine the "centrality" of religious beliefs before applying a "compelling interest" test in the free exercise field, than it would be for them to determine the "importance" of ideas before applying the "compelling interest" test in the free speech field. What principle of law or logic can be brought to bear to contradict a believer's assertion that a particular act is "central" to his personal faith . . . ?

If the "compelling interest" test is to be applied at all, then, it must be applied across the board, to all actions thought to be religiously commanded. Moreover, if "compelling interest" really means what it says, [. . .] many laws will not meet the test. Any society adopting such a system would be courting anarchy, but that danger increases in direct proportion to the society's diversity of religious beliefs, and its determination to coerce or suppress none of them. Precisely because "we are a cosmopolitan nation made up of people of almost every conceivable religious preference," *Braunfeld v. Brown* (1961), and precisely because we value and protect that religious divergence, we cannot afford the luxury of deeming presumptively invalid, as applied to the religious objector, every regulation of conduct that does not protect an interest of the highest order. The rule

respondents favor would open the prospect of constitutionally required religious exemptions from civic obligations of almost every conceivable kind. [. . .]

Values that are protected against government interference through enshrinement in the Bill of Rights are not thereby banished from the political process. Just as a society that believes in the negative protection accorded to the press by the First Amendment is likely to enact laws that affirmatively foster the dissemination of the printed word, so also a society that believes in the negative protection accorded to religious belief can be expected to be solicitous of that value in its legislation as well. It is therefore not surprising that a number of States have made an exception to their drug laws for sacramental peyote use. But to say that a nondiscriminatory religious-practice exemption is permitted, or even that it is desirable, is not to say that it is constitutionally required, and that the appropriate occasions for its creation can be discerned by the courts. It may fairly be said that leaving accommodation to the political process will place at a relative disadvantage those religious practices that are not widely engaged in; but that unavoidable consequence of democratic government must be preferred to a system in which each conscience is a law unto itself or in which judges weigh the social importance of all laws against the centrality of all religious beliefs.

Because respondents' ingestion of peyote was prohibited under Oregon law, and because that prohibition is constitutional, Oregon may, consistent with the Free Exercise Clause, deny respondents unemployment compensation when their dismissal results from use of the drug. [. . .]

Sandra Day O'Connor

Employment Division, Oregon Department of Human Resources v. Smith, Concurrence (1990)

Justice O'Connor, with whom Justice Brennan, Justice Marshall, and Justice Blackmun join as to Parts I and II, concurring in the judgment.

Although I agree with the result the Court reaches in this case, I cannot join its opinion. In my view, today's holding dramatically departs from well-settled First Amendment jurisprudence, appears unnecessary to resolve the question presented, and is incompatible with our Nation's fundamental commitment to individual religious liberty. [. . .]

II

The Court today extracts from our long history of free exercise precedents the single categorical rule that "if prohibiting the exercise of religion . . . is . . . merely the incidental effect of a generally applicable and otherwise valid provision, the First Amendment has not been offended." Indeed, the Court holds that where the law is a generally applicable criminal prohibition, our usual free exercise jurisprudence does not even apply. To reach this sweeping result, however, the Court must not only give a strained reading of the First Amendment but must also disregard our consistent application of free exercise doctrine to cases involving generally applicable regulations that burden religious conduct.

A

The Free Exercise Clause of the First Amendment commands that "Congress shall make no law . . . prohibiting the free exercise [of religion]." [. . .] Because the First Amendment does not distinguish between religious belief and religious conduct, conduct motivated by sincere religious belief, like the belief itself, must be at least presumptively protected by the Free Exercise Clause.

The Court today, however, interprets the Clause to permit the government to prohibit, without justification, conduct mandated by an individual's religious beliefs, so long as that prohibition is generally applicable. But a law that prohibits certain conduct—conduct that happens to be an act of worship for someone—manifestly does prohibit that person's free exercise of his religion. A person who is barred from engaging in religiously motivated conduct is barred from freely exercising his religion. Moreover, that person is barred from freely exercising his religion regardless of whether the law prohibits the conduct only when engaged in for religious reasons, only by members of that religion, or by all persons. It is difficult to deny that a law that prohibits religiously motivated conduct, even if the law is generally applicable, does not at least implicate First Amendment concerns.

The Court responds that generally applicable laws are "one large step" removed from laws aimed at specific religious practices. The First Amendment, however, does not distinguish between laws that are generally applicable and laws that target particular religious practices. Indeed, few States would be so naive as to enact a law directly prohibiting or burdening a religious practice as such. Our free exercise cases have all concerned generally applicable laws that had the effect of significantly burdening a religious practice. [. . .]

To say that a person's right to free exercise has been burdened, of course, does not mean that he has an absolute right to engage in the conduct. [. . .] Instead, we have respected both the First Amendment's express textual mandate and the governmental interest in regulation of conduct by requiring the government to justify any substantial burden on religiously motivated conduct by a compelling state interest and by means narrowly tailored to achieve that interest. [. . .] The compelling interest test effectuates the First Amendment's command that religious liberty is an independent liberty, that it occupies a preferred position, and that the Court will not permit encroachments upon this liberty, whether direct or indirect, unless required by clear and compelling governmental interests "of the highest order."

The Court attempts to support its narrow reading of the Clause by claiming that "[w]e have never held that an individual's religious beliefs excuse him from compliance with an otherwise valid law prohibiting conduct that the State is free to regulate." But as the Court later notes, as it must, in cases such as *Cantwell* [*v. Connecticut* (1940)] and *Yoder* we have in fact interpreted the Free Exercise Clause to forbid application of a generally applicable prohibition to religiously motivated conduct. Indeed, in *Yoder* we expressly rejected the interpretation the Court now adopts. [. . .]

The Court endeavors to escape from our decisions in *Cantwell* and *Yoder* by labeling them "hybrid" decisions, but there is no denying that both cases expressly relied on the Free Exercise Clause, and that we have consistently regarded those cases as part of the mainstream of our free exercise jurisprudence. Moreover, in each of the other cases cited by the Court to support its categorical rule, we rejected the particular constitutional claims before us only after carefully weighing the competing interests. [. . .]

B

In my view [. . .] the essence of a free exercise claim is relief from a burden imposed by government on religious practices or beliefs, whether the burden is imposed directly through laws that prohibit or compel specific religious practices, or indirectly through laws that, in effect, make abandonment of one's own religion or conformity to the religious beliefs of others the price of an equal place in the civil community. As we explained in *Thomas*:

> Where the state conditions receipt of an important benefit upon conduct proscribed by a religious faith, or where it denies such a benefit because of conduct mandated by religious belief, thereby putting substantial pressure on an adherent to modify his behavior and to violate his beliefs, a burden upon religion exists.

A State that makes criminal an individual's religiously motivated conduct burdens that individual's free exercise of religion in the severest manner possible, for it "results in the choice to the individual of either abandoning his religious principle or facing criminal prosecution." *Braunfeld*. [. . .]

Indeed, we have never distinguished between cases in which a State conditions receipt of a benefit on conduct prohibited by religious beliefs and cases in which a State affirmatively prohibits such conduct. The *Sherbert* compelling interest test applies in both kinds of cases. [. . .]

I would reaffirm that principle today. [. . .]

Legislatures, of course, have always been "left free to reach actions which were in violation of social duties or subversive of good order." *Reynolds*. Yet because of the close relationship between conduct and religious belief, "[i]n every case the power to regulate must be so exercised as not, in attaining a permissible end, unduly to infringe the protected freedom." *Cantwell*. Once it has been shown that a government regulation or criminal prohibition burdens the free exercise of religion, we have consistently asked the government to demonstrate that unbending application of its regulation to the religious objector "is essential to accomplish an overriding governmental interest," *Lee*, or represents "the least restrictive means of achieving some compelling state interest," *Thomas v. Review Bd. of Indiana Employment Security Div.* (1981). To me, the sounder approach—the approach more consistent with our role as judges to decide each case on its individual merits—is to apply this test in each case to determine whether the burden on the specific plaintiffs before us is constitutionally significant and whether the particular criminal interest asserted by the State before us is compelling. Even if, as an empirical matter, a government's criminal laws might usually serve a compelling interest in health, safety, or public order, the First Amendment at least requires a case-by-case determination of the question, sensitive to the facts of each particular claim. Given the range of conduct that a State might legitimately make criminal, we cannot assume, merely because a law carries criminal sanctions and is generally applicable, that the First Amendment never requires the State to grant a limited exemption for religiously motivated conduct. [. . .]

The Court today gives no convincing reason to depart from settled First Amendment jurisprudence. There is nothing talismanic about neutral laws of general applicability or general criminal prohibitions, for laws neutral toward religion can coerce a person to violate his religious conscience or intrude upon his religious duties just as effectively as laws aimed at religion. Although the Court suggests that the compelling interest test, as applied to generally applicable laws, would result in a "constitutional anomaly," the First Amendment unequivocally makes freedom of religion, like freedom from race discrimination and freedom of speech, a "constitutional nor[m]," not an "anomaly." [. . .] The Court's parade of horribles not only fails as a reason for discarding the compelling interest test, it instead demonstrates just the opposite: that courts have been quite capable of applying our free exercise jurisprudence to strike sensible balances between religious liberty and competing state interests.

Finally, the Court today suggests that the disfavoring of minority religions is an "unavoidable consequence" under our system of government and that accommodation of such religions must be left to the political process. In my view, however, the First Amendment was enacted precisely to protect the rights of those whose religious practices are not shared by the majority and may be viewed with hostility. The history of our free exercise doctrine amply demonstrates the harsh impact majoritarian rule has had on unpopular or emerging religious groups such as the Jehovah's Witnesses and the Amish. Indeed, the words of Justice Jackson in *West Virginia State Bd. of Ed. v. Barnette* (1943) are apt:

> The very purpose of a Bill of Rights was to withdraw certain subjects from the vicissitudes of political controversy, to place them beyond the reach of majorities and officials and to establish them as legal principles to be applied by the courts. One's right to life, liberty, and property, to free speech, a free press, freedom of worship and assembly, and other fundamental rights may not

be submitted to vote; they depend on the outcome of no elections.

The compelling interest test reflects the First Amendment's mandate of preserving religious liberty to the fullest extent possible in a pluralistic society. For the Court to deem this command a "luxury," is to denigrate "[t]he very purpose of a Bill of Rights."

III

The Court's holding today not only misreads settled First Amendment precedent; it appears to be unnecessary to this case. I would reach the same result applying our established free exercise jurisprudence. [. . .]

B

[T]he critical question in this case is whether exempting respondents from the State's general criminal prohibition "will unduly interfere with fulfillment of the governmental interest." Although the question is close, I would conclude that uniform application of Oregon's criminal prohibition is "essential to accomplish" its overriding interest in preventing the physical harm caused by the use of a Schedule I controlled substance. Oregon's criminal prohibition represents that State's judgment that the possession and use of controlled substances, even by only one person, is inherently harmful and dangerous. Because the health effects caused by the use of controlled substances exist regardless of the motivation of the user, the use of such substances, even for religious purposes, violates the very purpose of the laws that prohibit them. Moreover, in view of the societal interest in preventing trafficking in controlled substances, uniform application of the criminal prohibition at issue is essential to the effectiveness of Oregon's stated interest in preventing any possession of peyote. [. . .]

Harry Blackmun

Employment Division, Oregon Department of Human Resources v. Smith, Dissent (1990)

Justice Blackmun, with whom Justice Brennan and Justice Marshall join, dissenting.

This Court over the years painstakingly has developed a consistent and exacting standard to test the constitutionality of a state statute that burdens the free exercise of religion. Such a statute may stand only if the law in general, and the State's refusal to allow a religious exemption in particular, are justified by a compelling interest that cannot be served by less restrictive means.

Until today, I thought this was a settled and inviolate principle of this Court's First Amendment jurisprudence. The majority, however, perfunctorily dismisses it as a "constitutional anomaly." As carefully detailed in Justice O'Connor's concurring opinion, the majority is able to arrive at this view only by mischaracterizing this Court's precedents. The Court discards leading free exercise cases such as *Cantwell v. Connecticut* (1940) and *Wisconsin v. Yoder* (1972) as "hybrid." [. . .]

This distorted view of our precedents leads the majority to conclude that strict scrutiny of a state law burdening the free exercise of religion is a "luxury" that a well-ordered society cannot afford, and that the repression of minority religions is an "unavoidable consequence of democratic government." I do not believe the Founders thought their dearly bought freedom from religious persecution a "luxury," but an essential element of liberty—and they could not have thought religious intolerance "unavoidable," for they drafted the Religion Clauses precisely in order to avoid that intolerance.

For these reasons, I agree with Justice O'Connor's analysis of the applicable free exercise doctrine, and I join parts I and II of her opinion. As she points out, "the critical question in this case is whether exempting respondents from the State's general criminal prohibition 'will unduly interfere with fulfillment of the governmental interest.'" I do disagree, however, with her specific answer to that question.

Oren Lyons

Address at the Aboriginal Law Association Conference, McGill University (1991)

Sovereignty is a term that we hear being used all the time and particularly in relation to Indians. It is a term that should be applied to Indians. However, I have noticed in the past ten years or so a certain change in terminology. Nationally and internationally, the term "sovereignty" is often being replaced by the term

"autonomy." I have noticed this in relation to the Nicaraguan conflict and the Mesquitoe Indians.

What is the difference between the two terms? What is sovereignty? We have always taken a rather simplistic view. We said that sovereignty is the act thereof. You are as sovereign as you are able to be.

Generally, sovereignty is applied to nations and today, to nation-states. Indians have always perceived themselves to be nations, sovereign and independent. Further, we apply sovereignty even further than nations. We apply it to individuals in the form of respect. Indian People, of all people, understand the concept of freedom and being born free with rights. [. . .]

Since 1992 is a year of assessment, where we stand back and look at five hundred years of activity in the western hemisphere and assess what condition we are in. It can be a year of atonement for what happened to the Indigenous Peoples who caught the brunt of this invasion, or it can be a year of commitment to see that the next five hundred years are going to be better than the last five hundred.

This process of reflection will have to involve Indian nations. We have to make our own assessment of our condition. We have to present a position to challenge this idea of a celebration, to challenge this idea of a discovery. Discovery is a very arrogant perception; we were "discovered," sort of like the flora and fauna of North America. In truth, there were free nations here with a real understanding of government and community, of the process and great principles of life. In fact, on the landfall of Christopher Columbus, freedom was rampant in North, Central and South America. Everybody was free and living in a natural world economy where they had economic security in perpetuity. They had adjusted themselves to working with the land, and understood that every year that the land renewed itself.

Now, coming across the water were people with a different perception about economy. As a matter of fact, up to the present day, the Governments of Canada and the United States have spent their time trying to get our people involved in this economy. They have spent a lot of time trying to tell us about the importance of private property as opposed to community property. We hear terms like development, progressive development, sustainable development, but our perception is that if you do not operate around the real laws of the universe, you are challenging fundamental cycles that you depend on for life.

So, there was obviously a conflict between Christopher Columbus' perception, and the people that he met. All of the writing says the First Peoples were healthy, happy and well-fed, and not overly, inclined to warfare. Yet, the process of domination began immediately. He said: these would make good slaves. That was his first message back to the Queen: we can make slaves of these people since they are easily subjugated, and they do not know much about warfare. Any ten of my men can take over this island with the technology and weapons we have brought over.

The basic conflict relates to economy because Indian Nations operated on the basis of a natural world economy. They had Thanksgiving ceremonies that went around the clock and around the calendar year. Something was always coming up so there was always Thanksgiving in a land-based economy. It was part of the structure of a community. It was an instruction to respect what was growing. This was true across the Americas. Yet, our white brother kept telling us there was a better way: get rich. Our people had a hard time with that. They said, "No, our land is held in common, everyone owns the land. Water is free, air is free, everything you need for life sustenance is free." And he said, "I would like to buy your land." They said, "What do you mean by buying?" Now we have people "buying" his argument. We have people, our own people, who are now willing to "sell" long-term sovereignty for short-term personal gain.

As we sit back and assess these last five hundred years, let us look at what has happened to our people. How have the Indian Nations fared? How have our children? How are our institutions? Are they holding up? How are our principles? Are they holding up? We have to look at ourselves because as tough as these last five hundred years have been, the next five hundred or even fifty years are going to be tougher.

There is a fundamental issue here that we have to look at because human beings are displacing life around the world. Huge populations are displacing life whether it is trees, the elephants in Africa, the tigers in India or the buffalo in this country. They are not here anymore. Yet, there are more and more people. There is a displacement going on here of things a fundamental economy needs. The Indians understood one thing: they understood that the law of flesh, blood and bones is common to all living beings. We are under one common law here. We are animals, but we are animals with intellect. Intellect is what makes us dangerous because we have the foreknowledge of death. Animals know when death is coming, and they prepare for it. Yet, we know from a very young age that we are going to die. This is a tremendous knowledge, but how do you use that knowledge? How do you work with it?

When one speaks of generations the way the Indians speak of them, we must see that the next generations, those faces coming from the earth, have the same good that we have and can enjoy the same law that we do. Well, in assessing five hundred years in this country, we see that the next seven generations are not going to enjoy that. Every day, at least six species of life become extinct. So, when you talk about the philosophy of sovereignty, you must talk of longevity and the future. This is the common sense that comes from the long experience of Indian Nations being in one place: if you do not work with the laws that surround you, you will not survive. It is quite simple. We know that there is no mercy in the natural law whatsoever. It will exact retribution in direct ratio to violation. You cannot discuss this— there are no lawyers, only the retribution. The problem here is that we visit this retribution on our children and on our grandchildren. We leave them the problem of our excesses. What do we say to greedy individuals that say sovereignty is money?

I never believed the white man when he said his way was better. I never believed it. I always believed that our way was better, maybe just because I knew more about it. The truth is, if we sit back and really look at it, there is some hard news here for all of us no matter who we are.

When we speak of sovereignty, we have to have a large conceptualization of what it is we are talking about. With Indian Nations, it is not just a political term, it is also a spiritual term. It may be even be more spiritual than political. One of our people once said that spirituality is the highest form of politics. So, let us keep the parameters of what we are talking about clear.

The parameters are beyond the oceans that surround us, and they are beyond our time here on earth. The parameters we are discussing reverberate into the future. If your economy does not function within those parameters then you are shortchanging those future generations we talked about. Maybe it is only the Indians that talk about the seventh generation. I do not know. Since we have talked about it a lot, I have heard it again and again. I hear it from strangers, I hear it from strange places. Why not? It seems to us common law and common sense. So, let us say that sovereign is common sense in its most basic fundamental form: common sense and respect for all life.

Land is the issue, land has always been the issue. We cannot trade our jurisdiction over lands and territories for money. Our lands and our right to govern ourselves are all we have. If we gamble our lands for money, jurisdiction and taxation, we will lose because that is the white man's game.

DANIEL ELAZAR

Obligations and Rights in the Jewish Political Tradition: Some Preliminary Observations (1991)

Rights in the Contemporary World

The conventional wisdom in our rights-conscious age is that there is nothing quite as fixed and permanent as rights. The only changes that take place in connection with them are in connection with an expanded understanding of what constitute individual rights, their scope, and meaning.[1] Serious students of

---

1. Contemporary works on human rights include: Ronald S. Dworkin, *Taking Rights Seriously* (Cambridge,

the subject know that this is not exactly the case, that the very concept of rights as we understand it is a modern one developed in the seventeenth and eighteenth centuries as one of the foundation stones of modern democracy.[2]

We begin by trying to understand what we are looking for. Present understandings of rights are all derived from modernity; hence we can begin with the two most prominent modern formulations, that of Locke — "life, liberty and property" — and that of the U.S. Declaration of Independence — "life, liberty, and the pursuit of happiness." The last of the Declaration's triad subsumes the right of property while defining a broader right to pursue happiness which is not directly defined. Under modern and post-modern rights doctrine, at least these rights are inherent in all humans and inalienable. At most, humans can come together for collective action in such a way that they delegate some control over the expression and effectuation of these rights to their common association in which they retain a decision-making role, directly or indirectly.

These rights transcend civil society, which then translates them into constitutional, civil, criminal, and property rights. Throughout much of the modern period, the rights directly associated with the two triads were considered to be natural rights. In the postmodern epoch they are defined as human rights. In either case, the theory provides that humans start with those rights and assume obligations only as they agree to enter civil society. In that sense, at least, obligations are secondary to rights and so they have come to be treated in rights-based Western democracies. The notion that for every right there is a corresonding responsibility or duty is

not unknown and indeed is embodied in a number of contemporary constitutions, but it has been principally associated with less-than-democratic if not totalitarian regimes, offering them a means to pay obeisance to human rights while at the same time making it possible for the state to radically or drastically restrict their exercise.

Leo Strauss has taught us the difference between the modern and premodern philosophic understanding of rights and "right." Premodern classical philosophy understood natural right as part of natural law, a normative standard built into the universe. Classical natural right was related to the good life and the good commonwealth, which, while difficult of attainment by human beings, could be achieved with the right convergence of conditions and forces.

The good life within the good commonwealth was grounded in an appropriate understanding of the ideal public order and the duties of men in their efforts to achieve it. Modern natural rights, on the other hand, adhere exclusively to individuals and are derived from their natural psychology, "scientifically" discovered. Rights adhere to individuals qua individuals, and while their preservation is the highest norm, as rights they are not associated with normative goals but rather with the preservation of individual life and liberty as (close to) absolutes. Rooted in methodological individualism, they reflect the liberal principle that the individual is the only atom from which to begin the construction or analysis of civil society.

While early modern thought recognized and emphasized that all society is civil society, organized politically from its foundations (in contradistinction to premodern organic views, or nineteenth century views of the subject which sought the "automatic society" that existed independently of political organization), it also emphasizes that civil society's governmental dimension should be limited; indeed as limited as possible. For moderns of this school, civil society and government were instituted by individuals (solely) to protect their rights. Inevitably, in such a system, individual rights take precedence over all else, and every institution, including the commonwealth, ultimately is judged by how well it protects individual rights as defined. Since there is no other overarching conception of the good, there is no standard against which to measure individual behavior in

Mass.: University of Harvard Press, 1978); John Rawls, *A Theory of Justice* (Cambridge, Mass.: Harvard University Press, 1971); L. W. Sumner, *The Moral Foundation of Rights* (Oxford: Clarendon Press, 1987); Judith J. Thomson, *The Realm of Rights* (Cambridge, Mass.: Harvard University Press, 1990).

2.   Cf. Leo Strauss, *Natural Right and History* (Chicago: University of Chicago Press, 1953); Thomas Hobbes, *Leviathan* (London: J. M. Dent & Sons, 1947); John Locke, *Two Treatises of Government*, edited by Peter Laslett (Cambridge: Cambridge University Press, 1960).

riate exercise of individual rights other ᵫbiguous question of injury to others in ⸴se of one's own rights.

The entire edifice of modern political life, indeed, of modern civil society, is constructed on this modern conception of rights, first embodied constitutionally in the English Bill of Rights of 1689 and expanded in the declarations of rights of the American state constitutions beginning in 1776, the U.S. Bill of Rights and the French Declaration of the Rights of Man both drafted in 1789. Its most recent and far-reaching expressions to be found in the Universal Declaration of Human Rights.[3] This edifice is modified only to the extent that some would argue that every right has correlative responsibilities, a position which is viewed in certain quarters as less and less appropriate to postmodern democracy and to contemporary civil society.[4]

In the United States, for example, the conception of what constitutes rights among the thinking public has moved from the early seventeenth century conception of rights as liberties derived from prior obligations to modern individual rights to be protected by government in the spirit of John Locke, to natural rights as constitutional rights in the late eighteenth and nineteenth centuries, to the late twentieth century view of natural rights as human rights that take

precedence over all social concerns. That is where Americans are today.[5]

The Traditional Jewish View

The traditional Jewish view offers a somewhat different position on rights and obligations which is derived from the biblical sense of human obligation to God as a result of our covenants with Him. To explore the traditional Jewish conceptions of obligations and rights, we must be prepared to resolutely confront a reality that is often very different from contemporary theories. We must do so without apologetics and most especially without attempting to reconcile or harmonize Jewish views with contemporary views in every case, unless it is clearly appropriate to do so.

So problematic is the topic before us for contemporary humans that the Encyclopedia Judaica has no entry at all under rights and under obligations has entries only with regard to the talmudic laws of property. While some of the issues raised here are treated in that work by eminent experts such as Judges Haim Cohn and Menahem Elon, they are subsumed under other categories.[6] The Hebrew terms we use today to define rights are strictly modern ones whose usage was established within the last 100 years, as part of the development of modern Hebrew, in line with contemporary Western thought.[7]

After we complete our analysis we may be able to draw certain conclusions, but we must fully and frankly face the possibility that the Jewish tradition in this respect is radically different from the rights doctrines that we all have learned as normative. Our goal here as scholars is understanding. Whatever personal

3. Albert Blaustein, *Constitutions of the World* (Dobbs Ferry: Ocean Publications, 1990) and Albert Blaustein, Roger Clark, and Jay Sigler, *A Human Rights Sourcebook* (New York: Paragon, 1987); Donald Lutz, *The Origins of American Constitutionalism* (Baton Rouge: Louisiana University Press, 1988) and *Popular Consent and Popular Control* (Baton Rouge: Louisiana University Press, 1980). On the English Bill of Rights, see Maurice Ashley, *The Glorious Revolution of 1688* (London: Hodden and Stoughton, 1966), pp. 206–209 (Declaration of Rights) and pp. 183–191. Cf. also John Miller, *The Glorious Revolution* (London: Longman, 1983), pp. 34–38 and 114–116.

4. On rights and responsibilities, see James F. Childress, *Moral Responsibility in Conflicts* (Baton Rouge: Louisiana University Press, 1982); Ren Blanchard Edwards, *Freedom, Responsibility and Obligation* (The Hague: M. Nijhoff, 1969); William Horosz, *The Crisis of Responsibility* (Norman: University of Oklahoma Press, 1975); Hans Jonas, *The Imperative of Responsibility* (Chicago: University of Chicago Press, 1984); Ralph Ross, *Obligation* (Ann Arbor: University of Michigan Press, 1970).

5. Cf. forthcoming issue (1992) of *Publius* on rights.

6. Encyclopedia Judaica, Cf. Haim Colin, *Human Rights in Jewish Law* (New York: Ktav, 1984), especially the Introduction, "Rights and Duties"; Menachem Elon, *The Principles of Jewish Law* (Jerusalem: Encyclopedia Judaica, 1975) and *The Restraint of the Person as a Means in the Collection of Debts* (Jerusalem: Magnes Press, 1981).

7. Cf. Yaacov Canaani, *Otzar HaLashon Halvrit* (Tel Aviv: Masada, 1968); Abraham Ben Shoshan, *HaMilon HaHadash* (Jerusalem: Kiryat Sefer, 1957).

conclusions we draw from that understanding must be drawn separately.

We begin with the fact that Jewish tradition derives rights from the obligation of all humans to God as their creator, sovereign, and covenant partner. Fundamental to any Jewish conception here is the principle that God is the creator and sovereign of the universe, all of which ultimately belongs to Him—"*Ki li kol ha'aretz*" (because the whole earth is Mine)—including all life within it (Ex. 19:5; Lev. 25:23).

At the same time, since God's universe is founded on *tzedakah u'mishpat* (justice or right in the German sense of recht and law in the sense of right judgment), God's relations with His creatures must have a dimension of what have been called rights and liberties built in, as it were. Humans have what we call rights and liberties by the authority of our covenant with God. Whether or not *tzedakah u'mishpat* are built into the very fabric of the universe (i.e., represent the biblical equivalent of natural law) or are the products of covenant is a matter of some dispute among students of biblical and Jewish thought. This writer believes that while the potential for *tzedek* (justice) may be built into the universe, *tzedakah u'mishpat* exists by covenant and certainly must be actualized through covenants.

Tzedakah u'mishpat are of the essence in biblical rights terminology.[8] They are invoked by *tzaakah* (literally, calling out) or appeal, what appears in the Bible to be a formal step; that is to say, where *tzedakah u'mishpat* are violated the victims can appeal (*tzoak*) to God or to human kings for redress. (Contrast the situation where humans must appeal to God for mercy because they have no particular rights at stake.) Moshe Greenberg argues that, according to the Bible, government is instituted among men to protect the *tzedakah u'mishpat* of the weak and perhaps solely for that purpose.[9]

The special significance of this for our topic is that while humans have nothing other than what God grants or covenants with them, as God's possessions no human instrumentality, certainly no state, can legitimately interfere with their God-given rights, liberties, protections, or obligations. Once God has commanded or covenanted (and his commandments are based upon His covenants), no human authority or agency has the right to interpose itself without the consent of those commanded or those who are partners to the covenant. As we all know, this, indeed, is the foundation of the modern development of rights, growing out of sixteenth and seventeenth century Reformed Protestantism which took these matters very seriously indeed.[10]

While partnership with God is based upon humans' acceptance of their covenant obligations toward Him, those rest upon the establishment of a certain measure of equality between God and humans, itself a very daring idea. Only those with at least a minimum of equality can be partners. Since the Bible projects an omnipotent, omniscient and eternal God while all humans are mortal and limited, even after eating from the tree of knowledge, that partnership is essentially a functional one, confined to certain tasks of *yishuv ha-aretz* (the settlement of the earth) and *tikkun olam* (the repair of the world); in other words, the earthly tasks of this world where humans increasingly have played a major role in God's scheme of things. It is by virtue of that partnership and the obligations that flow from it that humans have rights that are real rights, not at all diminished by being derived from obligations. Nevertheless, because they are rights that flow from God's covenant with humans, they are to some extent conditional on humans' maintaining their part of the covenantal bargain. In the language of the Puritans, they have a federal (*foedus* is the Latin term

---

8. Moshe Greenberg, "Al Zekhuyot U'Hovot Ba Mikrah" (On Rights and Obligations in the Bible) presented to the Beit Vaad Seminar on Obligations and Rights in the Jewish Political Tradition, Jerusalem Center for Public Affairs, November 8, 1991 (Unpublished; transcript and working paper in the files of the Jerusalem Center for Public Affairs).

9. Ibid., p. 3.

10. See, e.g., Harold J. Laski, *A Defense of Liberty Against Tyrants*, a translation of the *Vindicae Contra Tyrannos* by Junius Brutus (New York: Burt Franklin, 1972); John Milton, *Areopagitica*, with a commentary by Sir Richard C. Jebb (Cambridge: Cambridge University Press, 1940) and *Paradise Lost*, edited by Alistair Fowler (London: Longman, 1971); J. Wayne Baker, *Heinrich Bullinger and the Covenant* (Athens, Ohio: Ohio University Press, 1980).

for covenant, a translation of brit) obligation, fulfillment of which guarantees their federal liberty, of which more below.[11]

The character of biblically-mandated obligations thus relates to the character of the covenant in question. Thus, humanity as a whole is bound by the Noahide covenant (Genesis 9), based on the common obligation of all to the recognition of God's sovereignty, the protection of human life, and the pursuit of justice on earth. For Jews, who are further bound by the covenant of Sinai, there is a further obligation of holiness (Deuteronomy 19–21) as the highest form of imitation of God. Whether or not the Jewish people in this respect were to be the pioneers for the rest of humanity or whether their holiness is forever exclusive is a question that has been the subject of some discussion. (Many Christians see themselves so bound but with a twist.) While it does have a bearing on rights of citizenship, what bearing it has on human rights is an open question. On basic matters of human right to life, sustenance, property (within limits), and justice, the Bible explicitly provides that "the stranger within thy gates" has the same rights as Israelites, even in the land of Israel (cf. Ex. 23:9; Lev. 25:23; Deut. 15:29). What the outer limits of those basic rights are has been a matter of some discussion over the years.[12]

What is critical about the relationship between rights and obligations in the biblical tradition and in subsequent Jewish tradition is that those covenanted with God are obligated to their fellows under the terms of the covenant to do them justice, from whence derives their right to justice. The covenant partners are obligated because they are covenant partners. For Jews the obligation is that they must do justice to the widow and the orphan and the stranger in order to be holy (Ex. 23:9; Deut. 15:29). So it is not that the widows, orphans and strangers have rights in an abstract sense, but that they can

call upon their fellow Israelites to live up to their obligations.

Is this merely a semantic point? I think not, because Israelites are equally obligated to do justice in the form of punishing those who are violators of God's covenant, who cannot claim some a priori natural or human right to be protected against such punishments. What they can claim on constitutional grounds is that the Israelites must live up to their obligations. In some respects that is an even stronger claim than a rights claim. But however it is perceived, it is a different one.

Even more than that, rights themselves are expressed as obligations. Thus humans have an obligation to remain alive and to preserve the lives of others. From this what moderns would refer to as the right to life can be inferred, but in classical Jewish sources it is expressed as the duty to maintain life—your own and that of others—a covenantal obligation, as it were. Thus the duty to preserve life is derived from the belief that it is God who bestows human life and therefore only He can prescribe the ways in which it can be taken away. Every human has a duty to preserve his or her life as part of his or her duties to God.

The issue is even more clearly joined in the case of property. The right of humans to own and use property can be derived from many scriptural statements of obligations, not the least of which is the commandment, "Thou shalt not steal" (Ex. 20:13; Deut. 5:17). Scripture also clearly states that all land and other property ultimately belongs to God who prescribes the parameters of its use by humans (Lev. 25:23). Thus, for example, people can own land. If that land is another Jew's *nahalah* (biblical inheritance) in Eretz Israel, it must be returned to the family of the original owners at the appropriate jubilee year (Lev. 25:8ff). While in a person's possession, agricultural land must be governed by rules providing for the poor to glean, the worker to eat of its produce, and the ox working the field not to be muzzled (Lev. 25:1–7).

Over the years these restrictions on property rights were interpreted broadly rather than narrowly to create a set of environmental rights that recognized the special needs of individual humans. These included protections of the right to sunlight that existed when a property was acquired, even at the expense of preventing another from building on his

---

11. On the biblical, talmudic and later Jewish views of covenant, see Daniel J. Elazar, ed., *Kinship and Consent: The Jewish Political Tradition and Its Contemporary Uses* (Jerusalem: Jerusalem Center for Public Affairs and University Press of America, 1983) and *The Covenant Tradition in Politics*, vol. 1 (forthcoming).

12. Cf. Cohen, *op. cit.*

adjacent property in such a way that would interfere with that sunlight, or a right to ventilation protected in the same way. Whether formally defined that way or not, these were essentially duties/rights of *re'ut*, that is to say, neighborly comity of the kind described in Deuteronomy (e.g., Deut. 23:25–26; 24:10; 27:17) constitutionally required of Israelites in the Torah. *Re'ut* is an extension of *hesed* and as such is an obligation of holiness on the part of covenant partners.

A different and more extensive set of rights developed in the area of criminal protections (Ex. 21–24). In that field the relevant biblical passages were built into a comprehensive system of protection of the civil rights of individuals accused of crimes. These protections were so extensive that at points they bordered on the ridiculous as, for example, when certain Sages suggested that only if a person was actually warned at the time against committing the crime for which he was accused could that person be held responsible.

This ideal talmudic world of protection of the rights of the accused was seized upon by many contemporary Jews to claim, not improperly, that the Jewish people had pioneered in that field of civil and communal rights protection.[13] Indeed, their writings even came to the attention of such bodies as the United States Supreme Court which cited talmudic precedents in some of their landmark cases.[14] In fact,

as we now know from the historical evidence available to us, it seems that there is a question as to whether these talmudic laws and standards were always enforced since the more extreme ones seem to have been developed after the autonomous Jewish authorities lost criminal law jurisdiction in the Roman Empire. In Babylonia, where the Resh Galuta acquired such jurisdiction, it was customary for accused criminals to be turned over to a parallel system of what might be called civil courts under his authority where trial procedures were more in conformity with the standards of the time, thereby preserving the talmudic principles intact while at the same time being able to administer a criminal justice system.[15] Nevertheless, it can be said that the right to life was well-protected at least for those humans deemed bound by the Noahide covenant.

The Torah tends to be uncompromising in its expression of the obligations of humans in general and Jews in particular. The other books of the Bible introduce loopholes, the most important of which are associated with the *mishpat hamelekh* or *mishpat hamelukhah* (the law of the king or of the kingdom), derived particularly from I Samuel 8 where the prophet Samuel warns Israelites against seeking a king because of the powers a king inevitably has. It seems that even in biblical times kings exercised power over and above Torah constraints. Subsequently the idea of the *mishpat hamelekh* as a loophole, especially against stringent aspects of the criminal law.[16]

What emerges out of the biblical approach are a series of protections and limitations which can roughly be translated into rights and obligations as

13. Cf. *inter alia*, Sol Roth, *Halakhah and Politics: The Jewish Idea of a State* (New York: Ktav, 1988); Louis Finkelstein, ed., *The Jews: Their History, Culture, and Religion* (New York: Schocken Books, 1970).

14. U.S. Supreme Court cases citing Jewish sources include: *County of Allegheny v. American Civil Liberties Union* (1989), 492 U.S. 573, 109 S. Ct. 3086; *Murray v. Curlett* (1963), 374 U.S. 203, 83 S. Ct. 1560; *McCollum v. Board of Education*, 333 U.S. 203 (1948); *Zorach v. Clauson* 343 U.S. 306 (1952); *Torcaso v. Watkins* 367 U.S. 488 (1961); *Engel v. Vitale* 370 U.S. 421 (1962); and *Nom. School District of Abington Township v. Schempp* 374 U.S. 203 (1963).

In *McCollum*, the Court ruled to allow a certain "released time" during which sectarian religious education could be offered during the school day. *Zorach* extended this "accommodation" by granting the use of public funds for religious instruction in schools. In *Torcaso*, Justice Black wrote the decision striking down a provision in the

Maryland constitution which required prospective public officials to take an oath of faith in God. In *Engel*, Justice Black again wrote the decision striking down the use of a non-sectarian prayer in New York schools. In *Schempp*, Bible-reading and the Lord's Prayer were prohibited from public school education.

15. Moshe Ber, *Amorai Bavel* (Ramat Gan: Bar-Ilan University Press, 1982) (Hebrew); and Shalom Albeck, *Batei HaDin BeYamei HaTalmud* (Ramat Gan: Bar-Ilan University Press, 1980).

16. Cf. Simon Federbush, *Mishpat HaMeluchah B'Yisrael* (Jerusalem: Mossad HaRav Kook, 1952) (Hebrew).

when the poor are given rights to glean the fields during the harvest. Thus, many of these protections and limitations become what we would call rights, as protected through the Torah as any constitutional right is today. The result, as already noted, are rights and obligations stemming from the federal relationship between humans and God, what John Winthrop, the great Puritan governor of Massachusetts, was later to define as "federal liberty."[17]

In the last analysis, while there may not be natural rights, there are fundamental rights in the sense that all humans are bound by covenant with God, at least through the Noahide covenant (some Christians would claim an earlier covenant with Adam as well). These fundamental rights are in that sense constitutional or federal rather than inherent. They certainly are not like the vulgar modern conception of rights as the individual's right to do whatever he or she pleases, perhaps limited only by how an individual's actions effect others, but maybe not even by that.

Who Can Be Obligated and How?

This leads to another question, namely, who can be obligated and how. We have already touched upon this question to some extent in the preceding paragraphs, but it deserves to be sharpened because it has to do with rights that are other than fundamental. For example, while all humans are obligated by the Noahide covenant to recognize God's sovereignty and pursue and do justice, only Jews are obligated by the Sinai covenant to maintain the more extensive norms—social and ritual—of that covenant, and among traditional Jews there are distinctions between men and women as to who is obligated to do what with regard to rituals.

No such distinctions prevail, however, with regard to those obligations associated with what we understand to be rights. There all are equally responsible. The talmudic sages raise the question as to whether those obligations extend only to fellow Jews or to all humans. Thus the famous discussion between Rabbi Akiva and Ben Azzai, in which Rabbi Akiva states that the most important verse in Torah is *veahavta l're'akha kamokha* (love thy neighbor as thyself) (Lev. 19:18), while Ben Azzai claims that even more important is the verse *elle toledot ha-adam* (these are the generations of Adam) because *rea* (neighbor) has been interpreted by some to apply only to fellow Jews while the second verse clearly refers to the common descent of all humans and hence their common equality before God (Gen. 5:1–2).

Re'ut (neighborliness) is a good example of a biblical concept related to what we could call rights. It is a very important covenant concept, dealing with those to whom we are obligated beyond the letter of the law, what in Anglo-American jurisprudence is referred to as comity and in German as *treu*. In that way it also reflects a certain right which *re'im* possess toward one another. Thus it is important to establish who is a *re'a* to determine the scope of our obligations toward him.

What is clear is that biblical terminology dealing with these concepts is not our terminology. The biblical term expressing obligation is *hesed*, which is appropriately translated "loving covenant obligation." *La'asot hesed* (to act out of loving covenant obligation) reflects the way the burden is on he who is obligated to do what he does because of his covenant obligations and is connected with holiness.[18] No other biblical word relates to what we call obligation. The contemporary word for obligation, *hovah*, comes into use only in the Middle Ages.

Hesed is a very powerful word and a very covenantal one. It cannot be understood apart from its

---

17. For Winthrop's speech in which he refers to federal liberty, see Sam Savage, ed., *History of New England, 1630–1649* (Boston: Harvard University Press, 1853), vol. 2, pp. 279–282. On federal liberty, see also Frederick Carney (trans. and ed.), *The Politics of Johannes Althusius* (Boston: Beacon Press, 1962); and Daniel J. Elazar, *The American Constitutional Tradition* (Lanham, Maryland: University Press of America, 1989), p. 167.

18. On *hesed*, see Elazar, *Kinship and Consent*; Nelson Glueck, *Hesed in the Bible* (New York: Ktav, 1975); Moshe Weinfeld, "Jeremiah and the Spiritual Metamorphosis of Israel" (Reprint from *Zeitschrift fur die Testamentlische Wissenschaft*, 1976); and Norman Snaith, *The Distinctive Ideas of the Old Testament* (New York: Schocken Books, 1964).

covenantal dimension and the moral authority embodied within it is a very heavy one. There are three related biblical terms that relate to the concept of rights: *yosher*, *tzedek*, and *mishpat*. *Yosher*, from *yashar*, has to do with being straight—with somebody or in one's own behavior. *Tzedek* is concerned with doing justice and *mishpat* with fulfilling the law. All three clearly refer more to the obligated party than to the possessor of the right. *Yosher* may possibly have some relationship to the latter as in Judges when Israelites are described as *kol ish asa et ha-yashar b'einav* (every man did what was right in his eyes), but that has to do more with what is defined as the straight path than with the possession of a right.

The one exception to all this lies in property rights as rights of citizenship. Every Jew has the right of *nahalah* (landed inheritance) which is a familial right that entitles every household to a permanent portion of the Land of Israel. The obligation of the Jubilee Year is designed to protect this right.

Transitions and Transformations

As elaborations of the Torah, both the Mishnah and the Gemarah attempted to elaborate specifics with regard to obligations and rights as in every other field. A new terminology began to develop with such words as *zekhut* and its derivatives (e.g., *zakhai*) and *reshut* and its derivatives (e.g., *rashai*) introduced (*kol sh'ani zakhai b'amirato, rashai ani l'hakhshikh alav* [Shabbat 23:3]; *Sh'ain doro zakkai l'kakh* [Sanhedrin 11]). Here we begin to get a conception of rights as such, albeit within the framework of the obligations imposed on humanity through God's covenants and on the Jews through the Torah. Still the terms are most frequently used in connection with property.

The Talmudic discussions go into details of the enforcement of obligations and, by implication, rights, often in an extremely formalistic way, although at the same time they provide for a sufficiently dynamic approach to include what Anglo-American law defines as equity. Based on Deuteronomy 6:18, "And thou shall do what is right and good in the sight of the Lord," "right and good" became the basis of equity in Talmudic jurisprudence.

In addition to the Bible and the Talmud, one finds the issues of rights treated in the medieval codes, the responsa, and commentaries on the Bible, Talmud and codes. All of these are particularly important after the closing of the Talmud at the end of the fifth and early sixth centuries and became particularly important from the eighth century onward. Their role in the case of obligations and rights, much like their role in other spheres of Jewish law, was to synthesize, elucidate, and apply accepted rules to new situations.

For our purposes, the greatest of the codes was Maimonides' Mishneh Torah which provides the most detailed and comprehensive listing of obligations and rights defined and explained. The Mishneh Torah has also served to bring together the *halakhah* and the *mishpat hamelukhah* under one roof, so to speak. Nevertheless, as important as it is, it is not simply authoritative. Different interpretations of the meaning of certain obligations and rights are to be found among different sources throughout the medieval period, even when normative Judaism was dominant.[19]

The Talmud also brought with it the beginnings of a rights terminology, although essentially in relationship to property, not to rights as we know them. That terminology was further developed and amplified in the medieval codes and commentaries. As to be expected, the Hebrew usage took its cues from common medieval usage and reflected a premodern

---

19. Cf. Gerald Blidstein, "Individual and Community in the Middle Ages," in Elazar, *Kinship and Consent*, pp. 217–258; and Menachem Elon, "On Power and Authority: Halachic Stance of the Traditional Community and Its Contemporary Implications," in *Kinship and Consent*, pp. 183–216. For an overview of medieval Jewish theories of rights, cf., *inter alia*, Saadia Gaon, *Book of Opinions and Beliefs*, translated by Samuel Rosenblatt (New Haven: Yale University Press, 1976); Maimonides, *Guide of the Perplexed*, translated with an introduction and notes by Shlomo Pines with an interpretive essay by Leo Strauss (Chicago: University of Chicago Press, 1963); Isadore Twersky, ed., *Explorations in Nachmanides' Religious and Literary Virtuousity* (Cambridge, Mass.: Harvard University Press, 1983); B. Netanyahu, *Don Isaac Abravanel: Statesman and Philosopher* (Philadelphia: Jewish Publication Society, 1953), esp. part II, ch. 3; and Yehudah HaLevi, *The Kuzari*, translated by Hartwig Hirschfeld (New York: P. Shalom, 1969).

European or Islamic conception of right rather than a modem conception of rights.

With the coming of the modem epoch in the mid-seventeenth century and the Jewish emancipation that followed in its wake, particularly after the American and French Revolutions, modern Jews began to think in terms of rights as preceding obligations. A rather unusual example of this was the actual inclusion of a bill of rights in the 1790 constitution of Congregation Shearith Israel, the oldest congregation in the United States.[20] While that was exceptional, congregational community constitutions did undergo changes as their ability to oblige their members to behave in acceptable ways diminished in the face of the increasingly voluntary character of membership. This happened first in the United States and, until the twentieth century, only to a lesser extent in Europe, but still it happened wherever Jews were emancipated.

A contemporary Hebrew terminology of rights dates from the modem epoch. For the most part it was developed by the *maskilim*, either in the German *haskalah* (Jewish enlightenment), which came at the time of the French and American Revolutions, or in some cases a hundred years later by the leaders of the Eastern European *haskalah*. In some cases the terminology was not developed until the twentieth century, either in the United States or in Eretz Israel as part of the revival of the Hebrew language at a time when Jews were consciously returning to the political arena. The principal term for rights, *zekhuyot*, was adapted from talmudic and medieval usage, but was rather substantially transformed. To indicate how recent these transformations took place, Yaakov Canaani's *Otzar Halashon Halvrit*, the most recent Hebrew dictionary on historical principles, identifies certain usages as coming from the Eastern European *haskalah* poet Y. L. Gordon, or from Daniel Persky, leader of the American Hebrew movement between the world wars.

In the last analysis, however, even under modern conditions Jewish doctrine begins with obligations from which rights are derived rather than vice versa. It may have become a matter of free choice as to whether to accept the obligations involved, but still the obligations take precedence. Thus in the most secular kind of situation a Jew is obligated to join a Jewish community and pay appropriate membership fees or taxes before being able to enjoy any of the rights or privileges of membership. While this is a pale reflection of the biblical covenantal tradition, it is still an extension of that tradition. The precedence of obligation continues to be part of the postmodern Jewish experience where issues such as the rights of women in ritual matters for some also hinge on acceptance of commensurate halakhic obligations. Thus even as Jews have become modern in their understanding of human rights, they have retained more traditional Jewish notions in connection with Jewish matters. [. . .]

Conclusion

If one were to try to summarize the basic Jewish theory from which rights are derived, I would suggest the following five points:

1. God is sovereign over all humans and the universe.
2. All humans are created equal and, through Adam and Eve, are descended from the same ancestors, so that no primordial distinctions can be made among them.
3. As equals all can covenant and assume partnership obligations with God.
4. All must covenant or accept being bound by covenant in order to have what we call rights, which are essentially obligations that either can be inferred from the terms of the covenant or are obligations that are themselves rights.
5. The result is federal liberty, that is to say, the liberty to live according to the terms and obligations of the covenant which in turn provides rights and protections.

---

20. Reprinted in Daniel J. Elazar, Jonathan Sarna and Rela G. Monson, eds., A *Double Bond: The Constitutional Documents of American Jewry* (Lanham, Maryland: University Press of America and Jerusalem Center for Public Affairs, 1992).

The system presented in the Bible is among those that try to accommodate the individual in the commonwealth without abandoning the fabric of the commonwealth as a collectivity with its own responsibilities. The basis for this effort is three-fold: first of all, the idea that every individual is created in the image of God, has a soul, and is holy. Second, that it is the task of the individual and the community, indeed the individual in the community, to strive to be holy by observing not only what are today referred to as prescribed religious rituals, but by doing justice, providing for the poor, maintaining human freedom and dignity, and assuring a basic economic floor for every household.

Third, every individual is morally autonomous and his or her consent is required for all acts, even in response to God's commandments. In biblical terminology, God commands but humans hearken (*shamoa*). That is to say, they listen to God's commandment and in essence decide whether or not to observe it. Biblical Hebrew has no word for obey. All human actions require hearkening.

Fourth, humans act together through covenants and covenanting, beginning with the foundation of existence, man's covenant with God, whereby God enters into a partnership with humans for the fulfillment and governance of this world. According to the terms of the constitution which He has set before them, all human organization flows from that original covenant and is ordered by the subsidiary covenants to which the parties must consent and which are morally binding under God who serves as partner, guarantor, or witness. All, of course, are based on consent and the ability of the partners to make autonomous moral commitments.

While we do not know exactly how this biblical system worked in practice in ancient Israel, we can gather some sense of its reality in the way it has shaped the Jewish people who are noted for their commitment to individual autonomy, liberty, and equality, and for their striving to achieve one or another moral end and the tendency to view public issues in moralistic terms even as they are among the most communal, even tribal, of peoples, tied together through a rich fabric of history and destiny.

What of the matter of rights? For the Bible, the question of rights is derived essentially from the question of justice and the human obligation of God to act justly. Politics provides the framework and the means to act justly and to do justice. Thus the fundamental associations of political community—public and private, civil and natural—are media for doing justice.

Beyond that, each form of association forms a particular kind of moral community within which justice is to be achieved and right or rights protected in a diferent way. One of the principal lessons of the biblical teaching for us today is that humans are organized in different moral communities, and right or rights with regard to each must be treated in a manner appropriate to it.

The modern worldview, by emphasizing the individual standing naked against civil society as represented by government, has increasingly come to emphasize the legal enforcement of legally defined rights. Originally applied to government alone, this approach to rights has been extended to other forms of civil associations and even more recently to natural associations, public and private, because of that oversimple and limited perception of the political relationship underlying civil society, what constitutes rights, and how they are to be enforced.

In a just society, there must be an appropriate conceptualization of right and rights for relationships within each different kind of moral community with appropriate means of enforcement. In ancient and medieval society, much justice was promised without sufficient means of enforcement. Modern political thought successfully attacked that problem by providing means of enforcement but, in the process, rejected a more complex view of what constitutes justice or right, a view based upon an understanding of the different forms of association in which humans are involved, recognizing the fact that all such associations being established on the basis of covenant includes the dimensions of justice and right and establishes or systematizes relationships upon which appropriate theories of rights and rights enforcement can be based.

We postmoderns understand the truth and vital importance of the revolutionary modern idea of rights. But we also understand that while it may be the truth it is not necessarily the whole truth. We may better understand that, while individual liberty is

essential for us all, so, too, are the institutions of family and community so that the public institutions of civil society will rest on the proper foundations; not only in the way that they are constituted but in terms of the private dimension in which they serve to function as they are intended to function. The character of the res publica (or commonwealth) depends on the character of the public it serves and just as there can be no res publica without a public so does the character of the res publica rest upon the kind of public within it.

William Rehnquist

United States v. Lopez (1995)

Chief Justice Rehnquist delivered the opinion of the Court.

In the Gun-Free School Zones Act of 1990, Congress made it a federal offense "for any individual knowingly to possess a firearm at a place that the individual knows, or has reasonable cause to believe, is a school zone." The Act neither regulates a commercial activity nor contains a requirement that the possession be connected in any way to interstate commerce. We hold that the Act exceeds the authority of Congress "[t]o regulate Commerce . . . among the several States. . . ." U.S. Const., Art. I, 8, cl. 3.

On March 10, 1992, respondent, who was then a 12th-grade student, arrived at Edison High School in San Antonio, Texas, carrying a concealed .38 caliber handgun and five bullets. Acting upon an anonymous tip, school authorities confronted respondent, who admitted that he was carrying the weapon. He was arrested and charged under Texas law with firearm possession on school premises. The next day, the state charges were dismissed after federal agents charged respondent by complaint with violating the Gun-Free School Zones Act of 1990.

A federal grand jury indicted respondent on one count of knowing possession of a firearm at a school zone. Respondent moved to dismiss his federal indictment on the ground that [. . .] "it is beyond the power of Congress to legislate control over our public schools." The District Court denied the motion, concluding that [the Act] "is a constitutional exercise of Congress' well-defined power to regulate activities in and affecting commerce, and the 'business' of elementary, middle and high schools . . . affects interstate commerce." Respondent waived his right to a jury trial. The District Court conducted a bench trial, found him guilty [. . .] and sentenced him to six months' imprisonment and two years' supervised release.

On appeal, respondent challenged his conviction based on his claim that [the Act] exceeded Congress' power to legislate under the Commerce Clause. The Court of Appeals for the Fifth Circuit agreed and reversed respondent's conviction. It held that, in light of what it characterized as insufficient congressional findings and legislative history, [the Act] "in the full reach of its terms, is invalid as beyond the power of Congress under the Commerce Clause." [. . .]

We start with first principles. The Constitution creates a Federal Government of enumerated powers. As James Madison wrote, "[t]he powers delegated by the proposed Constitution to the federal government are few and defined. Those which are to remain in the State governments are numerous and indefinite." *The Federalist* No. 45. [. . .]

The Constitution delegates to Congress the power "[t]o regulate Commerce with foreign Nations, and among the several States, and with the Indian Tribes." U.S. Const., Art. I, 8 3. The Court, through Chief Justice Marshall, first defined the nature of Congress' commerce power in *Gibbons v. Ogden* (1824):

Commerce, undoubtedly, is traffic, but it is something more: it is intercourse. It describes the

commercial intercourse between nations, and parts of nations, in all its branches, and is regulated by prescribing rules for carrying on that intercourse.

The commerce power "is the power to regulate; that is, to prescribe the rule by which commerce is to be governed. This power, like all others vested in Congress, is complete in itself, may be exercised to its utmost extent, and acknowledges no limitations, other than are prescribed in the Constitution." The *Gibbons* Court, however, acknowledged that limitations on the commerce power are inherent in the very language of the Commerce Clause.

It is not intended to say that these words comprehend that commerce, which is completely internal, which is carried on between man and man in a State, or between different parts of the same State, and which does not extend to or affect other States. Such a power would be inconvenient, and is certainly unnecessary

Comprehensive as the word "among" is, it may very properly be restricted to that commerce which concerns more States than one. . . . The enumeration presupposes something not enumerated; and that something, if we regard the language or the subject of the sentence, must be the exclusively internal commerce of a State.

For nearly a century thereafter, the Court's Commerce Clause decisions dealt but rarely with the extent of Congress' power, and almost entirely with the Commerce Clause as a limit on state legislation that discriminated against interstate commerce. [. . .] Under this line of precedent, the Court held that certain categories of activity such as "production," "manufacturing," and "mining" were within the province of state governments, and thus were beyond the power of Congress under the Commerce Clause. [. . .]

In 1887, Congress enacted the Interstate Commerce Act, and in 1890 Congress enacted the Sherman Antitrust Act. These laws ushered in a new era of federal regulation under the commerce power. When cases involving these laws first reached this Court, we imported from our negative Commerce Clause cases the approach that Congress could not regulate activities such as "production," "manufacturing," and "mining." See, e.g., *United States v. E. C. Knight Co.* (1895). [. . .] Simultaneously, however, the Court held that, where the interstate and intrastate aspects of commerce were so mingled together that full regulation of interstate commerce required incidental regulation of intrastate commerce, the Commerce Clause authorized such regulation.

In *A. L. A. Schecter Poultry Corp. v. United States* (1935), the Court struck down regulations that fixed the hours and wages of individuals employed by an intrastate business because the activity being regulated related to interstate commerce only indirectly. In doing so, the Court characterized the distinction between direct and indirect effects of intrastate transactions upon interstate commerce as "a fundamental one, essential to the maintenance of our constitutional system." Activities that affected interstate commerce directly were within Congress' power; activities that affected interstate commerce indirectly were beyond Congress' reach. The justification for this formal distinction was rooted in the fear that otherwise "there would be virtually no limit to the federal power and for all practical purposes we should have a completely centralized government."

Two years later, in the watershed case of *NLRB v. Jones & Laughlin Steel Corp.* (1937), the Court upheld the National Labor Relations Act against a Commerce Clause challenge, and in the process, departed from the distinction between "direct" and "indirect" effects on interstate commerce. The Court held that intrastate activities that "have such a close and substantial relation to interstate commerce that their control is essential or appropriate to protect that commerce from burdens and obstructions" are within Congress' power to regulate.

In *United States v. Darby* (1941), the Court upheld the Fair Labor Standards Act, stating:

The power of Congress over interstate commerce is not confined to the regulation of commerce among the states. It extends to those activities intrastate which so affect interstate commerce or the exercise of the power of Congress over it as to make regulation of them appropriate means to the attainment of a legitimate end, the exercise of the granted power of Congress to regulate interstate commerce.

In *Wickard v. Filburn*, the Court upheld the application of amendments to the Agricultural Adjustment

Act of 1938 to the production and consumption of home-grown wheat. The *Wickard* Court explicitly rejected earlier distinctions between direct and indirect effects on interstate commerce, stating:

> [E]ven if appellee's activity be local and though it may not be regarded as commerce, it may still, whatever its nature, be reached by Congress if it exerts a substantial economic effect on interstate commerce, and this irrespective of whether such effect is what might at some earlier time have been defined as "direct" or "indirect."

The *Wickard* Court emphasized that although Filburn's own contribution to the demand for wheat may have been trivial by itself, that was not "enough to remove him from the scope of federal regulation where, as here, his contribution, taken together with that of many others similarly situated, is far from trivial."

Jones & Laughlin Steel, *Darby*, and *Wickard* ushered in an era of Commerce Clause jurisprudence that greatly expanded the previously defined authority of Congress under that Clause. In part, this was a recognition of the great changes that had occurred in the way business was carried on in this country. Enterprises that had once been local or at most regional in nature had become national in scope. But the doctrinal change also reflected a view that earlier Commerce Clause cases artificially had constrained the authority of Congress to regulate interstate commerce.

But even these modern-era precedents which have expanded congressional power under the Commerce Clause confirm that this power is subject to outer limits. In *Jones & Laughlin Steel*, the Court warned that the scope of the interstate commerce power "must be considered in the light of our dual system of government and may not be extended so as to embrace effects upon interstate commerce so indirect and remote that to embrace them, in view of our complex society, would effectually obliterate the distinction between what is national and what is local and create a completely centralized government." [. . .] Since that time, the Court has heeded that warning and undertaken to decide whether a rational basis existed for concluding that a regulated activity sufficiently affected interstate commerce.

Similarly, in *Maryland v. Wirtz* (1968), the Court reaffirmed that "the power to regulate commerce, though broad indeed, has limits" that "[t]he Court has ample power" to enforce. In response to the dissent's warnings that the Court was powerless to enforce the limitations on Congress' commerce powers because "[a]ll activities affecting commerce, even in the minutest degree, [*Wickard*], may be regulated and controlled by Congress" (Douglas, J., dissenting), the *Wirtz* Court replied that the dissent had misread precedent as "[n]either here nor in *Wickard* has the Court declared that Congress may use a relatively trivial impact on commerce as an excuse for broad general regulation of state or private activities." Rather, "[t]he Court has said only that where a general regulatory statute bears a substantial relation to commerce, the *de minimis* character of individual instances arising under that statute is of no consequence."

Consistent with this structure, we have identified three broad categories of activity that Congress may regulate under its commerce power. First, Congress may regulate the use of the channels of interstate commerce. Second, Congress is empowered to regulate and protect the instrumentalities of interstate commerce, or persons or things in interstate commerce, even though the threat may come only from intrastate activities. Finally, Congress' commerce authority includes the power to regulate those activities having a substantial relation to interstate commerce.

Within this final category, admittedly, our case law has not been clear whether an activity must "affect" or "substantially affect" interstate commerce in order to be within Congress' power to regulate it under the Commerce Clause. We conclude, consistent with the great weight of our case law, that the proper test requires an analysis of whether the regulated activity "substantially affects" interstate commerce.

We now turn to consider the power of Congress, in the light of this framework, to enact [the Gun-Free School Zones Act]. The first two categories of authority may be quickly disposed of: [the Act] is not a regulation of the use of the channels of interstate commerce, nor is it an attempt to prohibit the interstate transportation of a commodity through the channels of commerce; nor can [it] be justified as a regulation by which Congress has sought to protect an instrumentality of interstate commerce or a thing in interstate commerce. Thus, if [it] is to be sustained, it must be under the third category as a regulation of an activity that substantially affects interstate commerce.

First, we have upheld a wide variety of congressional Acts regulating intrastate economic activity where we have concluded that the activity substantially affected interstate commerce. Examples include the regulation of intrastate coal mining, intrastate extortionate credit transactions, restaurants utilizing substantial interstate supplies, inns and hotels catering to interstate guests, and production and consumption of home-grown wheat. These examples are by no means exhaustive, but the pattern is clear. Where economic activity substantially affects interstate commerce, legislation regulating that activity will be sustained.

Even *Wickard*, which is perhaps the most far reaching example of Commerce Clause authority over intrastate activity, involved economic activity in a way that the possession of a gun in a school zone does not. Roscoe Filburn operated a small farm in Ohio, on which, in the year involved, he raised 23 acres of wheat. It was his practice to sow winter wheat in the fall, and after harvesting it in July to sell a portion of the crop, to feed part of it to poultry and livestock on the farm, to use some in making flour for home consumption, and to keep the remainder for seeding future crops. The Secretary of Agriculture assessed a penalty against him under the Agricultural Adjustment Act of 1938 because he harvested about 12 acres more wheat than his allotment under the Act permitted. The Act was designed to regulate the volume of wheat moving in interstate and foreign commerce in order to avoid surpluses and shortages, and concomitant fluctuation in wheat prices, which had previously obtained. The Court said, in an opinion sustaining the application of the Act to Filburn's activity:

> One of the primary purposes of the Act in question was to increase the market price of wheat and to that end to limit the volume thereof that could affect the market. It can hardly be denied that a factor of such volume and variability as home-consumed wheat would have a substantial influence on price and market conditions. This may arise because being in marketable condition such wheat overhangs the market and, if induced by rising prices, tends to flow into the market and check price increases. But if we assume that it is

never marketed, it supplies a need of the man who grew it which would otherwise be reflected by purchases in the open market. Home-grown wheat in this sense competes with wheat in commerce.

[The Gun-Free School Zones Act] is a criminal statute that, by its terms, has nothing to do with "commerce" or any sort of economic enterprise, however broadly one might define those terms. [It] is not an essential part of a larger regulation of economic activity, in which the regulatory scheme could be undercut unless the intrastate activity were regulated. It cannot, therefore, be sustained under our cases upholding regulations of activities that arise out of or are connected with a commercial transaction, which viewed in the aggregate, substantially affects interstate commerce. [. . .]

The Government's essential contention, *in fine*, is that we may determine here that [the Act] is valid because possession of a firearm in a local school zone does indeed substantially affect interstate commerce. The Government argues that possession of a firearm in a school zone may result in violent crime and that violent crime can be expected to affect the functioning of the national economy in two ways. First, the costs of violent crime are substantial, and, through the mechanism of insurance, those costs are spread throughout the population. Second, violent crime reduces the willingness of individuals to travel to areas within the country that are perceived to be unsafe. The Government also argues that the presence of guns in schools poses a substantial threat to the educational process by threatening the learning environment. A handicapped educational process, in turn, will result in a less productive citizenry. That, in turn, would have an adverse effect on the Nation's economic well-being. [. . .]

We pause to consider the implications of the Government's arguments. The Government admits, under its "costs of crime" reasoning, that Congress could regulate not only all violent crime, but all activities that might lead to violent crime, regardless of how tenuously they relate to interstate commerce. Similarly, under the Government's "national productivity" reasoning, Congress could regulate any activity that it found was related to the economic productivity of individual citizens: family law (including marriage, divorce, and child custody), for example. Under the theories that the Government presents . . . it is difficult to perceive any limitation on federal power, even in areas such as criminal law enforcement or education where States historically have been sovereign. Thus, if we were to accept the Government's arguments, we are hard-pressed to posit any activity by an individual that Congress is without power to regulate.

To uphold the Government's contentions here, we would have to pile inference upon inference in a manner that would bid fair to convert congressional authority under the Commerce Clause to a general police power of the sort retained by the States.

Admittedly, some of our prior cases have taken long steps down that road, giving great deference to congressional action. The broad language in these opinions has suggested the possibility of additional expansion, but we decline here to proceed any further. To do so would require us to conclude that the Constitution's enumeration of powers does not presuppose something not enumerated, and that there never will be a distinction between what is truly national and what is truly local. This we are unwilling to do.

For the foregoing reasons the judgment of the Court of Appeals is Affirmed.

CLARENCE THOMAS

United States v. Lopez, Concurrence (1995)

Justice THOMAS, *concurring.*

Although I join the majority, I write separately to observe that our case law has drifted far from the original understanding of the Commerce Clause. In a future case, we ought to temper our Commerce Clause jurisprudence in a manner that both makes sense of our more recent case law and is more faithful to the original understanding of that Clause.

We have said that Congress may regulate not only "Commerce . . . among the several states," U.S. Const., Art. I, 8, cl. 3, but also anything that has a "substantial effect" on such commerce. This test, if taken to its logical extreme, would give Congress a "police power" over all aspects of American life. Unfortunately, we have never come to grips with this implication of our substantial effects formula. Although we have supposedly applied the substantial effects test for the past 60 years, we always have rejected readings of the Commerce Clause and the scope of federal power that would permit Congress to exercise a police power; our cases are quite clear that there are real limits to federal power. [. . .]

While the principal dissent concedes that there are limits to federal power, the sweeping nature of

our current test enables the dissent to argue that Congress can regulate gun possession. But it seems to me that the power to regulate "commerce" can by no means encompass authority over mere gun possession, any more than it empowers the Federal Government to regulate marriage, littering, or cruelty to animals, throughout the 50 States. Our Constitution quite properly leaves such matters to the individual States, notwithstanding these activities' effects on interstate commerce. [. . .]

In an appropriate case, I believe that we must further reconsider our "substantial effects" test with an eye toward constructing a standard that reflects the text and history of the Commerce Clause without totally rejecting our more recent Commerce Clause jurisprudence. [. . .]

I

At the time the original Constitution was ratified, "commerce" consisted of selling, buying, and bartering, as well as transporting for these purposes. [. . .] In fact, when Federalists and Anti-Federalists discussed the Commerce Clause during the ratification period, they often used trade (in its selling/bartering sense) and commerce interchangeably. See *The Federalist* No. 4 (J. Jay) (asserting that countries will cultivate our friendship when our "trade" is prudently regulated by Federal Government); No. 7 (A. Hamilton) (discussing "competitions of commerce" between States resulting from state "regulations of trade"); No. 40 (J. Madison) (asserting that it was an "acknowledged object of the Convention . . . that the regulation of trade should be submitted to the general government"); Lee, *Letters of a Federal Farmer* No. 5. [. . .]

As one would expect, the term "commerce" was used in contradistinction to productive activities such as manufacturing and agriculture. Alexander Hamilton, for example, repeatedly treated commerce, agriculture, and manufacturing as three separate endeavors. See, e.g., *The Federalist* No. 36 (referring to "agriculture, commerce, manufactures"); No. 21 (distinguishing commerce, arts, and industry); No. 12 (asserting that commerce and agriculture have shared interests). [. . .]

Moreover, interjecting a modern sense of commerce into the Constitution generates significant textual and structural problems. For example, one cannot replace "commerce" with a different type of enterprise, such as manufacturing. When a manufacturer produces a car, assembly cannot take place "with a foreign nation" or "with the Indian Tribes." Parts may come from different States or other nations and hence may have been in the flow of commerce at one time, but manufacturing takes place at a discrete site. Agriculture and manufacturing involve the production of goods; commerce encompasses traffic in such articles. [. . .]

The Constitution not only uses the word "commerce" in a narrower sense than our case law might suggest, it also does not support the proposition that Congress has authority over all activities that "substantially affect" interstate commerce. The Commerce Clause does not state that Congress may "regulate matters that substantially affect commerce with foreign Nations, and among the several States, and with the Indian Tribes." In contrast, the Constitution itself temporarily prohibited amendments that would "affect" Congress' lack of authority to prohibit or restrict the slave trade or to enact unproportioned

direct taxation. Clearly, the Framers could have drafted a Constitution that contained a "substantially affects interstate commerce" clause had that been their objective.

In addition to its powers under the Commerce Clause, Congress has the authority to enact such laws as are "necessary and proper" to carry into execution its power to regulate commerce among the several States. But on this Court's understanding of congressional power under these two Clauses, many of Congress' other enumerated powers under Art. I, 8 are wholly superfluous. After all, if Congress may regulate all matters that substantially affect commerce, there is no need for the Constitution to specify that Congress may enact bankruptcy laws, or coin money and fix the standard of weights and measures, or punish counterfeiters of United States coin and securities. Likewise, Congress would not need the separate authority to establish post offices and post roads, or to grant patents and copyrights, or to "punish Piracies and Felonies committed on the high Seas." It might not even need the power to raise and support an Army and Navy, for fewer people would engage in commercial shipping if they thought that a foreign power could expropriate their property with ease. Indeed, if Congress could regulate matters that substantially affect interstate commerce, there would have been no need to specify that Congress can regulate international trade and commerce with the Indians. As the Framers surely understood, these other branches of trade substantially affect interstate commerce.

Put simply, much if not all of Art. I, 8 (including portions of the Commerce Clause itself) would be surplusage if Congress had been given authority over matters that substantially affect interstate commerce. An interpretation of cl. 3 that makes the rest of 8 superfluous simply cannot be correct. Yet this Court's Commerce Clause jurisprudence has endorsed just such an interpretation: the power we have accorded Congress has swallowed Art. I, 8.

Indeed, if a "substantial effects" test can be appended to the Commerce Clause, why not to every other power of the Federal Government? There is no reason for singling out the Commerce Clause for special treatment. Accordingly, Congress could regulate all matters that "substantially affect" the Army and Navy, bankruptcies, tax collection, expenditures, and so on. In that case, the clauses of 8 all mutually overlap, something we can assume the Founding Fathers never intended.

Our construction of the scope of congressional authority has the additional problem of coming close to turning the Tenth Amendment on its head. Our case law could be read to reserve to the United States all powers not expressly prohibited by the Constitution. Taken together, these fundamental textual problems should, at the very least, convince us that the "substantial effects" test should be reexamined. [. . .]

II

Early Americans understood that commerce, manufacturing, and agriculture, while distinct activities, were intimately related and dependent on each other — that each "substantially affected" the others. . . .

Yet, despite being well aware that agriculture, manufacturing, and other matters substantially affected commerce, the founding generation did not cede authority over all these activities to Congress. Hamilton, for instance, acknowledged that the Federal Government could not regulate agriculture and like concerns:

> The administration of private justice between the citizens of the same State, the supervision of agriculture and of other concerns of a similar nature, all those things in short which are proper to be provided for by local legislation, can never be desirable cares of a general jurisdiction. *The Federalist* No. 17. [. . .]

The comments of Hamilton and others about federal power reflected the well-known truth that the new Government would have only the limited and enumerated powers found in the Constitution. Agriculture and manufacture, since they were not surrendered to the Federal Government, were state concerns. See *The Federalist* No. 34 (A. Hamilton) (observing that the "internal encouragement of agriculture and manufactures" was an object of state expenditure). Even before the passage of the Tenth Amendment, it was apparent that Congress would possess only those powers "herein granted" by the rest of the Constitution. U.S. Const., Art. I, 1.

Where the Constitution was meant to grant federal authority over an activity substantially affecting interstate commerce, the Constitution contains an enumerated power over that particular activity. Indeed, the Framers knew that many of the other enumerated powers in 8 dealt with matters that substantially affected interstate commerce. Madison, for instance, spoke of the bankruptcy power as being "intimately connected with the regulation of commerce." *The Federalist* No. 42. Likewise, Hamilton urged that "[i]f we mean to be a commercial people or even to be secure on our Atlantic side, we must endeavour as soon as possible to have a navy." [*The Federalist*] No. 24.

In short, the Founding Fathers were well aware of what the principal dissent calls "'economic . . . realities.'" Even though the boundary between commerce and other matters may ignore "economic reality" and thus seem arbitrary or artificial to some, we must nevertheless respect a constitutional line that does not grant Congress power over all that substantially affects interstate commerce. [. . .]

IV

Apart from its recent vintage and its corresponding lack of any grounding in the original understanding of the Constitution, the substantial effects test suffers from the further flaw that it appears to grant Congress a police power over the Nation. When asked at oral argument if there were any limits to the Commerce Clause, the Government was at a loss for words. Likewise, the principal dissent insists that there are limits, but it cannot muster even one example. Indeed, the dissent implicitly concedes that its reading has no limits when it criticizes the Court for "threaten[ing] legal uncertainty in an area of law that . . . seemed reasonably well settled" (Breyer, J., dissenting). The one advantage of the dissent's standard is certainty: it is certain that under its analysis everything may be regulated under the guise of the Commerce Clause.

The substantial effects test suffers from this flaw, in part, because of its "aggregation principle." Under so-called "class of activities" statutes, Congress can regulate whole categories of activities that are not themselves either "interstate" or "commerce." In applying the effects test, we ask whether the class of activities as a whole substantially affects interstate commerce, not whether any specific activity within the class has such effects when considered in isolation.

The aggregation principle is clever, but has no stopping point. Suppose all would agree that gun possession within 1,000 feet of a school does not substantially affect commerce, but that possession of weapons generally (knives, brass knuckles, nunchakus, etc.) does. Under our substantial effects doctrine, even though Congress cannot single out gun possession, it can prohibit weapon possession generally. But one always can draw the circle broadly enough to cover an activity that, when taken in isolation, would not have substantial effects on commerce. Under our jurisprudence, if Congress passed an omnibus "substantially affects interstate commerce" statute, purporting to regulate every aspect of human existence, the Act apparently would be constitutional. Even though particular sections may govern only trivial activities, the statute in the aggregate regulates matters that substantially affect commerce.

V

This extended discussion [. . .] reveals that our substantial effects test is far removed from both the Constitution and from our early case law and that the Court's opinion should not be viewed as "radical" or another "wrong turn" that must be corrected in the future. [. . .]

Unless the dissenting Justices are willing to repudiate our long-held understanding of the limited nature of federal power, I would think that they too must be willing to reconsider the substantial effects test in a future case. If we wish to be true to a Constitution that does not cede a police power to the Federal Government, our Commerce Clause's boundaries simply cannot be "defined" as being "commensurate with the national needs" or self-consciously intended to let the Federal Government "defend itself against economic forces that Congress decrees inimical or destructive of the national economy" (Breyer, J., dissenting). Such a formulation of federal power is no test at all: it is a blank check.

WILLIAM KRISTOL

The Politics of Liberty, the Sociology of Virtue (1995)

The 1994 election marked the end of an era. In narrow political terms, it ended sixty-two years of Democratic Party dominance.[1] In a broader sense, it marked the end of the New Deal/Great Society era of big government liberalism. It would be too strong to say that the 1994 election represented a repudiation of that era, for much that was accomplished during those years will—and should—survive. But the election did mark the closing of a historic period—a

period whose roots in turn lie in the Progressive movement. In a sense, then, November 8, 1994, could be said to cap and conclude the Progressive Era of American history. We have fulfilled the "promise"of Herbert Croly's vision—and in doing so have brought to light its limitations and even its pathologies. We now have a chance to shape a new era, informed by a new promise.

It won't be easy. It is entirely possible that the Progressive Era will simply be followed by an era of deconstruction, and deconstruction not just of progressivism but of much that is solid in American life. We can all too easily imagine an American future consisting of a politics of dealignment, a culture of decomposition, and a society of disenchantment. But

---

1. This essay draws substantially on the Bradley Lecture delivered by the author at the American Enterprise Institute for Public Policy Research in December 1993.

perhaps not. Perhaps we can move on and up from progressivism, informed by a new vision that returns, with suitable modifications, to the principles and understandings of the Founders. In Federalist No. Thirty-Nine, Madison refers to "that honorable determination which animates every votary of freedom to rest all our political experiments on the capacity of mankind for self-government."[2] Vindicating the capacity of mankind for self-government implies a political system that protects our liberty, and a society that fosters in its citizens a character capable of self-government, in both the political and moral senses. Self-government therefore implies both a politics of liberty and a sociology of virtue.

The construction (or reconstruction) of a politics of liberty and a sociology of virtue is at the core of the promise of postprogressive America. For as the sociologist Robert Nisbet points out, "a conservative party (or other group) has a double task confronting it. The first is to work tirelessly toward the diminution of the centralized, omnipotent, and unitary state with its ever-soaring debt and deficit." This task—the relimiting of government—is the politics of liberty. "The second and equally important task," says Nisbet, "is that of protecting, reinforcing, nurturing, where necessary, the varied groups and associations which form the true building blocks of the social order."[3] This task—strengthening the institutions of civil society that attend to the character of the citizenry—is the sociology of virtue.

The Politics of Liberty

The phrase "politics of liberty" suggests that the preservation of liberty is a political task. Conservatives and libertarians have on occasion neglected the implications of this fact. We have sometimes acted as if making the theoretical case for liberty, and decrying restrictions on liberty, would convince our fellow citizens to relimit government. But we have given less thought to the matter of structuring institutions and incentives to preserve and strengthen the system of liberty. We have criticized big government's usurpations and lamented its continued growth. Many—a majority of Americans—share this criticism. But how do we go about relimiting government?

In the wake of the election of 1994, this question has come to the fore. It is now clear that there is far more popular support than before for rolling back the huge expansion of government of the past half-century. The American people now believe the federal government is too big, too intrusive, and too meddlesome. They are open to more than criticism of particular government policies; they are now willing to address the issue of the size and scope of government itself. And we have learned that it is not enough simply to make the case against big government; we have to think politically and institutionally about how to rally support and create incentives for limited government.

Such thinking begins with an appreciation of the institutional obstacles to cutting government policies and programs. Electing conservative or Republican presidents in recent years, after all, has not changed things very much. Nor, so far, has the movement of popular opinion toward greater skepticism about government policies and programs. This is because the liberal welfare state has built up sets of relationships and patterns of behavior that are hard to break once they have formed and congealed. George Bernard Shaw said early in this century, "A government that borrows from Peter to pay Paul can always depend on the support of Paul." And if the government doesn't rob Peter too much, and if there are a lot of Peters dispersed throughout the society and only a few Pauls, there will be an endless process of little robberies of Peter to give benefits to Paul. And if the Pauls are organized as an interest group, and are strong in several congressional districts, and if, in the name of "progress," the notion of principled limits on governmental action disappears, then the welfare stare just keeps on growing.

And yet it has become discredited. Poll data, and the recent election results, show that the American people now have a deep distrust of the federal government. In fact they believe, by substantial margins, that the government is more likely to do harm than good. We now have a public opinion that could

2. James Madison, *The Federalist Papers*, ed. Clinton Rossiter (New York: New American Library, 1961), 240.

3. Robert Nisbet, "Still Questing," *Intercollegiate Review*, Fall 1993, 45.

support a broad attack on unlimited government. But because particular policies have beneficiaries who will fight to keep them, while the opposition to these particular policies is often diffuse, the best strategy for containing and rolling back the liberal welfare state may be to look for ways to cut the Gordian knot, rather than trying to unwind it one string at a time. Thus the attraction of proposals such as a balanced budget amendment, term limits, tax and spending limitations at several levels of government, the devolution of power to states and localities, and the privatization of government functions. Such policies are radical in the sense that they do not seek simply to contain some of the damage done by the welfare state, or to address its particular pathologies one by one. Rather, they seek to change the patterns of behavior of the political system as a whole to make it more supportive of relimiting government.

Such institutional reforms are, of course, in the spirit of the Founding Fathers' attempts to create structures, incentives, and relationships that would preserve liberty. In this sense, the new politics of liberty is an attempt to find new remedies for diseases that have grown up over our progressive century, as we abandoned the older constraints on government. Some of these new remedies are in fact traditional ones—for example, federalism, or devolution of power. But what conservative reformers now understand is that we do not need more "New Federalism" efforts in which state and local governments simply become ever more dependent extensions of the federal octopus. We need *real* federalism, understood as part of a general program of relimiting government. And that means that the devolution effort must occur at the state level as well. State governments are no more immune to capture by interest groups than the federal government, though they are more constrained by the need to balance the budget and by popular pressure. Teachers' unions in Albany or Sacramento are as strong as they are in Washington, D. C. Thus, it is not enough to kill the federal Department of Education and return power to states and localities; that is but a *step* on the road to real devolution of power to citizens—in this case, to greater parental control of and choice in their children's schools. The point, after all, is not to get power back to the state governments; it is to get power back to parents and citizens.

Similarly, the new politics of liberty does not simply seek to *restore* the old ways of governing. In 1995, the accumulated departures from those ways have acquired such weight that we need to think more imaginatively about cutting through the jungle of the modern welfare state with fresh populist remedies. Most striking in this respect is the emergence of the movement for term limits. This idea, rejected at the Constitutional Convention had virtually disappeared from our politics for almost two centuries. Today, however, term limits may be the most popular movement in the country. Few in Washington like this idea very much—but voters in all twenty-two states where it has been on the ballot have passed such limits. If the Supreme Court now strikes down state-imposed term limits on federal officials, the issue will be driven to the national level, and could trigger a broader debate about what we want from our representatives and what their relationship to limited government is to be.

The reason for the interest in term limits, after all, is not simply a general belief that Congress will work better if there is greater turnover of its members. The case for term limits rests on a critique of what "representation" has become in the world of big-government/interest-group liberalism, in which "iron triangles" of politicians, bureaucrats, and interest groups establish and benefit from welfare-state and corporatist programs. This triangle seems at once virtually impervious to change from above—from a popular president—and to change from below—from public opinion. Term limits strike at the iron triangle. The incentives for individual congressmen will change under term limits, as the seniority system and committee baronies disintegrate and the balance of power changes within Congress, between Congress and the other branches of government, and between Congress and the electorate. Term limits thus offer the promise of addressing some of the pathological tendencies of interest-group liberalism.

The politics of liberty, therefore, goes beyond a politics informed by a generalized hostility to big government. It means thinking imaginatively about structural, legislative, and constitutional changes that would restore both the principle and the practice of limited government. Above all, the politics of liberty does not imply that we reinvent government; it requires that we relimit it.

We must relimit it not simply because big government is a threat to our economic well-being. It is a threat to free society, because it corrupts such a society by making its people less able to govern themselves. Self-government means that communities and citizens and families are able and willing to govern themselves. This requires the reassertion of the old-fashioned presumption that civil society should exist more or less free of government regulation, even regulation for desirable policy ends. The "pursuit of happiness" will be left primarily to citizens acting freely in civil society; government will secure some of the conditions of such a pursuit, but it will not try to make "happiness"—or even "security" in an extended sense—its direct object. And politicians in this new era will have to be able to articulate and live by this stern message of the limits to proper government action.

The Sociology of Virtue

The sternness of this message can be softened, however, by the hope embodied in the other pillar of the postprogressive agenda, the sociology of virtue. Critics of progressivism have long been concerned with the effect of modern political and social developments on our character, on our virtues. But we have tended to speak primarily of "preserving" our wasting moral capital from the depredations of modern life, of "defending" traditional ideas of law and morality against the assaults launched by a new doctrine of personal liberation, of "shoring up" old institutions that were under modernist assault. Our concern for virtue has been profoundly "conservative," even defensive.

Today's task—and possibility—is radical rather than conservative, proactive rather than defensive: it is to foster a sociology of virtue rather than merely stemming further erosion of virtue's moral capital; That erosion has today gone too far for a merely "conservative" approach. A new sociology of virtue thus implies a thinking through of the ways in which social institutions can be reinvented, restructured, or reformed to promote virtue and foster sound character. This won't happen merely because of a few political victories. Relimiting government would help us

deal with our social and moral problems; a successful politics of liberty would make a sociology of virtue easier to pursue. But even a sound political order will not be sufficient for a good society. Such a society also requires a resurgence of efforts within the private and voluntary spheres to grapple directly with our social problems, problems that are ultimately problems of character, problems of virtue.

Such efforts are in fact already happening. They are not waiting for the success of the politics of liberty. Despite all the social destructiveness around us, there is ample evidence of a resurgent sociology of virtue at work. There are efforts by inner-city pastors to relegitimize and redignify fatherhood, for example, as a beginning to solving the terrible problems of our inner cities. There is an authentic religious revival going on in the land, despite the continuing efforts of progressives in the public sphere to delegitimize religion and reduce its role. The right-to-life movement provides counseling and homes for unwed mothers, trying to convince women to shun the exercise of a right they have won thanks to a "progressive" Supreme Court. Citizens are banding together to deal with even so fundamental an area of government responsibility as crime. It is clear that we will see ever more such efforts to deal with our social problems through social and civic actions, efforts that simply leave government aside or incorporate it as one part of a larger enterprise.

These efforts will ultimately have a political effect, of course. Take the area of education. Following on the successful models in Indianapolis and Milwaukee, there are increasing numbers of privately funded voucher programs that enable students from lower-income families to go to a school of their parents' choice. Those who wanted to help young people at risk to escape from dreadful government schools decided they could not wait for the political system to act. But ultimately, this kind of nonpolitical activity does put pressure on the political system to allow school choice, for the evidence of the success of the private efforts is itself a powerful political argument. In fact, such activity in the private sphere may be the most effective way to spur efforts to reform government policies.

This approach might be called the Federal Express model of reform. Critics of the post office tried for decades to reform it, decrying it as an inefficient monopoly dominated by unions. Americans agreed that the post office did not work well, but it seemed impossible to make any progress legislatively or administratively. Then, in the early 1970s, Fred Smith started Federal Express. The post office and its allies made an effort to strangle this upstart in its cradle. But Federal Express prevailed, since it is politically easier to defend a small business from the government than to break up a huge government monopoly. Now, thanks also to technological developments (such as the fax machine), we have a situation where, with no real legal change, the delivery of mail in America has been transformed. The post office is still big, unwieldy, and sluggish, but it is not a major obstacle to American competitiveness; and it is now weaker politically, because of the growth of private-sector competitors and to the demonstrated superiority of the private sector. The opportunities for fundamental political reform are far greater today thanks to autonomous actions in the private sector.

A similar approach can be taken in many other areas. Instead of waiting for success in changing government institutions, citizens simply begin to go around them. As that happens, these institutions either have to reform themselves, or they become relics that ultimately lose political support. Now, as the Federal Express example suggests, political action is often necessary to protect these private-sector efforts from government attempts to suppress them. That is, after all, how religious conservatives became politically active. During the Carter administration the federal government seemed to threaten the tax-exempt status of Christian schools; as a response to this perceived threat, the Moral Majority was founded to protect these private-sector institutions from the government. As this example suggests, defensive efforts on behalf of the institutions of civil society can ultimately become proactive ones that seek also to reform the political system and the political culture.

So while the sociology of virtue implies pursuing virtue primarily in the private sector through our social institutions, it ultimately has political implications. At the very least, it requires the defense of sound social institutions from attempts by a "progressive"polity to suppress or reshape them.

Liberty, Virtue, and the Family

The politics of liberty and the sociology of virtue might be said to be the twin tracks for a postprogressive American politics. They are, on the whole, consistent and complementary tracks—and they influence each other. A politics of liberty can allow for new kinds of common pursuits in the space cleared by the retrenchment of government. Thus these tracks run parallel to one another for a considerable distance, allowing libertarians to limit government and social conservatives to attend to the sociology of virtue.

But the two tracks cannot be kept forever parallel; the two efforts—though basically complementary—do come into some tension, especially around a core set of issues involving the family. Here the politics of liberty runs up against the impossibility of neutrality about the fundamental arrangements of society; and the sociology of virtue runs up against the limits of what can be achieved in the civil sphere without some legal or policy support.

This can perhaps be made clear by reflecting briefly on Charles Murray's famous October 1993 *Wall Street Journal* article, "The Coming White Underclass."[4] Murray argued that the problems of crime, illiteracy, welfare, homelessness, drugs, and poverty all stem from a core problem, which is illegitimacy. Illegitimacy is therefore "the single most important social problem of our time." Doing something about it is not just one more item on the American political and social agenda; it should be at the top of the agenda. The broad and deep response to Murray's article suggests that it struck a chord—and, in fact, it has implications for both the politics of liberty and sociology of virtue.

Murray argues that we need a politics of liberty. We do not need additional progressive social engineering to solve a problem such engineering has in part created; we need the state to stop interfering with the social forces that kept the overwhelming majority of births within marriage for millennia. While Murray

---

4.   Charles Murray, "The Coming White Underclass," *Wall Street Journal*, October 29, 1993, A 14.

is pessimistic about how much government can do (except for getting out of the way), he is optimistic about how little it needs to do. Perhaps government could make the tax code friendlier to families with children; otherwise, a politics of liberty, presumably supplemented by a private-sector sociology of virtue, would seem to be Murray's recommendation.

But near the end of his article Murray adds this: "A more abstract but ultimately crucial step is to make marriage once again the sole legal institution through which parental rights and responsibilities are defined and exercised." Indeed, "a marriage certificate should establish that a man and woman have entered into a unique legal relationship. The changes that have blurred the distinctiveness of marriage are subtly but importantly destructive."[5]

Murray's suggestion that we reverse these changes goes beyond a mere "politics of liberty." It implies legal "discrimination" against illegitimacy or nontraditional family arrangements. In other words, a pure politics of liberty seems insufficient to Murray to combat "the single most important social problem of our time." State welfare policies, for example, cannot today discriminate against illegitimate children. Part of this problem could be solved by undoing welfare as we know it. But if it is essential that the law explicitly support marriage and the family—if we can't depend on civil society in a climate of legal neutrality simply to produce healthy families and to see to it that children are mostly born into intact families— then we come to the point where the politics of liberty and the sociology of virtue intersect. At this intersection, the politics of liberty would have to accommodate the special status of the family, and the sociology of virtue would have to acknowledge its need for political support for the family as a social institution. In other words, the political sphere, whose primary goal is liberty, cannot be entirely inattentive to the claims of virtue; and the social sphere, whose focus is virtue, requires some political support. For the two spheres to accommodate one another, a common view of what is right and just must ultimately underlie and inform both our politics and our society.

To support the family, one must hold a certain view of human nature and possibilities, a view different from that animating the sexual revolution, whose effects Murray laments. Murray thinks that our public policy should lean against the sexual revolution. But Murray also alludes to the (differing) expectations we need to have for "little boys" and "little girls"; he would seem to want our public policy to lean as well against the other powerful revolution of our time, the feminist revolution. For Murray emphasizes that the burden of preserving the family inevitably must fall primarily on women, and he believes public policy has to recognize this fact.

The sexual and feminist revolutions sprang up in civil society, so to speak. Politicians did not invent them. But the policy helped them along by legitimizing them and delegitimizing those who tried to resist them. No politics can simply be neutral between the sexual revolution and those who would resist it, or between radical feminism and those who would resist it. So even though our new American politics should be overwhelmingly a politics of liberty, and the pursuit of virtue should be primarily a "sociological" matter, at the intersection of politics and society—especially at the family—some judgments will have to be made. These judgments will always be more problematic than the relatively clear and mostly separate agendas of the politics of liberty and the sociology of virtue; but they cannot be avoided. We can pursue the politics of liberty and the sociology of virtue for quite a distance before we reach their intersection, but they do come together at a point at which neither our politics nor our sociology can be neutral as to the content of "the laws of Nature and Nature's God." Ultimately, the return to nature, an ascent from the progressive view of history, underlies both the politics of liberty and the sociology of virtue.

---

5. Ibid.

Anthony Kennedy

City of Boerne, Petitioner v. P. F. Flores, Archbishop of San Antonio, and United States (1997)

Justice Kennedy delivered the opinion of the Court:

A decision by local zoning authorities to deny a church a building permit was challenged under the Religious Freedom Restoration Act of 1993 (RFRA). The case calls into question the authority of Congress to enact RFRA. We conclude the statute exceeds Congress' power.

I

Situated on a hill in the city of Boerne, Texas, some 28 miles northwest of San Antonio, is St. Peter Catholic Church. Built in 1923, the church's structure replicates the mission style of the region's earlier history. The church seats about 230 worshippers, a number too small for its growing parish. Some 40 to 60 parishioners cannot be accommodated at some Sunday masses. In order to meet the needs of the congregation the Archbishop of San Antonio gave permission to the parish to plan alterations to enlarge the building.

A few months later, the Boerne City Council passed an ordinance authorizing the city's Historic Landmark Commission to prepare a preservation plan with proposed historic landmarks and districts. Under the ordinance, the Commission must preapprove construction affecting historic landmarks or buildings in a historic district.

Soon afterwards, the Archbishop applied for a building permit so construction to enlarge the church could proceed. City authorities, relying on the ordinance and the designation of a historic district (which, they argued, included the church), denied the application. The Archbishop brought this suit challenging the permit denial in the United States District Court for the Western District of Texas.

The complaint contained various claims, but to this point the litigation has centered on RFRA and the question of its constitutionality. The Archbishop relied upon RFRA as one basis for relief from the refusal to issue the permit. The District Court concluded that by enacting RFRA Congress exceeded the scope of its enforcement power under §5 of the Fourteenth Amendment. . . . [T]he Fifth Circuit reversed, finding RFRA to be constitutional. We granted certiorari and now reverse.

Congress enacted RFRA in direct response to the Court's decision in *Employment Div., Dept. of Human Resources of Ore. v. Smith* (1990). [. . .]

RFRA prohibits "[g]overnment" from "substantially burden[ing]" a person's exercise of religion even if the burden results from a rule of general applicability unless the government can demonstrate the burden "(1) is in furtherance of a compelling governmental interest; and (2) is the least restrictive means of furthering that compelling governmental interest." The Act's mandate applies to any "branch, department, agency, instrumentality, and official (or other person acting under color of law) of the United States," as well as to any "State, or . . . subdivision of a State." [. . .] RFRA "applies to all Federal and State law, and the implementation of that law, whether statutory or otherwise, and whether adopted before or after [RFRA's enactment]." In accordance with RFRA's usage of the term, we shall use "state law" to include local and municipal ordinances.

III

A

Under our Constitution, the Federal Government is one of enumerated powers. The judicial authority to determine the constitutionality of laws, in cases and controversies, is based on the premise that the "powers of the legislature are defined and limited; and that those limits may not be mistaken, or forgotten, the Constitution is written." *Marbury v. Madison* (1803).

Congress relied on its Fourteenth Amendment enforcement power in enacting the most far reaching and substantial of RFRA's provisions, those which impose its requirements on the States. The Fourteenth Amendment provides, in relevant part:

> Section 1. . . . No State shall make or enforce any law which shall abridge the privileges or immunities of citizens of the United States; nor shall any State deprive any person of life, liberty, or property, without due process of law; nor deny to any person within its jurisdiction the equal protection of the laws.
>
> Section 5. The Congress shall have power to enforce, by appropriate legislation, the provisions of this article.

The parties disagree over whether RFRA is a proper exercise of Congress' § 5 power "to enforce" by "appropriate legislation" the constitutional guarantee that no State shall deprive any person of "life, liberty, or property, without due process of law" nor deny any person "equal protection of the laws."

In defense of the Act respondent contends, with support from the United States as amicus, that RFRA is permissible enforcement legislation. Congress, it is said, is only protecting by legislation one of the liberties guaranteed by the Fourteenth Amendment's Due Process Clause, the free exercise of religion, beyond what is necessary under *Smith*. It is said the congressional decision to dispense with proof of deliberate or overt discrimination and instead concentrate on a law's effects accords with the settled understanding that §5 includes the power to enact legislation designed to prevent as well as remedy constitutional violations. It is further contended that Congress' § 5 power is not limited to remedial or preventive legislation.

All must acknowledge that § 5 is "a positive grant of legislative power" to Congress. In *Ex parte Virginia* (1880), we explained the scope of Congress' § 5 power in the following broad terms:

> Whatever legislation is appropriate, that is, adapted to carry out the objects the amendments have in view, whatever tends to enforce submission to the prohibitions they contain, and to secure to all persons the enjoyment of perfect equality of civil rights and the equal protection of the laws against State denial or invasion, if not prohibited, is brought within the domain of congressional power.

Legislation which deters or remedies constitutional violations can fall within the sweep of Congress' enforcement power even if in the process it prohibits conduct which is not itself unconstitutional and intrudes into "legislative spheres of autonomy previously reserved to the States." For example, the Court upheld a suspension of literacy tests and similar voting requirements under Congress' parallel power to enforce the provisions of the Fifteenth Amendment, see U.S. Const., Amdt. 15, § 2, as a measure to combat racial discrimination in voting, *South Carolina v. Katzenbach* (1966), despite the facial constitutionality of the tests under *Lassiter v. Northampton County Bd. of Elections* (1959). We have also concluded that other measures protecting voting rights are within Congress' power to enforce the Fourteenth and Fifteenth Amendments, despite the burdens those measures placed on the States. [. . .]

Congress' power under § 5, however, extends only to "enforc[ing]" the provisions of the Fourteenth Amendment. The Court has described this power as "remedial." The design of the Amendment and the text of § 5 are inconsistent with the suggestion that Congress has the power to decree the substance of the Fourteenth Amendment's restrictions on the States. Legislation which alters the meaning of the Free Exercise Clause cannot be said to be enforcing the Clause. Congress does not enforce a constitutional right by changing what the right is. It has been given the power "to enforce," not the power to determine what constitutes a constitutional violation. Were it not so, what Congress would be enforcing would no longer be, in any meaningful sense, the "provisions of [the Fourteenth Amendment]."

While the line between measures that remedy or prevent unconstitutional actions and measures that make a substantive change in the governing law is not easy to discern, and Congress must have wide latitude in determining where it lies, the distinction exists and must be observed. There must be a congruence and proportionality between the injury to be prevented or remedied and the means adopted to that end. Lacking such a connection, legislation may become substantive in operation and effect. History and our case law support drawing the distinction, one apparent from the text of the Amendment.

The Fourteenth Amendment's history confirms the remedial, rather than substantive, nature of the Enforcement Clause. The Joint Committee on Reconstruction of the 39th Congress began drafting what would become the Fourteenth Amendment in January 1866. The objections to the Committee's first draft of the Amendment, and the rejection of the draft, have a direct bearing on the central issue of defining Congress' enforcement power. In February, Republican Representative John Bingham of Ohio reported the following draft amendment to the House of Representatives on behalf of the Joint Committee:

> The Congress shall have power to make all laws which shall be necessary and proper to secure to the citizens of each State all privileges and immunities of citizens in the several States, and to all persons in the several States equal protection in the rights of life, liberty, and property. Cong. Globe, 39th Cong., 1st Sess., 1034 (1866).

The proposal encountered immediate opposition, which continued through three days of debate. Members of Congress from across the political spectrum criticized the Amendment, and the criticisms had a common theme: The proposed Amendment gave Congress too much legislative power at the expense of the existing constitutional structure. Democrats and conservative Republicans argued that the proposed Amendment would give Congress a power to intrude into traditional areas of state responsibility, a power inconsistent with the federal design central to the Constitution. Typifying these views, Republican Representative Robert Hale of New York labeled the Amendment "an utter departure from every principle ever dreamed of by the men who framed our Constitution," and warned that under it "all State legislation, in its codes of civil and criminal jurisprudence and procedures . . . may be overridden, may be repealed or abolished, and the law of Congress established instead." Senator William Stewart of Nevada likewise stated the Amendment would permit "Congress to legislate fully upon all subjects affecting life, liberty, and property," such that "there would not be much left for the State Legislatures,"

and would thereby "work an entire change in our form of government." Some radicals, like their brethren "unwilling that Congress shall have any such power . . . to establish uniform laws throughout the United States upon . . . the protection of life, liberty, and property," (statement of Rep. Hotchkiss), also objected that giving Congress primary responsibility for enforcing legal equality would place power in the hands of changing congressional majorities.

As a result of these objections having been expressed from so many different quarters, the House voted to table the proposal until April. The congressional action was seen as marking the defeat of the proposal. [. . .] The measure was defeated "chiefly because many members of the legal profession s[aw] in [it] . . . a dangerous centralization of power," and "many leading Republicans of th[e] House [of Representatives] would not consent to so radical a change in the Constitution." The Amendment in its early form was not again considered. Instead, the Joint Committee began drafting a new article of Amendment, which it reported to Congress on April 30, 1866.

Section 1 of the new draft Amendment imposed self executing limits on the States. Section 5 prescribed that "[t]he Congress shall have power to enforce, by appropriate legislation, the provisions of this article." Under the revised Amendment, Congress' power was no longer plenary but remedial. Congress was granted the power to make the substantive constitutional prohibitions against the States effective. Representative Bingham said the new draft would give Congress "the power . . . to protect by national law the privileges and immunities of all the citizens of the Republic . . . whenever the same shall be abridged or denied by the unconstitutional acts of any State." Representative Stevens described the new draft Amendment as "allow[ing] Congress to correct the unjust legislation of the States." The revised Amendment proposal did not raise the concerns expressed earlier regarding broad congressional power to prescribe uniform national laws with respect to life, liberty, and property. After revisions not relevant here, the new measure passed both Houses and was ratified in July 1868 as the Fourteenth Amendment.

The significance of the defeat of the Bingham proposal was apparent even then. During the debates over the Ku Klux Klan Act only a few years after the Amendment's ratification, Representative James Garfield argued there were limits on Congress' enforcement power, saying "unless we ignore both the history and the language of these clauses we cannot, by any reasonable interpretation, give to [§5] . . . the force and effect of the rejected [Bingham] clause." Scholars of successive generations have agreed with this assessment.

The design of the Fourteenth Amendment has proved significant also in maintaining the traditional separation of powers between Congress and the Judiciary. The first eight Amendments to the Constitution set forth self executing prohibitions on governmental action, and this Court has had primary authority to interpret those prohibitions. The Bingham draft, some thought, departed from that tradition by vesting in Congress primary power to interpret and elaborate on the meaning of the new Amendment through legislation. Under it, "Congress, and not the courts, was to judge whether or not any of the privileges or immunities were not secured to citizens in the several States." While this separation of powers aspect did not occasion the widespread resistance which was caused by the proposal's threat to the federal balance, it nonetheless attracted the attention of various Members. As enacted, the Fourteenth Amendment confers substantive rights against the States which, like the provisions of the Bill of Rights, are self executing. The power to interpret the Constitution in a case or controversy remains in the Judiciary.

The remedial and preventive nature of Congress' enforcement power, and the limitation inherent in the power, were confirmed in our earliest cases on the Fourteenth Amendment. In the *Civil Rights Cases* (1883), the Court invalidated sections of the Civil Rights Act of 1875 which prescribed criminal penalties for denying to any person "the full enjoyment of" public accommodations and conveyances, on the grounds that it exceeded Congress' power by seeking to regulate private conduct. The Enforcement Clause, the Court said, did not authorize Congress to pass "general legislation upon the rights of the citizen, but corrective legislation; that is, such as may be necessary and proper for counteracting such laws as the States may adopt or enforce, and which, by the amendment, they are prohibited from making

or enforcing . . . ." The power to "legislate generally upon" life, liberty, and property, as opposed to the "power to provide modes of redress" against offensive state action, was "repugnant" to the Constitution. Although the specific holdings of these early cases might have been superseded or modified, see, e.g., *Heart of Atlanta Motel, Inc. v. United States* (1964), their treatment of Congress' § 5 power as corrective or preventive, not definitional, has not been questioned.

Recent cases have continued to revolve around the question of whether § 5 legislation can be considered remedial. In *South Carolina v. Katzenbach* we emphasized that "[t]he constitutional propriety of [legislation adopted under the Enforcement Clause] must be judged with reference to the historical experience . . . it reflects." There we upheld various provisions of the Voting Rights Act of 1965, finding them to be "remedies aimed at areas where voting discrimination has been most flagrant," and necessary to "banish the blight of racial discrimination in voting, which has infected the electoral process in parts of our country for nearly a century." We noted evidence in the record reflecting the subsisting and pervasive discriminatory—and therefore unconstitutional—use of literacy tests. The Act's new remedies, which used the administrative resources of the Federal Government, included the suspension of both literacy tests and, pending federal review, all new voting regulations in covered jurisdictions, as well as the assignment of federal examiners to list qualified applicants enabling those listed to vote. The new, unprecedented remedies were deemed necessary given the ineffectiveness of the existing voting rights laws, and the slow costly character of case by case litigation.

After *South Carolina v. Katzenbach*, the Court continued to acknowledge the necessity of using strong remedial and preventive measures to respond to the widespread and persisting deprivation of constitutional rights resulting from this country's history of racial discrimination. [. . .]

Any suggestion that Congress has a substantive, non remedial power under the Fourteenth Amendment is not supported by our case law. In *Oregon v. Mitchell* (1970) a majority of the Court concluded Congress had exceeded its enforcement powers by enacting legislation lowering the minimum age of voters from 21 to 18 in state and local elections. The five Members of the Court who reached this conclusion explained that the legislation intruded into an area reserved by the Constitution to the States. [. . .]

If Congress could define its own powers by altering the Fourteenth Amendment's meaning, no longer would the Constitution be "superior paramount law, unchangeable by ordinary means." It would be "on a level with ordinary legislative acts, and, like other acts, . . . alterable when the legislature shall please to alter it." *Marbury v. Madison* (1803). Under this approach, it is difficult to conceive of a principle that would limit congressional power. Shifting legislative majorities could change the Constitution and effectively circumvent the difficult and detailed amendment process contained in Article V.

We now turn to consider whether RFRA can be considered enforcement legislation under § 5 of the Fourteenth Amendment.

B

Respondent contends that RFRA is a proper exercise of Congress' remedial or preventive power. The Act, it is said, is a reasonable means of protecting the free exercise of religion as defined by *Smith*. It prevents and remedies laws which are enacted with the unconstitutional object of targeting religious beliefs and practices. To avoid the difficulty of proving such violations, it is said, Congress can simply invalidate any law which imposes a substantial burden on a religious practice unless it is justified by a compelling interest and is the least restrictive means of accomplishing that interest. If Congress can prohibit laws with discriminatory effects in order to prevent racial discrimination in violation of the Equal Protection Clause, then it can do the same, respondent argues, to promote religious liberty.

While preventive rules are sometimes appropriate remedial measures, there must be a congruence between the means used and the ends to be achieved. The appropriateness of remedial measures must be considered in light of the evil presented. Strong measures appropriate to address one harm may be an unwarranted response to another, lesser one.

A comparison between RFRA and the Voting Rights Act is instructive. In contrast to the record which confronted Congress and the judiciary in the voting rights cases, RFRA's legislative record lacks examples of modern instances of generally applicable

laws passed because of religious bigotry. The history of persecution in this country detailed in the hearings mentions no episodes occurring in the past 40 years. The absence of more recent episodes stems from the fact that, as one witness testified, "deliberate persecution is not the usual problem in this country." House Hearings 334 (statement of Douglas Laycock). Rather, the emphasis of the hearings was on laws of general applicability which place incidental burdens on religion. Much of the discussion centered upon anecdotal evidence of autopsies performed on Jewish individuals and Hmong immigrants in violation of their religious beliefs, which as an incident of their normal operation, have adverse effects on churches and synagogues. It is difficult to maintain that they are examples of legislation enacted or enforced due to animus or hostility to the burdened religious practices or that they indicate some widespread pattern of religious discrimination in this country. Congress' concern was with the incidental burdens imposed, not the object or purpose of the legislation. This lack of support in the legislative record, however, is not RFRA's most serious shortcoming. Judicial deference, in most cases, is based not on the state of the legislative record Congress compiles but "on due regard for the decision of the body constitutionally appointed to decide." As a general matter, it is for Congress to determine the method by which it will reach a decision.

Regardless of the state of the legislative record, RFRA cannot be considered remedial, preventive legislation, if those terms are to have any meaning. RFRA is so out of proportion to a supposed remedial or preventive object that it cannot be understood as responsive to, or designed to prevent, unconstitutional behavior. It appears, instead, to attempt a substantive change in constitutional protections. Preventive measures prohibiting certain types of laws may be appropriate when there is reason to believe that many of the laws affected by the congressional enactment have a significant likelihood of being unconstitutional. Remedial legislation under § 5 "should be adapted to the mischief and wrong which the [Fourteenth] [A]mendment was intended to provide against."

RFRA is not so confined. Sweeping coverage ensures its intrusion at every level of government, displacing laws and prohibiting official actions of almost every description and regardless of subject matter.

RFRA's restrictions apply to every agency and official of the Federal, State, and local Governments. RFRA applies to all federal and state law, statutory or otherwise, whether adopted before or after its enactment. §2000bb–3(a). RFRA has no termination date or termination mechanism. Any law is subject to challenge at any time by any individual who alleges a substantial burden on his or her free exercise of religion.

The reach and scope of RFRA distinguish it from other measures passed under Congress' enforcement power, even in the area of voting rights. In *South Carolina v. Katzenbach*, the challenged provisions were confined to those regions of the country where voting discrimination had been most flagrant, and affected a discrete class of state laws, i.e., state voting laws. Furthermore, to ensure that the reach of the Voting Rights Act was limited to those cases in which constitutional violations were most likely (in order to reduce the possibility of overbreadth), the coverage under the Act would terminate "at the behest of States and political subdivisions in which the danger of substantial voting discrimination has not materialized during the preceding five years." The provisions restricting and banning literacy tests, upheld in *Katzenbach v. Morgan* (1966), and *Oregon v. Mitchell* (1970), attacked a particular type of voting qualification, one with a long history as a "notorious means to deny and abridge voting rights on racial grounds." In *City of Rome* (1980) the Court rejected a challenge to the constitutionality of a Voting Rights Act provision which required certain jurisdictions to submit changes in electoral practices to the Department of Justice for preimplementation review. The requirement was placed only on jurisdictions with a history of intentional racial discrimination in voting. Like the provisions at issue in, this provision permitted a covered jurisdiction to avoid preclearance requirements under certain conditions and, moreover, lapsed in seven years. This is not to say, of course, that § 5 legislation requires termination dates, geographic restrictions or egregious predicates. Where, however, a congressional enactment pervasively prohibits constitutional state action in an effort to remedy or to prevent unconstitutional state action, limitations of this kind tend to ensure Congress' means are proportionate to ends legitimate under § 5.

The stringent test RFRA demands of state laws reflects a lack of proportionality or congruence between the means adopted and the legitimate end to be achieved. If an objector can show a substantial burden on his free exercise, the State must demonstrate a compelling governmental interest and show that the law is the least restrictive means of furthering its interest. Claims that a law substantially burdens someone's exercise of religion will often be difficult to contest. Requiring a State to demonstrate a compelling interest and show that it has adopted the least restrictive means of achieving that interest is the most demanding test known to constitutional law. . . . Laws valid under *Smith* would fall under RFRA without regard to whether they had the object of stifling or punishing free exercise. We make these observations not to reargue the position of the majority in *Smith* but to illustrate the substantive alteration of its holding attempted by RFRA. Even assuming RFRA would be interpreted in effect to mandate some lesser test [. . .] the statute nevertheless would require searching judicial scrutiny of state law with the attendant likelihood of invalidation. This is a considerable congressional intrusion into the States' traditional prerogatives and general authority to regulate for the health and welfare of their citizens.

The substantial costs RFRA exacts, both in practical terms of imposing a heavy litigation burden on the States and in terms of curtailing their traditional general regulatory power, far exceed any pattern or practice of unconstitutional conduct under the Free Exercise Clause as interpreted in *Smith*. Simply put, RFRA is not designed to identify and counteract state laws likely to be unconstitutional because of their treatment of religion. In most cases, the state laws to which RFRA applies are not ones which will have been motivated by religious bigotry. If a state law disproportionately burdened a particular class of religious observers, this circumstance might be evidence of an impermissible legislative motive. RFRA's substantial burden test, however, is not even a discriminatory effects or disparate impact test. It is a reality of the modern regulatory state that numerous state laws, such as the zoning regulations at issue here, impose a substantial burden on a large class of individuals. When the exercise of religion has been burdened in an incidental way by a law of general application, it does not follow that the persons affected have been burdened any more than other citizens, let alone burdened because of their religious beliefs. In addition, the Act imposes in every case a least restrictive means requirement—a requirement that was not used in the pre-*Smith* jurisprudence RFRA purported to codify—which also indicates that the legislation is broader than is appropriate if the goal is to prevent and remedy constitutional violations.

When Congress acts within its sphere of power and responsibilities, it has not just the right but the duty to make its own informed judgment on the meaning and force of the Constitution. This has been clear from the early days of the Republic. In 1789, when a Member of the House of Representatives objected to a debate on the constitutionality of legislation based on the theory that "it would be officious" to consider the constitutionality of a measure that did not affect the House, James Madison explained that "it is incontrovertibly of as much importance to this branch of the Government as to any other, that the Constitution should be preserved entire. It is our duty." Were it otherwise, we would not afford Congress the presumption of validity its enactments now enjoy.

Our national experience teaches that the Constitution is preserved best when each part of the government respects both the Constitution and the proper actions and determinations of the other branches. When the Court has interpreted the Constitution, it has acted within the province of the Judicial Branch, which embraces the duty to say what the law is. When the political branches of the Government act against the background of a judicial interpretation of the Constitution already issued, it must be understood that in later cases and controversies the Court will treat its precedents with the respect due them under settled principles, including *stare decisis*, and contrary expectations must be disappointed. RFRA was designed to control cases and controversies, such as the one before us; but as the provisions of the federal statute here invoked are beyond congressional authority, it is this Court's precedent, not RFRA, which must control.

It is for Congress in the first instance to "determin[e] whether and what legislation is needed to secure the guarantees of the Fourteenth Amendment," and its conclusions are entitled to much deference. Congress' discretion is not unlimited, however, and the courts retain the power, as they have since *Marbury v. Madison*, to determine if Congress has exceeded its authority under the Constitution. Broad as the power of Congress is under the Enforcement Clause of the Fourteenth Amendment, RFRA contradicts vital principles necessary to maintain separation of powers and the federal balance. The judgment of the Court of Appeals sustaining the Act's constitutionality is reversed.

National Conference of Catholic Bishops/ United States Catholic Conference

Economic Justice for All (1997)

Pastoral Message

As followers of Jesus Christ and participants in a powerful economy, Catholics in the United States are called to work for greater economic justice in the face of persistent poverty, growing income gaps, and increasing discussion of economic issues in the United States and around the world. We urge Catholics to use the following ethical framework for economic life as principles for reflection, criteria for judgment, and directions for action. These principles are drawn directly from Catholic teaching on economic life:

1. The economy exists for the person, not the person for the economy.

2. All economic life should be shaped by moral principles. Economic choices and institutions must be judged by how they protect or undermine the life and dignity of the human person, support the family, and serve the common good.

3. A fundamental moral measure of any economy is how the poor and vulnerable are faring.

4. All people have a right to life and to secure the basic necessities of life (e.g., food, clothing, shelter, education, health care, safe environment, economic security).

5. All people have the right to economic initiative, to productive work, to just wages and benefits, to decent working conditions, as well as to organize and join unions or other associations.

6. All people, to the extent they are able, have a corresponding duty to work, a responsibility to provide for the needs of their families, and an obligation to contribute to the broader society.

7. In economic life, free markets have both clear advantages and limits; government has essential responsibilities and limitations; voluntary groups have irreplaceable roles, but cannot substitute for the proper working of the market and the just policies of the state.

8. Society has a moral obligation, including governmental action where necessary, to assure opportunity, meet basic human needs, and pursue justice in economic life.

9. Workers, owners, managers, stockholders, and consumers are moral agents in economic life. By our choices, initiative, creativity, and investment, we enhance or diminish economic opportunity, community life, and social justice.

10. The global economy has moral dimensions and human consequences. Decisions on investment, trade, aid, and development should protect human life and promote human rights, especially for those most in need wherever they might live on this globe.

According to Pope John Paul II, the Catholic tradition calls for a "society of work, enterprise and participation" which "is not directed against the market, but demands that the market be appropriately controlled by the forces of society and by the state to assure that the basic needs of the whole society are satisfied" (*Centesimus Annus*, 35). All of economic life should recognize the fact that we are all God's children and members of one human family, called to exercise a clear priority for "the least among us."

The sources for this framework include the *Catechism of the Catholic Church*, recent papal encyclicals, the pastoral letter *Economic Justice for All*, and other statements of the U.S. Catholic bishops. They reflect the Church's teaching on the dignity, rights, and duties of the human person; the option for the poor; the common good; subsidiarity and solidarity. [. . .]

The challenge of this pastoral letter is not merely to think differently, but also to act differently. A renewal of economic life depends on the conscious choices and commitments of individual believers who practice their faith in the world. . . . This letter calls us to conversion and common action, to new forms of stewardship, service, and citizenship. The completion of a letter such as this is but the beginning of a long process of education, discussion, and action. [. . .]

12. The pastoral letter is not a blueprint for the American economy. It does not embrace any particular theory of how the economy works, nor does it attempt to resolve the disputes between different schools of economic thought. Instead, our letter turns to Scripture and to the social teachings of the Church. There, we discover what our economic life must serve, what standards it must meet. Let us examine some of these basic moral principles.

13. *Every economic decision and institution must be judged in light of whether it protects or undermines the dignity of the human person.* The pastoral letter begins with the human person. We believe the person is sacred—the clearest reflection of God among us. Human dignity comes from God, not from nationality, race, sex, economic status, or any human

accomplishment. We judge any economic system by what it does *for* and *to* people and by how it permits all to *participate* in it. The economy should serve people, not the other way around.

14. *Human dignity can be realized and protected only in community.* In our teaching, the human person is not only sacred but also social. How we organize our society—in economics and politics, in law and policy—directly affects human dignity and the capacity of individuals to grow in community. The obligation to "love our neighbor" has an individual dimension, but it also requires a broader social commitment to the common good. We have many partial ways to measure and debate the health of our economy: Gross National Product, per capita income, stock market prices, and so forth. The Christian vision of economic life looks beyond them all and asks, Does economic life enhance or threaten our life together as a community? [. . .]

15. *All people have a right to participate in the economic life of society.* Basic justice demands that people be assured a minimum level of participation in the economy. It is wrong for a person or group to be excluded unfairly or to be unable to participate or contribute to the economy. For example, people who are both able and willing, but cannot get a job are deprived of the participation that is so vital to human development. For, it is through employment that most individuals and families meet their material needs, exercise their talents, and have an opportunity to contribute to the larger community. Such participation has a special significance in our tradition because we believe that it is a means by which we join in carrying forward God's creative activity.

16. *All members of society have a special obligation to the poor and vulnerable.* From the Scriptures and church teaching, we learn that the justice of a society is tested by the treatment of the poor. The justice that was the sign of God's covenant with Israel was measured by how the poor and unprotected—the widow, the orphan, and the stranger—were treated. The kingdom that Jesus proclaimed in his word and ministry excludes no one. Throughout Israel's history and in early Christianity, the poor are agents of God's transforming power. "The Spirit of the Lord is upon me, therefore he has anointed me. He has sent me to bring glad tidings to the poor"(Lk 4:18). This was Jesus' first public utterance. Jesus takes the side of those most in need. In the Last Judgment, so dramatically described in St. Matthew's Gospel, we are told that we will be judged according to how we respond to the hungry, the thirsty, the naked, the stranger. As followers of Christ, we are challenged to make a fundamental "option for the poor"—to speak for the voiceless, to defend the defenseless, to assess life styles, policies, and social institutions in terms of their impact on the poor. This "option for the poor" does not mean pitting one group against another, but rather, strengthening the whole community by assisting those who are most vulnerable. As Christians, we are called to respond to the needs of *all* our brothers and sisters, but those with the greatest needs require the greatest response.

17. *Human rights are the minimum conditions for life in community.* In Catholic teaching, human rights include not only civil and political rights but also economic rights. As Pope John XXIII declared, "all people have a right to life, food, clothing, shelter, rest, medical care, education, and employment." This means that when people are without a chance to earn a living, and must go hungry and homeless, they are being denied basic rights. Society must ensure that these rights are protected. In this way, we will ensure that the minimum conditions of economic justice are met for all our sisters and brothers.

18. *Society as a whole, acting through public and private institutions, has the moral responsibility to enhance human dignity and protect human rights.* In addition to the clear responsibility of private institutions, government has an essential responsibility in this area. This does not mean that government has the primary or exclusive role, but it does have a positive moral responsibility in safeguarding human rights and ensuring that the minimum conditions of human dignity are met for all. In a democracy, government is a means by which we can act together to protect what is important to us and to promote our common values.

19. These six moral principles are not the only ones presented in the pastoral letter, but they give an overview of the moral vision that we are trying to share. This vision of economic life cannot exist in a vacuum; it must be translated into concrete measures. Our pastoral letter spells out some specific

applications of Catholic moral principles. We call for a new national commitment to full employment. We say it is a social and moral scandal that one of every seven Americans is poor, and we call for concerted efforts to eradicate poverty. The fulfillment of the basic needs of the poor is of the highest priority. We urge that all economic policies be evaluated in light of their impact on the life and stability of the family. We support measures to halt the loss of family farms and to resist the growing concentration in the ownership of agricultural resources. We specify ways in which the United States can do far more to relieve the plight of poor nations and assist in their development. We also reaffirm church teaching on the rights of workers, collective bargaining, private property, subsidiarity, and equal opportunity.

20. We believe that the recommendations in our letter are reasonable and balanced. In analyzing the economy, we reject ideological extremes and start from the fact that ours is a "mixed" economy, the product of a long history of reform and adjustment. We know that some of our specific recommendations are controversial. As bishops, we do not claim to make these prudential judgments with the same kind of authority that marks our declarations of principle. But, we feel obliged to teach by example how Christians can undertake concrete analysis and make specific judgments on economic issues. The Church's teachings cannot be left at the level of appealing generalities.

21. In the pastoral letter, we suggest that the time has come for a "New American Experiment"—to implement economic rights, to broaden the sharing of economic power, and to make economic decisions more accountable to the common good. This experiment can create new structures of economic partnership and participation within firms at the regional level, for the whole nation, and across borders. [. . .]

23. We should not be surprised if we find Catholic social teaching to be demanding. The Gospel is demanding. We are always in need of conversion, of a change of heart. We are richly blessed, and as St. Paul assures us, we are destined for glory. Yet, it is also true that we are sinners; that we are not always wise or loving or just; that, for all our amazing possibilities, we are incompletely born, wary of life, and hemmed in by fears and empty routines. We are unable to entrust ourselves fully to the living God,

and so we seek substitute forms of security in material things, in power, in indifference, in popularity, in pleasure. The Scriptures warn us that these things can become forms of idolatry. We know that, at times, in order to remain truly a community of Jesus' disciples, we will have to say "no" to certain aspects in our culture, to certain trends and ways of acting that are opposed to a life of faith, love, and justice. Changes in our hearts lead naturally to a desire to change how we act. With what care, human kindness, and justice do I conduct myself at work? How will my economic decisions to buy, sell, invest, divest, hire, or fire serve human dignity and the common good? In what career can I best exercise my talents so as to fill the world with the Spirit of Christ? How do my economic choices contribute to the strength of my family and community, to the values of my children, to a sensitivity to those in need? In this consumer society, how can I develop a healthy detachment from things and avoid the temptation to assess who I am by what I have? How do I strike a balance between labor and leisure that enlarges my capacity for friendships, for family life, for community? What government policies should I support to attain the well-being of all, especially the poor and vulnerable?

24. The answers to such questions are not always clear—or easy to live out. But, conversion is a life-long process. And, it is not undertaken alone. It occurs with the support of the whole believing community, through baptism, common prayer, and our daily efforts, large and small, on behalf of justice. As a Church, we must be people after God's own heart, bonded by the Spirit, sustaining one another in love, setting our hearts on God's kingdom, committing ourselves to solidarity with those who suffer, working for peace and justice, acting as a sign of Christ's love and justice in the world. The Church cannot redeem the world from the deadening effects of sin and injustice unless it is working to remove sin and injustice in its own life and institutions. All of us must help the Church to practice in its own life what it preaches to others about economic justice and cooperation.

25. The challenge of this pastoral letter is not merely to think differently, but also to act differently. A renewal of economic life depends on the conscious choices and commitments of individual believers who practice their faith in the world. The road to

holiness for most of us lies in our secular vocations. We need a spirituality that calls forth and supports lay initiative and witness not just in our churches but also in business, in the labor movement, in the professions, in education, and in public life. Our faith is not just a weekend obligation, a mystery to be celebrated around the altar on Sunday. It is a pervasive reality to be practiced every day in homes, offices, factories, schools, and businesses across our land. We cannot separate what we believe from how we act in the marketplace and the broader community, for this is where we make our primary contribution to the pursuit of economic justice. [. . .]

27. The pursuit of economic justice takes believers into the public arena, testing the policies of government by the principles of our teaching. We ask you to become more informed and active citizens, using your voices and votes to speak for the voiceless, to defend the poor and the vulnerable, and to advance the common good. We are called to shape a constituency of conscience, measuring every policy by how it touches the least, the lost, and the left-out among us. This letter calls us to conversion and common action, to new forms of stewardship, service, and citizenship. [. . .]

The Church and the Future of the U.S. Economy

6. The United States is among the most economically powerful nations on earth. In its short history the U.S. economy has grown to provide an unprecedented standard of living for most of its people. The nation has created productive work for millions of immigrants and enabled them to broaden their freedoms, improve their families' quality of life, and contribute to the building of a great nation. Those who came to this country from other lands often understood their new lives in the light of biblical faith. They thought of themselves as entering a promised land of political freedom and economic opportunity. The United States is a land of vast natural resources and fertile soil. It *has* encouraged citizens to undertake bold ventures. Through hard work, self-sacrifice, and cooperation, families have flourished; towns, cities and a powerful nation have been created.

7. But we should recall this history with sober humility. The American experiment in social, political, and economic life has involved serious conflict and suffering. Our nation was born in the face of injustice to native Americans, and its independence was paid for with the blood of revolution. Slavery stained the commercial life of the land through its first two hundred and fifty years and was ended only by a violent civil war. The establishment of women's suffrage, the protection of industrial workers, the elimination of child labor, the response to the Great Depression of the 1930s, and the civil rights movement of the 1960s all involved a sustained struggle to transform the political and economic institutions of the nation.

8. The U.S. value system emphasizes economic freedom. It also recognizes that the market is limited by fundamental human rights. Some things are never to be bought or sold. This conviction has prompted positive steps to modify the operation of the market when it harms vulnerable members of society. Labor unions help workers resist exploitation. Through their government, the people of the United States have provided support for education, access to food, unemployment compensation, security in old age, and protection of the environment. The market system contributes to the success of the U.S. economy, but so do many efforts to forge economic institutions and public policies that enable *all* to share in the riches of the nation. The country's economy has been built through a creative struggle; entrepreneurs, business people, workers, unions, consumers, and government have all played essential roles.

9. The task of the United States today is as demanding as that faced by our forebears. Abraham Lincoln's words at Gettysburg are a reminder that complacency today would be a betrayal of our nation's history: "It is for us the living, rather to be dedicated here to the unfinished work they . . . have thus far so nobly advanced." There is unfinished business in the American experiment in freedom and justice for all.

10. The preeminent role of the United States in an increasingly interdependent global economy is a central sign of our times. The United States is still the world's economic giant. Decisions made here have immediate effects in other countries; decisions made abroad have immediate consequences for steelworkers

in Pittsburgh, oil company employees in Houston, and farmers in Iowa. U.S. economic growth is vitally dependent on resources from other countries and on their purchases of our goods and services. Many jobs in U.S. industry and agriculture depend on our ability to export manufactured goods and food.

11. In some industries the mobility of capital and technology makes wages the main variable in the cost of production. Overseas competitors with the same technology but with wage rates as low as one-tenth of ours put enormous pressure on U.S. firms to cut wages, relocate abroad, or close. U.S. workers and their communities should not be expected to bear these burdens alone.

12. All people on this globe share a common ecological environment that is under increasing pressure. Depletion of soil, water, and other natural resources endangers the future. Pollution of air and water threatens the delicate balance of the biosphere on which future generations will depend. The resources of the earth have been created by God for the benefit of all, and we who are alive today hold them in trust. This is a challenge to develop a new ecological ethic that will help shape a future that is both just and sustainable.

13. In short, nations separated by geography, culture, and ideology are linked in a complex commercial, financial, technological, and environmental network. These links have two direct consequences. First, they create hope for a new form of community among all peoples, one built on dignity, solidarity, and justice. Second, this rising global awareness calls for greater attention to the stark inequities across countries in the standards of living and control of resources. We must not look at the welfare of U.S. citizens as the only good to be sought. Nor may we overlook the disparities of power in the relationships between this nation and the developing countries. The United States is the major supplier of food to other countries, a major source of arms sales to developing nations, and a powerful influence in multilateral institutions such as the International Monetary Fund, the World Bank, and the United Nations. What Americans see as a growing interdependence is regarded by many in the less developed countries as a pattern of domination and dependence.

14. Within this larger international setting, there are also a number of challenges to the domestic economy that call for creativity and courage. The promise of the "American dream"—freedom for all persons to develop their God-given talents to the full—remains unfulfilled for millions in the United States today.

15. Several areas of U.S. economic life demand special attention. Unemployment is the most basic. Despite the large number of new jobs the U.S. economy has generated in the past decade, approximately 8 million people seeking work in this country are unable to find it, and many more are so discouraged they have stopped looking. Over the past two decades the nation has come to tolerate an increasing level of unemployment. The 6 to 7 percent rate deemed acceptable today would have been intolerable twenty years ago. Among the unemployed are a disproportionate number of blacks, Hispanics, young people, or women who are the sole support of their families. Some cities and states have many more unemployed persons than others as a result of economic forces that have little to do with people's desire to work. Unemployment is a tragedy no matter whom it strikes, but the tragedy is compounded by the unequal and unfair way it is distributed in our society.

16. Harsh poverty plagues our country despite its great wealth. More than 33 million Americans are poor; by any reasonable standard another 20 to 30 million are needy. Poverty is increasing in the United States, not decreasing. For a people who believe in "progress," this should be cause for alarm. These burdens fall most heavily on blacks, Hispanics, and Native Americans. Even more disturbing is the large increase in the number of women and children living in poverty. Today children are the largest single group among the poor. This tragic fact seriously threatens the nations future. That so many people are poor in a nation as rich as ours is a social and moral scandal that we cannot ignore.

17. Many working people and middle-class Americans live dangerously close to poverty. A rising number of families must rely on the wages of two or even three members just to get by. From 1968 to 1978 nearly a quarter of the U.S. population was in poverty part of the time and received welfare benefits in at least one year. The loss of a job, illness, or the breakup of a marriage may be all it takes to push people into poverty.

18. The lack of a mutually supportive relation between family life and economic life is one of the most serious problems facing the United States today. The economic and cultural strength of the nation is directly linked to the stability and health of its families. When families thrive, spouses contribute to the common good through their work at home, in the community, and in their jobs; and children develop a sense of their own worth and of their responsibility to serve others. When families are weak or break down entirely, the dignity of parents and children is threatened. High cultural and economic costs are inflicted on society at large.

19. The precarious economic situation of so many people and so many families calls for examination of U.S. economic arrangements. Christian conviction and the American promise of liberty and justice for all give the poor and the vulnerable a special claim on the nation's concern. They also challenge all members of the Church to help build a more just society.

20. The investment of human creativity and material resources in the production of the weapons of war makes these economic problems even more difficult to solve. Defense Department expenditures in the United States are almost $300 billion per year. The rivalry and mutual fear between superpowers divert into projects that threaten death, minds, and money that could better human life. Developing countries engage in arms races they can ill afford, often with the encouragement of the superpowers. Some of the poorest countries of the world use scarce resources to buy planes, guns, and other weapons when they lack the food, education, and health care their people need. Defense policies must be evaluated and assessed in light of their real contribution to freedom, justice, and peace for the citizens of our own and other nations. We have developed a perspective on these multiple moral concerns in our 1983 pastoral letter, *The Challenge of Peace: God's Promise and Our Response*. When weapons or strategies make questionable contributions to security, peace, and justice and will also be very expensive, spending priorities should be redirected to more pressing social needs. [. . .]

24. The quality of the national discussion about our economic future will affect the poor most of all, in this country and throughout the world. The life and dignity of millions of men, women, and children hang in the balance. Decisions must be judged in light of what they do *for* the poor, what they do to the poor, and what they enable the poor to do *for themselves.* The fundamental moral criterion for all economic decisions, policies, and institutions is this: They must be at the service of *all people, especially the poor.*

25. This letter is based on a long tradition of Catholic social thought, rooted in the Bible and developed over the past century by the popes and the Second Vatican Council in response to modern economic conditions. This tradition insists that human dignity, realized in community with others and with the whole of God's creation, is the norm against which every social institution must be measured.

26. This teaching has a rich history. It is also dynamic and growing. Pope Paul VI insisted that all Christian communities have the responsibility "to analyze with objectivity the situation which is proper to their own country, to shed on it the light of the Gospel's unalterable words and to draw principles of reflection, norms of judgment, and directives for action from the social teaching of the Church." Therefore, we build on the past work of our own bishops' conference, including the 1919 *Program of Social Reconstruction* and other pastoral letters. In addition many people from the Catholic, Protestant, and Jewish communities, in academic, business or political life, and from many different economic backgrounds have also provided guidance. We want to make the legacy of Christian social thought a living, growing resource that can inspire hope and help shape the future. [. . .]

The Christian Vision of Economic Life

28. The basis for all that the Church believes about the moral dimensions of economic life is its vision of the transcendent worth—the sacredness—of human beings. *The dignity of the human person, realized in community with others, is the criterion against which all aspects of economic life must be measured.* All human beings, therefore, are ends to be served by the institutions that make up the economy, not means to

be exploited for more narrowly defined goals. Human personhood must be respected with a reverence that is religious. When we deal with each other, we should do so with the sense of awe that arises in the presence of something holy and sacred. For that is what human beings are: we are created in the image of God (Gn 1:27). Similarly, all economic institutions must support the bonds of community and solidarity that are essential to the dignity of persons. Wherever our economic arrangements fail to conform to the demands of human dignity lived in community, they must be questioned and transformed. These convictions have a biblical basis. They are also supported by a long tradition of theological and philosophical reflection and through the reasoned analysis of human experience by contemporary men and women.

29. In presenting the Christian moral vision, we turn first to the Scriptures for guidance. Though our comments are necessarily selective, we hope that pastors and other church members will become personally engaged with the biblical texts. The Scriptures contain many passages that speak directly of economic life. We must also attend to the Bible's deeper vision of God, of the purpose of creation, and of the dignity of human life in society. Along with other churches and ecclesial communities who are "strengthened by the grace of baptism and the hearing of God's Word," we strive to become faithful hearers and doers of the word. We also claim the Hebrew Scriptures as common heritage with our Jewish brothers and sisters, and we join with them in the quest for an economic life worthy of the divine revelation we share. [. . .]

64. *The commandments to love God with all one's heart and to love one's neighbor as oneself are the heart and soul of Christian morality.* Jesus offers himself as the model of this all-inclusive love: ". . . love one another as I have loved you" (Jn 15:12). These commands point out the path toward true human fulfillment and happiness. They are not arbitrary restrictions on human freedom. Only active love of God and neighbor makes the fullness of community happen. Christians look forward in hope to a true communion among all persons with each other and with God. The Spirit of Christ labors in history to build up the bonds of solidarity among all persons until that day on which their union is brought to

perfection in the Kingdom of God. Indeed Christian theological reflection on the very reality of God as a trinitarian unity of persons—Father, Son, and Holy Spirit—shows that being a person means being united to other persons in mutual love.

65. What the Bible and Christian tradition teach, human wisdom confirms. Centuries before Christ, the Greeks and Romans spoke of the human person as a "social animal" made for friendship, community, and public life. These insights show that human beings achieve self-realization not in isolation, but in interaction with others. [. . .]

68. Biblical justice is the goal we strive for. This rich biblical understanding portrays a just society as one marked by the fullness of love, compassion, holiness, and peace. On their path through history, however, sinful human beings need more specific guidance on how to move toward the realization of this great vision of God's Kingdom. This guidance is contained in the norms of basic or minimal justice. These norms state the *minimum* levels of mutual care and respect that all persons owe to each other in an imperfect world. Catholic social teaching, like much philosophical reflection, distinguishes three dimensions of basic justice: commutative justice, distributive justice, and social justice.

69. *Commutative justice calls for fundamental fairness in all agreements and exchanges between individuals or private social groups.* It demands respect for the equal human dignity of all persons in economic transactions, contracts, or promises. For example, workers owe their employers diligent work in exchange for their wages. Employers are obligated to treat their employees as persons, paying them fair wages in exchange for the work done and establishing conditions and patterns of work that are truly human.

70. *Distributive justice requires that the allocation of income, wealth, and power in society be evaluated in light of its effects on persons whose basic material needs are unmet.* The Second Vatican Council stated: "The right to have a share of earthly goods sufficient for oneself and one's family belongs to everyone. The fathers and doctors of the Church held this view, teaching that we are obliged to come to the relief of the poor and to do so not merely out of our superfluous goods." Minimum material resources are an absolute necessity for human life. If persons are to

be recognized as members of the human community, then the community has an obligation to help fulfill these basic needs unless an absolute scarcity of resources makes this strictly impossible. No such scarcity exists in the United States today.

71. Justice also has implications for the way the larger social, economic, and political institutions of society are organized. *Social justice implies that persons have an obligation to be active and productive participants in the life of society and that society has a duty to enable them to participate in this way.* This form of justice can also be called "contributive," for it stresses the duty of all who are able to help create the goods, services, and other nonmaterial or spiritual values necessary for the welfare of the whole community. In the words of Pius XI, "It is of the very essence of social justice to demand from each individual all that is necessary for the common good." Productivity is essential if the community is to have the resources to serve the well-being of all. Productivity, however, cannot be measured solely by its output in goods and services. Patterns of production must also be measured in light of their impact on the fulfillment of basic needs, employment levels, patterns of discrimination, environmental quality, and sense of community.

72. The meaning of social justice also includes a duty to organize economic and social institutions so that people can contribute to society in ways that respect their freedom and the dignity of their labor. Work should enable the working person to become "more a human being," more capable of acting intelligently, freely, and in ways that lead to self-realization.

73. Economic conditions that leave large numbers of able people unemployed, underemployed, or employed in dehumanizing conditions fail to meet the converging demands of these three forms of basic justice. Work with adequate pay for all who seek it is the primary means for achieving basic justice in our society. Discrimination in job opportunities or income levels on the basis of race, sex, or other arbitrary standards can never be justified. It is a scandal that such discrimination continues in the United States today. Where the effects of past discrimination persist, society has the obligation to take positive steps to overcome the legacy of injustice. Judiciously administered affirmative action programs in education and employment can be important expressions of

the drive for solidarity and participation that is, at the heart of true justice. Social harm calls for social relief.

74. Basic justice also calls for the establishment of a floor of material well-being on which all can stand. This is a duty of the whole of society and it creates particular obligations for those with greater resources. This duty calls into question extreme inequalities of income and consumption when so many lack basic necessities. Catholic social teaching does not maintain that a flat, arithmetical equality of income and wealth is a demand of justice, but it does challenge economic arrangements that leave large numbers of people impoverished. Further, it sees extreme inequality as a threat to the solidarity of the human community, for great disparities lead to deep social divisions and conflict.

75. This means that all of us must examine our way of living in light of the needs of the poor. Christian faith and the norms of justice impose distinct limits on what we consume and how we view material goods. The great wealth of the United States can easily blind us to the poverty that exists in this nation and the destitution of hundreds of millions of people in other parts of the world. Americans are challenged today as never before to develop the inner freedom to resist the temptation constantly to seek more. Only in this way will the nation avoid what Paul VI called "the most evident form of moral underdevelopment," namely greed. [. . .]

86. *The obligation to provide justice for all means that the poor have the single most urgent economic claim on the conscience of the nation.* Poverty can take many forms, spiritual as well as material. All people face struggles of the spirit as they ask deep questions about their purpose in life. Many have serious problems in marriage and family life at some time in their lives, and all of us face the certain reality of sickness and death. The Gospel of Christ proclaims that God's love is stronger than all these forms of diminishment. Material deprivation, however, seriously compounds such sufferings of the spirit and heart. To see a loved one sick is bad enough, but to have no possibility of obtaining health care is worse. To face family problems, such as the death of a spouse or a divorce, can be devastating, but to have these lead to the loss of one's home and end with living on the streets is something no one should have to endure in a country as rich as ours. In developing

countries these human problems are even more greatly intensified by extreme material deprivation. This form of human suffering can be reduced if our own country, so rich in resources, chooses to increase its assistance.

87. As individuals and as a nation, therefore, we are called to make a fundamental "option for the poor." The obligation to evaluate social and economic activity from the viewpoint of the poor and the powerless arises from the radical command to love one's neighbor as one's self. Those who are marginalized and whose rights are denied have privileged claims if society is to provide justice for *all*. This obligation is deeply rooted in Christian belief. As Paul VI stated:

> In teaching us charity, the Gospel instructs us in the preferential respect due the poor and the special situation they have in society: the more fortunate should renounce some of their rights so as to place their goods more generously at the service of others.

John Paul II has described this special obligation to the poor as "a call to have a special openness with the small and the weak, those that suffer and weep, those that are humiliated and left on the margin of society, so as to help them win their dignity as human persons and children of God."

88. The prime purpose of this special commitment to the poor is to enable them to become active participants in the life of society. It is to enable *all* persons to share in and contribute to the common good. The "option for the poor," therefore, is not an adversarial slogan that pits one group or class against another. Rather it states that the deprivation and powerlessness of the poor wounds the whole community. The extent of their suffering is a measure of how far we are from being a true community of persons. These wounds will be healed only by greater solidarity with the poor and among the poor themselves.

89. In summary, the norms of love, basic justice, and human rights imply that personal decisions, social policies, and economic institutions should be governed by several key priorities. These priorities do not specify everything that must be considered in economic decision making. They do indicate the most fundamental and urgent objectives. [. . .]

[I]t is primarily through their daily labor that people make their most important contributions to economic justice. [. . .]

97. All work has a threefold moral significance. First, it is a principal way that people exercise the distinctive human capacity for self-expression and self-realization. Second, it is the ordinary way for human beings to fulfill their material needs. Finally, work enables people to contribute to the well-being of the larger community. Work is not only for one's self. It is for one's family, for the nation, and indeed for the benefit of the entire human family.

98. These three moral concerns should be visible in the work of all, no matter what their role in the economy: blue collar workers, managers, homemakers, politicians, and others. They should also govern the activities of the many different, overlapping communities and institutions that make up society: families, neighborhoods, small businesses, giant corporations, trade unions, the various levels of government, international organizations, and a host of other human associations including communities of faith.

99. Catholic social teaching calls for respect for the full richness of social life. The need for vital contributions from different human associations—ranging in size from the family to government—has been classically expressed in Catholic social teaching in the "principle of subsidiarity":

> Just as it is gravely wrong to take from individuals what they can accomplish by their own initiative and industry and give it to the community, so also it is an injustice and at the same time a grave evil and disturbance of right order to assign to a greater and higher association what lesser and subordinate organizations can do. For every social activity ought of its very nature to furnish help (*subsidium*) to the members of the body social, and never destroy and absorb them. [. . .]

100. This principle guarantees institutional pluralism. It provides space for freedom, initiative, and creativity on the part of many social agents. At the same time, it insists that *all* these agents should work in ways that help build up the social body. Therefore, in all their activities these groups should be working in ways that express their distinctive capacities for action, that help meet human needs, and that make true contributions to the common good of

the human community. The task of creating a more just U.S. economy is the vocation of all and depends on strengthening the virtues of public service and responsible citizenship in personal life and on all levels of institutional life. [. . .]

102. Though John Paul II's understanding of work is a very inclusive one, it fully applies to those customarily called "workers" or "labor" in the United States. Labor has great dignity, so great that all who are able to work are obligated to do so. The duty to work derives both from God's command and from a responsibility to one's own humanity and to the common good. The virtue of industriousness is also an expression of a persons dignity and solidarity with others. All working people are called to contribute to the common good by seeking excellence in production and service.

103. Because work is this important, people have a right to employment. In return for their labor, workers have a right to wages and other benefits sufficient to sustain life in dignity. As Pope Leo XIII stated, every working person has "the right of securing things to sustain life." The way power is distributed in a free market economy frequently gives employers greater bargaining power than employees in the negotiation of labor contracts. Such unequal power may press workers into a choice between an inadequate wage and no wage at all. But justice, not charity, demands certain minimum guarantees. The provision of wages and other benefits sufficient to support a family in dignity is a basic necessity to prevent this exploitation of workers. The dignity of workers also requires adequate health care, security for old age or disability, unemployment compensation, healthful working conditions, weekly rest, periodic holidays for recreation and leisure, and reasonable security against arbitrary dismissal. These provisions are all essential if workers are to be treated as persons rather than simply as a "factor of production."

104. The Church fully supports the right of workers to form unions or other associations to secure their rights to fair wages and working conditions. This is a specific application of the more general right to associate. In the words of Pope John Paul II, "The experience of history teaches that organizations of this type are an indispensable element of social life, especially in modern industrialized societies." Unions may also legitimately resort to strikes where

this is the only available means to the justice owed to workers. No one may deny the right to organize without attacking human dignity itself. Therefore, we firmly oppose organized efforts, such as those regrettably now seen in this country, to break existing unions and prevent workers from organizing. Migrant agricultural workers today are particularly in need of the protection, including the right to organize and bargain collectively. U.S. labor law reform is needed to meet these problems as well as to provide more timely and effective remedies for unfair labor practices. [. . .]

106. Along with the rights ot workers and unions go a number of important responsibilities. Individual workers have obligations to their employers, and trade unions also have duties to society as a whole. Union management in particular carries a strong responsibility for the good name of the entire union movement. Workers must use their collective power to contribute to the well-being of the whole community and should avoid pressing demands whose fulfillment would damage the common good and the rights of more vulnerable members of society. It should be noted, however, that wages paid to workers are but one of the factors affecting the competitiveness of industries. Thus, it is unfair to expect unions to make concessions if managers and shareholders do not make at least equal sacrifices. [. . .]

110. The economy's success in fulfilling the demands of justice will depend on how its vast resources and wealth are managed. Property owners, managers, and investors of financial capital must all contribute to creating a more just society. Securing economic justice depends heavily on the leadership of men and women in business and on wise investment by private enterprises. Pope John Paul II has pointed out, "The degree of well-being which society today enjoys would be unthinkable without the dynamic figure of the business person, whose function consists of organizing human labor and the means of production so as to give rise to the goods and services necessary for the prosperity and progress of the community." The freedom of entrepreneurship, business, and finance should be protected, but the accountability of this freedom to the common good and the norms of justice must be assured.

111. Persons in management face many hard choices each day, choices on which the well-being of

many others depends. Commitment to the public good and not simply the private good of their firms is at the heart of what it means to call their work a vocation and not simply a career or a job. We believe that the norms and priorities discussed in this letter can be of help as they pursue their important tasks. The duties of individuals in the business world, however, do not exhaust the ethical dimensions of business and finance. The size of a firm or bank is in many cases an indicator of relative power. Large corporations and large financial institutions have considerable power to help shape economic institutions within the United States and throughout the world. With this power goes responsibility and the need for those who manage it to be held to moral and institutional accountability.

112. Business and finance have the duty to be faithful trustees of the resources at their disposal. No one can ever own capital resources absolutely or control their use without regard for others and society as a whole. This applies first of all to land and natural resources. Short-term profits reaped at the cost of depletion of natural resources or the pollution of the environment violate this trust.

113. Resources created by human industry are also held in trust. Owners and managers have not created this capital on their own. They have benefited from the work of many others and from the local communities that support their endeavors. They are accountable to these workers and communities when making decisions. For example, reinvestment in technological innovation is often crucial for the long-term viability of a firm. The use of financial resources solely in pursuit of short-term profits can stunt the production of needed goods and services; a broader vision of managerial responsibility is needed. [. . .]

117. Business people, managers, investors, and financiers follow a vital Christian vocation when they act responsibly and seek the common good. We encourage and support a renewed sense of vocation in the business community. We also recognize that the way business people serve society is governed and limited by the incentives which flow from tax policies, the availability of credit, and other public policies.

118. Businesses have a right to an institutional framework that does not penalize enterprises that act responsibly. Governments must provide regulations and a system of taxation which encourage firms to preserve the environment, employ disadvantaged workers, and create jobs in depressed areas. Managers and stockholders should not be torn between their responsibilities to their organizations and their responsibilities toward society as a whole. [. . .]

120. Every citizen also has the responsibility to work to secure justice and human rights through an organized social response. In the words of Pius XI, "Charity will never be true charity unless it takes justice into account. . . . Let no one attempt with small gifts of charity to exempt himself from the great duties imposed by justice." The guaranteeing of basic justice for all is not an optional expression of largesse but an inescapable duty for the whole of society.

121. The traditional distinction between society and the state in Catholic social teaching provides the basic framework for such organized public efforts. The Church opposes all statist and totalitarian approaches to socioeconomic questions. Social life is richer than governmental power can encompass. All groups that compose society have responsibilities to respond to the demands of justice. We have just outlined some of the duties of labor unions and business and financial enterprises. These must be supplemented by initiatives by local community groups, professional associations, educational institutions, churches, and synagogues. All the groups that give life to this society have important roles to play in the pursuit of economic justice. [. . .]

A Commitment to the Future

326. Because Jesus' command to love our neighbor is universal, we hold that the life of each person on this globe is sacred. This commits us to bringing about a just economic order where all, without exception, will be treated with dignity and to working in collaboration with those who share this vision. The world is complex and this may often tempt us to seek simple and self-centered solutions; but as a community of disciples we are called to a new hope and to a new vision that we must live without fear and without oversimplification. Not only must we learn more about our moral responsibility for the larger economic issues that touch the daily life of each and every person on this planet, but we also want to help

shape the Church as a model of social and economic justice. [. . .]

328. The transformation of social structures begins with and is always accompanied by a conversion of the heart. As disciples of Christ each of us is called to a deep personal conversion and to "action on behalf of justice and participation in the transformation of the world." By faith and baptism we are fashioned into a "new creature"; we are filled with the Holy Spirit and a new love that compels us to seek out a new profound relationship with God, with the human family, and with all created things. Renouncing self-centered desires, bearing one's daily cross, and imitating Christ's compassion, all involve a personal struggle to control greed and selfishness, a personal commitment to reverence one's own human dignity and the dignity of others by avoiding self-indulgence and those attachments that make us insensitive to the conditions of others and that erode social solidarity. Christ warned us against attachments to material things, against total self-reliance, against the idolatry of accumulating material goods and seeking safety in them. We must take these teachings seriously and in their light examine how each of us lives and acts toward others. But personal conversion is not gained once and for all. It is a process that goes on through our entire life. Conversion, moreover, takes place in the context of a larger faith community: through baptism into the Church, through common prayer, and through our activity with others on behalf of justice. [. . .]

337. Some of the difficulty in bringing Christian faith to economic life in the United States today results from the obstacles to establishing a balance of labor and leisure in daily life. Tedious and boring work leads some to look for fulfillment only during time off the job. Others have become "workaholics," people who work compulsively and without reflection on the deeper meaning of life and their actions. The quality and pace of work should be more human in scale enabling people to experience the dignity and value of their work and giving them time for other duties and obligations. This balance is vitally important for sustaining the social, political, educational, and cultural structures of society. The family, in particular, requires such balance. Without leisure there is too little time for nurturing marriages, for developing parent-child relationships, and

for fulfilling commitments to other important groups: the extended family, the community of friends, the parish, the neighborhood, schools, and political organizations. Why is it one hears so little today about shortening the work week, especially if both parents are working? Such a change would give them more time for each other, for their children, and for their other social and political responsibilities.

338. Leisure is connected to the whole of one's value system and influenced by the general culture one lives in. It can be trivialized into boredom and laziness, or end in nothing but a desire for greater consumption and waste. For disciples of Christ, the use of leisure may demand being countercultural. The Christian tradition sees in leisure, time to build family and societal relationships and an opportunity for communal prayer and worship, for relaxed contemplation and enjoyment of God's creation, and for the cultivation of the arts which help fill the human longing for wholeness. Most of all, we must be convinced that economic decisions affect our use of leisure and that such decisions are also to be based on moral and ethical considerations. In this area of leisure we must be on our guard against being swept along by a lack of cultural values and by the changing fads of an affluent society. In the creation narrative God worked six days to create the world and rested on the seventh (Gn 2:14). We must take that image seriously and learn how to harmonize action and rest, work and leisure, so that both contribute to building up the person as well as the family and community. [. . .]

363. Confronted by this economic complexity and seeking clarity for the future, we can rightly ask ourselves one single question: How does our economic system affect the lives of people—all people? Part of the American dream has been to make this world a better place for people to live in; at this moment of history that dream must include everyone on this globe. Since we profess to be members of a "catholic" or universal Church, we all must raise our sights to a concern for the well-being of everyone in the world. Third World debt becomes our problem. Famine and starvation in sub-Saharan Africa become our concern. Rising military expenditures everywhere in the world become part of our fears for the future of this planet. We cannot be content if we see ecological neglect or the squandering of natural

resources. In this letter we bishops have spoken often of economic interdependence; now is the moment when all of us must confront the reality of such economic bonding and its consequences and see it as a moment of grace—a *kairos*—that can unite all of us in a common community of the human family. We commit ourselves to this global vision.

364. We cannot be frightened by the magnitude and complexity of these problems. We must not be discouraged. In the midst of this struggle, it is inevitable that we become aware of greed, laziness, and envy. No utopia is possible on this earth; but as believers in the redemptive love of God and as those who have experienced God's forgiving mercy, we know that God's providence is not and will not be lacking to us today.

365. The fulfillment of human needs, we know, is not the final purpose of the creation of the human person. We have been created to share in the divine life through a destiny that goes far beyond our human capabilities and before which we must in all humility stand in awe. Like Mary in proclaiming her *Magnificat*, we marvel at the wonders God has done for us, how God has raised up the poor and the lowly and promised great things for them in the Kingdom. God now asks of us sacrifices and reflection on our reverence for human dignity—in ourselves and in others—and on our service and discipleship, so that the divine goal for the human family and this earth can be fulfilled. Communion with God, sharing God's life, involves a mutual bonding with all on this globe. Jesus taught us to love God and one another and that the concept of neighbor is without limit. We know that we are called to be members of a new covenant of love. We have to move from our devotion to independence, through an understanding of interdependence, to a commitment to human solidarity. That challenge must find its realization in the kind of community we build among us. Love implies concern for all—especially the poor—and a continued search for those social and economic structures that permit everyone to share in a community that is a part of a redeemed creation (Rom 8:21–23).

GERTRUDE HIMMELFARB

Welfare and Charity: Lessons from Victorian England (1997)

The word "welfare" is ambiguous. Does it mean the well-being of the citizenry? Or does it mean relief—state-subsidized relief, which now goes by the euphemism of "welfare"? Perhaps I am especially sensitive to such euphemisms because they were conspicuously lacking in my own field of study, Victorian England. And the example of Victorian England has never been as pertinent as it is today.

More than a century and a half ago, a few years before Queen Victoria ascended the throne, a Royal Commission of Parliament proposed a major reform of the Poor Law. In its report, the Commission deplored "the mischievous ambiguity of the word 'poor'." The very name, Poor Law, was a misnomer; it was a pauper law, not a poor law. Most of the poor—which is to say, virtually all the working classes—were indeed poor, but they were not paupers. They were "independent"—that is, self-supporting—laborers. Unfortunately, the enormous expansion of relief in the preceding decades, including relief "in aid of wages" (to supplement wages), had confused the distinction between pauper and poor, thus contributing to the "pauperization of the poor."

In a passage strikingly reminiscent of the situation today, the report explained why the enemies of reform sought to perpetuate the ambiguity of pauper and poor:

> Such persons will, no doubt, avail themselves of the mischievous ambiguity of the word poor, and

treat all diminution of the expenditure for the relief of the poor as so much taken from the labouring classes; as if those classes were naturally pensioners on the charity of their superiors, and relief, not wages, were the proper fund for their support; as if the independent laborers themselves were not, directly or indirectly, losers by all expenditure on paupers; as if those who would be raised from pauperism to independence would not be the greatest gainers by the change; as if, to use the expression of one of the witnesses whom we have quoted, the meat of industry were worse than the bread of idleness.

At just this time, while the reform of the Poor Law was being debated, Tocqueville visited England and shortly afterward wrote a "Memoir on Pauperism" reflecting on his experiences. He started by commenting on the paradox that the poorest countries in Europe had the fewest paupers while the richest country, England, had the most. The explanation was simple: The richest country had the highest standard of living and thus, also, the highest standard of basic needs; and because it was at a higher stage of civilization, it aspired to meet that standard for all its citizens. This combination of affluence and compassion produced the most generous system of public relief and thus, the largest population of paupers.

Tocqueville admired the spirit behind the English Poor Law but deplored the consequences. Unlike private charity, he said, which depends on the goodwill of the benefactor, public relief is a matter of legal right. The recipient of charity has no assurance of assistance; the recipient of relief has that assurance. And it is that assurance, the right to relief, that undermines the incentive to work and thus tends to pauperize the poor. By guaranteeing the means of subsistence as a legal right to all, England relieved the poor of the obligation to work and thus made paupers of so many of the poor.

Rights in general are commendable, Tocqueville granted, but this right degrades the man who exercises it. Whereas most rights testify to the individual's superiority, the right to relief is a legal, public testimony to his inferiority. Relief is thus more demeaning than charity, for charity involves only a private acknowledgement of dependency, while relief is "a notarized manifestation of misery, of weakness, of misconduct." And the more prolonged the exercise of this right, the more degrading it becomes.

Moreover, charity, being individual and voluntary, establishes a "moral tie" between the donor and the recipient, between the rich and the poor. Relief, being impersonal and legal, destroys any sense of morality. The donor (the tax-payer) resents his involuntary contribution, and the recipient feels no gratitude for what he gets as a matter of right, which, in any case, he feels to be insufficient.

Tocqueville proves himself once again a prophet for our time as he went on to explain why relief is demoralizing, why public authorities cannot really judge the merit of individual claimants for relief, why schemes to put paupers to work generally fail, why well-intentioned policies often produce greater misery, and why future generations pay the cost of present follies. Most prescient is his description of the contrast between the improvement of the working classes and the deterioration of the pauper class—a class where "the number of illegitimate children and criminals grows rapidly and continuously, the indigent population is limitless, the spirit of foresight and of saving becomes more and more alien. . . ."

Tocqueville's essay ought to be required reading for all legislators, policy-makers, and commentators. As it happened, the English did not take Tocqueville's advice, which was to abolish the Poor Law. (They could not, in fact, have known of the "Memoir," which appeared in the proceedings of a French provincial academy a year after the passage of the New Poor Law.) Instead they reformed the law to remove its worst failing: the "mischievous ambiguity" of pauper and poor that contributed to the pauperization of the poor.

Victorian Principles of "Relief"

The New Poor Law of 1834 was based on the "principle of less eligibility," which stipulated that the condition of the "able-bodied pauper" on relief (it did not apply to the sick, aged, or children) be less "eligible"—that is, less desirable, less favorable—than the condition of the independent laborer. "Less-eligibility" meant not only that the pauper receive less by way of relief than the laborer did from his wages but also that he receive it in such a way (in the workhouse, for example) as to make pauperism less respectable than work—to "stigmatize" it, as we now say disapprovingly. Thus the laborer would be discouraged from lapsing into a state of dependency and the pauper would be encouraged to work.

In fact, it was not so much the actual conditions in the workhouse that discouraged pauperism. As contemporaries constantly pointed out, food and living conditions in the house were often no worse and sometimes even better than those of the very poor outside. But what made the workhouse unmistakably less-eligible was the demeaning, degrading fact of being in it. It was the very idea of it, the loss of respectability implied by it, that constituted the real deterrent. Indeed, the mere threat of the workhouse continued to stigmatize pauperism even though many parishes did not build workhouses and continued to provide outdoor relief for the able-bodied.

Obviously, no one today would propose reviving the workhouse (although that is probably what I shall be accused of doing). The principle of less-eligibility, as the term plainly signifies, is a relative one, and it should take no great ingenuity to find other ways of implementing that principle, well short of the workhouse. At the very least, it should be possible to reverse the present situation, which more nearly resembles that of "more-eligibility." Welfare recipients today are often in a more-eligible condition than workers earning a minimum or modest wage and thus have no incentive to try to get a job. Unwed mothers receive benefits that married mothers do not have, thus providing an incentive not to get married. And since there is no longer any stigma attached to relief (it is not even called that any more—*welfare* is the current term), that moral deterrent, too, is absent.

Victorian Principles of Charity

Just as the Victorians gave serious thought to the principles governing relief, so they did to the principles of charity. Somewhat later in the century, in 1869, the Charity Organization Society (COS) was established to coordinate the multitude of private charities and philanthropies that were being founded. (In London alone there were about seven hundred philanthropic societies, devoted to every conceivable human misery or affliction.)

The COS prided itself on being at the same time a "religion" of charity and a "science" of charity: a religion in satisfying the spiritual duty of the donors, as expressed in John Wesley's famous sermon: "Gain all you can . . . , save all you can . . . , give all you can . . ."; and a science in seeking to maximize the good effects of the giving and minimize the ill-effects. It was this combination of religiosity and rationality that characterized Victorian charity, in a period when charity flourished as never before—and perhaps never since.

Charity, the COS insisted, was not only different in nature from relief; it was aimed at different people. Relief was intended for those who were in a condition of destitution; charity for those "deserving poor" who were temporarily in need of help and for whom a timely and appropriate provision of help would prevent their falling into a state of pauperism. Charity would not duplicate relief; nor would it be "indiscriminate" or "promiscuous." Above all, it would require the recipient of charity to exercise the same self-discipline, the same virtues, required of all the poor.

The housing reformer, Octavia Hill, was one of that tribe of "governing and guiding women," as Beatrice Webb put it, who were so influential in the philanthropic movement. Hill renovated houses and rented them to the poor at somewhat less cost and with better facilities than they could otherwise afford; in return, she insisted upon the prompt payment of rent, reasonable decorum, and cleanliness. Similarly, Toynbee Hall, the prototype of the settlement house, provided classes and instruction of all kinds, at no cost, but in the expectation of regular attendance and in the hope that the poor would be intellectually and spiritually elevated. And the dispensers of other charitable funds and services did so on condition that the assistance would enable the beneficiaries to become self-supporting and to "better themselves."

If the beneficiaries were held to high standards, so were the benefactors. The great Victorian philanthropists were not Rockefellers or Carnegies who gave of their fortunes for worthy causes. This was not check-book philanthropy. Nor was it what Dickens and George Eliot satirized as "telescopic philanthropy"—the charity that "increases directly as the square of the distance," like that of Mrs. Jellyby in *Bleak House*, who was more concerned with the natives of Borrioboola-Gha than with her own children. The Victorians gave what they could by way of money, but more important, they gave of themselves, with their personal, sustained involvement in their work and their direct and immediate concern for those whom they were assisting.

In one sense, they were professional philanthropists; they took their work seriously and abided by professional standards—"scientific" principles, as they said. But they were, with rare exceptions, unpaid (or, if they had no other source of income, very modestly paid). Octavia Hill's rent collectors—in effect, social workers—were volunteers, as were the COS's "visitors" and the settlement house "residents." The latter, in fact, paid for the privilege of living in Toynbee Hall and spending all their spare time in communal work. Thus it was that charity was both a "science" and a "religion": a science in seeking the best way to help the beneficiaries to help themselves, and a religion in satisfying the spiritual need of the benefactors for public service.

When Beatrice Webb started work as a visitor for the COS (before she married Sidney Webb and became a Fabian socialist), she pondered on "the relationship of giver and receiver" and decided that the moral effect on the giver was as important as that on the receiver. It was "distinctly *advantageous to us*," she wrote, "to go amongst poor" not only to have a better understanding of their problems but also because "contact with them develops on the whole our finer qualities, disgusting us with our false and worldly application of men and things and educating in us a thoughtful benevolence."

I do not agree with Beatrice Webb about much else, but I do think she got that quite right. Charity is, or should be, the exercise of "a thoughtful benevolence." Not benevolence alone but a thoughtful benevolence—a reasoned, prudent, discriminating, even skeptical benevolence—a benevolence that is acutely aware of the often unintended consequences of goodwill, that knows that it is more important to do good than to feel good, that is morally and spiritually satisfying for the giver, and morally as well as materially beneficial to the receiver. It is this kind of charity that promotes welfare in the proper sense of that word—the well-being of the citizenry.

Roberto Unger and Cornel West

Progressive Politics and What Lies Ahead (1998)

The oldest element of American life is the religion of individual and collective possibility: the belief that citizens can remake themselves and their society, that they can make everything new. The American dream includes a middle-class standard of living for everyone, with economic independence and security, as well as opportunities for children to achieve what their parents failed to accomplish or obtain.

Today, however, at the apogee of the country's world power and in the midst of a thriving economy, most working Americans feel more squeezed than ever and are convinced that life will be harder for them than it was for their parents. Even politically active and educated elites feel incapable of addressing, much less solving, many of the basic problems of the country, from inadequate healthcare and education to the social and racial apartheid of inner-city poverty; from increasing inequality of wealth and income to abstention from the vote and indifference to politics. The practical consequence of this national failure is that Americans despair of collective solutions to their collective problems, and alternate between resenting the incapable politics of their country and blaming themselves for failure to succeed at a game that so often seems rigged against them.

At the same time, faith in the power of the individual to better his or her life—against all odds—is the most prominent element in the American religion of possibility. That religion also includes something more basic and ambitious: a belief in the unlimited potential of practical problem-solving and a faith in democracy as a terrain on which ordinary men and women can become strongly defined personalities, in full possession of themselves.

The United States is a country of tinkerers. To believe in the American religion of possibility is to hold that each of the problems that oppress, weaken and frighten us as individuals can be confronted, problem by problem, through human effort and ingenuity. Americans resist seeing particular problems as manifestations of hidden, hard constraints. They believe that the terrors of vast problems yield to the effects of many small solutions.

Motivated, sustained and cumulative tinkering with institutional arrangements is an indispensable tool of democratic experimentalism, of improvisational reform, of jazzlike public action. Americans, however, have been willing to use this tool only under the extreme pressure of crisis and catastrophe. There have been three great periods of institutional innovation in American history: the foundation of the Republic, the Civil War and Reconstruction, and the New Deal. In each, national leaders won support for institutional experiments from an energized majority. Nonetheless, ever since the first of these three periods of collective creation, the country has been attracted to the idea that it came close to the natural and necessary form of a free society. There were ordeals to undergo—the terrible burden of slavery and its aftermath, a massive economic failure and the outbreak of war in Europe—and crisis might require adjustment. But such innovations as were needed would result mainly from the independent initiative of people in their businesses or the voluntary association of individuals in their communities. Exceptions like the GI Bill or the Civil Rights Act—triggered by grassroots groups like the American Legion or black churches—prove the rule.

A small number of major thinkers like Thomas Jefferson, Abraham Lincoln, Henry George, W. E. B. Du Bois, Ida B. Wells-Barnett and John Dewey tried to convince Americans to lift the exemption from experimentalism they accorded to their institutions, and to trade in some bad American exceptionalism for some good American experimentalism. Their message, however, was only selectively heard, even by progressive movements whose rigid, ideological grids often overlook the complexity and experimental impulse of American life.

If American progressivism is to be reborn today and to carry forward its work, if it is to keep the religion of possibility alive and loosen the constraints that racial and gender oppression and class hierarchy impose upon our democracy, it must hear that message of democratic: experimentalism more clearly. Progressives must present to the country a reform program that looks neither backward to the perpetuation of the liberal social programs nor sideways to the softening of the conservative free-market agenda but forward to a practical vision of the re-energizing of democratic politics and the democratizing of the market economy in America.

Americans should use the tools of institutional experimentalism to rethink and rebuild each strand in their religion of possibility: the hope of social opportunity and mobility for the individual; the hope that practical ingenuity can resolve, one by one, the problems people face; and the hope that under democracy individual men and women can achieve the largeness of vision and experience that less democratic civilizations have reserved for the exceptional few.

But Americans have traditionally gone about solving problems one at a time. They have been distrustful of the idea that their problems at any given time fit into a single scheme. Thus, the temper of progressive movements in the United States has been simple and sincere: majorities against minorities, poor against rich, powerless against powerful. Such a sensibility is impatient with the idea of combined and cumulative institutional change. The obstacles it is willing to recognize are visible: forceful interests rather than hidden assumptions or unchallenged arrangements.

The attitudes of practical progressives are mirrored in the self-image of many a practical politician. They distrust, as romantic or dangerous, talk of ideologies, institutional alternatives and citizens' action. The policy discussion permitted by such a mentality takes the established institutions of the country for granted. Without ideas about institutional alternatives and without the political mobilization of once-passive majorities, politics degenerates into inconclusive bargaining among organized interest groups. Such a politics is incapable of addressing, much less solving, any of the major acknowledged problems of the country.

When American radicals have broken with the tradition of the sincere progressives and the disillusioned politicians, they have sometimes embraced a view that is equally paralyzing. It is the belief, recommended by European theories like Marxism, in the existence of a system out there—capitalism, for example—with its driving laws, its inner logic and its indivisible unity. Either you change the whole system, or you merely try to soften its harsh effects through reformism. The idea of fundamental social change has been associated with the picture of decisive crisis, triggering the total substitution of one way of organizing society by another.

We reject the choice between a view that would promote popular interests without reimagining and remaking institutional arrangements, and a view that sees such arrangements as pieces of a take-it-or-leave-it system. To understand the truth about political possibility, we need to jumble these categories, combining the idea of step-by-step reform with the idea that institutions matter. We have it in our power to reimagine and remake them. The institutions of a society are its fate. Transformative politics is, like art, an antifate, restoring to us a freedom we have renounced or forgotten.

Progressives do not need to create a blueprint to map out a path. The steps along the way can and should be described both at points close to present circumstances and at points farther away. The direction—and its effect upon people's understanding of their interests and identities as well as upon their practical problems—is what matters. Only when we fail to hold in our minds a credible view of social change do we fall back on a fake, surrogate standard of political realism: that a proposal is realistic according to its proximity to what exists.

It is easy to be a realist when you accept everything. It is easy to be a visionary when you confront nothing. To accept little and confront much, and to do so on the basis of an informed vision of piecemeal but cumulative change, is the way and the solution.

There is broad consensus in America about what the basic problems of the country are. The economy has failed to achieve growth in productivity that is either inclusive of all citizens or rapid enough. The innovative practices of the best firms—the turning of production into permanent innovation—have remained within relatively isolated, advanced parts of the economy. Vast wealth, privilege and power have accumulated in the hands of a tiny and self-serving corporate elite, which pays itself proportionately more—and pays workers proportionately less—than in any other industrial democracy. The present systems of education and healthcare impose a burden on growth and prosperity as well as upon social welfare.

In politics, where solutions must begin, there is less agreement about problems. Progressives, if not yet many of their fellow Americans, see problems with how money and moneyed interests exert an inordinate influence upon the outcome of elections and the direction of policy, an influence occasionally sanctified by the judiciary as if the ability of money to talk, magnifying the voices of the few and crowding out the voices of the many, were a principle rather than a wrong. Recent conservative administrations have succeeded in convincing Americans that they have little to hope for from the government or from political work. Progressive forces, in and outside the Democratic Party, have willingly resigned themselves to the humanization of the Republican as the outer limit of their transformative ambitions. The politically active minority of the country generally agrees that this surrender is the straightforward expression of political realism rather than the self-fulfilling consequence of a failure of ideas and nerve.

Only in moments of deep crisis—the Civil War, the Great Depression, the civil uprisings in the sixties—have Americans pursued national politics with democratic, innovative energy. When things have seemed under control, they have derided national politics as a barely respectable sideshow to their personal responsibilities. Americans must resolve their ambivalence about politics if they are to fashion the institutional improvements that would allow them to solve the admitted problems of the country and begin to address the major features of the emerging world economy that have made many of these problems both more urgent and more intractable.

The work of American progressivism today is to build the link between political reforms intended to quicken democratic politics in America and economic reforms designed to challenge the stark divisions between vanguard and rearguard—between advanced and backward sectors of the economy.

The program we support opposes such economic divisions, and proposes a deepening of democracy: strengthening the tools for the collective discussion and solution of collective problems. It is a productivist program, rooting a bias toward more equality of income and wealth in a set of economic arrangements and a strategy of economic growth, rather than merely attempting, through retrospective and compensatory tax-and-transfer, to undo part of what the economy has wrought. It rejects the simple contrast between governmental activism and free enterprise, not because it wants to have a little of each but because it insists upon having more of both.

Here, for example, are a few of its elements:

(1) We should develop a broad-based and market-friendly effort to lift up the economic rearguard. One component of this would be the broadening of access to finance and technology through the establishment of independently administered venture-capital funds chartered to invest in the rearguard and to conserve and grow the resources with which they would be endowed. Experience suggests that, with accountable but independent management and properly diversified investment portfolios, such funds can achieve high rates of return on their endowments. Different regimes of private and social property and decentralized initiative would begin to coexist experimentally within the economy. The outcome of such experiments is not the suppression of the market; it is the democratizing and diversification of the market.

(2) The law should develop standards to give a special push in schooling and employment—and therefore in admissions and hiring—to those who suffer from an accumulation of forms of disadvantage from which they cannot be expected to escape on their own. Prominent among these sources of subjugation are class, race, gender and handicap. Placed in this context, the offer of preferment loses its invidious, narrowly racial character.

(3) Society should be independently organized outside the government—a simple idea with complicated and controversial implications. One major site of organization is work. Labor laws need to be strengthened, not to deepen divisions between a minority of relatively privileged workers in traditional industries and everyone else but to facilitate unionization everywhere, particularly in the expanding area of temporary work. We must resist the entrenchment of stark divisions between insiders—relatively privileged, organized workers with jobs in the capital- and knowledge-rich sectors of the economy—and outsiders with unstable, dead-end jobs in the capital- and knowledge-poor sectors.

To advance such a program, we must encourage the master practice of democratic experimentalism: motivated, sustained and cumulative tinkering with institutional arrangements of the government and the economy, relying on a more engaged and informed citizenry rather than on a more enlightened technocratic elite. The gradual emergence of a lasting, transracial progressive majority in American politics is both the condition and the consequence of such democratizing changes. Ultimately, this project will move us not toward the humanization of the inevitable, but toward the alternative to an unnecessary and unacceptable fate.

Elie Wiesel

Speech at the White House on the Perils of Indifference
(1999)

April 12, 1999, Washington, D.C.

Mr. President, Mrs. Clinton, members of Congress, Ambassador Holbrooke, Excellencies, friends:

Fifty-four years ago to the day, a young Jewish boy from a small town in the Carpathian Mountains woke up, not far from Goethe's beloved Weimar, in a place of eternal infamy called Buchenwald. He was finally free, but there was no joy in his heart. He thought there never would be again. Liberated a day earlier by American soldiers, he remembers their rage at what they saw. And even if he lives to be a very old man, he will always be grateful to them for that rage, and also for their compassion. Though he did not understand their language, their eyes told him what he needed to know—that they, too, would remember, and bear witness.

And now, I stand before you, Mr. President— Commander-in-Chief of the army that freed me, and tens of thousands of others—and I am filled with a profound and abiding gratitude to the American people. Gratitude is a word that I cherish. Gratitude is what defines the humanity of the human being. And I am grateful to you, Hillary, or Mrs. Clinton, for what you said, and for what you are doing for children in the world, for the homeless, for the victims of injustice, the victims of destiny and society. And I thank all of you for being here.

We are on the threshold of a new century, a new millennium. What will the legacy of this vanishing century be? How will it be remembered in the new millennium? Surely it will be judged, and judged severely, in both moral and metaphysical terms. These failures have cast a dark shadow over humanity: two World Wars, countless civil wars, the senseless chain of assassinations (Gandhi, the Kennedys, Martin Luther King, Sadat, Rabin), bloodbaths in Cambodia and Nigeria, India and Pakistan, Ireland and Rwanda, Eritrea and Ethiopia, Sarajevo and Kosovo; the inhumanity in the gulag and the tragedy of Hiroshima. And, on a different level, of course, Auschwitz and Treblinka. So much violence; so much indifference.

What is indifference? Etymologically, the word means "no difference." A strange and unnatural state in which the lines blur between light and darkness, dusk and dawn, crime and punishment, cruelty and compassion, good and evil. What are its courses and inescapable consequences? Is it a philosophy? Is there a philosophy of indifference conceivable? Can one possibly view indifference as a virtue? Is it necessary at times to practice it simply to keep one's sanity, live normally, enjoy a fine meal and a glass of wine, as the world around us experiences harrowing upheavals?

Of course, indifference can be tempting—more than that, seductive. It is so much easier to look away from victims. It is so much easier to avoid such rude interruptions to our work, our dreams, our hopes. It is, after all, awkward, troublesome, to be involved in another person's pain and despair. Yet, for the person who is indifferent, his or her neighbor are of no consequence. And, therefore, their lives are meaningless. Their hidden or even visible anguish is of no interest. Indifference reduces the Other to an abstraction.

Over there, behind the black gates of Auschwitz, the most tragic of all prisoners were the "Muselmanner," as they were called. Wrapped in their torn blankets, they would sit or lie on the ground, staring vacantly into space, unaware of who or where they were—strangers to their surroundings. They no longer felt pain, hunger, thirst. They feared nothing. They felt nothing. They were dead and did not know it.

Rooted in our tradition, some of us felt that to be abandoned by humanity then was not the ultimate. We felt that to be abandoned by God was worse than to be punished by Him. Better an unjust God than an indifferent one. For us to be ignored by God was a harsher punishment than to be a victim of His anger. Man can live far from God—not outside God. God is wherever we are. Even in suffering? Even in suffering.

In a way, to be indifferent to that suffering is what makes the human being inhuman. Indifference, after all, is more dangerous than anger and hatred. Anger can at times be creative. One writes a great poem, a great symphony. One does something special for the sake of humanity because one is angry at the injustice that one witnesses. But indifference is never creative. Even hatred at times may elicit a response. You fight it. You denounce it. You disarm it.

Indifference elicits no response. Indifference is not a response. Indifference is not a beginning; it is an end. And, therefore, indifference is always the friend of the enemy, for it benefits the aggressor—never his victim, whose pain is magnified when he or she feels forgotten. The political prisoner in his cell, the hungry children, the homeless refugees—not to respond to their plight, not to relieve their solitude by offering them a spark of hope is to exile them from human memory. And in denying their humanity, we betray our own.

Indifference, then, is not only a sin, it is a punishment.

And this is one of the most important lessons of this outgoing century's wide-ranging experiments in good and evil.

In the place that I come from, society was composed of three simple categories: the killers, the victims, and the bystanders. During the darkest of times, inside the ghettoes and death camps—and I'm glad that Mrs. Clinton mentioned that we are now commemorating that event, that period, that we are now in the Days of Remembrance—but then, we felt abandoned, forgotten. All of us did.

And our only miserable consolation was that we believed that Auschwitz and Treblinka were closely guarded secrets; that the leaders of the free world did not know what was going on behind those black gates and barbed wire; that they had no knowledge of the war against the Jews that Hitler's armies and their accomplices waged as part of the war against the Allies. If they knew, we thought, surely those leaders would have moved heaven and earth to intervene. They would have spoken out with great outrage and conviction. They would have bombed the railways leading to Birkenau, just the railways, just once.

And now we knew, we learned, we discovered that the Pentagon knew, the State Department knew. And the illustrious occupant of the White House then, who was a great leader—and I say it with some anguish and pain, because, today is exactly 54 years marking his death—Franklin Delano Roosevelt died on April the 12th, 1945. So he is very much present to me and to us. No doubt, he was a great leader. He mobilized the American people and the world, going into battle, bringing hundreds and thousands of valiant and brave soldiers in America to fight fascism, to fight dictatorship, to fight Hitler. And so many of the young people fell in battle. And, nevertheless, his image in Jewish history—I must say it—his image in Jewish history is flawed.

The depressing tale of the *St. Louis* is a case in point. Sixty years ago, its human cargo—nearly 1,000 Jews—was turned back to Nazi Germany. And that happened after the Kristallnacht, after the first state-sponsored pogrom, with hundreds of Jewish shops destroyed, synagogues burned, thousands of people put in concentration camps. And that ship, which was already in the shores of the United States, was sent back. I don't understand. Roosevelt was a good man, with a heart. He understood those who needed help. Why didn't he allow these refugees to disembark? A thousand people—in America, the great country, the greatest democracy, the most generous of all new nations in modern history. What happened? I don't understand. Why the indifference, on the highest level, to the suffering of the victims?

But then, there were human beings who were sensitive to our tragedy. Those non-Jews, those Christians, that we call the "Righteous Gentiles," whose selfless acts of heroism saved the honor of their faith. Why were they so few? Why was there a greater effort to save SS murderers after the war than to save their victims during the war? Why did some of America's largest corporations continue to do business with Hitler's Germany until 1942? It has been suggested, and it was documented, that the Wehrmacht could not have conducted its invasion of France without oil obtained from American sources. How is one to explain their indifference?

And yet, my friends, good things have also happened in this traumatic century: the defeat of Nazism, the collapse of communism, the rebirth of Israel on its ancestral soil, the demise of apartheid,

Israel's peace treaty with Egypt, the peace accord in Ireland. And let us remember the meeting, filled with drama and emotion, between Rabin and Arafat that you, Mr. President, convened in this very place. I was here and I will never forget it.

And then, of course, the joint decision of the United States and NATO to intervene in Kosovo and save those victims, those refugees, those who were uprooted by a man, whom I believe that because of his crimes, should be charged with crimes against humanity.

But this time, the world was not silent. This time, we do respond. This time, we intervene.

Does it mean that we have learned from the past? Does it mean that society has changed? Has the human being become less indifferent and more human? Have we really learned from our experiences? Are we less insensitive to the plight of victims of ethnic cleansing and other forms of injustices in places near and far? Is today's justified intervention in Kosovo, led by you, Mr. President, a lasting warning that never again will the deportation, the terrorization of children and their parents, be allowed anywhere in the world? Will it discourage other dictators in other lands to do the same?

What about the children? Oh, we see them on television, we read about them in the papers, and we do so with a broken heart. Their fate is always the most tragic, inevitably. When adults wage war, children perish. We see their faces, their eyes. Do we hear their pleas? Do we feel their pain, their agony? Every minute one of them dies of disease, violence, famine. Some of them—so many of them—could be saved.

And so, once again, I think of the young Jewish boy from the Carpathian Mountains. He has accompanied the old man I have become throughout these years of quest and struggle. And together we walk towards the new millennium, carried by profound fear and extraordinary hope.

GEORGE W. BUSH

State of the Union Address (2002)

Thank you very much. Mr. Speaker, Vice President Cheney, members of Congress, distinguished guests, fellow citizens: As we gather tonight, our nation is at war, our economy is in recession and the civilized world faces unprecedented dangers. Yet the state of our Union has never been stronger.

We last met in an hour of shock and suffering. In four short months, our nation has comforted the victims, begun to rebuild New York and the Pentagon, rallied a great coalition, captured, arrested, and rid the world of thousands of terrorists, destroyed Afghanistan's terrorist training camps, saved a people from starvation, and freed a country from brutal oppression.

The American flag flies again over our embassy in Kabul. Terrorists who once occupied Afghanistan now occupy cells at Guantanamo Bay. And terrorist leaders who urged followers to sacrifice their lives are running for their own.

America and Afghanistan are now allies against terror. We'll be partners in rebuilding that country. And this evening we welcome the distinguished interim leader of a liberated Afghanistan: Chairman Hamid Karzai.

The last time we met in this chamber, the mothers and daughters of Afghanistan were captives in their own homes, forbidden from working or going to school. Today women are free, and are part of Afghanistan's new government. And we welcome the new Minister of Women's Affairs, Doctor Sima Samar.

Our progress is a tribute to the spirit of the Afghan people, to the resolve of our coalition, and to the might of the United States military. When I called our troops into action, I did so with complete confidence in their courage and skill. And tonight, thanks to them, we are winning the war on terror. The man and women of our Armed Forces have delivered a message now clear to every enemy of the United States: Even 7,000 miles away, across oceans and continents, on mountaintops and in caves—you will not escape the justice of this nation.

For many Americans, these four months have brought sorrow, and pain that will never completely go away. Every day a retired firefighter returns to Ground Zero, to feel closer to his two sons who died there. At a memorial in New York, a little boy left his football with a note for his lost father: Dear Daddy, please take this to heaven. I don't want to play football until I can play with you again some day.

Last month, at the grave of her husband, Michael, a CIA officer and Marine who died in Mazur-e-Sharif, Shannon Spann said these words of farewell: "Semper Fi, my love." Shannon is with us tonight.

Shannon, I assure you and all who have lost a loved one that our cause is just, and our country will never forget the debt we owe Michael and all who gave their lives for freedom.

Our cause is just, and it continues. Our discoveries in Afghanistan confirmed our worst fears, and showed us the true scope of the task ahead. We have seen the depth of our enemies' hatred in videos, where they laugh about the loss of innocent life. And the depth of their hatred is equaled by the madness of the destruction they design. We have found diagrams of American nuclear power plants and public water facilities, detailed instructions for making chemical weapons, surveillance maps of American cities, and thorough descriptions of landmarks in America and throughout the world.

What we have found in Afghanistan confirms that, far from ending there, our war against terror is only beginning. Most of the 19 men who hijacked planes on September the 11th were trained in Afghanistan's camps, and so were tens of thousands of others. Thousands of dangerous killers, schooled in the methods of murder, often supported by outlaw regimes, are now spread throughout the world like ticking time bombs, set to go off without warning.

Thanks to the work of our law enforcement officials and coalition partners, hundreds of terrorists have been arrested. Yet, tens of thousands of trained terrorists are still at large. These enemies view the entire world as a battlefield, and we must pursue them wherever they are. So long as training camps operate, so long as nations harbor terrorists, freedom is at risk. And America and our allies must not, and will not, allow it.

Our nation will continue to be steadfast and patient and persistent in the pursuit of two great objectives. First, we will shut down terrorist camps, disrupt terrorist plans, and bring terrorists to justice. And, second, we must prevent the terrorists and regimes who seek chemical, biological or nuclear weapons from threatening the United States and the world.

Our military has put the terror training camps of Afghanistan out of business, yet camps still exist in at least a dozen countries. A terrorist underworld—including groups like Hamas, Hezbollah, Islamic Jihad, Jaish-i-Mohammed—operates in remote jungles and deserts, and hides in the centers of large cities.

While the most visible military action is in Afghanistan, America is acting elsewhere. We now have troops in the Philippines, helping to train that country's armed forces to go after terrorist cells that have executed an American, and still hold hostages. Our soldiers, working with the Bosnian government, seized terrorists who were plotting to bomb our embassy. Our Navy is patrolling the coast of Africa to block the shipment of weapons and the establishment of terrorist camps in Somalia.

My hope is that all nations will heed our call, and eliminate the terrorist parasites who threaten their countries and our own. Many nations are acting forcefully. Pakistan is now cracking down on terror, and I admire the strong leadership of President Musharraf.

But some governments will be timid in the face of terror. And make no mistake about it: If they do not act, America will.

Our second goal is to prevent regimes that sponsor terror from threatening America or our friends and allies with weapons of mass destruction. Some of these regimes have been pretty quiet since September the 11th. But we know their true nature. North Korea is a regime arming with missiles and weapons of mass destruction, while starving its citizens.

Iran aggressively pursues these weapons and exports terror, while an unelected few repress the Iranian people's hope for freedom.

Iraq continues to flaunt its hostility toward America and to support terror. The Iraqi regime has plotted to develop anthrax, and nerve gas, and nuclear weapons for over a decade. This is a regime that has already used poison gas to murder thousands of its own citizens—leaving the bodies of mothers huddled over their dead children. This is a regime that agreed to international inspections—then kicked out the inspectors. This is a regime that has something to hide from the civilized world.

States like these, and their terrorist allies, constitute an axis of evil, arming to threaten the peace of the world. By seeking weapons of mass destruction, these regimes pose a grave and growing danger. They could provide these arms to terrorists, giving them the means to match their hatred. They could attack our allies or attempt to blackmail the United States. In any of these cases, the price of indifference would be catastrophic.

We will work closely with our coalition to deny terrorists and their state sponsors the materials, technology, and expertise to make and deliver weapons of mass destruction. We will develop and deploy effective missile defenses to protect America and our allies from sudden attack. And all nations should know: America will do what is necessary to ensure our nation's security.

We'll be deliberate, yet time is not on our side. I will not wait on events, while dangers gather. I will not stand by, as peril draws closer and closer. The United States of America will not permit the world's most dangerous regimes to threaten us with the world's most destructive weapons.

Our war on terror is well begun, but it is only begun. This campaign may not be finished on our watch—yet it must be and it will be waged on our watch.

We can't stop short. If we stop now—leaving terror camps intact and terror states unchecked—our sense of security would be false and temporary. History has called America and our allies to action, and it is both our responsibility and our privilege to fight freedom's fight.

Our first priority must always be the security of our nation, and that will be reflected in the budget. I send to Congress. My budget supports three great goals for America: We will win this war; we'll protect our homeland; and we will revive our economy.

September the 11th brought out the best in America, and the best in this Congress. And I join the American people in applauding your unity and resolve. Now Americans deserve to have this same spirit directed toward addressing problems here at home. I'm a proud member of my party—yet as we act to win the war, protect our people, and create jobs in America, we must act, first and foremost, not as Republicans, not as Democrats, but as Americans. [. . .]

During these last few months, I've been humbled and privileged to see the true character of this country in a time of testing. Our enemies believed America was weak and materialistic, that we would splinter in fear and selfishness. They were as wrong as they are evil.

The American people have responded magnificently, with courage and compassion, strength and resolve. As I have met the heroes, hugged the families, and looked into the tired faces of rescuers, I have stood in awe of the American people.

And I hope you will join me—I hope you will join me in expressing thanks to one American for the strength and calm and comfort she brings to our nation in crisis, our First Lady, Laura Bush.

None of us would ever wish the evil that was done on September the 11th. Yet after America was attacked, it was as if our entire country looked into a mirror and saw our better selves. We were reminded that we are citizens, with obligations to each other, to our country, and to history. We began to think less of the goods we can accumulate, and more about the good we can do.

For too long our culture has said, "If it feels good, do it." Now America is embracing a new ethic and a new creed: "Let's roll." In the sacrifice of soldiers, the fierce brotherhood of firefighters, and the bravery and generosity of ordinary citizens, we have glimpsed what a new culture of responsibility could look like. We want to be a nation that serves goals larger than self. We've been offered a unique opportunity, and we must not let this moment pass,

My call tonight is for every American to commit at least two years—4,000 hours over the rest of your lifetime—to the service of your neighbors and your nation. Many are already serving, and I thank you. If you aren't sure how to help, I've got a good place to start. To sustain and extend the best that has emerged in America, I invite you to join the new

USA Freedom Corps. The Freedom Corps will focus on three areas of need: responding in case of crisis at home; rebuilding our communities; and extending American compassion throughout the world.

One purpose of the USA Freedom Corps will be homeland security. America needs retired doctors and nurses who can be mobilized in major emergencies; volunteers to help police and fire departments; transportation and utility workers well-trained in spotting danger.

Our country also needs citizens working to rebuild our communities. We need mentors to love children, especially children whose parents are in prison. And we need more talented teachers in troubled schools. USA Freedom Corps will expand and improve the good efforts of AmeriCorps and Senior Corps to recruit more than 200,000 new volunteers.

And America needs citizens to extend the compassion of our country to every part of the world. So we will renew the promise of the Peace Corps, double its volunteers over the next five years—and ask it to join a new effort to encourage development and education and opportunity in the Islamic world.

This time of adversity offers a unique moment of opportunity—a moment we must seize to change our culture. Through the gathering momentum of millions of acts of service and decency and kindness, I know we can overcome evil with greater good. And we have a great opportunity during this time of war to lead the world toward the values that will bring lasting peace.

All fathers and mothers, in all societies, want their children to be educated, and live free from poverty and violence. No people on Earth yearn to be oppressed, or aspire to servitude, or eagerly await the midnight knock of the secret police.

If anyone doubts this, let them look to Afghanistan, where the Islamic "street" greeted the fall of tyranny with song and celebration. Let the skeptics look to Islam's own rich history, with its centuries of learning, and tolerance and progress. America will lead by defending liberty and justice because they are right and true and unchanging for all people everywhere.

No nation owns these aspirations, and no nation is exempt from them. We have no intention of imposing our culture. But America will always stand firm for the non-negotiable demands of human dignity: the rule of law; limits on the power of the state; respect for women; private property; free speech; equal justice; and religious tolerance.

America will take the side of brave men and women who advocate these values around the world, including the Islamic world, because we have a greater objective than eliminating threats and containing resentment. We seek a just and peaceful world beyond the war on terror.

In this moment of opportunity, a common danger is erasing old rivalries. America is working with Russia and China and India, in ways never before, to achieve peace and prosperity. In every region, free markets and free societies are proving their power to lift lives. Together with friends and allies from Europe to Asia, and Africa to Latin America, we will demonstrate that the forces of terror cannot stop the momentum of freedom.

The last time I spoke here, I expressed the hope that life would return to normal. In some ways, it has. In others, if never will. Those of us who have lived through these challenging times have been changed by them. We've come to know truths that we will never question: evil is real, and it must be opposed. Beyond all differences of race or creed, we are one country, mourning together and facing danger. Deep in the American character, there is honor, and it is stronger than cynicism. And many have discovered again that in tragedy—especially in tragedy—God is near.

In a single instant we realized that this will be a decisive decade in the history of liberty, that we've been called to a unique role in human events. Rarely has the faced a choice more clear or consequential.

Our enemies send other people's children on missions of suicide and murder. They embrace tyranny and death as a cause and a creed. We stand for a different choice. Made long ago, on the day of our founding. We affirm it again today. We choose freedom and the dignity of every life.

Steadfast in our purpose, we now press on. We have known freedom's price. We have shown freedom's power. And in this great conflict, my fellow Americans, we will see freedom's victory.

Thank you all. May God bless.

Second Inaugural Address (2005)

Vice President Cheney, Mr. Chief Justice,
President Carter, President Bush,
President Clinton, members of the
United States Congress, reverend clergy,
distinguished guests, fellow citizens:

On this day, prescribed by law and marked by ceremony, we celebrate the durable wisdom of our Constitution, and recall the deep commitments that unite our country. I am grateful for the honor of this hour, mindful of the consequential times in which we live, and determined to fulfill the oath that I have sworn and you have witnessed.

At this second gathering, our duties are defined not by the words I use, but by the history we have seen together. For a half century, America defended our own freedom by standing watch on distant borders. After the shipwreck of communism came years of relative quiet, years of repose, years of sabbatical—and then there came a day of fire.

We have seen our vulnerability, and we have seen its deepest source. For as long as whole regions of the world simmer in resentment and tyranny, prone to ideologies that feed hatred and excuse murder, violence will gather, and multiply in destructive power, and cross the most defended borders, and raise a mortal threat. There is only one force of history that can break the reign of hatred and resentment, and expose the pretensions of tyrants, and reward the hopes of the decent and tolerant, and that is the force of human freedom.

We are led, by events and common sense, to one conclusion: The survival of liberty in our land increasingly depends on the success of liberty in other lands. The best hope for peace in our world is the expansion of freedom in all the world.

America's vital interests and our deepest beliefs are now one. From the day of our founding, we have proclaimed that every man and woman on this earth has rights and dignity and matchless value, because they bear the image of the Maker of Heaven and earth. Across the generations we have proclaimed the imperative of self-government, because no one is fit to be a master, and no one deserves to be a slave.

Advancing these ideals is the mission that created our nation. It is the honorable achievement of our fathers. Now it is the urgent requirement of our nation's security, and the calling of our time.

So it is the policy of the United States to seek and support the growth of democratic movements and institutions in every nation and culture, with the ultimate goal of ending tyranny in our world.

This is not primarily the task of arms, though we will defend ourselves and our friends by force of arms when necessary. Freedom, by its nature, must be chosen and defended by citizens, and sustained by the rule of law and the protection of minorities. And when the soul of a nation finally speaks, the institutions that arise may reflect customs and traditions very different from our own. America will not impose our own style of government on the unwilling. Our goal instead is to help others find their own voice, attain their own freedom, and make their own way.

The great objective of ending tyranny is the concentrated work of generations. The difficulty of the task is no excuse for avoiding it. America's influence is not unlimited, but fortunately for the oppressed, America's influence is considerable, and we will use it confidently in freedom's cause.

My most solemn duty is to protect this nation and its people against further attacks and emerging threats. Some have unwisely chosen to test America's resolve, and have found it firm.

We will persistently clarify the choice before every ruler and every nation: The moral choice between oppression, which is always wrong, and freedom, which is eternally right. America will not pretend that jailed dissidents prefer their chains, or that women welcome humiliation and servitude, or that any human being aspires to live at the mercy of bullies.

We will encourage reform in other governments by making clear that success in our relations will require the decent treatment of their own people. America's belief in human dignity will guide our policies, yet rights must be more than the grudging concessions of dictators; they are secured by free dissent and the participation of the governed. In the long run, there is no justice without freedom, and there can be no human rights without human liberty.

Some, I know, have questioned the global appeal of liberty—though this time in history, four decades defined by the swiftest advance of freedom ever seen, is an odd time for doubt. Americans, of all people, should never be surprised by the power of our ideals. Eventually, the call of freedom comes to every mind and every soul. We do not accept the existence of permanent tyranny because we do not accept the possibility of permanent slavery. Liberty will come to those who love it.

Today, America speaks anew to the peoples of the world: All who live in tyranny and hopelessness can know: the United States will not ignore your oppression, or excuse your oppressors. When you stand for your liberty, we will stand with you.

Democratic reformers facing repression, prison, or exile can know: America sees you for who you are: the future leaders of your free country.

The rulers of outlaw regimes can know that we still believe as Abraham Lincoln did: "Those who deny freedom to others deserve it not for themselves; and, under the rule of a just God, cannot long retain it."

The leaders of governments with long habits of control need to know: To serve your people you must learn to trust them. Start on this journey of progress and justice, and America will walk at your side.

And all the allies of the United States can know: we honor your friendship; we rely on your counsel, and we depend on your help. Division among free nations is a primary goal of freedom's enemies. The concerted effort of free nations to promote democracy is a prelude to our enemies' defeat.

Today, I also speak anew to my fellow citizens: From all of you, I have asked patience in the hard task of securing America, which you have granted in good measure. Our country has accepted obligations that are difficult to fulfill, and would be dishonorable to abandon. Yet because we have acted in the great liberating tradition of this nation, tens of millions have achieved their freedom. And as hope kindles hope, millions more will find it. By our efforts, we have lit a fire as well—a fire in the minds of men. It warms those who feel its power, it burns those who fight its progress. And one day this untamed fire of freedom will reach the darkest corners of our world.

A few Americans have accepted the hardest duties in this cause—in the quiet work of intelligence and diplomacy, the idealistic work of helping raise up free governments, the dangerous and necessary work of fighting our enemies. Some have shown their devotion to our country in deaths that honored their whole lives, and we will always honor their names and their sacrifice.

All Americans have witnessed this idealism, and some for the first time. I ask our youngest citizens to believe the evidence of your eyes. You have seen duty and allegiance in the determined faces of our soldiers. You have seen that life is fragile, and evil is real, and courage triumphs. Make the choice to serve in a cause larger than your wants, larger than yourself, and in your days you will add not just to the wealth of our country, but to its character.

America has need of idealism and courage, because we have essential work at home—the unfinished work of American freedom. In a world moving toward liberty, we are determined to show the meaning and promise of liberty.

In America's ideal of freedom, citizens find the dignity and security of economic independence, instead of laboring on the edge of subsistence. This is the broader definition of liberty that motivated the Homestead Act, the Social Security Act, and the G.I. Bill of Rights. And now we will extend this vision by reforming great institutions to serve the needs of our time. To give every American a stake in the promise and future of our country, we will bring the highest standards to our schools, and build an ownership society. We will widen the ownership of homes and businesses, retirement savings and health insurance— preparing our people for the challenges of life in a free society. By making every citizen an agent of his or her own destiny, we will give our fellow Americans greater freedom from want and fear, and make our society more prosperous and just and equal.

In America's ideal of freedom, the public interest depends on private character—on integrity, and tolerance toward others, and the rule of conscience in our own lives. Self-government relies, in the end, on the governing of the self. That edifice of character is built in families, supported by communities with standards, and sustained in our national life by the truths of Sinai, the Sermon on the Mount, the words of the Koran, and the varied faiths of our people.

Americans move forward in every generation by reaffirming all that is good and true that came before—ideals of justice and conduct that are the same yesterday, today, and forever.

In America's ideal of freedom, the exercise of rights is ennobled by service, and mercy, and a heart for the weak. Liberty for all does not mean independence from one another. Our nation relies on men and women who look after a neighbor and surround the lost with love. Americans, at our best, value the life we see in one another, and must always remember that even the unwanted have worth. And our country must abandon all the habits of racism, because we cannot carry the message of freedom and the baggage of bigotry at the same time.

From the perspective of a single day, including this day of dedication, the issues and questions before our country are many. From the viewpoint of centuries, the questions that come to us are narrowed and few. Did our generation advance the cause of freedom? And did our character bring credit to that cause?

These questions that judge us also unite us, because Americans of every party and background, Americans by choice and by birth, are bound to one another in the cause of freedom. We have known divisions, which must be healed to move forward in great purposes, and I will strive in good faith to heal them. Yet those divisions do not define America. We felt the unity and fellowship of our nation when freedom came under attack, and our response came like a single hand over a single heart. And we can feel that same unity and pride whenever America acts for good, and the victims of disaster are given hope, and the unjust encounter justice, and the captives are set free.

We go forward with complete confidence in the eventual triumph of freedom—not because history runs on the wheels of inevitability; it is human choices that move events; not because we consider ourselves a chosen nation; God moves and chooses as he wills. We have confidence because freedom is the permanent hope of mankind, the hunger in dark places, the longing of the soul. When our Founders declared a new order of the ages, when soldiers died in wave upon wave for a union based on liberty, when citizens marched in peaceful outrage under the banner "Freedom Now," they were acting on an ancient hope that is meant to be fulfilled. History has an ebb and flow of justice, but history also has a visible direction, set by liberty, and the Author of Liberty.

When the Declaration of Independence was first read in public and the Liberty Bell was sounded in celebration, a witness said, "It rang as if it meant something." In our time it means something still. America, in this young century proclaims liberty throughout all the world, and to all the inhabitants thereof. Renewed in our strength, tested, but not weary, we are ready for the greatest achievements in the history of freedom.

May God bless you, and may he watch over the United States of America.

ANTHONY KENNEDY

John Geddes Lawrence and Tyron Garner, Petitioners v. Texas (2003)

Justice KENNEDY delivered the opinion of the Court.

Liberty protects the person from unwarranted government intrusions into a dwelling or other private places. In our tradition the State is not omnipresent in the home. And there are other spheres of our lives and existence, outside the home, where the State should not be a dominant presence. Freedom extends beyond spatial bounds. Liberty presumes an autonomy of self that includes freedom of thought, belief, expression, and certain intimate conduct. The instant case involves liberty of the person both in its spatial and more transcendent dimensions.

I

The question before the Court is the validity of a Texas statute making it a crime for two persons of the same sex to engage in certain intimate sexual conduct.

In Houston, Texas, officers of the Harris County Police Department were dispatched to a private residence in response to a reported weapons disturbance. They entered an apartment where one of the petitioners, John Geddes Lawrence, resided. The right of the police to enter does not seem to have been questioned. The officers observed Lawrence and another man, Tyron Garner, engaging in a sexual act. The two petitioners were arrested, held in custody over night, and charged and convicted before a Justice of the Peace.

The complaints described their crime as "deviate sexual intercourse, namely anal sex, with a member of the same sex (man)." The applicable state law is Tex. Penal Code Ann. §21.06(a) (2003). It provides: "A person commits an offense if he engages in deviate sexual intercourse with another individual of the same sex." The statute defines "[d]eviate sexual intercourse" as follows:

(A) any contact between any part of the genitals of one person and the mouth or anus of another person; or (B) the penetration of the genitals or the anus of another person with an object. §21.01(1).

The petitioners [. . .] challenged the statute as a violation of the Equal Protection Clause of the Fourteenth Amendment and of a like provision of the Texas constitution. Those contentions were rejected. The petitioners, having entered a plea of *nolo contendere*, were each fined $200 and assessed court costs of $141.25.

The Court of Appeals for the Texas Fourteenth District considered the petitioners' federal constitutional arguments under both the Equal Protection and Due Process Clauses of the Fourteenth Amendment. After hearing the case *en banc* the court, in a divided opinion, rejected the constitutional arguments and affirmed the convictions. The majority opinion indicates that the Court of Appeals considered our decision in *Bowers v. Hardwick* (1986), to be controlling on the federal due process aspect of the case. *Bowers* then being authoritative, this was proper.

We granted certiorari (2002), to consider three questions:

1. Whether Petitioners' criminal convictions under the Texas "Homosexual Conduct" law—which criminalizes sexual intimacy by same-sex couples, but not identical behavior by different-sex couples—violates the Fourteenth Amendment guarantee of equal protection of laws?
2. Whether Petitioners' criminal convictions for adult consensual sexual intimacy in the home violate their vital interests in liberty and privacy protected by the Due Process Clause of the Fourteenth Amendment?
3. Whether *Bowers v. Hardwick* (1986) should be overruled?

The petitioners were adults at the time of the alleged offense. Their conduct was in private and consensual.

II

We conclude the case should be resolved by determining whether the petitioners were free as adults to engage in the private conduct in the exercise of their liberty under the Due Process Clause of the Fourteenth Amendment to the Constitution. For this inquiry we deem it necessary to reconsider the Court's holding in *Bowers*. [. . .]

The facts in *Bowers* had some similarities to the instant case. A police officer, whose right to enter seems not to have been in question, observed Hardwick, in his own bedroom, engaging in intimate sexual conduct with another adult male. The conduct was in violation of a Georgia statute making it a criminal offense to engage in sodomy. One difference between the two cases is that the Georgia statute prohibited the conduct whether or not the participants were of the same sex, while the Texas statute, as we have seen, applies only to participants of the same sex. Hardwick was not prosecuted, but he brought an action in federal court to declare the state statute invalid. He alleged he was a practicing homosexual and that the criminal prohibition violated rights guaranteed to him by the Constitution. The Court, in an opinion by Justice White, sustained the Georgia law. [. . .]

The Court began its substantive discussion in *Bowers* as follows: "The issue presented is whether the Federal Constitution confers a fundamental right upon homosexuals to engage in sodomy and hence invalidates the laws of the many States that still make such conduct illegal and have done so for a very long time." That statement, we now conclude, discloses the Court's own failure to appreciate the extent of the liberty at stake. To say that the issue in *Bowers* was simply the right to engage in certain sexual conduct demeans the claim the individual put forward, just as it would demean a married couple were it to be said marriage is simply about the right to have sexual intercourse. The laws involved in *Bowers* and here are, to be sure, statutes that purport to do no more than prohibit a particular sexual act. Their penalties and purposes, though, have more far-reaching consequences, touching upon the most private human conduct, sexual behavior, and in the most private of places, the home. The statutes do seek to control a personal relationship that, whether or not entitled to formal recognition in the law, is within the liberty of persons to choose without being punished as criminals.

This, as a general rule, should counsel against attempts by the State, or a court, to define the meaning of the relationship or to set its boundaries absent injury to a person or abuse of an institution the law protects. It suffices for us to acknowledge that adults may choose to enter upon this relationship in the confines of their homes and their own private lives and still retain their dignity as free persons. When sexuality finds overt expression in intimate conduct with another person, the conduct can be but one element in a personal bond that is more enduring. The liberty protected by the Constitution allows homosexual persons the right to make this choice.

Having misapprehended the claim of liberty there presented to it, and thus stating the claim to be whether there is a fundamental right to engage in consensual sodomy, the *Bowers* Court said: "Proscriptions against that conduct have ancient roots."

In academic writings, and in many of the scholarly *amicus* briefs filed to assist the Court in this case, there are fundamental criticisms of the historical premises relied upon by the majority and concurring opinions in *Bowers*. We need not enter this debate in the attempt to reach a definitive historical judgment, but the following considerations counsel against adopting the definitive conclusions upon which *Bowers* placed such reliance.

At the outset it should be noted that there is no longstanding history in this country of laws directed at homosexual conduct as a distinct matter. Beginning in colonial times there were prohibitions of sodomy derived from the English criminal laws passed in the first instance by the Reformation Parliament of 1533. The English prohibition was understood to include relations between men and women as well as relations between men and men. Nineteenth-century commentators similarly read American sodomy, buggery, and crime-against-nature statutes as criminalizing certain relations between men and women and between men and men. The absence of legal prohibitions focusing on homosexual conduct may be explained in part by noting that according to some scholars the concept of the homosexual as a distinct category of person did not emerge until the late 19th century. Thus early American sodomy laws were not directed at homosexuals as such but instead sought to prohibit nonprocreative sexual activity more generally. This does not suggest approval of homosexual conduct. It does tend to show that this particular form of conduct was not thought of as a separate category from like conduct between heterosexual persons.

Laws prohibiting sodomy do not seem to have been enforced against consenting adults acting in private. A substantial number of sodomy prosecutions and convictions for which there are surviving records were for predatory acts against those who could not or did not consent, as in the case of a minor or the victim of an assault. As to these, one purpose for the prohibitions was to ensure there would be no lack of coverage if a predator committed a sexual assault that did not constitute rape as defined by the criminal law. Thus the model sodomy indictments presented in a 19th-century treatise addressed the predatory acts of an adult man against a minor girl or minor boy. Instead of targeting relations between consenting adults in private, 19th-century sodomy prosecutions typically involved relations between men and minor girls or minor boys, relations between adults involving force, relations between adults implicating disparity in status, or relations between men and animals. [. . .]

The policy of punishing consenting adults for private acts was not much discussed in the early legal literature. We can infer that one reason for this was the very private nature of the conduct. Despite the absence of prosecutions, there may have been periods in which there was public criticism of homosexuals as such and an insistence that the criminal laws be enforced to discourage their practices. But far from possessing "ancient roots," American laws targeting same-sex couples did not develop until the last third of the 20th century. The reported decisions concerning the prosecution of consensual, homosexual sodomy between adults for the years 1880–1995 are not always clear in the details, but a significant number involved conduct in a public place.

It was not until the 1970's that any State singled out same-sex relations for criminal prosecution, and only nine States have done so. Post-*Bowers* even some of these States did not adhere to the policy of suppressing homosexual conduct. Over the course of the last decades, States with same-sex prohibitions have moved toward abolishing them.

In summary, the historical grounds relied upon in *Bowers* are more complex than the majority opinion and the concurring opinion by Chief Justice Burger indicate. Their historical premises are not without doubt and, at the very least, are overstated.

It must be acknowledged, of course, that the Court in *Bowers* was making the broader point that for centuries there have been powerful voices to condemn homosexual conduct as immoral. The condemnation has been shaped by religious beliefs, conceptions of right and acceptable behavior, and respect for the traditional family. For many persons these are not trivial concerns but profound and deep convictions accepted as ethical and moral principles to which they aspire and which thus determine the course of their lives. These considerations do not answer the question before us, however. The issue is whether the majority may use the power of the State to enforce these views on the whole society through operation of the criminal law. "Our obligation is to define the liberty of all, not to mandate our own moral code." *Planned Parenthood of Southeastern Pa. v. Casey* (1992).

Chief Justice Burger joined the opinion for the Court in *Bowers* and further explained his views as follows: "Decisions of individuals relating to homosexual conduct have been subject to state intervention throughout the history of Western civilization. Condemnation of those practices is firmly rooted in Judeo-Christian moral and ethical standards." As with Justice White's assumptions about history, scholarship casts some doubt on the sweeping nature of the statement by Chief Justice Burger as it pertains to private homosexual conduct between consenting adults. In all events we think that our laws and traditions in the past half century are of most relevance here. These references show an emerging awareness that liberty gives substantial protection to adult persons in deciding how to conduct their private lives in matters pertaining to sex. [. . .]

This emerging recognition should have been apparent when *Bowers* was decided. In 1955 the American Law Institute promulgated the Model Penal Code and made clear that it did not recommend or provide for "criminal penalties for consensual sexual relations conducted in private." It justified its decision on three grounds: (1) The prohibitions undermined respect for the law by penalizing conduct many people engaged in; (2) the statutes regulated private conduct not harmful to others; and (3) the laws were arbitrarily enforced and thus invited the danger of blackmail. In 1961 Illinois changed its laws to conform to the Model Penal Code. Other States soon followed.

In *Bowers* the Court referred to the fact that before 1961 all 50 States had outlawed sodomy, and that at the time of the Court's decision 24 States and the District of Columbia had sodomy laws. Justice Powell pointed out that these prohibitions often were being ignored, however. Georgia, for instance, had not sought to enforce its law for decades.

The sweeping references by Chief Justice Burger to the history of Western civilization and to Judeo-Christian moral and ethical standards did not take account of other authorities pointing in an opposite direction. A committee advising the British Parliament recommended in 1957 repeal of laws punishing homosexual conduct. Parliament enacted the substance of those recommendations 10 years later.

Of even more importance, almost five years before *Bowers* was decided the European Court of Human Rights considered a case with parallels to *Bowers* and to today's case. An adult male resident in Northern Ireland alleged he was a practicing homosexual who desired to engage in consensual homosexual conduct. The laws of Northern Ireland forbade him that right. He alleged that he had been questioned, his home had been searched, and he feared criminal prosecution. The court held that the laws proscribing the conduct were invalid under the European Convention on Human Rights. Authoritative in all countries that are members of the Council of Europe (21 nations then, 45 nations now), the decision is at odds with the premise in *Bowers* that the claim put forward was insubstantial in our Western civilization.

In our own constitutional system the deficiencies in *Bowers* became even more apparent in the years following its announcement. The 25 States with laws prohibiting the relevant conduct referenced in the *Bowers* decision are reduced now to 13, of which 4 enforce their laws only against homosexual conduct. In those States where sodomy is still proscribed, whether for same-sex or heterosexual conduct, there is a pattern of nonenforcement with respect to consenting adults acting in private. The State of Texas admitted in 1994 that as of that date it had not prosecuted anyone under those circumstances.

Two principal cases decided after *Bowers* cast its holding into even more doubt. In *Planned Parenthood of Southeastern Pa. v. Casey* (1992), the Court reaffirmed the substantive force of the liberty protected by the Due Process Clause. The *Casey* decision again confirmed that our laws and tradition afford constitutional protection to personal decisions relating to marriage, procreation, contraception, family relationships, child rearing, and education. In explaining the respect the Constitution demands for the autonomy of the person in making these choices, we stated as follows:

> These matters, involving the most intimate and personal choices a person may make in a lifetime, choices central to personal dignity and autonomy, are central to the liberty protected by the Fourteenth Amendment. At the heart of liberty is the right to define one's own concept of existence, of meaning, of the universe, and of the mystery of human life. Beliefs about these matters could not define the attributes of personhood were they formed under compulsion of the State.

Persons in a homosexual relationship may seek autonomy for these purposes, just as heterosexual persons do. The decision in *Bowers* would deny them this right.

The second post-*Bowers* case of principal relevance is *Romer v. Evans* (1996). There the Court struck down class-based legislation directed at homosexuals as a violation of the Equal Protection Clause. *Romer* invalidated an amendment to Colorado's constitution which named as a solitary class persons who were homosexuals, lesbians, or bisexual either by "orientation, conduct, practices or relationships" and deprived them of protection under state antidiscrimination laws. We concluded that the provision was "born of animosity toward the class of persons affected" and further that it had no rational relation to a legitimate governmental purpose.

As an alternative argument in this case, counsel for the petitioners and some *amici* contend that *Romer* provides the basis for declaring the Texas statute invalid under the Equal Protection Clause. That is a tenable argument, but we conclude the instant case requires us to address whether *Bowers* itself has continuing validity. Were we to hold the statute invalid under the Equal Protection Clause some might question whether a prohibition would be valid if drawn differently, say, to prohibit the conduct both between same-sex and different-sex participants.

Equality of treatment and the due process right to demand respect for conduct protected by the substantive guarantee of liberty are linked in important respects, and a decision on the latter point advances both interests. If protected conduct is made criminal and the law which does so remains unexamined for its substantive validity, its stigma might remain even if it were not enforceable as drawn for equal protection reasons. When homosexual conduct is made criminal by the law of the State, that declaration in and of itself is an invitation to subject homosexual persons to discrimination both in the public and in the private spheres. The central holding of *Bowers* has been brought in question by this case, and it should be addressed. Its continuance as precedent demeans the lives of homosexual persons.

The stigma this criminal statute imposes, moreover, is not trivial. The offense, to be sure, is but a class C misdemeanor, a minor offense in the Texas legal system. Still, it remains a criminal offense with all that imports for the dignity of the persons charged. The petitioners will bear on their record the history of their criminal convictions. Just this Term we rejected various challenges to state laws requiring the registration of sex offenders. We are advised that if Texas convicted an adult for private, consensual homosexual conduct under the statute here in question the convicted person would come within the registration laws of a least four States were he or she to be subject to their jurisdiction. This underscores the consequential nature of the punishment and the state-sponsored condemnation attendant to the criminal prohibition. Furthermore, the Texas criminal conviction carries with it the other collateral consequences always following a conviction, such as notations on job application forms, to mention but one example.

The foundations of *Bowers* have sustained serious erosion from our recent decisions in *Casey* and *Romer*. When our precedent has been thus weakened, criticism from other sources is of greater significance. In the United States criticism of *Bowers* has been substantial and continuing, disapproving of its reasoning in all respects, not just as to its historical assumptions. The courts of five different States have declined to follow it in interpreting provisions in their own state constitutions parallel to the Due Process Clause of the Fourteenth Amendment.

To the extent *Bowers* relied on values we share with a wider civilization, it should be noted that the reasoning and holding in *Bowers* have been rejected elsewhere. The European Court of Human Rights has followed not *Bowers* but its own decision in *Dudgeon v. United Kingdom* (1981). Other nations, too, have taken action consistent with an affirmation of the protected right of homosexual adults to engage in intimate, consensual conduct. The right the petitioners seek in this case has been accepted as an integral part of human freedom in many other countries. There has been no showing that in this country the governmental interest in circumscribing personal choice is somehow more legitimate or urgent.

The doctrine of *stare decisis* is essential to the respect accorded to the judgments of the Court and to the stability of the law. It is not, however, an inexorable command. [. . .]

The rationale of *Bowers* does not withstand careful analysis. In his dissenting opinion in *Bowers* Justice Stevens came to these conclusions:

> Our prior cases make two propositions abundantly clear. First, the fact that the governing majority in a State has traditionally viewed a particular practice as immoral is not a sufficient reason for upholding a law prohibiting the practice; neither history nor tradition could save a law prohibiting miscegenation from constitutional attack. Second, individual decisions by married persons, concerning the intimacies of their physical relationship, even when not intended to produce offspring, are a form of "liberty" protected by the Due Process Clause of the Fourteenth Amendment. Moreover, this protection extends to intimate choices by unmarried as well as married persons.

Justice Stevens' analysis, in our view, should have been controlling in *Bowers* and should control here.

Bowers was not correct when it was decided, and it is not correct today. It ought not to remain binding precedent. *Bowers v. Hardwick* should be and now is overruled.

The present case does not involve minors. It does not involve persons who might be injured or coerced or who are situated in relationships where consent might not easily be refused. It does not involve public conduct or prostitution. It does not involve whether the government must give formal recognition to any relationship that homosexual persons seek to enter. The case does involve two adults who, with full and mutual consent from each other, engaged in sexual practices common to a homosexual lifestyle. The petitioners are entitled to respect for their private lives. The State cannot demean their existence or control their destiny by making their private sexual conduct a crime. Their right to liberty under the Due Process Clause gives them the full right to engage in their conduct without intervention of the government. [. . .]

Had those who drew and ratified the Due Process Clauses of the Fifth Amendment or the Fourteenth Amendment known the components of liberty in its manifold possibilities, they might have been more specific. They did not presume to have this insight. They knew times can blind us to certain truths and later generations can see that laws once thought necessary and proper in fact serve only to oppress. As the Constitution endures, persons in every generation can invoke its principles in their own search for greater freedom.

The judgment of the Court of Appeals for the Texas Fourteenth District is reversed, and the case is remanded for further proceedings not inconsistent with this opinion.

ANTONIN SCALIA

John Geddes Lawrence and Tyron Garner, Petitioners v. Texas, Dissent (2003)

Justice SCALIA, with whom the Chief Justice and Justice THOMAS join, dissenting.

I

I begin with the Court's surprising readiness to reconsider a decision rendered a mere 17 years ago in *Bowers v. Hardwick*. I do not myself believe in rigid adherence to *stare decisis* in constitutional cases; but I do believe that we should be consistent rather than manipulative in invoking the doctrine. [. . .]

Today's approach to *stare decisis* invites us to overrule an erroneously decided precedent (including an "intensely divisive" decision) *if:* (1) its foundations have been "eroded" by subsequent decisions; (2) it has been subject to "substantial and continuing" criticism; and (3) it has not induced "individual or societal reliance" that counsels against overturning. The problem is that *Roe* itself—which today's majority surely has no disposition to overrule—satisfies these conditions to at least the same degree as *Bowers*. [. . .]

I do not quarrel with the Court's claim that *Romer v. Evans* (1996) "eroded" the "foundations" of *Bowers*' rational-basis holding. But *Roe* and *Casey* have been equally "eroded" by *Washington v. Glucksberg* (1997), which held that *only* fundamental rights which are "'deeply rooted in this Nation's history and tradition'" qualify for anything other than rational basis scrutiny under the doctrine of "substantive due process." *Roe* and *Casey*, of course, subjected the restriction of abortion to heightened scrutiny without even attempting to establish that the freedom to abort *was* rooted in this Nation's tradition.

(2) *Bowers*, the Court says, has been subject to "substantial and continuing [criticism], disapproving of its reasoning in all respects, not just as to its historical assumptions." Exactly what those nonhistorical criticisms are, and whether the Court even agrees with them, are left unsaid, although the Court does cite two books. Of course, *Roe* too (and by extension *Casey*) had been (and still is) subject to unrelenting criticism, including criticism from the two commentators cited by the Court today.

(3) That leaves, to distinguish the rock-solid, unamendable disposition of *Roe* from the readily overrulable *Bowers*, only the third factor. "[T]here has been," the Court says, "no individual or societal reliance on *Bowers* of the sort that could counsel against overturning its holding. . . ." It seems to me that the "societal reliance" on the principles confirmed in *Bowers* and discarded today has been overwhelming. Countless judicial decisions and legislative enactments have relied on the ancient proposition that a governing majority's belief that certain sexual behavior is "immoral and unacceptable" constitutes a rational basis for regulation. See, *e.g., Williams v. Pryor*, 240 F. 3d 944, 949 (CA11 2001)

(citing *Bowers* in upholding Alabama's prohibition on the sale of sex toys on the ground that "[t]he crafting and safeguarding of public morality . . . indisputably is a legitimate government interest under rational basis scrutiny"). We ourselves relied extensively on *Bowers* when we concluded, in *Barnes v. Glen Theatre, Inc.*, (1991), that Indiana's public indecency statute furthered "a substantial government interest in protecting order and morality." State laws against bigamy, same-sex marriage, adult incest, prostitution, masturbation, adultery, fornication, bestiality, and obscenity are likewise sustainable only in light of *Bowers'* validation of laws based on moral choices. Every single one of these laws is called into question by today's decision; the Court makes no effort to cabin the scope of its decision to exclude them from its holding. The impossibility of distinguishing homosexuality from other traditional "morals" offenses is precisely why *Bowers* rejected the rational-basis challenge. "The law," it said, "is constantly based on notions of morality, and if all laws representing essentially moral choices are to be invalidated under the Due Process Clause, the courts will be very busy indeed."

What a massive disruption of the current social order, therefore, the overruling of *Bowers* entails. Not so the overruling of *Roe*, which would simply have restored the regime that existed for centuries before 1973, in which the permissibility of and restrictions upon abortion were determined legislatively State-by-State. *Casey*, however, chose to base its *stare decisis* determination on a different "sort" of reliance. "[P]eople," it said, "have organized intimate relationships and made choices that define their views of themselves and their places in society, in reliance on the availability of abortion in the event that contraception should fail." This falsely assumes that the consequence of overruling *Roe* would have been to make abortion unlawful. It would not; it would merely have *permitted* the States to do so. Many States would unquestionably have declined to prohibit abortion, and others would not have prohibited it within six months (after which the most significant reliance interests would have expired). Even for persons in States other than these, the choice would not have been between abortion and childbirth, but between abortion nearby and abortion in a neighboring State.

To tell the truth, it does not surprise me, and should surprise no one, that the Court has chosen today to revise the standards of *stare decisis* set forth in *Casey*. It has thereby exposed *Casey's* extraordinary deference to precedent for the result-oriented expedient that it is.

II

Having decided that it need not adhere to *stare decisis*, the Court still must establish that *Bowers* was wrongly decided and that the Texas statute, as applied to petitioners, is unconstitutional.

Texas Penal Code Ann. § 21.06(a) (2003) undoubtedly imposes constraints on liberty. So do laws prohibiting prostitution, recreational use of heroin, and, for that matter, working more than 60 hours per week in a bakery. But there is no right to "liberty" under the Due Process Clause, though today's opinion repeatedly makes that claim. The Fourteenth Amendment *expressly allows* States to deprive their citizens of "liberty," *so long as 'due process of law' is provided.* [. . .]

Our opinions applying the doctrine known as "substantive due process" hold that the Due Process Clause prohibits States from infringing *fundamental* liberty interests, unless the infringement is narrowly tailored to serve a compelling state interest. We have held repeatedly, in cases the Court today does not overrule, that *only* fundamental rights qualify for this so-called "heightened scrutiny" protection—that is, rights which are "'deeply rooted in this Nation's history and tradition'" *Washington v. Glucksberg* (1997). All other liberty interests may be abridged or abrogated pursuant to a validly enacted state law if that law is rationally related to a legitimate state interest.

Bowers held, first, that criminal prohibitions of homosexual sodomy are not subject to heightened scrutiny because they do not implicate a "fundamental right" under the Due Process Clause. Noting that "[p]roscriptions against that conduct have ancient roots," that "[s]odomy was a criminal offense at common law and was forbidden by the laws of the original 13 States when they ratified the Bill of Rights," and that many States had retained their bans on sodomy, *Bowers* concluded that a right to engage in homosexual sodomy was not "'deeply rooted in this Nation's history and tradition.'"

The Court today does not overrule this holding. Not once does it describe homosexual sodomy as a "fundamental right" or a "fundamental liberty interest," nor does it subject the Texas statute to strict scrutiny. Instead, having failed to establish that the right to homosexual sodomy is "'deeply rooted in this Nation's history and tradition,'" the Court concludes that the application of Texas's statute to petitioners' conduct fails the rational-basis test, and overrules *Bowers'* holding to the contrary.

I shall address that rational-basis holding presently. First, however, I address some aspersions that the Court casts upon *Bowers'* conclusion that homosexual sodomy is not a "fundamental right"— even though, as I have said, the Court does not have the boldness to reverse that conclusion.

III

The Court's description of "the state of the law" at the time of *Bowers* only confirms that *Bowers* was right. The Court points to *Griswold v. Connecticut* (1965). But that case *expressly disclaimed* any reliance on the doctrine of "substantive due process," and grounded the so-called "right to privacy" in penumbras of constitutional provisions *other than* the Due Process Clause. [. . .]

Roe v. Wade recognized that the right to abort an unborn child was a "fundamental right" protected by the Due Process Clause. The *Roe* Court, however, made no attempt to establish that this right was "deeply rooted in this Nation's history and tradition"; instead, it based its conclusion that "the Fourteenth Amendment's concept of personal liberty . . . is broad enough to encompass a woman's decision whether or not to terminate her pregnancy" on its own normative judgment that anti-abortion laws were undesirable. We have since rejected *Roe's* holding that regulations of abortion must be narrowly tailored to serve a compelling state interest, see *Planned Parenthood v. Casey* (1992).

After discussing the history of antisodomy laws, the Court proclaims that, "it should be noted that there is no longstanding history in this country of laws directed at homosexual conduct as a distinct matter." This observation in no way casts into doubt the "definitive [historical] conclusion" on which *Bowers* relied: that our Nation has a longstanding history of laws prohibiting *sodomy in general*—regardless of whether it was performed by same-sex or opposite-sex couples. [. . .] It is (as *Bowers* recognized) entirely irrelevant whether the laws in our long national tradition criminalizing homosexual sodomy were "directed at homosexual conduct as a distinct matter." Whether homosexual sodomy was prohibited by a law targeted at same-sex sexual relations or by a more general law prohibiting both homosexual and heterosexual sodomy, the only relevant point is that it *was* criminalized—which suffices to establish that homosexual sodomy is not a right "deeply rooted in our Nation's history and tradition." The Court today agrees that homosexual sodomy was criminalized and thus does not dispute the facts on which *Bowers actually* relied.

Next the Court makes the claim, again unsupported by any citations, that "[l]aws prohibiting sodomy do not seem to have been enforced against consenting adults acting in private." The key qualifier here is "acting in private"—since the Court admits that sodomy laws *were* enforced against consenting adults (although the Court contends that prosecutions were "infrequent"). I do not know what "acting in private" means; surely consensual sodomy, like heterosexual intercourse, is rarely performed on stage. If all the Court means by "acting in private" is "on private premises, with the doors closed and windows covered," it is entirely unsurprising that evidence of enforcement would be hard to come by.[. . .] Surely that lack of evidence would not sustain the proposition that consensual sodomy on private premises with the doors closed and windows covered was regarded as a "fundamental right," even though all other consensual sodomy was criminalized. There are 203 prosecutions for consensual, adult homosexual sodomy reported in the West Reporting system and official state reporters from the years 1880–1995. There are also records of 20 sodomy prosecutions and 4 executions during the colonial period. *Bowers'* conclusion that homosexual sodomy is not a fundamental right "deeply rooted in this Nation's history and tradition" is utterly unassailable.

Realizing that fact, the Court instead says: "[W]e think that our laws and traditions in the past half century are of most relevance here. These references show *an emerging awareness* that liberty gives substantial protection to adult persons in deciding how to conduct their private lives *in matters pertaining to sex*" (emphasis added). Apart from the fact that such an "emerging awareness" does not establish a "fundamental right," the statement is factually false. States continue to prosecute all sorts of crimes by adults "in matters pertaining to sex": prostitution, adult incest, adultery, obscenity, and child pornography. Sodomy laws, too, have been enforced "in the past half century," in which there have been 134 reported cases involving prosecutions for consensual, adult, homosexual sodomy. In relying, for evidence of an "emerging recognition," upon the American Law Institute's 1955 recommendation not to criminalize "consensual sexual relations conducted in private," the Court ignores the fact that this recommendation was "a point of resistance in most of the states that considered adopting the Model Penal Code."

In any event, an "emerging awareness" is by definition not "deeply rooted in this Nation's history and tradition[s]," as we have said "fundamental right" status requires. Constitutional entitlements do not spring into existence because some States choose to lessen or eliminate criminal sanctions on certain behavior. Much less do they spring into existence, as the Court seems to believe, because *foreign nations* decriminalize conduct. The *Bowers* majority opinion *never* relied on "values we share with a wider civilization," but rather rejected the claimed right to sodomy on the ground that such a right was not "deeply rooted in *this Nation's* history and tradition." *Bowers'* rational-basis holding is likewise devoid of any reliance on the views of a "wider civilization." The Court's discussion of these foreign views (ignoring, of course, the many countries that have retained criminal prohibitions on sodomy) is therefore meaningless dicta. [. . .]

IV

I turn now to the ground on which the Court squarely rests its holding: the contention that there is no rational basis for the law here under attack. This proposition is so out of accord with our jurisprudence—indeed, with the jurisprudence of *any* society we know—that it requires little discussion.

The Texas statute undeniably seeks to further the belief of its citizens that certain forms of sexual behavior are "immoral and unacceptable,"—the same interest furthered by criminal laws against fornication, bigamy, adultery, adult incest, bestiality, and obscenity. *Bowers* held that this *was* a legitimate state interest. The Court today reaches the opposite conclusion. The Texas statute, it says, "furthers *no legitimate state interest* which can justify its intrusion into the personal and private life of the individual." The Court embraces instead *Justice Stevens'* declaration in his *Bowers* dissent, that "the fact that the governing majority in a State has traditionally viewed a particular practice as immoral is not a sufficient reason for upholding a law prohibiting the practice." This effectively decrees the end of all morals legislation. If, as the Court asserts, the promotion of majoritarian sexual morality is not even a *legitimate* state interest, none of the above-mentioned laws can survive rational-basis review. [. . .]

Today's opinion is the product of a Court, which is the product of a law-profession culture, that has largely signed on to the so-called homosexual agenda, by which I mean the agenda promoted by some homosexual activists directed at eliminating the moral opprobrium that has traditionally attached to homosexual conduct. I noted in an earlier opinion the fact that the American Association of Law Schools (to which any reputable law school *must* seek to belong) excludes from membership any school that refuses to ban from its job-interview facilities a law firm (no matter how small) that does not wish to hire as a prospective partner a person who openly engages in homosexual conduct.

One of the most revealing statements in today's opinion is the Court's grim warning that the criminalization of homosexual conduct is "an invitation to subject homosexual persons to discrimination both in the public and in the private spheres." It is clear from this that the Court has taken sides in the culture war, departing from its role of assuring, as neutral observer, that the democratic rules of engagement are observed. Many Americans do not want persons who openly engage in homosexual conduct as partners in their business, as scoutmasters for their children, as teachers in their children's schools, or as boarders in their home. They view this as protecting themselves and their families from a lifestyle that they believe to be immoral and destructive. The Court views it as "discrimination" which it is the function of our judgments to deter. So imbued is the Court with the law profession's anti-anti-homosexual culture, that it is seemingly unaware that the attitudes of that culture are not obviously "mainstream"; that in most States what the Court calls "discrimination" against those who engage in homosexual acts is perfectly legal; that proposals to ban such "discrimination" under Title VII have repeatedly been rejected by Congress; that in some cases such "discrimination" is *mandated* by federal statute, see 10 U.S. C. §654(b)(1) (mandating discharge from the armed forces of any service member who engages in or intends to engage in homosexual acts); and that in some cases such "discrimination" is a constitutional right, see *Boy Scouts of America v. Dale* (2000).

Let me be clear that I have nothing against homosexuals, or any other group, promoting their agenda through normal democratic means. Social perceptions of sexual and other morality change over time, and every group has the right to persuade its fellow citizens that its view of such matters is the best. That homosexuals have achieved some success in that enterprise is attested to by the fact that Texas is one of the few remaining States that criminalize private, consensual homosexual acts. But persuading one's fellow citizens is one thing, and imposing one's views in absence of democratic majority will is something else. I would no more *require* a State to criminalize homosexual acts—or for that matter, display *any* moral disapprobation of them—than I would *forbid* it to do so. What Texas has chosen to do is well within the range of traditional democratic action, and its hand should not be stayed through the invention of a brand-new "constitutional right" by a Court that is impatient of democratic change. It is indeed true that "later generations can see that laws once thought necessary and proper in fact serve only to oppress," *ante,* at 18; and when that happens, later generations can repeal those laws. But it is the premise of our system that those judgments are to be made by the people, and not imposed by a governing caste that knows best.

One of the benefits of leaving regulation of this matter to the people rather than to the courts is that the people, unlike judges, need not carry things to their logical conclusion. The people may feel that their disapprobation of homosexual conduct is strong enough to disallow homosexual marriage, but not strong enough to criminalize private homosexual acts—and may legislate accordingly. The Court today pretends that it possesses a similar freedom of action, so that that we need not fear judicial imposition of homosexual marriage, as has recently occurred in Canada. At the end of its opinion—after having laid waste the foundations of our rational-basis jurisprudence—the Court says that the present case "does not involve whether the government must give formal recognition to any relationship that homosexual persons seek to enter." Do not believe it. More illuminating than this bald, unreasoned disclaimer is the progression of thought displayed by an earlier passage in the Court's opinion, which notes the constitutional protections afforded to "personal decisions relating to *marriage,* procreation, contraception, family relationships, child rearing, and education," and then declares that "[p]ersons in a homosexual relationship may seek autonomy for these purposes, just as heterosexual persons do" (emphasis added). Today's opinion dismantles the structure of constitutional law that has permitted a distinction to be made between heterosexual and homosexual unions, insofar as formal recognition in marriage is concerned. If moral disapproval of homosexual conduct is "no legitimate state interest" for purposes of proscribing that conduct; and if, as the Court coos (casting aside all pretense of neutrality), "[w]hen sexuality finds overt expression in intimate conduct with another person, the conduct can be but one element in a personal bond that is more enduring," what justification could there possibly be for denying the benefits of marriage to homosexual couples exercising "[t]he liberty protected by the Constitution?" Surely not the encouragement of procreation, since the sterile and the elderly are allowed to marry. This case "does not involve" the issue of homosexual marriage only if one entertains the belief that principle and logic have nothing to do with the decisions of this Court. Many will hope that, as the Court comfortingly assures us, this is so.

The matters appropriate for this Court's resolution are only three: Texas's prohibition of sodomy neither infringes a "fundamental right" (which the Court does not dispute), nor is unsupported by a rational relation to what the Constitution considers a legitimate state interest, nor denies the equal protection of the laws. I dissent.

CLARENCE THOMAS

John Geddes Lawrence and Tyron Garner, Petitioners v. Texas, Dissent (2003)

Justice THOMAS, dissenting.

I join Justice Scalia's dissenting opinion. I write separately to note that the law before the Court today "is . . . uncommonly silly." *Griswold v. Connecticut* (1965) (Stewart, J., dissenting). If I were a member of the Texas Legislature, I would vote to repeal it. Punishing someone for expressing his sexual preference through noncommercial consensual conduct with another adult does not appear to be a worthy way to expend valuable law enforcement resources.

Notwithstanding this, I recognize that as a member of this Court I am not empowered to help petitioners and others similarly situated. My duty, rather, is to "decide cases 'agreeably to the Constitution and laws of the United States.'" And, just like Justice Stewart, I "can find [neither in the Bill of Rights nor any other part of the Constitution a] general right of privacy," or as the Court terms it today, the "liberty of the person both in its spatial and more transcendent dimensions."

SANDRA DAY O'CONNOR

Hamdi et al. v. Rumsfeld (2004)

Justice O'CONNOR announced the judgment of the Court and delivered an opinion, in which the Chief Justice, Justice KENNEDY, and Justice BREYER join.

At this difficult time in our Nation's history, we are called upon to consider the legality of the Government's detention of a United States citizen on United States soil as an "enemy combatant" and to address the process that is constitutionally owed to one who seeks to challenge his classification as such. The United States Court of Appeals for the Fourth Circuit held that petitioner's detention was legally authorized and that he was entitled to no further opportunity to challenge his enemy-combatant label. We now vacate and remand. We hold that although Congress authorized the detention of combatants in the narrow circumstances alleged here, due process demands that a citizen held in the United States as an enemy combatant be given a meaningful opportunity to

contest the factual basis for that detention before a neutral decisionmaker. [. . .]

I

This case arises out of the detention of a man whom the Government alleges took up arms with the Taliban during this conflict. His name is Yaser Esam Hamdi. Born an American citizen in Louisiana in 1980, Hamdi moved with his family to Saudi Arabia as a child. By 2001, the parties agree, he resided in Afghanistan. At some point that year, he was seized by members of the Northern Alliance, a coalition of military groups opposed to the Taliban government, and eventually was turned over to the United States military. The Government asserts that it initially detained and interrogated Hamdi in Afghanistan before transferring him to the United States Naval Base in Guantanamo Bay in January 2002. In April 2002, upon learning that Hamdi is an American citizen, authorities transferred him to a naval brig in Norfolk, Virginia, where he remained until a recent transfer to a brig in Charleston, South Carolina. The Government contends that Hamdi is an "enemy combatant," and that this status justifies holding him in the United States indefinitely—without formal charges or proceedings—unless and until it makes the determination that access to counsel or further process is warranted.

In June 2002, Hamdi's father, Esam Fouad Hamdi, filed the present petition for a writ of habeas corpus under 28 U.S.C. § 2241 in the Eastern District of Virginia, naming as petitioners his son and himself as next friend. The elder Hamdi alleges in the petition that he has had no contact with his son since the Government took custody of him in 2001, and that the Government has held his son "without access to legal counsel or notice of any charges pending against him." The petition contends that Hamdi's detention was not legally authorized. It argues that, "[a]s an American citizen, . . . Hamdi enjoys the full protections of the Constitution," and that Hamdi's detention in the United States without charges, access to an impartial tribunal, or assistance of counsel "violated and continue[s] to violate the Fifth and Fourteenth Amendments to the United States Constitution." The habeas petition asks that the court, among other things, (1) appoint counsel for Hamdi; (2) order respondents to cease interrogating him; (3) declare that he is being held in violation of the Fifth and Fourteenth Amendments; (4) "[t]o the extent Respondents contest any material factual allegations in this Petition, schedule an evidentiary hearing, at which Petitioners may adduce proof in support of their allegations"; and (5) order that Hamdi be released from his "unlawful custody." Although his habeas petition provides no details with regard to the factual circumstances surrounding his son's capture and detention, Hamdi's father has asserted in documents found elsewhere in the record that his son went to Afghanistan to do "relief work," and that he had been in that country less than two months before September 11, 2001, and could not have received military training. The 20-year-old was traveling on his own for the first time, his father says, and

"[b]ecause of his lack of experience, he was trapped in Afghanistan once that military campaign began."

The District Court found that Hamdi's father was a proper next friend, appointed the federal public defender as counsel for the petitioners, and ordered that counsel be given access to Hamdi. The United States Court of Appeals for the Fourth Circuit reversed that order, holding that the District Court had failed to extend appropriate deference to the Government's security and intelligence interests. It directed the District Court to consider "the most cautious procedures first," and to conduct a deferential inquiry into Hamdi's status. It opined that "if Hamdi is indeed an 'enemy combatant' who was captured during hostilities in Afghanistan, the government's present detention of him is a lawful one."

On remand, the Government filed a response and a motion to dismiss the petition. It attached to its response a declaration from one Michael Mobbs (hereinafter "Mobbs Declaration"), who identified himself as Special Advisor to the Under Secretary of Defense for Policy. Mobbs indicated that in this position, he has been "substantially involved with matters related to the detention of enemy combatants in the current war against the al Qaeda terrorists and those who support and harbor them (including the Taliban)." He expressed his "familiar[ity]" with Department of Defense and United States military policies and procedures applicable to the detention, control, and transfer of al Qaeda and Taliban personnel, and declared that "[b]ased upon my review of relevant records and reports, I am also familiar with the facts and circumstances related to the capture of . . . Hamdi and his detention by U.S. military forces."

Mobbs then set forth what remains the sole evidentiary support that the Government has provided to the courts for Hamdi's detention. The declaration states that Hamdi "traveled to Afghanistan" in July or August 2001, and that he thereafter "affiliated with a Taliban military unit and received weapons training." It asserts that Hamdi "remained with his Taliban unit following the attacks of September 11" and that, during the time when Northern Alliance forces were "engaged in battle with the Taliban," "Hamdi's Taliban unit surrendered" to those forces, after which he "surrender[ed] his Kalishnikov assault rifle" to them. The Mobbs Declaration also states that, because al Qaeda and the Taliban "were and are hostile forces engaged in armed conflict with the armed forces of the United States," "individuals associated with" those groups "were and continue to be enemy combatants." Mobbs states that Hamdi was labeled an enemy combatant "[b]ased upon his interviews and in light of his association with the Taliban." According to the declaration, a series of "U.S. military screening team[s]" determined that Hamdi met "the criteria for enemy combatants," and "a subsequent interview of Hamdi has confirmed that he surrendered and gave his firearm to Northern Alliance forces, which supports his classification as an enemy combatant."

After the Government submitted this declaration, the Fourth Circuit directed the District Court to proceed in accordance with its earlier ruling and, specifically, to "'consider the sufficiency of the Mobbs Declaration as an independent matter before proceeding further.'" The District Court found that the Mobbs Declaration fell "far short" of supporting Hamdi's detention. It criticized the generic and hearsay nature of the affidavit, calling it "little more than the government's 'say-so.'" It ordered the Government to turn over numerous materials for *in camera* review, including copies of all of Hamdi's statements and the notes taken from interviews with him that related to his reasons for going to Afghanistan and his activities therein; a list of all interrogators who had questioned Hamdi and their names and addresses; statements by members of the Northern Alliance regarding Hamdi's surrender and capture; a list of the dates and locations of his capture and subsequent detentions; and the names and titles of the United States Government officials who made the determinations that Hamdi was an enemy combatant and that he should be moved to a naval brig. The court indicated that all of these materials were necessary for "meaningful judicial review" of whether Hamdi's detention was legally authorized and whether Hamdi had received sufficient process to satisfy the Due Process Clause of the Constitution and relevant treaties or military regulations.

The Government sought to appeal the production order, and the District Court certified the question of whether the Mobbs Declaration, "standing alone, is sufficient as a matter of law to allow meaningful judicial review of [Hamdi's] classification as an enemy combatant." The Fourth Circuit reversed, but did not squarely answer the certified question. It instead stressed that, because it was "undisputed that Hamdi was captured in a zone of active combat in a foreign theater of conflict," no factual inquiry or evidentiary hearing allowing Hamdi to be heard or to rebut the Government's assertions was necessary or proper. Concluding that the factual averments in the Mobbs Declaration, "if accurate," provided a sufficient basis upon which to conclude that the President had constitutionally detained Hamdi pursuant to the President's war powers, it ordered the habeas petition dismissed. The Fourth Circuit emphasized that the "vital purposes" of the detention of uncharged enemy combatants—preventing those combatants from rejoining the enemy while relieving the military of the burden of litigating the circumstances of wartime captures halfway around the globe—were interests "directly derived from the war powers of Articles I and II." In that court's view, because "Article III contains nothing analogous to the specific powers of war so carefully enumerated in Articles I and II," separation of powers principles prohibited a federal court from "delv[ing] further into Hamdi's status and capture." Accordingly, the District Court's more vigorous inquiry "went far beyond the acceptable scope of review."

On the more global question of whether legal authorization exists for the detention of citizen enemy combatants at all, the Fourth Circuit rejected Hamdi's arguments that 18 U.S.C. § 4001(a) and Article 5 of the Geneva Convention rendered any such detentions unlawful. The court expressed doubt as to Hamdi's argument that § 4001(a), which provides that "[n]o citizen shall be imprisoned or otherwise detained by the United States except pursuant to an Act of Congress," required express congressional authorization of detentions of this sort. But it held that, in any event, such authorization was found in the post-September 11 Authorization for Use of Military Force. Because "capturing and detaining enemy combatants is an inherent part of warfare," the court held, "the 'necessary and appropriate force' referenced in the congressional resolution necessarily includes the capture and detention of any and all hostile forces arrayed against our troops." The court likewise rejected Hamdi's Geneva Convention claim, concluding that the convention is not self-executing and that, even if it were, it would not preclude the Executive from detaining Hamdi until the cessation of hostilities.

Finally, the Fourth Circuit rejected Hamdi's contention that its legal analyses with regard to the authorization for the detention scheme and the process to which he was constitutionally entitled should be altered by the fact that he is an American citizen detained on American soil. Relying on *Ex parte Quirin* (1942), the court emphasized that "[o]ne who takes up arms against the United States in a foreign theater of war, regardless of his citizenship, may properly be designated an enemy combatant and treated as such." "The privilege of citizenship," the court held, "entitles Hamdi to a limited judicial inquiry into his detention, but only to determine its legality under the war powers of the political branches. At least where it is undisputed that he was present in a zone of active combat operations, we are satisfied that the Constitution does not entitle him to a searching review of the factual determinations underlying his seizure there." [. . .]

We now vacate the judgment below and remand.

II

The threshold question before us is whether the Executive has the authority to detain citizens who qualify as "enemy combatants." There is some debate as to the proper scope of this term, and the Government has never provided any court with the full criteria that it uses in classifying individuals as such. It has made clear, however, that, for purposes of this case, the "enemy combatant" that it is seeking to detain is an individual who, it alleges, was "part of or supporting forces hostile to the United States or coalition partners" in Afghanistan and who "engaged in an armed conflict against the United States" there. We therefore answer only the narrow question before us: whether the detention of citizens falling within that definition is authorized.

The Government maintains that no explicit congressional authorization is required, because the Executive possesses plenary authority to detain pursuant to Article II of the Constitution. We do not reach the question whether Article II provides such authority, however, because we agree with the Government's alternative position, that Congress has in fact authorized Hamdi's detention, through the AUMF.

Our analysis on that point, set forth below, substantially overlaps with our analysis of Hamdi's principal argument for the illegality of his detention. He posits that his detention is forbidden by 18 U.S.C. § 4001(a). Section 4001(a) states that "[n]o citizen shall be imprisoned or otherwise detained by the United States except pursuant to an Act of Congress." Congress passed § 4001(a) in 1971 as part of a bill to repeal the Emergency Detention Act of 1950, which provided procedures for executive detention, during times of emergency, of individuals deemed likely to engage in espionage or sabotage. Congress was particularly concerned about the possibility that the Act could be used to reprise the Japanese internment camps of World War II. The Government again presses two alternative positions. First, it argues that § 4001(a), in light of its legislative history and its location in Title 18, applies only to "the control of civilian prisons and related detentions," not to military detentions. Second, it maintains that § 4001(a) is satisfied, because Hamdi is being detained "pursuant to an Act of Congress"—the AUMF. Again, because we conclude that the Government's second assertion is correct, we do not address the first. In other words, for the reasons that follow, we conclude that the AUMF is explicit congressional authorization for the detention of individuals in the narrow category we describe (assuming, without deciding, that such authorization is required), and that the AUMF satisfied § 4001(a)'s requirement that a detention be "pursuant to an Act of Congress" (assuming, without deciding, that § 4001(a) applies to military detentions).

The AUMF authorizes the President to use "all necessary and appropriate force" against "nations, organizations, or persons" associated with the September 11, 2001, terrorist attacks. There can be no doubt that individuals who fought against the United States in Afghanistan as part of the Taliban, an organization known to have supported the al Qaeda terrorist network responsible for those attacks, are individuals Congress sought to target in passing the AUMF. We conclude that detention of individuals falling into the limited category we are considering, for the duration of the particular conflict in which they were captured, is so fundamental and accepted an incident to war as to be an exercise of the "necessary and appropriate force" Congress has authorized the President to use.

The capture and detention of lawful combatants and the capture, detention, and trial of unlawful combatants, by "universal agreement and practice," are "important incident[s] of war." *Ex parte Quirin.* The purpose of detention is to prevent captured individuals from returning to the field of battle and taking up arms once again.

There is no bar to this Nation's holding one of its own citizens as an enemy combatant. In *Quirin,* one of the detainees, Haupt, alleged that he was a naturalized United States citizen. We held that "[c]itizens who associate themselves with the military arm of the enemy government, and with its aid, guidance and direction enter this country bent on hostile acts, are enemy belligerents within the meaning of . . . the law of war." While Haupt was tried for violations of the law of war, nothing in *Quirin* suggests that his citizenship would have precluded his mere detention for the duration of the relevant hostilities. Nor can we see any reason for drawing such a line here. A citizen, no less than an alien, can be "part of or supporting forces hostile to the United States or coalition partners" and "engaged in an armed conflict against the United States;" such a citizen, if released, would pose the same threat of returning to the front during the ongoing conflict.

In light of these principles, it is of no moment that the AUMF does not use specific language of detention. Because detention to prevent a combatant's return to the battlefield is a fundamental incident of waging war, in permitting the use of "necessary and appropriate force," Congress has clearly and unmistakably authorized detention in the narrow circumstances considered here.

Hamdi objects, nevertheless, that Congress has not authorized the indefinite detention to which he is now subject. The Government responds that "the detention of enemy combatants during World War II was just as 'indefinite' while that war was being fought." We take Hamdi's objection to be not to the lack of certainty regarding the date on which the conflict will end, but to the substantial prospect of perpetual detention. We recognize that the national security underpinnings of the "war on terror," although crucially important, are broad and malleable.

As the Government concedes, "given its unconventional nature, the current conflict is unlikely to end with a formal cease-fire agreement." The prospect Hamdi raises is therefore not far-fetched. If the Government does not consider this unconventional war won for two generations, and if it maintains during that time that Hamdi might, if released, rejoin forces fighting against the United States, then the position it has taken throughout the litigation of this case suggests that Hamdi's detention could last for the rest of his life.

It is a clearly established principle of the law of war that detention may last no longer than active hostilities. [. . .]

Hamdi contends that the AUMF does not authorize indefinite or perpetual detention. Certainly, we agree that indefinite detention for the purpose of interrogation is not authorized. Further, we understand Congress' grant of authority for the use of "necessary and appropriate force" to include the authority to detain for the duration of the relevant conflict, and our understanding is based on longstanding law-of-war principles. If the practical circumstances of a given conflict are entirely unlike those of the conflicts that informed the development of the law of war, that understanding may unravel. But that is not the situation we face as of this date. Active combat operations against Taliban fighters apparently are ongoing in Afghanistan. The United States may detain, for the duration of these hostilities, individuals legitimately determined to be Taliban combatants who "engaged in an armed conflict against the United States." If the record establishes that United States troops are still involved in active combat in Afghanistan, those detentions are part of the exercise of "necessary and appropriate force," and therefore are authorized by the AUMF.

Ex parte Milligan (1866) does not undermine our holding about the Government's authority to seize enemy combatants, as we define that term today. In that case, the Court made repeated reference to the fact that its inquiry into whether the military tribunal had jurisdiction to try and punish Milligan turned in large part on the fact that Milligan was not a prisoner of war, but a resident of Indiana arrested while at home there. That fact was central to its conclusion. Had Milligan been captured while he was assisting Confederate soldiers by carrying a rifle against Union troops on a Confederate battlefield, the holding of the Court might well have been different. The Court's repeated explanations that Milligan was not a prisoner of war suggest that had these different circumstances been present he could have been detained under military authority for the duration of the conflict, whether or not he was a citizen.

Moreover, as Justice Scalia acknowledges, the Court in *Ex parte Quirin* (1942) dismissed the language of Milligan that the petitioners had suggested prevented them from being subject to military process. [. . .] *Quirin* makes undeniably clear that this is not the law today. Haupt [. . .] was accused of being a spy. The Court in *Quirin* found him "subject to trial and punishment by [a] military tribunal" for those acts, and held that his citizenship did not change this result.

Quirin was a unanimous opinion. It both postdates and clarifies *Milligan*, providing us with the most apposite precedent that we have on the question of whether citizens may be detained in such circumstances. Brushing aside such precedent—particularly when doing so gives rise to a host of new questions never dealt with by this Court—is unjustified and unwise. [. . .]

III

Even in cases in which the detention of enemy combatants is legally authorized, there remains the question of what process is constitutionally due to a citizen who disputes his enemy-combatant status. Hamdi argues that he is owed a meaningful and timely hearing and that "extra-judicial detention [that] begins and ends with the submission of an affidavit based on third-hand hearsay" does not comport with the Fifth and Fourteenth Amendments. The Government counters that any more process than was provided below would be both unworkable and "constitutionally intolerable." [. . .]

A

Though they reach radically different conclusions on the process that ought to attend the present proceeding, the parties begin on common ground. All agree that, absent suspension, the writ of habeas corpus remains available to every individual detained within the United States. Only in the rarest of circumstances has Congress seen fit to suspend the writ. At all other times, it has remained a critical check on the Executive, ensuring that it does not detain individuals except in accordance with law. All agree suspension of the writ has not occurred here. Thus, it is undisputed that Hamdi was properly before an Article III court to challenge his detention under 28 U.S.C. § 2241. Further, all agree that § 2241 and its companion provisions provide at least a skeletal outline of the procedures to be afforded a petitioner in federal habeas review. Most notably, § 2243 provides that "the person detained may, under oath, deny any of the facts set forth in the return or allege any other material facts," and § 2246 allows the taking of evidence in habeas proceedings by deposition, affidavit, or interrogatories.

The simple outline of § 2241 makes clear both that Congress envisioned that habeas petitioners would have some opportunity to present and rebut facts and that courts in cases like this retain some ability to vary the ways in which they do so as mandated by due process. The Government recognizes the basic procedural protections required by the habeas statute, but asks us to hold that, given both the flexibility of the habeas mechanism and the circumstances presented in this case, the presentation of the Mobbs Declaration to the habeas court completed the required factual development. It suggests two separate reasons for its position that no further process is due.

B

First, the Government urges the adoption of the Fourth Circuit's holding below—that because it is "undisputed" that Hamdi's seizure took place in a combat zone, the habeas determination can be made purely as a matter of law, with no further hearing or factfinding necessary. This argument is easily rejected. [. . .] [T]he circumstances surrounding Hamdi's seizure cannot in any way be characterized as "undisputed," as "those circumstances are neither conceded in fact, nor susceptible to concession in law, because Hamdi has not been permitted to speak for himself or even through counsel as to those circumstances." Further, the "facts" that constitute the alleged concession are insufficient to support Hamdi's detention. Under the definition of enemy combatant that we accept today as falling within the scope of Congress' authorization, Hamdi would need to be "part of or supporting forces hostile to the United States or coalition partners" and "engaged in an armed conflict against the United States" to justify his detention in the United States for the duration of the relevant conflict. The habeas petition states only that "[w]hen seized by the United States Government, Mr. Hamdi resided in Afghanistan." An assertion that one *resided* in a country in which combat operations are taking place is not a concession that one was "*captured* in a zone of active combat operations in a foreign theater of war," (emphasis added), and certainly is not a concession that one was "part of or supporting forces hostile to the United States or coalition partners" and "engaged in an armed conflict against the United States." Accordingly, we reject any argument that Hamdi has made concessions that eliminate any right to further process.

C

The Government's second argument requires closer consideration. This is the argument that further factual exploration is unwarranted and inappropriate in light of the extraordinary constitutional interests at stake. Under the Government's most extreme rendition of this argument, "[r]espect for separation of powers and the limited institutional capabilities of courts in matters of military decision-making in connection with an ongoing conflict" ought to eliminate entirely any individual process, restricting the courts to investigating only whether legal authorization exists for the broader detention scheme. At most, the Government argues, courts should review its determination that a citizen is an enemy combatant under a very deferential "some evidence" standard. Under this review, a court would assume the accuracy of the Government's articulated basis for Hamdi's detention, as set forth in the Mobbs Declaration, and assess only whether that articulated basis was a legitimate one.

In response, Hamdi emphasizes that this Court consistently has recognized that an individual challenging his detention may not be held at the will of the Executive without recourse to some proceeding before a neutral tribunal to determine whether the Executive's asserted justifications for that detention have basis in fact and warrant in law. He argues that the Fourth Circuit inappropriately "ceded power to the Executive during wartime to define the conduct for which a citizen may be detained, judge whether that citizen has engaged in the proscribed conduct, and imprison that citizen indefinitely," and that due process demands that he receive a hearing in which he may challenge the Mobbs Declaration and adduce his own counter evidence. The District Court, agreeing with Hamdi, apparently believed that the appropriate process would approach the process that accompanies a criminal trial. It therefore disapproved of the hearsay nature of the Mobbs Declaration and anticipated quite extensive discovery of various military affairs. Anything less, it concluded, would not be "meaningful judicial review."

Both of these positions highlight legitimate concerns. And both emphasize the tension that often exists between the autonomy that the Government asserts is necessary in order to pursue effectively a particular goal and the process that a citizen contends he is due before he is deprived of a constitutional right. The ordinary mechanism that we use for balancing such serious competing interests, and for determining the procedures that are necessary to ensure that a citizen is not "deprived of life, liberty, or property, without due process of law," is the test that we articulated in *Mathews v. Eldridge* (1976). *Mathews* dictates that the process due in any given instance is determined by weighing "the private interest that will be affected by the official action" against the Government's asserted interest, "including the function involved" and the burdens the Government would face in providing greater process. The *Mathews* calculus then contemplates a judicious balancing of these concerns, through an analysis of "the risk of an erroneous deprivation" of the private interest if the process were reduced and the "probable value, if any, of additional or substitute safeguards." We take each of these steps in turn.

1

It is beyond question that substantial interests lie on both sides of the scale in this case. Hamdi's "private interest . . . affected by the official action," is the most elemental of liberty interests—the interest in being free from physical detention by one's own government. [. . .]

Nor is the weight on this side of the *Mathews* scale offset by the circumstances of war or the accusation of treasonous behavior, for "[i]t is clear that commitment for *any* purpose constitutes a significant deprivation of liberty that requires due process protection," *Jones v. United States* (1983) (emphasis added), and at this stage in the *Mathews* calculus, we consider the interest of the *erroneously* detained individual. Indeed, as *amicus* briefs from media and relief organizations emphasize, the risk of erroneous deprivation of a citizen's liberty in the absence of sufficient process here is very real. Moreover, as critical as the Government's interest may be in detaining those who actually pose an immediate threat to the national security of the United States during ongoing international conflict, history and common sense teach us that an unchecked system of detention carries the potential to become a means for oppression and abuse of others who do not present that sort of threat. Because we live in a society in which "[m]ere public intolerance or animosity cannot constitutionally justify the deprivation of a person's physical liberty," our starting point for the *Mathews v. Eldridge* analysis is unaltered by the allegations surrounding the particular detainee or the organizations with which he is alleged to have associated. We reaffirm today the fundamental nature of a citizen's right to be free from involuntary confinement by his own government without due process of law, and we weigh the opposing governmental interests against the curtailment of liberty that such confinement entails.

2

On the other side of the scale are the weighty and sensitive governmental interests in ensuring that those who have in fact fought with the enemy during a war do not return to battle against the United States. As discussed above, the law of war and the realities of combat may render such detentions both necessary and appropriate, and our due process analysis need not blink at those realities. Without doubt, our Constitution recognizes that core strategic matters of warmaking belong in the hands of those who are best positioned and most politically accountable for making them.

The Government also argues at some length that its interests in reducing the process available to alleged enemy combatants are heightened by the practical difficulties that would accompany a system of trial-like process. In its view, military officers who are engaged in the serious work of waging battle would be unnecessarily and dangerously distracted by litigation half a world away, and discovery into military operations would both intrude on the sensitive secrets of national defense and result in a futile search for evidence buried under the rubble of war. To the extent that these burdens are triggered by heightened procedures, they are properly taken into account in our due process analysis.

3

Striking the proper constitutional balance here is of great importance to the Nation during this period of ongoing combat. But it is equally vital that our calculus not give short shrift to the values that this country holds dear or to the privilege that is American citizenship. It is during our most challenging and uncertain moments that our Nation's commitment to due process is most severely tested; and it is in those times that we must preserve our commitment at home to the principles for which we fight abroad.

With due recognition of these competing concerns, we believe that neither the process proposed by the Government nor the process apparently envisioned by the District Court below strikes the proper constitutional balance when a United States citizen is detained in the United States as an enemy combatant. That is, "the risk of erroneous deprivation" of a detainee's liberty interest is unacceptably high under the Government's proposed rule, while some of the "additional or substitute procedural safeguards" suggested by the District Court are unwarranted in light of their limited "probable value" and the burdens they may impose on the military in such cases.

We therefore hold that a citizen-detainee seeking to challenge his classification as an enemy combatant must receive notice of the factual basis for his classification, and a fair opportunity to rebut the Government's factual assertions before a neutral decisionmaker. [. . .] It is equally fundamental that the right to notice and an opportunity to be heard "must be granted at a meaningful time and in a meaningful manner." These essential constitutional promises may not be eroded.

At the same time, the exigencies of the circumstances may demand that, aside from these core elements, enemy combatant proceedings may be tailored to alleviate their uncommon potential to burden the Executive at a time of ongoing military conflict. Hearsay, for example, may need to be accepted as the most reliable available evidence from the Government in such a proceeding. Likewise, the Constitution would not be offended by a presumption in favor of the Government's evidence, so long as that presumption remained a rebuttable one and fair opportunity for rebuttal were provided. Thus, once the Government puts forth credible evidence that the habeas petitioner meets the enemy-combatant criteria, the onus could shift to the petitioner to rebut that evidence with more persuasive evidence that he falls outside the criteria. A burden-shifting scheme of this sort would meet the goal of ensuring that the errant tourist, embedded journalist, or local aid worker has a chance to prove military error while giving due regard to the Executive once it has put forth meaningful support for its conclusion that the detainee is in fact an enemy combatant. [. . .]

We think it unlikely that this basic process will have the dire impact on the central functions of warmaking that the Government forecasts. The parties agree that initial captures on the battlefield need not receive the process we have discussed here; that process is due only when the determination is made to *continue* to hold those who have been seized. The Government has made clear in its briefing that documentation regarding battlefield detainees already is kept in the ordinary course of military affairs. Any factfinding imposition created by requiring a knowledgeable affiant to summarize these records to an independent tribunal is a minimal one. Likewise, arguments that military officers ought not have to wage war under the threat of litigation lose much of their steam when factual disputes at enemy-combatant hearings are limited to the alleged combatant's acts. This focus meddles little, if at all, in the strategy or conduct of war, inquiring only into the appropriateness of continuing to detain an individual claimed to have taken up arms against the United States.

While we accord the greatest respect and consideration to the judgments of military authorities in matters relating to the actual prosecution of a war, and recognize that the scope of that discretion necessarily is wide, it does not infringe on the core role of the military for the courts to exercise their own time-honored and constitutionally mandated roles of reviewing and resolving claims like those presented here.

In sum, while the full protections that accompany challenges to detentions in other settings may prove unworkable and inappropriate in the enemy-combatant setting, the threats to military operations posed by a basic system of independent review are not so weighty as to trump a citizen's core rights to challenge meaningfully the Government's case and to be heard by an impartial adjudicator.

D

In so holding, we necessarily reject the Government's assertion that separation of powers principles mandate a heavily circumscribed role for the courts in such circumstances. Indeed, the position that the courts must forgo any examination of the individual case and focus exclusively on the legality of the broader detention scheme cannot be mandated by any reasonable view of separation of powers, as this approach serves only to condense power into a single branch of government. We have long since made clear that a state of war is not a blank check for the President when it comes to the rights of the Nation's citizens. Whatever power the United States Constitution envisions for the Executive in its exchanges with other nations or with enemy organizations in times of conflict, it most assuredly envisions a role for all three branches when individual liberties are at stake. Likewise, we have made clear that, unless Congress acts to suspend it, the Great Writ of habeas corpus allows the Judicial Branch to play a necessary role in maintaining this delicate balance of governance, serving as an important judicial check on the Executive's discretion in the realm of detentions. Thus, while we do not question that our due process assessment must pay keen attention to the particular burdens faced by the Executive in the context of military action, it would turn our system of checks and balances on its head to suggest that a citizen could not make his way to court with a challenge to the factual basis for his detention by his government, simply because the Executive opposes making available such a challenge. Absent suspension of the writ by Congress, a citizen detained as an enemy combatant is entitled to this process.

Because we conclude that due process demands some system for a citizen detainee to refute his classification, the proposed "some evidence" standard is inadequate. Any process in which the Executive's factual assertions go wholly unchallenged or are simply presumed correct without any opportunity for the alleged combatant to demonstrate otherwise falls constitutionally short. [. . .] This standard [. . .] is ill suited to the situation in which a habeas petitioner has received no prior proceedings before any tribunal and had no prior opportunity to rebut the Executive's factual assertions before a neutral decisionmaker.

Today we are faced only with such a case. Aside from unspecified "screening" processes, and military interrogations in which the Government suggests Hamdi could have contested his classification, Hamdi has received no process. An interrogation by one's captor, however effective an intelligence-gathering tool, hardly constitutes a constitutionally adequate factfinding before a neutral decisionmaker. [. . .]

There remains the possibility that the standards we have articulated could be met by an appropriately authorized and properly constituted military tribunal. Indeed, it is notable that military regulations already provide for such process in related instances, dictating that tribunals be made available to determine the status of enemy detainees who assert prisoner-of-war status under the Geneva Convention. In the absence of such process, however, a court that receives a petition for a writ of habeas corpus from an alleged enemy combatant must itself ensure that the minimum requirements of due process are achieved. Both courts below recognized as much, focusing their energies on the question of whether Hamdi was due an opportunity to rebut the Government's case against him. The Government, too, proceeded on this assumption, presenting its affidavit and then seeking that it be evaluated under a deferential standard of review based on burdens that it alleged would accompany any greater process. As we have discussed, a habeas court in a case such as this may accept affidavit evidence like that contained in the Mobbs Declaration, so long as it also permits the alleged combatant to present his own factual case to rebut the Government's return. We anticipate that a District Court would proceed with the caution that we have indicated is necessary in this setting, engaging in a factfinding process that is both prudent and incremental. We have no reason to doubt that courts faced with these sensitive matters will pay proper heed both to the matters of national security that might arise in an individual case and to the constitutional limitations safeguarding essential liberties that remain vibrant even in times of security concerns. [. . .]

The judgment of the United States Court of Appeals for the Fourth Circuit is vacated, and the case is remanded for further proceedings.

ANTONIN SCALIA

Hamdi et al. v. Rumsfeld, Dissent (2004)

Justice SCALIA, with whom Justice STEVENS joins, dissenting.

Petitioner, a presumed American citizen, has been imprisoned without charge or hearing in the Norfolk and Charleston Naval Brigs for more than two years, on the allegation that he is an enemy combatant who bore arms against his country for the Taliban. His father claims to the contrary, that he is an inexperienced aid worker caught in the wrong place at the wrong time. This case brings into conflict the competing demands of national security and our citizens' constitutional right to personal liberty. Although I share the Court's evident unease as it seeks to reconcile the two, I do not agree with its resolution.

Where the Government accuses a citizen of waging war against it, our constitutional tradition has been to prosecute him in federal court for treason or some other crime. Where the exigencies of war prevent that, the Constitution's Suspension Clause, Art. I, § 9, cl. 2, allows Congress to relax the usual protections temporarily. Absent suspension, however, the Executive's assertion of military exigency has not been thought sufficient to permit detention without charge. No one contends that the congressional Authorization for Use of Military Force, on which the Government relies to justify its actions here, is an implementation of the Suspension Clause. Accordingly, I would reverse the decision below.

I

The very core of liberty secured by our Anglo-Saxon system of separated powers has been freedom from indefinite imprisonment at the will of the Executive. Blackstone stated this principle clearly:

> Of great importance to the public is the preservation of this personal liberty: for if once it were left in the power of any, the highest, magistrate to imprison arbitrarily whomever he or his officers thought proper . . . there would soon be an end of all other rights and immunities. . . . To bereave a man of life, or by violence to confiscate his estate, without accusation or trial, would be so gross and notorious an act of despotism, as must at once convey the alarm of tyranny throughout the whole kingdom. But confinement of the person, by secretly hurrying him to gaol, where his sufferings are unknown or forgotten; is a less public, a less striking, and therefore a more dangerous engine of arbitrary government. . . .
>
> To make imprisonment lawful, it must either be, by process from the courts of judicature, or by warrant from some legal officer, having authority to commit to prison; which warrant must be in writing, under the hand and seal of the magistrate, and express the causes of the commitment, in order to be examined into (if necessary) upon a *habeas corpus.* If there be no cause expressed, the gaoler is not bound to detain the prisoner. For the law judges in this respect . . . , that it is

unreasonable to send a prisoner, and not to signify withal the crimes alleged against him. *Commentaries on the Laws of England.*

These words were well known to the Founders. Hamilton quoted from this very passage in *The Federalist* No. 84. The two ideas central to Blackstone's understanding—due process as the right secured, and habeas corpus as the instrument by which due process could be insisted upon by a citizen illegally imprisoned—found expression in the Constitution's Due Process and Suspension Clauses.

The gist of the Due Process Clause, as understood at the founding and since, was to force the Government to follow those common-law procedures traditionally deemed necessary before depriving a person of life, liberty, or property. When a citizen was deprived of liberty because of alleged criminal conduct, those procedures typically required committal by a magistrate followed by indictment and trial. [. . .]

These due process rights have historically been vindicated by the writ of habeas corpus. In England before the founding, the writ developed into a tool for challenging executive confinement. It was not always effective. For example, in *Darnel's Case* (1627), King Charles I detained without charge several individuals for failing to assist England's war against France and Spain. The prisoners sought writs of habeas corpus, arguing that without specific charges, "imprisonment shall not continue on for a time, but for ever; and the subjects of this kingdom may be restrained of their liberties perpetually." The Attorney General replied that the Crown's interest in protecting the realm justified imprisonment in "a matter of state . . . not ripe nor timely" for the ordinary process of accusation and trial. The court denied relief, producing widespread outrage, and Parliament responded with the Petition of Right, accepted by the King in 1628, which expressly prohibited imprisonment without formal charges.

The struggle between subject and Crown continued, and culminated in the Habeas Corpus Act of 1679, described by Blackstone as a "second *magna charta,* and stable bulwark of our liberties." The Act governed all persons "committed or detained . . . for any crime." In cases other than felony or treason plainly expressed in the warrant of commitment, the Act required release upon appropriate sureties (unless the commitment was for a nonbailable offense). Where the commitment was for felony or high treason, the Act did not require immediate release, but instead required the Crown to commence criminal proceedings within a specified time. If the prisoner was not "indicted some Time in the next Term," the judge was "required . . . to set at Liberty the Prisoner upon Bail" unless the King was unable to produce his witnesses. Able or no, if the prisoner was not brought to trial by the next succeeding term, the Act provided that "he shall be discharged from his Imprisonment." English courts sat four terms per year, so the practical effect of this provision was that imprisonment without indictment or trial for felony or high treason [. . .] would not exceed approximately three to six months.

The writ of habeas corpus was preserved in the Constitution—the only common-law writ to be explicitly mentioned. Hamilton lauded "the establishment of the writ of *habeas corpus*" [. . .] as a means to protect against "the practice of arbitrary imprisonments . . . in all ages, [one of] the favourite and most formidable instruments of tyranny." *The Federalist* No. 84. Indeed, availability of the writ under the new Constitution (along with the requirement of trial by jury in criminal cases, see Art. III, § 2, cl. 3) was his basis for arguing that additional, explicit procedural protections were unnecessary. See *The Federalist* No. 83.

II

The allegations here, of course, are no ordinary accusations of criminal activity. Yaser Esam Hamdi has been imprisoned because the Government believes he participated in the waging of war against the United States. The relevant question, then, is whether there is a different, special procedure for imprisonment of a citizen accused of wrongdoing by *aiding the enemy in wartime.*

A

Justice O'Connor, writing for a plurality of this Court, asserts that captured enemy combatants (other than those suspected of war crimes) have traditionally been detained until the cessation of hostilities and then released. That is probably an accurate description of wartime practice with respect to enemy aliens. The tradition with respect to American citizens, however, has been quite different. Citizens aiding the enemy have been treated as traitors subject to the criminal process.

As early as 1350, England's Statute of Treasons made it a crime to "levy War against our Lord the King in his Realm, or be adherent to the King's Enemies in his Realm, giving to them Aid and Comfort, in the Realm, or elsewhere." [. . .]

Subjects accused of levying war against the King were routinely prosecuted for treason. The Founders inherited the understanding that a citizen's levying war against the Government was to be punished criminally. The Constitution provides: "Treason against the United States, shall consist only in levying War against them, or in adhering to their Enemies, giving them Aid and Comfort"; and establishes a heightened proof requirement (two witnesses) in order to "convic[t]" of that offense. Art. III, § 3, cl. 1.

In more recent times, too, citizens have been charged and tried in Article III courts for acts of war against the United States, even when their noncitizen co-conspirators were not. For example, two American citizens alleged to have participated during World War I in a spying conspiracy on behalf of Germany were tried in federal court. A German member of the same conspiracy was subjected to military process. During World War II, the famous German saboteurs of *Ex parte Quirin* (1942) received military process, but the citizens who associated with them (with the exception of one citizen-saboteur, discussed below) were punished under the criminal process. [. . .]

[. . .] The only citizen other than Hamdi known to be imprisoned in connection with military hostilities in Afghanistan against the United States was subjected to criminal process and convicted upon a guilty plea.

B

There are times when military exigency renders resort to the traditional criminal process impracticable. English law accommodated such exigencies by allowing legislative suspension of the writ of habeas corpus for brief periods. Blackstone explained:

And yet sometimes, when the state is in real danger, even this [i.e., executive detention] may be a necessary measure. But the happiness of our Constitution is, that it is not left to the executive power to determine when the danger of the state is so great, as to render this measure expedient. For the parliament only, or legislative power, whenever it sees proper, can authorize the crown, by suspending the habeas corpus act for a short and limited time, to imprison suspected persons without giving any reason for so doing. . . . In like manner this experiment ought only to be tried in case of extreme emergency; and in these the nation parts with it[s] liberty for a while, in order to preserve it for ever.

Where the Executive has not pursued the usual course of charge, committal, and conviction, it has historically secured the Legislature's explicit approval of a suspension. In England, Parliament on numerous occasions passed temporary suspensions in times of threatened invasion or rebellion. Not long after Massachusetts had adopted a clause in its constitution explicitly providing for habeas corpus, it suspended the writ in order to deal with Shays' Rebellion.

Our Federal Constitution contains a provision explicitly permitting suspension, but limiting the situations in which it may be invoked: "The privilege of the Writ of Habeas Corpus shall not be suspended, unless when in Cases of Rebellion or Invasion the public Safety may require it." Although this provision does not state that suspension must be effected by, or authorized by, a legislative act, it has been so understood, consistent with English practice and the Clause's placement in Article I.

The Suspension Clause was by design a safety valve, the Constitution's only "express provision for exercise of extraordinary authority because of a crisis," *Youngstown Sheet & Tube Co. v. Sawyer* (1952). Very early in the Nation's history, President Jefferson unsuccessfully sought a suspension of habeas corpus to deal with Aaron Burr's conspiracy to overthrow the Government. During the Civil War, Congress passed its first Act authorizing Executive suspension of the writ of habeas corpus, to the relief of those many who thought President Lincoln's unauthorized proclamations of suspension unconstitutional. Later Presidential proclamations of suspension relied upon the congressional authorization. During Reconstruction,

Congress passed the Ku Klux Klan Act, which included a provision authorizing suspension of the writ, invoked by President Grant in quelling a rebellion in nine South Carolina counties. [. . .]

III

Of course the extensive historical evidence of criminal convictions and habeas suspensions does not *necessarily* refute the Government's position in this case. When the writ is suspended, the Government is entirely free from judicial oversight. It does not claim such total liberation here, but argues that it need only produce what it calls "some evidence" to satisfy a habeas court that a detained individual is an enemy combatant. Even if suspension of the writ on the one hand, and committal for criminal charges on the other hand, have been the only *traditional* means of dealing with citizens who levied war against their own country, it is theoretically possible that the Constitution does not require a choice between these alternatives.

I believe, however, that substantial evidence does refute that possibility. First, the text of the 1679 Habeas Corpus Act makes clear that indefinite imprisonment on reasonable suspicion is not an available option of treatment for those accused of aiding the enemy, absent a suspension of the writ. In the United States, this Act was read as "enforc[ing] the common law," and shaped the early understanding of the scope of the writ. As noted above, the Act specifically addressed those committed for high treason, and provided a remedy if they were not *indicted and tried* by the second succeeding court term. That remedy was not a bobtailed judicial inquiry into whether there were reasonable grounds to believe the prisoner had taken up arms against the King. Rather, if the prisoner was not indicted and tried within the prescribed time, "he shall be discharged from his Imprisonment." The Act does not contain any exception for wartime. [. . .]

Writings from the founding generation also suggest that, without exception, the only constitutional alternatives are to charge the crime or suspend the writ. In 1788, Thomas Jefferson wrote to James Madison questioning the need for a Suspension Clause in cases of rebellion in the proposed Constitution. His letter illustrates the constraints under which the Founders understood themselves to operate:

> Why suspend the Hab. corp. in insurrections and rebellions? The parties who may be arrested may be charged instantly with a well defined crime. Of course the judge will remand them. If the publick safety requires that the government should have a man imprisoned on less probable testimony in those than in other emergencies; let him be taken and tried, retaken and retried, while the necessity continues, only giving him redress against the government for damages.

A similar view was reflected in the 1807 House debates over suspension during the armed uprising that came to be known as Burr's conspiracy:

> With regard to those persons who may be implicated in the conspiracy, if the writ of habeas corpus be not suspended, what will be the consequence? When apprehended, they will be brought before a court of justice, who will decide whether there is any evidence that will justify their commitment for farther prosecution. From the communication of the Executive, it appeared there was sufficient evidence to authorize their commitment. Several months would elapse before their final trial, which would give time to collect evidence, and if this shall be sufficient, they will not fail to receive the punishment merited by their crimes, and inflicted by the laws of their country. 16 Annals of Congress, at 405 (remarks of Rep. Burwell).

The absence of military authority to imprison citizens indefinitely in wartime—whether or not a probability of treason had been established by means less than jury trial—was confirmed by three cases decided during and immediately after the War of 1812. In the first, *In re Stacy* (N.Y. 1813), a citizen was taken into military custody on suspicion that he was "carrying provisions and giving information to the enemy." Stacy petitioned for a writ of habeas corpus, and, after the defendant custodian attempted to avoid complying, Chief Justice Kent ordered attachment against him. Kent noted that the military was "without any color of authority in any military tribunal to try a citizen for that crime" and that it was "holding him in the closest confinement, and contemning the civil authority of the state."

Two other cases, later cited with approval by this Court in *Ex parte Milligan* (1866), upheld verdicts for false imprisonment against military officers. In *Smith v. Shaw* (N.Y. 1815), the court affirmed an award of damages for detention of a citizen on suspicion that he was, among other things, "an enemy's spy in time of war." The court held that "[n]one of the offences charged against Shaw were cognizable by a court-martial, except that which related to his being a spy; and if he was an American citizen, he could not be charged with such an offence. He might be amenable to the civil authority for treason; but could not be punished, under martial law, as a spy." "If the defendant was justifiable in doing what he did, every citizen of the United States would, in time of war, be equally exposed to a like exercise of military power and authority." Finally, in *M'Connell v. Hampton* (N. Y. 1815), a jury awarded $9,000 for false imprisonment after a military officer confined a citizen on charges of treason; the judges on appeal did not question the verdict but found the damages excessive, in part because "it does not appear that [the defendant] . . . knew [the plaintiff] was a citizen."

President Lincoln, when he purported to suspend habeas corpus without congressional authorization during the Civil War, apparently did not doubt that suspension was required if the prisoner was to be held without criminal trial. In his famous message to Congress on July 4, 1861, he argued only that he could suspend the writ, not that even without suspension, his imprisonment of citizens without criminal trial was permitted.

Further evidence comes from this Court's decision in *Ex parte Milligan*. There, the Court issued the writ to an American citizen who had been tried by military commission for offenses that included conspiring to overthrow the Government, seize munitions, and liberate prisoners of war. The Court rejected in no uncertain terms the Government's assertion that military jurisdiction was proper "under the 'laws and usages of war'":

> It can serve no useful purpose to inquire what those laws and usages are, whence they originated, where found, and on whom they operate; they can never be applied to citizens in states which have upheld the authority of the government, and where the courts are open and their process unobstructed.

Milligan is not exactly this case, of course, since the petitioner was threatened with death, not merely imprisonment. But the reasoning and conclusion of *Milligan* logically cover the present case. The Government justifies imprisonment of Hamdi on principles of the law of war and admits that, absent the war, it would have no such authority. But if the law of war cannot be applied to citizens where courts are open, then Hamdi's imprisonment without criminal trial is no less unlawful than Milligan's trial by military tribunal.

Milligan responded to the argument, repeated by the Government in this case, that it is dangerous to leave suspected traitors at large in time of war:

> If it was dangerous, in the distracted condition of affairs, to leave Milligan unrestrained of his liberty, because he "conspired against the government, afforded aid and comfort to rebels, and incited the people to insurrection," the law said arrest him, confine him closely, render him powerless to do further mischief; and then present his case to the grand jury of the district, with proofs of his guilt, and, if indicted, try him according to the course of the common law. If this had been done, the Constitution would have been vindicated, the law of 1863 enforced, and the securities for personal liberty preserved and defended.

Thus, criminal process was viewed as the primary means—and the only means absent congressional action suspending the writ—not only to punish traitors, but to incapacitate them.

The proposition that the Executive lacks indefinite wartime detention authority over citizens is consistent with the Founders' general mistrust of military power permanently at the Executive's disposal. In the Founders' view, the "blessings of liberty" were threatened by "those military establishments which must gradually poison its very fountain." *The Federalist* No. 45. No fewer than 10 issues of *The Federalist* were devoted in whole or part to allaying fears of oppression from the proposed Constitution's authorization of standing armies in peacetime. Many safeguards in the Constitution reflect these concerns. Congress's authority "[t]o raise and support Armies" was hedged with the proviso that "no Appropriation of Money to that Use shall be for a longer Term than two Years." Except for the actual command of military forces, all authorization for their maintenance and all explicit authorization for their use is placed in the control of Congress under Article I, rather than the President under Article II. [. . .]

A view of the Constitution that gives the Executive authority to use military force rather than the force of law against citizens on American soil flies in the face of the mistrust that engendered these provisions. [. . .]

V

It follows from what I have said that Hamdi is entitled to a habeas decree requiring his release unless (1) criminal proceedings are promptly brought, or (2) Congress has suspended the writ of habeas corpus. A suspension of the writ could, of course, lay down conditions for continued detention, similar to those that today's opinion prescribes under the Due Process Clause. But there is a world of difference between the people's representatives' determining the need for that suspension (and prescribing the conditions for it), and this Court's doing so.

The plurality finds justification for Hamdi's imprisonment in the Authorization for Use of Military Force. [. . . .] This is not remotely a congressional suspension of the writ, and no one claims that it is. Contrary to the plurality's view, I do not think this statute even authorizes detention of a citizen with the clarity necessary to satisfy the interpretive canon that statutes should be construed so as to avoid grave constitutional concerns; or with the clarity necessary to overcome the statutory prescription that "[n]o citizen shall be imprisoned or otherwise detained by the United States except pursuant to an Act of Congress." But even if it did, I would not permit it to overcome Hamdi's entitlement to habeas corpus relief. The Suspension Clause of the Constitution, which carefully circumscribes the conditions under which the writ can be withheld, would be a sham if it could be evaded by congressional prescription of requirements other than the common-law requirement of committal for criminal prosecution that render the writ, though available, unavailing. If the Suspension Clause does not guarantee the citizen that he will either be tried or released, unless the conditions for suspending the writ exist and the grave action of suspending the writ has been taken; if it merely guarantees the citizen that he will not be detained unless Congress by ordinary legislation says he can be detained; it guarantees him very little indeed.

It should not be thought, however, that the plurality's evisceration of the Suspension Clause augments, principally, the power of Congress. As usual, the major effect of its constitutional improvisation is to increase the power of the Court. Having found a congressional authorization for detention of citizens where none clearly exists; and having discarded the categorical procedural protection of the Suspension Clause; the plurality then proceeds, under the guise of the Due Process Clause, to prescribe what procedural protections it thinks appropriate. It "weigh[s] the private interest . . . against the Government's asserted interest," and—just as though writing a new Constitution—comes up with an unheard-of system in which the citizen rather than the Government bears the burden of proof, testimony is by hearsay rather than live witnesses, and the presiding officer may well be a "neutral" military officer rather than judge and jury. It claims authority to engage in this sort of "judicious balancing" from *Mathews v. Eldridge* (1976), a case involving . . . *the withdrawal of disability benefits!* Whatever the merits of this technique when newly recognized property rights are at issue (and even there they are questionable), it has no place where the Constitution and the common law already supply an answer.

Having distorted the Suspension Clause, the plurality finishes up by transmogrifying the Great Writ—disposing of the present habeas petition by remanding for the District Court to "engag[e] in a factfinding process that is both prudent and incremental." "In the absence of [the Executive's prior provision of procedures that satisfy due process], . . . a court that receives a petition for a writ of habeas corpus from an alleged enemy combatant must itself ensure that the minimum requirements of due process are achieved." This judicial remediation of executive default is unheard of. The role of habeas corpus is to determine the legality of executive detention, not to supply the omitted process necessary to make it legal. It is not the habeas court's function to make illegal detention legal by supplying a process that the Government could have provided, but chose not to. If Hamdi is being imprisoned in violation of the Constitution (because without due process of

law), then his habeas petition should be granted; the Executive may then hand him over to the criminal authorities, whose detention for the purpose of prosecution will be lawful, or else must release him.

There is a certain harmony of approach in the plurality's making up for Congress's failure to invoke the Suspension Clause and its making up for the Executive's failure to apply what it says are needed procedures—an approach that reflects what might be called a Mr. Fix-it Mentality. The plurality seems to view it as its mission to Make Everything Come Out Right, rather than merely to decree the consequences, as far as individual rights are concerned, of the other two branches' actions and omissions. Has the Legislature failed to suspend the writ in the current dire emergency? Well, we will remedy that failure by prescribing the reasonable conditions that a suspension should have included. And has the Executive failed to live up to those reasonable conditions? Well, we will ourselves make that failure good, so that this dangerous fellow (if he is dangerous) need not be set free. The problem with this approach is not only that it steps out of the courts' modest and limited role in a democratic society; but that by repeatedly doing what it thinks the political branches ought to do it encourages their lassitude and saps the vitality of government by the people.

VI

Several limitations give my views in this matter a relatively narrow compass. They apply only to citizens, accused of being enemy combatants, who are detained within the territorial jurisdiction of a federal court. This is not likely to be a numerous group; currently we know of only two, Hamdi and Jose Padilla. Where the citizen is captured outside and held outside the United States, the constitutional requirements may be different. Moreover, even within the United States, the accused citizen-enemy combatant may lawfully be detained once prosecution is in progress or in contemplation. The Government has been notably successful in securing conviction, and hence long-term custody or execution, of those who have waged war against the state.

I frankly do not know whether these tools are sufficient to meet the Government's security needs, including the need to obtain intelligence through interrogation. It is far beyond my competence, or the Court's competence, to determine that. But it is not beyond Congress's. If the situation demands it, the Executive can ask Congress to authorize suspension of the writ—which can be made subject to whatever conditions Congress deems appropriate, including even the procedural novelties invented by the plurality today. To be sure, suspension is limited by the Constitution to cases of rebellion or invasion. But whether the attacks of September 11, 2001, constitute an "invasion," and whether those attacks still justify suspension several years later, are questions for Congress rather than this Court. If civil rights are to be curtailed during wartime, it must be done openly and democratically, as the Constitution requires, rather than by silent erosion through an opinion of this Court.

The Founders well understood the difficult trade-off between safety and freedom. "Safety from external danger," Hamilton declared,

is the most powerful director of national conduct. Even the ardent love of liberty will, after a time, give way to its dictates. The violent destruction of life and property incident to war; the continual effort and alarm attendant on a state of continual danger, will compel nations the most attached to liberty, to resort for repose and security to institutions which have a tendency to destroy their civil and political rights. To be more safe, they, at length, become willing to run the risk of being less free. *The Federalist* No. 8.

The Founders warned us about the risk, and equipped us with a Constitution designed to deal with it.

Many think it not only inevitable but entirely proper that liberty give way to security in times of national crisis—that, at the extremes of military exigency, *inter arma silent leges*. Whatever the general merits of the view that war silences law or modulates its voice, that view has no place in the interpretation and application of a Constitution designed precisely to confront war and, in a manner that accords with democratic principles, to accommodate it. Because the Court has proceeded to meet the current emergency in a manner the Constitution does not envision, I respectfully dissent.

JOSEPH R. BIDEN, JR.

Learned Hand Dinner Address before the American Jewish Committee (2005)

Thank you very much. This is a very special evening, and it's an honor to be invited to speak here tonight.

As you all know, Learned Hand was best known for his tireless, determined and avid support of free speech.

"All discussion," he said, "all debate, all dissidence tends to question and, in consequence, to upset existing convictions; that is precisely its purpose and justification."

Indeed, it is that attitude of challenging the status quo, to have a moral compass rather than a finger to the wind, that characterizes the work and very purpose of the American Jewish Committee.

And it is why we are here tonight to honor the life and commitment and dedication of Bruce Ramer. I first met Bruce several years ago, and learned we share many things in common. And what I've come to admire most is that moral compass that guides him.

The leader of the American Jewish Committee who traveled to Macedonia to visit the displaced persons camps filled with Kosovar Muslims, and whose conscience compelled him to act, not as a leader of an organization, not even as a Jew looking into his soul, but as a human being shaken, troubled, and profoundly moved.

Bruce Ramer, a man who has sat with Kings and Emirs, Presidents and Prime Ministers—but who prefers to talk about the earthquake in India that impelled him to lend his efforts to help bring humanitarian assistance to people in desperate need, and to rebuild a Muslim school.

That spirit of Tikkun Olam—repairing the world—is what inspires Bruce and the raison d'etre of the AJC.

And that brings me to tonight's topic. The surprising, some would say amazing, things going on in the Middle East: are we witnessing the fruits of Tikkun Olam, or are we headed down a dark, dangerous path? Ladies and gentlemen, I believe we are witnessing—and I believe we can help shape—an extraordinary moment in the greater Middle East.

As President Bush put it this week, "a critical mass of events is taking the region in a hopeful new direction."

These events—Palestinian and Iraqi national elections; Saudi municipal elections; Egyptian President Mubarak's move to allow competitive elections for President; and the Lebanese people demanding Syria's withdrawal and free parliamentary elections raise this question:

Have we reached a democratic "tipping point" similar to the peaceful revolutions that brought down communist regimes in Eastern Europe?

That's what I'd like to talk to you about tonight.

Bush's Call for Democracy

Just two months ago, in his second inaugural address. President Bush spoke with great eloquence about expanding freedom.

I was a little frustrated by the negative reaction from some in my party . . . and some of our friends around the world. Here's the headline from the leading Green Party newspaper in Germany: "Bush Threatens More Freedom."

It seemed to me that distaste for the messenger obscured the power of the message.

Clearly, the President's speech struck a chord with many Americans. The benefits of freedom and the desire to share them with others go to who we are as a people to how we see ourselves and to our national experience.

The President is also right to link expanding freedom to our interests.

A world full of liberal democracies would not only be better for the people living in those countries—it would be better for us.

Liberal democracies tend not to attack one another. They tend not to abuse the rights of their people. They tend not to produce terrorists.

Of course, there are exceptions: Timothy McVeigh . . . the IRA . . . the ETA . . . the Red Brigades. But that's the point: these are exceptions, not the rule, in advanced democracies.

Conversely, we learned on 9/11 that the absence of democracy halfway around the world can do terrible harm to us here at home.

I don't believe in a clash of civilizations. I do believe of a clash within civilizations between those who want to move their societies forward and those who would retreat to the past.

Those who want to take their societies backwards have great allies in the autocratic leaders of the Middle East. The region has become a breeding ground for terror because of an almost total lack of political, economic and social openness.

In the absence of any productive outlets, dissent is channeled underground and into the Mosques, where it is captured by radical Islamic fundamentalists. When young people are alienated from their governments, they will fight, kill and die for their causes instead of living for them.

I also believe that history is on democracy's side. In 1775 there were no democracies. The American Revolution raised the number to one. Today, there are 117 electoral democracies—some 60 percent of the world's governments.

As the number of democracies increases still further, pressure will rise on the tyrannical outliers. We may be witnessing this very phenomenon in the Middle East.

But We Need a
Little Realism, Too

So I for one applaud President Bush's vision. But I do so without blinders on. First, President Bush is a Johnny-come-lately to the democratizers' club.

Remember, he arrived in Washington four years ago mocking the very notion of democracy promotion.

Nor was establishing democracy the rationale for his two signature initiatives—Afghanistan and Iraq. Rather, it was an ex-post-facto justification.

Second, there is a significant gap between the President's rhetoric and the reality of his administration's policies. That risks undermining our credibility.

The administration is tough on dictatorial adversaries like Iran and North Korea.

But it rarely sustains the heat on illiberal friends like Pakistan, Russia, Saudi Arabia and Egypt.

It temporarily recognized a coup against the misguided but democratically elected leader of Venezuela.

It has said little about the virtual coup in Nepal.

And it adopted an ultra-realist policy toward undemocratic Libya when Kaddafi agreed to give up his weapons.

Third, there is often a short term conflict between democracy promotion and our vital security interests.

We need China's help on North Korea, Russia's help on Iran, Pakistan's help on Al Qaeda, Egypt's help on the Middle East peace process and Iraq. Pushing too hard, too fast on democracy risks alienating governments whose help we need.

Finally, and perhaps most important, democracy promotion is hard work that must go beyond rhetorical support and the passion of one speech.

It's one thing to topple a tyrant, another to put something better in his place.

Our experience in Iraq demonstrates the unintended consequences of imposing democracy from the outside by force. Autocrats in the region have pointed to the post-Saddam chaos as a warning to their own people: you may not like me, but at least life is stable and predictable. Without me, you will reap the whirlwind.

Even where we simply lend our political and rhetorical support to democratizers, it is not enough to hold an election and declare victory. We must help build liberal institutions: political parties; an independent judiciary; independent media; modern education; a developed civil society and non-governmental organizations, a private sector.

Elections in the absence of these institutions favor the most organized groups in society, which also tend to be the most radical.

That was the case when Algeria held elections in the early 1990s. It could be the short term result in Lebanon, where Hezbollah already holds a dozen seats in parliament in Egypt, where the Muslim Brotherhood would probably poll well and even Iraq, where it remains to be seen what direction the victorious Shia take the country.

In short, because Arab rulers have long suppressed civil society and the development of liberal institutions, those best positioned to take advantage of elections are Islamists.

Is It Because of Bush?

Each of these caveats is important. And I want to come back to them in a few moments to suggest a third way between unbridled idealism and overly cynical realism.

But the fact remains that something important is happening in the greater Middle East.

And the question remains: to what extent are the policies we pursue responsible?

At first blush, we should proceed with great humility about our ability to write the future for others. Think about the catalysts for the change we're witnessing:

In the Palestinian territories, Arafat's death.

In Iraq, the Ayatollah Sistani insisting on elections, despite initial opposition from the US and UN.

In Lebanon, the assassination of Rafiq Hariri.

And throughout the region, including in Egypt and Saudi Arabia, long term disaffection with the stagnant political and economic status quo the gradual discrediting of alternative models like the Taliban's Afghanistan and the Cleric's Iran greater access to information through the internet and satellite television and a demographic youth explosion, as a result of which 60 percent of the population in the greater Middle East is under the age of 30.

The United States had no control over these specific incidents and trends.

But I believe President Bush's strong rhetorical support for democracy has made a difference by creating space for and emboldening modernizers and moderates. They are less fearful of reprisals when they believe the United States will hold their regimes to account.

In Egypt, Secretary Rice cancelled a planned visit to Cairo because of the detention of political leader Ayman Nour. And President Bush restated during his European trip: "the great and proud nation of Egypt, which showed the way toward peace in the Middle East, can now show the way toward democracy in the Middle East."

This sent an unmistakable signal to President Mubarak and at the very time Egypt is doing some heavy lifting for us in the Middle East peace process and in offering to train Iraqi security forces. Yes, Egypt may have been just as concerned about Congress cutting aid and about increasingly bold anti-Mubarak protests. But the administration did the right thing, and I believe it made a difference.

Elections in Iraq made a difference, too. No matter what you think about the war or the way we've mishandled the peace, the images of Iraqis lined up to vote, images that were beamed across the Middle East had to have had an impact, especially in Lebanon and Egypt. Most Arabs have been fed a steady diet of bad news on Iraq to the point that they believed the country was in complete shambles. Now, Arabs are asking: if elections can be held in a violence-torn country under occupation, why can't they be held in the generally stable countries in which they live.

Yes, in Iraq, the main mover behind elections was not President Bush, but Ayatollah Sistani. But the President does deserve credit for resisting calls to delay elections. He made the right call.

Elsewhere, the administration has done less to translate the President's rhetoric into action and progress is more the result of internal factors.

In the Palestinian territories, after Arafat's death the Palestinian Legislative Council considered appointing his successor. Some in the administration expressed support for such a process. The Palestinians themselves decided to follow their laws and hold elections within 60 days.

In Saudi Arabia, most of the pressure on the Royal Family to open up the system comes from domestic sources. I'm not aware of any evidence the Bush Administration compelled the Saudis to go forward with municipal elections. The real driver is internal pressure.

In Lebanon, the Administration was right to coordinate closely with the French. Franco-US cooperation has inspired a degree of confidence among the Lebanese and encouraged them as they stand up to the Syrians. And the fact that Saudi Arabia, which had close ties to Hariri, has called for Syrian withdrawal has placed unprecedented pressure on Syria.

The bottom line is that local conditions are the driving force behind change in the region, but outside pressure is critical particularly at key moments. Our policies did not start the process of reform, but they can help to accelerate it.

So What Should Be Done?

So let me end with a few thoughts on the policies we should pursue to help accelerate and sustain the movement toward openness and democracy.

As I suggested a few moments ago, we need to chart a course between unbridled idealism and overly cynical realism.

We should begin by acknowledging some hard truths.

For years, the United States has seemed, at best, indifferent to the plight of the oppressed and, at worst, complicit with corrupt and autocratic regimes—despite our generosity.

In the past, we've justified that support in different ways: the Cold War struggle against communism, the preference for stability over chaos, the need to ensure a steady supply of oil.

9/11 has taught America the hard way that we cannot afford such policies.

The great struggle of our times—the struggle between freedom and radical Islamic fundamentalism—is also a war of ideas.

To prevail, we must be strong. But we also have to be smart, wielding the force of our ideas and ideals together with the force of our arms.

The spread of democracy is crucial to us winning that war and undercutting the ideology of the radical Islamic fundamentalists.

But democracy is about much more than elections. Our goal must be to help build and support the institutions of liberal democracy.

Here, the Bush administration is falling well short of the mark. Just follow the money.

In the FY '06 budget, the administration requests $30 million less for the Middle East Partnership

Initiative—its signature democracy promotion fund for the region—than last year. It makes the same request as last year for the National Endowment for Democracy ($80 million). It zeroes out regional democracy funds for Africa, Asia and the Middle East.

And the administration continues to channel most of our non-economic assistance to illiberal friends like Egypt through the central government instead of directly to independent actors. That has to change. Two years ago, I proposed the establishment of a private, non-profit Middle East Foundation. It would provide grants to those in the region working to promote a vibrant civil society, independent media, political parties, the rule of law, modern education systems, human rights including women's rights, and the private sector.

The administration has embraced the idea and with a little luck, the legislation we need to create the foundation will become law this spring.

We should also leverage the energy and resources of our closest allies. The Administration has tried. For example, it launched a G-8 initiative for democratization in the so-called Broader Middle East and North Africa.

Thus far, the initiative has not borne much fruit. Many projects agreed upon have yet to be launched. And Europeans have made clear that they prefer to work in parallel, not jointly, lest they be tainted by association with this administration. That's where we pay a price for distrust of the messenger.

Europeans, no less than Americans, should heed Learned Hand's words, when he wrote, in 1932, "the condition of our survival in any but the meagerest existence is our willingness to accommodate ourselves to the conflicting interests of others, to learn to live in a social world." I would press our allies to do more, with us. The progress in Egypt, Lebanon, Iraq, and the Palestinian territories may help overcome their reluctance and their own cynicism.

In my judgment, freedom from fear and freedom from want are flip sides of the same democratic coin. We should work with our allies to help countries pursue both. Let me conclude by quoting one last time that wise judge, Learned Hand, from his famous "I Am an American" speech delivered in Central Park in NYC in the midst of WWII in 1944.

Like Americans today, he spoke about liberty, and he understood very well, and expressed very passionately, what freedom means:

"And what is this Liberty which must lie in the hearts of men and women? It is not the ruthless, the unbridled will; it is not freedom to do as one likes. That is the denial of liberty, and leads straight to its overthrow. A society in which men recognize no check upon their freedom soon becomes a society where freedom is the possession of only a savage few, as we have learned to our sorrow.

"What then is the spirit of liberty? It is the spirit which is not too sure that it is right, the spirit which seeks to understand the mind of other men and women; the spirit which weighs their interests alongside its own without bias.

"And now in that spirit, that spirit of an America which has never been, and which may never be; nay, which never will be except as the conscience and courage of Americans to create it; yet in the spirit of that America which lies hidden in some form in the aspirations of us all; in the spirit of that America for which our young men are at this moment fighting and dying; in that spirit of liberty and of America I ask you to rise and with me pledge our faith in the glorious destiny of our beloved country."

Thank you very much.

CREDITS

Saul Alinsky, excerpts from *Rules for Radicals*. Copyright © 1971 by Saul Alinsky. Reprinted with the permission of Random House, Inc.

Hannah Arendt, "Reflections on Little Rock" from *The Portable Hannah Arendt*, edited by Peter Baehr. Copyright © 1959 by Hannah Arendt. Reprinted by permission of Georges Borchardt, Inc., on behalf of the Estate of Hannah Arendt.

James Baldwin, "The Discovery of What It Means to Be an American" originally published in *The New York Times Book Review* (1959). Collected in *Nobody Knows My Name*, published by Vintage Books. Copyright © 1959 by James Baldwin. Copyright renewed. Used by arrangement with the James Baldwin Estate.

James Baldwin, "Fifth Avenue, Uptown: A Letter from Harlem" originally published in *Esquire*. Collected in *Nobody Knows My Name*. Copyright © 1960 by James Baldwin. Copyright renewed. Used by arrangement with the James Baldwin Estate.

James Baldwin and William F. Buckley, Jr., "Debate at Cambridge University" (1965) from *The New York Times Magazine* (March 1965). Copyright © 1965 by James Baldwin and William F. Buckley, Jr. Used by permission of the James Baldwin Estate and the Wallace Literary Agency, Inc.

Joseph R. Biden, Jr., "American Jewish Committee/Learned Hand Dinner" (March 10, 2005). Reprinted with the permission of The Honorable Joseph R. Biden, Jr.

Stokely Carmichael, "What We Want" from *The New York Review of Books* (22 September 1966). Reprinted with the permission of Mabel Carmichael.

Whittaker Chambers, "Foreword in the Form of a Letter to My Children" from *Witness* (New York: Random House, 1952). Copyright © 1952 by Whittaker Chambers. Reprinted with the permission of John Chambers.

Cesar Chavez, "Delano Plan and Statement" (1968). Reprinted with the permission of the Cesar E. Chavez Foundation.

Cesar Chavez, excerpt from interview with *The Observer*. Reprinted with the permission of the Cesar E. Chavez Foundation.

John Dewey, excerpts from "Renascent Liberalism" from *Liberalism and Social Action*. Copyright © 1991 by the Board of Trustees, Southern Illinois University. Reprinted with the permission of Southern Illinois University Press.

W. E. B. Du Bois, excerpt from "On the Talented Tenth" from *The Souls of Black Folk*. Reprinted with the permission of Penguin Books, Ltd.

W. E. B. Du Bois, "Of Booker T. Washington and Others" from *The Souls of Black Folk*. Reprinted with the permission of Penguin Books, Ltd.

W. E. B. Du Bois, "The Development of a People" from *International Journal of Ethics* (1904). Reprinted with the permission of the Estate of W. E. B. Du Bois.

Daniel Elazar, excerpt from "Obligations and Rights in the Jewish Tradition" (Jerusalem Center for Public Affairs, 1991), www.jcpa.org/dje/articles2/oblig-rights.htm. Reprinted with the permission of the author and the Jerusalem Center for Public Affairs.

Lawrence Ferlinghetti, "I Am Waiting" from *A Coney Island of the Mind: Poems*. Copyright © 1958 by Lawrence Ferlinghetti. Reprinted with the permission of New Directions Publishing Corporation.